ONE W

DISPUTE
RESOLUTION

ASPEN CASEBOOK SERIES

DISPUTE RESOLUTION

Beyond the Adversarial Model

Second Edition

Carrie J. Menkel-Meadow

Chancellor's Professor and Founding Faculty,
University of California Irvine Law School and
   A.B. Chettle Jr. Professor of Law, Dispute Resolution and Civil Procedure
Georgetown University Law Center

Lela Porter Love

Professor of Law and Director, Kukin Program for Conflict Resolution and the
   Cardozo Mediation Clinic
Benjamin N. Cardozo Law School,
Yeshiva University

Andrea Kupfer Schneider

Professor of Law and Director, Dispute Resolution Program
Marquette University Law School

Jean R. Sternlight

Saltman Professor of Law and Director, Saltman Center for Conflict Resolution
University of Nevada Las Vegas, Boyd School of Law

. Wolters Kluwer
Law & Business

AUSTIN   BOSTON   CHICAGO   NEW YORK   THE NETHERLANDS

To contact Customer Service, e-mail customer.care@aspenpublishers.com,
call 1-800-234-1660, fax 1-800-901-9075, or mail correspondence to:

> Aspen Publishers
> Attn: Order Department
> PO Box 990
> Frederick, MD 21705

Printed in the United States of America.

1 2 3 4 5 6 7 8 9 0

978-0-7355-8919-3

Library of Congress Cataloging-in-Publication Data

Dispute resolution : beyond the adversarial model / Carrie J. Menkel-Meadow...[et al.].—2nd ed.
    p. cm.
  Includes bibliographical references and index.
  ISBN 978-0-7355-8919-3 (alk. paper)
  1. Dispute resolution (Law)—United States. I. Menkel-Meadow, Carrie. II. Title.

  KF9084.A75D57 2011
  347.73'9—dc22

                          2010045593

About Wolters Kluwer Law & Business

Wolters Kluwer Law & Business is a leading provider of research information and work-flow solutions in key specialty areas. The strengths of the individual brands of Aspen Publishers, CCH, Kluwer Law International and Loislaw are aligned within Wolters Kluwer Law & Business to provide comprehensive, in-depth solutions and expert-authored content for the legal, professional and education markets.

CCH was founded in 1913 and has served more than four generations of business professionals and their clients. The CCH products in the Wolters Kluwer Law & Business group are highly regarded electronic and print resources for legal, securities, antitrust and trade regulation, government contracting, banking, pension, payroll, employment and labor, and healthcare reimbursement and compliance professionals.

Aspen Publishers is a leading information provider for attorneys, business professionals and law students. Written by preeminent authorities, Aspen products offer analytical and practical information in a range of specialty practice areas from securities law and intellectual property to mergers and acquisitions and pension/benefits. Aspen's trusted legal education resources provide professors and students with high-quality, up-to-date and effective resources for successful instruction and study in all areas of the law.

Kluwer Law International supplies the global business community with comprehensive English-language international legal information. Legal practitioners, corporate counsel and business executives around the world rely on the Kluwer Law International journals, loose-leafs, books and electronic products for authoritative information in many areas of international legal practice.

Loislaw is a premier provider of digitized legal content to small law firm practitioners of various specializations. Loislaw provides attorneys with the ability to quickly and efficiently find the necessary legal information they need, when and where they need it, by facilitating access to primary law as well as state-specific law, records, forms and treatises.

Wolters Kluwer Law & Business, a unit of Wolters Kluwer, is headquartered in New York and Riverwoods, Illinois. Wolters Kluwer is a leading multinational publisher and information services company.

For Robert Meadow,

    Peter Popov and Nicole Love Popov,
    Rodd, Joshua, Noah, and Zachary Schneider,
    Sylvia Lazos, Samuel Sternlight Lazos, and Benjamin Sternlight Lazos,

Our partners and children whose support, love and dispute resolution talents we appreciate and cherish, and

For our many students, past, present, and future, whom we learn from and hope will use these materials to make the world a better place, with both peace and justice.

Summary of Contents

Contents

Preface to the Second Edition

Since the publication of our first edition in 2005 there has been continued growth and diversification in the "process pluralism" we have described in both the older edition and now this new edition. Increasing use is being made of negotiation, mediation, and arbitration, and creative system designers are combining these processes in new ways in varied contexts. At the international level, more and more transnational disputes, conflicts, and transactions are drawing on dispute resolution processes,[1] which we hope soon to cover in a separate book on Transnational Dispute Resolution.

Nevertheless, since our last edition, the United States has been participating in two new wars and litigation and its concomitant fees and costs have continued to climb, even while an economic recession has altered the legal landscape. With the recession we have seen more housing foreclosures, a rise in financial fraud and complex business litigation, and additional banking, housing, employment and consumer disputes that have caused many people great personal and financial harm. There has also been a major realignment in the market for legal services.

Thus, we think the process pluralism of ADR has gained even more importance in our daily and professional lives, and remains at the core of what all law students (and lawyers) should learn as part of their basic legal education and experience. We see ADR in the courts, out of the courts in a myriad of forms, and increasingly, in areas of aggregated disputes and conflicts, within organizations and among peoples and nations, spawning the new separate field of dispute system design. We report here, in the last chapter, some of the newest empirical and other research, designed to test claims about ADR's usefulness in our (and other) societies.

As in the first edition, we continue to center dispute resolution processes in a context of problem solving for clients, including individuals, governmental agencies,

---

1. Carrie Menkel-Meadow, Why and How to Study Transnational Law, 1 University of California Irvine Law Review (2010).

groups, private entities, organizations, corporations and nations. In order to negotiate, arbitrate, or mediate, lawyers need to understand their clients' needs and interests
and those of the other parties, so interviewing, counseling, listening, communicating, and understanding are important constituent activities of dispute resolution
which are also covered in this book.

In this new edition we have listened to our readers and students and streamlined
(and shortened!) the materials we present to you. Instead of *Notes and Questions*, we
now provide you with clearly demarcated *Problems* found, (somewhat ironically, in a
book that is about "thinking outside of the box") inside grey boxes, which are easy to
read (if not always easy to solve). These problem boxes can be used as out-of-class
thinking and homework assignments or serve as discussion points for classes, whether
in large group or smaller task groups. The Teacher's Manual for both the earlier edition (and this one too) continue to supply the largest collection of shorter role-plays
and longer simulations for any ADR text, demonstrating our belief that the subjects
of negotiation, mediation, arbitration, and dispute resolution generally are learned
best *in action* where *theories in use*[2] can be tested for their efficacy, appropriateness, and
ability to solve clients' problems. Both this book and the companion shorter
"splits" — *Mediation: Practice Policy and Ethics* and *Negotiation: Processes for Problem Solving* can be used in both classroom (survey or specialized) courses or clinical settings,
both within and outside of the United States.

This new edition adds new materials, including a number of recently decided
cases, primarily on arbitration issues, from the highest courts in the land, and the latest
in commentary and scholarship on dispute resolution issues. We have also edited some
of the classic materials from our first edition to a more manageable length.

This book is presented in several sections. We offer two introductory chapters on
the history and jurisprudence of dispute processes, as well as the importance and
underlying value of problem solving for clients and the skills necessary to problem-
solve. Then in three separate chapters for each primary process of negotiation, mediation, and arbitration we cover concepts and models of that process, skills needed to be
both representatives and third party neutrals in that process, and the ethical, legal and
policy issues that are implicated in the use of those processes. Next, we provide a section of the book examining more complex issues in dispute resolution: variations and
combinations of dispute resolution processes in both private and public settings; uses
of dispute resolution in multi-party and transactional settings; and insights from dispute system design and related planning for dispute resolution processes. Finally, we
survey some of the issues in assessing the past uses and future possibilities of dispute
resolution, both for clients and for the larger society.

*   *   *

All of us remain grateful to our various institutions for support as teachers, schol-
ars, and practitioners: Georgetown University Law Center, the Center for Transna-
tional Legal Studies, and the University of California, Irvine Law School for Carrie
Menkel-Meadow, Benjamin N. Cardozo Law School and its Kukin Program for
Conflict Resolution at Yeshiva University for Lela Love, Marquette University Law
School and its Dispute Resolution Program for Andrea Kupfer Schneider and the

---

2. Donald Schön, The Reflective Practitioner (1983).

University of Nevada, Las Vegas and its Saltman Center for Dispute Resolution for Jean Sternlight. We thank our deans, colleagues, and our many students who have worked with these materials and given us useful feedback.

We thank the many authors and publishers who have allowed us to reprint their materials (as formally acknowledged in the Acknowledgments). We are especially grateful to those who allowed us to use their materials without exorbitant permissions or royalty payments, in the interest of dissemination of learning and education. And we are grateful for the continued inspiration of both our intellectual mentors and seniors (a smaller group as we join the ranks of the "senior mentors" ourselves), and our enthusiastic students, many of whom want to make full-time careers in this field, which we all helped create and foster.

Individually and specifically we thank:

Carrie thanks Katherine M. Hayes (at Georgetown) and Jean Su (at UCI) for superb research assistance, manuscript preparation, and student insights; Maike Kotterba (CTLS) and Charlene Anderson (UCI) (for administrative support) and Peter Reilly, Clark Freshman, and Bob Bordone for mentees who have become true peers, colleagues and friends in this work we all do.

Lela thanks Nicole and Peter for constant support (particularly Nicole's technical support) and research assistants Halley Anolik and Dan Liston who did excellent work with page proofs.

Andrea (and the rest of us) thanks Carrie Kratochvil who was there at the birth of this book and has been our constant star of minding, managing and maneuvering this edition to completion. She also thanks research assistants Erica Hayden, Erin Naipo, Amanda Tofias, Ben Scott, and Andrea Thompson for their excellent work.

Jean thanks her family for their tolerance and research assistants Kimberly DelMonico, Kathleen Wilden and Will Thompson for their excellent work.

All of us thank Aspen Publishers (again), especially Melody Davies who started with us, helped us with kindness and appreciation, and we hope is now enjoying retirement, John Devins who manages us, Troy Froebe who manages our manuscript, Tracy Metivier for permissions and related editorial work, and Enid Zafran for indexing.

We thank our students for teaching us, our colleagues for supporting and critiquing us, and most importantly, our families who continue to not only support us, but to love us, for which we are all eternally grateful.

Finally, all of us thank each other for continuing to work, learn, and collaborate with each other — often from scattered corners of the world as we continue to spread our hopes and dreams for a more peaceful and just world.

Carrie J. Menkel-Meadow
Lela Porter Love
Andrea Kupfer Schneider
Jean R. Sternlight

November 2010

Preface to the First Edition

This book is inspired by our conviction that study of a variety of different processes of dispute resolution, what we here call "process pluralism," will enable the lawyers of the future to be more creative and effective in their legal problem solving. We subtitle this book "Beyond the Adversarial Model" because we believe that while litigation, and the adversarial process that inspires it, has its place in the legal order, modern life requires additional processes that better meet the needs of parties in conflict, as well as of the larger societies within which legal and other disputes occur. We believe that these other processes will produce qualitatively better solutions, improve relationships between parties, and deliver both justice and peace, both effectively and meaningfully. We also care about efficiency, of course, but for us, that value must often bow to the others.

Two of us are of the founding generation of "alternative dispute resolution" (a field many now call "appropriate dispute resolution" or simply "dispute resolution"); the other two of us came fast behind with specialized knowledge of several of the processes we study in this book. We have all been teaching these processes for many years and thought it time to enter the field with a new textbook. (Note that we did not say "casebook," as "cases" are not all that our field is about.) This book is organized to provide a comprehensive treatment of the field of dispute resolution, whether taught with skills components (and use of the many simulations, role-plays, and problem sets found in the Teacher's Manual) or as a survey of the field's theoretical, practical, ethical, legal, or policy issues.

We begin with a theoretical and historical introduction to the field of dispute and conflict resolution, introducing readers to the basic concepts and their creative developers and pointing out innovations in social and legal problem solving. Important theorist and practitioner Professor Lon Fuller, whom we call "the jurisprude of ADR," introduces us to the idea of "process integrity" — the evaluation of each dispute resolution process for its own logic, function, purpose, and morality — a theme we follow throughout the book.

We then turn to the three foundational processes of dispute resolution: negotiation, mediation (as facilitated negotiation), and arbitration (party controlled adjudication). Each process is studied in three separate chapters. The first focuses on the concepts, frameworks, and approaches characterizing different conceptualizations of the process; another explores the skills and practices needed to conduct that process; and a third examines the legal, ethical, and policy issues the process raises. This section of the book is primarily concerned with how lawyers (whether as negotiators, mediators, representatives in mediation and arbitration, or arbitrators) can more effectively solve their clients' problems and the problems of those with whom their clients interact.

Each of these processes has become more complex, both in study and in practice, since the modern field was founded about thirty years ago. To help students cope with that complexity, we present materials for practice (role-plays and simulations are provided in the Teacher's Manual); for analysis (questions and problems are posed in the text's Notes and Questions sections, following each of the readings, drawn from law, social science, popular culture, and examples of the processes in use); and for speculation on future dispute resolution designs. Throughout these chapters, we focus on the multiple roles that lawyers can play and on the importance of the interaction, consultation, and participation lawyers should have with the parties and clients whose disputes and conflicts they are hoping to help resolve. We also suggest more active roles for parties and clients in participating with lawyers in the resolution of their own issues and problems. Our conception of these roles goes beyond what many have suggested before. We maintain that participation, empowerment, creativity, and self-determination are important values in the successful and satisfying resolution of disputes and conflicts.

Beyond the foundational processes, this book goes on to explore the sophisticated adaptations of these basic processes sometimes required by modern life. Beginning with Part III, we explore how the basic processes combine to form hybrid processes; how the addition of multiple parties and the introduction of more complex issues change our understanding of how these processes can be used; how we might anticipate and avoid disputes by using conflict resolution in transaction planning and contracts; and how international conflicts may differ from or require adaptation of the processes commonly used in domestic legal disputes.

Dispute resolution is no longer just about avoiding or settling lawsuits. It should be thought of before relationships are formed, throughout their duration, and then, if necessary, when things go bad. Since various forms of ADR have now been in use for at least three decades, we are in a position to present some important critiques of and challenges to ADR's use. A separate chapter in this text therefore asks practitioners and students to consider how the claims of dispute resolution processes in different fora can be properly assessed and evaluated. Our concluding chapter examines the issues involved in counseling clients on the most appropriate process to use to resolve their disputes and conflicts and to plan transactions.

Our goal in this book is to help you as lawyers and future lawyers to be as well educated and informed as possible about effective options for dispute resolution. From this basis, you will be better prepared to advise your clients about the many ways they can go about their dealings with others, both when putting things together and, sadly, when dealing with the consequences of relationships that fall apart.

*   *   *

This book is the culmination of many years of study, teaching, research, and writing by all of us, and we have many intellectual, personal, and work-related debts. We cannot begin to acknowledge all of those debts, but we would like to recognize a few.

First, our intellectual sources. In some ways, the field or "movement" of ADR is a continuation of earlier schools of legal thought, including both Legal Realism and the Legal Process school of the 1950s (see Henry M. Hart and Albert M. Sacks, *The Legal Process: Basic Problems in the Making and Application of Law* [1958, reissued in 1994, edited by Professors William N. Eskridge, Jr., and Philip P. Frickey]), both of which saw legal doctrine as insufficient to explain what lawyers did and how law is made, enforced, and lived. Both approaches sought to add people and processes to the study of law and its operations. The Law and Society field added empirical study of dispute processes by sociologists, anthropologists, psychologists, political scientists, and economists to the work of legal scholars, broadening the disciplinary reach of dispute processing studies during a period of both domestic and international conflict and ferment.

The 1960s and 1970s saw a tremendous explosion of legal rights, with many more laws added to the books than could easily be enforced in courts, no matter how actively managed. Those decades were further characterized by political movements that encouraged people with legal problems or issues to participate directly in the system, diminishing the involvement of professionals.

At the same time, two different schools of thought arose questioning the adequacy of lawsuits and traditional adversarialism to solve all social and legal problems. One group was concerned about finding qualitatively better solutions to conflicts and increasing parties' participation, while the other group was more concerned about efficiency and the costs in money and time of so much litigation. These two movements coalesced at a famous conference held in 1976 — "Causes of Popular Dissatisfaction with the Administration of Justice" — and a speech delivered there by Professor Frank Sander officially launched the field of ADR. Concurrently, some of us (including the authors of this book) asked lawyers to learn to "problem solve" rather than to "beat or best the other side" in legal negotiations (Menkel-Meadow, 1984).

The study of negotiation was institutionalized as several law schools began to teach and study negotiation processes related to a variety of settings, producing a founding generation of negotiation scholars, many of whose works are cited and explored in the pages that follow. The concept of third party neutrals was added to facilitate negotiation, and two of us were early mediators when mediation found its place in the law school curriculum. The adaptation of the mediation process to legal disputes and conflicts is also chronicled in this book, with excerpts from those who founded and elaborated that field as well.

The study, practice, and teaching of first negotiation and then mediation were part of another important movement in legal education: clinical legal education, which seeks to teach law students how to behave as well as to think like lawyers. While litigation was the focus of most early clinical programs, frustration with enforcement of winning lawsuits or with the inefficacy of lawsuits to effect both individual and social change led some early clinicians to look for other methods of legal and social problem solving, all while teaching law students to understand that there are many ways to serve one's clients and solve legal problems. The clinical movement, like the study of ADR, is an "experiential" field, and we also owe intellectual debts to those, like Donald Schön and Chris Arygris, who developed, in professional education, the concepts and practices of "theories-in-use." This book elaborates theories of dispute resolution, in various forms, and asks students to put those theories into use immediately, while learning about them.

We have all been supported greatly by the institutions at which we teach, including Georgetown University Law Center (and before that UCLA); Benjamin N. Cardozo School of Law/Yeshiva University; Marquette University Law School; and the University of Nevada, Las Vegas, Boyd Law School (and before that the University of Missouri-Columbia School of Law). We thank our respective deans, colleagues, and disbursers of research funds for their ample support in producing this book, and, more importantly, for encouraging our teaching, scholarship, and practice in this field. The William and Flora Hewlett Foundation has done much to support the field and indirectly supported much of the work of this book (both the publications in it and the work described therein).

We thank the many authors and their publishers whose work we have reprinted (see Acknowledgments, following this Preface). Knowledge in dispute resolution is only partially reflected in reported cases; most of what we know comes from other sources, including articles, transcripts, rules, practice manuals, and empirical studies.

Carrie thanks James Bond, Jaimie Kent, Ellen Connelly Cohen, and, especially, David Mattingly for superb research assistance, editorial work, and manuscript preparation; Rada M. Stojanovich Hayes, Carolyn Howard, Sylvia Johnson, Ronnie E. Rease, Jr., and Toni Patterson for administrative and moral support; and Anna Selden and John Showalter for masterful manuscript management and computer feats beyond the call of duty. She thanks Robert Meadow, Susan Gillig, and Vicki Jackson for being the best dispute resolution role models a professor ever had, and Peter Reilly for being the best hope for the next generation of negotiation teachers and scholars.

Lela thanks Roger Deitz, for his painstaking edits; and her wonderful research assistants, Clymer Bardsley, Malte Pendergast-Fischer, Barry Rosenhouse, Michael Stone, and Chelsea Teachout, for their cheerful and energetic contributions.

Andrea thanks her amazing administrative assistant Carrie Kratochvil (as do the rest of us for organizing us all); her research assistants Amy Koltz, Deanna Senske, Mindy Dummermuth, and Anna Coyer for their wonderful ideas and great work; and her colleague Joanne Lipo-Zovic.

Jean thanks and is grateful for the excellent research assistance of Alyson Carrel, Ann Casey, Jennifer Chierek, Michele Baron, and Mark Lyons.

We are all thankful for the wisdom, advice, guidance, and suggestions of Carol Liebman, Jennifer Gerada Brown, Michael Moffitt, Clark Freshman, and other anonymous reviewers of this book, long in birthing, and to a few more of you who ventured to teach this in page proofs and try it out.

We appreciate the Aspen team — Richard Mixter, who put us together, and Melody Davies, Elsie Starbecker, Lisa Wehrle, Elizabeth Ricklefs, Michael Gregory, Susan Boulanger, and Tracy Metivier, who kept us on track and together and worded and sewed and sold this book.

Most importantly, we want to publicly thank one another. We have been calling this "the girl" book, to mark the fact that still so few law casebooks are written by women, never mind totally written by women. (OK, so most of the authors in this edited volume are men. . . .) We hope this book will appeal to all genders, but still, we are proud that we have not only worked and played well together but that we also created life-time friendships and wonderful working relationships. We may have had some disputes (did we?), but we are proud to say that we have lived the words on these pages as we negotiated, mediated, and built consensus to bring you this book. We know this relationship will continue into many more editions (and the separate books on negotiation, mediation, and arbitration to be derived from this book).

Finally, we also want to thank our many students who worked with this book in draft and through its various stages of development. It is for you that this is written: May you all go forth and make the world a better place, using appropriate dispute processes to make more peace and justice in the world and to solve as many human problems as you possibly can.

Carrie J. Menkel-Meadow
Lela Porter Love
Andrea Kupfer Schneider
Jean R. Sternlight

October 2004

Acknowledgments

The authors wish to express their thanks to the following authors, periodicals, and publishers for their permission to reproduce materials from their publications:

Adler, Peter S., Protean Negotiation, in The Negotiator's Fieldbook (Andrea Kupfer Schneider & Christopher Honeyman eds., 2006).

Albin, Cecilia, The Role of Fairness in Negotiations, 9 Negot. J. 223 (1993). Reprinted with permission of John Wiley & Sons, Inc.

American Arbitration Association, Sample Arbitration Clause for General Commercial Transactions, from Drafting Dispute Resolution Clauses: A Practical Guide 7 (2004), *available at* http://www.adr.org/si.asp?id=2424.

American Arbitration Association/American Bar Association, AAA/ABA Code of Ethics for Arbitrators in Commercial Disputes, Reporter's Comments to RUAA Sec. 14 (a) (1977).

American Bar Association, Section of Dispute Resolution, Mediation and the Unauthorized Practice of Law on February 2, 2002, available at http://www.abanet.org/dispute/resolution 2002.pdf.

Arnold, Tom, 20 Common Errors in Mediation Advocacy, 13 Alternatives to the High Cost of Litig. 69 (1995). © 1995 CPR Institute for Dispute Resolution, 366 Madison Avenue, New York, NY 10017-3122; (212) 949-6490. Reprinted with permission from the May 1995 issue of ALTERNATIVES, a monthly newsletter published by the CPR Institute, a nonprofit initiative of general counsel of major corporations, leading law firms and prominent legal academics whose mission is to install alternative dispute resolution (ADR) into the mainstream of legal practice.

Axelrod, Robert, The Evolution of Cooperation (1984). Copyright © 2006 Robert Axelrod. Reprinted by permission of Basic Books, a member of the Perseus Books Group.

Bastress, Robert M., & Joseph D. Harbaugh, Interviewing, Counseling, and Negotiating: Skills for Effective Representation (1990). Reprinted with the permission of Aspen Publishers.

Binder, David, Paul Bergman & Susan Price, Lawyers as Counselors: A Client Centered Approach (1991). Reprinted with permission of Thomson West.

Birke, Richard, & Craig R. Fox, Psychological Principles in Negotiating Civil Settlements, Acad. of Mgmt. Rev., Oct. 1981, at 23-24, 48-50. Used with permission of Academy of Management Review; permission conveyed through Copyright Clearance Center, Inc.

Brown, Jennifer Gerarda, Creativity and Problem-Solving, 87 Marq. L. Rev. 697 (2004). Copyright © 2004. Reprinted with permission.

Brunet, Edward, Replacing Folklore Arbitration with a Contract Model of Arbitration. Originally published in 74 Tul. L. Rev. 39-86 (1999). Reprinted with the permission of the Tulane Law Review Association, which holds the copyright.

Burrese, Alain, Listen Up, Mont. Law., Sept. 2006, at 22.

Bush, Robert A. Baruch, Mediation and Adjudication, Dispute Resolution and Ideology: An Imaginary Conversation, 3 J. of Contemp. Legal Issues 1 (1990). Reprinted with permission.

Bush, Robert Baruch, & Joseph Folger, The Promise of Mediation: Responding to Conflict Through Empowerment and Recognition. Copyright © 2005 by Jossey-Bass, Inc. Reprinted by permission of John Wiley & Sons, Inc.

Center for Public Resources, The ABC's of ADR: A Dispute Resolution Glossary, 13 Alternatives to the High Cost of Litig. 147 (1995). © 1995 CPR Institute for Dispute Resolution, 366 Madison Avenue, New York, NY 10017-3122; (212) 949-6490. Reprinted with permission from the November 1995 issue of ALTERNATIVES, a monthly newsletter published by the CPR Institute, a nonprofit initiative of general counsel of major corporations, leading law firms and prominent legal academics whose mission is to install alternative dispute resolution (ADR) into the mainstream of legal practice.

Cialdini, Robert, Influence: The Psychology of Persuasion 15-16, 17-18, 36, 38, 40-42 (1993). Copyright © 1993 by Robert Cialdini. Reprinted by permission of HarperCollins Publishers, Inc.

Clinton, William J., Acceptance Speech, International Advocate for Peace Award, Benjamin N. Cardozo School of Law, Mar. 18, 2001. Reprinted with permission of Benjamin N. Cardozo School of Law, Yeshiva University.

Coben, James, A Sample Confidentiality Provision from an Agreement to Mediate. James Coben, Director and Associate Professor, Dispute Resolution Institute, Hamline University School of Law. Reprinted with permission.

Cohen, Jonathan R., Adversaries? Partners? How About Counterparts? On Metaphors in the Practice and Teaching of Negotiation and Dispute Resolution, 20 Conflict Resol. Q. 433. Copyright © 2003 by Jossey-Bass, Inc. This material is used by permission of John Wiley & Sons, Inc.

_____, When People Are the Means: Negotiating with Respect, 14 Geo. J. Legal Ethics 739 (2001). Reprinted with the permission of the publisher, Georgetown Journal of Legal Ethics © 2001.

Cosgrove, Rabbi Elliot, sermon. Reprinted with permission of Rabbi Elliot Cosgrove.

CPR-Georgetown Model Rule 4.5.4: Conflicts of Interest.

Dezalay, Yves, & Bryant Garth, Dealing in Virtue: International Commercial Arbitration and the Construction of a Transnational Legal Order 34-39 (1996). Reprinted with permission of the University of Chicago.

Ebner, Noam, Anita D. Bhappu, Jennifer Brown, Kimberlee K. Kovach & Andrea Kupfer Schneider, You've Got Agreement: Negotiation via Email, in Rethinking Negotiation Teaching 91, 94-106 (Christopher Honeyman, James Coben & Giuseppe de Palo eds., 2009).

Fisher, Roger, et al., Beyond Machiavelli: Tools for Coping with Conflict. Reprinted by permission of the publisher from Beyond Machiavelli: Tools for Coping with Conflict by Roger Fisher, pp. 32-35, Cambridge, Mass.: Harvard University Press, Copyright © 1994 by the President and Fellows of Harvard College.

Guthrie, Chris, Panacea or Pandora's Box? The Costs of Options in Negotiation. Reprinted with permission. Used with permission of Iowa Law Review, from Chris Guthrie, Panacea or Pandora's Box? The Costs of Options in Negotiation, 88 Iowa L. Rev. 601 (2003); permission conveyed through Copyright Clearance Center, Inc.

Harter, Philip, Negotiating Regulations: A Cure for Malaise, 71 Geo. L.J. 1 (1982). Reprinted with the permission of the publisher, Georgetown Law Journal © 1982.

Hensler, Deborah, A Glass Half Full, A Glass Half Empty: The Use of Alternative Dispute Resolution in Mass Personal Injury Litigation, 74 Tex. L. Rev. 1587. Copyright © 1985. Reprinted with permission.

Hinshaw, Art, & Jess K. Alberts, Doing the Right Thing: An Empirical Study of Attorney Negotiation Ethics, 16 Harv. Negot. L. Rev. (forthcoming, 2011).

Hofstadter, Douglas, Metamagical Themas: Questing for the Essence of Mind and Pattern (1985). Copyright © 1996 Douglas Hofstadter. Reprinted by permission of Basic Books, a member of the Perseus Books Group.

Hollander-Blumoff, Rebecca, & Tom R. Tyler, Procedural Justice in Negotiation: Procedural Fairness, Acceptance, and Integrative Potential, 33 Law & Soc. Inquiry 473. Copyright © 2008 by John Wiley & Sons. Reprinted with permission.

Kahneman, Daniel, & Amos Tversky, Conflict Resolution: A Cognitive Perspective. Excerpts from Barriers to Conflict Resolution, edited by Kenneth J. Arrow, et al. Copyright © 1995 by The Stanford Center on Conflict & Negotiation. Used by permission of W. W. Norton & Company, Inc.

Kakalik, James S., Terence Dunworth, Laural Hill, Daniel McCaffrey, Marian Oshiro, Nicholas Pace & Mary Vaiana, An Evaluation and Early Neutral Evaluation Under the Civil Justice Reform Act, pp. 57-66, Santa Monica, CA: RAND Corporation, 1996. Reprinted with permission.

Kaufmann-Kohler, Gabrielle, Arbitration and the Games or the First Experience of the Olympic Division of the Court of Arbitration for Sport, 12 Mealey's Int'l Arb. Rep. #2 (Feb. 1997). Reprinted with permission.

Kichaven, Jeff, Apology in Mediation: Sorry to Say, It's Much Overrated. Reproduced with permission of the publisher, International Risk Management Institute, Inc., Dallas, Texas from IRMI.COM. Further reproduction prohibited. Visit www.IRMI.com.

Korobkin, Russell, A Positive Theory of Legal Negotiation, 88 Geo. L.J. 1789 (2000). Reprinted with the permission of the publisher, Georgetown Law Journal © 2000.

Kruse, Katherine R., Beyond Cardboard Clients in Legal Ethics, 23 Geo. J. Legal Ethics 1, 20-22, 28, 31, 33-34, 36, 41, 44 (2010). Reprinted with permission of the publisher, Georgetown Journal of Legal Ethics © 2010.

Lax, David, & James Sebenius, The Manager as Negotiator: Bargaining for Cooperation and Competitive Gain (1986). Reprinted and edited with the permission of The Free Press, a Division of Simon & Schuster Adult Publishing Group, from The Manager as Negotiator: Bargaining for Cooperation and Competitive Gain by David A. Lax and James K. Sebenius. Copyright © 1986 by David A. Lax and James K. Sebenius. All rights reserved.

Lehman, Warren, The Pursuit of a Client's Interest, 77 Mich. L. Rev. 1078. Copyright © 1979 by The Michigan Law Review Association. Reprinted with permission.

Levin, Murray, The Propriety of Evaluative Mediation: Concerns about the Nature and Quality of an Evaluative Opinion. Reprinted with the permission of Murray Levin and the Ohio State Journal on Dispute Resolution. Originally published at 16 Ohio St. J. on Disp. Resol. 267 (2001).

Levy, J. S., & R. C. Prather, Fly on the Wall, Texas Practice Guide, Appendix A (1999). Reprinted from Texas Practice Guide: Alternative Dispute Resolution by Jerome Levy (Attorney-Mediator, Dallas) and Robert Prather, Sr. (Jordan, Dunlap, Prather & Harris in Dallas), with permission of West, a Thomson business.

Liebman, Carol, Mediation as Parallel Seminars: Lessons from the Student Takeover of Columbia University's Hamilton Hall, 16 Negot. J. 157 (2000). Reprinted with permission of John Wiley & Sons, Inc.

Love, Lela, Glen Cove: Mediation Achieves What Litigation Cannot, Consensus, Oct. 1993. Copyright © 1993 by MIT-Harvard Public Disputes Program. Reprinted with permission.

_____, Images of Justice, 1 Pepp. Disp. Resol. J. 29 (2000). Copyright © 2000 by Pepperdine Dispute Resolution Journal. Reprinted with permission.

_____, adapted from Training Mediators to Listen: Deconstructing Dialogue and Constructing Understanding, Agendas, and Agreements, 38 Fam. & Conciliation Cts. Rev. 27, 39-40. Copyright © 2000 by Sage Publications, Inc. Reprinted with permission.

Love, Lela, & Joseph Stulberg, Training Materials Targets and Techniques to Generate Movement. Reprinted with permission of the authors.

Luban, David, Settlement and the Erosion of the Public Realm, 83 Geo. L.J. 2619 (1995). Reprinted with the permission of the publisher, Georgetown Law Journal © 1995.

Macfarlane, Julie, The New Lawyer 1-2 (2008).

McAdoo, Bobbi, Nancy A. Welsh & Roselle L. Wissler, Institutionalization: What Do Empirical Studies Tell Us About Court Mediation?, Disp. Resol. Mag., Winter 2003, at 8-9.

McGovern, Francis, Toward a Functional Approach for Making Complex Litigation, 53 U. Chi. L. Rev. 440. Copyright © 1986. Reprinted with permission.

Menkel-Meadow, Carrie, Aha? Is Creativity Possible in Legal Problem Solving and Teachable in Legal Education?, 6 Harv. Negot. L. Rev. 97. Copyright © 2001 by Harvard Negotiation Law Review. Reprinted with permission.

_____, Are Cross Cultural Ethics Standards Possible or Desirable in International Arbitration? (Melanges pour Pierre Tercier), 9-10 (F. Werro, P. Pichonnaz & P. Gauch eds., 2008).

_____, Conflict Theory, in Encyclopedia of Community, Vol. 1, pp. 323-326, by Karen Christensen and David Levinson, eds. Copyright © 2003 by Sage Publications, Inc. Reprinted with permission.

_____, Dispute Resolution, in Oxford Handbook of Empirical Legal Research (Peter Cane & Herbert Kritzer eds., 2010).

_____, Ethics in Alternative Dispute Resolution: New Issues, No Answers from the Adversary Conception of Lawyers' Responsibilities, 38 S. Tex. L. Rev. 407, 409-410 (1997).

_____, Ethics Issues in Arbitration and Related Dispute Resolution Processes: What's Happening and What's Not, 56 Miami L. Rev. 949. Copyright © 2002 by the Miami Law Review. Reprinted with permission of the Miami Law Review.

_____, Ethics, Morality and Professional Responsibility in Negotiation, Dispute Resolution Ethics by Phyllis Bernard and Bryant Garth. Copyright © 2002 by the American Bar Association. Reprinted by permission.

_____, For and Against Settlement: The Uses and Abuses of the Mandatory Settlement Conference, 33 UCLA L. Rev. 485 (1985). Reprinted with permission of the author.

_____, The Lawyer's Role(s) in Deliberative Democracy, 5 Nev. L.J. 347 (2005).

_____, Mediation. Copyright © 2000 Carrie Menkel-Meadow. Reprinted with permission.

_____, Modes of Conflict Resolution (chart), from Carrie Menkel-Meadow, Introduction: From Legal Disputes to Conflict Resolution and Human Problem Solving, in Dispute Processing and Conflict Resolution. Copyright © 2003 Ashgate Publishing Limited. Reprinted with permission.

_____, Mothers and Fathers of Invention: The Intellectual Founders of ADR. Reprinted with the permission of Carrie Menkel-Meadow and the Ohio State Journal on Dispute Resolution. Originally published at 16 Ohio St. J. on Disp. Resol. 1 (2000).

_____, Peace and Justice: Notes on the Evolution and Purposes of Legal Processes, 94 Geo. L.J. 553, 555-556, 557, 576-579 (2006).

_____, Practicing "In the Interests of Justice" in the Twenty-First Century: Pursuing Peace and Justice, 70 Fordham L. Rev. 1761. Copyright © 2002. Reprinted with permission.

_____, Pursuing Settlement in an Adversary Culture: A Tale of Innovation Co-Opted or "The Law of ADR." Originally published in 19 Fla. St. U. L. Rev. 1. Copyright © 1991. Reprinted with permission.

_____, Toward Another View of Legal Negotiation: The Structure of Problem Solving, 31 UCLA L. Rev. 754 (1984). Reprinted with permission of the author.

_____, The Trouble with the Adversary System in a Postmodern, Multicultural World, 38 Wm. & Mary L. Rev. 5. Copyright © 2000 by the William and Mary Law Review. Reprinted with permission.

_____, Whose Dispute Is It Anyway? A Philosophical and Democratic Defense of Settlement (in some cases), 83 Geo. L.J. 2663 (1995). Reprinted with the permission of the publisher, Georgetown Law Journal © 1995.

Menkel-Meadow, Carrie, & Michael Wheeler, What's Fair? Ethics for Negotiators. Copyright © 2004 by Jossey-Bass, Inc. Reprinted by permission of John Wiley & Sons, Inc.

Mnookin, Robert, Strategic Barriers to Dispute Resolution: A Comparison and Bilateral and Multi-lateral Negotiations, 159 J. Institutional & Theoretical Econ. 200 (2003). Reprinted with permission.

Mnookin, Robert, & Lewis Kornhauser, Bargaining in the Shadow of the Law: The Case of Divorce, 88 Yale L.J. 950, 968-969, 978-979 (1979).

Mnookin, Robert H., Scott R. Peppet & Andrew S. Tulumello, Beyond Winning: Negotiating to Create Value in Deals and Disputes. Reprinted by permission of the publisher from Beyond Winning: Negotiating to Create Value in Deals and Disputes by Robert H. Mnookin, Scott Peppet & Andrew S. Tulumello, pp. 46-49, 75-76, 83-87, 90, Cambridge, Mass.: The Belkhap Press of Harvard University Press, Copyright © 2000 by the President and Fellows of Harvard College.

Model Standards of Conduct for Mediators: Standard 3. Conflicts of Interest.

Moffitt, Michael, Ten Ways to Get Sued, 8 Harv. Negot. L. Rev. 81 (2003). Copyright © 2003 by Harvard Negotiation Law Review. Reprinted with permission.

Moore, Christopher, Sphere of Conflict — Causes and Interventions (chart), from Christopher Moore, The Mediation Process. Copyright © 1986 by Jossey-Bass, Inc. Reprinted with permission of John Wiley & Sons, Inc.

Peppet, Scott R., Contract Formation in Imperfect Markets: Should We Use Mediators in Deals? Reprinted with the permission of Scott R. Peppet and the Ohio State Journal on Dispute Resolution. Originally published at 19 Ohio St. J. on Disp. Resol. 283 (2004).

Philbin, Donald R., Jr., The One Minute Manager Prepares for Mediation: A Multidisciplinary Approach to Negotiation Preparation, Harv. Negot. L. Rev., Spring 1999, at 281-283.

pneumonic "BADGER" from Joseph B. Stulberg & Lela P. Love, The Middle Voice: Mediating Conflict Successfully. Copyright © 2009. Used with permission of Carolina Academic Press, Durham.

Posner, Richard, The Summary Jury Trial and Other Methods of Alternative Dispute Resolution: Some Cautionary Observations, 53 U. Chi. L. Rev. 366. Copyright © 1986. Reprinted with permission.

Price, Marty, Personalizing Crime: Mediation Produces Restorative Justice for Victims and Offenders, 7 (1) Disp. Resol. Mag. 8. Copyright © 2000 by the American Bar Association. Reprinted by permission.

_____, Bargaining with the Devil without Losing Your Soul, from Bargaining for Advantage by G. Richard Shell, copyright © 1999 by G. Richard Shell. Used by permission of Viking Penguin, a division of Penguin Group (USA) Inc.

Sternlight, Jean, ADR Is Here: Preliminary Reflections on Where It Fits in a System of Justice, 3 Nev. L. Rev. 289, 291, 293, 294, 296, 299, 300, 301, 303-304 (2002/2003).

_____, Fixing the Mandatory Arbitration Problem: We Need the Arbitration Fairness Act of 2009, 16 Disp. Resol. Mag. 5 (2009).

_____, Lawyerless Dispute Resolution: Rethinking a Paradigm, 37 Fordham Urban L.J. 1-2, 11-13, 26-31 (2010).

_____, Lawyers' Representation of Clients in Mediation: Using Economics and Psychology to Structure Advocacy in a Nonadversarial Setting. Reprinted with the permission of Jean Sternlight and the Ohio State Journal on Dispute Resolution. Originally published at 14 Ohio St. J. on Dispute Resol. 269 (1999).

Sternlight, Jean R., & Jennifer Robbennolt, Good Lawyers Should Be Good Psychologists: Insights for Interviewing and Counseling Clients, 23 Ohio St. J. on Disp. Resol. 437, 437, 441-442, 538-544 (2008).

Stone, Douglas, Bruce Patton & Sheila Heen, Difficult Conversations: How to Discuss What Matters Most, copyright © 1999 by Douglas Stone, Bruce M. Patton & Sheila Heen. Used by permission of Viking Penguin, a division of Penguin Group (USA) Inc. and International Creative Management (ICM).

Stulberg, Joseph, The Theory and Practice of Mediation: A Reply to Professor Susskind, 6 Vt. L. Rev. 85 (1981). Reprinted with permission.

Stulberg, Joseph B., & Lela P. Love, The Middle Voice: Mediating Conflict Successfully. Copyright © 2009. Used with permission of Carolina Academic Press, Durham.

Sunstein, Cass, Deliberative Trouble? Why Groups Go to Extremes, 110 Yale L.J. 71, 73-78, 82-83, 85-86, 88-90, 98, 105, 106, 113, 115-116 (2000).

Susskind, Lawrence, An Alternative to Robert's Rules of Order for Groups, Organizations, and Ad Hoc Assemblies that Want to Operate by Consensus, in Lawrence Susskind, Sarah McKearnan and Jennifer Thomas-Larmer, eds., The Consensus Building Handbook, pp. 3-35, copyright (1999) by Sage Publications, Inc. Reprinted by Permission of Sage Publications, Inc.; permission conveyed via Copyright Clearance Center.

_____, Environmental Mediation and the Accountability Problem, 6 Vt. L. Rev. 1 (1981). Reprinted with permission.

Thomas, Kenneth, Conflict and Conflict Management, in Handbook of Industrial and Organizational Psychology, by Marvin D. Dunnette, ed. Reprinted with permission of the author.

Thompson, Leigh, The Mind and Heart of the Negotiator 2/e by Thompson Leigh, © 2001. Adapted by permission of Pearson Education, Inc., Upper Saddle River, NJ.

Uniform Mediation Act §§2-6.

Ury, William, Stephen Goldberg & Jeanne Brett, Getting Disputes Resolved: Designing Systems to Cut the Costs of Conflict. Copyright © 1988 by Jossey-Bass, Inc. This material is used by permission of John Wiley & Sons, Inc.

Waldman, Ellen, ed. Are There Limits to What Can Be Mediated? Problem taken from Practical Ethics for Mediators (Jossey-Bass 2010).

Watson, Lawrence, Jr., Effective Advocacy in Mediation: A Planning Guide to Prepare for a Civil Trial Mediation. Reprinted with permission of the author.

Weinstein, Janet, & Linda Morton, Stuck in a Rut: The Role of Creative Thinking in Problem Solving and Legal Education, 9 Clinical L. Rev. 835. Copyright © 2003. Reprinted with permission.

Welsh, Nancy A., Looking Down the Road Less Traveled: Challenges to Persuading the Legal Profession to Define Problems More Humanistically, 2008 J. Disp. Resol. 45, 49-54, 56-57.

_____, Remembering the Role of Justice in Resolution: Insights from Procedural and Social Justice Theories, 54 J. Legal Educ. 49, 51-53 (2004).

White, James, Machiavelli and the Bar: Ethical Limitations on Lying in Negotiation, 1980 Am. B. Found. Res. J. 926-928, 931-935. Reprinted with permission of the University of Chicago.

DISPUTE
RESOLUTION

PART I INTRODUCTION

Chapter 1 — Entering the Fields of Conflict and Dispute Resolution

The skillful management of conflicts, [is] among the highest of human skills.
— Stuart Hampshire, *Justice Is Conflict* 35 (2000)

The core mission of the legal profession is the pursuit of justice, through the resolution of conflict or the orderly and civilized righting of wrongs.
— Howard Gardner, Mihaly Csiksentmihali & William Damon,
Good Work: When Excellence and Ethics Meet 10 (2001)

Conflicts among human beings are as old as life itself. From the time we began to work and socialize with other people we have had to learn how to resolve conflicts. Using approaches ranging from negotiation to violence we have, in some eras, been more successful than in others in resolving our conflicts effectively and productively. Indeed, our degree of success in dealing with the conflicts inevitable to human interdependence is one mark of our success (or not) in achieving an advanced civilization.

In striving to deal with our differences, we often have focused on trying to establish fair processes to resolve these differences. Stuart Hampshire, the philosopher quoted above, has suggested that while we will never reach agreement about the substantive good in our culturally and politically diverse world, we can come close to achieving a human universal value by committing to "procedural fairness." Thus we have developed law, legal institutions, and other procedural mechanisms to try to regulate our conflicts or potential conflicts with one another. Both substantive law and legal processes are modes of conflict resolution. These processes include judicial, legislative, and executive entities. But it is also important to recognize that law and traditional legal institutions are not the only viable means for resolving human problems.

Because you are in law school, it probably now seems commonplace for you to think of all human problems as having a "legal" solution. Yet many problems, even when strictly legal, never go further than the lawyer's office. Instead, negotiation and drafting are used to resolve many problems, both small and complex, even when the disputes are bitterly contested. Sometimes such disputes are resolved in noncourt settings, such as employee grievance systems, internal ombuds or complaint services, with privately contracted dispute resolution professionals, or community action organizations. Even after a case has been filed with a court, the parties sometimes voluntarily choose some other means of dispute settlement or are assigned to one of the newer forms of dispute resolution you will study in this book. In addition, as both transactions and disputes increasingly transcend national boundaries, processes other than one nation's legal system may be needed to structure relationships and solve problems involving multiple parties of different legal systems. That is, the field of dispute resolution or alternative or "appropriate" dispute resolution (ADR) in law has grown out of recognition that the conventional legal systems of legislative enactments, litigation practices, trials, and court decisions are not always adequate to deal with all kinds of human problems.

This book uses the theory of "process pluralism" to explain why different kinds of matters may require different kinds of procedures or ways of dealing with the underlying conflict. If trial-by-court is an evolved form as compared to the trial-by-ordeal or trial-by-combat of medieval days, then our newer forms of dispute resolution may be thought of as an evolutionary improvement over trial-by-court. Recent empirical research has documented that, for many people, being treated fairly by being heard and acknowledged may be as important as achieving a good result or "winning" a dispute, known as the measure of "procedural justice" as distinguished from substantive justice.

Although not all disputes are legal, and not all legal disputes have to be "tried" in order to be resolved, lawyers play a key role in helping to resolve a broad array of conflicts in our society. To be effective in this role, you will need to expand your knowledge base and behavioral repertoires. That's why this book is called "beyond the adversarial model." This book presents a particular point of view that human relationships and well-being are improved by a greater number of choices about how to resolve human problems and that some choices are better than others in particular cases. Usually (though not always) the maximum participation of parties in the decisions that affect their lives should be an essential part of any choice about how decisions should be made. While adversary process has its place, modern life, with multiple parties and multiple issues present in almost every human endeavor, may not fit so easily in the casebook headings where often only one name appears on either side of the "v." Your job as a well-educated lawyer and citizen is to know about and assist others in making choices about what process is best for the particular matter at hand.

To perform well in your job of assisting with process choices, you need to *think outside of the box*, to be aware of many alternative modes of conflict resolution, and to communicate and consult well with your clients. In each chapter we will offer problems for you to solve (which, ironically, will appear *"inside the box"* to demarcate the problems from the text). Thus, this book exposes you to more varied forms of human problem solving (including negotiation, mediation, arbitration, and variants of these).

This book is organized to help you move from the simpler forms of conflict and dispute resolution to the more complex. This first chapter introduces some key concepts that describe the frameworks or theories human beings have developed to understand themselves and how they interact with each other, the history of these concepts, and the institutions and practices that have been built around them. The second chapter will introduce the key skills needed to solve problems for clients, including interviewing clients about their needs and goals, and counseling them about available processes and potential outcomes. Subsequent sections of this book then examine particular forms of dispute resolution. The focus initially is on the three foundational processes, other than litigation, that are most frequently used to resolve disputes in the United States and most parts of the world: negotiation, mediation, and arbitration. Later chapters explore the infinite possibilities of dispute resolution in our complex world. The chapter on hybrid processes shows how we can creatively combine aspects of negotiation, mediation, arbitration, and even adjudication to form other processes that may better serve the needs of disputants or society in particular situations. Next you will examine particular processes that are used to deal with multiparty disputes, conflicts arising in the transactional context, and some conflicts that cross international borders. Finally, we conclude with a few words about the future and potential of different means of dispute resolution.

As the book presents these various processes, it elaborates the *theories, frameworks, models, concepts,* and *basic premises* of a particular process; examines each process's *internal* or *institutional structures*; describes the *skills* and *practices* involved in each process; and explores the *policies, ethics,* and *issues* or *dilemmas* challenging the use of each particular process.

This book focuses on theory of process, with the hope that such a grounding will serve you in counseling clients, making and affecting policy and law, and structuring your own professional (and personal) life. In particular, the book is conceptualized to present "theories-in-use," as Donald Schön of MIT has defined that phrase in The Reflective Practitioner (1983). To practice good dispute resolution and problem solving, we need to have theories to inform our actions and assist the choices we make about what process is appropriate for a particular human problem. At the same time, our theories should be useful, so we should constantly test the assumptions on which we base our actions and correct them if they do not serve us well. In short, "theory-in-use" means we must have some reasons for what we are doing. If what we are doing cannot be understood or adequately explained, we need to refine our theories and practices.

To explore the theoretical underpinnings of process pluralism, this text looks to both law and other disciplines, drawing at times from such fields as economics, game theory, political science, psychology, sociology, anthropology, sociolegal studies, peace studies, communication, and urban planning and public policy studies.

As globalization increases our contacts with others — individuals, groups, organizations, nation-states, and cultures — we can see both the existence of other forms of conflict resolution embedded in other legal systems and cultures and the need for different forms to deal with our many human problems and interactions, in varied regional and worldwide interdependent political, economic, and legal regimes. Perhaps you will develop your own new form of dispute resolution or process for some human, social, or legal problem we have yet to confront.

A. THEORETICAL UNDERPINNINGS OF CONFLICT AND DISPUTE RESOLUTION

Although law school focuses on disputes or cases, the disputes that make it into case-books represent the tip of the iceberg of all the kinds of conflicts that people have. Lawyers are often called on not only to bring or defend lawsuits, but also to help prevent conflicts from arising or to deal with disputes other than in court. Thus it is useful for lawyers to have a broad understanding of the types of conflicts that may exist. Scholars in a wide variety of the social sciences have attempted to define and develop taxonomies of different kinds of conflicts so as to better understand the different possible treatments or interventions available in conflict settings. At the same time, it is important to realize that not all conflict is bad or ought to be avoided. Carrie Menkel-Meadow briefly explores these multiple aspects of conflict.

 Carrie Menkel-Meadow, **CONFLICT THEORY**

in Encyclopedia of Community: From the Village to the Virtual World
323-326 (Karen Christensen & David Levinson eds., 2003)

There are many reasons for conflicts to develop, at both the individual and at the group level. Some conflicts are based on belief systems or principles, some are based on personality differences, and others on conflicts about material goods or personal or group status or reputation. Because there are so many different reasons conflicts develop and because much conflict is dangerous and unproductive, the theory of conflict attempts to understand the different sources of conflict, the dynamics of how conflict develops, escalates or declines, and how conflict can be managed, reduced or resolved.

At the same time, it must be recognized that conflict can have social utility as well. Many important changes in human society, many for the betterment of human life, have come from hard-fought conflicts that resulted in the change of human institutions, relationships or ideas. The United States Civil War, for example, was a bloody and painful war in which over a million Americans died, but this war eliminated slavery in the United States and ushered in a long period of change in race relations. . . . Even small interpersonal conflicts (like between a husband and wife or parent and child) can lead to important changes, not only in relationships between the people in conflict, but in larger social movements, such as the women's rights or feminist movement and the children's rights movement. Conflicts with outsiders often clarify and reinforce commitments and norms of one's own group. And internal conflict within the individual can lead to changed views and intellectual and emotional growth.

Conflict theory tries to explain the types of conflicts that exist and whether they are productive or destructive and then goes on to attempt to explain the ways in which conflict proceeds or is structured . . . and how it can be managed or resolved.

A conflict can be experienced as a simple disagreement, a feeling of discomfort or opposition, and a perception of difference from others, or a competition or incompatibility with others. Conflicts, then, can be perceptual, emotional or behavioral. When a conflict is actually acted on it becomes a dispute with someone or a group of others. In order for a conflict to fully develop into a dispute we have to experience some sense of wrong to ourselves, someone else to "blame" for that wrong and some way to take action against those we think caused our difficulty — what one set of scholars have called, "naming, blaming and claiming."[1] How the conflict turns into a dispute and how it is labeled ("framing") then may affect how it progresses and how it may either escalate and get worse, leading in extreme cases to war, or how it can be handled, managed or resolved.

TYPES OF CONFLICTS

Conflict can exist on many different levels, including the intrapersonal, interpersonal, intragroup, intergroup, and international. Conflicts can exist about different subject matters — ideational or beliefs, values, materiel and resources, emotions, roles and responsibilities. Conflicts vary in terms of the social contexts in which they are located (two old friends, family members, neighbors, strangers, consumers and merchants, distant nation-states) and in the time span in which they are located ("one-off" or "one-shot" encounters and conflicts, long-standing or "embedded" conflicts, temporary or "repeated" conflicts in on-going relationships like families and employment settings). Conflicts vary, even within the same social environment or subject matter by how the disputants treat the conflict, in the strategies, tactics and behaviors they employ (avoidance, self-help, peaceful negotiation, argument, escalation, physical violence, peace seeking, mediation or settlement) and how the strategies chosen interact with each other. And conflicts are often classified by how they affect the parties in the conflict (the consequences of the conflict) and those outside of the conflict (the "externalities" of the conflict, like children in a marital argument or divorce and neighbors of warring states who accept refugees). . . .

Conflicts have also been classified by various social scientists and conflict theorists by virtue of what is at stake in the conflict such as:

> *Resources* (land, power, property, natural resources like water, oil, minerals, money);
> *Values or beliefs* (class, religious, nationality, political aspirations and codes that create systemic belief systems for groups or individual members);
> *Preferences or interests* (incompatible desires, wants or objectives of action);
> *Relationship* (differences in desires or objectives about relationships);
> *Identity* (concerns about recognition of and respect for group memberships).

The theory of such classifications is that if we can analyze different kinds of conflict, we can determine how they might enfold and whether a particular conflict is amenable to a positive outcome (whether harnessing the conflict to constructive

---

1. William L. F. Felstiner, Richard Abel & Austin Sarat, The Emergence and Transformation of Disputes: Naming, Blaming and Claiming . . . , 15 L. & Socy. Rev. 631-654 (1980-1981).

solutions or processes) or whether it is likely to become destructive (for the parties or others affected by the parties). . . .

Conflicts often take somewhat predictable turns ranging from precipitating event, response or reaction, development of in-group-out-group loyalties and the development of both offensive and defensive strategies, followed by escalation, impasse or stalemate and then, motivation for resolution, settlement, and solution seeking (or, in highly competitive or violent conflicts, victory or "annihilation" of the other). But while many think of conflicts as necessarily competitive and antagonistic, there really are a wider range of behaviors that occur in most conflict situations, many of them dependent on the situation and social and political environment of the conflict, as well as the sophistication of the parties in using multiple strategies.

Many of those who study conflict see a greater variety of possible conflict modes or strategies in handling conflict that can occur at individual, group, organizational, and even nation-state levels of actions. There are those who *compete* (or seek to maximize their own self-interest, even at the expense of others), those who *cooperate* (seeking to work with the other side(s) to find some middle or compromise grounds), those who *accommodate* (who may simply give in to the other party), those who *avoid* (by exiting or absenting themselves from the conflict) and those who *collaborate* (by seeking to work for joint and mutual gains for all parties, without unnecessary harm to others or needless compromise or giving in).[2]

What makes conflict processes so complex are the strategic interactions that occur when more than one party must interact to start, maintain, interrupt or resolve the conflict. These different conflict management strategies interact with each other and can produce reactive and unproductive responses, such as when competing leads to more competing and escalation of competitive behavior causes more violence, less information sharing and an inability to seek mutual gain possibilities. This "mirroring" effect, when each party merely returns the behavior that is offered to it, often leads to stalemates or the impossibility of achieving some resolution because the parties cannot even see or hear beyond the one strategy they have chosen.

Thus, much recent empirical work in conflict processes has been to study the conditions under which parties in conflict can alter their behavioral or strategy choices and open themselves up to new ways of communicating or testing the possibilities with other parties. Conflicts have been studied at the level of community relations, ethnic-racial conflicts, economic and resource competition, environmental disputes, lawsuits (both individual and class actions) and international conflicts. Parties in conflict are now asked to explore their underlying interests (apart from their conflict-producing "positions"), to consider the needs and interests of other parties ("role-reversals" and other communication technologies) and to develop strategies of collaborative and creative problem solving (by expanding and creating resources and alternatives, by trading non-mutually exclusive preferences or goods, by using contingent or "trial" agreements, rather

---

2. K. Thomas, Conflict and Conflict Management, in Handbook of Industrial Organizational Psychology (M. D. Dunnette ed., 1976).

than permanent solutions, by developing processes and rules for respectful co-existence, such as in Truth and Reconciliation Commissions in politically divided nations).

Both modern research and recent history have demonstrated the importance of third party interveners (mediators, conciliators, fact-finders and facilitators) who can effectively manage processes. These third party efforts have been effective at interpersonal (divorce and family), organizational (labor-management), and international (Northern Ireland, Mid-east) levels of conflict in developing both interim "cease-fires" and more permanent resolutions or agreements to end conflicts and to attempt to resolve larger and underlying problems and conflicts.

Problem 1-1.   *What Are the Conflicts?*

Look through a case reporter or one of your casebooks, or do a random search on a computer service, and choose a reported case. What dispute brought the parties to litigation? What underlying conflicts existed between the parties or between other people involved in or affected by the dispute? Where do these conflicts fit in the list provided by Menkel-Meadow describing what is at stake?

Now, read a newspaper or magazine and find a conflict that is reported. How might the disputants (or possibly attorneys) have avoided such a conflict in advance? Do you think that the conflict you identified has positive or negative aspects, or both? What are they?

Conflicts will always exist. While we may prevent and avoid some, clearly we will never succeed in eliminating all of them. The remainder of this section examines how to deal with conflicts that already exist.

In focusing on conflict, it is critically important to examine what it means to "win" in a conflict. While many people assume that someone must lose when another person wins, the following readings show that this either-or mentality is often fallacious. Thomas Schelling, a Harvard economist and Nobel prize winner, examines the nature of conflict from a game theoretic perspective. He explains that while a person who approaches conflict strategically always tries to "win" in the sense of doing as well as possible for herself, that does not mean that other disputants need to lose. The next excerpt is taken from the work of Mary Parker Follett who was an important early theorist in the field of conflict resolution. She was trained as a political scientist and worked as a social worker, as well as working in labor-management relations, administrative "science," and business management. Follett urges that conflict can lead to a creative process that allows constructive solutions to come from the friction created by conflict. Yet the win-lose attitude toward conflict has permeated our culture in general, and our concept of the legal system in particular. Popular writer and professor of linguistics, Deborah Tannen, critiques the adversarial mindset of our society, arguing that it limits the possibilities of better alternatives and also makes for an uncomfortable civil society. Finally, Carrie Menkel-Meadow outlines some of the problems that arise when the legal system is envisioned in purely binary win-lose terms.

Thomas C. Schelling, THE STRATEGY OF CONFLICT

3-5 (1960)

Among diverse theories of conflict — corresponding to the diverse meanings of the word "conflict" — a main dividing line is between those that treat conflict as a pathological state and seek its causes and treatment, and those that take conflict for granted and study the behavior associated with it. Among the latter there is a further division between those that examine the participants in a conflict in all their complexity — with regard to both "rational" and "irrational" behavior, conscious and unconscious, and to motivations as well as to calculations — and those that focus on the more rational, conscious, artful kind of behavior. Crudely speaking, the latter treat conflict as a kind of contest, in which the participants are trying to "win." A study of conscious, intelligent, sophisticated conflict behavior — of successful behavior is like a search for rules of "correct" behavior in a contest-winning sense. We can call this field of study the *strategy* of conflict. . . .

But, in taking conflict for granted, and working with an image of participants who try to "win," a strategy does not deny that there are common as well as con-flicting interests among the participants. . . . Pure conflict, in which interests of two antagonists are completely opposed is a special case. . . . For this reason, "winning" in a conflict does not have a strictly competitive meaning; it is not winning relative to one's adversary. It means gaining relative to one's own value system; and this may be done by bargaining, by mutual accommodation and by the avoidance of mutually damaging behavior.

   Mary Parker Follett, CONSTRUCTIVE CONFLICT

in Prophet of Management: A Celebration of Writings from the 1920's
67-69, 75, 77, 79, 82, 84-86 (Pauline Graham ed., 1995)

As conflict — difference — is here in the world, as we cannot avoid it, we should, I think, use it. Instead of condemning it, we should set it to work for us. Why not? What does the mechanical engineer do with friction? Of course, his chief job is to eliminate friction, but it is true that he also capitalizes friction. The transmission of power by belts depends on friction between the belt and the pulley. . . . The music of the violin we get by friction. . . . We talk of the friction of the mind on mind as a good thing. So in business too, we have to know when to try to eliminate friction and when to try to capitalize it, when to see what work we can make it do. That is what I wish to consider here, whether we can set conflict to work and make it *do* something for us.

There are three main ways of dealing with conflict: domination, compromise and integration. Domination, obviously, is a victory of one side over the other. This is the easiest way of dealing with conflict, the easiest for the moment but not usually successful in the long run. . . .

The second way of dealing with conflict, that of compromise, we understand well, for it is the way we settle most of our controversies; each side gives up a little in order to have peace, or, to speak more accurately, in order that the activity which has been interrupted by the conflict can go on. . . .

Yet no one really wants to compromise, because that means a giving up of something. Is there any other method of ending conflict? There is a way now beginning to be recognized at least, and even occasionally followed: when two desires are *integrated*, that means that a solution has been found in which both desires have found a place, that neither side has to sacrifice anything. Let us take some very simple illustration. In the Harvard Library one day, in one of the smaller rooms, someone wanted the window open, I wanted it shut. We opened the window in the next room, where no one was sitting. This was not a compromise because there was no curtailing of desire; we both got what we really wanted. For I did not want a closed room, I simply did not want the north wind to blow directly on me; likewise the other occupant did not want that particular window open, he merely wanted more air in the room. . . .

[T]he revaluing of interests on both sides may lead the interests to fit into each other, so that all find some place in the final solution. . . . If the first step is to uncover the real conflict, the next is to take the demands of both sides and break them up into their constituent parts. . . . On the other hand, one often has to do just the opposite; find the whole demand, the real demand, which is being obscured by miscellaneous minor claims or by ineffective presentation. . . .

Finally, let us consider the chief *obstacles to integration*. It requires a high order of intelligence, keen perception and discrimination, more than that, a brilliant *inventiveness*. . . . Another obstacle to integration is that our way of life has habituated many of us to enjoy domination. Integration seems a tamer affair, it leaves no "thrills" of conquest. . . . Finally, perhaps the greatest of all obstacles to integration is our lack of training for it. In our college debates we try always to beat the other side. . . .

I should like to emphasize our responsibility for integration. . . . One test of business administration should be: is the organization such that both employers and employees, or co-managers, co-directors, are stimulated to a reciprocal activity which will give more than mere adjustment, more than equilibrium? Our outlook is narrowed, our activity restricted, our chances of business success largely diminished when our thinking is constrained within the limits of what has been called an "either-or" situation. We should never allow ourselves to be bullied by an "either-or." There is always the possibility of something better than either of two given alternatives.

 Deborah Tannen, **THE ARGUMENT CULTURE: MOVING FROM DEBATE TO DIALOGUE**

3-4, 8, 10 (1998)

The argument culture urges us to approach the world — and the people in it — in an adversarial frame of mind. It rests on the assumption that opposition is the best way to get anything done: The best way to discuss an idea is to set up a debate; the best way to cover news is to find spokespeople who express the most extreme, polarized views and present them as "both sides"; the best way to settle disputes is litigation that pits one party against the other; the best way to begin an essay is to attack someone and the best way to show you're really thinking is to criticize. . . .

In a word the type of opposition I am questioning is what I call "agonism." I use this term, which derives from the Greek word for "contest," *agonia*, to mean an automatic war-like stance — not the literal fighting against an attacker or the unavoidable opposition that arises organically in response to conflicting ideas or actions. An agonistic response, to me, is a kind of programmed contentiousness — a prepatterned, unthinking use of fighting to accomplish goals that do not necessarily require it. . . .

Our determination to pursue truth by setting up a fight between two sides leads us to believe that every issue has two sides — no more, no less: If both sides are given a forum to confront each other, all the relevant information will emerge and the best case will be made for each side. But opposition does not lead to truth when an issue is not composed of two opposing sides but is a crystal of many sides. Often the truth is in the complex middle, not the oversimplified extremes.

 Carrie Menkel-Meadow, **THE TROUBLE WITH THE ADVERSARY SYSTEM IN A POSTMODERN, MULTICULTURAL WORLD**

38 Wm. & Mary L. Rev. 5, 6-10 (1996)

Binary, oppositional presentations of facts in dispute are not the best way for us to learn the truth; polarized debate distorts the truth, leaves out important information, simplifies complexity and often obfuscates rather than clarifies. More significantly, some matters — mostly civil, but occasionally even criminal, cases — are not susceptible to a binary (i.e., right/wrong, win/lose) conclusion or solution. The inability to reach a binary resolution of these disputes may result because in some cases we cannot determine the facts with any degree of accuracy. In other cases the law may be conflicting, though legitimate, legal rights giving some entitlement to both, or all, parties. And, in yet another category of cases, human or emotional equities cannot be sharply divided.

Modern life presents us with complex problems, often requiring complex and multifaceted solutions. Courts, with what I have called their "limited remedial imaginations," may not be the best institutional settings for resolving some of the disputes that we continue to put before them.

Even if some form of the adversary system was defensible in particular settings for purposes of adjudication, the "adversary" model employed in the courtroom has bled inappropriately into and infected other aspects of lawyering, including negotiation carried on both in the "shadow of the court" and outside of it in transactional work. . . .

Furthermore, the complexities of both modern life and modern lawsuits have shown us that disputes often have more than two sides in the sense that legal disputes and transactions involve many more than two parties. Procedures and forms like interpleader, joinder, consolidation, and class actions have attempted to allow for more than just plaintiffs' and defendants' voices to be heard, all the while structuring the discourse so that parties must ultimately align themselves on one side of the adversarial line or the other. Multiparty, multiplex lawsuits or disputes may be distorted when only two sides are possible. Consider all of the multiparty and complex policy issues that courts contend with in environmental clean-up and siting, labor disputes in the public sector, consumer actions, antitrust actions, mass torts, school financing and desegregation and other civil rights issues, to name a few examples.

Finally, scholars have criticized modern adversarialism for the ways it teaches people to act toward each other.

Problem 1-2.   *What Do You Do about Conflict?*

For the next 24 hours, keep a list of all the conflicts, disputes, or disagreements in which you get (or could get) involved. What did you do? Argue, compromise, accommodate (give in), get your way, avoid, or "integrate"? How? Why?

Problem 1-3.   *Framing Conflicts and Solutions*

Problem 1-1 asked you to examine a series of reported cases and consider what underlying conflicts brought the parties to litigation. Now consider the following with respect to these cases:

    a. Who were the "real parties in interest," whether they were named in the reported case or not? Who else might be affected by a judicial resolution or settlement of the matter at issue?

    b. How were the issues framed? In terms of perceived wrongs and rights? Legal entitlements? Were there any instances of cases where not all the wrongs or rights existed on one side?

    c. Consider what solutions, other than those ordered by the court, might have resolved the conflict among all interested parties.

B. FRAMEWORKS FOR HANDLING CONFLICTS AND DISPUTES

Now that you have briefly examined the nature of conflict and some nonadversarial approaches to conflict resolution, we consider how disputants, lawyers, or others should choose the most appropriate process for resolving a particular dispute. In other words, as William Felstiner, Richard Abel, and Austin Sarat explain, once a "perceived injurious experience" (PIE) (or a potential conflict) with someone else occurs, the next question is what to do about that perception.[3] In the background, of course, are social processes and psychological factors that lead us to identify an "experience" as "injurious" or not, and that leads us to blame someone other than ourselves for what has happened. But, taking as given a body of PIEs, one can, in any social or legal culture, create a pyramid of possible ways in which such disputes are handled. The size and shape of the pyramid differs from culture to culture or legal system to legal system, but no system treats all conflicts the same; most have developed hierarchical systems for dealing with conflicts and disputes. In our U.S. legal system and culture, for example, despite all the claims that we are so litigious,[4] most people avoid dealing with every little conflict they have. Imagine what your day would be like if you decided to file a lawsuit about everything that made you feel wronged.

Figure 1-1 shows our current U.S. legal system (which has been changing dramatically in the last few decades); at the top of the pyramid are those important disputes that go all the way to the Supreme Court and culminate in a reported decisional precedent. Note that most of your legal education has been about reading the reported cases from the top of the pyramid. From a social scientific perspective, this may be a very unrepresentative sample of the actual disputes or conflicts that people have since the vast percentage of PIEs are resolved outside of courtrooms, whether through the choice not to pursue the claim, settlements, or third-party assisted processes such as mediation or arbitration.

The pyramid of dispute resolution is not a "given" in any society, but rather the result of choices made by policy makers and individuals in that society. Policy makers decide which dispute resolution mechanisms should be made available for which kinds of disputes, and choose whether and how to fund or subsidize particular dispute resolution tools. Disputants and their attorneys then make choices about how to approach a particular dispute, given the options provided in the society.

How should societies or individuals approach the question of what processes are most useful for resolving particular kinds of disputes? To use the phrase coined by major negotiation theorist (and mathematician and decision scientist), Howard Raiffa,[5] there is both a science and an art to conflict resolution, problem solving, and decision making. The science involves understanding and analyzing the nature of the problem in these categories:

1. Who are the parties? (And who speaks for them — principals, agents? Are they unified or divided?)
2. What issues do they have with each other (scarce or divisible resources, building or maintaining a relationship)?
3. How many parties? (Two? More than two? With or without representatives?)
4. How many issues are there?

---

3. Felstiner et al., *supra* note 1, at 631.
4. Marc S. Galanter, Reading the Landscape of Disputes: What We Know and Don't Know (and Think We Know) About Our Allegedly Contentious and Litigious Society, 31 UCLA L. Rev. 4-71 (1983).
5. Howard Raiffa, Negotiation Analysis: The Science and Art of Collaborative Decision Making (2002) (with John Richardson and David Metcalf).

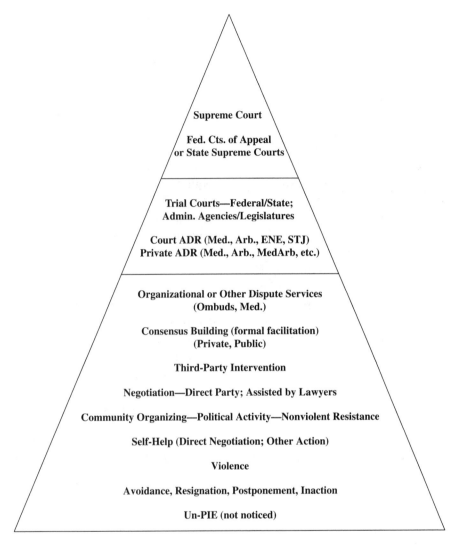

Figure 1-1
U.S. Legal System

5. How do the issues affect each other (intertwined, "linked" and dependent, or severable and independent)?

6. How do the parties "interact" with each other (long-term relationship, "one-off or one shot")?

7. What kind of a "solution" do the parties require (a precedent; a fast, temporary, or permanent decision; a contingent agreement; a modifiable agreement; a public announcement; a private arrangement)?

8. Can the parties solve their own problems, or do they need help (either to assist in the seeking of a solution (process) or to fund or create the substantive solution ("external" resources))? Do they share norms, rules, or a culture to resolve the conflict, or do they need to look outside or create their own rules and norms of process or substance or both?

9. What are the "stakes" for the parties? (How seriously do they need to resolve the problem or conflict? Who stands to gain or lose what and how much?)

Only once a problem has been analyzed for these (and possibly other) factors, can one consider which process might best effectuate the needs and interests of the parties to achieve their goals. (Of course, this becomes quite complicated when the parties don't agree on what their goals are or if they seek different things from the conflict before them.)

But the analysis does not stop there. The choice of a process itself shapes the outcomes. For example, the choice of an adjudicative process (litigation or binding arbitration) that results in a definitive ruling requires adversarial presentations and a win-lose result. The behaviors necessitated by such a process (presentation of evidence, witnesses, and arguments) reinforce the adversarial and competitive nature of the problem. Adversarial behaviors produce more conflict, making the likelihood greater that the parties will produce a "competitive" or "zero" or "negative-sum" result. Similarly, if the parties choose negotiation but use adversarial and competitive techniques (such as debate, argument, persuasion, and more extremely, lying, deception, threat, and intimidation), rather than a problem-solving approach, they may wind up either in a total loss or a stalemate (or at best, a coerced "compromise" or accommodation). Choosing a more "cooperative process" (explained in Chapters 3 and 4) can result in more joint gain, but it also presents the risks of being taken advantage of when one party openly reveals information, for example, and the other party "uses" this information against the other. Thus behaviors and processes cannot be chosen for themselves; they must be related to the analysis of what the problem looks like and what goals and outcomes are possible. You can also see that choices about process or behavior are "strategic" in the sense that they are necessarily affected by what the other parties do.

As individuals and policy makers choose appropriate dispute resolution processes, they must also consider the multiple ways in which people express themselves. One might call this "the art" of linking choice about process to particular behaviors so as to enhance the likelihood that desired goals and outcomes are achieved. Even in the traditional legal system and governmental institutions that you have studied in other courses, multiple "modes of discourse" are used. Political scientist Jon Elster,[6] for example, differentiates appeals to reason, argument, and principle (most familiar in law) from appeals to utilities, preferences, trading, and bargaining (which may be based on "wants," "needs," or "interests" but need not be "principled"). Added to this mix, other theorists suggest that claims of "passion," including not only emotion but also religious, moral, and political beliefs, form yet a third mode of discourse that is presented in conflict situations. Jürgen Habermas,[7] an important social philosopher of the twentieth century, has spent his lifetime exploring the requirements for "ideal speech conditions" under which citizens could come together to achieve legitimate decisions about their

---

6. Jon Elster, Strategic Uses of Argument in Barriers to Conflict Resolution (Kenneth Arrow et al. eds., 1995).
7. Jürgen Habermas, A Theory of Communicative Action (1984).

joint lives, even where they don't share substantive values. But even Habermas "privileges" reason and persuasion as the most appropriate mode of discourse for proper political problem solving. What if others disagree and think that arguments based on passion are just as valid? Conflict resolution professionals and political activists seeking to enact "legitimate" processes in the real world (such as in bitterly contested disputes about environmental justice, affirmative action, abortion, taxes, and welfare policy) have had to confront these issues of different "modes of discourse" in a wide variety of settings.[8] Are some processes better than others at generating both innovative and acceptable "solutions" to difficult conflicts? Where do our ideas about problem solving come from?

As you begin to think about which kinds of dispute resolution processes are best for resolving which kinds of disputes, or for engaging which kinds of "modes of discourse," it is appropriate to highlight the work of Lon Fuller. A legal scholar, philosopher, practitioner of law, and professor at Harvard Law School for many years, Fuller is considered by many the intellectual father of the jurisprudence of ADR. He wrote a series of articles on each of several different legal processes, including adjudication, arbitration, mediation, contracting, and legislation, in which he discussed the special moralities and structures of each of these separate processes. Fuller also wrote more broadly about other processes, such as elections and administration, and called this entire project "eumonics" — the study of good social arrangements. Because Fuller saw each process as unique, he was very uncomfortable with some of the combinations of processes that are common today. (These are discussed at length in Chapter 12, where we return to the question of whether such combinations are a good idea jurisprudentially and ethically.)

 Carrie Menkel-Meadow, **MOTHERS AND FATHERS OF INVENTION: THE INTELLECTUAL FOUNDERS OF ADR**

16 Ohio St. J. on Disp. Resol. 1, 15-21 (2000)

For Fuller, law was a "problem solving activity" purposively directed towards enabling voluntary transactions and contracts, preventing violence, defining ideals and standards for civic participation, as well as providing a means for settling disputes and preserving social harmony. Law was enacted in and enforced by a variety of different legal institutions, which is why some commentators refer to him as concerned, above all else, with "problems of institutional design," or as an "architect of social structure." Fuller saw that lawmaking and rulemaking occurred in the realms of private ordering — negotiating contracts and mediating solutions produced as much "law" as the public institutions of courts and legislatures. In his efforts to elaborate the different structures, functions, and moralities of different legal processes, Fuller wrote the first description of, and most sustained argument for, mediation. He said that this conciliatory process, which did not require a decision of state-made law, would "reorient the parties to each other" and "brin[g] about a more harmonious relationship between the parties, whether this be

8. See, e.g., Amy Gutmann & Dennis Thompson, Democracy and Disagreement (1996).

achieved through explicit agreement, through a reciprocal acceptance of 'social norms' relevant to their relationship or simply because the parties have been helped to a new and more perceptive understanding of one another's problems." For Fuller, as for other theorists of mediation, its principal functional strength lay in its release of the parties "from the encumbrances of rules and of accepting, instead, a relationship of mutual respect, trust and understanding that will enable them to meet shared contingencies without the aid of formal prescriptions laid down in advance." Mediation, in Fuller's words, is for "the administration and enforcement of rules or social norms" between parties, not for the creation of state-made law. . . .

For Fuller, each process of decision making, or as he preferred to say, "problem solving," had its own logic, morality, and function. Fuller acknowledged that not all legal disputes or social problems were similarly structured. Where a problem was like a "spider web" in which unraveling one thread of a "polycentric" problem (such as deciding a single legal issue in a web of relationships such as occurred in a factory among labor and management or in a marriage) might destroy the whole web, mediation, with its ability to work on many issues at the same time and focus the parties on their relationship concerns, would be better. . . .

Fuller's work is still best known for seeking to elucidate the particular moralities of particular process modalities. Fuller's strength as a theorist of process is that he fully elaborated the structures and functions and the "internal" moralities of each of the legal processes he studied. He gave us what probably still is the deepest and most "classic" statement of what mediation is. However, perhaps because he was somewhat encumbered by the structuralist-functionalist schools of both social science and the legal process school of jurisprudence of the 1950s and 1960s, structure and function were seldom rearranged or allowed to "mix" in his work on social ordering. Today's "hybrid" processes combine the structures of negotiation, mediation, and arbitration to attempt to perform a wide variety of functions, from relationship reorientation to dispute settlement to conflict resolution to administrative rulemaking and public policy decision making. It would be fascinating to see what Lon Fuller would make of these more flexible procedural institutions as the modern world of social ordering develops increasing complexity and reorganizes structures to meet the requirements of different functions. . . . Fuller's questions about process integrity and morality, as well as structural-functionalism, remain with us today.

 Lon L. Fuller, **THE FORMS AND LIMITS OF ADJUDICATION**

> **in The Principles of Social Order: Selected Essays of Lon L. Fuller**
> **105-106, 108-109, 113, 126-128, 133 (Kenneth I. Winston ed., rev. ed., 2001)**

It is customary to think of adjudication as a means of settling disputes or controversies. . . . More fundamentally, however, adjudication should be viewed as a form of social ordering, as a way in which the relations of men to one another are governed and regulated. . . . If . . . we start with the notion of a process of decision in which the affected party's participation consists of an opportunity to present proofs and reasoned arguments, the office of the judge or arbitrator and the requirement of impartiality follow as necessary implications. . . . Adjudication is, then, a device which gives formal and institutional expression to the influence of reasoned argument in human affairs. As such it assumes a burden of rationality not borne by other forms of social ordering. A decision which is the product of reasoned argument must be prepared itself to meet the test of reason. We demand of an adjudicative decision a kind of rationality that we do not expect of the results of contract or of voting. . . . The proper province of adjudication is to make authoritative determination of questions raised by claims of right and accusations of guilt. . . .

What kinds of tasks are inherently unsuited to adjudication? This . . . introduces a concept — that of the "polycentric" task. . . .

Some months ago a wealthy lady by the name of Timken died in New York leaving a valuable, but somewhat miscellaneous, collection of paintings to the Metropolitan Museum and the National Gallery "in equal shares," her will indicating no particular apportionment. When the will was probated the judge remarked something to the effect that the parties seemed to be confronted with a real problem. The attorney for one of the museums spoke up and said, "We are good friends. We will work it out somehow or other." What makes this problem of effecting an equal division of the paintings a polycentric task? It lies in the fact that the disposition of any single painting has implications for the proper disposition of every other painting. If it gets the Renoir, the Gallery may be less eager for the Cezanne but all the more eager for the Bellows, etc. If the proper apportionment were set for argument, there would be no clear issue to which either side could direct its proofs and contentions. Any judge assigned to hear such an argument would be tempted to assume the role of mediator or to adopt the classical solution: Let the older brother (here the Metropolitan) divide the estate into what he regards as equal shares, let the younger brother (the National Gallery) take his pick. . . .

We may visualize this kind of situation by thinking of a spider web. A pull on one strand will distribute tensions after a complicated pattern throughout the web as a whole. Doubling the original pull will, in all likelihood, not simply double each of the resulting tensions but will rather create a different complicated pattern of tensions. This would certainly occur, for example, if the double pull caused one or more of the weaker strands to snap. This is a polycentric situation because it is many centered — each crossing of strands is a distinct center for distributing tensions. . . . We are dealing with a situation of interacting points of influence and therefore with a polycentric problem beyond the proper limits of adjudication. . . . It may be said that problems in the allocation of economic resources present too strong a polycentric aspect to be suitable for adjudication. . . . When an attempt is made to deal by adjudicative forms with a problem that is essentially polycentric, what happens? . . . First, the adjudicative solution may fail. . . . Second, the purported arbiter ignores judicial proprieties — he "tries out" various solutions in posthearing conferences, consults parties not represented in the hearings, guesses at facts not proved and not properly matters for anything like judicial notice. Third, instead of accommodating his procedures to the nature of the problem he confronts, he may reformulate the problem so as to make it amenable to solution through adjudicative procedures.

One important theoretical question raised by students of conflict processes is the extent to which approaches to conflict resolution do or should cross cultural, temporal, or national lines. Do all humans have the same needs with respect to dispute resolution, or do different types of cultures and societies call for different dispute resolution processes? Social scientists such as anthropologists, historians, and sociologists have generally shed more light on this question than have legal scholars.

 Martin Shapiro, COURTS: A COMPARATIVE AND POLITICAL ANALYSIS

1-6, 9, 15-16 (1981)

Cutting across cultural lines, it appears that whenever two persons come into a conflict that they cannot themselves solve, one solution appealing to common sense is to call upon a third for assistance in achieving a resolution. So universal across time and space is this simple invention of triads that we can discover almost no society that fails to employ it. . . . [T]he triad for purposes of conflict resolution is the basic social logic of courts, a logic so compelling that courts have become a universal political phenomenon. The triad, however, involves a basic instability, paradox or dialectic that accounts for a large proportion of the scholarly quarrels over the nature of courts and the political difficulties that courts encounter in the real world. At the moment the two disputants find their third, the social logic of the court device is preeminent. A moment later when the third decides in favor of one of the two disputants, a shift occurs from the triad to a structure that is perceived by the loser as two against one. . . .

The most fundamental device for maintaining the triad is consent. . . . The almost universal reluctance of courts to proceed in the absence of one of the two parties is less a testimony to the appeal of adversary processes than it is a remnant of this emphasis on consent, of both parties choosing the triad as the appropriate device for conflict resolution. . . . Nearly every triadic conflict resolver adds another device to consent to avoid the breakdown into two against one. This device is the avoidance of the dichotomous, imposed solution. In examining triadic conflict resolution as a universal phenomenon, we discover that the judge of European or Anglo-American courts, determining that the legal right lies with one and against the other of the parties, is not an appropriate central type against which deviance can be conveniently measured. Instead, he lies at one end of a continuum. The continuum runs: go-between, mediator, arbitrator, judge. And placement on the continuum is determined by the intersection of the devices of consent and nondichotomous, or mediate, solution. . . . The key distinction between the mediator and arbitrator is that the arbitrator is expected to fashion his own resolution to the conflict rather than simply assisting the parties in shaping one of their own. . . . As societies become more complex, they tend to substitute law for the particular consent of the parties to a particular norm for their particular dispute. They also substitute office for their free choice of a particular third man to aid in resolution of their disputes. . . .

It would not be difficult to move about the world's legal systems endlessly multiplying the examples of the intermingling of mediation and judging. . . . In Western societies as well, firms that must maintain continuous relationships are not prone to litigation. . . . In short, if one were to review all societies, or even to confine oneself to modern industrial and commercial states where one would most expect to find the prototypic court, one discovers that legal processes are not necessarily or even entirely court processes, if we confine our definition to the prototype. For we frequently find intermediate rather than dichotomous resolutions. . . . A substantial share of the legal conflicts in most societies is resolved not by dichotomous but mediate decision, either rendered by a court itself or under the shadow of potential court proceedings. Much of what courts do is not adversarial in the sense of encouraging or requiring disputations between the two conflicting parties. It is enough that both parties present their views to one another with an option of going to a third. The style of interchange may be cooperative, benevolent, or even familial rather than one of ritualized trial by battle. Moreover, where courts preserve a more or less mediatory style, they may subtly mix preexisting legal rules with rules that emerge from the interaction of the parties. To the extent that there are preexisting rules, they may be ones created by the parties themselves in a contract. After the final settlement, less may depend on those rules than on a newly emerging agreement or understanding or set of subrules that is suggested or elicited in the very process of settling the dispute.

Problem 1-4.   *Choosing an Appropriate Process*

What kind of dispute process do you think would be appropriate for each of the following conflicts?

    a. Disagreement between the president and U.S. Congress over the federal budget;

    b. A grade dispute between you and your professor;

    c. A car accident between strangers involving only property damage;

    d. A parent-child dispute about going to school;

    e. A dispute between a fired high-tech employee and her former employer, when she takes the company source code with her, claiming she developed it and it is hers;

    f. Whether and how much the federal government should pay victims of terrorism against the United States.

C. INSTITUTIONS OF CONFLICT AND DISPUTE RESOLUTION

Now that you have examined theories of conflict and of dispute resolution processes, you are ready to examine the institutions that our society and others have used to resolve disputes. In thinking about such processes as litigation, arbitration, mediation, negotiation, and the many other processes we discuss in the pages that follow, you may find it useful to consider where each process falls on a variety of continua including the following:

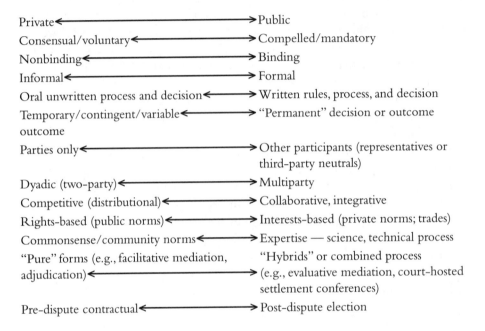

Private ⟷ Public
Consensual/voluntary ⟷ Compelled/mandatory
Nonbinding ⟷ Binding
Informal ⟷ Formal
Oral unwritten process and decision ⟷ Written rules, process, and decision
Temporary/contingent/variable outcome ⟷ "Permanent" decision or outcome
Parties only ⟷ Other participants (representatives or third-party neutrals)
Dyadic (two-party) ⟷ Multiparty
Competitive (distributional) ⟷ Collaborative, integrative
Rights-based (public norms) ⟷ Interests-based (private norms; trades)
Commonsense/community norms ⟷ Expertise — science, technical process
"Pure" forms (e.g., facilitative mediation, adjudication) ⟷ "Hybrids" or combined process (e.g., evaluative mediation, court-hosted settlement conferences)
Pre-dispute contractual ⟷ Post-dispute election

As societies or parties develop and choose different forms of conflict resolution, whether through laws or private contract, some of these forms become "institutionalized" and therefore formalized. Both public agencies (courts, administrative agencies, and even legislatures) and private organizations (such as the American Arbitration Association (AAA), the International Center for Conflict Prevention and Resolution (CPR), and the Judicial Arbitration and Mediation Services (JAMS)) offer (or in some cases require) particular forms of dispute resolution from a dispute resolution "menu." Thus whether through public or private action, it seems inevitable that dispute resolution processes become institutionalized, or some say "co-opted."[9] Consider the pros and cons of institutionalization as you study ADR.

---

9. Carrie Menkel-Meadow, Pursuing Settlement in an Adversary Culture: A Tale of Innovation Co-opted or the Law of ADR, 19 Fla. St. U. L. Rev. 1 (1991) (suggesting that processes that were intended to create flexibility now offer complex systems of rules, process, and decision).

Although most of your law school courses have focused until now on litigation, historically U.S. legal practice included a variety of dispute institutions, beginning in pre-colonial times. Some of the root values of modern dispute resolution ideology in the U.S. are found in early colonial "communitarianism." Early forms of mediation and arbitration generally were typically limited to culturally or religiously homogenous groups that presumedly shared values and goals. Many of these communities had different processes for resolving disputes with persons outside of the community and sometimes these were non-litigation processes as well. For example, the merchants of early America used commercial arbitration to resolve their disputes with one another.[10]

Modern dispute resolution in the United States began in the mid-1970s, as a host of complaints were leveled at the traditional legal system. These complaints can be divided into two categories: *efficiency* or "*quantitatively*" based arguments (that the legal system was overloaded, slow, inefficient and often prohibitively expensive); and more "*qualitatively*" based arguments (that litigation outcomes were inadequate to solve social, human, and legal problems and that the processes failed to permit parties to fully participate). Thus attempts to develop new forms of dispute resolution in the legal system emphasized speed, low cost, increased party participation, simplification of procedures, and more tailored and creative solutions. As new forms of dispute resolution were developed both outside of the formal legal system and eventually within the formal justice system itself, older forms of dispute resolution were also "rediscovered" and readapted for new uses (community mediation, industry specific arbitration). Together, these efforts eventually led to the development of new professions including mediators, arbitrators, early neutral evaluators, and facilitators.[11]

The "modern dispute resolution movement" is often formally dated to the 1976 Pound Conference on the Causes of Popular Dissatisfaction with the Administration of Justice, at which Professor Frank Sander of Harvard Law School delivered an address on the "Varieties of Dispute Processing." This speech was so influential that a number of court systems received funding to develop the "Multi-Door Courthouse" to attempt to enact Professor Sander's ideas and make them a functional reality.

---

10. Jerold Auerbach, Justice Without Law? Resolving Disputes Without Lawyers (1983).
11. See, e.g., Carrie Menkel-Meadow, The Lawyer as Consensus-Builder: Ethics for a New Practice, 70 Tenn. L. Rev. 63 (2002); Id., The Lawyer as Problem Solver and Third Party Neutral: Creativity and Non-Partisanship in Lawyering, 72 Temple L. Rev. 785 (1999).

Frank E. A. Sander, VARIETIES OF DISPUTE
PROCESSING

70 F.R.D. 79, 111-118, 120, 124-132 (1976)

[A] . . . way of reducing the judicial caseload is to explore alternative ways of resolving disputes outside the courts, and it is to this topic that I wish to devote my primary attention. By and large we lawyers and law teachers have been far too single-minded when it comes to dispute resolution. Of course, as pointed out earlier, good lawyers have always tried to prevent disputes from coming about, but when that was not possible, we have tended to assume that the courts are the natural and obvious dispute resolvers. In point of fact there is a rich variety of different processes, which, I would submit, singly or in combination, may provide far more "effective" conflict resolution.

Let me turn now to the two questions with which I wish to concern myself:

1. What are the significant characteristics of various alternative dispute resolution mechanisms (such as adjudication by courts, arbitration, mediation, negotiation, and various blends of these and other devices)?
2. How can these characteristics be utilized so that, given the variety of disputes that presently arise, we can begin to develop some rational criteria for allocating various types of disputes to different dispute resolution processes?

One consequence of an answer to these questions is that we will have a better sense of what cases ought to be left in the courts for resolution, and which should be "processed" in some other way. But since this inquiry essentially addresses itself to developing the most effective method of handling disputes it should be noted in passing that one by-product may be not only to divert some matters now handled by the courts into other processes but also that it will make available those processes for grievances that are presently not being aired at all. We know very little about why some individuals complain and others do not, or about the social and psychological costs of remaining silent. It is important to realize, however, that by establishing new dispute resolution mechanisms, or improving existing ones, we may be encouraging the ventilation of grievances that are now being suppressed. Whether that will be good (in terms of supplying a constructive outlet for suppressed anger and frustration) or whether it will simply waste scarce societal resources (by validating grievances that might otherwise have remained dormant) we do not know. The important thing to note is that there is a clear trade-off: the price of an improved scheme of dispute processing may well be a vast increase in the number of disputes being processed.

THE RANGE OF AVAILABLE ALTERNATIVES

There seems to be little doubt that we are increasingly making greater and greater demands on the courts to resolve disputes that used to be handled by other institutions of society. Much as the police have been looked to to "solve" racial, school and neighborly disputes, so, too, the courts have been expected to fill the void created by the decline of church and family. Not only has there been a waning of traditional dispute resolution mechanisms, but with the complexity of modern society, many new potential sources of controversy have emerged as a result of the immense growth of government at all levels, and the rising expectations that have been created.

Quite obviously, the courts cannot continue to respond effectively to these accelerating demands. It becomes essential therefore to examine other alternatives.

The chart reproduced [in Figure 1-2] attempts to depict a spectrum of some of the available processes arranged on a scale of decreasing external involvement.

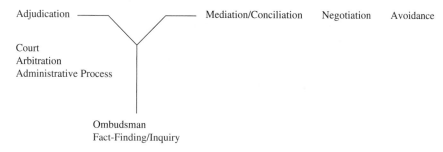

Figure 1-2
(Process Flow Chart)

At the extreme left is adjudication, the one process that so instinctively comes to the legal mind that I suspect if we asked a random group of law students how a particular dispute might be resolved, they would invariably say "file a complaint in the appropriate court." Professor Lon Fuller, one of the few scholars who has devoted attention to an analysis of the adjudicatory process, has defined adjudication as "a social process of decision which assures to the affected party a particular form of participation, that of presenting proofs and arguments for a decision in his favor." Although he places primary emphasis on process, I would like for present purposes to stress a number of other aspects — the use of a third party with coercive power, the usually "win or lose" nature of the decision, and the tendency of the decision to focus narrowly on the underlying relationship between the parties. Although mediation or conciliation also involves the use of a third party facilitation (and is distinguished in that regard from pure negotiation), a mediator or conciliator usually has no coercive power and the process in which he engages also differs from adjudication in the other two respects mentioned. Professor Fuller puts this point well when he refers to the "central quality of mediation, namely, its capacity to reorient the parties toward each other, not by imposing rules on them, but by helping them to achieve a new and shared perception of their relationship, a perception that will redirect their attitudes and disposition toward one another."

Of course quite a variety of procedures fit under the label of adjudication. Aside from the familiar judicial model, there is arbitration, and the administrative process. Even within any one of these, there are significant variations. Obviously there are substantial differences between the Small Claims Court and the Supreme Court. Within arbitration, too, although the version used in labor relations is generally very similar to a judicial proceeding in that there is a written opinion and an attempt to rationalize the result by reference to general principles, in some forms of commercial arbitration the judgment resembles a Solomonic pronouncement and written opinions are often not utilized. Another significant variant is whether the parties have any choice in selecting the adjudicator, as they typically do in arbitration. Usually a decision rendered by a person in whose selection the parties have played some part will, all things being equal, be less subject to later criticism by the parties.

There are important distinctions, too, concerning the way in which the case came to arbitration. There may be a statute (as in New York and Pennsylvania) requiring certain types of cases to be initially submitted to arbitration (so-called compulsory arbitration). More commonly arbitration is stipulated as the exclusive dispute resolution mechanism in a contract entered into by the parties (as is true of the typical collective bargaining agreement and some modern medical care agreements). In this situation the substantive legal rules are usually also set forth in the parties' agreement, thus giving the parties control not only over the process and the adjudicator but also over the governing principles.

As is noted on the chart, if we focus on the indicated distinctions between adjudication and mediation, there are a number of familiar hybrid processes. An inquiry, for example, in many respects resembles the typical adjudication, but the inquiring officer (or fact finder as he is sometimes called) normally has no coercive power; indeed, according to Professor Fuller's definition, many inquiries would not be adjudication at all since the parties have no right to any agreed-upon form of presentation and participation.

But a fact finding proceeding may be a potent tool for inducing settlement. Particularly if the fact finder commands the respect of the parties, his independent appraisal of their respective positions will often be difficult to reject. This is especially true of the Ombudsman who normally derives his power solely from the force of his position. These considerations have particular applicability where there is a disparity of bargaining power between the disputants (e.g., citizen and government, consumer and manufacturer, student and university). Although there may often be a reluctance in these situations to give a third person power to render a binding decision, the weaker party may often accomplish the same result through the use of a skilled fact finder.

There are of course a number of other dispute resolution mechanisms which one might consider. Most of these (e.g., voting, coin tossing, self-help) are not of central concern here because of their limited utility or acceptability. But one other mechanism deserves brief mention. Professor William Felstiner recently pointed out that in a "technologically complex rich society" avoidance becomes an increasingly common form of handling controversy. He describes avoidance as "withdrawal from or contraction of the dispute-producing relationship" (e.g., a child leaving home, a tenant moving to another apartment, or a businessman terminating a commercial relationship). He contends that such conduct is far more tolerable in modern society than in a "technologically simple poor society" because in the former setting the disputing individuals are far less interdependent. But, as was pointed out in a cogent response by Professors Danzig and Lowy, there are heavy personal and societal costs for such a method of handling conflicts, and this strongly argues for the development of some effective alternative mechanism. Moreover, even if we disregarded altogether the disputes that are presently being handled by avoidance — clearly an undesirable approach for the reasons indicated — we must still come to grips with the rising number of cases that do presently come to court and see whether more effective ways of resolving some of these disputes can be developed. . . .

CRITERIA

Let us now look at some criteria that may help us to determine how particular types of disputes might best be resolved.

1. Nature of Dispute

Lon Fuller has written at some length about "polycentric" problems that are not well suited to an adjudicatory approach since they are not amenable to an all-or-nothing solution. He cites the example of a testator who leaves a collection of paintings in equal parts to two museums. Obviously here a negotiated or mediated solution that seeks to accommodate the desires of the two museums is far better than any externally imposed solution. Similar considerations may apply to other allocational tasks where no clear guidelines are provided.

At the other extreme is a highly repetitive and routinized task involving application of established principles to a large number of individual cases. Here adjudication may be appropriate, but in a form more efficient than litigation (e.g., an administrative agency). Particularly once the courts have established the basic principles in such areas, a speedier and less cumbersome procedure than litigation should be utilized.

2. Relationship Between Disputants

A different situation is presented when disputes arise between individuals who are in a long-term relationship than is the case with respect to an isolated dispute. In the former situation, there is more potential for having the parties, at least initially, seek to work out their own solution, for such a solution is likely to be far more acceptable (and hence durable). Thus negotiation, or if necessary, mediation, appears to be a preferable approach in the first instance. Another advantage of such an approach is that it facilitates a probing of conflicts in the underlying relationship, rather than simply dealing with each surface symptom as an isolated event.

3. Amount in Dispute

Although, generally speaking, we have acted to date in a fairly hit-or-miss fashion in determining what problems should be resolved by a particular dispute resolution mechanism, amount in controversy has been an item consistently looked to to determine the amount of process that is "due." The Small Claims Court movement has taken as its premise that small cases are simple cases and that therefore a pared-down judicial procedure was what was called for. Next to the juvenile court, there has probably been no legal institution that was more ballyhooed as a great legal innovation. Yet the evidence now seems overwhelming that the Small Claims Court has failed its original purpose; that the individuals for whom it was designed have turned out to be its victims. Small wonder when one considers the lack of rational connection between amount in controversy and appropriate process. Quite obviously a small case may be complex, just as a large case may be simple. The need, according to a persuasive recent study, is for a preliminary investigative-conciliational stage (which could well be administered by a lay individual or paraprofessional) with ultimate recourse to the court. This individual could readily screen out those cases which need not take a court's time (e.g., where there is no dispute about liability but the defendant has no funds), and preserve the adjudicatory process for those cases where the issues have been properly joined and there is a genuine dispute of fact or law. Obviously such a screening mechanism is not limited in its utility to the Small Claims Court.

4. Cost

There is a dearth of reliable data comparing the costs of different dispute resolution processes. Undoubtedly this is due in part to the difficulty of determining what are the appropriate ingredients of such a computation. It may be relatively easy to determine the costs of an ad hoc arbitration (though even there one must deal with such intangibles as the costs connected with the selection of the arbitrator(s)). But determining the comparable cost of a court proceeding would appear to pose very difficult issues of cost accounting. Even more difficult to calculate are the intangible "costs" of inadequate (in the sense of incomplete and unsatisfactory) dispute resolution. Still, until better data become available one can probably proceed safely on the assumption that costs rise as procedural formalities increase.

The lack of adequate cost data is particularly unfortunate with respect to essentially comparable processes, such as litigation and arbitration. Assuming for the moment that arbitration would produce results as acceptable as litigation — a premise that is even more difficult to verify — would cost considerations justify the transfer (at least in the first instance) of entire categories of civil litigation to arbitration, as has been done in some jurisdictions for cases involving less than a set amount of money? One difficulty in this connection is that we have always considered access to the courts as an essential right of citizenship for which no significant charge should be imposed, while the parties generally bear the cost of arbitration. Thus although I believe, on the basis of my own arbitration experience, that process is, by and large, as effective as and cheaper than litigation, lawyers tend not to make extensive use of it (outside of special areas such as labor and commercial law), in part because it is always cheaper for the clients to have society rather than the litigants pay the judges. Perhaps if arbitration is to be made compulsory in certain types of cases because we believe it to be more efficient, then it should follow that society should assume the costs, unless that would defeat the goal of using costs to discourage appeals. . . .

5. Speed

The deficiency of sophisticated data concerning the costs of different dispute resolution processes also extends to the factor of speed. Although it is generally assumed — rightly, I believe — that arbitration is speedier than litigation, I am not aware of any studies that have reached such a conclusion on the basis of a controlled experiment that seeks to take account of such factors as the possibly differing complexity of the two classes of cases, the greater diversity of "judges" in the arbitration group, and the possibly greater cooperation of the litigants in the arbitration setting.

What I am thus advocating is a flexible and diverse panoply of dispute resolution processes, with particular types of cases being assigned to differing processes (or combinations of processes), according to some of the criteria previously mentioned. Conceivably such allocation might be accomplished for a particular class of cases at the outset by the legislature; that in effect is what was done by the Massachusetts legislature for malpractice cases. Alternatively one might envision by the year 2000 not simply a court house but a Dispute Resolution Center, where the grievant would first be channeled through a screening clerk who would then direct him to the process (or sequence of processes) most appropriate to his type of case. The room directory in the lobby of such a Center might look as follows:

Screening Clerk	Room 1
Mediation	Room 2
Arbitration	Room 3
Fact Finding	Room 4
Malpractice Screening Panel	Room 5
Superior Court	Room 6
Ombudsman	Room 7

Of one thing we can be certain: once such an eclectic method of dispute resolution is accepted there will be ample opportunity for everyone to play a part. Thus a court might decide of its own to refer a certain type of problem to a more suitable tribunal. Or a legislature might, in framing certain substantive rights, build in an appropriate dispute resolution process. Institutions such as prisons, schools, or mental hospitals also could get into the act by establishing indigenous dispute resolution processes. Here the grievance mechanism contained in the typical collective bargaining agreement stands as an enduring example of a successful model. Finally, once these patterns begin to take hold, the law schools, too, should shift from their preoccupation with the judicial process and begin to expose students to the broad range of dispute resolution processes.

Problem 1-5.   *Beyond the Multi-Door Courthouse*

Can you think of any process, other than those described by Sander above that might be useful for litigants generally? For particular classes of litigants? Can you think of any other function that a "screening clerk" should perform?

Now that you have had some exposure to the animating theories and history implicated in the use of various forms of dispute resolution, we look at the different forms these processes can take and where they can be used. The following excerpt offers a glossary of basic dispute resolution processes. We will study them all in greater detail in the chapters that follow.

 ## CENTER FOR PUBLIC RESOURCES, THE ABC'S OF ADR: A DISPUTE RESOLUTION GLOSSARY

13 (11) Alternatives (to the High Cost of Litigation) 1 (1995)

Experts know that ADR encompasses a wide range of practices for managing and quickly resolving disputes at modest cost and with minimal adverse impact on commercial relationships. These processes, marked by confidentiality when desired, significantly broaden dispute resolution options beyond litigation or traditional unassisted negotiation.

Some ADR procedures, such as binding arbitration and private judging, are similar to expedited litigation in that they involve a third-party decision-maker with authority to impose a resolution if the parties so desire. Other procedures, such as mediation and the minitrial, are collaborative: a neutral third party helps a group of individuals or entities with divergent views to reach a goal or complete a task to their mutual satisfaction.

Arbitration, mediation and the minitrial tend to be the mechanisms most often used and, for many people, are synonymous with the term, "ADR." But to respond to specific needs, parties often craft hybrid procedures that combine elements of one or more dispute resolution methods.

The following glossary is designed to help parties communicate about this rapidly changing field. Definitions are not standardized, but flexible and creative like ADR itself. And with all aspects of ADR it is most important not that the parties use exactly the same term, but that they understand each other.

We have divided the glossary into private and court-related ADR processes.

PRIVATE ADR PROCESSES

Arbitration   The most traditional form of private dispute resolution. It can be "administered" (managed) by a variety of private organizations, or "non-administered" and managed solely by the parties. It can be entered into by agreement at the time of the dispute, or prescribed in pre-dispute clauses contained in the parties' underlying business agreement. Arbitration can take any of the following forms:

Binding Arbitration   A private adversarial process in which the disputing parties choose a neutral person or a panel of three neutrals to hear their dispute and to render a final and binding decision or award. The process is less formal than litigation; the parties can craft their own procedures and determine if any formal rules of evidence will apply. Unless there has been fraud or some other defect in the arbitration procedure, binding arbitration awards typically are enforceable by courts and not subject to appellate review.

Non-Binding Arbitration   This process works the same way as binding arbitration except that the neutral's decision is advisory only. The parties may agree in advance to use the advisory decision as a tool in resolving their dispute through negotiation or other means.

"Baseball or Final-Offer" Arbitration   In this process, used increasingly in commercial disputes, each party submits a proposed monetary award to the arbitrator. At the conclusion of the hearing, the arbitrator chooses one award without modification. This approach imposes limits on the arbitrator's discretion and gives each party an incentive to offer a reasonable proposal in the hope that it will be accepted by the decision-maker. . . .

"Bounded" or "High-Low" Arbitration   The parties agree privately without informing the arbitrator that the arbitrator's final award will be adjusted to a bounded range. Example: P wants $200,000. D is willing to pay $70,000. Their high-low agreement would provide that if the award is below $70,000, D will pay at least $70,000; if the award exceeds $200,000, the payment will be reduced to $200,000. If the award is within the range the parties are bound by the figure in the award. . . .

Fact-Finding   A process by which the facts relevant to a controversy are determined. Fact-finding is a component of other ADR procedures and may take a number of forms.

In *neutral fact-finding,* the parties appoint a neutral third party to perform the function and typically determine in advance whether the results of the fact-finding will be conclusive or advisory only.

With *expert fact-finding,* the parties privately employ neutrals to render expert opinions that are conclusive or non-binding on technical, scientific or legal questions. In the latter, a former judge is often employed.

Federal Rules of Evidence 706 gives courts the option of appointing *neutral expert fact-finders.* And while the procedure was rarely used in the past, courts increasingly find it an effective approach in cases that require special technical expertise, such as disputes over high-technology questions. The neutral expert can be called as a witness subject to cross-examination.

In *joint fact-finding,* the parties designate representatives to work together to develop responses to factual questions.

Mediation   A voluntary and informal process in which the disputing parties select a neutral third-party to assist them in reaching a negotiated settlement. Parties can employ mediation as a result of a contract provision by private agreement made when disputes arise, or as part of a court-annexed program that diverts cases to mediation. Unlike a judge or arbitrator, a mediator has no power to impose a solution on the parties. Rather, mediators assist parties in shaping solutions to meet their interests and objectives. The mediator's role and the mediation process can take various forms, depending on the nature of the dispute and the approach of the mediator. The mediator can assist parties to communicate effectively; can identify and narrow issues; crystallize each side's underlying interests and concerns; carry messages between the parties; explore bases for agreement and the consequences of not settling; and develop a cooperative problem-solving approach. By learning the confidential concerns and positions of all parties, the mediator often can identify options beyond their perceptions. The process is sometimes referred to as "facilitation" to structure participation in the mediation process, or "conciliation" in the international arena.

The mediator's role can take various forms. Some mediators, who favor a "facilitative" style, encourage parties to generate their own settlement options, and will not suggest settlement terms. At the other end of the spectrum are "evaluative" mediators, who will propose settlement options and try to persuade parties to make concessions.

To guide negotiations in major commercial disputes, parties sometimes ask the mediator to assume an evaluative role. The mediator might assess the merits of claims or defenses, liability or damages, or predict the likely outcome of the case in court. Generally, mediators need substantive law background or expertise to make sound assessments.

Med-Arb   A short-hand reference to the procedure mediation-arbitration. In med-arb, the parties agree to mediate with the understanding that any issues not settled through the mediation will be resolved by arbitration asking the same mediator to act both as mediator and arbitrator. However, that choice may have a chilling effect on full participation in the mediation portion. A party might not believe that the arbitrator will be able to discount unfavorable information learned in mediation when making the arbitration decision. . . .

Minitrial   A structured process with two distinct components. Parties engage in an information exchange that provides an opportunity to hear the strengths and weaknesses of one's own case as well as the cases of the other parties involved, before negotiating the matter.

In the minitrial, an attorney for each party presents an abbreviated version of that side's case. The case is heard not by a judge, but by high-level business representatives from both sides with full settlement authority. It may be presided over by these representatives with or without a neutral advisor, who can regulate the information exchange. Following the presentations, the parties' representatives meet, with or without the neutral, to negotiate settlement. Frequently, the neutral will serve as a mediator during the negotiation phase or be asked to offer an advisory opinion on the potential court outcome, to guide negotiators. . . .

Multi-Step ADR   Parties may agree, either when a specific dispute arises, or earlier in a contract clause between business venturers, to engage in a progressive series of dispute resolution procedures. One step typically is some form of negotiation, preferably face-to-face between the parties. If unsuccessful, a second tier of negotiation between higher levels of executives may resolve the matter. The next step may be mediation or another facilitated settlement effort. If no resolution has been reached at any of the earlier stages, the agreement can provide for a binding resolution — through arbitration, private adjudication, or litigation.

One form of multi-step ADR is the *wise man* procedure, typically used when problems arise in long-term partnerships such as those in the oil and gas industry. Sometimes called "progressive negotiation" or "mutual escalation," this procedure refers matters first to a partnership committee which oversees the day-to-day operations of the project. If the problem cannot be resolved at that level, the wise-man option — the next ADR step — is employed.

The wise men (or women) are respected senior executives of each company who are uninvolved in the project. These officials are given a fairly short time frame (sometimes just 30 days) to investigate the dispute. If that fails, the matter goes to a third step, usually binding arbitration. While pioneered in the oil industry, the wise man approach could also be useful in the high-technology field and other areas involving close and continuing business relationships.

Negotiated Rule-Making   Also known as regulatory negotiation, this ADR method is an alternative to the traditional approach of U.S. government agencies to issue regulations after a lengthy notice and comment period. In reg-neg, as it is called, agency officials and affected private parties meet under the guidance of a neutral facilitator to engage in joint negotiation and drafting of the rule. The public is then asked to comment on the resulting, proposed rule. By encouraging participation by interested stakeholders, the process makes use of private parties' perspectives and expertise, and can help avoid subsequent litigation over the resulting rule.

Ombudsperson   An organizational dispute resolution tool. The ombudsperson is appointed by an institution to investigate complaints within the institution and either prevent disputes or facilitate their resolution. The ombudsperson may use various ADR mechanisms such as fact-finding or mediation in the process of resolving disputes brought to his or her attention.

Partnering   Typically used as a dispute-prevention method for large construction projects, this method is capable of being transposed in other settings, particularly in joint ventures. Before the work starts, parties to the project generally assemble for a several-day retreat away from their organizations. With the help of a third-party neutral, they get to know each other, discuss some of the likely rough spots in the project and even settle on a process to resolve misunderstandings and disputes as the project progresses.

Pre-Dispute ADR Contract Clause   A clause included in the parties' business agreement to specify a method for resolving disputes that may arise under that agreement. It may refer to one or more ADR techniques, even naming the third party that will serve as an arbitrator or mediator in the case. Pre-dispute agreements requiring arbitration of consumer disputes, or entered into as a condition of employment, have generated substantial backlash lately from people who argue that these clauses are adhesion contracts.

Two-Track Approach   Involves use of ADR processes or traditional settlement negotiations in conjunction with litigation. Representatives of the disputing parties who are not involved in the litigation are used to conduct the settlement negotiations or ADR procedure. The negotiation or ADR efforts may proceed concurrently with litigation or during an agreed-upon cessation of litigation. This approach is particularly useful in cases when it may not be feasible to abandon litigation while the parties explore settlement possibilities; or as a practical matter, the specter of litigation must be present in order for the opposing party to consider or agree to an alternative mechanism. It also is useful when the litigation has become acrimonious or when a suggestion of settlement would be construed as a sign of weakness.

COURT ADR PROCESSES

Court-Annexed Mediation   In mediation, a neutral third party — the mediator — facilitates negotiations among the parties to help them settle. The mediation session is confidential and informal. Disputants clarify their understanding of underlying interests and concerns, probe the strengths and weaknesses of legal positions, explore the consequences of not settling, and generate settlement options. . . . A hallmark of mediation is its capacity to help parties expand traditional settlement discussions and broaden resolution options, often by going beyond the legal issues in controversy.

Mediation works much the same in courts and in private settings, with a few important differences. A court mediation program may be based in the court, or may involve referral by the court to outside ADR programs run by bar associations, nonprofit groups, other local courts, or private ADR providers. Some courts require litigants to use mediation in what are known as mandatory mediation programs. The purpose of the mediation session is unchanged whether litigants enter the program voluntarily, or by court mandate. The court mediator may be a lawyer trained in mediation and compensated by the parties, or serve as a volunteer. Judges, magistrate judges, or court ADR professionals also serve as mediators in some court programs. . . .

Early Neutral Evaluation   Like mediation, ENE is applicable to many types of civil cases, including complex disputes. In ENE, a neutral evaluator — a private attorney expert in the substance of the dispute — holds a several hour confidential session with parties and counsel early in the litigation to hear both sides of the case. Afterwards, the evaluator identifies strengths and weaknesses of the parties' positions, flags areas of agreement and disputes, and issues a non-binding assessment of the merits of the case. . . .

Originally designed to make both case management and settlement more efficient, ENE has evolved into a pure settlement device in some courts. Used this way, ENE resembles evaluative mediation, in which the mediator uses case evaluation as a settlement tool.

Court-Annexed Arbitration   An adjudicatory dispute resolution process in which one or more arbitrators issue a non-binding judgment on the merits, after an expedited, adversarial hearing. The arbitrator's decision addresses only the disputed legal issues and applies legal standards. Either party may reject the non-binding ruling and proceed to trial.

Court-annexed arbitration is used mainly in small- and moderate-sized tort and contract cases when litigation costs are often disproportionate to the amounts at stake. . . . Once the premier court ADR process, it has lost popularity in recent years. Most court ADR development focuses on mediation.

Summary Jury Trial   The summary jury trial is a non-binding ADR process used to promote settlement in ready cases headed for protracted jury trials. Usually, a judge or magistrate judge presides over the SJT; occasionally, a neutral attorney conducts the process. Part or all of a complex dispute may be submitted to a summary jury trial. After an abbreviated hearing in which counsel presents evidence in summary form, the jury renders a verdict. Non-binding, it becomes the basis for subsequent settlement negotiations. If the parties do not reach a settlement, the case proceeds to trial. Because they are costly, SJTs are used relatively rarely. Typically, the SJT is reserved for large cases when settlement efforts have failed and litigants differ significantly about jury outcome.

Appellate ADR   Mediation programs have become increasingly popular among the nation's appeals courts. . . .[12]

In most programs, staff attorneys or outside lawyers conduct mandatory, pre-argument conferences in those cases that seem most likely to settle. Some appellate programs are geared exclusively toward settlement, while other programs also address case management and procedural issues.

Judge-Hosted Settlement Conferences   The most common form of ADR used in federal and state courts is the settlement conference presided over by a judge or magistrate judge. Almost all of the 94 federal district courts use judicial settlement conferences routinely, and now, one third of the courts assign this role almost exclusively to magistrate judges.

The classic role of the settlement judge is to articulate judgments about the merits of the case and to facilitate the trading of settlement offers. Some settlement judges and magistrate judges also use mediation techniques and the settlement conference to improve communication among the parties, probe barriers to settlement, and assist in formulating resolutions. In some courts, a special judge or magistrate judge is designated as settlement judge. In others, the assigned judge (or another judicial officer who will not hear the case) hosts settlement conferences at various points during the litigation, often directly before trial.

Court Minitrial   The minitrial is a flexible, non-binding settlement process primarily used out of court. During the past decade, some federal district judges

---

12. [All of the federal circuit courts of appeals now have appellate mediation programs, almost all of them using full-time staff mediators. — EDS.]

have used their own version of the minitrial. Like the summary jury trial the court minitrial is a relatively elaborate ADR method generally reserved for large disputes.

In a typical court minitrial, each side presents a shortened form of its best case to settlement-authorized client representatives — usually senior executives. The hearing is informal, with no witnesses and a relaxation of the rules of evidence and procedure. A judge, magistrate judge or non-judicial neutral presides over the one- or two-day hearing. Following the hearing, the client representatives meet, with or without the neutral advisor, to negotiate a settlement. At the parties' request, the neutral advisor may assist the settlement discussions by acting as a facilitator or by issuing an advisory opinion. If the talks fail, the parties proceed to trial.

Multidoor Courthouse or Multi-option ADR   This term describes courts that offer an array of dispute resolution options or screen cases and then channel them to particular ADR methods. Some multidoor courthouses refer all cases of certain types to particular ADR programs, while others offer litigants a menu of options in each case. Multidoor courthouses have been established in state courts in New Jersey, Texas, Massachusetts, and the District of Columbia. On the federal level, courts in the Western District of Missouri, the Northern District of California, the District of Rhode Island, and others now have multi-option ADR.

Settlement Week   In a typical settlement week, a court suspends normal trial activity and, aided by bar groups and volunteer lawyers, devotes itself to the mediation of long-pending civil cases. Mediation is the mainstay ADR method in a typical settlement week. . . .

Private Judging   Private judging is a general term used to describe a private or court-related process in which disputing parties empower a private individual to hear and decide their case. The procedure may be exclusively a matter of contract between the parties or may be undertaken in connection with an authorizing statute. When authorized by statute, the process is sometimes referred to by the colloquial term, "Rent-a-Judge."

The remainder of this book examines these and other processes in detail. But it is important to emphasize from the outset that no list of dispute resolution processes is ever complete. Creative disputants and their attorneys will always think of new processes and new variations on existing processes. At the same time, it is also important to remember that parties may not have a "choice" about what process is best for them. Increasingly courts or legislatures may require them to use a particular form of dispute resolution. It is also possible that legislatures or courts may proscribe the use of certain dispute resolution procedures in particular contexts.

There are obviously many jurisprudential, policy, and practical issues to be explored here from the perspective of both future policy makers and future attorneys. Thus the final section of this introduction turns to some fundamental questions regarding where these alternative procedural approaches fit in a system of justice.

D. ANIMATING VALUES FOR CONFLICT AND DISPUTE RESOLUTION: OF PEACE AND JUSTICE

As you have now seen, many arguments, claims, and justifications can be made for the use of a wide variety of dispute processes in addition to litigation. At the same time, it is important to consider critiques. Social and legal change do not come easily. While the various procedural developments documented or urged by Professor Sander have occurred, criticisms of the new forms of dispute resolution have also emerged. The critics challenged the "informalism," "de-legalization," "coercion," "privatization," and perceived unfairness of some of these new process innovations. You will explore these critiques more fully throughout this book, but below we present several of the classic critiques, including Owen Fiss' Against Settlement (1983). Although more flexible processes and more tailored solutions can seem to be more fair or just to particular disputants, critics claim that privatization of dispute resolution robs us of the ability to frame precedents from more public cases and thereby serve broader justice needs.

The tensions between formal legal systems and the alternatives to them likely will continue since each type of system serves different but important goals.[13] Indeed, the debate between formal and informal procedures can be analogized to the age-old debate in jurisprudence about the relative value of clear, but often, rigid "rules" versus the need for more tailored and nuanced judgment and legal "discretion." Some, including the authors of this book, are comfortable with this "creative" tension between formal and informal systems, believing that new developments in the alternatives, responsive to critiques of the formal legal system, may result in reforms in the formal justice system as well. Indeed, some have suggested that from a market perspective, the development of alternatives to the formal legal system provides an opportunity for "competition" in the provision of dispute resolution services.[14] Others, however, are more fearful that growth of informal processes will lead to a degradation of traditional legal structures and processes.[15] This debate can be seen as another version of the "Fullerian" question as to whether it is important to preserve as sacrosanct the moral integrity of particular processes. This debate also implicates one of the major issues of conflict and dispute resolution: For whom is the dispute process intended? The parties in conflict? Or the larger society that may desire public pronouncements of norms and enforcement of legal "peace"? Carrie Menkel-Meadow and David Luban debate this issue below.

---

13. Jean R. Sternlight, ADR is Here: Preliminary Reflections on Where it Fits in a System of Justice, 3 Nevada L. J. 289 (2003).

14. Bryant Garth, Privatization and the New Market for Disputes: A Framework for Analysis and a Preliminary Assessment, 12 Stud. L. Poly. & Socy. 367 (1992).

15. Deborah R. Hensler, Suppose It's Not True: Challenging Mediation Ideology, 2002 J. Disp. Resol. 81; Judith Resnik, Managerial Judges, 96 Harv. L. Rev. 76 (1982); Judith Resnik, Many Doors? Closing Doors? Alternative Dispute Resolution and Adjudication, 10 Ohio St. J. on Disp. Resol. 211 (1995).

Carrie Menkel-Meadow, WHOSE DISPUTE IS IT ANYWAY?
A PHILOSOPHICAL AND DEMOCRATIC DEFENSE OF
SETTLEMENT (IN SOME CASES)

83 Geo. L.J. 2663-2665, 2669-2670 (1995)

In the last decade or so, a polarized debate about how disputes should be resolved
has demonstrated to me once again the difficulties of simplistic and adversarial
arguments. . . . David Luban and Jules Coleman, among other philosophers, have
criticized the moral value of the compromises that are thought to constitute legal
settlements. On the other side, vigorous proponents of alternative dispute resolution,
including negotiation, mediation, arbitration and various hybrids of these forms of
preadjudication settlement, criticize the economic and emotional waste of adversarial processes and the cost, inefficiency, and political difficulties of adjudication, as
well as its draconian unfairness in some cases. . . . For me, the question is not "for
or against" settlement (since settlement has become the "norm" for our system),
but *when, how and under what circumstances* should cases be settled? When do our legal
system, our citizenry, and the parties in particular disputes need formal adjudication, and when are their respective interests served by settlement, *whether public or
private?* . . .

    Those who criticize settlement suffer from what I have called, in other contexts,
"litigation romanticism," with empirically unverified assumptions about what courts
can and will do. More important, those who privilege adjudication focus almost
exclusively on structural and institutional values and often give short shrift to those
who are actually involved in the litigation. I fear, but I am not sure, that this debate
can be reduced to those who care more about the people actually engaged in disputes versus those who care more about institutional and structural arrangements. I
prefer to think that we need both adjudication and settlement. . . . Settlement can
be justified on its own moral grounds — there are important values, consistent with
the fundamental values of our legal and political systems that support the legitimacy
of settlements of some, if not most, legal disputes. These values include consent,
participation, empowerment, dignity, respect, empathy and emotional catharsis,
privacy, efficiency, quality solutions, equity, access and, yes, even justice.

    Though some have argued that compromise itself can be morally justified,
I . . . argue here as well that compromise is not always necessary for settlement
and that in fact, some settlements, by not requiring compromise, may produce better
solutions than litigation. . . .

    To summarize, it seems to me that the key questions implicated in the ongoing
debate about settlement vs. adjudication are:

1. In a party-initiated legal system, when is it legitimate for the parties to settle
   their disputes themselves, or with what assistance from a court in which they
   have sought some legal-system support or service?
2. When is "consent" to settlement legitimate and "real," and by what standards
   should we (courts and academic critics) judge and permit such consent?
3. When, in a party-initiated legal system, should party consent be "trumped"
   by some other values — in other words, when should public, institutional,

and structural needs and values override parties' desire to settle or courts' incentives to promote settlement?

In short, when is the need for "public adjudication . . . or public settlement" more important (to whom?) than what the parties may themselves desire?

 David Luban, **SETTLEMENT AND THE EROSION OF THE PUBLIC REALM**

83 Geo. L.J. 2619, 2634-2635 (1995)

On the public-life conception, by contrast, the values realized in laws are a kind of public morality — objective spirit — and even ostensibly private disputes between apolitical citizens may have a public dimension engaging these values. Because the law is the visible residue of public action . . . , the law elevates private disputes into the public realm. Fiss defines adjudication as "the process by which the values embodied in an authoritative text, such as the Constitution, are given concrete meaning and expression," and he adds that these "public values" are "the values that define a society and give it its identity and inner coherence." As Fiss explains: "Courts exist to give meaning to our public values, not to resolve disputes." 93 Yale L. J. 1073 (1984).[16] Adjudication, then, is necessary to define and redefine the conditions of the public space. Furthermore, in line with the public-life conception's view of public life as reasoned deliberation, Fiss insists that the unique genius of the courts is their twin requirements of independence and dialogue. Independence guarantees an impartial use of reason, and dialogue guarantees that courts must listen to all comers and reply with reasoned opinions. . . .

The difference between the public-life and problem-solving pictures is that for the public-life conception all adjudications are public in significance — they are political, inevitably embroiling the meaning and legitimacy of government. In Fiss' words: "Civil litigation is an institutional arrangement for using state power to bring a recalcitrant reality closer to our chosen ideals."[17] For the problem-solving conception, by contrast, government gets involved only by unhappy necessity in the private ordering of human affairs. On this view, judicial involvement in a dispute is a necessary evil, whereas for the public-life conception it is an essential good.

 Owen M. Fiss, **AGAINST SETTLEMENT**

93 Yale L.J. 1073, 1075-1078, 1082-1083, 1085-1086, 1087-1088, 1089-1090 (1984)

The advocates of ADR . . . exalt the idea of settlement more generally because they view adjudication as a process to resolve disputes. They act as though courts arose to

---

16. See also, Owen Fiss, The Supreme Court 1978 Term, Foreword: The Forms of Justice, 93 Harv. L. rev. 29 (1979).
17. Fiss, 93 Yale L. J. 1075.

resolve quarrels between neighbors who had reached an impasse and turned to a stranger for help. Courts are seen as an institutionalization of the stranger and adjudication is viewed as the process by which the stranger exercises power. The very fact that the neighbors have turned to someone else to resolve their dispute signifies a breakdown in their social relations; the advocates of ADR acknowledge this, but nonetheless hope that the neighbors will be able to reach agreement before the stranger renders judgment. Settlement is that agreement. It is a truce more than a true reconciliation, but it seems preferable to judgment because it rests on the consent of both parties and avoids the cost of a lengthy trial.

In my view, however, this account of adjudication and the case for settlement rest on questionable premises. I do not believe that settlement as a generic practice is preferable to judgment or should be institutionalized on a wholesale and indiscriminate basis. It should be treated instead as a highly problematic technique for streamlining dockets. Settlement is for me the civil analogue of plea bargaining: Consent is often coerced; the bargain may be struck by someone without authority; the absence of a trial and judgment renders subsequent judicial involvement troublesome; and although dockets are trimmed, justice may not be done. Like plea bargaining, settlement is a capitulation to the conditions of mass society and should be neither encouraged nor praised.

THE IMBALANCE OF POWER

By viewing the lawsuit as a quarrel between two neighbors, the dispute-resolution story that underlies ADR implicitly asks us to assume a rough equality between the contending parties. It treats settlement as the anticipation of the outcome of trial and assumes that the terms of settlement are simply a product of the parties' predictions of that outcome. In truth, however, settlement is also a function of the resources available to each party to finance the litigation, and those resources are frequently distributed unequally. Many lawsuits do not involve a property dispute between two neighbors, or between AT&T and the government (to update the story), but rather concern a struggle between a member of a racial minority and a municipal police department over alleged brutality, or a claim by a worker against a large corporation over work-related injuries. In these cases, the distribution of financial resources, or the ability of one party to pass along its costs, will invariably infect the bargaining process, and the settlement will be at odds with a conception of justice that seeks to make the wealth of the parties irrelevant.

The disparities in resources between the parties can influence the settlement in three ways. First, the poorer party may be less able to amass and analyze the information needed to predict the outcome of the litigation, and thus be disadvantaged in the bargaining process. Second, he may need the damages he seeks immediately and thus be induced to settle as a way of accelerating payment, even though he realizes he would get less now than he might if he awaited judgment. All plaintiffs want their damages immediately, but an indigent plaintiff may be exploited by a rich defendant because his need is so great that the defendant can force him to accept a sum that is less than the ordinary present value of the judgment. Third, the poorer party might be forced to settle because he does not have the resources to finance the litigation, to cover either his own projected expenses, such as his lawyer's time, or the expenses his opponent can impose through the manipulation or procedural mechanisms such as discovery. It might seem that settlement benefits the plaintiff by allowing him to avoid the costs of litigation, but this is not so. The defendant can anticipate the plaintiff's costs if the case were to be tried fully and decrease his offer by that amount. The indigent plaintiff is a victim of the costs of litigation even if he settles. . . .

Of course, imbalances of power can distort judgment as well: Resources influence the quality of presentation, which in turn has an important bearing on who wins and the terms of victory. We count, however, on the guiding presence of the judge, who can employ a number of measures to lessen the impact of distributional inequalities. He can, for example, supplement the parties' presentations by asking questions, calling his own witnesses, and inviting other persons and institutions to participate as amici. These measures are likely to make only a small contribution toward moderating the influence of distributional inequalities, but should not be ignored for that reason. Not even these small steps are possible with settlement. There is, moreover, a critical difference between a process like settlement, which is based on bargaining and accepts inequalities of wealth as an integral and legitimate component of the process, and a process like judgment, which knowingly struggles against those inequalities. Judgment aspires to an autonomy from distributional inequalities, and it gathers much of its appeal from this aspiration. . . .

JUSTICE RATHER THAN PEACE

The dispute-resolution story makes settlement appear as a perfect substitute for judgment, as we just saw, by trivializing the remedial dimensions of a lawsuit, and also by reducing the social function of the lawsuit to one of resolving private disputes. In that story, settlement appears to achieve exactly the same purpose as judgment — peace between the parties — but at considerably less expense to society. The two quarreling neighbors turn to a court in order to resolve their dispute, and society makes courts available because it wants to aid in the achievement of their private ends or to secure the peace.

In my view, however, the purpose of adjudication should be understood in broader terms. Adjudication uses public resources, and employs not strangers chosen by the parties but public officials chosen by a process in which the public participates. These officials, like members of the legislative and executive branches, possess a power that has been defined and conferred by public law, not by private agreement. Their job is not to maximize the ends of private parties, nor simply to secure the peace, but to explicate and give force to the values embodied in authoritative texts such as the Constitution and statutes: to interpret those values and to bring reality into accord with them. This duty is not discharged when the parties settle. . . .

THE REAL DIVIDE

Someone like [former Harvard University President Derek] Bok sees adjudication in essentially private terms: The purpose of lawsuits and the civil courts is to resolve disputes, and the amount of litigation we encounter is evidence of the needlessly combative and quarrelsome character of Americans. Or as Bok put it, using a more diplomatic idiom: "At bottom, ours is a society built on individualism, competition, and success." I, on the other hand, see adjudication in more public terms: Civil litigation is an institutional arrangement for using state power to bring a recalcitrant reality closer to our chosen ideals. We turn to the courts because we need to, not because of some quirk in our personalities. We train our students in the tougher arts so that they may help secure all that the law promises, not because we want them to become gladiators or because we take a special pleasure in combat.

To conceive of the civil lawsuit in public terms as America does might be unique. I am willing to assume that no other country . . . has a case like *Brown v. Board of Education* in which the judicial power is used to eradicate the caste structure. I am willing to assume that no other country conceives of law and uses law in quite the way we do. But this should be a source of pride rather than shame. What is unique is not the problem that we live short of our ideals, but that we alone among the nations of the world seem willing to do something about it. Adjudication American-style is not a reflection of our combativeness but rather a tribute to our inventiveness and perhaps even more to our commitment.

Problem 1-6.   *Against "Against Settlement"*

How would you respond to the arguments made in "Against Settlement"? What might you say in response to Fiss' arguments about imbalances of power and resources, public values, judicial roles, and remedies and justice? Is Professor Fiss always "against settlement"?

See the recent Symposium on the legacy of this significant argument in Fordham Law Review: *Against Settlement: Twenty Five Years Later,* 78 Fordham L. Rev. 1117 (2009)

Fiss seems to argue that in dispute resolution it is difficult to achieve justice while seeking peaceful "settlement." This raises very important concerns and values for this course. Are peace and justice possible at the same time? Do we need justice to have peace? Must we have some kind of peace (or enough calm) to pursue justice? The final two excerpts explore this issue. Nancy Welsh summarizes an important literature that suggests that the experience of a fair process is an important element of "procedural justice" for parties engaged in dispute resolution. Carrie Menkel-Meadow suggests that peace and justice can and should be explored and practiced together.

Nancy A. Welsh, **REMEMBERING THE ROLE OF JUSTICE IN RESOLUTION: INSIGHTS FROM PROCEDURAL AND SOCIAL JUSTICE THEORIES**

54 J. of Legal Educ. 49, 51-53 (2004)

Over the years, we have revisited and debated the meaning of the A in ADR. It is now time, in this new world, to examine the sufficiency of the R. I offer a plea that we as law teachers begin and infuse our dispute resolution courses with a commitment to *both* resolution *and* justice.

If that is so, let us begin by examining the classic concept of procedural justice, which should be a part of every dispute resolution course — and part of the evaluation of every dispute resolution process. What is procedural justice? Is it enough to say that dispute resolution processes just ought to "feel" fair? . . .

Substantial research has been done in this area by social psychologists building on the pioneering work of John Thibaut and Laurens Walker[18] and on more recent research and theories developed by Allan Lind and Tom Tyler.[19] That research has revealed four procedural elements that reliably lead people to conclude that a dispute resolution process is procedurally fair: the process provides an opportunity for the disputants to express their views (generally described as "an opportunity for voice"); the third party demonstrates consideration of what the parties have said, the third party treats the disputants in an even-handed way and tries to be fair; and the third party treats the disputants with dignity and respect. Very recent research arising out of the U.S. Postal Service REDRESS employment mediation program (which uses a transformative model of mediation that focuses upon enhancing disputants' interaction rather than achieving resolution) has shown that the disputants also care very much about the procedural justice they receive *from each other*, perhaps even more than they care about the procedural justice offered by the third party mediator.[20] All of these results suggest that both the presence of a mediator and the mediator's guidance of the disputants interaction have the potential to bring procedural justice to the hard bargaining that often characterizes settlement negotiations.

The procedural justice literature further indicates that disputants' perceptions of procedural justice can have profound effects. The procedural elements described above do more than just make the disputants feel good. In fact, disputants are more likely to conclude that they have received *distributive* justice to the extent that they perceive that they have been treated in a procedurally just way. They are more likely to *comply* with the outcome of the dispute resolution process if they feel they have been treated fairly. And, if people perceive that a process was procedurally just, they are more likely to view the social institution that provided the process as *legitimate*. This last consequence of disputants' perceptions of procedural justice appears

18. Laurens Walker et al., Reactions of Participants and Observers to Modes of Adjudication, 4 J. Applied Soc. Pyschol. 295 (1975).
19. E. Allan Lind & Tom R. Tyler, The Social Psychology of Procedural Justice (1988).
20. Tina Nabatchi & Lisa Bingham, Expanding Our Models of Justice in Dispute Resolution: A Field Test of the Contribution of Interactional Justice (2003).

particularly important as formerly alternative processes for dispute resolution become imbedded within significant social institutions.

 Carrie Menkel-Meadow, **PRACTICING "IN THE INTERESTS OF JUSTICE" IN THE TWENTY-FIRST CENTURY: PURSUING PEACE AND JUSTICE**

70 Fordham L. Rev. 1761, 1764-1765, 1767-1770, 1773-1774 (2002)

In a recent address, . . . former President Clinton, upon accepting the Second Annual Cardozo International Advocate for Peace Award, said, "Throughout human history, tragically, we have seen more advances in tools for waging war than in the art of making peace." That comment, while certainly true of human behavior in general, is applicable to legal behavior as well. We have developed more and more sophisticated forms of legal warfare (discovery and the paper wars of attrition, and my personal favorite, the recent ad of the Los Angeles Intercontinental Hotel for a "litigation war room" available for lawyers planning strategy, taking depositions and developing their "battle plans," all in facilities with completely up to date technology and "close to the battlefield" — the courthouse). Fortunately, I think we have also seen some advances in developing some tools for "making peace" with the proliferation of mediation, problem solving and interest-based negotiation, negotiated rule-making and a variety of consensus building processes, as well as problem solving courts in a variety of substantive areas. These new tools are intended, in my view, to seek peace and justice simultaneously through the use of a variety of different forms of dialogue, policy-making, rule development, dispute settlement and conflict management. As I now tell my colleagues in a variety of substantive areas, if we cannot make enough peace and quiet to have a reasonable dialogue with each other (see by contrast the continuing violence in the troubled spots of the world) we will not be able to seek justice, let alone substantive solutions to any of our problems. Peace, of at least some minimal sort, is a prerequisite to the search for justice. And to the extent that peace-seeking tools are part of what I would call "process consciousness," lawyers should be — but are not yet, by disposition or training — at the forefront of practicing justice by considering and shaping processes that are more likely to lead to peaceful and better outcomes. . . .

"PEACE WORK" AND PROBLEM SOLVING WITH CLIENTS

. . . The work of the lawyer as a conflict resolver is to explore not only legal, but also other needs and interests of the parties (including economic, social, psychological, political, religious, moral and ethical concerns). Utilizing theories, not only of law, but of human behavior (sociology, psychology and economics), lawyers as conflict professionals look for situations where these diverse needs and interests do not compete with each other (the assumption of the legal system that "money is proxy" for all other, often non-economic, interests) but complement each other (the "Homans principle"). Complementary needs permit "efficient trades" (pareto-optimal in economic parlance) or "log-rolling" (in the language of political scientists) — positive-sum, rather than zero-sum results. Thus, at the level of substantive problem solving, lawyers seeking to achieve both maximum gain for individual clients and joint gain for all involved in a particular situation must employ different kinds of cognitive processes and different technologies and techniques in order to fashion good and lasting solutions to disputes and conflicts. At the relational level, where legal disputes and conflicts either begin with or accumulate a large emotional "residue" of resentment, anger and a sense of injustice (and, therefore, demand for both compensation and retribution), skilled lawyers as peace-makers must develop different kinds of communication skills than the traditional forms of argument, debate and adversarial claiming.

Lawyers interested in pursuing "resolution of human problems" as a dimension of justice (beyond the winning of a legal case) can perform such roles in different ways. Not all pursuers of justice in individual cases are mediators. Serving as the "representative" (restoring one of the lawyer's more conventional roles) in a mediation, a lawyer may still serve a client who needs assistance in stating a claim or articulating a need or interest, but will also have to develop a different mind-set of approaching the other side and seeking creative (perhaps beyond precedent and boilerplate) solutions to problems. For the jurisprudentially sensitive lawyer-conflict resolver, the question of justice in a mediative setting may be framed by asking the parties to reflect on what is "fair" to them. In the words of my friend and mediator-collaborator, Gary Friedman, "law may be relevant, but not determinative" of what is fair to each party. . . . The general law may not serve "justice" in an individual case and so, as long as not otherwise unlawful, individual or party-tailored solutions to legal disputes or problems may depart from particular legal formulations. Legal or "legislated justice" may not always be the same as personal or social justice between parties. Consider as examples: mutually agreed to departures from court-suggested spousal and child support guidelines, departures from sentencing guidelines, liquidated damages clauses in contracts and all future-oriented solutions to disrupted past dealings in both business and personal relationships. Lawyers seeking this kind of "individual" justice between parties (where no important public issue demands transparency or where the parties prefer a highly individualized and flexible, future-oriented solution to their problem) seek both a better quality solution and a more lasting "peace" between the parties than a "command" order of court is likely to accomplish.

This is not to say that all "alternative dispute resolution" is necessarily more individually just than traditional litigation. Indeed, I have been critical of very problematic distortions of the "ADR" process that inhibit several important justice values: access to justice and fairness, particularly in the form of mandatory arbitration clauses in a variety of settings, ranging from employment to consumer contracts to health care, which remove process choice, may be prohibitively costly and provide inadequate representation and remedies to harmed individuals. Claims about the fairness and "justice" of all forms of process must be considered both for what they promise and do internally, as well as in relation to what else is available — "the baseline" problem in evaluating relative fairness of legal processes to each other. The best and worst of different processes should not be compared to each other but best to best and worst to worst of each process. Ideally, we should be able to measure differences and understand the reasons for when and how justice is delivered in different settings (and sometimes differentially for different people). . . .

Lawyers, . . . may be particularly well suited to participating in these new processes. Lawyers have "process consciousness." Aware of procedural rules and concerned about "voice" and procedural fairness, with proper training (facilitation is quite different from argumentation), lawyers may make ideal process leaders of these new processes and institutions. To the extent that efforts at collaboration and community and democratic decision making still implicate legal requirements (siting disputes require zoning and environmental approvals from formal legal authorities), lawyers are well suited to spot the legal issues and provide for their appropriate coordination with less formal processes. To the extent that these new processes are experiments in constitution-making (as some legal scholars have named them) or simply more direct democratic enterprises than local and national and international government is accustomed to, law-trained individuals may be particularly well suited to serving in these processes, whether as "neutral-facilitators" or advocates or party representatives.

These new roles put lawyers in perhaps unfamiliar ways of functioning as they pursue justice. Focused not just on "winning" the case, but on meeting the needs of multiple sets of parties and affected third parties, and on looking for substantive solutions that will require marshaling new resources, drafting new regulations, creating new institutions (including public and private partnerships in some cases) and implementing and enforcing plans, lawyers will have to learn new skills and develop new conceptual frameworks. It will not be easy to do all of this, particularly in light of robust conventional frames and conceptual models through which we process the world, and because our system is more than several centuries old. It is clear we are living in a new world with new problems that will require new forms of processes and solutions if we are to achieve a peaceful and just world. If necessity is the mother of invention, we are certainly in need of the birth of some new ideas for pursuing justice, both at home and in the larger world we now all inhabit. Conventional approaches to pursuing "justice" like our "conventional" approaches of military solutions to international problems may destroy the very "res" we are fighting about (producing a "negative sum" game in negotiation parlance). Just as military solutions to "war" may not bring us peace, an exclusive focus on "legal" needs and interests may not bring us justice. This is true, whether we like it or not.

Problem 1-7.   *Promoting Peace and Justice?*

How would you define "justice"? How do you see conflict resolution processes in achieving your conception of justice? What specific behaviors will lawyers have to learn to promote "peace as well as justice"?

Write down three or four concrete skills that you would like to learn to be an effective conflict resolver. Why are these important things for you to know how to do?

As you proceed to study the specific processes of dispute resolution in this book, ask yourself the following questions:

a. What is the purpose of this process?

b. What is the historical context of the development of this process? What problem was it created to solve? What new problems are created by it?

c. What is the relation of process to the substantive problem to be solved?

d. Who should have decision-making authority or power in this process — the parties, their representatives, courts, legislatures, other people affected by the conflict or dispute?

e. What are the relations or tensions between "justice" or "fairness" and "peace" in individual cases and at the aggregate or system level?

f. How, if at all, has this process been institutionalized or formalized? What advantages or disadvantages are there to formalizing this process?

g. Why do we want and make process changes? What ills are we hoping to cure? What new problems do we create?

h. How should the success or effectiveness of a particular process be measured? What metrics are possible? Is party satisfaction enough, or should we look to some measures outside of the parties themselves?

i. What is the lawyer's proper role in dispute processes? As a representative of clients? As an officer of the court? Policy maker? Enacter?

j. What are the ethics of dispute resolution — both in the "macro" sense of systemic justice and in the "micro" sense of choosing particular processes and behaviors?

Further Reading

Jerold Auerbach. (1983). *Justice Without Law?* New York: Oxford University Press.

Jerome T. Barrett & Joseph Barrett. (2004). *A History of Alternative Dispute Resolution: The Story of a Political, Social and Cultural Movement.* San Francisco: Jossey-Bass.

Morton Deutsch. (1973). *The Resolution of Conflict: Constructive and Destructive Processes.* New Haven: Yale University Press.

Morton Deutsch & Peter T. Coleman (Eds.). (2000). *The Handbook of Conflict Resolution: Theory and Practice.* San Francisco: Jossey-Bass Publishers.

Mary Parker Follett. (1995). *Prophet of Management: A Celebration of Writings from the 1920s* (P. Graham, Ed.). Boston: Harvard Business School.

Lon L. Fuller. (2001). *The Principles of Social Order: Selected Essays of Lon L. Fuller* (Rev. ed.) (K.I. Winston, Ed.). Oxford: Hart Publishing.

Stuart Hampshire. (2000). *Justice Is Conflict.* Princeton: Princeton University Press.

Carrie Menkel-Meadow. (2003). *Dispute Processing and Conflict Resolution: Theory Practice and Policy.* Aldershot, UK and Burlington, Vt.: Ashgate Press.

Michael L. Moffitt & Robert C. Bordone. (2005). *The Handbook of Dispute Resolution.* San Francisco: Jossey-Bass Publishers.

Laura Nader, *The Recurrent Dialectic Between Legality and Its Alternatives: The Limitations of Binary Thinking*, 132 U. Pa. L. Rev. 621 (1984).

Joan C. Tonn. (2003). *Mary Parker Follett: Creating Democracy, Transforming Management.* New Haven: Yale University Press.

Chapter 2   The Lawyer as Problem Solver

In the Chinese language, the character for crisis is two different symbols — one means danger and the other means opportunity.

"Discourage litigation. Persuade your neighbors to compromise whenever you can. As a peacemaker the lawyer has superior opportunity of being a good man. There will still be business enough."

— Abraham Lincoln

This chapter focuses on the multiple roles that the lawyer may play in solving clients' problems and using various forms of dispute resolution to do so. In the first chapter you read about conflict theory and some of the frameworks for handling disputes in the United States, some of the issues it raises, as well as definitions of some of the processes available. You'll recall that some of what animated the creation of the ADR movement was a hope for justice, tailored to the parties' needs. In this chapter we will introduce you to some of the skills you will need to be that problem-solving lawyer. In order to try to accomplish both justice (for your clients and perhaps for the larger society as well) and satisfy your clients' instrumental, as well as affective, needs, you will have to have a deep repertoire of skills. Problem solvers are creative, look deeply into what their clients really need and hope to accomplish, have a special sensitivity to what the other parties need and hope to accomplish, and also consider what the situation permits (or can be enlarged to allow). This creates a tension that some dispute resolution scholars and practitioners have called the need to both "create" and "claim" value.[1] As a problem solver you will have to consider the other side as a possible solution to your problem, but also as someone whom you will have to persuade and advocate. You will need to be creative and listen to the other side to find out what they want to accomplish and what they can offer as well. At the same time you have to be ready to express clearly your clients' needs and goals too. How these conversations are conducted will be treated at length in this book in the chapters that follow. But, as you begin to learn how to listen to the other side, interview your own clients, and then put on your "thinking caps" to come up with rigorous

---

1. David A. Lax & James K. Sebenius, The Manager as Negotiator: Bargaining for Cooperation and Competitive Gain (1986).

and creative solutions to legal issues and disputes, we want you to realize you have to be open to new thoughts, ideas, and goals of the other side, following which you will also have to be an advocate (and an open one!) for a good solution to whatever problem you are negotiating, mediating, or arbitrating.

We will now turn to the skills which are essential for any good problem solver: considering client and social goals; exploring mind-sets and orientations toward goals and clients; listening to clients and parties; interviewing and counseling to determine interests, underlying needs and goals under those interests; and effective communication with all those you interact with in solving legal problems through dispute resolution methods.

In the first section of this chapter, we look specifically at the reasons that clients will hire lawyers to deal with their problems. What are the advantages and the pitfalls of having an agent working on a client's behalf using approaches other than litigation? Next, the second part of this chapter addresses the skill-sets we expect each lawyer to develop. When a client walks into your office, you will first interview him or her and find out why they have come to you. To adopt a problem-solving approach to their concerns, the lawyer needs to uncover more than the client's legal claim. We also examine client counseling skills — how do we advise a client in choosing among the different processes that you will be learning in this course? Because the goal of this book is to ensure you understand the many process options available to deal with the wide variety of client problems, we also want to make sure that you have the skills needed to explain these processes to your clients.

Problem 2-1. *What Is Your Purpose as a Lawyer?*

Before you read this chapter, spend some time thinking about your own expectations about what legal and conflict resolution processes should accomplish in the world, and about what you personally can contribute. What are your hopes and "higher aspirations"? What are your more "realistic expectations"?

A. THE CLIENT/LAWYER RELATIONSHIP

Why do clients need attorneys in disputes that take place outside the courtroom? The first article by Jeffrey Rubin and Frank Sander uses agency theory to explain the potential benefit of having a lawyer represent a client in a negotiation. The second article by Jean Sternlight continues and deepens the discussion of the role of attorneys in dispute resolutions settings. The final article by Robert Mnookin explores the normal tensions that may arise within the client/lawyer relationship.

Jeffrey Z. Rubin & Frank E. A. Sander, WHEN SHOULD WE USE AGENTS? DIRECT VS. REPRESENTATIVE NEGOTIATION

4 Negot. J. 395, 396-398 (1988)

EXPERTISE

One of the primary reasons that principals choose to negotiate through agents is that the latter possess expertise that makes agreement — particularly favorable agreement — more likely. This expertise is likely to be of three different stripes:

Substantive knowledge. A tax attorney or accountant knows things about the current tax code that make it more likely that negotiations with an IRS auditor will benefit the client as much as possible. Similarly, a divorce lawyer, an engineering consultant, and a real estate agent may have substantive knowledge in a rather narrow domain of expertise, and this expertise may redound to the client's benefit.

Process expertise. Quite apart from the specific expertise they may have in particular content areas, agents may have skill at the negotiation *process*, per se, thereby enhancing the prospects of a favorable agreement. A skillful negotiator — someone who understands how to obtain and reveal information about preferences, who is inventive, resourceful, firm on goals but flexible on means, etc. — is a valuable resource. Wise principals would do well to utilize the services of such skilled negotiators, unless they can find ways of developing such process skills themselves.

Special influence. A Washington lobbyist is paid to know the "right" people, to have access to the "corridors of power" that the principals themselves are unlikely to possess. Such "pull" can certainly help immensely, and is yet another form of expertise that agents may possess, although the lure of this "access" often outweighs in promise the special benefits that are confirmed in reality. . . .

DETACHMENT

Another important reason for using an agent to do the actual negotiation is that the principals may be too emotionally entangled in the subject of the dispute. A classic example is divorce. A husband and wife, caught in the throes of a bitter fight over the end of their marriage, may benefit from the "buffering" that agents can provide. Rather than confront each other with the depth of their anger and bitterness, the principals . . . may do far better by communicating only *indirectly*, via their respective representatives. . . . Stated most generally, when the negotiating climate is adversarial — when the disputants are confrontational rather than collaborative — it may be wiser to manage the conflict through intermediaries than run the risk of an impasse or explosion resulting from direct exchange.

Sometimes, however, it is the *agents* who are too intensely entangled. What is needed then is the detachment and rationality that only the principals can bring to the exchange. . . .

Note, however, that the very "detachment" we are touting as a virtue of negotiation through agents can also be a liability. For example, in some interpersonal negotiations, apology and reconciliation may be an important ingredient of any resolution. Surrogates who are primarily technicians may not be able to bring to bear these empathetic qualities.

TACTICAL FLEXIBILITY

The use of agents allows various gambits to be played out by the principals, in an effort to ratchet as much as possible from the other side. For example, if a seller asserts that the bottom line is $100,000, the buyer can try to haggle, albeit at the risk of losing the deal. If the buyer employs an agent, however, the agent can profess willingness to pay that sum but plead lack of authority, thereby gaining valuable time and opportunity for fuller consideration of the situation together with the principal. Or an agent for the seller who senses that the buyer may be especially eager to buy the property can claim that it is necessary to go back to the seller for ratification of the deal, only to return and up the price, profusely apologizing all the while for the behavior of an "unreasonable" client. The client and agent can thus together play the hard-hearted partner game.

Conversely, an agent may be used in order to push the other side in tough, even obnoxious, fashion, making it possible — in the best tradition of the "good cop/bad cop" ploy — for the client to intercede at last, and seem the essence of sweet reason in comparison with the agent. Or the agent may be used as a "stalking horse," to gather as much information about the adversary as possible, opening the way to proposals by the client that exploit the intelligence gathered.

Problem 2-2.   *Why Hire a Lawyer?*

As a lawyer, which of these reasons to use a lawyer-agent make the most sense to you? Which reasons would you use to persuade a skeptical client that you are useful?

As a client, what concerns might you have about hiring a lawyer? How would you decide when to hire a lawyer? On what factors would your decision depend?

While it is often easily understood why clients need lawyers to manage the complexity of litigation, this next excerpt from an article by Jean Sternlight suggests that lawyers can sometimes be equally or even more important to clients outside the courtroom in non-litigation processes.

Jean R. Sternlight, **LAWYERLESS DISPUTE RESOLUTION:
RETHINKING A PARADIGM**

37 Fordham Urban Law J. 1-2, 11-13, 26-31 (2010)

Do participants in mediation and arbitration have attorneys? Do they need them? Although the phenomenon of pro se litigation has received substantial attention in recent years, most commentators and policy makers have failed to focus on whether participants in mediation, arbitration, or other forms of alternative dispute resolution ("ADR") need legal assistance. Likely the failure to focus on the possible need for representation in proceedings is based on an often unstated premise that because ADR is non-adversarial or at least less adversarial than litigation, the need for representation in ADR is necessarily or at least typically less than the need for representation in litigation. . . .

WHY MIGHT ATTORNEYS BE NEEDED IN ADR?

Some might suggest that one of the goals of ADR is to avoid the need for attorneys. One of the virtues of purportedly simpler less adversarial dispute resolution process would seem to be that disputants would be fully capable of representing themselves, and not have to rely on expensive attorneys. . . .

The other reason some may believe attorneys are not necessary in mediation or arbitration is their sense that the typically adversarial mindset of attorneys do not fit with less adversarial ADR processes. . . . Specifically, attorneys in mediation may focus unduly on narrow monetary interests, may be overly argumentative, or may discourage their clients from addressing opposing disputants directly. . . . Some jurisdictions have gone so far as to prohibit attorneys from participating in certain categories of court-connected mediation. . . .

Yet, particularly as ADR has become mandatory in many contexts in many jurisdictions, the question of whether individuals can effectively represent themselves has become more pressing. . . . Moreover, upon reflection most people would probably agree that lawyers at least potentially can be extremely helpful in ADR proceedings. . . .

[L]awyers add value through imparting their procedural and strategic knowledge regarding the various processes, gathering and presenting legal and factual information, assisting specifically in negotiation, and empowering their clients. Thus, even to the extent arbitration and mediation are relatively simple and non-adversarial, which is often not the case, lawyers can provide a great deal of assistance with regard to these processes.

1. Knowledge and Strategy re: Processes

Lawyers can be very useful in helping disputants decide whether arbitration or mediation might be desirable. . . . If an ADR process is to be used, lawyers can help select the neutral. In purely voluntary processes lawyers rely on their networks to find names of mediators and arbitrators who they think would or would not be appropriate. . . . Once the neutral is selected the lawyer can be very helpful in coaching the client in such matters as what to expect in mediation/arbitration, who to bring to the mediation/arbitration as participants or witnesses, or what strategic moves might be desirable in either process. . . . One additional way attorneys can help clients to succeed in mediation is to help them better understand their own situation and goals. . . .

2. Gathering and Presenting Factual Information

Gathering and presenting legal and factual information is often a key aspect of both mediation and arbitration. No matter how informal the process, disputants typically need to explain such matters as what happened, what relief they are seeking or seeking to avoid providing, and why they believe they are in the right and someone else is in the wrong. . . .

Lawyers are accustomed to ferreting out information . . . and may be very useful to help parties prepare for a mediation or arbitration. . . . Having gathered the facts the lawyer can help make strategic arguments regarding which facts to disclose, as well as when and how such facts should be disclosed. . . . And, assuming facts will be presented, lawyers can typically prepare both verbal and written versions of the facts that are much clearer, better organized, and more persuasive than the client might be able to manage on her own. . . .

3. Researching and Presenting Legal Arguments

Although some may assume that legal arguments have no place or less of a place in ADR proceedings than in court, they would be wrong. Mediations often occur in the shadow of litigation, with disputants quite cognizant that the case may proceed to litigation if it does not settle in mediation. Thus, the strength and weakness of legal arguments is highly relevant to determine whether a disputant ought to settle on particular terms. . . . Arbitrations, of course, typically turn on legal arguments, merely substituting the arbitrator's legal determinations for those of a judge. Thus, in both forms of ADR lawyers can help a great deal in researching and presenting legal arguments.

4. Empowering Clients

In addition to the tasks outlined above, lawyers are poised to help their clients . . . specifically by providing emotional support and empowering their clients. Even in simpler ADR matters, that do not involve complex facts or law, it may be very important for clients to be accompanied and supported by a person who can help them emotionally to tell their own story. A large literature discusses this need as applied to minorities, women, and victims of domestic violence. But it seems that the empowerment issue is likely much bigger than that: many disputants can benefit substantially from the assistance of an attorney to help them tell their own story, even in matters that may seem relatively simple in terms of facts and law.

5. Drafting Agreements

If an agreement is reached in mediation the attorney can also help the client by drafting the actual mediation agreement. As with any contract, lawyers can add a great deal, ensuring that the terms of the contract are clear, fair and enforceable.

While we want clients to hire lawyers for all of the reasons listed above, we also think that it is useful for lawyers to recognize some of the classic problems that may occur between lawyers and clients. The next excerpt examines three sources of tensions between lawyers and clients, demonstrates how these tensions play out in the course of representation, and then provides mechanisms for dealing with these tensions.

 Robert H. Mnookin, Scott R. Peppet & Andrew S. Tulumello,
BEYOND WINNING

75-76, 83-87, 90 (2000)

THE SOURCES OF THE TENSION

Agency costs are not limited to the amount of money that a principal pays an agent as compensation for doing the job. They also include the money and time the principal spends trying to ensure that the agent does not exploit him but instead serves his interests well. To understand why agency costs exist, consider that principals and agents may differ in three general ways:

- Preferences
- Incentives
- Information

Different Preferences

First, the preferences, or interests, of an agent are rarely identical to those of the principal. Consider their economic interest. A real estate agent's primary economic interest is in her own earnings as a real estate agent. In this transaction, the seller's primary economic interest is in the net sale price for his house. The agent may have other interests as well. She has a strong interest in her reputation and in securing future clients. She has an interest in maintaining good relationships with other agents, banks, home inspectors, and insurance agencies. The agent is a repeat player in this game, while the seller, particularly if he intends to leave the community, is a one-shot player who might be more than willing to sacrifice the agent's reputation in order to get a better deal for himself. Conversely, the agent may be reluctant to bargain hard for certain advantages for the seller because of her desire to maintain a congenial relationship with the buyer's agent, who may be a source of future client referrals.

Different Incentives

Agency problems may also arise because the *incentives* of the principal and the agent are imperfectly aligned. The culprit is typically the agent's fee structure, which may create perverse incentives for the agent to act contrary to the principal's interests. This discrepancy is sometimes called an incentive gap.

For example, the seller wants an arrangement that maximizes his expected net sale proceeds after his agent's fee. The agent, on the other hand, wants a fee structure that yields her the highest expected return *for her time spent*. If they agree to a percentage fee, the agent may prefer a quick and easy sale at a lower price to a difficult sale at a higher price because with the former she will get more return for hours spent working. Indeed, a recent study suggests that when realtors put their *own* homes on the market, they tend to get higher-than-average prices, because they get the entire benefit of their additional hours of work, not just 6 percent of it.

Different Information

The information available to the principal and the agent may differ. We are speaking here of kinds of information that either side may have an incentive to keep to itself. The agent may know that market conditions are improving, for example, but she may be reluctant to share this with the seller for fear of inflating his expectations. Similarly, it may be difficult to know how much effort an agent is actually putting in on the principal's behalf. Because the principal cannot readily discover this information, the agent might shirk her responsibilities and earn pay without expending effort.

THE APPROACH: MANAGING THE TENSION

The central challenge in agency relationships is to capture the benefits while minimizing agency costs. Our approach requires the tension be acknowledged and managed explicitly; that principals and agents use the concept of comparative advantage to structure their roles and responsibilities; and that they aim to form a partnership based on reciprocal candor and respect. . . . Here, we outline general advice.

Create a Collaborative Relationship That Minimizes Agency Costs

The principal–agent tension should be acknowledged, not avoided, and treated as a shared problem. Fees and monitoring should be addressed explicitly, not left lurking under the table. . . . [P]rincipals and agents should search together for ways to reassure the principal without overburdening the agent. In our experience, openness and candor build trust. . . .

Consider Comparative Advantage and Strategy in Allocating Roles

A principal and agent may allocate negotiation roles in a variety of ways. At one extreme, the principal may do all the negotiating herself, using the agent as a coach and consultant behind the scenes. At the other extreme, the agent alone may be at the bargaining table and may not even disclose the principal's identity to the other side. There are many options in between. . . .

Consider the Incentives Created by Agency Relationships on the Other Side

In addition to thinking through principal-agent issues on your side, you should consider the relationships on the other side as well. Do not naively assume that the other side is a "unified actor" with a single set of interests. What are the agent's incentives? A broker or a sales agent may get paid only if the deal goes through. A contingent-fee lawyer who is very pressed for time because of other commitments may be eager to settle. An executive on the other side may either support or oppose a merger, depending on how his career will be affected. In crafting proposals, it is not enough to consider only the interests of the principal on the other side. The agent's incentives and interests should be taken into account as well.

Problem 2-3.   *Who Will You Trust?*

In the International War Crimes Tribunal for Former Yugoslavia, former Serbian leader Slobodon Milosevic insisted on representing himself. In addition to his numerous political reasons for doing this, what concerns about agency might he have had?

B. A CLIENT-CENTERED APPROACH

Now that you have a better grasp of why a client might hire a lawyer, as well as some of the challenges presented by the lawyer-client relationship, consider what skills a lawyer should have to advance his client's interests. The client-centered approach outlined in this book tries to avoid the common trap that can occur when a "lay" story becomes a "law" story. Often, a client tells his lawyer a broad story about the event, a "lay" story, and the lawyer will narrow or rephrase the story in his efforts to seek remediation. The lawyer will construct a story which is recognizable to the other lawyer, so that he can demand a stock remedial solution, a "law" story. The "law" story can be likened to a legal cause of action with prescribed elements which must be pleaded in a particular way in the legal system. If negotiation fails and the lawyer begins to craft a lawsuit, the dispute may be even further narrowed by the special language requirements of the substantive law, pleading rules, and rules of procedure. The next excerpt tells us how to avoid treating our clients as "law" stories and to see beyond the law.[2]

---

2. For more on the concept of "lay" versus "law" stories, see Carrie Menkel-Meadow, The Transformation of Disputes by Lawyers: What the Dispute Paradigm Does and Does Not Tell Us, 1985 Missouri J. Dispute Res. 25; G. Lopez, The Internal Structure of Lawyering: Lay Lawyering, 32 UCLA L. Rev. 1, 3 (1984); R. Nisbett & L. Ross, Human Inference: Strategies and Shortcomings of Social Judgment 32-41 (1980).

Katherine R. Kruse, BEYOND CARDBOARD CLIENTS IN
LEGAL ETHICS

23 Georgetown J. Legal Ethics 1, 20-22, 28, 31, 33-34, 36, 41, 44 (2010)

In the world of legal ethics, clients are most often constructed as cardboard figures
interested solely in maximizing their own wealth or freedom at the expense of
others. . . . The proliferation of these examples is no accident. Rather, it is a
consequence of a choice by early legal ethicists to focus on the dilemma faced by a
lawyer forced by professional duty to do something that would otherwise be
wrong. To generate this kind of dilemma, legal ethicists had to posit hypothetical clients impervious to ordinary moral considerations, unconcerned with
preserving their relationships with others and indifferent to their reputations in the
community. . . .

The focus on moral lawyers and cardboard clients prevented the early ethicists
from exploring the possibility that the real problems of legal professionalism might
originate — not primarily from selfish clients who push their lawyers to the limits
of the law — but primarily from lawyers who focus too narrowly on their clients'
legal interests and fail to view their clients as whole persons with a myriad of nonlegal concerns. . . .

The client-centered approach is directly responsive to the problem of legal
objectification. It urges lawyers to unlearn the professional habit of "issue-spotting"
their clients and to approach their clients as whole persons who are more than the
sum of their legal interests. The hallmarks of the client-centered approach include
understanding the client's problem from the client's point of view and shaping legal
advice around the client's values. Under the client-centered approach, hearing
clients' stories and understanding their values, cares and commitments is the first
step — and a continuing duty — of legal representation. . . .

In an early article on lawyer paternalism, David Luban . . . theoretically distinguished three different aspects of a client's objectives, as follows:

- *Wants* are those things a client subjectively desire in the moment; they are like
  facts that exist but cannot be disputed.
- *Values* are the desires with which a client most closely identify, playing an
  important role in defining a client's larger life-plans and self-conceptions.
- *Interests* are "generalizable means to any ultimate end." They include freedom,
  wealth, health, power, and control over other people's actions. Interests are not
  valuable in themselves, but as means by which we can satisfy our wants and
  actualize our values. . . .

When clients come to lawyers for legal advice and representation, their legal
issues are often entangled with values, projects, commitments, and relationships with
others. Sometimes getting legal help to start up a business a client has always
dreamed of having or helping a couple adopt a child. Sometimes legal action arises
because a client has been harmed by the actions of others: the client has been fired
from a job, hit by a car, or beaten by a spouse. Sometimes the client has been accused
of treating others unjustly: sexually harassing an employee, reneging on a deal,

negligently allowing harm to others, or committing a crime. Other times clients come to lawyers to overcome barriers to taking care of business as usual: a deal needs to be negotiated, property needs to be leased, or a permit needs to be obtained. . . .

The methods of client value clarification involve both actively listening to what the client wants and probing beneath the client's expressed desires. Client-centered interviewing literature, for example, suggests that the lawyer dedicate time early in a client's initial interview for open-ended questions and other active listening techniques that help the lawyer hear the client's problem in the client's own terms. Hearing the client's story — as the client chooses to tell it — is a key component of understanding what the client values and what it is about the legal representation that will threaten or further those values. . . .

The kind of moral neutrality that results from respect for another person's values helps to discipline lawyers' tendency to impose their own moral and value choices on their clients in the guise of legal advice. If we assume three-dimensional clients, it is respect for client values that ensures the good that moral activism hopes to achieve by importing moral considerations into legal representation without succumbing to the danger of moral overreaching. . . .

Lawyers, like clients, are morally complex three-dimensional persons who bring a mix of reputational interests, personal relationships, values, cares and commitments into the arena of legal representation. And, all of these factors may affect lawyers' decision making for better or for worse. . . .

In the arena of legal representation, lawyers and clients are thus differently situated, but it is difficult to conclude that one is better positioned than the other to engage in moral reasoning and decision making. The situations that lead clients to seek legal representation may incline clients to pursue their wants in favor of their values. Lawyers will generally have no particular investment in the situations in which their clients are embroiled. However, lawyers will inevitably have financial, reputational and personal interests that present their own form of temptation to transgress moral and professional values. The principles of partisan loyalty and moral neutrality — redefined as attention to and deference to client value choices — can help check lawyers' own self-interested motivations in legal representation. . . .

Problem 2-4.   *Goals in Representing a Drunk Driver*

You are a new associate in a firm and a partner whom you highly respect has just given you your first case. The case involves the daughter of a regular and important client. The daughter received a drunk-driving ticket and you are appointed as her defense counsel. Describe the wants, values, and interests of the daughter, the father, and you, as the attorney, involved in the case.

---

1. Identifying Clients' Interests

The following excerpt, from a major client counseling textbook, discusses the importance of uncovering the legal and nonlegal concerns of your client.

David A. Binder, Paul B. Bergman & Susan C. Price, LAWYERS
AS COUNSELORS: A CLIENT-CENTERED APPROACH

3-9, 11-12, 14-15 (1991)

Although law school perhaps gives a contrary impression, identifying and helping
clients resolve problems requires more than knowledge of relevant legal principles.
You also need to know about clients' individual circumstances if you are to help
them shape satisfactory solutions. Thus, two clients may have the same "legal" problem, but a solution that satisfies one may be unthinkable to the other. Accordingly,
effective counseling demands understanding of how each client's unique goals and
needs intertwine with legal issues.

Achieving this understanding requires that you acquire knowledge in at least
two broad areas not directly linked with legal principles. Skilled lawyers' knowledge
in each of these areas helps demonstrate why the practice of law requires much more
than knowledge of the law.

The first area concerns the context(s) in which clients' problems are embedded.
Helping fashion solutions to problems involving surgical malpractice requires
knowing something about medical diagnostic techniques, surgical procedures, and
hospital practices. Similarly, if a client's proposed business venture concerns marketing a new software program, you probably need some knowledge of software products, marketing practices and venture capital. This first "extralegal" area, then, is
principally content based; its focus is "industry knowledge" that you either have or
will need to acquire. . . .

The second extralegal area focuses more on process than content. Clients
come to you with differing degrees of knowledge, emotion and sophistication.
Some you will know personally; others will be strangers. Some will readily make
decisions; others will be in a continuous quandary. Accordingly, for legal principle
and contextual knowledge to lead to effective solutions, you need understanding
and skills in a variety of interpersonal spheres including interviewing, counseling
and negotiation. . . .

CLIENTS' TYPICAL NONLEGAL CONCERNS

As suggested above, lawyers' principal societal role is to help clients resolve problems,
not merely to identify and apply legal rules. Nonetheless, too often lawyers conceive
of clients' problems as though legal issues are at the problems' center, much as
Ptolemy viewed the Solar System as though the Earth were at the center of the
universe. But legal issues may be no more the essence of a client's problem than,
perhaps, religion might be its essence if a troubled client chose to talk to a minister
rather than to you, a lawyer. Whatever the legal aspects of a problem, nonlegal aspects
frequently are at the heart of a client's concerns. Effective counseling inevitably
requires that you elicit information about these nonlegal aspects and factor them
into a problem's resolution. . . .

Economic Consequences: Economic ramifications are the monetary effects of a
course of action. Almost every action will produce some economic ramifications.

Legal fees, damages and time spent preparing to testify are typical economic ramifications of litigation. In planning matters, typical economic consequences include
time spent in preparing for negotiation, legal fees and implementing the selected
course of action. . . .

Social Consequences: Social ramifications are those that affect a client's relations
with others. . . .

Psychological Consequences: Psychological ramifications are the internal personal
feelings that clients experience as the result of the choices they make. For example,
some litigation clients feel cowardly and cheated when they give up certain claims
as part of a settlement. Other clients feel anxious as long as a case remains unresolved. Similarly, some business clients are elated if their economic power produces
a final deal in which the price is better than the market price. Others are happiest
when a final agreement benefits both parties economically.

Moral, Political and Religious Consequences: Actions may create results or reactions
that implicate clients' moral, political and/or religious values. That is, choices often
arouse feelings based on clients' underlying personal values. For example a landlord's
decision not to evict a tenant during December may emanate from the landlord's
belief that people should not be made homeless during the holiday season. . . .

EVEN DESIRED SOLUTIONS TYPICALLY ENTAIL NEGATIVE NONLEGAL CONSEQUENCES

One factor that accounts for the prominence of nonlegal concerns is that typically,
in legal matters as in everyday life, achieving any benefit usually entails costs. Thus,
the legal and nonlegal benefits that any solution may create are typically accompanied by nonlegal costs. If a client is not already aware that the silverest of linings has
a cloud, having to make a decision typically causes a client to realize that every
option has potential nonlegal downsides. . . .

CHOOSING ONE SOLUTION MAY CUT OFF POSITIVE NONLEGAL CONSEQUENCES OF ALTERNATIVE SOLUTIONS

A second factor accounting for the prominence of nonlegal concerns is that by
opting for the positive nonlegal consequences of one choice, a client necessarily
forgoes the positive nonlegal consequences of others. . . .

CHOOSING A SOLUTION OFTEN REQUIRES A CLIENT TO TRADE ONE SET OF NEGATIVE CONSEQUENCES FOR ANOTHER

If clients find it difficult to choose between the positive nonlegal consequences of
alternative solutions, they typically find it even more difficult to do so when
alternative solutions each produce negative nonlegal consequences. . . .

NONLEGAL CONSEQUENCES ARE OFTEN DIFFICULT TO PREDICT

Uncertainty is another factor that commonly puts nonlegal consequences in the
forefront of client concerns. Nonlegal consequences are not prescribed by statutes

or Supreme Court decisions. Economic, social and psychological consequences vary considerably according to individual personalities, general social and economic conditions, and the like. Accordingly, when choosing between (or among) possible solutions, clients and lawyers need to predict the nonlegal consequences that are likely to flow from each. As the predictions are likely to be uncertain, clients often focus considerable time and energy on them. . . .

PROMINENCE OF NONLEGAL CONCERNS: COUNSELING IMPLICATIONS

The prominence of nonlegal aspects of client problems affects our entire view of counseling, from initial interview through problem resolution. To help clients effectively resolve their problems, you must continually take account of, and help clients think through, nonlegal as well as legal dimensions. When interviewing clients, gather information about all of their concerns, not merely evidence that might prove or disprove a legal claim or that may incline you to include a certain provision in an agreement. When developing potential resolutions to problems, take care that your suggestions respond to nonlegal as well as legal concerns. And when helping clients choose a course of action, discuss with them the possible nonlegal and legal impacts of available options.

In short, problem resolution is not guided by a "closed set" in which all that matters is statutes, regulations and court opinions. People's economic, social, psychological and moral concerns are as much a part of their problems as any worries about legal doctrine. The more you understand this reality, the better lawyer you will be.

———————————

In this next article, Warren Lehman outlines the concerns that we might have in counseling clients. Should we be morally neutral? What role should financial conditions and incentives (for both lawyer and client) play in client advising? Should the client's interest, *as the client defines it*, be the goal of the lawyer? When should a lawyer suggest particular solutions? Whose case it is anyhow?

 Warren Lehman, THE PURSUIT OF A CLIENT'S INTEREST

77 Mich. L. Rev. 1078, 1079, 1088-1089, 1091-1093 (1979)

Clients come to lawyers for help with important decisions in their business and private lives. How do lawyers respond to these requests, and how ought they? Doubtless many clients, thinking they know what they want — or wishing to appear to know — encourage the lawyer to believe he is consulted solely for a technical expertise, for a knowledge of how to do legal things, for his ability to interpret legal words, or for the objective way he looks at legal and practical outcomes. . . .

What I want to discuss in the balance of this Article is how utilitarianism in specific kinds of familiar counseling situations leads to giving clients bad advice, advice that sacrifices their humanity in the name of seemingly self-evident goods.

A practicing lawyer, call him Doe, who also teaches client counseling, said that he is very concerned, in doing estate matters, with the possibility that a client will be overborne by information about tax consequences. His tactic to avoid that result is to persuade his client — before there is any mention of those consequences — to expand in as much detail as possible upon what it is he wants to do. Only after that does Doe point out costs and mention ways the client's plan could be changed to save money. In teaching as well as practice, Doe is trying to take account of the power a lawyer has to impress upon a client the importance of his lawyerly considerations. The progress represented by Doe's concerned approach is the recognition that the client's values may not be the lawyer's, or more precisely, that the real, live client's interests may not match those of the "standard client" for whom lawyers are wont to model their services. . . .

I told Doe of a friend of mine, a widow recovering from alcoholism, who is fifty-four years old. Her house has become a burden to her, perhaps even a threat to her sobriety, although it might seem overly dramatic to say as much to a stranger. If she waits until she is fifty-five, the better part of a year, the large capital gain on the house will be tax free. She decided she did not want to go to a lawyer for fear he might talk her into putting off the sale. I asked Doe if that were realistic. He said her fear was well grounded; a lawyer might well give her the impression that another year in the house ought to be suffered for the tax saving. (I expect a lawyer's inclination to press the merits of his money-saving advice reflects, among other things, a desire to feel that his expertise is really useful. We may know no other way to judge our own usefulness.)

One possible analysis of these cases is that suggested by Doe: that the lawyer needs to be careful to discover what it is the client is really about, to give fullest possible opportunity for her interests to be explored, and to avoid the over-bearing assertion of simple money saving. . . .

The objection to utilitarian advice that we have been talking about is that there is a need to insert moral values into the calculation utilitarianism urges us to make. Once the choice of values comes out into the open, the question is whether it is to be done by the lawyer alone, by the client alone, or jointly. Once the choice comes out into the open the attractive apparent neutrality of utilitarian consequentialism disappears. The value questions must finally be faced. It is possible through self-awareness and honesty, which is the important basis of Doe's style of advice, to reduce the likelihood of the lawyer's imposing either his own values or the set presumed to be adopted by the standard, rationally self-interested ego. But there is an even more general problem with the utilitarian giving of advice that is independent of the values we assign to specific outcomes. That general problem is consequentialism itself: the idea that the way to decide how to act now is not to consider one's present disposition and the merit of the act in question, but to consider the value of the consequences of doing the act. . . .

So little are we allowed to regard the present that a client is likely to have difficulty even expressing the wise, human inclination to do the presently right-seeming and satisfying thing, especially if the lawyer is telling him how this or that will be saved or protected by deferral. The lawyer becomes an ally of the mean spirit that tells us we ought to live in and for the future; we ought to suffer and deprive ourselves of the only gratification possible — that which occurs presently. Present gratification in the law office is the prerogative of the eccentric client, the crotchety and willful. The solid everyday client does not do that kind of thing, and the lawyer will not let him.

Problem 2-5.   *What Would Be Your Advice?*

Further in the article, Lehman describes a story told to him by his father-in-law about two clients of his: "A husband and wife, who had been moved to give a sizeable gift to a friend who had shown them care and love. Mr. Wooster [the father-in-law] encouraged them to put off giving until the next year because a gift given that year would have been taxed less heavily. The following January, husband and wife were killed in the same accident, before the gift was delivered; there was thereafter no way to transfer the gift. The intended donee had lost out because of Mr. Wooster's tax advice. So, too, the donors had been denied the pleasure of bestowing the gift. The event suggests to a nice conscience that perhaps the advice had been wrong in the first place. Mr. Wooster was unhappy with the result, but could see nothing else — with the clients alive before him and no crystal ball — that would have been right for him to have done."

After reading this, what counsel would you give to a similarly situated couple — or their lawyer?

---

2. Interviewing

Interviewing skills are critical to learn what a case is about, help clients choose a dispute resolution process, and, once representation is underway, make sure client goals and needs are being met. An effective interview is essential to uncover your client's interests and needs, with appropriate attention to what happened in the past, what current interests are, and what future needs in relation to the matter might be. Without this knowledge, you may not be a good counselor, representative, or advocate for your client. In addition to initial interviewing, you can ensure that your client's goals, needs, and interests are being met through regular communication, as needs and interests may change during the course of representation. The lawyer who either assumes she knows what the client wants or, even more troublingly, substitutes her own judgment for the client's, may be failing the client. Yet communication between lawyer and client does not always occur as often or as well as it should.

David A. Binder, Paul B. Bergman & Susan C. Price, **LAWYERS AS COUNSELORS: A CLIENT-CENTERED APPROACH**

22-23, 35-40, 42-44 (1991)

THE ADVANTAGES OF A CLIENT-CENTERED APPROACH

[T]he client-centered approach encourages clients to participate actively in the description and resolution of their problems. As the discussion of the attributes suggests, the advantages of active client participation are substantial. Active client participation enhances the likelihood of producing satisfactory resolutions. It does so by (1) embracing both the legal and nonlegal dimensions of a client's problem; (2) employing the combined expertise of lawyer and client in identifying and evaluating potential solutions; and (3) encouraging decisions to be made by clients, who are generally better able than lawyers to assess whether solutions are likely to be satisfactory.

Moreover, active client participation respects the autonomy of the person who "owns" the problem. A client does not lose the right to make decisions which are likely to have a substantial impact on his or her life for having sought legal assistance. . . .

INHIBITORS

The seven inhibitors described below are common in lawyer-client dialogues. While other phenomena may also inhibit active client participation, these seven operate across a wide range of client personality types. Though the discussion treats each inhibitor as a separate phenomenon, in practice each often intertwines with others.

Of the seven inhibitors, the first two — ego threat and case threat — probably play the most pervasive role in blocking full communication.

A. Ego Threat

Clients tend to withhold information which they perceive as threatening to their self-esteem. The requested information may relate either to past or anticipated behavior, and the feelings that a question may arouse can range from mild embarrassment to a strong sense of guilt or shame. If a client believes that a truthful response will lead you to evaluate the client negatively, such a response threatens the client's self-esteem; the response is "ego threatening." Rather than risk your negative evaluation, the client may answer falsely, or become reluctant to participate in the conversation. . . .

B. Case Threat

A second major factor tending to inhibit client communication is "case threat." A client may believe that revealing information will "hurt my case." For example, an innocent criminal defendant may not want to reveal to you that she was near the scene of a crime because she fears that if the judge and jurors find it out she will lose. Alternatively, the client may fear that revealing the information will cause you to believe that the case is a loser and to fail to pursue it zealously. In either event, "case threat" is present. Similarly, assume that in a civil matter you ask a client about the whereabouts of a business document. If the client fears that information on the document contains damaging information, case threat may lead the client not to reveal its whereabouts. . . .

C. Role Expectations

Role expectations often affect communication between lawyers and clients. Most of us have sets of beliefs about what kind of behavior is appropriate within the confines of particular relationships. . . .

What does this phenomenon have to do with lawyers and clients? Clients will frequently enter your office with a set of expectations about what constitutes appropriate "client behavior." The expectations will vary from client to client; not all clients will have acquired their expectations from the same learning sources. In many instances, however, clients think of their lawyers as occupying positions of authority. Such clients may be somewhat reluctant to communicate fully in the belief that you know what subjects are deserving of inquiry. Thus, if you fail to broach a topic which a client feels is important, the client may assume (again, either consciously or intuitively) that the topic is not a significant one.

Interestingly, many clients have an opposite set of beliefs. This second group of clients tends to believe that a lawyer's role is limited to carrying out their wishes and that it is their privilege to speak their minds about any and all topics. In short, these clients see themselves in a dominant position vis à vis their counsel, and they are often not interested in fully responding to inquiries they perceive as unimportant. . . .

D. Etiquette Barrier

A fourth inhibitor is the "etiquette barrier." Often, an individual has information that he or she will freely provide to some persons but not to others. . . .

E. Trauma

This phenomenon occurs when you ask a client to recall an experience which evokes unpleasant feelings. Many events cause people to experience such negative feelings as fear, anger, humiliation, and sadness. When you ask clients to recall such events, they may re-experience the negative feelings. Consequently, a client may be motivated to avoid thinking and talking about unpleasant past events. . . .

F. Perceived Irrelevancy

This inhibitor is often more difficult to recognize, as it does not involve any feelings of discomfort or threat. The feeling involved here is one of "no reason to provide that data." A client feels that nothing will be gained by providing the information you request and so is reluctant to provide it. . . .

G. Greater Need

The last inhibitor is "greater need." This situation is characterized by a client's need or desire to talk about a subject other than that which is of immediate interest to you. . . .

FACILITATORS

The five facilitators described below encourage clients to participate fully in counseling dialogues. This chapter describes the facilitators but does not explore techniques for employing them. However, please note that you typically may employ facilitators without waiting for client reluctance to rear its annoying head. That is, you routinely incorporate the facilitators into all dialogues, whether the clients are enthusiastic or reluctant participants.

A. Empathic Understanding

Empathic understanding typically gives clients feelings of trust and confidence in an attorney-client relationship and thereby motivates clients to participate fully in conversations. Despite the motivational power of empathic understanding, lawyers commonly fail to utilize it when talking with clients.

Empathy probably cannot be defined or precisely described. Perhaps the following comments by Carl Rogers give some sense of what empathy involves:

> Empathy in its most fundamental sense . . . involves understanding the experiences, behaviors, and feelings of others as they experience them. It means that [lawyers] must, to the best of their abilities, put aside their own biases, prejudices, and points of view in order to understand as clearly as possible the points of view of their clients. It means entering into the experience of clients in order to develop a feeling for their inner world and how they view both this inner world and the world of people and [events] around them.

People have limited opportunities in our society to express their thoughts and feelings to someone who is willing to (1) listen, (2) understand, and (3) at the same time, not judge. . . .

B. Fulfilling Expectations

The phenomenon of "fulfilling expectations" refers to people's tendencies to want to satisfy the perceived expectations of those with whom they interact. Your simply communicating, verbally or nonverbally, your expectations will often be the catalyst that motivates a client to undertake a particular discussion.

This facilitator is especially useful when you sense that certain inhibitors are making a client reluctant to provide information. On sensing the reluctance, you can verbally convey a strong expectation that the sought data should be revealed. The client's need to conform to your expectations may well be stronger than whatever needs have given rise to the reluctance to respond. In such situations, the inhibitors will be overcome and the information revealed. . . .

C. Recognition

Human beings often need attention and recognition from people outside their close circle of family and friends. They enjoy feeling important and seek the attention and esteem of outsiders. Thus, giving an interviewee "recognition" motivates the interviewee to be more cooperative and open. . . .

D. Altruistic Appeals

People often need to identify with a high value or cause that is beyond their immediate self-interest. This need may be a form of identification with the objectives of a large social group. A person's performance of altruistic deeds usually increases the person's self-esteem. Thus, clients are often motivated to participate fully when doing so makes them feel altruistic. . . .

E. Extrinsic Reward

Realizing that certain behavior is in their self-interest usually motivates people to engage in that behavior. Thus, a person with the mind set, "what's in it for me?" at times is reluctant to provide information. Hence, you may facilitate disclosure of information that a client seems reluctant to discuss by pointing out why the sought data may aid in resolving the client's problem. You thereby indicate that providing the information is in the client's best interest. . . .

To succeed with a client-centered approach, the lawyer needs to listen carefully to their client. Indeed, listening is a key skill for lawyers in negotiation, mediation, arbitration, and life generally. Why does listening need to be taught as a separate skill? People spend plenty of time in life listening — listening in class, listening to their friends, listening to their family. But the difference between exercising a day-to-day skill and practicing to make this seemingly mundane skill more effective is significant. Listening well is actually hard to do.

The next excerpt, on how to listen to your client, continues from the Binder, Bergman & Price text on client-counseling.

 David A. Binder, Paul B. Bergman & Susan C. Price, **LAWYERS AS COUNSELORS: A CLIENT-CENTERED APPROACH**

46-48, 52-54, 56-57, 60-61 (1991)

Listening is a skill of paramount importance, and one which few lawyers employ successfully. Most lawyers are too busy asking questions and giving advice to take the time to listen. However, if you are to see problems from clients' perspectives, develop full information and involve clients fully in the decision-making process, you must become a good listener.

Just what is it a good listener will hear? Of course, a good listener will hear factual content. But a good listener will also hear the feelings that will accompany that content. When recalling an event, a client often describes not only what occurred, but also the feelings that the event aroused in the client. Moreover, a client's very act of recall may trigger still further emotional reactions: "At the time I was somewhat upset, but now just talking about it makes me really mad." Finally, proposed solutions almost inevitably generate emotional reactions for clients. For example, a client may say, "I'm nervous about leaving the terms of the payout provision so uncertain." Accordingly, good listeners hear both content and current and past feelings.

Your reaction may be that good listening is a very simple and easily accomplished task: "I just have to sit back and pay attention." In reality, listening requires enormous concentration and positive action. Far from being an intuitively simple task, listening is a skill. Like other skills, its mastery requires awareness and practice of specialized techniques. . . .

IDENTIFYING CONTENT AND FEELINGS

"Content" is the data that determines clients' legal rights or its relevance to their proposed transactions. "Feelings" are the labels that clients use to describe their emotional reactions to events or to contemplated transactions. Words typically used to describe feelings include happy, amused, excited, sad, angry, anxious, disappointed, frightened, irritated, and confused.

From a legal point of view, you may be primarily interested in content. However, you can usually provide empathic understanding only if you also identify and respond to a client's feelings. To develop your skill in recognizing both content and feelings, consider the following examples.

Client 1:

"My husband and I sat down years ago and wrote a will together, but I guess I never really thought we'd use it. Then they called to say my husband had had a heart attack at work. He died two days later. When he died, I felt overwhelmed. Lately, I've been worrying about our finances. It's hard to think of money at a time like this, but I feel like I should. I can't sleep at night, and I just sit around depressed all day. Other times, when I think about him, I start crying and it seems like it will never stop. On top of all this, the children are saying they are going to contest the will. They've already hired a lawyer. I'm really surprised, I never expected this."

What is the content of the client's situation?
What are the client's past and current feelings? . . .

Client 1:

Content: Husband died unexpectedly and wife must assume responsibility for family finances. Children plan to contest the will and have already hired a lawyer.

Feelings: Sad, overwhelmed, depressed, worried, surprised. . . .

ACTIVE LISTENING

Actively listening is the most effective talk tool that exists for demonstrating understanding and reducing misunderstanding. It is the process of picking up a client's message and sending it back in a reflective statement which mirrors what you have heard.

Client: "When I asked him for the money, he had the nerve to tell me not to be uptight."

Lawyer: "Rather than offering to pay you back, he suggested that you were somehow wrong for asking. You were angry."

Your reply is a classic active listening response. It demonstrates that you understand the content of the client's remark. Also, the reply reflects back to the client your understanding of the client's feelings that accompanied the incident. Further, the statement only mirrors the client's statement; it does not in any way "judge" it. And, though your statement reflects the client's feelings, you do not ask the client to explore those feelings in greater detail. Rather, the statement simply indicates your awareness that the client was angered.

Note that you do not simply repeat, or "parrot," what the client said. Rather, your reply reflects the *essence* of the content of the client's remark, as well as your perception, based both on the statement and on the client's non-verbal cues, of the client's feelings. You distill the information and emotion from the client's statement, and then convey back what you have heard and understood — hence the term "active listening." . . .

As a general rule, lawyers pay far too little attention to the feelings of their clients. Lawyers all too often see themselves as rational fact-gatherers and decision-makers. . . . This attitude towards the importance of feelings in the attorney-client relationship is wrong on at least two grounds. First, empathy is the real mortar of an attorney-client (indeed, *any*) relationship. To be empathic you need to hear, understand and accept a client's feelings, and to find a way to convey this empathic understanding to your clients. Second . . . [p]roblems evoke feelings, and feelings in turn shape problems. Lawyers can neither communicate fully with their clients nor help fashion satisfactory solutions if they ignore feelings . . .

We really have little formal training in listening for and articulating the human feelings that accompany events and future plans. . . . Therefore, you are likely to need to devote more effort to learning to reflect feelings than to learning to reflect content. . . .

RESPONDING TO VAGUELY EXPRESSED FEELINGS

By specifically labeling feelings, you can help a client understand her or his own emotions. The labeling helps bring the feelings out into the open, so that the feelings are explicitly included in the counseling process. . . .

Example:

Client: "I felt *bummed out* when I found out she was having an affair with him. I thought our marriage meant something. I *guess I was wrong*."

Lawyer: "You felt *hurt* and *disappointed* when you learned about the affair." . . .

RESPONDING TO UNSTATED FEELINGS

Sometimes you may be confident that a situation was an emotional one, but less confident about precisely what emotion was aroused. If so, you may doubt whether the feeling you identify in a reflective response will be completely accurate. As a result, you may shy away from verbalizing feelings when a client has not done so first.

However, a reflective response need not be "spot on" to provide empathy. For example, . . . your reflective response was "you sound pretty aggravated." If you are correct, your client may well validate the accuracy of your statement: "Yeah, I really am; given how we have helped these people for all this time, I can't believe they are doing this." But even if you are somewhat off the mark, a client may at most clarify the inaccuracy — "Well, I'm not aggravated yet, but I certainly am puzzled." . . .

RESPONDING TO NON-VERBAL EXPRESSIONS OF FEELINGS

Your everyday knowledge of how people are likely to react to situations is one basis for identifying unstated feelings. A second is a client's non-verbal cues. Non-verbal cues are generally of two types — auditory and visual. Auditory cues include such things as voice intonation, pitch, rate of speech, and pauses in conversation. Visual cues include posture; gestures; facial expressions; body movements such as fidgeting fingers and constantly shifting positions; and autonomic physiological responses such as sweating and blushing. When non-verbal cues indicate the presence of a particular emotion, an active listening response is often appropriate. . . .

NON-EMPATHIC (JUDGMENTAL) RESPONSES

Often, lawyers do respond to statements on an emotional level without providing the empathy of active listening responses. . . .

> Client: When the promotion list came out, I was not on it. And I know I had been on the preliminary list. To see such blatant discrimination made me realize it was finally time to do something about it.

> Lawyer:
> No. 1:   I don't blame you.
> No. 2:   But I guess after a while you calmed down.
> No. 3:   You finally acknowledged what you probably knew all along. You as well as many others were victims of discrimination, and would probably continue to be.

Lawyer No. 1 has judged the appropriateness of the reaction. Lawyer No. 2 has treated the feeling as irrelevant and shifted the discussion to another time frame. Lawyer No. 3 has played amateur psychologist, by attempting to analyze the reason for the reaction. None has simply mirrored back the client's likely emotions — "You were really furious," or "You feel wronged and want to take action." . . .

Problem 2-6.   *What Response Is Better?*

Another example from Binder, Bergman & Price is as follows:

Client: We've been working on landing this account for over two years. Our competitors were sure they were going to get it. I've got so many ideas for positioning the whole product line; I can't wait to finalize the contract and get going.

Lawyer:
No. 1:   You're probably happy because you feel you are achieving a potential you always knew you had.
No. 2:   That's great but you have to take your time and go over the contract carefully. If you don't you may regret it.
No. 3:   You have every right to gloat after pulling off a deal like this.

Assess the three lawyers' responses.

The following summary explains the goals of interviewing and how the actual interview progresses.

 Robert M. Bastress & Joseph D. Harbaugh, INTERVIEWING, COUNSELING AND NEGOTIATING: SKILLS FOR EFFECTIVE REPRESENTATION

66-68, 71, 77-78, 85-86, 92-97, 99, 101, 104, 106 (1990)

THE GOALS OF INTERVIEWING

1. Attorney-Client Rapport

From your first contact with a client, a relationship forms that will grow throughout the period of representation. The kind and quality of the relationship ultimately needed to effectively represent a client in a substantial case is likely beyond attaining in the initial interview. But the initial interview is essential to cementing the foundation for the lawyer-client relationship. If the job is poorly done, the foundation will be unable to support the construction of the complex professional relationship needed to conduct a long or emotionally difficult case. Therefore, your initial telephone contact or face-to-face meeting with the client is the moment to begin to establish the appropriate professional rapport.

"Rapport" here has a twofold significance. First, it connotes a certain personal regard between you and the client. . . . Rapport also means that the client respects you as a competent professional who is truly interested in the client's problem. . . .

Second, "rapport" means mutual trust. . . .

2. Goals of the Attorney-Client Relationship During the Interview Stage

In the initial phases of representation, you want to establish a relationship with the client that facilitates information flow, encourages assignment of responsibility, and fosters a willingness in the client to seriously consider your advice and engage in frank discussion of alternatives.

Information, whether it be helpful or damaging to the case, is the cornerstone of a lawyer's work and the primary goal of interviewing. . . . With an attitude that encourages, supports, and accepts the client, you make the client more comfortable and facilitate information flow. . . .

Assignment of responsibility in the client interview is a two-way street. Clients normally assign to you the overall handling of their legal problems. You, in turn, will more likely assign to the client additional information functions. . . . To facilitate this cross-assignment of duties, clients should have confidence in you as a competent professional and as a caring, considerate human being. With that confidence, clients are more likely to assign to you all facets of the legal problem and to accept your assignment of necessary fact-finding tasks.

Finally, lawyers are givers of advice. This advice, of course, is worthless if the client is unwilling to consider it seriously. . . . A relationship with the client must be established that encourages understanding of your role in advice-giving and the client's role in receiving and acting on that advice. Such a relationship demands your candor and honesty in evaluating alternatives and consequences and your patience and assistance as the client works through the available options. . . .

THE ANATOMY OF THE INITIAL CLIENT INTERVIEW

The initial interview with the client is an obviously important — and particularly difficult — stage of the lawyer-client relationship. . . . Because little or no information about the client's problem and goals has been exchanged, the lawyer must operate without a detailed agenda and the structure it provides.

Despite the apparent absence of information, you can nevertheless efficiently structure initial client interviews. . . . Those parts include planning for the interview, "ice-breaking," problem identification, problem overview, verification, and closure. . . .

Introductory Ice-Breaking

Most clients, from the experienced business client who routinely deals with attorneys to an unsophisticated person seeking a lawyer's advice for the first time, are apprehensive about the initial meeting with their new lawyer. Except for the most gregarious of us, people generally are discomforted by the process of formally meeting another person who, like a lawyer, represents power and authority. That discomfort is exacerbated by the fact that clients seeking legal counsel are usually troubled and concerned about the problem confronting them. Finally, because many clients visit a lawyer to seek help in a matter over which they have little control, they consciously or unconsciously experience a sense of dependency. The combination of these three factors produces people who approach their initial interviews with trepidation. . . .

By their very nature, feelings of apprehension, discomfort, and anxiety are inhibitors of open communication. Since these emotional conditions can interfere with the flow of information and the establishment of a trusting relationship between the attorney and the client, it is your responsibility to alleviate the apprehension and diminish the discomfort.

Effective use of your introductory interaction with the new (or old) client and the application of "ice-breaking" techniques should help to reduce client anxiety and allow the client to feel more comfortable in the professional setting. . . .

Problem Identification

Your goal during the problem identification stage of the initial interview is to obtain the client's perception of the problem without imposing your own structure on the client. To achieve this goal, begin with an open-ended question or statement that calls for a narrative response from the client and that contains only general guidance on the direction his or her response should take. . . .

First, the client is asked to identify the problem in his or her own terms. . . . Second, by suggesting there is a beginning of the problem, the client is reminded of the importance of chronological order. . . . By allowing the client to decide where along the time continuum to begin, you are more apt to get the client's uninfluenced view of which facts are critical. Third, the client should be told to isolate his or her preferred solutions to the identified problems. In this way, you obtain valuable information about the client's goals and are in a position to evaluate whether the client's expectations are realistic or unrealistic. . . .

Clients, from the most sophisticated businessperson with extensive experience with lawyers to the most naïve layperson with no prior legal contacts, usually have prepared for their initial encounter with counsel. Consciously or unconsciously, most clients review and organize the facts of their problems, think through their goals and options, and even select the words they will use in telling the lawyer about their problems and solutions. . . .

Given these likelihoods, you should listen carefully to the client's response to the initial open-ended question. . . . During your clients' narratives, you should encourage their elaboration with body language (maintaining eye contact, leaning forward slightly holding your arms in an open position, and nodding) and positive oral signals (e.g., "uh-huh" and "I see").

Lawyers often err in interviews by failing to allow the clients to complete their description of the problem, their perceptions, and their proposed solutions. Two reasons explain this common failure: premature diagnosis and fear of wasted time. . . .

If the attorney focuses too early on what appears to be the crux of the client's problem, the lawyer may impose this snap judgment on the rest of the interview. If this occurs, subtle facts can be missed, important emotions can be ignored, and unique solutions can be discarded. . . .

The first step in avoiding these interviewing errors is simple: Do not interrupt the client's rendition of the problem. . . .

Problem Overview

Once you gain an understanding of the problem as the client sees it and of the solution the clients wants, you are ready to move to the heart of the interview: the overview. . . . By overview, we mean you should carefully scrutinize the whole of the client's problem during this stage. . . .

You must determine three important issues during the problem overview portion of the initial client interview: (1) the sequencing of topics; (2) the nature of the questions put to the client; and (3) the techniques of following up initial topic questions. . . .

The process of topic identification involves determining which events mentioned by the client are significant to the solution of the client's problem. . . . The primary means of obtaining information during the overview phase of the interview is the posing of a series of questions to the client. . . . An inverted funnel approach begins with specific, narrow questions and leads toward inquiries of a broad, general nature. . . .

As the interview progresses, particularly during the later stages of the problem overview, you develop some tentative hypotheses about how the client's problem may be resolved. As these alternative solutions evolve in your mind, you encounter a growing need to confirm pivotal facts, corroborate the important feelings of the client, and clarify the client's real goals. In short, you must verify those factors upon which identification of likely alternatives will depend.

Problem 2-7. *Practice!*

With a partner, explore what ice-breaking moves are most comfortable.

Our last excerpt on interviewing points out that learning more about psychology can help attorneys be more effective at interviewing and counseling their clients.

 Jean R. Sternlight & Jennifer Robbennolt, **GOOD LAWYERS SHOULD BE GOOD PSYCHOLOGISTS: INSIGHTS FOR INTERVIEWING AND COUNSELING CLIENTS**

23 Ohio St. J. on Disp. Resol. 437, 437, 441-442, 538-544 (2008)

. . . To be effective in working with clients, witnesses, judges, mediators, arbitrators, experts, jurors, and other lawyers, attorneys must have a good understanding of how people think and make decisions, and must possess good people skills . . . even experienced lawyers can improve their approach to interviewing and counseling by drawing on relevant psychology. . . . In general, interviewing and counseling sessions have three main components. First, the attorney uses an interview to obtain information from the client. Second, the attorney uses the counseling portion of the initial session to provide information to the client. Third, throughout the session the attorney is concerned with establishing rapport between attorney and client. . . .

A. PREPARING FOR THE INTERVIEW

1. Pre-Interview Information

. . . From a psychological standpoint, brief preliminary phone conversations can potentially be helpful in beginning to establish a relationship and build rapport. Conversely, the use of surveys or screening interviews with paralegals may give the impression that the attorney does not care enough about the client to participate in a conversation, and may lead the attorney to pre-determine what kinds of issues are important. In-person interviews offer a better opportunity than phone conversations or certainly written surveys to impress the client, build rapport, learn from the client, minimize reliance on the attorney's prior conceptions, and assess the client's own credibility. If an attorney feels it is important to get a "heads up" on the subjects to be discussed, we suggest a brief and friendly phone call to probe the generalities of the problem . . .

2. Setting the Stage

For an attorney [who] keeps a neat and comfortable office with diplomas or other awards on the wall, the intimate office setting can be appropriate. Alternatively, attorneys who have messy or otherwise unimpressive offices may want to conduct interviews in a nice conference room. In either setting, the attorney may want to offer the client a choice of seating options, and ensure that physical distance is sufficient for the client to feel comfortable. . . .

Lawyers who work as sports agents or who represent entertainers may well want to dress more flamboyantly than lawyers who do estate planning for elderly widows in the Midwest. So, while we cannot prescribe a particular set of clothes or hairstyle that is best for all situations, we can say that appearances do matter. . . .

B. CONDUCTING THE INTERVIEW

1. Importance of Open-Ended Questions

. . . [Open-Ended] questions are useful, from a psychological standpoint, for a variety of reasons. First, they allow clients to tell the story in the order that makes sense to them. This will encourage clients to tell a more complete story, aid clients' recall, allow clients to provide a level of detail with which they are confident, allow clients to explain their non-legal concerns, and deter attorneys from putting their clients' stories into pre-existing schema. Allowing clients to speak fully in response to open-ended questions will also speak to clients' desire for procedural justice . . . [I]nterruptions may well cause clients to provide more limited information or to forget key details and is unlikely to make them feel respected.

2. Cultural Sensitivity and Avoidance of Stereotypes

As [an attorney] questions his clients he must be careful to avoid stereotypes. The mere fact that his client is dressed like a slob does not mean, for example, that his client is poor. Rather than make assumptions based on clients' appearance, race, ethnicity, gender, or other factors, the attorney should use his questions to allow his clients to tell their own stories. At the same time, the attorney should be attuned to the possibility that his clients' culture may lead them to have different preferences than might be natural to him. Some clients may, for example, be uncomfortable with the handshake, use of first names, and [a] straight gaze. . . .

3. Listening Effectively and Responding Encouragingly

In addition to asking appropriate questions of his clients, an attorney should . . . respond appropriately. Most people probably think they are fairly good listeners, but in fact many of us do not listen as effectively as we might. [We] may well be guilty of multi-tasking—letting [our] minds wander to other tasks while our clients describe their problems. Or, [we] may allow [ourselves] to be guided unduly by stereotypes and heuristics, placing [our] clients' problems into pre-determined categories. To battle these likely flaws [we] need to try to focus more attentively on [our] clients, and such effective listening includes not only hearing clients' words but also paying attention to their tone and body language.

[P]sychological studies have shown that interviewers can both obtain more information and also create better rapport by engaging in an effective and sympathetic back and forth with their clients. Similarly, [an attorney] must develop some comfort with interacting with his clients at an emotional level. If [he] attempts to completely avoid emotion, he will be unable to understand his clients' non-legal concerns, unable to build a solid rapport with his client, unable to encourage his client to provide all information pertinent to the legal issue, and unable to connect well to his client as a counselor.

4. Helping Clients Remember

. . . [An attorney] has at his disposal a number of helpful tools derived from the psychological literature that he can use to try to effectively trigger client memories. For example, he can use open-ended questions; ask his clients to retell their story in chronological or reverse chronological order; ask them to focus on details of the setting that may not be directly relevant to the legal problem; and try to get clients to focus more on facts. He also knows from the psychological literature that he will not have much success if he simply urges his clients to probe their memories better for all of the facts and understands that frequent interruptions can interfere with client memories.

5. Building Trust

. . . [T]he psychology literature shows that [an attorney] ought to care about creating trust because he will more readily obtain full information from a trusting client. Similarly, [an attorney] will be more effective as a counselor when his clients trust him. To gain his clients' trust, [an attorney] should not only continue to show clients that he is a competent and intelligent attorney, but also show clients that he cares about them as people and that he is willing to set aside his own personal interests, when necessary. Studies have shown that open communication, perspective taking, and willingness to explain can all be important to building a trusting relationship.

6. Being Aware of Clients' and One's Own Likely Cognitive Biases

. . . Both lawyers and clients tend to perceive the world through their schema and stereotypes, emphasize personal characteristics when they attribute causation, assume that others see the world the same way they do, are affected by an array of positive illusions, and show a tendency to do Monday morning quarterbacking. As clients report the "facts" as they understand them to their attorneys, the attorneys need to consider that their clients' discussions of these "facts" are undoubtedly affected by the psychology of cognition. Attorneys need to ask follow up questions and seek alternative perspectives to try to get beyond these biases. Similarly, attorneys need to be aware of the use of such heuristics in their own thinking.

7. Verifying Veracity

[An attorney] will be better off keeping an open mind and withholding judgment about veracity while seeking confirmation from other witnesses or documents. [He] also needs to remember that witnesses often report the same incident quite differently based on their different perceptions, construal, and memories, even though neither witness is lying.

8. Remembering the Interview

[An attorney's] own memory is no more infallible than that of his clients. [He] must take steps to ensure that he adequately recalls and records his discussions with his own clients, as absent special measures, surely his memory will fail.

Problem 2-8.   *Study with Your Own Mind*

Watch yourself as you listen in class or listen to another person. How many times does your mind wander? Are you thinking about what you will say next, what errands you need to run, the people you need to call, whether or not you fed the cat? If you are in an hour-long interview with a client what can you do to stay focused and actively listen? What note-taking or other recording techniques should you use in an interview?

---

3. Client Counseling

When the lawyer has successfully interviewed a client to learn what is really important to the client, then the lawyer may begin to counsel and advise the client about potential substantive "solutions" to the client's problem(s), and what processes might be most appropriate for achieving those solutions. The excerpts below provide some approaches for organizing these counseling tasks. We will discuss counseling specifically about dispute resolution processes at the end of the book after you have learned more about those processes.

David A. Binder, Paul B. Bergman & Susan C. Price, **LAWYERS AS COUNSELORS: A CLIENT-CENTERED APPROACH**

293-299, 303-304, 307-308 (1991)

[After Step One of clarifying objectives and step two of identifying alternatives,] the *third step* is to identify the likely consequences of each. Since, as you know, solutions carry nonlegal consequences, you must explore likely nonlegal as well as legal consequences. . . .

A. THE NECESSITY TO PREDICT

Assessing the consequences involves a prediction of what is likely to occur in the future. . . . Predictions are statements of probability. . . . The predictions that you and your clients make almost always center on people's behavior for which accurate data bases are not available. . . . Any data bases you and a client have individually acquired for predicting future consequences have usually been arrived at by a highly selective and intuitive process in which seeming similarities tend to mask important differences, and thus introduce uncertainty into your data base.

However, those imperfect data bases are often all that you and your clients will have available for making predictions. The question, then, is on whose data base should a prediction be made — yours or a client's?

B. PREDICTING LEGAL CONSEQUENCES

Predicting legal consequences is the essence of providing "legal advice." As you would imagine, responsibility for predicting legal consequences rests primarily on you. A client expects you to have a better data base for predicting such matters as how a jury is likely to rule, what legal consequences attach to doing business as a corporation rather than a sole proprietorship, how getting a trademark might protect a company's product, and whether a corporation's omission of information from a securities prospectus might subject the officers to criminal or civil liability.

C. PREDICTING NONLEGAL CONSEQUENCES

Nonlegal consequences, as you know, consist of the likely economic, social, psychological, political and moral ramifications that may flow from adopting a particular solution. And just as you generally have the better data base for predicting legal consequences, a client often has the better data base for predicting nonlegal ones. . . . Therefore, you often rely on clients to predict nonlegal consequences.

At the same time, your own experiences may enable you to predict (or at least inquire about) nonlegal consequences. . . .

D. ORGANIZING THE DISCUSSION OF CONSEQUENCES

Turn now to techniques for counseling clients with respect to likely consequences.

1. Review Options Separately

Many people have difficulty solving problems because they cannot focus on discrete options and their attendant advantages and disadvantages. . . . Thus, once Step Two has placed available options on the table, you should begin Step Three by focusing on a specific option.

2. Ask a Client to Choose a Starting Place

To maintain a client centered approach, ask clients which option they want to discuss first. . . . This approach builds on the advantages of neutrality, as you leave to a client the choice of which option to discuss first. It also tends to motivate a client to participate actively, since the client can select whichever option seems most appealing.

3. Adopt the Role of Information Seeker

After a client selects an option, you generally continue to place a client in the figurative limelight by asking the client to identify the pros and cons of that option. . . .

You can seek a client's thoughts about consequences in one of three ways. You can ask a client only about advantages, about both advantages and disadvantages, or only about disadvantages. . . .

4. The Cross Over Phenomenon

[R]arely will it be possible or desirable to systematically run through every alternative individually, taking up pros and then cons. Rather, clients tend to "cross over" from one alternative to another. Within a single alternative, they often jump back and forth between "pros" and "cons." . . .

5. Responding to Client Cross Over

The inevitability and frequency of cross over may entice you into abandoning any thoughts of an organized exploration of consequences. However, while cross over means that you must modify an "ideal" counseling dialogue, you should not abandon orderliness altogether.

The risk of cross over is that you fail to unearth all salient consequences. Crossing over is akin to the danger of "sidetracking" that you encounter when probing events for details. As clients jump back and forth, both of you are likely to lose track of how thoroughly consequences have been exhausted

6. Discuss Consequences You Foresee

As you will undoubtedly recognize, a Step Three discussion of likely consequences includes advising clients of potential legal and nonlegal consequences that you foresee. If, as will usually be the case, you first ask a client to predict consequences, you might then either (1) integrate the consequences you foresee into the client's discussion, or (2) wait until the client concludes and supplement the client's list with your own. . . .

7. Charting Alternatives and Consequences

We *strongly recommend* that during a Step Three discussion, you make a written chart of the advantages and disadvantages of every option. . . . Writing down consequences as they emerge is very important. First, a chart is often essential for carrying out the goal of fully exploring each alternative. Because of cross over, a discussion of alternatives and consequences rarely proceeds in a straightforward manner. Without a written record, it is hard for both you and a client to remember what territory has already been covered. Also, seeing consequences in writing may stimulate both you and a client to recall additional ones. . . .

With alternatives and consequences fully flushed out, you and a client are ready for *the fourth step*, making a decision. Often, you need do no more than ask for a client's choice. . . .

Sometimes you may have to re-review the options and their likely consequences, perhaps asking a client to think carefully about how likely a consequence really is and how much importance a consequence carries as you do so. Referring to a chart and summarizing its contents will often help you carry out the re-review.

This next excerpt returns to psychology to help us better understand how to counsel clients effectively.

 Jean R. Sternlight & Jennifer Robbennolt, GOOD LAWYERS SHOULD BE GOOD PSYCHOLOGISTS: INSIGHTS FOR INTERVIEWING AND COUNSELING CLIENTS

23 Ohio St. J. on Disp. Resol. 437, 437, 441-442, 538-544 (2008)

Providing advice to clients, or for that matter to anyone, can be tricky. No matter whether [an attorney] seeks to be directive or client-centered in his approach, he will need to overcome a variety of psychological hurdles to be effective as a counselor.

[An attorney] helps his clients think through their options, he needs to remember that many clients will have a craving for justice—procedural, distributive, and retributive. To some degree, [an attorney] can fulfill his clients' desire for procedural justice through the ways in which he interviews them. [Clients experience procedural justice when they have an opportunity to describe their concerns to a respectful and intelligent listener. . . .] But, as [he] counsels clients about their options, he should recall that his clients may have a strong interest in having their voice heard or in presenting their claims to a neutral, and not just in receiving a particular substantive outcome. Of course [an attorney] should also consider his clients' desire for distributive justice [a distribution of those things in dispute that accords with the equities of the situation], while recognizing that this may mean something more than just getting the most one can for oneself. In addition, clients may have needs based on their sense of retributive justice—such as a need to punish or to receive an apology. . . .

Dealing with clients' cognitive biases is also challenging. Given clients' tendency to be overoptimistic, attorneys need to make a special effort to explain potential risks and downsides clearly, and to try to make sure that clients are not just hearing the positive and tuning out the negative. At the same time, an attorney who beats her client over the head with negative risks may well have a difficult time establishing a good rapport. Clients look to their attorneys to be their advocates, and may feel that an attorney who spends too much time warning of downsides is not an effective advocate. Walking this fine line between optimism and pessimism is tricky, and no single strategy will work for all clients. The attorney needs to try to communicate risks while at the same time maintaining her role as a strong advocate for the client. . . .

The attorney also needs to be careful in the way that she frames a client's options. We have seen that the attractiveness of a particular option varies substantially depending upon the way it is presented. Grouping one option with certain others may lessen or heighten its attractiveness. Characterizing an option as a gain rather than a loss relative to the status quo will make that option more attractive. Similarly, the attorney needs to be careful about providing early assessments or other information that may tend to "anchor" clients' perceptions or expectations. So, what is the conscientious, psychologically aware attorney to do? One temptation may be to take a vow of silence, in that astute attorneys will realize that they cannot help but influence their clients every time they open their mouths. Yet, silence is not an option because the attorney has been hired to provide good counsel. Thus, our best advice is that the attorney be conscious of the significance of the terms she uses, and try to vary her advice accordingly. . . .

As clients respond to the advice afforded by their attorneys, psychologically educated attorneys can be prepared to address common phenomena that may affect the client's decisions: a tendency to gather irrelevant information, difficulty predicting future emotional reactions generally, and a tendency to make decisions based on regret aversion. The psychologically attuned attorney can try to counter all of these phenomena by addressing them head on.

Counseling clients involves, in part, acting as a teacher. Thus, the vast psychological literature on learning theory is highly relevant to attorneys. That literature shows that people learn in different ways, and that effective teachers use multiple methods to convey their messages. Thus, whereas the typical attorney may rely substantially on oral communication with the client, the psychologically attuned attorney will know to use different approaches [perhaps the client communicates more clearly via email, for example] as well. Good teachers also know that important lessons often need to be repeated, so attorneys should not assume that their clients heard and retained everything that was said at a prior session. . . .

> ## Problem 2-9.   *Delivering Reality*
>
> A client comes to you and is insistent that he wants to go to court to sue his place of employment for discrimination. After carefully listening to your client and going over all the information, you realize he has a very weak case. How do you present the reality of litigation to your client? What do you say to him if he still wants to pursue litigation?

This last excerpt by Nancy Welsh discusses one last concern to a client-centered approach, namely the attorney. It is probably not shocking to you that attorneys may be resistant to moving disputes outside the courtroom. Once the "battle" is no longer in the courtroom, are attorneys even necessary? Earlier in this chapter you read articles explaining why attorneys are often necessary in all areas of dispute resolution; attorneys bring knowledge, research, detachment, support, and empowerment. Still, there is resistance by the legal profession to make a move to a more "humanistic" approach to legal problems, and this excerpt seeks to explain why lawyers continue to focus on the legal and not on the human aspect of the problems.

 Nancy A. Welsh, LOOKING DOWN THE ROAD LESS TRAVELED: CHALLENGES TO PERSUADING THE LEGAL PROFESSION TO DEFINE PROBLEMS MORE HUMANISTICALLY

2008 J. Disp. Resol. 45, 49-54, 56-57

[W]hy does court-connected mediation, often involving newer lawyers as representatives of their clients, . . . still appear so unlikely to reflect a broader, more humanistic orientation to problem definition? . . . This essay will focus on three factors that may help to explain why it seems to be so difficult for many lawyers to escape the confines of a narrow, legalistic framing of issues . . .

THE PSYCHES AND PSYCHOLOGICAL NEEDS OF LAW STUDENTS AND LAWYERS

Research reveals that law students (and thus future lawyers) have some unique psychological needs and characteristics that may help explain the persistent narrowness of lawyers' definition of problems to be resolved. Not surprisingly, law students tend to have a strong focus on academics. In addition, though, research has found that law students are generally characterized by [and have] a high need for dominance, leadership, and attention; they experience severe discomfort with feelings of inferiority. Research also shows that though law students may have good social skills, most demonstrate a "low interest in emotions or others' feelings." Perhaps consistent with this aversion to focusing on emotions or feelings, law students also are much more likely than the general population to gather information and make decisions based on general standards or rules, rather than relational values. . . .

These needs and characteristics comprise the "typical" law student profile. This does not mean that *every* law student (and thus *every* future lawyer) fits the profile. In fact, there is research affirming that a hefty minority of law students do *not* fit this profile. But the exceptions are also less likely to remain in law school and become lawyers.

The psychological tendencies revealed by research should make it relatively unsurprising that the people who have chosen to enter the legal profession dominate mediation sessions and anchor any discussion of the issues in the application of litigation's rules and standards, rather than in the emotional, psychological, or moral needs of the people in the room. For this psychological profile, feeling like a lawyer may mean feeling in control, central to the action, adept at finding the appropriate analytical box to fit an unruly reality. It is also likely to mean substantial discomfort at the prospect of risking a human connection with people in pain or trying to respond constructively to the confusing and uncomfortable emotions that are often part of litigation. Such discomfort is not irrational. The degree of the discomfort, however, may present a significant impediment to the adoption of innovations that are explicitly humanistic.

THE REQUIREMENTS OF SUSTAINING A PROFESSION

As we assess law students' and lawyers' reluctance to frame problems to include their emotional, psychological, and moral elements, we also must consider lawyers' understandable interest in sustaining their right to call themselves "professionals . . . ". [S]ociologists have found that the privileges of professionalism are earned only by those groups that effectively demonstrate their possession of three attributes: (1) the unique, abstract body of knowledge..; (2) skillful application of this knowledge base; and (3) application that assists those members of society who have encountered physical or moral problems that involve significant risks. . . .

People in trouble seek out lawyers to learn the relevant rule of law and what they are entitled to expect. Indeed, if lawyers were to abandon skillful legal analysis, particularly in a country guided (at least aspirationally) by the rule of law, they would lose their unique ability to help the members of society caught in risky physical, financial, and moral situations navigate their way. Viewed from this perspective, lawyers' insistence on maintaining their focus on relevant legal principles in mediation is not just understandable but socially beneficial. . . .

It should not be surprising that lawyers prefer to continue "thinking like a lawyer" in court-connected mediation. The question is whether lawyers can maintain their professional privileges, role, and autonomy while also inviting the consideration of emotions, moral concerns, and underlying interests in appropriate cases. . . .

THE DEMANDS OF THE BUSINESS OF LAW

The demands of the business of law — both the demands of entering practice and the demands of practice itself — also may contribute to lawyers' hesitation to expand their focus much beyond the law and "litigation and persuasion issues". . . .

Law students' and lawyers' need or desire for money is likely to influence how they understand their own value in the marketplace. Their knowledge of the law, rather than their ability or willingness to feel a human connection, is what they have to sell. The new lawyers who are insecure about their role in a firm and face the repayment of huge law school loans, as well as those new lawyers who expect a quick ascension to a high standard of living, may be particularly hesitant to add human or moral considerations to the technical advice that the firm or the client has requested. Increasingly, too, profit-maximizing considerations have led segments of legal practice to emulate corporate employment, making one-on-one, personal interaction with real, individual clients less likely and thus humanistic practice less attainable. . . .

[W]hat do clients expect from lawyers? On one hand, there is evidence that both individual and corporate clients appreciate lawyers who show that they care, communicate well and are committed to helping their clients through difficult times. . . . On the other hand, good communication and caring take time, and many clients do not want to (or cannot) pay as much as many lawyers would like to (or must) charge for their services and time. In addition, there is evidence that clients expect lawyers to be smart, knowledgeable, and dominant. They are much less likely to expect care and compassion. . . .

THE ROLE OF LEGAL EDUCATION

Legal education, with its current primary focus on "thinking like a lawyer," reflects and reinforces the dominant psychological profile of its students, the desire of the legal profession to sustain its privileges, and the business of legal practice. Importantly, legal education's focus on logic, rules, and standards also serves an important social purpose.

Should legal education also try to help students care about *feeling* like lawyers? Should we prepare our students to make meaningful — and sometimes difficult — human connections as they provide legal services to people caught in significant physical, moral, and financial dilemmas? . . .

[P]rofessional schools are incorporating the development of "emotional intelligence" into their curricula, researchers are exploring the revision of law school admissions practices to include consideration of humanistic factors that predict effective lawyers. . . .

These encouraging developments suggest that both thinking and feeling like a lawyer can enable lawyers to identify issues in a variety of useful ways — in terms of legal analysis and litigation issues, but also in terms of human and ethical needs, including many clients' emotional and psychological need to experience something that feels like justice when they meet with their lawyers. These developments also suggest that despite the significant psychological, professional, and business hurdles identified in this essay, a growing number of lawyers are searching for constructive means to bring a caring, humanistic element to their practices.

———————————————

Braced with a fuller understanding of the client's needs, interests and goals — thanks to active listening skills and thoughtful interviewing and counseling techniques — lawyers often proceed to the most direct form of legal problem solving: negotiation. Negotiation is a process likely to be used in every transaction or dispute that comes to a lawyer. The next three chapters explore this process.

Further Reading

John Barkai, *How to Develop the Skill of Active Listening*, 30 PRAC. LAW. (June, 1984).

Robert F. Cochran, Jr., *Introduction: Three Approaches to Moral Issues in Law Office Counseling*, 30 PEPP. L. REV. 592 (2003).

Stephen Ellmann, Robert D. Dinerstein, Isabelle R. Gunning, Katherine R. Kruse & Ann C. Shalleck (2009). *Lawyers and Clients: Critical Issues in Interviewing and Counseling*. Eagan, MN: West.

Stephen Ellmann, Isabelle Gunning, Robert Dinnerstein & Ann Shalleck, *Legal Interviewing and Counseling: An Introduction*, 10 CLINICAL L. REV. 281 (2003).

Linda F. Smith, *Was It Good for You Too? Conversation Analysis of Two Interviews*, 96 KENTUCKY L. J. 579 (2007).

Paul R. Tremblay, *"Pre-Negotiation" Counseling: An Alternative Model*, 13 CLINICAL L. REV. 541 (2006).

PART II THE BASIC PROCESSES: NEGOTIATION, MEDIATION, AND ARBITRATION

Chapter 3 | Negotiation: Concepts and Models

When one door closes another door opens; but we so often look so long and so regretfully upon the closed door that we do not see the ones which open for us.

— Alexander Graham Bell

A pessimist sees the difficulty in every opportunity, an optimist sees the opportunity in every difficulty.

— Winston Churchill

If asked to draw a picture of a negotiation, many people likely would draw a table with two or more people sitting on opposite sides engaged in something akin to arm wrestling. This chapter expands and offers alternate pictures of negotiation. While it is true that many negotiations occur across large tables in conference rooms, many others occur in the hallways, on the phone, in the car, and at other everyday locations. Roger Fisher, author of the bestselling book *Getting to YES* and a well-known negotiation professor, says that a negotiation occurs every time that a person tries to influence someone else to do something. So, as you are reading this first chapter on negotiation, think about negotiations in which you have been regularly involved — with a parent, spouse, roommate, friend, neighbor, boss, or child — and how you think about these negotiations. How do they start? How do they proceed? What makes one successful and another the quintessential example of "if I had to do it again . . ."?

Negotiation is a process for resolving conflict and solving problems. It has, therefore, both conceptual and behavioral components, or, as negotiation scholar Howard Raiffa has described it, both a "science" (of substantive ideas for solutions and outcomes) and an "art" (the behavioral and skills aspects of approaching others to jointly accomplish some goal). Before we turn to the behaviors, skills, and processes (how to do negotiations), we need to spend some time thinking about how to think about or analyze what we hope to accomplish. As many negotiation scholars and practitioners have suggested, and as we will elaborate below, how one behaves in negotiation (what model or approach we choose to use) will depend on what we are trying to accomplish (what goals we are hoping to achieve) in the particular negotiation. And, in different kinds of negotiations, with different issues at stake, or different kinds of parties, we might choose different models or approaches to negotiation.

It is common for many to think of negotiation as an adversarial, competitive, or distributive (allocating scarce resources) exercise. Others prefer to see negotiation as an opportunity to resolve problems and seek joint gain, where possible, while remaining realistic about how the possibilities may be limited by what is at stake and who the parties are. It is useful to consider one's goals regarding both the process and the outcome of a negotiation, which will determine the orientation, mind-set, and behaviors chosen. These, in turn, will affect the outcomes produced. Some of the possibilities are illustrated below:[1]

Models of Negotiation

	GOAL	MODEL	BEHAVIOR	OUTCOMES
I.	Win (maximizing individual gain)	*Adversarial Distributive*	• Competitive or positional debate • Argue • Hide information • Make demands	• Win/lose • Impasse
II.	Compromise (relationship preserving)	*Soft Accommodative Sharing*	• Cooperate • Give in • Make unnecessary concessions	• Compromise • Split the difference • Lose
III.	Problem Solve (maximizing joint gain)	*Integrative Problem-solving Principled Interest-based*	• Collaborative • Ask questions • Listen • Explore needs/ interests • Find trades of complementary interests and needs • Use objective criteria	• Creative solutions • Expanded issues and opportunities • Contingent outcomes
IV.	Allocate created resources/solutions	*Mixed*	Create, then "claim"	Pareto optimal sharing gain

In this chapter we explore some of these basic models and approaches to negotiation with the hope that you will learn to conceptualize how best to handle your client's issues. You might think of negotiation as a complex process of first, conceptualizing what the problem or dispute is about (what is at stake), what you might need to resolve the matter (the "res" or resources needed for resolution), and whom (the parties) you might need to help you negotiate to good solution. Second, you

---

1. This chart is derived from Carrie Menkel-Meadow, Toward Another View of Legal Negotiation: The Structure of Problem Solving, 31 UCLA L. Rev. 754 (1983-1984) and ideas developed in Howard Raiffa, The Art and Science of Negotiation (1982) and David A. Lax & James K. Sebenius, The Manager as Negotiator: Bargaining for Cooperation and Competitive Gain (1986).

will make choices about how to achieve those goals (what behaviors to choose), as your negotiation counterpart also makes choices to which you will have to respond. And hopefully, if you are successful, you will seek to reach an agreement or solution that you should then evaluate for its ability to satisfy your client's needs and goals, as well as making the other side satisfied enough with the solution ("joint gain") so that there will be compliance with the agreement reached. Negotiation (whether direct or as mediated by a third party in mediation) involves both cognitive and behavioral skills. As an effective negotiator you should be able to analyze problems, plan for and prepare ideas for good resolutions, and choose behaviors that fit the situation and the parties to accomplish your goals.

When looking at the process of negotiation, scholars describe it in a variety of ways. One classic approach is to think of negotiation as linear — occurring in stages. For example, Professor Gerald Williams (looking at a conventional adversarial model) defines the process in four stages: (1) orientation and positioning; (2) argumentation; (3) emergence and crisis; and (4) agreement or final breakdown. The first step describes the way in which a negotiator thinks about the basic approach and style of the other negotiator. This negotiating relationship or orientation will dictate the approach, strategies, and tactics utilized by the negotiator. Positioning refers to the opening position or the beginning point that the negotiator establishes while he or she attempts to make further evaluations of the case and gain information. Generally, this stage continues over a longer period of time than other stages. During argumentation, stage two, legal and factual issues as well as strengths and weakness are more clearly outlined to each other, and the parties may go back and forth with offers. The third stage of emergence and crisis takes place as the deadline for settlement approaches. The parties need to determine if a deal is going to be made and on what terms. As a "final offer" is made, parties are faced with the choice of taking it, leaving it, or alternately, coming up with something else. Finally, the parties either reach a settlement, or the case goes forward to trial for resolution. In the case of settlement, the parties still face the task of working out the details of the settlement agreement that are important and deserve appropriate attention.

Another way of thinking about negotiation is more of a cyclical process, as explained by Phillip Gulliver. The process is not always directly linear but may require several moves (or cycles) to move forward. As he writes, "In negotiation, . . . there is a cyclical process comprising the repetitive exchange of information between the parties, its assessment, and the resulting adjustments of expectations and preferences; there is also a developmental process involved in the movement from the initiation of the dispute to its conclusion — some outcome — and its implementation. . . ."[2]

Other models described below suggest other forms of process that include reciprocal questioning and sharing of information, time for non-evaluative brainstorming of new ideas and solutions, presentation of multiple "interests" and "needs," framed differently than single or rigid positions or demands, and either direct or facilitated trading and sharing of ideas, rationales, and proposals for negotiated solutions. With negotiations varying in type and media (whether in person, in

---

2. Phillip H. Gulliver, Disputes and Negotiations: A Cross-Cultural Perspective 82 (1979).

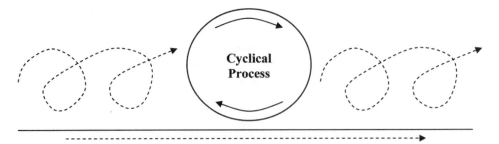

Developmental Process

e-mail, on the telephone, or through written drafts of documents), there are likely to be great variations in how stages and processes of negotiations develop, whether in single, specially designated negotiation meetings or in frequent, and interrupted, communications using a variety of media and negotiator representatives.

Problem 3-1. *House Hunting*

Imagine that you are house hunting. You find a house that looks like it meets your needs and is priced fairly based on your look at other houses in the neighborhood. It has the number of bedrooms you need and a lovely backyard. It is listed for $290,000, but your realtor thinks that it probably will go for less. You give an opening bid of $270,000. The realtor for the owners does not respond immediately but instead invites you to come back to see the house again. While there, the owner's realtor points out the newly refurbished kitchen with new appliances and a new floor. Also, he mentions that the owners recently redid much of the outdoor landscaping (which you cannot see because it is winter). You note, and point out to the realtor, that the driveway needs repaving soon. It also appears that the roof needs to be replaced within the next five years. When you ask for a response to your bid, the owners reply with a counteroffer of $285,000. You take your time to counteroffer and note that the house has been on the market for some time. You counteroffer at $280,000 and strongly let the realtor know this is your final bid. The owners accept.

Using Williams's stages, at which point does each stage commence in the above scenario? What issues are left for stage four? How is Gulliver's model relevant?

A. APPROACHES TO NEGOTIATION

This section discusses different approaches to negotiation, and the readings that follow highlight differences among these various approaches.

The first approach (and one you are probably most familiar with if you are a law student in our American culture) is called competitive bargaining or, sometimes, adversarial, distributive, or positional. Most of these labels refer to a negotiator who is primarily concerned with "winning" the negotiation for the client and for him- or herself. A competitive negotiator is often seen as more likely to engage in negative tactics, less likely to be interested in the other side's point of view, and perhaps, but not always, more unpleasant. This approach is often used by those who assume that what is being bargained for must be distributed between the parties — such as in simple two-party, "pricing" situations. A higher price gives the seller additional gain at the expense of the buyer.

At the other end of the spectrum is so-called "soft" bargaining, also known as accommodating, or cooperative. As the readings highlight, this approach focuses on relationships and on working with the other side. A cooperative negotiator is likely to be more pleasant and friendly. The risk for a cooperative negotiation approach is being taken advantage of by the competitive negotiator who values gain in the negotiation more than the relationship between the negotiators.

A third approach is problem solving, also called integrative, collaborative, or principled bargaining. A problem-solving approach to a negotiation is one in which the negotiator is interested in doing well for herself and her client and in working with the other side to meet that party's interests. Some call this the "joint gain" model of negotiation.

In the first excerpt below, two other styles are also discussed. A sharing or compromising approach is a splitting-the-difference style of negotiation. The final approach is avoiding. Avoiding is exactly as it sounds — a negotiator who tries to avoid conflict. This person either does not raise the conflict at all or tries to avoid discussing it if approached; if forced to deal with the conflict, an avoider tries to resolve it as quickly as possible.

 Kenneth Thomas, **CONFLICT AND CONFLICT MANAGEMENT**

in Handbook of Industrial and Organizational Psychology 889, 900-902 (Marvin D. Dunnette ed., 1976)

Conflict, like power, is one of those fascinating but frequently abused and misunderstood subjects. Like any potent force, conflict generates ambivalence by virtue of its ability to do great injury or, if harnessed, great good. Until recently, social scientists have been most aware of conflict's destructive capability — epitomized by strikes, wars, interracial hostility, and so on. This awareness seems to have given conflict an overwhelming connotation of danger and to have created a bias toward harmony and peacemaking in the social sciences. However, a more balanced view of conflict seems to be emerging. More and more, social scientists are coming to realize — and to demonstrate — that conflict itself is no evil, but rather a phenomenon which can have constructive or destructive effects depending upon its management. . . .

[P]arty's perceptions of stakes and conflict of interest have an important influence on his behavior. . . .

Orientation.   The model categorizes a party's orientation on the basis of the degree to which he would like to satisfy his own concern and the degree to which he would like to satisfy the concern of the other. Figure 4 uses the joint outcome space to plot five such orientations — competitive, collaborative, avoidant, accommodative, and sharing — together with their preferred outcomes. . . .

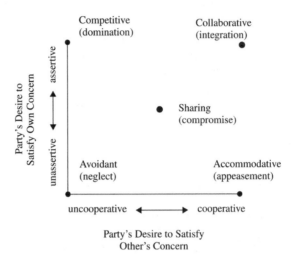

Figure 4.
Five Conflict Handling Orientations

Before discussing the orientations in Figure 4 individually, some comments on the complexity of this scheme are in order. A five-category scheme is obviously more complicated and difficult to master than a dichotomous differentiation like cooperative-uncooperative. The latter is appealing in its simplicity and is still used extensively in the experimental game approach to conflict research. However, the cooperative-uncooperative dichotomy appears to greatly oversimplify the more complex range of options available to the conflict party.

A stronger case can be made for the present two-dimensional scheme. The cooperative-uncooperative distinction represents one dimension which might accurately reflect the thinking of Party's opponent: "Does he want to cooperate and help me satisfy my concerns, or doesn't he?" However, a different distinction is more likely to be reflected in the thinking of Party and his constituents, namely, "Does Party actively strive to achieve his own concerns, or doesn't he?" Both distinctions in fact reflect important dimensions which are analytically independent: the degree to which one attempts to satisfy the other's concern and the degree to which one assertively pursues one's own concerns.

A great deal of unnecessary sacrifice or competition seems to stem from confusing these two dimensions or reducing them to a single dimension. When cooperation is assumed to be in opposition to pursuing one's own concerns, cooperation comes to mean sacrifice, and asserting one's needs ("standing up for one's rights") comes to mean putting up a fight.

Returning to the five orientations in Figure 4, the competitive orientation represents a desire to win one's own concerns at the other's expense, namely, to dominate. . . . Blake . . . refer[s] to such relationships as "win–lose power struggles."[3]

By contrast, an accommodative orientation focuses upon appeasement — satisfying the other's concerns without attending to one's own. Under such an orientation, a party may be generous or self-sacrificing for the sake of their relationship. . . .

The sharing orientation is intermediate between domination and appeasement. It is a preference for moderate but incomplete satisfaction for both parties — for compromise. Party gives up something and keeps something. . . . Blake . . . refer[s] to this as "splitting the difference," since Party seeks an outcome which is intermediate between the preferred outcomes of both parties.

In contrast to sharing, the collaborative orientation represents a desire to *fully* satisfy the concerns of both parties — to integrate their concerns. . . .

The remaining orientation, avoidance, reflects indifference to the concerns of either party. Blake . . . describe[s] this orientation as an instance of withdrawal, isolation, indifference, ignorance, or reliance upon fate. The words "evasion," "flight," and "apathy" have also been used to describe this orientation. . . .

Let us now consider the cooperative dimension in Figure 4 in more detail. . . . Cooperation involves movement toward the other — attempts to satisfy other's concerns. Collaboration and accommodation are certainly cooperative in this regard. By contrast, competition and avoidance are uncooperative, involving movement against and away from the other, respectively. Sharing is moderately cooperative, since it contains a limited amount of movement toward the other as well as a limited amount of competitive movement against. . . .

The cooperativeness of Party toward Other is to a large extent a function of his identification with Other. Party's identification may range from positive identification through indifference to hostility. Attention to Other's satisfaction through collaboration or accommodation appears to be a manifestation of identification. If two parties have agreed upon important issues in the past or agree on common ends, then they may feel sufficient goodwill toward each other to approach disagreement cooperatively. An uncooperative orientation, on the other hand, may stem from indifference to the other's outcomes or from a desire to injure the other. . . .

The second dimension in Figure 4, assertiveness . . . represents the extent to which Party is interested in satisfying his own concerns. The assertiveness of Party's orientation is in part a result of the strength of Party's concern, or [the] Party's "stakes" in the conflict. The most assertive orientations, competition and collaboration, require the greatest immediate outlay of energy — to compete and problem-solve, respectively. Hence, they require some degree of commitment to one's concern. By contrast, avoidance and accommodation require less energy — Party has only to do nothing or go along with Other. In matters of little import to Party, he is, therefore, apt to drift into avoidance or accommodation. Sharing is intermediate in assertiveness and energy expenditure.

---

3. R. R. Blake, H. A. Shepard & J. S. Mouton, Managing Intergroup Conflict in Industry (1964).

> **Problem 3-2.** *Your Conflict Orientation*
>
> Which orientation do you use when negotiating with your family? With your friends? With your romantic interest? With someone at work?

> **Problem 3-3.** *Changing Orientations*
>
> Should your orientation change depending on what's at stake? Where someone has been very generous or very selfish in the past, would it influence your negotiation approach?

1. Distributive Approaches to Negotiation

In this section we review strategies and tactics used to divide the limited resources at stake in a negotiation. Howard Raiffa notes that "[t]wo-party bargaining can be divided into two types: distributive and integrative. . . . In the distributive case one single issue, such as money, is under contention and the parties have almost strictly opposing interests on that issue: the more you get, the less the other party gets, and — with some exceptions and provisos — you want as much as you can get."

a. Competitive Bargaining

We first review the competitive approach to negotiation. Goodpaster provides an overview on the competitive approach and the motivations and attitudes of a competitive negotiator. In understanding the motivations behind this behavior, you will better be able to understand how to counter this positional bargaining in the future.

 Gary Goodpaster, **A PRIMER ON COMPETITIVE BARGAINING**

1996 J. Disp. Resol. 325, 326, 341-342

Competitive bargaining, sometimes called hard, distributive, positional, zero-sum or win-lose bargaining, has the purpose of maximizing the competitive bargainer's gain over the gain of those with whom he negotiates. He is, in effect, trying to "come out ahead of," or "do better than," all other parties in the negotiation. For this reason, we sometimes refer to this competitive bargaining strategy as a *domination* strategy, meaning that the competitive bargainer tends to treat negotiations as a kind of contest to win.

The competitive negotiator tends to define success in negotiation rather narrowly. It is simply getting as much as possible for himself: the cheapest price, the most profit, the least cost, the best terms and so on. In its simplest form, this strategy focuses on immediate gain and is not much concerned with the relationship between the negotiating parties. A more complex version of this strategy focuses on long-term gain. This focus usually requires some effort to maintain or further a relationship and usually moderates the competitive, often aggressive, behavior that jeopardizes relationships and possibilities of long-term gain. . . .

> "Trades would not take place unless it were advantageous to the parties concerned. Of course, it is better to strike as good a bargain as one's bargaining position permits. The worst outcome is when, by overreaching greed, no bargain is struck, and a trade that could have been advantageous to both parties does not come off at all."
>
> ~Benjamin Franklin

People bargain competitively essentially for three reasons, which often overlap. First, by inclination or calculation, they view the negotiation as a kind of competition, in which they wish to win or gain as much as possible. Secondly, they do not trust the other party. Where parties are non-trusting, they are non-disclosing and withhold information, which leads to further distrust and defensive or self-protective moves. Parties may be non-trusting because they are unfamiliar with the other party or because they are generally or situationally non-trusting. Finally, a party may bargain competitively as a defense to, or retaliation for, competitive moves directed at it.

---

b. *Accommodating and Cooperative Approaches to Negotiation*

A second approach to a negotiation when there are limited resources to divide is to be more concerned with the other sides' needs. Kenneth Thomas, earlier in this chapter, describes this orientation as "accommodative." Other authors refer to this approach as "soft bargaining" or as "cooperative." While this approach is completely different from the adversarial approach, it often shares the assumption that a distributional negotiation exists. This soft approach is used when the relationship is *so* important that accommodating your counterpart is more important than your own interests, for example, letting the bride choose the wedding date.

This next excerpt from Donald Gifford explains the theory behind a cooperative strategy and the skills available to the cooperative negotiator working through a conflict.

 Donald G. Gifford, **A CONTEXT-BASED THEORY OF STRATEGY SELECTION IN LEGAL NEGOTIATION**

46 Ohio St. L.J. 41, 52-54 (1985)

A view of human nature different than that upon which the competitive strategy is premised, with its emphasis on undermining the confidence of opposing counsel, underlies most collaborative interaction. In everyday events, even when they are deciding how to divide a limited resource between them, two negotiators often seek to reach an agreement which is fair and equitable to both parties and seek to build an interpersonal relationship based on trust. This approach to negotiation can be designated the cooperative strategy. The cooperative negotiator initiates granting concessions in order to create both a moral obligation to reciprocate and a relationship built on trust that is conducive to achieving a fair agreement.

The cooperative negotiator does not view making concessions as a necessity resulting from a weak bargaining position or a loss of confidence in the value of her case. Rather, she values concessions as an affirmative negotiating technique designed to capitalize on the opponent's desire to reach a fair and just agreement and to maintain an accommodative working relationship. Proponents of the cooperative strategy believe that negotiators are motivated not only by individualistic or competitive desires to maximize their own utilities, but also by collectivistic desires to reach a fair solution. Cooperative negotiators assert that the competitive strategy often leads to resentment between the parties and a breakdown of negotiations.

According to Professor Otomar Bartos, an originator of the cooperative strategy, the negotiator should begin negotiations not with a maximalist position, but rather with a more moderate opening bid that is both favorable to him and barely acceptable to the opponent. Once two such opening bids are on the table, the negotiators should determine the midpoint between the two opening bids and regard it as a fair and equitable outcome. External facts, such as how large a responsive concession the negotiator expects from the opponent, whether she is representing a tough constituency that would view large concessions unfavorably, and whether she is under a tight time deadline and wants to expedite the process by making a large concession, affect the size of the negotiator's first concession. According to Professor Bartos, the negotiator should then expect the opponent to reciprocate with a concession of similar size so that the midpoint between the parties' positions remains the same as it was after the realistic opening bids were made. The concessions by the parties are fair, according to Bartos, as long as the parties do not need to revise their initial expectations about the substance of the agreement.

The term *cooperative strategy* embraces a larger variety of negotiation tactics than Bartos' detailed model. Cooperative strategies include any strategies that aim to develop trust between the parties and that focus on the expectation that the opponent will match concessions ungrudgingly. Endemic to all cooperative strategies is the question of how the negotiator should respond if the opponent does not match her concessions and does not reciprocate her goodwill. The major weakness of the cooperative approach is its vulnerability to exploitation by the competitive negotiator. The cooperative negotiator is severely disadvantaged if her opponent fails to reciprocate her concessions. Cooperative negotiation theorists suggest a variety of responses when concessions are not matched. Professor Bartos recommends that the negotiator "stop making further concessions until the opponent catches up."[4]

Because of its vulnerability to exploitation, the cooperative theory may not initially appear to be a viable alternative to the competitive strategy. As mentioned

---

4. Otomar Bartos, Simple Model of Negotiation: A Sociological Point of View, in The Negotiation Process: Theories & Applications 23 (I. Zartman ed., 1978).

previously, in tightly controlled experiments with simulated negotiations, the competitive strategy generally produces better results. However, in actual practice, the competitive approach results in more impasses and greater distrust between the parties. Furthermore, most people tend to be cooperative in orientation and trusting of others. Professor Williams found that sixty-five percent of the attorneys he surveyed used a cooperative approach.[5] This, of course, means that in a majority of cases the cooperative negotiator will not be exploited by her opponent, because the opponent also uses a cooperative approach. Most cooperative negotiators probably would not feel comfortable using the competitive negotiators' aggressive tactics, which are designed to undermine the opponent and his case. Nor would they relish living and working in the mistrustful milieu which may result from the use of the competitive strategy.

Problem 3-4.   *"Peace in Our Time"*

Many historians use British Prime Minister Neville Chamberlain's 1938 appeasement of Hitler as a worst-case example of the possible consequences of accommodating. To avoid war, Chamberlain agreed not to defend Czechoslovakia against a German invasion if Hitler agreed to end his territorial ambitions at that point. Although Chamberlain kept his promise, Hitler, as history tells us, did not.[6] Can you think of other positive or negative examples of hard or soft bargaining?

---

2. Integrative or Problem-Solving Negotiation

"It's not that I'm so smart, it's just that I stay with problems longer"
— Albert Einstein

Many beginning negotiators assume that the distributive approaches presented in the previous section — adversarial or cooperative — are the primary choices of strategy in a negotiation. *This is a false choice.* Both strategies focus only on one part of the negotiation — dividing the "pie" of services or goods that are the subject

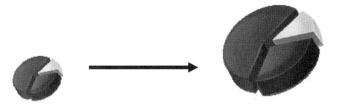

---

5. Gerald R. Williams, Legal Negotiation and Settlement 53 (1983).
6. Carrie Menkel-Meadow, Compromise, Negotiation and Morality, 26 Negotiation Journal 481 (2010) (exploring further the issues of appeasement and negotiations during WW II).

Problem 3-5.   *Why We Cooperate*

Researchers recently have found a biological reason for why people cooperate:

> What feels as good as chocolate on the tongue or money in the bank but won't make you fat or risk a subpoena from the [SEC]?
>
> Hard as it may be to believe in these days of infectious greed and sabers unsheathed, scientists have discovered that the small, brave act of cooperating with another person, of choosing trust over cynicism, generosity over selfishness, makes the brain light up with quiet joy.
>
> Studying neural activity in young women who were playing a classic laboratory game called the Prisoner's Dilemma, in which participants can select from a number of greedy or cooperative strategies as they pursue financial gain, researchers found that when the women chose mutualism over "meism," the mental circuitry normally associated with reward-seeking behavior swelled to life.
>
> And the longer the women engaged in a cooperative strategy, the more strongly flowed the blood to the pathways of pleasure.

Natalie Angier, Why We're So Nice: We're Wired to Cooperate, N.Y. Times, July 23, 2002, at 1.

The researchers had actually expected that the subjects would feel more emotion when one person cooperated and the other defected. In fact, the subjects were most responsive when patterns of cooperation occurred. Although the experiment was performed only on women, the researchers predicted that these findings would be the same for both genders. The researchers thought that this push to cooperate might explain why humans behave better than other species (assuming you think that). What do you think? If you have participated in a Prisoner's Dilemma game, how did you feel?

---

of negotiation — rather than on other activities that can expand the resources available to the parties before they may have to be allocated or divided. Problem solving or integrative negotiation looks for more creative solutions to problems that may lie outside of what the parties assume are available to them under a more distributive approach. This section focuses on these other activities and discusses the various ideas and approaches that fall under integrative negotiation (also called "problem solving" and "principled negotiation").

This first excerpt is from Carrie Menkel-Meadow's early article on the problem-solving concept of negotiation. This perspective is aligned with integrative and principled bargaining and focuses on the needs of the parties when negotiating a resolution to a dispute.

Carrie Menkel-Meadow, TOWARD ANOTHER VIEW OF
LEGAL NEGOTIATION: THE STRUCTURE OF
PROBLEM SOLVING

31 UCLA L. Rev. 754-759, 794-801 (1984)

INTRODUCTION

When people negotiate they engage in a particular kind of social behavior; they seek
to do together what they cannot do alone. Those who negotiate are sometimes
principals attempting to solve their own problems, or, more likely in legal negotiation, they are agents acting for clients, within the bounds of the law.

When lawyers write about this frequent social activity they join commentators
from other disciplines in emphasizing an adversarial or zero-sum game approach to
negotiation. In their view, what one party gains the other must lose. Resources are
limited and must be divided. Information about one's real preferences must be jeal-
ously guarded. If the negotiation fails, the court will declare one party a winner,
awarding money or an injunction. Successful negotiations represent a compromise
of each party's position on an ordinal scale of numerical (usually monetary) values.
This Article suggests that writers and negotiators who take such an adversarial
approach limit themselves unnecessarily because they have not fully examined their
assumptions.

Recently, several analysts have suggested that another approach to negotiation,
an approach I will call problem solving, might better accomplish the purposes of
negotiation. This problem-solving model seeks to demonstrate how negotiators, on
behalf of litigators or planners, can more effectively accomplish their goals by
focusing on the parties' actual objectives and creatively attempting to satisfy the
needs of both parties, rather than by focusing exclusively on the assumed objectives
of maximizing individual gain. . . .

In order to contrast the adversarial model with the problem-solving model
several key concepts must be defined and criteria for evaluation of the models
made explicit. The negotiation models described here may seem unduly polarized,
yet they represent the polarities of approach exemplified both by the conceptions
of negotiation we construct as well as by the strategies and behaviors we choose.
The models described here are based on orientations to negotiation, that is, how
we approach our purpose in negotiation, rather than on the particular strategies or
tactics we choose. It must be noted, however, that the tactics and strategies we
choose may well be affected by our conception of negotiation. A general model
demonstrates the relationship of negotiation orientations to negotiation results:

Orientation ⟶ Mind-set ⟶ Behavior ⟶ Results

The orientation (adversarial or problem solving) leads to a mind-set about what can
be achieved (maximizing individual gain or solving the parties' problem by satisfying their underlying needs) which in turn affects the behavior chosen (competitive
or solution searching) which in turn affects the solutions arrived at (narrow compromises or creative solutions).

The primary, but not exclusive, criterion for evaluation of a negotiation model is the quality of the solution produced. This includes the extent to which the process utilized contributes to or hinders the search for "quality" solutions.

In elaborating on approaches to negotiation I shall consider the following criteria of evaluation:

1. Does the solution reflect the client's total set of "real" needs, goals and objective, in both the short and the long term?
2. Does the solution reflect the other party's full set of "real" needs, goals and objectives, in both the short and long term?
3. Does the solution promote the relationship the client desires with the other party?
4. Have the parties explored all the possible solutions that might either make each better off or one party better off with no adverse consequences to the other party?
5. Has the solution been achieved at the lowest possible transaction costs relative to the desirability of the result?
6. Is the solution achievable, or has it only raised more problems that need to be solved? Are the parties committed to the solution so it can be enforced without regret?
7. Has the solution been achieved in a manner congruent with the client's desire to participate in and affect the negotiation?
8. Is the solution "fair" or "just"? Have the parties considered the legitimacy of each other's claims and made any adjustments they feel are humanely or morally indicated?

Criteria one through seven are all based on a utilitarian justification of negotiation. By satisfying these criteria, a negotiation may produce results which are more satisfactory to the parties, thus enhancing commitment to and enforcement of the agreement. The final criterion is applicable to those negotiators who wish to consider the effects of their solution on the other party from a humanitarian or ethical perspective. . . .

Problem solving is an orientation to negotiation which focuses on finding solutions to the parties' sets of underlying needs and objectives. The problem-solving conception subordinates strategies and tactics to the process of identifying possible solutions and therefore allows a broader range of outcomes to negotiation problems. . . .

The Underlying Principles of Problem Solving: Meeting Varied and Complementary Needs

Parties to a negotiation typically have underlying needs or objectives — what they hope to achieve, accomplish, and/or be compensated for as a result of the dispute or transaction. Although litigants typically ask for relief in the form of damages, this relief is actually a proxy for more basic needs or objectives. By attempting to uncover those underlying needs, the problem-solving model presents opportunities for discovering greater numbers of and better quality solutions. It offers the possibility of meeting a greater variety of needs both directly and by trading off different needs, rather than forcing a zero-sum battle over a single item.

The principle underlying such an approach is that unearthing a greater number of the actual needs of the parties will create more possible solutions because not all needs will be mutually exclusive. As a corollary, because not all individuals value the same things in the same way, the exploitation of differential or complementary needs will produce a wider variety of solutions which more closely meet the parties' needs.

A few examples may illustrate these points. In personal injury actions courts usually award monetary damages. Plaintiffs, however, commonly want this money for specific purposes. For instance, an individual who has been injured in a car accident may desire compensation for any or all of the following items: past and future medical expenses, rehabilitation and compensation for the cost of rehabilitation, replacement of damaged property such as a car and the costs of such replacement, lost income, compensation for lost time, pain and suffering, the loss of companionship with one's family, friends and fellow employees and employer, lost opportunities to engage in activities which may no longer be possible, such as backpacking or playing basketball with one's children, vindication or acknowledgment of fault by the responsible party, and retribution or punishment of the person who was at fault. In short, the injured person seeks to be returned to the same physical, psychological, social and economic state she was in before the accident occurred. Because this may be impossible, the plaintiff needs money in order to buy back as many of these things as possible. . . .

Some of the parties' needs may not be compensable, directly or indirectly. For example, some injuries may be impossible to fully rehabilitate. A physical disability, a scar, or damage to a personal or business reputation may never be fully eradicated. Thus, the underlying needs produced by these injuries may not be susceptible to full and/or monetary satisfaction. The need to be regarded as totally normal or completely honorable can probably never be met, but the party in a negotiation will be motivated by the desire to satisfy as fully as possible these underlying human needs. Some parties may have a need to get "as much X as possible," such as in demands for money for pain and suffering. This demand simply may represent the best proxy available for satisfying the unsatisfiable desire to be made truly whole — that is to be put back in the position of no accident at all. It also may represent a desire to save for a rainy day or to maximize power, fame or love.

It is also important to recognize that *both* parties have such needs. For example, in the personal injury case above, the defendant may have the same need for vindication or retribution if he believes he was not responsible for the accident. In addition, the defendant may need to be compensated for his damaged car and injured body. He will also have needs with respect to how much, when and how he may be able to pay the monetary damages because of other uses for the money. A contract breaching defendant may have specific financial needs such as payroll, advertising, purchases of supplies, etc.; defendants are not always simply trying to avoid paying a certain sum of money to plaintiffs. In the commercial case, the defendant may have needs similar to those of the plaintiff: lost income due to the plaintiff's failure to pay on the contract, and, to the extent the plaintiff may seek to terminate the relationship with the defendant, a steady source of future business. . . .

To the extent that negotiators focus exclusively on "winning" the greatest amount of money, they focus on only one form of need. The only flexibility in tailoring an agreement may lie in the choice of ways to structure monetary solutions, including one shot payments, installments, and structured settlements. By looking, however, at what the parties desire money for, there may be a variety of solutions that will satisfy the parties more fully and directly. For example, when an injured plaintiff needs physical rehabilitation, if the defendant can provide the plaintiff directly with rehabilitation services, the defendant may save money and the plaintiff may gain the needed rehabilitation at lower cost. In addition, if the defendant can provide the plaintiff with a job that provides physical rehabilitation, the plaintiff may not only receive income which could be used to purchase more rehabilitation, but be further rehabilitated in the form of the psychological self-worth which accompanies such employment. Admittedly, none of these solutions may fully satisfy the injured plaintiff, but some or all may be equally beneficial to the plaintiff, and the latter two may be preferable to the defendant because they are less costly.

Understanding that the other party's needs are not necessarily as assumed may present an opportunity for arriving at creative solutions. Traditionally, lawyers approaching negotiations from the adversarial model view the other side as an enemy to be defeated. By examining the underlying needs of the other side, the lawyer may instead see opportunities for solutions that would not have existed before based upon the recognition of different, but not conflicting, preferences.

An example from the psychological literature illustrates this point.[7] Suppose that a husband and wife have two weeks in which to take their vacation. The husband prefers the mountains and the wife prefers the seaside. If vacation time is limited and thus a scarce resource, the couple may engage in adversarial negotiation about where they should go. The simple compromise situation, if they engage in distributive bargaining, would be to split the two weeks of vacation time spending one week in the mountains and one week at the ocean. This solution is not likely to be satisfying, however, because of the lost time and money in moving from place to place and in getting used to a new hotel room and locale. In addition to being happy only half of the time, each party to the negotiation has incurred transaction costs associated with this solution. Other "compromise" solutions might include alternating preferences on a year to year basis, taking separate vacations, or taking a longer vacation at a loss of pay. Assuming that husband and wife want to vacation together, all of these solutions may leave something to be desired by at least one of the parties.

By examining their underlying preferences, however, the parties might find additional solutions that could make both happy at less cost. Perhaps the husband prefers the mountains because he likes to hike and engage in stream fishing. Perhaps the wife enjoys swimming, sunbathing and seafood. By exploring these underlying

---

7. Pruitt & Lewis, The Psychology of Interactive Bargaining, in Negotiations: Social-Psychological Perspectives 169-170 (D. Druckman ed., 1977).

preferences the couple might find vacation spots that permit all of these activities: a mountain resort on a large lake, or a seaside resort at the foot of mountains. By examining their underlying needs the parties can see solutions that satisfy many more of their preferences, and the "sum of the utilities" to the couple as a whole is greater than what they would have achieved by compromising.

In addition, by exploring whether they attach different values to their preferences they may be able to arrive at other solutions by trading items. The wife in our example might be willing to give up ocean fresh seafood if she can have fresh stream or lake trout, and so, with very little cost to her, the couple can choose another waterspot where the hikes might be better for the husband. By examining the weight or value given to certain preferences the parties may realize that some desires are easily attainable because they are not of equal importance to the other side. Thus, one party can increase its utilities without reducing the other's. This differs from a zero-sum conception of negotiation because of the recognition that preferences may be totally different and are, therefore, neither scarce nor in competition with each other. In addition, if a preference is not used to "force" a concession from the other party (which as the example shows is not necessary), there are none of the forced reciprocal concessions of adversarial negotiation.

The exploitation of complementary interests occurs frequently in the legal context. For example, in a child custody case the lawyers may learn that both parties desire to have the children some of the time and neither of the parties wishes to have the children all of the time. It will be easy, therefore, to arrange for a joint custody agreement that satisfies the needs of both parties. Similarly, in a commercial matter, the defendant may want to make payment over time and the plaintiff, for tax purposes or to increase interest income, may desire deferred income.

This next excerpt is from *Getting to YES*, a worldwide bestseller on principled or interest-based negotiation. Fisher and his co-authors cite why adversarial and accommodating approaches produce unwise agreements, inefficient agreements, or agreements that have damaged the parties' relationship. They then outline four points that will guide a negotiator to a better agreement.

   Roger Fisher, William Ury & Bruce Patton, **GETTING TO YES**

4-7, 10-14 (2d ed. 1991)

Any method of negotiation may be fairly judged by three criteria: It should produce a wise agreement if agreement is possible. It should be efficient. And it should improve or at least not damage the relationship between the parties. (A wise agreement can be defined as one that meets the legitimate interests of each side to the extent possible, resolves conflicting interests fairly, is durable, and takes community interest into account.) . . .

Taking positions, as the customer and storekeeper do, serves some useful purposes in a negotiation. It tells the other side what you want; it provides an anchor in an uncertain and pressured situation; and it can eventually produce the terms of an acceptable agreement. But those purposes can be served in other ways. And positional bargaining fails to meet the basic criteria of producing a wise agreement, efficiently and amicably.

ARGUING OVER POSITIONS PRODUCES UNWISE AGREEMENTS

When negotiators bargain over positions, they tend to lock themselves into those positions. The more you clarify your position and defend it against attack, the more committed you become to it. The more you try to convince the other side of the impossibility of changing your opening position, the more difficult it becomes to do so. Your ego becomes identified with your position. You now have a new interest in "saving face" — in reconciling future action with past positions — making it less and less likely that any agreement will wisely reconcile the parties' original interests. . . .

ARGUING OVER POSITIONS IS INEFFICIENT . . .

Bargaining over positions creates incentives that stall settlement. In positional bargaining you try to improve the chance that any settlement reached is favorable to you by starting with an extreme position, by stubbornly holding to it, by deceiving the other party as to your true views, and by making small concessions only as necessary to keep the negotiation going. The same is true for the other side. Each of those factors tends to interfere with reaching a settlement promptly. . . .

ARGUING OVER POSITIONS ENDANGERS AN ONGOING RELATIONSHIP

Positional bargaining becomes a contest of will. . . . Anger and resentment often result as one side sees itself bending to the rigid will of the other while its own legitimate concerns go unaddressed. Positional bargaining thus strains and sometimes shatters the relationship between the parties. . . .

THERE IS AN ALTERNATIVE . . .

The answer to the question of whether to use soft positional bargaining or hard is "neither." Change the game. At the Harvard Negotiation Project we have been developing an alternative to positional bargaining: a method of negotiation explicitly designed to produce wise outcomes efficiently and amicably. This method, called *principled negotiation* or *negotiation on the merits*, can be boiled down to four basic points.

These four points define a straightforward method of negotiation that can be used under almost any circumstance. Each point deals with a basic element of negotiation, and suggests what you should do about it.

People:	Separate the people from the problem.
Interests:	Focus on interests, not positions.
Options:	Generate a variety of possibilities before deciding what to do.
Criteria:	Insist that the result be based on some objective standard.

[E]motions typically become entangled with the objective merits of the problem. Taking positions just makes this worse because people's egos become identified with their positions. Hence, before working on the substantive problem, the "people problem" should be disentangled from it and dealt with separately. Figuratively if not literally, the participants should come to see themselves as working side by side, attacking the problem, not each other. Hence the first proposition: *Separate the people from the problem.*

The second point is designed to overcome the drawback of focusing on people's stated positions when the object of a negotiation is to satisfy their underlying interests. A negotiating position often obscures what you really want. Compromising between positions is not likely to produce an agreement which will effectively take care of the human needs that led people to adopt those positions. The second basic element of the method is: *Focus on interests, not positions.*

The third point responds to the difficulty of designing optimal solutions while under pressure. Trying to decide in the presence of an adversary narrows your vision. Having a lot at stake inhibits creativity. So does searching for the one right solution. You can offset these constraints by setting aside a designated time within which to think up a wide range of possible solutions that advance shared interests and creatively reconcile differing interests. Hence the third basic point: Before trying to reach agreement, *invent options for mutual gain.* . . .

[S]ome fair standard such as market value, expert opinion, custom, or law [should] determine the outcome. By discussing such criteria rather than what the parties are willing or unwilling to do, neither party need give in to the other; both can defer to a fair solution. Hence the fourth basic point: *Insist on using objective criteria.* . . .

To sum up, in contrast to positional bargaining, the principled negotiation method of focusing on basic interests, mutually satisfying options, and fair standards typically results in a *wise agreement.* The method permits you to reach a gradual consensus on a joint decision *efficiently* without all the transactional costs of digging into positions only to have to dig yourself out of them. And separating the people from the problem allows you to deal directly and emphatically with the other negotiator as a human being, thus making possible an *amicable* agreement.

PROBLEM		SOLUTION
Positional Bargaining: Which Game Should You Play?		Change the Game — Negotiate on the Merits

SOFT	HARD	PRINCIPLED
Participants are friends.	Participants are adversaries	Participants are problem-solvers.
The goal is agreement.	The goal is victory.	The goal is a wise outcome reached efficiently and amicably.
Make concessions to cultivate the relationship.	Demand concessions as a condition of the relationship.	*Separate the people from the problem.*
Be soft on the people and the problem.	Be hard on the problem and the people.	Be soft on the people, hard on the problem.
Trust others.	Distrust others.	Proceed independent of trust.
Change your position easily.	Dig in to your position.	*Focus on interests, not positions.*
Make offers.	Make threats.	Explore interests.
Disclose your bottom line.	Mislead as to your bottom line.	Avoid having a bottom line.
Accept one-sided losses to reach agreement.	Demand one-sided gains as the price of agreement.	*Invent options for mutual gain.*
Search for the single answer: the one *they* will accept.	Search for the single answer: the one *you* will accept.	Develop multiple options to choose from; decide later.
Insist on agreement.	Insist on your position.	*Insist on using objective criteria.*
Try to avoid a contest of will.	Try to win a contest of will.	Try to reach a result based on standards independent of will.
Yield to pressure.	Apply pressure.	Reason and be open to reason; yield to principle, not pressure.

Problem 3-6.   *Dealing with Hard Bargaining*

What concepts or strategies does principled bargaining suggest using with hard bargainers? Which ideas would be easiest for you to implement?

Problem 3-7. *Splitting an Orange*

A classic example of value creation is the story of two siblings fighting over an orange. They agree to split it in half. One throws out the peel and eats her half of the orange. The other uses her half of the peel in a recipe and throws out the rest of the orange. How could these siblings have better resolved this dispute?

The final excerpt in this section is based on an empirical study, conducted by Andrea Kupfer Schneider, which asked lawyers how they perceived the other side's negotiation strategy in a negotiation. Lawyers rated their counterpart attorneys using 89 adjectives, 60 negotiation techniques, and 14 goals. The attorneys also rated their counterparts for effectiveness.

The excerpt below discusses the division of attorneys into three groups — true problem solvers, cautious problem solvers, and adversarials. It outlines the differences among the groups, both in the description of the groups and each group's respective effectiveness. Note particularly the difference between true problem-solving negotiators, those who truly engage in the behavior described in the previous excerpts on integrative bargaining; cautious problem solvers, those who don't quite fully use the range of problem-solving behavior; and adversarial negotiators. Also, think about what adjectives most closely describe your approach to negotiation.

 Andrea Kupfer Schneider, **SHATTERING NEGOTIATION MYTHS: EMPIRICAL EVIDENCE ON THE EFFECTIVENESS OF NEGOTIATION STYLE**

7 Harv. Negot. L. Rev. 143, 171-175 (2002)

[We] can separate negotiation styles into three clusters, which I have labeled true problem-solving, cautious problem-solving, and adversarial. . . . [L]awyers were divided . . . evenly among the three clusters with approximately 36% in the true problem-solving group, 36% in the cautious problem-solving group, and 28% in the adversarial group. . . .

An interesting result in this analysis is the middle category [See table on following page]. Clearly this middle group is comprised of "good" lawyers in that all of the adjectives are positive. Again, all nine are included in the true problem-solving group. In comparison, however, the true problem-solving group had forty-nine highly rated adjectives. Consequently, I have labeled the middle group "cautious problem-solvers" to highlight the fact that most of these traits are problem-solving, yet this group seems hesitant to utilize all of the problem-solving

Top 20 Adjectives for Three Clusters			
	TRUE PROBLEM-SOLVING	**CAUTIOUS PROBLEM-SOLVING**	**ADVERSARIAL**
1	Ethical	Ethical	Irritating
2	Personable	Experienced	Headstrong
3	Experienced	Confident	Stubborn
4	Trustworthy	Personable	Arrogant
5	Rational	Self-controlled	Egotistical
6	Agreeable	Rational	Argumentative
7	Fair-minded	Sociable	Assertive
8	Communicative	Dignified	Demanding
9	Realistic	Trustworthy	Quarrelsome
10	Accommodating		Confident
11	Perceptive		Ambitious
12	Sociable		Manipulative
13	Adaptable		Experienced
14	Confident		Hostile
15	Dignified		Forceful
16	Self-controlled		Tough
17	Helpful		Suspicious
18	Astute about the law		Firm
19	Poised		Complaining
20	Flexible		Rude

attributes. By "cautious," I do not mean to suggest that these negotiators are themselves cautious, but rather they are cautious about adopting a completely problem-solving approach to the negotiation.

The true problem-solving negotiator understands the case well (reasonable, prepared, accurate representation of client's position, did own factual investigation) and wanted to work with the other side (friendly, tactful, cooperative, facilitated the negotiation, viewed the negotiation process as one with mutual benefits, understood my client's interests). This negotiator was flexible (movable position, did not use take it or leave it) and did not engage in manipulative tactics (did not make unwarranted claims, did not use threats, avoided needless harm to my client). The true problem-solving negotiator believed in the good faith exchange of information (cooperative, forthright, trustful, sincere, shared information, probed). . . .

The cautious problem-solving group, as in the adjectives ratings, did not stand out in most of the characteristics and is only rated more than slightly characteristic in eight descriptions. These eight are all positive and also appear on the problem-solving list, but the cautious problem-solving category lacks twenty-two descriptions that true problem-solvers display. As described above, these absent characteristics describe negotiation qualities that add depth and breadth to a negotiator's skills. . . .

Number of Lawyers Per Group by Effectiveness

	Ineffective	Average	Effective
True Problem-Solving	1%	24%	75%
Cautious Problem-Solving	13%	62%	25%
Adversarial	58%	33%	9%

First, approximately 25% of the negotiators in the new cautious problem-solving group are effective, whereas 75% of the true problem-solvers are described as effective. The missing negotiation elements between the groups must cause this difference. Adjectives found in true problem-solving but not in cautious problem-solving highlight empathy (communicative, accommodating, perceptive, helpful), option creation (adaptable, flexible), personality (agreeable, poised), and preparation (fair-minded, realistic, astute about the law). These skills make the difference between average skills and truly effective skills. Contrary to popular belief, behaviors described by these adjectives are not risky at all. The traditional fear of problem-solving is that problem-solvers will be taken advantage of by more adversarial bargainers, yet only 1% of true problem-solving negotiators were considered ineffective.

Problem 3-8. *Too Cautious?*

What seem to be the primary differences between true and cautious problem solvers? How do you think these differences matter in terms of effectiveness? Which of these do you think is the most important?

B. CHOOSING NEGOTIATION APPROACHES

In the real world, negotiations are rarely only distributive or only integrative. Most negotiations are a mix of both. The first excerpt from Jonathan Cohen shows how alternative negotiation styles and the metaphors associated with those styles reflect the balance between distributive or integrative approaches. The next part of this section examines the classic scenario called the Prisoner's Dilemma, an economic game theory that is often applied to the negotiation context. Third, we examine the Negotiator's Dilemma, similar to a Prisoner's Dilemma, where the choice of which strategy to choose affects the outcome of the negotiation. Finally, the last excerpt suggests that you can be a flexible negotiator, move between the many approaches, and use different skills to be a superior negotiator. And we suggest some factors you might consider in deciding which approach is most appropriate for what you are trying to achieve.

 Jonathan R. Cohen, **ADVERSARIES? PARTNERS? HOW ABOUT COUNTERPARTS? ON METAPHORS IN THE PRACTICE AND TEACHING OF NEGOTIATION AND DISPUTE RESOLUTION**

20 Conflict Resol. Q. 433, 433-436, 438-439 (2003)

A student of negotiation — or of its cousin, the assisted negotiation called mediation — will soon find herself awash in a sea of metaphors. Has she entered the animal kingdom, a dog-eat-dog world where hawks prey on doves and lions occasionally lie down with lambs? Or the kitchen, with pies to be baked and their slices cut, and oranges to be separated peel from fruit? Is she attending a music concert, where discord will be replaced by harmony, or embarking on a journey replete with speed bumps, road blocks, and detours, the negotiation "bicycle" at risk of falling if sufficient momentum is not maintained? Perhaps she is a carpenter carrying a toolbox of options, an engineer building bridges to span differences, or an architect designing a multidoor courthouse. . . .

If she is like most students, she will soon arrive at the competitive metaphors that dominate the field of negotiation, if not our culture. Negotiation is a game of poker in which players must hold the cards close to the chest. Negotiation is a sport like football, where a "level playing field" is required; mediators are thus "umpires" or "referees." Or like basketball, where "timeouts" are sometimes taken, or like baseball where parties sometimes play "hardball." . . .

The student may then realize that there is more to negotiation than competition. Although the adversarial metaphors capture an important piece of negotiation, they do not capture the whole of it. Competition is part of negotiation, but so is cooperation. Negotiation involves both give and take. As Schelling wrote, "the richness of the subject arises from the fact that . . . there is mutual dependence as well as opposition. Pure conflict, in which the interests of two antagonists are completely opposed, is a special case[.] . . . Concepts like . . . negotiation are concerned with the common interest and mutual dependence that can exist between participants in a conflict."

The student may now switch to a second set of metaphors within our field, those of cooperation. Whether through stumble or leap, she may well arrive at the metaphor of dance. The other party in the negotiation is not one's adversary, but one's *partner.* The dance occurs in steps and stages. As with empathy and assertiveness, skill in following one's partner is as important as skill in leading. It is essential to "put yourself in [the other side's] shoes," but hopefully without stepping on their toes. What is needed is to be shoulder to shoulder, side by side. Movement, balance, and trust are critical. Before an impasse is reached, perhaps a "trip to the balcony" can reveal new steps to be taken. As to third-party neutrals, the mediator is no longer an umpire at a sports event, but a choreographer.

Yet using solely cooperative metaphors is also problematic. Recall that when the dance metaphor is invoked, it is usually not the waltz but the aggressive and spicy tango, as in, "It takes two to tango." Schelling's point was that *both* competition and cooperation are present in negotiation. Disclosing one's interests, preferences, and resources may help to "expand the pie" (value creation), but it can also result in one getting a sliver (value distribution). On the other hand, if one refuses to disclose any information one may end up with the lion's share of a minuscule pie, also a poor outcome. Thus, most negotiation involves a blend of competition and cooperation.

How, then, is one to proceed? What language should be used to describe negotiation? If the goal is descriptive accuracy, since most negotiation is neither pure competition nor pure cooperation, I suggest using language that reflects the inherent tensions between competition and cooperation in negotiation and other forms of dispute resolution. Consider . . . what to call the other party to the negotiation. . . .

Parties to negotiations are often unsure of how to refer to one another. Those with largely competitive views of negotiation tend to label the other party as their "opponent" or "adversary." Those with largely cooperative views tend to label the other party their "partner." Yet what is needed is a word that captures the tension between these two roles. I suggest the word *counterpart*. As with competition, in negotiation the other party is against, or *counter* to, oneself. As with cooperation, the other party is in *partnership* with oneself. Negotiation involves an element of tension or paradox in one's relationship to the other party, and our language should reflect it. Using *counterpart* to describe such a mixed role has no less than biblical (though quite sexist) precedent. The second creation narrative in Genesis describes the creation of woman to be an "ezer c'negdo" to man. *Ezer* means "helper" and *c'negdo* means "against him." This term is sometimes well-translated as "counterpart." The language seems to suggest that being a good intimate partner involves both supportive and oppositional roles.

Game theories have made important contributions to negotiation literature as it impacts the choices of negotiation approaches. Probably the most famous "game" is the Prisoner's Dilemma. We have, in fact, been watching the Prisoner's Dilemma for years on television in police shows where the joint offenders are separated and asked to rat on each other in exchange for lower prison sentences. Game theorists took this model during the Cold War and applied it on a larger scale to understand the choices of cooperating or defecting between countries engaged in political and military contests. And, if you watched the movie *A Beautiful Mind*, you could see how mathematician John Nash conceptualized the dilemma regarding which woman to approach in a bar! In this excerpt, Douglas Hofstadter defines the Prisoner's Dilemma through the use of a simple scenario. In the second excerpt, Robert

Axelrod provides more detail in the inner workings of the dilemma. In a study involving both computer and game theorists as participants, he tested the application of different approaches to the game. As a result, Axelrod produced four suggestions to a player who finds himself involved in a Prisoner's Dilemma.

1. Prisoner's Dilemma

 Douglas R. Hofstadter, **METAMAGICAL THEMAS: QUESTING FOR THE ESSENCE OF MIND AND PATTERN**

716 (1985)

In case you're wondering why it is called "Prisoner's Dilemma," here's the reason. Imagine that you and an accomplice (someone you have no feelings for one way or the other) committed a crime, and now you've both been apprehended and thrown in jail, and are fearfully awaiting trials. You are being held in separate cells with no way to communicate. The prosecutor offers each of you the following deal (and informs you both that the identical deal is being offered to each of you — and that you both know *that* as well!): "We have a lot of circumstantial evidence on you both. So if you both claim innocence, we will convict you anyway and you'll both get two years in jail. But if you will help us out by admitting your guilt and making it easier for us to convict your accomplice — oh, pardon me, your *alleged* accomplice — why, then, we'll let you out free. And don't worry about revenge — your accomplice will be in for five years! How about it?" Warily you ask, "But what if we *both* say we're guilty?" "Ah, well, my friend — I'm afraid you'll both get four-year sentences, then."

Now you're in a pickle! Clearly, you don't want to claim innocence if your partner has sung, for then you're in for five long years. Better you should both have sung — then you'll only get four. On the other hand, if your partner claims innocence, then the best possible thing for you to do is sing, since then you're out scot-free! So at first sight, it seems obvious what you should do: Sing! But what is obvious to you is equally obvious to your opposite number, so now it looks like you both ought to sing, which means — Sing Sing for four years! At least that's what *logic* tells you to do. Funny, since if both of you had just been *illogical* and maintained innocence, you'd both be in for only half as long! Ah, logic does it again.

> **Problem 3-9.** *Alleged Prisoner Advice*
>
> If one of the prisoners was your client, how would you advise him or her? If both of the prisoners were your clients, how would you advise them? Does your advice differ? Why or why not? Assume that the prisoners know each other. How would you advise your client now? Is this different advice than above? Why or why not? Assume that the prisoners are married. How would you advise your client now?

What if the prisoners in the Prisoner's Dilemma were going to find themselves in the same situation next week? Does the idea of repeat interactions change behavior? The next excerpt explains a computer tournament run on that assumption and the lessons that can be drawn from the winning entry.

 Robert Axelrod, **THE EVOLUTION OF COOPERATION**

3, 7, 9, 30-31, 40-42, 54, 110-122 (1984)

In the Prisoner's Dilemma game, there are two players. Each has two choices, namely cooperate or defect. Each must make the choice without knowing what the other will do. No matter what the other does, defection yields a higher payoff than cooperation. The dilemma is that if both defect, both do worse than if both had cooperated. . . .

The way the game works is shown in figure 1. One player chooses a row, either cooperating or defecting. The other player simultaneously chooses a column, either cooperating or defecting. Together, these choices result in one of the four possible outcomes shown in that matrix. If both players cooperate, both do fairly well. Both get *R*, the *reward for mutual cooperation*. In the concrete illustration of figure 1 the reward is 3 points. This number might, for example, be a payoff in dollars that each player gets for that outcome. If one player cooperates but the other defects, the defecting player gets the *temptation to defect*, while the cooperating player gets the *sucker's payoff*. In the example, these are 5 points and 0 points respectively. If both defect, both get 1 point, the *punishment for mutual defection*.

What should you do in such a game? Suppose you are the row player, and you think the column player will cooperate. This means that you will get one of the two outcomes in the first column of figure 1. You have a choice. You can cooperate as well, getting the 3 points of the reward for mutual cooperation. Or you can defect, getting the 5 points of the temptation payoff. So it pays to defect if you think the other player will cooperate. But now suppose that you think the other player will defect. Now you are in the second column of figure 1, and you have a choice between cooperating, which would make you a sucker and give you 0 points, and defecting, which would result in mutual punishment giving you 1 point. So it pays to defect if you think the other player will defect. This means that it is better to defect if you think the other player will cooperate, *and* it is better to defect if you think the other player will defect. So no matter what the other player does, it pays for you to defect.

Figure 1
The Prisoner's Dilemma

		Column Player	
		Cooperate	*Defect*
Row Player	Cooperate	$R = 3, R = 3$ Reward for mutual cooperation	$S = 0, T = 5$ Sucker's payoff and temptation to defect
	Defect	$T = 5, S = 0$ Temptation to defect and sucker's payoff	$P = 1, P = 1$ Punishment for mutual defection

Note: The payoffs to the row chooser are listed first.

So far, so good. But the same logic holds for the other player too. Therefore, the other player should defect no matter what you are expected to do. So you should both defect. But then you both get 1 point which is worse than the 3 points of the reward that you both could have gotten had you both cooperated. Individual rationality leads to a worse outcome for both than is possible. Hence the dilemma. . . .

Wanting to find out what would happen [in an iterated game], I invited professional game theorists to send in entries to just such a computer tournament. It was structured as a round robin, meaning that each entry was paired with each other entry. As announced in the rules of the tournament, each entry was also paired with its own twin and with RANDOM, a program that randomly cooperates and defects with equal probability. . . .

TIT FOR TAT . . . won the tournament. This was the simplest of all submitted programs and it turned out to be the best! TIT FOR TAT, of course, starts with a cooperative choice, and thereafter does what the other player did on the previous move. . . .

The analysis of the tournament results indicate[s] that there is a lot to be learned about coping in an environment of mutual power. Even expert strategists from political science, sociology, economics, psychology, and mathematics made the systematic errors of being too competitive for their own good, not being forgiving enough, and being too pessimistic about the responsiveness of the other side.

The effectiveness of a particular strategy depends not only on its own characteristics, but also on the nature of the other strategies with which it must interact. For this reason, the results of a single tournament are not definitive. Therefore, a second round of the tournament was conducted.

The results of the second round provide substantially better grounds for insight into the nature of effective choice in the Prisoner's Dilemma. The reason is that the entrants to the second round were all given the detailed analysis of the first round, including a discussion of the supplemental rules that would have done very well in the environment of the first round. . . .

The second round was also a dramatic improvement over the first round in sheer size of the tournament. The response was far greater than anticipated. There was a total of sixty-two entries from six countries. . . . The contestants ranged from a ten-year-old computer hobbyist to professors of computer science, physics, economics, psychology, mathematics, sociology, political science, and evolutionary biology. . . .

TIT FOR TAT was the simplest program submitted in the first round, and it won the first round. It was the simplest submission in the second round, and it won the second round. Even though all the entrants to the second round knew that TIT FOR TAT had won the first round, no one was able to design an entry that did any better. . . .

TIT FOR TAT won the tournament because it did well in its interactions with a wide variety of other strategies. On average, it did better than any other rule with the other strategies in the tournament. Yet TIT FOR TAT never once scored better in a game than the other player! In fact, it can't. It lets the other player defect first, and it never defects more times than the other player has defected. Therefore, TIT FOR TAT achieves either the same score as the other player, or a little less. TIT FOR TAT won the tournament, not by beating the other player, but by eliciting behavior from the other player which allowed both to do well. TIT FOR TAT was so consistent at eliciting mutually rewarding outcomes that it attained a higher overall score than any other strategy. . . .

The purpose of this chapter is to translate these findings into advice for a player.

The advice takes the form of four simple suggestions for how to do well in a durable iterated Prisoner's Dilemma:

1. Don't be envious.
2. Don't be the first to defect.
3. Reciprocate both cooperation and defection.
4. Don't be too clever.

1. Don't Be Envious . . .

People tend to resort to the standard of comparison that they have available — and this standard is often the success of the other player relative to their own success. This standard leads to envy. And envy leads to attempts to rectify any advantage the other player has attained. In this form of Prisoner's Dilemma, rectification of the other's advantage can only be done by defection. But defection leads to more defection and to mutual punishment. So envy is self-destructive.

Asking how well you are doing compared to how well the other player is doing is not a good standard unless your goal is to destroy the other player. In most situations, such a goal is impossible to achieve, or likely to lead to such costly conflict as to be very dangerous to pursue. When you are not trying to destroy the other player, comparing your score to the other's score simply risks the development of self-destructive envy. A better standard of comparison is how well you are doing relative to how well someone else could be doing in your shoes. Given the strategy of the other player, are you doing as well as possible? Could someone else in your situation have done better with this other player? This is the proper test of successful performance. . . .

2. Don't Be the First to Defect

Both the tournament and the theoretical results show that it pays to cooperate as long as the other player is cooperating. . . .

The single best predictor of how well a rule performed was whether or not it was nice, which is to say, whether or not it would ever be the first to defect. In the first round, each of the top eight rules were nice, and not one of the bottom seven were nice. In the second round, all but one of the top fifteen rules were nice (and that one ranked eighth). Of the bottom fifteen rules, all but one were not nice. . . .

Of course, one could try to "play it safe" by defecting until the other player cooperates, and only then starting to cooperate. The tournament results show, however, that this is actually a very risky strategy. The reason is that your own initial defection is likely to set off a retaliation by the other player. This will put the two of you in the difficult position of trying to extricate yourselves from an initial pattern of exploitation or mutual defection. If you punish the other's retaliation, the problem can echo into the future. And if you forgive the other, you risk appearing to be exploitable. Even if you can avoid these long-term problems, a prompt retaliation against your initial defection can make you wish that you had been nice from the start. . . .

The lesson is that not being nice may look promising at first, but in the long run it can destroy the very environment it needs for its own success.

3. Reciprocate Both Cooperation and Defection

The extraordinary success of TIT FOR TAT leads to some simple, but powerful advice: practice reciprocity. After cooperating on the first move, TIT FOR TAT simply reciprocates whatever the other player did on the previous move. . . .

In responding to a defection from the other player, TIT FOR TAT represents a balance between punishing and being forgiving. TIT FOR TAT always defects exactly once after each defection by the other. . . . What is clear is that extracting more than one defection for each defection of the other side risks escalation. On the other hand, extracting less than one-for-one risks exploitation. . . .

The moral of the story is that the precise level of forgiveness that is optimal depends upon the environment. In particular, if the main danger is unending mutual recriminations, then a generous level of forgiveness is appropriate. But, if the main danger is from strategies that are good at exploiting easygoing rules, then an excess of forgiveness is costly. While the exact balance will be hard to determine in a given environment, the evidence of the tournament suggests that something approaching a one-for-one response to defection is likely to be quite effective in a wide range of settings. Therefore it is good advice to a player to reciprocate defection as well as cooperation.

4. Don't Be Too Clever

The tournament results show that in a Prisoner's Dilemma situation it is easy to be *too* clever. The very sophisticated rules did not do better than the simple ones. In fact, the so-called maximizing rules often did poorly because they got into a rut of mutual defection. A common problem with these rules is that they used complex methods of making inferences about the other player — and these inferences were wrong. . . .

In deciding whether to carry an umbrella, we do not have to worry that the clouds will take our behavior into account. We can do a calculation about the chance of rain based on past experience. Likewise in a zero-sum game, such as chess, we can safely use the assumption that the other player will pick the most dangerous move that can be found, and we can act accordingly. Therefore it pays for

---

Noise

What happens in a Prisoner's Dilemma when communication between the parties is unclear? Researchers hypothesize that the Soviet shooting down of a South Korean airliner in 1983 (killing all 269 people aboard) could have been a result of this miscommunication (or "noise" as it is called in a Prisoner's Dilemma game). Why did the airliner stray off course? What was the Soviet Union conveying when it shot it down? Jianzhong Wu and Robert Axelrod conducted additional experiments in 1995 to determine the most effective strategy in Prisoner's Dilemma when there is noise. Their conclusion is that it still pays to reciprocate provided that it is accompanied by either some generosity (immediately forgiving a defection rather than responding in kind) or contrition (cooperating after the other player defects in response to *your* own defection). Generosity allows for the correction of the other player's errors and contrition corrects for your own errors in communication. Jianzhong Wu & Robert Axelrod, How to Cope with Noise in the Iterated Prisoner's Dilemma, 39 J. Conflict Resol. 183 (1995).

---

us to be as sophisticated and as complex in our analysis as we can.

Non-zero-sum games, such as the Prisoner's Dilemma, are not like this. Unlike the clouds, the other player can respond to your own choices. And unlike the chess opponent, the other player in a Prisoner's Dilemma should not be regarded as someone who is out to defeat you. The other player will be watching your behavior for signs of whether you will reciprocate cooperation or not, and therefore your own behavior is likely to be echoed back to you.

Rules that try to maximize their own score while treating the other player as a fixed part of the environment ignore this aspect of the interaction, no matter how clever they are in calculating under their limiting assumptions. Therefore, it does not pay to be clever in modeling the other player if you leave out the reverberating process in which the other player is adapting to you, you are adapting to the other, and then the other player is adapting to your adaptation and so on. . . .

In other words, too much complexity can appear to be total chaos. If you are using a strategy which appears random, then you also appear unresponsive to the other player. If you are unresponsive, then the other player has no incentive to cooperate with you. So being so complex as to be incomprehensible is very dangerous. . . .

What accounts for TIT FOR TAT's robust success is its combination of being nice, retaliatory, forgiving, and clear. Its niceness prevents it from getting into unnecessary trouble. Its retaliation discourages the other side from persisting whenever defection is tried. Its forgiveness helps restore mutual cooperation. And its clarity makes it intelligible to the other player, thereby eliciting long-term cooperation.

Problem 3-10. *Prisoner's Dilemma Lessons?*

What lessons do you draw from Tit for Tat? How would you use those lessons in the litigation discovery scenario? How would you prepare for your next negotiation?

---

2. Negotiator's Dilemma

The Prisoner's Dilemma is a highly stylized interaction. Yet some legal scholars have analogized this situation to discovery prior to trial.[8] Each side has the choice whether to cooperate in discovery (to turn over requested documents easily, to schedule depositions conveniently, to answer interrogatories fully) or to be more adversarial (to fight document requests, to make depositions a true inconvenience, to evade answering interrogatories). If both sides cooperate, discovery moves forward quickly and relatively inexpensively. If both sides are adversarial, discovery is delayed and is far more costly as the parties file additional motions. If one side is cooperative while the other is adversarial, then the cooperative side ends up spending more money and getting less information. The adversarial side saves money and gets the information it needs. The balance of information exchange, trust, and defection is also seen in negotiation as discussed below where the choice to claim value or create value is called the Negotiator's Dilemma or the "mixed model" of negotiation, as described above.

 David A. Lax & James K. Sebenius, **THE MANAGER AS NEGOTIATOR: BARGAINING FOR COOPERATION AND COMPETITIVE GAIN**

29-30, 32, 38-40 (1986)

Negotiators and analysts tend to fall into two groups that are guided by warring conceptions of the bargaining process. In the left-hand corner are the "value creators" and in the right-hand corner are the "value claimers." Value creators

---

8. See Ronald J. Gilson & Robert H. Mnookin, Disputing Through Agents: Cooperation and Conflict Between Lawyers in Litigation, 94 Colum. L. Rev. 509 (1995).

tend to believe that, above all, successful negotiators must be inventive and cooperative enough to devise an agreement that yields considerable gain to each party, relative to no-agreement possibilities. Some speak about the need for replacing the "win-lose" image of negotiation with "win-win" negotiation, from which all parties presumably derive great value. . . .

Value claimers, on the other hand, tend to see this drive for joint gain as naïve and weak-minded. For them, negotiation is hard, tough bargaining. The object of negotiation is to convince the other guy that he wants what you have to offer much more than you want what he has. . . . To "win" at negotiation — and thus make the other fellow "lose" — one must start high, concede slowly, exaggerate the value of concessions, minimize the benefits of the other's concessions, conceal information, argue forcefully on behalf of principles that imply favorable settlement, make commitments to accept only highly favorable agreements, and be willing to outwait the other fellow. . . .

Both of these images of negotiation are incomplete and inadequate. Value creating and value claiming are linked parts of negotiation. Both processes are present. No matter how much creative problem solving enlarges the pie, it must still be divided; value that has been created must be claimed. And, if the pie is not enlarged, there will be less to divide; there is more value to be claimed if one has helped create it first. An essential tension in negotiation exists between cooperative moves to create value and competitive moves to claim it. . . .

Consider two negotiators (named Ward and Stone) each of whom can choose between two negotiating styles: creating value (being open, sharing information about preferences and beliefs, not being misleading about minimum requirements, and so forth) and claiming value (being cagey and misleading about preferences, beliefs, and minimum requirements; making commitments and threats, and so forth). Each has the same two options for any tactical choice. If both choose to create value, they each receive a good outcome, which we will call GOOD for each. If Ward chooses to create value and Stone chooses to claim value, then Stone does even better than if he had chosen to create value — rank this outcome GREAT for Stone — but Ward does much worse — rank this outcome TER-RIBLE for him. Similarly, if Stone is the creative one and Ward is the claimer, then Ward does well — rank this outcome for him as GREAT — while Stone's outcome is TERRIBLE. If both claim, they fail to find joint gains and come up with a mediocre outcome, which we call MEDIOCRE for both. . . . In each box, Ward's payoff is in the lower left corner and Stone's is in the upper right. Thus, when Ward claims and Stone creates, Ward's outcome is GREAT while Stone's is TERRIBLE. [See Figure 2.1.]

Figure 2.1
Negotiator's Dilemma

		Stone's Choice		
		Create		Claim
Ward's Choice Create		GOOD		GREAT
	GOOD		TERRIBLE	
Claim		TERRIBLE		MEDIOCRE
	GREAT		MEDIOCRE	

The lower left entry in each cell is Ward's outcome; the second entry is Stone's.

Now, if Ward were going to create, Stone would prefer the GREAT outcome obtained by claiming to the GOOD outcome he could have obtained by creating; so, Stone should claim. If, on the other hand, Ward were going to claim, Stone would prefer the MEDIOCRE outcome from claiming to the TERRIBLE outcome he would receive from creating. In fact, no matter what Ward does, it seems that Stone would be better off trying to claim value!

Similarly, Ward should also prefer to claim. By symmetric reasoning, if Stone chooses to create, Ward prefers the GREAT outcome he gets by claiming to the GOOD outcome he gets from creating. If Stone claims, Ward prefers the MEDIOCRE outcome he gets from claiming to the TERRIBLE outcome he gets from creating.

Both negotiators choose to claim. They land in the lower-right-hand box and receive MEDIOCRE outcomes. They leave joint gains on the table, since both would prefer the GOOD outcomes they could have received had they both chosen to create value and ended up in the upper-left-hand box.

This is the crux of the Negotiator's Dilemma. Individually rational decisions to emphasize claiming tactics by being cagey and misleading lead to a mutually undesirable outcome. As described, this situation has the structure of the famous "Prisoner's Dilemma." In such situations, the motivation to protect oneself and employ tactics for claiming value is compelling.

Problem 3-11. *Negotiator's Dilemma*

How is the Negotiator's Dilemma similar to the Prisoner's Dilemma? How is it different? How would you apply the lessons learned in Tit for Tat to the Negotiator's Dilemma?

3. The Solution — Be Flexible

This final excerpt from Peter S. Adler is an article that suggests that you can be a flexible negotiator — you can move between the many approaches and techniques that exist in the field of negotiation. The author compares the skilled negotiator to the Greek god Proteus. Proteus embodied the powers of mysticism and shape-shifting, but would only foretell the future to those who could capture him. Many gods tried to capture him, but he usually escaped by changing shapes. Like Proteus, a skilled negotiator is aware of all of the different concepts and strategies and is able to shift between them — a Protean negotiator.

 Peter S. Adler, **PROTEAN NEGOTIATION**

in The Negotiator's Fieldbook 17-27 (Andrea Kupfer Schneider & Christopher Honeyman eds., 2006)

ANCIENT IMPERATIVES

. . . Around the world, in classrooms, board rooms, and airport waiting rooms, the theory and practice of negotiation is awash with advice. Much of it is simplistic and some of it contradictory. One writer implores us to know our bottom line. Another urges us to ignore it and focus on needs. A third says to wait until the last moment to do a deal when the situation is ripe. A fourth counsels us to get in early. At best, the many lists of "dos" and "don'ts" serve as reference points and modest road maps for certain situations. At worst, they misdirect us into thinking there is some grand unified field theory or universal paradigm that, if we master it, will carry us seamlessly through every deal and dispute. . . .

While there are many different styles, schools, and brands, . . . most of these seem to devolve to four basic schools of thinking about how humans behave in the face of real or imagined conflict, how they negotiate, and how we might help them. One presupposes that all of us are fundamentally competitive. A second assumes we are, at core, cooperative. A third takes for granted that all of us will seek to do what is morally correct. A fourth assumes we are rational and pragmatic. These four impulses . . . . . . seem to have evolutionary roots that date back to our origins on the African savannah. . . . But there is also a fifth way, one that acknowledges the universality and importance of all of them but is not explicitly and strictly any of them. It too has ancient roots. Let's call it "Protean Negotiation." . . .

POLARITY AND PARADOX

It doesn't matter if you are a tenant talking to your landlord, an ambassador pressing for security measures on the Indian and Pakistani border, or Amalgamated and Pulsar testing the waters for a joint venture in Brazil: competition and cooperation form a paradox. So too do the pressures of acting ethically and pragmatically. Not every negotiation embodies every tension, nor are these four the only predicaments that come up when people struggle to reconcile different ideas. . . .

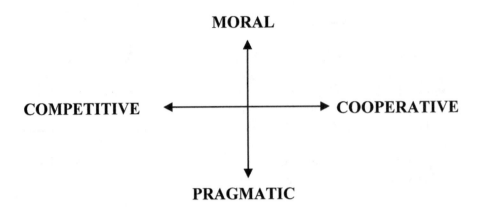

"An effective negotiator," says Robert Benjamin "requires a thinking frame that is adaptive, dynamic, fluid, and shifting and a model of negotiation that can house a variety of negotiation rituals." As the following schematic suggests, the Protean negotiator is not a polymath but more of a dancer.

He or she can dance the competitor's jitterbug, the collaborator's tango, the moralist's waltz, and the pragmatist's four step. One dance may be more comfortable than the others, and the dances can be sequenced, but they are all in the repertoire. The Protean negotiator adapts.

Like Proteus, skilled negotiators seem to be able to reconcile the tensions of inconsistent and confusing impulses that may attend cooperative, competitive, moral, or pragmatic approaches to negotiation. . . .

ANCIENT IMPERATIVES — REVISITED

In 1950 John Marshall, an anthropologist and film maker, received funding from the Smithsonian Institution and Harvard University to study one of the last migratory bands of the Kung people, also known as the Bushmen or San People. . . .

In a slow but mounting drama, it chronicles the story of a hunting expedition by four men from a particular band who have set off to find large game at a time when the group desperately needs a major infusion of protein. . . .

Although all of them hunt, one man among them is more skilled than the others. He is strong and highly competitive, able to pick up scents and follow trails when the others seem baffled. In these moments, the others cede leadership to his knowledge and prowess. The second is a craftsman. He is the technician, the one who fashions the small, intricate, and lethal poison-tipped arrows they use, the one who repairs spears and belts and bows. At certain moments, others cede leadership to his knowledge and skill. The third is the shaman, the man who performs small ceremonies along the way and who reminds the others of the rituals that must be done if harmony in the world is to be maintained. At key moments, he leads. And the last is the headman, the man who insists on cooperation when the others are quarreling, the one who wears the weight of their many failures on his shoulder, the one who urges them to work together until their goal is accomplished.

Four men, four styles of leadership, four approaches to the negotiation of their work, four ancient imperatives that permeate our work as problem solvers in dimly understood ways. . . .

Either way, Marshall's film hints at something older and more mysterious that permeates the negotiations we are all engaged in. If there is a deep imperative here, perhaps it is a constant reminder that negotiation is an all too human craft and that like so many other human endeavors, our greatest individual and collective strengths, taken to excess, inevitably become our greatest weaknesses. . . .

Choosing an Approach

How can you choose what model or approach to negotiation to use in a particular setting? Carrie Menkel-Meadow has suggested that the following factors might influence which model of negotiation we might choose in particular situations:

- *Subject matter* (Dispute vs. transaction, the material of the negotiation — is it limited expandable? Is there a need for a definitive, precedential ruling?)
- *Content of the issues* (What are the underlying interests of the parties — latent, manifest, short term, long term? Do the parties value the issues equally?)
- *Voluntariness* (Do the parties have a choice about negotiating?)
- *Visibility* (Will negotiations be conducted privately or publicly?)
- *Relationship* (Parties, negotiators, long term or one-shot)
- *Accountability* (To what constituencies is the negotiator responsible — a single client? an organizational client? a family? a labor union?)
- *Stake* (Who stands to "win or lose" most from the negotiation?)
- *Routineness* (How is the negotiation limited by frequency and norms of the problem, e.g., plea bargaining?)
- *Power* (How do parties assess their relative power in terms of fact, law, economic resources, and or moral righteousness?)
- *Personal characteristics of the negotiator* (Psychological "orientations")
- *Medium of the negotiation* (Face-to-face encounter vs. telephonic or written or computer-assisted negotiations)
- *Alternatives to negotiation* (Trial, transaction not consummated?)

— from Carrie Menkel-Meadow, Legal Negotiation: A Study of Strategies in Search of a Theory, 1983 A.B.F. Res. J. 905, 927-928.

Whatever choices about your approach you make as a negotiator, be sure to be mindful that different choices lead to different results. In the next chapter, we look at the behaviors that will also lead to being effective as a negotiator.

Further Reading

David B. Falk, *The Art of Contract Negotiation*, 3 MARQ. SPORTS L.J. 1 (1992).
Roger Fisher, William Ury & Bruce Patton. (2d ed. 1991). *Getting to YES*. New York: Penguin.

Roger Fisher, Elizabeth Kopelman & Andrea Kupfer Schneider. (1996). *Machiavelli, Beyond Machiavelli: Tools for Coping with Conflict*. New York: Penguin.

P.H. Gulliver. (1979). *Disputes and Negotiations: A Cross-Cultural Perspective (Studies on Law and Social Control)*. New York: Academic Press.

Russell Korobkin, *A Positive Theory of Legal Negotiation*, 88 Geo. L.J. 1789 (2000).

David A. Lax & James K. Sebenius. (1986). *The Manager as Negotiator*. New York: Free Press.

David A. Lax & James K. Sebenius. (2006). *3D Negotiation*. Cambridge: Harvard Business Press.

Gary Lowenthal, *A General Theory of Negotiation Process, Strategy and Behavior*, 31 Kansas L. Rev. 96 (1982).

Avishai Margalit. (2010). *On Compromise and Rotten Compromises*. Princeton, NJ: Princeton University Press.

Carrie Menkel-Meadow, *Legal Negotiation: A Study of Strategies in Search of a Theory*, 1983 American Bar Foundation Research Journal 905-937.

Carrie Menkel-Meadow, *Compromise, Negotiation and Morality*, 26 Negotiation Journal, 481-497 (2010).

Michael Meltsner & Philip G. Schrag (1974). "Negotiation," in *Public Interest Advocacy: Materials for Legal Education*. Boston: Little, Brown.

Robert H. Mnookin, Scott R. Peppet & Andrew S. Tulumello. (2000). *Beyond Winning: Negotiating to Create Value in Deals and Disputes*. Cambridge: Belknap Press of Harvard University Press.

Howard Raiffa, with John Richardson & David Metcalfe. (2007). *Negotiation Analysis*. Cambridge: Belknap Press of Harvard University Press.

Frank E. A. Sander & Jeffrey Rubin, *The Janus Quality of Negotiation: Dealmaking and Dispute Settlement*, 4 Negot. J. 109 (1988).

G. Richard Shell. (2d ed. 2006). *Bargaining for Advantage*. New York: Viking.

Chapter 4   Skills and Practices in Negotiation

Moderate your desire of victory over your adversary, and be pleased with the one over yourself.

— Benjamin Franklin, *The Morals of Chess* (1750)

In the first two chapters you were introduced to conflict theory and the framework and institutions that house the theory. You learned some of the reasons people hire lawyers, including: to avoid conflict, to distance themselves from emotional situations, to achieve justice, to win as much as possible, and to resolve disputes. You were also introduced to some of the skills an effective lawyer needs — one of the most important being the skill of listening. This chapter delves further into the many skills you will need to be an effective negotiator and to employ the approaches outlined in the previous chapter.

The most effective negotiators are able to choose among different approaches depending on the context, client, and the party on the other side. Yet to have that ability to choose — to be a Protean negotiator — you need to have an array of skills that allow you to engage in the different approaches. Without the ability to persuasively present your client's optimistic goals, it is rather challenging to assume a competitive approach to a negotiation. Similarly, without the ability to listen carefully and understand the other side's interests, it is harder to accommodate them. And, when engaging in problem solving, you'll need both of those skill sets in addition to the skill of finding more creative and flexible solutions that better meet both sides' interests.

The skills presented in this chapter are organized, first, how to most persuasively present your client's goals in the negotiation — preparing you and your client, how to frame your client's goals and tell their story to the other side, and how fairness and standards underlie the most effective arguments. The next section discusses the skills necessary to work with the other side — gathering information about them, understanding their perspective, listening to them, and building trust. Finally, the last section focuses on some of the most sophisticated thinking about the negotiation process — how parties can create better solutions and how lawyers can help their clients avoid some common mistakes.

A. PREPARING AND PRESENTING YOUR "CASE"

1. Set Your Goals

In Chapter 2 we discussed how interviewing your client to determine his or her goals is a crucial part of helping them address their situation. The lawyer's role is to think about those goals, both concrete and intangible, and then work with the client to set goals and aspirations for a negotiation. As we outlined in the previous chapter, these goals may vary depending on what approach to the negotiation you choose. Regardless of approach, however, working with your client to set goals is an important first step in which to engage. Thinking about how to set optimistic and realistic goals — and why that is important — is the subject of this first excerpt from business school professor G. Richard Shell.

 ### *G. Richard Shell*, BARGAINING FOR ADVANTAGE: NEGOTIATION STRATEGIES FOR REASONABLE PEOPLE

31-34 (1999)

SET AN OPTIMISTIC, JUSTIFIABLE TARGET

When you set goals, think boldly and optimistically about what you would like to see happen. Research has repeatedly shown that people who have higher aspirations in negotiations perform better and get more than people who have modest or "I'll do my best" goals, provided they really believe in their targets.

In one classic study, psychologists Sydney Siegel and Lawrence Fouraker set up a simple buy-sell negotiation experiment. They allowed the negotiators to keep all the profits they achieved but told the subjects they could qualify for a second, "double-their-money" round if they met or exceeded certain specified bargaining goals. In other words, Siegel and Fouraker gave their subjects both concrete *incentives* for hitting a certain specified level of performance and, perhaps unintentionally, a hint that the assigned target levels were realistically attainable (why else would subjects be told about the bonus round?). One set of negotiators was told they would have to hit a modest $2.10 target to qualify for the bonus round. Another set of negotiators was told they would have to hit a much more ambitious target of $6.10. Both sides had the same bottom line: They could not accept any deal that involved a loss. The negotiators with the more ambitious $6.10 goal achieved a mean profit of $6.25, far outperforming the median profit of $3.35 achieved by those with the modest $2.10 goal.

My own research has confirmed Siegel's and Fouraker's findings. In our experiment, unlike the one Siegel and Fouraker conducted, negotiation subjects set their own bargaining goals. And instead of letting everyone keep whatever profits they earned, we gave separate $100 prizes to the buyer and the seller with the best individual outcomes. The result was the same, however. Negotiators who reported

higher prenegotiation expectations achieved more than
those who entered the negotiation with more modest
goals.

Why are we tempted to
set modest bargaining goals
when we can achieve more
by raising our sights? There
are several possible reasons.
First, many people set modest
goals to protect their self-
esteem. We are less likely to
fail if we set our goals low, so
we "wing it," telling ourselves
that we are doing fine as long
as we beat our bottom line.
Modest goals thus help us
avoid unpleasant feelings of
failure and regret.

Second, we may not have
enough information about

> **Gender and Goal-Setting**
>
> Some studies have shown that women are less
> likely to set high goals in a negotiation or view
> some interactions as negotiations.
>
> - What is the impact of the kind of mindset in
>   these studies?
> - Have you seen this happen? Or experienced
>   it?
>
> Note that subsequent studies on lawyers have
> revealed no gender differences regarding negotia-
> tions on behalf of clients or in initial salary
> negotiations on behalf of themselves.
>
> See generally, Linda Babcock & Sara
> Laschever (2003), Women Don't Ask: Negotia-
> tion and the Gender Divide. Princeton: Princeton
> University Press; Andrea Kupfer Schneider et al.,
> Likeability v. Competence: The Impossible
> Choice Faced by Female Politicians, Evaded by
> Lawyers, Duke J. Gender L. & Pol'y (forth-
> coming 2010).

the negotiation to see the full potential for gain; that is, we may fail to appreciate
the true worth of what we are selling, not do the research on applicable standards,
or fail to note how eager the buyer is for what we have to offer. This usually means
we have failed to prepare well enough.

Third, we may lack desire. If the other person wants money, control, or power
more urgently than we do, we are unlikely to set a high goal for ourselves. Why look
for conflict and trouble over things we care little about?

Research suggests that the self-esteem factor plays a more important role in
low goal setting than many of us would care to admit. We once had a negotiation
speaker who said that the problem with many reasonable people is that they
confuse "win-win" with what he called a "wimp-win" attitude. The "wimp-win"
negotiator focuses only on his or her bottom line; the "win-win" negotiator has
ambitious goals.

I see further evidence of this in negotiation classes. As students and executives
in negotiation workshops start setting more ambitious goals for themselves and
strive to improve, they often report feeling more *dissatisfied and discouraged* regarding
their performance — even as their objective results get better and better. For this
reason, I suggest raising one's goals incrementally, adding risk and difficulty in small
steps over a series of negotiations. That way you can maintain your enthusiasm for
negotiation as you learn. Research shows that people who succeed in achieving new
goals are more likely to raise their goals the next time. Those who fail, however, tend
to become discouraged and lower their targets.

Once you have thought about what an optimistic, challenging goal would look
like, spend a few minutes permitting realism to dampen your expectations. *Optimistic*

goals are effective only if they are feasible; that is, only if you believe in them and they can be justified according to some standard or norm. . . . [N]egotiation positions must usually be supported by some standard, benchmark, or precedent, or they lose their credibility. No amount of mental goal setting will make your five-year-old car worth more than a brand-new version of the same model. You should also adjust your goal to reflect appropriate relationship concerns.

But do not let your ideas of what is appropriate or realistic take over completely. Simply note the reasons you come up with that explain why your optimistic goal may not be possible and look for the next highest, *defendable* target. Your old car may not be worth the same as a new one, but you should be able to find a used-car guide that reports the "average" price for your model. With that foundation, you can justify asking for a premium over that standard based on the tip-top condition of your vehicle.

One danger with being too realistic with your goals is that you may be making unwarranted assumptions about the values and priorities the other side will bring to the deal. Until you know for sure what *the other side* has for goals and what *the other side* thinks is realistic, you should keep your eyes firmly on your own defendable target. The other party will tell you if your optimistic deal isn't possible, and you will not offend him or her by asking for your goal so long as you have some justification to support it, you advance your ideas with courtesy, and you show a concern for his or her perspective.

Keep this point in mind as you progress toward higher goals: A certain amount of dissatisfaction is a good thing when you first start thinking seriously about improving how you negotiate. Dissatisfaction is a sign that you are setting your goals at a high enough level to encounter resistance from other parties and to take the risk that they may walk away. Eventually, you will learn to set targets that are challenging without being unduly discouraging.

BE SPECIFIC

The literature on negotiation goal setting counsels us to be as specific as possible. Clarity drives out fuzziness in negotiations as in many other endeavors. With a definite target, you will begin working on a host of psychological levels to get the job done. For example, when you land your new job, don't just set a goal to "negotiate a fair salary." Push yourself to take aim at a specific target — go for a 10 percent raise over what you made at your last job. Your specific goal will start you thinking about other, comparable jobs that pay your target salary, and you will begin to notice a variety of market standards that support a salary of that amount.

Be especially wary of goals such as "I'll do the best I can" or, worst of all, "I'll just go in and see what I can get." What we are really saying when we enter a negotiation with goals such as these is, "I do not want to take a chance on failing in this negotiation." Fear of failure and our natural desire to avoid feelings of disappointment and regret are legitimate psychological self-protection devices. But effective negotiators do not let these feelings get in the way of setting specific goals.

Problem 4-1. *Justify It*

What does Shell mean by "justifiable target"? Why should your goal be justifiable? How do you make your goal justifiable (or legitimate)?

Problem 4-2. *Dealing with Regret*

In empirical experiments of aspirations in negotiations, Russell Korobkin finds that setting aspiration levels can affect key "settlement levers" including reservation points, the definition of fairness, increased patience at the bargaining table, and rejection of barely acceptable offers. At the same time, Korobkin writes, high aspiration levels can increase the likelihood of impasse and reduce satisfaction with the outcome. Russell Korobkin, Aspirations and Settlement, 88 Cornell L. Rev. 1 (2002). Shell notes above that negotiators may set modest goals to avoid feelings of regret. Is it worth setting high aspiration levels if you are more likely to be disappointed?

---

2. Set Your Limits

Planning and preparation involve practices that every successful negotiator considers key skills. Integral to these skills is an understanding of the other side's position, their strengths and weaknesses. Of course, it is also crucial that you have a clear picture of your own strengths and weaknesses, your walk-a-way point, and your best alternative.

This section explains two key concepts that you will hear repeatedly in dispute resolution theory — BATNA and Reservation Point. *Getting to YES* first introduced the idea of BATNA — Best Alternative to a Negotiated Agreement. The phrase, now used freely in negotiation jargon, is a mechanism to ensure that you never make an agreement that you should not make. If the alternative to this agreement is preferable, you should walk away.

Using your BATNA to protect yourself from unwise agreements takes several steps. First, you need to brainstorm all of your alternatives to an agreement. This might include going to court in certain kinds of situations. Or your alternatives might include making an agreement with another company or buying a different house. Second, you choose your best alternative — the one that leaves you in the best situation. Finally, you convert this BATNA into a reservation price, point, or value. This number is the point at which you would be better off going to your BATNA.

For example, assume you are purchasing a home. Your first choice home is priced at $300,000. Your second choice is priced at $250,000, and you assume that you could probably purchase it for $240,000. How do you decide when buying your second choice makes more sense? You need to value the difference between the homes — what makes your first choice home your preferred choice. List these factors: (1) attached garage; (2) better school district; (3) larger back yard; and (4) does not need to be painted before moving in. Next, attach values to each of these items. For some differences between the properties, like the garage and the back yard, you might check with your realtor to get a sense of how others might value particular items. For others, like the school district, you are attaching a tangible number to an intangible item. Ask yourself how much more you would pay for the exact same house in one neighborhood versus the other. For the last item, painting, you can price this with some research of your own.

Assume you've attached the following values for your items: (1) attached garage ($10,000); (2) better school district ($15,000); (3) larger back yard ($5,000); and (4) not having to paint ($5,000 — for paint, the painter, and the inconvenience). The first choice home is worth about $35,000 more to you. Therefore, your reservation price is $240,000 plus $35,000 = $275,000. This means that if you can't negotiate the price on the more expensive house down to $275,000, you would be better off, given your preferences, buying the less expensive home.

In negotiations one of the largest difficulties negotiators face is working without knowing the other party's BATNA or reservation values. To overcome this lack of information, negotiators often estimate the values after conducting more research about the other party, primarily by looking for past behaviors, interests, needs, and values. We discuss learning more about the other side later in this chapter.

The value created by the difference between the two reservation values is a critical concept of negotiation theory. It becomes the surplus when the parties make an agreement. If the difference between the reservation values of the two parties is large, then there will be a relatively large amount of potential surplus to be divided between the parties. The parties lose this potential value if either side walks away.

The next excerpt is from Professor Russell Korobkin. This excerpt provides more specific advice on how to use your BATNA to ensure you achieve a wise agreement. Your BATNA and reservation price, as well as the BATNA and reservation price of the other party, should set the parameters of the bargaining zone.

 ### *Russell Korobkin,* A POSITIVE THEORY OF LEGAL NEGOTIATION

88 Geo. L.J. 1789, 1794-1798 (2000)

[S]uppose Esau, looking to get into business for himself, is willing to pay up to $200,000 for Jacob's catering business, while Jacob, interested in retiring, is willing to sell the business for any amount over $150,000. This difference between Esau's and Jacob's RPs creates a $50,000 bargaining zone. At any price between $150,000 and $200,000, both parties are better off agreeing to the sale of the business than they are reaching no agreement and going their separate ways.

The same structure used to describe a transactional negotiation can be used to describe a dispute resolution negotiation. Suppose that Goliath has filed suit against

David for battery. David is willing to pay up to $90,000 to settle the case out of court — essentially, to buy Goliath's legal right to bring suit — while Goliath will "sell" his right for any amount over $60,000. These RPs create a $30,000 bargaining zone between $60,000 and $90,000. Any settlement in this range would leave both parties better off than they would be without a settlement.

★ ★ ★

[P]ainstaking preparation is critical to success at the bargaining table. . . . [T]horough preparation is a prerequisite for the negotiator to accomplish zone definition as advantageously as possible. . . . "Internal" preparation refers to research that the negotiator does to set and adjust his own RP [Reservation Price]. "External" preparation refers to research that the negotiator does to estimate and manipulate the other party's RP.

INTERNAL PREPARATION

A negotiator cannot determine his RP without first understanding his substitutes for and the opportunity costs of reaching a negotiated agreement. This, of course, requires research. . . .

After identifying the various alternatives to reaching a negotiated agreement, the negotiator needs to determine which alternative is most desirable. Fisher and his coauthors coined the appropriate term "BATNA" — "best alternative to a negotiated agreement" — to identify this choice. The identity and quality of a negotiator's BATNA is the primary input into his RP.

If the negotiator's BATNA and the subject of the negotiation are perfectly interchangeable, determining the reservation price is quite simple: the reservation price is merely the value of the BATNA. For example, if Esau's BATNA is buying another catering business for $190,000 that is identical to Jacob's in terms of quality, earnings potential, and all other factors that are important to Esau, then his RP is $190,000. If Jacob will sell for some amount less than that, Esau will be better off buying Jacob's company than he would pursuing his best alternative. If Jacob demands more than $190,000, Esau is better off buying the alternative company and not reaching an agreement with Jacob.

In most circumstances, however, the subject of a negotiation and the negotiator's BATNA are not perfect substitutes. If Jacob's business is of higher quality, has a higher earnings potential, or is located closer to Esau's home, he would probably be willing to pay a premium for it over what he would pay for the alternative choice. For example, if the alternative business is selling for $190,000, Esau might determine he would be willing to pay up to a $10,000 premium over the alternative for Jacob's business and thus set his RP at $200,000. On the other hand, if Esau's BATNA is more desirable to him than Jacob's business, Esau will discount the value of his BATNA by the amount necessary to make the two alternatives equally desirable values for the money; perhaps he will set his RP at $180,000 in recognition that his BATNA is $10,000 more desirable than Jacob's business, and Jacob's business would be equally desirable only at a $10,000 discount. . . .

The relationship between a party's BATNA and his RP can be generalized in the following way. A party's RP has two components: (1) the market value of his BATNA;

and (2) the difference to *him* between the value of his BATNA and the value of the subject of the negotiation. A seller sets his RP by calculating (1) and either *subtracting* (2) if the subject of the negotiation is more valuable than his BATNA (and therefore he is willing to accept less to reach and agreement) or *adding* (2) if the BATNA is more valuable than the subject of the negotiation (and therefore, he would demand more to reach an agreement and give up his BATNA). A buyer sets his RP by calculating (1) and either *adding* (2) if the subject of the negotiation is more valuable than his BATNA (and therefore he would pay a premium to reach an agreement) or *subtracting* (2) if his BATNA is more valuable than the subject of the negotiation (and therefore he would demand a discount to give up the BATNA). . . .

By investigating an even wider range of alternatives to reaching agreement, and by more thoroughly investigating the value of obvious alternatives, the negotiator can alter his RP in a way that will shift the bargaining zone to his advantage. . . .

EXTERNAL PREPARATION

External preparation allows the negotiator to estimate his opponent's RP . . . [t]o accurately predict Jacob's RP and therefore pinpoint the low end of the bargaining zone. This information will also prepare Esau to attempt to persuade Jacob during the course of negotiations to lower his RP. . . .

It is worth noting that in the litigation context both parties often have the same alternatives and the same BATNA. If plaintiff Goliath determines that his BATNA is going to trial, then defendant David's only alternative — and therefore his BATNA default — is going to trial as well. In this circumstance, internal preparation and external preparations merge. . . .

Race, Gender, and the Perception of a Bad BATNA

In the mid-1990s, a study was performed concerning negotiations for the purchase of a new car. "More than 180 independent negotiations at ninety dealerships were conducted in the Chicago area to examine how dealerships bargain. Testers of different races and genders entered new car dealerships separately and bargained to buy a new car, using a uniform negotiation strategy. The study tests whether automobile retailers react differently to this uniform strategy when potential buyers differ only by gender or race.

The tests reveal that white males receive significantly better prices than blacks and women. . . . [W]hite women had to pay forty percent higher markups than white men; black men had to pay more than twice the markup, and black women had to pay more than three times the markup of white male testers. Moreover, the study reveals that testers of different race and gender are subjected to several forms of nonprice discrimination. Specifically, testers were systematically steered to salespeople of their own race and gender (who then gave them worse deals) and were asked different questions and told about different qualities of the car." Ian Ayres, Fair Driving, 104 Harv. L. Rev. 817, 818-819 (1991).

One hypothesis suggested by the author was that in making offers to white women, and to black men and women, salespeople assumed that these groups of people had poor BATNAs because these negotiators were unwilling or unable to negotiate, and had less ability to search and find a better deal. See Ian Ayres, Further Evidence of Discrimination in New Car Negotiations and Estimates of Its Cause, 94 Mich. L. Rev. 109 (1995).

Problem 4-3. *BATNA Research*

Assume that a local sandwich shop is negotiating with a national coffee franchise, Morebucks, to serve Morebucks coffee. The sandwich shop is interested in serving Morebucks so that it can bring in more customers and make more money.

- What else can the sandwich shop do to improve its financial situation? Note that your answers are all alternatives to a negotiated agreement; and that some of these alternatives may make sense to do anyway.
- What type of research would you perform in advance of the negotiations with Morebucks? Based on your research and your alternatives to this agreement, choose your BATNA. The BATNA is an action plan.
- Next, translate this BATNA into a reservation price. For example, assume you find out that (1) the other national coffee franchise, Coffeebest, usually charges $3 per pound of coffee to its franchisees; (2) the standard price from Morebucks to outside vendors is usually $4 per pound; and (3) Morebucks has been known to give discounts for long-term contracts, for large volume, and in new areas where it is trying to get a niche. How do you set your reservation price?

Problem 4-4. *Mistaken Estimates*

What if, in the course of the negotiation, you find out that your estimates of your counterpart's BATNA are mistaken? What if, for example, you thought the people placing a bid on your house also were very interested in another house? How would that affect your negotiation? What if you found out, instead, they loved your house?

In addition to determining your BATNA in a negotiation, it is equally important to find your WATNA — Worst Alternative to a Negotiated Agreement — and your ATNA(s) — All the Alternative(s) to a Negotiated Agreement. While a negotiator's BATNA is a mechanism that prevents him from making an unwise agreement, a WATNA can serve as a reality check for a negotiator who may find himself straying far from his goals or risking impasse. All alternatives that are not designated as the BATNA and the WATNA remain in the ATNA category — alternatives that may be visited throughout the course of the negotiation. In decision tree analysis people often look only at best- or worst-case scenarios. The good negotiator (and wise counselor to clients) will try to analyze all the alternatives that might be possible in both negotiation and other forms of dispute resolution (e.g., litigation) in order to evaluate what might best be accomplished in a negotiation. Often, the WATNA might be litigation (the possibility of "losing" completely), but then the chances or possibilities of losing will have to be assessed as a matter of probabilities, based on legal, factual, and discretionary factors.

3. Speaking Persuasively

After setting your goals and limits, it is now time to make your case for trying to solve the problem in a way that best meets your client's objectives. This section discusses some of the communication techniques that can make you persuasive. Before making your presentation to your counterpart in the negotiation, you need to think about how to make the most persuasive case. This is not unlike a trial lawyer's task when preparing to make arguments in front of a jury. What is likely to convince them that you are making good suggestions for a good resolution of a negotiation problem or set of issues.

One of the ways to make your presentation more persuasive is to tell a coherent story about what your client desires. For example, in addition to your legal arguments, you might also base your argument on good policy, a principle to be upheld, the better consequences of your agreement, an appeal to justice or morality, the needs and interests of the other side, or the general custom in that type of business or situation.

Additional methods to deepen your presentations and suggestions include framing and analogy. Negotiators sometimes use metaphors and labeling to make their arguments more persuasive. In a negotiation are we *partners* or *opponents*? When trying to motivate U.S. involvement in Kosovo, was this another Vietnam or was Milosevic another Hitler? Similar metaphors were used with the Iraq war in 2003. In another case were the people who took 700 hostages in a Moscow theater in October 2002 "terrorists" or Chechen "freedom fighters"? The use of labels simplifies a complex situation to convince and persuade the recipient. How you view the situation clearly affects what action you think is appropriate.

Other framing occurs through the use of specifics and detail. You can use statistics or expert authority to provide specific support for your argument. Sometimes this experience is personal or "anecdotal," often appealing to notions of justice, emotion, empathy, or morality — if you can tell a story about how your motorcycle helmet saved your life, you might be better able to persuade a legislator to change the law. Many congressional hearings focus on this type of framing. Other times you can tell a story using vivid detail to describe what has happened and bring the listener into the situation. Excellent trial attorneys often use this type of framing with a jury. In fact, in a study comparing the use of pallid information ("The defendant staggered against a serving table, knocking a bowl to the floor") versus vivid information ("The defendant staggered against a serving table, knocking a bowl of guacamole dip to the floor and splattering guacamole on the white shag carpet"), members of the mock jury were more likely to find the latter defendant guilty.[1]

---

1. R. M. Reyes, W. C. Thompson & G. H. Bower, Judgmental Biases Resulting from Differing Availabilities of Arguments, 39 J. Personality & Soc. Psychol. 2 (1980), cited in Scott Plous, The Psychology of Judgment and Decision Making 127-128 (1993).

Problem 4-5. *More Money*

Assume that you are arguing for increased funding of art and music programs in the public education system in your hometown. What arguments would you make from the perspective of policy? Of principle? Of consequences? What details or statistics might you want to know?

Speaking to be Heard

The following is a classic example of what happens when people are talking past one another or when they are not sufficiently clear or forthcoming with critical information. This is one version of a story that is based on a radio transcript released by the Chief of Naval Operations from October 10, 1995.

Station 1: Please divert your course 15 degrees to the North to avoid a collision.

Station 2: Recommend you divert YOUR course 15 degrees to the South to avoid a collision.

Station 1: This is the Captain of a U.S. Navy ship. I say again, divert YOUR course.

Station 2: No, I say again, you divert *your* course.

Station 1: This is the Aircraft Carrier Enterprise, we are a large warship of the U.S. Navy. Divert your course now!

Station 2: This is the Puget Sound Lighthouse. It's your call.

Problem 4-6. *Forget the Law*

Robert Condlin states that legal arguments tend to be the least persuasive to law students or practicing attorneys. Robert Condlin, Cases on Both Sides: Patterns of Argument in Legal Dispute Negotiation, 44 Md. L. Rev. 65 (1985). Why do you think this might be the case? Do you think this is a good thing? See Robert Condlin, Bargaining Without Law, *http://ssrn.com/abstract=1649467* (2010).

Reader's Report from the Parent of a College Coed

Dear Mother and Dad:

Since I left for college I have been remiss in writing and I am sorry for my thoughtlessness in not having written before. I will bring you up to date now, but before you read on, please sit down. You are not to read any further unless you are sitting down, okay?

Well, then, I am getting along pretty well now. The skull fracture and the concussion I got when I jumped out the window of my dormitory when it caught on fire shortly after my arrival here is pretty well healed now. I only spent two weeks in the hospital and now I can see almost normally and only get those sick headaches once a day. Fortunately, the fire in the dormitory, and my jump, was witnessed by an attendant at the gas station near the dorm, and he was the one who called the Fire Department and the ambulance. He also visited me in the hospital and since I had nowhere to live because of the burntout dormitory, he was kind enough to invite me to share his apartment with him. It's really a basement room, but it's kind of cute. He is a very fine boy and we have fallen deeply in love and are planning to get married. We haven't got the exact date yet, but it will be before my pregnancy begins to show.

Yes, Mother and Dad, I am pregnant. I know how much you are looking forward to being grandparents and I know you will welcome the baby and give it the same love and devotion and tender care you gave me when I was a child. The reason for the delay in our marriage is that my boyfriend has a minor infection which prevents us from passing our pre-marital blood tests and I carelessly caught it from him.

Now that I have brought you up to date, I want to tell you that there was no dormitory fire, I did not have a concussion or skull fracture, I was not in the hospital, I am not pregnant, I am not engaged, I am not infected, and there is no boyfriend. However, I am getting a "D" in American History, and an "F" in Chemistry and I want you to see those marks in their proper perspective.

Your loving daughter,
Sharon

Sharon may be failing chemistry, but she gets an "A" in psychology. The author of the preceding letter, sent to author Robert Cialdini, masterfully frames her message. The context, placing, and timing of information become critical to how the listeners receive the information. Robert B. Cialdini, Influence: The Psychology of Persuasion, 15-16 (1993).

Next, psychology professor Robert Cialdini shows how the idea of reciprocity — one of the basic concepts of fairness — can be used positively and negatively to persuade people. He also shares some ideas about how to avoid getting trapped by reciprocity when it is not warranted.

Robert B. Cialdini, **INFLUENCE: THE PSYCHOLOGY OF PERSUASION**

17-18, 36, 38, 40-42 (1993)

The rule [of reciprocation] says that we should try to repay, in kind, what another person has provided us. If a woman does us a favor, we should do her one in return; if a man sends us a birthday present, we should remember his birthday with a gift of our own; if a couple invites us to a party, we should be sure to invite them to one of ours. By virtue of the reciprocity rule, then, we are *obligated* to the future repayment of favors, gifts, invitations, and the like. So typical is it for indebtedness to accompany the receipt of such things that a term like "much obliged" has become a synonym for "thank you," not only in the English language but in others as well.

The impressive aspect of the rule for reciprocation and the sense of obligation that goes with it is its pervasiveness in human culture. It is so widespread that after intensive study, sociologists such as Alvin Gouldner can report that there is no human society that does not subscribe to the rule. . . .

I was walking down the street when I was approached by an eleven- or twelve-year-old boy. He introduced himself and said that he was selling tickets to the annual Boy Scouts circus to be held on the upcoming Saturday night. He asked if I wished to buy any at five dollars apiece. Since one of the last places I wanted to spend Saturday evening was with the Boy Scouts, I declined. "Well," he said, "if you don't want to buy any tickets, how about buying some of our big chocolate bars? They're only a dollar each." I bought a couple and, right away, realized that something noteworthy had happened. I knew that to be the case because: (a) I do not like chocolate bars; (b) I do like dollars; (c) I was standing there with two of his chocolate bars; and (d) he was walking away with two of my dollars. . . .

Because the rule for reciprocation governs the compromise process, it is possible to use an initial concession as part of a highly effective compliance technique. The technique is a simple one that we can call the rejection-then-retreat technique. Suppose you want me to agree to a certain request. One way to increase your chances would be first to make a larger request of me, one that I will most likely turn down. Then, after I have refused, you would make the smaller request that you were really interested in all along. Provided that you have structured your requests skillfully, I should view your second request as a concession to me and should feel inclined to respond with a concession of my own, the only one I would have immediately open to me — compliance with your second request. . . .

It seems that certain of the most successful television producers, such as Grant Tinker and Gary Marshall, are masters of this art in their negotiations with network censors. In a candid interview with *TV Guide* writer Dick Russell, both admitted to "deliberately inserting lines into scripts that a censor's sure to ax" so that they could then retreat to the lines they really wanted included. Marshall appears especially active in this regard. Consider, for example, the following quotes from Russell's article:

But Marshall . . . not only admits his tricks . . . he seems to revel in them. On one episode of his [then] top-rated *Laverne and Shirley* series, for example, he says, "We had a situation where Squiggy's in a rush to get out of his apartment and meet some girls upstairs. He says: 'Will you hurry up before I lose my lust?' But in the script we put something even stronger, knowing the censors would cut it. They did; so we asked innocently, well, how about 'lose my lust'? 'That's good,' they said. Sometimes you gotta go at 'em backward."

On the *Happy Days* series, the biggest censorship fight was over the word "virgin." That time, says Marshall, "I knew we'd have trouble, so we put the word in seven times, hoping they'd cut six and keep one. It worked. We used the same pattern again with the word 'pregnant.' " . . .

If I want you to lend me five dollars, I can make it seem like a smaller request by first asking you to lend me ten dollars. One of the beauties of this tactic is that by first requesting ten dollars and then retreating to five dollars, I will have simultaneously engaged the force of the reciprocity rule and the contrast principle. Not only will my five-dollar request be viewed as a concession to be reciprocated, it will also look to you like a smaller request than if I had just asked for it straightaway.

Problem 4-7.   *Reciprocity*

Cialdini explains that the reciprocity technique is used in hundreds of different contexts.

1. Have you seen this technique yourself? Did you feel compelled to reciprocate (the invitation, the gift, help on homework, the free address labels, and so on)?
2. How can the concept of reciprocal concessions be used in a negotiation?
3. How can you protect yourself against conceding too much if this is used unfairly?

Problem 4-8.   *Start High?*

This reading makes an argument for the often-used competitive bargaining tactic of starting with an outrageously high demand. In fact, some research supports that further. Why is such a move dangerous? Why might it be counterproductive even if your opponent does not walk away? What about the ethics of false demands?

Although not every negotiation ends up being difficult, negotiators need a set of tools to deal with more challenging situations as they arise. Three negotiation trainers and researchers advise in the next excerpt how to deal with or even prevent a difficult conversation.

Douglas Stone, Bruce Patton & Sheila Heen, **DIFFICULT CONVERSATIONS: HOW TO DISCUSS WHAT MATTERS MOST**

195-200 (1999)

TELLING YOUR STORY WITH CLARITY: THREE GUIDELINES

Obviously, how you express yourself makes a difference. How you say what you want to say will determine, in part, how others respond to you, and how the conversation will go. So when you choose to share something important, you'll want to do so in a way that will maximize the chance that the other person will understand and respond productively. Clarity is the key.

1. Don't Present Your Conclusions as the Truth

Some aspects of difficult conversations will continue to be rough even when you communicate with great skill: sharing feelings of vulnerability, delivering bad news, learning something painful about how others see you. But presenting your story as the truth — which creates resentment, defensiveness, and leads to arguments — is a wholly avoidable disaster. . . .

Some words — like "attractive," "ugly," "good," and "bad" — carry judgments that are obvious. But be careful with words like "inappropriate," "should," or "professional." The judgments contained in these words are less obvious, but can still provoke the "Who are you to tell me?!" response. If you want to say something is "inappropriate," preface your judgment with "My view is that . . ." Better still, avoid these words altogether.

2. Share Where Your Conclusions Come From

The first step toward clarity, then, is to share your conclusions and opinions as *your* conclusions and opinions and not as the truth. The second step is to share what's beneath your conclusions — the information you have and how you have interpreted it. . . .

3. Don't Exaggerate with "Always" and "Never": Give Them Room to Change

In the heat of the moment, it's easy to express frustration through a bit of exaggeration: "Why do you *always* criticize my clothes?" "You *never* give one word of appreciation or encouragement. The only time anyone hears anything from you is when there's something wrong!"

"Always" and "never" do a pretty good job of conveying frustration, but they have two serious drawbacks. First, it is seldom strictly accurate that someone criticizes *every* time, or that they haven't at some point said *something* positive. . . .

"Always" and "never" also make it harder — rather than easier — for the other person to consider changing their behavior. In fact, "always" and "never" suggest that change will be difficult or impossible. The implicit message is, "What is wrong with you such that you are driven to criticize my clothes?" or even "You are obviously incapable of acting like a normal person." . . .

The key is to communicate your feelings in a way that invites and encourages the recipient to consider new ways of behaving, rather than suggesting they're a schmuck and it's too bad there's nothing they can do about it. . . .

The secret of powerful expression is recognizing that you are the ultimate authority on you. You are an expert on what you think, how you feel, and why you've come to this place. If you think it or feel it, you are entitled to say it, and no one can legitimately contradict you. You only get in trouble if you try to assert what you are *not* the final authority on — who is right, who intended what, what happened. Speak fully the range of your experience and you will be clear. Speak for yourself and you can speak with power.

4. Using Appeals to Justice and Fairness

A crucial part of setting your limits and goals and of convincing others to respect them, as discussed in the preceding section, depends on establishing relevant criteria for assessing possible negotiation claims and outcomes. The next excerpt from research scholar Cecilia Albin focuses broadly on different types of fairness in a negotiation. As you prepare for a negotiation, the development of theories of fairness is critical.

 Cecilia Albin, **THE ROLE OF FAIRNESS IN NEGOTIATIONS**

9 Negot. J. 223, 225-228, 233-239 (1993)

[T]he actual practice of negotiation . . . suggests that concepts of fairness are often an influential factor. They influence the "give-and-take" in the bargaining process, help parties to forge agreement, and help to determine whether a particular outcome will be viewed as satisfactory, and thus be honored in the long run. Notions of fairness may create a motivation to resolve a particular problem through negotiation in the first place, and thus have an impact on the positions and expectations which parties bring to the table. . . .

This study identifies and analyzes four types of fairness which have an impact on negotiation: structural fairness, process fairness, procedural fairness, and outcome fairness. In any one case, all four types of fairness will not necessarily be significant nor even present. While concerns about outcome fairness are commonly thought to dominate negotiations, in some contexts no outcome can be quite fair — e.g., in the allocation of a single indivisible good or burden for which there is no adequate compensation, such as a death mission or a child in a custody dispute. Parties may then agree to use a procedure viewed as fair for settling the issue, and to accept whatever (unfair) solution it produces. Similarly, when a negotiation process cannot be fair in important respects (e.g., permit participation by all parties or public scrutiny), greater demands will often be advanced regarding the fairness of its outcome.

STRUCTURAL FAIRNESS

We commonly think of fairness as relating to the outcome, and perhaps also the process, of negotiations. Yet an important class of fairness issues concerns the overarching structure of the negotiation process which, in turn, reflects more or less the structure of the dispute and overall relations between parties. . . .

A major set of structural components concerns the parties to the negotiations, including any third parties: their identity; number; attributes (e.g., interests, amount of resources); representation; and relations, including the distribution of resources between them. . . . The idea that every major party to a conflict, or groups most affected by the outcome should be given a genuine opportunity to be represented in the negotiations is regarded as a key element of fairness which significantly influences perceptions of the legitimacy of the outcome and the chances of its implementation.

A second group of structural elements concerns the issues to be negotiated — their number and grouping as they appear on the agenda when negotiations begin; their complexity and "sums" (degree to which they are, or are perceived as, zero-sum or positive sum); and relationships between them (e.g., degree to which they are separate or intertwined). . . .

Another category of structural fairness elements is the rules and codes of conduct to govern the negotiations, and ways in which these are established. These elements include agenda-setting (e.g., issues to be negotiated, their order on the agenda, and time allowed for each issue); communication procedures between parties and with the outside world (e.g., use of press conferences to report on progress or deadlocks); voting procedures; and the use of deadlines and other time limits. A common notion of fairness is that parties, whether equal or not in power, should have an *equal* chance to determine the agenda, equal control over the use of deadlines, and so forth.

Finally, a major set of structural elements involving fairness issues concerns the physical features of the negotiations: the location; the presence and degree of access of various audiences to the negotiations; the availability of communication channels between parties; and access to information and technical support. . . .

PROCESS FAIRNESS

Process fairness concerns two broad issues: the extent to which parties in the process of negotiating relate to and treat each other "fairly"; and how parties' notions of (outcome) fairness influence the dynamics of the negotiation process, including their choice of procedures for arriving at an agreement.

Mind Your Manners

A study of libel litigation found that the primary goals of plaintiffs — restoring reputation, correcting a falsehood, and vengeance — had little to do with money or even their chance of success. The way that plaintiffs were treated when they called to complain of libel was directly connected to whether they chose to sue. The Iowa study of libel litigation found that some plaintiffs who were initially unsure about whether to sue only initiated lawsuits after being treated rudely by the media defendant. Randall Bezanson et al., Libel Law and the Press: Myth and Reality, 29-53 (1987).

"Fair behavior" in negotiations can be defined as the extent to which parties actually honor agreements reached on many structural issues before the process began and the degree to which they use procedures without deception in the effort to find a solution.

PROCEDURAL FAIRNESS

Procedural fairness concerns specific mechanisms used for arriving at an agreement. These mechanisms are considered fair because of some intrinsic value (e.g., they give parties an equal chance to "win" or demand equal concessions from them), because they tend to produce fair outcomes, or because of both of the qualities. Thus procedural fairness concerns the features of the mechanisms themselves, while process fairness refers to larger issues, such as how the mechanisms are actually used in the negotiation process (e.g., if in good faith, without bluffing) and the substance of parties' concessions.

These kinds of procedures are often used when parties cannot agree on a fair solution; when no solution can be quite fair (e.g., the allocation of a mission involving high risks of death); when a solution is needed quickly; when the stakes are relatively low so that it is not worth using a more time consuming procedure; when the stakes are so high that full-fledged bargaining would seem inappropriate or involve too many pressures and pain; and when the greater ambiguity or manipulability of other procedures are to be avoided.

OUTCOME FAIRNESS

Outcome fairness refers to the principles underlying the allocation (exchange or division) of benefits and burdens in negotiated agreements, and the extent to which parties actually consider that allocation fair after the fact.

Three major principles will be discussed, with brief references to ethnic conflict in which outcome fairness issues figure prominently: equity, equality, and need.

Equity.   Originating in Aristotle's notion of justice as rooted in "balance" and "proportion," the equity principle holds that resources (rewards) should be distributed proportionally to relevant contributions (inputs). Fairness is achieved when each party's ratio of inputs to rewards is the same, and injustice is experienced in relation to these ratios rather than in absolute terms. Relevant contributions may be qualities and endowments (e.g., status, power, skills, wealth, intelligence), or actions and efforts (e.g., hours worked, tasks completed, leadership exercised). . . .

Equality.   The principle of equality, also termed "impartial justice," holds that parties should receive the same or comparable rewards, irrespective of their contributions or needs. The norm finds its origins in the Enlightenment and the philosophy of Jean-Jacques Rousseau, which regarded individual differences as environmental products and equal treatment of all people as the natural and preferred type of human relationships. . . .

Need.   A third major principle of outcome fairness is need, also termed compensatory or redistributive justice. This principle stipulates that resources should be allocated proportionally based on the strength of need alone, so that the least endowed party gets the greatest share.

Problem 4-9. *Buy My Car*

One student shared the following story in class. It is a great example of a negotiation based on criteria of fairness. "I was selling my used car and the person I was dealing with was more of a haggling than problem-solving type. She asked if the car passed emission standards. I said I didn't know because it was never tested. She didn't believe me. Instead of arguing with her about whether or not I was lying, I offered to take her to the emissions test center so we would both know whether it passed. It did and she bought it." Which of Albin's fairness issues is raised here? How do the parties resolve it?

Problem 4-10. *Nuclear Waste*

There has been a long-running national debate over where to locate the nation's nuclear waste. In 2002, Congress approved burying the nuclear waste in Yucca Mountain in Nevada close to Las Vegas. The State of Nevada filed a lawsuit to block this. What issues of fairness does this raise? Who should determine where the waste is buried? Who should be at the table?

Start Walking!

A favorite story about this phenomenon of caring about the treatment of the other side comes from Steve Lubet's story of his family trip to Petra in Jordan. Tourists can either walk over a mile to the ruins at Petra or hire a Bedouin guide and horse for the ride. Tourists can either hire a horse round trip (for 7 dinars) or one way (guides would demand 7 dinars and would reluctantly lower to 4 dinars). In an experiment over three days, Professor Lubet tried unsuccessfully to negotiate a lower price than 4 dinars for just the return trip each day from Petra. His theory was that (a) by the end of the day there were more horses than tourists and that (b) guides would prefer to use their horses as much as possible in order to make money. As he wrote, "So we walked. Four of us. Three times. . . . The result was clearly suboptimal. My family walked instead of riding; the horses idled instead of working." Why did the Bedouin horse owners refuse to bargain lower with Lubet? Lubet asked his children why. " 'Because you didn't offer them enough money Daddy, and they thought that you didn't respect them.' 'But they still should have preferred the money to just standing around not working.' 'No, Daddy, they would rather stand around than take less than they thought they were worth.' " Steven Lubet, Notes on the Bedouin Horse Trade or "Why Won't the Market Clear Daddy?," 74 Tex. L. Rev. 1039 (1996).

Problem 4-11. *The Cold Shoulder*

Assume your landlord failed to repair your broken heater in the dead of winter — after you made multiple calls to him. Would it matter to you if you later found out that the landlord had left the country for a family emergency rather than just ignored your calls? See Russell Korobkin & Chris Guthrie, Psychological Barriers to Litigation Settlement: An Experimental Approach, 93 Mich. L. Rev. 107, 144-146 (1994), for more explanation of how people respond.

Problem 4-12. *Apologize?*

Would you, as the attorney, suggest that your client apologize if he or she were involved in a car accident? Why or why not? What if your client was a doctor who made a medical error? For more on apologies, see Jennifer Robbennolt, Apologies and Settlement Levers, 3 J. Empirical Stud. 333 (2006).

B. WORKING WITH THE OTHER SIDE

1. Learning About Them

One of the most important practices for an effective negotiator begins, and can be completed, before the negotiation takes places — preparation. Without adequate preparation, a negotiator is limiting his abilities as a negotiator, and doing a disservice to his client. In this first short excerpt, Carrie Menkel-Meadow provides a list of topics or categories that a negotiator should investigate before meeting with the other side.

 Carrie Menkel-Meadow, **KNOW WHEN TO SHOW YOUR HAND**

10 Negotiation Newsletter 6, 2-3 (June 2007)

Before talks begin — and, if possible, even before your initial contact with your counterpart — list the information you need to resolve your dispute or to build a strong deal. Also anticipate the information the other side will want from you and consider how you'll respond to these queries.

Information typically falls into these categories:

- Facts: Information about relevant past events, goods, and services; ongoing obligations and liabilities; parties needed to conclude talks; and so forth.

- Opinions, values, and predictions: Information subject to different interpretations, such as a company's value, the likely outcome from a new product, the outcome of a future court decision, or whether the dollar will rise or fall.
- Preferences: Information that negotiators express as their needs, interests, goals, objectives, desires, bottom lines, and reservation points.

***

Unfortunately, even with adequate preparation, a negotiator still may be thrown off track when he is told contrary information by the other side during the negotiation. The following excerpt outlines several key steps that negotiators can take in order to gather and test information about your counterpart in a negotiation.

 Peter Reilly, WAS MACHIAVELLI RIGHT? LYING IN NEGOTIATION AND THE ART OF DEFENSIVE SELF-HELP

24 Ohio St. J. on Disp. Resol. 3, 483-484, 486-493, 496-497, 499, 502-503
(2009)

[I]nformation is the lifeblood of any negotiation, and therefore, the mindsets, strategies, and techniques that influence if, when, and how information is obtained and/ or exchanged (and that influence how complete and accurate that information will be) are extremely important in the process of defending one's self (or one's client) against lying and deception.

A. CONDUCT THOROUGH BACKGROUND RESEARCH

Conducting a search on various Internet search engines (such as Yahoo! or Google) can often yield large amounts of information about other parties to the negotiation. Websites established by private companies, government entities, and various non-profit groups are available for criminal, financial, and other background checks. If possible, speaking with groups or individuals who have previously worked with or negotiated with one's potential negotiation counterparts can be very illuminating. It can be surprising how much of a "reputation" people develop, sometimes favorable and sometimes unfavorable, based on previous negotiation behavior. . . .

B. NETWORK FOR POTENTIAL NEGOTIATION COUNTERPARTS

There are times when one has no control over who will sit on the other side of the negotiation table. However, in those instances when one can play a role in selecting negotiation counterparts, one should attempt to do so through referrals, recommendations, or outside introductions. This is a compliment to the party being approached, which can generate feelings of goodwill and help solidify new working relationships should the negotiation process move forward. Initial meetings through referrals and introductions also signal that there is a greater prospect for the development of long-term relationships. Research suggests that, in general, even the prospect of a long-term relationship raises people's ethical standards and reduces exploitative conduct such as lying. . . .

C. CREATE RAPPORT

A cordial and supportive environment (one infused with sincerity, understanding, impartiality, empathy, and expressions of genuine concern for the other party) will probably not magically prevent lies or encourage people to disclose their deceitful behavior. However, research suggests that such an environment can lead to these individuals relaxing their defenses and providing information that may be used to secure the truth in the future. . . . Research shows that people are more inclined to lie by omission (not revealing the whole truth) than by commission (falsely answering a question when asked), so when they are asked to elaborate and thereby make direct statements that are lies, some people cannot do it and will back away from earlier statements. Finally, one can neutralize the harshness of asking a negative question by implying the question is a playful one. For example, "May I play the devil's advocate for a moment?" is one way to blunt the harshness of a request for information. . . .

D. DEMAND THE USE OF OBJECTIVE STANDARDS — BUT AVOID BEING HAMSTRUNG BY THEM

Asking questions such as, "What do you base that number on? or "Is that according to industry standard?" is essentially asking the other party to justify their position using objective standards. People will be less likely to attempt to lie and deceive if they know from the start of the negotiation that objective criteria and standards will constantly be sought from other parties, as well as outside sources.

E. STRATEGICALLY LIMIT INFORMATION REVELATION

Before the negotiation, one should brainstorm and list specific questions that will likely be asked by the other party. With enough preparation, many (if not most) questions can be anticipated. One might practice aloud how specific questions will be responded to and addressed, especially difficult and controversial questions. Practicing aloud can make it easier to arrive at word and phrase choices that will prevent or limit the revelation of strategic information. Preparation should also include deciding upon which tactic to employ in responding to questions about information that one does not wish to disclose. For example, should one decide to ignore the question all together? Or pretend to misconstrue the question and answer a less intrusive, specific, or direct question? . . .

F. RECOGNIZE AND THWART TACTICS OF EVASION

The simplest way to get information is to ask for it, yet it is sometimes the most obvious (and crucial) questions that do not get asked (or answered) during a negotiation. Prior to negotiating, one should write out a list of all the questions he or she wants answered, in order of importance. During the negotiation, one should listen carefully to the responses provided; many will be mere attempts to evade answering the question. Evasion techniques are abundant and varied (ignoring the question; offering to return to the question later; answering only part of the question; answering a related but less intrusive, specific, or direct question; calling the question unfair or inappropriate and therefore not entitled to a response, etc.). These or similar evasion techniques will likely be employed throughout the negotiation, and the most effective antidote is careful listening to determine if one's question is being addressed in full, in part, or not at all. One must continue grilling until the information being sought is either revealed or protected in a very different manner. Thus one might continue asking the same question (along with reasonable follow-up questions to probe even deeper) until the question (1) can be "checked off" as having been responded to in a (reasonably) complete and forthcoming manner, or (2) is met by the other party saying something to the effect of, "I simply cannot tell you that," or "I cannot speak about that issue at all."

G. ESTABLISH LONG-TERM RELATIONSHIPS AND WATCH FOR SIGNS OF DECEPTION

If one were skilled at detecting liars upon meeting them, one could simply walk away from the negotiation. Unfortunately, research indicates that people are very poor at such immediate detection. This is true even among the so-called "experts" (such as police investigators) who are more confident, but not more accurate, in their determinations of who is lying and who is not. . . . This conclusion underscores the importance of developing long-term relationships with potential negotiation partners, where baseline behaviors can be established, where changes in those normal behaviors can be observed, and where possible deception can thereby be detected.

H. USE "COME CLEAN" QUESTIONS STRATEGICALLY

Used at critical moments in the negotiation (often toward the conclusion of covering an important topic within the context of a larger negotiation), one can ask the "come clean" question: "Is there something known to you, but not to me, that needs to be reveled at this point?"

---

2. Understanding Their Point of View

We don't see things as they are, we see things as we are.

— Anaïs Nin

This section provides ideas for understanding the other side's, or even your own client's, point of view. The first excerpt discusses the skill of empathy — one of the key ingredients in effective negotiation. The second provides further tools for creating this empathy and double-checking your assumptions.

Robert H. Mnookin, Scott R. Peppet & Andrew S. Tulumello,
BEYOND WINNING

46–49 (2000)

In our experience, the most effective negotiators try . . . to both empathize and assert in their interactions with others. For purposes of negotiation, we define *empathy* as the process of demonstrating an accurate, nonjudgmental understanding of the other side's needs, interests, and perspective. There are two components to this definition. The first involves a skill which psychologists call *perspective-taking* — trying to see the world through the other negotiator's eyes. The second is the nonjudgmental *expression* of the other person's viewpoint in a way that is open to correction.

Defined in this way, empathy requires neither sympathy nor agreement. Sympathy is feeling for someone — it is an emotional response to the other person's predicament. Empathy does not require people to have sympathy for another's plight — to "feel their pain." Nor is empathy about being nice. Instead, we see empathy as a "value-neutral mode of observation," a journey in which you explore and describe another's perceptual world without commitment. Empathizing with someone, therefore, does not mean agreeing with or even necessarily liking the other side. Although it may entail being civil, it is not primarily about civility. Instead, it simply requires the expression of how the world looks to the other person. . . .

Three main points about empathy and assertiveness are central:

- Problem-solving negotiations go better for everyone when each side has well-honed empathy and assertiveness skills.
- Problem-solving negotiations go better for an individual negotiator if she both empathizes and asserts, even if the other side does not follow her lead.
- Empathy and assertiveness make problem-solving easier in both the value-creation and the value-distribution aspects of negotiation.

. . . Empathy and assertiveness are aspects of good communication. When people communicate well with each other, problem-solving is easier. . . .

First, [in a dispute between Susan and Martin] regardless of how Susan is behaving, Martin really *does* need to understand her point of view. . . . This will help him both when he's trying to create value from the deal and when he faces any dispute over how that value should be distributed. . . . [T]o the extent that Martin can clarify *for himself* what Susan's motives and goals are, he will be better equipped to find value-creating trades. Indeed, research confirms that negotiators with higher perspective-taking ability negotiate agreements of higher value than those with lower perspective-taking ability.

. . . The better Martin understands Susan's thinking, the better he will be able to anticipate the strategic problems and opportunities that may crop up in the negotiation — and to prepare for them.

A second benefit of empathy is that it allows Martin to correct any misperceptions *he* may have about Susan's thinking. . . . Indeed, regardless of the emotional content of a negotiation, research has shown that negotiators routinely jump to mistaken conclusions about their counterparts' motivations, usually because their information is limited. Such mistakes are a major reason why negotiations and relationships break down. For example, negotiators often make *attributional* errors — they attribute to their counterparts incorrect or exaggerated intentions or characteristics. If a counterpart is late to a meeting, we might assume either that he intended to make us wait or that he is chronically tardy, even though we may be meeting him for the first time. . . .

A third benefit of combining assertion with empathy is that Martin may be able to loosen Susan up — and gain her trust. . . . Most people have a need to tell their story and to feel that it has been understood. Meeting this need can dramatically shift the tone of a relationship. . . . Even if you are not interested in sharing a deeply soulful moment with your counterpart, remember that empathizing has highly practical benefits. It conveys concern and respect, which tend to defuse anger and mistrust, especially where these emotions stem from feeling unappreciated or exploited.

Finally, your empathy may inspire openness in others and may make you more persuasive.

Problem 4-13.   *What About You?*

Mnookin et al. write about empathy in tension with the skill of assertiveness. Why might there be tension between empathy and assertiveness? Which skill, empathy or assertiveness, are you more comfortable with? What does this tell you about yourself as a negotiator?

The Wedding Albums

This rabbi's sermon points out, in a very funny way, how people each can interpret the same events differently:

"If you were to walk into our home, the first book you would see on the coffee table is our wedding album. That's right, finally, after three years of marriage, two children, a change of city and much procrastination, the proofs were distributed to me, to my wife's parents, to my parents — and at long last the albums are finally complete. Over this past summer, as I have had a chance to review the completed copies in my home, my parents' home and the edition in my in-laws' home, I have discovered something very interesting about these albums — each one tells a very different story. Let me explain:

"If you were to look at our edition — the first page is a photograph of our wedding invitation, followed by a picture of Debbie and then me. This is followed by pictures of our families, me and Debbie under the huppah, the party, and a final picture of the happy couple. However, if you went to Pittsburgh to see the album at my in-laws, you would begin with a picture of Debbie, then Debbie and her mother, then Debbie and her siblings and then her Grandmother, and eventually around page six — you catch a glimpse of me — the groom.

"And, the rewriting of history is no less startling at my parents' place in Los Angeles. It begins with the primary male/female relationship . . . the groom and his mother; followed by the mother and the father, and then almost as an afterthought you meet the son stealer — my bride. And so it is throughout. . . .

"And as I looked at these albums this past summer — I was struck by their differences, which until now I kept to myself. It is fascinating really, I am positive I was at the wedding, and yet there exist very different records of the event. Each tells a different story, each constructs a different reality. Each family had the identical set of pictures to choose from and yet each book, the order, the emphasis, the beginnings and the endings lead to very different narratives of that wonderful day."

Courtesy of Rabbi Elliott Cosgrove.

 Roger Fisher, Elizabeth Kopelman & Andrea Schneider, **BEYOND MACHIAVELLI: TOOLS FOR COPING WITH CONFLICT**

32-35 (1994)

OBSERVE FROM DIFFERENT POINTS OF VIEW

To understand a conflict in which we are a party, we will want to observe it from at least three points of view. First, we want to be aware of ourselves (Are we angry?

Losing control? Reacting? Drifting?) and to consider the conflict from our own point of view (What are our goals? What are our interests? What risks do we see? And so forth). Our point of view is an important starting point. It is, however, only a starting point.

We will also want to observe the situation from the point of view of the other parties to this conflict. Putting ourselves hypothetically in their shoes, what would we see? How does everything look from that vantage point? If we were there, what would be our goals, our interests, our concerns? Would we feel justifiably angry? How does the conflict look from there?

And finally, to gain a more balanced view, how would the situation look from the point of view of a neutral third party? How would a "fly on the wall" describe things? How are the parties behaving? Do they seem to be quarreling, debating, scoring points, bickering, and attacking each other, or are they jointly attacking the problem? Are they wasting time or using it well?

To understand conflict well we want to observe it from all three positions. (If there are several parties to a conflict, we will want to understand how each sees it.) One who is skilled at dealing with conflict is likely to be adept at jumping back and forth, observing what is going on from each of these three positions, even "on line," while participating in a discussion. . . .

Three Positions for Observing a Conflict

First Position (Mine): How I see the problem, from my own perspective.

Second Position (Theirs): How I see the problem when I stand in the shoes of the other party to the dispute.

Third Position ("Fly on the Wall"): How a neutral third party would assess the conflict.

These three distinct points of view illuminate a variety of dimensions of a conflict.

TO GAIN EMPATHY, REVERSE ROLES

Understanding is not simply an intellectual activity. Feeling empathetically how others may feel can be as important as thinking clearly about how others may think.

There is a lot of truth in the old saying that "where you stand depends upon where you sit." Another way of trying to understand the other side's perceptions is literally to sit in a different chair, pretend to be someone on the other side, and try to see the situation from that vantage point.

The chairman of a company held liable for a patent infringement had called in a consultant to advise about the negotiation of a possible settlement on the dollar amount of damages. The case had been in litigation for years. The chairman had been told that if the worst happened, and he should be held liable, he could always settle — but he had little appreciation of how much the other side would expect.

Encouraged by the consultant, the executive agreed to switch seats, moving from his own chair to a chair the consultant had designated as that of the president of the plaintiff company. While the executive initially resisted "playing games," he was eventually persuaded to assume the role of that president and to state the plaintiff's case in the first person as forcefully as he could. Within a few minutes he was playing the role well. Asked how much he might accept in settlement (an amount that, in real life, would be paid out by this executive's own company) he replied (still in his role as the opposing company's president), "Why, I wouldn't take their whole damn company!" Shaken by this experience, and with new insight into what might be required to settle this case, his company raised its settlement offer by one hundred fold. It was rejected, and the judgment was ultimately for even more. An earlier attempt to appreciate the other side's partisan perceptions would no doubt have led him to pursue a wiser strategy from the outset. . . .

To gain insight by reversing roles, we first identify the person whom we expect to be attempting to persuade (the "absent party") and find a friend or colleague to help us. Our helper is someone who either already knows our side of the conflict or will quickly learn the points we currently plan to make. Then we sit in the chair labeled "absent party," and with the assistance of the helper, come to think of ourselves as being that person. Finally, our helper sits in our chair, assumes our role, and presents our side of the case. While playing the part of someone on the other side of a conflict, we hear our own arguments come back at us. Through such role reversal we can often gain insight and empathy for the other side — sometimes dramatically so — in a way that helps us tailor our arguments to make them more persuasive.

Profile: Success of Southwest Airlines

Treating the other side well was much of the explanation given for Southwest Airlines' success in dealing with its union. While other airlines face bankruptcy from high labor costs, labor slowdowns, and strikes, Southwest Airlines continues to be successful. In an interview on National Public Radio with Southwest President Colleen Barrett, reporter Wade Goodwyn noted that: "It surprises many to learn that Southwest is among the most unionized airlines in the industry. But Barrett and other top management have avoided the bloody battles that have crippled other carriers. Barrett sees to it that the unions understand they're not considered the enemy."

Barrett explained: "When I came up here, one of the first things that I did, anytime that we had an event, a company event — a Christmas party, a chili cook-off, whatever — I always assured that the union folks were invited. I mean, to me, we are one family. It's an extended family member, perhaps, but nevertheless, I wanted them to say 'we' when they talked about Southwest. That really was my thinking." NPR, Morning Edition, Profile: Success of Southwest Airlines, Dec. 4, 2002.

3. Listening

Conversation in the United States is a competitive exercise in which the first person to draw breath is considered the listener.

— Nathan Miller

As we previously discussed in Chapter 2, listening is essential in counseling and interviewing clients. It is also an important skill needed to understand the other party's point of view, values, and interests. The next excerpt, by attorney and mediator Alain Burrese, offers a list of skills negotiators can work on to improve their listening skills.

 Alain Burrese, LISTEN UP

Mont. Law. 22 (Sept. 2006)

Effective communication skills are crucial to negotiation success. You must be able to convince people that your position is reasonable, and do so against adversaries who are convincing in their own right. Additionally, you must be able to control your emotions under pressure, absorb and decipher the opposition's arguments, know when to talk, and sometimes most importantly, know when to listen.

In fact, if you're going to convince someone to agree to your terms in negotiations, the first step is to listen.

It is not good enough to just listen. You should engage in empathetic listening. You want to convey your interests in what they have to say and your understanding of their needs.

The components that make up the Chinese character for "to listen" include ear, eyes and heart. Remember these as you listen to someone. Do not just hear the words, but see what nonverbal signals they are communicating and use your heart to really understand their needs.

Additionally, showing you have respect for opposing viewpoints will help earn reciprocal respect for yours. This makes negotiations much easier when you encounter difficult hurdles on the path toward agreement.

Most people believe they are proficient at listening. After all, we do it all the time. In fact, many people would say they are good listeners. Unfortunately, these claims seem to exceed performance. If people were listening as well as they claimed, there would be far fewer misunderstandings and communication blunders in daily life.

The first rule to good listening is to stop talking. You need to know when to be quiet and listen to the message your opponent is sending through the words spoken and the nonverbal communication that is present. In "The Negotiator's Handbook," George Fuller lays out a few simple steps to enhance one's listening skills at the bargaining table. Using that list as a catalyst to expand upon, here are some skills to work on before your next negotiation:

- *Always be attentive.* During lengthy negotiation sessions it may become difficult to remain alert at all times. However, if you don't, you may miss important issues. You must pay attention to detail, and that requires being attentive.

  However, there are exceptions. During negotiations there may be times when you want to let the other negotiator know that what he is saying is nonsense. Being inattentive by looking elsewhere, looking through papers, or such other action, may help you get that message across. This is a purposeful inattentiveness, not daydreaming due to weariness or boredom.
- *Show you are paying attention.* You can send the message that you are paying attention and listening through eye contact, nods, smiles and so forth. Not only does this let your opponent know you are listening, it actually helps force you to pay attention and listen yourself.
- *Ask questions.* Ask questions to clarify what you have heard, but do so in a non-threatening manner. Do not show skepticism, but rather ask in a neutral tone of voice. Use questions to clarify and illustrate that you are listening, not to convey skepticism of what is being said.
- *Listen for nonverbal signs.* Part of listening is to pick up the nonverbal signals that may be being transmitted as part of the message. Signs such as nervousness may indicate the person is not secure in what is being said, or that the person is hiding something. Don't focus on just the words, but on the entire message, and that can be given by body language, tone of voice and other indicators besides the actual words being spoken.
- *Do not interrupt.* This is very difficult for some of us, but it is critical for good listening and effective communication. Often we will jump on an inconsistent statement catching our opponent and "proving" our position. Remember, the goal of listening is not to catch your opponent with the "Ah ha, I got you," but to learn as much as you can that can later support your negotiation position during the argument and help illustrate why your position is the more substantive one.
- *Be patient.* Resist the temptation to fill in blanks or help your opposition make a point, even if they seem to be having a difficult time clarifying an issue or substantiating their position. First of all, your assistance may be resented. More importantly, you never know what valuable information you may learn if you sit back patiently and allow your opposition the opportunity to ramble on and possibly inadvertently blurt out more than they intended.
- *Ask questions.* If you do not understand something, ask for clarification. We all know what assuming does. Summarize what you believe was being said and provide the speaker the opportunity to confirm that you understand what was presented. This also provides the opportunity to clarify or correct something that you may have misunderstood. In addition, ask questions regarding points that were not covered. What is not said can be as important as what is. If you don't ask, you will never know.

Negotiators require keen listening skills, and like skills in many other areas, the more you practice, the better you will become. Take the time and make the effort to become a better listener. The dividends from increasing your skill in this area will far surpass the investment.

4. Building Trust

Any negotiation involves an element of trust — whether to trust the other side, how to verify their statements, how to get over hurdles of mistrust, how to continue to build trust. In the Prisoner's Dilemma, discussed in Chapter 3, trust is at the core of the dilemma: With trust, we cooperate to reach mutual goals; without trust, we enter into a cycle of defection and lost opportunity.

In the best relationships, the relationship helps facilitate the negotiation and makes the negotiation itself more efficient. In the best negotiations, the negotiation improves the relationship.

In this excerpt Professor Jonathan Cohen discusses the moral responsibility of lawyers to respect other parties in a negotiation and how that can affect the lawyer's understanding of all the parties, including one's own self perception.

 Jonathan Cohen, **WHEN PEOPLE ARE THE MEANS: NEGOTIATING WITH RESPECT**

14 Geo. J. Legal Ethics 739, 741-743, 760-763, 766-767 (2001)

To introduce this domain, consider the following question: What distinguishes negotiation from interpersonal interactions generally? A basic difference is that in negotiation, each party attempts to get the other party to do something, or at least explores that possibility. Put differently, in negotiation the other party is a potential means towards one's ends. If two people are chatting about the weather, rarely will their conversation end with an exchange of promises. If they are negotiating the sale of a car, it very well may.

This basic difference between negotiation and most social interactions points to a core question, or tension, lying within the domain of orientation ethics. Usually we think of other people as, well, people. Yet negotiation may pull us towards seeing others as mere instruments for achieving our purposes. To borrow from the language of Martin Buber, in negotiation we are drawn towards reducing the other person from a "Thou" to an "It." Negotiation thus presents an apparent ethical tension that I call the object-subject tension: *when negotiating, how is one to reconcile the impulse to treat the other person as a mere means towards one's ends with general ethical requirements for treating people?* In response, I argue that in negotiation one should see the other party both as a means towards one's ends *and* as a person deserving respect. More specifically, the act of negotiation does not relieve one of the moral duties to respect others. This duty of respect implicates both the traditional negotiation ethics topics of deception, disclosure and fairness and also topics such as manipulation, coercion, listening, and autonomy. . . .

Respect, in its deepest form, is a choice of how one wants to see other people. It is the process of striving to recognize the fundamental dignity of the other person and to act in accordance with that orientation. Though we often think of respect as a noun signifying certain actions (e.g., "Did he treat me with respect?") or feelings (e.g., "She felt respect for her parents"), the core of respect is best understood as a verb. As the word itself suggests, *respect is the process we undertake when we "look again" — when we challenge ourselves about how we want to see, and thus treat, others.* This is not to negate the nounal aspects of respect when that process instantiates into particular external signs (e.g., courtesies) or internal feelings (e.g., esteem), but rather to identify its core. . . .

If in a negotiation I see you as no more than a means, then I have not only defined you as an object, but I have also defined myself as a manipulator. How one negotiates helps define one's identity. . . .

Where one party to a negotiation does not treat the other party with respect, we can draw a negative inference. Either the first party does not view the second party as an equal — a position to which few would admit, though many implicitly harbor these views — or the first party has a very low assessment of the dignity of all people. . . .

How I see and treat you in a negotiation also helps to define who *we* are. People are not just individuals. They are also members of groups. If I deceive you to get what I want, then *we* do not have an honest relationship. If I intimidate you to get what I want, *we* lack mutual respect. Irrespective of whether our interests are largely convergent or divergent (and divergent interests can result in beneficial exchanges too), how we negotiate with one another is critical to [how] we define ourselves and how others perceive us (e.g., how the public perceives lawyers). . . .

I recently gave a guest lecture in a colleague's professional responsibility class. At one point I asked the students, "How many of you think it's wrong to manipulate other people?" Most of the hands shot up. I then asked, "How many of you think that manipulating other people is a significant part of lawyering?" Most of the hands again shot up. "What do you make of this?" I asked. There was dead silence. . . .

Given both the moral responsibility to respect others in negotiation and (what I take as) the fact that many of us commonly fall short of this goal, objectifying the other person and simultaneously, though unwittingly, diminishing ourselves, one may at first see a dismal, pessimistic picture. If we had no capacity for change, then pessimism might be warranted. However, if one accepts a capacity for human change, then a more optimistic image of human existence can emerge.

It turns out that treating your counterpart fairly in a negotiation costs a lawyer nothing and has the potential to improve your outcome. In an empirical study described below, Professors Rebecca Hollander-Blumoff and Tom Tyler explain how procedural fairness in negotiation can make a negotiator more effective.

Rebecca Hollander-Blumoff & Tom R. Tyler, PROCEDURAL JUSTICE IN NEGOTIATION: PROCEDURAL FAIRNESS, OUTCOME ACCEPTANCE, AND INTEGRATIVE POTENTIAL

33 Law & Soc. Inquiry 473, 474, 492-494 (2008)

Lawyers are trained and steeped in the adversary system. This system, with its duty of zealous representation, encourages attorneys to exalt their client's interests while ignoring or denigrating those of their opponent. Indeed, the popular saying "nice guys finish last" reflects a general perception, not limited to the legal context, that treating others in a fair manner may be a display of weakness that will lead to personal loss. In the context of being a lawyer, such weakness may be deemed unprofessional or even potential malpractice. But if acting fairly does not hurt, and perhaps even helps, one's ability to represent his or her clients, then lawyers need not fear that fair treatment of an adversary is irresponsible. . . .

What does procedural justice in negotiation entail? Procedural justice literature has identified four factors that typically play an important role in assessment of procedural justice: input, neutrality, respect/politeness, and trust. First, it is important to allow parties opportunities to state their arguments and to make clear that those arguments are being listened to by acknowledging them. Second, people value having an unbiased and factual decision-making process in which the rules are applied in a consistent manner. Third, they want to be treated with dignity and courtesy and to have their rights acknowledged. Finally, people want to deal with people whose motives they trust. That is, they value people who act in good faith.

The findings suggest that when negotiators act in procedurally fair ways, they lose nothing at all in their "bottom line" in a zero-sum setting, expand the negotiation pie in a setting in which there is integrative potential, and in fact gain other important advantages in terms of agreement acceptance. Study 1 suggests that in a largely zero-sum situation in which the primary gain is realized by reaching a mutually acceptable agreement, procedural justice could help to encourage such acceptance. Study 2 replicates those findings, as well as showing that, when integrative potential exists but the parties are not jointly aware of the possibility, procedural justice could encourage the disclosure of information that could lead to the value-creating opportunity and indeed could encourage agreements that both expand the negotiation pie and split the surplus more equally, Thus, the wise negotiator, to achieve successful outcomes, may want to act in procedurally just ways when dealing with others in order to foster greater acceptance of the agreement and more disclosure of value-creating opportunities.

First, in order to obtain the best potential negotiation outcomes (settlement over nonsettlement, as in Study 1, or value-creating integrative over nonintegrative bargaining, as in Study 2), a rational actor should treat other in a fair manner. Second, and perhaps more striking, this research challenges the premise at the heart of the rational actor model: what drives people in their assessments of outcome is not just the gain maximizing/loss minimizing analysis of the economic results that they achieve, but also how fairly they feel they have been treated in the negotiation process. Thus, the real-world negotiator evaluates his or her outcome not in purely economic terms of gain and loss but in process terms of fairness.

In this excerpt, business school professor Leigh Thompson provides some specific advice on how to build the rapport that makes relationships work and how to rebuild trust if it has been broken.

 Leigh Thompson, **THE MIND AND HEART OF THE NEGOTIATOR**

109, 126-130, 133 (2001)

Superagent and attorney Leigh Steinberg negotiated quarterback Drew Bledsoe's multiyear contract with New England Patriots owner Bob Kraft. The two of them were sitting in a loud, crowded hotel lobby during the National Football League (NFL) Owners' Conference. As they led up to their bargaining positions, other people were interrupting them, thus making it difficult to talk or build a connection. In the midst of the interruptions and chaos, Kraft proposed $29 million over 7 years. Steinberg countered with $51 million. Insulted, angry, and shaking his head, Kraft got up and walked out. Steinberg had made a mistake, but instead of inflaming the situation, he gave it more time. Six months later, Steinberg asked Kraft to dinner at a quiet Italian restaurant. He let Kraft vent anger and frustration over Bledsoe's proposed salary. It came out that Kraft had interpreted the high counteroffer as a signal that Bledsoe wanted nothing to do with the team and instead wanted to be a free agent. Calmly, Steinberg assured Kraft that Bledsoe wanted to stay. He explained that in the hubbub of the lobby six months earlier, Steinberg had not been able to create the solid rapport that that they had that evening and had not been able to establish an atmosphere of trust. That night, they settled on $42 million. Says Steinberg, "The key to successful negotiations is to develop relationships, not conquests." . . .

BUILDING TRUST: IMPLICIT EMOTIONAL MECHANISMS

There are a variety of psychologically based ways of enhancing and building trust between people. . . .

People who are similar to each other like one another. The *similarity-attraction effect* occurs on the basis of very little, and sometimes downright trivial, information. . . . The process of searching for similarities often has the effect of making people feel that they have more in common than would be expected by chance. . . .

The more we are exposed to something — a person, object, or idea — the more we come to like it. . . . Savvy negotiators increase their effectiveness by making themselves familiar to the other party. Instead of having a single-shot negotiation, they suggest a preliminary meeting over drinks and follow with a few phone calls and unexpected gifts. . . .

People form both personal and business relationships to others who are literally physically close to them. For example, even when students are seated alphabetically in a classroom, friendships are significantly more likely to form between those whose last names begin with the same or nearby letter. . . . This may not seem important until you consider the fact that you may meet some of your closest colleagues, and perhaps even a future business partner, merely because of an instructor's seating chart! . . .

Small talk often seems to serve no obvious function. . . . However, on a *preconscious* level, schmoozing has a dramatic impact on our liking and trust of others. . . .

We like people who appreciate us and admire us. This means that we will tend to trust people more who like us. . . .

People involved in a face-to-face interaction tend to mirror one another in posture, facial expression, tone of voice, and mannerisms. This phenomenon, known as *social contagion*, is the basis for the development of rapport between people. . . .

Self-disclosure means sharing information about oneself with another person. It is a way of building a relationship with another person by making oneself vulnerable, in that the self-disclosing negotiator is providing information that could potentially be exploited. . . .

Steps Toward Repairing Broken Trust

Step 1: Insist on a personal meeting right away

Step 2: Tell the other party that you value the relationship

Step 3: Apologize for your behavior

Step 4: Let them vent

Step 5: Do not get defensive, no matter how wrong you think they are

Step 6: Ask for clarifying information

Step 7: Say that you understand their perspective

Step 8: Let them tell you what they need

Step 9: Paraphrase your understanding of what they need

Step 10: Think about ways to prevent a future problem

Step 11: Do an evaluation of the situation at a scheduled date

Step 12: Plan a future together

Problem 4-14.   *Shortcuts*

All of us have done damage to the trust in at least one relationship that we have tried to repair. Did you follow any of Thompson's twelve steps in your efforts? Is there a way to repair the relationship without all twelve steps? Which do you think you can skip, but still obtain a good result?

C. APPLYING THE PROCESS

1. Creating Better Solutions

As parents of young children know, children are far better at being creative than their parents. What to adult eyes looks like a basic shoebox is actually a house for dinosaurs, a bookcase for baby books, the first block in a tower, or a hat, all depending on how you look at it. After years of being told to color inside the lines (and that the grass should be green and the sky should be blue), to answer only the question asked, and to play games only by the rules printed on the box, we all lose much of our natural creativity. Yet the need to be creative hardly decreases with age. In fact, certain successful companies incorporate "creative conflict" into the very structure of the company.[2] Procter & Gamble, for example, fosters competition among its various brands. Nissan uses this method for designing new car models. Other companies use the model of brainteaser questions in their interviewing process to find creative people.[3]

Lehman Brothers used to follow this methodology of asking interviewees tough questions. In response to an interviewer's request to open a window in an office on the forty-third floor, the interviewee tossed a chair through the window![4] While we don't recommend this approach to law students and others, we do appreciate the ability of this particular person to let no barrier to creativity stand in their way.

The value of creative thinking also applies to effective negotiation, where the ability to "think outside the box" is quite valuable. Without this particular skill — often overlooked in legal education — problem solving or integrative solutions to negotiation become far more difficult. Often, the difference between simple compromise — splitting the orange — and a more collaborative or integrative solution — peel and fruit — is being sufficiently creative and flexible. This section focuses on the advantages that creative thinking brings to a negotiation and then provides some specific ideas to increase creativity.

Carrie Menkel-Meadow first discusses the importance of creativity in successful problem solving and then highlights past examples of legal creativity and what that means.

 Carrie Menkel-Meadow, AHA? IS CREATIVITY POSSIBLE IN LEGAL PROBLEM SOLVING AND TEACHABLE IN LEGAL EDUCATION?

6 Harv. Negot. L. Rev. 97, 106, 122-123, 125, 127-128, 131, 133, 135-136 (2001)

Dispute negotiation too often looks for its solutions among legal precedents or outcomes thought likely in the "shadow of the courthouse" (these days most often [a]

---

2. Sy Landau, Barbara Landau & Daryl Landau, From Conflict to Creativity 97-98 (2001).

3. Microsoft's brainteaser methodology not only has spawned a book, William Poundstone's How Would You Move Mount Fuji? (2003), but also multiple Web sites to help potential employees prepare for the interview.

4. Michael Lewis, Liar's Poker (1989).

compromise of some monetary values), and deal negotiations too often seek solutions in the boilerplate language of form contracts for transactions. Ironically, these litigated outcomes and boilerplate clauses were once the creative ideas of some lawyers who developed a new reading of a statute, a novel argument before a common law or Constitutional court, developed a new scheme of risk allocation, or found a new source of capital or drafted a new clause for a deal document.

Solutions to legal problems, then, come from creative lawyers, as well as legal or practice precedent. The challenge for negotiation theorists, practitioners and teachers is to find systematic ways to teach solution devising, short of reading thousands of cases, transactional documents, statutes or other legal documents that will show us not only what already has been done, but also what might be done. Are there ways of learning or thinking about solutions to legal problems that are generic or are there only substantive (domain based) solutions? Here the teachings of other disciplines may be useful. Some researchers focus on the positive solution-seeking side of cognition and creativity; others focus on the negative side of impediments to good or, as they define it, rational decision making or problem solving. . . .

In this literature, the following techniques are suggested as formal ways of enhancing creativity, solving problems and suggesting new ideas, some as separate individual cognitive processes, and others as structured processes to be used in multiparty settings.

1. Uses of analogy (direct, fanciful) and use of metaphor;
2. Aggregation/disaggregation/re-combination of elements of a problem;
3. Transfer (cross-disciplinary use of concepts, ideas, information, solutions from other fields);
4. Reversal (either extreme polarization or gradual modification of ideas) — which is done both in cognitive and in personal forms (as in role-reversal efforts to understand the point of view of others in the situation);
5. Extension — extending a line of reasoning, principle or solution beyond its original purpose;
6. Challenging assumptions — re-examining givens or problem statements and unpacking clichéd, conventional solutions or stereotypes;
7. Narrative — fully describing facts and problems to elaborate on complexity, and producing alternative endings;
8. Backward/forward thinking — focusing on how we came to a particular situation (reasons why, causes) in order to figure out how we get to desired end-state(s);
9. Design — plan for desired future end-state, structures, means;
10. Random stimulation/brainstorming — separation of idea generation, randomly generated, from judgment and evaluation. . . . ;
11. Visualization — use of different competencies and modes of thinking and processing information; this includes efforts at altered states (e.g., retreats and meditations); and
12. Entry points — explicit reframing of problems and solutions from different perspectives. . . .

Law as a discipline has contributed to the solution of human problems with the creation of institutions designed to preserve order and reduce or eliminate violence through the development of both governing principles and processes. Whether particular regimes or institutions are legitimate within a particular society, law and the institutions it creates are the glue which holds the society together by resolving disputes at both system-wide and individual levels. . . .

Lawyers work with words, so most of our creative acts involve the construction of new language and interpretation of existing language, creating new concepts from whole cloth or from the interstices of statutory, regulatory or contractual gaps. Our words have the force of law behind them, however, so that powerfully creative words in law have been known to create whole new institutions. Examples of new legal and real entities that have been created are corporations, trusts, regulatory agencies, condominiums, unions and tax shelters. In addition, our words have created new legal rights and constructs like leases, sexual harassment, probation — and also have recognized (sometimes from conflicting ideologies) new claims like civil rights, privacy, free speech and emotional distress. . . .

A form of creativity somewhat unique to legal reasoning, though similar to our related linguistic intelligences, is the process of characterization or argumentation in which we use our words to re-categorize facts, claims, arguments and rules, which disturb the linguistic purity desired by those outside of our domain. Consider how patent lawyers successfully assimilated the architecture of software to the vocabulary of a machine in order to obtain patent protection for what were thought to be unpatentable "mental processes, abstract intellectual concepts" or ideas. . . .

Similarly, alterations (in the form of aggregations or disaggregations) of concepts is a common legal trope, particularly in transactional legal work. Using basic property principles which combine space and time (time bounded estates in land), creative lawyers created co-ops, condominiums and time shares. . . .

Law's creativity may be somewhat limited by the bounds of law and legal ethics rules, but there still remains a fair amount of problem space to be manipulated within our adversarial culture. At the same time, the adversarial culture may also constrain and cabin our thinking unnecessarily by structuring it in polarized and oppositional terms. Are transactional lawyers more creative by being less constrained? Corporations and trusts, for example, were created legally to accomplish many different goals, some adversarial (tax delay, minimization or avoidance), but also to permit different power and control arrangements and to bundle and unbundle interests of wealth, time and assets to permit great flexibility of action. . . .

Legal creativity is necessarily limited by its need to work within the law, or at least within the foreseeable boundaries of legal change, but for optimal problem solving it would seem we should try to push the boundaries of little "c" creativity as much as we can to produce at least a greater number of choices about how best to accomplish legal results.

In this next excerpt, Professor Brown explains several different creativity techniques that can be useful in negotiation.

Jennifer Gerarda Brown, **CREATIVITY AND PROBLEM-SOLVING**

87 Marq. L. Rev. 697-705 (2004)

Negotiation experts seem to agree that creative solutions are often the key to reaching value-maximizing outcomes in integrative, interest based bargaining. Sticking to the problem as it is initially framed and considering only the solutions that most readily present themselves will sometimes yield the optimal result, but more often the situation will require the parties and their representatives to think more expansively. This process of thinking more expansively — thinking "that ventures out from the accustomed way of considering a problem, to find something else that might work" — is often referred to as creativity or creative thinking. Some commentators distinguish creative thinking from creativity, arguing that creativity "is more value-laden and tends to be often linked with art (in its broad sense)." Creativity might seem to resemble any other artistic quality, something people lack or possess as much as a matter of genetics as anything else. And yet, like other artistic qualities (observation, hand-eye coordination, vocabulary, or writing skills), creativity may be teachable — or at least, whatever quantity one has as a matter of natural endowment might be enhanced with the right training. On the theory that both creativity and creative thinking can be enhanced with some training and work, this essay will use the terms interchangeably. . . .

I. BEYOND BRAINSTORMING

Most teachers and trainers of interest-based negotiation will spend some time teaching creative thinking. Following the template set forth in *Getting to YES*, they will encourage their students to "brainstorm." Brainstorming . . . is a somewhat formalized process in which participants work together to generate ideas. I say that it is formalized because it proceeds according to two important ground rules: participants agree not to evaluate the ideas while they are brainstorming, and they agree not to take "ownership" of the ideas. They strive to generate options and put them on the table, no matter how wacky or far-fetched they may seem. The "no evaluation" rule encourages participants to suspend their natural urge to criticize,

> **Stuck, Stuck, Stuck**
>
> Stuck, stuck, stuck in a rut;
> Solving a problem's like cracking a nut.
> Without the right tools
> You can't do the work —
> You'll stress and waste time
> And look like a jerk.
> It's time we admit our long-standing denial.
> Treading one path will impede our survival.
> By connecting synapses
> We'll end mental lapses,
> So in rut-jumping we'll not have a rival.
>
> Janet Weinstein & Linda Morton, Stuck in a Rut: The Role of Creative Thinking in Problem Solving and Legal Education, 9 Clinical L. Rev. 835 (2003).

edit, or censor the ideas. Evaluation can come later, but the notion here is that solutions will flow more easily if people are not assessing even as they articulate them. The "no ownership" rule also facilitates innovation because participants are encouraged to feel free to propose an idea or solution without endorsing it — no one can later attribute the idea to the person who proposed it, or try to hold it against that person. People can therefore propose ideas that might actually disadvantage them and benefit their counterparts without conceding that they would actually agree to such proposals in the final analysis. The ground rules for brainstorming constrain the natural inclination to criticize, so that participants are free to imagine, envision, and play with ideas, even though these processes come less easily to them.

Why is brainstorming so popular, both in practice and in negotiation training? Perhaps the answer lies not so much in what it activates, but in what it disables. What I mean is that it may be easier to teach people what *not* to do — rather than what to do affirmatively — in order to enhance their creative thinking. We may not know much about how to unleash new sources of creativity for negotiators, but we are pretty sure about some things that impede creative thinking. Theory and practice suggest that creative thinking is difficult when people jump to conclusions, close off discussion, or seize upon an answer prematurely. Indeed, the very heuristics that make decisionmaking possible — those pathways that permit people to make positive and sometimes normative judgments — can also lead people astray. One of the ways they may be led astray is that the heuristic prompts them to decide too quickly what something is or should be. Once judgment has occurred, it is tough to justify the expenditure of additional energy that creative thinking would require. Creativity could be considered the "anti-heuristic"; it keeps multiple pathways of perception and decision-making open, even when people are tempted to choose a single, one-way route to a solution. If we do nothing else, we can attempt to delay this kind of judgment until negotiators have considered multiple options. Brainstorming provides the structure for this kind of delay. . . .

A. Wordplay

Once an issue or problem is articulated, it is possible to play with the words expressing that problem in order to improve understanding and sometimes to yield new solutions.

1. Shifting Emphasis

To take a fairly simple example, suppose that two neighbors are in a dispute because cigarette butts and other small pieces of trash, deposited by Mr. Smith in his own front yard, are blowing into Mr. Jones's yard, and those that remain in Mr. Smith's yard are detracting from the appearance of the neighborhood (at least as Mr. Jones sees it). Mr. Jones might ask himself (or a mediator at the neighborhood justice center), "How can I get Mr. Smith to stop littering in his yard?" Shifting the emphasis in this sentence brings into focus various aspects of the problem and suggests possible solutions addressing those specific aspects. Consider the different meanings of the following sentences:

"How can *I* get Mr. Smith to stop littering in his yard?"
"How can I get *Mr. Smith* to stop littering in his yard?"
"How can I get Mr. Smith to stop *littering* in his yard?"
"How can I get Mr. Smith to stop littering in *his* yard?"
"How can I get Mr. Smith to stop littering in his *yard*?"

As the focus of the problem shifts, so too different potential solutions might emerge to address the problem as specifically articulated.

2. Changing a Word

Sometimes changing a word in the sentence helps to reformulate the problem in a way that suggests new solutions. In the example above, Mr. Jones might change the phrase "littering in his yard" to something else, such as "neglecting his yard" or "hanging out in his yard." It may be that something besides littering lies at the root of the problem, and a solution will be found, for example, not in stopping the littering, but in more regularized yard work.

3. Deleting a Word

Through word play, parties can delete words or phrases to see whether broadening the statement of the problem more accurately or helpfully captures its essence. Mr. Jones might delete the phrase "Mr. Smith" from his formulation of the problem, and thereby discover that it is not just Mr. Smith's yard, but the entire street, that is looking bad. Focusing on Mr. Smith as the source of the problem may be counterproductive; Mr. Jones might discover that he needs to organize all of the homeowners on his block to battle littering in order to make a difference. Deleting words sometimes spurs creativity by removing an overly restrictive focus on the issue or problem.

4. Adding a New Word

A final form of word play that can spur creative thinking is sometimes called "random word association." Through this process, participants choose a word randomly and then think of ways to associate it with the problem. Suppose Mr. Jones and Mr. Smith were given the word "work" and asked how it might relate to their dispute. Here are some possible results:

> *Work (time, effort)*: Mr. Smith will try to work harder to keep his yard looking nice, and he will check Mr. Jones's yard every Saturday to make sure there are no cigarette butts or other pieces of trash in it.
>
> *Work (being operational or functional)*: What the neighborhood needs is a sense of cohesion; Mr. Jones and Mr. Smith will organize a neighborhood beautification project to try to instill a sense of community among their neighbors.
>
> *Work (job)*: Although Mr. Smith's odd working hours sometimes lead him to smoke on his front porch and chat with his friends or family late at night (after Mr. Jones has gone to bed), Mr. Smith will stay in the back of his house after 10 P.M., further from Mr. Jones's bedroom window.

As the different meanings and resulting associations of "work" are explored by the parties, they discover new ways to solve their shared problem. Other seemingly unrelated words might trigger still more associations and more potential solutions. . . .

C. De Bono's "Six Hats" Technique

Edward de Bono has proposed a technique he calls "Six Thinking Hats," in which six aspects of a problem are assessed independently. As problem solvers symbolically don each of six differently colored hats, they focus on an aspect of the problem associated with each color: red for emotions, white for facts, yellow for positive aspects of the situation, green for future implications, black for critique, and blue for process.[5] As Weinstein and Morton point out, the technique of isolating the black/critique hat may be especially important for lawyers, whose tendency to move quickly into a critical mode may prevent them from seeing other important aspects of a problem. If the black hat is worn at or near the end of the process, the Six Hats technique displays a characteristic shared by brainstorming: it delays critique and judgment until other approaches can be tried. And shutting down judgment may enable creativity, as suggested above. By forcing themselves to address separately the emotional, factual, and process issues at stake in a problem, parties may discover room for creative solutions. Similarly, creative solutions are sometimes found in the terms of a future relationship between the parties. Wearing the green hat may force participants to come to terms with a future they would rather ignore.

The prospect of changing hats, even (perhaps especially) if it is done symbolically, could make some participants uncomfortable. Negotiators and neutrals should bear in mind that age, sex, ethnicity and other cultural specifics may create dignitary interests for some participants that would be threatened or compromised by some techniques for boosting creative thought. Some people would feel embarrassed or humiliated if they were asked to engage in the theatrics required by some of these exercises. For others, the chance to pretend or play might be just the prod they need to open new avenues of thought. In a spirit of flexibility (surely a necessary condition for creativity), therefore, one should be thinking of ways to modify these techniques to fit other needs of the parties.[6]

D. Atlas of Approaches

Another technique for stimulating creative ideas about a problem from a variety of perspectives is called the "Atlas of Approaches." Roger Fisher, Elizabeth Kopelman and Andrea Kupfer Schneider propose this approach in Beyond Machiavelli, their book on international negotiation.[7] Using the Atlas of Approaches technique, participants adopt the perspectives of professionals from a variety of fields. By asking themselves, for example, "What would a journalist do?," "What would an economist do?," "How would a psychologist view this?," and so on, negotiators are able to form a more interdisciplinary view of their problem. With this more complete picture of the issues and potential outcomes, they might be able to connect disciplines in ways that give rise to creative solutions. . . .

---

5. Edward de Bono, Six Thinking Hats (1999).

6. For example, the Six Hats technique could be transformed into a "Six Flip Charts" exercise, still using differently colored paper or markers to signal the different focus of each inquiry.

7. Roger Fisher et al., Beyond Machiavelli: Tools for Coping with Conflict 67 (1996).

F. "WWCD": What Would Croesus[8] Do?

This process requires a participant to take the perspective of an unconstrained actor. What solutions suggest themselves if we assume no limit to available money, time, talent, technology, or effort? In some ways, one could think of the WWCD method as a more specific application of brainstorming. As the proponents of brainstorming are quick to point out, creativity and the free flow of ideas can be impeded by criticism or assessment. WWCD takes off the table any assessment based on constraints — financial, technological, etc. If we assume that we can afford and operationalize any solution we can come up with, what might we discover?

A second phase of this approach requires participants to think about the extent to which their unconstrained solution might be modified to make it workable given the existing constraints. . . .

H. Flipping or Reversal

With this technique, one asks whether flipping or reversing a given situation will work. As Edward de Bono explains:

> In the reversal method, one takes things as they are and then turns them round, inside out, upside down, back to front. Then one sees what happens . . . one is not looking for the right answer but for a different arrangement of information which will provoke a different way of looking at the situation.

Chris Honeyman sometimes uses this technique in his work as a neutral when he asks the parties to put forward some really *bad* ideas for resolving the conflict. When people offer ideas in response to a call for "bad" ideas, they may free themselves to offer the ideas they partially or secretly support; again, as in brainstorming, they disclaim ownership of the ideas. It is also possible that the instruction to offer bad ideas stimulates creative thinking because it can seem *funny* to people. Humor is a good stimulant for creativity.

This next excerpt from psychology professor Dean Pruitt focuses on how parties' seemingly opposing demands may be reconciled into an agreement. Pruitt describes five methods that can be used to achieve integrative agreements: (1) expanding the pie, (2) nonspecific compensation, (3) logrolling, (4) cost cutting, and (5) bridging.

---

8. Nalebuff and Ayers explain: "Croesus (rhymes with Jesus) was the supremely rich king of Lydia (modern Turkey), reigning from 560 to 546 b.c. His wealth came from mining gold. . . . His lavish gifts and sacrifices made his name synonymous with wealth. Even today we say 'rich as Croesus.' " Barry Nalebuff & Ian Ayres, Why Not? How to Use Everyday Ingenuity to Solve Problems Big and Small (2003).

Dean Pruitt, **ACHIEVING INTEGRATIVE AGREEMENTS**

in Negotiation in Organizations 36-41 (Max Bazerman & Roy Lewicki eds., 1983)

METHODS FOR ACHIEVING INTEGRATIVE AGREEMENTS

Five methods for achieving integrative agreements will now be described. These are means by which the parties' initially opposing demands can be transformed into alternatives that reconcile their interests. They can be used by one party, both parties working together, or a third party such as a mediator. Each method involves a different way of refocusing the issues under dispute. Hence potentially useful refocusing questions will be provided under each heading. Information that is useful for implementing each method will also be mentioned, and the methods will be listed in order of increasing difficulty of getting this information.

The methods will be illustrated by a running example concerning a husband and wife who are trying to decide where to go on a two-week vacation. [Also used by Carrie Menkel-Meadow in her article Legal Problem-Solving in Chapter 3.] The husband wants to go to the mountains, his wife to the seashore. They have considered the compromise of spending one week in each location but are hoping for something better. What approach should they take?

Expanding the Pie

Some conflicts hinge on a resource shortage. For example, time, money, space, and automobiles are in short supply but long demand. In such circumstances, integrative agreements can be devised by increasing the available resources. This is called expanding the pie. For example, our married couple might solve their problems by persuading their employers to give them four weeks of vacation so that they can take two in the mountains and two at the seashore. . . .

Expanding the pie is a useful formula when the parties reject one another's demands because of opportunity costs; for example, if the husband rejects the seashore because it keeps him away from the mountains and the wife rejects the mountains because they deny her the pleasure of the seashore. But it is by no means a universal remedy. Expanding the pie may yield strikingly poor benefits if there are inherent costs in the other's proposal, e.g., the husband cannot stand the seashore or the wife the mountains. Other methods are better in such cases.

Expanding the pie requires no analysis of the interests underlying the parties' demands. Hence its information requirements are slim. However, this does not mean that a solution by this method is always easy to find. There may be no resource shortage, or the shortage may not be easy to see or to remedy.

Refocusing questions that can be useful in seeking a solution by pie expansion include: How can both parties get what they want? Does the conflict hinge on a resource shortage? How can the critical resource be expanded?

Nonspecific Compensation

In nonspecific compensation, one party gets what he or she wants and the other is repaid in some unrelated coin. Compensation is nonspecific if it does not deal with the precise costs incurred by the other party. For example, the wife in our example might agree to go to the mountains, even though she finds them boring, if her husband promises her a fur coat. Another example would be giving an employee a bonus for going without dinner.

Compensation usually comes from the party whose demands are granted. But it can also originate with a third party or even with the party who is compensated. An example of the latter would be an employee who pampers him- or herself by finding a nice office to work in while going without dinner.

Two kinds of information are useful for devising a solution by nonspecific compensation: (a) information about what is valuable to the other party; for example, knowledge that he or she values love, attention, or money; (b) information about how badly the other party is hurting by making concessions. This is useful for devising adequate compensation for these concessions. If such information is not available, it may be possible to conduct an "auction" for the other party's

> ### Ticket to Success
>
> An example of nonspecific compensation is provided by Leigh Thompson: Phil Jones, managing director of Real Time, the London-based interactive design studio, recalls an instance where he used nonspecific compensation in his negotiations. The problem was that his client, a Formula 1 motor-racing team, wanted to launch Internet Web sites but did not have the budget to pay him. However, in Jones's eyes, the client was high profile and had creative, challenging projects that Real Time wanted to get involved with. Formula 1 came up with a nonspecific compensation offer to make the deal go through: tickets to some of the major Formula 1 meetings. It worked. Says Jones: "The tickets are like gold dust . . . and can be used as a pat on the back for staff or as an opportunity to pamper existing clients or woo new ones." Leigh Thompson, The Mind and Heart of the Negotiator 163-164 (2001).

acquiescence, changing the sort of benefit offered or raising one's offer, in trial-and-error fashion, until an acceptable formula is found.

Refocusing questions that can help locate a means of compensation include: How much is the other party hurting in conceding to me? What does the other party value that I can supply? How valuable is this to the other party?

Logrolling

Logrolling is possible in complex agendas where several issues are under consideration and the parties have differing priorities among these issues. Each party concedes on low priority issues in exchange for concessions on issues of higher priority to itself. Each gets that part of its demands that it finds most important. For example, suppose that in addition to disagreeing about where to go on vacation, the wife in our example wants to go to a first-class hotel while her husband prefers a tourist home. If accommodations are a high priority issue for the wife and location for the husband, they can reach a fairly integrative solution by agreeing to go to a first-class hotel in the mountains. Logrolling can be viewed as a variant of nonspecific compensation in which both parties instead of one are compensated for making concessions desired by the other.

To develop solutions by logrolling, it is useful to have information about the two parties' priorities so that exchangeable concessions can be identified. But it is not necessary to have information about the interests (e.g., the aspirations, values) underlying these priorities. Solutions by logrolling can also be developed by a process of trial and error in which one party moves systematically through a series of possible packages, keeping his or her own outcomes as high as possible, until an alternative is found that is acceptable to the other party.

Refocusing questions that can be useful for developing solutions by logrolling include: Which issues are of higher and lower priority to myself? Which issues are of higher and lower priority to the other party? Are some of my high-priority issues of low priority to the other party and vice versa?

Cost Cutting

In solutions by cost cutting, one party gets what he or she wants and the other's costs are reduced or eliminated. The result is high joint benefit, not because the first party has changed his or her demands but because the second party suffers less. For instance, suppose that the husband in our example dislikes the beach because of the hustle and bustle. He may be quite willing to go there on vacation if his costs are cut by renting a house with a quiet inner courtyard where he can read while his wife goes out among the crowds.

Cost cutting often takes the form of specific compensation in which the party who concedes receives something in return that satisfies the precise values frustrated. For example, the employee who must work through dinner time can be specifically compensated by provision of a meal in a box. Specific compensation differs from nonspecific compensation in dealing with the precise costs incurred rather than providing repayment in an unrelated coin. The costs are actually canceled out rather than overbalanced by benefits experienced in some other realm.

Information about the nature of one of the parties' costs is, of course, helpful for developing solutions by cost cutting. This is a deeper kind of information than knowledge of that party's priorities. It involves knowing something about the interests — the values, aspirations, and standards — underlying that party's overt position.

Refocusing questions for developing solutions by cost cutting include: What costs are posed for the other party by our proposal? How can these costs be mitigated or eliminated?

Bridging

In bridging, neither party achieves its initial demands but a new option is devised that satisfies the most important interests underlying these demands. For example, suppose that the husband in our vacation example is mainly interested in fishing and hunting and the wife in swimming and sunbathing. Their interests might be bridged by finding an inland resort with a lake and a beach that is close to woods and streams. . . .

Bridging typically involves a reformulation of the issue(s) based on an analysis of the underlying interests on both sides. For example, a critical turning point in our vacation example is likely to come when the initial formulation, "Shall we go to the mountains or the seashore?" is replaced by "Where can we find fishing, hunting, swimming, and sunbathing?". . . . This new formulation can be done by either or both parties or by a third party who is trying to help.

People who seek to develop solutions by bridging need information about the nature of the two parties' interests and their priorities among these interests. . . . More often, higher-priority interests are served while lower-priority interests are discarded. For example, the wife who agrees to go to an inland lake may have forgone the lesser value of smelling the sea air and the husband may have forgone his preference for spectacular mountain vistas.

In the initial phase of search for a solution by bridging, the search model can include all of the interests on both sides. But if this does not generate a mutually acceptable alternative, some of the lower-priority interests must be discarded from the model and the search begun anew. The result will not be an ideal solution but, it is hoped, one that is mutually acceptable. Dropping low-priority interests in the development of a solution by bridging is similar to dropping low-priority demands in the search for a solution by logrolling. However, the latter is in the realm of concrete proposals, while the former is in the realm of the interests underlying these proposals.

Refocusing questions that can be raised in search of a solution by bridging include: What are the two parties' basic interests? What are their priorities among these interests? How can the two sets of high priority interests be reconciled?

Problem 4-15.   *Bake Sale*

There once was a law student with chronic medical problems. Unfortunately, she was also uninsured. The good news was that she was a fabulous cook. The first time she saw the doctor she explained her financial situation. She was able to work out with her doctor a payment plan for services over time. What kind of solution is this? After they negotiated the first time, she delivered a chocolate chip cheesecake to the doctor in appreciation for his understanding. The next time she needed the doctor, the doctor requested payment in cheesecakes! What kind of solution is this?

Problem 4-16.   *Problems with Options*

Chris Guthrie writes that the creation of too many options may actually hinder clear decision making based on four phenomena:

> The first phenomenon [*option devaluation*] arises when a choice set grows from one option to two or more options. When a choice set expands from the original option under consideration to more than one option, negotiators tend to devalue the initial option. . . . The second phenomenon [*context dependence*] arises when a choice set consisting of two or more options grows by one. . . . [N]egotiators tend to reconsider their relative ranking of the options already under consideration even when the additional option sheds no new light on those options. Negotiators do *not*, in other words, make context-*in*dependent decisions. . . . The third phenomenon [*partial decision making*] arises when a choice set grows to include a large number of options. . . . [N]egotiators tend to abandon compensatory decision-making strategies that take all options and attributes into account in favor of simplified decision strategies that consider only some of the available information. . . . The fourth and final phenomenon [*decision regret*] arises after the decision has been made . . . [when] negotiators tend to feel greater regret when they have selected one option over another than when they have simply selected the sole available option.

Although the prescriptive literature on negotiation is certainly correct that option generation offers potential benefits to negotiators, the four phenomena identified above . . . suggest that option generation poses potential costs as well. Negotiators who generate multiple options may be induced by the very availability of those options to make decisions that run contrary to their true preferences and that induce negative post-decision emotions.

Chris Guthrie, Panacea or Pandora's Box: The Costs of Options in Negotiation, 88 Iowa L. Rev. 601, 607-608 (2003).

What do you think about Professor Guthrie's perspective on option creation? How can lawyers help their clients avoid these pitfalls?

2. Avoiding Common Mistakes and Errors of Judgment

Now that we have discussed the skills that effective negotiators bring to the table, we turn to how to avoid many of the common mistakes and judgment errors that negotiators make. These mistakes occur for a variety of reasons, and often negotiators are not even aware of the thinking processes that lead them into common traps.

Being able to recognize these traps often requires the ability to step back — to take the fly-on-the-wall perspective — and analyze the negotiation process itself. What is working and what is not? Am I or my counterpart falling into a typical negotiation trap? How can we get out of this? Recognizing the mistakes we might make is the first step. Avoiding them, of course, is more complex and often will require a combination of working with your clients, working with experts for better information, and even bringing in a mediator (as we discuss in the next several chapters) who can help both parties minimize some of these judgment errors that negotiators can make.

The final part of this chapter discusses the role of culture in negotiation and points out that, like other incorrect assumptions we make, cultural assumptions can limit a negotiator's effectiveness.

a. Judgment Errors

Status quo barriers refer to the mistakes or assumptions that negotiators make because they like the status quo. They like the items they have in their possession and fear losing them. Economics professor Daniel Kahneman and psychology professor Amos Tversky discuss a phenomenon called the "endowment effect," which occurs when negotiators value what they own more than what they do not. This effect also brings in the element of risk. What are we willing to risk to avoid losing something we have? In 2002, Kahneman won the Nobel Prize in economics for his work on the endowment effect, also known as loss aversion.

 Daniel Kahneman & Amos Tversky, **CONFLICT RESOLUTION: A COGNITIVE PERSPECTIVE**

in Barriers to Conflict Resolution 54-55 (Kenneth Arrow et al. eds., 1995)

Loss aversion refers to the observation that losses generally loom larger than the corresponding gains. This notion may be captured by a value function that is steeper in the negative than in the positive domain. In decisions under risk, loss aversion entails a reluctance to accept even-chance gambles, unless the payoffs are very favorable. For example, many people will accept such a gamble only if the gain is at least twice as large as the loss. . . .

The following classroom demonstration illustrates the principle of loss aversion. An attractive object (e.g., a decorated mug) is distributed to one third of the students. The students who have been given mugs are *sellers* — perhaps better described as owners. They are informed that there will be an opportunity to exchange the mug for a predetermined amount of money. The subjects state what their choice will be for different amounts, and thereby indicate the minimal amount for which they are willing to give up their mug. Another one-third of the students are *choosers*. They are told that they will have a choice between a mug like the one in the hands of their neighbor and an amount of cash; they indicate their choices for different amounts. The remaining students are *buyers:* they indicate whether they would pay each of the different amounts to acquire a mug. In a representative experiment, the median price set by sellers was $7.12, the median cash equivalent set by the choosers was $3.12, and the median buyer was willing to pay $2.88 for the mug.

The difference between the valuations of owners and choosers occurs in spite of the fact that both groups face the same choice: go home with a mug or with a prespecified sum of money. Subjectively, however, the choosers and owners are in different states: the former evaluate the mug as a gain, the latter as something to be given up. Because of loss aversion, more cash is required to persuade the owners to give up the mug than to match the attractiveness of the mug to the choosers. In the same vein, Thaler tells of a wine lover who will neither sell a bottle that has gained value in his cellar nor buy another bottle at the current price.[9] The experimental studies of the discrepant valuation of owners, choosers, and buyers demonstrate that loss aversion can be induced instantaneously; it does not depend on a progressive attachment to objects in one's possession.

Problem 4-17.   *Betting the Farm*

- Why are negotiators willing to risk more to avoid a loss? Is this just denial?
- Why do you think people value what they have in their possession more than other items? What implications for negotiation does this theory have?
- What can the lawyer do to help the client deal with these tendencies (or the lawyer's own tendencies)? How does framing the offer from the other side matter?

Problem 4-18.   *Buy My Car, Take 2*

Russell Korobkin and Chris Guthrie conducted an experiment in which a hypothetical car accident causes damages of $28,000. The other (negligent) driver's insurance company offers $21,000 to settle. In one set of facts, however, the driver is driving a $14,000 car with $14,000 of medical bills. In the other set of facts, the driver is driving a $24,000 car with $4,000 of medical bills. In both cases, the driver's health insurance already covers the medical expenses (although a jury would not be informed of that fact). The owners of the $14,000 car are more likely to accept the settlement than the owners of the $24,000 car. Russell Korobkin & Chris Guthrie, Psychological Barriers to Litigation Settlement: An Experimental Approach, 93 Mich. L. Rev. 107 (1994).

    Why do you think this is so? How is a $21,000 settlement perceived as a loss or a gain?

This chapter has already discussed the importance of gathering information to prepare for the negotiation and the key roles that listening and understanding play in seeking information from the client and the other side. This section examines problems with information gathering. What happens when negotiators do not share

---

9. Richard Thaler, Toward a Positive Theory of Consumer Choice, 1. J. Econ. Behav. & Org. 1, 39–60 (1980).

useful information? What happens when negotiators get too wedded to the information they already have?

The next two excerpts explore two informational barriers: anchoring and overconfidence. Awareness of barriers, such as these, will help you identify barriers when you encounter them in yourself and when you encounter them with others. This awareness will help you navigate these barriers in future negotiations.

Dan Orr & Chris Guthrie, ANCHORING, INFORMATION, EXPERTISE, AND NEGOTIATION: NEW INSIGHTS FROM META-ANALYSIS

Ohio St. J. on Disp. Resol. 597-598, 608-609 (2006)

Suppose that we asked you whether the average temperature in San Francisco was higher or lower than 558 degrees. Do you think this question would influence your estimate of the average temperature in the city? Suppose instead that we asked you whether the average price of a college textbook was higher or lower than $7,128.53. Would this question have an impact on your estimate of the average price of such a text? What if we asked you whether the number of "top 10" Beatles' records was higher or lower than 100,025? Would this affect your estimate of the number of Beatles' albums that did make the top 10?

You wouldn't think so, but you would probably be wrong. Due to a phenomenon that psychologists call "anchoring," we are often unduly influenced by the initial figure we encounter when estimating the value of an item. This initial value serves as a kind of reference point or benchmark that anchors our expectations about the item's actual value.

Negotiation and dispute resolution scholars have observed that this phenomenon could have an impact on negotiation. In a number of studies, researchers have shown that opening offers and demands, insurance policy caps, statutory damage caps, negotiator aspirations, and other "first numbers" can influence negotiation outcomes in transactions and settlements. . . .

Donald R. Philbin, Jr., THE ONE MINUTE MANAGER PREPARES FOR MEDIATION: A MULTIDISCIPLINARY APPROACH TO NEGOTIATION PREPARATION

Harv. Negot. L. Rev. 281-283 (Spring 1999)

OPTIMISTIC OVERCONFIDENCE: THE LAKE WOBEGON EFFECT

Life would be tough without optimists and they are often risk-takers. "'A common feature of human behavior is overoptimism,' scholars have noted, including in the litigation context." Faced with a nasty lawsuit, we all want lawyers to champion our cause. That is their job. As repeat players with a portfolio of cases, lawyers instinctively value cases. Economic analyses may test and extend those instinctive valuations. But when the tests come, the client probably does not want their champion to be the one poking holes in their case and they sure do not want the other side to point out their shortcomings. Most are, however, open to questions by impartial third-parties based on a rounded view of the case. The answers to those questions may impact their valuation. If the spread between assumptions is wide enough to eliminate a zone of agreement, the parties raise the risk of negotiation impasse and may end up surrendering the decision to someone else.

Overconfidence leads us to discount small probabilities, assume luck runs in our favor, and distort unattractive consequences. It is human nature to place more emphasis on "facts that are consistent with our desired outcomes" and to make self-serving assessments of our own ability. Over 80% of interviewed entrepreneurs described their chances of success as 70% or better, and 33% described them as "certain." That compares with a five-year survival rate for new firms around 33%. Couples about to be married estimated their chances of later divorcing at zero, even though most know that the divorce rate is between 40% and 50%. Negotiators in final arbitrations overestimated the chance that their offer would be chosen by 15%. Surveys find the Lake Wobegon above-average effect across demographics — college professors, high school students, truck and taxi drivers, and even negotiators.

Although most negotiators believe that they are more "fair" than average, in specific mediations they tend to overestimate their trial alternatives. Advocates naturally focus attention on case assets while under-appreciating the weaker issues. Myopically focusing on the strengths of a case blurs our focus on less favorable points. Focusing tightly on the merits of the case also increases the risk of undervaluing the transaction costs associated with continuing to trial. While overconfidence is prevalent among negotiators, it is not constant. So we cannot just cut the probabilities on both sides by 15% and balance the decision trees. What we can do is prepare alternative scenarios looking through different ends of the same telescope. Some scenarios will be rosy and others thorny, but together they are more likely to cover the range of potential outcomes — worst case to best case. Disciplining ourselves to articulate specific explanations for various outcomes can break our single-minded focus on a single scenario.

Problem 4-19.   *Anchors Away*

- If parties can get anchored by information, should you make the first offer in a negotiation? What are the risks? What are the benefits?
- How does the concept of setting aspirations tie in with the concept of anchoring? Can you also anchor yourself?
- How can you protect yourself from the anchoring phenomenon? How can lawyers assist their clients in this?

> **Problem 4-20.** *Buy My Car, Take 3*
>
> A couple plans to buy a car for the husband's parents who live in New York. They research the car cost very carefully, know there is a year-end sale, and even talk to a friend who is a dealer in Wisconsin about the best price they could negotiate. When they arrive in New York, they also talk to a friend who had just purchased the same model to confirm the price she paid. They again call their friend in Wisconsin to check the price. In fact, he says that he cannot match that price. (He wonders out loud whether the company bonuses for dealers in New York are more than in Wisconsin.) So the couple walks into a New York dealership and offers $200 under the price paid by their friend in New York several weeks before. They say that they would buy the car today if the dealer meets their price. The dealer checks with the manager and then agrees. The wife is thrilled. The husband worries for weeks that if the dealer took their opening price, the dealer would have taken less. What has happened?

This last excerpt discusses two common barriers that arise because negotiators are too concerned with winning the "game" of negotiation. Instead of concentrating on their own interests, negotiators become focused on how the other party is doing compared to themselves (escalation of commitment), and they may devalue a good offer just because it came from the other party (reactive devaluation). Both these barriers can cause a negotiator to become destructive to themselves and the negotiation, which means no one wins the "game" in the end.

 Richard Birke & Craig R. Fox, **PSYCHOLOGICAL PRINCIPLES IN NEGOTIATING CIVIL SETTLEMENTS**

Acad. of Mgmt. Rev. 23-24, 48-50 (Oct. 1981)

[A] psychological phenomenon that may contribute to overdiscovery is the tendency to *escalate commitment* to an initial course of action. This is especially likely to occur in situations in which the decisionmaker has not set an initial limit or budget, as is often the case in litigation.

A striking example of the irrational escalation of commitment is Shubik's dollar auction game. In such an auction the top bidder pays his bid and receives the prize — say, a twenty-dollar bill — while the second-place bidder pays his bid and receives nothing. The outcome is typically as follows: several bidders join the fray early on, angling to capitalize on an opportunity to obtain twenty dollars at a discount. Bids escalate. As the bids approach ten dollars, the number of bidders usually winnows to two. As the first bids exceed ten dollars, everyone realizes that the auctioneer has made a profit. The remaining bidders continue, until one participant bids twenty dollars, preferring to break even than to lose his prior bid amount (which would have been eighteen dollars assuming bids were restricted to whole dollars), and confident that no rational participant would bid more than twenty dollars for a twenty-dollar-bill. However, the other bidder will usually up the ante to at least $21, preferring a loss of $1 to a loss of $19. Typically the winning bid is significantly more than $20 (as is the losing second-place bid), and the auctioneer makes a tidy profit.

Shubik's auction is an apt model for some instances of civil litigation with escalating costs. A client who has spent a great deal of money on pretrial motions and discovery may be very reluctant to settle a case for less than costs or to walk away from the case, even when information obtained through the discovery process suggests that the case is worth less than the amount she has spent pursuing it. . . .

PSYCHOLOGY OF REACTIVE DEVALUATION

Fixed-pie bias (i.e., the assumption that what is good for my counterpart must be bad for me) may contribute to reactive devaluation, which is a tendency to evaluate proposals less favorably after they have been offered by one's adversary. In one classic study conducted during the days of Apartheid, researchers solicited students' evaluations of two university plans for divestment from South Africa. The first plan called for partial divestment, and the second increased investments in companies that had left South Africa. Both plans, which fell short of the students' demand for full divestment, were rated before and after the university announced that it would adopt the partial divestment plan. The results were dramatic: students rated the university plan less positively after it was announced by the university and the alternative plan more positively.

We hasten to note that the source of an offer may be diagnostic of its quality. It may be reasonable to view an offer more critically when the source is one's opponent, particularly if there is an unpleasant history between the parties. However, evidence from the aforementioned studies suggests that people tend to experience a knee-jerk overreaction to the source of the offer. If negotiators routinely undervalue concessions made their counterparts, it will inhibit their ability to exploit tradeoffs that might result in more valuable agreements.

Consider an example of how reactive devaluation might manifest itself in a negotiation between lawyers. Imagine a simplified environmental cleanup action in which the parties are a governmental enforcement agency (represented by a single person) and a single responsible polluter. There may be two solutions to their problem. In one, the government effectuates the cleanup and sends a bill to the polluter. In the second, the polluter does the cleanup and the government inspects. Perhaps solution one meets more of the polluters' interests than solution two. One might suppose that the polluter would prefer this solution regardless of how it emerges as the agreed method. However, studies of reactive devaluation suggest that once the government tentatively agrees to that particular solution, the polluter may view the alternative solution more favorably. The apparent thought process is "if they held it back, it must be worse for them and therefore better for me than the one offered." The polluter may irrationally reorder her priorities and reject a deal simply because it was offered freely by an opponent. . . .

. . . Resisting the destructive effects of reactive devaluation will require negotiators to unlearn a pervasive assumption that most people carry with them. Negotiations are rarely fixed-sum and it is simply not true that what is good for one side is necessarily bad for the other. As mentioned above, both parties often have congruent interests or a mutual interest in exploiting tradeoffs on issues that they prioritize differently. To resist reactive devaluation, one must short-circuit a deeply ingrained habit. It is natural to react against freedom to choose, and when an opponent holds back one offer in favor of another, its natural to yearn for the alternative option. However, it would be wise to critically examine this natural impulse and ask if this impulse is a rational response to a truly inferior offer or an emotional reaction against the other side's initiative.

Even if a lawyer can restrain herself from reactive devaluation, it may be very difficult to buffer this response in his counterpart. Certainly, it first may help to cultivate a cordial relationship with one's counterpart to the extent that this is possible, so that offers are regarded with less suspicion. Second, it may be helpful to ask a mutually trusted intermediary to convey a proposal. Some commentators have suggested that reactive devaluation can be overcome with the help of a mediator. Finally, if a party crafts a settlement package that would be mutually beneficial, it may be helpful to work with opposing counsel to make them feel as if the solution was jointly initiated or even that it was the opposing counsel's idea.

Returning to the hypothetical, the client may be experiencing reactive devaluation. It may behoove the attorney to counsel her client to consider whether her change of heart was a result of the fact that her original package was offered by her opponent in the litigation or is a result of other factors. If her reaction was driven by its source, the attorney should make sure she understands that she is rejecting her formerly-preferred deal solely because it was offered by an adversary, and not necessarily because it fails to meet her interests.

Problem 4-21.   *Bowing to Authority*

Can you think of an instance where, in negotiating with a parent or other authority figure, you automatically dismissed an otherwise "good" offer?

A phenomenon related to reactive devaluation is an elevated willingness to accept proposals — regardless of their objective or rational value or cost — if the proposal comes from someone loved or admired. Are there some people to whom you say "yes" before hearing even what they propose? Knowing that negotiators can gain power from being liked and trusted, how would that influence your strategy as an attorney negotiator?

---

b. Culture

Advice on dealing with cultural differences in negotiation runs the risk of either being too simplistic (don't cross your legs in certain cultures) or being so general that it is not helpful (there may be different assumptions about how negotiations are conducted). This next excerpt points out some common cultural differences in negotiation while also reminding negotiators that cultural differences may or may not explain any one individual's approach to negotiations. Much like gender and race, culture can be an obvious difference between negotiators but perhaps not the determining one in how each party approaches the negotiation. Some people, in fact, suggest that just learning about negotiation, like you are in this course, creates its own culture of people who know about negotiation across cultures, perhaps with some common strategies and vocabulary.

 Jeffrey Z. Rubin & Frank E.A. Sander, **CULTURE, NEGOTIATION, AND THE EYE OF THE BEHOLDER**

7 Neg. J. 249, 251-253 (1991)

The purpose of this brief column is to draw attention to several considerations that should be borne in mind in any analysis of culture and negotiation. Our thesis is that, although differences in culture clearly *do* exist and have a bearing on the style of negotiation that emerges, some of the most important effects of culture are felt even before the negotiators sit down across from one another and begin to exchange offers. Culture, we believe, is a profoundly powerful organizing prism, through which we tend to view and integrate all kinds of disparate interpersonal information. . . .

Robert Rosenthal and his colleagues have demonstrated the power of expectations and labels in an important series of experimental studies. In one of these experiments,[10] teachers were told that some of the children in their elementary school classes had been identified as "intellectual bloomers," children who were likely to grow and develop substantially in the coming year. About other children (who had been privately matched with the "bloomers" in terms of measured aptitude) nothing was said. When an achievement test was administered at the end of the academic year, a shocking and important discovery was made: those children who had been labeled as intellectual bloomers scored significantly higher than those with whom they had been matched. In explanation, the researchers hypothesized that children who were expected to do very, very well were given more attention by their teachers; this increased attention, organized by hypothesis that the child in question was a talented individual, created a self-fulfilling prophecy.

The label of culture may have an effect very similar to that of gender or intellectual aptitude; it is a "hook" that makes it easy for one negotiator (the perceiver) to organize what he or she sees emanating from that "different person" seated at the other side of the table. To understand how culture may function as a label, consider the following teaching exercise, used during a two week session on negotiation. . . . During one class session, the fifty or so participants were formed into rough national groups, and were asked to characterize their national negotiating style — as seen by others. That is, the task was *not* to describe true differences that may be attributable to cultural or nationality, but to characterize the stereotypic perceptions that others typically carry around in their heads.

This exercise yielded a set of very powerful, albeit contradictory, stereotypic descriptions of different nationalities. To give a couple of examples, British

---

10. [Robert Rosenthal & Lenore Jacobson, Pygmalion in the Classroom (1968). — EDS.]

participants characterized others' stereotypic characterization of the British as "reserved, arrogant, old-fashioned, eccentric, fair, and self-deprecating" . . . And a cluster of Central Americans listed other's stereotypes of them as negotiators as "idealistic, impractical, disorganized, unprepared, stubborn in arguments, and flowery in style."

Now imagine that you have begun to negotiate with someone from another culture, who at some point in the proceedings simply insists that he or she can go no further, and is prepared to conclude without an agreement if necessary; in effect, says this individual, his BATNA has been reached, and he can do just as well by walking away from the table. How should you interpret such an assertion? If you share the general cluster of stereotypes described by the students, your interpretation will probably depend on the other person's culture or nationality. Thus, if the other negotiator is British, and (among other things) you regard the British as "fair," you may interpret this person's refusal to concede further as an honest statement of principle. The same behavior issuing from a Central American, however (someone you suspect of being "stubborn in arguments"), may lead you to suspect your counterpart of being stubborn and perhaps deceitful. Wouldn't you therefore be more likely to strike an agreement with a British than a Central American negotiator — despite the fact that each has behaved in the identical way?

If there is any truth to our surmise, you can see how powerful the effects of culture may prove to be, leading us (even before we have had a chance to gather information about our counterpart) to hold a set of expectations that guide and inform our judgments. Moreover, once our "hypotheses" about others are in place, it becomes very difficult to disprove them. We tend to gather interpersonal information in such a way that we pay attention only to the "facts" that support our preconceived ideas, ignoring or dismissing disconfirming data. . . .

[P]robably the wisest thing any of us can do to prepare for such negotiations is to: be aware of our biases and predispositions; acquire as much information as possible about our counterpart as an individual; and learn as much as we can about the norms and customs (of all kinds) that are to be found in our counterpart's home country.

Problem 4-22.   *Your Stereotypes?*

Perform the same exercise the authors above write about in the article. Identify yourself culturally (again, regional or other identifying characteristics will work too). What are the typical stereotypes of your culture? Do they actually apply to you?

> **Problem 4-23.**   *Negotiating Within Cultures*
>
> Do you think that it will be easier in your career to negotiate with lawyers who have gone to the same law school as you? Who have taken negotiation courses? How might these types of professional cultures be the same or different than other types of "culture"?

Further Reading

Ian Ayres, *Fair Driving*, 104 HARV. L. REV. 817 (1991).

Ian Ayres, *Further Evidence of Discrimination in New Car Negotiations and Estimates of Its Cause*, 94 MICH L. REV. 109 (1995).

Max H. Bazerman & Margaret A. Neale. (1992). *Negotiating Rationally*. NewYork: The Free Press.

David Binder, Paul Bergman & Susan Price. (2d ed. 2004). *Lawyers as Counselors: A Client Centered Approach*. St. Paul: West Pub. Co.

Steven J. Brams & Alan D. Taylor. (1996). *Fair Division*. Cambridge: Cambridge University Press.

Jeanne Brett. (2001). *Negotiating Globally*. San Francisco: Jossey-Bass Publishers.

Jennifer Gerarda Brown. (2006). Creativity and Problem-Solving, in Andrea Kupfer Schneider & Christopher Honeyman (Eds.), *The Negotiator's Fieldbook* (pp. 407-414). Washington, D.C.: ABA Section on Dispute Resolution.

Clark Freshman, Adele Hayes & Greg Feldman, *The Lawyer-Negotiator as Mood Scientist: What We Know and Don't Know About How Mood Relates to Successful Negotiation*, J. DISP. RESOL. 1, 55 (2002).

Bee Chen Goh. (2006). Typical Errors of Westerners, in Andrea Kupfer Schneider & Christopher Honeyman (Eds.), *The Negotiator's Fieldbook* (pp. 293-300). Washington, D.C.: ABA Section on Dispute Resolution.

Sheila Heen & Douglas Stone. (2006). Perceptions and Stories, in Andrea Kupfer Schneider & Christopher Honeyman (Eds.), *The Negotiator's Fieldbook* (pp. 343-350). Washington, D.C.: ABA Section on Dispute Resolution.

Loretta Kelly. (2006). Indigenous Experiences in Negotiation, in Andrea Kupfer Schneider & Christopher Honeyman (Eds.), *The Negotiator's Fieldbook* (pp. 301-314). Washington, D.C.: ABA Section on Dispute Resolution.

Russell Korobkin & Chris Guthrie. (2006). Heuristics and Biases at the Bargaining Table. In Andrea Kupfer Schneider & Christopher Honeyman (Eds.), *The Negotiator's Fieldbook* (pp. 351-359). Washington, D.C.: ABA Section on Dispute Resolution.

Roy J. Lewicki & Barbara Benedict Bunker. (1995). Trust in Relationships: A Model of Development and Decline. In Barbara Bunker, Jeffrey Rubin et al. (Eds.), *Conflict in Cooperation and Justice* (p. 133). San Francisco: Jossey-Bass Publishers.

Robert Mnookin, *Why Negotiations Fail: An Exploration of Barriers to Conflict Resolution*, 8 OHIO ST. J. ON DISP. RESOL. 235 (1993).

Barry Nalebuff & Ian Ayres. (2003). *Why Not?* Boston: Harvard Business School Press.

Linda L. Putnam. (2006). Communication and Interaction Patterns. In Andrea Kupfer Schneider & Christopher Honeyman (Eds.), *The Negotiator's Fieldbook* (pp. 385-394). Washington, D.C.: ABA Section on Dispute Resolution.

Lee Ross. (1995). Reactive Devaluation in Negotiation and Conflict Resolution. In Kenneth Arrow et al. (Eds.), *Barriers to Conflict Resolution*. New York: W.W. Norton & Co.

Andrea Kupfer Schneider. (2006). Aspirations. In Andrea Kupfer Schneider & Christopher Honeyman, (Eds.), *The Negotiator's Fieldbook* (pp. 271-276). Washington, D.C.: ABA Section on Dispute Resolution.

Jeffrey M. Senger, *Decision Analysis in Negotiation*, 87 Marq. L. Rev. 721-725 (2004).

Daniel L. Shapiro. (2006). Untapped Power: Emotions in Negotiation. In Andrea Kupfer Schneider & Christopher Honeyman (Eds.), *The Negotiator's Fieldbook* (pp. 263-269). Washington, D.C.: ABA Section on Dispute Resolution.

Donna Shestowsky. (2006). Psychology and Persuasion. In Andrea Kupfer Schneider & Christopher Honeyman (Eds.), *The Negotiator's Fieldbook* (pp. 361-370). Washington, D.C.: ABA Section on Dispute Resolution.

Chapter 5

Negotiation Law & Ethics

This chapter covers the legal and ethical issues in negotiation. The first part of the chapter briefly reviews rules regarding settlements, including a lawyer's duty to inform his or her client about settlements, when settlements can be confidential, and how settlements are enforced. The second part of the chapter examines case law on successful challenges to negotiated agreements. Part three of the chapter reviews ethical rules regarding negotiation behavior and the ethical obligations of lawyers in negotiated settlements. Finally, part four looks at different approaches to thinking about appropriate conduct for lawyers as they represent clients in negotiation.

A. RULES REGARDING NEGOTIATED SETTLEMENTS

1. Duty to Inform and Gain Approval of Settlements

A lawyer is required to inform her client of any settlement offer in a negotiation and, according to Model Rule 1.2, also must educate the client sufficiently so that the client can make an informed decision about whether to accept the offer. Model Rule 1.2 states that the lawyer must abide by the client's decisions concerning the objectives of representation, but the requirement to inform the client about settlement and to gain approval of any settlement is much more specific. In fact, lawyers have faced sanctions, including disbarment, when this particular requirement of client representation is overlooked. For example, in In re Brown, 453 P.2d 958 (Ariz. 1969), Attorney Brown failed to communicate a settlement offer to his client for $600 in a dog bite case. After the client lost (and had to pay costs and jury fees), Brown was disbarred for this and a collection of other problematic law practices. (The great movie, *The Verdict,* portrays Paul Newman turning down an offer on behalf of his clients without communicating it to them, but this is only acceptable in the movies.)

An attorney is similarly only able to accept an offer on the client's behalf when he or she has specific authorization from the client to do so. A general authorization as part of an agreement to retain the lawyer's services, for example, is insufficient. "An attorney who is clothed with no other authority than that arising from his employment as attorney has no implied authority by virtue of his general retainer to compromise and settle a claim of his client." Cross v. State, 643 P.2d 39, 43 (1982). Clients also retain the right to change their mind. *Restatement (Third) on the Law Governing Lawyers* §22(3) says the client can revoke any authorization he or she previously had given the lawyer. In re Lewis, 463 S.E.2d 862 (Ga. 1995) is an example of a client revoking the broad authorization she had previously given Lewis, her attorney, to act in her best interest. When Lewis accepted a settlement without consulting her, she repudiated the settlement and filed a complaint against Lewis. The court held that a broad authorization is not adequate; there must be specific authorization to accept a settlement offer.

2. Keeping Settlements Confidential

Another relevant body of law covering negotiation is confidentiality. As discussed further in Chapter 8, settlement discussions must be kept confidential, unless there is an evidentiary exception or contrary legal policy.

A combination of four basic mechanisms provides confidentiality protections in the context of dispute resolution (and all of these are discussed in more detail in Chapter 8).

1. Evidentiary exclusions ("If the only place you heard it was during our settlement efforts, you can't use it in court.")
2. Contract ("We have a deal to keep our mouths shut.")
3. Privilege ("You can't make me testify. You can't even make me produce information in discovery.")
4. Protective order ("Under penalty of contempt, you have to keep your mouth shut.")

Each of these mechanisms *sometimes* assures disputants that their conversations in negotiations will remain confidential.

The most pertinent law regarding settlement offers and confidentiality is Federal Rule of Evidence 408, which states that settlement discussions cannot be revealed in litigation to demonstrate liability. However, courts have differed as to the extent of protection provided by Rule 408. Compare, for example, Thomas v. Resort Health Related Facility, 539 F. Supp. 630 (E.D.N.Y. 1982), where an ex-employee's rejection of a reinstatement offer was admissible because it fell outside Rule 408, with Affiliated Mfrs. v. Alcoa, 56 F.3d 521 (3d Cir. 1995), in which the court interpreted the scope of the term "dispute" to include less formal stages of a dispute that occurred before litigation, keeping an earlier dispute confidential. Settlements themselves can also impose confidentiality as part of the agreement. In some cases such as consumer safety, sexual harassment, and similar situations, in which others might face the same danger as a settling plaintiff, this confidentiality could be troubling for public policy reasons. A recent case in California highlights this dilemma. A court reviewed (and remanded) a settlement agreement that included a "fake arbitration" in which the arbitrator would rule for the defendant and the defendant could issue a press release claiming innocence from the sexual harassment claims. After the arbitrator and the plaintiff refused to participate in the sham arbitration, the court remanded some claims back to arbitration. See Nelson v. American Apparel, (Cal App. LA County, No. BC333028) (remanding for arbitration on some issues, but not to be published in official reports, as per California's unique "de-publication" procedure), available in full text at *www.onpointnews.com/docs/charney2.pdf.* Some jurisdictions' laws limit the enforceability of confidentiality provisions in certain contexts. For more information on the confidentiality of settlements and other concerns about these issues, see Carrie Menkel-Meadow, Public Access to Private Settlements: Conflicting Legal Policies, 11 Alternatives 85 (1993) and Carrie Menkel-Meadow, Maintaining ADR Integrity, 27 (1) Alternatives 1, 7-9 (2009).

Problem 5-1. *I Want to Know!*

In what types of cases might the parties agree to confidentiality? When do you think that public policy should prohibit confidentiality?

---

3. Enforcement of Settlements

Most settlement agreements are enforced just like any other contract. Settlements, however, incorporated into court decrees (antitrust violation settlements, mass torts, class actions, and institutional reforms such as school desegregation, environmental regulation, and housing reform, as well as all cases involving minors and others who are legally incapacitated) often receive judicial oversight of their enforcement. For example, in the well-known case of Spaulding v. Zimmerman, 263 Minn. 346, 116 N.W.2d 704 (1962), the judge overturned a settlement on behalf of a minor where the defendant's doctor had not disclosed his discovery of the plaintiff's aneurysm to the plaintiff prior to settlement.

Settlements can also be overturned by a court using typical contract defenses like coercion, duress, unconscionability, and mutual mistake. These familiar contract doctrines apply in a negotiation context as well. This section highlights just two of these — duress and unconscionability — for a brief review of what you learned in your contracts class.

Duress in a negotiation has been found when there is an illegitimate use of power by one side to coerce the other side into an agreement. Coercion might derive from a threat of physical power, a threat of criminal prosecution, or even a threat to reveal unpleasant information.

Generally, unconscionability is found in situations of unequal bargaining power resulting in grossly unfair settlement terms. As the court outlined in Williams v. Walker-Thomas Furniture, 350 F. 2d 445 (D.C. Cir. 1965), where a furniture store's credit agreement with its customer was voided, "[u]nconscionability has generally been recognized to include an absence of meaningful choice on the part of one of the parties together with contract terms which are unreasonably favorable to the other party." Unconscionability is typically reviewed in two parts — procedural unconscionability and substantive unconscionability — and a court will usually look for evidence of both kinds to overturn a contract.

B. HOW LAWYERS (SHOULD) BEHAVE IN NEGOTIATIONS

As we turn to this next section of the chapter, some might legitimately ask why not have a good-faith standard in negotiations in order to regulate lawyer behavior? Good faith could require that lawyers show up for a scheduled meeting, exchange reasonable offers, and treat each other with some amount of courtesy. The problem with suggesting a good-faith standard is two-fold. First, in the negotiation context (as opposed to the mediation context discussed in Chapter 8), good faith is rather difficult to define. While it is true that courts have found violations of good faith in specific instances where parties have unreasonably delayed negotiations, failed to seek approval of an agreement, and breached an agreement, these cases are more rarities than the norm, and definitions remain vague. Second, even if we could define good faith, it is unclear that there really is any duty to engage in good-faith negotiations. Although both the UCC and *Restatement of Contracts* refer to a duty of good faith in performance, neither specifies a duty of good faith in negotiations. In one of the more famous cases finding a violation of good faith (Hoffman v. Red Owl Stores, 26 Wis. 2d 683 (1965)), the plaintiff, Mr. Hoffman, relied on and acted upon Red Owl's negotiated promises of a franchise — selling his previous business, gathering his savings, and moving to a new town — and the court found sufficient reliance on Red Owl's promises to find a violation of good faith on their part. However, only in certain narrow contexts, for example, after preliminary agreements are made or when negotiations are conducted under court order or in the labor-management context, can we generally expect that a duty to negotiate in good faith exists. In labor negotiations, although there is a duty to "bargain in good faith," under the National Labor Relations Act, 29 U.S.C. §§151 *et seq.*, decisional law has made it rare and unlikely for courts to actually review whether the parties have substantively engaged with each other, except in certain limited "mandatory bargaining" areas, and limiting some unilateral negotiation behaviors (such as "Boulwarism"[1] or take it or leave it offers).

Instead, negotiation behavior is more often constrained through ethics rules and case law concerning fraud or deceit. There are, in fact, numerous cases in which the law has regulated negotiation behavior, often by refusing enforcement of an agreement reached by fraud, involving some form of deceit, or containing elements that are unconscionable. Whereas existing ethics rules regarding negotiation seem to leave some room for strategic behavior and deception, the negotiation lawyer who

---

1. Named for Lemeul R. Boulware of General Electric who used this practice in collective bargaining negotiations, which was held to be an unfair labor practice, NLRB v. General Electric Co., 418 F.2d 736 (2d Cir. 1969), *cert. denied*, 397 U.S. 965 (1970)

relies solely on those interpretations will be in trouble. The common law requires truthfulness in many elements of negotiation. The deceptive negotiator lies, deceives, or misrepresents at the risk of having a negotiated agreement later declared unenforceable, with sanctions against the lawyer (and the client) also possible. This next excerpt outlines some of the issues for lawyers' behavior in negotiation.

 Carrie Menkel-Meadow, **WHAT'S FAIR IN NEGOTIATION? WHAT IS ETHICS IN NEGOTIATION?**

in What's Fair: Ethics for Negotiators xiii-xvi (Carrie Menkel-Meadow & Michael Wheeler eds., 2004)

What do we owe other human beings when we negotiate for something that we or our clients want? How should we behave toward our "adversaries" — opponents, partners, clients, friends, family members, strangers, third parties and future generations — when we know what we do affects them, beneficially, adversely or unpredictably? How do we think about the other people we interact with in negotiations? Are they just means to our ends or people like us, deserving of respect or aid (depending on whether they are our equals or more or less enabled than ourselves)? How do we conceive of our goals when we approach others to help us accomplish together what we cannot do alone?

Perhaps after the question "What should I do?" in negotiation (seeking strategic or behavioral advice), the next most frequently asked question is, "What may I do?" (seeking advice, permission, or approval for particular goals, strategies, and tactics that comprise both the conceptualizations and behaviors of the human strategic interaction that we call negotiation). . . .

"What's fair" in negotiation is a complex and multi-faceted question, asking us to consider negotiation ethics on many different levels simultaneously. First, there are the concerns of the individual negotiator: What do I aspire to? How do I judge my own goals and behavior? What may I do? How will others judge me (my counterpart in a two-party negotiation, others in a multi-lateral negotiation, those with whom I might do business in the future, those who will learn of and judge my behavior or results in any negotiation that might become more public than the involved parties)? How do I calibrate my actions to those of the others with whom I am dealing? (Should I have a "relative" ethics that is sensitive, responsive, or malleable to the context, circumstances, customs or personalities of the situation at hand?) What limits are there on my goals and behavior, set from within (the "mirror" test [how do I appear to myself at the end of the day?]) or without, either informally, (the "videotape test" [what would my mother, teacher, spouse, child or clergy person think of me if they could watch this?]) or formally (rules, laws, ethics standards, religious or moral principles to which I must or choose to adhere)? With what sensibility should I approach each negotiation I undertake?

For those who negotiate as agents, there is the added dimension of what duty is owed a client or principal. When do agent and principal goals properly align? When are they different . . . and how are differences to be reconciled? When do legal rules (like the creation of fiduciary relationships) define the limits and obligations of negotiator-principal interactions?

Third, there is the question of duty, responsibility or relationship to the Other (call him "counterpart," "opponent," "adversary," "partner," "boss" or "subordinate," spouse, lover, child or parent). . . . Do we follow some version of the Golden Rule and treat others as we would hope to be treated by them (a norm of aspirational reciprocity), or does the Golden Rule tarnish a bit on application in particular contexts? . . .

How do those outside of a negotiation judge its ethical "externalities" or social effects? Has a particular negotiation done more good than harm? For those inside the negotiation? Those affected by it (employees, shareholders, vendors and clients, consumers and the public)? And, to what extent must any negotiation be morally accountable for impacts on third parties (children in a divorce, customers in labor-management negotiation, similarly situated claimants in mass torts and for its intergenerational effects (future generations in environmental disputes)?

In this chapter, we address some of these questions by examining formal rules, standards, case law, and other sources of ethical guidance on negotiation behavior. But, as you will learn, formal standards do not cover many situations, and some rules may seem to contradict other rules, so that, in the end, you will form your own ethical practice and reputation as a negotiator.

RESTATEMENT (SECOND) OF TORTS §525 (1977)

§525   Liability for Fraudulent Misrepresentation

One who fraudulently makes a misrepresentation of fact, opinion, intention or law for the purpose of inducing another to act or to refrain from action in reliance upon it, is subject to liability to the other in deceit for pecuniary loss caused to him by his justifiable reliance upon the misrepresentation.

RESTATEMENT (SECOND) OF CONTRACTS §§161, 164 (1981)

§161   When Non-Disclosure Is Equivalent to an Assertion

A person's non-disclosure of a fact known to him is equivalent to an assertion that the fact does not exist in the following cases only:

(a) where he knows that disclosure of the fact is necessary to prevent some previous assertion from being a misrepresentation or from being fraudulent or material.

(b) where he knows that disclosure of the fact would correct a mistake of the other party as to a basic assumption on which that party is making the contract and if non-disclosure of the fact amounts to a failure to act in good faith and in accordance with reasonable standards of fair dealing.

(c) where he knows that disclosure of the fact would correct a mistake of the other party as to the contents or effect of a writing, evidencing or embodying an agreement in whole or in part.

(d) where the other person is entitled to know the fact because of a relation of trust and confidence between them.

§164   When a Misrepresentation Makes a Contract Voidable

(1) If a party's manifestation of assent is induced by either a fraudulent or material misrepresentation by the other party upon which the recipient is justified in relying, the contract is voidable by the recipient. . . .

Understanding the definition of a fraudulent statement is useful, but what does this mean for a practicing attorney? Examining court cases can further clarify and define the elements of misrepresentation, material fact, reliance, and damages.

1. Misrepresentation

A misrepresentation clearly includes a deliberate lie. The law, however, goes further so that uncorrected mistakes are also included under knowing misrepresentation.

 STARE v. TATE

---

21 Cal. App. 3d 432, 98 Cal. Rptr. 264 (1971)

Justice KAUS delivered the Opinion of the Court. . . .

FACTS

The agreement in question was signed by both parties on February 21, 1968. . . .

In the negotiations both sides apparently agreed that the community property was to be evenly divided. They did not agree, however, on the value of certain items and on the community property status of certain stocks which stood in the husband's name alone.

These disagreements centered principally on items which, it was understood, were to be retained by the husband. . . .

In January, 1968, Joan's attorney prepared a document entitled "SECOND PROPOSAL FOR A BASIS OF SETTLEMENT — TATE v. TATE" which, among other things, arrived at a suggested figure of $70,081.85 for the value of Joan's share in the Holt property. This value was arrived at by a computation set forth in the proposal. It is copied in the footnote.[2]

---

2. "888 East Holt Avenue, Pomona
(Note: value as per previous offer)

Total value	$550,000.00
Less encumbrance	−308,362.99
Net value	$141,637.01
One-half community	$70,081.85"

It is obvious that Joan's attorney arrived at the figure of $70,081.85 for the community equity in the property only by making two substantial errors. First, the net value after deducting the encumbrances from the asserted gross value of $550,000 is $241,637.01, not $141,637.01; second, one-half of $141,637.01 is substantially more than $70,081.85. The correct figure for the equity should have been $120,818.50 or, roughly $50,000 more.

The mistake did not escape Tim's accountant who discovered it while helping Tim's attorney in preparing a counter-offer. He brought it to the attention of the attorney who, in his own words, reacted as follows:

"I told him that I had been arguing with [the wife's attorney] to use the value that was on the real property tax statement, but I knew that that was low and [he] would never go for it, that the appraisal had been $425,000.00 when the building had been purchased by said owners, and I thought that until we got it, that we would use something like a $450,000.00 value, and he said, 'Fine.' It is my recollection that I said to him, 'You know, you might as well use the figure that Walker has there because his mistake is a hundred thousand dollars and we value it at a hundred thousand dollars less, so it is basically the same thing, so give it a $70,000.00 equity.' And that is what he did and that is how it came about."

A counter-offer was then submitted to Joan and her lawyer. It lists all of the community assets, with the property in question being valued at $70,082.00, rounding up the erroneous figure in Joan's offer to the nearest dollar. There can be no reasonable doubt that the counter-offer was prepared in a way designed to minimize the danger that Joan or her attorney would discover the mistake. . . .

On February 16, 1968, the parties and their attorneys had a settlement conference. The counter-offer was the basis for the discussion. There was no mention that the figure of $70,082 for the equity in the Holt property was based on an agreed value of $550,000 or any other figure. . . .

The mistake might never have come to light had not Tim desired to have that exquisite last word. A few days after Joan had obtained the divorce he mailed her a copy of the offer which contained the errant computation. On top of the page he wrote with evident satisfaction: "PLEASE NOTE $100,000.00 MISTAKE IN YOUR FIGURES. . . . " The present action was filed exactly one month later. . . .

DISCUSSION

There is really no substantial conflict in the evidence and it is hard to understand how the trial court could do anything but grant Joan's prayer for relief.

Section 3399 of the Civil Code provides:

> "When, through fraud or a mutual mistake of the parties, *or a mistake of one party, which the other at the time knew or suspected,* a written contract does not truly express the intention of the parties, it may be revised on the application of a party aggrieved, so as to express that intention, so far as it can be done without prejudice to rights acquired by third persons, in good faith and for value." (Emphasis added.)

Clearly there was a mistake, Joan and her attorney thinking that a $550,000 value resulted in a community equity about $70,000. . . . Inasmuch as the error was discovered by Tim's attorney, it is, of course, no defense that it was negligently made by Joan's attorney. . . .

The case was fully tried and, as we said at the outset of our discussion, the record supports nothing but a judgment for the plaintiff as prayed.

The judgment is reversed with directions to make findings and conclusions and to enter a judgment in conformity with this opinion.

Problem 5-2.   *Misrepresentation & Mistake*

What if the mistake in *Stare v. Tate* had been a mistake of law rather than of math? Is there a duty to correct this? What about a situation when one side intentionally shields itself from the truth so that it does not "know"?

---

2. Omissions

Many negotiators' instincts may be that they can't be found liable for misrepresentation if they merely remain silent. However, omissions *can* be fraudulent, as outlined in *Restatement Second (Contracts)* §161. This next excerpt reviews the four exceptions outlined in the *Restatement* and further explains a lawyer's duties in negotiation.

  G. Richard Shell, **BARGAINING FOR ADVANTAGE: NEGOTIATION STRATEGIES FOR REASONABLE PEOPLE**

208-209 (1999)

Surprisingly, there are circumstances when it may be fraudulent to keep your peace about an issue *even if the other side does not ask about it.* When does a negotiator have a duty to voluntarily disclose matters that may hurt his bargaining position? American law imposes affirmative disclosure duties in the following four circumstances:

1. *When the negotiator makes a partial disclosure that is or becomes misleading in light of all the facts.* If you say your company is profitable, you may be under a duty to disclose whether you used questionable accounting techniques to arrive at that statement. You should also update your prior statement if you show a loss in the next quarter and negotiations are still ongoing.

2. *When the parties stand in a fiduciary relationship to each other.* In negotiations between trustees and beneficiaries, partners in a partnership, shareholders in a small corporation, or members of a family business, parties may have a duty of complete candor and cannot rely on the "be silent and be safe" approach.

3. *When the nondisclosing party has vital information about the transaction not accessible to the other side.* A recent case applying this exception held that an employer owed a duty of disclosure to a prospective employee to disclose contingency plans for shutting down the project for which the employee was hired. In general, sellers

have a greater duty to disclose hidden defects about their property than buyers do to disclose "hidden treasure" that may be buried there. Thus, a home seller must disclose termite infestation in her home,[3] but an oil company need not voluntarily disclose that there is oil on a farmer's land when negotiating to purchase it.[4] This is a slippery exception; the best test is one of conscience and fairness.

4. *When special codified disclosure duties, such as those regarding contracts of insurance or public offerings of securities, apply.* Legislatures sometimes impose special disclosure duties for particular kinds of transactions. In the United States, for example, many states now require home sellers to disclose all known problems with their houses.

If none of these four exceptions applies, neither side is likely to be found liable for fraud based on a nondisclosure. Each party can remain silent, passively letting the other proceed under its own assumptions.

Problem 5-3.   *Sellers or Buyers Beware?*

Do you think home buyers should carefully inspect and inquire or that sellers with "superior information" should inform regarding non-obvious defects connected with house sales?

If your neighbors are unpleasant, are you required to reveal this to potential purchasers of your house? If your neighbors belong to a rock band that practices late into the night, are you required to disclose this? If you are selling a home in which a murder occurred, are you required to reveal this?

In Reed v. King, 145 Cal. App. 3d 261 (1983), the seller of a house who represented it as fit for an elderly woman living alone had a duty to disclose that the house was the site of a multiple murder ten years ago!

An example of an omitted fact deemed a material misrepresentation arose in the case of Kentucky Bar Ass'n v. Geisler, 938 S.W.2d 578 (Ky. 1997). Geisler represented a pedestrian who was struck by an automobile. In the course of Geisler's negotiations with defense counsel, Geisler's client died. The attorneys eventually reached a settlement, but only following the settlement did the defendants learn that Geisler's client had died. When she faced a Bar disciplinary action, Geisler argued that she was under no affirmative duty to disclose the information and that the information was immaterial. The Supreme Court of Kentucky was unmoved by these arguments. It found the client's death to be plainly material to the settlement of a tort claim for injuries to the client. Citing the Kentucky equivalent of Model Rule 4.1, it also pointed out that "misrepresentations can occur by failure to act." In issuing its order publicly reprimanding Geisler and ordering her to pay the costs associated with her reprimand, the Kentucky Supreme Court wrote:

---

3. See, e.g., Miles v. McSwegin, 388 N.E.2d 1367 (Ohio 1979).
4. See, e.g., Zaschak v. Travers Corp., 333 N.W.2d 191 (Mich. App. 1983).

[T]his Court fails to understand why guidelines are needed for an attorney to understand that when their client dies, they are under an obligation to tell opposing counsel such information. This seems to be a matter of common ethics and just plain sense. However, because attorneys such as respondent cannot discern such matters and require written guidelines so as to figure out their ethical convictions, this Court [affirms the ABA Formal Opinion on this matter].

3. Material Facts

In examining whether action or inaction amounts to fraud, it is also important whether the facts under discussion are material. In negotiations in which puffing and bluffing are seen as part of the game, could a lawyer get in trouble for stretching too far? The answer is that it depends on what you are talking about in the negotiation. When the parties are of equal bargaining power, courts have permitted a certain amount of puffing and predictions of quality. The following case highlights some traditional ways that courts have examined sales promises.

 VULCAN METALS CO. v. SIMMONS MANUFACTURING CO.

248 F. 853, 856-857 (2d Cir. 1918)

Judge Learned HAND delivered the Opinion of the Court.

The first question is of the misrepresentations touching the quality and powers of the patented machine. These were general commendations, or, in so far as they included any specific facts, were not disproved; e.g., that the cleaner would produce 18 inches of vacuum with 25 pounds water pressure. They raise, therefore, the question of law how far general "puffing" or "dealers' talk" can be the basis of an action for deceit.

The conceded exception in such cases has generally rested upon the distinction between "opinion" and "fact"; but that distinction has not escaped the criticism it deserves. An opinion is a fact, and it may be a very relevant fact; the expression of an opinion is the assertion of a belief, and any rule which condones the expression of a consciously false opinion condones a consciously false statement of fact. When the parties are so situated that the buyer may reasonably rely upon the expression of the seller's opinion, it is no excuse to give a false one. And so it makes much difference whether the parties stand "on an equality." For example, we should treat very differently the expressed opinion of a chemist to a layman about the properties of a composition from the same opinion between chemist and chemist, when the buyer had full opportunity to examine. The reason of the rule lies, we think, in this: There are some kinds of talk which no sensible man takes seriously, and if he does he suffers from his credulity. If we were all scrupulously honest, it would not be so; but, as it is, neither party usually believes what the seller says about his own opinions, and each knows it. Such statements, like the claims of campaign managers before election, are rather designed to allay the suspicion which would attend their absence than to be understood as having any relation to objective truth. It is quite true that they induce a compliant temper in the buyer, but it is by a much more subtle process than through the acceptance of his claims for his wares. . . .

In the case at bar, since the buyer was allowed full opportunity to examine the cleaner and to test it out, we put the parties upon an equality. It seems to us that general statements as to what the cleaner would do, even though consciously false, were not of a kind to be taken literally by the buyer. As between manufacturer and customer, it may not be so; but this was the case of taking over a business, after ample chance to investigate. Such a buyer, who the seller rightly expects will undertake an independent and adequate inquiry into the actual merits of what he gets, has no right to treat as material in his determination statements like these. . . . We therefore think that the District Court was right in disregarding all these misrepresentations.

As respects the representation that the cleaners had never been put upon the market or offered for sale, the rule does not apply; nor can we agree that such representations could not have been material to Freeman's decision to accept the contract. The actual test of experience in their sale might well be of critical consequence in his decision to buy the business, and the jury would certainly have the right to accept his statement that his reliance upon these representations was determinative of his final decision. . . .

Problem 5-4.   *Types of Lies*

1. What type of lie was the lie about whether the vacuum cleaners had been *marketed*? Do you agree with the court that this type of lie should be illegal? What was the court's reasoning?
2. What type of lie was the lie about the *performance* of the vacuum cleaners? Do you agree with the court that this type of lie should be permitted (and expected)? What was the court's reasoning?

Courts have distinguished between opinion and fact as a way to determine when there is material misrepresentation of fact. A demand — "my client will only accept X" — is not deemed to be material as a matter of law. This type of statement is seen as an opinion rather than fact. Similarly, the reservation price — "my client won't settle for less than X" — is also viewed as an opinion. However, other types of tactics in a negotiation could be problematic if you start to inflate your own alternatives. The following case is a good example of what can happen with too much bluffing.

BEAVERS v. LAMPLIGHTERS REALTY

556 P.2d 1328, 1329-1331 (Okla. Ct. App. 1976)

BRIGHTMIRE, Judge.

It was sometime in January 1974 plaintiff saw a Lamplighters' for sale sign in front of an attractive Spanish style house at 4912 Larissa Lane. He liked the storybook looks of the abode, called the telephone number printed on the sign, and eventually was shown the house by agent Norma Ray. Shortly thereafter, on February 11, 1974, plaintiff's offer of $34,500 for the dwelling was rejected.

Plaintiff still wanted the place, however. He let a day or two pass and again called Lamplighters. This time a "Mr. Taylor came on the phone" and asked if plaintiff was still interested in the home. "Yes," said plaintiff, "but doggone it . . . they were asking too much."

"If you are going to do anything, you had better do it pretty quick, because I've got a buyer for it," said the realtor.

"You do?" responded plaintiff.

"Yes," said Taylor, "it [is] the original builder and he is coming in."

"Paul Good?" asked plaintiff.

"Yes," answered Taylor, adding that Good was coming in with a check right away.

"How much is it?" plaintiff asked concerning the check.

"Thirty-seven thousand dollars" was the answer.

"Well, he's bought it."

"No," retreated Taylor, "[i]f you want to put in a bid, he's going to be here within the hour. I just talked to him."

The high pressure tactic worked. Said plaintiff, "I [don't] know whether 'panicked' [is] the [right] word or not, but I figured . . . that [if] the original builder would pay thirty-seven thousand for the home, that maybe . . . it absolutely should be worth that much to me . . . and I just increased it [the fictitious offer] two hundred and fifty dollars. And the next thing I know I bought myself a home" for $37,250 by executing a contract dated February 15, 1974.

It was a while before plaintiff found out he had been a victim of a gross deception. One day, after he had moved into the house — and found, incidentally, that the agent Ray had made false representations about the condition of the house, requiring him to expend about $6,000 for repairs — he chanced to meet builder Paul Good at a neighbor's home, got to talking to him about plaintiff's house and came upon some interesting facts. Good said he had earlier looked at the house "but it was out of the ball park as far as he was concerned" and that he "would have given in the . . . lower thirties."

"Well," said plaintiff, "I'd offered thirty-four five to start."

"That should have bought it," said Good.

"Didn't you offer thirty-seven thousand?" plaintiff asked Good.

"No," he answered. . . .

In the instant case the evidence so far adduced establishes that realtor Taylor, upon becoming aware of plaintiff's desire for the Spanish villa, undertook to bring about a rather rapid resolution of the price problem by using, as it were, a dynamite sales technique to blast an immediate positive response out of plaintiff. The deliberate lie did indeed achieve the intended and expected effect and induced plaintiff to purchase the property for a figure higher than he would have had to pay absent the fraud. [The court held that this was fraudulent inducement.]

Problem 5-5. *Going Too Far or Right On!*

Does the court in *Beavers* set the bar too high? In Kabatchnick v. Hanover–Elm Bldg. Corp., 103 N.E.2d 692 (Mass. 1952), another court held that a landlord's lie that he had another, much higher, offer to rent was fraud. If you were selling a home and wanted to make it look like it was very popular and likely to be sold soon, what might you say to a potential buyer without risking violating the law?

C. ETHICAL RULES

In addition to case law on misrepresentation, ethical rules provide guidelines for how lawyers should behave in negotiations. Below, we have excerpted a selection from the Delaware Lawyers' Rules of Professional Conduct, which mirror the Model Rules of Professional Conduct. But please refer to the applicable rules in your own state. In the selection that follows, Carrie Menkel-Meadow reviews the most important of these rules and explains the impact of these ethical rules on negotiation conduct.

RULE 1.2   SCOPE OF REPRESENTATION

(a) [A] lawyer shall abide by a client's decisions concerning the objectives of representation and . . . shall consult with the client as to the means by which they are to be pursued. A lawyer shall abide by a client's decision whether to settle a matter. . . .

(d) A lawyer shall not counsel a client to engage, or assist a client, in conduct that the lawyer knows is criminal or fraudulent, but a lawyer may discuss the legal consequences of any proposed course of conduct with a client and may counsel or assist a client to make a good faith effort to determine the validity, scope, meaning or application of the law.

RULE 1.4 COMMUNICATION

(a) A lawyer shall:

(3) keep the client reasonably informed about the status of the matter;

(b) A lawyer shall explain a matter to the extent reasonably necessary to permit the client to make informed decisions regarding the representation.

RULE 1.6 CONFIDENTIALITY OF INFORMATION

(a) A lawyer shall not reveal information relating to the representation of a client unless the client gives informed consent, the disclosure is impliedly authorized in order to carry out the representation, or the disclosure is permitted by paragraph (b).

(b) A lawyer may reveal information relating to the representation of a client to the extent the lawyer reasonably believes necessary:

(1) to prevent reasonably certain death or substantial bodily harm; . . .

(2) to prevent the client from committing a crime or fraud that is reasonably certain to result in substantial injury to the financial interest or property of another and in furtherance of which the client has used or is using the lawyer's services; . . .

(5) to establish a claim or defense on behalf of the lawyer in a controversy between the lawyer and the client, to establish a defense to a criminal charge or civil claim against the lawyer based upon conduct in which the client was involved, or to respond to allegations in any proceeding concerning the lawyer's representation of the client;

RULE 4.1 TRUTHFULNESS IN STATEMENTS TO OTHERS

In the course of representing a client a lawyer shall not knowingly:

(a) make a false statement of material fact or law to a third person; or

(b) fail to disclose a material fact when disclosure is necessary to avoid assisting a criminal or fraudulent act by a client, unless disclosure is prohibited by Rule 1.6.

COMMENT

Misrepresentation

[1] A lawyer is required to be truthful when dealing with others on a client's behalf, but generally has no affirmative duty to inform an opposing party of relevant facts. A misrepresentation

can occur if the lawyer incorporates or affirms a statement of another person that the lawyer knows is false. Misrepresentations can also occur by partially true but misleading statements or omissions that are the equivalent of affirmative false statements. For dishonest conduct that does not amount to a false statement or for misrepresentations by a lawyer other than in the course of representing a client, see Rule 8.4.

Statements of Fact

[2] This Rule refers to statements of fact. Whether a particular statement should be regarded as one of fact can depend on the circumstances. Under generally accepted conventions in negotiation, certain types of statements ordinarily are not taken as statements of material fact. Estimates of price or value placed on the subject of a transaction and a party's intentions as to an acceptable settlement of a claim are ordinarily in this category, and so is the existence of an undisclosed principal except where nondisclosure of the principal would constitute fraud. Lawyers should be mindful of their obligations under applicable law to avoid criminal and tortious misrepresentation.

Crime or Fraud by Client

[3] Under Rule 1.2(d), a lawyer is prohibited from counseling or assisting a client in conduct that the lawyer knows is criminal or fraudulent. Paragraph (b) states a specific application of the principle set forth in Rule 1.2(d) and addresses the situation where a client's crime or fraud takes the form of a lie or misrepresentation. Ordinarily, a lawyer can avoid assisting a client's crime or fraud by withdrawing from the representation. Sometimes it may be necessary for the lawyer to give notice of the fact of withdrawal and to disaffirm an opinion, document, affirmation or the like. In extreme cases, substantive law may require a lawyer to disclose information relating to the representation to avoid being deemed to have assisted the client's crime or fraud. If the lawyer can avoid assisting a client's crime or fraud only by disclosing this information, then under paragraph (b) the lawyer is required to do so, unless the disclosure is prohibited by Rule 1.6.

RULE 4.4   RESPECT FOR RIGHTS OF THIRD PERSONS

(a) In representing a client, a lawyer shall not use means that have no substantial purpose other than to embarrass, delay or burden a third person, or use methods of obtaining evidence that violate the legal rights of such a person.

RULE 5.6   RESTRICTIONS ON RIGHT TO PRACTICE

A lawyer shall not participate in offering or making:

(a) a partnership, shareholders, operating, employment, or other similar type of agreement that restricts the rights of a lawyer to practice after termination of the relationship, except an agreement concerning benefits upon retirement; or

(b) an agreement in which a restriction on the lawyer's right to practice is part of the settlement of a client controversy.

RULE 8.3   REPORTING PROFESSIONAL MISCONDUCT

(a) A lawyer who knows that another lawyer has committed a violation of the Rules of Professional Conduct that raises a substantial question as to that lawyer's honesty, trustworthiness or fitness as a lawyer in other respects, shall inform the appropriate professional authority.

(b) A lawyer who knows that a judge has committed a violation of applicable rules of judicial conduct that raises a substantial question as to the judge's fitness for office shall inform the appropriate authority.

(c) This Rule does not require disclosure of information otherwise protected by Rule 1.6.

RULE 8.4   MISCONDUCT

It is professional misconduct for a lawyer to:

(a) violate or attempt to violate the Rules of Professional Conduct, knowingly assist or induce another to do so or do so through the acts of another; . . .

(c) engage in conduct involving dishonesty, fraud, deceit or misrepresentation;

(d) engage in conduct that is prejudicial to the administration of justice;

 Carrie Menkel-Meadow, **ETHICS, MORALITY AND PROFESSIONAL RESPONSIBILITY IN NEGOTIATION**

in Dispute Resolution Ethics 131-139 (Phyllis Bernard & Bryant Garth eds., 2002)

Most discussions of negotiation ethics begin with Model Rule of Professional Conduct 4.1(a) and (b) which provides that a lawyer shall not, in the course of representing a client,

> make a false statement of material fact or law to a third person; or fail to disclose a material fact to a third person when disclosure is necessary to avoid assisting a criminal or fraudulent act by a client, unless disclosure is prohibited by Model Rule 1.6 [client confidentiality rule].

What the black-letter rule appears to require (a fair amount of candor) is in fact greatly modified by the Comments. For example, Comment 2 states that this rule applies only to "statements of fact," and "whether a particular statement should be regarded as one of fact can depend on the circumstances." "Opinions" (of value, of interpretations of facts or of case law) are not considered "facts" under this rubric. Most significantly, the Comment goes on to exempt from the operation of the rule three particular kinds of statements made in negotiation. According to the Comment, there are "generally accepted conventions in negotiation" (a nod to the sociological phenomenology of negotiation) in which no one really expects the "truth" because these statements are not "material" statements of fact. These are (1) estimates of price or value placed on the subject of the transaction, (2) a party's intentions as to an acceptable settlement of a claim and (3) the existence of an undisclosed principal, except where non-disclosure of the principal would otherwise (by other law) constitute fraud.

Thus, the exception in the Comment defines away, as not material, several key notions of how negotiations are conducted, including inflated offers and demands (otherwise known as "puffing" and "exaggeration"), failure to disclose "bottom lines" or "reservation prices," and non-disclosure of a principal (say Donald Trump or Harvard University) where knowledge of who the principal is might raise a price or demand, on the assumption that the principal has deep pockets. In addition, as discussed more fully below, Comment 1 suggests that while a negotiating lawyer "is required to be truthful when dealing with others on a client's behalf," a lawyer does not have an *affirmative duty* to inform an opposing party of relevant facts (subject to some further qualifications that failure to act or to correct may sometimes constitute a misrepresentation and that substantive law may, in fact, sometimes require affirmative disclosure — see Comment 3).

A simple reading of these provisions demonstrates how indeterminate and unhelpful the formal rules of professional responsibility are. First, the claim that there are "generally accepted conventions" is an empirical one, without substantiation in the text of the Comments. Who, in fact, generally "accepts" these conventions? All lawyers? Lawyers who subscribe to the conventional, adversarial and distributive models of negotiation? Many lawyers would probably "accept" even more classes of "untruthful" or less-than-full-disclosure statement in negotiations. . . .

In an important test of these "generally accepted conventions," Larry Lempert asked 15 legal and ethics experts how — under these rules — they would resolve several important disclosure dilemmas, including lying about authorized limits given by the client, lying about the extent of a personal injury as a plaintiff's lawyer during a litigation negotiation, exaggerating an emotional distress claim in a torts negotiation, and failing to correct the other side's misimpression about the extent of injuries. Not surprisingly, there was relatively little consensus among the experts about how far a lawyer-negotiator could go in lying about, deceiving or misrepresenting these issues, all of which could be argued to be within the three "generally accepted conventions" excluded from the general non-misrepresentation rule.

Recently, I have added to this list the following negotiator's ethical dilemmas in a variety of lawyer-negotiator ethics CLE programs. Consider what you would do in the following situations, in addition to those four listed above.

1. Just before the closing of a sale of a closely held business, a major client of the business terminates a long-term commercial relationship, thereby lessening the value of the firm being purchased and you represent the seller. Do you disclose this information to the buyer?

2. On the morning of a scheduled negotiation about a litigation matter, you receive notice that your request for a summary judgment has been denied. The lawyer for the other side is coming to your office and clearly has no notice of the judge's ruling. Do you disclose it before negotiating or seek to "close the deal" quickly with an offer before the other side finds out about the summary judgment decision?

3. You receive, by mistake, a fax addressed to all of the counsel on the other side of a multi-party litigation. It contains important and damaging-to-the-other-side information that would enhance your bargaining position. What do you do? . . .

7. In a hotly contested contractual negotiation the other side demanded the inclusion of a particular clause that your client did not want to agree to but finally did when it was made a "deal-breaker." The final draft of the contract, prepared by the other side, arrives at your office without the disputed clause, which you know the other side really wants included in the final deal. What do you do? . . .

Remarkably, time after time, use of these hypotheticals reveals exactly the opposite of what Comment 2 to Model Rule 4.1 so baldly states. In my experience, there are virtually no "generally accepted conventions" with respect to what should be done in these situations. Different negotiators bring to the table different assumptions of what they are trying to do, and with those assumptions come different ethical orientations.

Thus, for those who are "tough negotiators" or who see legal negotiation as an individual maximization game, whether in the litigation or transactional context, most of the deceptions above can be justified by reference either to "expectations" about how the legal-negotiation game is played, or to the lawyer's obligation to be a zealous advocate and not to "do the work" of the other side. For those lawyers who are concerned about making a good agreement "stick" — the instrumentalists — some disclosure is considered desirable (for example, in the scenarios above that describe the omission of a contract provision or the failure to correct misimpressions) because of a concern that some failures to disclose might lead to a post-hoc attack on the agreement (fraud, negligent misrepresentation, unilateral mistake).

Still others regard negotiations as opportunities for problems to be solved and so are more likely to thoughtfully consider the later impact of doing some of the things suggested above. These lawyers ask questions such as these: What would be gained or lost by revealing to the landlord's lawyer that you know he is lying? How can you honestly return the helpful fax and honestly disclose what you now know, but perhaps shouldn't use? When should clients be consulted about these ethical choices, as Model Rule 1.2 suggests they should be, at least about some matters? And those who value their reputations and/or see negotiations as a method for achieving some modicum of justice outside of courtrooms or in deals would disclose (as some ethics opinions and fraud cases say they must) the omitted contract clause and the diminished value of the purchased company (is it a material matter?).

Thus, there are no "generally accepted conventions" in negotiation practice, especially as more and more lawyers and law students are trained in the newer canon of *Getting to YES*, collaborative, integrative and problem-solving negotiation models. Who decides what "generally accepted conventions" are? The drafters of the ethics rules, without empirical verification? And, more importantly, why should "generally accepted conventions" prevail in an ethics code? Are we looking at "generally accepted conventions" in other areas of the Rules? . . . The answer is usually "no" — we require lawyers appearing before tribunals to reveal adverse authority without regard to what "accepted conventions" of advocacy might suggest, e.g. that each side should do its own research and it is up to the judge or her clerk to find the cases. . . .

Do Lawyers Do the Right Thing in Practice?

[A] certain degree of dissembling and misdirection is to be expected in the negotiation realm. Consistent with these expectations, Model Rule 4.1 legitimizes some deceitful negotiation techniques and only prohibits fraudulent misrepresentations about material matters. Rule 4.1's truthfulness standard has been a fertile topic of discussion since its adoption. . . .

[W]e surveyed 734 practicing lawyers and asked them what they would do if a client asked them to assist him in a fraudulent pre-litigation settlement scheme. [The plaintiff asked the lawyer to not reveal his current healthy disease-free status when the other side wrongly assumed that she was responsible for infecting him with a fake deadly disease.] Nearly one-third indicated they would agree to one of the client's two requests to engage in the fraudulent scheme. Half of the respondents indicated that they would refuse both of the client's overtures. And the remaining twenty percent of respondents either indicated that they were not sure how to respond to both requests or refused one request and indicated that they were not sure how they would respond to the other request. . . .

[T]he study explored the respondents' reasons for agreeing or disagreeing with the client's requests. . . . First, there appears to be substantial misunderstanding as to what constitutes a misrepresentation, the standard that sets the boundary between acceptable and unacceptable negotiation behavior under the Rule. Second, the findings suggest substantial confusion surrounding the rule's operative term "material fact." Third, the respondents who agreed to the client's most egregious request appear to believe that other legal rules, including other portions of the Model Rules, either gave them permission or required them to engage in the fraudulent scheme.

Art Hinshaw & Jess K. Alberts, Doing the Right Thing: An Empirical Study of Attorney Negotiation Ethics, 16 Harvard Negotiation Law Review (forthcoming, 2011)

Model Rule 4.1, however, is not the only rule that might be seen to govern negotiation ethics. Model Rule 1.2, defining the scope of legal representation, has implications for negotiation behavior in several respects. First, Model Rule 1.2

provides for allocation of decision-making responsibility between lawyers and clients in any representation. Clients are to make decisions about the "objectives of representation," and lawyers, in consultation with clients, may make decisions about the "means" of representation. Some states now require, and others recommend, that this consultation about "means" should include counseling about and consideration of the forms of dispute resolution that should be considered in any representation, including negotiation, mediation, arbitration or other forms of "appropriate dispute resolution." Some might think that such consideration of "means" should extend to the different models of negotiation or different strategies now possible within the growing sophistication about different approaches to negotiation.

Second, and most importantly, Model Rule 1.2 requires the lawyer to "abide by a client's decision whether to settle a matter" and thus requires the lawyer to transmit settlement offers to the client, especially in conjunction with the requirements of Model Rule 1.4(a) that a lawyer "shall keep the client reasonably informed about the status of the matter" and Model Rule 1.4(b) that a lawyer "shall explain a matter to the extent reasonably necessary to permit the client to make informed decisions regarding the representation." Model Rule 1.2(d) also admonishes lawyers not to counsel a client to engage in and not to assist the client in conduct the lawyer knows is fraudulent or criminal, and thus, once again, the Rule implicates the substantive law of fraud and crimes. Lawyers may not assist clients in such activities, and thus, what constitutes a misrepresentation in a negotiation is dependent on tort and criminal law, outside the rules of professional responsibility. The lawyer may, then, be more restricted in 1.2(d) by what other laws prohibit clients from doing than by what the lawyer might be restricted from in 4.1.

Beyond these more specific requirements, Model Rules 8.3 and 8.4 can be and have been invoked with respect to the lawyer's duty to be honest and fair in negotiation. Model Rule 8.4 states that "it is professional misconduct for a lawyer to . . . (c) engage in conduct involving dishonesty, fraud, deceit or misrepresentation," once again incorporating by reference not only substantive standards of legal fraud and misrepresentation, but also suggesting that certain forms of dishonesty or breach of trust or "serious interference with the administration of justice" (especially when a "pattern of repeated offenses" exists) may subject a lawyer to discipline for his deceptive or other fraudulent actions in negotiations. Model Rule 8.3 requires a lawyer who "knows that another lawyer has committed a violation of the Rules of Professional Conduct that raises a substantial question as to the lawyer's honesty, trustworthiness or fitness as a lawyer" to report such misconduct to the appropriate professional authority. Thus, lawyers who repeatedly deceive or play some versions of negotiation "hardball" or "hide and seek" may be subject to discipline for their professional misconduct, though such misconduct is rarely reported.

Several other ethics rules, seldom invoked, also have possible applicability to the conduct of negotiations. Model Rule 4.4 prohibits lawyers from using means that have "no substantial purpose other than to embarrass, delay, or burden a third person," and thus requires lawyers to exercise some degree of "care" toward third parties (such as opposing parties in a negotiation, whether in litigation or transactional settings).

Finally, Model Rule 5.6 prohibits any agreement "in which a restriction on the lawyer's right to practice is part of the settlement of a client controversy." This section is intended to prevent a common practice of defense counsel settling favorably with one plaintiff under the condition that the plaintiff's lawyer be barred from representing similarly situated plaintiffs, or alternatively, be prevented from using evidence or other information acquired in one representation in another, as a condition of the settlement. Despite this rule, many civil settlements, including those in class-action and mass-torts settings, have utilized such conditions. Despite this ethics rule, a variety of case rulings now place substantial restraints on what some lawyers can negotiate for in settlements of civil matters, such as statutory attorneys fees.

Problem 5-6.   *Zealous Advocate or Diligent Negotiator?*

The article above outlines how lawyers believe that they have a purported duty to be a zealous advocate. Yet, the actual phrase "zealous advocacy" is no longer used in the Model Rules. This used to be the requirement under the Model Code of Professional Responsibility Canon 7, entitled "A Lawyer Should Represent a Client Zealously Within the Bounds of the Law," adopted in 1969, but was taken out with the adoption of the Model Rules in 1983. The closest language to the requirement for zealous advocacy is found in current Rule 1.3 on Diligence, Comment 1: "A lawyer should pursue a matter on behalf of a client . . . and take whatever lawful and ethical measures are required to vindicate a client's cause or endeavor. A lawyer must also act with commitment and dedication to the interests of the client and with zeal in advocacy upon the client's behalf. . . ."

How do you think the view of the lawyer's role as a zealous advocate versus a dedicated, diligent advocate potentially changes how a lawyer approaches negotiation?

D. APPROACHES TO ETHICAL DILEMMAS

The excerpts that follow take alternative approaches to conceptualizing negotiation, both in terms of how they view negotiation obligations and duties and in terms of how they set out the lawyer's behavioral role in negotiation. The first excerpt from Professor Richard Shell outlines three different ethical orientations to negotiation and is followed by Professor James White's classic article on ethical dilemmas and Professor Patrick Schlitz's reflection on what law practice does to our personal ethics.

G. Richard Shell, **BARGAINING FOR ADVANTAGE: NEGOTIATION STRATEGIES FOR REASONABLE PEOPLE**

215-220 (1999)

I want to challenge you to identify what *your* beliefs are. To help you decide how you feel about ethics, I will briefly describe the three most common approaches to bargaining ethics I have heard expressed in conversation with literally hundreds of students and executives. See which shoe fits — or take a bit from each approach and construct your own.

As we explore this territory, remember that nearly everyone is sincerely convinced that they are acting ethically most of the time, whereas they often think others are acting either naively or unethically, depending on their ethical perspective and the situation. Thus, a word of warning is in order. Your ethics are mainly your own business. They will help you increase your level of confidence and comfort at the bargaining table. But do not expect others to share your ethics in every detail. Prudence pays.

THREE SCHOOLS OF BARGAINING ETHICS

The three schools of bargaining ethics I want to introduce for your consideration are (1) the "It's a game" Poker School, (2) the "Do the right thing even if it hurts" Idealist School, and (3) the "What goes around, comes around" Pragmatist School.

Let's look at each one in turn. As I describe these schools, try to decide which aspects of them best reflect your attitudes. After you figure out where you stand today, take a moment and see if that is where you ought to be. My advice is to aim as high as you can, consistent with your genuinely held beliefs about bargaining. In the pressured world of practice, people tend to slide down rather than climb up when it comes to ethical standards.

The "It's a Game" Poker School

The Poker School of ethics sees negotiation as a "game" with certain "rules." The rules are defined by the law. . . . Conduct within the rules is ethical. Conduct outside the rules is unethical.

The modern founder of the Poker School was Albert Z. Carr, a former Special Consultant to President Harry Truman. Carr wrote a book in the 1960s called, appropriately enough, *Business as a Game*. In a related article that appeared in the *Harvard Business Review*, Carr argued that bluffing and other misleading but lawful negotiation tactics are "an integral part of the [bargaining] game, and the executive who does not master [these] techniques is not likely to accumulate much money or power."

People who adhere to the Poker School readily admit that bargaining and poker are not exactly the same. But they point out that deception is essential to effective play in both arenas. Moreover, skilled players in both poker and bargaining exhibit a robust and realistic distrust of the other fellow. Carr argues that good players should ignore the "claims of friendship" and engage in "cunning deception and conceal-ment" in fair, hard bargaining encounters. When the game is over, members of the Poker School do not think less of a fellow player just because that person success-fully deceived them. In fact, assuming the tactic was legal, they may admire the deceiver and vow to be better prepared (and less trusting) next time.

We know how to play poker, but how exactly does one play the bargaining "game"? Stripped to its core, it looks like this: Someone opens, and then people take turns proposing terms to each other. Arguments supporting your preferred terms are allowed. You can play or pass in each round. The goal is to get the other side to agree to terms that are as close as possible to your last proposal.

In the bargaining game, it is understood that both sides might be bluffing. Bluffs disguise a weak bargaining hand, that is, the limited or unattractive alternatives you have away from the table, your inability to affect the other side's alternatives, and the arguments you have to support your demands. Unlike poker players, negotiators always attempt to disclose a good hand if they have one in a bargaining game. So the most effective bluffs are realistic, attractive, difficult-to-check (but false) alterna-tives or authoritative (but false) supporting standards. Experienced players know this, so one of the key skills in the bargaining game is judging when the other party's alternatives or arguments are really as good as he or she says. If the other side calls you on your bargaining bluff by walking away or giving you a credible ultimatum, you lose. Either there will be no deal when there should have been one, or the final price will be nearer to their last offer than to yours.

As mentioned above, the Poker School believes in the rule of law. In poker, you are not allowed to hide cards, collude with other players, or renege on your bets. But you are expected to deceive others about your hand. The best plays come when you win the pot with a weak hand or fool the other players into betting heavily when your hand is strong. In bargaining, you must not commit outright, actionable fraud, but negotiators must be on guard for anything short of fraud.

The Poker School has three main problems as I see it. First, the Poker School presumes that everyone treats bargaining as a game. Unfortunately, it is an empirical fact that people disagree on this. For a start, neither the idealists nor the pragmatists (more on these below) think bargaining is a game. This problem does not deter the Poker School, which holds that the rules permit its members to play even when the other party disagrees about this premise.

Second, everyone is supposed to know the rules cold. But this is impossible, given that legal rules are applied differently in different industries and regions of the world. Finally, as you now know (having read about the legal treatment of fraud), the law is far from certain even within a single jurisdiction. So you often need a sharp lawyer to help you decide what to do.

The "Do the Right Thing Even if it Hurts" Idealist School

The Idealist School says that bargaining is an aspect of social life, not a special activ-ity with its own unique set of rules. The same ethics that apply in the home should carry over directly into the realm of negotiation. If it is wrong to lie or mislead in normal social encounters, it is wrong to do so in negotiations. If it is OK to lie in special situations (such as to protect another person's feelings), it is also OK to lie in negotiations when those special conditions apply.

Idealists do not entirely rule out deception in negotiation. For example, if the other party assumes you have a lot of leverage and never asks you directly about the situation as you see it, you do not necessarily have to volunteer the information weakening your position. And the idealist can decline to answer questions. But such exceptions are uncomfortable moments. Members of the Idealist School prefer to be candid and honest at the bargaining table even if it means giving up a certain amount of strategic advantage.

The Idealist School draws its strength from philosophy and religion. For example, Immanuel Kant said that we should all follow the ethical rules that we would wish others to follow. Kant argued that if everyone lied all the time, social life would be chaos. Hence, you should not lie. Kant also disapproved of treating other people merely as the means to achieve your own personal ends. Lies in negotiation are selfish acts designed to achieve personal gain. This form of conduct is therefore unethical. Period. Many religions also teach adherents not to lie for personal advantage.

Idealists admit that deception in negotiation rarely arouses moral indignation unless the lies breach a trust between friends, violate a fiduciary responsibility, or exploit people such as the sick or elderly, who lack the ability to protect themselves. And if the only way you can prevent some terrible harm like a murder is by lying, go ahead and lie. But the lack of moral outrage and the fact that sometimes lying can be defended does not make deception in negotiations right.

Idealists strongly reject the idea that negotiations should be viewed as "games." Negotiations, they feel, are serious, consequential communication acts. People negotiate to resolve their differences so social life will work for the benefit of all. People must be held responsible for all their actions, including the way they negotiate, under universal standards.

Idealists think that the members of the Poker School are predatory and selfish. For its part, the Poker School thinks that idealists are naïve and even a little silly. When members of the two schools meet at the bargaining table, tempers can flare.

Some members of the Idealist School have recently been trying to find a philosophical justification for bluffs about bottom lines. There is no agreement yet on whether these efforts have succeeded in ethical terms. But it is clear that outright lies such as fictitious other offers and better prices are unethical practices under idealist principles.

The big problem for the idealist is obvious: Their standards sometimes make it difficult to proceed in a realistic way at the bargaining table. Also, unless adherence to the Idealist School is coupled with a healthy skepticism about the way other people will negotiate, idealism leaves its members open to exploitation by people with standards other than their own. These limitations are especially troublesome when idealists must represent others' interests at the bargaining table.

Despite its limitations, I like the Idealist School. Perhaps because I am an academic, I genuinely believe that the different parts of my life are, in fact, whole. I aspire to ethical standards that I can apply consistently. I will admit that I sometimes fall short of idealism's strict code, but by aiming high I am leaving myself somewhere to fall that maintains my basic sense of personal integrity.

I confess my preference for the Idealist School so you will know where I am coming from in this discussion. But I realize that your experience and work environment may preclude idealism as an ethical option. That's ok. As I hope I am making clear, idealism is not the only way to think about negotiation in ethical terms.

The "What Goes Around Comes Around" Pragmatist School

The final school of bargaining ethics, the Pragmatist School, includes some original elements as well as some attributes of the previous two. In common with the Poker School, this approach views deception as a necessary part of the negotiation process. Unlike the Poker School, however, it prefers not to use misleading statements and overt lies if there is a serviceable, practical alternative. Uniquely, the Pragmatist School displays concern for the potential negative effects of deceptive conduct on present and future relationships. Thus, lying and other questionable tactics are bad not so much because they are "wrong" as because they cost the user more in the long run than they gain in the short run.

As my last comment suggests, people adhere to this school more for prudential than idealistic reasons. Lies and misleading conduct can cause serous injury to one's credibility. And credibility is an important asset for effective negotiators both to preserve working relationships and to protect one's reputation in the market or community. The latter concern is summed up in what I would call the pragmatist's credo: What goes around comes around. The Poker School is less concerned with reputation and more focused on winning each bargaining encounter within the rules of the "game."

What separates the Pragmatist School from the Idealist School? To put it bluntly, a pragmatist will lie a bit more often than will an idealist. For example, pragmatists sometimes will draw fine distinctions between lies about hard-core facts of a transaction, which are always imprudent (and often illegal), and misleading statements about such things as the rationales used to justify a position. A pragmatic car salesman considers it highly unethical to lie about anything large or small relating to the mechanical condition of a used car he is selling. But this same salesman might not have a problem saying "My manager won't let me sell this car for less than $10,000" even though he knows the manager would sell the car for $9,500. False justifications and rationales are marginally acceptable because they are usually less important to the transaction and much harder to detect as falsehoods than are core facts about the object being bought and sold.

Pragmatists are also somewhat looser within the truth when using so called blocking techniques — tactics to avoid answering questions that threaten to expose a weak bargaining position. For example, can you ethically answer "I don't know" when asked about something you *do* know that hurts your position? An idealist would refuse to answer the question or try to change the subject, not lie by saying "I don't know." A pragmatist would go ahead and say "I don't know" if his actual state of knowledge is hard to trace and the lie poses little risk to his relationships.

James J. White, **MACHIAVELLI AND THE BAR: ETHICAL LIMITATIONS ON LYING IN NEGOTIATION**

1980 Am. B. Found. Res. J. 926-928, 931-935 (1980)

[I]n negotiation, more than in other contexts, ethical norms can probably be violated with greater confidence that there will be no discovery and punishment. Whether one is likely to be caught for violating an ethical standard says nothing about the merit of the standard. However, if the low probability of punishment means that many lawyers will violate the standard, the standard becomes even more difficult for the honest lawyer to follow, for by doing so he may be forfeiting a significant advantage for his client to others who do not follow the rules. . . .

On the one hand the negotiator must be fair and truthful; on the other he must mislead his opponent. Like the poker player, a negotiator hopes that his opponent will overestimate the value of his hand. Like the poker player, in a variety of ways he must facilitate his opponent's inaccurate assessment. The critical difference between those who are successful negotiators and those who are not lies in this capacity both to mislead and not to be misled.

Some experienced negotiators will deny the accuracy of this assertion, but they will be wrong. I submit that a careful examination of the behavior of even the most forthright, honest, and trustworthy negotiators will show them actively engaged in misleading their opponents about their true position. . . . To conceal one's true position, to mislead an opponent about one's true settling point, is the essence of negotiation.

Of course there are limits on acceptable deceptive behavior in negotiation, but there is the paradox. How can one be "fair" but also mislead? Can we ask the negotiator to mislead, but fairly, like the soldier who must kill, but humanely? . . .

FIVE CASES

To test these limits, consider five cases. Easiest is the question that arises when one misrepresents his true opinion about the meaning of a case or a statute. Presumably such a misrepresentation is accepted lawyer behavior both in and out of court and is not intended to be precluded by the requirement that the lawyer be "truthful." . . .

A second form of distortion that the Comments plainly envision as permissible is distortion concerning the value of one's case or of the other subject matter involved in the negotiation. Thus the Comments make explicit reference to "puffery." . . . [T]his . . . generally means that the seller of a product has the right to make general statements without having the law treat those statements as warranties and without having liability if they turn out to be inaccurate estimates of the value. . . .

A third case is related to puffing but different from it. This is the use of the so-called false demand. It is a standard negotiating technique in collective bargaining negotiation and in some other multiple-issue negotiations for one side to include a series of demands about which it cares little or not at all. . . . Such behavior is untruthful in the broadest sense; yet at least in collective bargaining negotiation its use is a standard part of the process and is not thought to be inappropriate by any experienced bargainer.

Two final examples may be more troublesome. The first involves the response of a lawyer to a question from the other side. Assume that the defendant has instructed his lawyer to accept any settlement offer under $100,000. Having received that instruction, how does the lawyer respond to the plaintiff's question, "I think $90,000 will settle this case. Will your client give $90,000?" Do you see the dilemma that question poses for the defense lawyer? . . . A truthful answer to it concludes the negotiation and dashes any possibility of negotiating a lower settlement even in circumstances in which the plaintiff might be willing to accept half of $90,000. Even a moment's hesitation in response to the question may be a nonverbal communication to a clever plaintiff's lawyer that the defendant has given such authority. Yet a negative response is a lie. . . .

[C]onsider a final example recently suggested to me by a lawyer in practice. There the lawyer represented three persons who had been charged with shoplifting. Having satisfied himself that there was no significant conflict of interest, the defense lawyer told the prosecutor that two of the three would plead guilty only if the case was dismissed against the third. Previously those two had told the defense counsel that they would plead guilty irrespective of what the third did, and the third said that he wished to go to trial unless the charges were dropped. Thus the defense lawyer lied to the prosecutor by stating that the two would plead only if the third were allowed to go free. . . .

Taken together, the five foregoing cases show me that we do not and cannot intend that a negotiator be "truthful" in the broadest sense of that term. At the minimum we allow him some deviation from truthfulness in asserting his true opinion about cases, statutes, or the value of the subject of the negotiation in other respects. In addition some of us are likely to allow him to lie in response to certain questions that are regarded as out of bounds, and possibly to lie in circumstances where his interest is great and the injury seems small. It would be unfortunate, therefore, for the rule that requires "fairness" to be interpreted to require that a negotiator be truthful in every respect and in all of his dealings. It should be read to allow at least those kinds of untruthfulness that are implicitly and explicitly recognized as acceptable in this forum, a forum defined both by the subject matter and by the participants.

Problem 5-7.   *The White School*

From which of Professor Shell's negotiation schools does Professor White come? What does this mean in terms of a lawyer's role in negotiation? Review the Model Rules of Professional Conduct at the beginning of this section. Do you agree with White's analysis about what the rules permit?

> ## Problem 5-8.   *When Can You Lie?*
>
> A district attorney was sanctioned by the Colorado state disciplinary board for deception when, during a hostage negotiation, the district attorney pretended that he was a public defender acting on behalf of the murder suspect to encourage him to surrender. In affirming the sanctions, the Colorado Supreme Court held that "Purposeful deception by an attorney licensed in our state is intolerable. . . ." In the Matter of Paulter, 47 P.3d 1175, 1176 (Colo. 2002). If the Colorado Supreme Court would not condone deceiving a murder suspect during a hostage negotiation, do you think there is any lying of which it might approve?

This next excerpt takes quite a different view on legal ethics generally and how to practice as an ethical lawyer. Former big firm partner and now professor Patrick Schlitz wrote this article as both advice and guidance to law students about to enter the profession.

 Patrick J. Schlitz, ON BEING A HAPPY, HEALTHY AND ETHICAL MEMBER OF AN UNHAPPY, UNHEALTHY, AND UNETHICAL PROFESSION

52 Vand. L. Rev. 871, 906-912, 915-918 (1999)

THE ETHICS OF LAWYERS

[T]he legal profession is widely perceived — even by lawyers — as being unethical. Only one American in five considers lawyers to be "honest and ethical," and "the more a person knows about the legal profession and the more he or she is in direct personal contact with lawyers, the lower [his or her] opinion of them." This should concern you.

There are many reasons why ethics courses are so unpopular, but the most important is probably that law students do not think that they will become unethical lawyers. Students think of unethical lawyers as the sleazeballs who chase ambulances (think Danny DeVito in *The Rainmaker*) or run insurance scams (think Bill Murray in *Wild Things*) or destroy evidence (think Al Pacino's crew in *The Devil's Advocate*). Students have a hard time identifying with these lawyers. When students think of life after graduation, they see themselves sitting on the 27th floor of some skyscraper in a freshly pressed dark suit (blue, black, or gray) with a starched blouse or shirt (white or light blue) doing sophisticated legal work for sophisticated clients. Students imagine — wrongly — that such lawyers do not have to worry much about ethics, except, perhaps, when the occasional conflict of interest question arises.

If you think this — if you think that you will not have any trouble practicing law ethically — you are wrong. Dead wrong. In fact, particularly if you go to work for a big firm, you will probably begin to practice law unethically in at least some respects within your first year or two in practice. This happens to most young lawyers in big firms. It happened to me, and it will happen to you, unless you do something about it.

A. Practicing Law Ethically

Let's first be clear on what I mean by practicing law ethically. I mean three things. First, you generally have to comply with the formal disciplinary rules — either the Model Rules of Professional Conduct, the Model Code of Professional Responsibility, or some state variant of one or the other. As a law student, and then as a young lawyer, you will often be encouraged to distinguish ethical from unethical conduct solely by reference to the formal rules. Most likely, you will devote the majority of the time in your professional responsibility class to studying the rules, and you will, of course, learn the rules cold so that you can pass the Multi-State Professional Responsibility Exam ("MPRE"). In many other ways, subtle and blatant, you will be encouraged to think that conduct that does not violate the rules is "ethical," while conduct that does violate the rules is "unethical." . . .

I don't have anything against the formal rules. Often, they are all that stands between an unethical lawyer and a vulnerable client. You should learn them and follow them. But you should also understand that the formal rules represent nothing more than "the lowest common denominator of conduct that a highly self-interested group will tolerate." For many lawyers, "[e]thics is a matter of steering, if necessary, just clear of the few unambiguous prohibitions found in rules governing lawyers." But complying with the formal rules will not make you an ethical lawyer, any more than complying with the criminal law will make you an ethical person. Many of the sleaziest lawyers you will encounter will be absolutely scrupulous in their compliance with the formal rules. In fact, they will be only too happy to tell you just that. . . .

The second thing you must do to be an ethical lawyer is to act ethically in your work, even when you aren't required to do so by any rule. To a substantial extent, "bar ethical rules have lost touch with ordinary moral intuitions." To practice law ethically you must practice law consistently with those intuitions. . . .

The third thing you must do to be an ethical lawyer is to live an ethical life. Many big firm lawyers — who can be remarkably "smug[ ] about the superiority of the ethical standards of large firms" — ignore this point. So do many law professors who, when writing about legal ethics, tend to focus solely on the lawyer at work. But being admitted to the bar does not absolve you of your responsibilities outside of work — to your family, to your friends, to your community, and, if you're a person of faith, to your God. To practice law ethically, you must meet those responsibilities, which means that you must live a balanced life. If you become a workaholic lawyer, you will be unhealthy, probably unhappy, and, I would argue, unethical.

Now I recognize that we live in an age of moral relativism — an age in which "behavior is neither right nor wrong but a matter of personal choice." Your reaction to my claim that an unbalanced life is an unethical life may very well be, "That's just your opinion." It is my opinion, but it is surely not *just* my opinion. I would be surprised if the belief system to which you subscribe — whether it be religiously or secularly based — regards a life dominated by the pursuit of wealth to the exclusion of all else as an ethical life, or an attorney who meets only his responsibilities to his clients and law partners as an ethical person.

B. Big Firm Culture

It is hard to practice law ethically. Complying with the formal rules is the easy part. The rules are not very specific, and they don't demand very much. You may, on rare occasions, confront an extremely difficult conflict of interest problem that will require you to parse the rules carefully. You may even confront a situation in which some ethical or moral imperative compels you to violate the rules. But by and large, you will have no trouble complying with the rules; indeed, you are unlikely to give the rules much thought. . . .

But even practicing law ethically in the sense of being honest and fair and compassionate is difficult. To understand why, you need to understand what it is that you will do every day as a lawyer. Most of a lawyer's working life is filled with the mundane. It is unlikely that one of your clients will drop a smoking gun on your desk or ask you to deliver a briefcase full of unmarked bills or invite you to have wild, passionate sex (or even un-wild, un-passionate sex). These things happen to lawyers only in John Grisham novels. Your life as a lawyer will be filled with the kind of things that drove John Grisham to write novels: dictating letters and talking on the phone and drafting memoranda and performing "due diligence" and proofreading contracts and negotiating settlements and filling out time sheets. And because your life as a lawyer will be filled with the mundane, whether you practice law ethically will depend not upon how you resolve the one or two dramatic ethical dilemmas that you will confront during your entire career, but upon the hundreds of little things that you will do, almost unthinkingly, each and every day.

Because practicing law ethically will depend primarily upon the hundreds of little things that you will do almost unthinkingly every day, it will not depend much upon your thinking. You are going to be busy. The days will fly by. When you are on the phone negotiating a deal or when you are at your computer drafting a brief or when you are filling out your time sheet at the end of the day, you are not going to have time to reflect on each of your actions. You are going to have to act almost instinctively.

What this means, then, is that you will not practice law ethically — you *cannot* practice law ethically — unless acting ethically is *habitual* for you. You have to be in the habit of being honest. You have to be in the habit of being fair. You have to be in the habit of being compassionate. These qualities have to be deeply ingrained in you, so that you can't turn them on and off — so that acting honorably is not something you have to *decide* to do — so that when you are at work, making the thousands of phone calls you will make and writing the thousands of letters you will write and dealing with the thousands of people with whom you will deal, you will *automatically* apply the same values in the workplace that you apply outside of work, when you are with family and friends.

Here is the problem, though: After you start practicing law, nothing is likely to influence you more than "the culture or house norms of the agency, department, or firm" in which you work. If you are going into private practice — particularly private practice in a big firm — you are going to be immersed in a culture that is hostile to the values you now have. The system does not *want* you to apply the same values in the workplace that you do outside of work (unless you're rapaciously greedy outside of work); it wants you to replace those values with the system's values. The system is obsessed with money, and it wants you to be, too. The system wants you — it *needs* you — to play the game.

Now, no one is going to say this to you. No one is going to take you aside and say, "Jane, we here at Smith & Jones are obsessed with money. From this point forward the most important thing in your life has to be billing hours and generating business. Family and friends and honesty and fairness are okay in moderation, but don't let them interfere with making money." No one will tell you, as one lawyer told another in a Charles Addams cartoon, "I admire your honesty and integrity, Wilson, but I have no room for them in my firm." Instead, the culture will pressure you in more subtle ways to replace your values with the system's. . . .

C. Becoming Unethical

As the values of an attorney change, so, too, does her ability to practice law ethically. . . .

Unethical lawyers do not start out being unethical; they start out just like you — as perfectly decent young men or women who have every intention of practicing law ethically. They do not become unethical overnight; they become unethical just as you will (if you become unethical) — a little bit at a time. And they do not become unethical by shredding incriminating documents or bribing jurors; they become unethical just as you are likely to — by cutting a corner here, by stretching the truth a bit there.

Let me tell you how you will start acting unethically: It will start with your time sheets. One day, not too long after you start practicing law, you will sit down at the end of a long, tiring day, and you just won't have much to show for your efforts in terms of billable hours. It will be near the end of the month. You will know that all of the partners will be looking at your monthly time report in a few days, so what you'll do is pad your time sheet just a bit. Maybe you will bill a client for ninety minutes for a task that really took you only sixty minutes to perform. However, you will promise yourself that you will repay the client at the first opportunity by doing thirty minutes of work for the client for "free." In this way, you will be "borrowing," not "stealing."

And then what will happen is that it will become easier and easier to take these little loans against future work. And then, after a while, you will stop paying back these little loans. You will convince yourself that, although you billed for ninety minutes and spent only sixty minutes on the project, you did such good work that your client should pay a bit more for it. After all, your billing rate is awfully low, and your client is awfully rich.

And then you will pad more and more — every two minute telephone conversation will go down on the sheet as ten minutes, every three hour research project will go down with an extra quarter hour or so. You will continue to rationalize your dishonesty to yourself in various ways until one day you stop doing even that. And, before long — it won't take you much more than three or four years — you will be stealing from your clients almost every day, and you won't even notice it.

You know what? You will also likely become a liar. A deadline will come up one day, and, for reasons that are entirely your fault, you will not be able to meet it. So you will call your senior partner or your client and make up a white lie for why you missed the deadline. And then you will get busy and a partner will ask whether you proofread a lengthy prospectus and you will say yes, even though you didn't. And then you will be drafting a brief and you will quote language from a Supreme Court opinion even though you will know that, when read in context, the language does not remotely suggest what you are implying it suggests. And then, in preparing a client for a deposition, you will help the client to formulate an answer to a difficult question that will likely be asked — an answer that will be "legally accurate" but that will mislead your opponent. And then you will be reading through a big box of your client's documents — a box that has not been opened in twenty years — and you will find a document that would hurt your client's case, but that no one except you knows exists, and you will simply "forget" to produce it in response to your opponent's discovery requests.

Do you see what will happen? After a couple years of this, you won't even notice that you are lying and cheating and stealing every day that you practice law. None of these things will seem like a big deal in itself — an extra fifteen minutes added to a time sheet here, a little white lie to cover a missed deadline there. But, after a while, your entire frame of reference will change. You will still be making dozens of quick, instinctive decisions every day, but those decisions, instead of reflecting the notions of right and wrong by which you conduct your personal life, will instead reflect the set of values by which you will conduct your professional life — a set of values that embodies not what is right or wrong, but what is profitable, and what you can get away with. The system will have succeeded in replacing your values with the system's values, and the system will be profiting as a result.

Problem 5-9. *The Schlitz School*

Within which of Richard Shell's negotiation schools does Professor Schlitz most closely fit? Why? How exactly does Professor Schlitz define "ethical"? What do you think about his definition and your susceptability to it?

A Trust Land Mine

In any negotiation, you're likely to have information about the other party or about the deal (industry facts, economic health, new products, and so on) that he might not know you have. To gain some measure of your counterpart's trustworthiness, plant a "trust land mine": ask some questions to which you already know the answers. If someone avoids your information requests, or if he lies outright, that's one sign that you should be careful about what you reveal — or even call off talks altogether. Of course, someone who answers a few questions truthfully might not always behave honestly. Nonetheless, trust landmines offer a reasonably good way of determining if a person is leveling with you and what approach to negotiation your counterpart is using.

Carrie Menkel-Meadow, Know When to Show Your Hand, 10 Negotiation Newsletter 1 (June 2007)

Problem 5-10. *Wise Master*

A wise master once wanted to test his students. The temple where they studied was run down, and students normally begged for food in the nearby town. One day the master told the students that each of them was to go into the town and steal something they could sell to raise money. "In order not to defile our excellent reputation by committing illegal and immoral acts, please be certain to steal when no one is looking. I do not want anyone to be caught." After some hesitation, the group of students set out, except for one young boy. When the master asked him why he did not go, the boy responded, "I cannot follow your instructions to steal where no one will see me. Wherever I go, *I* am always there watching. My *own* eyes will see me steal." The boy was the only one who passed the test. Adapted from Heather Forest, The Wise Master, Wisdom Tales from Around the World 15-16 (1996). How is this folktale similar to Schlitz's advice?

When it is difficult to negotiate directly, the parties often seek help, for their substantive, process, and ethical problems, from a third-party neutral. The next few chapters explore how mediators can facilitate negotiation and help the parties resolve their problems.

Further Reading

Arthur Isak Applbaum. (1999). *Ethics for Adversaries*. Princeton, N.J.: Princeton University Press.

Phyllis Bernard & Bryant Garth (Eds.). (2002). *Dispute Resolution Ethics: A Comprehensive Guide.* Washington, D.C.: American Bar Association Section on Dispute Resolution.

Warren Burger, *The Necessity for Civility*, 52 F.R.D. 211 (1971).

Jonathan Cohen, *When People Are the Means: Negotiating with Respect*, 14 GEO. J. LEGAL ETHICS 739 (2001).

David Luban. (1988). *Lawyers and Justice.* Princeton, N.J.: Princeton University Press.

Carrie Menkel-Meadow, *Compromise, Negotiation and Morality*, 26 NEGOTIATION JOURNAL 481-497 (2010).

Carrie Menkel-Meadow & Michael Wheeler. (2004). *What's Fair: Ethics for Negotiators.* San Francisco: Jossey-Bass Publishers.

Deborah L. Rhode. (2000). *In the Interests of Justice: Reforming the Legal Profession.* New York: Oxford University Press.

Chapter 6 Mediation: Concepts and Models

Summum ius. Summa iniuria. (The strictest following of the law can lead to the greatest injustice.)

— Marcus Tullius Cicero

There is no intractable problem.

— Desmond Tutu

Conflicts are created and sustained by human beings. They can be ended by human beings.

— George J. Mitchell (referring to conflicts in Northern Ireland and the Middle East)

This chapter explores the foundations of mediation, the historical context for current perspectives on different types of mediation, and the place mediation holds in the array of dispute resolution processes. As mediation has developed, different orientations, goals, and strategies relating to the process have been propounded and debated. Using stories of actual mediations as background, a sampling of major approaches and varying descriptions of the mediation process are presented. The chapter concludes by reflecting on the direction that mediation will or should take as it becomes more central to human problem solving, legal practice, and courts.

A. INTRODUCTION TO MEDIATION

1. What Is Mediation?

Mediation is a process in which an impartial third party acts as a catalyst to help others constructively address and perhaps resolve a dispute, plan a transaction, or define the contours of a relationship. A mediator facilitates negotiation between the parties to enable better communication, encourage problem solving, and develop an agreement or resolution by consensus among the parties.

Mediators intervene in a wide array of disputes — from family and community to commercial and international. Mediation is useful for parties facing an actual dispute, trying to reconcile competing interests, or planning for the possibility of conflict. For example, a mediator can help divorcing couples determine parenting arrangements and asset division or help people who are contemplating marriage negotiate a prenuptial agreement. A mediator can help settle a controversy over liability and damages related to an environmental disaster, such as an oil spill, or can help a community determine a site for a highway or garbage facility.

In mediation, as in negotiation, the parties retain control over the outcome of their dispute, in some cases through their attorneys. This central feature of mediation — self-determination by the parties — is a facet of the promise of democratic process — that the voice and wisdom of people can shape novel outcomes responsive to particular situations. In this respect mediation is fundamentally different from adjudication, where power to determine the outcome is ceded to a judge, jury, or arbiter.

Adjudication and the rule of law can clarify and develop public norms. Adjudication supports the stability and predictability inherent in having laws and methods of evenhanded application of published rules. Litigation gives society precedents that promote order by guiding similarly situated actors. Mediation, on the other hand, enhances communication, fosters collaboration, and encourages problem solving, all suitably tailored to particular, not general, populations. While negotiation can also do these things, negotiation lacks the assistance of an impartial professional charged with making the process constructive. These different goals of consensus-based processes are also important to achieving individual and community well-being. If, for example, landlords and tenants, minority groups and school boards, or employers and employees can resolve an existing controversy through mediation, they not only can achieve a creative resolution tailored to their specific situation but also can bank their success in problem solving to help resolve, if not prevent, future disputes. The very success of their ability to problem-solve together can provide a precedent of process for resolving other issues that may come out of the relationship or transactions.

In comparing and contrasting adjudication and mediation, two very different approaches to addressing disputes, it is important to note that they serve different goals and objectives and have their own logic and integrity. In adjudication, with ideals embedded in concepts of evolving law and precepts for ordering society, a decision maker (whether judge, jury, or arbiter) determines facts and applies rules to determine rights and liabilities with respect to past acts. In mediation, a structuring of the future is possible to avoid past pitfalls and build new opportunities. The spotlight moves from evidence of past conduct and historic facts to parties' interests and possibilities for optimal balancing of those interests. Where, for example, a supplier and a customer have taken a matter to court to determine damages for a shipment that was nonconforming under a contract, those same parties in mediation might adjust their differences by arrangements in future contracts, making allowances for wrongs experienced by parties with respect to past conduct.

2. The Advantages of Mediation

To understand the various rationales for mediation, examine the fictional case of Jarndyce v. Jarndyce, the focal point of Charles Dickens' novel, *Bleak House*. The case involves a will contest that consumes several generations in a family. The family members become so obsessed and absorbed by the legal contest that they lose their way in life and become divided one against the other. The legal issues in the fictional case are so complicated that even the lawyers cannot explain or agree on them. Ultimately, the legal costs consume the estate, and the lawsuit ends with everyone (except the lawyers who retain their fees) a loser.

In a variety of ways, the story illustrates many of the common shortcomings of litigation: prohibitive expense, heart-breaking delay, a lack of party participation and control of the process, unsatisfactory outcomes from a party's perspective, and an adversarial orientation that makes parties enemies. Mediation can address each of these shortcomings.

Jarndyce v. Jarndyce

Jarndyce v. Jarndyce . . . has, in the course of time, become so complicated, that no man alive knows what it means. The parties to it understand it least; but it has been observed that no two Chancery lawyers can talk about it for five minutes, without coming to a total disagreement as to all the premises. Innumerable children have been born into the cause; innumerable young people have married into it; innumerable old people have died out of it. Scores of persons have deliriously found themselves made parties in Jarndyce v. Jarndyce, without knowing how or why; whole families have inherited legendary hatreds with the suit. The little plaintiff or defendant, who was promised a new rocking-horse when Jarndyce and Jarndyce should be settled, has grown up, possessed himself of a real horse, and trotted away into the other world. Fair wards of court have faded into mothers and grandmothers; a long procession of Chancellors has come in and gone out; the legion of bills in the suit have been transformed into mere bills of mortality; there are not three Jarndyces left upon the earth perhaps, since old Tom Jarndyce in despair blew his brains out at a coffee-house in Chancery Lane; but Jarndyce and Jarndyce still drags its dreary length before the Court, perennially hopeless.

— Charles Dickens, *Bleak House*

---

a. Settlement: Avoiding the Expense, Delay, and Risk of Adjudication

The success mediators have in settling cases in a satisfactory and efficient manner is a key reason that many lawyers advise clients to mediate, even though there is always the chance that mediation will not resolve the situation. Compared to the risky undertaking of adjudication — whether litigation or arbitration — mediation, when successful, offers parties the possibility of an acceptable conclusion, one that they have crafted and endorsed themselves. In litigation, a judge or jury decides the matter, checked only by the appeal process. In binding arbitration, an individual decision maker (or a panel of decision makers), chosen by the parties, renders a final decision. Whenever a party gives another person the power to decide a controversy, the outcome is inherently unpredictable and may produce a very unhappy surprise.

The benefits of speedy closure to conflict are financial, practical, and psychological. Litigation tends to be slow and expensive. Centuries ago William Shakespeare's *Hamlet* complained about "the law's delay." "The parties in Jarndyce v. Jarndyce grew old before the litigation whimpered to an end." In Jarndyce v. Jarndyce it is clear that *any settlement* — before the estate was exhausted — would have provided greater benefit to the parties than the failed litigation. While the procedural aspect of the arbitration process, created by the parties in their agreement to arbitrate, can be fast, arbitration can also be crafted to resemble litigation, in which case it too becomes slow and costly. Many disputes need prompt address. At least one side will want to resolve a patent dispute before the patent expires or someone begins to profit from abusing someone else's intellectual property. A benefit to resolving an allegation of discrimination in the workplace through prompt mediation is that it may prevent the employee from becoming embittered and infecting others in the office or before a similar act of discrimination occurs. Solutions, different from those courts can order, such as transfer to another job in the same company, can solve the problem without the need to adjudicate the legal claim. Businesses embroiled in conflict are diverted from the pursuit of business goals. A mediation can be scheduled quickly, and sessions can take as little as a few hours or one to two days to complete, preserving time, profit, and ongoing relationships.

Mediation can temper unrealistic positions, unwarranted assumptions, and demonization of another party. Overblown and overconfident views of a case and the dynamics of adversarial behavior can box parties into unproductive assertions and claims. Face-to-face interaction between the parties can allow each side to hear the presentation of one another and to take into account the other's perspectives.

> Justice delayed is justice denied.
>
> — attributed to William E. Gladstone

Finally, settlement benefits the court system. While there is no consensus among scholars or administrators regarding the ability of alternative dispute resolution processes to relieve court dockets, in offering a variety of methods to resolve disputes, courts can serve the various interests of disputing parties and may unclog their dockets as well.

b. Participation and Self-Determination: Giving Parties Voice and Choice

A central value of mediation is self-determination by the parties. Self-determination in this context means that parties retain control over both their participation in the process of dispute resolution and the outcome of their dispute.

Parties in adjudicative processes must fit their story within the narrow frame of a legal "cause of action" or an allowable arbitral claim, confine themselves to evidence that the decision maker will consider probative and persuasive, and give control over both process and outcome to a judge, jury, or arbiter. Because of these constraints, parties often do not feel they have had a chance to express themselves and be heard. In Jarndyce v. Jarndyce, both parties and lawyers were confused about the legal case, and no one seemed capable of controlling the delay (which exceeded the lives of many of the disputants) or the costs (which exceeded the assets being contested). A fundamental lack of control — or self-determination — can be the price of obtaining a third-party decision. Similarly, remedies in adjudicative processes are those prescribed by the particular forum, rather than remedies tailored for and by parties.

Mediators, at least ideally, promote party empowerment and self-determination by carving out space and time for each side to tell their story and be heard in a meaningful way. This feature alone can be important to clients. Mediators also seek party involvement in crafting proposals that are responsive to each side's needs. Participation in finding, and power in choosing, the solution means the parties are invested in the outcome, and hence the resolution is more durable when the parties have been properly involved. Apologies and other amends and benefits that will "satisfy the heart" can be both more valuable and less costly than outcomes dictated by third parties.

If only the family in *Bleak House* had sat down with each other, talked through their perspectives, and explored what they could do for one another, the family members may have found some satisfactory resolution to their differences that would have benefited someone other than the attorneys.

c. *Better Outcomes: Generating Creative Problem Solving*

Many proponents of mediation emphasize its ability to engage participants in a forward-looking exercise of developing options and optimal outcomes. Mediators try to get parties out of an adversarial contest and into the exercise of creating a better future. Custom-tailored outcomes, developed to maximize benefits for all sides, can create more value for parties than the standardized remedies provided in adjudicative forums. Agreements can be finely calibrated to balance out equities arising from past (mis)conduct and thus be reparative from a justice perspective. At the same time, the outcome must be better than the litigation (or other) alternatives of each party, since either party can "veto" the agreement (of course, this assumes that the parties are adequately informed and not strong-armed into settlement). Such "quality" solutions will likely be perceived as fairer by the parties. From a societal perspective, community value flows from maximizing individual benefit and from reducing the disaffection costs of conflict, such as poor health, social friction, and aggression.

Mediation can produce outcomes that litigation or arbitration cannot. For example, in commercial settings, compensatory damages can be replaced by profitable deals that take into account past wrongs. Agreements to communicate in a certain way, to write letters of reference, to refrain from contact or conduct can be valuable. Apologies can allow parties to "let go" and move on with their lives. Such results are not generally part of the remedies available to an arbitrator or judge.

Additionally, party-crafted and voluntary agreements that are responsive to the interests and values parties articulate are more durable than judgments that the "losing" party may find unfair and attempt to avoid by using an appeals process or simply making it difficult to collect the judgment. Parties in mediation can also create procedures for resolving whatever new conflicts they might have and for resolving issues that can occur when interpretations differ on what agreements actually mean.

No efforts to find a creative and consensual outcome were made in Jarndyce v. Jarndyce. An infinite array of possibilities might have worked in that case had mediation been tried. Unfortunately, as the estate in Jarndyce v. Jarndyce shrinks as a result of the litigation, so does the set of possible beneficial outcomes.

d. Relationship, Community, and Harmony: Building Bridges Between People

Many societies see conflict as a potential threat to the social fabric. These cultures value processes that rebuild connection between parties and bring both individual well-being and community harmony. Navajo peacemaking tribunals and mediation in China and Japan are examples. Any process such as mediation

> **"A Contempt for His Own Kind"**
>
> The receiver in the cause has acquired a goodly sum of money by it, but has acquired too a distrust of his own mother, and a contempt for his own kind.
>
> — Charles Dickens, *Bleak House*

that allows parties to recognize each other's perspectives and interests — even when these parties are strangers to each other — has a significant value in a world where strife and conflict threaten to tear families, communities, and nations apart. Society's interest in promoting healing relationships is measured, in part, by the costs of disaffection evident in depression, crime, productivity loss, and, ultimately, war.

The benefit of using mediation radiates beyond a single dispute to the larger system. In the context of a family, school, agency, workplace, or industry, mediation is used not only to resolve specific disputes but also to promote understanding and collaboration, for example, among parents and children, students from different ethnic groups, supervisors and employees, or customers and suppliers. As parties sit down and listen to each other, stereotypes can be shattered and more responsible, responsive, and profitable citizens, communities, and governments can emerge.

Problem 6-1.   *The Relation Between Case Type and Process*

Are the benefits discussed above relevant to all case types? For example, are relationship and community as important in a construction case as they might be in a probate matter? Can you make an argument that all of these advantages might be useful aspirations in a variety of case types?

Problem 6-2. *It's All About Money!*

In the context of civil litigation, some commentators believe that disputes are "all about money." Do you agree? Do you think that lawyers and their clients might have a different perspective on this question? See Tamara Relis, Perceptions in Litigation and Mediation: Lawyers, Defendants, Plaintiffs and Gendered Parties (Cambridge University Press).

---

3. The History of the U.S. Mediation Movement

a. Roots

The resolution of conflict by both adversarial contest and peacemaking activities has ancient origins. History chronicles parallel movements, as well as tension, between justice as embodied in the imposition of law backed by force and justice inherent in voluntary agreement and reconciliation. Various religious groups have long traditions of mediation, from Jewish rabbinical courts to mediative mechanisms used by Puritan, Quaker, Muslim, and other religious groups.

Professor David Luban describes an early reported settlement of a case that could have become an adversarial contest among the gods:

> The first trial in Greek literature occurs in the Homeric *Hymn to Hermes*. The infant Hermes, on the night of his birth, steals the cattle of Apollo, who eventually tracks him down. Hermes in the meantime has climbed back into his crib and donned his swaddling clothes. He indignantly denies the deed and swears mighty oaths of innocence: "I will swear the great oath on my father's head. I vow that I myself am not the culprit and that I have seen no one else stealing your cows — whatever these cows are" . . . Apollo takes Hermes before Zeus for judgment. Zeus is more amused than angered at Hermes' prodigious theft; he commands the two gods "to come to an accord and search for the cattle." Hermes shows Apollo where he has hidden them, then he placates Apollo with the gift of a splendid tortoise shell lyre, together with the secret

---

King Solomon — Mediator or Arbitrator?

Many people know the story about King Solomon and the two mothers — two women claiming they were the mother of the same child. King Solomon offers to settle the dispute by cutting the baby in half with his sword. When he lifts his sword to do so, one of the women cries out "No, don't cut the baby — give it to her" (the other woman). "Ah," says King Solomon, "then you must be the real mother for you do not want harm to come to the child." If you see this as a clever way for a judge to get evidence, what might a mediator have done?

> of playing it. The delighted Apollo reciprocates by granting Hermes "a beautiful staff of wealth and prosperity"; and the two gods become eternal allies. This delightful comic poem inaugurates a theme of profound importance. It is noteworthy that

Zeus is concerned above all with harmony and friendship among the Olympians, and not with punishment for Hermes' crime or for his violation of a sacred oath. The dispute between Apollo and Hermes is resolved by an amicable settlement and not a judgment.[1]

Mediation is not a new approach to dispute resolution. What follows is an examination of some recent developments in the United States.

b. Labor

Formal institutionalization of mediation in the United States first occurred in the labor field. The U.S. Department of Labor created a panel in 1913 to handle labor-management conflicts. In 1947, this panel evolved into the Federal Mediation and Conciliation Service, which is charged with maintaining stability in industries through mediation.

Two types of mediation characterize labor and employment disputes: collective bargaining mediation and the mediation of individual employee grievances. In collective bargaining mediation, where the terms and conditions of employment are negotiated, participants are generally experienced professionals representing large constituencies. Mediators must be knowledgeable about workplace issues and special bargaining dynamics. Where mediators help to address individual employee grievances — including claims of discrimination — the parties describe the issues that have affected them personally. The discussion can be therapeutic insofar as parties feel heard, and indirectly, the workplace may be improved by individuals getting responsive treatment to their concerns or reparations for their injuries.

c. Community

The Civil Rights Act of 1964 created the Community Relations Service (CRS) of the U.S. Department of Justice to help resolve disputes involving discrimination through negotiation and mediation and to restore disrupted racial and ethnic harmony. The CRS has intervened in a variety of controversies, including disruptions around desegregation orders, marches of the Ku Klux Klan, and tensions resulting from a lack of cultural awareness of, for example, Arab and Muslim cultural and religious practices. Today, mediation programs in state and federal agencies still respond to disputes concerning discrimination.

Neighborhood justice centers (also called community dispute resolution centers), where volunteer mediators intervene in community cases or "minor disputes," have been funded by state and federal budgets since the 1960s. Community centers receive case referrals both from the courts and from other agencies and institutions, as well as serve "walk-in" clients. These centers typically address disputes between landlords and tenants, neighbors, family members, persons involved in love triangle or work place situations, and a variety of other matters. Developed to be responsive to disputes that the litigation system could not handle effectively, community mediation centers have thrived on the simple premise that parties can solve their

---

1. David Luban, Some Greek Trials: Order and Justice in Homer, Hediod, Aeschylus and Plato, 54 Tenn. L. Rev. 279, 280 (1986).

problems with the help of trained interveners and, in so doing, achieve better outcomes and alleviate the tensions that conflict engenders in communities.

d. Family

One of the major growth areas for mediation has been in family disputes. The acrimony and expense surrounding divorce and the breakup of families has had such an adverse impact on parents, children, extended families, and society generally that courts, clients, and practitioners have sought "a better way" than litigation. Many states now mandate mediation in cases involving child custody and visitation before litigation is permitted. Some courts mandate or encourage mediation of property and partner support, sometimes separately and sometimes in conjunction with custody issues. Private practitioners, as well as court programs, provide mediation services to families. Success in divorce mediation has encouraged the development of mediation programs in other family situations such as probate disputes and mediation between parents and children in PINS (persons in need of supervision) proceedings.

Family mediators come to the field from a variety of backgrounds, including psychology, mental health, and social work, as well as law. It is not uncommon for co-mediation teams to work with divorcing parties. One mediator may be expert in psychology and the other in law and financial issues. Such teams are often gender-balanced as well.

e. Civil Cases

In 1976 many eminent jurists and scholars gathered at the Pound Conference on the Causes of Popular Dissatisfaction with the Administration of Justice. As Chapter 1 explores in more detail, at the conference, Professor Frank Sander described a different vision of a justice system in which courts "have many doors," some leading to litigation and others leading to alternative processes. Many legal scholars trace the modern U.S. alternative dispute resolution (ADR) movement to this event.

A purported "litigation boom" in the late 1970s and 1980s spurred on overloaded judges to find ways to reduce court dockets. By 1988 Florida authorized civil trial court judges to refer almost any civil case to mediation. Other state and federal courts followed suit, and today mediation is a predictable step in the pre-litigation process in many venues.

f. Cybermediation

A variety of providers offer online mediation mechanisms, including the American Arbitration Association Online (*https://services.adr.org/eroom*) and the Mediation Room (*www.themediationroom.com*). Cyberspace offers speed and the convenience of operating from your home computer. Such efficiencies are particularly appealing to parties residing in different countries. However, in the case of mediation services, the lack of face-to-face communication has been criticized as compromising one of mediation's key hallmarks of promoting better understanding between disputants, though improved video capabilities might change this calculus.

g. Other Arenas

It is hard to find an area where mediation is not used for resolving disputes. Mediation is an important resolution tool today in organizations, schools, government agencies, the criminal and civil justice system, and for environmental, construction, police-civilian, international, and intellectual property disputes.

In business matters, the International Institute for **C**onflict **P**revention and **R**esolution (CPR) has obtained commitments from many Fortune 500 companies to use mediation and other ADR processes rather than (or at least before) litigation. Mediation, with its forward-looking aspect, appeals to businesspeople who want to avoid the costs and risks of litigation and also want to preserve ongoing business relationships.

4. Mediation's Core Values

The following two excerpts capture critical features of the essence and origins of mediation. Note how mediation does not lend itself to a simple, mechanical description.

 Carrie Menkel-Meadow, INTRODUCTION

in Mediation: Theory, Practice and Policy xiii-xiv, xvi-xvii, xxix (2000)

Mediation is both a legal process and more than a legal process, used for thousands of years by all sorts of communities, families and formal governmental units. . . . [It] has become a sort of aspirational ideology for those who see its promise in promoting more productive ways of expressing and dealing with human conflict. . . . Mediation, in this larger sense, represents a political theory about the role of conflict in society, the importance of equality, participation, self-determination and a form of leaderless leadership in problem-solving and decision-making. Mediation, as a theory, is aspirational and utopian. In its most grandiose forms, mediation theorists and proponents expect mediation, as a process, to achieve the transformation of warring nation-states, differing ethnic groups, diverse communities, and disputatious workplaces, families and individuals and to develop new and creative human solutions to otherwise difficult or intractable problems. For some, it is a process for achieving interpersonal, intrapersonal and intrapsychic knowledge and understanding. . . .

Mediation, as a structured form of conflict resolution, challenges the Anglo-American idea of adversarial dispute resolution, which presumes that two sides must argue their case to a third-party neutral who will make rule-based, often binary, decisions about who is right and wrong. Instead, it offers the possibility of party-crafted solutions to problems, disputes, conflicts, transactions and relationships, which are facilitated by a third party with no authority to decide anything or to impose any rules. Parties to mediation may engage in other legalistic processes,

developing party-specific rules or understandings, even legislating or creating constitutions for their relationships in the future, all on a voluntary and consensual,
rather than coercive, basis. Thus mediation's authority is derived from the voluntary
commitment of the parties and their facilitator, rather than the coercion of rules, a
judge or the state (with some modern exceptions . . . as when courts sometimes
"mandate" mediation). . . .

The forms that mediation takes are themselves subject to debate. While most
definitions of mediation conclude that a third-party *neutral* should facilitate the
negotiation among parties, many mediation processes — historically and with
cultural variations — in fact involve a third party who is quite enmeshed in the
community as a "wise elder" or, in more recent times, as a substantive expert who
may promise *impartiality* to the parties but who may know quite a bit about the
disputants or the subject matter of the dispute. Mediation's forms, then, are variable
across cultures, times and different political systems. . . . To the extent that mediation privileges certain forms of communication ("talking cures") its use and its
forms may be varied in different settings by culture, nationality, ethnicity, gender,
race and class. . . . As anthropologists and other scholars have discovered, there is no
cultural uniformity to the practice or form of mediation, and different social
groupings and political configurations may re-form or deform the mediation mode
to respond to their particular interests. Some have suggested that mediation, with
its focus on words, communications and interpersonal competence, may be ethno-
centrically based in cultures that privilege such forms of problem-solving. . . .

THE FUTURE HOPE AND PROMISE OF MEDIATION

Theorists and practitioners of mediation claim a central core of functions for
mediation:

1. that it is a consensual process, both in participation and in agreements
   reached;
2. that it is, at its core, voluntarily engaged in (subject to recent efforts to mandate mediation in some contractual or court settings);
3. that it is participatory by the principals engaged in whatever problem or
   issue is presented at the mediation (who may have representatives who
   appear as well);
4. that it is "facilitated" by a third party "outside" the immediate dispute or
   conflict (the "neutrality" principle reframed to reflect some of the recent
   developments in use of expert facilitators);
5. that it seeks to develop solutions to problems or resolutions of conflicts or
   disputes on terms of mutual agreement and fairness to the parties; and
6. that it seeks to facilitate mutual understanding and apprehension of the other
   parties' needs, interests and situations.

These core functions are located within an ideology or belief system, held by
most theorists and practitioners of mediation, that such a process will reduce unnecessary conflict or acrimony among and between people in conflict, will lead to
increased learning and knowledge about others and, where possible, will facilitate

the creation of mutually satisfactory solutions to problems or resolutions of conflict that are better than what the parties might have achieved in other fora.

> ### Problem 6-3.   *The Relation Between Values and Approach*
> As you consider the story of Zeus' intervention in the dispute between Hermes and Apollo, what values were served by the approach Zeus took? What arguments could you make that judgment and punishment of Hermes would be a more prudent approach?

The excerpt that follows also analyzes the central values of mediation. In Chapter 1, the writing of Lon Fuller explored core values in different processes. Themes raised here by Fuller — how mediation builds a different relationship among parties and hence affects the resolution of future controversies — emphasize the more expansive potential of mediation beyond settlement of specific controversies.

 ### Lon L. Fuller, MEDIATION — ITS FORMS AND FUNCTIONS

44 S. Cal. L. Rev. 305, 307-309, 325-327 (1971)

Casual treatments of the subject in the literature of sociology tend to assume that the object of mediation is to make the parties aware of the "social norms" applicable to their relationship and to persuade them to accommodate themselves to the "structure" imposed by these norms. From this point of view the difference between a judge and a mediator is simply that the judge orders the parties to conform themselves to the rules, while the mediator persuades them to do so. But mediation is commonly directed, not toward achieving conformity to norms, but toward the creation of the relevant norms themselves. This is true, for example, in the very common case where the mediator assists the parties in working out the terms of a contract defining their rights and duties toward one another. In such a case there is no pre-existing structure that can guide mediation; it is the mediational process that produces the structure.

It may be suggested that mediation is always, in any event, directed toward bringing about a more harmonious relationship between the parties, whether this be achieved through explicit agreement, through a reciprocal acceptance of the "social norms" relevant to their relationship, or simply because the parties have been helped to a new and more perceptive understanding of one another's problems. The fact that in ordinary usage the terms "mediation" and "conciliation" are largely interchangeable tends to reinforce this view of the matter.

But at this point we encounter the inconvenient fact that mediation can be directed, not toward cementing a relationship, but toward terminating it. In a form of mediation that is coming to be called "marriage therapy," mediative efforts between husband and wife may be undertaken by a psychoanalyst, a psychiatrist, a social worker, a marriage counselor, or even a friendly neighbor. In this situation it will not infrequently turn out that the most effective use of mediation will be in assisting the parties to accept the inevitability of divorce. In a radically different context one of the most dramatically successful uses of mediation I ever witnessed involved a case in which an astute mediator helped the parties rescind a business contract. Two corporations were entrapped by a long-term supply contract that had become burdensome and disadvantageous to both. Canceling it, however, was a complicated matter, requiring a period of "phasing out" and various financial adjustments back and forth. For some time the parties had been chiefly engaged in reciprocal threats of a law suit. On the advice of an attorney for one of the parties, a mediator (whose previous experience had been almost entirely in the field of labor relations) was brought in. Within no time at all a severance of relations was accomplished and the two firms parted company happily.

Thus we find that mediation may be directed toward, and result in discrepant and even diametrically opposed results. This circumstance argues against our being able to derive any general structure of the mediational process from some identifiable goal shared by all mediational efforts. We may, of course, indulge in observations to the effect that the mere presence of a third person tends to put the parties on their good behavior, that the mediator can direct their verbal exchanges away from recrimination and toward the issues that need to be faced, that by receiving separate and confidential communication from the parties he can gradually bring into the open issues so deep-cutting that the parties themselves had shared a tacit taboo against any discussion of them and that, finally, he can by his management of the interchange demonstrate to the parties that it is possible to discuss divisive issues without either rancor or evasion. . . . [This] analysis . . . has dealt only inferentially and indirectly with what may be said to be the central quality of mediation, namely, its capacity to reorient the parties toward each other, not by imposing rules on them, but by helping them to achieve a new and shared perception of their relationship, a perception that will redirect their attitudes and dispositions toward one another.

This quality of mediation becomes most visible when the proper function of the mediator turns out to be, not that of inducing the parties to accept formal rules for the governance of their future relations, but that of helping them to free themselves from the encumbrance of rules and of accepting, instead, a relationship of mutual respect, trust and understanding that will enable them to meet shared contingencies without the aid of formal prescriptions laid down in advance. Such a mediational effort might well come into play in any of the various forms of mediation between husband and wife associated with "family counseling" and "marriage therapy." In the task of reestablishing the marriage as a going concern the mediator might find it essential to break up formalized conceptions of "duty" and to substitute a more fluid sense of mutual trust and shared responsibility. In effect, instead of working toward achieving a rule-oriented relationship he might devote his efforts, to some degree at least, in exactly the opposite direction.

. . . The negotiation of an elaborate written contract, such as that embodied in a collective bargaining agreement between an employer and a labor union, does indeed present a special set of problems for the mediator. . . . [I]t should be remembered that the primary function of the mediator in the collective bargaining situation is not to propose rules to the parties and to secure their acceptance of them, but to induce the mutual trust and understanding that will enable the parties to work out their own rules. The creation of rules is a process that cannot itself be rule-bound; it must be guided by a sense of shared responsibility and a realization that the adversary aspects of the operation are part of a larger collaborative undertaking. The primary task of the arbitrator [sic] is to induce this attitude of mind and spirit, though to be sure, he does this primarily by helping the parties to perceive the concrete ways in which this shared attitude can redound to their mutual benefit.

It should also be noted that the benefits of a collective bargaining agreement do not lie simply in the aptness of the numbered paragraphs that appear over the parties' signatures, but derive also from the mutual understanding produced by the process of negotiation itself. I once heard an experienced and perceptive lawyer observe, speaking of complex business agreements, "If you negotiate the contract thoroughly, explore carefully the problems that can arise in the course of its administration, work out the proper language to cover the various contingencies that may develop, you can then put the contract in a drawer and forget it." What he meant was that in the exchange that accompanied the negotiation and drafting of the contract the parties would come to understand each other's problems sufficiently so that when difficulties arose they would, as fair and reasonable men, be able to make the appropriate adjustments without referring to the contract itself.

> ### Problem 6-4.   *Providing a Fish or Making Fishermen*
> After studying Fuller's excerpt, what are the prime benefits of mediation? Is it more important that the process can settle a given dispute? Or that it can realign relationships so that parties can resolve disputes themselves without the need for outside intervention?

> ### Problem 6-5.   *The Effect of Means on Ends*
> In light of the benefits that Fuller articulates, consider some reported case you have studied. In what ways might mediation have served the parties differently than litigation?

5. Mediation's Place in the Justice System

Although mediation may be an excellent dispute resolution process for many disputes, it is just one among an array of processes that complement each other and serve different goals. The following excerpts illuminate how mediation fits into the landscape of major processes comprising our justice system. In the first, an idealized, simplified description of litigation, arbitration, and mediation illustrates how each of these processes has a legitimate claim to the delivery of justice. The second article delineates various rationales a court might consider when including a mediation component and explores the contrasting purposes of litigation and mediation.

 Lela P. Love, IMAGES OF JUSTICE

1 Pepp. Disp. Resol. L.J. 29, 29-32 (2000)

. . . In an effort to capture the vision behind the three major dispute resolution processes, this essay will present an image of a judge, an arbiter and a mediator. . . .

LITIGATION

Standing straight and tall in public places, a blindfolded woman holds up scales. Since she is blindfolded, she cannot be swayed by gender, race, wealth, or other influences or advantages that one party might hold. On her scales, disputing parties rest their case: the best they can muster for themselves and the worst they can present about the other side. The matter is weighed on these scales in public view, and the balance resolves the matter.

The scales themselves get more precisely balanced after each weighing, after each case. The weight and moment of precise and particular factors are calibrated, and the blindfolded lady announces how much factors weigh, this time, and for all time.

Should a party suspect that the scales were out of balance or the blindfold had been lifted, he may appeal to higher authorities to test the integrity of the process.

This lady is accessible to all, rich and poor alike. Like the other commanding woman standing at the Golden Door in NYC harbor with a torch of liberty, she says, "Give me your tired, your poor, your humbled masses yearning . . .". And if one party invokes her aid, the other must answer and counter-weight the scale, or risk an unfavorable verdict. He must also risk the power behind this blindfolded figure — the power of the state to take and give property and liberty. . . .

ARBITRATION

Wise, sophisticated, trusted, and honored in his community, the arbitrator is chosen by the parties who can agree that whatever such a person decides is just. The arbitrator does not wear blindfolds because the parties trust his discretion. On the other hand, the arbitrator cannot meet privately with a party, because the parties do not trust each other.

The arbitrator stands, aloof from the parties, arms folded in skepticism, but listening attentively for each clue which will piece together the puzzle of facts he must see clearly.

The gift the arbitrator gives the parties is a prompt decision informed by his expertise in the particular arena. His decision is bound to favor one party over the other, but his quick and precise award will allow the parties to move on with their lives and their businesses.

There is no appeal from this arbitrator because, in choosing him, the parties chose to live with what he decides. Thus, the power of the arbitrator is immense, once conferred by the parties, and is further bolstered by the blindfolded lady who will ensure that his awards are honored. . . .

MEDIATION

In this image one sees a figure sitting with the parties, her hands reaching towards each of them as if to support them in telling their tale or to caution them in listening to each other to weigh the matter more carefully. It is also possible that her outreached hands are pointing to the parties to remind them of their responsibility for dealing thoughtfully with their situation and each other, understanding the opportunities and risks inherent in various choices, and summoning their creativity in addressing the conflict.

The figure is not alone or aloof. Her outstretched arms form a bridge between the parties, so that communication and positive energy can flow again. Her presence is a catalyst setting in motion the potential that the parties hold.

Unlike the blindfolded lady, the mediator sees all that is offered unprotected by formal procedure or rules of evidence. Unlike the arbitrator or the judge, the mediator may meet with the parties together or listen to them privately so that each nuance of meaning and each atom of possibility are captured and offered back, in their most palatable form, for the parties.

The mediator's features are hazy, since the focus and light remains on the disputing parties. Her presence, however, exudes optimism, respect, and confidence in the parties' capacity. She brings an energetic and urgent sense that justice can be done by the parties' own hands.

Problem 6-6.   *The Ideal vs. the Real*

When reality diverges from the ideal, problems can arise. In Jarndyce v. Jarndyce the reality of the court system diverged in important ways from the ideal. Can you articulate the ways? If you have participated in a mediation, how did it differ from the ideal described here?

Problem 6-7.   *The Ideal?*

You will see in the following mediation chapters that mediation is often different from the ideal described above. Similarly, arbitration does not always (or even usually) follow this ideal. Isn't flexibility and customization to individual disputes also an "ideal" that Appropriate Dispute Resolution should advance?

In the following excerpt, Professor Robert Baruch Bush explores the underlining rationale for litigation and mediation and examines whether and how mediation should become part of court-sponsored dispute resolution.

Robert A. Baruch Bush, **MEDIATION AND
ADJUDICATION, DISPUTE RESOLUTION AND
IDEOLOGY: AN IMAGINARY CONVERSATION**

3 J. Contemp. Legal Issues 1, 1-6, 12 (1990)

The setting for the conversation is as follows. A judge has been empowered by a state statute to refer cases from his civil docket to mediation. The statute says that he can, in his discretion, refer any and all cases; the decision is his, and the parties cannot refuse mediation without showing good cause. The judge can send all his cases to mediation on a blanket basis or certain categories of cases, or individual cases on a case by case basis, whichever he decides. This is what the statute empowers him to do, and the Supreme Court has set up rules enabling him and other judges to do it. The problem is that the judge is uncertain how to exercise this new power. He has no clear idea which cases, if any, he should refer to the mediation process.

So, he picks six representative cases from his civil docket: a divorce case with a custody question, a complex commercial litigation, a landlord-tenant case, a discrimination suit, a consumer case, and a personal injury litigation. He sends copies of the case files, with names deleted, to four individuals who are friends or associates: his law clerk, his court administrator, his former law professor, and a practicing mediator who is a friend of his. The judge asks each of them for their advice. Should he send any of these cases to mediation? All of them? None of them? What should he do?

He is a bit startled when he gets back the results of this survey, because he gets four completely different recommendations. From the law professor, he gets the recommendation that he should send no cases to mediation; all the cases should stay in court. The law clerk gives him a more complex recommendation. He says that the discrimination case, the consumer case, and the personal injury case should be kept in court, but the divorce, the landlord-tenant, and the commercial cases should go to mediation. The court administrator says he should send them all to mediation, unless both parties to the dispute object; if both parties object, he shouldn't refer them to mediation, whatever the type of case. Finally, the mediator tells him that he should send all the cases to mediation, whether or not the parties object.

The judge is puzzled by this set of responses [and] . . . does what judges are very good at doing. He calls all four advisors and says, "I'd like you to argue this out in front of me. I want to hear what you have to say in the presence of one another. That way you can present the reasons for your recommendations, and I can hear some kind of response from you towards one another."

So, the four advisors come together with the judge in an informal meeting over lunch. The court administrator goes first. "Judge," she begins, "I'll tell you the reason for my recommendation. As far as I'm concerned, the most important goal we have here is saving time and money. That's the main goal that we want to keep in mind in using your powers under this new mediation statute. I suspect that was the legislature's main reason for enacting this law. The courts are heavily backlogged, delay is epidemic, and adding new judges and courtrooms appears fiscally — and politically — impossible. Settlements are the only solution. Settling cases is going to save public and private expense. It's also going to increase public satisfaction with the system. Now, since all cases have some potential to settle," she continues, "and we don't know which ones will and which ones won't, it makes sense to refer them all to mediation, unless we have a clear indication in advance that there's no real settlement possibility. For example, if both parties show a clear desire not to go to mediation, not to negotiate, then in that case it makes no sense to waste the time." She concludes, "That is the reason for my recommendation. Refer to mediation, unless it's clear that there's opposition on both sides to settlement."

The law clerk then is called upon. He says, "Judge, as you know, I disagree, and the reason for my recommendation is the following. In my view, the main goal is not saving time and money, regardless of what the legislature may have had in mind. There are other goals of dispute resolution that are much more important.

"Generally, it, seems to me," the law clerk continues, "protecting individual rights and ensuring some kind of substantive fairness to both sides in the resolution of the dispute are the most important goals. And when rights and substantive fairness are most important, adjudication in court is the best tool we have to accomplish those goals. However, there are cases, where rights and fairness are not the only or the most important goals. For example, if there is an ongoing relationship between the parties, preserving that relationship may be very important both to the parties and to the public. In that case, mediation would be desirable, because preserving relationships is something that mediation does much better than the adjudication process. Therefore, I think that you can distinguish between cases on the basis of the ongoing relationship factor. When you have such a relationship, refer to mediation; otherwise, keep the case in court. That's the way I've split up the cases you sent us. I'm not sure that it's immediately obvious from the way I've divided them, but that was my criterion, and I think it's the best one for you to use."

Next it is the mediator's turn. "I both agree and disagree with the administrator and the law clerk, your Honor," she explains. "Saving time and money must be considered important, and preserving relationships, in certain cases, is also a very important goal. But both of these are really just part of a more general goal that I consider the most important aim of dispute resolution: that is, to reach the best possible substantive result or solution to the parties' problem. Sometimes the best solution will be one that saves the parties time and money; sometimes it will be one that preserves the relationship. Sometimes it will be one that does neither of these. That will depend on many details of the case."

"But whatever the details, there is plenty of evidence now that, in terms of achieving the best results for the individual case in question, mediation is a process that has tremendous advantages over adjudication. The process is flexible, issues can be framed more effectively and discussed more fully, a greater variety of possible solutions can be considered, and unique, innovative and integrative solutions are possible, even likely. Therefore, mediation ought to be tried first in all cases because the potential to arrive at superior substantive results is always greater in mediation than in adjudication. If mediation doesn't work, if there's no resolution, then the parties can go back to court. But, in the first instance, achieving superior results is the most important goal to strive for in every single case. And mediation is the best vehicle we have for doing this. That's why I recommended referring all your cases to mediation, without exceptions."

Finally the law professor speaks. "Your Honor," he begins, "I'm sorry to have to disagree. But all of your other friends here have missed the point. I say this because they're all talking about goals that don't really pertain to your function, the function of a court. A court is a public institution, and the goal of a court as a public institution is not to save time and money; nor is it to help private parties secure private benefits in individual cases. Your goal as a public institution is to promote important public values. That ought to be your primary concern: the promotion and the securing of important public values through the dispute resolution process. That is what distinguishes your function from that of a mere private arbitrator, and justifies the public support — legal and fiscal — given uniquely to the courts."

"I submit to you, your Honor, that the most important public values at stake in dispute resolution are basically four. There may be others; but I think that these four have widely been recognized as the most important ones. First is the protection of the fundamental civil rights of the parties as individuals. Second is the pursuit of substantive or social justice, as between different classes represented by the parties in the case, and especially as between rich and poor, strong and weak, haves and have-nots. Third is the promotion of what the economists call efficiency — that is, the greatest possible level of aggregate societal welfare — through encouragement of activities that make the best use of our limited societal resources. And fourth is the establishment and articulation of public values that give us a sense of social solidarity in our society as a whole, which is of course a very pluralistic one and therefore requires the cement of shared values. . . ."

"Your Honor," the professor continues, "adjudication serves every one of these values. It does so because it operates by using and generating both procedural and substantive rules — using them in the instant case, and generating them for future cases. Indeed the rules themselves are often related to and based upon these values. Substantive rules promote economic welfare by signaling economic actors how to use resources efficiently. Substantive and procedural rules promote social justice by reducing the advantage of the powerful, in the aggregate and in the individual case. Procedural rules protect directly against violations of fundamental civil rights. And substantive rules foster solidarity by giving meaning to shared public values. Therefore, the rule-based, public adjudication process is an excellent — an unparalleled — instrument for accomplishing these values. Mediation, on the other hand, weakens and undermines every single one of these values. Why? Because, simply, it neither uses in the instant case, nor generates for the future, rules, whether procedural or substantive, based on these values or any other values. Mediation rests solely on the expedient of compromise. Therefore it cannot help but undermine all of these important, rule-dependent values."

"This brings me to the heart of my argument, your Honor," says the professor. "First, we can't sacrifice public values of this stature solely to save time and money. Certainly, we can't do so as a matter of public policy. If, as a matter of necessity, the courts can't handle all cases, that's one thing. But to adopt a public policy saying that values like rights protection and social justice are less important than saving money and judicial economy would be inexcusable. Second, there's no way of neatly dividing up cases on the basis that some involve these public values and others do not. That simply isn't true. All six of the kinds of cases that you submitted to us involve one or more of these public values. Indeed, most of them involve several. The same would be true for any other disputes we might examine." Here the professor went into a lengthy analysis of how this was so, which for the sake of brevity we will not reproduce. "Therefore," he concluded, " 'channeling' of different cases to different processes is undesirable."

"Finally, you cannot, as the mediator suggested, consider the value of better results for the parties in the individual case superior to these *public* values. You cannot do so, your Honor, as a matter of public policy. Why not? Because this would be to put private benefit over public values, over the public good, and as a public servant you cannot legitimately do so. . . . Therefore, your Honor, I say all of these cases should remain in court, unless perhaps a petition is submitted by both parties to adjourn pending voluntarily initiated settlement discussions or mediation." . . .

Before the judge has a chance to adjourn and consider arguments more thoroughly, however, the mediator asks the judge for one more minute. "Judge," she says, "I have another point to make. The reason I didn't make it before is that it's a little hard to articulate. But I see I will have to try. The truth is that the concern for better results in individual cases is not all that makes mediation important, in my view, even though I admit that most advocates of mediation emphasize this as the primary advantage of mediation. But there's more involved, and it goes far beyond expediency and private benefit. When I say mediation ought to be used in all these cases, my reason is also based on promoting public values, public values which are important to all of the cases you sent us, public values, different from and more important than the ones that the professor mentioned. In other words, like the professor's argument for adjudication, my argument for mediation is also a public values argument, but it is based on a different view of public values than the view he presented."

"Now, my problem is that it is hard to articulate clearly what these different public values are. I think they're evoked or implied by concepts like reconciliation, social harmony, community, interconnection, relationship, and the like. Mediation does produce superior results, as I argued earlier. But it also involves a non-adversarial process that is less traumatic, more humane, and far more capable of healing and reconciliation than adjudication. Those are the kinds of concerns that make me feel that these cases ought to be handled in mediation, not for private benefit reasons and not for expediency reasons, but because of these reconciliatory public values promoted by mediation. . . ."

"How can I define this public value? Simply put, it is the value of providing a moral and political education for citizens, in responsibility for themselves and respect for others. In a democracy, your honor, that must be considered a crucial public value and it must be considered a public function. As far as I'm concerned, there's the potential for that kind of direct and experiential education in every single one of these cases that you sent to us; and that potential can only be realized in mediation. It cannot be accomplished in adjudication. . . . In my view, this civic education value is more important than the values that the professor is concerned about. . . . Finally, I just want to clarify an important connection between my argument here and our earlier discussion. On reflection, I've realized that the 'superior results' argument that I mentioned at our first meeting is also based, at least in part, on the public value I'm talking about here. That is, many of us place value on the integrative, 'win/win' solutions that mediation helps produce precisely because such solutions embody in concrete terms the kind of respect for others that is the essence of the civic education value. So the 'superiority' of results we speak of is not only, or primarily, that the results better serve the individual interests of the parties — a private benefit — but that they express each individual's considered choice to respect and accommodate the other to some degree — a democratic public value. In short, both the experience of the mediation process and the kind of results it produces serve the public value of civic education in self-determination and respect for others."

Problem 6-8.   *You Be the Judge*

If you were the judge, what would you decide? What would be your rationale for choosing to refer or not refer cases (and certain case types) to mediation? Why were some of the characters more persuasive than others?

Problem 6-9.   *Promoting Law or Fostering Relationship*

Returning to the case of Hermes and Apollo, Zeus missed an opportunity to underline and elaborate on the importance of honoring sacred oaths and not stealing. If you were Zeus, does what happened between Hermes and Apollo after your intervention illustrate the values described by Bush's mediator? As you read the case examples that follow, keep asking which of Bush's characters — the law clerk, court administrator, law professor, or mediator — becomes more persuasive.

B. EXAMPLES OF MEDIATIONS

The following accounts of actual and fictional mediations illustrate the variety of practices and outcomes possible in the mediation of real cases. The first case is an appeal by shareholders against a large corporation, which was referred to the mediation program of the U.S. Court of Appeals for the Second Circuit. The second case involves a minority group, a town, and a lawsuit that raised constitutional questions. The third case involves the settlement of a damage claim in a personal injury case. The final example is a medical negligence case.

These provide only a small window into the universe of cases that benefit from mediation. Nonetheless, you will find here examples of (1) outcomes that are more custom-tailored than litigation can provide and a process that leads parties to a deeper appreciation of the other side's perspective (the Sisters and Bristol); (2) outcomes that address a far broader range of issues than litigation and achieve a higher level of cooperation and community among the parties (the Glen Cove case); (3) an account of distributive bargaining and raw compromise, where settlement saves the parties further disputing costs of litigation (the personal injury scenario); and (4) an outcome that provides both the closure and cost savings of a settlement and the personal connection and healing available from direct interaction between parties (the medical malpractice case).

As you read about these situations, imagine how the stories would have come out differently if mediation had not been used.

1. Sisters of the Precious Blood and Bristol-Myers

 Frank J. Scardilli, **SISTERS OF THE PRECIOUS BLOOD v. BRISTOL-MYERS CO.: A SHAREHOLDER-MANAGEMENT DISPUTE**

Presentation at a Harvard Faculty Seminar on negotiation on April 13, 1982

This case was on appeal to the U.S. Court of Appeals for the Second Circuit from a grant of summary judgment in favor of Bristol-Myers Co., defendant-appellee (hereinafter "Bristol") and against the Sisters of the Precious Blood, plaintiff-appellant (hereinafter "Sisters"). The latter, who owned 500 shares of Bristol stock, started a lawsuit against Bristol under the proxy solicitation section of the Securities Exchange Act of 1934 alleging that a shareholder resolution they proposed was defeated because Bristol's stated opposition to the resolution in the proxy materials distributed to the shareholders was based on serious misrepresentations of fact.

The Sisters were concerned that the company's sales practices in the third world of its infant baby formula were contributing to serious illness, malnutrition and death of infants because of the unsanitary conditions often prevailing there. Frequently the formula is mixed with contaminated water, there is no refrigeration and its use discourages breastfeeding which is clearly healthier in most instances than is the formula.

The Sisters' proposed resolution requested that management report to the shareholders the full extent of its marketing practices of the infant formula in the third world to alert other shareholders to what they perceived was irresponsible business behavior. Their lawsuit was aimed at getting the company to come up with a corrected proxy solicitation to be submitted to a special meeting of the shareholders to be called specifically for that purpose rather than await the next annual meeting of shareholders.

The court declined to grant the relief sought by the Sisters. . . .

MEDIATION EFFORTS ON APPEAL

The first of four conferences seeking to mediate this dispute was held on July 19, 1977. . . . Apparently because they believed no amicable resolution was possible, counsel who appeared for the parties were very able but had virtually no settlement authority. . . .

As is customary, I first explored the arguments of counsel relative to the strengths and weaknesses of their legal positions on appeal. The parties seemed genuinely far apart in their assessment of the likely outcome in our court. The issue on appeal involved some complexity because of the rather technical requirements for suits under Section 14 of the Securities Exchange Act of 1934. While generally appellees have a distinct advantage, if for no other reason than that only about one out of eight cases is reversed on appeal in our court, the outcome of this particular case was hard to predict. Even if the district court decision were deemed technically correct, this could have disturbing policy implications because the decision appeared to create a license for management to lie with impunity whenever it sought to defeat a proposed shareholder resolution. . . . The SEC was apparently disturbed by this implication and advised me it was seriously considering filing a brief amicus curiae urging our court to reverse the decision below. . . .

Predictably, the parties' respective positions on what might constitute a satisfactory settlement were far apart. The Sisters were adamant on the principle that no settlement terms could be discussed unless Bristol openly admitted that it had lied in its earlier proxy solicitation and that this fact had to be communicated through new proxy solicitations at a special meeting of the shareholders to be convened solely for that purpose. Bristol, of course, insisted it had been truthful all along. It offered, however, to permit the Sisters to make any written statement they wished at the next annual shareholders' meeting, and Bristol would simply state its opposition to the proposal without elaboration. This was unacceptable to the Sisters. Because it was clear I needed parties with more authority and flexibility, I set up a second conference requiring senior counsel to come in with their clients.

The second conference held in the middle of August, 1977, was attended by senior counsel for both sides, the inside General Counsel of Bristol, and a representative of the Advisory Committee of the Interfaith Group for Corporate Responsibility, which was the real moving force behind the Sisters' litigation.

It soon became apparent that there was very deep hostility and profound distrust between the parties. Each was convinced the other was acting in bad faith. The Sisters were outraged by Bristol's insistence that it had not lied. Its distrust of Bristol was total and uncompromising. At this conference, the Sisters, for the first time, insisted that they would have to be reimbursed for their litigation expenses of approximately $15,000 before any settlement could be effected. After checking with top management, counsel for management flatly refused to pay anything at all to the Sisters. . . .

It became clear that the respective parties' self-image was significantly at variance with the image each had of the other.

Bristol regarded itself as by far the most responsible marketer of infant formula in the third world, far more so than its three major American competitors and the giant Swiss company Nestle. It claimed it put out a quality nutritional product that was very useful when mothers either could not or chose not to breast feed their infants; that it did not advertise its infant formulas directly to consumers in the third world; that the company policy already sought to minimize the danger of improper use by its labeling. In short, it was convinced that its business practices were both prudent and responsible. Therefore, they were furious that they had been singled out as "baby killers" by the Sisters who had so testified before a Congressional committee and who had lost few opportunities to criticize them in the media. It was clear they viewed the Sisters as wild-eyed, misguided religious fanatics who were themselves engaging in a distortion of the facts and reckless character assassination.

The Sisters, on the other hand, had spent years accumulating data in affidavits taken throughout the world regarding the enormous peril to infants created by the indiscriminate use of infant formula in the third world. They had witnessed suffering and death and were suffused with the self-righteousness of avenging angels. To them Bristol was a monster who cared only about profits and not at all about the lives and health of infants. . . .

As negotiations proceeded, it became apparent that no meaningful communication could take place until each of the parties realized that its view of the other was a grossly distorted caricature and counter-productive.

I struck often at the theme that it was dangerous to assume that one with whom you disagree violently is necessarily acting in bad faith. Moreover, I stressed to both that I had become fully and firmly convinced that each of the parties was acting in complete good faith, albeit from a different perspective. I strove to get each to view the matter through the eyes of the other. . . .

It was necessary to convince each that its interests were not nearly as incompatible as they perceived them and that the interest of each would be best served by a cooperative problem-solving attitude rather than a litigious one.

I stressed that neither party's true interest would be served by "winning" the appeal. A "win" by Bristol would not be likely to stop the public attacks in the media which so angered and disturbed them. Likewise, a "win" by the Sisters could mean a remand for an expensive trial with no assurance whatever thereafter that Bristol's marketing practices would be altered in any way.

The point was made forcibly to the Sisters that their insistence that Bristol admit that it had lied was totally unrealistic and that progress was impossible so long as they insisted on humiliating the company's management. They were reminded that their real interest lay in effecting marketing changes in the third world and they could best achieve this in a climate of cooperative good will with management. So long as management perceived them as vindictive it was likely to simply dig in its heels and refuse to budge. I urged that a softening of their attitude would in turn create a more flexible attitude in management.

Bristol in turn was forced to concede that notwithstanding what they viewed as the distasteful stridency of the Sisters there was indeed a real moral issue to be faced and they had a real interest in being perceived as highly ethical, responsible businessmen who were not insensitive to the human tragedy which could result from the improper use of their product in the third world. . . .

After considerable negotiation in four face-to-face conferences supplemented by numerous telephone conferences over a period of nearly six months, in the course of which Bristol voluntarily changed some of its marketing practices, the parties finally agreed to resolve their differences as follows:

1. The Sisters were satisfied that Bristol had already changed some of its marketing practices which the Sisters had regarded as particularly offensive.
2. The Sisters would be given direct access to Bristol's Board of Directors and other representatives of the company at various times for the purpose of maintaining a first-hand continuing dialogue on the problems of marketing infant formula in the third world.
3. Bristol and the Sisters would each prepare a separate written statement of its views not to exceed 1500 words to be presented to the shareholders in the next quarterly report of the Company. This would be preceded by an agreed-upon joint preamble which would recite the background of the litigation, its resolution by the parties and that the Sisters and Bristol planned to continue to exchange views in an atmosphere of mutual respect for each other's good faith.

To insure that the statements would not be inflammatory each side was given the right to veto the statement of the other. Agreeing on the principle, however, was easier than its implementation. Numerous drafts were exchanged and when appropriate I mediated between their respective versions. The final agreement on language was arrived at as a result of a 4.5 hour drafting session involving 8 people sitting around a conference table in the court in the afternoon of Christmas Eve of 1977. In a sense of relief and elation, the Chairperson of the Interfaith Group for Corporate Responsibility stated: "It is fitting and perhaps prophetic that we have finally resolved our differences on how best to protect tender infants on this [Christmas] eve. . . ."

Problem 6-10.   *Private vs. Public Benefit?*

It is usually easy to see how a settlement achieves private benefit, as parties do not usually settle unless the settlement is better than the anticipated legal outcome and its related costs. Using this case as an example, is there *public* benefit from private parties settling a case? And, if something is gained for the public, what is lost? How do you think the professor in the imaginary conversation by Professor Baruch Bush above would react to this mediation description? Remember that the professor is concerned about litigation's role in protecting individual rights, promoting social justice for the poor and weak, maximizing aggregate societal welfare, and articulating public norms.

The case that follows, like the case of the Sisters and Bristol, has the potential for broad societal impact on groups of relatively weak and disenfranchised parties. As you read the case, reflect on the benefits of mediation to the parties in the case and on the impact of taking constitutional issues out of the litigation stream.

2. Glen Cove

 Lela P. Love, GLEN COVE: MEDIATION ACHIEVES
WHAT LITIGATION CANNOT

20 Consensus 1, 1-2 (Oct. 1993)

The city of Glen Cove, Long Island, and Central American refugees who sought day labor at a "shaping point" (a locale in the city where employers go to find day workers) experienced a bitter and protracted controversy with no end in sight — despite nearly two years of litigation — when the parties decided to attempt to work out their differences in mediation. Mediation resolved not only the issues which were being litigated, but also many other issues that, although not causes for legal action, were nonetheless extremely important to the individuals and groups involved in the controversy. . . .

BACKGROUND: TENSIONS BUILD

In 1988 tensions began to build between Glen Cove officials and the Central American immigrants (some of whom were undocumented aliens) who congregated in front of Carmen's Deli to find employment. More than 100 men, many from other towns, would gather on a given day to seek odd jobs from landscapers and other contractors.

Local merchants and neighbors expressed concerns about disorderly and noisy behavior at the shaping point, including cat-calling to women, and littering and urinating in public. City officials were also concerned about traffic safety, since employers would stop on a major road to negotiate with and pick up day workers. There also was a sentiment that it was illegal for those who were undocumented to seek employment.

Salvadoran workers, on the other hand, were interested in their survival, since the day labor was their means of livelihood, and a "shaping point" was essential for finding work. Many who gathered were political refugees from El Salvador, to whom a return home might mean a death sentence. There were those who felt that, since the laborers serviced the lawns and country clubs of the wealthy, the effort to remove them from gathering in public was unfair.

In addition to issues about the shaping point itself, the perception among the Hispanic community that the City — particularly the police — were hostile, created problems for both sides: poor channels of communication to cope with the host of problems; and a lack of resources for Central Americans when they were preyed upon by criminal elements in the community (a pressing problem).

ORDINANCES PROPOSED TO DEAL WITH PROBLEM

Tensions heightened in 1989 when the city, in an effort to curb the size of the gatherings, successfully urged the Immigration and Naturalization Service to round up and detain illegal aliens gathering in front of Carmen's Deli. This was followed by the city's proposing first an ordinance making it illegal for groups of five or more persons to assemble publicly to seek employment and later an ordinance which prohibited any "illegal undocumented alien" from soliciting work in a public or private place. These ordinances engendered a strident debate, although neither was adopted. In 1990, the City Council did adopt an ordinance which prohibited standing on a street or highway and soliciting employment from anyone in a motor vehicle and also prohibited occupants of a stopped or parked motor vehicle from hiring or attempting to hire workers.

The Hispanic community and civil libertarians saw the ordinance(s) as specifically targeted against Hispanics, as well as unconstitutional. Several months after the ordinance was adopted, advocacy groups for Cental American refugees filed a three million dollar class action suit against Glen Cove, alleging violation of Hispanic persons' First Amendment right of freedom of speech and 14th Amendment right of equal protection.

WHAT MEDIATION ACHIEVED

Two full days of mediation, spaced a week apart to give the parties time to come up with innovative proposals to address the concerns raised the first day, were sufficient to achieve consensus on an outline of an acceptable accord. This agreement was refined over several months and adopted in late 1992, providing for the dismissal of the lawsuit and the enforcement of the terms of the agreement by the federal court.

The significant achievements of the mediation process in this case were:

- The parties recognized their mutual interest in improving communications with each other.
- Greater accessibility to the city soccer field for the Salvadoran community was arranged.
- The City agreed to help find alternative sites for a shaping point (including possible use of Industrial Development Agency funds) or to support alternatives to meet the Hispanic community's employment needs. The Central American Refugee Center (CARECEN) agreed to educate day laborers who congregate in public places about their responsibilities to the community.
- Relations between the police and the Salvadoran community were addressed by CARECEN's agreement to host community meetings giving the police a platform to educate Salvadorans about community interests and concerns and undertaking such education themselves. The police in turn agreed to: cultural awareness training for all city police officers; appointing a liaison to the Salvadoran community who would attend CARECEN-organized community meetings; training two officers in conversational Spanish; taking ability in Spanish into account in hiring officers; adopting a policy barring officers from inquiring about immigration status under certain circumstances; and instituting a written protocol (in consultation with CARECEN) for the police handling of situations where a party does not speak English.
- The Ordinance was amended to a form acceptable to all parties and designed to promote the City's interest in traffic safety without singling out the Salvadoran Community or infringing upon Constitutional rights.

Perhaps most importantly, the mediation created a respectful dialogue between the parties, which should result in an enhanced ability to confront new problems as they arise. . . . Alan Levine, the Director of the Hofstra Constitution Law Clinic, which represented CARECEN, was quoted as saying, "If everyone lives up to their obligations under this agreement, it promises to establish the kinds of relationships between a municipal government and a minority population that one would hope for."

The town of Glen Cove has enjoyed improved relations between town officials and the Salvadoran community, arguably, in part, as a byproduct of the mediation. A shaping point, with toilet facilities provided by the city and a variety of supportive services for day laborers, was ultimately put into place. If mediation can set new precedents with respect to community interaction and constructive problem solving, do those results counterbalance the loss of a legal precedent in a case with important constitutional issues?

Problem 6-11.   *What's at Stake?*

Compare the issues addressed in the litigation and mediation of the Glen Cove case:

LITIGATION	MEDIATION
The ordinance	*Communication* between town officials and Salvadorans
Discrete incidents of *alleged police misconduct* at the shaping point	*A shaping point*
	Police interactions with non-English speaking individuals and groups (protocols when language barriers are present, cultural awareness and sensitivity, and opportunities for communication)
	Concerns regarding *public conduct of Salvadorans* ("cat-calling," public urination, blocking entryways)
	Use of the *city soccer field*
	The ordinance

Is a case about the legal causes of action it presents or all the concerns the parties have? What public utility derives from addressing the parties' concerns? In this situation, the plaintiffs' lawyers — prominent civil rights attorneys — had their own agenda regarding creating legal precedent. Would it be ethical for lawyers to ignore their clients' concerns in pursuit of such a goal?

3. Fly on the Wall

The following account of a fictional but representative personal injury mediation is an example of a settlement-oriented process where the mediator uses a joint session only at the beginning for making opening statements and at the end of the mediation for bringing the parties together to confirm agreements. The rest of the process is conducted in caucuses (separate meetings with each side). As you will see, the focus is on arriving at a mutually acceptable dollar amount rather than on exploring the parties' underlying interests or encouraging creative problem solving, a more cynical account of mediation than in the preceding two examples.

 J. S. Levy & R. C. Prather, **FLY ON THE WALL**

Texas Practice Guide: ADR App. A (1999)

To set the stage for the following, it is necessary to establish a factual predicate. Assume that the dispute arose following an intersectional automobile collision that happened approximately three years earlier. Suit was filed a little more than a year ago shortly before the Statute of Limitations barred any recovery. Most of the discovery and other pre-trial work has been completed. Last month the judge ordered the parties to mediate. . . . [After the mediator's opening remarks, each side gives an opening presentation and then are separated into separate caucus rooms. The Plaintiff and his counsel are in one room and the Insurance Adjuster who represents the insurance company is with his counsel in the other room. Here is a slice of what happens in those rooms.]

SCENE ONE: THE PLAINTIFF'S ROOM

Mediator: The door is closed and everything that is said in this room is confidential. Nothing leaves here unless you expressly authorize it. Let's talk. . . . (turning to the Plaintiff) Did you understand what the Adjuster said during the joint session about the most likely jury range?

Plaintiff: No I didn't. How can someone price such a painful injury the way that you price a used car? I don't believe that it can be quantified by some mechanistic formula. . . .

Mediator: Before proceeding, let me repeat one comment that I made a few minutes ago during the joint session: you listen to your attorney and not me. Your counsel is here to represent your best interests, while I am an advocate for settlement.

Having said that, let me continue by observing that there is a certain fiction in our jury system. To illustrate, the loss of a leg has a jury value today in this county of "X" number of dollars, plus or minus 20%. No sane person would "sell" a leg for that amount, but there is a sufficient statistical track record of jury awards to reflect that amount as being the most likely outcome.

From my perspective as the mediator/negotiator, this figure of "X" dollars, plus or minus 20%, is known as the "range of settlement." It is possible that the plaintiff who lost a leg could have a "home run" jury award in the "run away" amount of double or triple "X" dollars. That happens around ten percent of the time. Keep in mind the fact that, at the same time, it is equally logical that the jury in about ten percent of such cases would only award in the area of half of "X" dollars.

I know my remark sounds callous but that is the real world of jury trial. In virtually every personal injury case that I mediate, this county's jury reports are argued as a negotiating tool. It is irrelevant whether you think the Adjuster is a prince or a cretin. The sole issue is whether you can get the Adjuster to make an offer you can accept. . . . (turning to the Counsel for the Plaintiff) Have there been any settlement talks?

Counsel for the Plaintiff: Prior to suit, I offered to settle for the policy limits of $100,000 and the Adjuster responded with an offer of $8,000. The Adjuster said that if I would drop my offer to a "more realistic amount" — whatever . . . that means — that a higher offer would be forthcoming.

After talking with my client, I moved to $70,000 and the Adjuster then made an offer of $12,000. At that point, I asked the Adjuster to double the $12,000 offer and the response was a comment to the effect that my mother wore a flea collar. Suffice it to say that discussions broke down then so I filed suit. There have been no settlement talks subsequently. . . .

Mediator (to the counsel for the Plaintiff): I know that you have a good reputation as a trial attorney. However, let me ask you to momentarily step out of the role of an advocate and let's talk about the most likely jury award if this case were ever to go to trial.

Counsel: Why? Aren't you going to be able to settle this case for me?

Mediator: No, I don't settle anything. It's the parties that cause settlement. I help in the communications. It's y'all who settle a case.

Let me phrase my question a little differently. If you were to try this case a hundred times for a hundred consecutive weeks in that same court with that judge, what would be the probable, objective range of jury awards? Of course, this case can only be tried once. For purposes of your evaluation, disregard the 10% "Armageddon" scenario on the low end and the 10% "home run" result on the other end of the spectrum, since no case ever settles at mediation in either of those areas.

Counsel for the Plaintiff: The numbers would be between $25,000 on the low end and $35,000 on the high end. However, understand that I have a really good Plaintiff. The jury will like the Plaintiff. For that reason, the jury award will be at the top end of that range, so I don't want you to try later today into talking about a settlement in the $25,000 to $30,000 area. Do you understand me! . . .

Mediator: You know that the Adjuster is not going to pay $70,000 on this claim, since if the Adjuster were going to do so, we would not be here today. By your own analysis, the case is worth no more than half that figure. Finally, you can safely assume that the other side thinks the jury value of the case is a figure lower than your projection of $25,000 to $35,000.

Plaintiff (angrily to the Counsel for the Plaintiff): Stop for a moment. If my case is worth only $35,000, why did we initially demand $100,000 and then offered to settle at $70,000? I was planning on walking away after all fees, medical bills and expenses with a net of more than $35,000. Something is wrong with this equation! I feel like a chihuahua surrounded by a pack of pit bulls.

Counsel for Plaintiff (turning to Plaintiff): Perhaps I need to refresh your memory. You and I spoke about the most likely outcome at trial before I reduced our settlement offer from $100,000 to $70,000. . . .

Mediator (turning to Counsel for the Plaintiff): Realistically speaking, where would you like the Adjuster to be on the next round of offers? . . .

Plaintiff (to the Mediator): What do you mean "on the next round"?

Mediator (to the Plaintiff): A mediation is not the type of function where someone can leave the engine running and quickly go inside to pick up a check. According to one study done on the topic of mediation, there usually are six to eight sets of offers and counteroffers until the parties either agree to a settlement or agree that an impasse has been reached. In short, today's negotiation is a give and take process, with a certain element of a battle of attrition. . . .

Plaintiff: Then let's go to $65,000. . . .

Mediator: Keeping in mind the Adjuster has the checkbook, it may not be wise to anger him. Look at the issue this way, his previous offer was $12,000, which is $13,000 from the bottom of your own jury range. At the same time, the $65,000 figure that you suggest is $30,000 above the top end of your range. . . .

Counsel for Plaintiff (to the Mediator): What figure would you propose to take to the Adjuster?

Mediator: I propose nothing, as that is not my role. However, if you want a suggestion, let me throw out the idea that you reduce your demand to $50,000, along with a message that the Adjuster needs to double the $12,000 offer.

Plaintiff (to the Mediator): Tell the Adjuster that I will settle for $60,000.

Counsel for Plaintiff (to the Mediator): That's our decision.

Mediator: Will do. Thank you. . . .

SCENE TWO: THE ADJUSTER'S ROOM

Mediator: Thank you for being patient. Usually the first meeting with the Plaintiff is the longest. . . . The Plaintiff has now moved to $60,000.

Adjuster: That's double where the Plaintiff should be! Why in the world would the Plaintiff think this is a sasquatch-sized claim?

Mediator: If for purposes of discussion the Plaintiff were to go to $30,000, would you pay that amount?

Adjuster: Hell no! I meant that if the Plaintiff is serious about settling this case, the settlement has to be below $30,000.

Mediator: I'm not wishing to put words in your mouth, but please clarify one thing for me. Am I hearing that this case can settle in the 20's?

Adjuster: Perhaps.

Counsel for the Defendant (turning to the Mediator): Do you think that the Plaintiff would accept a settlement figure between $20,000 and $30,000?

Mediator: I don't know. What I do know is that the Plaintiff has moved from $70,000 to $60,000. That isn't where you wanted the Plaintiff to be but — at the risk of sounding patronizing — the Plaintiff is moving in your direction.

You would have liked the Plaintiff to drop from $70,000 to $30,000, but you and I know that a move of that magnitude is not possible. Matter of fact, if I had walked into this room and told you that the Plaintiff had dropped the demand from $70,000 to $30,000, both of you would have had a coronary on the spot. Am I right or am I right?

Adjuster: You're right. . . .

Counsel for the Defendant: What are you trying to do?

Mediator: In the course of the average mediation, I drop more seeds than Johnny Appleseed did in his entire career. Right now, I'm dropping seeds. At the same time, I believe that a reality check needs to be made.

I have twice asked the question about a settlement value between $20 and $30 thousand and neither of you has told me to get lost. That implicitly says to me that you are willing to entertain the idea.

Obviously the Plaintiff is not going to accept your $12,000 offer. Let's talk about jury ranges if the case were to go to trial. . . .

Counsel for the Defendant: Somewhere between $20,000 and $26,000.

Mediator (turning to the Adjuster): Do you agree?

Adjuster: That's about right. . . .

Mediator (turning to the Adjuster): Perhaps this isn't the Enchanted Forest after all, but — correct me if I am wrong — when I add to the $23,000 judgment roughly $7,000 in pre-judgment interest and $10,000 in expenses, it totals $40,000. That doesn't even consider reimbursement for the Plaintiff's taxable court costs. If my math is correct, it would appear that the moment that the Plaintiff drops below $40,000, you are ahead of the proverbial curve.

Adjuster: Your math is accurate but your logic is flawed. I am not paying more than $30,000 to settle this case.

Mediator: Fair, 'nuf. Now throwing caution to the wind, what are you willing to authorize me to take to the Plaintiff at this point in the discussion?

Adjuster: $16,000.

Mediator: May I ask a question. Would you be willing for me to tell the Plaintiff that you would be willing to discuss a settlement in the range of $20,000 to $29,000 if the Plaintiff would?

Adjuster: No, but on second thought offer $18,000 and tell the Plaintiff that if the Plaintiff's offer is cut in half and dropped from $60,000 to $30,000, we can probably settle this case fairly quickly.

Mediator: I commend your negotiating acuity. I will do just that. Thank you. . . .

[After the mediator talked with each side many more times, a settlement was reached. The negotiation dance went like this: The Plaintiff lowered his demand to $55,000, and the Adjuster responded with $20,000 coupled with a commitment to leave if the next offer was over $40,000. The Plaintiff agreed to drop his demand to $35,000 contingent on the Adjuster raising his offer to $25,000; the Adjuster agreed to raise his offer to $25,000 contingent on the Plaintiff lowering his $35,000 demand; the Plaintiff lowered his demand to $32,500; the Adjuster came back with an offer of $27,500; the Plaintiff responded with $30,000 provided that it be paid within two weeks and that the Adjuster also pay $765 to reimburse Plaintiff for mediation fees and taxable court costs; the Adjuster agreed.]

. . . [T]he story . . . depicted a typical mediation, with the usual undercurrents of emotion, humor, greed, manipulation and disappointment. Nothing about the mediation process was romanticized. In short, it was a typical mediation, one in which — due to the different personalities and agendas in the two caucus rooms — the mediator consciously employed somewhat differing styles in handling the negotiations. It worked.

Problem 6-12.   *Right Mediator Approach?*

What discrete moves does the mediator make to bring the parties closer together? Can you imagine this same scenario being pursued in a more interest-based, problem-solving manner?

Problem 6-13.   *Right Process?*

Some commentators suggest that personal injury cases of this sort are more suited to neutral evaluation (a process where the neutral's primary role is to give an opinion or assessment) than mediation. What do you think?

---

4. A Medical Negligence Case

The case described below illustrates a settlement-oriented approach that nonetheless allows the parties to have a meaningful closure to their conflict. Note how the recognition and personal closure generated by mediation was nearly undermined by the lawyers involved.

 Eric Galton, **MEDIATION OF MEDICAL NEGLIGENCE CLAIMS**

---

28 Cap. U. L. Rev. 321, 324-325 (2000)

During the joint session, it became apparent that both the physician and the parents had been instructed by counsel not to speak during joint session, despite my repeated attempts to engage the parties. Only the lawyers spoke during the joint session.

The case involved the following general facts. The wife was pregnant with the couple's third child. The couple's first two children were born with no complications. The physician caring for the mother delivered the couple's first two children.

The third pregnancy was unremarkable with appropriate prenatal care. The mother goes into labor and is instructed to go to the hospital. She arrives at 6:00 A.M. Although it is the physician's day off, the physician is called when the fetal monitor strips show some signs of distress. The physician arrives and during the fifteen minutes he is attending to the mother, the strips seem to return to normal. The physician leaves.

Thirty minutes later, the strips begin to show even greater evidence of distress. Attempts to locate the physician are initially futile, although the parents hear a nurse say, "Try the golf course." The physician is located on the golf course fifty minutes later, arrives at the hospital, and orders an emergency C-section. The baby is born, barely alive, and dies twenty minutes later.

Counsel for both sides agree to mediation after paper discovery is exchanged, but before depositions are taken. During the joint session, the lawyers make benign, constructive opening presentations. When engaged by the mediator during the joint session, neither the physician nor the husband and wife elect to speak.

The parties are split into different rooms and the mediator begins to caucus, privately, with each side. Negotiations commence and are productive. Five hours later the matter resolves with a written agreement, signed by all parties and counsel, in which the family is to receive $400,000.

As I walk into the physician's room with copies of the executed memorandum of agreement, I sense that the physician has something on his mind. I ask the physician if he wants an opportunity to meet with the family before he leaves. Immediately, the physician's lawyers state that such a meeting is unnecessary, would be awkward, and is something the physician is not required to do. The physician states (and these are *his* words almost verbatim), "I would like to meet with the family. I need some closure."

I next ask the mother and father whether they wish to meet with the physician. Similarly, the lawyers tell the parents they do not have to meet and that such a meeting would be awkward. The mother declares, "Yes, I would very much like to meet with *my* doctor."

The physician is escorted to the parents' room. As the physician enters the room, he stops just outside the door. The mother is seated ten feet away.

For several minutes, no words are exchanged. No one even moves. Suddenly, the mother gets up, tears begin to flow, and she holds out her arms. The physician goes over to the mother. As they embrace, the physician says, "I'm sorry. I'm so sorry." The mother, patting the physician's back responds, "It's okay, we forgive you." The husband comes over and joins the embrace. The lawyers, standing on the opposite end of the room, appear mystified. The physician, father, and mother sit together and talk for ten minutes.

No doubt, the economic settlement was important and a legitimate goal of the mediation process. But, for the parties, the opportunity for conciliation and closure was at least equally important. In cases where the parties desire such closure, the process must provide such an opportunity. In the case described above, the parties, without such opportunity, would have received neither the full benefits of the process nor what they needed or wanted.

It is equally clear in this, and in other instances, that the needs and goals of the parties in mediation are not necessarily the same as their lawyers. In fact, lawyers, because they often fail to either value or recognize or understand such needs, may even discourage a process that attempts to meet their clients' needs.

Problem 6-14. *The Lawyer's Role*

Think about the most important moments in your life. Can you put a monetary value on those moments? Obviously, there are a host of critically important events — an apology, a handshake, a smile — that cannot be financially valued but have an immense impact. Shouldn't lawyers be in tune with the whole range of interests of their clients and capable of furthering interests in respect, recognition, healing, connection, and communication? The lawyers in the example above do not encourage their clients to participate but rather try to protect their clients from contact with the other side. Is this a mistake? Chapter 7 explores these and other issues related to representation in mediation.

C. APPROACHES TO MEDIATION

Mediation takes various forms depending on variables such as culture, context, mediator goals and strategies, and party participation and preferences. The case descriptions above illustrate some of the range. This section explores a variety of different approaches that arguably fall within the family group of mediation. As Chapter 7 reveals, a lively debate about the proper boundaries of the mediation process itself exists. Also consider that the variety and flexibility of mediator approaches is cited as among the strengths of the mediation process.

1. Narrow or Broad Problem Definition, Evaluative or Facilitative

The various mediator orientations described by Professor Leonard Riskin below on his grid are often-cited descriptors of key mediator orientations.

 Leonard L. Riskin, **MEDIATOR ORIENTATIONS, STRATEGIES AND TECHNIQUES**

12 Alternatives 111, 111-113 (1994)

Almost every conversation about "mediation" suffers from ambiguity. People have disparate visions of what mediation is or should be. Yet we lack a comprehensive system for describing these visions. This causes confusion when people try to choose between mediation and another process or grapple with how to train, evaluate, regulate, or select mediators.

I propose a system for classifying mediator orientations. Such a system can help parties select a mediator and deal with the thorny issue of whether the mediator should have subject-matter expertise. The classification system starts with two principal questions: 1. Does the mediator tend to define problems *narrowly* or *broadly*? 2. Does the mediator think she should *evaluate* — make assessments or predictions or proposals for agreements — or *facilitate* the parties' negotiation without evaluating?

The answers reflect the mediator's beliefs about the nature and scope of mediation and her assumptions about the parties' expectations.

PROBLEM DEFINITION

Mediators with a *narrow* focus assume that the parties have come to them for help in solving a technical problem. The parties have defined this problem in advance through the *positions* they have asserted in negotiations or pleadings. Often it involves a question such as, "Who pays how much to whom?" or "Who can use such-and-such property?" As framed, these questions rest on "win-lose" (or "distributive") assumptions. In other words, the participants must divide a limited resource; whatever one gains, the other must lose.

The likely court outcome — along with uncertainty, delay and expense — drives much of the mediation process. Parties, seeking a compromise, will bargain adversarially, emphasizing positions over interests.

A mediator who starts with a *broad* orientation, on the other hand, assumes that the parties can benefit if the mediation goes beyond the narrow issues that normally define legal disputes. Important interests often lie beneath the positions that the participants assert. Accordingly, the mediator should help the participants understand and fulfill those interests — at least if they wish to do so.

THE MEDIATOR'S ROLE

The *evaluative* mediator assumes that the participants want and need the mediator to provide some direction as to the appropriate grounds for settlement — based on law, industry practice or technology. She also assumes that the mediator is qualified to give such direction by virtue of her experience, training and objectivity.

The *facilitative* mediator assumes the parties are intelligent, able to work with their counterparts, and capable of understanding their situations better than either their lawyers or the mediator. So the parties may develop better solutions than any that the mediator might create. For these reasons, the facilitative mediator assumes that his principal mission is to enhance and clarify communications between the parties in order to help them decide what to do.

The facilitative mediator believes it is inappropriate for the mediator to give his opinion, for at least two reasons. First, such opinions might impair the appearance of impartiality and thereby interfere with the mediator's ability to function. Second, the mediator might not know enough — about the details of the case or the relevant law, practices or technology — to give an informed opinion.

Each of the two principal questions — Does the mediator tend toward a narrow or broad focus? and Does the mediator favor an evaluative or facilitative role? — yield responses that fall along a continuum. Thus, a mediator's orientation will be more or less broad and more or less evaluative.

STRATEGIES AND TECHNIQUES OF EACH ORIENTATION

Each *orientation* derives from assumptions or beliefs about the mediator's role and about the appropriate focus of a mediation. A mediator employs *strategies* — plans — to conduct the mediation. And he uses *techniques* — particular moves or behaviors — to effectuate those strategies. Here are selected strategies and techniques that typify each mediation orientation.

The following grid shows the principal techniques associated with each mediator orientation, arranged vertically with the most evaluative at the top and the most facilitative at the bottom. The horizontal axis shows the scope of problems to be addressed, from the narrowest issues to the broadest interests.

EVALUATIVE

• Urges/pushes parties to accept narrow (position-based) settlement	• Urges/pushes parties to accept broad (interest-based) settlement	
• Develops and proposes narrow (position-based) settlement	• Develops and proposes broad (interest-based) settlement	
• Predicts court outcomes	• Predicts impact (on interests) of not settling	
• Assesses strengths and weaknesses of legal claims	• Probes parties' interests	
NARROW Problem Definition	Litigation Issues Other Distributive Issues	Business (Substantive) Issues Business Personal Societal Interests Interests Interests **BROAD** Problem Definition
• Helps parties evaluate proposals	• Helps parties evaluate proposals	
• Helps parties develop narrow (position-based) proposals	• Helps parties develop broad (interest-based) proposals	
• Asks parties about consequences of not settling	• Helps parties develop options	
• Asks about likely court outcomes	• Helps parties understand issues and interests	
• Asks about strengths and weaknesses of legal claims	• Focuses discussion on underlying interests (business, personal, societal)	

FACILITATIVE

While the terminology of the original Riskin grid has been widely used and debated, in a more recent article, Professor Riskin replaces the "facilitative-evaluative" dichotomy with "elicitive-directive."[2] The new terminology may prove more helpful and less controversial, though Riskin expresses reservations about the static quality of the grid and its oversimplification as an accurate "map" of the mediation process. His "New New Grid" is a far more complex system that maps not only the predispositions, intentions, and influences of the mediator, but also those of parties and their attorneys.

Problem 6-15.   *Subject Matter Expertise?*

Imagine you are called on to recommend a mediator for a client. If the client wants the mediator to give evaluative input, would you require that the mediator have subject-matter expertise in lieu of process expertise? Or would you find someone with both? If your client cares about his relationship with his counterpart, how would you strike the balance between process and subject-matter expertise?

Problem 6-16.   *Matching Theory to Practice*

Look back at the four case studies in Section B — the Sisters versus Bristol, the Glen Cove case, the personal injury case, and the medical malpractice case. Do the mediators in those cases define the problem presented by the dispute narrowly or broadly? Can you tell whether the mediators are evaluative or facilitative? Do you see evidence that mediators move among quadrants in Riskin's Grid in a given case?

---

2. Facilitative Mediation: Problem-Solving, Understanding-Based, or Transformative

a. *Problem-Solving Approach*

The problem-solving approach to mediation, most clearly aligned with what has been called facilitative-broad mediation in Riskin's Grid above, seeks to assist parties to understand their interests, the issues, and each other more fully and to generate options and ultimately solutions or agreements.

b. *Understanding-Based Model*

The understanding-based model incorporates knowledge of law by inviting lawyers to bring legal perspectives into the mediation while retaining an emphasis

---

2. Leonard L. Riskin, Decisionmaking in Mediation: The New Old Grid and the New New Grid System, 79 Notre Dame L. Rev. 1 (2003).

on parties working together to find a resolution ideal for them — and doing that using joint sessions only where all parties and their attorneys participate. This use of joint sessions only is a marked departure from other models that use a caucus (private meetings with less than all participants) on either an as-needed or an exclusive basis.

 ***Gary Friedman & Jack Himmelstein*, CHALLENGING CONFLICT: MEDIATION THROUGH UNDERSTANDING**

xxvii, xxviii (2008)

Understanding-based mediation offers people in conflict a way to *work together* to make decisions that resolve their dispute. This non-traditional approach to conflict is based on a simple premise: *The people ultimately in the best position to determine the wisest solution to a dispute are those who created and are living the problem.* They may well need support, and we seek to provide them support in helping them find a productive and constructive way to work together, to understand their conflict and the possibilites for resolving it, and to reach a resolution. . . .

To pursue this path, we work from a base of four interrelated core principles.

- First, we rely heavily on the power of **understanding** rather than the power of coercion or persuasion to drive the process.
- Second, the primary **responsibility** for whether and how the dispute is resolved needs to be with the parties.
- Third, the parties are best served by **working together** and making decisions together.
- Fourth, conflicts are best resolved by **uncovering what lies under** the level at which the parties experience the problem.

———

Two special features of the understanding-based model flow from its core principles: first, the non-caucus approach, as it is the parties, not the mediator, who should gain the fullest picture of their problem; and second, the invitation to lawyers to participate, so that parties can understand possible legal outcomes and decide themselves what importance to give to the law. In other forms of facilitative mediation, the caucus is a tool that can be used for specific purposes and, in some cases, is used to the exclusion of joint sessions. In some mediation programs and approaches, lawyers are excluded in order to make the process less adversarial, and, in others, lawyers become the central participants, speaking for their clients, rather than being present to enhance party understanding as in the Friedman-Himmelstein model.

c. Transformative Model

While problem-solving and understanding-based mediations include creative problem solving, along with enriched understanding, as a goal of mediation, Robert

Baruch Bush and Joseph Folger, in their transformative mediation model, reject problem solving as a goal of mediation and add party empowerment to that of enhanced understanding between parties. This model of mediation aims not at solving the problem or finding a resolution, but rather at changing the parties in the midst of conflict — making the parties stronger themselves ("empowerment") and more open to an understanding of each other ("recognition"). Since transformative mediation facilitates empowerment and recognition — rather than resolution — arguably it is not on Riskin's Grid at all.

 Robert A. Baruch Bush & Joseph P. Folger, THE PROMISE OF MEDIATION: THE TRANSFORMATIVE APPROACH TO CONFLICT

45-46, 65-66 (Revised ed. 2005)

. . . The transformative theory of conflict starts by offering its own answer to the foundational question of what conflict means to the people involved. According to transformative theory, what people find most significant about conflict is not that it frustrates their satisfaction of some right, interest, or pursuit, no matter how important, but that it leads and even forces them to behave toward themselves and others in ways that they find uncomfortable and even repellent. More specifically, it alienates them from their sense of their own strength and their sense of connection to others, thereby disrupting and undermining the interaction between them as human beings. This crisis of deterioration in human interaction is what parties find most affecting, significant — and disturbing — about the experience of conflict.

. . . [I]n the transformative model [m]ediation is defined as a process in which a third party works with parties in conflict to help them change the quality of their conflict interaction from negative and destructive to positive and constructive, as they explore and discuss issues and possibilities for resolution. The mediator's role is to help the parties make positive interactional shifts (empowerment and recognition shifts) by supporting the exercise of their capacities for strength and responsiveness, through their deliberation, decision making, communication, perspective taking, and other party activities. The mediator's primary goals are (1) to support empowerment shifts, by supporting — but never supplanting — each party's deliberation and decision making, at every point in the session where choices arise (regarding either process or outcome) and (2) to support recognition shifts, by encouraging and supporting — but never forcing — each party's freely chosen efforts to achieve new understandings of the other's perspective.

The goals of a transformative mediator — empowerment and recognition — are at odds with the goals of a problem-solving mediator and of an understanding-based mediator to some degree. However, to solve a problem or understand a situation, it is helpful to have the parties both strong individually ("empowered") and responsive to each other ("recognition"). Consequently, there may be some overlap between the purposes, strategies, and techniques of transformative, understanding-based, and facilitative mediators. On the other hand, if the mediator has "problem-solving" in mind, she may be less inclined to keep the focus on empowerment and recognition.

Providing a living laboratory for a particular mediation model, the U.S. Postal Service, one of the largest employers in the United States, adopted a transformative model for workplace disputes involving allegations of discrimination. The program, which is probably the largest employment mediation program in the world, uses outside mediators with specialized training in transformative mediation and provides a forum for supervisors and employees to mediate during their working hours. Noted scholar Lisa Bingham has collected data since the program's inception in 1994. Her findings include high levels of participant satisfaction with both the mediation process (91 percent) and the mediators (96 percent), high levels of satisfaction with the mediation outcome (from 64 percent for complainants to 72 percent for management), a significant drop in the number of formal discrimination complaints at the Postal Service, and evidence of improved communication between employers and supervisors during mediation.[3] Perhaps most significantly, findings suggest there is a positive impact on the workplace itself as a result of the transformative mediation program.

3. Evaluative and Directive Mediation

A number of approaches to mediation envision a central role for the mediator of importing information that will influence, if not determine, the outcome.

a. *Trashing and Bashing*

Studying mediator approaches in civil court cases, including personal injury, construction, commercial, contract, and real estate, Professor James Alfini describes two approaches that place the mediator in a role of considerable outcome influence. A "**trasher**" tears apart the case of each party, pointing out weaknesses that each side will face at trial, to encourage them to make more realistic and acceptable settlement offers. "to get them to a point where they will put realistic settlement figures on the table." In other words, the trasher will point out weaknesses that each side will face at trial. A "**basher**" does not engage in case evaluation but spends "most of the session bashing away at . . . [parties'] initial offers in an attempt to get the parties to agree to a figure somewhere in between."[4] Recall how the mediator in A Fly on the Wall above kept moving the parties closer and closer to one another.

---

3. See Lisa B. Bingham, Mediation at Work: Transforming Workplace Conflict at the United States Postal Service, IBM Center for the Bus. of Govt. (2003), available at *http://www.businessofgovernment .org/pdfs/Bingham_Report.pdf.*
4. James J. Alfini, Trashing, Bashing, and Hashing It Out: Is This the End of "Good Mediation", 19 Fla. St. U. L. Rev. 47, 69 (1991)

b. *Norm-educating and Norm-advocating*

Professor Ellen Waldman describes forms of mediation she calls "**norm-educating**" and "**norm-advocating.**" Norm-educating mediation is akin to "trashing" described by Professor Alfini. The norm-educating mediator insures that party decision making is informed by relevant legal and social norms — either by educating parties himself or making sure that each party's lawyer does that. Like the trasher, such a mediator would dissect weaknesses in each disputant's case, using legal or other norms. While a norm-educating mediator would allow the parties to make decisions contrary to prevailing norms (once they were properly educated), a norm-advocating mediator would not. A norm-advocating mediator would provides information about norms to insure secure norms were obeyed. Professor Waldman asserts that the norm-advocating model is used in "a variety of conflicts, including bioethical, environmental, zoning, and, in some instances, discrimination disputes."[5]

c. *Community-enhancing and Community-enabling*

Similarly, Professor Clark Freshman describes two forms of mediation that place responsibility on the mediator to import information about community values. In "**community-enhancing mediation**," a mediator helps individuals make decisions about and resolving their disputes in keeping with the values of some relevant community," for example, in rabbinical courts or the Islamic community. In "**community-enabling mediation**," assisted by the mediator, individuals make choices in right of the values of a variety of communities to which they might belong and they determine what weight, if any, to give to the norms at a given community. The mediator has responsibility to discuss the norms of relevant communities — for example, the norms of same-sex couples, or Jewish couples, or simply the legal norms. "[C]ommunity-enabling mediation should be designed to allow individuals to make informed decisions about how to organize their lives and intimate relationships by exposing them to competing norms, including competing communities."[6]

---

5. Ellen A. Waldman, *Identifying the Role of Social Norms in Mediation: A Multiple Model Approach*, 48 Hastings L.J. 703, 746 (1997)

6. Clark Freshman, Privatizing Same-Sex "Marriage" Through Alternative Dispute Resolution: Community-Enhancing Versus Community-Enabling Mediation, 44 UCLA L. Rev. 1687, 1697 (1997).

> ## Problem 6-17.   *What Is Essential to Mediation?*
>
> The central aspects of mediation, outlined by Carrie Menkel-Meadow earlier in this chapter, are that it is: (1) consensual, (2) voluntary, (3) participatory, (4) facilitated by a third party outside the dispute, (5) seeking solutions and resolutions acceptable to all parties, and (6) seeking enhanced understanding among parties. Do all the variants described above comport with those core aspects? If your answer is no, would you amend the list or exclude the variant from the mediation family? Consider particularly whether evaluative-narrow mediation (Riskin), transformative mediation (Bush and Folger), "trashing" and "bashing" (Alfini), norm-advocating mediation (Waldman), and community-enhancing mediation (Freshman) arguably fall outside at least one of Menkel-Meadow's parameters.

D. TRENDS: THE FUTURE OF MEDIATION IN THE LEGAL ARENA

1. Challenges Ahead

a. *The Demise of Party Participation and a Broad Problem-Definition in Court Contexts*

Professor Nancy Welsh suggests that the powerful and simple vision of mediation as a process to foster party participation and self-determination is "thinning." To put the concern more boldly, mediation may be gutted in the process of its adoption into the adversarial world of attorneys and courts. Mediators, many of them attorneys and retired judges, have a conception of mediation built on judicial settlement conferences where the neutral often provides reasoned evaluation. Parties (as clients) take the back seat, "largely limited to selecting from among the settlement options developed by their attorneys," allowing their attorneys to drive the mediation. Caucusing, rather than joint sessions, dominate the process.[7] What this means is that mediation may shift towards an adversarial and lawyer-focused process — at least in court-based contexts.

In more recent research Professors Welsh and Leonard Riskin, examining mediation in court-oriented, civil (non-family) cases, found that mediations are tending to focus very narrowly on the legal claim. The bargaining revolves around the likely court outcome and discounts off the litigation prediction that each side might accept to avoid litigation costs and risks. While this narrow focus might serve the repeat players — attorneys and other court regulars, like insurance adjusters — it can ignore the interests of "one shot" participants in the legal

---

7. Nancy A. Welsh, The Thinning Vision of Self-Determination in Court-Connected Mediation: The Inevitable Price of Institutionalization, 6 Harv. Negot. L. Rev. 1 (2001).

system, who may have broader interests and concerns than a "cause of action" encompasses.[8] Remember Riskin's Grid, presented earlier in this chapter? One of the exciting potentials of mediation is a party-centered problem definition where the process addresses all negotiable concerns raised, including personal, business, and societal issues that go beyond the legal cause of action.

b. Mediator Conduct

Professor James Coben, who has done exhaustive studies on lawsuits involving mediation, writes: "mediation's dirty little secret is the degree to which mediators . . . routinely and unabashedly engage in manipulation and deception to foster settlements, albeit under the rationale of fostering self-determination. Sophisticated consumers have come to know and expect it. Unsophisticated consumers are not so lucky."[9] As examples of mediator manipulation, Coben points to: skipping or delaying meals to increase pressure, conveying false demands, reframing, the use of neuro-linguistic programming to increase party comfort, over-reporting progress — or the opposite, overly pessimistic predictions of stalemate — to generate movement, strategically setting out Kleenex to encourage emotional expression, and the like. Some of these "manipulations" are arguably part of a mediator's job; others are unethical. In any case, the regulation of mediator conduct is one of the issues for the field that lies ahead.

2. The Promise of Mediation

We return, however, to the simple vision of mediation: enabling parties to work together to resolve their dispute as they see best. How can we insure that that vision stays vital?

The next chapter asks: What is the role — the tasks and skills — of the attorney in mediation and of the mediator? What practical challenges does the mediator face? If the incoming generation of lawyers and mediators attends to those questions, then mediation can keep its simple promise of party self-determination.

Further Reading

Robert A. Baruch Bush & Joseph P. Folger. (2005). *The Promise of Mediation.* San Francisco: Jossey-Bass Publishers.

Gary Friedman & Jack Himmelstein. (2008). *Challenging Conflict: Mediation Through Understanding.* Washington, D.C.: ABA.

Kolb & Associates. (1994). *When Talk Works: Profiles of Mediators.* San Francisco: Jossey-Bass Publishers.

---

8. Leonard L. Riskin & Nancy A. Welsh, Is That All There Is? 'The Problem' in Court-Oriented Mediation, 15 Geo. Mason L. Rev. 863 (2008).
9. James R. Coben, Mediation's Dirty Little Secret: Straight Talk About Mediation Manipulation and Deception, 2 J. Alternative Disp. Resol. Emp. 4, 4-6 (2000).

Bernard Mayer. (2000). *The Dynamics of Conflict Resolution: A Practitioner's Guide.* San Francisco: Jossey-Bass Publishers.

Carrie Menkel-Meadow (Ed.). (2000). *Mediation: Theory Practice and Policy.* Aldershot, UK and Burlington, Vt.: Ashgate Press.

Christopher Moore. (2003). *The Mediation Process.* San Francisco: Jossey-Bass Publishers.

Joseph B. Stulberg & Lela P. Love. (2009). *The Middle Voice: Mediating Conflict Successfully.* Durham, NC: Carolina Academic Press.

John Winslade & Gerald Monk. (2001). *Narrative Mediation: A New Approach to Conflict Resolution.* San Francisco: Jossey-Bass Publishers.

Chapter 7 | Mediation: Skills and Practices for the Mediator and the Attorney in Mediation

Leaders must . . . create an attitude of success, the belief that problems can be solved, that things can be better. Not in a foolish or unrealistic way, but in a way that creates hope and confidence.

— George Mitchell

Our task now is not to fix the blame for the past, but to fix the course for the future.
— John F. Kennedy

The significant problems we face cannot be solved at the same level of thinking we were at when we created them.

— Albert Einstein

The very first requirement in a hospital is that it should do the sick no harm.
— Florence Nightingale

A mediation is successful if it accomplishes any of the following goals: giving disputing parties an enhanced understanding of their dispute and of each other's perspective, enabling parties to develop options responsive to issues raised by the dispute, and bringing closure to the dispute on terms that are mutually agreeable. Conversely, the mediation process should not make negotiations more difficult, nor should it generate an outcome worse than outcomes available elsewhere. In other words, at a minimal level, the process should do no harm. This chapter explores skills mediators and any attorneys involved in mediation should possess to achieve success.

Both the mediator and any attorney representatives share the goal of helping disputants advance their interests. This chapter first examines mediator skills and strategies to enable parties to achieve a successful outcome. Even if you have no intention of practicing as a mediator, attorneys need to understand what a mediator does and how they think in order to utilize their services to best advantage. It then identifies best practices — and practices to avoid — for the attorney representative who wants to maximize the good that mediation might do for his client.

A. THE MEDIATOR

> *[C]areful as someone crossing an iced-over stream.*
> *Alert as a warrior in enemy territory.*
> *Courteous as a guest.*
> *Fluid as melting ice.*
> *Shapeable as a block of wood.*
> *Receptive as a valley.*
> *Clear as a glass of water.*
>
> Tao te Ching 15 (Steven Mitchell trans., 1991)

The *Tao* describes Masters who lead in subtle ways so people believe they have achieved results on their own. This invisible leadership that supports parties in determining an appropriate outcome is one vision of the mediation process.

1. Mediator Traits

What personality traits serve a mediator? Generally, a mediator must be able to stay in the middle — that is, be neutral, impartial, and nonjudgmental. Other often-cited attributes of a good mediator include being a good listener; displaying intelligence; having the ability both to take charge and to recede into the background when the parties are engaging in constructive conversation; and having the energy, optimism, and dogged perseverance to press on when hope fades. Confidence, decisiveness, flexibility, creativity, reliability, nondefensiveness, a sense of humor, and empathy are other important traits. Some mediators are naturally more blessed with these traits than others. However, nurture and support, training and mentoring, and self-reflection can go a long way in developing these qualities.

> **"An Endless Supply of Patience"**
>
> *[T]here must be an endless supply of patience and perseverance. Sometimes the mountains seem so high and rivers so wide that it is hard to continue the journey. . . . Seeking an end to conflict is not for the timid or the tentative. . . .*
>
> *We had 700 days of failure and 1 day of success.*
>
> — George J. Mitchell (describing negotiations in Northern Ireland)

Working with these traits, what tasks do mediators perform?

2. Mediator Tasks

Organization: Imagine a *host* who provides for your comfort and safety and a meeting *chair* who convenes the meeting and organizes the discussion so it is efficient and meaningful.

Communication: Picture a master *communicator* who helps parties speak clearly and listen to each other, who clarifies, summarizes, translates, and reframes so everyone understands what is said, and who captures and records understandings and agreements.

Education: Envision a *teacher* who explains the process and who encourages parties to get helpful information and advice, a *coach* and *model* for effective negotiation behaviors and attitudes, and someone who urges evaluation and reality-testing of every attitude and option.

Negotiation: Consider a master *negotiator* who elicits common interests, frames negotiable issues, inspires the parties to develop options, conveys offers and counteroffers, and makes sure that agreements are clear and doable.

Protection: Think about a *sentinel* who will prevent misuse of the process and a *referee* who ensures an equal place at the table.

3. Qualifications for Mediators

With these traits and tasks framing the challenge of mediation service, this chapter explores the knowledge, strategies, and skills necessary for the competent mediator. Keep in mind that there is no universal consensus on one correct method for mediation practice. Courts and other institutions have tried to determine how to measure competence and qualify persons for mediation service on their panels. A typical formula includes: a certain number of hours of training (from 4 hours for civil cases in some jurisdictions to 60 hours in others); experience observing and co-mediating cases under supervision (from 3 cases in some jurisdictions to 125 hours for some credentialing associations); and continuing education requirements. Some court-annexed panels also rely on educational degree requirements, mandating a college degree or, in some cases, a law (or other graduate) degree, or, in a few cases, having been a practicing member of the bar in a particular state for a number of years. There is little data to indicate which of these approaches (training-based, experience-based, or degree-based) assure quality. Perhaps the most promising approach involves combining training and experience requirements with skills-based evaluation, using videotapes, for example, that are reviewed by an appointed expert. This last approach, while more difficult to develop and administer, holds more promise for ensuring that mediators are capable of high-quality performance.

No licensing of mediators currently exists. Compare this to licensing requirements for hair dressers where states require from 1,500 to 2,000 hours of training or apprenticeship! In the quest to ensure quality mediation services, a primary challenge is to maintain the current professional and practice diversity in the field and not unnecessarily disqualify competent individuals by setting inappropriate bars and standards.

4. Mediator Strategies and Skills for Stages in the Mediation Process

This section breaks the mediation process into discrete segments and analyzes theory and strategies for each. Keep in mind that mediation scholars and theorists have developed various ways of describing the process — from no stages at all to approaches similar to those described below. Professors Joseph Stulberg and Lela Love use the pneumonic "BADGER" to describe the stages of the mediation process:[1]

Begin the discussions;
Accumulate information;
Develop the discussion strategy;
Generate movement;
Elect separate sessions;
Reach closure.

BADGER signifies that the mediator's role is energetic, proactive, and persistent, while the mediator proceeds through each stage of the process the letters represent. Christopher Moore, a noted writer and trainer, describes a twelve-stage process beginning with pre-session contacts and decisions and culminating in formal settlement.[2] Whatever the process description, there is general consensus that even where one conceptualizes a linear "map" of stages, the reality of mediation is not a linear lock-step process. Rather, it is a more unpredictable process where a linear map may serve as a useful guide for both the mediator and the attorney representatives, but where there is constant movement forward, backward, and in circles between and among the so-called stages.

a. Beginning

The mediator must consider and help the parties resolve a variety of issues prior to the start of a mediation session. Among those issues are choosing participants, assessing whether participants have special needs, deciding what preliminary and procedural issues need to be addressed, and setting the stage.

---

1. Joseph B. Stulberg & Lela P. Love, The Middle Voice: Mediating Conflict Successfully (Carolina Academic Press 2009).
2. Christopher Moore, The Mediation Process (3d ed., Jossey-Bass 2003).

i. Who Should Participate in the Mediation?

For each case, while the parties ultimately determine who participates, the mediator helps analyze this critical factor. The following chart outlines some potential mediation participants, generalizes about whether they should participate in mediation, and suggests a rationale for inclusion.

PARTICIPANT	INCLUDE?	RATIONALE FOR INCLUSION/EXCLUSION
Party	Yes	The parties are in the best position to examine underlying interests, to develop creative proposals, and to determine whether commitment to a proposal is possible and optimal.
Attorney(s) or other representative	Yes	If a party to the dispute wants a representative — to help articulate the legal case, to be a negotiation coach or protector, to assist in listening, persuading, and developing and analyzing options — then she should be allowed such support. Where attorneys import an adversarial climate, mediators may seek to limit their role to advising the client about the legal consequences of proposed settlement terms and helping draft a settlement agreement.
Interpreter	Yes, if needed	Since understanding is a central goal of mediation, an interpreter is critical if there are language issues.
Expert	Maybe	An expert may be needed to inform or educate the other side or to expand settlement options. Mutually acceptable experts can also be brought in to provide information where data is lacking.
Witness	Maybe	A witness may be helpful to persuade the other side to consider another perspective. Sometimes a witness will be more persuasive than the party, or the cumulative impact of another voice will be helpful.
Support person	Maybe	A general rule is "to keep it simple" where possible. On the other hand, some parties cannot operate effectively without a support person — for example, a spouse, significant family member, or business partner. It is wise to exclude "extra" persons who have their own agendas and may derail discussions, but it is critical to include support people whose presence is helpful for emotional, data, decisional, or other support.

General guidelines, however, do not answer all questions. For example, situations arise where a party cannot be present and an attorney or other representative attends as a surrogate negotiator. Additionally, unlike litigation, where parties are named in the papers filed with the court, in many situations in mediation it is hard to tell who the parties are. For example, a litigated custody dispute typically has as the parties those persons — often the husband and wife — named in the complaint. However, in the mediation of a situation concerning parenting arrangements, the parties may include a much broader potential array — grandparents, aunts, uncles, or the children themselves.

Although the same people may participate in mediation and adjudication, their role in each process is quite different. In adjudication, parties, attorneys, experts, and witnesses all work for one side or the other to persuade a neutral decision maker. In mediation, on the other hand, all participants increase the common information base and operate to shift parties' perspective and develop proposals responsive to the situation.

Problem 7-1.   *Who Should Participate?*

Recall a dispute with which you have been involved. Whom would you want to attend the mediation? Does it depend on your goals? If the same dispute were brought to court, who would be the named parties? Now examine a case you have studied in other law school courses — *Brown v. Board of Education*, for example. Who should be the parties in a mediation of that situation?

---

ii. What Procedural Issues Must Be Addressed?

In addition to the participant mix, issues about allocating mediation costs, determining necessary information exchange, and deciding the nature of pre-mediation submissions, if any, must be addressed. The excerpt that follows discusses the challenges of setting the procedural framework for a mediation.

 Joseph B. Stulberg & Lela P. Love, THE MIDDLE VOICE

49-50 (2009)

Where will people meet? How many will be there? When will they meet? How long will the session last? Will there be food? Who will talk first? Who will sit where?

The mediator wants to ensure that meeting arrangements and procedures do not disrupt the discussions. She wants them handled well so that people feel comfortable as they start to talk with one another.

The mediator begins by taking care of these important details. Usually, after having consulted with the parties, she simply announces the framework and makes appropriate arrangements. Sometimes, however, these matters become issues of fierce debate among the parties and end up as the first topic for mediated discussion. In any event, no mediator thinks they are trivial. The procedural framework creates a space within which people must feel safe, and the mediator must construct it with care. Like any host, the mediator will receive no compliments for handling arrangements well but will invite interminable haggling and destructive exchanges for botching them. . . .

Although these seem straightforward enough, they can be devilishly compli-cated. If a mediator schedules a meeting for 11:00 A.M., does that mean the meeting will last only until lunch at noon? If only one party has to travel seventy miles to attend a meeting in the city where all of the other parties live and work, should the mediator change the meeting site so that everyone must travel thirty-five miles, or should she alternate meeting sites so as not to favor one group? If one group has only two negotiators, but the other has five negotiating team members and thirty "observers and supporters," should the mediator arrange a meeting site that accom-modates eight or thirty-eight persons? The mediator must develop guidelines with a keen sensitivity to the impact that choices will have on the parties' interaction and the way in which the guidelines might affect her own image as neutral.

---

iii. How Is the Stage Set?

Sometimes when I consider what tremendous consequences come from little things . . . I am tempted to think . . . there are no little things.

— Bruce Barton, in Stephen R. Covey, The Seven Habits of Highly Effective People 287 (1989)

We shape our buildings: thereaf-ter they shape us.

— Winston Churchill

In determining how to choose and arrange a room for a media-tion, key mediation goals must be kept in mind: to enhance com-munication between the parties, to ensure safety, to maximize comfort, to support mediator neutrality, and to set a stage or create an atmosphere that is conducive to creativity and to inspiration.

Mediators must consider what artwork to place on the walls to create a positive atmosphere, what sort of furniture would be most helpful — a round, rect-angular, square, or some other shaped table? No table? And, of

Israel-PLO Agreement Ceremony

Sometimes getting the atmosphere right is the most important thing. When we signed the Israel-PLO agreement in 1993 on the White House lawn, I had a tough time. First Arafat wanted to bring his gun — he said he didn't go anywhere without his gun. Well I said, "This isn't about guns. If you want to walk away from a televised audi-ence of a billion people because you won't leave your six shooter at the door, I'll be happy to tell them that." So he left his gun.

Then I said to Rabin, "He left his gun. You've got to shake hands with him." He said, "I am signing the agreement, I have to shake his hand?" We are laughing today, but this was a tough thing for him. These guys had fought for decades. How many young Israelis had Rabin put in body bags? He lived and they died. . . . He was considering all that. Finally I said to him, "Yitzhak you have made all these steps and you have taken all these risks and the whole world will be look-ing at you. And I have to shake hands with Arafat; so you do too." And he looked at me and he said, "Well I suppose you do not make peace with your friends." And then he smiled at me and said, "but no kissing."

— William J. Clinton, Acceptance Speech, International Advocate for Peace Award, Benjamin N. Cardozo School of Law, Mar. 19, 2001 available at http://www.cardozojcer.com/iap/2001.html.

course, the mediation space should have extra rooms for caucuses, kitchen facilities, telephones, computers, photocopy and fax machines, internet access, and printing capabilities.

Food and beverages are inextricably linked to the success of meetings. In setting the stage for a mediation that may go all day, food will play an important role. Keep in mind that hunger is related to energy, creativity, irritability, and patience, and consequently the mediator should keep a sharp eye on parties' needs for food and drink. What opportunities and dangers lie in arranging opportunities for parties to "break bread together"?

Problem 7-2.   *How Should You Seat the Parties?*

Would you sit parties side by side to emphasize that they are facing a common problem and must work together or sit them across the table from each other where direct eye contact is easy and the security of a table between them may provide safety and psychological comfort? Should an attorney be seated nearest the mediator or should the party be given that place with his attorney by his side (on the side away from the mediator)? How might differences in the nature of the dispute or in the personalities or backgrounds of the disputants affect your handling of these issues?

---

iv. How Does the Mediator Open the Session?

Typically, the mediator begins the session by making opening remarks. These remarks have multiple goals: to develop trust and rapport with the parties, to educate the parties about the mediation process, to ensure that everyone (mediator and parties) has compatible goals, and to develop guidelines for the process.

What follows is a sample opening statement by a mediator in a community mediation center, which primarily handles neighbor, landlord-tenant, and family-related disputes. Keep in mind that the statement might look very different in other contexts, but it would still address the goals set out above.

Good morning. Welcome to mediation. My name is Kabi Jorgensen, and I have been assigned to assist you.

Please check that I have your names and addresses recorded correctly. Am I pronouncing your names correctly?

I want you both to know that I have never met either of you before, and I know very little about the concerns that brought you here today. I look forward to your explaining this matter to me. I am telling you this because it is my job not to take sides, but rather remain in the middle, as a neutral — both as we begin and throughout the session. I am not a judge. A judge would decide who was wrong or right with respect to conduct that happened in the past. I am here to help you work out how you want the future to be.

Before you tell me what brought you here, I want to explain the goals of this process and suggest some guidelines for our conversation. My first job is to understand your concerns and to be sure that you understand each other. To do that, it is important that each person has the opportunity to speak without being interrupted. I know you will want to comment about what the other person says and perhaps remember some points that are new to you, so I have given you paper and a pen to make notes. When it is your turn to speak, you will have a full opportunity to explain your concerns and respond to one another. Can you agree not to interrupt each other and not to interrupt me? Are there other conversation guidelines that might be helpful?

After we explore the situation and your goals, I will encourage you to work together to come up with proposals to address the concerns you raised. If you are able to reach an agreement that resolves your concerns, if you wish and at your request, I will assist you in writing up your commitments to each other.

I will be taking notes as we proceed to help me remember the concerns you raise and the understandings you reach. However, I will destroy my notes at the end of this session. I am telling you this so you will feel comfortable to speak freely here. This session is private and confidential. That means I am under a duty not to reveal what is said in this room to anyone outside this room. There are some exceptions to confidentiality, however. For example, there is an exception for allegations of child abuse. From time to time I do consult with the staff about questions I might have regarding your situation, but the staff here are under the same duty as I am to keep confidential what is said in mediation. The only record of what happened in this session will be the agreement you make to resolve your concerns, and that document will not be confidential.

There may come a time when I feel it would be helpful to meet individually with each of you. If that happens, I will explain that process — which is called caucusing — in more detail.

Sessions here generally take two hours. They can also be shorter or longer as you require. I am committed to work with you as long as necessary.

Do you have any questions?

Mr. Chin, since you brought this matter to the attention of the Center, would you please begin and relate what brought you here.

Observe the language in the opening. The mediator refers to *concerns, interests, priorities, proposals, options,* and *agreements,* rather than using adversarial or potentially abrasive words such as *parties, allegations, claim, position,* or *problem.*

> **Problem 7-3.**   *Practice Delivering an Opening!*
>
> How would you change this opening if attorneys were present? If you were conducting a mediation between fellow law students? Note that every opening statement should include the following: introductions, disclaiming of mediator partiality or bias, explanation of the mediation process and the mediator's role, development of ground rules (including understandings regarding courtesy), note taking, confidentiality, the length of the session, the use of separate meetings or caucuses, and an opportunity to ask questions.
>
>   Choose a context and in groups of three, practice giving an opening statement. In turn, each student in the group should be the mediator and the other students should be parties. Note that even if three people use the same words, the opening may have very different impacts. Give your colleagues feedback on their body language and eye contact (which should not favor either party), whether they created a tone of trust and optimism, and whether they conveyed confidence and competence.

b. Understanding the Conflict and Developing the Information Base

Once the mediator has set the stage and delivered an opening statement, she asks the parties to describe the matter that brought them to mediation. As the mediator listens to the parties and urges them to listen to each other, she is looking for elements of the conflict that will be constructive in developing a better understanding among the parties, that may generate ideas for resolutions, and that may become agreements resolving the matter. You have seen that listening is a critical skill for the negotiator. The excerpts that follow show how a mediator will (or should) help advance good listening.

i. "Looping"

One mediator technique for listening is called "looping," which is taught in the understanding-based model of mediation introduced in Chapter 6. The essence of looping is a genuine commitment of the mediator to understanding each party and demonstrating that understanding. As you read this section, remember the other aspects of good listening discussed in the context of counseling and negotiation, as the mediator should also be displaying those skills.

Gary Friedman & Jack Himmelstein, THE LOOP OF UNDERSTANDING

(2004)[3]

Central to the Understanding-Based approach to mediation is the search for understanding. The "Loop of Understanding," as we have come to call it, gives form and substance to that effort. "*Looping*" is a technique, but it is also much more than a technique. The goal is to *Develop Understanding* systematically, authentically and compassionately throughout the mediation.

Looping builds on the mediator's intention. Just as successful mediation ultimately must build on the parties' intention to work through their conflict together, looping proceeds from the mediator's intention to understand the parties and to build a ground of understanding between the mediator and the parties.

THE STEPS OF LOOPING

Although the approach is similar to and borrows much from what others have referred to as "active listening," "looping" captures a fuller sense of it for us. We term it the "loop" of understanding because the goal is to complete a loop.

For the mediator, the simple steps are to try within him or herself to understand each party, to try to express that understanding to that party, and to seek and receive confirmation from the party that he/she feels understood. The last step is crucial. When a party confirms that the mediator understands what he or she has been trying to express, that loop is complete. Until then, it is not.

Step 1:	**M inquires of**	→	**P**
Step 2:	**P responds, asserts**	→	**M**
Step 3:	**M demonstrates and confirms Understanding**	→	**P**
Step 4:	**P responds**	→	**M**

      If yes, loop is complete.

      If no, go back to Step 1 and ask: "What am I missing?"

By bringing *looping* to the exchange between him/herself and each of the principal antagonists to the conflict, the mediator has begun to understand each of them. And while they likely do not feel understood by each other, they feel at least somewhat understood by the mediator. He has also begun to clarify the essence of the dispute.

The goal is to understand the speaker *and* to demonstrate that you understand. Already this is much more than many mediators (and others) will do in the effort to listen. Even when we make a sincere effort to understand another, that effort is often evidenced by silent attention, a nod of agreement, or a statement such as: "I understand what you are saying." These are not bad. But when it comes to

---

3. A fuller discussion of the technique of looping can be found in G. Friedman & J. Himmelstein, Challenging Conflict: Mediation Through Understanding (2008) at 68-76.

the goal of resolving conflict through understanding, much more is possible. Stating what you hear the other to have said goes further. It shows that you understand (if you do).

So far we have a partial loop — statement by the loopee and response (restatement) by the looper. The next step begins to close the loop. If done with the intent of fostering understanding, it tests whether the mediator has truly understood. The mediator asks the party whether the response captured the meaning of what he was trying to communicate.

The loopee's response can close the loop. If "yes" — if the speaker confirms that he/she feels understood — this one loop is complete. If the speaker does not feel fully understood by the looper's words (whether because the looper missed something or simply because the speaker has the need to clarify what he/she meant), the loop is not complete. The party can then clarify what he/she meant), the mediator loops back and again seeks confirmation. When the party confirms that the mediator correctly has understood, that loop is complete.

The point is not to convince, nor to contradict, nor to take exception to, nor explain away. The point is to understand. . . .

The honest attempt by the mediator to understand each party begins to point to an alternative to the confines of a most basic element that keeps people ensnared in a Conflict Trap. For when people are locked in conflict, they typically tend to want to defend their position, blame the other, and try to convince a third party that they are right and the other wrong. The mode is one of defense, persuasion, coercion.

When conflict takes that form, understanding is at a minimum. Misunderstanding prevails. The more the parties to conflict feel blamed or vilified by the other, the more they feel misunderstood. The more that they feel misunderstood, the more they tend to justify, blame and vilify. The cycle is well known and yet, once within its grasp, very powerful. Understanding, from the get-go, can help begin to soften the strictures and be the beginning of pointing the way out.

A caution: our recommendation for looping from the start applies to the mediator looping the parties, not to asking the parties to loop each other. Many mediators, drawn by the desire to increase understanding, will turn to the parties early on and ask: what did you understand the other to say? Our advice, generally, is: NOT YET. People are much more willing and able to understand [one] another when they feel understood themselves. To put it another way, being mired in feelings of being misunderstood is not a good place from which to be asked to understand another. And parties to conflict are often mired in just such feelings. By establishing some understanding at the start (by the mediator of the parties), the mediator can begin to help break the cycle of misunderstanding. The invitation to the parties to loop each other can also prove essential, but it rarely comes at the start.

LOOPING FROM THE INSIDE OUT

As the description we have been giving about *looping* may suggest, it is both a skill and much more than a skill. To understand *looping* and its place in this approach to mediation is to realize that understanding has an inner life. And it is in that inner life that the essential spirit of looping is grounded. The mediator needs to want to loop (and learn to loop) as more than a useful skill. The hard work is to truly want to understand the people before you — to reach inside oneself when each speaker is speaking and make the effort to understand how the other (each of them) really experiences the situation — even (and particularly) when you find it difficult to understand them. That inner desire to understand is key.

Focusing too much on the outer skill, on getting the words right, on learning to rephrase or reframe (which are important skills to learn) can miss the essential point. *That point* is truly *to want to* understand — to connect within oneself to one's own intention to do that. If the inner intent is there, you may at times miss some of the basic steps and still move toward understanding.

---

ii. Reframing

In the next excerpt Lela Love describes another listening skill — that of reframing. Love urges mediators to translate accusations, put-downs, and threats into "building blocks" for moving forward and helping parties shift their perspectives.

 Lela P. Love, **TRAINING MEDIATORS TO LISTEN: DECONSTRUCTING DIALOGUE AND CONSTRUCTING UNDERSTANDING, AGENDAS, AND AGREEMENTS**

adapted from 38 Fam. & Concil. Cts. Rev. 27 (2000)

Much as a miner looks for gold, a mediator listens to the often hostile, accusatory and adversarial dialogue between parties, gleaning the constructive elements — the "heart of gold" — that are being expressed. Amidst the put-downs, insults, and threats that are frequently exchanged by people in conflict, the mediator must extract solid building blocks which will allow disputants to construct different perspectives, clearer understandings and ultimately agreements. The mediator must hear and identify those elements, and also enable the parties to hear each other. This task is difficult because parties in conflict typically experience fear, confusion, anger, hate, frustration, and hopelessness; and the expression of these feelings can be so loud that other elements are drowned out. The mediator must be optimistic that "gold" exists and be able to selectively and thoughtfully frame constructive components at appropriate times in the session.

What are the building blocks of constructive dialogue and how would the mediator translate these building blocks into language that might reorient the parties toward the dispute and toward each other? The "heart of gold" or building blocks of constructive dialogue are each discussed below.

INTERESTS AND NEEDS

Interests are the underlying and inescapable human motivators that press us into action. When interests are frustrated by actions or inactions of others, frequently a conflict ensues. Examples of interests include: survival, security, reputation, financial well-being, respect, career, and health. Recognition of these important matters at stake can be motivating.

In many cases, mediators find common interests among the disputants. In an employment scenario, frequently both a supervisor and an employee share an interest in their respective reputations, careers and financial security. In a landlord-tenant situation, both disputants often have a common interest in: a safe, clean and serviceable dwelling and responsive and respectful treatment. Divorcing parents share an interest in the well-being, health and happiness of their children. A common interest provides a useful foundation upon which to build.

ISSUES

Issues are those distinct and negotiable matters or behaviors that are frustrating a party's interests. Issues are the critical components of the negotiating agenda. Since mediators are generally charged with helping craft a discussion agenda that is right "on target" with respect to concerns raised, a mediator's ability to mine the conversation for issues and to label them in neutral language is key. One of the unique strengths of mediation compared to litigation or arbitration is its ability to address the infinitely wide range of concerns that disputing parties have with each other.

Legal issues or causes of action are distinct from negotiable issues. In a probate dispute, for example, the litigated issues might be: whether undue influence was exerted on the testator or whether the testator had testamentary capacity. These legal questions might never be resolved in mediation. Rather, though parties might discuss the legal cause of action, the negotiable issues, often broader than the legal ones, would be targeted for resolution: the disposition of the art collection; the division of the residuary estate; the division of photographs, albums and family memorabilia; the hosting of holiday events; interaction between aunts, uncles, nieces and nephews; and so on.

The mediator pays attention to how issues are framed. In a labor-management context, frequent issues that arise include: wages, benefits, vacations, and overtime. Note that those descriptions of the issues do not take sides. In a divorce context, financial and parenting arrangements are frequently central. In a litigation context, the negotiable issue of "parenting arrangements" would be described as "custody" and "visitation" — a framing that invites adversarial positioning rather than problem-solving. In a landlord-tenant situation where back rent is contested, if the mediator framed the issue as "the delinquent rent owed by the tenant" she is inviting a hostile reaction from the tenant. Identifying the issue simply as "the rent" serves better.

PROPOSALS

Proposals are offers or suggestions for the resolution of particular issues or of the dispute. Like other elements which require mining, proposals are rarely neatly and attractively packaged by the parties. Disputants frequently embed a proposal in a threat or insult, and mediators must be attuned to extract and display the proposal. A supervisor might say to an employee, for example: "If you didn't have such a nasty attitude, the company might help you. As it is, you're going to walk." From a mediator's perspective, that may be a proposal! The mediator would want to know what specifically the employee might do to display a different attitude and what sort of "help" might ensue.

Opening proposals (often called "positions") tend to be extreme and unworkable, since workable proposals would have led to resolution and avoided the need for a mediator. However, they are nonetheless an important indication of what each party sees as an interest-satisfying outcome.

LEGEND: Common interests→ **Bold**;
Issues→underscore;
Mutually Acceptable Proposals→*italics*

Employer and Employee want to end their employment relationship in an amicable manner. To that end, they agree:

1. <u>Employment Relationship.</u>
    A. <u>Employee's Employment Status.</u> **Both Employer and Employee would like to facilitate Employee's smooth transition to a new job. Consequently, they agree:**
        i. that Employee shall remain at the company for three months with full pay and benefits, retaining her current office, telephone and e-mail privileges, and job title. During that period Employee shall look for other employment and shall have no job-related responsibilities. At the end of that period, Employee shall resign; and
        ii. that Employer shall provide Employee with outplacement services at a provider chosen by Employee for one year or until Employee is hired (whichever occurs sooner). . . .

Consequently, a mediator must be encouraged to pay sharp attention to proposals, even though he may not relay or reframe each proposal, as some may be so extreme that they would result in further alienation of the parties.

The relationship of interests, issues and proposals to agreements is the following. Agreements begin with a purpose clause (common interests), they employ headings (the issues in dispute) and they entail understandable and precise arrangements and undertakings between the parties (proposals that are mutually acceptable). Hence the mediator, even as he listens to the opening presentations of the parties, is actually beginning to construct an agreement from the articulated interests, issues and proposals he hears (see box above).

FEELINGS

Both recipients of and witnesses to put-downs and insults tend naturally to react with alarm, heightened adrenalin and, especially for the recipient, an attack response. Mediators must hear, and at appropriate points reframe, the feelings that generate such statements: the speaker is angry; the speaker is scared; the speaker is frustrated. It is often the case that all parties to a conflict have similar feelings of anger and frustration. In many cases, a vitriolic insult is the tip of an iceberg of a history of hurt feelings, waiting to be heard and acknowledged. Sometimes the venting and acknowledgment alone can shift the feelings themselves. Mediators should be trained to hear insults and reframe the statement to acknowledge the feelings underneath.

PRINCIPLES, VALUES AND RULES

Parties govern themselves in accordance with certain principles and values they hold dear. A sense of entitlement and need for "justice" and setting things right grows out of parties' understanding of family, industry, community, religious or legal rules and norms. Exposing and clarifying the parties' (and sometimes their attorneys' or other experts') operating principles, values, norms and rules are part of the mediator's task. This is so for several reasons: (1) behavior becomes more understandable when the parties understand the important principles, values and rules governing the other party's behavior; and (2) proposals generally will not work for a party unless they comport with the party's operating norms.

In court-annexed settings or for disputes involving legal claims and lawyers, the law and the parties' perceptions and positions with respect to their legal rights and obligations may play a critical role. If counsel are present in the mediation session, their presentations regarding the legal posture of the case will be a key element in framing the parties' perceptions of legal norms. Such presentations will assist the parties re-evaluate their understanding of the litigation alternative. The mediator should encourage a discussion and analysis of the weaknesses and strengths of elements of each party's case. Risk assessment (or conversely, opportunity analysis) with respect to litigation may provide a key piece to the puzzle of what would provide a meaningful settlement in court-connected cases. It is up to the mediator to encourage the attorneys to make presentations about legal norms, risks and opportunities, which are persuasive in terms of making the other side re-evaluate their litigation option, but are not personally offensive to the other side such that a climate for constructive negotiation is undermined.

Lawyers, however, can overemphasize the importance of the role of law. Remember that it is usual for legal analysis to result in widely different assessments of likely litigation outcomes. Also, other values and interests come into play for many parties. The power of an apology, for example, and the recognition it entails, is typically underestimated by lawyers. Moral, religious, family or community values can play a more decisive role, in some cases, than legal norms.

VISIONS

A vision in this context is a picture that a party may have of an ideal state. Often the frustration and high tension in a conflict setting is due to the fact that the status quo is so far from where a party would like it to be. Interestingly, "visions" often do not conflict, and sometimes are complementary. For example, in disputes between neighbors parties often say: "I just want peace when I come home"; or "I want my building to feel welcoming"; or "I want to be left alone, not bothered." In an employment situation, parties might say: "I want a friendly workplace"; or "I want co-workers who pull together"; or "I want my employees to care about the business." The mediator can explore these pictures by asking: "Tell me more about how you would like your building to be"; or "Describe how you would like the office to be" (asking both parties, of course). Such an exploration can result in a target status quo that is appealing to both parties. Having some clarity about the ideal makes it easier to dream up intermediate steps to achieve such an ideal.

STORIES

Allowing parties to tell their stories (often a story of a wrong they have experienced) is critical to each party being able to move beyond that experience of wrong and to listen to the other party's story, frequently a quite different story or viewpoint on the same "facts" and invariably expanding the picture or "reality" which informs each individual party's perception of events. Mediators need to understand that they must listen to each party's story and be able to see how that party views events, but — unlike a judge or an arbitrator — they need not judge or determine which version of events constitutes "facts." By preserving for each party an uninterrupted platform for speech, the mediator gives each party voice and respect and encourages a heightened level of understanding. Unlike an arbitrator or neutral expert who must find "facts," a mediator gives each party the storytelling floor so that the parties can be shifted by the power of the other's narrative (sometimes assisted by advocates and the translating function of the mediator). The telling of the story may shift the speaker; the hearing of the story may shift the listener; from a mediator's perspective, the parties, as first-hand participants, are in the best position to judge the "truth" around the events related to their conflict.

BATNAs (Best Alternative to a Negotiated Agreement)

A party's BATNA represents their favored or default option if mediation is unsuccessful in resolving the conflict. How the mediator uses BATNAs can be very important. BATNAs are frequently expressed as a threat, for example: "I will pursue this all the way to the Supreme Court"; "I have friends" (sometimes meaning "my friends will injure you"); "we will send in troops"; and "I will tell Mom." Such statements may be expressions of options a party may have, and the mediator will urge the parties to explore and evaluate the realistic costs and opportunities available through each option. Each party's perspective will be informed by the evaluation of the other side. In that manner, the process enables decision-making to take place in an environment providing enriched information. In its least ambitious form, mediation can be seen as an opportunity to "beat the BATNA" of each party through the negotiation process.

Problem 7-4.   *Finding the Gold!*

Ask a colleague to describe a conflict that is distressing him. As you listen, identify and reframe for the speaker the interests, issues, feelings, proposals, principles, visions, and any BATNA expressed. If these elements are not described, ask questions to elicit them.

---

c. Constructing a Discussion Agenda

As any chair of a meeting would do, the mediator must help the parties build a constructive discussion agenda. The agenda items — the issues — are those matters that require negotiation. After identifying those matters and framing them in a neutral manner, the final challenge is to order the agenda in a way most conducive to collaboration, which Joseph Stulberg discusses in the excerpt below.

 Joseph B. Stulberg, **THE THEORY AND PRACTICE OF MEDIATION: A REPLY TO PROFESSOR SUSSKIND**

6 Vt. L. Rev. 85, 99-103 (1981)

An important consideration for the mediator when trying to structure effective communication is the order in which the parties will discuss the issues. To those unfamiliar with the negotiation-mediation process, this matter might appear to be a trivial house-keeping point. Frequently, however, stalemates and impasses occur not because parties disagree on all matters but because they have failed to structure discussions so that they can distinguish those matters on which they agree from those on which they do not.

. . . A mediator could adopt one of several approaches in structuring the discussion of issues. He could start by discussing the easy issues first. Everyone can assess matters in terms of degree of importance. If the mediator focuses discussions on those less important matters (i.e. the matters perceived as enhancing the parties' relationship without in any way jeopardizing their substantive interests), then he can help the parties begin to forge some agreements.

Using this approach serves two purposes. First, it begins to develop a pattern of agreement and momentum of progress between the parties. Confidence in the talks grows as agreement is reached on some items, and the parties obtain a limited basis for believing it possible to resolve the more difficult issues. Second, by building a series of small agreements, the mediator has laid a settlement foundation. As the parties reach more difficult issues, the cost of not settling increases since that cost would include relinquishing all agreements which had been reached. That fact alone might give the parties a strong incentive to reconsider any resistance to the remaining matters.

Another approach would involve dividing issues and proposals according to their common subject-matter. The mediator could categorize the proposals [in a labor dispute] into such subjects as vacation, wages, hours of work, and the like and then discuss each party's proposal(s) that falls within that category. The starting point of the discussion would be the category of issues that seems most susceptible to prompt resolution. . . .

[T]he mediator could approach the discussion of the issues and proposals according to existing time constraints. The mediator could suggest that the parties first address those matters requiring prompt attention and defer discussion on the other matters until they could be addressed at a more leisurely pace. . . .

The most effective approach depends on the context of the discussions and the individual parties. What must be underscored is that the approach to the discussion of issues can be deliberate rather than haphazard; it is the mediator's job to ensure that the discussions are intelligently ordered.

> **Problem 7-5.** *How Do You Structure the Agenda?*
>
> Another approach is to allow the parties to negotiate about the order of the agenda. The mediator might, for example, lay out issues she has heard, check that the list fully represents the topics that must be addressed, and then ask, "What would you like to talk about first?" What are the advantages of the more directive approach that Stulberg suggests? The disadvantages?
>
> Imagine that you are a mediator faced with parties disputing over the amount of damages a defendant will pay, the timing of the payment, the method of payment, and the type of release that plaintiff will give. In what order would you address these issues? Analyze the advantages and disadvantages of different choices. Wherever you start, having the ability to shelve an issue and get movement elsewhere by moving to another issue can keep the mediation dynamic.

d. Generating Movement: Developing Options and Agreements

Mediator responsibility for "generating movement" and overcoming impasse is frequently portrayed as the use of strategies to find a compromise between two extreme positions that disputants take. For example, if one party demands "$1 million" to compensate for damaged reputation, and the response is "I've done nothing wrong. I'll give you nothing. Everything I said was true!", then a "compromise" might be the payment of any amount between $0 and $1 million.

However, the idea of movement — and strategies for achieving movement — is a much richer study than simply techniques to encourage compromise, accommodation, and trade-off. Movement of any sort can engender movement of every sort. Consequently, it is helpful to think of movement from a variety of angles.

Mediators create a safe space where both listening and being heard can encourage softening of extreme positions, lessen demonization of the other party, and abate some of the blame and anger disputing parties often experience. Sometimes parties need to be understood before they can move on. Any movement towards understanding and "letting go" is potentially impasse-breaking movement. Other times disputants need to confront the cost of being stuck in recriminations, blame, and extreme, unworkable positions before they can move into a collaborative posture to attempt to find mutually acceptable resolutions.

Former President Bill Clinton describes accompanying Nelson Mandela to the South African prison cell where Mandela slept on the floor for the first 14 years of his incarceration without heat, toilet, or faucet. Clinton asked whether Mandela was bitter and angry as he walked away from that cell after 27 years of imprisonment. Mandela replied that he felt anger rising up, but he said to himself: "Mandela, they had you 27 years. If you are still angry with them when you get out the gate, they will still have you. . . . I wanted to be free, and so I let it go."[4] Mandela thoughtfully weighed the cost of carrying his anger, and he moved beyond it. This internal movement of "letting go" of anger can have powerful consequences, as Mandela's career exemplifies. When negotiating parties relinquish some of their bitterness and animosity, possibilities for resolution emerge.

In your study of negotiation, you learned methods of generating flexibility, creativity, and "out-of-the-box" thinking in the context of negotiation. You also examined psychological barriers to "rational" resolutions and methods to address such barriers. The mediator — really a negotiation moderator — must be aware of and use those same strategies and skills. The mediator is charged with jump-starting the process of option generation and tries to bring negotiators up to speed, with respect to both a constructive perspective and awareness of productive strategies. The mediator has the advantage of being impartial, providing a lightning rod for frustration, and having a fresh outlook on the situation.

Where substantive resolutions cannot be found, the mediator can assist with a search for procedural resolutions. For example, if disputants agree that Party A should compensate Party B for a piece of antique furniture but cannot agree on the value of the furniture, they might agree to accept the valuation of a neutral expert. Tossing a coin to decide an issue is another example of a procedural resolution.

What follows is a short list of techniques to generate movement that are specifically targeted at mediators. They are divided into three categories. The first and second categories highlight strategies that strengthen the individual negotiating parties and enable them to understand each other's perspective. The third category highlights techniques that may be helpful in developing agreements. Even though this list was developed for mediator training, see how the ideas for effective mediator strategies parallel approaches for negotiators.

 Lela P. Love & Joseph B. Stulberg, **TARGETS AND TECHNIQUES TO GENERATE MOVEMENT**

in Training Materials (2004)

POSITIVE PSYCHOLOGICAL STANCE, EMPOWERMENT, STRENGTH

1. <u>Compliment productive behavior.</u> (*"Thank you both for coming to mediation." "You did a good job explaining your concerns, Ms. A, and you in listening patiently, Mr. B." "I'd like to commend you both for developing a variety of options. Let's try to find one that works for both of you."*) Behavior that is commended tends to be repeated. Sincere praise is empowering. As well as being empowering, this move is aimed at educating parties about constructive conduct.

2. <u>Use a "paradoxical intervention."</u> Offer the parties a choice. (*"It seems as if you keep returning to the question of who was at fault for the project's failure. We can certainly*

---

4. William J. Clinton, Acceptance Speech, International Advocate for Peace Award, Benjamin N. Cardozo School of Law, Mar. 19, 2001, available at http://www.cardozojcr.com/iap/2001.html#speech.

spend our time together exploring that question if you think that discussion would be useful. Or, in the hour we have remaining today, we could examine how you would like to structure future arrangements to address what happened. It's up to you. How would you like to spend the time?") This intervention is "paradoxical" because typically when people are offered the choice as to whether they would like to continue attacking and blaming each other or to move on, they will choose the latter, while, absent the offer, they will continue to attack and blame.

3. Appeal to principles and ideals. If disputants both agree that, for example, avoiding unnecessary harm or dividing a family's assets so that children share equally or treating men and women equally are shared principles or ideals, then those common goals can shape various elements of the discussion.

UNDERSTANDING. RECOGNITION. PERSPECTIVE TAKING

1. Highlight common interests, common values and common feelings. (*"You both seem to care deeply about the happiness of your child." "If I understand you correctly, you both would like to find a way to end your partnership while preserving the value of the business you have created and also preserving your reputations."*) Interests, values and feelings are powerful. When parties discover they share an interest or value or feeling it can become a common motivator and bridge.

2. Build information base regarding each party's interests, assumptions, aspirations, values, priorities, legal analysis and past practices. (*"Tell me more about . . ."*). Information is frequently the lever that shifts parties in meaningful ways.

3. Try role reversal. This technique comprises a variety of methods to challenge a party to see the situation from the point of view of another party or person. A mediator could actually ask the parties to switch seats or to imagine how the other person is feeling or conceive a solution that the other party would find desirable. (*"Putting yourself for a moment in X's chair and considering what he has said here this morning about . . . how would you see this situation?" "Can you propose a solution that might be regarded favorably by X?"*)

BUILDING SETTLEMENTS AND AGREEMENTS

1. Explore the costs of no agreement on both quality of life (*"What will it be like going home this evening and facing the same situation?"*) and process costs (*"Have you explored the costs — in terms of time, money and stress — of litigation?"*). Using decision tree formulas, for example, a mediator can assist parties to develop an analysis of the expected value of a litigated outcome (likely court outcome times % likelihood of that court outcome minus costs of litigation and discounted by the time it will take to get outcome) and to compare that figure to proposals on the table.

2. Use deadlines to move participants. (*"The building closes at midnight. Up to this point we have achieved x, y, and z. Would you like to bring closure to this in this session? Any ideas?"*) One reason deadlines may be effective is that loss aversion comes into play. That is, the opportunity to bring closure may be lost forever if movement does not occur.

3. <u>Seek accommodations to priority proposals of the other side.</u> ("*Ms. A, you have said you need money immediately, and Ms. B you are most concerned about the amount of the payment, is there any amount between $10,000, Ms. B's first offer, and $100,000, requested by Ms. A, that, Ms. A, you would be willing to accept if the money was paid immediately?*").

Problem 7-6.   *Should You Be Transparent?*

Do you think mediators should explain *why* they are using a particular strategy or technique? Professor Michael Moffit explores the advantages of a transparent approach. One example he uses is that a mediator, instead of simply asking a party why the party is making a proposal that the lease run for no more than three years, might say: "I'm hoping you'll change the way you're thinking about your demands. Right now, you seem to be fixed on the idea that there is only one way you can be satisfied in this dispute, and that seems unlikely to me. I think it would be more productive for you and for this process if you (and the rest of us) were better able to understand the things that are motivating you to make these demands. Why is the duration of the lease important to you?" Michael Moffit, 13 Ohio St. J. on Disp. Resol. 1, 13 (1997). What are the potential benefits and dangers of a transparent approach? Try it out as a mediator!

In the pie chart that follows, Christopher Moore provides another approach for thinking about generating movement. Inside the circle he shows the impediments that cause impasse in a given dispute. For each type of conflict, outside the circle, he gives a variety of mediator interventions that would be responsive or appropriate to overcome the given impasse.

 Christopher W. Moore, **THE MEDIATION PROCESS**

60-61 (1996)

Sphere of Conflict—Causes and Interventions

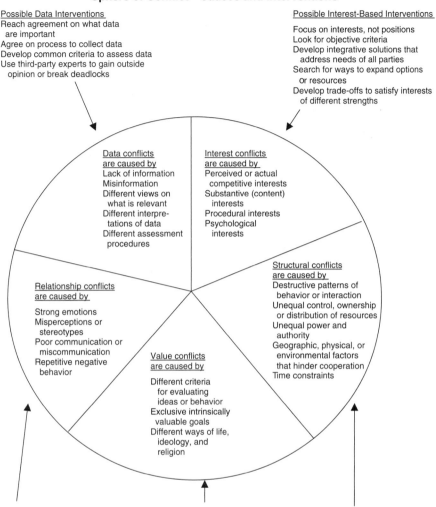

Possible Data Interventions
Reach agreement on what data
  are important
Agree on process to collect data
Develop common criteria to assess data
Use third-party experts to gain outside
  opinion or break deadlocks

Possible Interest-Based Interventions

Focus on interests, not positions
Look for objective criteria
Develop integrative solutions that
  address needs of all parties
Search for ways to expand options
  or resources
Develop trade-offs to satisfy interests
  of different strengths

Data conflicts
are caused by
Lack of information
Misinformation
Different views on
  what is relevant
Different interpre-
  tations of data
Different assessment
  procedures

Interest conflicts
are caused by
Perceived or actual
  competitive interests
Substantive (content)
  interests
Procedural interests
Psychological
  interests

Structural conflicts
are caused by
Destructive patterns of
  behavior or interaction
Unequal control, ownership
  or distribution of resources
Unequal power and
  authority
Geographic, physical, or
  environmental factors
  that hinder cooperation
Time constraints

Relationship conflicts
are caused by

Strong emotions
Misperceptions or
  stereotypes
Poor communication or
  miscommunication
Repetitive negative
  behavior

Value conflicts
are caused by

Different criteria
  for evaluating
  ideas or behavior
Exclusive intrinsically
  valuable goals
Different ways of life,
  ideology, and
  religion

Possible Relationship Interventions
Control expression of emotions'
  through procedure, ground rules,
  caucuses, and so forth
Promote expression of emotions
  by legitimizing feelings and
  providing a process
Clarify perceptions and build
  positive perceptions
Improve quality and quantity
  of communication
Block negative repetitive
  behavior by changing structure
Encourage positive problem-
  solving attitudes

Possible Value-Related
Interventions
Avoid defining problem
  in terms of value
Allow parties to agree
  and to disagree
Create spheres of influence
  in which one set of
  values dominates
Search for superordinate
  goal that all parties
  share

Possible Structural Interventions
Clearly define and change roles
Replace destructive behavior patterns
Reallocate ownership or control
  of resources
Establish a fair and mutually acceptable
  decision-making process
Change negotiation process from
  positional to interest-based bargaining
Modify means of influence used by
  parties (less coercion, more persuasion)
Change physical and environmental
  relationships of parties (closeness
  and distance)
Modify external pressures on parties
Change time constraints (more or
  less time)

e. Using the Caucus

Among the strategies to generate movement, perspective taking, and a more creative approach to a dispute is to invite parties to meet separately with the mediator. After the mediator and each side give an opening statement — and at each juncture for the remainder of the mediation — a choice can be made about whether to stay in joint session or move to caucus. A joint session is where all the participants meet together with the mediator. A caucus is where the mediator meets individually with one side or some subset of the entire participant group (for example, one side only, lawyers only, clients only, kids without parents). In a caucus, parties are invited to speak openly with the assurance that the mediator will not share information conveyed unless given permission to do so. Practically speaking, this means that once a caucus is used the mediator must keep track of what he knows *and* how he learned what he knows *and* the constraints regarding use of the information if obtained in a caucus.

Different philosophies guide mediators in determining their preferred approach to using the caucus. Three dominant approaches are followed: caucus selectively, never caucus, or mostly caucus. As you read about each of these, consider what goals each approach is most likely to advance: understanding, problem-solving, or settlement?

i. Caucus Selectively

In the first approach, caucus selectively, most meetings are conducted in joint session unless there is a particular reason to caucus. Mediators following this approach might conduct an entire mediation without ever using a caucus. Such mediators view the caucus as a tool used only for particular applications. Reasons *not* to caucus include the belief that direct communication between parties is superior to using an intermediary and that parties benefit from working out matters themselves. A "selective caucus" mediator might suggest a caucus when, for example, communication becomes so heated or the parties so volatile that constructive progress is threatened; an apparent power imbalance suggests that individual explorations of the underlying dynamic is necessary; the mediator believes that more information is available but it will not be shared with all present; the parties need space to reflect about proposals; or the mediator wants to "reality check" that proposals being considered are doable and optimal.

ii. Never Caucus

Mediators using a never caucus approach believe that private meetings can taint the mediator's neutrality, create undue reliance on the mediator, cut off the parties' direct communication, and undermine the opportunity for collaboration. The Understanding-Based model, discussed in Chapter 6, follows this "non-caucus" approach:

The mediator holds all matters confidential as to outsiders, but holds nothing confidential between the parties. If the mediator speaks with either of the parties separately, which we believe is not the preferred way to proceed, that information is available to the other party. . . . [T]he goal [is] that all parties understand all relevant information rather than the mediator putting him or herself in the position of being the only one who has the whole picture. The mediator will also not speak with the parties' lawyers unless both parties give permission.[5]

iii. Mostly Caucus

In the mostly caucus approach, parties typically meet jointly at the beginning of the mediation and at the end when a resolution is reached. In the middle, the mediator conducts a series of caucuses. Proceeding in this manner ensures that hostilities between the parties do not escalate the dispute and maximizes mediator control over the flow of information and over the way proposals are developed and presented. The caucus, to the extent parties share information about their bottom line, also maximizes the potential benefit of mediation in preventing impasse where there is a positive zone of agreement. However, the approach also takes power and control away from the parties, as the mediator becomes the source of information and the person who holds the key to movement. With some mediators, the mostly caucus approach can become the always caucus approach where *all* joint sessions are eliminated.

f. Drafting Agreements and Closing the Session

Sessions can end: without an agreement, with a written agreement, with a verbal agreement, with a partial agreement regarding substantive issues, with an agreement to return for another session, or with an agreement to use some other procedure to address the dispute. One of the final tasks of a mediator is to help parties capture and memorialize their commitments to each other if they have been able to resolve their dispute and, in every case, formulate a plan going forward. This is an important mediator function for several reasons. First, the mediator must ensure the parties have a clear — and the same — understanding about the agreement so that a dispute does not arise about its terms. Reviewing the terms of agreement (if it is verbal) or reducing the agreement to a writing (if the parties want a written agreement) can aid that task. Second, helping bring closure with an agreement can be important both psychologically and practically. Psychologically, leaving mediation with an agreement means that the matter is put to rest, that closure is achieved. The internal debate about agreement terms can cease. Practically speaking, the parties can move on with their lives, and the momentum achieved in the session will not be lost by the passage of time and intervening events. If the matter is in litigation, the litigation can end.

---

5. Gary Friedman & Jack Himmelstein, Center for Mediation in Law, Memo No. 2, Elements of Mediator-Parties Contract (2003).

Drafting agreements, however, is a task closely connected with the practice of law. Some mediators hesitate to draft agreements or even memoranda of understanding for fear they are engaging in the unauthorized practice of law or may otherwise expose themselves to liability. In business and employment cases where parties have their own attorneys, a mediator may well avoid drafting a detailed and comprehensive agreement, but rather leave that to the parties' attorneys. Many mediators, however, will draft a "bare-bones" memorandum of understanding at the parties' request, capturing essential features of the agreement.

In situations where the parties do not have lawyers and ask the mediator to draft an agreement, the mediator can provide valuable service by capturing agreement terms. In community cases, for example, mediators routinely draft agreements, as agencies and parties expect this service in order to bring effective closure to the mediation.

The safest posture for the mediator, to avoid a charge of engaging in the unauthorized practice of law, is to view herself as a scribe, capturing the parties' undertakings, using the parties' words, avoiding additional provisions, and advising the parties to get legal advice prior to signing the agreement.

Principles of good agreement drafting include being sure that agreement terms are understandable and precise. Using the parties' own words and "plain English," making sure that payment terms, the time frame and methods of performance are precise will contribute to those goals. Also, mediators want to make an agreement appealing. To that end, they will: begin with a statement of common interests and goals, put mutual obligations first, balance the agreement (for example, if party A agrees to pay money then Party B agrees to provide a receipt). An agreement, until it is signed, is merely a draft or proposal. Whether or not it matures into an agreement that is durable will depend in part on the quality of the drafting.

In every case, whether or not any agreement is achieved, the mediator must end on as positive a note as possible, commending the parties for their efforts and acknowledging any constructive movement that has been made. The mediator will want both parties to leave the session at the same time, avoiding the appearance of partiality that may be created where one side lingers for a private conversation with the mediator. The mediator will also want to ensure there is an exit strategy so that parties who are still uncomfortable in each other's presence do not find themselves together in a small elevator.

Problem 7-7. *Should You Draft the Parties' Agreement?*

In response to the unauthorized practice of law issue, the ABA Section of Dispute Resolution adopted a resolution on Mediation and the Unauthorized Practice of Law on February 2, 2002 (*available at* http://www.abanet.org/dispute/resolution2002.pdf). With respect to agreement drafting, the resolution advises:

> When an agreement is reached in a mediation, the parties often request assistance from the mediator in memorializing their agreement. The preparation of a memorandum of understanding or settlement agreement by a mediator, incorporating the terms of settlement specified by the parties, does not constitute the practice of law. If the mediator drafts an agreement that goes beyond the terms specified by the parties, he or she may be engaged in the practice of law. However, in such a case, a mediator shall not be engaged in the practice of law if (a) all parties are represented by counsel and (b) the mediator discloses that any proposal that he or she makes with respect to the terms of settlement is informational as opposed to the practice of law, and that the parties should not view or rely upon such proposals as advice of counsel, but merely consider them in consultation with their own attorneys.

Note, however, that this resolution is not controlling on courts or local Bar associations.

If you were a divorce mediator without legal training with a background in psychology would you feel comfortable drafting an agreement in light of this resolution? If you were an attorney-mediator authorized to practice in the relevant jurisdiction would you feel comfortable adding "boiler plate" terms to the parties' agreement?

---

5. Other Mediator Approaches

The models and strategies presented above assume that the mediator is chairing a negotiation process where negotiable issues are targeted and the parties are accompanied and supported in a problem solving quest to find resolutions to those issues. As Chapter 6 discusses, there are other approaches to mediation. For example, transformative mediation rejects problem solving as a goal, seeking instead party empowerment and recognition. Since the goals of transformative mediation differ, at least in some respects, from other types of mediation, practitioner skills also vary. The transformative mediator will focus on practices that empower parties and support recognition between them. The opening statement of a transformative mediator will lay out these goals, indicating that settlement is only one of the possible outcomes of the mediation. All critical choices about process and outcome will be strictly left to the parties, and the mediator will consistently follow, rather than lead, the parties.

The evaluative mediator, mentioned in Riskin's Grid in Chapter 6, uses many of the facilitative skills discussed above and *also* must be adept at evaluation — skills discussed in the arbitration chapters. Additional to finding facts and applying legal rules or industry customs, mediators who evaluate must do it in a way that, ideally, makes parties feel nondefensive and that is least likely to impact mediator neutrality.

B. THE ATTORNEY REPRESENTATIVE

If lawyers are not leaders in marshaling cooperation and designing mechanisms that allow it to flourish, they will not be at the center of the most creative social experiments of our time.

> — Derek Bok, former president of Harvard University

In section A above, you examined how a mediator prepares for and strategizes about various steps in the mediation process. Now change your perspective to an attorney representing a client in mediation. All of the negotiation skills you studied, and many of the mediator skills, are relevant for the attorney representative too. We will look now at add-on considerations for the attorney operating in a mediation context. Professor Harold Abramson provides attorneys a formula for representing clients in mediation urging them to make use of the presence of the mediator to advance their client's interests at six critical junctures: selecting the mediator, preparing pre-mediation submissions, participating in the pre-mediation conference, presenting opening statements, participating in joint sessions, and participating in caucuses. At each of these junctures Professor Abramson urges a creative problem-solving approach.[6] What follows is an analysis of the problem-solving perspective, followed by advice about how to put the perspective into action — as well as what actions the attorney representative should avoid.

1. The Problem-Solving Perspective

In the excerpt that follows, Professor Leonard Riskin describes an attitude and perspective shift — a new orientation that lawyers need to adopt to be constructive mediation advocates. Given the prevalence of mediation, comfort with this new approach is increasingly important.

 Leonard L. Riskin, **MEDIATION AND LAWYERS**

43 Ohio St. L.J. 29, 43-45 (1982)

E. F. Schumacher begins his Guide for the Perplexed with the following story:

---

6. Harold I. Abramson, Mediation Representation: Advocating as a Problem-Solver in Any Country or Culture (2d ed., NITA 2010).

On a visit to Leningrad some years ago, I consulted a map . . . but I could not make it out. From where I stood, I could see several enormous churches, yet there was no trace of them on my map. When finally an interpreter came to help me, he said: "We don't show churches on our maps." Contradicting him, I pointed to one that was very clearly marked. "That is a museum," he said, "not what we call a 'living church.' It is only the 'living churches' we don't show." It then occurred to me that this was not the first time I had been given a map which failed to show many things I could see right in front of my eyes. All through school and university I had been given maps of life and knowledge on which there was hardly a trace of many of the things that I most cared about and that seemed to me to be of the greatest possible importance to the conduct of my life.

The philosophical map employed by most practicing lawyers and law teachers, and displayed to the law student — which I will call the lawyer's standard philosophical map — differs radically from that which a mediator must use. What appears on this map is determined largely by the power of two assumptions about matters that lawyers handle: (1) that disputants are adversaries — i.e., if one wins, the others must lose — and (2) that disputes may be resolved through application, by a third party, of some general rule of law. These assumptions, plainly, are polar opposites of those which underlie mediation: (1) that all parties can benefit through a creative solution to which each agrees; and (2) that the situation is unique and therefore not to be governed by any general principle except to the extent that the parties accept it.

The two assumptions of the lawyer's philosophical map (adversariness of parties and rule-solubility of dispute), along with the real demands of the adversary system and the expectations of many clients, tend to exclude mediation from most lawyers' repertoires. They also blind lawyers to other kinds of information that are essential for a mediator to see, primarily by riveting the lawyers' attention upon things that they must see in order to carry out their functions. The mediator must, for instance, be aware of the many interconnections between and among disputants and others, and of the qualities of these connections; he must be sensitive to emotional needs of all parties and recognize the importance of yearnings for mutual respect, equality, security, and other such non-material interests as may be present.

On the lawyer's standard philosophical map, however, the client's situation is seen atomistically; many links are not printed. The duty to represent the client zealously within the bounds of the law discourages concern with both the opponents' situation and the overall social effect of a given result.

Moreover, on the lawyer's standard philosophical map, quantities are bright and large while qualities appear dimly or not at all. When one party wins, in this vision, usually the other party loses, and, most often, the victory is reduced to a money judgment. This "reduction" of nonmaterial values — such as honor, respect, dignity, security, and love — to amounts of money, can have one of two effects. In some cases, these values are excluded from the decision makers' considerations, and thus from the consciousness of the lawyers, as irrelevant. In others, they are present but transmuted into something else — a justification for money damages. Much like the church that was allowed to appear on the map of Leningrad only because it was a museum, these interests — which may in fact be the principal motivations for a lawsuit — are recognizable in the legal dispute primarily to the extent that they have monetary value or fit into a clause of a rule governing liability.

The rule orientation also determines what appears on the map. The lawyer's standard world view is based upon a cognitive and rational outlook. Lawyers are trained to put people and events into categories that are legally meaningful, to think in terms of rights and duties established by rules, to focus on acts more than persons. This view requires a

> ### "The True Practice of the Law"
>
> Mahatma Gandhi relates that after he persuaded his victorious client to agree to accept installment payments instead of a lump sum, which the defendant would have been unable to deliver, "[b]oth were happy over the result, and both rose in the public estimation. My joy was boundless. I had learnt the true practice of the law. I had learnt to find out the better side of human nature and to enter men's hearts. I realized that the true function of a lawyer was to unite parties riven asunder."
>
> Riskin at 54 (quoting Mohandas Gandhi, Autobiography, The Story of My Experiments with Truth 168 (1948)).

strong development of cognitive capabilities, which is often attended by the undercultivation of emotional faculties. This combination of capacities joins with the practice of either reducing most nonmaterial values to amounts of money or sweeping them under the carpet, to restrict many lawyers' abilities to recognize the value of mediation or to serve as mediators.

The lawyer's standard philosophical map is useful primarily where the assumptions upon which it is based — adversariness and amenability to solution by a general rule imposed by a third party — are valid. But when mediation is appropriate, these assumptions do not fit.

---

2. Strategies and Skills of the Attorney Representative

a. Prescriptions for the Attorney

Adding to this perspective shift advocated by Professor Riskin, Larry Watson, a former litigator and seasoned mediator of civil trial cases provides practical guidance for attorneys representing clients in various stages of the mediation process.

 Lawrence M. Watson, Jr., EFFECTIVE ADVOCACY IN MEDIATION: A PLANNING GUIDE TO PREPARE FOR A CIVIL TRIAL MEDIATION

(prepared for various Continuing Legal Education programs) (2002)

. . . With the expansion of mediation as the leading ADR process, it is clear that the civil trial counsel's role must thus also expand to include proficiency in reaching acceptable mediated settlements for their clients. The growth of ADR is redefining the role of the American trial lawyer. . . .

STEP ONE: PREPARING THE CLIENT FOR THE MEDIATION EXPERIENCE

It is critically important to have the clients understand that the outcome of the mediation process contemplates "win-win," not "win-lose." Mediation is a process that seeks to *reconcile* disputes. Mediation is not a process that seeks to *adjudicate* disputes. The outcome of reconciliation is an *agreement* with the other side. The outcome of adjudication is a *judgment* against the other side. There are big differences between the two. . . .

Clients should therefore understand that the mediation program does not dwell on who may be proven right or wrong in court — it is a factor, but not a controlling factor. To be successful at mediation, the client must understand the focus must ultimately come to mutually satisfying the interests of all parties to the dispute. Simply stated, the process involves compromise — giving as well as getting. . . .

Bear in mind, one salient difference between resolving disputes through adjudication and resolving disputes through reconciliation is the range of settlement options available to the parties. With the exception of some limited equitable relief that might [be] available in some cases, the judicial resolution of a dispute will be restricted to money judgments. An important benefit offered to parties agreeing to reconcile their differences is the broad range of settlement options that can be deployed. Thinking through and developing contingent plans to utilize these options in advance, doing feasibility research on settlement alternatives before the mediation starts, can dramatically increase the potential for a successful outcome. . . .

STEP TWO: DEFINING THE OVERALL GOALS OF MEDIATION

The first step of any journey is to decide where you want to go. In a civil trial mediation, that step is taken by simply sitting down with the client and mutually agreeing, in concept, on a range of acceptable outcomes to the mediation process. As noted above, every effort should be made to avoid "bottom line" dollar amount absolutes. To the contrary the client should be impressed and thinking about the wide range of objectives which could become available through a well-structured and prepared mediation session. . . .

STEP THREE: DECIDING WHEN, WHERE, WHO AND HOW WE WILL MEDIATE THIS CASE

Although a bit dated, an attitude still exists among many trial lawyers (and litigation clients) that being the first one to suggest mediation — or any settlement process — is a sign of weakness to be avoided. A "macho mind set" about the case would suggest that even discussing reconciliation signals a lack of confidence in the merits of one's position, and involves an immediate loss of face. There are a number of ways to get past this problem.

In jurisdictions where mediation is mandatory, the problem can be avoided by simply noting that going to mediation is an inevitable circumstance and both sides would be better off attempting to take the initiative to control the process. The argument that both parties are better served by deciding on a mutually agreeable mediator, picking a time and location of their choosing, and defining the format for the process themselves rather than allowing the judge or a court administrator to do it for them is compelling. . . .

Another approach is to attribute the idea to the economics. Once a litigation plan is roughly sketched, it is natural for both sides to note the costs involved in legal fees and expenses.

A. Selection of the Mediator . . .

In preparing the initial list, or in making the final selection from the list, it is wise to take the time to complete some level of research on each mediator under consideration. Ask the mediators under consideration to submit resumes and, more importantly, the names of other counsel with whom they have worked in the past. Contact those lawyers and ask about the proposed mediator's style, energy, creativity and success rate. Network with other lawyers in your own firm or in the field to see if they have had any experience with the proposed mediator as well. Prepare a short report on each and include the client in the final determination. In particularly significant cases where the proposed mediators are unknown, arrange for a short interview session to meet with the proposed mediators in advance. Again, including the client in those sessions will go a long way to help determine the best person for the job.

The overall goal in selecting the mediator should be to find an individual who can truly serve as a neutral, who demonstrates a capacity to work hard, and who will command the respect of both sides.

B. Location, Duration and Timing

The choice of location for a mediation session should be driven solely by the physical requirements necessary to stage the event. Appropriate considerations would thus include reasonable travel accessibility, ample room for attendees in joint and caucus sessions, adequate secured storage space for files and materials, overnight lodging opportunities and some separation from other distractions. Choice of location should never be allowed to become a positional issue involving a "home court" advantage of one party or another.

The duration and timing for a mediation is, perhaps, more important than the location. Sufficient time should be allotted for a mediation to allow for adequate presentations by all parties followed by ample time to privately caucus and develop alternative resolution options. Obviously, the number of parties, complexity of issues, and dollar amounts involved will play into defining an appropriate time to reserve for the mediation. The decision-making temperament of the parties — the amount of time the individuals involved in the dispute will need to make up their minds — is also an important factor in scheduling mediations. Creating situations in which the parties are rushed to judgment, or forced to endure exhausting marathon sessions into the late hours of the night can compromise the validity of the agreement reached. Scheduling or conducting a mediation in a manner that adversely affects the parties' self determination is tantamount to abusing the process. "Mediation remorse" should be carefully avoided. . . .

PREPARATION FOR MEDIATION

The presentation of the client's case in the opening phase of a mediation is a task that must meet two, often conflicting, needs.

First, the client must feel his or her story has been told. Any anger, frustration, and discontent stemming from the events leading to the dispute must be relieved before focused attention can be given to reconciliation considerations. To one extent or another, therefore, the client must be given the chance to vent. In all occasions, the client must feel that the merits of . . . his or her position in the debate have been fairly presented and understood.

Secondly (and often in contradiction of satisfying the client's "venting" needs) there is a need for the opening presentations to clearly and effectively communicate the "other side of the story" to the opposition. Many clients to a dispute might be quite pleased with a lawyer that relieves built up feelings and relates their positions in ominous, scolding, or even threatening terms. An overly aggressive tone or demeanor to an opening presentation in a mediation, however, can serve to "turn off" the opposition and the critical task of expanding their understanding of the dispute is not achieved. . . .

One acceptable method of satisfying both needs is to simply allow the client an opportunity to participate in the opening presentations to satisfy whatever venting needs exist. In that event, counsel would prepare and execute an opening presentation geared toward communicating the reality of the dispute to the opposition in a tone and manner best suited to complete that task. The client could then add the emotive element to the presentation while satisfying his or her need to vent.

Accordingly, the best overall theme and tone of opening presentation in mediation would probably be a matter of fact description of the case to be presented at trial — firmly and unequivocally stated. It should clearly set forth the principal contentions underlying the position asserted, and the facts, principal documents, and expert opinions that support those contentions. There should be minimal argument — let the facts do the arguing. . . .

SOMETHING OTHER THAN MONEY — PREPARING SETTLEMENT OPTIONS

. . . In commercial cases, a systematic search for settlement options other than money should be conducted before the mediation commences. . . . If there is any way to convert a business dispute to a business opportunity, careful consideration should be given to that option in advance. The objective of any advance consideration of "other than money" settlement options is to make sure that they are potentially doable — that there are no legal, contractual, political or physical barriers to including such terms to the final agreement. The ultimate decision whether or not to include these terms in a final arrangement can be made later. The settlement negotiations themselves should be entered with an, "anything is possible" frame of mind. . . .

Problem 7-8. *Non-Monetary Settlements and Legal Fees*

Attorneys tend to assume that most disputes turn on money, whereas studies have shown that clients' interests are often much broader. Yet, one of the difficulties of other-than-money settlements can be the fee arrangements between lawyers and clients. If the plaintiff's lawyer's fee is based on a percentage of the settlement, then that lawyer has a built-in incentive to maximize settlement dollars. An apology, for example, provides no tangible benefit to a lawyer operating with a contingency fee. If the defense attorney's fee is based on an hourly charge the defense attorney may have an incentive to allow the dispute to continue rather than resolve. How might lawyers, clients and mediators deal with these potential conflicts of interest?

---

b. Customizing Representation

In the next excerpt, Jean Sternlight suggests a case-by-case approach to attorney strategy for representation in mediation, particularly sensitive to various barriers to negotiation that arise in particular cases.

 Jean R. Sternlight, **LAWYERS' REPRESENTATION OF CLIENTS IN MEDIATION: USING ECONOMICS AND PSYCHOLOGY TO STRUCTURE ADVOCACY IN A NONADVERSARIAL SETTING**

14 Ohio St. J. on Disp. Resol. 269, 274, 291-292, 295-296, 354-360, 365
(1999)

While no single lawyer's role in mediation is always proper, lawyers need to be particularly vigilant in guarding against their own tendencies to behave in mediation exactly as they would in litigation. Instead, to serve their clients' interests, and in light of the conflicts of interest and perception between lawyers and their own clients, attorneys should often encourage their clients to play an active role in the mediation, allow the discussion to focus on emotional as well as legal concerns, and work toward mutually beneficial rather than win-or-lose solutions. Those lawyers who, seeking to advocate strongly on behalf of their clients, take steps to dominate the mediation, focus exclusively on legal issues, and minimize their clients' direct participation, will often ill serve their clients' true needs and interests. Such overly zealous advocates are frequently poor advocates. . . .

If advocacy is defined broadly as supporting or pleading the cause of another, there is no inconsistency between advocacy and mediation. Permitting an attorney to act as an advocate for her client simply allows that attorney to speak and make arguments on her client's behalf and to help her client achieve her goals. . . . Nor is it clear why "adversarial" behavior, at least broadly defined, is necessarily inconsistent with mediation. To the extent that acting adversarially means advocating only on behalf of one's own client and not on behalf of any other party or on behalf of the process or system, the conduct is easy to reconcile with mediation. The problem-solving that works well in mediation does not require sacrifice of one's self-interest, but rather allows parties to search for solutions that are mutually beneficial. . . .

Yet, while attorneys may appropriately advocate for their clients in mediation, it is certainly true that those attorneys who attempt to employ traditional "zealous" litigation tools when representing their clients in mediation may frequently (but not always) fail either to fulfill their clients' wishes or to serve their clients' interests. Those who would hoard information, rely solely on legal rather than emotional arguments, or refuse to let their clients speak freely will often have little success in mediation. This is not because attorneys ought not to advocate for their clients, but rather because attorneys ought not to advocate poorly on behalf of their clients. . . .

PROPOSED GUIDELINES FOR DETERMINING THE RESPECTIVE ROLES OF LAWYER AND CLIENT

While a lawyer should consult with her client in determining how best to divide mediation responsibilities, the lawyer should still play a key role in helping the client to make this decision. As the lawyer does in other contexts, she should facilitate the client's choice by helping to lay out the advantages and disadvantages of various options. . . . To aid attorneys in this endeavor, . . . attorneys [should] ask themselves the following two interrelated questions to help determine how to divide mediation responsibilities: (1) who is this particular client and (2) what barriers seem to be preventing the case from settling.

1. Who Is This Client?

Attorneys should not assume that all clients are the same, but rather should focus on the potential differences between clients. Nor should they assume that all clients involved in a particular kind of lawsuit — e.g., personal injury, commercial, or employment termination — have the same concerns. They should instead try to determine not only the clients' goals and interests but also the clients' capabilities and even to some degree the clients' psychological makeup. They should recognize that clients and their attorneys often have very different incentives and psychologies.

a. *Is This a Client Who Would Benefit from Playing an Active Role in the Mediation?*

. . . Although attorneys often think about cases primarily in terms of likelihood of success on the merits and consequential dollar value, either in court or in a settlement, they should recognize that clients' interests are not necessarily so narrow. Sometimes the client's interests are such that she would benefit from playing an active role in the mediation, even assuming for the sake of argument that such participation might lower the dollar value of the case. For example, the client may have nonmonetary interests or psychological needs such that she seeks an opportunity to voice her concerns or sense of injury to the opposing attorney. Or, the client may feel a strong need to apologize to the opposing party. Alternatively, the client may seek to preserve her relationship with the opposing party. In these and many other situations, it may be beneficial for the client to be provided with extensive opportunities to speak and listen in the mediation, even when such behavior might not be desirable from a purely financial perspective.

b. Is This a Client Who Requires Protection by the Attorney?

. . . The attorney should ask herself whether this particular client would benefit by having the attorney speak for her. Is the client inarticulate? Shy? Prone to anger quickly in a context when such anger would be detrimental to the client's interests or wishes? Alternatively, is the client incapable of providing the analysis that is required? Is she likely to say things she later regrets or that jeopardize her case? Some clients may have some of these characteristics. Certainly, they are not shared by all clients.

As well, the attorney should ask herself whether the client would benefit by having the attorney protect her from the opposing party. Although, ideally, mediation should be an opportunity for clients to communicate directly with one another, sometimes such direct communication by clients or their attorneys may be undesirable. At one extreme, if the client has been subjected to domestic abuse by the opposing party, it may be not only emotionally distressing but also coercive and even unsafe for the victim to converse directly with her abuser. A victim of sexual harassment may similarly be unable to bargain as an equal with her harasser. Even in personal injury or commercial disputes, certain clients may be subject to browbeating or coercion by the opposing party or attorney. Where a client's attorney fears that direct confrontations would have such an impact, she should at least recommend setting up the mediation so as to minimize such problems. For example, the attorney might request that the parties break into caucus immediately, or the attorney might attempt to interrupt the opposing party's presentation or to prevent certain presentations from being made.

In answering these questions, the attorney should be sure to approach them separately. A client who is not good at speaking up for herself might well be perfectly capable of hearing directly from the opposing party or vice versa.

2. What Are the Barriers to Negotiation?

Once having considered who the client is, an attorney can best analyze how to divide mediation responsibilities with her client by attempting to determine what, if any, barriers are preventing the case from settling in a way that would serve the client's interests. If a case goes to mediation, it is because the parties and their attorneys have not yet reached a mutually acceptable agreement. Why have they not? What has stopped them from predicting how a court would resolve the dispute and reaching the same solution on their own? Or, what has prevented them from reaching an even better solution than the one the court might impose? By focusing on the dispute in this fashion, clients and their attorneys will begin to see how they ought to divide their responsibilities so as to best overcome the barriers to a negotiated agreement. The following discussion organizes potential barriers to settlement in terms of which participant is the primary obstacle to settlement. To clarify the discussion, it uses the following nomenclature: the primary client is labeled "A," her lawyer "AL," her opponent "B," and her opponent's lawyer "BL." . . . [Sternlight proceeds to examine barriers created by each type of participant and appropriate attorney responses. The analysis with respect to barriers created by the opposing party follows.]

i. B Has Unrealistic Expectations Based on Lack of Information.   If B is blocking a fair settlement because she has unrealistically high expectations regarding her likelihood of success at trial, AL and A should attempt to convince B that B's expectations are overblown. Each may have a role to play, depending on the nature of the misinformation. For example, sometimes a party may refuse to settle because she believes the opposing party will be a terrible witness who will therefore lose big at trial. In this situation, it may be desirable to allow that supposedly terrible witness, A, to play a very active role in the mediation to disprove B's false belief. Alternatively, if B thinks she has a sure winner in terms of the law, it may be important to have AL make a lengthy legal presentation to convince B that she is being over-optimistic. Usually AL will be better suited than A to convince B that her case is problematic in terms of the law.

ii. B Is Engaging in Strategic Behavior.   If B is blocking a settlement by engaging in strategic behavior, such as hoarding information or bluffing, then A and AL must attempt to convince B to engage in a more problem-solving approach that will allow for the possibility of creative and mutual gains. Roger Fisher, William Ury, and Bruce Patton, in *Getting to YES*, have offered a series of practical suggestions on how one may convince her opponent to move from competitive to problem-solving negotiation. The gist of their advice is to attempt to move the discussion to the merits and to look behind mere positions to the underlying ideas. Either A or AL may be the person who is better situated to attempt to earn B's trust and convince B to change her orientation. Thus, A and AL should jointly consider which of them, or perhaps both, are most likely to be successful in such a venture and divide their responsibilities accordingly.

If, however, it appears impossible to convince B to approach the negotiation with a positive, problem-solving attitude, it may be necessary for AL to encourage her own client not to share too much information or case strategy. Where one party insists on behaving competitively and the other is attempting to cooperate, the cooperating party may be disadvantaged.

iii. B Has Unmet Nonmonetary Goals.   If B is blocking a fair settlement because she has nonmonetary goals that are not being met, A and AL should consider whether it is desirable and possible for them to attempt to meet these goals. For example, B may be greatly injured because A chose to sue her, and an apology or explanation might go a long way toward healing the rift. In this event, if A is willing to apologize, it is important that she and her attorney divide responsibilities so she can do so. Alternatively, it may be that B feels the need to really tell A off, face-to-face. If A and AL decide that this would not be too damaging to A, they should again divide responsibilities to provide B with this opportunity. Perhaps A and B were business partners, and perhaps B would like to renew or continue the relationship. If such a result has possible appeal to A, and assuming A would be more capable of working out such an arrangement than her attorney, it is critical that A be provided with the opportunity to play a very active role in the mediation. . . .

[Sternlight goes on to examine how an attorney (AL) can constructively respond to barriers created by the opposing attorney (BL), her own client (A), and also to barriers that the attorney may be creating herself. She concludes:] Anyone who says they have a simple answer to the question of how lawyers and clients should divide their responsibilities in a mediation must be wrong. Either their answer is not simple or their answer is not right. The answer is complicated because the division of responsibilities should vary substantially depending upon who the client is, who the lawyer is, and what factors appear to be blocking a reasonable and fair settlement of the dispute. . . .

c. Avoiding Mistakes as a Representative in Mediation

With advice in hand on what you should do as an attorney in mediation, the following excerpt highlights some things you should *not* do.

   Tom Arnold, 20 COMMON ERRORS IN MEDIATION ADVOCACY

13 Alternatives 69, 69-71 (1995)

Trial lawyers who are unaccustomed to being mediation advocates [make] common errors. . . .

WRONG CLIENT IN THE ROOM

CEOs settle more cases than vice presidents, house counsel or other agents. Why? For one thing, they don't need to worry about criticism back at the office. Any lesser agent, even with explicit "authority," typically must please a constituency which was not a participant in the give and take of the mediation. That makes it hard to settle cases.

A client's personality also can be a factor. A "Rambo," who is aggressive, critical, unforgiving, or self-righteous doesn't tend to be conciliatory. The best peacemakers show creativity, and tolerance for the mistakes of others. Of course, it also helps to know the subject. . . .

ADDRESSING THE MEDIATOR INSTEAD OF THE OTHER SIDE

Most lawyers open the mediation with a statement directed at the mediator, comparable to opening statements to a judge or jury. Highly adversarial in tone, it overlooks the interests of the other side that gave rise to the dispute.

Why is this strategy a mistake? The "judge or jury" you should be trying to persuade in a mediation is not the mediator, but the adversary. If you want to make the other party sympathetic to your cause, don't hurt him. . . .

FAILURE TO USE ADVOCACY TOOLS EFFECTIVELY

You'll want to prepare your materials for maximum persuasive impact. Exhibits, charts, and copies of relevant cases or contracts with key phrases highlighted can be valuable visual aids. A 90-second video showing key witnesses in depositions making important admissions, followed by a readable size copy of an important document with some relevant language underlined, can pack a punch.

TIMING MISTAKES

Get and give critical discovery, but don't spend exorbitant time or sums in discovery and trial prep before seeking mediation.

Mediation can identify what's truly necessary discovery and avoid unnecessary discovery. One of my own war stories: With a mediation under way and both parties relying on their perception of the views of a certain vice president, I leaned over, picked up the phone, called the vice president, introduced myself as the mediator, and asked whether he could give us a deposition the following morning. "No," said he, "I've got a Board meeting at 10:00." "How about 7:30 a.m., with a one-hour limit?" I asked. "It really is pretty important that this decision not be delayed." The parties took the deposition and settled the case before the 10:00 board meeting. . . .

HURTING, HUMILIATING, THREATENING, OR COMMANDING

Don't poison the well from which you must drink to get a settlement. That means you don't hurt, humiliate or ridicule the other folks. Avoid pejoratives like "malingerer," "fraud," "cheat," "crook," or "liar." You can be strong on what your evidence will be and still be a decent human being.

All settlements are based upon trust to some degree. If you anger the other side, they won't trust you. This inhibits settlement.

The same can be said for threats, like a threat to get the other lawyer's license revoked for pursuing such a frivolous cause, or for his grossly inaccurate pleadings.

Ultimatums destroy the process, and destroy credibility. Yes, there is a time in mediation to walk out — whether or not you plan to return. But a series of ultimatums, or even one ultimatum, most often is very counterproductive.

FAILURE TO TRULY CLOSE

Unless parties have strong reasons to "sleep on" their agreement, to further evaluate the deal, or to check on possibly forgotten details, it is better to get some sort of enforceable contract written and signed before the parties separate. Too often, when left to think overnight and draft tomorrow, the parties think of new ideas that delay or prevent closing.

LACK OF PATIENCE AND PERSEVERANCE

The mediation "dance" takes time. Good mediation advocates have patience and perseverance.

MISUNDERSTANDING CONFLICT

A dispute is a problem to be solved together, not a combat to be won. To prepare for mediation, rehearse answers to the following questions, which the mediator is likely to ask:

- How do you feel about this dispute? Or about the other party?
- What do you really want in the resolution of this dispute?
- What are your expectations from a trial? Are they realistic?
- What are the weaknesses in your case?
- What law or fact in your case would you like to change?
- What scares you most?
- What would it feel like to be in your adversary's shoes?
- What specific evidence do you have to support each element of your case?
- What will the jury charge and interrogatories probably be?
- What is the probability of a verdict your way on liability?
- What is the range of damages you think a jury would return in his case if it found liability?
- What are the likely settlement structures, from among the following possibilities: terms, dollars, injunction, services, performance, product, recision, apology, costs, attorney fees, releases?
- What constituency pressures burden the other party? Which ones burden you?

———————————————

Simeon Baum, another accomplished attorney and mediator, urges advocates in mediation not to balk at emotion.[7] Seasoned mediator Jeff Kichaven, in the excerpt below, chastises attorneys for failure to recognize the importance of civility, acknowledgment and apology.

 Jeff Kichaven, **APOLOGY IN MEDIATION**

International Risk Management Institute (2003)

. . . [M]ediation provides an oasis in the litigation desert where [the] heart's hunger [for feeling important and appreciated] may yet be sated. There are hundreds of things you can do at a mediation to make others feel important and appreciated. Arrive on time. Bring the right people. Dress respectfully. Listen attentively. Apologize. But don't apologize in the conventional way.

Apologize in a way that admits no liability or fault. Self-flagellation is not required. Any sentence that begins with "I'm sorry" and continues with some recognition of the other side's human condition will do. It will be more than adequate to make the other side feel important and appreciated.

———————————————

7. Simeon H. Baum, Top 10 Things Not To Do in Mediation, NYLJ, Apr. 25, 2005, at col. 78.

In a medical malpractice case, it might start out as, "I'm sorry the operation had a bad outcome."

In an employment case, "I'm sorry you have not yet found another job."

In any case, "I'm sorry this has reached the point where you felt it necessary to sue me. I did not intend you any suffering." What defendant, after all, is not sorry that he or she has been sued? Do we really intend that others suffer? This kind of apology is sincere, it acknowledges the plaintiff as a human being, it places everyone on a small tuft of common ground, and it sets the stage for tremendous progress in the conversation.

Where the opportunity for such an apology is missed, a mediation can end in disaster. Where the opportunity is seized, success is still not guaranteed, but the chances of a successful resolution are greatly increased. An example of each type of case, from my own experience, makes the lesson clear.

First, the nightmare.

A community bank offers free safe deposit boxes to depositors. An elderly couple takes advantage of the offer. Eventually, the husband dies and the widow, in her 80s, and her daughter, in her 50s, come in to sign new signature cards. The bank takes the new signature cards and does not file them, but rather loses them. At year end, the bank considers the box abandoned, drills it with appropriate witnesses, records its contents as "empty," and life goes on.

Until the widow pays the bank a visit, that is. She is shocked to learn that her safe deposit box is no longer there, and feels that she is not treated appropriately by the bank personnel to whom she complains. Her distress grows so great that she consults a lawyer and a lawsuit is filed.

At the mediation, plaintiff's counsel begins an initial joint session by explaining that the widow does not exactly remember the last time she and her husband visited the deposit box, or just what was in it. The lawyer recounts that the widow thinks there may have been some envelopes there, sealed of course, but perhaps with cash, perhaps with a lock of their children's baby hair, perhaps with a love letter from the husband, to be read after he died. How tragic, the lawyer concludes, that the poor widow will have to go to her grave never knowing what was left behind in that precious safe deposit box.

I paused and counted to ten. Defense counsel was a highly-placed partner in a major law firm. I turned to her and said, "You know, I'm glad you're here in mediation. Because your law firm runs a business, I run a business, your client runs a business. We all have clients, or customers, and we all want to keep our clients happy. Here you have a customer who had been with your client's bank for over 20 years. Now she's a former customer. Nobody wants to have an unhappy customer. Here in mediation, you have a chance to do something you could never do in court. I know you don't believe your client has done anything wrong, and I'd never ask you to acknowledge any such thing. But here you have the unique opportunity to look across the table at this nice woman, and respecting the fact that you don't think your client did anything wrong, you can still tell her how sorry you are that she got so upset that she took the extraordinary steps of hiring a lawyer and filing a lawsuit against you."

Litigator X straightened up in her chair, looked down at her notes, and responded to what I thought was a big fat softball pitch thusly: "I will do no such thing! I am here to explain why all appropriate banking regulations were followed, why my client did nothing wrong, why we are extremely likely to obtain summary judgment in this case and why we think it has at best nuisance value for settlement purposes."

A nuisance! Talk about the antithesis of making someone feel important! Or that their patronage over 20 years was the least bit appreciated! This was the worst mediation advocacy I had ever seen, and the result was predictable. By day's end, the president of the bank had seen fit to offer $30,000 in settlement, an amount in excess of the anticipated future defense fees. But the case did not settle. No matter what the number had been, it could not have been high enough to make up for the manifest disrespect Litigator X had shown the widow and her daughter hours before.

Now the dream. As if to prove how rarely an appropriate apology is used effectively, this anecdote comes from a simulated mediation rather than a real one.

In 2001, we presented the mediation of Palsgraf v. Long Island Railroad as a CLE program for the ABA's Tort Trial and Insurance Practice Section at the Association's Annual Meeting in Chicago. Robin Westerfield of Walnut Creek, California's Bowles & Verna played the role of trial counsel for the LIRR.

As we were walking on stage into the mythical mediation room, before we were even seated, Westerfield turned to Rene Ellis of Duke Law School, who played Mrs. Palsgraf, and said: "Mrs. Palsgraf, before we actually begin the mediation, I just want to let you know how sorry we are that the explosion occurred and how sorry we are that you were caught in the middle of it. We pride ourselves on keeping our passengers safe, and we're sorry that you were hurt while you were standing on the platform of one of our stations."

Did that ever put magic in the air! No admission of liability or fault. Not for any consideration, because Westerfield characterized his apology as taking place "before we actually begin the mediation." A recognition of the facts that Mrs. P. was important as a customer, that her patronage was appreciated, and that she had in fact suffered as a result of all this. Not surprisingly, at the end of our little play, Westerfield and his opposing counsel, Honolulu's Richard Turbin, got the case settled.

A myth? Maybe. But the players were deeply "in role" that day, and really put me through my paces in the role of mediator. It worked for us, and it may well work for you. A well-constructed apology in a mediation, or any other negotiation, is something for which you will never have to say you're sorry.

A full apology that accepts responsibility will probably have a more favorable impact on willingness to settle than a partial, "safe" apology that expresses sympathy. A full apology, however, may be risky if the case does not settle. Nonetheless, given the data, attorneys should help their clients weigh the likely costs and benefits of a partial or full apology.

C. THE IMPACT OF DIFFERENCES AND DIVERSITY

A thread running through all discussions of skills and strategies — for both neutrals and attorneys — is the importance of differences and diversity. Gender, age, ethnicity, religion, education, social standing, profession, nationality, and a variety of other factors will all impact the conduct of negotiation. They play an equal role in mediation. Psychological differences among parties (for example, extroverts versus introverts) and cultural norms of different groups will require different approaches to mediation. The mediator's cultural and other norms will also be a factor.

Choice of mediator may be influenced by culture. Certain cultures have specific requirements and preferences with respect to mediators and the process generally. A North American view of mediator qualifications typically focuses on neutrality, training, and experience. Other cultures might prefer a "wise elder" who is inextricably linked to the community, is not a stranger to the parties, and will lead — rather than follow — the parties to a resolution. A student from Ghana, when asked what key mediator trait would engender confidence and acceptability in his country, answered "old." Every feature of the mediation process — when and where parties meet, how the session is opened, how the seating is arranged, and who attends — is shaped by culture.

Isabelle Gunning explores different mediation approaches for different cultures.

 Isabelle R. Gunning, DIVERSITY ISSUES IN MEDIATION: CONTROLLING NEGATIVE CULTURAL MYTHS

1995 J. Disp. Resol. 55, 83-84

Mediation, as a method of resolving disputes, has a long tradition that is not exclusively American. The American emphasis on non-intervention as the mark of neutrality is a product of the culture. Other cultures have made different choices on the "activism" of mediators. For example in both the Navajo Peacemaker Court and the Filipino Katarungang Pambarangay system, traditional methods of non-adversarial dispute resolution are kept alive which involve "mediators," called peacemakers or barangay captains, who intervene much more actively than their American counterparts even though they too are not decision-makers for the parties. In both these kinds of mediations, the mediators have confidence in their own knowledge of the community values which all participants are assumed to share. Two aspects of these mediations mark them especially: (1) the mediators openly inject concerns larger than the participants themselves; for example, community harmony and even spiritual guidance which they understand the parties share; and (2) the mediators are rarely ever strangers or unknown volunteers or professionals even though they are not to be biased towards one side or the other.

The Navajo peacemaker does not make American style claims of neutrality. He will often be a relative of the disputing parties and his role will involve teaching and even "lecturing" the parties on Navajo values and "how their behavior comports with shared values." The ground rules for a peace making session are steeped in ceremony and tradition, beginning and ending with prayers. Filipino mediators, somewhat like Navajo peacemakers, are comfortable making strong recommendations to the participants on how they should resolve their disputes. Like Navajo peacemakers, Filipino mediators often know the parties. The mediator is not likely to be a relative, but as the local barangay captain [an elected village leader] . . . they will often be familiar with the parties or their situation. Also similar to the Navajo peacemaker, the Filipino mediator, with his familiarity with the community, will have an interest in maintaining the peace within the larger community. The attitude is reflected in the practice of the mediator getting personally involved with helping the disputants achieving agreement. The session does include a spiritual component, like the Navajo Peacemaker Court, and often begins with prayer.

Problem 7-9.   *The American Way*

What in American culture explains why American mediation emphasizes a non-intervention approach and strict mediator neutrality? Is mediation's emphasis on a "talking cure" particularly "American"?

Professor Phyllis Bernard highlights issues in developing countries that make the job of an international mediator highly sensitive, including complex webs of duties owed in traditional village structures, repercussions in rural areas from business transactions in cities, power structures that may not be visible to an outsider, and dangerous military realities and reactions that might lead to dire consequences. Mediators and trainers cannot blithely transport their familiar process to foreign lands without care and appropriate adjustment. In a similar vein, working in the United States with parties from different backgrounds, a mediator must continually strive to be culturally sensitive.

In addition to these concerns, a mediator must understand her own cultural (and other) biases in order to act impartially. In fact, many scholars point out that neutrality and impartiality — while something to be strived for — is not, in any pure form, attainable. Consider these examples of mediator bias from Professor Trina Grillo.

 Trina Grillo, THE MEDIATION ALTERNATIVE: PROCESS DANGERS FOR WOMEN

100 Yale L.J. 1545, 1585-1586 (1991)

Mediators . . . exert a great deal of power. When two people are in conflict, having a third, purportedly neutral person take the viewpoint of one or the other results in a palpable shift of power to the party with whom the mediator agrees. The mediator also can set the rules regarding who talks, when they may speak, and what may be said. The power of the mediator is not always openly acknowledged but is hidden beneath protestations that the process belongs to the parties. This can make the parties feel less, not more, in control of the process and its consequences for their lives. There is much room for, but little acknowledgment of, the possibility of the mediator's exhibiting partiality or imposing a hidden agenda on the parties. . . .

> *George, a Black man, is in the process of divorcing Michelle, a white woman. During the course of the mediation, the mediator asks a number of times whether there is a history of domestic violence. She seems not to believe George or his wife when each insists that although Michelle occasionally has attacked George, he has never fought back.*
>
> *Elaine is a Black woman, who has worked herself up in the ranks of the local telephone company from an entry level position to her new job, in which she supervises a number of employees. She handles herself with calm and poise, but also a certain coolness. Joe, her husband, who is also Black, is a friendly, gregarious man who has not been reliable in meeting his support obligations or in taking regular responsibility for their two sons. In mediation, Elaine immediately senses that the mediator favors her husband and does not like her. This intuition is confirmed when the mediator permits her husband to interrupt her constantly, but quickly stops her with a sharp lecture when she tries to interrupt him. At one point, the mediator turns to her and says, "I was a single parent too, and I did not have the luxury of an ex-husband who was willing to help me with the children." Five minutes later, the mediator repeats the same statement. When Elaine mentions her debilitating health problems, the mediator laughs and says, "You don't have to act sick to get what you want."*

George and Elaine are encountering extreme examples of what is, to some degree, a troublesome aspect of any mediation: the process introduces a third party who is held out to be, but is not, impartial.

Some scholars have concluded that formal processes, like litigation, are more advantageous for minority disputants because more formality deters prejudice by — among other factors — putting people on their best behavior.[8] Additionally, serious questions have been raised about whether minority or female disputants fare as well in mediation in terms of the monetary outcome as white male participants, particularly if the mediator is not of the same ethnicity as the minority disputant.[9] Another generation of research is needed to address these critical concerns. In the meantime, mediators and attorneys must be acutely aware of these issues and make appropriate adjustments where necessary. They must also strive to understand their own personal and cultural biases and to act impartially.

---

8. Richard Delgado, Chris Dunn, Pamela Brown, Helena Lee & David Hubbert, Fairness and Formality: Minimizing The Risk of Prejudice in Alternative Dispute Resolution, 1985 Wis. L. Rev. 1359.
9. Gary LaFree & Christine Rack, The Effects of Participants' Ethnicity and Gender on Monetary Outcomes in Mediated and Adjudicated Civil Cases, 30 L. & Soc'y Rev. 767 (1996).

> **Problem 7-10.** *Know Thyself*
>
> Reflect on your family of origin — an important aspect of your identity. Recall meals and gatherings. Were they begun with prayer or animated discussion? Did family members interrupt each other or wait for a turn to speak? Recall conflicts in the family. What was the process for resolving conflicts? Whatever your answers, you are probably describing biases you will need to appreciate to serve as either an impartial mediator or an effective representative.

D. THE SELF-REFLECTIVE PRACTITIONER

Whether you serve as the mediator or the attorney representative in mediation, an important indicia of your competence and your potential for growth is your regular practice of thoughtful reflection. While anyone can make mistakes (and everyone does), it is unfortunate to spend a lifetime making the same mistakes over and over. Consequently, viewing oneself as a lifelong learner is critical to successful performance. After each engagement, ask, "What happened and why? What did I do well? What could I improve?" In this final excerpt, Carol Liebman, a master mediator, reflects about her service as a mediator between student groups and the administration at Columbia University. The mediation succeeded in ending a student hunger strike and building takeover and in developing responsive agreements about curricula reform at Columbia. Note the mediator's capacity to be both reflective about the process and constructively self-critical.

 Carol B. Liebman, **MEDIATION AS PARALLEL SEMINARS: LESSONS FROM THE STUDENT TAKEOVER OF COLUMBIA UNIVERSITY'S HAMILTON HALL**

16 Negot. J. 157, 163, 165-168, 170, 179 (2000)

In April of 1996, a faculty colleague and I spent four days and all of one night mediating the student takeover of Hamilton Hall at Columbia University. The building takeover was the culmination of a year-long debate about whether or not Ethnic Studies should become a formal part of the university's curriculum. When I was called in (by the university) to mediate, three students had been on a hunger strike for twelve days and were approaching what I was told was the point at which they began to be in danger of long-term damage to their health. Two days earlier, the University had called the New York City Police, which resulted in the arrest of 22 demonstrators at another of the university's main buildings. In short, the debate over Ethnic Studies was rapidly escalating. . . .

THE MEDIATION . . .

Mediation as Parallel Seminars

Once the agreement [to mediate] was signed, Carlton [my co-mediator] and I indicated that we intended to start by having everyone who wanted to speak tell us their view of the situation. This request was greeted with a fair amount of eye rolling by members of both teams. I had the sense they were thinking they had already told their stories ad nauseam. They were right but, as in so many mediations, stories had been told but not heard. A great deal of what we did as mediators during the first few hours was basic clarification of exactly what the parties intended by various phrases or actions. We asked the students such questions as, "When you say Ethnic Studies what do you mean? Why is it important to you?" We asked the university representatives questions like, "When you say 'it (Ethnic Studies as a department) can't happen in the university,' tell us how the university works." We were really conducting two parallel seminars the whole four days, but especially that first evening. In one, the members of the university team taught us how universities are governed, how change comes about in the university, and how faculty get appointed. In the other seminar, the members of the student team taught us what they mean by Ethnic Studies, why it is important to them as a way of addressing the alienation they feel, and why it should be important to the university. . . .

Building Trust

. . . While earning the trust of the student team was an underlying issue throughout the process, it became an explicit issue early in the mediation. We had taken a break so that the student team could confer. I had gone to my office in the law school, where the mediation sessions were being held. Carlton was elsewhere. The students . . . came to my office and asked to meet with me. One student said that they thought that I had cut him off when he tried to take the discussion in a certain direction, saying that we were not ready to talk about that topic. He charged that, fifteen minutes later, another student had brought the same topic up and I had not objected. He accused me of trying to split the student group.

Frankly, I did not remember the exchange, and said so. I also said I was sorry if I had given that impression. I acknowledged that sometimes mediators looked for differences within a negotiating team, but told them I had realized early that that was not going to be a useful approach in this situation. I paused, and then my mediator instincts took over: I addressed an underlying issue by saying to the student who had challenged me, "If what you are really asking me is, 'Have I heard about you as a controversial student?' the answer is 'Yes, I have.' I have been told that you can be pretty wild, but I haven't seen that here and I am going on what I have seen." I had felt the tension in the room go down a little when I said I was sorry if I had given the student the impression I was trying to split the group. However, when I acknowledged the underlying reputation issue, the decrease in tension was remarkable. I knew I had made a small inroad toward establishing trust. Mediators talk about the importance of addressing underlying issues. And we talk about how discussing explosive issues can make them less scary. But I was still stunned by the impact on my interactions with the students of the use of those basic techniques. . . .

Lessons Learned and Relearned

Saturday was the kind of day most mediators would expect — joint sessions, caucuses with the mediators present, caucuses without the mediators. On Saturday, I learned one important lesson and relearned another. The lesson I learned was about the importance of food in mediation, while the lesson I relearned was about ways in which a mediator's personal stake in the outcome of a dispute can interfere with her effectiveness.

A Lesson Learned — The Role of Food.   Before the Hamilton mediation, the only time I had thought about the role of food in mediation was when a student from the Middle East mentioned, in a class discussion about cultural differences and conflict, that in his culture, if you broke bread in public with someone with whom you had been having a dispute, it was a signal that the dispute was over. When Carlton and I began the Hamilton Hall mediation, we had been authorized to order refreshments as needed. We had a local provider (the aptly named Hamilton Deli) send over soda, juice, chips, cookies, and fruit. I had been on a weight loss program for several months and decided to see if I could stick with that regime during the mediation instead of doing what would have been more typical for me — going for the chocolate and junk food. As a result, I ended up (until Monday afternoon) staying away from junk food and sweets, instead eating a piece of fruit, a yogurt, or half a sandwich every two or three hours to maintain a steady energy level. Also, in the months before the mediation, I had not been drinking much caffeine; so, when I started to drag, a Coke or cup of tea had much more than the normal impact.

Once the mediation sessions began, normal eating schedules for all the participants disappeared. I realized the first night that, when members of the negotiation teams had not eaten for a long time, their morale dropped, they became pessimistic, and it was difficult to get them to consider new options. Then they would eat and would experience a surge of energy which let us make some progress for about an hour before they began to sag again. Often the two teams were eating on different schedules. We would break for caucuses or meetings with constituents. During the break, one team would grab a bite while the other would return to the table hungry and dragging.

As mediators, we had to be aware of where the teams were in terms of their energy level. We needed to pay attention to when people were eating and manage the additional tension that was created when one team returned to the table full of energy after a meal while the other was dragging. If both teams had "refueled" at about the same time, we had the opportunity to take on tough issues and make progress. When they were eating at different times, we needed to use caucuses to take advantage of the opportunities for movement presented by the high energy team while encouraging the team that was dragging.

An Old Lesson Relearned — The Risks When the Mediator Has a Stake in the Outcome.   The principle of mediator impartiality is one of the first lessons in any basic mediation training. On Saturday afternoon, I gained new insight into the reason that an impartial mind-set can be so important. As the day progressed, I was getting resistance from both teams. At first I could not figure out what was going on. Then I realized that I had been pushing both teams too hard, and that the pushing was occurring because I had a stake in the outcome.

One of my standard "lines" to the parties when a mediation seems stuck is, "I am here to try to help you work out a solution to the situation that brought you to mediation. I have no stake in the outcome. If we work it out, I'll be pleased. If we don't work it out, you will go on living with the dispute, while I shall feel a bit sad but then just move on with the rest of my life." I finally realized that was not the situation I was in during the Hamilton mediation. As part of the university community, I had a stake in the outcome and as a result I had been pushing too hard to reach an agreement. Once I realized what was happening, I actually told the negotiators from both teams what my standard line was. However, I went on to say that this situation was different, that as a member of the university community I had a stake in finding a solution that would resolve the crisis. I told them that because I did care a great deal about finding a way to resolve the situation, I had been leaning on them, and that I would try to back off.

Articulating what was going on for me, first to myself and then to the negotiators, enabled me to back off and lower the temperature of the mediation. While the voicing of these feelings was in no way intended as a mediator tactic, in retrospect my admission did help me establish credibility, especially with the members of the student team who identified me with the administration. I simply told the truth — that I cared very much about helping find a solution. It may have built another layer of trust. . . .

The Final Day

At 6 A.M. on Monday morning, we reached a tentative agreement. . . . The student team members needed to sell the deal to the 180 demonstrators occupying Hamilton Hall, but were not prepared for that difficult role. This is another area where I think we mediators fell short. Even though it would have been difficult, given the limited trust between the mediators and the students, we should have tried to talk to the students about the difficult role they were facing, and offered to brainstorm with them about how to handle it. Those with experience in the labor field are familiar with the phenomenon where the workers are in the streets or on the picket line riled up and demonstrating. The negotiator gets the best deal she can at the bargaining table, using the noise in the streets as one of her persuasive tools. Then she has to go back and calm the troops down, tell them she has gotten far less than they were demanding, but that it is a fabulous deal. The student negotiators had no experience in this role. They were tired and, while they knew (given what they had heard during the mediation) that they had obtained a reasonable package, they went to meet with a core group of the demonstrators feeling what they had achieved was not a victory or even close to a victory. The student team met at the law school with a core group of about thirty or forty of the Hamilton demonstrators.

More on the Role of Food.   While the university team was meeting with the university leadership and the students were beginning their meeting with the core group, Carlton and I went off and bought five dozen bagels, along with juice and a big urn of coffee, and delivered it to the students. At that point, I was wishing that we had someone staffing the mediation whom we could have sent out to do the shopping. In retrospect, I think that being the person who was lugging the bagels and cream cheese to the student meeting gave a message of commitment to the students. During mediation sessions, mediators often have a nurturing function. They encourage participants to deal with underlying issues, reframe so that the parties can hear each other, and validate feelings and create a safe setting in which to wrestle with highly charged issues. Buying breakfast put us in a different sort of nurturing role which may have been another important trust-building gesture. . . .

FINAL THOUGHTS

The takeover of Hamilton ended Monday night. Wednesday morning, I had an early morning meeting on the main campus. I had to go to my office before the meeting and left the law school building at 117th Street since the main entrance at 116th was closed because of renovations. There was a gate to the main campus directly in front of me across Amsterdam Avenue. Out of habit developed during the five days of demonstrations when only the two main gates to the campus were open, I started to turn left toward the main entrance at 116th. Then I realized that the 117th Street gate was again open. It struck me that much of what we do as mediators is opening gates. When mediators help people talk to each other and hear each other and understand their own and others' interests, they symbolically aid the participants in unlocking the positional or emotional gates that have stood as a bar to settlement. . . .

Problem 7-11.   *What Did You Learn?*

Recall a mediation where you served as a mediator or a party representative (either in the context of this course or in real life). What lessons can you extract and pass on to others? State the lesson, and, like Carol Liebman, provide vivid examples. What did you do well in your role? What would you change — why and how?

Whether you are serving as a mediator or an attorney in mediation, the combination of attention to best practices and constant self-reflection are the keys to improve your practice. We turn now to policy issues, confidentiality, and legal and ethical questions.

Further Reading

Harold I. Abramson. (2d ed. 2010). *Mediation Representation: Advocating as a Problem-Solver in Any Country or Culture*. National Institute for Trial Advocacy.

Laurence J. Boulle, Michael T. Colatrella Jr. & Anthony P. Picchioni. (2008). *Mediation: Skills and Techniques.* LexisNexis.

John W. Cooley. (2005). *Creative Problem Solver's Handbook for Negotiators and Mediators* (Volumes 1 and 2). Washington, D.C.: ABA Section of Dispute Resolution.

Morton Deutsch & Peter Coleman. (2000). *The Handbook of Conflict Resolution.* San Francisco: Jossey-Bass Publishers.

Gary Friedman & Jack Himmelstein. (2008). *Challenging Conflict: Mediation Through Understanding.* Washington, D.C.: ABA Section of Dispute Resolution.

Joseph P. Folger & Robert A. Baruch Bush, *Transformative Mediation and Third-Party Intervention: Ten Hallmarks of a Transformative Approach to Practice,* 13 MEDIATION Q. 263 (1996).

Dwight Golann. (1996). *Mediating Legal Disputes: Effective Strategies for Lawyers and Mediators.* New York: Aspen Law and Business.

John Haynes. (1993). *The Fundamentals of Family Mediation* Albany, NY: State University of NY Press.

Jennifer K. Robbennolt, *Apologies and Legal Settlement: An Empirical Examination,* 102 MICH. L. REV. 201 (2003).

J. Edward Russo & Paul J.H. Schoemaker. (1990). *Decision Traps: The Ten Barriers to Brilliant Decision-Making and How to Overcome Them.* Fireside.

Andrea Schneider & Chris Honeyman (Eds.). (2006). *The Negotiator's Fieldbook.* Washington, D.C.: ABA Section of Dispute Resolution.

Chapter 8

Mediation: Law, Policy, and Ethics

It must be remembered that there is nothing more difficult to plan, more doubtful of success, nor more dangerous to manage, than the creation of a new system. For the initiator has the enmity of all who would profit by the preservation of the old institutions and merely lukewarm defenders in those who would gain by the new ones.

— Niccolo Machiavelli

Many innovations that start as a simple idea become more complex as their use grows. This natural process of maturation has affected mediation as well. Compounding the growing pains as mediation moves into the courts, the more familiar adversarial paradigm has exerted a gravitational pull, shifting mediation towards litigation with less party participation and interaction, more attorney control, and greater influence of legal norms, sometimes overriding party interests and values. While studying this chapter on legal, policy, and ethical questions, keep in mind that mediation springs from the simple — yet radical — idea of assisting disputing parties to resolve issues themselves. Part A examines the interaction between law and mediation and the development of law about mediation. In Part B, four policy issues that continue to be regularly debated are explored. Part C looks at ethical questions for mediators, parties, and their representatives in mediation.

A. MEDIATION AND THE LAW

1. The Relationship Between Law and Mediation

a. The Law's Long Shadow

Particularly where mediation is taking place under the roof of a courthouse or in the context of a litigated case, there can be tension between the rule of law and party choice. For example, when a mediator helps an employer and employee negotiate in the context of a Title VII discrimination claim, should a mediator let an employee trade his right to freedom from discrimination for some other benefit the employer offers? Should the mediator at least raise the law's prohibition on discrimination? Or, if a contract claim is being pursued and the statute of limitations has run, should the mediator alert the parties to the fact that a legal claim is barred? Would it make a difference if the mediator were operating in a court-sponsored or mandated program? If the agreement were subject to court approval?

Even where legal principles are not explicitly raised, public values and norms may influence the process. The landmark article below suggests that people do not bargain in a vacuum but rather in "the shadow of the law." Law, then, plays a significant role in mediation, as do other norms, even without the mediator being charged with injecting such norms or ensuring a "fair" settlement. Legal and other norms affect the assumptions, expectations, BATNAs, and proposals of bargaining parties and hence shape negotiated outcomes.

 Robert H. Mnookin & Lewis Kornhauser, **BARGAINING IN THE SHADOW OF THE LAW: THE CASE OF DIVORCE**

88 Yale L.J. 950, 968-970 (1979)

Divorcing parents do not bargain over the division of family wealth and custodial prerogatives in a vacuum; they bargain in the shadow of the law. The legal rules governing alimony, child support, marital property, and custody give each parent certain claims based on what each would get if the case went to trial. In other words, the outcome that the law will impose if no agreement is reached gives each parent certain bargaining chips — an endowment of sorts.

A simplified example may be illustrative. Assume that in disputed custody cases the law flatly provided that all mothers had the right of custody of minor children and that all fathers only had the right to visitation two weekends a month. Absent some contrary agreement acceptable to both parents, a court would order this arrangement. Assume further that the legal rules relating to marital property, alimony, and child support gave the mother some determinate share of the family's economic resources. In negotiations under this regime, neither spouse would ever consent to a division that left him or her worse off than if he or she insisted on going to court. The range of negotiated outcomes would be limited to those that leave both parents as well off as they would be in the absence of a bargain.

If private ordering were allowed, we would not necessarily expect parents to split custody and money the way a judge would if they failed to agree. The father might well negotiate for more child-time and the mother for less. This result might occur either because the father made the mother better off by giving her additional money to compensate her for accepting less child-time, or because the mother found custody burdensome and considered herself better off with less custody. Indeed, she might agree to accept less money, or even to pay the father, if he agreed to relieve her of some child-rearing responsibilities. In all events, because the parents' tastes with regard to the trade-offs between money and child-time may differ, it will often be possible for the parties to negotiate some outcome that makes both better off than they would be if they simply accepted the result a court would impose. . . .

Legal rules are generally not as simple or straightforward as is suggested by the last example. Often, the outcome in court is far from certain, with any number of outcomes possible. Indeed, existing legal standards governing custody, alimony, child support, and marital property are all striking for their lack of precision and thus provide a bargaining backdrop clouded by uncertainty. The almost universal judicial standard for resolving custody disputes is the "best interests of the child." Except in situations when one parent poses a substantial threat to the child's well-being, predicting who will get custody under this standard is difficult indeed, especially given the increasing pressure to reject any presumption in favor of maternal custody. Similarly, standards governing alimony and child support are also extraordinarily vague and allow courts broad discretion in disputed cases. . . .

Problem 8-1.   *The Shadow of the Law*

When you bargain with a landlord over repairs or with a merchant over defective goods you have purchased, do you feel empowered by your understanding of the law? Are there other situations where the law — or your belief about the law — has an impact on your negotiations?

---

b. Informed Consent

What if the law's shadow does not reach all parties, and some bargain in ignorance of legal norms? Should parties to a court-mandated mediation negotiate without knowledge of the relevant law? This issue is less troubling when parties are represented by attorneys because the attorneys have the responsibility of informing their clients about the law and legal entitlements. With respect to pro se parties, however, Professor Jacqueline Nolan-Haley states that courts requiring unrepresented parties to mediate should insure that those parties have a basic knowledge of their legal rights.[1] If you agree with this proposition, how could courts or administrative tribunals sponsoring mediation programs insure that parties have knowledge of their rights? Some courts, for example, make a court attorney available for that service. Others offer literature explaining basic legal information. Many mediators would inquire whether parties would prefer to adjourn a session until they have legal — or other expert — representation or advice.

Another solution for parties who do not understand their legal rights is placing the burden on mediators to inform them of such rights. This is fraught with problems. Such a task risks impinging on a mediator's neutrality since legal information often favors one party over another. Parties with information about the law often ask how the law applies to them. If the mediator begins to interpret the law, such conduct quickly becomes the practice of law, and the mediator risks liability for engaging in that activity. The mediator may not be an attorney, and even if he is, he may not have expertise in the law at issue or be positioned to do appropriate research.

---

1. Jacqueline M. Nolan-Haley, Informed Consent in Mediation: A Guiding Principle for Truly Educated Decisionmaking, 74 Notre Dame L. Rev. 775, 780 (1999).

Clearly, informed parties are preferable to ignorant ones. However, assuring that parties have full information may not be possible, even if it were desirable. Different counselors, after all, have different opinions, and considerations of the psychological, economic, and social impacts of various options might be as important as the relevant legal norms. Lawyer mediators may overrate the importance of law. Therapist mediators may focus on theories of healing and group dynamics that they use in therapy. Mediators with multiple professions are well advised not to confuse their professional roles. Arguably, the principle of self-determination requires the parties to determine the amount and type of information they wish to obtain when making a decision.

> ### Problem 8-2.   *Legal Information*
> Imagine that free or low-cost legal aid and public defenders were readily available to all — analogous to free health care. Would the concern about informed consent evaporate? Does the availability of information on the Internet change the calculus? Or, is it that when people go to court — like when the sick go to a hospital — we expect a higher level of informed consent?

c. Sources of "Law" and Justice

Lawyers tend to think of law — and the related concept of justice — as the body of legal precedents and legislation that govern legal entitlements and duties. In adjudication, justice norms come from these public pronouncements.

In regulating conduct in every sphere of life, however, there are many more norms and expectations that govern an individual's idea of proper conduct. These norms include, for instance, family and community values, religious and moral codes, and practical considerations. Robin Hood was said to be a champion of distributive justice — a belief that resources should be allocated among people in a way that is fair. And he was a criminal in the eyes of the law. In considering distributive justice, principles such as equality, equity, and need come into play. All of those notions might justify Robin Hood's "illegal" conduct in stealing from the rich to give to the poor. At both an individual and societal level, good relationships, peace, harmony, and the maintenance of stability are values that can impact the outcome of a dispute, but these values may not be reflected in legal doctrine or a court-governed outcome.

Whether or not we assume that parties take into account their legal rights as they bargain, there are contexts where even the courts prefer that the parties determine their own outcome regardless of legal entitlements. For example, in Card v. Card, 706 So. 2d 409, 410 (Fla. Dist. Ct. App. 1998), the court articulated a preference for party self-determination over third-party decision making for parenting decisions:

> When divorcing parents cede to the judicial branch of government the duty to decide the most intimate family issues, it is not unlikely that one or both parents

will be less than satisfied with the decision. The bench and bar have for years now encouraged divorcing parents to resolve their differences through mediation. In effect, parents have been urged to make their own law, in the hope that they can better live with a decision that is their own, rather than a decision that is externally imposed. Where attempts at mediation or other settlement fail, or are not seriously undertaken, a court must decide.

This proposition is in keeping with the notion that in mediation the fair outcome is that which the parties themselves find fair and best for their circumstances. According to this view, the application of public norms and the use of public processes is the default option when parties cannot agree. When developing their own agreement, parties are not guided solely by those values articulated by courts and legislatures. Rather they may aspire to guide their conduct by values that the public does not require — values of generosity, forgiveness, and connection, for example. Or they may be driven by practical considerations: their priorities, personal cost-benefit analysis, and the like.

Problem 8-3. *What Drives Decisions?*

Examine an important decision you have made about a dispute in which you were (or are) involved. What drove the decision? How important was the "law"?

---

2. Litigation About Mediation

In some ways the proliferation of issues and case law surrounding mediation is an alarming development. If mediation is, at its heart, about parties finding a way to resolve their own dispute, often supported by their lawyers and with the help of a mediator, why is this effort to avoid the costs and limited outcomes of lawsuits spawning its own litigation? The answer is probably that growth and use breed complexity. Below is a short, and not exhaustive, survey of issues unique to mediation — that is, questions that arise because mediation has been chosen by or imposed upon the parties or because a neutral intervener has been added to the negotiation process. Section 3 that follows also examines law, but focuses on one issue — confidentiality — a legal issue that dwarfs others in the mediation context in sheer volume of statutes and cases.

a. The Effect of a Duty to Mediate

Generally, courts will enforce obligations to mediate as a prerequisite to allow-ing access to arbitration or litigation — whether the obligation arises from a court order, a statutory mandate, or a pre-dispute agreement of the parties. A variety of rationales support courts' power to compel mediation. In In Re Atlantic Pipeline Corp., 304 F.3d 135 (1st Cir. 2002), the court lays out the sources of court authority to compel mediation — court rule, applicable statutes, the rules of civil procedure, and the court's inherent power — and affirms the court's power to do so. In an unusual opinion, Annapolis Professional Firefighters Local 1926 v. City of Annapolis, 642 A.2d 889, 895 (Md. Ct. Spec. App. 1994), the court noted that it would enforce an agreement to mediate "to the same extent that it would be enforced if the chosen method were arbitration." In an amusing footnote, the opinion said the court might not enforce an agreement to resolve a dispute by trial by combat or ordeal but that it did not "wish to put a straightjacket on the creative development of new forms of alternative dispute resolution that individual parties, or industries, find useful and preferable to litigation." Id. at 895, n.6.

Non-compliance with a contractual duty to mediate could result in a stay of proceedings or a dismissal of the claim, as courts will keep the door shut to arbitration and litigation if parties do not comply with agreements to mediate. For example, in In Re Pisces Foods, LLC, 228 S.W.3d 349 (Tex. App. 2007), where mediation was a precondition to arbitration and neither party had submitted the dispute to mediation, the trial court refused to compel arbitration. The lesson is that dispute resolution clauses that obligate parties to engage in mediation are likely to be enforced — drafters should take note and should consider defining the contours of the duty they impose and the mechanism to enforce it!

Courts, legislators, and lawyers in preparing contracts must weigh the possible burden of adding a mediation obligation against the benefits that might follow from the use of mediation.

b. The Enforceability of Mediated Agreements

Once an agreement has been reached in mediation, will it be enforced? In many cases a mediated agreement is simply a contract between the parties, enforceable like other contracts but with no special standing by virtue of the mediator's participation. In some situations, however, where mediation is part of the court process, a judge or arbitrator will enter the mediation agreement as an order of the court or an arbitral award.

You will see in the section on confidentiality below that confidentiality and privilege intersect with the enforcement of mediated agreements in multiple ways. For example, if mediation is confidential and communications are privileged, how can a party prove a contract defense like fraud, duress, and mistake when challenging an agreement? With respect to enforceability, are oral agreements enforceable if you cannot prove them due to confidentiality? While these questions are explored in the material on confidentiality, take note that the assertion of an oral agreement or a contract defense may have a different outcome where an agreement arises from mediation.

However, while confidentiality can pose challenges to enforceability of mediated agreements, also realize that mediated agreements have their own strengths where they are the product of an exploration of parties' interests, a thoughtful weighing of options, and mediator-driven reality testing. Those features of the mediation process arguably make mediation agreements more durable than many contracts, and also more durable than court awards where one side seeks to avoid judgment.

Increasingly, legislation is being developed that makes mediation agreements easier to enforce, like arbitration awards. For example, the recent European Union Directive on Mediation requires that: "Member States shall ensure that . . . the parties, or for one of them with the explicit consent of the others, [can] request that the content of a written agreement resulting from mediation be made enforceable . . . by a court or other competent authority in a judgment or decision or in an authentic instrument in accordance with the law of the Member State where the request is made." Directive 2008/52/EC of the European Parliament and of the Council of 21 May 2008 on certain aspects of mediation in civil and commercial matters.

c. Special Requirements of Mediated Agreements

Sometimes it is unclear whether a memorandum of understanding or an agreement entered into during a mediation session was intended to bind the parties, as a contract would. Particularly where mediation is compelled by courts, scholars and legislatures have worried that the momentum created by the process would unduly pressure parties into agreements. Wanting to ensure that mediated agreements are entered into with care, some legislatures have imposed special requirements on mediated agreements. For example, in Haghighi v. Russian-American Broadcasting Co., 173 F.3d 1086, 1087 (8th Cir. 1999), because a settlement agreement did not contain the magic words required by Minnesota statute that "it was binding," the courts refused to enforce an otherwise fair agreement signed by the parties and their attorneys. The lesson of *Haghighi* is that drafters of mediated agreements must be on guard for special requirements imposed by legislatures to make agreements binding in the mediation context.

3. Confidentiality in Mediation

Since the beginning of the modern mediation movement, confidentiality offered to the parties has been a hallmark of mediation. The promise of confidentiality, in turn, has created complex legal and policy issues, some of which remain unsettled. This section explores those issues.

Similar to speaking with an attorney, a priest, a psychiatrist, or a doctor, most people expect that their conversation with a mediator will be kept in confidence. In most cases such special relationships are protected by legal privileges, which are created by statute and evidence rules. Additionally, many professionals may have ethical duties, imposed by professional standards of conduct, not to disclose those communications where privacy is expected or promised. Contracts can also protect communications between parties and professionals from disclosure.

Confidentiality is deemed necessary in relationships where parties might not otherwise share information and where furthering the particular relationship, activity, or service is important to society. Settling disputes is important to both courts and communities. Since, arguably, parties would not be candid with mediators without confidentiality protections, confidentiality is thought by many to be critical to mediation. Further, calling mediators to testify raises issues about their neutrality since the mediator's testimony will most likely favor one party over another. Proponents of confidentiality point out that confidentiality also helps protect mediators and mediation programs from being bombarded by subpoenas. Fairness considerations also argue for confidentiality, since a more sophisticated party might use mediation to obtain information and then use the information to harm or take advantage of the more forthcoming party.

However, opponents of confidentiality raise important concerns. There is always tension between the public's right to obtain the "truth" or "every person's testimony" in adjudicative proceedings and the public good furthered by confidentiality. Where important matters are being resolved out of public view, concerns arise about coercion, misconduct, and a loss of societal protections for the less powerful. Confidentiality interferes with public oversight. Some have argued that confidentiality is not necessary for mediation to succeed, and indeed, programs have operated successfully without confidentiality protections.

Different balances have been struck between the need for mediation confidentiality and the need for disclosure about what occurred in mediation. In striking that balance, both common law and statutes have been used both to protect confidentiality as well as to delineate exceptions. The discussion that follows outlines the legal sources of confidentiality protections and exceptions to confidentiality laws and privileges. In doing so, this section reviews a variety of decisions applying statutory and common law. However, state-by-state variation in the law (not to mention international differences) and conflicting court opinions make this area murky. At the end of this section you will see an attempt to bring coherence: the Uniform Mediation Act.

a. Sources of Confidentiality

i. Common Law and Evidentiary Exclusions

Traditionally, evidence concerning offers of settlement and

Federal Rule of Evidence 408

COMPROMISE AND OFFERS TO COMPROMISE

(a) <u>Prohibited uses.</u> Evidence of the following is not admissible on behalf of any party, when offered to prove liability for, invalidity of, or amount of a claim that was disputed as to validity or amount, or to impeach through a prior inconsistent statement or contradiction:

(1) furnishing or offering or promising to furnish — or accepting or offering or promising to accept — a valuable consideration in compromising or attempting to compromise the claim; and

(2) conduct or statements made in compromise negotiations regarding the claim, except when offered in a criminal case and the negotiations related to a claim by a public office or agency in the exercise of regulatory, investigative, or enforcement authority.

(b) <u>Permitted uses.</u> This rule does not require exclusion if the evidence is offered for purposes not prohibited by subdivision (a). Examples of permissible purposes include proving a witness' bias or prejudice; negating a contention of undue delay; and proving an effort to obstruct a criminal investigation or prosecution.

compromise of disputed claims has been excluded in judicial proceedings on the grounds of it being not probative as an admission with respect to the amount or validity of a claim. Parties, for example, might make a settlement offer simply to get rid of a claim, or perhaps out of sympathy for the other side even where they do not feel legally responsible. However, statements of fact — "I am to blame because I was texting when I crossed into your lane" — made in settlement discussions would be admissible under the common law.

Federal Rule of Evidence 408 and similar state counterparts broaden the common law protection. In addition to settlement offers, Rule 408 protects evidence of conduct or statements made in compromise negotiations as well. While Rule 408 provides more protection for settlement discussions, the protection is still quite limited. Evidence from settlement discussions may be introduced to show bias or prejudice, impeach credibility, or prove a material matter other than liability. To be excluded, the evidence must have a sufficient relationship to discussions of settlement. Furthermore, the rule applies only to subsequent litigation (not administrative or legislative hearings or other types of public disclosure), and there must be a disputed civil claim (that is, negotiations over matters that are not a legal cause of action may not be protected).

Imagine you are a mediator explaining to parties the protection that Rule 408 provides. The Rule and its many exceptions do not inspire confidence about mediation confidentiality.

ii. Discovery Limitations

In addition to Rule 408, mediation communications might receive protection under the Federal Rules of Civil Procedure and comparable state rules. Discovery Rule 26(c) has been invoked to protect a party from harm that might be caused by divulging information learned in mediation. That rule would allow a party to seek, and a court to issue, a protective order to protect a party "from annoyance, embarrassment, oppression, or undue burden or expense."

iii. Contracts

In agreements to mediate, parties can, and frequently do, agree not to disclose information conveyed in the mediation and not to subpoena the mediator to testify about what happened. Mediators, both in their opening statements to parties and in agreements to mediate, typically promise not to disclose information that arose in the mediation. Such agreements may provide additional protection for confidentiality.

For example, in Princeton Insurance Company v. Vergano, 883 A.2d 44 (Del. Ch. 2005), where medical malpractice defendants sought the mediator's testimony that plaintiff's representations in mediation about her pain and suffering were inconsistent with surreptitious post-mediation surveillance videos, the court refused to force the mediator to testify. The court pointed both to public policy and to the terms of the parties' own mediation agreement. Their agreement specified that the mediator would not be called on to testify and that statements at the mediation would remain confidential and could not be used in any judicial proceeding.

However, courts may refuse to enforce a confidentiality agreement because suppression of evidence needed in litigation is contrary to public policy. Hence, legal protection for such agreements is not certain. Even if the confidentiality agreement

---

A Sample Confidentiality Provision from an Agreement to Mediate

Confidentiality. The parties and mediator agree to the following confidentiality provisions:

a. Without the consent of all parties and an order of the court, no evidence that there has been a mediation or any fact concerning the mediation may be admitted in a trial de novo or in any subsequent proceeding involving any of the issues or parties to the mediation.

b. Statements made and documents produced in this mediation which are not otherwise discoverable are not subject to discovery or other disclosure and are not admissible into evidence for any purpose, including impeachment.

c. The mediator will not discuss the mediation process or disclose any communications made during the mediation process except as authorized by the parties, or required by law or other applicable professional codes. If either party seeks to subpoena the mediator or the mediator's records, that party shall be liable for, and shall indemnify the mediator against, any liabilities, costs or expenses, including reasonable attorneys' fees, which the mediator may incur in resisting such compulsion.

Agreement provision provided by Professor James Coben

---

is upheld for those signing it, third parties may have access to the information through discovery and subsequent use in trial. In Hauzinger v. Hauzinger, 892 N.E.2d 849 (N.Y. 2008), the NY Court of Appeals held that a mediator could be subpoenaed to testify despite the parties' pre-mediation agreement that the mediation was private and confidential, that nothing said in or prepared for the mediation could be used in a subsequent legal action, and that the parties would not subpoena the mediator. The court found that the parties waived confidentiality in the case.

iv. Statutory and Judicially Created Privileges

A privileged communication is protected from being divulged in court. Privileges, the strongest protection of confidentiality in mediation, can be created by statutes or by court decisions.

An example of a statutory privilege, from the California Evidence Code, may be seen in the adjacent boxes. Yet even such seemingly clear statutes do not necessarily yield predictable answers regarding mediation privilege. Later in this chapter several cases construing this California statutory privilege reach different outcomes. In the *Foxgate* case, which follows in the policy section on "good faith," the privilege is upheld. Following *Foxgate*, in Eisendrath v. Superior Court, 134 Cal. Rptr. 2d 716 (Cal. Ct. App. 2003), the court also upheld the privilege in the context of mediation communications between a husband and wife, holding that no evidence of such communications was admissible even if the communications were made outside the presence of the mediator, as long as they were materially related to the mediation. However, the *Olam* case discussed later in this chapter creates an exception to the confidentiality privilege, holding that the statutorily created privilege yields to a claim of undue influence where there is an express waiver of confidentiality by the parties. Reading these cases together, you will see a struggle to balance various policies.

> **California Evidence Code §703.5. Judges, arbitrators or mediators as witnesses; subsequent civil proceeding**
>
> No person presiding at any judicial or quasi-judicial proceeding, and no arbitrator or mediator, shall be competent to testify, in any subsequent civil proceeding, as to any statement, conduct, decision, or ruling, occurring at or in conjunction with the prior proceeding, except as to a statement or conduct that could (a) give rise to civil or criminal contempt, (b) constitute a crime, (c) be the subject of investigation by the State Bar or Commission on Judicial Performance, or (d) give rise to disqualification proceedings.

> **California Evidence Code §1119 (Written or oral communications during mediation process; admissibility) provides:**
>
> (a) No evidence of anything said or any admission made for the purpose of, in the course of, or pursuant to, a mediation or a mediation consultation is admissible or subject to discovery, and disclosure of the evidence shall not be compelled, in any arbitration, administrative adjudication, civil action, or other noncriminal proceeding in which, pursuant to law, testimony can be compelled and given." and
> "[c] All communications, negotiations, or settlement discussions by and between participants in the course of a mediation . . . shall remain confidential.

In addition to statutory privileges, some courts have created common law privileges for mediation communications. The case below explores the costs and benefits of a mediation privilege and the essential elements in the creation of a privilege. In *Folb*, the plaintiff (Folb), in a discrimination action against his former employer (the Plans), is seeking information from a mediation session between the Plans and another employee (Vasquez) whom Folb allegedly sexually harassed. As you will see, applying the federal common law of privilege, the court denied Folb access to mediation information — information that might have exonerated him from the charge by his employer — and created a federal mediation privilege — at least in those federal courts bound by this decision.

 ## FOLB v. MOTION PICTURE INDUSTRY PENSION & HEALTH PLANS

16 F. Supp. 2d 1164, 1167, 1170-1181 (C.D. Cal. 1998)

. . . In approximately February 1997, Vasquez and the Plans attended a formal mediation with a neutral in an attempt to settle Vasquez' potential claims against defendants arising out of the alleged sexual harassment [by Folb]. Vasquez and the Plans signed a contract agreeing to maintain the confidentiality of the mediation and all statements made in it. . . . Folb sought to compel production of (1) Vasquez' mediation brief; (2) correspondence between Vasquez' counsel and counsel for the Plans regarding mediation or other settlement discussions; and (3) notes to the file prepared by Vasquez' counsel regarding settlement communications. Folb argues that the Plans are trying to take a position in this litigation that is inconsistent with the position he believes they took in settlement negotiations with Vasquez. Folb suggests that the Plans will argue that he was properly terminated for sexually harassing Vasquez, despite the fact that they may have argued in mediation or settlement negotiations with Vasquez that she was never sexually harassed at all. . . .

FEDERAL MEDIATION PRIVILEGE

The federal courts are authorized to define new privileges based on interpretation of "common law principles . . . in the light of reason and experience." *Jaffee*, 518 U.S. at 8. . . . Nonetheless, that authority must be exercised with caution because the creation of a new privilege is based upon considerations of public policy. In general, the appropriate question is not whether a federal mediation privilege should exist in the abstract, but whether "(1) the need for that privilege is so clear, and (2) the desirable contours of that privilege are so evident, that it is appropriate for this court to craft it in common law fashion, under Rule 501." In re Grand Jury, 103 F.3d 1140, 1154 (3d Cir. 1997) (quoting *Jaffee*, 518 U.S. at 35

> **Federal Rule of Evidence 501**
>
> Except as otherwise required by the Constitution of the United States or provided by Act of Congress or in rules prescribed by the Supreme Court pursuant to statutory authority, the privilege of a witness, person, government, State, or political subdivision thereof shall be governed by the principles of the common law as they may be interpreted by the courts of the United States in the light of reason and experience. However, in civil actions and proceedings, with respect to an element of a claim or defense as to which State law applies the rule of decision, the privilege of a witness, person, government, State, or political subdivision thereof shall be determined in accordance with State law.

(Scalia, J., dissenting)), cert. denied, Roe v. U.S., 520 U.S. 1253 (1997).

The general rule is that the public is entitled to every person's evidence and that testimonial privileges are disfavored. Id. Consequently,

> we start with the primary assumption that there is a general duty to give what testimony one is capable of giving. . . . Exceptions from the general rule disfavoring testimonial privileges may be justified, however, by a "public good transcending the normally predominant principle of utilizing all rational means for ascertaining the truth." *Jaffee*, 518 U.S. at 9 (quoting *Trammel*, 445 U.S. 40 at 50).

To determine whether an asserted privilege constitutes such a public good, in light of reason and experience, the Court must consider (1) whether the asserted privilege is "rooted in the imperative need for confidence and trust"[;] (2) whether the privilege would serve public ends; (3) whether the evidentiary detriment caused by exercise of the privilege is modest; and (4) whether denial of the federal privilege would frustrate a parallel privilege adopted by the states. Id. at 9-13.

Need for Confidence and Trust

. . . To determine whether there is a need for confidentiality in mediation proceedings, the Court looks first to judicial and Congressional pronouncements on the issue. No federal court has definitively adopted a mediation privilege as federal common law under Rule 501. In one of the leading cases on the treatment of confidential communications in mediation, however, the Ninth Circuit approved revocation of a subpoena that would have required a Federal Mediation and Conciliation Service ("FMCS") mediator to testify in a National Labor Relations Board ("NLRB") enforcement proceeding. National Labor Relations Board v. Joseph Macaluso, Inc., 618 F.2d 51, 52 (9th Cir. 1980). . . .

The Ninth Circuit's conclusion that requiring a federal mediator to disclose information about the mediation proceedings would inevitably impair or destroy the usefulness of the FMCS in future proceedings is equally applicable in the context of private mediation. Admittedly, the express federal interest in preserving a labor mediation system establishes a stronger basis for a mediator privilege in the context of NLRB proceedings. Nonetheless, mediation in other contexts has clearly become a critical alternative to full-blown litigation, providing the parties a more cost-effective method of resolving disputes and allowing the courts to keep up with ever more unmanageable dockets. . . .

Whether information divulged in mediation proceedings is disclosed through the compelled testimony of a mediator or the compelled disclosure of documents conveyed to or prepared by the mediator, the side most forthcoming in the mediation process is penalized when third parties can discover confidential communications with the mediator. Refusing to establish a privilege to protect confidential communications in mediation proceedings creates an incentive for participants to withhold sensitive information in mediation or refuse to participate at all.

Today, the Court is faced with a somewhat more attenuated concern: whether the "imperative need for confidence and trust" that would support creation of a privilege protecting confidential communications with a mediator should extend so far as to protect all oral and written communications between the parties to a mediation. Before delving into the heart of the matter, we must also clarify what constitutes "mediation" for purposes of the Court's analysis today. Given the facts presented by the parties before the Court, we need only consider whether communications between parties who agreed in writing to participate in a confidential mediation with a neutral third party should be privileged and whether that privilege should extend to communications between the parties after they have concluded their formal mediation with the neutral.

Several commentators have suggested that successful mediation requires open communication between parties to a dispute. See, e.g., Alan Kirtley, The Mediation Privilege's Transition from Theory to Implementation: Designing a Mediation Privilege Standard to Protect Mediation Participants, the Process and the Public Interest, 1995 J. Disp. Resol. 1, 8, 16 (collecting sources indicating weight of scholarly authority suggests confidentiality is essential to mediation). Kirtley argues that

> [w]ithout adequate legal protection, a party's candor in mediation might well be "rewarded" by a discovery request or the revelation of mediation information at trial. A principal purpose of the mediation privilege is to provide mediation parties protection against these downside risks of a failed mediation. Id. at 9-10.

In general, however, the academic literature provides little analysis of whether communications disclosed to the opposing party in the course of mediation proceedings should be accorded the same level of protection as private communications between one party and the mediator.

One self-described "heretical" commentator has expressed doubt over the need for a mediation privilege to protect confidentiality in mediation.

> Although most mediators assert that confidentiality is essential to the process, there is no data of which I am aware that supports this claim, and I am dubious that such data could be collected. Moreover, mediation has flourished without recognition of a privilege, most likely on assurance given by the parties and the mediator that they agree to keep mediation matters confidential, their awareness that attempts to use the fruits of mediation for litigation purposes are rare, and that courts, in appropriate instances, will accord mediation evidence Rule 408 and public policy-based protection. Eric D. Green, A Heretical View of the Mediation Privilege, 2 Ohio St. J. Disp. Resol. 1, 32 (1986) (arguing campaign to obtain blanket mediation privilege rests on "faulty logic, inadequate data, and shortsighted professional self-interest").

. . . Legal authority on the necessity of protecting confidential communications between the parties to a mediation is sparse. In an early decision by the Second Circuit, the court stated:

> [i]f participants cannot rely on the confidential treatment of everything that transpires during [mediation] sessions then counsel of necessity will feel constrained to conduct themselves in a cautious, tight-lipped, noncommittal manner more suitable to poker players in a high-stakes game than adversaries attempting to arrive at a just solution of a civil dispute. This atmosphere if allowed to exist would surely destroy the effectiveness of a program which has led to settlements and withdrawals of some appeals and to the simplification of issues in other appeals, thereby expediting cases at a time when the judicial resources of this Court are sorely taxed. Lake Utopia Paper Ltd. v. Connelly Containers, Inc., 608 F.2d 928 (2d Cir. 1979). . . .

At least one district court has concluded that confidential information disclosed in alternative dispute resolution ("ADR") proceedings is privileged. See United States v. Gullo, 672 F. Supp. 99, 104 (W.D.N.Y. 1987). In *Gullo*, the court found that the confidentiality provision in New York's Community Dispute Resolution Centers Program served to ensure the effectiveness and continued existence of the program. Id. Looking to Rule 501, the court concluded, on balance, that the privilege afforded under New York law should be recognized by the federal court. Id. Having concluded that the information was protected, the *Gullo* court suppressed evidence in a criminal proceeding of all statements made during the dispute resolution process, as well as the terms and conditions of the settlement. Id. . . .

Taking the foregoing authorities en masse, the majority of courts to consider the issue appear to have concluded that the need for confidentiality and trust between participants in a mediation proceeding is sufficiently imperative to necessitate the creation of some form of privilege. This conclusion takes on added significance when considered in conjunction with the fact that many federal district courts rely on the success of ADR proceedings to minimize the size of their dockets. . . .

Public Ends

A new privilege must serve a public good sufficiently important to justify creating an exception to the "general rule disfavoring testimonial privileges." *Jaffee*, 518 U.S. at 9. . . . The proposed blanket mediation privilege would serve public ends by encouraging prompt, consensual resolution of disputes, minimizing the social and individual costs of litigation, and markedly reducing the size of state and federal court dockets. . . .

Evidentiary Detriment

In assessing the necessity of adopting a new privilege, the courts must consider whether "the likely evidentiary benefit that would result from the denial of the privilege is modest." *Jaffee*, 518 U.S. at 11-12. . . .

Where, as here, an employer is sued by one employee claiming wrongful termination based on false allegations of sexual harassment and by another employee asserting a claim for sexual harassment perpetrated by the other employee, a blanket mediation privilege might permit an unscrupulous employer to garner the benefit of the two employees' opposing positions. In open mediation proceedings, the employer would be forced to strike a balance between the two parties' positions rather than taking one employee's side in the first case and then shifting to the other side when defending against charges by the second employee. Despite the potential moral implications of fostering such duplicity, however, there is very little evidentiary benefit to be gained by refusing to recognize a mediation privilege.

First, evidence disclosed in mediation may be obtained directly from the parties to the mediation by using normal discovery channels. For example, a person's admission in mediation proceedings may, at least theoretically, be elicited in response to a request for admission or to questions in a deposition or in written interrogatories. In addition, to the extent a party takes advantage of the opportunity to use the cloak of confidentiality to take inconsistent positions in related litigation, evidence of that inconsistent position only comes into being as a result of the party's willingness to attend mediation. Absent a privilege protecting the confidentiality of mediation, the inconsistent position would presumably never come to light. . . .

Mediation Privilege in the 50 States

In assessing a proposed privilege, a federal court should look to a consistent body of state legislative and judicial decisions adopting such a privilege as an important indicator of both reason and experience. *Jaffee*, 518 U.S. at 12-13. Put simply, "the policy decisions of the States bear on the question whether federal courts should recognize a new privilege or amend the coverage of an existing one." Id. Practically speaking, the confidential status accorded to mediation proceedings by the states will be of limited value if the federal courts decline to adopt a federal mediation privilege. See id. at 13. . . .

At the forefront of the inquiry, however, is the fact that every state in the Union, with the exception of Delaware, has adopted a mediation privilege of one type or another.

Contours of the Privilege

. . . On the facts presented here, the Court concludes that communications to the mediator and communications between parties during the mediation are protected. In addition, communications in preparation for and during the course of a mediation with a neutral must be protected. Subsequent negotiations between the parties, however, are not protected even if they include information initially disclosed in the mediation. To protect additional communications, the parties are required to return to mediation. A contrary rule would permit a party to claim the privilege with respect to any settlement negotiations so long as the communications took place following an attempt to mediate the dispute. . . .

CONCLUSION

. . . In short, the Court concludes that encouraging mediation by adopting a federal mediation privilege under Fed. R. Evid. 501 will provide "a public good transcending the normally predominant principle of utilizing all rational means for ascertaining the truth." *Jaffee*, 518 U.S. at 9.

The analysis in *Folb* was followed in Sheldone v. Pennsylvania Turnpike Commn., 104 F. Supp. 2d 511 (W.D. Pa. 2000). In *Sheldone*, workers and union members (plaintiffs) sought admission of statements made by their employer (defendant) in the mediation of a related matter. Plaintiffs argued that the mediation communications would show a motive for retaliation and rebut the employer's defense that it was acting in the good-faith belief that it was not violating the law.

The government employer sought a protective order to preclude use of the mediation communications and documents, and the court held that the federal mediation privilege would be adopted and excluded the evidence. The *Sheldone* court noted, however, that the privilege would not protect evidence independently discoverable merely because it was presented in a mediation.

v. Ethical Norms

Finally, ethical norms about confidentiality are yet another source of confidentiality regulation. The Model Standards of Conduct for Mediators, sponsored by the American Bar Association, the American Arbitration Association, and the Association for Conflict Resolution (*http://www.abanet.org/dispute/news/Model StandardsofConductforMediatorsfinal05.pdf*) provides that: "A mediator shall maintain the confidentiality of all information obtained by the mediator in mediation, unless otherwise agreed to by the parties or required by applicable law." This code of conduct, and others like it, means that mediators could be challenged in ADR-provider proceedings and professional license and discipline proceedings (if they are lawyers or other professionals with disciplinary bodies) and that parties can try to use ethical rules to protect confidentiality in other settings, like malpractice lawsuits.

b. Exceptions to Confidentiality

While a number of exceptions to confidentiality are discussed below, perhaps the biggest exception is the fact that mediation evidence is regularly considered by courts without confidentiality being raised either by the court or the participants, leading to the conclusion that "the walls of the mediation room are remarkably transparent."[2]

i. Criminal or Quasi-Criminal Cases

In criminal or quasi-criminal cases, where the defendant's constitutional rights and personal liberty are at stake, there is more momentum to admit mediation communications. In Florida v. Castellano, 460 So. 2d 480 (Fla. Dist. Ct. App. 1984), the court held that privileges in Florida had to be established by the legislature and could not be judicially created. In that case, a criminal defendant in a murder case, to support a contention of self-defense, sought the testimony of a community mediator that the murder victim had made life-threatening statements to the defendant in the course of a mediation. Despite the mediator's assurance to the parties of confidentiality, the court ordered the mediator to testify and stated that: "If confidentiality is essential to the success of the CDSP [Citizens Dispute Settlement Program] program, the legislature is the proper branch of government from which to obtain the necessary protection." Id. at 482. In addition to rejecting the privilege argument, the court rejected an argument that the mediation communications were protected under the Federal Rules of Evidence as "offers to compromise," noting

---

2. James R. Coben & Peter N. Thompson, Disputing Irony: A Systematic Look at Litigation About Mediation, 11 Harv. Neg. L. Rev. 43, 59 (2006).

that the "plain language of the provision only excludes evidence of an offer of compromise presented to prove liability or the absence of liability for a claim or its value . . . [which is] simply not relevant to the situation where a mediator testifies in a criminal proceeding regarding an alleged threat made by one party to another in a prior CDSP setting." Id. at 481.

However, courts have also upheld confidentiality in criminal contexts. In People v. Snyder, 492 N.Y.S.2d 890 (Sup. Ct. 1985), where a defendant in a murder case also sought the testimony of a community mediator to support his claim of self-defense, confidentiality was upheld. A New York Supreme Court held that the statute establishing the Community Dispute Resolution Center's program provided for confidentiality, which could not be waived by parties. Similarly, in State v. Williams, 877 A.2d 1258 (N.J. 2005), where a defendant sought to support his self-defense claim in an assault action with testimony from a mediator, the court held that the state interest in protecting mediation confidentiality outweighed the defendant's need for evidence, particularly where the defendant had other evidence to support his self-defense claim and there were concerns about mediator neutrality.

Juvenile cases provide more likelihood that courts will pierce confidentiality to protect the youth rather than the mediation process. In Rinaker v. Superior Court of San Joaquin County, 62 Cal. App. 4th 155 (3d Dist. 1998) (discussed in *Olam* below), a California appellate court found that inconsistent statements made by a witness in a confidential mediation proceeding could be admitted when balanced against the competing goals of preventing perjury and preserving the integrity of the truth-seeking process of a juvenile delinquency hearing. In this context, the *Rinaker* court found that:

> neither the witness nor the mediator had a reasonable expectation of privacy in inconsistent statements made by the witness during confidential mediation because it has long been established that, when balanced against the competing goals of preventing perjury and preserving the integrity of the truth-seeking process of a juvenile delinquency proceeding, the interest in promoting settlements (in this case through confidential mediation of a civil harassment action against the minors) must yield to the minors' constitutional right to effective impeachment. Id. at 161.

Inconsistencies like this gave rise to the Uniform Mediation Act (UMA), discussed below. In Section 6 of the UMA, court proceedings involving a felony are exceptions to a confidentiality privilege if the need for the evidence substantially outweighs the interest in protecting the privilege.

ii. Mediation Documents

Will documents produced in or for mediation be usable in later litigation? The answer is unclear and will vary by jurisdiction.

In In re Grand Jury Proceedings, 148 F.3d 487 (5th Cir. 1998), the court held that mediation documents could be subpoenaed for grand jury investigation. Construing the Agricultural Credit Act, which provides that mediation sessions shall be confidential in order to qualify for federal funding, the court declined to infer a privilege for documents sought by a grand jury.

However, in Rojas v. Los Angeles Superior Court, 93 P.3d 260 (Cal. 2004), the California Supreme Court decided that evidence prepared for a mediation in an action for construction defects, including photographs, expert witness reports, and raw test data, was not discoverable in a subsequent action, even though the repairs in question had been made so the evidence was otherwise unobtainable. In the first suit, owners of an apartment complex sued contractors and settled in mediation. In the second suit, residents of the apartments sued the building owners and sought to obtain evidence the owners had compiled in the course of securing their settlement in mediation with the contractors. The California Supreme Court held that the evidence was not discoverable, pursuant to California's Evidence Code, section 1119(b), which provides: "No writing, as defined in section 250, that is prepared for the purpose of, in the course of, or pursuant to, a mediation . . . is admissible or subject to discovery. . . ." Id. at 265. Citing *Foxgate*, the Court gave great deference to the statutory confidentiality privilege and the importance of the legislative policy protecting mediation confidentiality, noting that the legislature, not the courts, should create exceptions to mediation confidentiality or privilege.

This section may well encourage you to consider stamping documents used in mediation "For mediation only" to attempt to preserve an objection to the use of the documents in subsequent litigation.

iii.   *Contract Defenses*

Recall the prior section on the enforceability of agreements arising in mediation. Since mediation is a negotiation process that most often moves towards an agreement, or contract, traditional contract defenses — mistake, duress, fraud, undue influence, technical failings of the document — are raised in the context of enforcing mediated settlement agreements. Courts resolve these cases using general contract law principles. However, confidentiality protections could make such cases difficult, if not impossible, to prove. Consequently, many courts are reluctant to impose bright-line rules regarding confidentiality that would result in unfairness.

So, for example, a contract defense of mutual mistake might open the door to mediation communications. In DR Lakes Inc. v. Brandsmart U.S.A., 819 So. 2d 971, 972 (Fla. Dist. Ct. App. 2002), where a party claimed that a settlement agreement entered into after mediation contained a $600,000 clerical error, the court allowed evidence as to what transpired in the mediation, holding that the privilege for mediation confidentiality must yield in such instances.

The contract defense of duress has opened the door to breaching mediation confidentiality. In FDIC v. White, 76 F. Supp. 2d 736 (N.D. Tex. 1999), a party tried to avoid a mediation settlement agreement by alleging that threats of criminal prosecution made in mediation were coercive. In light of these allegations of duress, a federal district court in Texas allowed into evidence otherwise privileged mediation communications, ultimately finding that the written settlement agreement was not the result of duress. Or consider McKinlay v. McKinlay, 648 So. 2d 806 (Fla. Dist. Ct. App. 1995), where a wife in a divorce action, in an effort to avoid a mediation settlement agreement, alleged she was badgered and intimidated by her husband's counsel, given inaccurate information and pressured by the mediator, and also pressured by her own counsel to settle. The wife also asserted she was under severe emotional distress at the time of the mediation. The court held that these allegations waived her statutory privilege to preclude mediation communications and testimony from the mediator and that it was "a breach of fair play to deny husband the opportunity to present rebuttal testimony." Id. at 810.

The defense of incapacity has, at least in one jurisdiction, pierced confidentiality. The Georgia Supreme Court, in Wilson v. Wilson, 282 Ga. 728, 732 (Ga. 2007), created an exception to confidentiality where a party contended that he was incompetent to sign an agreement, allowing the mediator to testify as to whether a party had the mental capacity to enter a settlement agreement.

In the *Olam* case below, despite the mediation privilege created by the California Evidence Code, the court admits evidence of mediation communications. The plaintiff, who was 65 years old and suffering from high blood pressure, was represented by an attorney in a court-sponsored, voluntary mediation. She asserted that she had signed a Memorandum of Understanding (MOU) under duress and hence sought to avoid its enforcement. Both parties expressly waived their statutory mediation privilege. After finding that the parties' waiver of confidentiality was not a sufficient basis to order the mediator to testify, the court conducted a two-stage balancing analysis and concluded that the mediator should testify. Judge Wayne Brazil, a noted scholar in the ADR field, thoughtfully lays out pertinent considerations in the opinion. In this case, in contrast to *Foxgate*, *Folb*, *Macaluso*, and *Sheldone*, the need for mediator testimony is found to trump the need to protect mediation confidentiality.

OLAM v. CONGRESS MORTGAGE CO.

68 F. Supp. 2d 1110, 1118, 1131-1134, 1136-1139 (N.D. Cal. 1999)

. . . [P]laintiff alleges that at the time she signed the MOU she was suffering from physical pain and emotional distress that rendered her incapable of exercising her own free will. She alleges that after the mediation began during the morning of September 9, 1998, she was left *alone* in a room *all* day and into the early hours of September 10, 1998, while all the other mediation participants conversed in a nearby room. She claims that she did not understand the mediation process. In addition, she asserts that she felt pressured to sign the MOU — and that her physical and emotional distress rendered her unduly susceptible to this pressure. As a result, she says, she signed the MOU against her will and without reading and/or understanding its terms. . . .

We turn to the issue of whether, under California law, we should compel the mediator to testify — despite the statutory prohibitions set forth in sections 703.5 and 1119 of the Evidence Code. The most important opinion by a California court in this arena is Rinaker v. Superior Court, 62 Cal. App. 4th 155 (3d Dist. 1998). In that case the Court of Appeal held that there may be circumstances in which a trial court, over vigorous objection by a party and by the mediator, could compel testimony from the mediator in a juvenile delinquency proceeding (deemed a "civil" matter under California law). The defendant in the delinquency proceeding wanted to call the mediator to try to impeach testimony that was expected from a prosecution witness. That witness and the delinquency defendant had earlier participated in a mediation — and the delinquency defendant believed that the complaining witness had made admissions to the mediator that would substantially undermine the credibility of the complaining witness' testimony — and thus would materially strengthen the defense. In these circumstances, the *Rinaker* court held that the mediator could be compelled to testify if, after *in camera* consideration of what her testimony would be, the trial judge determined that her testimony might well promote significantly the public interest in preventing perjury and the defendant's fundamental right to a fair judicial process.

In essence, the *Rinaker* court instructs California trial judges to conduct a two-stage balancing analysis. The goal of the first stage balancing is to determine whether to compel the mediator to appear at an *in camera* proceeding to determine precisely what her testimony would be. In this first stage, the judge considers all the circumstances and weighs all the competing rights and interests, including the values that would be threatened not by public disclosure of mediation communications, but by ordering the mediator to appear at an *in camera* proceeding to disclose only to the court and counsel, out of public view, what she would say the parties said during the mediation. At this juncture the goal is to determine whether the harm that would be done to the values that underlie the mediation privileges simply by ordering the mediator to participate in the *in camera* proceedings can be justified — by the prospect that her testimony might well make a singular and substantial contribution to protecting or advancing competing interests of comparable or greater magnitude.

The trial judge reaches the second stage of balancing analysis only if the product of the first stage is a decision to order the mediator to detail, *in camera*, what her testimony would be. A court that orders the *in camera* disclosure gains precise and reliable knowledge of what the mediator's testimony would be — and only with that knowledge is the court positioned to launch its second balancing analysis. In this second stage the court is to weigh and comparatively assess (1) the importance of the values and interests that would be harmed if the mediator was compelled to testify (perhaps subject to a sealing or protective order, if appropriate), (2) the magnitude of the harm that compelling the testimony would cause to those values and interests, (3) the importance of the rights or interests that would be jeopardized if the mediator's testimony was not accessible in the specific proceedings in question, and (4) how much the testimony would contribute toward protecting those rights or advancing those interests — an inquiry that includes, among other things, an assessment of whether there are alternative sources of evidence of comparable probative value. . . .

If a party to the mediation were objecting to compelling the mediator to testify we would be faced with a substantially more difficult analysis. But the absence of such an objection does not mean that ordering the mediator to disclose, even *in camera*, matters that occurred within the mediation does not pose some threat to values underlying the mediation privileges. As the *Rinaker* court pointed out, ordering mediators to participate in proceedings arising out of mediating imposes economic and psychic burdens that could make some people reluctant to agree to serve as a mediator, especially in programs where that service is pro bono or poorly compensated.

This is not a matter of time and money only. Good mediators are likely to feel violated by being compelled to give evidence that could be used against a party with whom they tried to establish a relationship of trust during a mediation. Good mediators are deeply committed to being and remaining neutral and non-judgmental, and to building and preserving relationships with parties. To force them to give evidence that hurts someone from whom they actively solicited trust (during the mediation) rips the fabric of their work and can threaten their sense of the center of their professional integrity. These are not inconsequential matters.

Like many other variables in this kind of analysis, however, the magnitude of these risks can vary with the circumstances. Here, for instance, all parties to the mediation want the mediator to testify about things that occurred during the mediation — so ordering the testimony would do less harm to the actual relationships developed than it would in a case where one of the parties to the mediation objected to the use of evidence from the mediator.

We acknowledge, however, that the possibility that a mediator might be forced to testify over objection could harm the capacity of mediators in general to create the environment of trust that they feel maximizes the likelihood that constructive communication will occur during the mediation session. But the level of harm to that interest likely varies, at least in some measure, with the perception within the community of mediators and litigants about how likely it is that any given mediation will be followed at some point by an order compelling the neutral to offer evidence about what occurred during the session. I know of no studies or statistics that purport to reflect how often courts or parties seek evidence from mediators — and I suspect that the incidence of this issue arising would not be identical across the broad spectrum of mediation programs and settings. What I can report is that this case represents the first time that I have been called upon to address these kinds of questions in the more than fifteen years that I have been responsible for ADR programs in this court. Nor am I aware of the issue arising before other judges here. Based on that experience, my partially educated guess is that the likelihood that a mediator or the parties in any given case need fear that the mediator would later be constrained to testify is extraordinarily small.

That conviction is reinforced by another consideration. As we pointed out above, under California law, and this court's view of sound public policy, there should be no occasion to consider whether to seek testimony from a mediator for purpose of determining whether the parties entered an enforceable settlement contract unless the mediation produced a writing (or competent record) that appears on its face to constitute an enforceable contract, signed or formally assented to by all the parties. Thus, it is only when there is such a writing or record, and when a party nonetheless seeks to escape its apparent effect, that courts applying California law would even consider calling for evidence from a mediator for purposes of determining whether the parties settled the case. Surely these circumstances will arise after only a tiny fraction of mediations.

. . . [T]he kind of testimony sought from the mediator in this case poses less of a threat to fairness and reliability values than the kind of testimony that was sought from the mediator in *Rinaker*. During the first stage balancing analysis in the case at bar, the parties and I assumed that the testimony from the mediator that would be most consequential would focus not primarily on what Ms. Olam said during the mediation, but on how she acted and the mediator's perceptions of her physical, emotional, and mental condition. The purpose would not be to nail down and dissect her specific words, but to assess at a more general and impressionistic level her condition and capacities. That purpose might be achieved with relatively little disclosure of the content of her confidential communications. As conceded above, that does not mean that compelling the testimony by the mediator would pose no threat to values underlying the privileges — but that the degree of harm to those values would not be as great as it would be if the testimony was for the kinds of impeachment purposes that were proffered in *Rinaker*. And in a balancing analysis, probable degree of harm is an important consideration.

What we have been doing in the preceding paragraphs is attempting, as the first component of the first stage balancing analysis, to identify the interests that might be threatened by ordering the mediator, in the specific circumstances presented here, to testify under seal — and to assess the magnitude of the harm that ordering the testimony would likely do to those interests. Having assayed these matters, we turn to the other side of the balance. We will identify the interests that ordering the testimony (under seal, at least initially) might advance, assess the relative importance of those interests, and try to predict the magnitude of the contribution to achieving those interests that ordering the testimony would likely make (or the extent of the harm that we likely would do to those interests if we did not compel the testimony).

The interests that are likely to be advanced by compelling the mediator to testify in this case are of considerable importance. Moreover, as we shall see, some of those interests parallel and reinforce the objectives the legislature sought to advance by providing for confidentiality in mediation.

The first interest we identify is the interest in doing justice. Here is what we mean. For reasons described below, the mediator is positioned in this case to offer what could be crucial, certainly very probative, evidence about the central factual issues in this matter. There is a strong possibility that his testimony will greatly improve the court's ability to determine reliably what the pertinent historical facts actually were. Establishing reliably what the facts were is critical to doing justice (here, justice means this: applying the law correctly to the real historical facts). It is the fundamental duty of a public court in our society to do justice — to resolve disputes in accordance with the law when the parties don't. Confidence in our system of justice as a whole, in our government as a whole, turns in no small measure on confidence in the courts' ability to do justice in individual cases. So doing justice in individual cases is an interest of considerable magnitude.

When we put case-specific flesh on these abstract bones, we see that "doing justice" implicates interests of considerable importance to the parties — all of whom want the mediator to testify. From the plaintiff's perspective, the interests that the defendants' motion threatens could hardly be more fundamental. According to Ms. Olam, the mediation process was fundamentally unfair to her — and resulted in an apparent agreement whose terms are literally unconscionable and whose enforcement would render her homeless and virtually destitute. To her, doing justice in this setting means protecting her from these fundamental wrongs.

From the defendants' perspective, doing justice in this case means, among other things, bringing to a lawful close disputes with Ms. Olam that have been on-going for about seven years — disputes that the defendants believe have cost them, without justification, at least scores of thousands of dollars. The defendants believe that Ms. Olam has breached no fewer than three separate contractual commitments with them (not counting the agreement reached at the end of the mediation) — and that those breaches are the product of a calculated effort not only to avoid meeting legitimate obligations, but also to make unfair use, for years, of the defendants' money.

Defendants also believe that Ms. Olam has abused over the years several of her own counsel — as well as the judicial process and this court's ADR program (for which she has been charged nothing). Through their motion, the defendants ask the court to affirm that they acquired legal rights through the settlement agreement that the mediation produced. They also ask the court to enforce those rights, and thus to enable the defendants to avoid the burdens, expense, delay, and risks of going to trial in this matter. These also are matters of consequence.

And they are not the only interests that could be advanced by compelling the mediator to testify. According to the defendants' pre-hearing proffers, the mediator's testimony would establish clearly that the mediation process was fair and that the plaintiff's consent to the settlement agreement was legally viable. Thus the mediator's testimony, according to the defendants, would reassure the community and the court about the integrity of the mediation process that the court sponsored.

That testimony also would provide the court with the evidentiary confidence it needs to enforce the agreement. A publicly announced decision to enforce the settlement would, in turn, encourage parties who want to try to settle their cases to use the court's mediation program for that purpose. An order appropriately enforcing an agreement reached through the mediation also would encourage parties in the future to take mediating seriously, to understand that they represent real opportunities to reach closure and avoid trial, and to attend carefully to terms of agreements proposed in mediating. In these important ways, taking testimony from the mediator could strengthen the mediation program.

In sharp contrast, refusing to compel the mediator to testify might well deprive the court of the evidence it needs to rule reliably on the plaintiff's contentions — and thus might either cause the court to impose an unjust outcome on the plaintiff or disable the court from enforcing the settlement. In this setting, refusing to compel testimony from the mediator might end up being tantamount to denying the motion to enforce the agreement — because a crucial source of evidence about the plaintiff's condition and capacities would be missing. Following that course, defendants suggest, would do considerable harm not only to the court's mediation program but also to fundamental fairness. If parties believed that courts routinely would refuse to compel mediators to testify, and that the absence of evidence from mediators would enhance the viability of a contention that apparent consent to a settlement contract was not legally viable, cynical parties would be encouraged either to try to escape commitments they made during mediating or to use threats of such escapes to try to re-negotiate, after the mediation, more favorable terms — terms that they never would have been able to secure without this artificial and unfair leverage.

In sum, it is clear that refusing even to determine what the mediator's testimony would be, in the circumstances here presented, threatens values of great significance. But we would miss the main analytical chance if all we did was identify those values and proclaim their importance. In fact, when the values implicated are obviously of great moment, there is a danger that the process of identifying them will generate unjustified momentum toward a conclusion that exaggerates the weight on this side of the scale. Thus we emphasize that the central question is not which values are implicated, but how much they would be advanced by compelling the testimony or how much they would be harmed by not compelling it.

We concluded, after analysis and before the hearing, that the mediator's testimony was sufficiently likely to make substantial contributions toward achieving the ends described above to justify compelling an exploration, under seal, of what his testimony would be. While we did not assume that there were no pressures or motivations that might affect the reliability of the mediator's testimony, it was obvious that the mediator was the only source of presumptively disinterested, neutral evidence. The only other witnesses with personal knowledge of the plaintiff's condition at the mediation were the parties and their lawyers — none of whom were disinterested. And given the foreseeable testimony about the way the mediation was structured (with lots of caucusing by the mediator with one side at a time), it was likely that the mediator would have had much more exposure to the plaintiff over the course of the lengthy mediation than any other witness save her lawyer. . . .

In short, there was a substantial likelihood that testimony from the mediator would be the most reliable and probative on the central issues raised by the plaintiff in response to the defendants' motion. And there was no likely alternative source of evidence on these issues that would be of comparable probative utility. So it appeared that testimony from the mediator would be crucial to the court's capacity to do its job — and that refusing to compel that testimony posed a serious threat to every value identified above. In this setting, California courts clearly would conclude the first stage balancing analysis by ordering the mediator to testify *in camera* or under seal — so that the court, aided by inputs from the parties, could make a refined and reliable judgment about whether to use that testimony to help resolve the substantive issues raised by the pending motion.

The ultimate outcome in the *Olam* case, after Judge Brazil examined the mediator *in camera*, was admission of the mediator's testimony and a finding that the agreement was not the product of duress. The mediator's testimony substantially and critically differed from Ms. Olam's account of events and was particularly probative to the court.

However, subsequent cases, while not overruling *Olam*, have limited the reach of its holding. In Kieturakis v. Kieturakis, 41 Cal. Rptr. 3d 119 (Cal. Ct. App. 2006), the court held that a party seeking to set aside a mediated settlement agreement on the grounds of fraud or duress must waive confidentiality to proceed (as the parties in *Olam* did), which could mean that a challenge based on fraud, duress, or undue influence would fail if the other side refused to waive the confidentiality privilege, thereby preventing a mediated settlement from being effectively challenged. The *Kieturakis* court noted that whether *Olam* "remains a viable precedent" is an open question after *Foxgate* and *Rojas*. Id. at 147.

iv. Settlement Agreements

Written settlement agreements are generally exempt from confidentiality protections. Though, in some cases, parties have confidentiality provisions specified in the agreements.

However, courts are divided over whether evidence of oral settlement agreements should be admissible. Under contract law, oral agreements are generally enforceable — with exceptions for Statute of Frauds scenarios (for example, agreements to transfer an interest in land or agreements that cannot be performed in one year). Confidentiality protections could effectively make an oral agreement reached in mediation impossible to prove. The Indiana Supreme Court in Vernon v. Acton, 732 N.E.2d 805 (Ind. 2000), concluded that confidentiality — the protection of Indiana Rule of Evidence 408 — would encompass oral agreements, and therefore, testimony about such agreements would be precluded. Similarly, in Simmons v. Ghaderi, 44 Cal. 4th 570 (Cal. 2008), the California Supreme Court held that statutory mediation confidentiality precluded the plaintiffs from proving an oral settlement agreement. The Utah Supreme Court also refused to enforce an oral mediated settlement agreement in Tingey Construction v. LWP Claims Solutions, 177 P.3d 605 (Utah 2008). In GLN Compliance Group v. Aviation Manual Solutions, 203 P.3d 595 (Colo. App. 2008), the Colorado Court of Appeals held that despite there being a written transcript made of a mediated oral settlement agreement, the written transcript was not admissible, and hence the contract was not enforceable. The result of this line of cases is that, to be enforceable, mediation agreements must be written and signed.

However, in Kaiser Found. Health Plan of the Northwest v. Doe, 903 P.2d 375 (Or. Ct. App. 1995), an oral settlement agreement reached in mediation was enforced, creating an exception to mediation confidentiality. Similarly, in Few v. Hammack Enters., 511 S.E.2d 665 (N.C. Ct. App. 1999), testimony and other evidence arising in a mediation was found admissible solely for purposes of determining if a settlement was reached and, if so, what the terms of that settlement were.

Sometimes parties develop a Memorandum of Understanding in mediation with the intention that this understanding will subsequently be expanded into a detailed agreement. The effect of such a memorandum — whether or not it is a binding contract — depends on party intent but will be influenced by confidentiality restrictions too. Also, the agreement must be sufficiently detailed and complete.

In Chappell v. Roth, 548 S.E.2d 499 (N.C. 2001), the court held that the failure of the parties to reach agreement on specific terms of a release precluded enforcement of the agreement because a valid agreement requires a meeting of the minds on all terms.

v. Mediator Misconduct

Allegations of mediator misconduct have resulted in "opening the door" shut by confidentiality in order to allow a mediator to defend himself. In Allen v. Leal, 27 F. Supp. 2d 945 (S.D. Tex. 1998), the court held that a mediator could testify to defend himself against charges of misconduct. In that case the mother of a child shot by a police officer was attempting to avoid the settlement agreement, which she claimed was coerced by the mediator. The court noted that the plaintiffs " 'opened the door' by attacking the professionalism and integrity of the mediator and the mediation process, [hence] the Court was compelled, in the interests of justice, to breach the veil of confidentiality." Id. at 947.

vi. Other Issues Surrounding Exceptions to Confidentiality

Many other questions arise in the complicated arena of confidentiality exceptions. For example:

- What is mediation itself, for purposes of analyzing whether a privilege applies? Some statutes require a court order to mediate; others require that a "mediator" have a certain amount of training and experience; others require a written agreement to mediate. Are other professionals functioning in a mediator-like role, like ombuds, "mediators" for purposes of confidentiality?
- When does mediation begin? Is the "beginning" the first formal session or the first point of contact between a party and mediator's office staff? When does mediation end?
- Who is covered by the mediation privilege? Typically, statements by parties, their attorneys, and the mediator are covered, but what about statements of witnesses, support persons, and other types of advocates?
- Are the protections of a privilege limited to court proceedings, or are they broader?
- Who holds the privilege, and who can waive the privilege? Parties only? Does the mediator independently hold the privilege (remember here the analysis in *Olam*)?

Case law and statutes give various, sometimes conflicting, answers to these questions. As you will see immediately below, the creation of the Uniform Mediation Act (UMA) was a response to this lack of consistency. As you read the UMA, see whether you can answer these questions. A simple lesson to be taken away from this section on confidentiality is that confidentiality in mediation is not simple!

c. The Uniform Mediation Act

As is evident from the questions above and the different views of mediation confidentiality, this subject is riddled with confusion and controversy. In an effort to promote uniformity, in 2001 the National Conference of Commissioners on Uniform State Laws and the American Bar Association approved and recommended for enactment in all states the Uniform Mediation Act (UMA) after a lengthy and careful process. The purpose of uniform laws is to bring coherency, consistency, and predictability to an area of practice, but, as of 2010, only 11 states have adopted the Act. As you read selected sections of the UMA that follow, consider why it has not been more universally embraced.

THE UNIFORM MEDIATION ACT, SECTIONS 2-6

Section 2.   Definitions

In this [Act]:

(1) "Mediation" means a process in which a mediator facilitates communication and negotiation between parties to assist them in reaching a voluntary agreement regarding their dispute.

(2) "Mediation communication" means a statement, whether oral or in a record or verbal or nonverbal, that occurs during a mediation or is made for purposes of considering, conducting, participating in, initiating, continuing, or reconvening a mediation or retaining a mediator.

(3) "Mediator" means an individual who conducts a mediation.

Section 3.   Scope

(a) Except as otherwise provided in subsection (b) or (c), this [Act] applies to a mediation in which:

(1) the mediation parties are required to mediate by statute or court or administrative agency rule or referred to mediation by a court, administrative agency, or arbitrator;

(2) the mediation parties and the mediator agree to mediate in a record that demonstrates an expectation that mediation communications will be privileged against disclosure; or

(3) the mediation parties use as a mediator an individual who holds himself or herself out as a mediator, or the mediation is provided by a person that holds itself out as providing mediation. . . . [Section 3 goes on to note mediations where the Act does not apply: collective bargaining, judicial, school or correctional institution mediations.]

Section 4.   Privilege against disclosure; admissibility; discovery

(a) Except as otherwise provided in Section 6, a mediation communication is privileged as provided in subsection (b) and is not subject to discovery or admissible in evidence in a proceeding unless waived or precluded as provided by Section 5.

(b) In a proceeding, the following privileges apply:

(1) A mediation party may refuse to disclose, and may prevent any other person from disclosing, a mediation communication.

(2) A mediator may refuse to disclose a mediation communication, and may prevent any other person from disclosing a mediation communication of the mediator.

(3) A nonparty participant may refuse to disclose, and may prevent any other person from disclosing, a mediation communication of the nonparty participant.

(c) Evidence or information that is otherwise admissible or subject to discovery does not become inadmissible or protected from discovery solely by reason of its disclosure or use in a mediation.

Section 5.   Waiver and preclusion of privilege

(a) A privilege under Section 4 may be waived in a record or orally during a proceeding if it is expressly waived by all parties to the mediation and:

(1) in the case of the privilege of a mediator, it is expressly waived by the mediator; and

(2) in the case of the privilege of a nonparty participant, it is expressly waived by the nonparty participant.

(b) A person that discloses or makes a representation about a mediation communication which prejudices another person in a proceeding is precluded from asserting a privilege under Section 4, but only to the extent necessary for the person prejudiced to respond to the representation or disclosure.

(c) A person that intentionally uses a mediation to plan, attempt to commit or commit a crime, or to conceal an ongoing crime or ongoing criminal activity is precluded from asserting a privilege under Section 4.

Section 6.   Exceptions to privilege

(a) There is no privilege under Section 4 for a mediation communication that is:

(1) in an agreement evidenced by a record signed by all parties to the agreement;

(2) available to the public under [insert statutory reference to open records act] or made during a session of a mediation which is open, or is required by law to be open, to the public;

(3) a threat or statement of a plan to inflict bodily injury or commit a crime of violence;

(4) intentionally used to plan a crime, attempt to commit a crime, or to conceal an ongoing crime or ongoing criminal activity;

(5) sought or offered to prove or disprove a claim or complaint of professional misconduct or malpractice filed against a mediator;

(6) except as otherwise provided in subsection (c), sought or offered to prove or disprove a claim or complaint of professional misconduct or malpractice filed against a mediation party, nonparty participant, or representative of a party based on conduct occurring during a mediation; or

(7) sought or offered to prove or disprove abuse, neglect, abandonment, or exploitation in a proceeding in which a child or adult protective services agency is a party. . . .

(b) There is no privilege under Section 4 if a court, administrative agency, or arbitrator finds, after a hearing in camera, that the party seeking discovery or the proponent of the evidence has shown that the evidence is not otherwise available, that there is a need for the evidence that substantially outweighs the interest in protecting confidentiality, and that the mediation communication is sought or offered in:

> (1) a court proceeding involving a felony [or misdemeanor]; or
>
> (2) except as otherwise provided in subsection (c), a proceeding to prove a claim to rescind or reform or a defense to avoid liability on a contract arising out of the mediation.

(c) A mediator may not be compelled to provide evidence of a mediation communication referred to in subsection (a)(6) or (b)(2).

(d) If a mediation communication is not privileged under subsection (a) or (b), only the portion of the communication necessary for the application of the exception from nondisclosure may be admitted. Admission of evidence under subsection (a) or (b) does not render the evidence, or any other mediation communication, discoverable or admissible for any other purpose.

Problem 8-4.   *The* Olam *Case Under a UMA Regime?*

If the *Olam* case (above) had been decided in a jurisdiction that adopted the UMA, what would the outcome have been?

Problem 8-5.   *Does the UMA Make it All Come Clear?*

Professor Scott Hughes opined that some of the UMA's provisions would "decimate predictability." Can you now answer the questions that precede the UMA above? Imagine a mediation participant asks you to explain confidentiality in a state where the UMA is adopted. What would you say? For one very amusing answer to this question, see *http://law.hamline.edu/mediationlawvideoslisting.aspx?id=222/taxId=180* (go to confidentiality and then Uniform Mediation Act video).

---

d. Sanctions for Breach of Confidentiality

Breaches of confidentiality have yielded an array of outcomes in different courts ranging from monetary sanctions (attorney's fees, mediator's fees, and costs) to the dismissal of an action.

Monetary sanctions were awarded in Bernard v. Galen Group, 901 F. Supp. 778 (S.D.N.Y. 1995), where the plaintiff's lawyer, in an unsolicited letter to the judge, divulged specific terms of settlement offers. The lawyer was fined $2,500.

Courts have split on whether a new trial is necessary where confidential information is divulged. In Hudson v. Hudson, 600 So. 2d 7 (Fla. Dist. Ct. App. 1992), the court held that admitting evidence about an oral mediation agreement taints the subsequent judgment and ordered a new trial where this error was made. However, in Enterprise Leasing Co. v. Jones, 789 So. 2d 964 (Fla. 2001), the Florida Supreme Court held that where a party reveals mediation settlement offers to a judge, it does not automatically disqualify the judge absent proof that the confidential communication results in actual prejudice.

The severe sanction of case dismissal with prejudice is also possible. In Paranzino v. Barnett Bank, 690 So. 2d 725 (Fla. Dist. Ct. App. 1997), where the plaintiff breached mediation confidentiality by divulging to a newspaper specific terms of defendant's settlement offer, the court dismissed her case with prejudice.

B. FOUR POLICY QUESTIONS AT THE INTERSECTION OF LAW, JUSTICE, AND MEDIATION

Judges and juries rely on law — the complex web of statutes and cases — to decide cases. Arbitrators apply whatever norms — law, custom, tradition, contractual and legal rules — parties dictate in their agreement to arbitrate. Mediators, however, elicit principles and standards from the parties and cannot prescribe the governing norms or determine the outcome. Given these fundamental differences among processes, the relationship of law and justice to mediation raises challenging questions. This section explores four policy questions that generate vigorous debate about mediation among scholars and practitioners.

1. Mandatory Mediation

Given the benefits of mediation both to parties and society, mediation is now routinely required as a preliminary step to getting into court. Benefits of mandating mediation include disposing of matters clogging court dockets, overcoming the hurdle that a party proposing mediation may be perceived as weak by the other side, educating parties and attorneys about mediation, creating a body of skilled neutrals, providing parties who are uneducated about mediation the benefits the process can provide, and encouraging the voluntary use of mediation. However, since mediation is often described as a voluntary and consensual process that promotes party self-determination, mandated participation seems contradictory. Despite the contradiction, studies suggest that mandating mediation does not reduce the rate of settlement as compared to voluntary mediation (or does so only marginally), nor does it adversely impact the parties' experience in mediation.

The next two excerpts examine this issue. Dr. Roselle Wissler addresses some concerns about mandatory mediation and concludes that, on balance, it is worthwhile. Professor Trina Grillo raises serious concerns about mandating mediation in the context of divorce and custody cases, which is one of the arenas where mediation has been regularly required as a prerequisite to court action.

Roselle L. Wissler, THE EFFECTS OF MANDATORY MEDIATION: EMPIRICAL RESEARCH ON THE EXPERIENCE OF SMALL CLAIMS AND COMMON PLEAS COURTS

33 Willamette L. Rev. 565-566 (1997)

Although parties tend to be satisfied with their experience in mediation, voluntary mediation programs consistently report low rates of utilization. In order to divert more cases from the courts and to expose more parties to the benefits associated with mediation, many states have adopted mandatory mediation programs for a variety of disputes. Critics have raised the concern that coercion into the mediation process translates into coercion in the mediation process, creating undue settlement pressures that produce unfair outcomes. In cases involving an imbalance of power, the weaker party is thought to be particularly vulnerable to such pressures. However, studies of divorce mediation that examine the effects of mandatory mediation and that explore gender differences in evaluations of the process tend not to support such concerns.

This Article reports research on the effects of mandatory mediation in two different court settings: small claims courts and common pleas courts. . . . [I]t reports the findings of two studies that compare mandatory and voluntary mediation in terms of case outcomes and parties' and attorneys' evaluations. These studies reveal few differences between mandatory and voluntary mediation and between the assessments of male versus female litigants and white versus nonwhite litigants in mandatory mediation. Thus, there is little support for concerns about pressures to accept unfair settlements in mandatory mediation. The findings of these and prior studies suggest that costs associated with mandatory mediation are relatively few, compared to the benefits that mediation provides as an alternative to adjudication.

 Trina Grillo, THE MEDIATION ALTERNATIVE: PROCESS DANGERS FOR WOMEN

100 Yale L.J. 1545, 1549-1550, 1582-1583 (1991)

. . . [M]andatory mediation provides neither a more just nor a more humane alternative to the adversarial system of adjudication of custody, and, therefore, does not fulfill its promises. In particular, quite apart from whether an acceptable result is reached, mandatory mediation can be destructive to many women and some men because it requires them to speak in a setting they have not chosen and often imposes a rigid orthodoxy as to how they should speak, make decisions, and be. This orthodoxy is imposed through subtle and not-so-subtle messages about appropriate conduct and about what may be said in mediation. It is an orthodoxy that often excludes the possibility of the parties' speaking with their authentic voices.

Moreover, people vary greatly in the extent to which their sense of self is "relational" — that is, defined in terms of connection to others. If two parties are forced to engage with one another, and one has a more relational sense of self than the other, that party may feel compelled to maintain her connection with the other, even to her own detriment. For this reason, the party with the more relational sense of self will be at a disadvantage in a mediated negotiation. Several prominent researchers have suggested that, as a general rule, women have a more relational sense of self than do men, although there is little agreement on what the origin of this difference might be. Thus, rather than being a feminist alternative to the adversary system, mediation has the potential actively to harm women.

Some of the dangers of mandatory mediation apply to voluntary mediation as well. Voluntary mediation should not be abandoned, but should be recognized as a powerful process which should be used carefully and thoughtfully. Entering into such a process with one who has known you intimately and who now seems to threaten your whole life and being has great creative, but also enormous destructive, power. Nonetheless, it should be recognized that when two people themselves decide to mediate and then physically appear at the mediation sessions, that decision and their continued presence serve as a rough indication that it is not too painful or too dangerous for one or both of them to go on.

. . . Proponents of [mandatory mediation] seldom recognize that, even though an agreement might not be required, a person might agree to something because of the pressures of the situation; or that, even if no agreement is reached, the process itself might be traumatic.

It is presumptuous to assume that the state has a better idea than the parties themselves about whether mediation will work in their particular case. A party may know something the mediator does not: that her spouse is a pathological, but convincing, liar; that years of living with a man have resulted in a pattern in which the woman consistently accommodates him, even when she does not want to; that the woman will lose sight of her own needs in the attempt to appear a cooperative female; or that the woman will sacrifice many of her interests in order to end what may be a psychologically painful process. In sum, there may be an internal wisdom, one that needs to be honored, that mediation is inappropriate in a particular situation. It is true that mandatory mediation may serve the interests of women who do not wish to enter the adversary process; if opting out of mediation is permitted, some women (as well as some men) will be forced to litigate when their preference would have been to mediate. There is no way around this unfortunate situation. Either some women will be forced to litigate against their will, or some women will be forced to mediate against their will. Mediation poses such substantial dangers, and provides so few benefits to unwilling female participants, however, that to my mind it is indefensible to require mediation, notwithstanding that such a requirement would help women who do want to mediate. . . .

> **Problem 8-6.**   *Would You Welcome an Order to Mediate?*
>
> Imagine that you have been married for ten years and have two young children, but are now getting a divorce. Your spouse tells you that he or she will seek custody of the children in court. Would you welcome a mandate to mediate? Would it make a difference if you were the victim of domestic violence?

What level of participation does mandatory mediation require? Do Trina Grillo's concerns seem less pressing if a woman is free to leave once she finds mediation will not serve her needs? How does the answer to this question affect your views on the relative advantages and disadvantages of a court-annexed program? As you read the section below on good-faith participation, keep this question in mind.

2. A "Good Faith" Requirement

Connected to the growth of court-ordered mediation and of contracts that require the use of mediation prior to adjudication, commentators have advocated, and some legislatures and courts have required, "good faith" participation in mediation. The call for good faith in mediation is premised on the need to ensure that the court-ordered process is not a waste of time, that it is at least possible to achieve a collaborative resolution, and that mediation is not misused. Furthermore, some suggest that to the extent that courts order participation and parties devote resources to it, society should protect the integrity of the process.

One of the problems with a good-faith requirement is the difficulty in defining "good faith." It is easier to identify what is indicative of bad faith than to define good faith. A list of such indicators might include: failure to attend mediation; failure to bring the client or an organizational representative with settlement authority to the mediation; failure to exchange information, bring data, or bring a key expert; failure to prepare a requested pre-mediation memorandum; and failure to participate seriously or to make suitable offers in mediation. Some items on the list are objective, and others are highly subjective. Attendance arguably falls into the objective category; serious participation is certainly open to differences of opinion and thus harder to enforce.

There are other challenges with a good-faith requirement. Placing the burden on mediators to report bad faith can compromise their facilitative role and neutral posture. It could create an incursion into mediation confidentiality since allegations or evidence of bad faith would require disclosure of otherwise confidential mediation proceedings and mediator testimony. This could increase adversarial behavior of the parties — who now have a new weapon against each other — and undermine confidence in the mediator. Similarly, creating a cause of action for bad-faith participation could encourage satellite litigation and spawn more procedural costs and delay for litigants — an ironic outcome since mediation ideally reduces costs and delays.

The *Foxgate* case below illustrates the struggle between upholding a good-faith standard on the one hand and maintaining mediation confidentiality on the other. As you read this case, consider whether the court found the correct balance.

 ## FOXGATE HOMEOWNERS' ASSOCIATION v. BRAMALEA

25 P.3d 1117, 1119-1121, 1124-1129 (Cal. 2001)

The questions we address here are independent of the issues in the underlying lawsuit. Instead, we face the intersection between court-ordered mediation, the confidentiality of which is mandated by law, and the power of a court to control proceedings before it and other persons "in any manner connected with a judicial proceeding before it," by imposing sanctions on a party or the party's attorney for statements or conduct during mediation. . . .

We conclude that there are no exceptions to the confidentiality of mediation communications or to the statutory limits on the content of mediator's reports. Neither a mediator nor a party may reveal communications made during mediation. . . . We also conclude that, while a party may do so, a mediator may not report to the court about the conduct of participants in a mediation session. . . .

BACKGROUND

The underlying litigation is a construction defects action in which the defendants are the developers Bramalea. . . . The plaintiff is a homeowners association made up of the owners of a 65-unit Culver City condominium complex developed and constructed by defendants. In a comprehensive January 22, 1997 case management order (C.M.O.) . . . the superior court appointed Judge Peter Smith, a retired judge, as a special master to act as both mediator and special master for ruling on discovery motions. Judge Smith was given the power to preside over mediation conferences and to make orders governing attendance of the parties and their representatives at those sessions. The C.M.O. specifically provided that Judge Smith was to "set such . . . meetings as [he] deems appropriate to discuss the status of the action, the nature and extent of defects and deficiencies claimed by Plaintiffs, and to schedule future meetings, including a premediation meeting of all experts to discuss repair methodology and the mediation. . . ." Defendants were ordered to serve experts' reports on all parties prior to the first scheduled mediation session. The order confirmed that privileges applicable to mediation and settlement communications applied. The parties were ordered to make their best efforts to cooperate in the mediation process.

Bramalea . . . was (and continues to be) represented by Ivan K. Stevenson. . . . The record reflects that, on the morning of September 16, 1997, the first day of a five-day round of mediation sessions of which the parties had been notified and to which the court's notice said they should bring their experts and claims representatives, plaintiff's attorney and nine experts appeared for the session. Stevenson was late and brought no defense experts. Subsequent mediation sessions were cancelled after that morning session because the mediator concluded they could not proceed without defense experts.

Plaintiff filed its first motion . . . for the imposition of sanctions of $24,744.55 on Bramalea and Stevenson . . . for their failure to cooperate in mediation. The sanctions sought reflected the cost to plaintiff of counsel's preparation for the sessions, the charges of plaintiff's nine experts for preparation and appearance at the mediation session, and the payment to the mediator, which was no longer refundable. Plaintiff's memorandum of points and authorities and declaration of counsel in support of the motion for sanctions recited a series of actions by Bramalea and Stevenson that, plaintiff asserted, reflected a pattern of tactics pursued in bad faith and solely intended to cause unnecessary delay. The actions described included objections to the schedule and attempts to postpone the mediation sessions, and culminated with Stevenson's appearance without experts at the mediation session at which architectural and plumbing issues were to be discussed. The motion recited that when asked by plaintiff's counsel if he would have expert consultants present for the future mediation sessions, Stevenson replied that "I can't answer that." When asked why he had arrived without expert consultants, Stevenson replied: "This is your mediation, you can handle it any way you want. I'm here, you can talk to me." . . .

On September 18, two days after the aborted mediation session, Judge Smith filed the report that is the object of this dispute with the superior court. The report recited that on June 13, 1997, plaintiff's counsel requested that the mediation be continued to a later date to accommodate Stevenson. It was then continued to the September 16-22 dates. On July 16, 1997, the mediator denied as untimely a request by Stevenson for changes to the C.M.O. and for another postponement. On August 15, 1997, Stevenson challenged the mediator pursuant to Code of Civil Procedure section 170.6. The Superior Court struck the challenge on September 8, 1997, and on September 15, 1997, Stevenson sought a writ of mandate in the Court of Appeal. That court denied Stevenson's request for stay two days later and subsequently summarily denied the petition.

The report of the mediator stated: "Mr. Stevenson has spent the vast majority of his time trying to derail the mediations scheduled for September 16 through 22, 1997. . . . On September 16, 1997, Mr. Stevenson arrived 30 minutes late. Even though the purpose of the mediation session was to have Bramalea's expert witnesses interact with plaintiff's experts on construction defect issues, Mr. Stevenson refused to bring his experts to the mediation. Mr. Stevenson stated on several occasions that he did not need experts because of his vast knowledge in the field of construction defect litigation. . . . As a result of Mr. Stevenson's obstructive bad faith tactics, the remainder of the mediation sessions were canceled at a substantial cost to all parties. . . ."

The mediator's report recommended, inter alia, that Bramalea/Stevenson be ordered to reimburse all parties for expenses incurred as a result of the cancelled September 16-22 mediation sessions. . . . Judge Smith then resigned as of the September 18, 1997, date of his report. . . .

DISCUSSION

. . . Section 1121 provides: "Neither a mediator nor anyone else may submit to a court or other adjudicative body, and a court or other adjudicative body may not consider, any report, assessment, evaluation, recommendation, or finding of any kind by the mediator concerning a mediation conducted by the mediator, other than a report that is mandated by court rule or other law and that states only whether an agreement was reached, unless all parties to the mediation expressly agree otherwise in writing, or orally in accordance with Section 1118."

Section 1119, subdivision (c), enacted at the same time (Stats. 1997, ch. 772, §3) provides: "All communications, negotiations, or settlement discussions by and between participants in the course of a mediation or a mediation consultation shall remain confidential." . . .

The language of sections 1119 and 1121 is clear and unambiguous, but the Court of Appeal reasoned that the Legislature did not intend these sections to create "an immunity from sanctions, shielding parties to court-ordered mediation who disobey valid orders governing their participation in the mediation process, thereby intentionally thwarting the process to pursue other litigation tactics." The court therefore crafted the exception in dispute here. As stated and as applied, the exception created by the Court of Appeal permits reporting to the court not only that a party or attorney has disobeyed a court order governing the mediation process, but also that the mediator or reporting party believes that a party has done so intentionally with the apparent purpose of derailing the court-ordered mediation and the reasons for that belief.

Appellants contend that the legislative policies codified in sections 1119 and 1121 are absolute except to the extent that a statutory exception exists. The only such exception they acknowledge is the authority of a mediator to report criminal conduct. They argue that the report of the mediator, which plaintiff submitted to the court with its motion for sanctions and which the court considered, was a form of testimony by a person made incompetent to testify by section 703.5, and violated the principle that mediators are to assist parties in reaching their own agreement, but ordinarily may not express an opinion on the merits of the case. In permitting consideration of any part of the report, the Court of Appeal has created a vague and inconsistent exception to the mandate of confidentiality, one that the Legislature did not authorize. . . .

Thus, we . . . must determine if the mediation confidentiality statutes then applicable admit of any exceptions. . . . The statutes are clear. Section 1119 prohibits any person, mediator and participants alike, from revealing any written or oral communication made during mediation. Section 1121 also prohibits the mediator, but not a party, from advising the court about *conduct* during mediation that might warrant sanctions. It also prohibits the court from considering a report that includes information not expressly permitted to be included in a mediator's report. The submission to the court, and the court's consideration of, the report of Judge Smith violated sections 1119 and 1121.

Because the language of sections 1119 and 1121 is clear and unambiguous, judicial construction of the statutes is not permitted unless they cannot be applied according to their terms or doing so would lead to absurd results, thereby violating the presumed intent of the Legislature. . . .

As all parties and *amici curiae* recognize, confidentiality is essential to effective mediation, a form of alternative dispute resolution encouraged and, in some cases required by, the Legislature. Implementing alternatives to judicial dispute resolution has been a strong legislative policy since at least 1986. In that year the Legislature enacted provisions for dispute resolution programs, including but not limited to mediation, conciliation, and arbitration, as alternatives to formal court proceedings which it found to be "unnecessarily costly, time-consuming, and complex" as contrasted with noncoercive dispute resolution. . . .

To carry out the purpose of encouraging mediation by ensuring confidentiality, the statutory scheme . . . unqualifiedly bars disclosure of communications made during mediation absent an express statutory exception. . . .

The mediator and the Court of Appeal here were troubled by what they perceived to be a failure of Bramalea to participate in good faith in the mediation process. Nonetheless, the Legislature has weighed and balanced the policy that promotes effective mediation by requiring confidentiality against a policy that might better encourage good faith participation in the process. Whether a mediator in addition to participants should be allowed to report conduct during mediation that the mediator believes is taken in bad faith and therefore might be sanctionable under Code of Civil Procedure section 128.5, subdivision (a), is a policy question to be resolved by the Legislature. Although a party may report obstructive conduct to the court, none of the confidentiality statutes currently makes an exception for reporting bad faith conduct or for imposition of sanctions under that section when doing so would require disclosure of communications or a mediator's assessment of a party's conduct although the Legislature presumably is aware that Code of Civil Procedure section 128.5 permits imposition of sanctions when similar conduct occurs during trial proceedings.

. . . The Legislature has decided that the policy of encouraging mediation by ensuring confidentiality is promoted by avoiding the threat that frank expression of viewpoints by the parties during mediation may subject a participant to a motion for imposition of sanctions by another party or the mediator who might assert that those views constitute a bad faith failure to participate in mediation. Therefore, even were the court free to ignore the plain language of the confidentiality statutes, there is no justification for doing so here. . . . No evidence of communications made during the mediation may be admitted or considered.

---

a. Tests for Good Faith

Professor John Lande, in an exhaustive summary of the status of good-faith cases, concludes that courts have consistently found bad faith where a party failed to attend mediation or to provide a required pre-mediation memorandum; have split in cases involving allegations that organizational parties, such as corporations, have provided representatives without sufficient settlement authority; and in other types of cases involving more subjective allegations of bad faith have generally rejected claims of bad faith.[3]

However, no generalization is without exceptions. In In re A.T. Reynolds & Sons, Inc., 424 B.R. 76 (Bankr. S.D.N.Y. 2010), the United States Bankruptcy Court of the Southern District of NY, after ordering parties to mediate, found the creditor in bad faith, despite its sending a representative with full settlement authority to the mediation, because it refused to engage in risk analysis. The court sanctioned the creditor the amount of the mediation's costs. In Carlsbad Hotel v. Patterson-Uti Drilling Company, 199 P.3d 288 (N.M. Ct. App. 2008), a defendant was sanctioned for bad faith because he came to a mediation with no intent of settling, made an offer of $1,000 only after the mediator threatened him with sanctions, then refused to make a higher offer. In *Carlsbad*, the defendant was ordered to pay plaintiff's costs, including attorneys' fees, for the mediation because defendant put all parties through "an exercise in futility." Id. at 294.

b. *Corporate Representatives and Good Faith*

With respect to corporate parties, it is sometimes difficult to ascertain who is best fitted to participate in mediation to satisfy a requirement that a representative "with settlement authority" attend. In G. Heileman Brewing Co. v. Joseph Oat Corp., 871 F.2d 648 (7th Cir. 1989), the court affirmed the district court's conclusion that the company had failed to send a representative in an appropriate position to the settlement conference. The court ruled that the corporate representative attending a pre-trial conference must "hold a position within the corporate entity allowing him to speak definitively and to commit the corporation to a particular position in the litigation." Id. at 653. In that case, a corporate representative was sent with authority to speak for a party, but the only instruction he had was to make no offer. Similarly, in Nick v. Morgan's Foods, 99 F. Supp. 2d 1056 (E.D. Mo. 2000), *aff'd.* 270 F.3d 590 (8th Cir. 2001), the defendant was sanctioned for sending a corporate representative (the regional manager) who had no independent knowledge of the case, nor the authority to reconsider Morgan Food's position on settlement. The manager's authority was limited to $500, after which the general counsel, who was not present, had to be consulted.

Of course, beyond the minimum necessary for "good faith," the more authority the corporate representative has, the more flexible and creative they can be. Having someone high on the corporate ladder can make a critical difference in terms of a good settlement.

c. *Is Attendance by Telephone in Good Faith?*

The meaning of "attendance" has also been challenged. In Raad v. Wal-Mart Stores, 1998 WL 272879 (D. Neb. 1998), Wal-Mart was sanctioned — ordered to pay

---

3. John Lande, Using Dispute System Design Methods to Promote Good-Faith Participation in Court-Connected Mediation Programs, 50 UCLA L. Rev. 69 (2002).

$4,950, representing plaintiff's costs for the mediation — for failing to bring a corporate representative to a court-ordered mediation even though the representative was available by phone. The court said:

> There are several reasons for requiring the presence of authorized representatives at a settlement conference. During the conference, counsel for both sides are given an opportunity to argue their clients' respective positions to the court, including pointing out strengths and weaknesses of each party's case. In this discussion, it is often true that client representatives and insurers learn, for the first time, the difficulties they may have in prevailing at a trial. They must, during the conference, weigh their own positions in light of the statements and arguments made by counsel for the opposing parties. It is often true that as a result of such presentations, the clients' positions soften to the extent that meaningful negotiation, previously not seriously entertained, becomes possible. This dynamic is not possible if the only person with authority to negotiate is located away from the courthouse and can by reached only by telephone, if at all. The absent decision-maker learns only what his or her attorney conveys by phone, which can be expected to be largely a recitation of what has been conveyed in previous discussions. At best, even if the attorney attempts to convey the weakness of that client's position as they have been presented by opposing counsel at the settlement conference, the message, not unlike those in the children's game of "telephone," loses its impact through repetition, and it is simply too easy for that person to reject, out of hand, even a sincere desire on the part of counsel to negotiate further. At worst, a refusal to have an authorized representative in attendance may become a weapon by which parties with comparatively greater financial flexibility may feign a good faith settlement posture by those in attendance at the conference, relying on the absent decision-maker to refuse to agree, thereby unfairly raising the stakes in the case, to the unfair disadvantage of a less wealthy opponent. In either case, the whole purpose of the settlement conference is lost, and the result is an even greater expenditure of the parties' resources, both time and money, for naught. Id. at 6.

As technology makes "virtual" meetings more readily available, the meaning of "attendance" may shift!

d. Sanctions for Bad Faith

Sanctions for bad faith can range from the award of the other side's costs of participation in mediation, including attorneys' fees, to an ordered apology or remedial education, or to a default judgment or dismissal against the party acting in bad faith. In Brooks v. The Lincoln Nat'l. Life Ins. Co., 2006 WL 2487937 (D. Neb. 2006), an attorney was ordered to send letters of apology to all participants, complete an educational course on representation in mediation, and notify his client of this sanction. The attorney in *Brooks* had rejected his opponent's initial settlement offers, refusing to give the mediator an opportunity to explain the opponent's reasoning, and demanded a serious offer "in five minutes." Id. at 2. Not getting an offer he thought serious, he peremptorily left the mediation. In Toon v. Wackenhut Corrections Corp., 250 F.3d 950 (5th Cir. 2001), the court found that plaintiffs' counsel violated confidentiality provisions in the mediation settlement agreement by not filing its motion to enforce under seal. The case involved abuse of young girls in a juvenile justice center and settled for $1.5 million, and the unsealed motion resulted in a newspaper article regarding the agreement. For this bad faith conduct, plaintiffs' counsel were sanctioned as follows: Their contingency fee was reduced from 40 percent to 30 percent; they were precluded from representing other plaintiffs in related claims against defendants without the leave of court; and they were ordered to pay a $15,000 fine to the district court. Courts have imposed the extreme sanction for failing to attend mediation without good cause of a dismissal against the plaintiff or default judgment against the defendant. For example, in Garcia v. Mireles, 14 S.W.3d 839 (Tex. App. 2000), and despite the plaintiff's protest that "death penalty" sanctions were not justified, the case was dismissed for the failure of plaintiff and her counsel to appear for a court-ordered mediation after rescheduling the mediation twice.

Problem 8-7.   *The Court Gone Wild?*

In a civil action against Joseph Francis (and his companies), Doe v. Francis, No. 5.03cv260-RS-WCS, 2003 WL 24073307 (N.D. Fla.) (2003), the founder of the lucrative soft porn videos *Girls Gone Wild*, alleging the enticement of underage girls to perform sexual acts on film, the parties were ordered to mediation by U.S. District Judge Smoak.

Francis's actions at the court-ordered mediation included: arriving four hours late and keeping out-of-town plaintiffs waiting; wearing sweat shorts, a backwards baseball cap, and no shoes; placing his bare, dirty feet on the table, facing plaintiffs' counsel; interrupting plaintiff's counsel to yell repeatedly, "Don't expect to get a fucking dime — not one fucking dime!"; threatening, as the plaintiffs and their counsel left the room, "We will bury you and your clients! I'm going to ruin you, your clients, and all of your ambulance-chasing partners!"; and, as a farewell, saying to plaintiffs' counsel, "Suck my dick." Pitts v. Francis, 2007 WL 4482168 (N.D. Fla. 2007) at 11-12. After this outburst, the mediation continued for 13 hours.

The sanctions for Francis's conduct included paying plaintiffs' attorneys' fees and costs and serving time in jail until he mediated in good faith. The judge, finding that the mediation was essentially a sham, specified that proper participation in mediation would include Francis arriving on time, dressed and groomed appropriately. The Court elaborated that Francis would wear "a business suit and a tie, business shoes and socks and he will conduct himself and communicate in a manner during the mediation with the demeanor and courtesy expected in serious business transactions and appearances before the court." Id. at 6. Upon the mediator's certification that Francis participated in good faith, Francis would be released from incarceration.

Is this an example of a good case making bad law? Or, was Judge Smoak correct to find Francis in civil contempt and to order him to be jailed until he mediated in good faith?

3. Mediator Evaluation and Assessment

Another heated debate is whether a mediator should offer the parties assessments about positions parties are taking, the likely adjudicated outcome, or other matters in dispute. This evaluative function is clearly the domain of neutral experts, arbiters, and judges. Should it also be a service provided by mediators? As mediation has been brought into the courts, the practice of evaluative mediation has grown, perhaps because lawyers and clients are most comfortable in adversarial processes and with neutrals who give opinions. The Riskin grid shown in Chapter 6 depicts a mediation universe split into evaluative and facilitative spheres. An evaluative mediator, according to Leonard Riskin, has an evaluative orientation and does some or all of the following: develops and proposes settlement terms, urges parties to accept a particular settlement, predicts court outcomes, and assesses strengths and weaknesses of legal claims. While a facilitative mediator may be very energetic in urging parties to reevaluate their positions and legal analysis, she would not give her own opinion of the merits of claims or defenses or of the likely outcome of a case. Some scholars claim that evaluative mediation is an oxymoron, just as facilitative arbitration would be.[4] In the excerpt that follows, Murray Levin reflects on this question.

 Murray S. Levin, **THE PROPRIETY OF EVALUATIVE MEDIATION: CONCERNS ABOUT THE NATURE AND QUALITY OF AN EVALUATIVE OPINION**

16 Ohio St. J. on Disp. Resol. 267, 270-271 (2001)

Proponents of evaluative mediation assert that disputants [need] help in understanding the law and how their case is affected by the law, and that lawyers want mediators to provide direction regarding appropriate settlement figures. Additionally, proponents claim that because settlement negotiation takes place in the context of the alternative of litigation, the alternative outcome is highly relevant and therefore evaluation should be considered a valuable and proper component of mediation. Included within this group of proponents are commentators who do not advocate evaluative mediation, per se, but believe it should be available when chosen by the disputants.

Opponents of evaluative mediation counter that the tenor of the mediation process changes dramatically when the mediator assumes an evaluative role, because evaluation reduces mediator impartiality and disputant self-determination. When the mediator interjects an opinion, the disputant's ability to fashion a resolution based on their own needs is compromised. Understanding that the mediator will be evaluative, the disputants will not be as forthright with the mediator. A foremost goal will be a favorable mediator evaluation, and a disputant will not be willing to share information that could have an adverse effect on that evaluation. Under these circumstances it is more likely that the mediator will not learn about important

---

4. Kimberlee K. Kovach & Lela P. Love, "Evaluative" Mediation Is an Oxymoron, 14 Alternatives 31 (1996).

information that could be relevant to assisting the disputants and should be relevant to forming a valid evaluation. This is especially likely if the mediation occurs at an early point in time prior to discovery. Evaluation turns the process away from problem solving toward an adversarial contest — sharing turns to posturing. Facilitative mediators view the potential for sharing of information through mediation as a chief means to assist the parties in recognizing opportunities to create new value and find win-win solutions. Moreover, too much emphasis on a likely legal outcome overlooks the possibility that the legal solution is not necessarily the best solution. Critics also express concern about the directive and coercive nature of the process when evaluation occurs. Some have gone so far as to characterize evaluative mediators as "Rambo mediators" who are out to "knock some sense" into the disputants by "banging their heads together" or "twisting their arms." Even if the evaluative mediator does not pressure, but merely opines, it is hard to deny a preferential effect, for there is a natural tendency to rely on the ideas, opinions, and predictions of the mediator. Undeniably, any opinion or evaluation will favor one side and disfavor the other. One may then ponder whether this influence is justified — whether the evaluative mediator's evaluation is valid and proper.

Elsewhere in his article, Levin notes the lack of empirical research testing the quality or validity of mediator evaluative opinions. He points to data from studies regarding negotiation outcomes between highly regarded lawyer negotiators, case evaluations by lawyers and claims adjusters, and mock jury experiments displaying — with remarkable ranges of outcomes — the difficulty of predicting negotiation or litigation outcomes. This difficulty is compounded by the fact that mediation takes place under the umbrella of confidentiality, and consequently, the protections of a public process and the right of appeal are absent. Concerns about mediator opinions are allayed to some extent by the fact that such opinions are not binding on the parties.

Proponents of mediators being willing to give a neutral assessment when requested by the parties point to its value in providing a reality check to reduce unrealistic expectations and bridge final gaps. Its use may be particularly appropriate as a last step when all else has failed.

> ## Problem 8-8.   *Does Case Type Matter?*
>
> Is evaluation appropriate in some cases but not others? If you think so, what cases would call for evaluative mediation? Cases involving constitutional or statutory rights? Commercial cases? Divorce cases? Personal injury cases? Environmental cases? Is your answer supported by the examples of mediation in Chapter 6?

There is agreement that combining evaluative and facilitative dispute resolution services can be useful in particular cases where requested by informed parties. Indeed, the principle of self-determination suggests that parties should be free to pursue the approach to dispute resolution that best suits their needs. Nonetheless, the debate continues about what to call a combination of facilitation and evaluation. Should evaluative mediation be called mediation or mediation *plus* neutral evaluation?

Proponents of careful labeling of processes argue that calling evaluative mediation "mediation *plus* neutral evaluation" would: make the services to be provided by the neutral clearer (a benefit both for providers and participants); help educate consumers about choices with respect to dispute resolution options; and forewarn advocates and parties about the best approach to information sharing and advocacy in a blended process where the neutral's opinion might have a decisive impact on negotiations. Furthermore, insuring a meaningful array of processes — rather than one process labeled "mediation" but consisting of a variety of approaches — is more likely to generate thoughtful choice about process options. In New York, qualification requirements for neutrals are different for those serving as mediators, arbitrators, and neutral evaluators — indicating that distinct processes have significant differences in practice and training norms and cannot be blended unless all criteria for insuring quality are met.[5] Finally, the benefits of a multi-door courthouse may be lost if the courthouse has only two doors: litigation and "mediation" — an amorphous process that means whatever works to resolve the dispute.

On the other hand, as you have seen from Riskin's Grid in Chapter 6, since a considerable portion of the mediation world is already evaluative, the word "mediation" has come to include this blended process. Advocates of mediator flexibility note that mediation has been characterized by fluidity and creativity, and mediators should not be constrained by excessive rules or constricting labels.

Problem 8-9.   *Impacts of a Blended Process?*

If you were responsible for a panel of mediators where evaluative mediation was the norm, what impact would that have on: the qualification criteria for panelists? the description of the panel's services? accountability for erroneous conclusions of mediators? training for panelists? whether the program encouraged — or allowed — the use of caucuses and ex parte communications? ethical rules?

---

4. Mediator Responsibility for the Quality of the Parties' Agreement

Self-determination by the parties is the hallmark of mediation. This means that the parties' sense of fairness usually trumps other arguably applicable norms. The following two excerpts explore mediator accountability for the quality of mediated

---

5. Part 146.4, Rules of the Chief Administrative Judge, New York State Unified Court System.

outcomes. Does a high quality outcome mean that the parties' agreement is in keeping with applicable norms — law, industry norms and best practices, and the interests of third parties and future generations? Or, is a high quality agreement in the mediation context one with which the parties are satisfied and to which they are committed? Two prominent professors reach remarkably different conclusions about the nature and scope of the mediator's job with respect to mediated outcomes.

 ### *Lawrence Susskind*, ENVIRONMENTAL MEDIATION AND THE ACCOUNTABILITY PROBLEM

6 Vt. L. Rev. 1, 6-8, 18, 42, 46-47 (1981)

. . . The success of most mediation efforts tends to be measured in rather narrow terms. If the parties to a labor dispute are pleased with the agreement they have reached voluntarily, and the bargain holds, the mediator is presumed to have done a good job. In the environmental field, there are reasons that a broader definition of success is needed — one that is more attentive to the interests of all segments of society.

If the parties involved in environmental mediation reach an agreement, but fail to maximize the joint gains possible, environmental quality and natural resources will actually be lost. If the key parties involved in an environmental dispute reach an agreement with which they are pleased, but fail to take account of all impacts on those interests not represented directly in the negotiations, the public health and safety could be seriously jeopardized. If the key parties to a dispute reach an agreement, but selfishly ignore the interests of future generations, short term agreements could set off environmental time bombs that cannot be defused. Although the key stakeholders in an environmental dispute may pay only a small price for failing to reach an agreement, their failure could impose substantial costs on many groups, who may be affected indefinitely. Finally, the parties to environmental disputes must be sensitive to the ways in which their agreements set precedents; even informal settlements have a way of becoming binding on others who find themselves in similar situations. . . .

[E]nvironmental mediators ought to accept responsibility for ensuring (1) that the interests of parties not directly involved in negotiation, but with a stake in the outcome, are adequately represented and protected; (2) that agreements are as fair and stable as possible; and (3) that agreements reached are interpreted as intended by the community-at-large and set constructive precedents. . . .

Effective environmental mediation may require teams composed of some individuals with technical backgrounds, some specialized in problem-solving or group dynamics and some with political clout. . . .

Environmental mediators ought to be concerned about (1) the impacts of negotiated agreements on underrepresented or unrepresentable groups in the community; (2) the possibility that joint net gains have not been maximized; (3) the long-term or spill-over effects of the settlements they help to reach, and (4) the precedents that they set and the precedents upon which agreements are based. To be effective, an environmental mediator will need to be knowledgeable about the substance of disputes and intricacies of the regulatory context within which decisions are embedded. An environmental mediator should be committed to procedural fairness — all parties should have an opportunity to be represented by individuals with the technical sophistication to bargain effectively on their behalf. Environmental mediators should also be concerned that the agreements they help to reach are just and stable. To fulfill these responsibilities, environmental mediators will have to intervene more often and more forcefully than their counterparts in the labor-management field. Although such intervention may make it difficult to retain the appearance of neutrality and the trust of the active parties, environmental mediators cannot fulfill their responsibilities to the community-at-large if they remain passive.

 Joseph B. Stulberg, **THE THEORY AND PRACTICE OF MEDIATION: A REPLY TO PROFESSOR SUSSKIND**

6 Vt. L. Rev. 85, 85-88, 108-109, 112-115 (1981)

. . . Paradoxically, while the use of mediation has expanded, a common understanding as to what constitutes mediation has weakened. . . . It is important . . . to identify and clarify the principles and dynamics which together constitute mediation as a dispute settlement procedure. . . . Susskind's argument is novel in that he asserts that the mediator of environmental disputes, unlike his counterpart in labor management, community, or international disputes, should not be neutral and should be held accountable for the mediated outcome. Since most mediators believe that a commitment to impartiality and neutrality is the defining principle of their role, Susskind's argument carries significant consequences for mediation.

. . . Susskind's demand for a non-neutral intervenor is conceptually and pragmatically incompatible with the goals and purposes of mediation. The intervenor posture that Susskind advocates is not anchored by any principles or obligations of office. The intervenor's conduct, strategies or contribution to the dispute settlement process is, therefore, neither predictable nor consistent. It is precisely a mediator's commitment to neutrality which ensures responsible actions on the part of the mediator and permits mediation to be an effective, principled dispute settlement procedure. . . .

On a substantive level, Susskind argues that the mediator must ensure that the negotiated agreements are fair. The most dramatic example of the difference between the traditional neutral mediator and Susskind's environmental mediator is the person Susskind describes and endorses as a mediator with "clout." For Susskind, the term "clout" applies to a mediator publicly committed to a particular substantive outcome with the power to move the contesting parties toward an agreement. In contrast, the traditional mediator would view that public commitment as the signal reason for disqualifying himself from service.

It is more than a mere terminological quibble to analyze whether a mediator must be someone who is committed to a posture of neutrality. Such a commitment enables both the mediation process and the mediator to operate effectively. A commitment of neutrality provides the mediator with a principled rather than opportunistic basis for service. As a result, the parties will use his services in ways that would be foreclosed to the "mediator with clout." Susskind's analysis has practical implications for mediator selection, training, scope of service, and financing of services. Clarifying this matter is of no small moment for those interested in the continued experimentation and use of mediation.

One disclaimer is in order. Arguing that a mediator's role requires a commitment to impartiality and neutrality is not to claim that Susskind's "mediator with clout" could not be an effective intervenor. There are many types of "intervenors with clout," a police officer, parent, government regulatory agency, psychologist, marriage counselor, meeting facilitator, corporate executive, and school principal. For certain kinds of dispute settings, those persons intervene with clout in much the same way that Susskind proposes for his environmental dispute mediator. Such a description does not make these persons mediators nor does it make their intervention ineffective or less effective than service rendered by a mediator. It simply constitutes a different kind of intervention posture from that of a mediator. One purpose served by conceptual analysis is to distinguish among different functions served by various types of intervenor postures, allowing those involved to become more sensitive to the types of intervention which are appropriate to different disputes.

. . . At issue is an understanding of, and respect for, what the parties to the mediation session are entitled to expect from the intervenor. Will confidences be honored? Who sets the agenda in terms of issues to be discussed? Will the order in which the issues are discussed be skewed so as to insure the mediator's desired outcome? Will meeting times be scheduled for the convenience of the parties or might they be arranged by the intervenor in order to make it difficult for some (i.e. "obstreperous") parties to attend and voice objections to the intervenor's preferred position? Will the mediator refuse to schedule meetings if the one party whose position the mediator supports demands that future meetings be conditional upon the other parties having made particular concessions? . . . Is it appropriate, for example, for the "mediator with clout" to threaten a recalcitrant party with political retaliation? If not, why not? . . . To suggest that an environmental mediator assume the responsibility of protecting the public's interest within the mediation context is comparable to suggesting that the way to avoid impasses in mediation is to authorize the mediator to impose dispositive, enforceable decisions on the parties.

Such a proposal is not simply adding a different twist to the mediation process; it is converting it from mediation to arbitration in the interest of promoting finality. Susskind has yet to meet the burden of justifying how the environmental mediator can assume this particular responsibility to the "public" without simultaneously converting the dispute settlement procedure into something other than mediation.

. . . Susskind suggests that "environmental mediators ought to be concerned . . . about . . . the possibility that joint net gains have not been maximized [and about] . . . the long-term or spillover effects of the settlements they help to reach." Susskind proposes that it is the mediator's responsibility as an objective observer to insure that the final solution secures the greatest overall net benefits for each party, without leaving any party worse off than it was in its original configuration (the Pareto-optimal principle). He further suggests that the solution agreed upon should have the least possible adverse impact on other aspects of present or future community life. Simply stating the proposed responsibility for the mediator in this way reveals how awesome the task is that Susskind is proposing for the environmental mediator. To insure that the Pareto principle is met, the environmental mediator must be able to generate, or at least guarantee, consideration of every possible technical solution to the environmental problem. He must secure demographic information on all persons affected by the dispute and factor their interests, desires, aspirations, preferences and values into the solution. He must project alternative development plans for jobs, tax bases, population trends, aesthetic values, school development and recreational needs for each possible solution. He must calculate the advantages and disadvantages of each solution against retaining the status quo, including the costs involved in using alternative dispute settlement procedures. And the list goes on. . . . Although these tasks might constitute a city planner's dream, they [raise] the serious possibility that Pareto-optimal outcomes in the context of an environmental dispute are not, in principle, possible. As such, Susskind's proposal that the mediator ought to insure such an outcome must, charitably speaking, be held in abeyance.

A more troublesome question arises, however, regarding the justification for a mediator to block an agreement that fails to meet the requirements of the Pareto principle. Who authorized the mediator to design or insure the attainment of the "optimal" outcome so conceived? Clearly, it is preferable for persons to act as rational agents and do the "right" thing. Even conceding, however, the dubious proposition that the mediator could identify the "right" course of action as defined by the Pareto principle, on what basis does the mediator assume as an obligation of office that he help parties do only what is "right" and not necessarily that which is possible? . . .

If we were to accept the obligations of office that Susskind ascribes to the environmental mediator with regard to insuring Pareto-optimal outcomes, then the environmental mediator is simply a person who uses his entry into the dispute to become a social conscience, environmental policeman, or social critic and who carries no other obligations to the process or the participants beyond assuring Pareto-optimality. It is, in its most benign form, an invitation to permit philosopher-kings to participate in the affairs of the citizenry. . . .

The potential range of services for Susskind's environmental mediator, versus that of a traditional mediator committed to a posture of neutrality, is so importantly different that it is seriously misleading to use the same label to describe these respective intervention postures.

Problem 8-10.   *Achieving Pareto Superior Outcomes*

The Pareto principle (named after an Italian economist) — or a "Pareto superior" outcome — means that the agreement maximizes the available utilities or good for all the parties involved. Said another way, Pareto-efficient situations are those in which it is impossible to improve one person's outcome without making someone else's worse. For example, in a case involving the termination of an employee, the employer may agree to provide a positive reference for the employee, which costs the employer nothing and provides an enormous benefit to the employee. This is a Pareto superior outcome to a severance package without provision for a reference, assuming the employer has positive things to say. While Stulberg rejects placing responsibility on the mediator for insuring a Pareto superior result, what mediator tools have you studied that encourage movement in a Pareto superior direction?

Problem 8-11.   *What's Your Opinion?*

With a group of five colleagues, consider one of the questions posed from the point of view of a mediator, a judge, a participant in mediation, a legislator, and a member of a bar committee. How would you answer these questions?

1. Should mediation be mandatory?
2. Should courts enforce a "good faith" requirement?
3. Should the mediator provide evaluations or assessments for the parties?
4. Should the mediator bear responsibility for the quality of the parties' agreement?

At the end of this chapter, there are suggestions for further readings on some of these topics.

C. ETHICS IN MEDIATION

Like all professionals, mediators face many ethical choices in their practice. Dilemmas that arise often result from conflicting obligations or aspirations. As you have seen in the discussions above, conflicts abound between the rule of law and the goal of party choice or the aspiration of good-faith conduct and the promise of confidentiality. Michael Moffitt describes different scenarios below that raise ethical issues for mediators and possibly could lead to mediator liability. Read these examples in light of the Model Standards of Conduct for Mediators (the Model Standards) developed by the American Bar Association, the American Arbitration

Association, and the Association for Conflict Resolution (*http://www.abanet.org/ dispute/news/ModelStandardsofConductforMediatorsfinal05.pdf*).

The Model Standards provide guideposts that articulate the fundamental values and mediator duties associated with mediation. Those values are: party self-determination, mediator impartiality, mediator disclosure and avoidance of conflicts of interest, mediator competence, mediator maintenance of the confidentiality and quality of the process, truth in advertising, disclosure of fees, and the mediator's duty to improve the practice of mediation. However, ethics codes rarely give bright-line boundaries and indisputable answers. Rather, they help develop a moral compass for reflective practitioners and a guide to the outer limits of permissible conduct. Pinpoint for each scenario what, if anything, about the mediator's conduct arguably violates a duty to the process or parties or society. Then double-check your answers against the prescriptions in the Model Standards.

 Michael Moffitt, TEN WAYS TO GET SUED: A GUIDE FOR MEDIATORS

8 Harv. Negot. L. Rev. 81, 86, 95-96, 111, 113-114, 116-117, 120, 122, 125 (2003)

[Eight of ten dilemmas posed by Moffitt follow.]

1. Melissa Mediator is a member of a small consulting firm specializing in corporate dispute resolution. One of the firm's clients is a large, multi-national conglomerate. Unlike most of her colleagues, Melissa has never done work for the conglomerate. A dispute arises between one of the subsidiaries of the conglomerate and a local business. Melissa agrees to mediate the dispute and discloses nothing about the relationship between the conglomerate and her firm.

2. After considerable efforts to facilitate an agreement, and at the request of the disputants, Marjorie Mediator examines the evidence each side has compiled and develops her best assessment of a court's likely disposition of the case. The parties then quickly agree to basic settlement terms. Again at the parties' request, Marjorie drafts a formal contract to capture the terms of the parties' agreement.

3. Plaintiffs brought suit seeking injunctive relief to force a change in a particular policy at the defendant corporation and seeking modest monetary damages. During a private caucus, Marsha Mediator learns that the defendant has already decided to change the policies in question, in a way the plaintiffs will embrace. When Marsha asks defense counsel why they have not told the plaintiffs about the corporation's plans, they indicate that they hope to use the change in policies as a "trade-off concession" in order to minimize or eliminate any financial payment. In a subsequent private meeting with the plaintiffs, without the consent of the defendant, Marsha says, "Look, the defendants have already told me that they're going to make the policy change, the only issue is money."

4. Maurice Mediator learns during a conversation with a divorcing couple that the children are regularly subjected to living arrangements tantamount to abuse or neglect. Maurice mentions his concern, but both of the parents swear that the circumstances will change once they can finalize the divorce. Maurice says nothing to anyone outside of the mediation and proceeds to assist the parties in finalizing the terms of the divorce.

5. Mitchell Mediator's website touts his mediation services as "expert." In part, it says, "Over 1,000 cases of experience. Certified and sanctioned by the State and by prominent national mediation organizations." Mitchell is a former judge who presided over more than a thousand civil cases during his years on the bench. He has formally mediated, however, only a few dozen cases. Furthermore, neither the state nor the national mediation organizations to which Mitchell belongs certifies or sanctions mediators. Mitchell is simply a member of the mediation rosters each body maintains.

6. During the mediation, Muriel Mediator adopts an aggressive approach to creating settlement. As always, she had told the parties, a divorcing couple, "Bring your toothbrushes when you show up to my mediation." The divorcing wife, unrepresented by counsel, is visibly worn down by Muriel's relentless efforts at "persuasion." When the wife protests and indicates a desire to leave, Muriel threatens to report to the judge that the wife did not participate in mediation in good faith. Muriel further indicates that such a report would "all but guarantee that you'll lose your claim for custody of the children."

7. In a private caucus, the plaintiffs tell Manuel Mediator that they would be able to break this case wide open if only they could get some cooperation from a few important executives in the defendant corporation. They admit, however, that they have had no luck so far in their efforts. Manuel then sits down privately with the general counsel for the defendant and says, "Look, I spoke with the plaintiffs. They have just lined up some key insider witnesses, including a couple members of your management team. It's time for you to end this." The general counsel looks surprised but increases the defendants' offer considerably. The mediator takes the new offer to the plaintiffs, who quickly agree to it.

8. Michael Mediator misses an opportunity to improve the parties' understanding of each other and of the relevant issues. Michael creates an unhelpful agenda and refuses to adapt his approach. Michael misreads the parties' primary concerns. He makes inappropriate suggestions. Michael is unprepared. He listens horribly. Michael oversees a lengthy process that produces no agreement and worsens the parties' relationship.

Wrestling with these eight scenarios should develop an appreciation of major dilemmas that have informed the development of mediation ethical codes. Recurring issues, many of which have no definitive resolution, include: conflicts of interest that impact mediator neutrality or create the appearance of mediator bias; mediator evaluation and agreement drafting that raise questions about unauthorized practice of law; mediator responsibilities to maintain party confidences and simultaneously promote settlement; mediator duties to endangered third parties, as such duties impact mediation confidentiality; consumers' rights to truthfulness in advertising and parties' rights to honesty and integrity from the mediator; the line between energizing parties to move forward and improperly pressuring them into settlement; and the contours of minimal competence.

Three of these areas that have generated recurring issues — conflicts of interest, mediator immunity, and unauthorized practice of law — are explored below.

1. Conflicts of Interest

Look back to the first dilemma posed by Professor Moffitt in the excerpt above regarding Melissa Mediator. Here are examples of two courts dealing with conflict-of-interest cases. In Fields-D'Arpino v. Restaurant Assocs., 39 F. Supp. 2d 412 (S.D.N.Y. 1999), the court held that counsel for defendants–employer were disqualified from representing defendants because a partner in the firm had served as a neutral mediator in trying to resolve plaintiff-employee's discrimination claim against her employer. Similarly, in Poly Software Intl. v. Su, 880 F. Supp. 1487 (D. Utah 1995), the mediator-attorney who had previously settled a dispute between two parties involving the same software was disqualified from representing one of the parties, as were other members of his law firm.

Courts tend to take seriously the presence of conflicts of interest, particularly coupled with failure of the mediator to disclose the conflict. In Furia v. Helm, 4 Cal. Rptr. 3d 357 (Cal. Ct. App. 2003), the California Court of Appeals found that an attorney who acted as a mediator between his own homeowner clients and a construction business owner was potentially liable for legal malpractice because he did not fully and fairly disclose to the business owner that he did not intend to be entirely impartial as a mediator. While the court ultimately found the error harmless, it emphasized the importance of complete disclosure and said that a "party to mediation may well give more weight to the suggestions of the mediator if under the belief that the mediator is neutral." Id. at 365.

Can you identify the rationale for these decisions? Compare the rule on conflicts of interest in the Model Standards of Conduct for Mediators and that of the CPR-Georgetown Commission on Ethics and Standards in ADR Proposed Model Rule of Professional Conduct for the Lawyer as Third Party Neutral (CPR-Georgetown Model Rule) (*http://www.cpradr.org/Portals/0/CPRGeorge-ModelRule.pdf*) below. The CPR-Georgetown Model Rule, promulgated in 2002 after many years of deliberation, was proposed for adoption to regulate conduct of lawyers serving as neutrals.

MODEL STANDARDS OF CONDUCT FOR MEDIATORS **Standard 3. Conflicts of Interest**	CPR-GEORETOWN MODEL RULE **4.5.4: Conflicts of Interest**
A. A mediator shall avoid a conflict of interest or the appearance of a conflict of interest during and after a mediation. A conflict of interest can arise from involvement by a mediator with the subject matter of the dispute or from any relationship between a mediator and any mediation participant, whether past or present, personal or professional, that reasonably raises a question of a mediator's impartiality.	(a) Disqualification of Lawyer-Neutrals (1) A lawyer who is serving as a third-party neutral shall not, during the course of an ADR proceeding, seek to establish any financial, business, representational, neutral or personal relationship with or acquire an interest in, any party, entity or counsel who is involved in the matter in which the lawyer is participating as a neutral, unless all parties consent after full disclosure.
B. A mediator shall make a reasonable inquiry to determine whether there are any facts that a reasonable individual would consider likely to create a potential or actual conflict of interest for a mediator. A mediator's actions necessary to accomplish a reasonable inquiry into potential conflicts of interest may vary based on practice context.	(2) A lawyer who has served as a third-party neutral shall not subsequently represent any party to the ADR proceeding (in which the lawyer-neutral served as a neutral) in the same or a substantially related matter, unless all parties consent after full disclosure.
C. A mediator shall disclose, as soon as practicable, all actual and potential conflicts of interest that are reasonably known to the mediator and could reasonably be seen as raising a question about the mediator's impartiality. After disclosure, if all parties agree, the mediator may proceed with the mediation.	(3) A lawyer who has served as a third-party neutral shall not subsequently represent a party adverse to a former ADR party where the lawyer-neutral has acquired information protected by confidentiality under this Model Rule, without the consent of the former ADR party.
D. If a mediator learns any fact after accepting a mediation that raises a question with respect to that mediator's service creating a potential or actual conflict of interest, the mediator shall disclose it as quickly as practicable. After disclosure, if all parties agree, the mediator may proceed with the mediation.	(4) Where the circumstances might reasonably create the appearance that the neutral had been influenced in the ADR process by the anticipation or expectation of a subsequent relationship or interest, a lawyer who has served as a third-party neutral shall not subsequently acquire an interest in or represent a party to the ADR proceeding in a substantially unrelated matter for a period of one year or other reasonable period of time under the circumstances, unless all parties consent after full disclosure.
E. If a mediator's conflict of interest might reasonably be viewed as undermining the integrity of the mediation, a mediator shall withdraw from or decline to proceed with the mediation regardless of the expressed desire or agreement of the parties to the contrary.	

F. Subsequent to a mediation, a mediator shall not establish another relationship with any of the participants in any matter that would raise questions about the integrity of the mediation. When a mediator develops personal or professional relationships with parties, other individuals or organizations following a mediation in which they were involved, the mediator should consider factors such as time elapsed following the mediation, the nature of the relationships established, and services offered when determining whether the relationships might create a perceived or actual conflict of interest.

(b) Imputation of Conflicts to Affiliated Lawyers and Removing Imputation
(1) If a lawyer is disqualified by section (a), no lawyer who is affiliated with that lawyer shall knowingly undertake or continue representation in any substantially related or unrelated matter unless the personally disqualified lawyer is adequately screened from any participation in the matter; is apportioned no fee from the matter; and timely and adequate notice of the screening has been provided to all affected parties and tribunals, provided that no material confidential information about any of the parties to the ADR proceeding has been communicated by the personally disqualified lawyer to the affiliated lawyer or that lawyer's firm. . . .
(d) If a lawyer serves as a neutral at the request of a court, public agency or other group for a de minimis period and pro bono publico, the firm with which the lawyer is associated is not subject to imputation under section (b).

These rules and cases make service as a mediator more complicated in the United States than in a developing country where, in some situations, a village elder (who probably knows everyone in town) is called on to serve in the mediator's role.

> ### Problem 8-12.   *What Do the Experts Think?*
> Imagine a situation where a colleague asks you whether she can accept an appointment as an estate administrator where, after serving as a mediator, the parties to the mediation ask the mediator to take on this role. After answering yourself, see what the experts say by looking at the National Clearinghouse for Mediation Ethics Opinions created by the ABA Section of Dispute Resolution: *http://www.abanet.org/dispute/clearinghouse.html* and search for: NC-2008-15.

2. Mediator Liability and Immunity

What happens to a mediator who breaches an ethical duty?

Mediators operating under the umbrella of a court-annexed or court-sponsored ADR program may be protected by quasi-judicial immunity. In Wagshal v. Foster,

28 F.3d 1249 (D.C. 1994), the court held that a mediator's actions in communicating to the judge — and breaching confidentiality prescribed for his role — when he recused himself from a case were within the scope of his official duties and hence entitled to absolute immunity. Some scholars and practitioners feel that mediators should not enjoy immunity; rather, like other professionals, they should be liable for malpractice. Professor Michael Moffitt argues that "a mediator who engages in egregious behavior, violates contractual or statutory obligations, or breaches separately articulated duties should enjoy no legal or de facto immunity from lawsuits."[6] Similarly, well-known mediator Jeff Kichaven argues that mediators should not absolve themselves from liability for their own poor performance in agreements to mediate, but rather, like other professionals, should be responsible for malpractice and carry appropriate insurance.

Even absent immunity, there are other ways in which mediators are virtually immune from liability. Because there are no bright-line standards for mediator conduct, it is difficult to prove that a mediator has been negligent. A party may not be able to establish that an unfavorable settlement amounts to an actionable injury or appropriate damages for that injury. Further, parties often agree in their agreements to mediate to hold mediators harmless from future actions. Finally, these hurdles are compounded by the evidentiary restrictions related to confidentiality discussed earlier in this chapter.

3. Unauthorized Practice of Law

Model Standard 6 urges mediators to "refrain from providing professional advice." This simple directive, however, is undercut by the fact that "evaluative mediation" has grown, particularly in the arena of civil court cases, and there is significant market demand for this service. There is a similar demand for mediators to bring closure to cases by assisting with agreement drafting. Both of these activities are arguably the practice of law and give rise to questions of unauthorized practice when done by a mediator.

In response to the issue of unauthorized practice, the Dispute Resolution Section of the American Bar Association has promulgated a resolution on Mediation and the Unauthorized Practice of Law (*http://www.abanet.org/dispute/webpolicy .html*), essentially defining away the issue. The statement asserts that mediation is *not* the practice of law and that mediators' discussions with parties about legal issues do not constitute legal advice. The same resolution provides that the preparation of a memorandum of understanding or a settlement agreement by a mediator, incorporating the terms of settlement specified by the parties, does not constitute the practice of law, provided that the mediator does not go beyond the party dictated terms. (A portion of this resolution is in Chapter 7, Problem 7-7.)

---

6. Michael Moffitt, Suing Mediators, 83 B.U. L. Rev. 147, 207 (2003).

However, Professor Carrie Menkel-Meadow argues that the evaluation of the merits of a case or the drafting of settlement agreements *is* the practice of law, and some measures should be put into place to ensure quality and competence when these services are rendered, particularly in light of the fact that mediators often enjoy quasi-judicial immunity.[7]

Lawyers who are not admitted in the jurisdiction where they are serving as representatives in mediation may also face an unauthorized practice problem. For example, in In re Non-Member of State Bar of Arizona, 152 P.3d 1183 (Ariz. 2007), a lawyer who was licensed to practice in Florida and Virginia was found to have engaged in unauthorized practice of law by representing sellers in a private mediation of a real estate transaction dispute in Arizona.

4. Attorney Representative and Mediator Malpractice

For the most part a lawyer representative's ethical duties in mediation will track his duties as a negotiator when there is no mediator. A lawyer cannot misrepresent a material fact, but there remains room for "puffing and bluffing" in mediated negotiations. Lawyers must be as diligent in mediation as they are in other areas of legal service and follow the Rules of Professional Conduct. For example, an attorney was found in violation of the rules of professional conduct where he arrived an hour late at two mediation sessions and was unprepared. Attorney Grievance Comm'n of Md. v. Steinberg, 910 A.2d 429 (Md. 2006). Can you think of any other ethical responsibilities a lawyer representing a party in a mediation should have, that might be different from a representative role in litigation?

Claims of mediator misconduct are most likely to come up in the context of parties trying to avoid an agreement made in mediation. For example, in Vitakis v. Valchine, 793 So. 2d 1094 (Fla. Dist. Ct. App. 2001), a mediator's alleged misconduct in a court-ordered mediation created an exception to the general rule that coercion and duress by a third party is insufficient to invalidate an agreement between principals. The mediator's alleged misconduct included: telling the wife that she would never get custody of her embryos, that he would report to the judge that she caused the settlement to fail, that her litigation costs would consume any benefits she might receive from mediation, and placing her under extreme time pressure. While, on remand, the trial court did not find that the allegations of mediator misconduct were supported and upheld the settlement agreement, the case stands for the proposition that the court has inherent power to maintain the integrity of its processes, and mediator's must follow ethical guidelines.

Multiple models of mediation and mediation's rapid growth raise concerns about maintaining a core consistency to the process and safeguarding consumers. At

---

7. Carrie Menkel-Meadow, Is Mediation the Practice of Law?, 14 Alternatives 57 (1996).

the same time, proponents of mediation want to preserve its flexibility and creativity. For one attempt to specify some general principles of "ethical practice" in this new field, Professor Carrie Menkel-Meadow has proposed a "credo" of basic principles for mediators and neutral consensus builders or facilitators. She suggests that all third-party neutrals should:

- insure broad party and "stakeholder" participation
- provide opportunities for participants to agree on procedural and ground rules, as well as on decision rules for agreements
- encourage participant recognition of both individual and joint needs and interests
- encourage parties to express reasons and justifications for their views, needs, and offers
- facilitate creative and tailored solutions to meet parties' needs and objectives
- provide a place of fair hearing and respect for all parties
- facilitate capacity building of parties to negotiate on their own behalf
- consider the practicality and enforceability of agreements reached
- be themselves free from bias and conflicts of interests and
- avoid unjust, unfair, or unconscionable agreements, wherever possible.[8]

Problem 8-13. *Are There Limits to What Can Be Mediated?*

Seventeen-year-old Ziba and her 44-year-old husband Ahmed, who have been married for four years, have come to you for mediation. They have two sons, ages three and two. Ziba wants a divorce, but, like her husband, is anxious to remain part of the local mosque and surrounding community. To that end, Ziba and Ahmed met with their Imam to learn how to resolve their marriage contract in accord with Islamic law.

Their Imam advised them that while a husband can obtain a divorce for any reason, he is obliged to support his children until they reach the age of majority, regardless of who has primary custody. In addition he is obliged to pay the amount stipulated in the marriage contract that must be paid if the marriage comes to an end. Ziba and Ahmed's marriage contract calls for a payment of $40,000. The Imam also tells Ziba that she cannot receive a divorce without Ahmed's consent. And, if she initiates the divorce, she will lose her right to the marriage contract payment, although Ahmed's financial obligations toward the children will still stand. As far as custody of the children goes, the young children should stay with their mother until the boys reach their seventh birthday, when custody reverts to the father.

---

8. Carrie Menkel-Meadow, The Lawyer as Consensus Builder: Ethics for a New Practice, 70 Tenn. L. Rev. 63, 106-110 (2002).

Ziba is miserable in the marriage. Ahmed is controlling and rigid in his notions of what Ziba can do, monitoring her movements and only occasionally allowing her outside. In addition, he has taken a second wife (in accord with his privileges pursuant to Islamic law) and pays little attention to both Ziba and their children. Angry and humiliated, Ziba seeks permission for the divorce from Ahmed. Ahmed says that he will not grant her request unless she forfeits her marriage dissolution payment and any other financial support for herself and agrees to give up custody of each child at age five. Ahmed says that by asking for a divorce, Ziba is demonstrating that she is an unfit mother and that his sons should thus revert to his care at the earlier age. Ahmed wants his sons raised by his female relatives.

At the mediation, Ziba capitulates and tearfully says she will waive all rights to financial support and agree to his requests regarding custody if Ahmed grants her request for a divorce. Although Ziba has agreed to relinquish her children two years earlier than traditional Islamic law would warrant, privately negotiated deviations from default rules are not uncommon. Ahmed is very unhappy with the prospect of divorce and strongly feels Ziba's behavior compromises her ability to parent. He has stated to you in private that the only reason he is not demanding immediate transfer is that he doesn't think Ziba will agree and doesn't believe he would receive support from his community. He is confident, however, that the agreement, as contemplated, is broadly supportable and within the norms of the Iranian community in which they live.

Would you help Ziba and Ahmed with their divorce?[9] Why or Why not?

The policy, legal, and ethical concerns and complexities addressed in this chapter are only a subset of all the concerns that have been raised about mediation. In Chapter 1, Owen Fiss argued that settlement may offer peace but not justice, that mediation robs our public litigation system of opportunities to clarify the law and consequently develop public values, and that power imbalances and distributional inequalities may be exacerbated in private and consensual processes. Other critics point out that ADR can (ironically) increase state control over private matters;[10] that exporting U.S.-style ADR may have unexpected adverse consequences in other cultures and may interfere with the development of the rule of law in emerging democracies;[11] that there may be process dangers for women and minorities in

---

9. Problem from Practical Ethics for Mediators (Ellen Waldman ed., Jossey-Bass 2010).
10. Richard L. Abel, The Contradictions of Informal Justice, The Politics of Informal Justice: The American Experience 270-272 (Richard L. Abel ed., 1982).
11. Laura Nader & Elisabetta Grande, Current Illusions and Delusions about Conflict Management — In Africa and Elsewhere, 27 Law & Soc. Inquiry 573 (2002).

mediation and other informal processes;[12] that mediator manipulation may be unprincipled;[13] that mediators exert more control and direction than is advertised;[14] and that some of the claims of ADR in terms of efficiency, cost-savings, and relief to court dockets may be unfounded.[15]

While grappling with these questions, keep in mind the enormous promise of mediation, a process geared towards helping parties communicate more effectively, tap into human creativity, and bring about consensual and durable resolutions. As Abraham Lincoln said in his first inaugural address: "Why should there not be a patient confidence in the ultimate justice of the people? Is there any better or equal hope in the world?"

Further Reading on Law and Mediation

James R. Coben & Peter N. Thompson, *Disputing Irony: A Systematic Look at Litigation About Mediation*, 11 Harv. Neg. L. Rev. 43 (2006).

Jonathan M. Hyman & Lela P. Love, *If Portia Were a Mediator*, 9 Clinical L. Rev. 157 (2002).

Joseph B. Stulberg, *Fairness and Mediation*, 13 Ohio St. J. on Disp. Resol. 909 (1998).

Further Reading on Informed Consent

Lela P. Love & John W. Cooley, *The Intersection of Evaluation by Mediators and Informed Consent: Warning the Unwary*, 21 Ohio St. J. on Disp. Resol. 45 (2005).

Further Reading on Evaluative Mediation

Marjorie Corman Aaron, *ADR Toolbox: The Highwire Art of Evaluation*, 14 Alternatives 62 (1996).

Deborah R. Hensler. (2000). In Search of "Good Mediation." In J. Sanders & V.L. Hamilton (Eds.), *Handbook of Justice Research in Law* (p. 231). Springer US.

Lela P. Love & Kimberlee K. Kovach, *ADR: An Eclectic Array of Processes, Rather Than One Eclectic Process*, 2000 J. Disp. Resol. 295.

Lela P. Love, *The Top Ten Reasons Why Mediators Should Not Evaluate*, 24 Fla. St. U. L. Rev. 937 (1997).

---

12. Trina Grillo, The Mediation Alternative: Process Dangers for Women, 100 Yale L.J. 1545 (1991); Gary LaFree & Christine Rack, The Effects of Participants' Ethnicity and Gender on Monetary Outcomes in Mediated and Adjudicated Civil Cases, 30 Law & Socy. Rev. 767 (1996).

13. James R. Coben, Mediation's Dirty Little Secret: Straight Talk about Mediator Manipulation and Deception, 2 J. Alt. Disp. Resol. Emp. 4 (2000).

14. David Greatbatch & Robert Dingwall, Selective Facilitation: Some Preliminary Observations on a Strategy Used by Divorce Mediators, 23 Law & Socy. Rev. 613 (1989).

15. James S. Kakalik et al., An Evaluation of Mediation and Early Neutral Evaluation under the Civil Justice Reform Act (RAND Institute for Civil Justice, 1996).

Jeffrey W. Stempel, *The Inevitability of the Eclectic: Liberating ADR from Ideology*, 2000 J. Disp. Resol. 247.

Further Reading on Mandatory Mediation

Mary G. Marcus, Walter Marcus, Nancy A. Stilwell & Neville Doherty, *To Mediate or Not to Mediate: Financial Outcomes in Mediated Versus Adversarial Divorces*, 17 Conflict Resol. Q. 143 (1999).

Further Reading on Good Faith

American Bar Association, *Resolution on Good Faith Requirements for Mediators and Mediation Advocates in Court-Mandated Mediation Programs*, available at *http://www.abanet.org/dispute/webpolicy.html#9/*.

Carol L. Izumi & Homer C. La Rue, *Prohibiting "Good Faith" Reports Under the Uniform Mediation Act: Keeping the Adjudication Camel Out of the Mediation Tent*, 2003 J. Disp. Resol. 67.

Kimberlee K. Kovach, *Good Faith in Mediation — Requested, Recommended or Required? A New Ethic*, 38 S. Tex. L. Rev. 575 (1997).

Edward Sherman, *Court Mandated Alternative Dispute Resolution: What Form of Participation Should Be Required?*, 46 SMU L. Rev. 2079 (1993).

Maureen A. Weston, *Checks on Participant Conduct in Compulsory ADR: Reconciling the Tension in the Need for Good-Faith Participation, Autonomy, and Confidentiality*, 76 Ind. L.J. 591 (2001).

Michael Young, *Mediation Gone Wild: How Three Minutes Put an ADR Party Behind Bars*, 25 Alternatives 97 (2010).

Further Reading on Confidentiality

Ellen E. Deason, *Enforcing Mediated Settlement Agreements: Contract Law Collides with Confidentiality*, 35 U.C. Davis L. Rev. 33 (2001).

Scott H. Hughes, *The Uniform Mediation Act: To the Spoiled Go the Privileges*, 85 Marq. L. Rev. 9 (2001).

Pamela A. Kentra, *Hear No Evil, See No Evil, Speak No Evil: The Intolerable Conflict for Attorney-Mediators between the Duty to Maintain Mediation Confidentiality and the Duty to Report Fellow Attorney Misconduct*, 1997 B.Y.U. L. Rev. 715 (1997).

Further Reading on Ethics

Phyllis Bernard & Bryant Garth (Eds.). (2002). *Dispute Resolution Ethics: A Comprehensive Guide*. American Bar Association.

Carrie Menkel-Meadow, *Ethics and Professionalism in Non-Adversarial Lawyering*, 27 FLA. ST. U. L. REV. 153 (1999).

Carrie Menkel-Meadow, *Ethics in ADR: The Many "Cs" of Professional Responsibility and Dispute Resolution*, 28 FORDHAM URB. L.J. 979 (2001).

Carrie Menkel-Meadow, *Is Mediation the Practice of Law?*, 14 ALTERNATIVES 57 (1996).

Carrie Menkel-Meadow, *The Lawyer as Consensus Builder: Ethics for a New Practice*, 70 TENN. L. REV. 63 (2002).

Robert Moberly, *Ethical Standards for Court-Appointed Mediators and Florida's Mandatory Mediation Experiment*, 21 FLA. ST. U. L. REV. 701 (1994).

Scott Peppet, *ADR Ethics*, 54 J. LEGAL EDUC. 72 (2004).

Scott Peppet, *Contractarian Economics and Mediation Ethics: The Case for Customizing Neutrality Through Contingent Fee Mediation*, 82 TEX. L. REV. 227 (2003).

Charles Pou, Jr., *"Embracing Limbo": Thinking About Rethinking Dispute Resolution Ethics*, 108 PENN. ST. L. REV. 199 (2003).

Leonard Riskin, *Toward New Standards for the Neutral Lawyer in Mediation*, 26 ARIZ. L. REV. 329 (1984).

Further Reading on Mediator Immunity

Scott H. Hughes, *Mediator Immunity: The Misguided and Inequitable Shifting of Risk*, 83 OR. L. REV. 107 (2004).

Judith Maute, *Public Values and Private Justice: A Case for Mediator Accountability*, 4 GEO. J. LEGAL ETHICS 503 (1991).

Michael Moffitt, *Suing Mediators*, 83 B.U. L. REV. 147 (2003).

Chapter 9 Arbitration: Concepts and Models

Equity bids us: to settle a dispute by negotiation and not by force; to prefer arbitration to litigation — for an arbitrator goes by the equity of a case, a judge by the strict law, and arbitration was invented with the express purpose of securing full power for equity.

— Aristotle

A. AN INTRODUCTION TO ARBITRATION

Arbitration is a process in which a third party who is not acting as a judge renders a decision in a dispute. Disputants have used arbitration for many thousands of years. Before societies had created the kinds of courts and judges with which we are familiar, disputants often brought their problems to a wise elder who helped them work things out. Indeed, in the biblical story when two women asked King Solomon to decide which of them could keep the baby, he acted not as an officially appointed judge, deciding the matter according to predetermined rules and procedures, but rather as an arbitrator to whom they voluntarily brought their dispute. Similarly, various ancient societies used arbitration not only to resolve disputes within a given society, but also to resolve border disputes and other issues between two or more nations. This practice was common in ancient Greece. Arbitration was also used for commercial disputes in the Anglo-Saxon and early Norman periods in Europe.

Today, arbitration is still commonly used both domestically and internationally. Indeed, it is used more frequently than litigation to resolve international business disputes and many other types of commercial and labor matters.

Beyond the simple definition of arbitration articulated above, there are immense variations among arbitration processes. Thus, while one often hears that arbitration is quicker and cheaper than litigation, this will not always be true. Perhaps the biggest mistake a student of arbitration can make is to assume that all arbitration is the same, or even similar. The nature of arbitration varies, often predictably, depending on the subject matter of the dispute. A person who is familiar with labor arbitration does not necessarily know what to expect from commercial arbitration, and a person who is familiar with commercial arbitration may be surprised to learn how arbitration works in the diamond industry. International and domestic arbitrations may look different from one another, and even international arbitration varies substantially. The differences among the many forms of arbitration are crucial because the advantages and disadvantages of arbitration depend on the nature of the process.

For example, a critical distinction exists between binding and non-binding arbitration. Binding arbitration is a process whereby the third party renders a decision that is final and binding on the disputants. Although a disputant who is dissatisfied with the award may have some opportunity to vacate that award, typically it is more difficult to vacate an arbitral award than it is to overturn a judicial decision on appeal. In contrast, non-binding arbitral awards can be merely advisory opinions. If either party is dissatisfied with the award, the party can reject it and elect to proceed with litigation or some other form of dispute resolution. When the non-binding award is not challenged, however, it will become binding. Binding arbitration is far more common than non-binding arbitration and is the focus of Chapters 9-11. We will discuss non-binding arbitration later, in Chapter 12, on hybrid processes.

Arbitration also varies according to its source of origin. Most arbitration is elected privately by the disputing parties, usually in a contract before the specific dispute has arisen. Such contracts are called "pre-dispute arbitration agreements." In the United States pre-dispute arbitration agreements can be broken down into two main subcategories: those that are negotiated, knowingly, between two businesses or knowledgeable persons; and those that are imposed by a business on a consumer or employee in a boilerplate nonnegotiable contract. As is discussed infra, in Chapter 10, some commentators argue that it is unjust, unfair, or even unconstitutional for binding arbitration to be imposed in this manner on consumers, employees, or other less powerful parties. Alternatively, some arbitration is mandated by a statute, court rule, or treaty. In the United States the vast majority of arbitration that is governmentally mandated is non-binding rather than binding arbitration, as courts would typically find it unconstitutional to mandate binding arbitration by statute, rule, or treaty.

In addition to these critical distinctions, there are many other important variations in the nature of arbitration. First, arbitrations vary depending on the choice of arbitrator. Sometimes a single arbitrator is used; other times a panel of three or possibly more arbitrators is used. At times the arbitrators are kings, former judges, or lawyers; but often arbitrators are instead chosen on the basis of business expertise or common sense knowledge. In some cases the arbitrators are all expected to be completely neutral, but in other contexts (rarely outside the United States) each side picks an arbitrator who is to some degree an advocate for that side's position. The two partial arbitrators pick a third neutral arbitrator who chairs the panel.

Second, the degree of formality within arbitration varies substantially. One of the key features of arbitration is that the disputants determine their own rules of procedure and evidence; thus it is not surprising that the nature of these rules may vary. Traditionally, arbitration was far less formal than litigation. Rules of evidence were relaxed, if used at all. Parties could represent themselves rather than rely on a lawyer. A minimal amount of discovery or pre-arbitration preparation was used, and arbitrators issued few, if any, pre-hearing rulings. While such informality is still common in many contexts, in some settings arbitration is now virtually indistinguishable from litigation in terms of its formality. Arbitrations can involve extensive discovery; arbitrators can rule on numerous pre-hearing motions; arbitral hearings can be extremely formal, legalistic, and time-consuming; and lawyers can make arguments and introduce testimony and exhibits in arbitration just as they might at a trial. Occasionally, class actions have even been used in arbitration. And, while arbitration is often a private process, it may be public as well.

Third, there is no set rule on how arbitration decisions are announced. Most arbitral awards are written, but some are oral. Among written awards, some are extremely short and simply state which disputant prevailed; others include lengthy reasoned analysis. Similarly, whereas many arbitral awards are private and distributed only to the disputants, others are published.

Fourth, the way in which arbitrations are administered varies substantially. The administrator of the arbitration is the person or group who performs such tasks as helping to select the arbitrator, arranging the location, and exchanging any pre-hearing documents. Binding arbitration is frequently administered by a special arbitral organization. Some of the best-known U.S. providers include the American Arbitration Association (AAA), JAMS,[1] the National Arbitration Forum (NAF),[2] and the National Association of Securities Dealers (NASD). Also, the CPR Institute for Dispute Resolution,[3] while not technically a provider because it does not "administer" hearings, offers rules and provides names of potential arbitrators.

Fifth, there are multiple possible conceptions of the appropriate arbitral role. Should arbitrators apply law to facts, as judges do? Should they simply strive for fair solutions or solutions that will maximize disputants' satisfaction? Alternatively, in "final offer" arbitrations, arbitrators are required to choose between the positions of one side or the other, rather than to come up with an independent decision. Below, noted jurisprude Lon Fuller discusses alternative conceptions of the arbitrator's proper role. (As you will recall from Chapter 1, Fuller has also opined on the appropriate "morality" of each of the other major dispute resolution processes.)

 Lon L. Fuller, **COLLECTIVE BARGAINING AND THE ARBITRATOR**

1963 Wis. L. Rev. 3, 3-4

One conception of the role of the arbitrator is that he is essentially a judge. His job is to do justice according to the rules imposed by the parties' contract, leaving the chips to fall where they may. He decides the controversy entirely on the basis of arguments and proofs presented to him "in open court" with the parties confronting one another face to face. He does not attempt to mediate or conciliate, for to

---

1. "JAMS" originally stood for Judicial Arbitration and Mediation Service, but the organization is now known only by its acronym.
2. NAF was recently accused of misconduct and subsequently shrank the scope of its business. This is discussed in more detail in Chapter 11.B.2.
3. "CPR" originally stood for Center for Public Resources, but the organization is now known only by its acronym.

do so would be to compromise his role as an adjudicator. He will strictly forego any private communication with the parties after the hearing. . . .

The opposing conception expects the arbitrator to adapt his procedures to the case at hand. Indeed, in its more extreme form it rejects the notion that his powers for good should be restrained at all by procedural limitations. By this view the arbitrator has a roving commission to straighten things out, the immediate controversy marking the occasion for, but not the limits of, his intervention. If the formal submission leaves fringes of dispute unsettled, he will gladly undertake to tidy them up. If the arguments at the hearing leave him in doubt as to the actual causes of the dispute, or as to what the parties really expect of him, he will not scruple to hold private consultations for his further enlightenment. If he senses the possibility of a settlement, he will not hesitate to step down from his role as arbitrator to assume that of mediator. If despite his conciliatory skill negotiations become sticky, he will follow Harry Shulman's advice and — with an admonitory glance toward the chair just vacated — "exert the gentle pressure of a threat of decision" to induce agreement.[4]

B. THE ATTRACTIONS AND LIMITS OF ARBITRATION

Given the tremendous variation within the dispute resolution technique known as arbitration, disputants are attracted to arbitration for a range of reasons. In fact, arbitration is probably most popular precisely because of its flexibility. To a large extent, disputants can design exactly the process they want under the rubric of arbitration. Disputants who are primarily looking for a speedy, low-cost dispute resolution technique can meet these goals by making their arbitration quite informal and virtually nonappealable. Disputants who want a decision maker with a particular background or expertise can write those requirements into the arbitration agreement. If disputants want a private, nonpublished decision, they can call for that in their agreement; but if the disputants prefer a process that is open to the public and results in a reasoned written award, that too can be arranged. In the international arena, arbitration is desirable because it allows disputants to pick a forum and decision makers who are likely more predisposed to be neutral than the home court of any disputant. Also, as a result of international treaties, arbitral awards are often more enforceable internationally than is a court decision. Thus, depending on the context, disputants may choose arbitration over other forms of dispute resolution because, for example, it can potentially be cheap, quick, private, neutral, expert, and/or enforceable. The disputants can also set up a process that, as compared to litigation, is more likely to restore or improve future relationships. Binding arbitration offers the additional benefit of finality. In contrast to mediation or negotiation, which may or may not resolve a particular dispute, one is assured that binding arbitration will result in a decision that ends the immediate controversy.

---

4. Harry Shulman, Reason, Contract, and Law in Labor Relations, 68 Harv. L. Rev. 999, 1023 (1955).

From the public standpoint, arbitration can be advantageous precisely because the disputants themselves find it desirable. In addition, to the extent disputes are resolved privately, the public saves money it otherwise would have expended on courthouses and judges.

As this book emphasizes, no dispute resolution technique is appropriate for all disputes all of the time. Thus, depending on the terms of arbitration, some disputants may find arbitration too costly or too slow; they may prefer a more public forum; they may regret the loss of opportunity for full appeal; or they may opt for a process, such as mediation, that leaves the final determination in their own hands. Where one side uses a contract of adhesion to compel an opponent to arbitrate, that opponent may find that the stronger party has designed arbitration terms that create a disadvantage for the opponent. From a public standpoint, the desirability of arbitration often turns not only on the type of arbitration, but also on the particular disputes that are being arbitrated. Even when private parties find arbitration desirable, the public may prefer to have certain disputes resolved in a public forum such as litigation. Arbitration is sometimes criticized because it typically allows decisions to be made privately and thus usually does not create public precedents that are important to support the development of law and inculcation of societal values.

> **Problem 9-1.** *Differentiating Arbitration and Mediation*
>
> Imagine that you are a new associate at a law firm. One of the partners says, "Hey kid, I understand you recently took a course in alternative dispute resolution. I have to admit, I am old school, and I have never quite understood the difference between arbitration and mediation. Can you explain it to me?" What would you say to the partner?

C. EXAMPLES OF ARBITRATION

Section A provided a list of the dimensions along which arbitration may vary. This section makes the discussion more concrete, illustrating how arbitration is used in a variety of contexts. At the same time, remember that while it may be traditional to use particular variations of arbitration in particular contexts, it is at least theoretically possible to use any of the variations in any of the contexts.

1. Commercial Arbitration

Historically, arbitration has been extremely popular as a method of resolving disputes within particular industries. In medieval Europe, guilds often used arbitration. More recently, particular specialized U.S. industries such as construction and shipping have often chosen to resolve disputes through arbitration rather than litigation. In these contexts, arbitration was especially attractive because it offered expertise, speed, and privacy that would not be available in court. Arbitrators, who were familiar with the industry in question but were not necessarily lawyers, could use industry norms to resolve disputes. Often the claims would be resolved on the basis of technical knowledge and industry practice, rather than law. Edward Brunet calls this the "folklore" version of commercial arbitration. While arbitration is still very common among businesses, Brunet points out in the excerpt below that the modern contractual version of commercial arbitration can be far more judicialized and formal than the "folklore" version of arbitration.

One important variation among commercial arbitration awards in the United States has to do with whether those awards contain extensive recitation of the facts and legal reasoning underlying the dispute. Typically, commercial awards are neither reasoned nor published. That is, the decision usually simply states who won and who lost, and how much money (if any) the respondent owes to the claimant. Thus, in most cases the arbitrators do not provide the kind of written analysis that would be afforded by a judge. In particular industries, however, arbitrators may choose to write more extensive decisions.

Commercial arbitration clauses typically are based on sample clauses provided by such providers as the American Arbitration Association, JAMS, or the National Arbitration Forum. Such rules typically incorporate rules prepared by the provider for use in the commercial context. Alternatively, drafters of commercial arbitration clauses can come up with their own clause and/or rules.

   Edward Brunet, **REPLACING FOLKLORE ARBITRATION WITH A CONTRACT MODEL OF ARBITRATION**

74 Tul. L. Rev. 39, 42-47 (1999)

Unlike the competing models of arbitration, folklore arbitration is both a mythical perception and a reality. The oversimplified perception is that folklore arbitration is the only type of arbitration that exists. It is speedy, cheap, informal, and equitable. In arbitration orthodoxy, the results of folklore arbitration leave no room for the courts because arbitration awards are final. The partners to an arbitration contract have intentionally opted out of the court system. The expert arbitrator fashions a result by applying Solomon-like principles of equity and eschewing the rigidity of doctrinal formalism. Folklore arbitrators decide disputes based upon factual context and avoid application of substantive legal rules.

The historical roots of folklore arbitration lie in the use of arbitration to resolve intra-industry disputes in the late nineteenth and early twentieth centuries. Garment or textile industry arbitration, one of the earliest industry-wide examples of arbitration use, is illustrative. Under this procedure, two textile merchants, each of whom had previously contracted with the other, agreed to a supply contract containing an arbitration clause. While each party was pleased to employ a simple, informal process that would probably be a less expensive way to resolve a dispute than conventional litigation, it is likely that the popularity of folklore arbitration grew because of the selection of the arbitrator. Rather than allowing a judge, a stranger who knew little or nothing about the matter, to resolve their dispute, the parties selected one of their own fellow textile merchants to be their arbitrator. This selection of a trusted and expert decision maker dominated the arbitration process. The choice of an intra-industry arbitrator guaranteed a knowledgeable decision maker who was likely to rule on the equities of the factual context in an informal manner. The selection of a knowledgeable expert with credentials within the same group also satisfied a strong need for industry self-governance.

In early twentieth-century textile arbitration, the facts were likely to matter much more than the law to the nonlawyer expert experienced in the textile business of each of the parties. Law played a truly subordinate role. While it is possible that the arbitrator could use the law as a basis for decision, the reality was that the parties selected the arbitrator hoping and even knowing that this particular arbitrator was prone to make equitable, fact-based decisions. Compromise results, fair to each party, were the order of the day and played a major role in the ability of arbitrators to obtain repeat business and the parties' selection of the arbitration process. . . .

Privacy is also a prime characteristic of folklore arbitration. The textile businesses that opted for arbitration desired as little publicity as possible regarding any future controversies. Just as their contract was a private matter, any disputes between the textile merchants were conducted in private. The disputants had no wish to conduct their disputes in public where negative publicity might occur. The public nature of courts and juries was incompatible with a strong desire for privacy.

In the historic folklore arbitrations, informal procedures dominated. There was little or no discovery. Evidence rules were inapplicable, in part because the expert arbitrator selected by the partners was not a lawyer. The fact that these lay arbitrators were untrained in the law helps explain why there were no written opinions. In addition, the need for private dispute resolution made formal written opinions (which would generate publicity) seem imprudent. . . .

While folklore arbitration still exists, it is far less common than thought and increasingly difficult to detect. Instead, parties now contract to select a form of arbitration that can often be a very different process than folklore arbitration.

Today, many arbitrations resemble litigation. The characteristics of what some may label a "judicialized model of arbitration" include (1) routine discovery, (2) motion practice, (3) application of substantive legal rules, (4) written, discursive awards with findings of fact and conclusions of law or reasons, and (5) enhanced judicial review pursuant to arbitration clauses that require courts to evaluate awards for legal error. Such procedures are a far cry from the historical, hypothetical textile arbitration.

The evolution of modern arbitration to include judicialized features has been accomplished through contract. In a sense, a "contract model" of arbitration has emerged in which the parties craft their own private disputing procedures. The parties now exercise party autonomy by writing their own style of arbitration into the agreement. They select the procedure they think appropriate and need not follow the template of prior arbitration adversaries.

This is not to suggest that the contract model of arbitration bears no resemblance to folklore arbitration. Contract model arbitration continues to draw on selected elements of folklore arbitration. Arbitrators in a contract model arbitration are still likely to temper their awards with the rough justice of equity. Similarly, contract model arbitration and folklore arbitration share the use of the expert arbitrator who is knowledgeable in the subject matter of the dispute and avoids the potential arbitrariness of a jury. Contract model arbitration is not totally differentiated from folklore arbitration. These models share a place in the continuum of arbitration and are not always polar opposites.

Folklore arbitration, an agreement to arbitrate on the assumption that the arbitration procedures will be settled and definite without any particular contract language setting forth specific arbitration features, can still be found. Its existence may be due to the contracting parties' lack of experience or knowledge regarding arbitration. . . . Experienced parties with a background in arbitration are more likely to carefully constrain the ambiguity inherent in a loose agreement to "arbitrate."

Even parties who dislike the expense of a judicialized type of arbitration may employ the contract model. For example, contracting parties who want the features of folklore arbitration can agree to prohibit discovery, set a quick hearing date, and forbid the arbitrator from holding a preliminary hearing or issuing a written decision containing reasons. By specifying their procedural desires, the parties constrain the discretion of the arbitrator and the arbitration-sponsoring organization.

Of course, if courts held to a static folklore model of arbitration, arbitration parties could not contract for procedures that differ from folklore arbitration. . . . [T]he Supreme Court has interpreted the Federal Arbitration Act to make parties the masters of their own disputes and to create a framework in which the courts enforce the procedures selected in the disputants' arbitration clause.

Problem 9-2.   *Drafting a Commercial Arbitration Clause*

You represent a company, Barging Inc., which ships grain up and down the Mississippi River. Barging Inc. wants you to draft a form contract that will be used as the starting point for the contracts Barging Inc. enters into with the various grain shippers along the river. The president of Barging Inc. has asked you to consider (1) what are the pros and cons of including an arbitration clause and (2) if an arbitration clause is used, what should it require?

---

2. International Arbitration

Arbitration is used internationally in a variety of ways. Most frequently, international arbitration grows out of commercial disputes. Sometimes arbitration is also used internationally to resolve political disputes among two or more countries, or among feuding groups within and among countries. Although the line between commercial and public international arbitration sometimes blurs, it is still useful to discuss international arbitration in both categories.

a. International Commercial Arbitration

Internationally, most business transactions are based on contracts that include binding arbitration clauses. To understand why international arbitration is so popular, you must understand why companies find international litigation so undesirable.

International commercial litigation is highly problematic for many reasons. First, disputes often arise regarding what jurisdiction can appropriately hear the claim. Disputants are likely to be very suspicious of a hearing held in the national court of their opponent and thus are likely to fight lengthy expensive battles over what forum is appropriate. Apart from the risk of losing and having to appear in a hostile forum, fights over such issues as sovereignty and jurisdiction are often very expensive. Sometimes parties end up litigating their disputes in multiple fora concurrently. Even once a single forum is selected, travel costs to that forum are often high. Second, disputes often arise with respect to choice of substantive and procedural law. If a contractual dispute arises between French and Egyptian companies with respect to a construction project in Saudi Arabia, whose law of contracts governs? What rules of evidence and procedure are used? Choice-of-law clauses can solve some but not all of these issues. Third, how can judgments obtained in one country's court be enforced in another country? Assuming that an Egyptian company prevails against a French company in an Egyptian court, how does that Egyptian company recover assets that are all located in France? Will or must a French court honor the Egyptian judicial decision? Most often, one country is not required by treaty or any other provision to enforce the decisions issued by another country's court.

Arbitration offers a solution to many of these problems. Parties can use their arbitration provision to designate that the dispute be heard in a neutral or a mutually convenient location. They can also specify the qualifications and nationality of the arbitrator or panel of arbitrators. Often each disputant is permitted to select an arbitrator, and these two arbitrators together must select a third arbitrator who will chair the panel. Substantive law and procedural law can also be specified in the arbitration provision, which means that parties will have greater trust in the process and that they will spend less time and money fighting about procedural issues. Finally, although it may come as a surprise to some, a country's court is far more frequently required to enforce an arbitration award issued elsewhere than it is to enforce a similarly issued judicial decision because several existing treaties require countries' courts to enforce each others' arbitration awards. The most important of these treaties is the 1958 Convention on Recognition and Enforcement of Foreign Arbitral Awards, better known as the New York Convention, 21 U.S.T. 2517 (1970). At latest count, that Convention has been ratified by 144 countries. In contrast, while some treaties also require countries to enforce each others' judicial awards, such treaties are far less widely adopted than the New York Convention. Although international commercial parties may also select arbitration because it offers flexibility, privacy, and expertise, the primary reasons for the popularity of arbitration in the international commercial setting are the limits of international litigation as set out above.

The nature of international commercial arbitration varies substantially, depending on the terms of the arbitration agreement and rules, on the norms that exist in a particular industry, and on the nationality of the arbitrators. Some international arbitrations are resolved using the substantive laws of a particular country; some are resolved according to equitable principles, *ex aequo et bono* (in justice and fair dealing); and still others (though not too many) are resolved according to an international commercial common law, *lex mercatoria* (mercantile law). International commercial arbitrations can be fairly formal. Indeed, some arbitrators and attorneys from outside the United States complain that U.S. litigators are bringing their concepts of cross-examination and discovery to the world of international arbitration. Typically, awards issued in international commercial arbitrations are written and reasoned.

International commercial arbitrations are often handled by well-established arbitration providers. The best known and respected is the Paris-based International Chamber of Commerce, which sponsors arbitrations all over the world. Other well-known international arbitration providers include the World Bank's International Center for the Settlement of Investment Disputes, the London Court of International Arbitration, the China International Economic Trade Arbitration Commission, the Arbitration Institute of the Stockholm Chamber of Commerce, the Cairo Regional Center for International Commercial Arbitration, the International Centre for Dispute Resolution (an arm of the American Arbitration Association), and the Permanent Court of Arbitration.

The United Nations has played an important role in furthering the use of international commercial arbitration. The U.N. Commission on International Trade Law (UNCITRAL) has issued a Model Law on International Commercial Arbitration, designed to be implemented by countries throughout the world and thereby support and harmonize the use of arbitration. In addition, UNCITRAL has issued a set of arbitration rules that disputants may choose to adopt in ad hoc commercial arbitrations. These rules seek to harmonize conflicts that have arisen traditionally between companies from countries with conflicting traditions or economic interests, and have proved quite popular.

Problem 9-3.   *Drafting an International Commercial Arbitration Provision*

You represent a U.S. construction company, Jaberini Brothers Inc., which is being hired by a Saudi Arabian general contractor to build some hotels in Saudi Arabia. Other aspects of the job (e.g., design, landscaping, interior decoration) will be done by other companies, some from other countries. Your client has asked you to review a proposed contract that includes an arbitration provision. How will you advise your client as to the pros and cons of including an arbitration provision, and what would you hope to see included in such a provision?

b. Public International Arbitration

Arbitration is also used internationally to resolve more public disputes. Several important treaties, such as the North America Free Trade Agreement (NAFTA), call for arbitration to be used to resolve certain kinds of disputes between two countries or between one country's investor and another country.

For example, in Metalclad Corp. v. United Mexican States, 40 I.L.M. 36 (Aug. 30, 2000), Metalclad, a U.S. company, alleged that respondent Mexico "interfered with its development and operation of a hazardous waste landfill" in violation of Chapter 11 of NAFTA. Pursuant to Article 1120(1)(b), Metalclad submitted the matter to be arbitrated through the offices of the ICSID. A panel of three arbitrators sitting in Vancouver, British Columbia, Canada, heard the matter over a period of several years. After reviewing a great deal of evidence and considering numerous motions, the panel found in favor of the U.S. investor, Metalclad, ruling it had not been treated fairly and equitably as required by NAFTA. The panel ordered that Mexico pay Metalclad $16.7 million.

Arbitration was also used to resolve claims arising out of the disputes that arose between U.S. and Iranian interests in the 1980s after the hostage crisis and the confiscation of assets that followed. Pursuant to the 1981 Algiers Accords, such claims were resolved through arbitration held at The Hague in the Netherlands. In 20 years this special tribunal has awarded more than $2 billion, likely operating more efficiently than would have been possible in national courts, and also avoiding the political tensions that would have been caused through alternative attempts to recover confiscated assets.

Two countries involved in a dispute have sometimes agreed to arbitration on an ad hoc basis to resolve land disputes or other matters. For example, Ethiopia and Eritrea arbitrated a border dispute, which had previously led to war, before a special Boundary Commission under the auspices of the Permanent Court of Arbitration. The commission consisted of two members appointed by each country, together with a neutral chair. Following nine years of hearings the Commission issued final damages awards in April 2009, and the two countries are still at peace.

Another well-known public international arbitration involved a colorful dispute between France and New Zealand over the destruction of a Greenpeace ship, the Rainbow Warrior. In the 1980s, to protest France's engagement in nuclear testing, the activist organization Greenpeace dispatched the Rainbow Warrior to observe the testing being conducted on some French South Pacific islands. Disturbed by the adverse publicity, France sent two spies to New Zealand where the Rainbow Warrior was in port being repaired. The spies, posing as a married couple, blew up the ship and also killed a Dutch national who was on board at the time. The incident led to a major dispute between France and New Zealand, which was ultimately brought to then U.N. Secretary-General Perez de Cuellar as arbitrator for resolution. He issued an award requiring France to apologize, pay $7 million compensation to New Zealand, withdraw economic sanctions it had previously imposed, and require its two spies to spend three years in prison on the French island of Hao, in the South Pacific. The decision also required both countries to agree to arbitrate any future disputes that arose out of the U.N.-initiated agreement.[5] Shortly after issuance of the U.N. decision, France withdrew both its agents from Hao, and New Zealand initiated arbitration. In 1990 an arbitral tribunal issued an award holding that while France had clearly violated the 1986 agreement, the panel could not order specific performance. Instead, the tribunal ordered that France pay $2 million into a France-New Zealand friendship fund. Rainbow Warrior Arbitration (New Zealand v. France), 82 I.L.R. 499 (1990). Although it may be more difficult to enforce arbitration awards arising out of political disputes than commercial awards, in this case at least the country complied with the arbitrator's order.

Problem 9-4.   *Using Arbitration to Resolve International Boundary Disputes*

For many years fishermen from Maine and Canada have argued over fishing boundary lines between the United States and Canada. You are an attorney in the U.S. Department of State, which has been asked (again) by U.S. fishermen to get involved in trying to resolve this dispute. From the government's perspective what do you see as the pros and cons of trying to take this dispute to an international tribunal of some sort where it would be arbitrated?

---

c. International Arbitrators

As international arbitral institutions and rule systems have proliferated and evolved, so have the actors. European lawyers and academics dominated the field of international arbitration for a long time, but recent studies note the increasing competition between lawyers and decision makers from different legal regimes, including legal systems (common law versus civil law) and competitions over economic hegemonies (American versus European or Third World practice, customs, rules, and players).

In the following excerpt, Yves Dezalay, a French sociologist, and Bryant Garth, an American legal scholar, report on their study of how international arbitration is changing from domination by a few "grand old men" from Europe to a younger, more "technocratic" (and more American litigation-like) generation of specialists with technical and commercial competence. Their study examines how this change will affect the nature of international arbitration.

---

5. U.N. Secretary General: Ruling Pertaining to the Differences between France and New Zealand arising from the Rainbow Warrior Affair, 26 I.L.M. 1346, 1372-1373 (1987).

Yves Dezalay & Bryant G. Garth, **DEALING IN VIRTUE:**
INTERNATIONAL COMMERCIAL ARBITRATION AND
THE CONSTRUCTION OF A TRANSNATIONAL
LEGAL ORDER

34-39 (1996)

OPPOSITIONS AND COMPLEMENTARITIES IN THE FIELD
OF INTERNATIONAL COMMERCIAL ARBITRATION

The field of international commercial arbitration is given its structure and its logic of transformation through oppositions and complementarities that we shall now begin to map. The key source of conflict, and also of transformation, is that between two generations — "grand old men" versus "technocrats." We therefore begin this section by showing what this conflict and the symbolic battles around it reveal about international commercial arbitration. . . .

Grand Old Men and Technocrats

The starting point of the generational warfare is diverging ideas of arbitral competence — the characteristics that qualify one to be an arbitrator. For the pioneers of arbitration, exemplified especially, but not only, by very senior European professors imbued with the traditional values of the European legal elites, the dominant opinion has been that arbitration should not be a profession: "Arbitration is a duty, not a career." For true independence of judgment, in the words of another senior insider, "The person who goes into this business as an arbitrator to make a living should not be encouraged." Arbitrators, they insist, should render an occasional service, provided on the basis of long experience and wisdom acquired in law, business, or public service. Those who hold this opinion are, indeed, individuals who have risen to the top of their national legal professions and gained financial independence before being asked to serve as arbitrators. . . .

To the aura or the charisma of their elders, these new arrivals oppose their specialization and technical competence. In the words of a Swiss member of the new generation, "Arbitration was characterized by a limited, small group of impeccable, outstanding professionals — characters known around the world. . . . Today I have difficulty in seeing the outstanding personality [among] a big crowd of people." Put in more aggressive terms by a member of the same cohort, an arbitrator cannot now just step in "with all . . . [the] glorious past" and provide the "great old man's opinion." Indeed, charisma is said even to be a source of error. In the words of an ICC insider, "Some of the biggest problems that we see are probably with some of the big names." Why? "They're probably just more full of themselves than other people." Furthermore, "Sometimes an eminent arbitrator feels he doesn't have to explain things." A leading figure of the younger generation thus describes his generation as "technically better equipped in procedure and substance."

They present themselves in this new generation as international arbitration professionals, and also as entrepreneurs selling their services to business practitioners, contrasting their qualities to the "amateurism" or "idealism" of their predecessors. . . .

Indeed, now that arbitration has become accepted in commercial international mores, they assert, even citing Max Weber in one instance, that the time has come for the "routinization of charisma" essential to the transition from the stage of artisans to that of mass production. This transition requires the "rationalization" of arbitration know-how.

These technocrats play key roles now in institutions like the International Chamber of Commerce, which they not only have come to direct but also have used for their education in arbitration. The quick route to arbitration expertise is through the major institutions, which hire young lawyers to administer the arbitrations. These organizations, which the pioneers used for evangelical purposes to promote arbitration, now have added a more technical involvement in the administration of the arbitrations themselves.

The large Anglo-American law firms, which dominate the international market of business law, are also central to this conflict between grand old men and technocrats. With the growth of trade and the success of the pioneers in building international arbitration, they now consider it important to include this specialty in the gamut of services that they put at the disposition of their multinational clients. The attitude of the large law firms has been to favor overtly this "banalization" and rationalization of arbitration, which permits them to introduce themselves into the closed "club" and to introduce the legal techniques that are at the basis of their preeminence. . . .

This opposition between grand old men and young technocrats — supported by Anglo-American firms — is one of the keys that permits decoding a great number of the debates and the fights — in scholarship as well as in institutions — that affect this field of practice. One controversy . . . is whether the major institutions, the ICC notably, are now too involved in the actual work of the arbitrators. A second is whether arbitration is becoming too much like litigation. The perspective of the senior generation is highly critical of both of these trends. . . .

But beyond the contest between generations about what and whose characteristics should be at the center of international commercial arbitration, this fight for power contains the true transformation that is taking place — the passage from one mode to another for the production of arbitration and the legitimation of arbitrators. As is the case for the entire field of business law, the Anglo-American model of the business enterprise and merchant competition is tending to substitute itself for the Continental model of legal artisans and corporatist control over the profession. In the same way, international commercial arbitration is moving from a small, closed group of self-regulating artisans to a more open and competitive business.

3. Labor Arbitration

Labor arbitration has evolved along a separate path from commercial arbitration in the United States. During the Great Depression of the 1930s and the subsequent war years of the 1940s, labor unions and management in various industries engaged in numerous battles. These battles included debilitating strikes and lockouts that were perceived to harm the nation as a whole, as well as the particular affected industries and workers. In an attempt to improve workplace relationships and prevent or limit strikes and lockouts, many unions and managers began to include grievance arbitration provisions as part of their collective bargaining agreements. According to these clauses, if an employee felt that she was not being afforded the benefits required by the collective bargaining agreement such as seniority, compensation, or protection against discipline or termination, she was to arbitrate her claim against the company, rather than litigate that claim in court. Stephen Hayford reports, "By the mid-1950's, binding arbitration provisions were included in ninety to ninety-five percent of collective bargaining agreements in the United States."[6] If anything the percentage is probably higher today.

a. *Purpose of Labor Arbitration*

In a series of decisions known as the "Steelworkers' Trilogy," the Supreme Court explained that it viewed such labor arbitration as serving highly laudable purposes, and that it saw those purposes as being quite different from those served by commercial arbitration. Thus, in United Steelworkers of America v. Warrior & Gulf Navigation Co., 363 U.S. 574 (1960), the Court stated: "The present federal policy is to promote industrial stabilization through the collective bargaining agreement. A major factor in achieving industrial peace is the inclusion of a provision for arbitration of grievances in the collective bargaining agreement." It explained that whereas "[i]n the commercial case, arbitration is the substitute for litigation . . . [h]ere arbitration is the substitute for industrial strife." The distinction was significant because, at the time, commercial arbitration was not necessarily looked upon with favor by the courts. "Since arbitration of labor disputes has quite different functions from arbitration under an ordinary commercial agreement, the hostility evinced by courts toward arbitration of commercial agreements has no place here." Id. at 578.

b. *Function of Labor Arbitrators*

The Court explained in the Steelworkers' Trilogy that whereas the function of the commercial arbitrator is to interpret existing statutes or contract provisions and apply them to the dispute at hand, labor arbitrators have a broader function of trying to create appropriate rules and solutions in situations that may not have been specifically envisioned by union and management when they entered into the collective bargaining agreement.

---

6. Stephen L. Hayford, Unification of the Law of Labor Arbitration and Commercial Arbitration: An Idea Whose Time Has Come, 52 Baylor L. Rev. 781, 786 (2000).

> The collective bargaining agreement . . . is more than a contract; it is a generalized code to govern a myriad of cases which the draftsmen cannot wholly anticipate. . . . The collective agreement covers the whole employment relationship. It calls into being a new common law — the common law of a particular industry or of a particular plant. . . . A collective bargaining agreement is an effort to erect a system of industrial self-government.

United Steelworkers of America v. Warrior & Gulf Navigation Co., 363 U.S. 574 at 578-80.

The Court goes on to explain that because collective bargaining agreements must deal with such a broad range of issues over an extended period of time "[g]aps may be left to be filled in by reference to the practices of the particular industry and of the various shops covered by the agreement." Id. at 580. Thus,

> [a]rbitration is the means of solving the unforeseeable by molding a system of private law for all the problems which may arise and to provide for their solution in a way which will generally accord with the variant needs and desires of the parties. The processing of disputes through the grievance machinery is actually a vehicle by which meaning and content are given to the collective bargaining agreement. . . . The grievance procedure is, in other words, a part of the continuous collective bargaining process. It, rather than a strike, is the terminal point of a disagreement.

Id. at 581. As a result,

> [t]he labor arbitrator performs functions which are not normal to the courts. . . . The labor arbitrator's source of law is not confined to the express provisions of the contract, as the industrial common law — the practices of the industry and the shop — is equally a part of the collective bargaining agreement although not expressed in it.

Id. at 581-82.

c. Selection of Labor Arbitrators

Given the unique function of labor arbitrators, it is not surprising that labor arbitrators are also selected in a special way and for a special type of expertise. Typically, management selects one member of a grievance panel and the union selects one member of a grievance panel, and these two arbitrators together select a third arbitrator to chair the panel. The Supreme Court explains:

> The labor arbitrator is usually chosen because of the parties' confidence in his knowledge of the common law of the shop and their trust in his personal judgment to bring to bear considerations which are not expressed in the contract as criteria for judgment. The parties expect that his judgment of a particular grievance will reflect not only what the contract says but, insofar as the collective bargaining agreement permits, such factors as the effect upon productivity of a particular result, its consequence to the morale of the shop, his judgment whether tensions will be heightened or diminished. For the parties' objective in using the arbitration process is primarily to further their common goal of uninterrupted production under the agreement, to make the agreement serve their specialized needs. The

ablest judge cannot be expected to bring the same experience and competence to bear upon the determination of a grievance, because he cannot be similarly informed.

United Steelworkers of America v. Warrior & Gulf Navigation Co., 363 U.S. 574, 582. Management and unions typically select arbitrators either from among persons with whom they are already acquainted or from lists provided by an arbitration provider such as the Federal Mediation and Conciliation Service or the American Arbitration Association.

d. Logistics of Labor Arbitration

Julius Getman explains how labor arbitrations come about:

When an employee or the union feels that rights under an agreement have been violated, a grievance may be filed. Once filed, the grievance is handled by the union through shop stewards and the grievance committee. If pursued, it is dealt with by successively higher levels of management in consultation with their union counterparts.

. . . If the grievance is not resolved through negotiation, the union has the option of demanding arbitration. Thus, only cases that are not winnowed out by the process of day-to-day negotiation proceed to arbitration. The agreement typically provides a technique for choosing the arbitrator and declares that his decision will be final and binding. Each party pays for his own witnesses and representative. The parties share the arbitrator's fees and the expense of the hearing.[7]

As Getman details, it is typically the union rather than the employee who decides whether a particular grievance is worth bringing to arbitration. Thus, not infrequently, employees who believe they were treated improperly under the collective bargaining agreement do not generally have the opportunity to either litigate or arbitrate against their employer. Instead, the only recourse for such employees is to bring a lawsuit against both union and employer simultaneously; arguing both that the employer violated the contract and that the union violated its duty of fair representation towards the employee. See Teamsters Local 391 v. Terry, 494 U.S. 558 (1990). This type of suit, which requires the plaintiff to prevail against both defendants to prevail against either, is among the most difficult to win in all of American jurisprudence.

Labor arbitrations tend to be fairly formal in nature. Employees are typically represented by a "shop steward" (an employee who also works for the union), and employers are typically represented by someone who works in the human relations department. Such representatives may or may not be attorneys, but in any event are experienced advocates who are expert in the art of presenting testimony, conducting cross-examination, and making arguments to the arbitrators. Advocates in arbitrations typically cite as precedent decisions that have been made in prior arbitrations. These advocates often prepare written briefs to accompany their oral advocacy.

---

7. Julius G. Getman, Labor Arbitration and Dispute Resolution, 88 Yale L.J. 916, 919-20 (1979).

e. Issues that Can be Addressed in Labor Arbitrations

For many years it was believed that union members could be required to arbitrate their claims with respect to the collective bargaining agreement, but that union members could still litigate statutory claims against the employer under anti-discrimination statutes such as the federal Title VII. In 1974 the Supreme Court's decision in Alexander v. Gardner-Denver Co., 415 U.S. 36, 59-60(1974), held that a union member who had arbitrated a contractual claim for unjust discharge could not be subsequently barred from litigating a claim of race discrimination arising out of the same event. However, in 14 Penn Plaza LLC v. Pyett, 129 S. Ct. 1456, 1469 (2009), the Supreme Court held that employees could be required to arbitrate statutory claims for discrimination as well as claims under the collective bargaining agreement, at least so long as the employee would have the opportunity to arbitrate such claim, regardless of the preference of the union. The decision is excerpted and discussed infra, in Chapter 10. Without purporting to overrule *Alexander*, the Court has now made clear that arbitrators can be expected to rule on union members' statutory claims, as well as their claims under the collective bargaining agreement. Id. at 1471. Any binding arbitral ruling on such statutory claim would preclude the union member from separately litigating that statutory claim.

f. Access to Labor Arbitration Decisions

The typical labor arbitration decision is reasoned, written, and published. Such decisions are often available, for example, in Lexis and Westlaw databases. As Jules Getman explains:

> The advantages of utilizing precedent make it desirable that arbitrators write opinions. Written opinions also serve to explain to the losing side why it lost and may convince a rejected grievant that he has at least "had his day in court." A written opinion helps to ensure that the arbitrator will consider the opposing contentions and formulate a coherent resolution. It also affords an arbitrator a way to demonstrate his intelligence, fairness, and good judgment, all of which may help him to be chosen in the future.[8]

In the commercial context, by contrast, many arbitrators do not write lengthy decisions or provide the reasoning underlying their decisions, fearing that extensive reasons may simply support efforts to vacate their awards. One explanation for the difference between labor and commercial awards is likely that labor arbitrators are very conscious that they are providing guidance, not only for the grievant and the company but also for other employees. Commercial arbitrators, by contrast, are focused primarily on the disputants themselves.

g. Interest Arbitrations

In addition to the "grievance" arbitrations described above, another type of arbitration is also used in the labor context. When labor and management are unable to negotiate a contract successfully, arbitrators are sometimes used to write the terms

---

8. Julius G. Getman, Labor Arbitration and Dispute Resolution, 88 Yale L.J. 916, 920, (1979).

of the future contract. In particular, a number of states have statutes that prohibit public employees from going on strike and instead require labor and management to take unresolved disputes regarding new contract terms to arbitration. Here, the arbitrator is not interpreting an existing contract term, as is described above, but rather is helping to draft a new one. This form of arbitration is known as interest arbitration. Federal legislation was proposed in 2009 that would have mandated interest arbitration where newly certified unions and employers failed to negotiate an agreement within a certain period of time. See Employee Free Choice Act, H.R. 1409, S. 560, 111th Cong. (Introduced Mar. 10, 2009). To date the legislation has not been adopted.

Problem 9-5. *Differentiating Commercial and Labor Arbitration*

You are an associate at a law firm. One of the partners tells you she is generally quite familiar with commercial arbitration but knows next to nothing about labor arbitration. Write a short memo (no more than one page) explaining to the partner the key differences between labor and commercial arbitration.

---

4. Sports Arbitration

Arbitration is frequently used in a variety of sports contexts. For example, certain salary disputes between major league baseball players and team owners are resolved though a specialized form of arbitration called "baseball arbitration" or "final offer arbitration." In this type of arbitration, the arbitrator is required to select either the salary offered by management or that demanded by the player, but not to issue a compromise decision. One of the benefits of this form of arbitration is said to be that it encourages disputants to negotiate their own resolution rather than risking that the arbitrator may choose the other side's number. Baseball arbitrations are private, although the results ultimately are made public. The baseball collective bargaining agreement contains rules on how such arbitrations are to be run.

Other popular sports including football, hockey, and professional cycling use arbitration as well. Football player Terrell Owens famously arbitrated a four-week suspension imposed by the Philadelphia Eagles. When Tour de France cycling winner (2006) Floyd Landis was accused of having cheated his way to victory by using a testosterone supplement, the claim and his defenses were heard by a panel of three arbitrators according to rules set out by the North American Court of Arbitration for Sport (run through the American Arbitration Association). His arbitration was unusual in that it was held at Pepperdine Law School and was open to the press and the public. When the arbitrators found that Landis had engaged in illegal doping, he filed an appeal to the Court of Arbitration for Sport, based in Switzerland.

Arbitration is also frequently used to resolve disputes that arise in connection with the Olympics. The Olympic Division of the Court of Arbitration for Sport handles disputes ranging from eligibility to doping to misconduct to conflicts over results. The author of the following excerpt is a Swiss attorney and law school lecturer who played an active role in establishing the Olympic Division and served as president of that Division.

 Gabrielle Kaufmann-Kohler, **ARBITRATION AND THE GAMES, OR THE FIRST EXPERIENCE OF THE OLYMPIC DIVISION OF THE COURT OF ARBITRATION FOR SPORT**

12 Mealey's Int. Arb. Rep. 2, 20-25, 27-29 (Feb. 1997)

1. GOAL: FAIR, FAST AND FREE . . .

In creating the Olympic Division, the CAS was pursuing the objective of providing athletes and other participants (Federations, National Olympic Committees, officials, trainers, doctors, etc.) with a body able to resolve disputes occurring during the Games in a final manner within time limits appropriate to the pace of the competition. In order for the decisions to be final, a "real" arbitration tribunal was required, i.e., an independent tribunal following the fundamental principles of procedure. In order for decisions to be made quickly, it was necessary to have an appropriate procedure and organizational structure as well as arbitrators who knew the subject. Furthermore, in order for the body to be accepted by the sporting community, it was desirable that it reflected the diversity of this community and included former athletes. Finally, the free nature of the procedure and the existence of a legal aid fund could only serve to further improve the attractiveness and the quality of the services thus offered to the sporting community. . . .

2. STRUCTURE

The structure put in place to reach this goal included twelve arbitrators (judges, practicing lawyers and law professors), all of whom had experience in sport (some were even former athletes themselves, such as the American lawyer who won a medal for wrestling at the Barcelona Olympics, and the German dressage champion Rainer Klimke, also a lawyer, who has six Olympic gold medals to his credit). In addition to Americans, one Canadian and some Europeans, the Division included one member from Australia, one from Senegal and one from China. . . .

3. LEGAL FRAMEWORK

3.1 Jurisdiction

As regards the individuals and organizations taking part in one way or another in the Olympic Games, the jurisdiction of the CAS stems from the following provisions:

- firstly, since 1995 the Olympic Charter has contained an Article 74 under which "any dispute arising on the occasion of or in connection with the

Olympic Games shall be submitted exclusively to the Court of Arbitration for Sport, in accordance with the Code of Sports-related Arbitration";

- in addition, the entry form for the Atlanta Games signed by all athletes, judges, trainers, medical staff, etc. included an express acceptance of the jurisdiction of the CAS;
- also, a large number of [International Federations] IFs provide for the jurisdiction of the CAS in their bylaws or regulations. . . .

Consequently, the Olympic Division may be called upon to resolve all forms of disputes if they occur between the opening and the closing of the Games. In most cases, . . . these are disputes involving the challenge of a decision taken by a sports body ([International Olympic Committee] IOC, IF, National Olympic Committee or NOC). The Division's jurisdiction could, however, also encompass "first instance" disputes, for example a tort action brought by an athlete against the organizing committee or the IOC. . . .

3.3 Rules Applicable to Merits of the Dispute

The Rules provide that the arbitration panel resolve the dispute "pursuant to the Olympic Charter, the applicable regulations, general principles of law and the rules of law, the application of which it deems appropriate."

The applicable regulations include primarily the IOC Medical Code relating to doping and the IF regulations regarding the practice of each sport and the organization of events. . . .

4. COURSE OF THE ARBITRATION . . .

The arbitration procedure is triggered when an application is filed with the Court Office of the Division, preferably on a standard form prepared for this purpose. . . . The President of the Division then forms a Panel of three arbitrators and appoints the President of the Panel. To save time and to reduce the risk of arbitrators being challenged, the Rules do not grant the parties the right to choose their arbitrator. . . .

While allowing the Panel broad discretion to shape the procedure and, in particular, the evidentiary proceedings as it sees fit considering the needs of a specific dispute, the Rules provide that, in principle, the Panel calls one single hearing, during which each party presents its case (with or without the assistance of counsel or other persons) and produces all its evidence (witnesses, documents, experts).

After the hearing, the Panel renders a decision within 24 hours following the filing of the application, except if the President of the Division exceptionally grants an extension. As a rule, the decision (rendered by majority or, failing a majority, by the President of the Panel) contains brief reasons. It is forthwith served on the parties. . . .

6. CASES SUBMITTED TO THE OLYMPIC DIVISION

The Olympic Division handled six arbitrations in 1996 . . . [two of which are summarized below].

6.4 Mendy v. AIBA

On July 31 at 4.20 P.M., the French boxer Christophe Mendy lodged an application challenging the decision of the International Amateur Boxing Association (in French, Association Internationale de Boxe Amateur, AIBA), which confirmed his disqualification for punching his opponent below the belt during a quarter final match in the heavyweight titles. The French Boxing Federation supported Mendy's application. The result of the arbitration had an impact on the participation in the semi-final and the outcome was therefore urgent.

At the time when the case was tried, the competitions were in progress and the representatives of the federations were not free to attend a hearing. Making use of the procedural flexibility available under the Rules, the Panel (composed of Luc Argand, Switzerland; Youssoupha Ndiaye, Senegal; and Jan Paulsson, Sweden) decided therefore not to hold a formal hearing. With the parties' consent, they heard the parties separately, one of them just by telephone. They then watched the video recording supporting the application during their deliberation.

This accelerated procedure made it possible to give a decision 3 hours and 40 minutes after the application had been filed, the reasons being notified the morning of the day after, again within the 24-hour time limit.

This case raised an issue of arbitrability, which the respondent did not put forward, but which the arbitrators addressed ex officio. Indeed, the dispute hinged on the application of a purely technical sports rule: was the punch a low blow or not? For years, the Swiss Supreme Court (before which an award could be challenged) has consistently held that the application of a technical rule, or a game rule as opposed to a rule of law, cannot be reviewed by a court or arbitral tribunal, because the game rules are outside the reach of the law. . . .

The scope of the game rule not subject to court review has dwindled away over the years. In addition, recent scholarly writings have challenged the very distinction between the rules of the game and the rule of law . . . [asserting that] top competition sport is not a game at all any more. It is an unremitting battle for enormous stakes in some cases. "Sport is war" was the headline in an edition of a major European monthly paper before the Atlanta Games. . . . And war cannot — must not — be outside of the reach of the law.

In addition, the Swiss Supreme Court's position is an isolated one in comparative law. If the CAS intends to be accepted as *the* body for resolving sports disputes throughout the world, it cannot base its decisions exclusively on comparatively unusual Swiss legal rules.

This thinking led the Panel to decide that the dispute was arbitrable despite the fact that it involved the application of a technical rule. Therefore, the arbitrators considered that they had jurisdiction over the Mendy application.

Even though it had jurisdiction, the Panel held that it should exercise a definite restraint in assessing the application which the sports referee had made of the technical rule. Indeed, the sports referee is closer to the facts and more familiar with the day-to-day handling of the technical rules. He is thus in a better position to decide on the application of a technical rule than the legal arbitrator. Hence, it makes sense that the referee's view prevails, unless there is a gross violation of the athlete's rights, or in the Panel's words "an error of law, a wrong or a malicious act." The precise meaning of these terms will obviously require refinement in the future.

6.5   Korneev and Russian NOC v. IOC; Gouliev and Russian v. IOC

On July 29, 1996, two Russian athletes, the swimmer, Korneev, and the wrestler, Gouliev, filed applications challenging an IOC decision, whereby they were stripped of their medals following a positive drug test. The test had revealed that they had taken bromantan, a still relatively unknown substance, which the IOC Medical Commission had classified as a stimulant as defined by the Medical Code and therefore as a banned substance. Before the Olympics Division, the Russian NOC alleged that it had recommended the use of this product to all its athletes in order to strengthen their immune system which was particularly put to the test by the humid and hot Atlanta climate, and not for the purpose of enhancing their performance.

Subsequently, other Russian athletes tested positive to bromantan, which lead to further sanctions by the IOC. The sanctions were not, however, brought before the Olympic Division, the Korneev/Gouliev proceedings apparently being considered to be test cases which would in practice dispose of the further sanctions as well.

As the two applications raised the same issue, the proceedings were consolidated. After a first hearing of the parties, the arbitrators (Vince Bruce, Australia; Gerard Rasquin, France; and Barbara Shycoff, USA) appointed a scientific expert not without having given the parties a prior opportunity to comment on the person and the assignment of this expert. The expert produced a report within 24 hours and was then heard on two occasions over the following days. During these hearings, where interpreters were used in three languages and which generated hundreds of pages of transcripts, the Panel also heard the witnesses called by the parties. In parallel, it set the parties various time limits to produce documentary evidence, such as scientific reports and notes, and minutes of the sessions of the IOC Medical Commission.

Having completed such fact finding, the arbitrators held that the scientific evidence on record did not support the conclusion that bromantan had been used as a stimulant with a sufficient degree of certainty to justify such a serious sanction as the withdrawal of an Olympic medal. In fact, the expert was not able to rule out the possibility that the product had been absorbed for the sole purpose of strengthening the athletes' immune system. The Panel thus gave the athletes the benefit of the doubt, [and restored the medals] but not without restating the overriding importance of the fight against doping and the principle of strict liability for doping offenses, a principle which is well established in the case law of the CAS.

Despite the complexity of the scientific problems raised, the decision was rendered on the last day of the competitions. The uncertainty about the final winners of the medals was thus lifted before the closing of the Games.

Problem 9-6. *Propriety of Mandatory Sports Arbitration*

You are an attorney working for the House of Representatives' Judiciary Committee. The Chair of the committee, a cycling fan, has received a lengthy complaint from his constituent Floyd Landis regarding the length, cost, and fairness of the arbitration process he went through to try to prove he had not engaged in blood doping when he won the Tour de France. You have been assigned to write a memo discussing whether it is appropriate for athletes like Landis or like Olympics competitors to be required to resolve their disputes through arbitration. Would it be desirable for Congress to pass legislation seeking to protect such athletes from being required to arbitrate their disputes?

You may find the following cases useful as you ponder this question: *Michels v. United States Olympic Comm.*, 741 F.2d 155, 159 (7th Cir. 1984) ("There can be few less suitable bodies than the federal courts for determining the eligibility, or the procedures for determining eligibility, of athletes to participate in the Olympic games.") (Posner, J.); *Slaney v. International Amateur Athletic Fed'n*, 244 F.3d 580, 590 (7th Cir. 2001) (finding that runner Mary Decker Slaney was precluded by the New York Convention (on arbitration) from challenging an arbitral award that found she had engaged in blood doping). Also, you may want to consider Maureen A. Weston, Doping Control, Mandatory Arbitration, and Process Dangers for Accused Athletes in International Sports, 10 Pepp. Disp. Res. L.J. 5 (2009).

---

5. Online Arbitration

In online arbitration, the arbitrator and parties do not meet in person but rather exchange documents and arguments online, in virtual space. One obvious advantage of resolving disputes online is that disputants can save the time and money they would have expended in order to be present in the same physical space. Particularly for smaller disputes, where the travel costs may well exceed the value of the dispute, this potential is very appealing. Furthermore, as the extreme poplarity of texting demonstrates, some people prefer written to verbal or in-person communications, at least for some issues. On the other hand, sometimes the benefits of person-to-person communication may exceed its costs. Psychologists have found that a great deal of communication is done through body language, looks, and verbal subtleties that may not be captured online. Most, if not all, of us have fallen victim to e-mail miscommunications. As well, the use of online technologies may raise additional privacy and confidentiality concerns, as it may be difficult to guarantee that the online communications won't be intercepted.

Currently, most online arbitrations involve only written statements (documents and e-mail). The online conversations can be synchronous, if the disputants choose to participate in a chat room simultaneously or commit to an e-mail conversation at a particular time. Alternatively, such communications can be, and often are, asynchronous, meaning that there is a delay between when one party sends a communication and another responds. The arbitrator then reviews the materials that have been presented and makes a determination.

As technology evolves, online arbitrations may come to resemble live arbitrations more closely. For example, video conferencing tools such as Skype can be used so that disputants, albeit not in the same physical space, can speak to one another more directly. Perhaps one day video conferencing related technology will evolve to a point where we actually feel all disputants are physically present.

Currently, online arbitration is used most frequently for disputes arising with respect to online activities. Many online marketers offer online dispute resolution mechanisms that may include arbitration. Similarly, the Internet Corporation for Assigned Names and Numbers (ICANN) has issued a Uniform Domain Name Dispute Resolution Policy requiring that disputes over ownership of a particular domain name be heard initially through arbitration, preferably online arbitration. Online arbitration, of course, can also be used for disputes that do not arise over the Internet.

Some online arbitrations use a computer rather than a live person to arbitrate disputes. For example, cybersettle.com offers a blind bidding process to resolve insurance disputes. Each side submits its actual bottom line offer or demand. If there is an overlap the case resolves for the average of the amount offered and the amount demanded. Other similar computerized processes may use a different algorithm to resolve the dispute, but the idea is similar — a computer "arbitrates" a resolution to the dispute.

Problem 9-7.   *Using Online Arbitration to Decide Casino-Related Disputes*

You are in-house counsel for a large casino in Las Vegas. The casino may sometimes be involved in disputes as a plaintiff and sometimes as a defendant. These disputes may pertain to goods and services provided to the casino (construction, maintenance, upkeep of slot machines, third-party vendors like shops and restaurants), to labor disputes with casino employees, or to personal injury claims brought by casino visitors. Some of these disputes may be covered by pre-dispute arbitration agreements, and others may not. You have been asked to write a memo discussing when it would be desirable for the casino to seek to use online arbitration to resolve such disputes. As appropriate, set out the factors counsel would want to consider in deciding whether online arbitration might or might not be appropriate for a particular claim.

6. "Mandatory" Arbitration (Employment and Consumer)

As has been noted, arbitration may take on a very different look when it is imposed on consumers or employees by companies using small print provisions or other means. The legality and desirability (or not) of this type of arbitration will be discussed infra, in Chapter 10.

D. EXAMPLES OF ARBITRATION CLAUSES

As you now know, arbitration varies tremendously from context to context. You will not be surprised to learn, therefore, that arbitration clauses also vary substantially. Here are just a few samples, but recognize that the potential variations are infinite. Also, note that even when an arbitration clause appears sparsely written, it may incorporate an institution's arbitration rules that include many more specifics.

1. Sample Arbitration Clause for General Commercial Transactions

The following clause is suggested by the AAA for general commercial use:

"Any controversy or claim arising out of or relating to this contract, or the breach thereof, shall be settled by arbitration administered by the American Arbitration under its Commercial Arbitration Rules and judgment on the award rendered by the arbitrator(s) may be entered in any court having jurisdiction thereof."[9]

2. AT&T Arbitration Clause

In Ting v. AT&T, 319 F.3d 1126, 1133 n.4 (9th Cir. 2003), the court set out the arbitration clause imposed by AT&T on some of its customers. The court noted that the clause was provided in approximately eight-point font (replicated below). Section 7(a) provided in part:

THIS SECTION PROVIDES FOR RESOLUTION OF DISPUTES THROUGH FINAL AND BINDING ARBITRATION BEFORE A NEUTRAL ARBITRATOR INSTEAD OF IN A COURT BY A JUDGE OR JURY OR THROUGH A CLASS ACTION. YOU CONTINUE TO HAVE CERTAIN RIGHTS TO OBTAIN RELIEF FROM A FEDERAL OR STATE REGULA- TORY AGENCY. NO DISPUTE MAY BE JOINED WITH ANOTHER LAWSUIT, OR IN AN ARBITRATION WITH A DISPUTE OF ANY OTHER PERSON, OR RESOLVED ON A CLASS WIDE BASIS.

---

9. AAA, Drafting Dispute Resolution Clauses: A Practical Guide (2004) at 7, available at *http:// www.adr.org/si.asp?id=2424.*

THE ARBITRATOR MAY NOT AWARD DAMAGES THAT ARE NOT EXPRESSLY AUTHO-
RIZED BY THIS AGREEMENT AND MAY NOT AWARD PUNITIVE DAMAGES OR
ATTORNEYS' FEES UNLESS SUCH DAMAGES ARE EXPRESSLY AUTHORIZED BY A
STATUTE. YOU AND AT&T BOTH WAIVE ANY CLAIMS FOR AN AWARD OF DAMAGES
THAT ARE EXCLUDED UNDER THIS AGREEMENT.[10]

3. Sample Ad Hoc International Arbitration Clause

The following clause is proposed by attorney Lucy F. Reed for use in an international business transaction. The clause is "ad hoc," meaning that the disputants are
designing their own clause and administering their own arbitration, rather than
using the help of an established arbitration provider:

1. Any dispute, difference, controversy or claim arising out of or in connection with
    this agreement shall be referred to and determined by arbitration in [place].
2. The arbitral tribunal (hereinafter referred to as "the tribunal") shall be composed
    of three arbitrators appointed as follows:

    (i)   each party shall appoint an arbitrator, and the two arbitrators so appointed
          shall appoint a third arbitrator who shall act as president of the tribunal;
    (ii) if either party fails to appoint an arbitrator within 30 days of receiving
          notice of the appointment of an arbitrator by the other party, such arbitra-
          tor shall at the request of that party be appointed by [appointing authority];
    (iii) if the two arbitrators to be appointed by the parties fail to agree upon a third
          arbitrator within 30 days of the appointment of the second arbitrator, the
          third arbitrator shall be appointed by [appointing authority] at the written
          request of either party;
    (iv) should a vacancy arise because any arbitrator dies, resigns, refuses to act, or
          becomes incapable of performing his functions, the vacancy shall be filled
          by the method by which that arbitrator was originally appointed. When a
          vacancy is filled the newly established tribunal shall exercise its discretion to
          determine whether any hearings shall be repeated.

3. As soon as practicable after the appointment of the arbitrator to be appointed by
    him, and in any event no later than 30 days after the tribunal has been consti-
    tuted, the claimant shall deliver to the respondent (with copies to each arbitra-
    tor) a statement of case, containing particulars of his claims and written
    submissions in support thereof, together with any documents relied on.
4. Within 30 days of the receipt of the claimant's statement of case, the respondent
    shall deliver to the claimant (with copies to each arbitrator) a statement of case
    in answer, together with any counterclaim and any documents relied upon.

---

10. The Ninth Circuit went on to affirm in relevant part the district court ruling that had voided the
clause as unconscionable. The courts were particularly troubled by the fact that the clause prevented
arbitrators from awarding compensatory damages, punitive damages, and attorneys' fees that might have
been awarded in court, and also prevented the plaintiffs from proceeding by way of a class action. *Ting,*
319 F.3d at 1148-1152. Chapter 10 discusses such unconscionability attacks on purportedly unfair
arbitration clauses.

5. Within 30 days of the receipt by the claimant of any statement of counterclaim by the respondent, the claimant may deliver to the respondent (with copies to each arbitrator) a reply to counterclaim together with any additional documents relied upon.

6. As soon as practicable after its constitution, the tribunal shall convene a meeting with the parties or their representatives to determine the procedure to be followed in the arbitration.

7. The procedure shall be as agreed by the parties or, in default of agreement, as determined by the tribunal. However, the following procedural matters shall in any event be taken as agreed:

   (i)   the language of the arbitration shall be [language];
   (ii) the tribunal may in its discretion hold a hearing and make an award in relation to any preliminary issue at the request of either party and shall do so at the joint request of both parties;
   (iii) the tribunal shall hold a hearing, or hearings, relating to substantive issues unless the parties agree otherwise in writing;
   (iv) the tribunal shall issue its final award within 60 days of the last hearing of the substantive issues in dispute between the parties.

8. In the event of default by either party in respect of any procedural order made by the tribunal, the tribunal shall have power to proceed with the arbitration and to make its award.

9. If an arbitrator appointed by one of the parties fails or refuses to participate in the arbitration at any time after the hearings on the substance of the dispute have started, the remaining two arbitrators may continue the arbitration and make an award without a vacancy being deemed to arise if, in their discretion, they determine that the failure or refusal of the other arbitrator to participate is without reasonable excuse.

10. Any award or procedural decision of the tribunal shall if necessary be made by a majority and, in the event that no majority may be formed, the presiding arbitrator shall proceed as if he were a sole arbitrator.

Lucy F. Reed, Drafting Arbitration Clauses, 670 Practicing L. Inst. 553, 600-602 (2002).

Now that you have been introduced to a variety of concepts and models of arbitration, Chapter 10 will provide you with a sense of the complex law underlying arbitration. Then, Chapter 11 will give you guidance on the skills, practices, and ethics of arbitration.

Further Reading on Commercial Arbitration

Jerold S. Auerbach. (1983). *Justice Without Law?* New York: Oxford University Press.
Lisa Bernstein, *Opting Out of the Legal System: Extralegal Contractual Relations in the Diamond Industry*, 21 J. Legal Stud. 115 (1992).

Morton J. Horwitz. (1977). *The Transformation of American Law, 1780-1860.* Cambridge, MA: Harvard University Press.

William Catron Jones, *Three Centuries of Commercial Arbitration in New York*, 1956 WASH. U. L.Q. 193 (1956).

Bruce H. Mann, *The Formalization of Informal Law: Arbitration Before the American Revolution*, 59 N.Y.U. L. REV. 443 (1984).

Soia Mentschikoff, *Commercial Arbitration*, 61 COLUM. L. REV. 846 (1961).

Thomas Stipanowich, *Arbitration: "The New Litigation,"* 2010 ILL. L. REV. 1. (2010).

Further Reading on International Arbitration

Gary B. Born. (2009). *International Commercial Arbitration*. Alphen aan den Rijn: Kluwer Law International.

Yves Dezalay & Bryant G. Garth. (1996). *Dealing in Virtue: International Commercial Arbitration and the Construction of a Transnational Legal Order.* Chicago, IL: University of Chicago Press.

Christopher R. Drahozal, *Contracting Out of International Law: An Empirical Look at the New Law Merchant,* 80 NOTRE DAME L. REV. 523 (2005).

PricewaterhouseCoopers. (2008). *International Arbitration: Corporate Attitudes and Practices 2008.* Available at *http://www.pwc.co.uk/pdf/PwC_International_Arbitration_2008.pdf.*

Further Reading on Online Arbitration

Ethan Katsh & Janet Rifkin. (2001). *Online Dispute Resolution: Resolving Conflicts in Cyberspace.* San Francisco: Jossey-Bass Publishers.

David Larson, *Robots, Avatars, and the Demise of the Human Mediator*, 25 OHIO STATE J. ON DISP. RES. 105 (2010).

Colin Rule. (2002). *Online Dispute Resolution for Business: B2B, Ecommerce, Consumer, Employment Insurance, and Other Commercial Conflicts.* San Francisco: Jossey-Bass Publishers.

Symposium: *ADR in Cyberspace*, 15 OHIO ST. J. ON DISP. RESOL. 589 (2000).

Further Reading on Labor Arbitration

Frank Elkouri. (2003). *How Arbitration Works.* Washington, D.C.: Bureau of National Affairs.

Julius G. Getman, *Labor Arbitration and Dispute Resolution*, 88 YALE L.J. 916 (1979).

Stephen Hayford, *Unification of the Law of Labor Arbitration and Commercial Arbitration: An Idea Whose Time Has Come*, 52 BAYLOR L. REV. 781 (2000).

Harry Shulman, *Reason, Contract, and Law in Labor Relations*, 68 HARV. L. REV. 999, 1004-1005 (1955).

Further Reading on Sports Arbitration

Roger I. Abrams. (2000). *The Money Pitch: Baseball Free Agency and Salary Arbitration.* Philadelphia, PA: Temple University Press.

Maureen A. Weston, *Doping Control, Mandatory Arbitration, and Process Dangers for Accused Athletes in International Sports*, 10 PEPPERDINE DISP. RES. L.J. 5 (2009).

Further Reading on Drafting Arbitration Clauses

Neal Blacker, *Drafting the Arbitration/ADR Clause: A Checklist for Practitioners.* 46 PRAC. LAW, 55 (2000).

Kathleen M. Scanlon. (2002). *CPR Institute for Dispute Resolution, Drafter's Deskbook for Dispute Resolution Clauses.* New York: CPR Institute.

Terry L. Trantina, *How to Design ADR Clauses that Satisfy Clients' Needs and Minimize Litigation Risk*, 19 ALTERN. HIGH COST LITIG. 137 (2001).

Chapter 10   Arbitration: Law and Policy

One might well think that the primary point of agreeing to arbitration would be to avoid litigation and courts of law. Yet, it turns out that the law and courts are often very important to the world of arbitration. This chapter is divided into three sections to explore three sets of issues: when and how arbitration *clauses* are enforced; how arbitrators' *powers* are defined and limited; and how arbitral *awards* are enforced or vacated. The last portion of the chapter will discuss the most controversial policy debate currently pertaining to arbitration in the United States: whether companies should be permitted to impose "mandatory" binding arbitration on consumers, employees, or others who have not meaningfully consented to resolve future disputes through arbitration. You will see that this debate draws on the existing law discussed in the first three sections of the chapter.

A. ENFORCEMENT OF ARBITRATION CLAUSES

An agreement to arbitrate a future dispute is called a "*pre-dispute arbitration agreement*." Often, when two parties have entered into such an agreement they willingly take a dispute covered by the clause to arbitration. But what if, despite the pre-dispute arbitration agreement, one party decides it does not want to arbitrate after all? In that event, must the party who still prefers arbitration resign itself to no arbitration? What means can the pro-arbitration party use to insist that the dispute be resolved through arbitration? On what grounds might the party resisting arbitration be able to have the pre-dispute arbitration agreement voided or eliminated? One method of assuring adherence to pre-dispute arbitration agreements is social pressure or coercion. Historically, when arbitration was used in small business or other close communities, a party that sought to avoid agreed-to arbitration might be ostracized by the group. The fear of being ostracized would likely push the party into complying with the clause after all. Today, however, as the number of potential trading and social partners has increased, such social pressures have weakened in most contexts. Thus, in lieu of either giving up or threatening ostracism or even violence, the most common means for seeking to enforce arbitration agreements is litigation. We will see that courts' attitudes towards such enforcement efforts have changed substantially over the years, due to legislative reforms and to changing judicial attitudes about the value and docket-clearing implications of arbitration.

1. The History of United States Arbitration Law

a. Courts' Historical Reluctance to Enforce Pre-Dispute Arbitration Agreements

In the reading that follows, Richard Reuben explains that British courts were historically reluctant to use equitable measures to enforce pre-dispute arbitration agreements. The subsequent excerpt from Justice Story's decision in *Tobey v. Bristol* shows that early U.S. courts initially adopted this reluctance as well. Throughout the world, some countries still refuse to enforce pre-dispute arbitration agreements — although that attitude is no longer common.

 Richard C. Reuben, PUBLIC JUSTICE: TOWARD A STATE ACTION THEORY OF ALTERNATIVE DISPUTE RESOLUTION

85 Cal. L. Rev. 577, 598-601 (1997)

[Q]uestions over the enforceability of private agreements to arbitrate disputes, particularly those involving pre-dispute agreements, have dominated the historical relationship between arbitration and the courts over many centuries. . . . Simply stated, without a mechanism for enforcing the agreements to arbitrate, such promises were seen as essentially illusory; either party could walk away from the agreement with impunity. . . .

Enforceability was not a problem during arbitration's formative years in medieval England, where it was used primarily by traveling crafters' guilds and merchants to resolve commercial disputes quickly. In that setting, arbitration awards were largely enforced through communitarian norms. But, as England became more sophisticated and the use of arbitration expanded, disputants increasingly looked to courts of law to enforce private agreements to arbitrate, first through mutually signed written instruments called "deeds," and then through conditional bonds that required each of the parties submitting a dispute to arbitration to include a bond under seal that was enforceable by the obligee whenever any of the conditions in it were not met. As a compliance incentive, English courts often set these bonds at high values, even double the amount of the debt, which would be redeemable in full upon noncompliance with the arbitrator's decision.

The earliest English judicial decisions, however, demonstrate the reluctance of courts to enforce these private agreements. The theory behind this reticence was first articulated by an eighteenth-century King's Bench court in Kill v. Hollister,[1] which bluntly ruled that such agreements wrongly "oust" properly constituted

---

1. 95 Eng. Rep. 532 (K.B. 1746).

courts of their jurisdiction. Commentators have advanced two primary reasons for the existence of what has come to be known as the "ouster doctrine." The first of these has suggested that judges were wary of the fact that arbitration could result in miscarriages of justice because the process included no procedural safeguards to prevent bias in the determination of rights and duties and could easily lead to many different forms of abuse. A more cynical theory, however, pinned judicial reluctance to enforce arbitration agreements on greed, arguing that private arbitration was seen as an economic threat to English judges, whose incomes often depended on fees from disputants. In any case, Parliament responded to commercial interests by enacting in 1684 an arbitration statute that authorized judicial enforcement of agreements to arbitrate as rules of court. This made properly executed agreements irrevocable and enforceable through the courts' contempt powers.

The history of ADR in the United States involved both arbitration and mediation, and tracked the English evolution in many ways. Both techniques were commonly used in the colonial period. While some arbitrations were litigated, some scholars have suggested that enforcement during this time was a lesser issue because of cultural considerations; the socio-religious structure of religiously-based covenant communities, mutual trust, interdependence, and good faith made non-compliance impractical.

However, as the collection of independent colonies matured into the United States, disputes and their resolution became more sophisticated, and communitarian norms proved ineffective at securing compliance. Once again, disputants began looking to courts to enforce private promises to arbitrate. While the courts were willing to enforce arbitration awards, American judges, like their English counterparts, were reluctant to enforce the actual agreement to arbitrate. State courts readily embraced the ouster doctrine in the early nineteenth century; the United States Supreme Court did the same in 1874. Overwhelmingly, however, American judges seemed to be motivated by concerns for fairness of the judicial process, rather than by their personal financial gain.

The ouster doctrine remained the common law rule in the United States until the early twentieth century, when the nation's established commercial and legal communities united to bring down the doctrine through legislative means.

 TOBEY v. COUNTY OF BRISTOL

23 F. Cas. 1313, 1319-1323 (D. Mass. 1845)

STORY, Circuit Justice.

[Jonathan Tobey was hired by Bristol County to build a road from Taunton to New Bedford, Massachusetts. He brought a claim for damages against the county, alleging that the county officials' delay in procuring a site for the road had cost him substantial time and money. Tobey brought an equity action in court seeking to compel arbitration of his claim by injunction or otherwise.]

The grave question is, whether this court, as a court of equity, does possess juris-diction to compel the defendants to submit the claims of the plaintiff to arbitration, under the circumstances of the present case.

. . . [C]an such an agreement be enforced by a court of equity? . . . [N]o case has been cited by counsel, or has fallen within the scope of my researches, in which an agreement to refer a claim to arbitration, has ever been specifically enforced in equity. So far as the authorities go, they are altogether the other way. The cases are divided into two classes. One, where an agreement to refer to arbitration has been set up as a [defense] to a suit at law, as well as in equity; the other, where the party as plaintiff has sought to enforce such an agreement in a court of equity. Both classes have shared the same fate. The courts have refused to allow the former as a bar or [defense] against the suit; and have declined to enforce the latter as ill-founded in point of jurisdiction. . . .

The two general grounds on which [this doctrine] rests, belong to other branches of equity jurisprudence as well as this. . . . The first ground is, that a court of equity ought not to compel a party to submit the decision of his rights to a tribunal, which confessedly, does not possess full, adequate, and complete means, within itself, to investigate the merits of the case, and to administer justice. . . . [W]hen [courts] . . . are asked to proceed farther and to compel the parties to appoint arbitrators whose award shall be final, they necessarily pause to consider, whether such tribunals possess adequate means of giving redress, and whether they have a right to compel a reluctant party to submit to such a tribunal, and to close against him the doors of the common courts of justice, provided by the government to protect rights and to redress wrongs. One of the established principles of courts of equity is, not to entertain a bill for the specific performance of any agreement, where it is doubtful whether it may not thereby become the instrument of injustice, or to deprive parties of rights which they are otherwise fairly entitled to have pro-tected. . . . Now we all know, that arbitrators, at the common law, possess no authority whatsoever, even to administer an oath, or to compel the attendance of witnesses. They cannot compel the production of documents, and papers and books of account, or insist upon a discovery of facts from the parties under oath. They are not ordinarily well enough acquainted with the principles of law or equity, to administer either effectually, in complicated cases; and hence it has often been said, that the judgment of arbitrators is but *rusticum judicium*. Ought then a court of equity to compel a resort to such a tribunal, by which, however honest and intel-ligent, it can in no case be clear that the real legal or equitable rights of the parties can be fully ascertained or perfectly protected?

It has been said at the bar, that in modern times, most nations, and especially commercial nations, not only favor arbitrations, but in many instances make them compulsive. But in considering this point, two circumstances are important to be kept in view. In the first place, whenever arbitrations are made compulsive, it is by legislative authority, which at the same time, arms the arbitrators with the fullest powers to ascertain the facts, to compel the attendance of witnesses, to require dis-covery of papers, books and accounts, and generally, also, to compel the parties to submit themselves to examination under oath. In the next place, these arbitrations are never, or at least not ordinarily, made compulsive to the extent of excluding the jurisdiction of the regular courts of justice; but are instituted as mere preliminaries to an appeal to those courts, from the award of the arbitrators, if either party desires it, so that the law, and in many cases, the facts also, if disputed, are re-examinable there. . . . It is certainly the policy of the common law, not to compel men to submit their rights and interests to arbitration, or to enforce agreements for such a purpose. Nay, the common law goes farther, and even if a submission has been made to arbitrators, who are named, by deed or otherwise, with an express stipulation, that the submission shall be irrevocable, it still is revocable and countermandable, by either party, before the award is actually made, although not afterwards. This was decided as long ago as in Vynior's Case, 8 Coke, 81b. The reason there given, is, that a man cannot, by his act, make such authority, power, or warrant not countermandable, which is by law, and of its own nature, countermandable; . . . But where an award has been made before the revocation, it will be held obligatory, and the parties will not be allowed to revoke it, and the courts of law as well as of equity will enforce it. . . . [I]n the second place, . . . it is an established principle of courts of equity never to enforce the specific performance of any agreement, where it would be a vain and imperfect act, or where a specific performance is from the very nature and character of the agreement, impracticable or inequitable, to be enforced. 2 Story, Eq. Jur. §959a. . . . From their very nature, all such contracts must depend for their due execution, upon the skill, and will, and honor of the contracting party. Now this very reasoning applies with equal force to the case at bar. How can a court of equity compel the respective parties to name arbitrators; and a fortiori, how can it compel the parties mutually to select arbitrators, since each much [sic], in such a case, agree to all the arbitrators? If one party refuses to name an arbitrator, how is the court to compel him to name one? If an arbitrator is named by one party, how is the court to ascertain, if the other party objects to him, whether he is right or wrong in his objection? If one party names an arbitrator, who will not act, how can the court compel him to select another? If one party names an arbitrator not agreed to by the other, how is the court to find out what are his reasons for refusing? If one party names an arbitrator whom the other deems incompetent, how is the court to decide upon the question of his competency? Take the present case, where the arbitrators are to be mutually selected, when and within that time are they to be appointed? How many shall they be, — two, three, four, five, seven, ten, or even twenty? The resolve is silent as to the number. Can the court fix the number, if the parties do not agree upon it? That would be doing what has never yet been done. If either party should refuse to name any arbitrator, or to agree upon any named by the other side, has the court authority, of itself, to appoint arbitrators, or to substitute a master for them? That would . . . bind the parties contrary to their agreement. . . . So that we abundantly see, that the very impracticability of compelling the parties to name arbitrators, or upon their default, for the court to appoint them, constitutes, and must forever constitute, a complete bar to any attempt on the part of a court of equity to compel the specific performance of any agreement to refer to arbitration. It is essentially, in its very nature and character, an agreement which must rest in the good faith and honor of the parties, and like an agreement to paint a picture, or to carve a statue, or to write a book, or to invent patterns for prints, must be left to the conscience of the parties, or to such remedy in damages for the breach thereof, as the law has provided. . . .

Without going more at large into the subject, it appears to me, that the present is not a case in which this court can afford any relief whatsoever to the plaintiff, however strong his claims may be upon the justice of the county and its public functionaries. I shall, therefore, order the bill to be discharged, but without costs to the defendants.

Problem 10-1.   *Were Early Courts Hostile to Arbitration?*

The Supreme Court and some commentators have summarized early American courts' attitude toward arbitration as "hostile." Others, however, argue that this is an overstatement. What argument can you craft to defend the early courts from the charge that they were hostile to arbitration? For help in structuring such an argument see Michael H. Leroy & Peter Feuille, Judicial Enforcement of Predispute Arbitration Agreements: Back to the Future, 18 Ohio St. J. on Disp. Resol. 249, 259-277 (2003); and Ian R. Macneil, American Arbitration Law: Reformation, Nationalization, Internationalization (1992) at 19.

---

b. *Birth of Modern Arbitration Law*

i. *Commercial Entities Lobby for Change*

The effort to modernize U.S. arbitration laws commenced in New York, in the 1920s. Frustrated by courts' unwillingness to order specific performance of agreements to arbitrate in many business to business transactions, a number of business and commercial entities joined together to lobby for legislative change. Specifically, Charles L. Bernheimer, president of a cotton-goods business and chair of the New York Chamber of Commerce Arbitration Committee, led the reform efforts, together with Julius H. Cohen, general counsel for the New York Chamber of Commerce. Cohen's book, Commercial Arbitration and the Law, published in 1918, proved to be influential and helped fuel the reform. Joining forces with the New York State Bar Association, the Chamber of Commerce drafted a bill that was enacted by the New York legislature in 1920. This statute provided that a written contract to arbitrate future disputes was valid and established a right to petition the courts for an order compelling arbitration to proceed. A similar bill was passed in New Jersey in 1923. Meanwhile, parallel efforts were being made in Europe. In 1919 American and European business interests founded the International Chamber of Commerce in Paris and in the early 1920s it began to offer private arbitration services for transborder business disputes.

Below, Julius Henry Cohen and co-author Kenneth Dayton, explain why business interests were eager to obtain statutory reform to support arbitration.

Julius Henry Cohen & Kenneth Dayton, THE NEW FEDERAL
ARBITRATION LAW

12 Va. L. Rev. 265, 269-270 (1926)

[T]he evils which arbitration is intended to correct are three in number: (1) The
long delay usually incident to a proceeding at law, in equity or in admiralty, especially in recent years in centers of commercial activity, where there has arisen great
congestion of the court calendars. This delay arises not only from congestion of the
calendars, which necessitates each case awaiting its turn for consideration, but also
frequently from preliminary motions and other steps taken by litigants, appeals
therefrom, which delay consideration of the merits, and appeals from decisions upon
the merits which commonly follow the decision of any case of real importance.
(2) The expense of litigation. (3) The failure, through litigation, to reach a decision regarded as just when measured by the standards of the business world. This
failure may result either because the courts necessarily apply general rules which do
not always fit a specific case, or because, in the ordinary jury trial, the parties do not
have the benefit of the judgment of persons familiar with the peculiarities of the
given controversy.

Making an agreement to arbitrate is not always sufficient, however. If both parties are strictly honorable and if there is no misunderstanding between them as to
the scope and effect of the agreement which they have made, they will carry out
the contract to arbitrate and perform the award entered upon it, and there is no
necessity for a statute. Unfortunately, this situation does not commonly exist. The
party refusing to proceed may believe in good faith that for one reason or another
his agreement to arbitrate does not bind him (i.e., he may assert that he made no
such agreement or that it was not intended to cover the particular controversy).
Even without this, after a dispute has arisen, one party or the other ordinarily has a
certain technical advantage which may be impaired if he submits the controversy
to arbitration rather than to the courts. It may be in the application of a settled
rule of law. It may be in some procedural peculiarity, or it may be merely in the
delay of which he is assured by the congestion of the courts before he has to meet
his obligation. The result is that this party is usually loath to surrender his supposed
advantage. His unwillingness is not necessarily due to dishonesty or bad faith.
Unfortunately, business has become so used to the doctrine of revocability of
arbitration agreements that these clauses are not regarded in the same light as other
contractual obligations, and the party who refuses to perform his agreement
frequently does not realize that he is violating his plighted word. He has no
conscious intention of defaulting upon his agreement, but the rule of law has
blinded him to the fact this is an agreement. While our American courts have usually declared a friendly attitude toward arbitration they have felt themselves bound
by the long standing decisions holding that arbitration agreements were revocable
at will and would not be enforced by the courts. The result has been that any party
who wished to avoid an agreement which he had made to arbitrate had only to
declare his refusal to proceed and the courts would not order specific performance
of the contract while the alternative of a damage suit was inadequate.

ii. Federal Arbitration Act

Following the lead of New York and New Jersey, Congress in 1925 passed the Federal Arbitration Act (FAA), 9 U.S.C. §§1-16. (Note that this initial FAA is now Chapter 1 of a larger statute, also including Chapters 2 and 3 dealing with international arbitration, 9 U.S.C. §§201-307.) A key portion of the FAA is §2.

Federal Arbitration Act Section 2 (1925)

A written provision in any maritime transaction or a contract evidencing a transaction involving commerce to settle by arbitration a controversy thereafter arising out of such contract or transaction . . . shall be valid, irrevocable, and enforceable, save upon such grounds as exist at law or in equity for the revocation of any contract.

The passage of the FAA was noncontroversial. Virtually no interest group or legislator rose to speak in opposition to the bill. However, when a few persons did question whether the FAA might allow businesses to use form contracts to impose arbitration on unwilling persons such as employees or insurance customers, the advocates of the bill assured Congress that this was not the intent of the legislation. Following two sets of congressional hearings, it was signed into law by President Coolidge on February 12, 1925.

Reading through Chapter 1 of the FAA, you may be amazed at the brevity of this important statute. In just a few pages, however, the FAA accomplishes a great deal. As we have noted, Section 2, the "guts" of the statute, provides that pre-dispute agreements to arbitrate are enforceable and must be treated like any other contractual promise. Sections 3 and 4 operationalize this provision, calling on courts to stay litigation that is covered by a valid arbitration provision and to issue orders compelling arbitration where it is required by agreement. Taken together, these provisions explicitly require courts to use their injunctive powers to enforce pre-dispute agreements to arbitrate. The Supreme Court has made clear (as will be discussed infra) that Section 2 applies in both federal and state courts. When a party wants a federal court to issue a Section 4 motion to compel arbitration they must show that the court has independent jurisdiction because the Supreme Court has held that the FAA does not create independent federal jurisdiction. That is, a federal court must "look through" the Section 4 petition to determine whether the underlying claim arises from party diversity or raises an independent federal question. Vaden v. Discover Bank, 129 S. Ct. 1262, 1273 (2009). Alternatively, a party may file its motion to compel arbitration under the FAA in state court.

In addition to mandating the enforceability of pre-dispute arbitration agreements, the FAA also sets out the manner in which arbitral awards are to be enforced. Section 9 provides that the prevailing party may "confirm" an award by filing it in the appropriate court within a year. Once the award has been confirmed, it will have the same force and effect as any judgment entered by the court. 9 U.S.C. §13. If a party feels that the arbitrator's award was erroneous, it may move to modify or vacate the arbitral award. However, as will be discussed in section C, the grounds set out in §§10 and 11 for vacation and modification are extremely limited, making it far more difficult to overturn an arbitral decision than to reverse a trial court's award on appeal. Neither errors of law nor errors of fact are listed as among the grounds for vacating an arbitral decision. While the FAA leaves most of the details of arbitration to the parties' own agreement, it does require courts to appoint the arbitrator in the absence of party agreement, 9 U.S.C. §5, and it permits arbitrators to compel witnesses to attend proceedings and to bring certain documents. 9 U.S.C. §7.

Problem 10-2. *Enforcement of Arbitration Clauses*

You are representing Company X, which has entered into a pre-dispute arbitration agreement with Company Y. A dispute that appears to be covered by the arbitration agreement arises between the two companies.

1. Notwithstanding the clause, Company Y has filed a lawsuit in federal court against Company X with respect to the claim. What are Company X's procedural options? What difference would it make if Company Y had filed its lawsuit against Company X in state court?

2. Alternatively, Company X discusses the issue with Company Y, and asserts that Company X's claim against Company Y should be resolved through arbitration. Company Y states that it will not agree to resolve the claim through arbitration. What are Company X's procedural options?

---

iii. State Arbitration Laws

Having achieved success in New York and New Jersey, with the passage of state arbitration laws, requiring recognition and enforcement of agreements to arbitrate, the arbitration reformers turned their attention to the remaining states. Focusing their efforts on the National Conference of Commissioners on Uniform State Laws ("NCCUSL"), the reformers sought to convince the commissioners to adopt a "modern" arbitration statute that other states would then enact.[2] Here, their campaign was met with a great deal more resistance than it had in New York, New Jersey, or than it soon would meet in Congress. Opponents of the reform expressed substantial concern about the potential for adhesive arbitration contracts that would require persons to give up their rights to go to court. Despite substantial lobbying by Julius Cohen and others, the commissioners passed a Uniform Arbitration Act in

---

2. "Modern" in this context means a statute that requires enforcement of pre-dispute arbitration agreements.

1924 that excluded enforcement of future agreements to arbitrate. In other words, the 1924 Uniform Arbitration Act was not a modern arbitration statute.

Still, over time, the reformers eventually won out at the state level. Despite the 1924 Uniform Act, many states began to enact modern arbitration statutes. Eventually the Commissioners withdrew the 1924 Uniform Arbitration Act and, in 1955, NCCUSL passed a modern Uniform Arbitration Act, subsequently adopted by most states. A Revised Uniform Arbitration Act was adopted by the same body in 2000, substantially lengthening and complicating the original Act, but most states have not yet adopted the revision. Today, virtually all of the states have modern arbitration laws that require courts to enforce most pre-dispute arbitration agreements. One exception to the modern approach is Alabama, whose statute still provides that an agreement to submit a controversy to arbitration cannot be specifically enforced. Code of Ala. §8-1-41 (2009).

Although almost all states generally require courts to enforce arbitration agreements, many also exempt arbitration clauses dealing with certain subjects. For example, some state laws provide that pre-dispute arbitration agreements are not enforceable with respect to contracts dealing with certain subjects such as employment, medical claims, insurance, or franchisees. Some state laws also impose procedural requirements that are not included in the FAA, such as that an arbitration clause must be displayed in a particular font or location within the contract. In California, judicial rules and legislation impose disclosure requirements with respect to arbitrators and arbitral organizations. Because federal and state arbitration laws may differ, one of the important legal issues that must be resolved when arbitration is disputed is which law applies to a particular claim. This is one of the many thorny arbitration legal issues that are discussed later in this chapter.

iv. The New Field of Labor Arbitration

As is discussed above, in Chapter 9, it became extremely common to include arbitration clauses in collective bargaining agreements in the mid 1900s, as a tool to help ensure labor peace. Nonetheless, the enforceability of these clauses initially was not clear.

> Even though labor arbitration was the "king of the collective bargaining relation," its legal status remained uncertain. The National Labor Relations Act (NLRA) made no mention of the process. Similarly, the Labor Management Relations Act, enacted in 1947, contained no explicit reference to arbitration. However, . . . the Supreme Court would find in the [Labor Management Relation] Act's section 301(a) provision for enforcement of collective bargaining agreements in the federal courts and its section 203(d) sanction of employer-union fashioned dispute resolution devices, a springboard from which to fashion what amounts to a federal "common law" of labor arbitration.[3]

---

3. Stephen L. Hayford, Unification of the Law of Labor Arbitration and Commercial Arbitration: An Idea Whose Time Has Come, 52 Baylor L. Rev. 781, 786-787 (2000).

The Supreme Court, in Textile Workers Union v. Lincoln Mills, 353 U.S. 448, 451 (1957), first enunciated the federal common law of labor arbitration. In that case, holding that §301 of the Labor Management Relations Act "authorizes federal courts to fashion a body of federal law for the enforcement of these collective bargaining agreements," the Court found that the Act granted federal district courts jurisdiction to hear suits alleging violation of collective bargaining agreements. Explaining that federal policy supports the enforcement of agreements to arbitrate grievance disputes, the Court held that a district court would have jurisdiction to compel a company to engage in arbitration required by the collective bargaining agreement.

> Plainly the [employer's] agreement to arbitrate grievance disputes is the *quid pro quo* for an agreement [by the union] not to strike. Viewed in this light, the legislation does more than confer jurisdiction in the federal courts over labor organizations. It expresses a federal policy that federal courts should enforce these agreements on behalf of or against labor organizations and that industrial peace can be best obtained only in that way.

Id. at 455. In the *Steelworkers' Trilogy*, discussed earlier in Chapter 9.C.3.a, the Supreme Court further supported courts' enforcement of arbitration agreements contained in collective bargaining contracts. How far the Supreme Court would go in compelling arbitration in employment contracts, in both union and non-union contexts, became one of the most important legal issues in the field at the end of the twentieth century and into the twenty-first, as more fully explored below.

The relationship between the law of labor arbitration and the law of commercial (including employment) arbitration is somewhat confusing. Historically commercial arbitration was governed by the FAA and labor arbitration was governed mostly by common law. More recently, however, the Supreme Court has begun to cite labor precedent in commercial cases and vice versa, so the two bodies of law are increasingly blending together, e.g., Granite Rock Co. v. Int'l Bhd. of Teamsters, 130 S. Ct. 2847, 2857 at n.6 (2010).

2. The Supreme Court's Change of Heart Regarding Arbitration

a. The Supreme Court's Initial Reluctance to Enforce Agreements to Arbitrate Statutory Claims

Even after the FAA was passed and labor arbitration was becoming popular, a question remained as to which commercial and other non-labor disputes should be arbitrable, and thus, which arbitration agreements should be enforceable. In most countries, a distinction has been drawn between matters which are and are not appropriate for arbitration. At least for a time this same distinction was drawn in the United States.

For example, two of the leading advocates behind passage of the FAA in 1925 drew a distinction between arbitrable and non-arbitrable matters in a law review article they wrote in 1926. (Another portion of this article was excerpted earlier in this chapter.) Pay particular attention to the question of whether and which statutory or constitutional claims should be subject to arbitration.

 Julius Henry Cohen & Kenneth Dayton, **THE NEW FEDERAL ARBITRATION LAW**

12 Va. L. Rev. 265, 281 (1926)

Not all questions arising out of contracts ought to be arbitrated. It is a remedy peculiarly suited to the disposition of the ordinary disputes between merchants as to questions of fact — quantity, quality, time of delivery, compliance with terms of payment, excuses for non-performance, and the like. It has a place also in the determination of the simpler questions of law which arise out of these daily relations between merchants as to the passage of title, the existence of warranties, or the questions of law which are complementary to the questions of fact which we have just mentioned. It is not the proper method for deciding points of law of major importance involving constitutional questions or policy in the application of statutes. Speaking generally, it is a proper remedy for the determination of those classes of disputes which arise day by day in the common experience of the disputants and the individuals to whom the dispute is to be referred, where all meet upon a common ground. It is not a proper remedy for what we may call casual questions — questions with which the arbitrators have no particular experience and which are better left to the determination of skilled judges with a background of legal experience and established systems of law. . . .

Following Cohen's and Dayton's reasoning, for a time the Supreme Court and lower courts hesitated to grant motions to compel arbitration in circumstances they felt were not appropriate, such as those involving arbitration of statutory claims as opposed to contractual matters. The Supreme Court's 1953 decision in Wilko v. Swan, 346 U.S. 427, excerpted below, provides an example of courts' failure to embrace commercial arbitration of statutory claims. But it is critical to note that *Wilko*'s holding was subsequently overruled in 1989 by Rodriguez de Quijas v. Shearson/American Express, Inc., 490 U.S. 477 (1989), as part of the Supreme Court's current embrace of arbitration. See section A.2.b, below. Today the Supreme Court's view seems to be that all types of disputes are potentially arbitrable, unless Congress specifically provides that a particular type of dispute should not be arbitrated.

> **Problem 10-3.   *What Kinds of Disputes Should Be Arbitrable?***
>
> Does the distinction Cohen and Dayton drew between arbitrable and
> non-arbitrable disputes make sense to you? How does their reasoning
> relate to the different types of arbitration, described in Chapter 9? Does
> the question of what kinds of disputes ought to be arbitrable relate to the
> qualifications and training of the arbitrator, or to the degree to which
> arbitration awards are subject to court review?

 WILKO v. SWAN

346 U.S. 427, 430-438 (1953)

Mr. Justice REED delivered the opinion of the Court. Mr. Justice FRANKFURTER and
Mr. Justice MINTON, dissented.

[Plaintiff, a securities brokerage customer, brought suit in federal court under
§12(2) of the Securities Act of 1933 against the partners of the brokerage firm for
securities fraud. He claimed the firm made various misrepresentations and omissions
about stock that he purchased. Defendant responded by seeking a stay of the litigation under §3 of the FAA, pointing out that the margin agreement required the
customer to arbitrate all disputes with the brokerage. The district court denied the
stay on the ground that the arbitration agreement deprived plaintiff of the advantageous court remedy afforded by the Securities Act. The court of appeals reversed.]

The question is whether an agreement to arbitrate a future controversy is a
"condition, stipulation, or provision binding any person acquiring any security
to waive compliance with any provision" of the Securities Act which section 14
declares "void."[4] . . .

In response to a Presidential message urging that there be added to the ancient
rule of *caveat emptor* the further doctrine of "let the seller also beware," Congress
passed the Securities Act of 1933. Designed to protect investors, the Act requires
issuers, underwriters, and dealers to make full and fair disclosure of the character of
securities sold in interstate and foreign commerce and to prevent fraud in their sale.
To effectuate this policy, section 12(2) created a special right to recover for misrepresentation which differs substantially from the common-law action in that the seller
is made to assume the burden of proving lack of scienter. The Act's special right is
enforceable in any court of competent jurisdiction — federal or state — and
removal from a state court is prohibited. . . .

The United States Arbitration Act[5] establishes by statute the desirability of arbitration as an alternative to the complications of litigation. The reports of both
Houses on that Act stress the need for avoiding the delay and expense of litigation,

---

4. 48 Stat. 84, 15 U.S.C. §77n (2003). Section 14 provides: "Any condition, stipulation, or provision
binding any person acquiring any security to waive compliance with any provision of this subchapter
or of the rules and regulations of the Commission shall be void."
5. In early decisions, the FAA is usually referred to as the United States Arbitration Act.

and practice under its terms raises hope for its usefulness both in controversies based on statutes or on standards otherwise created. This hospitable attitude of legislatures and courts toward arbitration, however, does not solve our question as to the validity of petitioner's stipulation by the margin agreements, set out below, to submit to arbitration controversies that might arise from the transactions.

Petitioner argues that section 14 [n. 4, supra] shows that the purpose of Congress was to assure that sellers could not maneuver buyers into a position that might weaken their ability to recover under the Securities Act. He contends that arbitration lacks the certainty of a suit at law under the Act to enforce his rights. He reasons that the arbitration paragraph of the margin agreement is a stipulation that waives "compliance with" the provision of the Securities Act, set out in the margin, conferring jurisdiction of suits and special powers.

Respondent asserts that arbitration is merely a form of trial to be used in lieu of a trial at law, and therefore no conflict exists between the Securities Act and the United States Arbitration Act either in their language or in the congressional purposes in their enactment. Each may function within its own scope, the former to protect investors and the latter to simplify recovery for actionable violations of law by issuers or dealers in securities. . . .

The words of section 14 void any "stipulation" waiving compliance with any "provision" of the Securities Act. This arrangement to arbitrate is a "stipulation," and we think the right to select the judicial forum is the kind of "provision" that cannot be waived under section 14 of the Securities Act. . . . While a buyer and seller of securities, under some circumstances, may deal at arm's length on equal terms, it is clear that the Securities Act was drafted with an eye to the disadvantages under which buyers labor. Issuers of and dealers in securities have better opportunities to investigate and appraise the prospective earnings and business plans affecting securities than buyers. It is therefore reasonable for Congress to put buyers of securities covered by that Act on a different basis from other purchasers.

When the security buyer, prior to any violation of the Securities Act, waives his right to sue in courts, he gives up more than would a participant in other business transactions. The security buyer has a wider choice of courts and venue. He thus surrenders one of the advantages the Act gives him and surrenders it at a time when he is less able to judge the weight of the handicap the Securities Act places upon his adversary.

Even though the provisions of the Securities Act, advantageous to the buyer, apply, their effectiveness in application is lessened in arbitration as compared to judicial proceedings. Determination of the quality of a commodity or the amount of money due under a contract is not the type of issue here involved. This case requires subjective findings on the purpose and knowledge of an alleged violator of the Act. They must be not only determined but applied by the arbitrators without judicial instruction on the law. As their award may be made without explanation of their reasons and without a complete record of their proceedings, the arbitrators' conception of the legal meaning of such statutory requirements as "burden of proof," "reasonable care" or "material fact," . . . cannot be examined. Power to vacate an award is limited. While it may be true, as the Court of Appeals thought, that a failure of the arbitrators to decide in accordance with the provisions of the

Securities Act would "constitute grounds for vacating the award pursuant to section 10 of the Federal Arbitration Act," that failure would need to be made clearly to appear. In unrestricted submission, such as the present margin agreements envisage, the interpretations of the law by the arbitrators in contrast to manifest disregard are not subject, in the federal courts, to judicial review for error in interpretation. The United States Arbitration Act contains no provision for judicial determination of legal issues such as is found in the English law. As the protective provisions of the Securities Act require the exercise of judicial direction to fairly assure their effectiveness, it seems to us that Congress must have intended section 14 to apply to waiver of judicial trial and review.

. . . By the terms of the agreement to arbitrate, petitioner is restricted in his choice of forum prior to the existence of a controversy. While the Securities Act does not require petitioner to sue, a waiver in advance of a controversy stands upon a different footing.

Two policies, not easily reconcilable, are involved in this case. Congress has afforded participants in transactions subject to its legislative power an opportunity generally to secure prompt, economical and adequate solution of controversies through arbitration if the parties are willing to accept less certainty of legally correct adjustment. On the other hand, it has enacted the Securities Act to protect the rights of investors and has forbidden a waiver of any of those rights. Recognizing the advantages that prior agreements for arbitration may provide for the solution of commercial controversies, we decide that the intention of Congress concerning the sale of securities is better carried out by holding invalid such an agreement for arbitration of issues arising under the Act.

Reversed.

Wilko was far from the only case in which the Court expressed reluctance to enforce arbitration agreements with respect to statutory claims. For example, in Alexander v. Gardner-Denver Co., 415 U.S. 36 (1974), the Court held that employees whose union contracts contained arbitration clauses could nonetheless bring discrimination claims in court, even if they had already lost on related claims in arbitration. Subsequently, in Barrentine v. Arkansas-Best Freight Sys. Inc., 450 U.S. 728 (1981), the Court allowed employees to bring minimum wage claims under the Fair Labor Standards Act, even though they had unsuccessfully submitted wage claims based on the same underlying facts to a grievance committee. See also McDonald v. City of West Branch, 466 U.S. 284 (1984) (permitting discharged police officer to raise claim of violation of constitutional rights, even though he had previously lost at arbitration on the claim of improper discharge). However, as will be shown below, the Court has dramatically changed its tune.

b. The Supreme Court Embraces Arbitration Agreements

Beginning in the early 1980s, the Supreme Court's attitude toward commercial arbitration changed substantially from suspicion or even hostility to enthusiasm. In Moses H. Cone Memorial Hosp. v. Mercury Constr., 460 U.S. 1 (1983), the Court considered the validity of an arbitration provision that was part of a construction contract. The party opposing arbitration argued that its opponent had waived any right it would have had to arbitrate by delaying the dispute resolution process. In the course of the opinion, Justice Brennan and the majority opined:

> [Q]uestions of arbitrability must be addressed with a healthy regard for the federal policy favoring arbitration. . . . The Arbitration Act establishes that, as a matter of federal law, any doubts concerning the scope of arbitrable issues should be resolved in favor of arbitration, whether the problem at hand is the construction of the contract language itself or an allegation of waiver, delay, or a like defense to arbitrability.

460 U.S. at 24-25.

Although the Court presented this policy "favoring" commercial arbitration as if it were a longstanding judicial philosophy, in fact the policy had never previously been enunciated. Jean Sternlight characterizes the Court's announcement of the new philosophy as the espousal of a "myth that commercial arbitration served a substantial public purpose and should be favored regardless of the parties' intentions."[6] She goes on to explain:

> Significantly, the Court did not provide an explicit rationale for *why* arbitration should be favored over litigation. Most of the lower court cases it cited as favoring arbitration also provided no rationale for this favoritism. . . . In the absence of any other rationale, it appears that the Court was swayed or at least influenced by a desire to conserve judicial resources.[7]

Sternlight notes that at least two of the Justices, Burger and Rehnquist, were at the time writing articles and giving talks praising arbitration for being cost-effective and reducing court delay.[8]

In subsequent cases, the Court has frequently referred to the federal policy "favoring" arbitration, although it has never explicitly explained whether this policy means only that arbitration agreements are looked upon with favor or whether it really means that arbitration is to be favored *over* litigation. For example, in Scherk v. Alberto-Culver, 417 U.S. 506, 518-519 (1974) the Court held that a securities claim that might not be ordered to arbitration if brought domestically would be ordered to arbitration if the contract had international implications, because arbitration is favored in the international context. In Mitsubishi Motors Corp. v. Soler Chrysler-Plymouth, Inc., 473 U.S. 614, 629 (1985) the Court similarly held that even if arbitration of antitrust claims could not be compelled domestically it could be compelled in the context of international transactions, where arbitration is favored. Subsequently, building on these cases, the Court began to issue decisions rejecting one purported public policy exception to the enforcement of arbitration agreements after another. See Shearson/American Express, Inc. v. McMahon, 482 U.S 220 (1987) (holding that a consumer could be compelled to arbitrate claims

---

6. Jean R. Sternlight, Panacea or Corporate Tool? Debunking the Supreme Court's Preference for Binding Arbitration, 74 Wash. U. L.Q. 637, (1996).
7. Id. at 660-661.
8. Id. at 660 n.126, citing Warren E. Burger, Isn't There a Better Way?, 68 A.B.A. J. 274 (1982), and William Rehnquist, A Jurist's View of Arbitration, Arb. J., Mar. 1977, at 1.

against a brokerage under both §10(b) of the Securities Exchange Act of 1934 and RICO). Ultimately, in Rodriguez de Quijas v. Shearson/American Express, Inc., 490 U.S. 477, 479-890 (1989), the Court explicitly overruled *Wilko*, stating it was unduly hostile to arbitration, and held that a brokerage customer could be compelled to arbitrate claims brought under the Securities Act of 1933. Most recently, Granite Rock Co. v. Int'l Bhd. of Teamsters, 130 S. Ct. 2847, 2859-2860 (2010), clarified that arbitration is favored only when agreed to by the parties.

One landmark case that illustrates how far the Court has moved from the suspicion it exhibited in *Wilko* is *Gilmer v. Interstate/Johnson Lane Corp.* Although many had assumed that companies could not mandate arbitration of disputes implicating important public policy issues such as discrimination, the Supreme Court found otherwise.

GILMER v. INTERSTATE/JOHNSON LANE CORP.

500 U.S. 20, 22-35 (1991)

WHITE, J., delivered the opinion of the Court, in which REHNQUIST, C.J., and BLACKMUN, O'CONNOR, SCALIA, KENNEDY, and SOUTER, JJ., joined. STEVENS, J., filed a dissenting opinion, in which MARSHALL, J., joined.

The question presented in this case is whether a claim under the Age Discrimination in Employment Act of 1967 (ADEA) . . . can be subjected to compulsory arbitration pursuant to an arbitration agreement in a securities registration application. The Court of Appeals held that it could, 895 F.2d 195 (4th Cir. 1990), and we affirm.

I

Respondent Interstate/Johnson Lane Corporation (Interstate) hired petitioner Robert Gilmer as a Manager of Financial Services in May 1981. As required by his employment, Gilmer registered as a securities representative with several stock exchanges, including the New York Stock Exchange (NYSE). . . . His registration application . . . provided, among other things, that Gilmer "agree[d] to arbitrate any dispute, claim or controversy" arising between him and Interstate "that is required to be arbitrated under the rules, constitutions or by-laws of the organizations with which I register." . . . Of relevance to this case, NYSE Rule 347 provides for arbitration of "[a]ny controversy between a registered representative and any member or member organization arising out of the employment or termination of employment of such registered representative." . . .

Interstate terminated Gilmer's employment in 1987, at which time Gilmer was 62 years of age. After first filing an age discrimination charge with the Equal Employment Opportunity Commission (EEOC), Gilmer subsequently brought suit in . . . [court] alleging that Interstate had discharged him because of his age, in violation of the ADEA. In response to Gilmer's complaint, Interstate filed . . . a motion to compel arbitration of the ADEA claim. . . . The District Court denied Interstate's motion, based on this Court's decision in Alexander v. Gardner-Denver

Co., 415 U.S. 36 (1974), and because it concluded that "Congress intended to protect ADEA claimants from the waiver of a judicial forum." . . . The United States Court of Appeals for the Fourth Circuit reversed, finding "nothing in the text, legislative history, or underlying purposes of the ADEA indicating a congressional intent to preclude enforcement of arbitration agreements." 895 F.2d, at 197. We granted certiorari . . . to resolve a conflict among the Courts of Appeals regarding the arbitrability of ADEA claims.

II

The FAA was originally enacted in 1925. . . . Its purpose was to reverse the long-standing judicial hostility to arbitration agreements that had existed at English common law and had been adopted by American courts, and to place arbitration agreements upon the same footing as other contracts . . . Its primary substantive provision states that "[a] written provision in any maritime transaction or a contract evidencing a transaction involving commerce to settle by arbitration a controversy thereafter arising out of such contract or transaction . . . shall be valid, irrevocable, and enforceable, save upon such grounds as exist at law or in equity for the revocation of any contract." 9 U.S.C. §2. The FAA also provides for stays of proceedings in federal district courts when an issue in the proceeding is referable to arbitration, section 3, and for orders compelling arbitration when one party has failed, neglected, or refused to comply with an arbitration agreement, section 4. These provisions manifest a "liberal federal policy favoring arbitration agreements." Moses H. Cone Memorial Hospital v. Mercury Construction Corp., 460 U.S. 1, 24 (1983).

It is by now clear that statutory claims may be the subject of an arbitration agreement, enforceable pursuant to the FAA. Indeed, in recent years we have held enforceable arbitration agreements relating to claims arising under the Sherman Act, . . . the Securities Exchange Act of 1934; . . . the civil provisions of the Racketeer Influenced and Corrupt Organizations Act (RICO); . . . and section 12(2) of the Securities Act of 1933. . . . In these cases we recognized that "[b]y agreeing to arbitrate a statutory claim, a party does not forgo the substantive rights afforded by the statute; it only submits to their resolution in an arbitral, rather than a judicial, forum." Mitsubishi Motors Corp. v. Solar Chrysler-Plymouth, Inc., 473 U.S. 614, 628 (1985).

Although all statutory claims may not be appropriate for arbitration, "[h]aving made the bargain to arbitrate, the party should be held to it unless Congress itself has evinced an intention to preclude a waiver of judicial remedies for the statutory rights at issue." Id. In this regard, we note that the burden is on Gilmer to show that Congress intended to preclude a waiver of a judicial forum for ADEA claims. . . . If such an intention exists, it will be discoverable in the text of the ADEA, its legislative history, or an "inherent conflict" between arbitration and the ADEA's underlying purposes. . . . Throughout such an inquiry, it should be kept in mind that "questions of arbitrability must be addressed with a healthy regard for the federal policy favoring arbitration." *Moses H. Cone,* 460 U.S. at 24.

III

Gilmer concedes that nothing in the text of the ADEA or its legislative history explicitly precludes arbitration. He argues, however, that compulsory arbitration of

ADEA claims pursuant to arbitration agreements would be inconsistent with the statutory framework and purposes of the ADEA. Like the Court of Appeals, we disagree.

A

Congress enacted the ADEA in 1967 "to promote employment of older persons based on their ability rather than age; to prohibit arbitrary age discrimination in employment; [and] to help employers and workers find ways of meeting problems arising from the impact of age on employment." 29 U.S.C. §621(b). To achieve those goals, the ADEA, among other things, makes it unlawful for an employer "to fail or refuse to hire or to discharge any individual or otherwise discriminate against any individual with respect to his compensation, terms, conditions, or privileges of employment, because of such individual's age." 29 U.S.C. §623(a)(1). This proscription is enforced both by private suits and by the EEOC. . . .

As Gilmer contends, the ADEA is designed not only to address individual grievances, but also to further important social policies. . . . We do not perceive any inherent inconsistency between those policies, however, and enforcing agreements to arbitrate age discrimination claims. It is true that arbitration focuses on specific disputes between the parties involved. The same can be said, however, of judicial resolution of claims. Both of these dispute resolution mechanisms nevertheless also can further broader social purposes. The Sherman Act, the Securities Exchange Act of 1934, RICO, and the Securities Act of 1933 all are designed to advance important public policies, but, as noted above, claims under those statutes are appropriate for arbitration. "[S]o long as the prospective litigant effectively may vindicate [his or her] statutory cause of action in the arbitral forum, the statute will continue to serve both its remedial and deterrent function." *Mitsubishi,* 473 U.S. at 637.

We also are unpersuaded by the argument that arbitration will undermine the role of the EEOC in enforcing the ADEA. An individual ADEA claimant subject to an arbitration agreement will still be free to file a charge with the EEOC, even though the claimant is not able to institute a private judicial action. Indeed, Gilmer filed a charge with the EEOC in this case. In any event, the EEOC's role in combating age discrimination is not dependent on the filing of a charge; the agency may receive information concerning alleged violations of the ADEA "from any source," and it has independent authority to investigate age discrimination. See 29 C.F.R. §§1626.4, 1626.13 (1990). Moreover, nothing in the ADEA indicates that Congress intended that the EEOC be involved in all employment disputes. Such disputes can be settled, for example, without any EEOC involvement. . . . Finally, the mere involvement of an administrative agency in the enforcement of a statute is not sufficient to preclude arbitration. For example, the Securities Exchange Commission is heavily involved in the enforcement of the Securities Exchange Act of 1934 and the Securities Act of 1933, but we have held that claims under both of those statutes may be subject to compulsory arbitration. . . .

Gilmer also argues that compulsory arbitration is improper because it deprives claimants of the judicial forum provided for by the ADEA. Congress, however, did not explicitly preclude arbitration or other nonjudicial resolution of claims, even in its recent amendments to the ADEA. "[I]f Congress intended the substantive protection afforded [by the ADEA] to include protection against waiver of the right to a judicial forum, that intention will be deducible from text or legislative history." *Mitsubishi,* 473 U.S. at 628. Moreover, Gilmer's argument ignores the ADEA's flexible approach to resolution of claims. The EEOC, for example, is directed to pursue "informal methods of conciliation, conference, and persuasion," 29 U.S.C. §626(b), which suggests that out-of-court dispute resolution, such as arbitration, is consistent with the statutory scheme established by Congress. In addition, arbitration is consistent with Congress' grant of concurrent jurisdiction over ADEA claims to state and federal courts, see 29 U.S.C. §626(c)(1) (allowing suits to be brought "in any court of competent jurisdiction"), because arbitration agreements, "like the provision for concurrent jurisdiction, serve to advance the objective of allowing [claimants] a broader right to select the forum for resolving disputes, whether it be judicial or otherwise." Rodriguez de Quijas v. Shearson/American Express, Inc., 490 U.S. 477, 483 (1989).

B

In arguing that arbitration is inconsistent with the ADEA, Gilmer also raises a host of challenges to the adequacy of arbitration procedures. Initially, we note that in our recent arbitration cases we have already rejected most of these arguments as insufficient to preclude arbitration of statutory claims. Such generalized attacks on arbitration "res[t] on suspicion of arbitration as a method of weakening the protections afforded in the substantive law to would-be complainants," and as such, they are "far out of step with our current strong endorsement of the federal statutes favoring this method of resolving disputes." *Rodriguez de Quijas,* 490 U.S. at 481. Consequently, we address these arguments only briefly.

Gilmer first speculates that arbitration panels will be biased. However, "[w]e decline to indulge the presumption that the parties and arbitral body conducting a proceeding will be unable or unwilling to retain competent, conscientious and impartial arbitrators." *Mitsubishi,* 473 U.S. at 634. In any event, we note that the NYSE arbitration rules, which are applicable to the dispute in this case, provide protections against biased panels. The rules require, for example, that the parties be informed of the employment histories of the arbitrators, and that they be allowed to make further inquiries into the arbitrators' backgrounds. . . . In addition, each party is allowed one peremptory challenge and unlimited challenges for cause. . . . Moreover, the arbitrators are required to disclose "any circumstances which might preclude [them] from rendering an objective and impartial determination." . . . The FAA also protects against bias, by providing that courts may overturn arbitration decisions "[w]here there was evident partiality or corruption in the arbitrators." 9 U.S.C. §10(b). There has been no showing in this case that those provisions are inadequate to guard against potential bias.

Gilmer also complains that the discovery allowed in arbitration is more limited than in the federal courts, which he contends will make it difficult to prove discrimination. It is unlikely, however, that age discrimination claims require more extensive discovery than other claims that we have found to be arbitrable, such as RICO and antitrust claims. Moreover, there has been no showing in this case that the NYSE discovery provisions, which allow for document production, information requests, depositions, and subpoenas . . . will prove insufficient to allow ADEA claimants such as Gilmer a fair opportunity to present their claims. Although those procedures might not be as extensive as in the federal courts, by agreeing to arbitrate, a party "trades the procedures and opportunity for review of the courtroom for the simplicity, informality, and expedition of arbitration." *Mitsubishi,* 473 U.S. at 628. Indeed, an important counterweight to the reduced discovery in NYSE arbitration is that arbitrators are not bound by the rules of evidence. . . .

A further alleged deficiency of arbitration is that arbitrators often will not issue written opinions, resulting, Gilmer contends, in a lack of public knowledge of employers' discriminatory policies, an inability to obtain effective appellate review, and a stifling of the development of the law. The NYSE rules, however, do require that all arbitration awards be in writing, and that the awards contain the names of the parties, a summary of the issues in controversy, and a description of the award issued. . . . In addition, the award decisions are made available to the public. . . . Furthermore, judicial decisions addressing ADEA claims will continue to be issued because it is unlikely that all or even most ADEA claimants will be subject to arbitration agreements. Finally, Gilmer's concerns apply equally to settlements of ADEA claims, which, as noted above, are clearly allowed.[9]

It is also argued that arbitration procedures cannot adequately further the purposes of the ADEA because they do not provide for broad equitable relief and class actions. As the court below noted, however, arbitrators do have the power to fashion equitable relief. . . . Indeed, the NYSE rules applicable here do not restrict the types of relief an arbitrator may award, but merely refer to "damages and/or other relief." . . . The NYSE rules also provide for collective proceedings. . . . But "even if the arbitration could not go forward as a class action or class relief could not be granted by the arbitrator, the fact that the [ADEA] provides for the possibility of bringing a collective action does not mean that individual attempts at conciliation were intended to be barred." . . . Finally, it should be remembered that arbitration agreements will not preclude the EEOC from bringing actions seeking class-wide and equitable relief.

C

An additional reason advanced by Gilmer for refusing to enforce arbitration agreements relating to ADEA claims is his contention that there often will be unequal bargaining power between employers and employees. Mere inequality in bargaining power, however, is not a sufficient reason to hold that arbitration agreements are never enforceable in the employment context. Relationships between securities dealers and investors, for example, may involve unequal bargaining power, but we nevertheless held in *Rodriguez de Quijas* and *McMahon* that agreements to arbitrate in that context are enforceable. See 490 U.S. at 484; 482 U.S. at 230. As discussed

---

9. Gilmer also contends that judicial review of arbitration decisions is too limited. We have stated, however, that "although judicial scrutiny of arbitration awards necessarily is limited, such review is sufficient to ensure that arbitrators comply with the requirements of the statute" at issue. Shearson/American Express Inc. v. McMahon, 482 U.S. 220, 232 (1987).

above, the FAA's purpose was to place arbitration agreements on the same footing as other contracts. Thus, arbitration agreements are enforceable "save upon such grounds as exist at law or in equity for the revocation of any contract." 9 U.S.C. §2. "Of course, courts should remain attuned to well-supported claims that the agreement to arbitrate resulted from the sort of fraud or overwhelming economic power that would provide grounds 'for the revocation of any contract.'" *Mitsubishi*, 473 U.S. at 627. There is no indication in this case, however, that Gilmer, an experienced businessman, was coerced or defrauded into agreeing to the arbitration clause in his registration application. As with the claimed procedural inadequacies discussed above, this claim of unequal bargaining power is best left for resolution in specific cases. . . .

IV

In addition to the arguments discussed above, Gilmer vigorously asserts that our decision in Alexander v. Gardner-Denver Co., 415 U.S. 36 (1974), and its progeny . . . preclude arbitration of employment discrimination claims. Gilmer's reliance on these cases, however, is misplaced.

In *Gardner-Denver*, the issue was whether a discharged employee whose grievance had been arbitrated pursuant to an arbitration clause in a collective-bargaining agreement was precluded from subsequently bringing a Title VII action based upon the conduct that was the subject of the grievance. In holding that the employee was not foreclosed from bringing the Title VII claim, we stressed that an employee's contractual rights under a collective-bargaining agreement are distinct from the employee's statutory Title VII rights . . .

We also noted that a labor arbitrator has authority only to resolve questions of contractual rights. . . . By contrast, "in instituting an action under Title VII, the employee is not seeking review of the arbitrator's decision. Rather, he is asserting a statutory right independent of the arbitration process." Id., at 54. We further expressed concern that in collective-bargaining arbitration "the interests of the individual employee may be subordinated to the collective interests of all employees in the bargaining unit." Id., at 58, n.19.[10] . . .

There are several important distinctions between the *Gardner-Denver* line of cases and the case before us. First, those cases did not involve the issue of the enforceability of an agreement to arbitrate statutory claims. Rather, they involved the quite different issue whether arbitration of contract-based claims precluded subsequent judicial resolution of statutory claims. Since the employees there had not agreed to arbitrate their statutory claims, and the labor arbitrators were not authorized to resolve such claims, the arbitration in those cases understandably was held not to preclude subsequent statutory actions. Second, because the arbitration in those cases occurred in the context of a collective-bargaining agreement, the claimants there were represented by their unions in the arbitration proceedings. An important concern therefore was the tension between collective representation and

---

10. The Court in *Alexander* also expressed the view that arbitration was inferior to the judicial process for resolving statutory claims. Id., at 57-58. That "mistrust of the arbitral process," however, has been undermined by our recent arbitration decisions. . . .

individual statutory rights, a concern not applicable to the present case. Finally, those cases were not decided under the FAA, which, as discussed above, reflects a "liberal federal policy favoring arbitration agreements." *Mitsubishi*, 473 U.S., at 625. Therefore, those cases provide no basis for refusing to enforce Gilmer's agreement to arbitrate his ADEA claim.

V

We conclude that Gilmer has not met his burden of showing that Congress, in enacting the ADEA, intended to preclude arbitration of claims under that Act. Accordingly, the judgment of the Court of Appeals is *Affirmed*.

Even after the *Gilmer* decision was issued it was unclear for a time whether arbitration agreements contained in employment contracts would be enforceable under the FAA. (Although *Gilmer* involved a dispute between an employer and an employee, from a technical standpoint the arbitration clause was not mandated in an employment contract but rather in rules propounded by the stock exchanges in which the employee agreed to work. 500 U.S. at 25 n.2.). Citing Section 1 of the FAA, many argued that employees could not be required to arbitrate disputes with their employers.

Federal Arbitration Act Section 1 (1925)

[B]ut nothing herein contained shall apply to contracts of employment of seamen, railroad employees, or any other class of workers engaged in foreign or interstate commerce.

The Supreme Court resolved the dispute in Circuit City Stores, Inc. v. Adams, 532 U.S. 105 (2001), holding that the Section 1 exclusion applies narrowly to transportation workers (those workers who are directly engaged in interstate commerce) and that all other types of employees are potentially covered by the Federal Arbitration Act.

Problem 10-4. *Was* **Circuit City Stores v. Adams** *Correctly Decided?*

After reviewing the language of the FAA prepare to discuss whether the *Circuit City* case was correctly decided. Scholars have disagreed as to the meaning of Section 1. Compare Samuel Estreicher, Predispute Agreements to Arbitrate Statutory Employment Claims, 72 N.Y.U. L. Rev. 1345, 1365-1372 (1997) (arguing that Section 1 applies only to transportation workers) with Matthew W. Finkin, Employment Contracts Under the FAA — Reconsidered, 48 Lab. L.J. 328 (1997) & Jeffrey W. Stempel, Reconsidering the Employment Contract Exclusion in Section 1 of the Federal Arbitration Act: Correcting the Judiciary's Failure of Statutory Vision, 1991 J. Disp. Res. 259 (arguing that Section 1 excludes all employment claims from FAA).

Another important question that lingered after *Gilmer* and *Circuit City* was whether a unionized employer could require its employees to resolve all claims, including statutory discrimination claims, through arbitration rather than in litigation. That is, if a labor union entered a collective bargaining agreement that required its members to arbitrate rather than litigate all claims, could such an agreement cover statutory discrimination claims, as well as more traditional matters such as overtime, seniority, and work conditions. Attorneys and commentators noted a tension between *Gilmer* (holding that individuals could be required to arbitrate age discrimination claims) and *Alexander* (holding that a union member who participated in contractual arbitration was not foreclosed from bringing subsequent statutory discrimination claims in court). After all, the Supreme Court had distinguished rather than overturned *Alexander* in Section IV of its decision in *Gilmer*, excerpted above.

Those opposing the extension of *Gilmer* to unionized workers argued that it would not be fair or just to let unions bargain away their members' right to litigate, particularly since the union typically need not arbitrate all of its members' claims but rather can tell members they have no right to arbitrate a particular claim, if the union decides the claim is not worthy (as long as the union does not violate the duty of fair representation, a separate labor law doctrine). Those favoring the extension of *Gilmer* to unionized workers asserted that arbitrators are perfectly competent to resolve discrimination claims made by unionized employees, just as they do those of non-unionized employees.

The Supreme Court first took on this question in Wright v. Universal Maritime Serv. Corp., 525 U.S. 70, 79-80 (1998), but did not fully resolve the question in that case. Instead the Court in *Wright* held that a collective bargaining agreement could only be interpreted to require an employee to waive litigation of statutory claims if that waiver was "clear and unmistakable," and found the *Wright* waiver did not meet that test.

Then, in 2009, the Court in 14 Penn Plaza v. Pyett, 129 S. Ct. 1456 (2009) held in a 5-4 decision that union members, like non-unionized employees, can be contractually required to arbitrate statutory as well as contractual claims. However, the

Court's decision in *Pyett* still does not address a situation in which an employee might be deprived of the right both to arbitrate or litigate the claim, rather leaving such factual and legal issues for another day. 129 S. Ct. at 1474. Thus, in light of *Pyett,* employers can indeed use their collective bargaining agreement to require unionized workers to resolve all statutory discrimination claims through arbitration, at least so long as the worker has the opportunity to arbitrate the claim, regardless of the wishes of the union.

   14 PENN PLAZA v. PYETT

129 S. Ct. 1456, 1465, 1466, 1468-1469, 1472, 1474 (2009)

THOMAS, J., delivered the opinion of the Court, in which ROBERTS, C.J., and SCALIA, KENNEDY, and ALITO, JJ., joined. STEVENS, J., filed a dissenting opinion. SOUTER, J., filed a dissenting opinion, in which STEVENS, GINSBURG, and BREYER, JJ., joined.

The *Gilmer* Court's interpretation of the ADEA fully applies in the collective-bargaining context. Nothing in the law suggests a distinction between the status of arbitration agreements signed by an individual employee and those agreed to by a union representative. . . .

The [National Labor Relations Act] provided the Union and the [Realty Advisory Board on Labor Relations Inc.] with statutory authority to collectively bargain for arbitration of workplace discrimination claims, and Congress did not terminate that authority with respect to federal age-discrimination claims in the ADEA. . . .

The CBA's arbitration provision is also fully enforceable under the *Gardner-Denver* line of cases. . . . *Gardner-Denver* and its progeny . . . do not control the outcome where, as is the case here, the collective-bargaining agreement's arbitration provision expressly covers both statutory and contractual discrimination claims.

We recognize that apart from their narrow holdings, the *Gardner-Denver* line of cases included broad dicta that was highly critical of the use of arbitration for the vindication of statutory antidiscrimination rights. That skepticism, however, rested on a misconceived view of arbitration that this Court has since abandoned. . . .

[T]he Court in *Gardner-Denver* raised in a footnote a "further concern" regarding "the union's exclusive control over the manner and extent to which an individual grievance is presented." 415 U.S. at 58, n. 19. The Court suggested that in arbitration, as in the collective bargaining process, a union may subordinate the interests of an individual employee to the collective interests of all employees in the bargaining unit. . . .

We cannot rely on this judicial policy concern as a source of authority for introducing a qualification to the ADEA that is not found in its text. . . . Until Congress amends the ADEA to meet the conflict-of-interest concern identified in the *Gardner-Denver* dicta, and seized on by respondents here, there is "no reason to color the lens through which the arbitration clause is read" simply because of an alleged conflict of interest between a union and its members. Mitsubishi Motors Corp., 473 U.S. at 628. . . .

Respondents also argue that the CBA operates as a substantive waiver of their ADEA rights because it not only precludes a federal lawsuit, but also allows the Union to block arbitration of these claims. . . . Petitions contest this characterization of the CBA . . . and offer record evidence suggesting that the Union has allowed respondents to continue with the arbitration even though the Union has declined to participate. . . . But not only does this question require resolution of contested factual allegations, it was not fully briefed to this or any court and is not fairly encompassed within the question presented. . . . Thus, although a substantive waiver of federally protected civil rights will not be upheld, . . . we are not positioned to resolve in the first instance whether the CBA allows the Union to prevent respondents from "effectively vindicating" their "federal statutory rights in the arbitral forum." Green Tree Financial Corp.-Ala. v. Randolph, 531 U.S. 79, 90 (2000). Resolution of this question at this juncture would be particularly inappropriate in light of our hesitation to invalidate arbitration agreements on the basis of speculation.

Equal Employment Opportunity Commission & Arbitration

Note that according to the Supreme Court's decision in EEOC v. Waffle House, 534 U.S. 279, 294 (2002) employers cannot use arbitration to prevent employees from filing claims of discrimination with the Equal Employment Opportunity Commission, nor to prevent the EEOC from filing its own actions to protect employees' rights. The mere fact that an employee is covered by an arbitration agreement does not limit the remedies available to EEOC, though an employee's resolution of his claim through arbitration or settlement may limit the availability of other personal remedies. Id. at 296-297.

Problem 10-5.   *Reversing* 14 Penn Plaza v. Pyett

Some are now arguing that Congress should take action to effectively reverse the Court's decision in *14 Penn Plaza v. Pyett*. What, if any, legislation do you think should be adopted regarding union members' right to bring statutory claims in court? Can you draft such a statute?

After *Gilmer, Circuit City*, and *Pyett* it is generally recognized that absent an explicit prohibition, the Supreme Court will find all types of disputes to be arbitrable. Nonetheless, as will be discussed infra, specific clauses can still be challenged on contractual or other grounds.

Problem 10-6.   *Treatment of Arbitration in Other Countries*

Imagine that you have been retained to represent Widget Inc., a U.S. corporation that sells its products in many countries around the world. The company has instructed you to use arbitration agreements in the company's contracts whenever possible, but you want to make sure the contracts would be enforceable. While Americans may tend to assume that other countries' laws are similar to those of the U.S., this is not always true. With regard to arbitration, many countries' laws and public policies provide that certain kinds of claims are not subject to arbitration, even if the parties seemingly contracted for arbitration. That is, "some disputes are treated as non-arbitrable or not objectively arbitrable, relieving states from otherwise applicable obligations to recognize and enforce agreements to arbitrate such disputes." Gary B. Born, International Commercial Arbitration (vol. 1) 767 (2009). Some claims that are commonly exempted include labor and employment, antitrust, and domestic relations. Also, within the European Union, companies are not permitted to require consumers to arbitrate their claims. See Jean R. Sternlight, Is the U.S. Out on a Limb? Comparing the U.S. Approach to Mandatory Consumer and Employment Arbitration to That of the Rest of the World, 56 Miami L. Rev. 831 (2002) and Matthew Finkin, Privatization of Wrongful Dismissal Protection in Comparative Perspective, 37 Indust. L.J. 149 (2008). How would you go about researching when it would be possible to include arbitration clauses in Widget's contracts?

Problem 10-7.   *Should Congress Prohibit Pre-Dispute Arbitration Agreements as to Any Category of Dispute?*

Although the Supreme Court, in the last twenty years, has refused to find any category of dispute non-arbitrable, it has repeatedly stated that Congress has the power to declare any category of dispute off-limits, if it wishes. Alternatively, even if Congress does not rule whole categories of disputes entirely off-limits to arbitration, Congress could provide that *pre-dispute* arbitration agreements are not valid with respect to certain categories of disputes. To date, Congress has, in two instances, provided that pre-dispute arbitration agreements are not valid. The Motor Vehicle Franchise Contract Arbitration Fairness Act of 2001 protects car dealers from arbitration imposed by car manufacturers, but interestingly does nothing to prohibit car dealers from requiring their customers to arbitrate future disputes, as has become common. Another piece of legislation protects members of the military from arbitration imposed by payday lenders. It is "unlawful for any creditor to extend consumer credit to a covered member or a dependent of such member with respect to which . . . the creditor requires the borrower to submit to arbitration or imposes onerous legal notice provisions in the case of a dispute." 10 U.S.C. §987(e)(3) (2000). As will be discussed infra, in section D.4, legislation known as the Arbitration Fairness Act has recently been introduced in Congress that would prevent courts from enforcing pre-dispute arbitration agreements with respect to consumer, employment, civil rights, or franchise disputes. Do you think Congress should pass this or any other legislation rendering certain kinds of disputes non-arbitrable?

3. The Enforcement of Mandatory Arbitration Provisions

As arbitration became more popular with the Supreme Court in the 1980s and as companies increasingly used form contracts to require that their consumers and employees resolve future disputes through arbitration, rather than in litigation, attorneys and commentators began to question whether such mandatory imposition of arbitration violated the U.S. Constitution or could otherwise be attacked. While, in theory, some of the arguments discussed below might also be used to attack arbitration that was agreed to knowingly and voluntarily by all parties, in reality the challenges have primarily been geared to attack mandatory provisions. We will discuss policy aspects of the mandatory arbitration debate infra, in section D.

a. *Is Mandatory Contractual Imposition of Arbitration on Consumers, Employees or other "Little Guys" Unconstitutional?*

Although many law students and scholars find the constitutionality arguments intuitively appealing, to date, courts have not generally accepted these arguments. To establish a violation of the Due Process Clause, arbitration opponents must first demonstrate the existence of state action, a requirement that has proved very difficult. When two private parties contractually "agree" to arbitrate future disputes, whether knowingly or alternatively in a small print adhesive contract, most courts have found no state involvement sufficient to rise to the level of state action.[11] On the other hand, where Congress, a state legislature, or a court imposes the arbitration requirement, the challenger should have no problem establishing the existence of state action. But even once state action is established, the challenger must also demonstrate that the arbitration process is sufficiently unfair as to violate the norms of due process. Courts have not typically gotten to this step, but even if they did courts would not likely strike down typical arbitration provisions as lacking due process.

Challengers may also argue that a binding arbitration provision violates their rights to a jury trial under the Seventh Amendment or a state constitutional clause. The Seventh Amendment argument is potentially valid only in cases in which a Seventh Amendment right would otherwise have applied, that is, cases brought in federal court, "at common law," claiming damages of at least $20. The state clauses apply more broadly. On their face, the jury trial arguments seem promising. No state action need be proven, and in the non-arbitration context, courts have upheld jury trial waivers only when the waivers are made knowingly, voluntarily, and intelligently. Many mandatory arbitration provisions arguably would not pass this test. Nonetheless, constitutional jury trial rights have rarely defeated contractual arbitration clauses as courts tend to find that, by "agreeing" to arbitration, the parties waived any jury trial rights they would have had.[12] Jury trial arguments will likely be effective, however, where legislatures or courts, rather than private parties, replace litigation with binding arbitration.

b. *Contractual and Statutory Arguments that Arbitration Agreements Are Not Enforceable*

Once parties have agreed to arbitrate future disputes, most frequently the process proceeds smoothly, without the need for court intervention. Typically, the

---

11. For a discussion and defense of this position see Sarah Rudolph Cole, Arbitration and State Action, 2005 B.Y.U. L. Rev. 1. Compare Richard C. Reuben, Public Justice: Toward a State Action Theory of Alternative Dispute Resolution, 85 Cal. L. Rev. 577, 615-619 (1997) (arguing that intertwining of public and private processes in enforcement of contractual arbitration gives rise to state action) and Jean R. Sternlight, Rethinking the Constitutionality of the Supreme Court's Preference for Binding Arbitration: A Fresh Assessment of Jury Trial, Separation of Powers, and Due Process Concerns, 72 Tul. L. Rev. 1, 40-47 (1997) (arguing that state action exists at least to the extent courts rely on a preference for arbitration over litigation to interpret validity and scope of arbitration agreements).
12. See Jean R. Sternlight, Mandatory Binding Arbitration and the Demise of the Seventh Amendment Right to a Jury Trial, 16 Ohio St. J. on Disp. Resol. 669 (2001).

arbitrators are selected, relevant documents are exchanged, and the arbitration proceeds. In the minority of cases, however, one or more party argues that it should not, in fact, be required to arbitrate its claims or defenses. Although the U.S. Supreme Court has made clear that virtually any type of dispute can be arbitrated (absent Congressional language to the contrary), and although Constitutional attacks on arbitration have largely failed, it remains true that courts or potentially arbitrators themselves will hold some arbitration agreements to be unenforceable.[13] The two primary arguments that still may be used to defeat an arbitration agreement are (1) standard contract arguments; and (2) arguments that the wording of the specific clause would prevent a party from protecting their rights under federal law.

The most successful means for challenging arbitration clauses have been contractual and other common law attacks. As §2 of the FAA makes clear and as the Supreme Court has frequently stated, arbitration clauses can be invalidated on standard common law grounds. See, e.g., Allied-Bruce Terminix Cos. v. Dobson, 513 U.S. 265, 281 (1995) (stating "[s]tates may regulate contracts, including arbitration clauses, under general contract law principles and they may invalidate an arbitration clause 'upon such grounds as exist at law or in equity for the revocation of any contract' "). For example, the challenger may argue that the clause was unconscionable, invalid due to lack of consideration, invalid due to fraud, that it lacked mutuality or that the clause did not cover the particular claim.

Of the contractual arguments, unconscionability has been the most successful. In considering whether a particular arbitration clause is so grossly unfair that it ought to be held unconscionable, courts apply state law that may vary somewhat by jurisdiction. Typically, such law looks to both the procedural aspects of the clause (how it was imposed, e.g. print size, actual negotiation, relative bargaining power of the parties) and the substance of the clause (specific nature of the arbitration called for by the clause). Courts do not typically strike down run-of-the-mill arbitration clauses as unconscionable. Instead, courts only tend to strike down the clauses that appear most unfair (e.g., because they impose excessive costs, require claimants to travel to distant locations, limit remedies, or impose a biased arbitrator).[14] The Supreme Court recently granted certiorari in AT&T Mobility v. Concepcion, 130 S. Ct. 3322 (2010), in which it appears the Court will examine whether certain unconscionability determinations may be preempted by the FAA.

Courts and commentators are currently paying a great deal of attention to the question of whether arbitration clauses that expressly prohibit claimants from joining together in class actions ought to be held unconscionable on that basis. This is an extremely important question because companies are increasingly using arbitration clauses that include such class action prohibitions, particularly in the consumer setting. Indeed, some say that one of companys' primary motivations for imposing arbitration is to insulate themselves from potential class action exposure. A number

---

13. The question of whether courts or instead arbitrators should decide on the validity and scope of arbitration clauses will be discussed infra in Section B of this chapter.

14. For discussion of the applicability of unconscionability arguments to arbitration clauses see Charles L. Knapp, Unconscionability as a Signaling Device, 46 San Diego L. Rev. 609 (2009) and Jeffrey W. Stempel, Arbitration Unconscionability and Equilibrium: The Return of Unconscionability Analysis as a Counterweight to Arbitration Formalism, 19 Ohio St. J. on Disp. Resol. 757 (2004).

of courts have found that class action prohibitions can be unconscionable, reasoning that such prohibitions may effectively insulate a company from being called to account for its allegedly illegal conduct.[15] On the other hand, other federal and state courts have found the use of arbitration to eliminate class actions unproblematic.[16]

The Supreme Court has shown great interest of late regarding the intersection between arbitration and class actions. Stolt-Nielsen SA v. AnimalFeeds Intern., 130 S. Ct. 1758 (2010), found that classwide arbitration is permissible only when all parties to an arbitration agreement have agreed to that form of arbitration. Those who believe that it is not unconscionable to use arbitration to eliminate class actions will argue that *Stolt-Nielsen* supports their position, and indeed that the FAA pre-empts findings that class action waivers are unconscionable. Subsequent to *Stolt-Nielsen*, in American Express v. Italian Colors Restaurant, 130 S. Ct. 2410 (2010), the Supreme Court vacated and remanded for reconsideration a Second Circuit decision that had found a class action waiver unenforceable in that it would deprive plaintiffs of the opportunity to present their antitrust claim. 554 F.3d 300 (2009). While the Second Circuit may, on remand, find that its prior decision still stands, at minimum the Court has sent a message that the many decisions voiding arbitral class action waivers are in some jeopardy. Finally, as noted, the Supreme Court recently granted certiorari in AT&T Mobility v. Concepcion, 130 S. Ct. 3322 (2010). This case considers whether a decision voiding an arbitral class action as unconscionable was preempted by the FAA where the lower courts were arguably applying a different and stricter test for unconscionability to arbitration clauses than they were to other kinds of contracts.

One well-known example of a case in which a court struck down an arbitration clause as both unconscionable and in violation of state statutory provisions is Armendariz v. Foundation Health Psychare Services, 6 P.3d 669 (Cal. 2000). Plaintiffs had brought an employment action for wrongful termination and the employer sought to require them to bring their claim in arbitration, rather than in litigation. Examining the particulars of the arbitration clause, the California Supreme Court held that the clause was inherently unfair, and severed those portions of the clause that it found improper. The Court emphasized the clause's lack of mutuality and the fact that it limited the damages employees could recover.

Perhaps because unconscionability challenges have worked so well, companies that are imposing arbitration on their employees and consumers are now beginning to argue that arbitrators rather than courts should resolve such challenges. The Supreme Court recently held in Rent-a-Center West v. Jackson, 130 S. Ct. 2772 (2010), that parties can draft arbitration clauses to require that arbitrators, rather than judges, decide such claims. This case will be discussed infra in section B of this chapter.

---

15. E.g., Kristian v. Comcast Corp., 446 F.3d 25 (1st Cir. 2006).
16. E.g., Jenkins v. First Am. Cash Adv., 400 F.3d 868 (11th Cir. 2005), cert den. 126 S. Ct. 1457 (2006). For general discussion of this matter see Myriam Gilles, Opting Out of Liability: The Forthcoming, Near Total Demise of the Modern Class Action, 104 Mich L. Rev. 373 (2005) and Jean R. Sternlight & Elizabeth J. Jensen, Using Arbitration to Eliminate Consumer Class Actions: Efficient Business Practice or Unconscionable Abuse?, 67 Law & Contemp. Probs. 75 (2004).

Although consumers and employees have been successful in striking down some arbitration clauses on unconscionability and other grounds, these cases are often expensive to litigate and win. As the challengers bear the burden of proving that a particular clause is grossly unfair, the challengers must often conduct substantial discovery and retain expert witnesses to prove their point. Thus, somewhat ironically, the battle over arbitration can be quite expensive and time consuming. To the extent the challengers prevail, the court may well sever just that portion of the clause rather than entirely void the arbitration provision.

Also, as state law varies substantially with regard to the enforceability of arbitration clauses, companies are now increasingly inserting choice of law clauses that require the arbitration clause to be considered under the law of a jurisdiction where it is more likely to be enforced. Thus, the extent to which such choice of law provisions are themselves enforceable is being hotly contested. E.g., Hoffman v. Citibank, 546 F.3d 1078 (9th Cir. 2008).

Problem 10-8.   *Avoiding Arbitration in Post-Gilmer Discrimination Claim*

You represent a securities broker, Julie Jackson, who was hired for the position from which Mr. Gilmer (see *Gilmer v. Interstate/Johnson Lane Corp.*) was terminated. Ms. Jackson, a 57-year-old African American female, who was subsequently fired, believes she was terminated on the basis of her race, age and gender. She wishes to present these claims in court, but like Mr. Gilmer she is covered by an arbitration clause. The clause has some different terms than did Mr. Gilmer's clause. Ms. Jackson wants to know whether there are any contractual arguments she might make that she is entitled to litigate her claims, even though Mr. Gilmer's attempt to litigate his claim of age discrimination was unsuccessful. What are your thoughts? What kind of research would you need to do to answer Ms. Jackson's question?

---

c. As-Applied Federal Statutory Challenges

Although the Supreme Court has found that claims under most federal statutes are generally subject to arbitration, the Court has also explained that "[b]y agreeing to arbitrate a statutory claim, a party does not forgo the substantive rights afforded by the statute; it only submits to their resolution in an arbitral, rather than a judicial, forum." Mitsubishi Motors Corp. v. Soler Chrysler-Plymouth, Inc., 473 U.S. 614, 628 (1985). Thus, where a challenger can show that the arbitration clause was written in such a way as to effectively prevent the challenger from vindicating her rights under a particular federal statute, the Court has found that the arbitration clause should not be enforced. So, although the facial attack made by plaintiffs in *Gilmer* failed, the Court left open the possibility that future age discrimination plaintiffs could void a particular arbitration clause if plaintiffs could show it prevented them from adequately vindicating their rights due to specific failings in the arbitration process (for example, non-neutral arbitrators, insufficient discovery, or inadequate appeal opportunities). In the following case, plaintiffs attempted to show that they could not effectively vindicate their rights under federal law because the costs of arbitration were too high. You will see that although the Court rejected plaintiffs' claim due to an inadequate factual showing, the Court recognized that this attack on arbitration could potentially be valid if a stronger factual showing could be made.

 GREEN TREE FINANCIAL CORP.-ALABAMA v. RANDOLPH

531 U.S. 79, 82-84, 89-97 (2000)

Chief Justice R EHNQUIST delivered the opinion of the Court.

[The Court first determined that an order compelling arbitration and dismissing a party's underlying claims is a "final decision with respect to an arbitration" within the meaning of §16(a)(3) of the Federal Arbitration Act, 9 U.S.C. §16(a)(3), and thus is immediately appealable.]

Respondent Larketta Randolph purchased a mobile home from Better Cents Home Builders, Inc., in Opelika, Alabama. She financed this purchase through petitioner[ ] Green Tree Financial Corporation. . . . Petitioners' Manufactured Home Retail Installment Contract and Security Agreement . . . provided that all disputes arising from, or relating to, the contract, whether arising under case law or statutory law, would be resolved by binding arbitration.

Randolph later sued petitioners, alleging that they violated the Truth in Lending Act . . . [and] the Equal Credit Opportunity Act by requiring her to arbitrate her statutory causes of action. She brought this action on behalf of a similarly situated class. In lieu of an answer, petitioners filed a motion to compel arbitration, to stay the action, or, in the alternative, to dismiss. The District Court granted petitioners' motion to compel arbitration . . . [and] denied her request to certify a class. . . .

The [Court of Appeals] then determined that the arbitration agreement failed to provide the minimum guarantees that respondent could vindicate her statutory rights under the TILA . . . [in that] the arbitration agreement was silent with respect to payment of filing fees, arbitrators' costs, and other arbitration expenses. On that basis, the court held that the agreement to arbitrate posed a risk that respondent's ability to vindicate her statutory rights would be undone by "steep" arbitration costs, and therefore was unenforceable. . . .

We now turn to the question whether Randolph's agreement to arbitrate is unenforceable because it says nothing about the costs of arbitration, and thus fails to provide her protection from potentially substantial costs of pursuing her federal statutory claims in the arbitral forum. . . .

In determining whether statutory claims may be arbitrated, we first ask whether the parties agreed to submit their claims to arbitration, and then ask whether Congress has evinced an intention to preclude a waiver of judicial remedies for the statutory rights at issue. In this case, it is undisputed that the parties agreed to arbitrate all claims relating to their contract, including claims involving statutory rights. Nor does Randolph contend that the TILA evinces an intention to preclude a waiver of judicial remedies. She contends instead that the arbitration agreement's silence with respect to costs and fees creates a "risk" that she will be required to bear prohibitive arbitration costs if she pursues her claims in an arbitral forum, and thereby forces her to forgo any claims she may have against petitioners. Therefore, she argues, she is unable to vindicate her statutory rights in arbitration.

It may well be that the existence of large arbitration costs could preclude a litigant such as Randolph from effectively vindicating her federal statutory rights in the arbitral forum. But the record does not show that Randolph will bear such costs if she goes to arbitration. Indeed, it contains hardly any information on the matter.[17] As the Court of Appeals recognized, "we lack . . . information about how claimants fare under Green Tree's arbitration clause." 178 F.3d 1149 at 1158. The record reveals only the arbitration agreement's silence on the subject, and that fact alone is plainly insufficient to render it unenforceable. The "risk" that Randolph will be saddled with prohibitive costs is too speculative to justify the invalidation of an arbitration agreement.

To invalidate the agreement on that basis would undermine the "liberal federal policy favoring arbitration agreements." . . . It would also conflict with our prior holdings that the party resisting arbitration bears the burden of proving that the claims at issue are unsuitable for arbitration. We have held that the party seeking to avoid arbitration bears the burden of establishing that Congress intended to preclude arbitration of the statutory claims at issue. Similarly, we believe that where, as here, a party seeks to invalidate an arbitration agreement on the ground that arbitration would be prohibitively expensive, that party bears the burden of showing the likelihood of incurring such costs. Randolph did not meet that burden. How detailed the showing of prohibitive expense must be before the party seeking arbitration

---

17. In Randolph's motion for reconsideration in the District Court, she asserted that "[a]rbitration costs are high" and that she did not have the resources to arbitrate. But she failed to support this assertion. She first acknowledged that petitioners had not designated a particular arbitration association or arbitrator to resolve their dispute. Her subsequent discussion of costs relied entirely on unfounded assumptions. She stated that "[f]or the purposes of this discussion, we will assume filing with the [American Arbitration Association], the filing fee is $500 for claims under $10,000 and this does not include the cost of the arbitrator or administrative fees." Randolph relied on, and attached as an exhibit, what appears to be informational material from the American Arbitration Association that does not discuss the amount of filing fees. She then noted: "[The American Arbitration Association] further cites $700 per day as the average arbitrator's fee." For this proposition she cited an article in the Daily Labor Report, February 15, 1996, published by the Bureau of National Affairs, entitled Labor Lawyers at ABA Session Debate Role of American Arbitration Association. Plaintiff's Motion for Reconsideration, Record Doc. No. 53, pp. 8-9. The article contains a stray statement by an association executive that the average arbitral fee is $700 per day. Randolph plainly failed to make any factual showing that the American Arbitration Association would conduct the arbitration, or that, if it did, she would be charged the filing fee or arbitrator's fee that she identified. These unsupported statements provide no basis on which to ascertain the actual costs and fees to which she would be subject in arbitration.

In this Court, Randolph's brief lists fees incurred in cases involving other arbitrations as reflected in opinions of other Courts of Appeals, while petitioners' counsel states that arbitration fees are frequently waived by petitioners. None of this information affords a sufficient basis for concluding that Randolph would in fact have incurred substantial costs in the event her claim went to arbitration.

must come forward with contrary evidence is a matter we need not discuss; for in this case neither during discovery nor when the case was presented on the merits was there any timely showing at all on the point. The Court of Appeals therefore erred in deciding that the arbitration agreement's silence with respect to costs and fees rendered it unenforceable.

The judgment of the Court of Appeals is affirmed in part and reversed in part.

Justice GINSBURG, with whom Justice STEVENS and Justice SOUTER join, and with whom Justice BREYER joins as to Parts I and III, concurring in part and dissenting in part. . . .

II

The Court today deals with a "who pays" question, specifically, who pays for the arbitral forum. The Court holds that Larketta Randolph bears the burden of demonstrating that the arbitral forum is financially inaccessible to her. Essentially, the Court requires a party, situated as Randolph is, either to submit to arbitration without knowing who will pay for the forum or to demonstrate up front that the costs, if imposed on her, will be prohibitive. As I see it, the case in its current posture is not ripe for such a disposition.

The Court recognizes that "the existence of large arbitration costs could preclude a litigant such as Randolph from effectively vindicating her federal statutory rights in the arbitral forum." . . . But, the Court next determines, "the party resisting arbitration bears the burden of proving that the claims at issue are unsuitable for arbitration" and "Randolph did not meet that burden." . . . In so ruling, the Court blends two discrete inquiries: First, is the arbitral forum *adequate* to adjudicate the claims at issue; second, is that forum *accessible* to the party resisting arbitration.

Our past decisions deal with the first question, the *adequacy* of the arbitral forum to adjudicate various statutory claims. These decisions hold that the party resisting arbitration bears the burden of establishing the inadequacy of the arbitral forum for adjudication of claims of a particular genre. It does not follow like the night the day, however, that the party resisting arbitration should also bear the burden of showing that the arbitral forum would be financially inaccessible to her. . . .

III

. . . As a repeat player in the arbitration required by its form contract, Green Tree has superior information about the cost to consumers of pursuing arbitration. In these circumstances, it is hardly clear that Randolph should bear the burden of demonstrating up front the arbitral forum's inaccessibility, or that she should be required to submit to arbitration without knowing how much it will cost her. . . .

For the reasons stated, I dissent from the Court's reversal of the Eleventh Circuit's decision on the cost question. I would instead vacate and remand for further consideration of the accessibility of the arbitral forum to Randolph.

Problem 10-9. *Voiding an Arbitration Clause in an Antitrust Suit*

Your firm represents a restaurant that seeks to bring an antitrust claim against American Express. The restaurant owner is upset because the contract it has entered with American Express states that if the restaurant accepts American Express charge cards it must also accept American Express credit and debit cards. The restaurant believes that this contract calls for "tying," which is proscribed by antitrust law. The restaurant seeks to join with other restaurants covered by the clause to sue American Express in a class action in court. However, the restaurant's contract contains an arbitration clause. The partner at your firm has asked you to consider whether you might successfully have a court void the arbitration clause on the ground that it prevents the restaurant from adequately vindicating its right under the antitrust law. What do you think? What would you need to investigate to be able to fully answer this question? See generally In re American Express Merchant's Litigation, 554 F.3d 300 (2d Cir. 2009), vacated for reconsideration, 130 S. Ct. 2410 (2010).

Problem 10-10. *Voiding an Arbitration Clause in Post-Randolph Consumer Suit*

A. Sara Valdez has come to consult you with respect to her potential claim against Bank of the Angels, a company from which she obtained a home loan. Sara believes that the loan was illegal under federal law in various respects. However, the loan agreement clearly requires Sara to arbitrate all disputes pertaining to the loan. According to the arbitration clause, Sara must bring her arbitration claim to the Banking Arbitration Board, an entity which has offices only in Chicago and which requires claimants to pay $200 per hour for the arbitrator's time, as well as to pay a filing fee which varies from $500 to $50,000, depending on the size of the claim. Sara is not wealthy and you both believe these charges are excessive. In light of *Randolph*, what kind of evidence do you think would be sufficient to convince a court that your client could not vindicate her rights? How would you go about gathering that evidence? What would be the cost, and to whom, of gathering that evidence? Blair v. Scott Specialty Gases, 283 F.3d 595,

604-610 (3d Cir. 2002) (discussing the extensive showing it thought a plaintiff would have to make to defeat an arbitration clause as too costly). For an empirical summary of some cost cases, see Michael H. Leroy & Peter Feuille, When Is Cost an Unlawful Barrier to Alternative Dispute Resolution? The Ever Green Tree of Mandatory Employment Arbitration, 50 UCLA L. Rev. 143 (2002) (finding that 77 percent of trial courts and 50 percent of appellate courts ordered arbitration when plaintiffs challenged the arbitration as unduly expensive). Note that Justice Ginsburg's concurrence and dissent in *Randolph* emphasizes burden of proof. What is the practical significance of the burden of proof issue?

B. What if the arbitration clause covering Sara Valdez and Bank of the Angels also limits Sara's right to recover particular relief that otherwise might have been available, such as punitive damages or compensatory damages? Or, what if the clause shortened the statute of limitations that would otherwise apply to Sara's claims? Some courts have struck clauses that include these sorts of terms. For a discussion of courts' treatment of remedy-stripping arbitration clauses, and of how preclusion principles relate to courts' treatment of such provisions, see David S. Schwartz, Understanding Remedy-Stripping Arbitration Clauses: Validity, Arbitrability and Preclusion Principles, 38 U.S.F. L. Rev. 49 (2003). At times, rather than void a remedy-stripping arbitration provision, courts have mandated that the dispute be arbitrated, leaving the arbitrator to determine how to handle the remedy-stripping aspect of the clause. See, e.g., Hawkins v. Aid Ass'n for Lutherans, 338 F.3d 801, 807 (7th Cir. 2003). The issue of whether courts or instead arbitrators should decide challenges to arbitration clauses will be discussed in section B.

When courts find that a particular arbitration clause would prevent plaintiff from vindicating her rights under the relevant federal statute, they differ as to the appropriate remedy. Some courts invalidate the entire arbitration clause on this ground.[18] Other courts merely sever the offending portion of the arbitration provision and permit arbitration to proceed under modified terms.[19]

---

18. E.g., Alexander v. Anthony Crane Int'l, 341 F.3d 256, 270-273 (3d Cir. 2003) (voiding entire clause, rather than severing unfair portions, because unfair portions so permeated the entire agreement rendering it fundamentally unfair).

19. E.g., Booker v. Robert Half Int'l Inc., 413 F.3d 77, 84 (D.C. Cir. 2005) (holding that the punitive damages clause in arbitration agreement should be severed).

d. Can States Deem Certain Disputes Non-Arbitrable?

If neither the Supreme Court nor Congress has found certain types of disputes non-arbitrable, can state legislatures do so? This seemingly simple issue raises three big questions regarding federalism and the scope of the Federal Arbitration Act: (1) Does the Federal Arbitration Act apply to actions brought in state court?; (2) What test should be used to decide if a transaction involves sufficient interstate commerce such that the FAA applies?; and (3) if the FAA does apply, when does it preempt state arbitration legislation? After these questions are answered, below, you will see that states are left with relatively little opportunity to regulate arbitration.

i. The FAA Applies to Actions Brought in State Court

The Supreme Court has clearly held, now on multiple occasions, that the FAA was intended to apply in state as well as federal courts so long as the relevant transaction involves interstate commerce. The Court first faced the issue in Southland v. Keating, 465 U.S. 1 (1984), and ruled 6-3 that Section 2 does apply in state court. Justice O'Connor penned a highly critical dissent and most academics who have opined on the issue share her view that the language and legislative history of the FAA should be interpreted to limit the scope of the statute to federal court. In subsequent decisions several sitting Justices have expressed skepticism towards the *Southland* decision.[20] Twenty state attorneys general signed an amicus brief urging the Court to reverse itself. Nonetheless, despite dissents and criticism, in Allied-Bruce Terminix Cos. v. Dobson, 513 U.S. 265, 281 (1995) and Circuit City Stores v. Adams, 532 U.S. 105, 122 (2001) the Court proclaimed again and again that Section 2 of the FAA applies to state court proceedings.

ii. The FAA Applies to the Broadest Possible Definition of Interstate Commerce

In Allied-Bruce Terminix Cos. v. Dobson, 513 U.S. 265 (1995), the Supreme Court found that the FAA should be interpreted to apply to the broadest possible definition of interstate commerce, specifically all "commerce in fact." 513 U.S. at 278. The effect of the Court's ruling was to severely limit the scope of an Alabama statute providing that no pre-dispute arbitration agreements can be specifically enforced. Ala. Code Section 8-1-41 (2009).

Terminix involved Alabama homeowners who had hired the local Terminix termite extermination company to spray their home for termites. When the treatment proved unsuccessful, and substantial damage transpired, the homeowners

---

20. See David S. Schwartz, Correcting Federalism Mistakes in Statutory Interpretation: The Supreme Court and the Federal Arbitration Act, 67 Law & Contemp. Probs 5 (2004). But see Christopher R. Drahozal, In Defense of *Southland*: Reexaming the Legislative History of the Federal Arbitration Act, 78 Notre Dame L Rev. 101 (2002).

asserted that the Alabama law quoted above trumped their arbitration agreement and gave them the right to bring a claim in court rather than in arbitration. However, Terminix successfully argued that the FAA preempted the Alabama statute, in that the arbitration clause was a "written provision in . . . a contract evidencing a transaction involving commerce" and thus covered by Sections 1 and 2 of the FAA. Thus, regardless of whether parties believe their transaction involves interstate commerce or want the FAA to apply, it does apply to any transaction Congress would have the power to regulate directly under its commerce power. In light of this decision, almost no transactions have been found so purely local that the FAA does not apply. While one Supreme Court decision, Volt Information Sciences, Inv. v. Board of Trustees of Leland Stanford Junior University, 489 U.S. 468 (1989), seemingly allows parties to choose to be governed by state, rather than federal, arbitration law, so long as the two don't conflict, the case has not exempted many transactions from FAA coverage.

iii.   *Extent of FAA Preemption*

In light of *Southland*, *Terminix* and their progeny, it is clear that the FAA has a very broad application, and the Supreme Court's subsequent decision in Doctor's Assocs. v. Casarotto, 517 U.S. 681 (1996), shows that the FAA preempts rather than coexists with much state arbitration law. In *Casarotto* an 8-1 majority held that the FAA preempted a Montana statute requiring that arbitration clauses in franchise agreements be "typed in underlined capital letters on the first page of the contract." Id. at 683. The Justices explained that "[c]ourts may not . . . invalidate arbitration agreements under state laws applicable only to arbitration provisions." Id. at 687. Thus, although some might have argued that the Montana Code ought to be permitted to coexist with the FAA, in that it merely ensured that franchisees be afforded adequate notice as to arbitration, instead the Court found such a requirement was inconsistent with and preempted by the FAA.[21]

Given the Court's decisions, it is clear that states cannot prohibit arbitration altogether, except to the extent they are regulating either purely local transactions or insurance transactions, where a separate federal law has ceded regulatory power to the states. The McCarran Ferguson Act, 15 U.S.C. §1012(b), gives states the right to invalidate the use of arbitration to resolve insurance claims. This statute in effect "reverse-preempts" the FAA by providing in relevant part that "no Act of Congress shall be construed to invalidate, impair, or supersede any law enacted by any State for the purpose of regulating the business of insurance."

---

21. Those interested in relationships between federal and state courts may want to look at the prior history of *Casarotto*, in which the Montana Supreme Court initially voided the clause, the Supreme Court vacated that decision and remanded for reconsideration, the Montana Supreme Court then reinstated its original decision, and finally the Supreme Court vacated and reversed, finding the clause was valid. Justice Treiweiler's special concurrence in the first Montana Supreme Court decision is particularly colorful. Casarotto v. Lombardi, 886 P.2d 931, 939 (1994).

It is also clear that states cannot require that disputes be resolved administratively, rather than through arbitration. In Preston v. Ferrer, 552 U.S. 346 (2008), the Court ruled that a dispute between television Judge Alex and his attorney must be resolved through arbitration, as provided in their contract, even though California law arguably provided that disputes pertaining to entertainment contracts should instead be resolved by the California Labor Commissioner.

However, many open issues remain regarding the extent of FAA preemption. For example, the California Code of Civil Procedure requires substantial disclosures by arbitrators and arbitration providers. Cal. Code Civ. Proc. Section 1281.5. Is that preempted? New Mexico's version of the Uniform Arbitration Act provides that arbitration clauses are voidable where they impose certain burdens on consumers, borrowers, tenants, or employees. N.M. Unif. Arbitration Act, ch. 44, §§7A-1 & 7A-5 (2003). While the New Mexico Supreme Court noted, in passing, that the statute may be preempted by the FAA, it did not actually reach a conclusion on this issue. Fiser v. Dell Computer Corp., 188 P.3d 1215, 1219 (N.M. 2008). Is that legislation preempted by the FAA? Are courts' rulings that certain arbitration clauses are unconscionable or otherwise invalid preempted by the FAA? See AT&T Mobility v. Concepcion, cert. granted 130 S. Ct. 3322 (2010) (raising question whether decision finding class action waiver unconscionable was preempted by the FAA). Would a state's refusal to conduct business with companies that require mandatory arbitration of their employees or consumers be preempted?[22]

Problem 10-11.   *How Can States Restrict Mandatory Arbitration?*

You are an attorney working for a committee of the state legislature. The committee Chair has told you that many legislators are concerned about unfair aspects of mandatory binding arbitration and would like to pass legislation prohibiting or restricting the practice. She has asked you to discuss what steps your state might take in this regard.

B. WHAT POWERS DO ARBITRATORS HAVE?

Section A has examined which kinds of disputes are subject to arbitration. Section B will look at the scope of arbitrators' powers. Specifically, it will first consider an arbitrator's power to determine the scope of the arbitrator's own jurisdiction, by ruling on the validity and meaning of the contract that gives rise to arbitration. It

---

22. For a good discussion on the scope of FAA preemption, see Christopher R. Drahozal, Federal Arbitration Act Preemption, 79 Ind. L.J. 393 (2004).

will then look at the extent to which the parties can contractually define arbitrators' powers, as well as arbitrators' ability to certify class actions, compel discovery, and award various types of damages.

1. Arbitrators' Power to Determine Meaning and Validity of Contracts, Including the Arbitration Clause Itself

One of the most litigated issues pertaining to arbitration is the question whether arbitrators or instead courts should decide particular issues. While the question may seem academic, arcane, or frankly even boring, it has substantial real world significance and has spawned numerous U.S. Supreme Court decisions. In the 2009 term alone the Court decided two cases that directly turn on this issue,[23] and a third that raises the question indirectly.[24] Over the last ten years the Court has decided many other cases raising this "who decides" issue. Why so many cases? In part, the Court may have taken many cases because the issue is confusing. Arbitrators' power to determine the scope of their own jurisdiction has been analogized by some as a person's ability to pull himself up by his own bootstraps. Second, parties keep raising these issues not to fuel academics' fire but because they believe it really makes a difference which issues are resolved by courts, and which by arbitrators. In the cases discussed below readers may notice that the side seeking to void arbitration clauses invariably argues that the court should make the decision, whereas the side contending that the arbitration clause is valid always asserts that the arbitrator ought to resolve this question. Likely, this is not coincidence, but rather reflects real world suspicion that arbitrators, consciously or not, will be more apt than courts to make a ruling that extends their own jurisdiction (and allows them to get paid!). Perhaps it also reflects a suspicion that remnants of the "ouster" doctrine may cause some judges to be hostile to arbitration.

a. *Who Decides Whether a Contract That Contains an Arbitration Clause Is Valid?*

Arbitration clauses are typically contained in larger contracts that include a variety of terms such as the nature of goods or services, price, and delivery terms. What happens if one of the parties argues that this container contract, which includes an arbitration clause, itself is void or voidable? Should this question be resolved by a court, or instead by an arbitrator? Enunciating a doctrine variously known as "separability" or "severability," the Supreme Court has repeatedly stated that when disputants challenge only the larger container contract, and not the validity of the arbitration clause itself, the arbitrator rather than a court should decide whether the contract is valid.

---

23. Granite Rock Co. v. Int'l Bhd. of Teamsters, 130 S. Ct. 2847 (2010); Rent-a-Center, West v. Jackson, 130 S. Ct. 2772 (2010).
24. Stolt-Nielsen S.A. v. AnimalFeeds Int'l, 130 S. Ct. 1758 (2010).

In Prima Paint Corp. v. Flood & Conklin Mfg. Co., 388 U.S. 395 (1967), the Supreme Court dealt with a contract dispute between Prima Paint and its consultant, Flood & Conklin (F&C). The consulting agreement between the two companies included a broad arbitration provision. However, Prima Paint sought to rescind the entire contract, including the arbitration provision, on grounds of fraud in the inducement. The Court found that the arbitrator must resolve this question and stated: "[I]f the claim is fraud in the inducement of the arbitration clause itself — an issue which goes to the 'making' of the agreement to arbitrate — the federal court may proceed to adjudicate it. But the statutory language [of the FAA] does not permit the federal court to consider claims of fraud in the inducement of the contract generally." 388 U.S. at 400-401. The *Prima Paint* decision has been harshly criticized by some, including Justice Black, dissenting, who called the decision "fantastic" but not in the flattering sense of the word. 388 U.S. at 407. Critics like Justice Black are puzzled how an invalid contract could give rise to a valid arbitration provision.

Notwithstanding criticism leveled at *Prima Paint* the Court has recently reiterated the doctrine multiple times. In Buckeye Check Cashing Inc. v. Cardegna, 546 U.S. 440 (2006), plaintiff consumers sued Buckeye in state court, arguing that Buckeye's interest rates were usurious and violated state civil and criminal laws. Buckeye filed a motion to compel arbitration, pointing to an arbitration agreement contained in the agreements signed by plaintiffs, but plaintiffs argued that a court should hold the entire agreement invalid because the usurious provisions rendered the contract void under state law. An 8-1 Court rejected plaintiffs' arguments, instead holding that under *Prima Paint* an arbitrator rather than a court should decide the validity of the container agreement. 546 U.S. at 449. In so holding, the Supreme Court made clear that *Prima Paint* applies to cases brought in state as well as federal courts, and that it applies even to contracts that are allegedly void or even criminal in nature. 546 U.S. at 448. The Court also re-endorsed the doctrine in Rent-a-Center West v. Jackson, 130 S. Ct. 2772, 2778 (2010), and Granite Rock Co. v. Int'l Bhd. of Teamsters, 130 S. Ct. 2847, 2858 (2010).

b. *Who Decides the Validity and Applicability of an Arbitration Clause?*

In Granite Rock Co. v. International Brotherhood of Teamsters, 130 S. Ct. 2847 (2010) the Supreme Court attempted to set out some clear rules on which decisions are to be made by arbitrators, and which by courts. It stated:

> It is well settled in both commercial and labor cases that whether parties have agreed to submit a particular dispute to arbitration is typically an issue for judicial determination. (citations and quotations omitted). . . . It is similarly well settled that where the dispute at issue concerns contract formation, the dispute is generally for courts to decide. . . . [C]ourts should order arbitration of a dispute only where the court is satisfied that neither the formation of the parties' arbitration agreement *nor* . . . its enforceability or applicability to the dispute is in issue.

Id. at 2855.

Whereas some of the Court's prior decisions had enunciated a federal policy favoring arbitration, the Court in *Granite Rock* made clear "we have never held that this policy overrides the principle that a court may submit to arbitration only those disputes that the parties have agreed to submit." Id. at 2859 (quotation omitted). Thus, such questions as whether the arbitration agreement was offered, accepted, imposed through duress or fraud, or imposed unconscionably are typically assumed to be questions for the court. See also First Options of Chicago, Inc. v. Kaplan, 514 U.S. 938 (1995) (holding that the court rather than the arbitrator should decide whether Manuel and Carol Kaplan, as opposed to merely their wholly owned company, MK Investments, had contracted to arbitrate future disputes with First Options of Chicago). *Granite Rock* also reiterates that courts rather than arbitrators should decide the "scope" of an arbitration clause, that is whether a valid arbitration clause applies to a particular dispute. Id. at 2855. However, as discussed below the Court has also set out an important exception to these rulings in that decisions initially assumed to be for the court can sometimes be "delegated" to the arbitrator.

c. *Who Decides the Meaning of an Arbitration Clause?*

i. *Allegedly Time-Barred Claims*

The Court has found that once the validity and applicability of an arbitration clause is clear, the arbitrator rather than the court should make various interpretive decisions. Thus, in Howsam v. Dean Witter Reynolds, Inc., 537 U.S. 79 (2002), the Court found that the question of whether a claim was time-barred by an arbitration provider's rule should be resolved by the arbitrator, not the court. The Court explained that this kind of issue involves "procedural" rather than "substantive" arbitrability, and that parties would expect such decisions to be made by arbitrators. The Court similarly stated that arbitrators should typically be the ones to decide questions pertaining to notice, laches, estoppel, and other conditions precedent.

ii. *Available Damages*

The Supreme Court has held that an arbitrator rather than a court should decide what type of relief is available according to the arbitration provision. Pacifi-Care Health Sys. Inc. v. Book, 538 U.S. 401 (2003), involved an action brought by physicians against a health care provider. The physicians sued in part under RICO, the federal racketeering statute. The court of appeals had held that because the RICO statute allows for the recovery of treble damages, and because the arbitration clause prohibited recovery of "punitive damages," the doctors would not be able to fully vindicate their RICO rights in arbitration and thus should not be compelled to arbitrate the claim. The Supreme Court reversed and remanded, holding that the arbitration clause was ambiguous as to whether treble damages were precluded, and that the arbitrator should first interpret the contract before the doctors would be in a position to argue they could not fully vindicate their rights in arbitration. The Court made no ruling regarding whether, assuming the damages were not available, a court or arbitrators should decide whether the arbitration was still valid.

d. Permissibility of Arbitral Class Actions

The interrelationship between arbitration and class actions is complex, controversial, and very important. As discussed at the end of this chapter, critics of mandatory arbitration argue that one important reason companies have imposed arbitration on consumers is to prevent consumers from joining together to bring claims against companies in class actions. For a time, companies' clauses did not explicitly reference class actions and companies often asked courts to rule that such "silent" arbitration clauses implicitly proscribed consumers from bringing class claims in either arbitration or litigation. More recently some companies have begun to put provisions in their arbitration clauses that explicitly prohibit consumers or others from bringing class claims against the company in arbitration or litigation. These practices raise many legal issues, among them, some "who decides" questions.

The Court first addressed this important issue in Green Tree Financial Corp. v. Bazzle, 539 U.S. 444 (2003), in which a four-member plurality of the Court found that an arbitrator, rather than a court, could interpret an arbitration agreement to determine whether an arbitral class action was permitted by the language of the contract. Following the issuance of *Bazzle* a number of arbitrators went on to rule that class actions could be permissible or even certified the class. The AAA even sponsored rules for arbitral class actions and published statistics on how arbitral class actions were being handled.

However, in Stolt-Nielsen SA v. AnimalFeeds Intern., 130 S. Ct. 1758 (2010), the Court took on the question of how a silent arbitration clause should be interpreted with respect to class actions. The case involved an antitrust dispute between two business entities. Although a panel of three arbitrators had interpreted the silent clause to potentially permit plaintiffs to bring a class action, the Supreme Court found that decision must be vacated in that it exceeded the arbitrators' powers. The Court found that "a party may not be compelled under the FAA to submit to class arbitration unless there is a contractual basis for concluding that the party agreed to do so." Finding that neither the silent agreement nor any bargaining history could support a finding that the companies had agreed to classwide arbitration, the Court ruled that the arbitrators' interpretation was based on public policy rather than interpretation of the contract and thus must be vacated. Thus, arbitrators can decide whether classwide arbitration is permitted but must limit the basis of their decision to interpretation of the parties' agreement. As a matter of practical reality *Stolt-Nielsen* is likely to lead to the demise of classwide arbitrations because few if any arbitration agreements are or will be written to allow for arbitral class actions.

e. Can Interpretive Questions Be Delegated to the Arbitrator?

The Court has explained that while there may be certain default rules as to which decisions are made by courts, and which by arbitrators, parties can also draft their arbitration agreement to provide that decisions ordinarily expected to be made by courts instead be made by arbitrators. In First Options of Chicago, Inc. v. Kaplan, 514 U.S. 938 (1995), writing for the Court, Justice Breyer stated: "Just as the arbitrability of the merits of a dispute depends upon whether the parties agreed to arbitrate that dispute, so the question 'who has the primary power to decide arbitrability' turns upon what the parties agreed about *that* matter. Did the parties agree to submit the arbitrability question itself to arbitration?" Id. at 943. However, explained Justice Breyer, "[c]ourts should not assume that the parties agreed to arbitrate arbitrability unless there is "clea[r] and unmistakabl[e]" evidence that they did so. . . ." Id. at 944. The Court went on to conclude that "because the [parties] . . . did not clearly agree to submit the question of arbitrability to arbitration, the Court of Appeals was correct in finding that the arbitrability of the Kaplan/First Options dispute was subject to independent review by the courts." Id. at 947. That is, the court, rather than the arbitrator, should decide whether the issue of contractual applicability should be decided by a court or by an arbitrator. Scholars disagree as to whether *Prima Paint* and *First Options* are consistent with one another, and whether they were correctly decided.[25]

Subsequently, in Rent-a-Center West v. Jackson, 130 S. Ct. 2772 (2010) the Court addressed the question of whether an arbitration agreement could delegate to the arbitrator the question of whether the arbitration agreement itself was unconscionable. Mr. Jackson, an employee, sought to have his employment discrimination claim heard by a court rather than an arbitrator and urged that the discovery limits and fee-splitting provisions made the arbitration clause unconscionable. In a 5-4 decision Justice Scalia, writing for the Court, found that the unconscionability decision could indeed be delegated so long as the delegation clause itself was not unconscionable. Analogizing to the *Prima Paint* case, in which, as discussed above, the Court had ruled that attacks on a contract as a whole were to be decided by arbitrators, rather than courts, the Court in *Jackson* found that delegation of the unconscionability decision to the arbitrator was valid because plaintiff never argued that the delegation itself was unconscionable. Id. at 2780. In so ruling Justice Scalia expressly reocognized that it will typically be much more difficult to show that a delegation provision is unconscionable than to show that the arbitration clause itself is unconscionable. Id. Dissenting, Justice Stevens and three other Justices stated that "[i]n applying *Prima Paint* the Court has unwisely extended a 'fantastic' and likely erroneous decision." Id. at 2785. The dissenters urged that parties should not have the power to take unconscionability decisions away from the court, given that Section 2 of the FAA assigns arbitrability issues to the courts. Id. at 2782.

From a practical standpoint the outcome in *Rent-a-Center* is highly significant. Companies that impose arbitration on consumers and employees will now likely draft their clauses to provide that arbitrators rather than courts should hear unconscionability and perhaps other challenges to arbitration clauses. If arbitrators prove less willing than courts to invalidate arbitration clauses this will give companies greater license to draft arbitration clauses in ways beneficial to the company, but not necessarily to the consumer or employee.

---

25. See, e.g., Richard Reuben, *First Options*, Consent to Arbitration, and the Demise of Separability: Restoring Access to Justice for Contracts with Arbitration Provisions, 56 SMU L. Rev. 819, 841-848 (2003) (attacking *Prima Paint* and promoting actual party consent to arbitration, similar to that endorsed in *First Options*) and Alan Scott Rau, Everything You Really Need to Know About "Separability" in Seventeen Simple Propositions, 14 Am. Rev. Intl. Arb. 1 (2003) (defending *Prima Paint* and arguing that *First Options* is consistent with that decision).

Problem 10-12.   *Who Decides What?*

Given all the decisions discussed above, how clear do you find the line distinguishing which issues are decided by courts, and which by arbitrators? Do you find the Court's distinction between substantive and procedural arbitrability to be clear, or instead circular? Make a list of the issues each body should decide and then try to think of some issues the court has not ruled on and how those ought to be resolved.

Problem 10-13.   *Who Decides Unconscionability?*

You represent Sigmoid Wireless, a cellphone provider. The company has a form arbitration agreement with its customers providing that all claims made by customers against the company shall be decided in arbitration, rather than litigation. The clause also provides that customers can recover no punitive damages against the company, and must bring their claims individually, rather than as a class. The partner for whom you work has asked you to draft a memo discussing the pros and cons of whether the company should revise the clause to expressly state that any unconscionability challenges to the arbitration provision shall be resolved by the arbitrator rather than a court.

Assuming that a particular dispute is subject to arbitration, additional questions may arise regarding whether arbitrators possess the powers to issue injunctions, to award punitive damages, to decide motions, and to supervise class actions. Parties can control arbitrators' powers to a large degree by using the language of the arbitration clause. Federal and state statutes also provide certain default rules regarding arbitrators' powers. Both points are discussed below.

2. Parties' Ability to Regulate Arbitrators' Powers

In general, parties can use their arbitration agreement to determine the scope of the arbitrators' powers. In section B.1.e, above, we discussed parties' ability to delegate arbitrability issues to arbitrators. Discussing the broader question of parties' ability to regulate arbitrators, Judge Posner colorfully stated the following in Baravati v. Josephthal, Lyon & Ross, Inc., 28 F.3d 704, 709 (7th Cir. 1994):

> short of authorizing trial by battle or ordeal or, more doubtfully, by a panel of three monkeys, parties can stipulate to whatever procedures they want to govern the arbitration of their disputes; parties are as free to specify idiosyncratic terms of arbitration as they are to specify any other terms in their contract.

Such agreements can be used either to empower or to disempower arbitrators from engaging in particular conduct. Thus, where parties want their arbitrators to have the power to issue particular kinds of orders, they should so state; where they do not want the arbitrators to engage in particular conduct, they should also so state. As has been discussed, many parties' arbitration agreements adopt the rules of a particular administrative organization, such as the American Arbitration Association. These rules may provide for pre-hearing conferences or permit arbitrators to rule on preliminary matters. The Revised Uniform Arbitration Act, §15(a), similarly provides that "[a]n arbitrator may conduct an arbitration in such manner as the arbitrator considers appropriate for a fair and expeditious disposition of the proceeding," subject to the specifics of the parties' agreement. Some parties therefore specify in their arbitration agreements whether arbitrators may award certain forms of damages, hear class actions, hear claims for injunctive relief, decide cases on summary judgment, or apply particular rules of evidence or procedure.

There are, however, a few constraints on the extent to which parties can use their arbitration agreement to control the arbitrators' actions. First, some arbitration statutes, such as §4 of the Revised Uniform Arbitration Act, may limit parties' ability to draft around the mandatory terms of such a statute.[26] Second, as discussed earlier, if a court (or perhaps arbitrator) finds the definition of arbitral powers to be unconscionable or in violation of a federal statute, it may void the entire arbitration agreement or sever the problematic portion of the clause. Third, the Constitution may impose certain constraints on arbitrators, just as it does on courts. For example, in the court setting, awards for punitive damages may be vacated if they are not adequately supported. See, e.g., State Farm Mut. Auto. Ins. Co. v. Campbell, 538 U.S. 408 (2003). Perhaps Due Process or other constraints apply to arbitrators, as they would to courts? However, as noted earlier, courts have not typically found that private arbitration gives rise to state action, thus the Due Process Clause may not typically apply.

3. Requiring the Presence of Parties and Production Documents

The FAA's §7 affords arbitrators the power to summon persons to attend arbitration hearings and to bring designated documents to those hearings. If persons so summoned fail to obey the summons, the federal district court is empowered to compel their attendance and to use its contempt power to enforce the summons. 9 U.S.C. §7. Section 17(a) of the Revised Uniform Arbitration Act (RUAA) similarly empowers arbitrators to issue subpoenas. ("An arbitrator may issue a subpoena for the attendance of a witness and for the production of records and other evidence at any hearing.") Yet, questions remain, such as whether an arbitrator may compel non-parties to produce documents. See Hay Group, Inc. v. E. B. S. Acquisition Corp., 360 F.3d 404 (3d Cir. 2004). Arbitrators customarily permit disputants to conduct discovery, using such tools as interrogatories, document requests, and depositions, but the scope of discovery may not be as broad as that which a court might permit

---

26. See Christopher R. Drahozal, Contracting Around RUAA: Default Rules, Mandatory Rules, and Judicial Review of Arbitral Awards, 3 Pepperdine Disp. Resol. L. J. 419 (2003).

in litigation. Arbitration clauses or rules often provide that arbitrators shall permit a "reasonable" amount of discovery, which many interpret to be less discovery than might be available in court.

4. Arbitrators' Award of Damages and Attorneys' Fees

Absent prohibitive language in the agreement or in a relevant statute, most U.S. courts have held arbitrators may award punitive damages, exemplary damages, attorneys' fees, and other types of monetary relief. Section 21 of the RUAA explicitly provides:

(a) An arbitrator may award punitive damages or other exemplary relief if such an award is authorized by law in a civil action involving the same claim and the evidence produced at the hearing justifies the award under the legal standards otherwise applicable to the claim.

(b) An arbitrator may award reasonable attorney's fees and other reasonable expenses of arbitration if such an award is authorized by law in a civil action involving the same claim or by the agreement of the parties to the arbitration proceeding.

(c) As to all remedies other than those authorized by subsections (a) and (b), an arbitrator may order such remedies as the arbitrator considers just and appropriate under the circumstances of the arbitration proceeding. The fact that such a remedy could not or would not be granted by the court is not a ground for refusing to confirm an award under Section 22 or for vacating an award under Section 23.

In Mastrobuono v. Shearson Lehman Hutton, Inc., 514 U.S. 52 (1995), the Supreme Court examined the question of whether arbitrators can award punitive damages. The defendant argued that the punitive damages portion of the arbitral award must be vacated because the arbitration agreement called for application of New York law, which barred arbitrators from awarding punitive damages. The Supreme Court found that because the arbitration agreement permitted arbitrators to award punitive damages the award should stand. The Court emphasized that "[a]rbitration under the Act is a matter of consent, not coercion, and parties are generally free to structure their arbitration agreements as they see fit. Just as they may limit by contract the issues which they will arbitrate, so too may they specify by contract the rules under which that arbitration will be conducted." 514 U.S. at 57.

5. Injunctive Relief

U.S. courts differ in how they view arbitrators' ability to award injunctive relief. Courts applying the FAA have generally recognized the authority of arbitrators to grant injunctions. See, e.g., Saturday Evening Post Co. v. Rumbleseat Press, Inc., 816 F.2d 1191, 1194 (7th Cir. 1987) (affirming the confirmation of an arbitration award enjoining company from making or selling porcelain dolls covered by copyright).

However, some have raised a concern that because arbitrators would not be able to retain jurisdiction to revise an injunction, if necessary, they should not be able to issue injunctions in the first place. The California Supreme Court has not entirely prohibited arbitrators from issuing injunctive relief but has limited arbitrators' power to issue injunctions in one context. Specifically, that Court has ruled that certain claims for injunctive relief brought on behalf of the public are non-arbitrable, absent statutory language specifically permitting arbitration of such claims. Cruz v. PacifiCare Health Sys., Inc., 66 P.3d 1157 (2003).

As a practical matter, even when arbitrators issue injunctions, they might be harder to enforce than injunctions issued by courts. Arbitrators do not retain jurisdiction over cases they have handled. While a party seeking enforcement of an arbitral injunction might turn to a judge, it is unclear how courts would handle such suits.

6. Provisional Relief

Most U.S. jurisdictions also permit arbitrators to award provisional relief, including orders for replevin, sequestration, and preliminary injunctions. Section 8 of the RUAA expressly provides arbitrators with these powers, to the same extent as they would be possessed by a judge. Comment 4 to that section sets out the rationale:

> The case law, commentators, rules of arbitration organizations, and some state statutes are very clear that arbitrators have broad authority to order provisional remedies and interim relief, including interim awards, in order to make a fair determination of an arbitral matter. This authority has included the issuance of measures equivalent to civil remedies of attachment, replevin, and sequestration to preserve assets or to make preliminary rulings ordering parties to undertake certain acts that affect the subject matter of the arbitration proceeding.

However, as a practical matter arbitrators are not necessarily available on the expedited basis that would be needed to issue temporary restraining orders or preliminary injunctions. For that reason, arbitration agreements sometimes permit disputants to request such relief from the courts. The RUAA allows parties to arbitration agreements to seek relief from courts either prior to the appointment of the arbitrators or subsequent to their appointment, stating "a party to an arbitration proceeding may move the court for a provisional remedy only if the matter is urgent and the arbitrator is not able to act timely or the arbitrator cannot provide an adequate remedy." Revised Unif. Arbitration Act §8(b)(2).

C. JUDICIAL REVIEW OF ARBITRAL AWARDS

1. Confirming Arbitral Awards

Having discussed which kinds of disputes can be arbitrated and what powers arbitrators possess, the third major legal issue we will examine is judicial review of arbitral awards. In general, once an arbitration award has been issued, the parties comply with it. Where the prevailing party fears noncompliance it can file a motion under federal or state law to have the arbitral award "confirmed" by a court. See Federal Arbitration Act, 9 U.S.C. §9. Such motions typically must be filed fairly quickly, e.g., within one year. With respect to international arbitration, the FAA contains a similar provision. 9 U.S.C. §207. A confirmed award has the same force as the judgment of a court.

2. Vacating Arbitral Awards

Parties do not typically seek to vacate arbitral awards. This is true internationally as well as domestically. One experienced international arbitrator has stated that voluntary compliance with International Chamber of Commerce arbitration awards exceeds 90 percent.[27] The typically low rate of challenges is due in part to the fact that once an arbitrator has issued an award, it is quite difficult to vacate. Unlike lower court awards, which can successfully be appealed for either errors of law or significant misinterpretation of the facts, arbitral decisions can usually be vacated only on far more limited grounds. While it may be somewhat easier to vacate arbitral awards today than it was a number of years back, it is still quite difficult to upset either a commercial or labor award in the United States.

With respect to commercial arbitration, §10(a) of the FAA spells out a set of limited grounds for vacating the arbitral award.

Federal Arbitration Act, 9 U.S.C. §10(a) (1925)

In any of the following cases the United States court in and for the district wherein the award was made may make an order vacating the award upon the application of any party to the arbitration —

(1) where the award was procured by corruption, fraud, or undue means;

(2) where there was evident partiality or corruption in the arbitrators, or either of them;

(3) where the arbitrators were guilty of misconduct in refusing to postpone the hearing, upon sufficient cause shown, or in refusing to hear evidence pertinent and material to the controversy; or of any other misbehavior by which the rights of any party have been prejudiced; or

(4) where the arbitrators exceeded their powers, or so imperfectly executed them that a mutual, final, and definite award upon the subject matter submitted was not made.

---

27. Pierre Lalive, Enforcing Awards, in 60 Years of ICC Arbitration: A Look at the Future 317, 319 (1984).

Section 23 of the Revised Uniform Arbitration Act similarly lists a very few grounds on which arbitral awards may be vacated. The New York Convention also limits the grounds on which arbitral awards can be vacated in the international context, although Article V provides a few grounds in addition to those allowed under the FAA. Specifically, Article V(2) provides:

New York Convention, Article V(2) (1958)

Recognition and enforcement of an arbitral award may also be refused if the competent authority in the country where recognition and enforcement is sought finds that:

(a) The subject matter of the difference is not capable of settlement by arbitration under the law of that country; or

(b) The recognition or enforcement of the award would be contrary to the public policy of that country.

In practice, it is often even more difficult to vacate an arbitral award than these narrow grounds suggest. Domestic courts have repeatedly made statements such as " '[f]actual or legal errors by arbitrators — even clear or gross errors — do not authorize courts to annul awards.' " Flexible Mfg. Sys. Pty. Ltd. v. Super Prods. Corp., 86 F.3d 96, 100 (7th Cir. 1996) (quotation omitted) (7th Cir. 1995).

As to labor arbitrations, courts similarly tend to confirm most awards. In United Paperworkers Intl. Union, AFL-CIO v. Misco, Inc., 484 U.S. 29, 36 (1987) the Court stated, "the Court made clear almost 30 years ago that the courts play only a limited role when asked to review the decision of an arbitrator. The courts are not authorized to reconsider the merits of an award even though the parties may allege that the award rests on errors of fact or on misinterpretation of the contract."[28] Similarly, in Hill v. Norfolk & W. Ry., 814 F.2d 1192 (7th Cir. 1987), Judge Posner explained:

> [W]hether the award is made under the Railway Labor Act, the Taft-Hartley Act, or the United States Arbitration Act — [the question] is not whether the arbitrator or arbitrators erred in interpreting the contract; it is not whether they clearly erred in interpreting the contract; it is not whether they grossly erred in interpreting the contract. . . . A party can complain if the arbitrators don't interpret the contract — that is, if they disregard the contract and implement their own notions of what is reasonable and fair. . . . But once the court is satisfied that they were interpreting the contract, judicial review is at an end, provided there is no fraud or corruption and the arbitrators haven't ordered anyone to do an illegal act.

Id. at 1195. However, note that a recent study showed that state courts did in fact vacate arbitral awards in the employment area at a fairly significant rate, but only when the motion to vacate was brought by the employer, and not the employee.[29]

---

28. See also Major League Baseball Players Assn. v. Garvey, 532 U.S. 1015 (2001) (reversing Ninth Circuit's reversal of arbitrator's award and observing that court had failed to apply proper narrow review standard).

29. Michael H. LeRoy, Do Courts Create Moral Hazard? When Judges Nullify Employer Liability In Arbitrations: An Empirical Analysis, 93 Minn. L Rev. 998 (2009).

On the other hand, the language of the FAA is sufficiently open-ended that it will sometimes support a more searching review. In Stolt-Nielsen S.A. v. Animal-Feeds Int'l, 130 S. Ct. 1758 (2010), the Supreme Court recently considered whether an arbitration panel's decision potentially allowing a matter to proceed as a class action should be allowed to stand. The panel's decision purported to consider the language of the arbitration clause and relevant case law. However, rather than simply accept the decision, under a deferential standard of review, the Court vacated the panel's award on the ground that the arbitrators had exceeded their powers in violation of Section 10(a)(4) of the FAA. Specifically, the Court stated that "what the arbitration panel did was simply to impose its own view of sound policy regarding class arbitration." Id. at 1767-1768. The Court went on to find that by imposing its own policy choice instead of "identifying and applying a rule of decision derived from the FAA or other . . . law," id. at 1770, the arbitrators exceeded their powers. Rather than remand the matter to the arbitrators for further consideration the Court found that no classwide arbitration could be permitted given the evidence presented by the parties. It is possible that the Court's recent decision in *Stolt-Nielsen* will lead to somewhat less deference being afforded to arbitral decisions.

Some courts have also vacated arbitral awards for a few reasons outside of the list provided in FAA §10. At least with respect to labor arbitrations, the Supreme Court has expressly recognized that arbitral awards may be vacated where they violate public policy. Although this might sound like a broad basis for appeal, in fact, the Court has enunciated that this ground for vacating an award may be used only in very narrow circumstances. The Court explained in Eastern Associated Coal Corp. v. United Mine Workers of Am., 531 U.S. 57, 62 (2000), that arbitral awards may be vacated on grounds of public policy only if "any such public policy [is] . . . 'explicit,' 'well defined,' and 'dominant.' . . . It must be 'ascertained "by reference to the laws and legal precedents and not from general considerations of supposed public interests.'" Id. at 62. Rejecting an employer's attempt to vacate an arbitral award that reinstated a truck driver who had twice tested positive for marijuana, the Court stated: "of course, the question to be answered is not whether [the employee's] drug use itself violates public policy, but whether the agreement to reinstate him does so." Id. at 62-63. The Court went on to hold that considerations of public policy, as expressed in the Omnibus Transportation Employee Testing Act of 1991 and the Department of Transportation implementing regulations, did not preclude enforcement of the award. Id. at 65.

Many federal courts have also stated that arbitral awards can be vacated when they reflect "manifest disregard of the law." This language comes from dictum in the Supreme Court's decision in Wilko v. Swan, 346 U.S. 427 (1953), stating "the interpretations of the law by the arbitrators in contrast to manifest disregard are not subject, in the federal courts, to judicial review for error." Id. at 436. However, the continued viability of the "manifest disregard" ground for vacating arbitral awards is now in some question. In Hall Street Assocs. v. Mattel, 128 S. Ct. 1396 (2008), excerpted below, the Supreme Court recently cast substantial doubt on the status of this ground for review. Subseqently, in Stolt-Nielsen S.A. v. AnimalFeeds Int'l, 130 S. Ct. 1758 (2010) the Court again refused to decide whether manifest disregard is an independent ground for vacating arbitral awards. Id. at 1768 n.3.

Faced with such limited statutory grounds for appeal, some parties have tried to draft arbitration agreements that make it easier to vacate arbitral awards. Some parties and certainly some lawyers would prefer an arbitration process that allows appeals from errors of fact or law to a process that makes most arbitral awards unappealable. However, in *Hall Street*, the Supreme Court found that to the extent parties seek review of arbitration under the FAA they are limited to the statutory grounds for vacating arbitral awards. That is, the Section 10 grounds are not mere default rules, that parties can contract around, but rather are the exclusive means for challenging arbitral awards under the FAA. On the other hand, to the extent parties seek to use means other than the FAA to enforce their arbitral awards, perhaps parties can contract for broader grounds for review.

 HALL STREET ASSOCIATES v. MATTEL

552 U.S. 576 (2008)

SOUTER, J., delivered the opinion of the Court, in which ROBERTS, C.J., and THOMAS, GINSBURG, and ALITO, JJ., joined, and in which SCALIA, J., joined as to all but footnote 7. STEVENS, J., filed a dissenting opinion, in which KENNEDY, J., joined. BREYER, J., filed a dissenting opinion.

[The convoluted facts involve a lease dispute between landlord Hall Street Associates and its tenant, Mattel. After a portion of the dispute was resolved in litigation the parties agreed (with judicial encouragement or some might say duress) to have an arbitrator resolve an indemnification issue. One paragraph of the arbitration agreement provided that:]

> . . . "[t]he United States District Court for the District of Oregon may enter judgment upon any award, either by confirming the award or by vacating, modifying or correcting the award. The Court shall vacate, modify or correct any award: (i) where the arbitrator's findings of facts are not supported by substantial evidence, or (ii) where the arbitrator's conclusions of law are erroneous."

[After a series of lower court decisions and arbitral awards the Supreme Court] . . . granted certiorari to decide whether the grounds for vacatur and modification provided by §§10 and 11 of the FAA are exclusive. . . . We agree with the Ninth Circuit that they are, but vacate and remand for consideration of independent issues.

Hall Street makes two main efforts to show that the grounds set out for vacating or modifying an award are not exclusive, taking the position, first, that expandable judicial review authority has been accepted as the law since Wilko v. Swan, 346 U.S. 427 (1953). This, however, was not what *Wilko* decided, which was that §14 of the Securities Act of 1933 voided any agreement to arbitrate claims of violations of that Act . . . , a holding since overruled by Rodriguez de Quijas v. Shearson/American Express, Inc., 490 U.S. 477, 484 (1989). Although it is true that the Court's discussion includes some language arguably favoring Hall Street's position, arguable is as far as it goes.

The *Wilko* Court was explaining that arbitration would undercut the Securities Act's buyer protections when it remarked (citing FAA §10) that "[p]ower to vacate an [arbitration] award is limited," 346 U.S. at 436, and went on to say that "the interpretations of the law by the arbitrators in contrast to manifest disregard [of the law] are not subject, in the federal courts, to judicial review for error in interpretation," id. at 436-437. Hall Street reads this statement as recognizing "manifest disregard of the law" as a further ground for vacatur on top of those listed in §10, and some Circuits have read it the same way. . . . Hall Street sees this supposed addition to §10 as the camel's nose: if judges can add grounds to vacate (or modify), so can contracting parties.

But this is too much for *Wilko* to bear. . . . Maybe the term "manifest disregard" was meant to name a new ground for review, but maybe it merely referred to the §10 grounds collectively, rather than adding to them. . . .

Second, Hall Street says that the agreement to review for legal error ought to prevail simply because arbitration is a creature of contract, and the FAA is "motivated, first and foremost, by a congressional desire to enforce agreements in to which parties ha[ve] entered." Dean Witter Reynolds Inc. v. Byrd, 470 U.S. 213, 220 (1985). But again, we think the argument comes up short. Hall Street is certainly right that the FAA lets parties tailor some, even many features of arbitration by contracting, including the way arbitrators are chosen, what their qualifications should be, which issues are arbitrable, along with procedure and choice of substantive law. But to rest this case on the general policy of treating arbitration agreements as enforceable as such would be to beg the question, which is whether the FAA has textual features at odds with enforcing a contract to expand judicial review following the arbitration.

To that particular question we think the answer is yes, that the text compels a reading of the §§10 and 11 categories as exclusive. To begin with, even if we assumed §§10 and 11 could be supplemented to some extent, it would stretch basic interpretive principles to expand the stated grounds to the point of evidentiary and legal review generally. Sections 10 and 11, after all, address egregious departures from the parties' agreed-upon arbitration. . . .

[E]xpanding the detailed categories would rub too much against the grain of the §9 language, where provision for judicial confirmation carries no hint of flexibility. . . . Instead of fighting the text, it makes more sense to see the three provisions, §§9-11, as substantiating a national policy favoring arbitration with just the limited review needed to maintain arbitration's essential virtue of resolving disputes straightaway. Any other reading opens the door to the full-bore legal and evidentiary appeals that can "rende[r] informal arbitration merely a prelude to a more cumbersome and time-consuming judicial review process," . . . and bring arbitration theory to grief in post-arbitration process." . . .

In holding that Sections 10 and 11 provide exclusive regimes for the review provided by the statute, we do not purport to say that they exclude more searching review based on authority outside the statute as well. The FAA is not the only way into court for parties wanting review of arbitration awards: they may contemplate enforcement under statute statutory or common law, for example, where judicial review of different scope is arguable. But here we speak only to the scope of the expeditious judicial review under Sections 9, 10 and 11, deciding nothing about other possible avenues for judicial enforcement of arbitration awards. . . .

The parties' supplemental arguments on the subject in this Court implicate issues of waiver and the relation of the FAA both to Rule 16 and the Alternative Dispute Resolution Act of 1998, 28 U.S.C. §51 et seq. none of which has been considered previously in this litigation, or could be well addressed for the first time here. We express no opinion on these matters beyond leaving them open for Hall Street to press on remand. . . .

Problem 10-14.   *Continued Viability of "Manifest Disregard" as Grounds to Vacate*

Following issuance of *Hall Street*, federal courts have split on whether "manifest disregard of the law" still exists as an independent ground for vacating arbitral awards, but in any event it is, at most, a narrow ground for vacating arbitral awards. From a policy perspective do you think the "manifest disregard" concept should be used to supplement the grounds FAA Section 10 provides for vacating arbitral awards?

Problem 10-15.   *Challenging Arbitrator's Award of Punitive Damages*

You represent Lawnmowers Inc., a large franchisor that sells lawnmowers through franchisees based around the United States. The franchise agreement contains a provision requiring that disputes between franchisor and franchisees be resolved through binding arbitration. One of your franchisees brought a breach of contract claim against your client in arbitration. The arbitrator awarded the franchisee $249,000 on the breach of contract claim and also awarded franchisee $3,000,000 in punitive damages. You believe that the arbitrator's award was erroneous as a matter of fact and law, and that the punitive damages award was particularly egregious. Normally breach of contract awards are not accompanied by punitive damages. You also feel that such a high punitive damages award violates your client's rights to due process under the Constitution. How might you try to protect your client from this arbitration award that you believe to be erroneous?

Problem 10-16.   *Allowing Arbitrators to Review Other Arbitrators' Decisions*

Many attorneys who draft arbitration agreements are nervous about the typical finality of arbitration awards. One option available to such attorneys is to draft an agreement providing that arbitral awards can be appealed to a second arbitral body rather than to a court. What do you see as the pros and cons of this approach from both the public and private perspective?

---

3. Suing Arbitrators

To the extent that parties seek to bring claims against arbitrators, in lieu of or in addition to trying to vacate their awards, they likely will fail. Most jurisdictions, either by statute or common law, afford arbitrators the same scope of immunity to which judges are entitled. Section 14(a) of the Revised Uniform Arbitration Act affords judicial immunity not only to arbitrators but also to arbitral organizations. ("An arbitrator or an arbitration organization acting in that capacity is immune from civil liability to the same extent as a judge of a court of this State acting in a judicial capacity.") However, one commentator has argued that the nature and scope of arbitral immunity ought to be reexamined and reined in, given recent changes in the nature of arbitration such as the growth of mandatory arbitration. See Maureen A. Weston, Reexamining Arbitral Immunity in an Age of Mandatory and Professional Arbitration, 88 Minn. L. Rev. 449 (2004).

Problem 10-17.   *Changing the Statutory Grounds for Vacating Arbitral Awards*

In some other countries, arbitral awards can be vacated more easily than in the United States. For example, in Great Britain, unless otherwise agreed by the parties, arbitral awards can be vacated where they are founded on errors of law. See Arbitration Act, 1996, c. 23, §69 (Eng.). The Argentine National Code of Civil and Commercial Procedure, art. 758, provides that "all means of recourse available against court decisions can be raised against an arbitral award, if not waived in the terms of reference." Do you think the FAA should be amended to allow for a more searching standard of review? Are there any particular categories of cases (e.g., statutory disputes) that you think would particularly warrant a tougher appellate standard? Should the FAA be amended to allow parties to draft an enforceable arbitration clause that would permit courts to review arbitrators more strictly?

D. POLICY ISSUES REGARDING MANDATORY BINDING ARBITRATION

In the United States, the key policy issue that has arisen with respect to binding arbitration is whether, and if so, how and when, companies should be permitted to use form contracts to require consumers and employees to resolve future disputes with the company through binding arbitration, rather than through litigation. Both critics and defenders of mandatory arbitration agree that the practice has become increasingly common in the United States. Using small-print contracts, envelope stuffers, and computer click-through agreements companies increasingly require customers and employees to agree in advance to arbitrate future disputes. Indeed, you yourself can empirically investigate the prevalence of mandatory arbitration by checking the extent to which providers of goods and services in your own life (e.g., credit cards, phones, computers, leases, and contracts with doctors, gyms, nursing homes) require you to resolve future disputes through arbitration rather than litigation. One study conducted in Los Angeles with respect to a hypothetical "average Joe" showed that one-third of the consumer transactions in his life were covered by arbitration clauses. See Linda J. Demaine & Deborah R. Hensler, "Volunteering" to Arbitrate Through Predispute Arbitration Clauses: The Average Consumer's Experience, 67 Law & Contemp. Probs. 55 (2004). Indeed, some major law firms are now seeking to require their associates and other employees to agree to arbitrate rather than litigate any disputes they may have with the firm. See Davis v. O'Melveny & Myers, 485 F.3d 1066 (9th Cir. 2007) (holding a particular clause unconscionable and thus unenforceable).

The growth of mandatory arbitration is directly linked to the changing Supreme Court jurisprudence on binding arbitration. Recall that whereas the Court initially prevented companies from imposing binding arbitration on consumers and employees in such cases as Wilko v. Swan, 346 U.S. 427 (1953), and Alexander v. Gardner-Denver Co., 423 U.S. 1058 (1976), the Court's subsequent decisions in such cases as Rodriguez de Quijas v. Shearson/American Express, Inc., 490 U.S. 477 (1989) and Gilmer v. Interstate/Johnson Lane Corp., 500 U.S. 20 (1991) make clear that with certain exceptions discussed earlier, companies are generally free to require their customers or employees to resolve future disputes through binding arbitration. However, while the Supreme Court has permitted mandatory arbitration under existing law, the question remains whether such laws should be changed.

1. Attacks on Mandatory Arbitration

Critics of "mandatory" or "cram down" arbitration assert that it is unfair to individuals and bad as a matter of public policy. In brief, the critics argue that companies are using arbitration not merely to change the procedural venue of claims, but also — for example by proscribing class actions — to prevent consumers or employees from bringing claims at all. The critics argue that arbitration clauses are often drafted in an overreaching manner that is stacked against the "little guy" consumers and employees. Critics point to particular clauses that have required consumers to appear in front of biased arbitrators; forced them to pay high fees or travel to distant locations; deprived them of such remedies as attorneys' fees, compensatory, or punitive damages; shortened their statute of limitations; or eliminated their right to bring class claims. From the public perspective, critics complain that private arbitration will prevent the public-at-large from learning about defective products or widespread discrimination, and that the lack of public precedent will impede the development of law.

Critics urge the passage of federal legislation, such as the Arbitration Fairness Act of 2009 (which will be discussed in further detail below) to eliminate mandatory binding arbitration. Professor Sternlight's defense of the Arbitration Fairness Act also sets out a critique of mandatory binding arbitration.

 Jean R. Sternlight, **FIXING THE MANDATORY ARBITRATION PROBLEM: WE NEED THE ARBITRATION FAIRNESS ACT OF 2009**

16 Disp. Resol. Mag. 5 (2009)

U.S. companies are increasingly requiring their consumers and employees, whom I refer to here as "little guys," to arbitrate rather than litigate disputes with the company. With envelope stuffers, computerized click-through agreements, or just small print companies can eliminate "little guys' " opportunity to litigate, even if the "little guys" did not knowingly or intelligently agree, and even if they never signed the provision.

The U.S. Supreme Court has held that the 1925 Federal Arbitration Act requires that courts enforce such "agreements," called "mandatory" binding arbitration by their critics. Although such clauses usually affect potential plaintiffs, sometimes they also affect "little guys" as defendants. Credit card companies are increasingly using mandatory arbitration clauses to bring collection actions against their customers in arbitration rather than in court.

Pointing to the often inaccessible litigation system, some argue that consumers are better off in mandatory arbitration than in litigation. Defenders assert that most arbitrators are fair, that the purportedly cheaper process will benefit keep wages higher and prices lower, and that empirical studies prove mandatory arbitration is better than litigation. Some even contend that mandatory arbitration is necessary to protect companies from "predatory" litigation by consumers or employees.[30]

But empirical studies don't resolve this dispute. Few have been done, as arbitration providers are unwilling to provide open access to their files. Moreover, to the extent studies look only at who prevails in an arbitration hearing they miss most of the empirical picture. Much of mandatory arbitration's impact is that it deters people from bringing claims at all, and causes them to settle on unfavorable terms.

---

30. Alan S. Kaplinsky & Mark J. Levin, Excuse Me, but Who's the Predator? Banks Can Use Arbitration Clauses as a Defense, Bus. L. Today (May-June 1998) at 24.

Defenders of mandatory arbitration play a rhetorical game when they suggest critics should have the burden of proving the practice is unfair, instead of requiring defenders to prove the practice is fair. Yet, without definitive proof either way, we know that companies have an incentive to eke out every advantage in battles against consumers and employees. Companies want to prevent "little guys" from bringing claims against the company and then want to maximize companies' opportunities to prevail if claims are brought. When courts enforce "agreements" that studies show few will read or understand, companies have every opportunity to skew the clauses to their own advantage. Even the rare consumer or employee who reads and understands the clauses usually can't avoid them because all the other industry companies are imposing similar clauses.

Sometimes, companies try to use arbitration to gain blatant advantage over consumers and employees — such as by eliminating claims for punitive or compensatory damages, shortening statutes of limitations, or imposing biased arbitrators. The Minnesota Attorney General recently brought a claim alleging that one provider, the National Arbitration Forum, was actually owned in part by a company that also owned the very debt collection companies that regularly sued consumers in NAF arbitration. In settlement of this claim NAF has now ceased handling consumer arbitrations. Sometimes, the skewing is less blatant but equally detrimental — like preventing "little guys" from bringing class actions when that would be the only economically feasible means of presenting a small claim affecting numerous consumers.

In addition to adversely impacting individuals, mandatory arbitration clauses may have a detrimental impact on the public. Such clauses ensure that disputes will be resolved behind closed doors, rather than through public precedent.

Theoretically, a company could set up an even-handed mandatory binding arbitration program. Some companies and many arbitrators do their best to give consumers and employees justice, and sometimes they succeed. But, human nature and the profit motive ensure that many companies will take advantage of the opportunity to use mandatory arbitration to treat the "little guys" unfairly.

If unfairness or potential unfairness is the problem, what is the solution? Some say courts already have the power to knock out unfair clauses using standard contract doctrines such as unconscionability. Yet, although courts have voided some of the most blatantly unfair clauses, these case-by-case reviews are insufficient to ensure justice. First, many "little guys" will never attempt to challenge unfair clauses. Many won't even realize a challenge could be possible. Second, it is time consuming and expensive for challengers to meet their burden to prove unconscionability. Successful challenges often take years, and more than $100,000 may be needed to pay for discovery and experts. Third, many unfair clauses have survived court challenge because the law only targets the most blatantly unfair provisions.

State legislators and regulators have no ability to rein in abusive arbitration practices. Numerous Supreme Court decisions have held that state attempts at regulation are preempted by the FAA.[31]

Unless the Supreme Court chooses to reverse 20 years of arbitration precedents, a highly unlikely short-term prospect, federal legislation is needed to protect ordinary Americans from mandatory arbitration. Note that other countries, including members of the European Union, have ensured that companies cannot use mandatory binding arbitration to secure unfair advantage over consumers and employees. We in the United States ought to protect ourselves as well.

Congress could protect Americans by enacting either of two types of legislation: prohibitive or regulatory. Prohibitive legislation, of which the proposed 2009 Arbitration Fairness Act ("AFA") is an example, would prohibit mandatory pre-dispute arbitration altogether with respect to consumers, employees, and civil rights claimants.[32] Regulatory legislation, on the other hand, would eliminate only the most egregious forms of mandatory arbitration, allowing companies to continue to mandate arbitration for consumers and employees so long as it meets minimal fairness requirements. For example, companies might be barred from using biased arbitrators or using arbitration to eliminate remedies available in court.

Upon reflection, there are two significant problems with the seemingly reasonable regulatory approach. First, how will unfair/impermissible arbitration practices be defined? In the past, with providers' voluntary Due Process protocols, the definition of unfair practices has proven to be a moving target. Just as one unfair practice is restricted, companies creatively devise another unfair arbitration provision, such as prohibiting all class actions so as to insulate the company from smaller claims. As long as companies have the incentive and ability to define arbitration in a way that is beneficial to them, attempts to regulate such practices may resemble that famous Dutch boy trying to put his fingers in the holes in the dike. No sooner is one hole blocked than another springs up.

Second, a regulatory approach is only as effective as the regulator. How vigorously would a statute prohibiting unfair arbitration practices be enforced? If the statute requires individual "little guys" to prove particular arbitration clauses are unfair under the new federal law, they will suffer the same high burdens of proof and expense that they already face as they try to prove particular arbitration clauses are unconscionable. Alternatively, the Consumer Financial Protection Agency could be empowered to police all arbitration clauses. But, as we have seen with other federal regulatory efforts in this country, inadequate funding will likely cause enforcement to fall short of the aspiration.

---

31. E.g., Doctors Associates Inc. v. Casarotto, 517 U.S. 681 (1996) (holding that the FAA preempted Montana law specifying that an arbitration clause be printed at page one of a contract and be provided in capital letters and underlined).
32. The currently pending bills, S. 931 and H.R. 1020, would also prohibit franchisors from imposing mandatory arbitration on franchisees, on the theory that many franchisees require protection from the more powerful franchisors.

The proposed AFA is a far preferable means to protect consumers, employees and civil rights claimants. Its direct prohibition on the imposition of mandatory pre-dispute arbitration in these settings would be simple to enforce. The prohibition would protect persons who, realistically, will not read or understand the meaning of an arbitration provision prior to when a dispute has even arisen. Yet, the statute would allow members of those groups to voluntarily opt for binding arbitration on a post-dispute basis, thereby permitting disputants to select arbitration over litigation once they can meaningfully compare the costs and benefits of the two processes.

Some have criticized the AFA as overly broad in that it would outlaw even pre-dispute agreements that are entered knowingly, voluntarily, and intelligently. It is true that a broad prohibition no doubt catches up at least a small number of persons who could capably draft a pre-dispute arbitration agreement. However, it is better that this statute be a bit overly broad than significantly overly narrow. It simply is not possible to draft a statute that would perfectly distinguish between knowing consensual and non-consensual pre-dispute arbitration agreements without imposing impossibly high regulatory costs. To the extent parties are precluded from entering enforceable pre-dispute arbitration agreements, they always have the option to agree to arbitration post-dispute. Although defenders of mandatory arbitration typically assert post-dispute agreements are infeasible, both sides would have every incentive to agree to a process that was truly better and more efficient for all.

In the end, the most practical way to ensure that arbitration is fair is to make it voluntary on a post-dispute basis. Once a dispute has arisen consumers, employees and other "little guys" will be able to make knowledgeable determinations as to whether the proposed arbitration is efficient and fair for all concerned. The proposed Arbitration Fairness Act in this sense would use the free market to ensure that arbitration is fair and just.

―――――――――――――――

2. Defenses of Mandatory Arbitration

Defenders of the practice typically reject the "mandatory" label, urging that consumers and employees accept arbitration voluntarily, even if it is contained in form contracts. Such defenders point out that most contracts in our complex economy are form contracts, and that form contracts are routinely enforced by courts. Pointing to the high cost and slow speed of our litigation system, the defenders of "mandatory" arbitration assert that binding arbitration is beneficial not only for the companies that impose it, but also, for individual consumers and employees and for society as a whole. They argue that when companies include arbitration in form contracts, they help consumers and employees by providing them with a forum that is cheaper, quicker, and more accessible than litigation. Such defenders also argue that to the extent companies reduce their own dispute resolution costs, market forces will ensure that they pass on such savings to their workers in the form of higher wages and to their customers in the form of lower prices. They contend that while it may be appropriate to proscribe egregiously unfair mandatory arbitration, it would be a mistake to prohibit the practice altogether. Below, Peter Rutledge argues that the Arbitration Fairness Act should not be adopted.

 Peter B. Rutledge, **THE CASE AGAINST THE ARBITRATION FAIRNESS ACT**

16 Disp. Resol. Mag. 4 (2009)

The Arbitration Fairness Act is a well-intended but ultimately misguided attempt to address a system of dispute resolution that has largely worked well. The bill currently being considered by Congress rests on a series of flawed empirical premises. This article addresses three. First, though the bill posits that arbitration leaves consumers and employees worse off, data demonstrate individuals overall are often better off under a system with enforceable pre-dispute arbitration agreements than a system without them. Second, although the bill promises improved access to justice, the proposal actually erects more impediments. Third, though the bill suggests that post-dispute arbitration will provide a continued outlet for this system of dispute resolution, it fails to recognize the significant structural impediments to a successful system of postdispute arbitration.

First, it now appears to be common ground that the policy debate over the Arbitration Fairness Act should focus on empirical data. We all can harness our success stories and horror stories about arbitration (or any other system of dispute resolution). Yet the Arbitration Fairness Act does not simply address the bad cases while preserving the good. Instead, it proposes a systemic overhaul that categorically bans predispute agreements entirely. Thus, to assess the bill's impact, a systematic view of the empirical data is appropriate.

Interestingly, the data frequently show that predispute arbitration in general produces better outcomes for individuals. In March, the Searle Institute of Northwestern University Law School published a thorough study of consumer arbitrations conducted by the American Arbitration Association. Contrary to the cries of arbitration's critics, individuals fared quite well, prevailing in a significant number of arbitrations and recovering a reasonable share of the damages that they sought. This study represents simply the latest chapter in a growing body of empirical literature suggesting that arbitration largely reaches a fair result for individuals in their disputes against companies.

To be sure, not all studies are as sanguine. Some research suggests that low-income individuals in arbitrations under promulgated (as opposed to individually negotiated) arbitration agreements fare poorly. Such results, though, simply beg the question about what causes such outcomes. Is it that arbitration is stacked against the individual? Or something in the nature of the claim that gives rise to a low likelihood of success, whether in arbitration, litigation, or some other forum?

Not only are the data mixed, but they are also incomplete. Although the Arbitration Fairness Act broadly addresses employment, consumer, and franchise arbitration, gaps exist in all three areas, especially franchise arbitration, in which few studies are available and almost none address outcomes.

The upshot here is simply that Congress should tread cautiously when contemplating a systematic overhaul of a system that, by some measures, produces favorable results and, in other important respects, has an incomplete empirical record.

Second, eliminating predispute arbitration agreements impedes rather than improves an individual's access to justice. For one thing, individuals may find it more difficult to find a lawyer if they are forced to litigate their claims. The high costs of our civil litigation system mean that lawyers generally will demand high recoveries and a high prospect of success before they are willing to undertake a case. By contrast, the lower costs of arbitration and the procedural flexibility enable an individual to obtain judgment at a lower cost.

Apart from access to counsel, arbitration improves access to justice in another respect. Individuals achieve results faster. Every major empirical study on arbitration has found that it produces results faster than litigation. For individuals who seek recovery, the speed to resolution may be a valuable advantage of this system of alternative dispute resolution. By eliminating predispute arbitration, Congress may worsen access to justice and end up hurting the very classes of people whom it purports to protect.

For society as a whole, the costs of resolving disputes without arbitration would rise. Consider the thousands of disputes currently resolved by arbitration. If those disputes no longer were arbitrable, where would they go? "To the courts" is the obvious answer. But any self-respecting lawyer or judge would tell us that the court dockets are already overburdened. Shuttling these cases out of arbitration simply lengthens the line at the courthouse for everyone.

Some defenders of the Arbitration Fairness Act try to turn these arguments on their head by arguing that arbitration deprives plaintiffs of the ability to bring class actions and thereby deprives those plaintiffs "access to justice." There is some surface appeal to this argument, but it ultimately does not support adoption of the Arbitration Fairness Act. For one thing, the argument assumes the widespread adoption of class action waivers, and although some evidence suggests its use in certain industries (such as the cellular telephone industry), I am unaware of any systemwide evidence on this point. For another thing, even assuming the problem is widespread, the argument further assumes that a large number of cases exist that would satisfy Federal Rule of Civil Procedure 23's exacting standards — again, I am unaware of any empirical evidence on this point. Finally, even assuming that these two preceding hurdles can be overcome, the argument does not support the wholesale invalidation of arbitration clauses — a more calibrated solution would simply invalidate class action waivers but not the arbitration clauses themselves. Organizations such as the American Arbitration Association have begun to develop extensive experience administering class arbitrations, and there is no principled reason why the purported benefits of a class action cannot also be realized through the mechanism of an arbitration. Thus, at bottom, the class action argument is a bit of a ruse — at best it is an argument for the invalidation of class action waivers; at worst, it is self-interested politicking by class action plaintiffs' lawyers masquerading as policy making in the public interest.

Third, defenders of the Arbitration Fairness Act often argue that postdispute arbitration mitigates these and other risks of eliminating enforceable agreements. Yet postdispute arbitration is not a viable alternative to predispute arbitration agreements. One problem is psychological — parties are simply far more willing to agree on matters before a dispute has arisen; once a dispute arises, the opportunities for cooperation dwindle. The second problem is structural: the parties' incentives in the postdispute context fundamentally differ from the predispute context. Postdispute parties have more information, which enables them to make more calculated decisions regarding which form of dispute resolution better promotes their interests or effectively hinders the individual's interests. Conversely, in the predispute context, parties have an incentive to enter into arbitration. An individual's incentive is that arbitration is an affordable forum with superior chances for a favorable result. A company's incentive is that arbitration can lower the company's litigation costs.

At bottom, the Arbitration Fairness Act applies a meat cleaver to an issue that requires a scalpel. The solution is not for Congress to prohibit predispute arbitration agreements in employment, consumer, and franchise contracts. Instead, Congress should encourage and await additional empirical research. Research may show minor additions to the regulatory repertoire are necessary. However, wholesale, retroactive elimination of predispute arbitration agreements would effectively make worse off the individuals whom Congress, through this legislation, seeks to protect.

Problem 10-18.   *The Policy Arguments Regarding Mandatory Arbitration*

You are a member of the staff of a U.S. Senator who has heard complaints about mandatory arbitration. Summarize both the critiques and the defenses of this practice. Discuss how the Court's most recent decisions, including particularly Rent-a-Center, West v. Jackson, 130 S. Ct. 2772 (2010) may influence this debate.

You may find it useful to refer to the following scholarly critiques of mandatory arbitration: David S. Schwartz, Mandatory Arbitration and Fairness, 84 Notre Dame L. Rev. 1247 (2009); Jean R. Sternlight, Creeping Mandatory Arbitration: Is It Just?, 57 Stan. L. Rev. 1631 (2005); Jean R. Sternlight & Elizabeth J. Jensen, Using Arbitration to Eliminate Consumer Class Actions: Efficient Business Practice or Unconscionable Abuse?, 67 Law & Contemp. Probs. 75 (2004); Katherine Van Wezel Stone, Mandatory Arbitration of Individual Employment Rights: The Yellow Dog Contract of the 1990s, 73 Denv. U. L. Rev. 1017 (1996); and Jean R. Sternlight, Panacea or Corporate Tool?: Debunking the Supreme Court's Preference for Binding Arbitration, 74 Wash. U. L.Q. 637 (1996).

For popular press critiques of mandatory arbitration see Robert Berner & Brian Grow, Banks vs. Consumers (Guess Who Wins), Business Week, June 5, 2008; Margaret Mannix, No Suits for You — Mad at a Firm? Arbitration Could Be Your Only Recourse, U.S. News & World Rep., June 7, 1999, at 58; Barry Meier, In Fine Print, Customers Lose Ability to Sue, N.Y. Times, Mar. 10, 1997, at A1.

Public interest groups and consumer activists have also launched projects seeking to defeat the practice of mandatory arbitration. For example, Public Citizen has authored a report entitled "The Arbitration Trap: How Credit Card Companies Ensnare Consumers." Public Justice devotes an entire division of its organization, the Mandatory Arbitration Abuse Prevention Project, to trying to defeat mandatory arbitration clauses.

For scholarly defenses of mandatory arbitration, see Stephen J. Ware, Paying the Price of Process: Judicial Regulation of Consumer Arbitration Agreements, 2001 J. Disp. Resol. 89; Samuel Estreicher, Saturns for Rickshaws: The Stakes in the Debate over Predispute Employment Arbitration Agreements, 16 Ohio St. J. on Disp. Resol. 559 (2001); Peter B. Rutledge, Who Can Be Against Fairness? The Case Against the Arbitration Fairness Act, 9 Cardozo J. Conflict Resol. 267 (2008); and Stephen J. Ware, The Case for Enforcing Adhesive Arbitration Agreements — with Particular Consideration of Class Actions and Arbitration Fees, 5 J. Am. Arb. 251 (2006).

Problem 10-19. *Voluntary Post-Dispute Arbitration*

Critics of mandatory arbitration assert that if arbitration were truly better, quicker, and cheaper for all concerned, the disputants would agree to it voluntarily on a post-dispute basis. Defenders of mandatory arbitration claim that this position is naïve at best, or perhaps just a rhetorical ploy. Such defenders assert that although binding arbitration might seem desirable to all pre-dispute, on a post-dispute basis one side or the other will often prefer litigation, thus making post-dispute agreements unlikely. For example, represented plaintiffs with strong claims and the potential for high damages would purportedly prefer litigation, and companies opposing plaintiffs with weaker or smaller value claims would prefer litigation because they know litigation would not be viable for such a plaintiff. Do you have a sense regarding the likely viability of voluntary post-dispute arbitration?

Problem 10-20.   *Ethics of Mandatory Arbitration*
If a company's attorney is fairly certain that consumers/employees will not read and or understand a binding arbitration provision, is it ethical for the attorney to draft such a provision on the company's behalf?

3. Empirical Studies Regarding Mandatory Arbitration

Given the fierce controversy over mandatory arbitration, one would hope that empirical studies could be used to evaluate the process objectively. Unfortunately, researchers have found it very difficult to evaluate mandatory arbitration. One significant impediment to research is that to a large extent, researchers cannot obtain access to the data they need to perform good studies. As we have seen, one of the fundamental traits of arbitration is that it is typically private. Thus, researchers can obtain data on arbitration only to the extent that disputants or arbitration providers make the data available, which they often do not. When data is provided to researchers it sometimes is not made available to the public or other researchers in order that they might verify the first researcher's results.

Researchers face a number of other significant hurdles as well. First, even if they have data regarding results of claims filed in arbitration and in court, it is difficult to know how to compare that data. After all, the same case is never brought in both processes, and one cannot simply assume that claims brought in arbitration are otherwise identical to those brought in litigation. Differences in the nature and cost of the processes are likely going to mean that the kinds of disputes that go to court are different from those that go to arbitration. Second, to the extent researchers look only at who wins or loses and how much they obtain when a claim goes to trial/arbitration, they are missing a large part of the dispute resolution picture. For example, it seems likely that the choice between arbitration and litigation may also affect such things as whether a disputant chooses to bring a claim at all, whether a disputant can obtain a lawyer, whether a claim settles and, if so, for how much, and whether a claim is resolved by motion prior to a hearing. Studies that focus only on results at trial/arbitration miss this bigger picture. Third, to the extent one can reach conclusions about uses of mandatory arbitration in one context, such as nondiscrimination employment claims presented to AAA arbitrators, there is no reason to believe that these results would also apply in other arbitration contexts. Arbitration results may vary tremendously depending on how the arbitration is done, the type of claim, whether the arbitration was entered voluntarily or involuntarily, the background of the arbitrator, the nature of the arbitral provider organization if any, whether the disputants were represented, and an array of other factors. Thus, it is often improper to extend results gained in one context to a different context.

For these reasons, and because the debate over mandatory arbitration is so pitched, those empirical studies that have been done have not brought the two sides closer together. Rather, critics of mandatory arbitration tend to cite certain studies and defenders of mandatory arbitration cite other studies. For example, critics of mandatory arbitration often cite a study done by Public Citizen: "The Arbitration Trap: How Credit Card Companies Ensnare Consumers" (9/27/07). Defenders of mandatory arbitration often cite a study done by the Searle Civil Justice Institute at Northwestern Law School: "Consumer Arbitration Before the American Arbitration Association" (2009). For additional discussions of some of the most recent empirical work see Symposium, Empirical Studies of Mandatory Arbitration, 41 U. Mich. J. L. Reform 777 (2008) and David S. Schwartz, Mandatory Arbitration and Fairness, 84 Notre Dame L. Rev. 1247 (2009).

Those academics who have done empirical studies of mandatory arbitration spend a great deal of time critiquing each others' conclusions and debating the burden of proof. For example compare Theodore Eisenberg & Geoffrey Miller, The Flight from Arbitration: An Empirical Study of Ex Ante Arbitration Clauses in the Contracts of Publicly Held Companies, 56 DePaul L. Rev. 335 (2007) (drawing on data from publicly held companies' filings with SEC to conclude that such companies are fleeing from arbitration in their transactions with one another) with Christopher Drahozal & Quentin R. Wittrock, Is There a Flight from Arbitration?, 37 Hofstra L. Rev. 71 (2008) (concluding, based on study of franchise agreements, that there has been no flight from arbitration in that arena). In short, as one author puts it "while in this essay I review some of the recent studies on the uses of ADR, my theme is one of skepticism that we can ever truly measure, with any degree of accuracy, whether one particular process is ever "better" or "worse" than another in a particular case."[33] See more discussion of this issue in Chapter 14, section B. Evaluating ADR.

4. Responses to the Public Policy Debate over Mandatory Arbitration

Despite numerous criticisms of mandatory arbitration by academics and journalists, courts continue to enforce many arbitration clauses that are imposed on consumers, employees, and others in contracts of adhesion. While, as discussed earlier, courts do void some clauses on grounds, such as unconscionability, for the most part only the most egregious mandatory arbitration provisions are being struck down.

Faced with this situation, critics of mandatory arbitration are attacking the practice in two ways. First, working within the system, critics are urging that arbitrators and arbitration providers regulate themselves to eliminate the excesses of mandatory arbitration. Second, the critics of mandatory arbitration are seeking help from Congress and, to a much lesser degree, state legislatures.

a. Due Process Protocols

Beginning in 1995, a number of arbitration providers began to adopt policies known collectively as "due process protocols." Although the phrase "due process" is

---

33. Carrie Menkel-Meadow, ADR: What Is It and What Is It Compared To?: The Baseline Problem, in P. Cane & H. Kritzer, eds., Oxford Handbook on Empirical Legal Research (2010).

used, it is meant to denote general fairness and not technical compliance with the Due Process Clause of the Constitution. Some of the protocols are known by other names. For example, the National Arbitration Forum has its equivalent, the Arbitration Bill of Rights.

In general, providers' protocols do not prohibit the practice of mandatory arbitration but instead require that if a company imposes arbitration, it meets minimal fairness criteria. The protocols address such issues as neutrality, cost, location, and availability of remedies. The protocol that has received the most widespread attention is A Due Process Protocol for Mediation and Arbitration of Statutory Disputes Arising Out of the Employment Relationship, released in 1995. The AAA played a key role in drafting the protocol, though representatives of labor, management and individual employees, arbitration providers, and arbitrators also collaborated in its development. Adopted by a broad range of organizations from all these perspectives, this Employment Protocol stops short of disapproving mandatory pre-dispute employment arbitration clauses.

Subsequent protocols cover arbitration in the consumer and health areas. The Health Care Due Process Protocol is unique. Unlike any of the others, it proscribes mandatory arbitration of certain disputes. Principle 3 states: "In disputes involving patients, binding forms of dispute resolution should be used only where the parties agree to do so after a dispute arises." In deference to this policy, the AAA announced that effective January 1, 2003, "it will no longer accept the administration of cases involving individual patients without a post-dispute agreement to arbitrate." See AAA Web site, *http://www.adr.org*. The Consumer Protocol, like the Employment Protocol, allows mandatory arbitration subject to certain conditions.

Because the protocols are simply policies adopted by arbitration providers, there is no clear enforcement mechanism. While a disputant may bring a supposed violation of a protocol to the attention of a provider, the disputant has limited recourse if the provider chooses to administer the clause, notwithstanding the violation of the protocol. However, a recent study of AAA found that it was at least fairly good in screening out non-compliant clauses. Consumer Arbitration Before the American Arbitration Association (Searle Civil Justice Institute 2009). In addition, many have raised the concern that even if major and reputable arbitration providers all choose to adopt and enforce fairness protocols, other less reputable companies may enter the field, offering companies an alternative that is beneficial to the company but not to its opponents. That is, the protocols could prompt a classic "race to the bottom."

b. Federal Legislation

For those who seek to eliminate mandatory binding arbitration, new federal legislation is their best hope. As discussed earlier, Congress has already passed legislation preventing automobile franchisors from imposing mandatory arbitration on automobile franchisees, and protecting members of the military.

The proposed Arbitration Fairness Act of 2009 would eliminate the practice of mandatory arbitration by prohibiting companies from using pre-dispute arbitration agreements to require employees, consumers, franchisees, or persons asserting civil rights claims to resolve their disputes in arbitration. The proposed legislation would, however, allow parties to agree to binding arbitration post-dispute.

The following is an excerpt of the key provisions of the proposed Arbitration Fairness Act of 2009, S. 931 as of September 2010.

Proposed Arbitration Fairness Act of 2009, S. 931

. . .

CHAPTER 4 — ARBITRATION OF EMPLOYMENT, CONSUMER, FRANCHISE, AND CIVIL RIGHTS DISPUTES

. . .

Sec. 402. Validity and enforceability

(a) In General — Notwithstanding any other provision of this title, no predispute arbitration agreement shall be valid or enforceable if it requires arbitration of an employment, consumer, franchise, or civil rights dispute.

(b) Applicability —

(1) IN GENERAL — An issue as to whether this chapter applies to an arbitration agreement shall be determined under Federal law. The applicability of this chapter to an agreement to arbitrate and the validity and enforceability of an agreement to which this chapter applies shall be determined by the court, rather than the arbitrator, irrespective of whether the party resisting arbitration challenges the arbitration agreement specifically or in conjunction with other terms of the contract containing such agreement.

(2) COLLECTIVE BARGAINING AGREEMENTS — Nothing in this chapter shall apply to any arbitration provision in a contract between an employer and a labor organization or between labor organizations, except that no such arbitration provision shall have the effect of waiving the right of an employee to seek judicial enforcement of a right arising under a provision of the Constitution of the United States, a State constitution, or a Federal or State statute, or public policy arising therefrom.

As this book goes to press, it is unclear whether Congress will pass this law.

Further Reading*

Gary Born. (2009). *International Commercial Arbitration: Commentary and Materials.* The Hague, The Netherlands: Kluwer Law International.

Edward Brunet, Richard E. Speidel, Jean R. Sternlight & Stephen J. Ware. (2006). *Arbitration Law in America: A Critical Assessment.* New York, NY: Cambridge U. Press.

---

* Because this chapter is filled with many citations to books, articles, and cases, we will only highlight a few additional references. — EDS.

Thomas E. Carbonneau. (2004). *The Law and Practice of Arbitration.* Huntington, NY: JurisNet, LLC.

Laura J. Cooper, Dennis Nolan & Richard A. Bales. (2005). *ADR in the Workplace.* St. Paul, Minn. The West Group.

Christopher R. Drahozal. (2006). *Commercial Arbitration: Cases and Problems.* Newark, NJ: LexisNexis/Matthew Bender.

John T. Dunlop & Arnold M. Zack. (1997). *Mediation and Arbitration of Employment Disputes.* San Francisco: Jossey-Bass Publishers.

Alan Miles Ruben, Frank Elkouri & Edna Asper Elkouri. (2003). *How Arbitration Works: Elkouri & Elkouri.* Washington, D.C.: Bureau of National Affairs.

Chapter 11   Arbitration: Skills, Practices, and Ethics

This chapter examines the skills that are necessary to be a good arbitrator, or a good representative of a disputant in arbitration. Although skills and ethics issues are inextricably linked in real life, for ease of presentation, we focus first on skills and then on ethics.

A. THE SKILLS OF ARBITRATION

Persons who work as arbitrators or arbitral representatives may require some specialized skills. Because, as we have seen, arbitration varies tremendously from context to context, the skills needed to be a good arbitrator or arbitral representative will also vary according to the context. An arbitrator who is handling a complex domestic commercial matter will no doubt want to do some things differently than would an arbitrator handling a collective bargaining issue, an international business dispute, or a Better Business Bureau claim. Similarly, an attorney who is representing a disputant in each of those situations will need different skills because the various arbitrations will not be handled in the same manner. At the same time, there will be an overlap of skills and approaches in many contexts.

1. Skills of Arbitrators

To be a good arbitrator requires many of the same skills needed to be a good judge. But what are these skills? Socrates purportedly said: "Four things belong to a judge: to hear courteously; to answer wisely; to consider soberly; to decide impartially." Moses gave a similar charge to the judges he appointed as the Jews began their long trek through the desert: "Hear the cases between your brethren, and judge righteously between a man and his brother or the stranger that is with him. You shall not be partial in judgment; you shall hear the small and the great alike." *Deuteronomy* 1:16-17.

Arbitrators, like judges, must seek to do justice in the cases over which they preside. Their decisions may affect not only the disputants who immediately appear before them, but also society at large. Yet it may not be easy for arbitrators to make just decisions of the highest quality. Arbitrators, like judges, are necessarily influenced by their past experiences. As Judge Jerome Frank explained: "[Judges] may first arrive at [a decision] intuitively and, then only, work backward to a major 'rule' premise and a minor 'fact' premise to see whether or not that decision is logically defective."[1] Whether or not one believes that the "gestalt" process described by Judge Frank is proper, it is difficult to disagree that it is common practice. Judge Frank concludes that in recognizing the way judges often decide cases, we need to have special training for judges. He urges that this training ought to focus particularly on how to find facts, how to keep judges' minds open to new impressions, how to be patient and attentive, and how to be aware of judges' hidden internal biases. Id. at 247-253. This is good advice for arbitrators as well. Arbitrators must strive to be open-minded so that they can adjust or completely change their initial reaction based on the evidence and law that is presented at the hearing.

As arbitrators listen to the parties' arguments they should keep in mind that psychologists have shown that humans are not as rational and fair as we think we are. Rather, we are often controlled by predictable biases. Social science suggests, that to the extent that arbitrators and judges become more aware of their biases, they may be better able to counter their effects.[2]

Arbitrators should also strive to perform their duties in such a way that the parties feel and perceive that they have been treated justly. As we discussed in Chapter 1, a body of work known as the "procedural justice" literature has shown that disputants often care at least as much about procedural fairness as they do about the substantive resolution of their dispute. Ideally, therefore, arbitrators will try to ensure that the process provides the voice, consideration, even-handedness, and dignity such that participants will feel they were treated justly.

Finally, in seeking to both render just decisions and also provide parties with the feeling that they have been treated justly, arbitrators must be careful to comply with the terms of the agreement that led to their appointment as an arbitrator. Often the agreement and the rules that it incorporates will provide arbitrators with quite specific guidance on how they should handle themselves. The following are some suggestions as to how arbitrators should deal with particular stages of the arbitration process.

a. Appointment as an Arbitrator

The method by which an arbitrator is appointed will vary, depending on the terms of the arbitration agreement or relevant court rules. Where the agreement calls for a particular organization to administer the arbitration process, the arbitrator will typically not know that she has been considered for appointment until after the disputants have had the opportunity to have input regarding whom they do or do not want as an arbitrator. These selections are usually based on qualifications and fees set out in the arbitrator's resume or other documents. Among other things, the arbitral organization typically screens for potential conflicts of interest. Arbitrators must

---

1. Jerome Frank, Courts on Trial (1950) at 184.
2. See, e.g., Jeffrey J. Rachlinski et al., Does Unconscious Racial Bias Affect Trial Judges?, 84 Notre Dame L. Rev. 1195 (2009).

be scrupulous in providing all information requested by the parties, arbitral organization, or required by law to ensure that a proper conflicts check can be done. When in doubt as to whether certain information should be disclosed, the arbitrator should err on the side of disclosure.

If the disputants are administering the arbitration themselves, potential arbitrators may have much more extensive involvement in the appointment process. For example, they will sometimes meet with one or both disputants to discuss the nature of the arbitral services they might provide. In this case it is critical that the potential arbitrator comply with all relevant ethical guidelines, such as any rules that may preclude ex parte communications. (Ex parte communications are those made by one side to the neutral, outside the hearing of the other side.)

In most cases, neutrality is one of the fundamental attributes that an arbitrator should possess. There is, however, an exception to this general rule. Sometimes in the United States, arbitrators are selected as party-appointed non-neutral arbitrators. This highly controversial practice will be discussed in greater detail later in this chapter. To the extent that an arbitrator is being appointed as a non-neutral arbitrator, she must be sure that all disputants understand equally the role that she will play in the arbitration. Note that not all party-selected arbitrators are expected to be non-neutral, so it is critically important that both arbitrator and parties understand the terms of appointment.

No matter what the appointment process, the arbitrator should ensure that she is working toward a just decision and toward a process with which all disputants will feel comfortable. Courtesy, timeliness, and good organization are essential. It is crucial that an arbitrator not accept an appointment if she does not meet the parties' minimal qualifications, or if she will not be able to handle the claim in the manner desired by the disputants.

b. Initial Meetings with the Parties

Once appointed, arbitrators often hold preliminary hearings with the disputants or their attorneys, if they are represented, to discuss how the arbitration will be handled and to resolve preliminary issues. The meeting, typically held jointly with all disputants or attorneys, can be conducted in person but is sometimes done by conference call, video conference, or even online. Depending on how the dispute is administered, the content of this meeting may vary. The arbitrators may use the preliminary meeting to discuss the scope of the issues to be resolved, to set deadlines, to discuss potential discovery, or even to resolve preliminary evidentiary issues. In the case of small disputes, or where speed or cost is a high priority, the arbitrators or parties may determine that a preliminary meeting is not desirable. In International Chamber of Commerce (ICC) arbitrations, a preliminary meeting is used to establish the "terms of reference" by which the remainder of the arbitration will proceed, focusing on such matters as the issues that will be considered and the manner in which they will be handled.

c. Arbitrator's Role in Encouraging Settlement

The extent to which arbitrators become involved in settlement or mediation varies substantially. Some arbitrators encourage parties to resolve their dispute amicably before commencing the arbitration process. Such arbitrators may themselves offer to conciliate or mediate the dispute. In some contexts, however, it would be thought inappropriate for the arbitrator to take too active a role in trying to help the disputants resolve their issues amicably. One rationale for restricting arbitrators' involvement in settlement is that exposure to settlement discussions may improperly influence a decision maker. For example, Rule 9 of the AAA Commercial Rules of Arbitration permits parties to request mediation at any time but provides that "the mediator shall not be an arbitrator appointed to the case." Thus, the arbitrator should be careful not to offer her services as a mediator or conciliator without first checking that such a role is permissible given the terms of relevant statutes, rules, and any arbitral agreement.

d. Ruling on Discovery and Other Pre-trial Motions

Before making any rulings on discovery, and before ruling on any pre-trial motions, the arbitrator should check to see whether the arbitration agreement or relevant arbitration rules expressly discuss these matters. Assuming that the agreement and rules are not determinative, the arbitrator should consider discovery requests and motions in light of the overarching goals of providing a process that is just from both procedural and substantive perspectives.

Certain forms of discovery, particularly depositions and interrogatories, are far more common in U.S. litigation than in the litigation of many other countries. Thus, U.S. disputants may assume that they have a "right" to certain forms of discovery that are quite foreign to many non-U.S. litigants.

Although pre-trial motions were not traditionally considered part of arbitration, because it was designed to be simple and quick, they are more commonly found in arbitration now that the process is also being used to handle increasingly complex business disputes. To the extent that arbitrators conclude that motions to dismiss, motions for summary judgment, or motions *in limine* are permitted by the relevant rules and also promote justice, the arbitrators may choose to decide such motions in appropriate situations. Given disputants' desire for procedural justice, arbitrators should be cautious about dismissing claims without giving disputants an opportunity to at least state their arguments fully.

In short, a tension often exists between the traditional promise of arbitration — a fast, efficient, less formal process — and the goals of some litigators to provide their arbitration clients with all the same protections and accommodations as litigation. The skillful arbitrator will look for ways to balance these divergent pulls, often in consultation with the parties and their representatives.

e. Setting Up

Arbitrators will often have an opportunity to influence the parties' perception of the arbitration process by adjusting the physical setup of the hearing room. Appropriate seating can enhance communications among the participants; can affect the safety or perceived safety of the participants; can influence the extent to which the arbitrator is perceived as a neutral or viewed with respect; and influence the comfort of participants.

No single seating arrangement is always best. When an informal atmosphere is desired, it may be appropriate to seat all participants at a conference table, perhaps placing the arbitrator at the head of the table, the parties at either side of the arbitrator, and the representatives next to their own clients. On the other hand, sometimes a more formal look may be better, with the arbitrator sitting in the front of a room as might a judge, and with parties and their attorneys seated at counsel tables. In all cases, the arbitrator should be careful that the seating does not appear to favor one side or the other. Any accommodation given to one side should be given to both, and the arbitrator should be equidistant from the parties.

f. The Opening Statement

Like mediations, arbitrations typically begin with an opening statement from the neutral. In making preliminary introductions, the arbitrator should take care to pronounce names correctly, to shake hands with all disputants as well as with their representatives (unless that seems culturally inappropriate), and to treat all persons equally. Unintended small slights, such as having informal conversations with just one side, might have a dramatically negative impact. The arbitrator must ensure that her neutrality and perceived neutrality are preserved at all times.

The arbitrators should take the time to describe the arbitration process, and what role each party and representative will play in that process. Even if disputants are generally acquainted with arbitration, they may not be familiar with the particular form of arbitration or with the styles of the particular arbitrators. As part of their opening, arbitrators should typically emphasize their neutrality (party-appointed non-neutral arbitrators are an exception, as noted earlier). If potential conflicts have not already been disclosed, the arbitrator should be sure to reveal them in the introduction, erring on the side of over-disclosure. If the arbitrator's neutrality is challenged by a party, she should generally withdraw.

Arbitrators should also use their opening statements to make sure that parties and their attorneys have been provided with copies of the rules that will govern the proceeding. It is usually a good idea to remind participants that they will not be permitted to interrupt one another. In some cases it will also be advisable to let parties know that they will be provided with an opportunity to supplement the statements made by their attorneys. After asking the parties and their attorneys if they have any questions, typically the arbitrator will end her opening by administering an oath of truthfulness to the prospective witnesses.

Below is a sample of an opening statement that might be given by an arbitrator in a fee dispute arbitration. Note that not all arbitrators would offer the binding consent order option discussed in this sample opening and that an attorney is the claimant and a client a respondent in the fee dispute matter.

Sample Arbitrator Opening Statement

Good afternoon. My name is Christina Chavez and I have been appointed to serve as your arbitrator. (My name is Christina Chavez; Mike Jones is on my right; Cindy Kowalski is on my left. We have been appointed to serve as your arbitrators).

I (we) want to be sure I (we) have everyone's name accurately, and I (we) am (are) pronouncing your names correctly. You are? . . .

I (we) want you both to know that I (we) have never met either one of you before, and I (we) know nothing about the matters that brought you here except for the complaint and response that you have filed. (Is that correct, Mr. Jones? Ms. Kowalski?)

My (our) role today is to listen to and consider what you have to say and to examine the evidence you have to present and then make a decision that will resolve the matter. Whatever decision I (we) make will be final and binding and cannot be appealed. Your task is to present to me (us) your claim or response, and any evidence you have to support the claim or response.

Have you tried to resolve this matter by talking to each other? It is more likely that you will be satisfied with a resolution you adopt yourself, than with a resolution I (we) impose. Would you like a chance to talk to each other now? (If yes) Why don't you step out into the hall for a few moments. If you are able to work out a resolution, I (we) will write it up as a binding consent award, and it can be enforced just like an arbitrator's award. (If no) I (We) will give you another opportunity before we are done today to work this out yourselves. As we proceed, you might be thinking about ways that this could be resolved to your mutual satisfaction.

There are several ground rules that we will follow today.

1. *I (We) ask that you not interrupt each other. After each of you has presented your case, the other may ask questions and make a response. Take notes about questions you have or comments you want to make, and save them until it is your turn to speak.*
2. *I (We) may ask questions too after you have each presented your case.*
3. *Ms. Attorney will begin today, and Mr. Client has the privilege of making the final reply.*
4. *I (We) have cleared my (our) calendar(s) until 6 p.m. If we need more time, we can reschedule for another day. Do you have any time constraints we should be aware of?*

From your submissions, I (we) understand that, Ms. Attorney, you are claiming. . . . And, Mr. Client, you are claiming. . . .

Before we begin, I (we) would like each of you to take an oath to tell the truth. Please raise your right hand. Do you swear or affirm that you will tell the truth, the whole truth and nothing but the truth?

Ms. Attorney, please begin.

---

g. Parties' Presentations

In arbitration, as in litigation, the plaintiff and/or her attorney typically commences the presentation by calling witnesses and presenting documents. However, the arbitrator is the one who will decide the order of presentation and could structure the hearing differently. Depending on the context, defendant's attorney may cross-examine the plaintiff's witnesses before commencing presentation of her own case. The arbitrators may also choose to question witnesses directly.

In considering how to run the arbitration hearing, arbitrators should be careful not to let interests in speed and efficiency diminish the importance of allowing all sides to present their cases fully, while being accorded dignity and respect. For example, cross examination should not be rude or disrespectful. Also, arbitrators should be careful in the way that they interject their own questions into the process. Those arbitrators who frequently interrupt direct examinations to pose their own questions may cause witnesses to feel that they have not had a full and just opportunity to present their own version of the facts. Interruptions also disturb the train of thought of the speaker and can thus erode the quality of the evidence.

h. Arbitrator's Evidentiary Rulings

In making evidentiary rulings it is essential that the arbitrator consider what evidentiary standards have been chosen by the disputants or mandated by any relevant statute or rules. Traditionally, arbitrators applied more "relaxed" rules of evidence than are typically applied in court, but recently some parties have expressed a preference that arbitrators apply rules similar to those that would be applied by a court.

In the traditional practice, often an arbitrator will respond to an evidentiary challenge by stating "I'll admit it for what it's worth." The rationale for this relaxed approach has been that strict adherence to evidentiary rules would bog down a process that was supposed to be quick and simple, and that arbitrators would be sufficiently sophisticated to disregard or discount evidence that was admitted, but in fact had little real value. In addition, the FAA provides that an arbitral award can be vacated if the arbitrator improperly failed to admit evidence, but does not provide that the award can be vacated if the arbitrator admitted evidence that should not have been allowed. See 9 U.S.C. §10. When the arbitrator states that she will admit evidence "for what it's worth," she is implicitly assuring the objecting party that she understands the purported defect in the evidence, while simultaneously allowing the other side to present its case fully.

If the arbitration agreement or rules call upon the arbitrator to make the same kinds of evidentiary rulings that would be made by a judge, then the arbitrator will be responsible for determining if proposed evidence is irrelevant, inadmissible hearsay, or unduly prejudicial. To the extent that the relevant rules leave the arbitrator free to either admit or reject a particular piece of evidence, the arbitrator should remember, throughout, the goal of issuing a high quality decision. There are reasons why certain types of evidence, such as hearsay, are not typically admitted in court. Thus, even if the arbitrator chooses to admit hearsay, she should recall that it may not be reliable. But, the arbitrator should also consider that if she chooses to exclude a piece of evidence that one party feels is crucial, that party may never feel that her claim has been adequately considered.

i. Parties' Closing Statements

Even if the arbitrator believes she already has a complete understanding of the issues, she generally should give both sides the chance to sum up, to ensure that the parties and lawyers feel they have had every chance to persuade the arbitrator. Closing statements also provide an opportunity to balance out any advantages one side may have had. By permitting the defendant to give the final closing statement, the arbitrator can potentially balance the advantage plaintiff may have secured by being permitted to make the initial opening argument. This is so because what is said first and what is said last can have particularly significant impact on a decision maker.

j. The Award or Decision

The arbitrator must take the responsibility of issuing an award very seriously and weigh the disputants' arguments and facts carefully before coming to a conclusion. At the same time, it is also essential for the arbitrator to issue the award in a timely fashion. Initially, the arbitrator must consult the relevant arbitration agreement and rules. Most likely, they will require a written decision, but occasionally oral awards may be permitted. The FAA only requires courts to confirm written arbitration awards. 9 U.S.C. §§2, 9.

As was discussed in Chapter 9, there is wide variation as to whether arbitrators issue *reasoned* awards, which contain findings of fact and conclusions of law, or whether they instead issue decisions that simply state which party won, which lost, and what, if any, relief must be afforded to the winner by the loser. Simple awards may not even specify which of several claims plaintiff won or whether the money that was awarded represented contractual damages, compensatory damages, or punitive damages. These sorts of awards are regularly issued in securities arbitrations, even though large sums of money are at stake. If issuance of a reasoned award is left to the arbitrator's discretion, she should consider competing policies. In the United States, many commercial arbitrators believe it is unwise to issue reasoned awards, unless the parties have expressly requested such a decision, on the theory that by providing the reasoning underlying the decision the arbitrator is simply inviting the loser to search for flaws in the reasoning and to ask a court to vacate the award. In contrast, reasoned awards are the norm in the labor arbitration context in the United States, and are typically also used in the international commercial setting. Advocates of reasoned awards urge that by providing findings of fact and conclusions of law the arbitrator will afford a more understandable result to the disputants and a more useful result to others who might be guided by the precedent, however informal. Some believe that disputants who are frustrated by an award that simply states who won and who lost might be more likely to seek to vacate such an award.

Publication is a separate question. Whereas most arbitration awards are kept private and provided only to the parties, in some fields publication is expected. For example, in the United States, labor arbitration awards are frequently published, and their reasoning serves as precedent for other workers, unions, and companies facing issues similar to those dealt with in the reasoned award. Securities arbitration awards are also published, but as they are not typically accompanied by reasoning, they are less useful as precedent.

Whether or not the award is reasoned or published, the arbitrator should ensure that it meets certain other minimal requirements. The award should state its conclusions clearly and definitely, it should be signed by all or a majority of the arbitrators, it should state where and when it was rendered, and in some jurisdictions it should be notarized. Of course, the award should deal only with matters that were submitted to arbitration and should resolve the claims only of persons or companies that were covered by the arbitration agreement or order. Further, the award should be provided to the parties in an even-handed fashion, rather than, for example, provided to one party in advance of the other. The award should also be issued in a timely fashion, though the time needed for a decision will vary according to the complexity of the matter in dispute. Note that some arbitration clauses may require that decisions be issued in a particular time period, such as 30 days.

Problem 11-1. *Process for Selecting Additional Arbitrators*

You have been selected by an auto workers' union to serve as an arbitrator in a labor dispute. The auto manufacturer has also selected one arbitrator. Under the parties' arbitration agreement, the two of you are responsible for selecting three additional arbitrators that meet with your mutual approval. What process might you propose be followed? What types of qualifications would you look for in selecting additional arbitrators? What concerns do you foresee the manufacturer's arbitrator might have? What concerns might you have? Do you think this is a good way to select a panel?

Problem 11-2. *Pre-Hearing Discussion with Disputant*

You are an arbitrator. You have been contacted by an attorney representing a plaintiff in a legal malpractice action. The attorney explains that her client agreed to arbitrate future claims against her former attorney, but that the clause does not specify how the arbitrator would be selected. She has called you because of your impeccable reputation for ethical behavior and hopes that if you are amenable to serving as an arbitrator, the opposing side might also accept you. What concerns does this call raise, what questions would you ask, and how would you handle this inquiry?

Problem 11-3. *Arbitrator's Role in Encouraging Settlement*

Do you believe it is appropriate for an arbitrator to help the disputants reach a settlement? If you were arbitrating a contractual dispute that you felt ought to be settled, what would you do?

Problem 11-4.   *Arbitral Discovery*

You are serving as the chair of a panel of three arbitrators hearing a sexual harassment claim brought by a woman who worked as a securities broker. Her lawyer has requested extensive discovery, including the files of plaintiff and the supervisor who allegedly harassed her, as well as the files of male co-workers who allegedly received superior treatment despite inferior work. Plaintiff's lawyer also seeks to depose the supervisor, the supervisor's supervisor, and two male co-workers. The arbitration clause provides that the parties shall be entitled to "such discovery as the arbitrators deem necessary." How would you handle the request?

Problem 11-5.   *Arbitration Room Set-Up*

You will be arbitrating a Better Business Bureau complaint brought by an unrepresented consumer against an unrepresented merchant. The arbitration will take place in your conference room. How would you set up the room?

Problem 11-6.   *Arbitration Motions* In Limine

You are arbitrating a claim brought by plaintiff against her ex-husband for non-payment of child support. (The divorce settlement called for such disputes to be arbitrated). Both the plaintiff and defendant are represented by counsel. Plaintiff's attorney has asked that her client be permitted to give an opening statement, separate from that of her attorney. The defendant's counsel has objected that this would be redundant and prejudicial. How would you rule?

Problem 11-7.   *Arbitration Motions for Summary Judgment*

You have been appointed to serve as an arbitrator in a complex intellectual property dispute. This matter has been pending for 18 months, and you have already reviewed several thousand pages of evidence. Defendant has now filed a motion for summary judgment, asserting that the material that was allegedly misappropriated was in fact in the public domain. The arbitration agreement and relevant rules do not mention the possibility of summary judgment motions. Plaintiff argues that no summary judgment motion should be permitted in this case. What would you do?

2. Skills of Arbitration Representatives

In some contexts, disputants represent themselves in arbitration. Indeed, one of the purported advantages of arbitration is that it can be simple enough and non-threatening enough that disputants need not turn to an attorney or other representative for assistance. When this is possible, the disputant saves the money she would otherwise have had to pay to an advocate.

In many situations, however, a disputant will want or need to be represented in arbitration, as is true in mediation as well. Often, but not always, it is attorneys who represent disputants in arbitration. In labor arbitrations, union members may sometimes be represented by a shop steward who is not an attorney. Whether or not the arbitration advocate is an attorney, she will need to draw on a variety of skills.

The role of an attorney advocate in arbitration bears many similarities to that of the attorney advocate in litigation. However, while certainly there are many commonalities between these roles depending on the type of arbitration, there can also be substantial differences between the work of a litigator and the work of a representative in arbitration.

Probably the most important thing for the arbitration advocate to realize is that being a representative in arbitration requires substantial knowledge, skill, and care. The biggest mistake the arbitration advocate can make is to think that because arbitration is often less formal than litigation, little attention or preparation is required. Arbitration advocates who try to "wing it" will discover that that strategy works just as poorly in arbitration as it does in litigation. The sections that follow provide some advice to attorneys with respect to particular stages of the arbitration.

In applying this advice attorneys should remember above all that taking a hard-nose, win-lose adversarial approach is not necessarily best for one's clients. Rather, like attorneys representing clients in negotiation, mediation, or, for that matter, litigation, the attorney advocate in arbitration should be sure she is helping the client to consider all her economic and non-economic interests. A client may have many interests that are more important than winning a particular claim in arbitration. Thus, attorneys should remember that their own personal attitudes and goals are not necessarily shared by their clients.[3]

a. *Initial Pleadings*

To learn how to commence an arbitration, the advocate must carefully read the arbitration clause, together with any referenced arbitration rules. Typically, such rules require the claimant or her attorney to send a demand for arbitration to the opposing disputant and to the arbitration provider, if one has been pre-selected. As in litigation, it is critical to comply with any stated deadlines and procedural requirements. To the extent the agreement does not specify how arbitration should be commenced, state arbitration law may be helpful. Section 9 of the Revised Uniform Arbitration Act (RUAA) outlines a default process for how to demand

---

3. See Jean R. Sternlight, Lawyers' Representation of Clients in Mediation: Using Economics and Psychology to Structure Advocacy in a Nonadversarial Setting, 14 Ohio St. J. on Disp. Resol. 269 (1999).

arbitration. It is also important to use the initial demand to tell a clear and compelling story as to why the claimant is entitled to prevail. Usually arbitration demands are simpler and shorter than complaints filed in court. In some large commercial arbitrations, the arbitration complaint will resemble a complaint that might have been used in court.

If no agreement to arbitrate exists, the attorney representing the claimant can contact the opposing party's attorney or, if unrepresented, the opposing party, to discuss whether she would be amenable to arbitration. If both sides agree to arbitration, they can submit the claim and response to arbitration. This is called a "submission" agreement.

Once a demand for arbitration is asserted, the representative of the responding party must carefully read any relevant arbitration clause and rules to determine what, if any, response is required. Unlike in court, where failure to answer a complaint almost always results in the plaintiff securing a default judgment, arbitration rules do not necessarily require the responding party to file the equivalent of an answer. Responses are typically short documents, but, again, responding parties must read the rules to be sure what defenses must be included and how any counterclaims should be asserted.

b. Selection of the Arbitrator

One of the advocate's most important roles is often to help select the arbitrator or arbitrators. Depending on the arbitration agreement and rules, the parties may suggest or veto names forwarded by the arbitration provider or opposing party. If the agreement does not specify how the arbitrator should be selected, §5 of the FAA and §11 of the RUAA each provide default mechanisms that may be relevant.

It is critical that the advocate do a good job of researching the background of potential arbitrators, as their predispositions could influence their decisions. Some background information may be supplied by the arbitrator or arbitration provider. The attorney should not only review such disclosures carefully but also attempt to do additional backgrounding, for example by contacting organizations of which the attorney is a member. Members of such organizations may be able to provide the attorney with information on past decisions made by the potential arbitrator or information regarding whether that arbitrator tends to be liberal in granting discovery or willing to grant dispositive motions.

In the international context, attorneys should pay close attention to the country affiliation of the proposed arbitrators. Attorneys in the United States are used to a common law litigation style including discovery, substantial reliance on live testimony, and cross examination. By contrast, many other countries use civil law litigation systems that have little or no pre-hearing exchange of information, rely more heavily on documents than on live testimony, and sometimes prohibit cross examination. If the U.S. attorney is comfortable with the U.S. approach and wants to be sure the arbitrators will adopt it, he either has to write such requirements into the arbitral rules or else select arbitrators from countries such as the United States or Britain, who are likely to feel comfortable with the common law approach. If an attorney is uncomfortable with the U.S. approach, she should keep that concern in mind when selecting rules and arbitrators.

While an advocate is sometimes tempted to select an arbitrator who is in the client's corner, this strategy often backfires if a panel of arbitrators is used. An arbitrator will not be effective in influencing the other arbitrators if it is clear that he came into the case with preconceived notions. By contrast, if an advocate picks an arbitrator who has some links to the opposing party, and then convinces the arbitrator of the strength of the advocate's position, that arbitrator can become a very powerful advocate.

c. Preliminary Hearing

If the arbitrator elects to hold preliminary hearings or conferences prior to commencement of the actual arbitration, the attorney needs to take such conferences seriously. You never have a second chance to make a first impression, and attorneys should be mindful at every stage of the arbitration that they are potentially influencing the decision maker. Thus, whether such hearings are conducted live or by phone, the attorney must come prepared to discuss all issues that may arise. She should plan for the meeting, in part, by asking those familiar with the particular type of arbitration what kinds of issues will likely arise and how resolution of those issues might impact her case. A preliminary hearing in a labor arbitration might well be handled differently than a preliminary hearing in an international commercial arbitration.

d. Discovery

As has been discussed, although traditional arbitration would not have involved much, if any, discovery, the use of discovery is increasing significantly in many arbitration contexts. Thus, the advocate should be aware that it may be possible to use interrogatories, document requests, or depositions in arbitration. It may also be possible to conduct on-site visits of the respondent's property. As with other issues, the arbitral agreement and rules are the first place to check to determine what discovery is permitted. Often, these documents do not discuss the issue, which means not that discovery is prohibited or permitted, but rather that it will be up to the parties either to mutually agree to discovery or else to seek discovery rulings from the arbitrators.

The arbitration advocate who seeks discovery should remember two things. First, to convince the arbitrator that discovery on a particular issue is needed, the advocate should explain, in common-sense terms, why the information that is sought is important to her case. Rhetoric is far less effective than facts, and arbitrators are not likely to be supportive of requests that are perceived to be mere fishing expeditions. Second, the advocate should carefully consider whether the particular discovery is really needed before initiating a discovery request. If attorneys engage in knee-jerk, all-out discovery campaigns similar to those sometimes encountered in litigation, the costs of arbitration will soon equal or exceed those of litigation. After all, in arbitration one must not only pay one's advocate but also the arbitrator. Moreover, once one side begins bombarding the other with discovery requests, the opponent usually returns the favor. Discovery is an important tool and should be requested when needed, but attorneys should think through the pros and cons before seeking extensive discovery.

Arbitration statutes are also relevant to some discovery issues. Section 7 of the FAA, for example, allows arbitrators proceeding under that statute to summon the attendance of witnesses and to require those witnesses to bring documents to a hearing. If the summons is disobeyed, the U.S. district court may be petitioned to compel the attendance of the person and the production of documents, or to punish non-compliance with the arbitrator's order.

e. Motions

As with discovery, pre-trial motions were not typically thought of as part of the arbitration process. However, motions have become increasingly common, particularly in complex commercial arbitrations. Arbitrators, if they are willing, can decide motions to dismiss and motions for summary judgment just as a court might do. For example, §15 of the RUAA allows arbitrators to make summary dispositions of claims either if all parties agree or if one party makes the motion and the opponent has had adequate opportunity to respond.

In filing or responding to motions in arbitration, the advocate should follow many of the same practices that would be followed in court. Motions should be well written and compelling, should be based on properly researched law and properly stated facts, and should not be overly rhetorical. Motions filed in arbitration should typically be shorter and simpler than those that might be filed in court in a comparable case.

While it is not customary to hold oral argument on a motion filed in arbitration, it is possible. If an advocate feels that it would be important to present certain concerns orally, she may request at least a telephonic oral argument.

f. Arbitration Hearings

As you have seen in Chapter 9, arbitration proceedings vary tremendously in their degree of formality. At the formal extreme, some arbitrations are actually held in a court room. Even if they take place in a conference room, the arbitrators may sit at one end of the room; attorneys may stand to make opening and closing arguments; witnesses may be sworn; direct examination, cross examination, and formal rules of evidence may be used; and a court reporter may record all that transpires. At the less formal extreme, arbitrations may take place in a conference room, with all parties and their representatives sitting around the table. Witnesses need not be sworn; attorneys (if present) might not make formal opening or closing arguments; rules of evidence need not be employed; and evidence can be given narratively rather than using formal questioning. Sometimes testimony is presented solely through advocates' summaries of what witnesses would say, rather than through live witness testimony. In some cases, the arbitration "hearing" is not live at all. Arbitrations can be resolved solely based on documents, and arbitrations can also be conducted telephonically or online. Whereas in the United States the system of adjudication relies on a single, though often multi-day, live hearing, many other countries instead use a system of adjudication whereby evidence is submitted piecemeal, in writing, over a long period of time. If one or more live hearings occur, their purpose may be to allow arbitrators to ask questions raised by the written documents, rather than to start fresh with a presentation of evidence.

The arbitration advocate's key task is to be prepared for the kind of hearing that will be held in her particular case. The advocate fails her client if she simply assumes that the arbitration will resemble the kind of litigation — or, for that matter, arbitration — with which she is familiar. Arbitration advocates who do not do their homework can meet with extremely rude surprises: They may be precluded from introducing evidence they had counted on using; prohibited from cross-examining adverse witnesses; asked to give opening or closing arguments for which they did not prepare; or required to contend with adverse evidence they wrongly assumed was inadmissible. U.S. lawyers, well trained in U.S. litigation, sometimes find that their fundamental assumptions are completely invalid. Their war stories can be funny, but the results may not be and can include malpractice. For example, some countries draw a sharp distinction between parties and witnesses, and do not permit parties to testify as witnesses in their own cases. Their potential testimony is essentially dismissed in advance as self-serving and biased, and their statements are permitted only as the equivalent of lawyers' summary arguments at most. Thus, an attorney who is relying on his own client as his key witness could find himself devoid of evidence. Similarly, non-U.S. rules on sequestration of witnesses are sometimes different than U.S. norms. Of course, the non-U.S. lawyer can have equivalent problems when required to arbitrate U.S.-style. Imagine being forced to contend with cross examination, for the first time, when your country views the technique as inherently unfair and unlikely to lead to truth.

Another important task of an advocate is to try to ensure that the arbitration is conducted in a manner that benefits her client and is consistent with her own strengths. The advocate should not assume that how the arbitration is conducted is a foregone conclusion. Either through agreement with opposing counsel or through discussion with the arbitrator, the advocate may be able to influence the style of the arbitration. In attempting to influence the arbitration process, however, the advocate should be careful not to push for a particular process simply because it is more familiar. Perhaps the U.S. arbitrator may realize that live testimony or cross examination are not in fact necessary, or even desirable, in a particular case. If, for example, the arbitrators are not likely to find information obtained through cross examination to be credible, it may make little sense to insist upon a right to conduct cross examination.

Once having done her best to learn how the arbitration is likely to be conducted and to influence it, if possible, the advocate must prepare carefully for the particular style of arbitration that will ensue. When the arbitration is going to be formal and similar to U.S.-style litigation, the advocate should typically follow the same kinds of rules of good practice that advocates conducting a bench trial would follow. The trial plan should be carefully constructed; opening arguments should be drafted in advance; witnesses should be prepared for testimony; documents should be organized and pre-marked; evidentiary objections should be made; and rhetorical excesses should be avoided.

When the arbitration is going to be less formal, or when it is going to be based on documents or online exchanges, the arbitration representative must not cease to be an advocate for her client. Whether one speaks informally or presents direct and cross examination, it is critically important to be well versed on the specifics of the dispute.

At the same time, as we have seen already with negotiation and mediation, being a good advocate does not mean being unduly adversarial or hostile to the opposing party or attorney. One of the potential advantages of arbitration is that it can allow parties to resolve their disputes in a more amicable and long-lasting fashion, as compared to litigation. The potentially quicker and less formal nature of arbitration, combined with the greater finality of arbitration as compared to litigation, can lead to fewer appeals and collateral attacks. Moreover, an arbitral hearing can provide an opportunity for disputants to reconsider their positions and to examine whether a solution might be available that would improve both sides' positions.

g. *Post-Hearing Advocacy*

Once again, the advocate must be familiar with the relevant statutes and arbitral rules to be an effective post-hearing advocate. Some arbitrators expect or request carefully prepared post-hearing briefs to help guide them in their decision making. After the arbitrators have issued their decision, advocacy need not cease. Rather, in appropriate circumstances, arbitrators can be requested to reconsider or modify their decision; arbitration providers may be requested to revise the award; or courts may be asked to either vacate or confirm the arbitral award.

> **Problem 11-8.   *How to Be an Advocate in a Construction
> Arbitration***
>
> Imagine that as a recent law school graduate you are retained to represent a client in a construction arbitration. How would you go about researching what rules apply and what you should do as an arbitration advocate?

B. KEY ETHICAL ISSUES IN ARBITRATION

Good practice requires ethical practice. Moreover, from a public policy perspective, because arbitration is an important element of our system of justice, it is crucial that arbitrators, disputants involved in arbitration, representatives in arbitration, and arbitral organizations behave ethically. Professor Menkel-Meadow examines ethical issues raised by arbitration for each of these players in the reading below.

Carrie Menkel-Meadow, ETHICS ISSUES IN ARBITRATION
AND RELATED DISPUTE RESOLUTION PROCESSES:
WHAT'S HAPPENING AND WHAT'S NOT

56 U. Miami L. Rev. 949, 951-53 (2002)

The use of arbitration presents a variety of different kinds of ethical issues, ranging from the particular ethical behavioral choices made by the actors inside an arbitration, including the arbitrators, lawyers (or other representatives), parties and witnesses, to the institutions who choose, administer and promote arbitration (such as courts, the American Arbitration Association, the Center for Public Resources, the International Chamber of Commerce, and many other "provider" organizations), to the parties or entities who place arbitration clauses in contracts of sale, or provision of services, sometimes without fully knowing what they are drafting. In addition to behavioral choices in the conduct of arbitration there are larger, macro or systemic justice issues in how arbitral choices and decisions are made in conjunction with other possible methods of dispute resolution (comparisons to formal legal justice in courts, foregoing conflict), whether disputing should be public or private, how real or deep the consent in consensual dispute resolution should be and what kind of formal governmental or other scrutiny there ought to be of privately arranged dispute resolution.

In developing taxonomies of ethical issues it is common to divide such issues, as I often have, into "micro" or individual behavioral issues and "macro" or institutional or social justice issues. In examining the ethical issues that have emerged in the use of arbitration, we are beginning to see proposed rules that attempt to provide formal regulations or suggested "guidelines" and "best practices" at both of these levels — for the individuals involved in arbitration, including both third party neutrals (arbitrators) and advocates or representatives of parties in arbitration and the institutions that administer or construct the process. In examining the kinds of ethical issues that emerge from the practice of arbitration and the bodies that have chosen to attempt to address those issues it is interesting, instructive and sometimes ironic to view both the content of the proposed ethical guidelines and the chosen forms of sanctioning, regulation or "policing." At the level of enforcement there are important questions about whether the field of arbitration, like the legal profession, should be self-regulating (like the fox guarding the hen house, as some might argue, as when the AAA determines its own conflicts of interest or that of its arbitrators) or whether some outside bodies (courts) or greater public scrutiny of the process might be desirable.

I have come to use a simple mnemonic device to delineate the ethics issues presented by the use of arbitration as a device for dispute resolution: the 10 C's of dispute resolution ethics. I present them below, more or less in order of their current importance and controversy.

[The 10C's of dispute resolution ethics identified by Menkel-Meadow are:

(1)   choice/consent/coercion (Is it ethically improper to impose arbitration on persons who have not really chosen it?);

(2)   courts or contracts (Is it ethical for courts to mandate arbitration and if so, what ethical rules apply?);

(3)   conflicts of interest (Do arbitrators face improper conflicts of interest to the extent they are trying to please repeat-player clients or serve as party-appointed arbitrator advocates?);

(4)   confidentiality (Although parties may seek confidentiality, is it ethical from a public perspective?);

(5)   competence and credentialing (Should competency and credentials be governed by an ethical code?);

(6)   corporate-organizational liability (To what extent should arbitration providers be governed by ethical rules?);

(7)   communication and counseling (Should lawyers be ethically required to counsel their clients about arbitration or other forms of ADR?);

(8)   costs and fees (Do the costs and fees associated with arbitration raise ethical concerns?);

(9)   complaints and grievance systems (From an ethical standpoint, should parties be provided with a forum in which they can complain about alleged arbitration improprieties?); and

(10) conflicts of laws (Whether and, if so, how should the many sometimes conflicting statutes, rules, and codes of arbitration ethics be reconciled).[4]]

Menkel-Meadow identifies many ethical issues that arise with respect to arbitration. However, as her tenth "C" emphasizes, no single set of ethical rules applies to all arbitrators, disputants, representatives, or arbitration organizations. Indeed, some might suggest that because arbitration is a private process, the state should not seek to regulate the ethics of the process, but rather should leave such regulation to private parties and the marketplace.

The ethical regulation of arbitration can be seen as a glass that is either half full or half empty. On the one hand, it is clear that no single set of ethical rules applies to any of the many participants in arbitration. Neither arbitrators nor arbitration organizations are regulated or certified to the same extent as lawyers, accountants, or even hairdressers. While attorneys are, of course, regulated, no rules apply specifically to their conduct as representatives in arbitration. Yet, on the other hand, there are an abundance of statutes, rules, and codes that have at least precatory authority in these areas.

In the international realm, the ethical regulation of arbitration is even more problematic. Background differences among various countries' approach to litigation, for example, distinctions among adversarial and inquisitorial emphases, lead countries to take vastly different approaches to such issues as the propriety of ex

---

4. See also Carrie Menkel-Meadow, Ethics In ADR: The Many "Cs" of Professional Responsibility and Dispute Resolution, 28 Fordham Urb. L.J. 979 (2001).

parte conversations with judges, whether parties can testify, the degree of zeal attorneys should use to represent their clients, the extent to which attorneys should prepare their clients to testify, and whether parties can hear each other's testimony. These and

> *International arbitration dwells in an ethical no-man's land.*
>
> — Catherine A. Rogers, Fit and Function in Legal Ethics: Developing a Code of Conduct for International Arbitration, 23 Mich. J. Int'l L. 341, 342 (2002).

other differences in litigation lead to great ethical confusion in the world of international arbitration.

Both domestically and internationally, the problem is often less a dearth of regulation than a conflict of regulations. Some of the key sets of rules regulating or advising arbitrators, arbitration providers, and attorneys representing clients in arbitration are discussed next.

1. Arbitrator Ethics

a. Arbitral Bias and the Duty to Disclose

We expect arbitrators to behave fairly, justly, impartially, and also to provide the appearance of these characteristics. At the same time, because arbitrators are typically selected by the parties, realists or cynics among us recognize that arbitrators may consciously or unconsciously feel some pressure to please the parties who have selected them in order to maximize their chances of being chosen as arbitrators again in the future. It is this tension that has led some to suspect that some arbitrators "split the baby" in an effort to please both sides. When both parties play an equally active role in selecting arbitrators, perhaps market pressures will discourage the arbitrator from unduly favoring one side or the other. However, when one disputant is a "repeat player" who will choose many arbitrators and is quite familiar with the arbitrators' backgrounds, and the other disputant is not a "repeat player," perhaps the arbitrator may have an incentive to favor the repeat player. These fears underlie many of our ethical rules.

The Supreme Court addressed the issue of arbitral bias in Commonwealth Coatings Corp. v. Continental Casualty Co., 393 U.S. 145 (1968), but unfortunately issued a split decision that leaves open many issues.

 COMMONWEALTH COATINGS CORP. v. CONTINENTAL CASUALTY CO.

393 U.S. 145 (1968)

Mr. Justice BLACK delivered the opinion of the Court.

At issue in this case is the question whether elementary requirements of impartiality taken for granted in every judicial proceeding are suspended when the parties agree to resolve a dispute through arbitration.

The petitioner, Commonwealth Coatings Corporation, a subcontractor, sued the sureties on the prime contractor's bond to recover money alleged to be due for a painting job. . . . Pursuant to th[e] agreement [to arbitrate] petitioner appointed one arbitrator, the prime contractor appointed a second, and these two together selected the third arbitrator. This third arbitrator, the supposedly neutral member of the panel, conducted a large business in Puerto Rico, in which he served as an engineering consultant for various people in connection with building construction projects. One of his regular customers in this business was the prime contractor that petitioner sued in this case. This relationship with the prime contractor was in a sense sporadic in that the arbitrator's services were used only from time to time at irregular intervals, and there had been no dealings between them for about a year immediately preceding the arbitration. Nevertheless, the prime contractor's patronage was repeated and significant, involving fees of about $12,000 over a period of four of five years, and the relationship even went so far as to include the rendering of services on the very projects involved in this lawsuit. An arbitration was held, but the facts concerning the close business connections between the third arbitrator and the prime contractor were unknown to petitioner and were never revealed to it by this arbitrator, by the prime contractor, or by anyone else until after an award had been made. Petitioner challenged the award on this ground, among others, but the District Court refused to set aside the award. The Court of Appeals affirmed. . . .

Section 10 [of the FAA] . . . sets out the conditions upon which awards can be vacated. The two courts below held, however, that §10 could not be construed in such a way as to justify vacating the award in this case. We disagree and reverse. Section 10 does authorize vacation of an award where it was "procured by corruption, fraud, or undue means" or "[w]here there was evident partiality . . . in the arbitrators." These provisions show a desire of Congress to provide not merely for *any* arbitration but for an impartial one. It is true that petitioner does not charge before us that the third arbitrator was actually guilty of fraud or bias in deciding this case, and we have no reason, apart from the undisclosed business relationship, to suspect him of any improper motives. But neither this arbitrator nor the prime contractor gave to petitioner even an intimation of the close financial relations that had existed between them for a period of years. We have no doubt that if a litigant could show that a foreman of a jury or a judge in a court of justice had, unknown to the litigant, any such relationship, the judgment would be subject to challenge. This is shown beyond doubt by Tumey v. State of Ohio, 273 U.S. 510 (1927), where this Court held that a conviction could not stand because a small part of the judge's income consisted of court fees collected from convicted defendants. Although in *Tumey* it appeared the amount of the judge's compensation actually depended on whether he decided for one side or the other, that is too small a distinction to allow this manifest violation of the strict morality and fairness Congress would have expected on the part of the arbitrator and the other party in this case. Nor should it be at all relevant, as the Court of Appeals apparently thought it was here, that "[t]he payments received were a very small part of (the arbitrator's) income. . . ."[5] For in *Tumey* the Court held that a decision should be set aside where there is "the slightest pecuniary interest" on the part of the judge, and specifically rejected the State's contention that the compensation involved there was "so small that it is not to be regarded as likely to influence improperly a judicial officer in the discharge of his duty. . . ."[6] Since in the case of courts this is a *constitutional* principle, we can see no basis for refusing to find the same concept in the broad statutory language that governs arbitration proceedings and provides that an award can be set aside on the basis of "evident partiality" or the use of "undue means." . . . It is true that arbitrators cannot sever all their ties with the business world, since they are not expected to get all their income from their work deciding cases, but we should, if anything, be even more scrupulous to safeguard the impartiality of arbitrators than judges, since the former have completely free rein to decide the law as well as the facts and are not subject to appellate review. We can perceive no way in which the effectiveness of the arbitration process will be hampered by the simple requirement that arbitrators disclose to the parties any dealings that might create an impression of possible bias. . . .

[A]ny tribunal permitted by law to try cases and controversies not only must be unbiased but also must avoid even the appearance of bias. We cannot believe that it was the purpose of Congress to authorize litigants to submit their cases and controversies to arbitration boards that might reasonably be thought biased against one litigant and favorable to another.

Reversed.

Mr. Justice WHITE, with whom Mr. Justice MARSHALL joins, concurring.

The Court does not decide today that arbitrators are to be held to the standards of judicial decorum of Article III judges, or indeed of any judges. It is often because they are men of affairs, not apart from but of the marketplace, that they are effective in their adjudicatory function. . . . This does not mean the judiciary must overlook outright chicanery in giving effect to their awards; that would be an abdication of our responsibility. But it does mean that arbitrators are not automatically disqualified by a business relationship with the parties before them if both parties are informed of the relationship in advance, or if they are unaware of the facts but the relationship is trivial. I see no reason automatically to disqualify the best informed and most capable potential arbitrators.

The arbitration process functions best when an amicable and trusting atmosphere is preserved and there is voluntary compliance with the decree, without need for judicial enforcement. This end is best served by establishing an atmosphere of frankness at the outset, through disclosure by the arbitrator of any financial transactions which he has had or is negotiating with either of the parties. In many cases the arbitrator might believe the business relationship to be so insubstantial that to make a point of revealing it would suggest he is indeed easily swayed, and perhaps a partisan of that party. But if the law requires the disclosure, no such imputation can

---

5. 382 F.2d 1010, 1011.
6. 273 U.S. at 524.

arise. And it is far better that the relationship be disclosed at the outset, when the parties are free to reject the arbitrator or accept him with knowledge of the relationship and continuing faith in his objectivity, than to have the relationship come to light after the arbitration, when a suspicious or disgruntled party can seize on it as a pretext for invalidating the award. The judiciary should minimize its role in arbitration as judge of the arbitrator's impartiality. That role is best consigned to the parties, who are the architects of their own arbitration process, and are far better informed of the prevailing ethical standards and reputations within their business.

Of course, an arbitrator's business relationships may be diverse indeed, involving more or less remote commercial connections with great numbers of people. He cannot be expected to provide the parties with his complete and unexpurgated business biography. But it is enough for present purposes to hold, as the Court does, that where the arbitrator has a substantial interest in a firm which has done more than trivial business with a party, that fact must be disclosed. If arbitrators err on the side of disclosure, as they should, it will not be difficult for courts to identify those undisclosed relationships which are too insubstantial to warrant vacating an award.

Mr. Justice FORTAS, with whom Mr. Justice HARLAN and Mr. Justice STEWART join, dissenting.

The facts in this case do not lend themselves to the Court's ruling. The Court sets aside the arbitration award despite the fact that the award is unanimous and no claim is made of actual partiality, unfairness, bias, or fraud.

The arbitration was held pursuant to provisions in the contracts between the parties . . .

Each party appointed an arbitrator and the third arbitrator was chosen by those two. The controversy relates to the third arbitrator.

The third arbitrator was not asked about business connections with either party. Petitioner's complaint is that he failed to volunteer information about professional services rendered by him to the other party to the contract, the most recent of which were performed over a year before the arbitration. Both courts below held, and petitioner concedes, that the third arbitrator was innocent of any actual partiality, or bias, or improper motive. There is no suggestion of concealment as distinguished from the innocent failure to volunteer information.

The third arbitrator is a leading and respected consulting engineer who has performed services for "most of the contractors in Puerto Rico." He was well known to petitioner's counsel and they were personal friends. Petitioner's counsel candidly admitted that if he had been told about the arbitrator's prior relationship "I don't think I would have objected because I know Mr. Capacete [the arbitrator]."

Clearly, the District Judge's conclusion, affirmed by the Court of Appeals for the First Circuit, was correct, that "the arbitrators conducted fair, impartial hearings; that they reached a proper determination of the issues before them, and that plaintiff's objections represent a 'situation where the losing party to an arbitration is now clutching at straws in an attempt to avoid the results of the arbitration to which it became a party.'"

The Court nevertheless orders that the arbitration award be set aside. It uses this singularly inappropriate case to announce a *per se* rule that in my judgment has no basis in the applicable statute or jurisprudential principles: that, regardless of the agreement between the parties, if an arbitrator has any prior business relationship with one of the parties of which he fails to inform the other party, however innocently, the arbitration award is always subject to being set aside. This is so even where the award is unanimous; where there is no suggestion that the nondisclosure indicates partiality or bias; and where it is conceded that there was in fact no irregularity, unfairness, bias, or partiality. Until the decision today, it has not been the law that an arbitrator's failure to disclose a prior business relationship with one of the parties will compel the setting aside of an arbitration award regardless of the circumstances.

I agree that failure of an arbitrator to volunteer information about business dealings with one party will, prima facie, support a claim of partiality or bias. But where there is no suggestion that the nondisclosure was calculated, and where the complaining party disclaims any imputation of partiality, bias, or misconduct, the presumption clearly is overcome.

I do not believe that it is either necessary, appropriate, or permissible to rule, as the Court does, that, regardless of the facts, innocent failure to volunteer information constitutes the "evident partiality" necessary under §10(b) of the Arbitration Act to set aside an award. "Evident partiality" means what it says: conduct — or at least an attitude or disposition — by the arbitrator favoring one party rather than the other. This case demonstrates that to rule otherwise may be a palpable injustice, since all agree that the arbitrator was innocent of either "evident partiality" or anything approaching it.

Arbitration is essentially consensual and practical. The United States Arbitration Act is obviously designed to protect the integrity of the process with a minimum of insistence upon set formulae and rules. The Court applies to this process rules applicable to judges and not to a system characterized by dealing on faith and reputation for reliability. Such formalism is not contemplated by the Act nor is it warranted in a case where no claim is made of partiality, of unfairness, or of misconduct in any degree.

Problem 11-9.   *Implications of Recent Supreme Court Recusal Decision*

In Caperton v. A.T. Massey Coal Co., 129 S. Ct. 2252 (2009), the Supreme Court found, in a 5-4 decision, that the Due Process Clause required a judge who had received a very substantial campaign contribution from one of the parties to recuse himself from the case. The Court reasoned that even if there was no actual bias, there was at least an appearance of impropriety in that the circumstances were such as to pose a temptation to the average judge "not to hold the balance nice, clear and true." Id. at 2264 (citation omitted). The Court explained that "fears of bias can arise when — without the other parties' consent — a man chooses the judge in his own cause." Id. at 2265. Do you believe that this new decision might have any implications for arbitration jurisprudence? See Nancy A. Welsh, What Is "Impartial Enough" in a World of Embedded Neutrals, 52 Arizona L. Rev. 395 (2010).

In addition to the statutory background provided by *Commonwealth Coatings*, numerous ethical rules and codes spell out the expectations of fairness and impartiality that govern arbitrators' actions. These various rules and codes may or may not apply, depending on the terms of the parties' contract, and depending in some cases on whether or not the arbitrators are attorneys. Internationally, the International Bar Association in 2004 promulgated a set of Guidelines on Conflicts of Interest in International Arbitration.

Domestically, the AAA/ABA Code of Ethics for Arbitrators in Commercial Disputes, revised in 2003, is frequently cited by courts. It includes canons requiring arbitrators to "uphold the integrity and fairness of the arbitration process," "disclose any interest or relationship likely to affect impartiality or . . . create an appearance of partiality," conduct proceedings "fairly and diligently," avoid impropriety or its appearance in communicating with the parties, make decisions in a "just, independent and deliberate manner," and "be faithful to the relationship of trust and confidentiality inherent in that office." Details of each of these responsibilities are spelled out in the AAA/ABA Code.[7]

Another frequently cited ethical document is the Code of Professional Responsibility for Arbitrators of Labor-Management Disputes. It focuses on special issues arising in the labor-management context and is sponsored by the National Academy of Arbitrators, the American Arbitration Association, and the Federal Mediation and Conciliation Service.[8] In addition, the CPR-Georgetown Commission on Ethics and Standards in ADR has published a code entitled "Model Rules for The Lawyer as Third-Party Neutral." This Code focuses on the special responsibilities of lawyers who serve as arbitrators or other kinds of third-party neutrals.[9] In addition, individual arbitration providers such as the American Arbitration Association, JAMS, the International Chamber of Commerce, and the London Court of International Arbitration frequently have their own internal rules that discuss such issues as what information regarding possible conflicts must be disclosed by arbitrators and whether ex parte contacts are permitted. As you learn about these codes, consider whether they are adequate to ensure arbitrators act ethically.

Next, Section 12 of the Revised Uniform Arbitration Act lays out a set of ethical duties that is similar to many of the various codes mentioned above. Although the RUAA has to date been adopted by just 14 jurisdictions, its discussion of arbitrators' ethical responsibilities, and its accompanying Reporter's notes, are informative.

---

7. See *http://www.adr.org.*
8. See *http://www.naarb.org/code.html.*
9. See *http://www.cpradr.org/Portals/0/CPRGeorge-ModelRule.pdf.*

REVISED UNIFORM ARBITRATION ACT SECTION 12 (2005)

§12.   Disclosure by Arbitrator

(a) Before accepting appointment, an individual who is requested to serve as an arbitrator, after making a reasonable inquiry, shall disclose to all parties . . . and to any other arbitrators any known facts that a reasonable person would consider likely to affect the impartiality of the arbitrator in the arbitration proceeding, including:

> (1) a financial or personal interest in the outcome of the arbitration proceeding; and

> (2) an existing or past relationship with any of the parties to the agreement to arbitrate or the arbitration proceeding, their counsel or representatives, a witness, or another arbitrators.

(b) An arbitrator has a continuing obligation to disclose to all parties . . . and to any other arbitrators any facts that the arbitrator learns after accepting appointment which a reasonable person would consider likely to affect the impartiality of the arbitrator.

(c) If an arbitrator discloses a fact required by subsection (a) or (b) to be disclosed and a party timely objects to the appointment or continued service of the arbitrator based upon the fact disclosed, the objection may be a ground . . . for vacating an award made by the arbitrator.

(d) If the arbitrator did not disclose a fact as required by subsection (a) or (b), upon timely objection by a party, the court . . . may vacate an award.

(e) An arbitrator appointed as a neutral arbitrator who does not disclose a known, direct, and material interest in the outcome of the arbitration proceeding or a known, existing, and substantial relationship with a party is presumed to act with evident partiality. . . .

(f) If the parties to an arbitration proceeding agree to the procedures of an arbitration organization or any other procedures for challenges to arbitrators before an award is made, substantial compliance with those procedures is a condition precedent to a [motion] to vacate an award on that ground. . . .

While the ethical responsibilities laid out in RUAA Section 12 might seem fairly obvious, arbitration experts have recognized that a tension exists between the expectation of impartiality and the goal of party control over the arbitration process. As discussed by the dissent in *Commonwealth Coatings*, excerpted earlier, when parties have consented to a particular form of arbitration and have accepted certain individuals as their arbitrators, is it appropriate to use ethical rules to undercut their intentions?

The drafters of the RUAA addressed these competing policies in the Reporter's Comment to Section 12. The Comment observes that while lower court decisions following *Commonwealth Coatings* have taken various tacks, a great number of such courts have "placed a higher burden on those seeking to vacate awards on grounds of arbitrator interests or relationships. . . ." Reporter's Comment to Revised Unif. Arbitration Act §12, 7 U.L.A. 44 (2005).

When one reviews lower court decisions with respect to purported arbitrator bias, one learns that the decisions are very fact specific, and that courts are quite diverse in their approach to bias. Thus, although courts tend to be reluctant to vacate arbitral awards, it is difficult to predict the result in any particular case. It is certainly safest for arbitrators to err on the side of too much — rather than too little — disclosure.

b. Party-Appointed Non-Neutral Arbitrators

In the United States, both in the commercial and labor contexts, parties sometimes elect a process in which each selects one or more non-neutral arbitrators. These party-appointed arbitrators then select a neutral arbitrator who serves as the Chair of the panel. Typically, the non-neutral arbitrator is supposed to serve as a sort of advocate for the side that appointed her. While such an arbitrator would not directly present evidence at the hearing, she might be expected to make sure that the other arbitrators fully understood the evidence that had been presented. It is often considered permissible for non-neutral party-appointed arbitrators to have conversations about the case with the party that appointed them, outside of the hearing of the other parties or arbitrators. Although in theory the non-neutral arbitrator could ultimately rule against the party that appointed him or her, this does not usually occur.

The practice of appointing non-neutral arbitrators has been very controversial, particularly outside the United States, because many persons find the concept of a non-neutral arbitrator to be abhorrent. One concern is that the lack of clarity with respect to the role of the non-neutral arbitrator can lead to problems. For these reasons, some ethical codes proscribe the practice. For example, the CPR Rules for Non-Administered Arbitration of International Disputes (2007), Rules 7.1 and 7.4, provide that arbitrators shall be "independent and impartial" and prohibit ex parte communications.[10] Similarly, the International Bar Association, Ethics for International Arbitrators, paragraph 3.1, provides that "[t]he criteria for assessing questions relating to bias are impartiality and independence," and further states that "[p]artiality arises where an arbitrator favours one of the parties."[11] Article 7 of the Rules of Arbitration of the International Chamber of Commerce (1998) states: "Every

---

10. See *http://www.cpradr.org*.
11. See *http://www.int-bar.org/images/downloads/pubs/Ethics_arbitrators.pdf*.

arbitrator must be and remain independent of the parties involved in the arbitration."[12]

In contrast, some U.S. arbitrator ethical codes contain provisions allowing and explaining this form of arbitration. Comment 5 to §12 of the RUAA specially discusses the phenomenon of non-neutral party-appointed arbitrators. It states:

> The integrity of the process demands that the non-neutral arbitrators chosen by the parties, like neutral arbitrators, disclose pertinent interests and relationships to all parties as well as other members of the arbitration panel. It is particularly important for the neutral arbitrator to know the interest of the arbitrator selected by each of the parties if, for example, such non-neutral arbitrator is being paid on a contingent-fee basis.

7 U.L.A. 46 (2005).

The 2004 AAA/ABA Code of Ethics for Arbitrators in Commercial Disputes states a preference against the use of non-neutral arbitrators while nonetheless allowing the practice. The Code's prefatory "Note on Neutrality" subjects non-neutrals to additional ethical guidelines. On the other hand, the non-neutral arbitrators are permitted to engage in conduct that would normally be proscribed, such as ex parte contacts with the appointing party. See AAA/ABA Code of Ethics for Arbitrators in Commercial Disputes Canon X (2004).

Problem 11-10.   *Appointing Neutral or Non-Neutral Arbitrators*

You are the attorney for Flash!, a company specializing in website design. Your company is about to enter a major website design contract with a large online retailer. The contract has mostly been agreed to by the parties. It will include an arbitration clause requiring all disputes in excess of $100,000 to be resolved by a panel of three arbitrators. Each side will appoint one arbitrator, and those arbitrators will appoint the Chair. However, the parties have not yet agreed whether the party-appointed arbitrators should be neutral or not. The president of Flash! has asked you to explain what the difference is between neutral and non-neutral arbitrators and why it might matter.

---

c. Enforcement of Ethical Codes

Assuming an arbitrator has violated an ethical code, what can be done? Alleged ethical violations are most frequently raised by the losing party in an arbitration, who attempts to vacate the arbitral award on that basis. However, many courts have found that the "mere" violation of an ethical code is not necessarily sufficient to void an arbitral award. See, e.g., Merit Insurance Co. v. Leatherby Insurance Co., 714 F.2d 673, 680 (7th Cir. 1983) ("Although we have great respect for the Commercial Arbitration Rules and the Code of Ethics for Arbitrators, they are not the proper starting point for an inquiry into an award's validity under section 10 of the United

---

12. See *http://www.iccwbo.org/uploadedFiles/Court/Arbitration/other/rules_arb_english.pdf.*

States Arbitration Act and Rule 60(b) of the Federal Rules of Civil Procedure."). Thus, while a party who believes an arbitrator has violated ethical standards can report that arbitrator to a relevant provider, seeking to have that arbitrator disqualified from future arbitrations, the ethical lapse will not necessarily lead to the award being vacated.

Problem 11-11.   *Providers' Internal Review Panels*

Some arbitral providers have internal processes variously known as courts or committees or tribunals whereby disputants can file a challenge as to arbitrators they believe are not sufficiently neutral or independent. See Rules of Arbitration of the International Chamber of Commerce, Art. 11 (1998); American Arbitration Association Commercial Arbitration Rules and Mediation Procedures, R-17 (2009); CPR-Principles for ADR Provider Organizations, Principle VI (2002). Do you think these internal processes are likely to be adequate to ensure that arbitrators act ethically? What features of the provider or of the internal process itself do you think would be important in deciding whether an internal review process were likely to be adequate?

As difficult as it is for a losing party to vacate an arbitral award based on the arbitrator's unethical behavior, it is even more difficult to convince a court to force the withdrawal of an arbitrator prior to the dispute being heard. See, e.g., Smith v. American Arbitration Ass'n, 233 F.3d 502, 506 (7th Cir. 2000) (Posner, J.) (rejecting challenge to panel's lack of gender diversity and stating "The time to challenge an arbitration on whatever grounds, including bias, is when the arbitration is completed and an award is rendered."). For a contrary view, see Borst v. Allstate Ins. Co., 717 N.W.2d 42 (Wis. 2006) (concluding that pre-arbitration challenge to arbitrator was appropriate).

An alternative way of approaching the issue of arbitrator ethics is to use credentialing or certification processes to regulate who can become an arbitrator. You will recall that this issue was previously discussed with respect to mediation in Chapter 7. While there are no national or international rules as to who is qualified to be an arbitrator, some providers, such as the National Academy of Arbitrators, CPR, and AAA, create lists of arbitrators who are said to possess particular qualifications or expertise. Traditionally, disputants often sought arbitrators with specialized expertise in business or science, but not necessarily in law. Today, in some contexts, the arbitrators who are sought are lay people or have a background in consumer issues. For example, non-lawyers or non-industry representatives may be appropriate for "lemon law" arbitration involving automobiles, for claims against securities dealers, or for claims against attorneys over billing disputes.

> ### Problem 11-12. *Credentialing Arbitrators — Pros and Cons*
>
> What do you see as the pros and cons of requiring that arbitrators be certified or credentialed? If certification or credentialing of arbitrators were to be required, what should be the criteria? Do you think that "experts" always make better arbitrators, or might experts have an inclination to be poor listeners, jump to conclusions, and thus give less procedural satisfaction to disputants? Where do these factors leave your thinking about the propriety of credentialing arbitrators? Does it depend on the context?

Finally, if an arbitrator does behave unethically, a party can attempt to bring a lawsuit against that arbitrator. However, as noted in Chapter 10.C.3, the arbitrator is generally protected by quasi-judicial immunity. While immunity won't protect an arbitrator who engaged in deliberate or intentional misconduct, it will make it quite difficult to establish most claims of ethical impropriety. See, e.g., Austern v. Chicago Board Options Exchange, Inc., 898 F.2d 882, 886 (2d Cir. 1990) (observing that "the Courts of Appeals that have addressed the issue have uniformly immunized arbitrators from civil liability for all acts performed in their arbitral capacity"). *Austern* explained that "[a]s with judicial and quasi-judicial immunity, arbitral immunity is essential to protect the decision-maker from undue influence and protect the decision-making process from reprisals by dissatisfied litigants.'" Id. (quotation omitted).

> ### Problem 11-13. *Dealing with Arbitrator Bias*
>
> You are an attorney representing a plaintiff in a medical malpractice claim that is being handled through arbitration according to the terms of a pre-dispute arbitration clause. The relevant provider, the Medical Arbitration Association, has selected an arbitrator who is a doctor with the same expertise as the defendant. You believe that such an arbitrator is likely to be biased in defendant's favor.
>
> What are your options in dealing with this situation?

2. Arbitral Provider Ethics

Increasingly it is recognized that ADR provider organizations, such as the American Arbitration Association (AAA), JAMS, the International Chamber of Commerce (ICC), and the National Arbitration Forum (NAF),[13] play a critically

---

13. As discussed below, the NAF has recently eliminated a substantial portion of its business, consumer arbitration. Nonetheless, we discuss NAF here because it remains a provider of arbitration services in other areas including domain name disputes, personal injury protection claims, and cargo disputes.

important role in delivering arbitration to the public. Together these entities administer numerous cases worth many millions of dollars. This administrative function typically includes helping to select the arbitrators, performing clerical duties, and arranging hearing dates and times. Some providers, in particular the ICC, play an even more active role by reviewing arbitral awards. These organizations may also be big businesses. NAF and JAMS are both for-profit entities. AAA, the largest U.S. provider, although technically a not-for-profit corporation, listed its assets for 2007 as over $131 million and its revenues as over $72 million.[14] Thus, it is critical that these organizations, as well as individual arbitrators, be held to high ethical standards.

One provider, NAF, was sued in several high profile suits by local governmental entities. In 2008, the San Francisco City Attorney brought suit in state court against NAF on various claims of consumer fraud, citing statistics showing that companies overwhelmingly prevail against consumers in NAF-sponsored arbitrations. Subsequently, in 2009, the Minnesota Attorney General brought an action against NAF asserting that the entity had committed consumer fraud by claiming neutrality when in fact the provider was owned in substantial part by a company that also owned many of the collection agencies that frequently appeared in front of NAF in claims against consumers. A few days after the Minnesota suit was filed, NAF stated that it would "voluntarily cease to administer consumer arbitration disputes as of Friday, July 24, 2009, as part of a settlement agreement with the Minnesota Attorney General."[15] As this book goes to press, NAF has been sued in several class actions by consumers who participated in NAF arbitrations. The status of consumer arbitration awards that were secured in NAF arbitrations remain in some doubt.

The scope of provider ethical responsibilities under current law is not clear. Nor is it clear how any such responsibilities can be enforced. Providers often argue that they, like arbitrators, should have quasi-judicial immunity, and this argument has often been accepted. See, e.g., International Medical Group, Inc. v. American Arbitration Ass'n, 312 F.3d 833 (7th Cir. 2002). Section 14(a) of the RUAA provides that "(a) An arbitrator *or an arbitration organization* acting in that capacity is immune from civil liability to the same extent as a judge of a court of this State acting in a judicial capacity." (emphasis added). The Reporter's Notes to Section 14 explain:

> Section 14(a) also provides the same immunity as is provided to an arbitrator to an arbitration organization. Extension of judicial immunity to those arbitration organizations is appropriate to the extent that they are acting "in certain roles and with certain responsibilities" that are comparable to those of a judge. Corey v. New York Stock Exch., 691 F.2d 1205, 1209 (6th Cir. 1982). This immunity to neutral arbitration organizations is appropriate because the duties that they perform in administering the arbitration process are the functional equivalent of the roles and responsibilities of judges administering the adjudication process in a court of law. There is substantial precedent for this conclusion.

National Arbitration Forum, The FORUM Continues to Administer Domain Name Disputes (Aug. 5, 2009), *http://www.adrforum.com/newsroom.aspx?itemID=1534.*

14. AAA 2007 Annual Report available at *http://www.adr.org/annual_reports.*

15. National Arbitrator Forum, National Arbitration Forum to Cease Administering All Consumer Arbitrations in Response to Mounting Legal and Legislative Challenges (July 19, 2009), *http://www.adrforum.com/newsroom.aspx?itemID=1528.*

Yet, the practice of providing broad immunity to arbitral providers can be critiqued by those who believe the analogy between judges (who are afforded full immunity) and arbitrators breaks down. Such critics note that arbitration may lack the procedural safeguards of court (such as full appeal), arbitrations are conducted out of the public eye, arbitrators are often sufficiently compensated that they could purchase malpractice insurance, arbitration may be mandatorily imposed, and that some enforcement mechanism such as suits against arbitrators is needed in order that ethical restrictions have teeth.[16]

In May 2002, the CPR-Georgetown Commission on Ethics and Standards of Practice in ADR issued a set of "Principles for ADR Provider Organizations."[17] Although these principles do not have the force of law, the promulgators hoped that arbitral providers would voluntarily agree to be bound by their terms. Focusing primarily on disclosure, the Principles are founded on the idea that "[c]onsumers of dispute resolution services are entitled to sufficient information about ADR Provider Organizations, their services and affiliated neutrals to make well-informed decisions about their dispute resolution options." Id. at Preamble. The goal is that such providers "should foster and meet the expectations of consumers, policy makers and the public generally for fair, impartial and quality dispute resolution services and processes." Id.

To meet these goals, the Principles require, *inter alia*, that providers should "take all reasonable steps to maximize the quality and competence of its services, absent a clear and prominent disclaimer to the contrary"; "take all reasonable steps to provide clear, accurate and understandable information about . . . [their] services, operations and fees"; "ensure that ADR processes provided under its auspices are fundamentally fair"; "take all reasonable steps . . . to provide access to their services at reasonable cost to low-income parties"; "disclose the existence of any interests or relationships which are reasonably likely to affect the impartiality or independence of the Organization or which might reasonably create the appearance that the Organization is biased . . . including a contractual stream of referrals, a *de facto* stream of referrals, or a funding relationship between a party and the organization"; and "require affiliated neutrals to subscribe to a reputable internal or external ADR code of ethics." Id. at Principles I-V, VII.

One controversial aspect of these principles is the requirement that organizations disclose information regarding interests or relationships that might be perceived to constitute a conflict of interest. Id. at Principle V. This Principle could be interpreted to require providers to disclose information about ownership of the provider by an interested party, provider's investments, membership fees paid by persons to whom neutral services are provided, consulting services provided to disputants, and long-term contracts entered into with disputants that provide repeat business to the provider.

---

16. See Maureen A. Weston, Reexamining Arbitral Immunity in an Age of Mandatory and Professional Arbitration, 88 Minn. L. Rev. 449 (2004).

17. CPR-Georgetown Commission on Ethics and Standards of Practice in ADR, Principles for ADR Provider Organizations (May 1, 2002), *http://www.cpradr.org/Portals/0/finalProvider.pdf.*

The CPR–Georgetown Principles have not been generally accepted. The President of the AAA, although a member of the drafting committee, "declined to fully endorse the . . . Principles, . . . stating that he does not believe the Principles are fully applicable to the AAA because of its 'unique size and complexity.' " Principles at p. 3 n.5. Moreover, some suggest that the Principles, in any event, do not go far enough, asserting for example that "[u]nethical marketing and administrative practices by the providers taint the neutrality of the arbitrators and the entire process," that "[s]elf regulation of the arbitration industry has been a dismal failure," and that when providers market themselves to repeat player parties, such as credit card issuers, for whom they will handle many disputes with individual borrowers, they may explicitly or implicitly assure favorable results to that party.[18] Although the CPR–Georgetown principles were written substantially before NAF's alleged misconduct was uncovered, it almost seems that they could have been written to deal with future situations of that sort.

Problem 11-14.   *Dealing with Arbitrator Bias*

You are a junior partner in a firm that has become very involved in ADR practice over the past decade. In fact, your firm is one of a very few in this particular region that provide a full range of ADR representation options for clients. Due to this reputation, other lawyers consult your firm regularly when trying to find qualified arbitrators and mediators within the region. A senior partner has come to you with the idea that perhaps the referral process should become more formalized. She floats ideas that range from publishing a guide to marketing this service, and she hopes that this could become a stream of revenue for the firm. What rules would govern your options? Can you provide official referrals, with or without charging fees, without changing the firm's current practice? Is the firm breaching any ethical principles simply by providing informal referrals?

---

3. Ethics for Attorney Representatives in Arbitration

Do lawyers who represent clients in arbitration have the same ethical responsibilities as lawyers representing clients in litigation? In negotiation? In mediation? Unfortunately, policy makers have not provided substantial guidance regarding whether attorney advocates in arbitration should follow the same rules as attorney advocates in other contexts.

---

18. Cliff Palefsky, Only A Start: ADR Provider Ethics Principles Don't Go Far Enough, 7 No. 3 Disp. Resol. Mag. 18, 20 (2001).

For the most part attorneys' rules of professional conduct do not contain clear rules for those engaged as advocates in arbitration. Internationally, the ethical rules governing advocates' conduct in arbitration are even more fuzzy.

Nonetheless, we must consult those rules for the guidance they can provide. Below, we have excerpted a selection from the Delaware Lawyers' Rules of Professional Conduct, which mirror the Model Rules of Professional Conduct. But please refer to the applicable rules in your own state.

One issue that is clear in many jurisdictions in the United States, thanks to a fairly recent amendment to the ABA Model Rules of Professional Conduct, is that attorneys owe the same duty of candor to an arbitrator in a binding arbitration as they would to a judge. Model Rule 1.0(m) now includes binding arbitration in the definition of "tribunal." So, Model Rule 3.3's requirements that attorneys be truthful with respect to tribunals apply to attorneys' conduct as representatives in binding arbitration. (Note that the term "tribunal" does not cover mediation.)

> *To put it at its most concrete, as I have asserted in debate with many legal ethicists, the Model Rules of Professional Conduct (still based on an adversarial conception of the advocate's, including "counselor's", role) is not responsive to the needs, duties, and responsibilities of one seeking to be a "non-adversarial" problem-solver and the Code of Judicial Conduct, while perhaps helpful for arbitrators, is not responsive to the particular needs, duties and responsibilities of the now wide variation in third-party neutral practices.*

Carrie Menkel-Meadow, Ethics in Alternative Dispute Resolution: New Issues, No Answers from the Adversary Conception of Lawyers' Responsibilities, 38 S. Tex. L. Rev. 407, 409-410 (1997).

> *There remain virtually no rules for the conduct of lawyers, parties, witnesses, etc. in international arbitration, in contrast to the growing attention to rules of ethics and professional responsibility for lawyers, litigators and other professionals in domestic settings and increasing analysis and pleas for the same in international settings.*

Carrie Menkel-Meadow, Are Cross Cultural Ethics Standards Possible or Desirable in International Arbitration? (Mélanges pour Pierre Tercier), 891-892 (F. Werro, P. Pichonnaz & P. Gauch eds., 2008).

RULE 1.0(m) TERMINOLOGY

"Tribunal" denotes a court, an arbitrator in a binding arbitration proceeding or a legislative body, administrative agency or other body acting in an adjudicative capacity. A legislative body, administrative agency or other body acts in an adjudicative capacity when a neutral official, after the presentation of evidence or legal argument by a party or parties, will render a binding legal judgment directly affecting a party's interests in a particular matter.

RULE 3.3 CANDOR TOWARD THE TRIBUNAL

(a) A lawyer shall not knowingly:

(1) make a false statement of fact or law to a tribunal or fail to correct a false statement of material fact or law previously made to the tribunal by the lawyer; (2) fail to disclose to the tribunal legal authority in the controlling jurisdiction known to the lawyer to be directly adverse to the position of the client and not disclosed by opposing counsel; or (3) offer evidence that the lawyer knows to be false. If a lawyer, the lawyer's client, or a witness called by the lawyer, has offered material evidence and the lawyer comes to know of its falsity, the lawyer shall take reasonable remedial measures, including, if necessary, disclosure to the tribunal. A lawyer may refuse to offer evidence, other than the testimony of a defendant in a criminal matter, that the lawyer reasonably believes is false. . . .

The application of some of the other Rules remains unclear. For example, is it impermissible for an attorney to seek to influence an arbitrator by means prohibited by law, or to communicate with an arbitrator on an ex parte basis? See Rule 3.5.

RULE 3.5 IMPARTIALITY AND DECORUM OF THE TRIBUNAL

A lawyer shall not:

(a) seek to influence a judge, juror, prospective juror or other official by means prohibited by law;

(b) communicate ex parte with such a person during the proceeding unless authorized to do so by law or court order; . . .

Similarly, does Rule 3.6 apply to arbitration when it limits an attorney "who is participating or has participated in the investigation or litigation of a matter" from publicizing matters in certain ways?

Are attorneys prohibited, by Rule 3.7, from serving as witnesses in arbitration matters in which they are representing a disputant? The Rule states that, subject to certain exceptions, lawyers "shall not act as advocate at a trial in which the lawyer is likely to be a necessary witness."

Also, how do the professional conduct rules defining "unauthorized practice of law" apply to arbitration? Recent revisions to ABA Model Rule 5.5 seem to permit an attorney who customarily represents a client in one jurisdiction (and in which she is licensed) to represent a client in a related arbitration in another jurisdiction. However, the wording of the Rule is not entirely clear (see Delaware Lawyers' Rule 5.5 below, which mirrors the Model Rule), and not all jurisdictions have adopted the ABA language.

RULE 5.5 UNAUTHORIZED PRACTICE OF LAW; MULTIJURISDICTIONAL PRACTICE OF LAW

(a) A lawyer shall not practice law in a jurisdiction in violation of the regulation of the legal profession in that jurisdiction, or assist another in doing so.

(b) A lawyer who is not admitted to practice in this jurisdiction shall not:

(1) except as authorized by these Rules or other law, establish an office or other systematic and continuous presence in this jurisdiction for the practice of law; or

(2) hold out to the public or otherwise represent that the lawyer is admitted to practice law in this jurisdiction.

(c) A lawyer admitted in another United States jurisdiction, and not disbarred or suspended from practice in any jurisdiction, may provide legal services on a temporary basis in this jurisdiction that: . . .

(3) are in or reasonably related to a pending or potential arbitration, mediation, or other alternative dispute resolution proceeding in this or another jurisdiction, if the services arise out of or are reasonably related to the lawyer's practice in a jurisdiction in which the lawyer is admitted to practice and are not services for which the forum requires pro hac vice admission;
. . . .

Prior to the revision of Rule 5.5, several courts found that persons who represented others in arbitration engaged in unauthorized practice of law if they were not licensed attorneys in the relevant jurisdiction. The California Supreme Court held that attorneys licensed in New York engaged in unauthorized practice of law in California by pursuing settlement discussions and making preliminary arbitration arrangements on behalf of their client.[19] As well, the Florida Supreme Court enjoined an attorney, not licensed in Florida, from representing Floridians in securities arbitration.[20]

Outside the United States, ethical rules governing the role of attorneys in arbitration may vary greatly, just as the ethical responsibilities of attorneys in litigation vary substantially from country to country. For example, other jurisdictions' rules may be quite different than those in the United States with respect to whether attorneys can prepare witnesses for an arbitration, whether attorneys need

---

19. Birbrower v. Super. Ct., 949 P.2d 1 (Cal. 1998).
20. Florida Bar v. Rapoport, 845 So. 2d 874 (Fla. 2003).

to disclose clients' intent to commit perjury at an arbitration hearing, whether parties or their attorneys can engage in ex parte communications with arbitrators, whether arbitrators can try to settle cases, whether witnesses must be excluded from the hearing when they are not testifying, whether in-house attorneys are treated as attorneys, whether attorneys owe responsibility to the government as well as to their clients, how loyalty to clients is defined, and how client confidences are protected.[21]

> ## Problem 11-15. *Regulation of Arbitration*
>
> Now that you have considered various ethical regulations, where do you come out on the question of whether arbitration should be regulated at all? Should it be regulated differently than litigation? Should lying be restricted more heavily in arbitration than in litigation? When disputants have consented to have disputes resolved through arbitration, are ethical rules necessary? Are ethical concerns greater where arbitration is less clearly consensual, as with "mandatory" arbitration? How should regulation of ethics be handled in the international setting?

4. Non-Attorney Representatives in Arbitration

Thus far, our ethical discussion has assumed that the persons who are representing others in arbitration are attorneys, but this need not be the case. As noted earlier, in the collective bargaining context, it is quite common for both sides to be represented by non-lawyer representatives. Although these representatives have no formal legal training, they often have a great deal of familiarity with the union contract and company work rules, as well as substantial experience serving as an advocate in arbitration hearings. As well, non-attorneys often represent consumers bringing claims in arbitration against securities brokers. However, the Florida Supreme Court held that it was impermissible for a person not licensed as an attorney in Florida to represent Floridians in securities arbitrations, for compensation.

---

21. See Catherine A. Rogers, Fit and Function in Legal Ethics: Developing a Code of Conduct for International Arbitration, 23 Mich. J. Int'l L. 341, 357-378 (2002).

Supreme Court of Florida, Florida Bar re: Advisory Opinion on Nonlawyer Representation in Securities Arbitration, 696 So. 2d 1178, 1183 (Fla. 1997)

Although we recognize that arbitration was set up to be a nonjudicial alternative for dispute resolution, it is clear that, in light of our caselaw thoroughly discussing the activities that constitute the practice of law, the services provided by nonlawyer representatives in the alternative but still adversarial context of securities arbitration constitutes the practice of law. As the Committee pointedly and accurately notes in its proposed opinion, nonlawyer representatives give specific legal advice and perform the traditional tasks of the lawyer at every stage of the arbitration proceeding in an effort to protect the investor's important legal and financial interests. We cannot ignore such a situation. Because such activities — when performed by nonlawyers — are wholly unregulated and unsanctionable, we further agree with the proposed opinion that these activities must be enjoined. In these circumstances, the public faces a potential for harm from incompetent and unethical representation by compensated nonlawyers which cannot otherwise be remedied.[22]

Problem 11-16.   *Regulation of Non-Attorney Representation in Arbitration*

You are the member of a state bar association that has been asked to consider whether non-lawyers should be permitted to represent persons in arbitration. What are the factors you would consider? What variables do you think are important, for example, does it matter if the representative is being paid? Is related to the disputant? Should all types of arbitration be treated the same? Consider how this question relates to the more general subject of unauthorized practice of law, discussed supra, in Chapter 7, with respect to mediation.

You have now learned a great deal about different kinds of arbitration, how arbitration is regulated through litigation, and how arbitrators and representatives in arbitration ought to conduct themselves. In the next chapter we examine how arbitration, mediation, negotiation, and even litigation can be combined to form new modes of dispute resolution.

---

22. But see Williamson v. John D. Quinn Const. Corp. 537 F. Supp. 613, 616 (S.D.N.Y. 1982) (holding that a non-New York lawyer participating in an arbitration in New York did not commit unauthorized practice under New York law).

Further Reading

Harold I. Abramson, *Protocols for International Arbitrators Who Dare to Settle Cases*, 10 AM. REV. INT'L ARB. 1 (1999).

John W. Cooley & Steven Lubet. (2003). *Arbitration Advocacy*. Notre Dame, IN: National Institute for Trial Advocacy.

Marvin F. Hill, Jr., Anthony V. Sinicropi & Amy L. Evenson. (1997). *Winning Arbitration Advocacy*. Washington, DC: Bureau of National Affairs.

Catherine A. Rogers. (forthcoming 2011). *Ethics in International Arbitration*. New York: Oxford University Press.

PART III

PROCESS PLURALISM: ADAPTATIONS AND VARIATIONS OF PROCESSES

We have now studied the three foundational processes used as alternatives to litigation in resolving disputes: negotiation, mediation, and arbitration. The fourth foundational process, litigation, is the focus of your studies in civil procedure and most of the rest of your law school courses. In addition, while traditional thinking about legal disputes separates disputants into plaintiff and defendant, modern life often presents situations that involve multiple issues in which there are more than two parties and sides to a dispute.

In the past 30 years, the foundational processes of negotiation, mediation, arbitration, and adjudication have been modified, expanded, and transformed. Courts and administrative agencies frequently order parties to use non-litigative processes. Mediators are increasingly asked to make evaluations, and judges and arbitrators increasingly try to settle disputes. New processes are invented to deal with complex issues of multiple causation and responsibility, pre-dispute negotiation, public policy making, and transaction planning.

Part III of this book explores multiple aspects of these new forms of dispute resolution. Chapter 12 examines the ways in which the foundational processes are combined or adapted to create variations on original themes. It looks first at how private parties sometimes choose to blend dispute resolution processes and then moves on to examine how public entities adopt new forms of dispute resolution. Chapter 13 focuses on multiparty disputes, looking at how the foundational processes must be adjusted as disputes become more complex, both in number of parties and numbers of issues. This chapter also considers how dispute resolution systems should be designed for those with complex disputes or those in ongoing relationships and organizations. We also take a look at how dispute resolution methods can be useful in transaction planning and negotiation. Finally, having provided you with substantial information about each of these processes, Chapter 14 helps you to understand where the field of dispute resolution is heading in the future, what are some of its promises, some of its limits, how you can help clients to choose between and among processes, and what processes you might help design in the future that meet your clients' needs. You will see that, in the design of conflict handling, "one size *does not* fit all."

Chapter 12   Private and Public Hybrid Processes

Can the whole be greater than the sum of its parts?

— Anonymous

The foundational processes of negotiation, mediation, arbitration, and litigation are often combined or modified to reflect the demands and desires of private individuals, organizations, and policy makers seeking to create or redesign transactions and relationships. Whether creating new legal arrangements, preventing disputes, or resolving disputes, these mixed processes rely on the negotiation principle of direct engagement and on the use of third-party neutrals to create new forms of conflict resolution and multiparty decision making. This chapter first examines hybrid processes in private settings. It then moves on to public hybrids offered or mandated by court rules or government agencies or regulations. And, while we often associate ADR processes with civil matters, alternative processes are also used in criminal cases, including "restorative justice" efforts, mediated victim-offender "healing," community and specialized courts (such as drug courts), and "sentencing circles." Such processes typically yield new conceptions of remedial possibilities such as rehabilitation and restitution. You will note how many ideas flow from the private sector to the public and vice versa. The final section of the chapter examines problems posed by the institutionalization of ADR processes.

As you examine how these processes are redesigned to deal with particular kinds of disputes, conflicts, decision-making processes, and policy issues, consider the following questions:

1. What foundational (primary) processes are used? How have these processes been modified? With what effects?
2. Can multiple processes be combined without sacrificing the special "morality" or "integrity" of each process?
3. What is the role of third-party neutrals? Facilitative, evaluative, or decisional?
4. Who has designed the particular hybrid process? The parties themselves? A process expert? Another party or institution, such as a court or an administrative agency?
5. Is this ADR process ad hoc (designed for a particular dispute, transaction, rule making, or other "event") or more formal, permanent, or institutionalized (contractual, rule-based, common practice)?

6. What is the "authority" for creation of this particular process? A contract (private ADR)? A court rule, judge's recommendation or suggestion, law, or administrative regulation (public ADR)?
7. Is entrance to this process consensual or more directed or "coerced"?
8. What are the goals or intended purposes of this process, and how might it differ from other possible processes?
9. What special areas of concern apply to the use of this process (for example, notice, fairness, ethics, inclusion, publicity, confidentiality)?
10. What other adaptations or variations of this process might be available?

A. PRIVATE HYBRIDS

One of the most attractive aspects of various forms of ADR is that they can be crafted to meet the particular needs and interests of the disputants. The sections that follow discuss some particular combinations that are now common, but remember that the potential variations are really infinite. You may be asked to design your own special processes some day for particular client needs.

1. Variations on Arbitration

In Chapters 9, 10, and 11 we looked at conventional arbitration processes in a variety of settings. What makes arbitration "conventional" is its reliance on a binding decision by a third-party decision maker, backed up by the force of court enforcement through either the Federal Arbitration Act (domestic) or the NY Convention for Recognition and Enforcement of Foreign Arbitral Awards (international). But arbitration itself has become a much hybridized process, in both public and private spheres, as variations have developed with respect to how awards are reached ("final offer") and whether they are binding or not, depending on how parties tailor the processes to their needs.

a. Binding Offer Arbitration

Although binding offers can be structured in many ways, two variations warrant special attention: *final-offer* and *high-low arbitration*.

Final-offer arbitration is also known as *baseball arbitration* because it is used to resolve salary disputes among many baseball players and their teams.[1] However, this form of arbitration is also used outside the baseball or sports context.

With final-offer arbitration, the arbitrator does not have the power to reach any conclusion she wants. Instead, the two opposing parties submit sealed offers or requests to the arbitrator, and the arbitrator must choose only one of these offers. The goal of limiting arbitrators' discretion through the final-offer process is to

---

1. Roger I. Abrams, Inside Baseball's Salary Arbitration Process, 6 U. Chi. L. Sch. Roundtable 55 (1999).

encourage disputants to take more reasonable positions. When arbitrators are free to select whatever result they think is best, parties have some incentive to take extreme positions in arguing their case to the arbitrator. This is particularly true to the extent one believes arbitrators typically reach compromise or "split the baby" results. In contrast, if the arbitrator is permitted to select only the offer of one side or the other, each side has an incentive to be reasonable. If the plaintiff is too greedy, the arbitrator will feel compelled to select the defendant's offer; if the defendant is too stingy, the arbitrator will select the plaintiff's offer. Thus, the final-offer process encourages both sides to be reasonable and, in a sense, to bid against themselves. The final-offer process also proves very effective as a means to encourage settlement. As each side fears that the arbitrator may choose the other side's offer, the two parties often opt for settlement to avoid that risk, usually moving closer and closer to a "mid-point" evaluation of the real value.

The reason that final-offer arbitration is popular in professional baseball is for many of the reasons outlined above. First, extensive use of statistics makes comparisons easy among players, and therefore, offers can be based on objective criteria. Second, the mix of player egos, owners' financial constraints, and fan loyalties, all conducted under the glare of extensive media coverage, make reaching a negotiated settlement (in which one side might be perceived as caving to the other) much harder than an arbitration award in which a third party decides. Of course, arbitration can be a problem if the costs are too high, if relationships between players and managers are damaged, and if opportunities to create more detailed and tailored packages of compensation and other benefits are lost.

One non-baseball context in which final-offer arbitration is commonly used is public employee collective bargaining disputes. As noted in Chapter 9.C.3.g, some states' laws require the use of interest arbitration to help labor and management write their contract terms. Sometimes these interest arbitrations are done on a final-offer basis so that the arbitrator is required to choose either the labor or management position on a particular dispute. In some jurisdictions, the arbitrators consider each of several issues (such as salary, overtime, pension, and vacation) separately; in some, each side is required to put together a single package offer. In the latter jurisdictions, arbitrators are required to choose either the union or management package, rather than to select terms from each side's packages.

Another variation on final-offer arbitration is sometimes called *"night baseball"* arbitration. Here, the arbitrator holds a hearing and makes a tentative ruling without having reviewed either side's offer. However, the arbitrator examines the offers submitted previously by both sides and is required to select whichever offer is closest to her own tentative ruling. The purported advantage of this approach is that although the arbitrator makes a tentative decision she thinks is fair, without being influenced by the parties' offers, her actual decision is reined in by the parties' reasonable positions.

High-low contracts, which can be used in litigation as well as arbitration, are another means of constraining the decision makers' discretion and limiting the parties' exposure to risk. With high-low agreements, parties agree in advance that no matter what the fact finder's actual award is, plaintiff will not receive more than X or less than Y. That is, the award is bracketed between a minimum and a maximum figure. Such agreements can be attractive to plaintiffs because they are assured at least a set minimum award, and they can be attractive to defendants because defendants can limit their maximum exposure. In addition, high-low agreements can save both sides time and expense because less time needs to be devoted to arbitrating the damages portion of the case, and no appeal of the amount of the award is permitted.

b. Non-Binding Arbitration

Another and quite different type of arbitration is non-binding arbitration, in which the arbitrator's award becomes binding only if it is accepted voluntarily by the disputants. Here, the purpose of the arbitration is not to guarantee a final resolution of the dispute but rather to give the disputants a good prediction of how the claim would be resolved if it went to trial. The hope is that once the disputants learn this prediction and have the opportunity to go through a process that is similar to what they might obtain in court, they will voluntarily abide by the arbitrator's decision. Although non-binding arbitration sometimes is agreed to contractually, most non-binding arbitration that takes place in the United States occurs pursuant to court order, rule, or statute.

In addition, many courts have adopted non-binding arbitration programs with the hope that they will provide a quicker, cheaper form of justice than litigation. We will look at these arbitration programs in section B.6 below.

Problem 12-1.   *What Type of Arbitration?*

If you were drafting a contractual arbitration clause mandating arbitration, what variations of arbitration might you consider? What kinds of matters would lend themselves to different kinds of treatments in arbitration? Would it matter if the parties were disputing only monetary amounts or had other issues? Would it be advisable to specify the form of arbitration in advance or let the parties choose at the time of the dispute? Why?

---

2. Med–Arb and Arb–Med

One of the first-used types of hybrid processes was med-arb — mediation, followed by arbitration if the parties fail to reach agreement. This practice began in labor contexts, but has spread to family (child custody conciliation) and commercial matters. In the original form of med-arb, the parties select an individual to facilitate the negotiation of their dispute (using all the usual ground rules of mediation, such as confidentiality and private caucusing). If that process fails the mediator is empowered to turn into an arbitrator who then makes a decision. Med-arb can be varied in a number of interesting ways, each of which has its own advantages and disadvantages. In one version of med-arb, two neutrals are used. If the mediation fails to result in agreement, the mediator is replaced by a second neutral who arbitrates the dispute. In another version of med-arb, the arbitrator issues a non-binding rather than binding determination.[2] Sometimes the order of the processes is reversed in a process known as arb-med. Here an arbitrator hears the parties' presentations on the legal merits and then tries to help settle, rather than decide, the case. In some cases the arbitrator may make a sealed award before or during settlement discussions, which is revealed only after mediation or negotiation fails. Arb-med has become common practice in many settings, including labor, employment, and commercial cases. Alternatively, the arbitrator can issue a non-binding award and then allow the parties to shift to a mediation process to try to "improve" on the award.[3]

Some argue that combining arbitration and mediation blends the best aspects of each process. The speed, efficiency, and consensual aspects of mediation are combined with the efficient finality of arbitration. It is certainly more efficient to have the same person hear the facts and interests of the case, so as to avoid duplication of effort, time, and disclosure. For example, some labor arbitrators find it beneficial to use mediation in situations that were formerly allocated to arbitration, such as "grievances" under collective bargaining agreements, because of the greater flexibility of mediation and the possibility of resolving more than a single issue at once.[4]

Yet critics of med-arb assert that the practice is problematic because mediators typically urge parties to be forthcoming and honest about their needs, interests, and facts, in settings where the disputants are assured the mediators have no power over them. If the mediators then turn into decision makers, unwary parties may find their confidences used against them. One example of this occurs in California, where family court conciliators (mediators) transform into decision-advising probation officers who sometimes reveal facts told to them in confidence during the mediation and who make arbitral-like recommendations to the court. This role switching may undermine participant trust in the whole system. Also, knowledge that the mediator may change roles allows savvy parties to rethink what they tell mediators, potentially undermining the effectiveness of the mediation. Similarly, critics of arb-med argue that the parties may resent the arbitrator's effort to force a "compromise" of the dispute, when what the parties seek is a clear-cut decision, assignment of liability or blame, enforcement of a rule, precedential value, or one of the other underlying reasons for choosing arbitration.

The classic work discussing "role confusion" when mediation and arbitration are combined was written by Lon Fuller.

---

2. Sherry Landry, Med-Arb: Mediation with a Bite and an Effective ADR Model, 63 Def. Couns. J. 263 (1996).

3. See Lawrence D. Connor, How to Combine Facilitation with Evaluation, 14 Alternatives High Cost Litig. 15 (1996).

4. Stephen B. Goldberg, Grievance Mediation: A Successful Alternative to Labor Arbitration, 5 Negot. J. 9, 11 (1989) (urging that two different persons perform the mediation and arbitration roles).

Lon L. Fuller, COLLECTIVE BARGAINING AND THE ARBITRATOR

in Collective Bargaining and the Arbitrator's Role: Proceedings of the Fifteenth Annual Meeting, National Academy of Arbitrators 8, 29-30, 32-33 (Mark L. Kahn ed., 1962)

Mediation and arbitration have distinct purposes and hence distinct moralities. The morality of mediation lies in optimum settlement, a settlement in which each party gives up what he values less, in return for what he values more. The morality of arbitration lies in a decision according to the law of the contract. The procedures appropriate for mediation are those most likely to uncover that pattern of adjustment which will most nearly meet the interests of both parties. The procedures appropriate for arbitration are those which most securely guarantee each of the parties a meaningful chance to present arguments and proofs for a decision in his favor. Thus, private consultations with the parties, generally wholly improper on the part of an arbitrator, are an indispensable tool of mediation.

Not only are the appropriate procedures different in the two cases, but the facts sought by those procedures are different. [There] is no way to define "the essential facts" of a situation except by reference to some objective. Since the objective of reaching an optimum settlement is different from that of rendering an award according to the contract, the facts relevant in the two cases are different, or, when they seem the same, are viewed in different aspects. If a person who has mediated unsuccessfully attempts to assume the role of arbitrator, he must endeavor to view the facts of the case in a completely new light, as if he had previously known nothing about them. This is a difficult thing to do. It will be hard for him to listen to proofs and arguments with an open mind. If he fails in this attempt, the integrity of adjudication is impaired. . . .

What, then, are the objections to an arbitrator's undertaking mediative efforts after the hearing and before rendering the award, this being often so advantageous a time for settlement? Again, the objection lies essentially in the confusion of role that results. In seeking a settlement the arbitrator turned mediator quite properly learns things that should have no bearing on his decision as an arbitrator. For example, suppose a discharge case in which the arbitrator is virtually certain that he will decide for reinstatement, though he is striving to keep his mind open until he has a chance to reflect on the case in the quiet of his study. In the course of exploring the possibilities of a settlement he learns that, contrary to the position taken by the union at the hearing, respectable elements in the union would like to see the discharge upheld. Though they concede that the employee was probably innocent of the charges made by the company, they regard him as an ambitious troublemaker the union would be well rid of. If the arbitrator fails to mediate a settlement, can he block this information out when he comes to render his award?

It is important that an arbitrator not only respect the limits of his office in fact, but that he also *appear* to respect them. The parties to an arbitration expect of the arbitrator that he will decide the dispute, not according to what pleases the parties, but by what accords with the contract. Yet as a mediator he must explore the parties' interests and seek to find out what would please them. He cannot be a good mediator unless he does. But if he has then to surrender his role as mediator to resume that of adjudicator, can this award ever be truly free from the suspicion that it was influenced by a desire to please one or both of the parties?

Problem 12-2.   *Med-Arb or Arb-Med?*

To what extent are Fuller's criticisms of combining mediation and arbitration valid when two different persons perform the mediation and arbitration roles? As noted in the beginning of this section, mediation and arbitration are sometimes combined in different orders. What advantages and disadvantages do you see with how the order is established — med-arb or arb-med?

---

3. The Mini-Trial

Other combinations and variations of the basic ADR processes flourished creatively in the early years of ADR experimentation and practice after the historic 1976 conference on Causes of Popular Dissatisfaction with Justice, discussed in Chapter 1. Some of these processes, like the mini-trial discussed below and its public analogue, the summary jury trial, discussed in Section B.4, are less frequently used now, but still serve as useful illustrations of how the different ADR processes can be combined and modified for different disputant needs.

In 1977, a group of creative lawyers were faced with a complex and expensive patent infringement lawsuit that threatened to cost millions of dollars and to publicly reveal trade secrets.[5] These lawyers designed a special new legal process called the "mini-trial." The process took several months to plan but only two days to conduct. A settlement in principle was reached within a half hour after the proceeding ended. What the parties arranged was an informal (private, outside of the pending litigation) process that combined elements of many different dispute resolution processes. Through a negotiated agreement on procedural rules, the parties in *Telecredit, Inc. v. TRW, Inc.* engaged in expedited discovery for several months, deposed key witnesses, and exchanged a limited number of documents. During the two-day proceeding, retained counsel presented, in structured but abbreviated time, their "best case" in arguments, along with their supporting evidence, to the top management of both companies. The proceeding was presided over by a neutral advisor, former Federal Court of Claims Judge James Davis, an expert in patent infringement matters. His official duties, as negotiated by the parties, were to moderate the proceedings and to keep order, but not to rule in any way on the

---

5. This description of the process is taken from The CPR Legal Program Mini-Trial Handbook, in 1982 CPR Corporate Dispute Management, at MH-5 (Eric D. Green et al. eds., 1982). For further analysis of *Telecredit* by some of the lawyers involved, see Eric D. Green, Jonathan B. Marks & Ronald L. Olsen, Settling Large Case Litigation: An Alternative Approach, 11 Loy. L.A. L. Rev. 493 (1978).

outcome. As the parties agreed in advance, if they did not reach a negotiated agreement at the end of the information exchange, Judge Davis was to supply a non-binding opinion discussing the strengths and weaknesses of each party's case and predict how a court might rule on the merits. The parties agreed that everything exchanged during this special proceeding would be inadmissible at any subsequent trial. Parties, lawyers, and the neutral advisor all asked questions of each other, and all participants later disclosed that they learned new things from the proceeding. After the information exchange, the top management officials negotiated without their lawyers. Management resolved the matter according to business interests, not just legal principles.

As described above, the mini-trial uses negotiation, non-binding evaluation (arbitration), and some aspects of mediation (in the role of the neutral advisor). What is most unusual about the mini-trial is that top management negotiates directly without lawyers. These negotiations are founded on the companies' business interests, as well as the executives' perspectives on their litigation prospects. They form their view of these prospects after hearing the positions of the other side directly from the other side, rather than as filtered through their own lawyers.

For some years after this first mini-trial, the process was used often in high stakes cases. It was particularly attractive in cases where the parties sought to avoid the high costs of litigation, get informal advice from noted experts, keep the subject matter of their disputes private, or avoid the inevitable vagaries of having issues resolved by "lay" juries or judges who were presumed not to know enough about complex business disputes or complicated legal issues. The mini-trial was especially valued for getting clients (especially CEOs or high-level government officials) to pay close attention to a particular matter. In part, the idea was that concentrated and focused attention at an early stage of a dispute would prevent economic waste by avoiding protracted discovery, longer trials, expensive expert witnesses, and lost management time from company officials spending time in court.

Over time, however, use of the mini-trial has diminished, perhaps because if high-level officials spend too much time in "direct and focused" attention on disputes, they do not spend enough time managing. Some also think mini-trials are quite expensive to run, after taking into account attorneys' fees, high neutral advisor fees, and lost work time for key corporate or government officials.

Perhaps the greatest strength of the mini-trial is indirect in that it demonstrates that parties can develop alternatives to both courts and the more conventional alternatives to courts on an informal, ad hoc basis. The concept of a negotiated process resulting in a dispute resolution agreement or protocol, crafted for a particular purpose, dispute, or transaction, continues to be an important part of ADR. As you will see in later chapters, professionals in dispute resolution now counsel clients about the appropriateness of particular processes for their matters, tailor-make processes for single matters, or serve as "system designers" who develop dispute resolution mechanisms for classes of disputes or for whole entities, including government agencies, corporations, and other organizations.

4. Private Judges and Juries

Some private disputants are attracted by many aspects of the public litigation system but put off by others, such as its public nature, high cost, or slow speed. Thus both bench and jury trials have been occasionally recreated as private dispute resolution processes.

a. Private Judges

A number of states permit "referral" or "reference" to private (often retired) judges who have the full authority of public judges, either by authorizing statute or by constitutional provision. While similar to arbitration, private judging uniquely treats the judge's determination just like a public judge's award. That is, the private judgment can be enforced and executed like any other judgment and appealed through regular public processes, when authorized by statute or other legal authority. In contrast, as you will recall, there is usually no effective appeal from binding arbitration awards. In addition, parties may choose the private judge and arrange fees, timing, and scheduling on their own, as in a private dispute resolution process. Of all the states, California probably has the most well-developed private judging program.[6]

From the disputants' standpoint, private judging offers many potential advantages over public litigation: privacy (no public courtrooms), speed (self-scheduled), and choice of decision maker. For example, many corporations and celebrities have chosen private judging to keep matters out of the public eye (as in divorces and claims of corporate misfeasance). Costs in private judging can be higher (with private judges receiving fees much higher than public judges and fees for facilities, etc.), but the process can also be more efficient since parties can control scheduling better than with public dockets.

Although quite popular in some states, private judging is criticized by many as introducing a system of tiered justice in which those who can afford it are able to buy their way out of the public justice system, which often takes longer, and to choose their own decision makers.[7] Because of increased scrutiny of this form of ADR by consumer advocates and others, the California Judicial Council has promulgated rules that attempt to regulate some aspects of the process of "compensated judges."

Private judging has had an interesting impact on the career of some sitting judges. One of the first private provider organizations of dispute resolution services, JAMS,[8] was founded in 1979 by a retiring California judge, Warren Knight. Other judges soon joined the organization and offered arbitration and

---

6. See Cal. Civ. Proc. Code §§638-645. Florida has also adopted a private judging program, known as "voluntary trial resolution." Fla. Stat. Ann. §44.104.

7. See, e.g., Barlow F. Christensen, Private Justice: California's General Reference Procedure, 1982 Am. B. Found. Res. J. 79; Ann S. Kim, Note: Rent-a-Judges and the Cost of Selling Justice, 44 Duke L.J. 166 (1994). But see Richard Chernick, Helen I. Bendix & Robert C. Barrett, Private Judging: Privatizing Civil Justice (1997), for a defense of this process

8. "JAMS" originally stood for Judicial Arbitration and Mediation Services, but the organization is now known only by its acronym.

mediation services privately for a fee. JAMS now has offices in 20 cities and is a multimillion-dollar-a-year business. Indeed, some say that the career of private judging has become so attractive that it is hard to keep public judges from retiring at a young age to go private. In the early 1990s, another group of active judges in Connecticut formed an organization, STAFED, that would have allowed sitting judges to moonlight by offering their services outside of court time for a private fee. However, widespread concern about the ethics of publicly sitting judges earning private fees for their services caused this group to disband. Some leading states (for example, California, Florida, and Texas) regulate who may serve as court-appointed mediators or arbitrators. In some instances, states apply their regulations (ethics, fees, conflicts of interests, confidentiality, liability, and immunity) to those working as private judges as well as to court-sanctioned dispute resolvers.[9]

b. Private Juries

Private jury trials can be attractive to disputants who want lay fact finders but don't want to wait or pay for the expensive, time-consuming, public version of the jury trial. In response to this need, some private dispute resolution providers offer their own private jury trials. The private jurors, recruited through help-wanted advertisements, are paid a daily fee to perform typical juror duties. The disputants and their lawyers have the opportunity to use typical voir dire procedures to choose among the potential jurors. To the extent the parties agree, the demographics of the jury pool can be adjusted to meet their particular needs, such as for a more or less highly educated jury. The parties can agree, by contract, to be bound by the jury's verdict. Or, with the acquiescence of the court, private jury verdicts can be appealed on the same grounds as regular jury verdicts.

Some critics of the private jury trial argue that it is inappropriate to decide matters of public concern (such as police abuse, for which private juries have been used) outside the viewing of the public eye. Some complain of the "vanishing civil jury trial" in the public system, the result of which is to privatize civil justice and reduce lay decision making and fact finding.[10] It can also be argued that it is inappropriate to tamper with the natural demographics of the jury pool and that using this private tool may erode public confidence in the public jury trial.[11]

---

9. For one attempt to study what private judges do in comparison to judges who mediate within the public courts, see Stacy Lee Burns, Making Settlement Work: An Examination of the Work of Judicial Mediators (2000).

10. See, e.g., ADR and the Vanishing Trial, Disp. Resol. Mag. 3-21 (Summer 2004); and Symposium, The Vanishing Trial, 1 (3) J. of Empirical Studies (2004); see also Carrie Menkel-Meadow, Is the Adversary System Really Dead? Dilemmas of Legal Ethics as Legal Institutions and Roles Evolve, in Current Legal Problems (Jane Holder ed., 2005).

11. Margaret A. Jacobs, Legal Beat: Private Jury Trials: Cheap, Quick, Controversial, Wall St. J., July 7, 1997, at B1.

Problem 12-3. *Are Private Processes Good for the Public?*

Should private parties be able to recreate the public justice system on a private basis? Does this recreation harm the public in any way? Does your answer depend on whether the parties recreate bench or jury trials? Would you be willing to serve on a private jury? Why or why not?

What downsides, if any, are there to allowing private judicial determinations to be enforced and appealed as if they had been made by public judges? Should parties who have filed formal court proceedings be permitted to agree on any kind of private process they want to resolve their dispute? In a divorce case? In a personal injury case? In a stockholder derivative suit? Explain your answer.

---

5. Dispute Resolution and Large Organizations: Ombuds

Private organizations such as corporations and universities have long looked for ways to resolve disputes efficiently within their own structures, to avoid the fees and often the publicity and complexity of public courts.

One tool that private organizations have used is the Ombuds (formerly known as ombudsman), meaning, from the original Swedish, "agent." Ombuds serve as counselors, problem solvers, and mediators of issues and disputes involving persons employed by or working with companies or organizations. Disputes handled by Ombuds may be internal (such as employment) or external (involving clients, students, or customers of the organization). The concept of the Ombuds was originally distilled from a form of neutral public office, used in Scandinavia, to which citizens could seek individualized redress with respect to government action. Today, the role of Ombuds has taken many forms in modern American life, in both the public and private sectors. There are many tensions in defining the position, and even Ombuds themselves disagree on such issues as the extent to which the Ombuds must be independent of management; whether the Ombuds is an advocate for citizen-claimants or instead a counselor or a mediator; and whether the Ombuds possesses legal protections, such as confidentiality, that apply to others in similar professional roles. Today, Ombuds worry about whether their primary responsibility is to the grievants who seek them out for advice and help or to the organization for whom they work. Some Ombuds are working to use their casework experience to document patterns of problems that may then be used to improve organizational policies and practices.[12] Below, Howard Gadlin, a leading founding Ombuds (currently at the National Institutes of Health), defines some of the key terms and practices of different forms of Ombuds.

---

12. Susan Sturm & Howard Gadlin, Conflict Resolution and Systemic Change, 2007 J. Disp. Resol. 2; Cathy Costantino, Second Generation Organizational Conflict Management Systems Design: A Practitioner's Perspective on Emerging Issues, 14 Harv. Negot. L. Rev. 81, 93-96 (2009).

Howard Gadlin, THE OMBUDSMAN: WHAT'S IN A NAME?

16 Negot. J. 37-43 (2000)

In North America, the ombudsman role emerged late in the 1960s during a period of tremendous social turmoil, amidst a growing demand for protections of citizen's rights, and a demand for mechanisms by which people could address maladministration by government, educational, and corporate bureaucracies. . . .

All ombudsmen give voice to people who might otherwise be disadvantaged in their dealings with the management and bureaucracy of the institution within which the ombudsman functions. In the state, the ombudsman serves citizens; in corporations, employees; in the academic world, students, staff, and faculty; in newspapers, the readers; in health care, the patients; in prisons, the inmates. However, there are seemingly enormous differences in the way in which that purpose is served and the manner in which the ombudsman function is established in these different settings. Not only do these differences lead to confusion in the public about what an ombudsman is, they have also engendered a considerable amount of disputing among ombudsmen themselves. . . .

In one camp were those who saw themselves as direct descendants of what has come to be called the "classical ombudsman" tradition. The first modern ombudsmen were established . . . by the Swedish parliament in the early 1800s to provide citizens a means to pursue grievances against the executive and administrative offices of the government. The classical ombudsman emphasizes statutory independence from governmental control, the power to investigate complaints, and the authority to publish findings and recommendations. Almost all of their offices are established by legislation, although there are also executive ombudsmen, meant to serve a similar function but called into being and appointed by a governmental executive, such as a mayor. . . .

In the other camp were the "organizational ombudsmen," at first found mostly in universities and corporations, but also including ombudsmen serving the employees of government agencies. Although they, too, emphasized independence from the managerial hierarchy of the institutions within which they functioned, they were not established by statute, but rather from within the governance structure of their institutions. In universities, this often meant upon the recommendation of some combination of the faculty senate, the student government, and the university administration. In Canada, university ombudsmen were given specific terms of reference which spelled out their authority and responsibility. In corporations, upper management typically established this position in response to a variety of internal and external pressures, especially in companies that were moving away from traditional notions of managerial authority and rigid hierarchical organization. . . .

It should be noted that, in actuality, there have emerged many varieties of the ombudsman role. In addition to the classical ombudsmen in government, and the organizational ombudsmen in education, government and the corporate world, there are: (1) executive ombudsmen who are similar to the classicals but lacking the same independence since they are appointed directly by a governmental executive;

(2) citizen advocacy ombudsmen established by statute whose authority is limited to dealing with the issues of designated populations such as the long-term care ombudsmen or children's ombudsmen; and (3) ombudsmen like the human rights ombudsman springing up in some South American and African countries who have responsibility for oversight of democratic rights in their countries. Often these ombudsmen have the authority to bring suit and make binding decisions. Finally there are, unfortunately, many people who are designated as ombudsmen but who really function more like ethics officers or other functionaries. However, the major dividing line in the way ombudsmen think about and define themselves is still between the classical and the organizational interpretations of the role. . . .

Other social factors also shaped the direction of the profession. From within corporations and universities, there was growing concern about employee complaints regarding managerial power abuse, the complexities of managing an increasingly diverse workforce, recognition of the limitations of hierarchical management structures, and similar issues. Externally, developments in tort law, as well as the possibility of scrutiny by regulatory agencies addressing matters such as safety, equal opportunity, environmental hazards (and the need for channels through which possible violations might be safely brought to the attention of management), also contributed to the recognition of a need for systems to address grievances and conflicts within corporations. Concerns about protecting a confidentiality privilege that was asserted by organizational ombudsmen but not directly protected in law also influenced practices in the field. For the most part, the organizational ombudsmen, especially in corporations, began to place less emphasis on conducting formal investigations than did the classical ombudsmen and they generally eschewed written reports and recommendations. Many practitioners began to severely limit their note-taking and record keeping. Unless they were fortunate enough to have protections in their terms of reference (as do many of the Canadian university ombudsmen), the norm in the field for organizational ombudsman became to keep no records beyond a data base within which the identity of individual complainants could not be discovered. . . .

The classical ombudsman notion is located for the most part, but with some important deviations, within the tradition of adversarial dispute resolution. The classical ombudsman can compel cooperation with an investigation whereas a mediator, in most instances, depends upon voluntary cooperation of the parties with the mediation process. Also unlike a mediator, the classical ombudsman is an adjudicator. A citizen initiates a complaint about some sort of maladministration and an ombudsman investigates the complaint and renders a judgment about whether the complaint is warranted or not. If the complaint is warranted, the classical ombudsman then makes recommendations for appropriate remedies. However, the classical ombudsman idea contains within it some features of the ADR perspective as well. That is, although the classical ombudsman may render a judgment about right and wrong, the classical ombudsman lacks the authority to enforce that judgment. Although the classical ombudsman may make recommendations regarding solutions, she or he must attempt to achieve voluntary compliance with the judgment and recommendation. Reason and persuasion are as much tools of the classical ombudsman as are criticism and embarrassment.

Obviously, with no formal authority to compel compliance, the effectiveness of the ombudsman's advocacy depends to a very large extent on the respect that the office and the person command as well as on the independence of the office — its ability to be free of direct attempts at political influence. . . .

Many of the organizations that established ombudsman programs did so in the hope of creating nonauthoritative, nonjudgmental approaches to addressing grievances and disputes. They did so not because they were intent on shortchanging the rights of those who participate in their organizations, but because they were concerned with addressing the *interests* that underlie many grievances and disputes. Among other things, this meant expanding enormously the range of concerns that could be addressed within the context of the organization, especially those for which there were not, and could not be, formal policies, procedures, and guidelines. And, just as the critics of mediation clash with mediators about the possible limitations and dangers of the mediation sensibility, so too organizational ombudsmen and their classical counterparts have clashed.

The classicals are concerned that the approach of organizational ombudsman will compromise the rights of those who turn to them, as well as possibly leave unaddressed important issues of justice and injustice. In turn, the organizationals are wary of the classical insistence on an approach that is fundamentally judgmental in the face of issues whose complexity and mutuality defy clear-cut judgments of right and wrong. In addition, organizational ombudsmen often see themselves as functioning as they do precisely to provide an alternative to other formal investigatory programs that exist within their organizations. Ethics officers, compliance officers, EEO officers, and, in the case of federal workforce ombudsmen, inspectors general, all have the power to investigate, issue reports, and make recommendations.

The House of Delegates of the American Bar Association, in February 2004, approved standards for appropriate behavior for public and private ombuds. These standards emphasize three key characteristics of the ombuds: impartiality, independence, and confidentiality. The standards also distinguish between three different types of ombuds: classical (within government), organizations (in educational and private corporate settings), and advocacy (giving advice and counseling to grievants). These standards are reproduced on the website of the ABA Section of Dispute Resolution, *http://www.abanet.org/dispute.*

Note that whether the ombuds treats the information acquired in the course of his work as confidential may differ in traditional and legal understandings of the ombuds role. In Carman v. McDonnell Douglas Corp., 114 F.3d 790 (8th Cir. 1997), the plaintiff in a civil rights claim sought to obtain notes and documents in possession of a corporate ombuds; the company claimed that the documents were protected by an "ombudsman privilege." The Eighth Circuit found that the district court lacked sufficient justification for creating an ombudsman privilege and therefore reversed and remanded the district court's denial of plaintiff's discovery request. The appellate court explained that the company failed to make the factual showing necessary to justify a new evidentiary privilege. It stated:

First, McDonnell Douglas has failed to present any evidence, and indeed has not even argued, that the ombudsman method is more successful at resolving workplace disputes than other forms of alternative dispute resolution, nor has it even pointed to any evidence establishing that its own ombudsman is especially successful at resolving workplace disputes prior to the commencement of litigation. . . . Second, McDonnell Douglas has failed to make a compelling argument that most of the advantages afforded by the ombudsman method would be lost without the privilege. Even without a privilege, corporate ombudsmen still have much to offer employees in the way of confidentiality, for they are still able to promise to keep employee communications confidential from management. Indeed, when an aggrieved employee or an employee-witness is deciding whether or not to confide in a company ombudsman, his greatest concern is not likely to be that the state-ment will someday be revealed in civil discovery. More likely, the employee will fear that the ombudsman is biased in favor of the company, and that the ombudsman will tell management everything that the employee says. The denial of an ombuds-man privilege will not affect the ombudsman's ability to convince an employee that the ombudsman is neutral, and creation of an ombudsman privilege will not help alleviate the fear that she is not. We are especially unconvinced that "no present or future [McDonnell Douglas] employee could feel comfortable in airing his or her disputes with the Ombudsman because of the specter of discovery." . . . McDonnell Douglas also argues that failure to recognize an ombudsman privilege will disrupt the relationship between management and the ombudsman's office. In cases where management has nothing to hide, this is unlikely.

Carman, 114 F.3d at 793-794 (citation omitted).

Note that several courts have gone the other way and sustained an ombuds privilege. Is development of a uniform definition or uniform rules desirable? Should states adopt statutes affording legal confidentiality or an evidentiary privilege to work undertaken by ombuds? See Chapter 8 for a discussion of confidentiality and privilege with respect to mediation. To protect information given to ombuds or mediators, should it make a difference whether the case is in the private sector or the public sector (where other rules, like the Freedom of Information Act, sunshine laws, or criminal prohibitions might apply)?

Problem 12-4.   *Confidentiality and the Ombuds*

An ombuds has been asked by a member of an organization to investigate a claim of fraudulent use of funds by her supervisor. The employee asks the ombuds to hold her identity confidential for fear she will be retaliated against, and the ombuds assures her that everything she says will be kept confidential. Shortly after the internal meeting occurs, a criminal investi-gation is launched by public authorities. The court subpoenas the records of the ombuds. The ombuds refuses to turn over the records on the ground he has promised confidentiality to the employee, and he claims an eviden-tiary privilege on this basis. How should the court rule on a motion to quash the subpoena? See In Re Grand Jury Subpoena Dated December 17, 1996, 148 F.3d 487 (5th Cir. 1998).

6. Online Dispute Resolution Mechanisms

Some of the most innovative forms of dispute resolution are those developed for use on the Internet. Variously called EDR (electronic dispute resolution), Technology Mediated Dispute Resolution, or ODR (online dispute resolution), these online processes vary enormously. Some ODR directly involves the Internet (such as claims relating to sales made on the Internet or relating to rights over Web site addresses). Other ODR resolves disputes having nothing to do with the Internet, such as automobile accidents. Sometimes the ODR consists simply of taking conventional forms of mediation or arbitration and conducting the process through words and e-mails rather than face-to-face. At other times more unusual methods are used, including auctions, blind-bidding, or a "behind the screen" mediation conducted by an unseen moderator, either in real time or with sequential discussion. ODR will change quickly as technology changes. For example, as Web-based cameras become more common, the line between online and live hearings may become fuzzier. For an excellent overview of ODR, see *http://www.odr.info* (The Center for Information Technology and Dispute Resolution). Some of the best-known online providers include *http:// www.squaretrade.com* (which handles many disputes relating to eBay); *http://www. cybersettle.com* (which uses a double-blind bidding system to resolve many personal injury claims involving insurance); *http://www.hamaar.com* (which handles insurance and other commercial disputes); and the World Intellectual Property organization, *http://arbiter.wipo.int* (which handles intellectual property disputes). You can view decisions pertaining to conflicts over domain name ownership at *http://www.icann.org/udrp*.

The use of ODR raises unique issues of both over- and under-use of the technology. Does the absence of a "real" person, whether neutral or participant, incite parties to more conflict, or does the necessity of using written words slow down communication and require people to think before they write, encouraging more rational discourse than might occur in person? The following article discusses some of the advantages and challenges of online communication.

 Noam Ebner, Anita D. Bhappu, Jennifer Brown, Kimberlee K. Kovach & Andrea Kupfer Schneider, YOU'VE GOT AGREEMENT: NEGOTI@TING VIA EMAIL

in Rethinking Negotiation Teaching (Christopher Honeyman, James Coben & Giuseppe de Palo eds., 2009) 91, 94-106

NEGOTIATION VIA EMAIL: YES, IT IS DIFFERENT!

In negotiation, communication media influence not only what information is shared and how that information is communicated, but also how information is received and interpreted. Some information may be easy to communicate face-to-face, but difficult to convey in an email. Other information might be laid out clearly in an email message but misconstrued in a face-to-face setting. We can understand these differences more clearly by comparing face-to-face and email negotiations with reference to two dimensions of communication media: *media richness* and *interactivity*. Media richness is the capacity of the medium to transmit visual and verbal cues, thus providing more immediate feedback and facilitating communication of personal information. Interactivity is the potential of the medium to sustain a seamless flow of information between two or more negotiators. Both characteristics account for differences across media in the structure of information exchanged, the number of social context cues transmitted, and the social presence of negotiators . . .

Media Effects: Implications of Email Communication for Negotiation

The foregoing comparison of face-to-face negotiation and email negotiation gives rise to five major implications — incorporating both challenges and opportunities for parties negotiating by email:

1) Increased contentiousness
2) Diminished information sharing
3) Diminished process cooperation
4) Diminished trust
5) Increased effects of negative attribution

1) *Increased Contentiousness*

Even before the advent of Internet-based e-communication, research showed that communication at a distance via technological means is more susceptible to disruption than face-to-face dialogue. . . .

In Internet-based communication, these findings not only hold true, they are intensified. Communication in cyberspace tends to be less inhibited; parties ignore the possible adverse consequences of negative online interactions because of physical distance, reduced social presence, reduced accountability and a sense of anonymity. The lack of social cues in e-communication causes people to act more contentiously than they do in face-to-face encounters, resulting in more frequent occurrences of swearing, name calling, insults, and hostile behavior.

Research shows that these findings on e-communication also hold true in e-negotiation. Early research showed that negotiators are apt to act tough and choose contentious tactics when negotiating with people at a distance. As researchers began to focus on e-negotiation, they discovered the effects of diminished media richness in e-negotiation: the social presence of others is reduced and the perceived social distance among negotiators increases. Thus, negotiators' social awareness of each other may be seriously diminished when communicating through email. This might explain why e-negotiators feel less bound by normatively appropriate behavior than face-to-face negotiators apparently do. This weakening of the normative fabric translates into an increased tendency to make threats and issue ultimata to adopt contentious, "squeaky wheel" behavior, to lie or deceive, to confront each other negatively, and to engage in flaming.

Hence, email negotiators are contending on a much rougher playing field than face-to-face negotiators. Still, the better we understand the nature of email as described in the previous section, the greater our abilities to turn the potentially hazardous characteristics of email to good use — i.e., *reducing* contentiousness. Used properly, lean media may facilitate better *processing* of social conflict exactly because these media do *not* transmit visual and verbal cues. First, the visible, physical presence of an opponent can induce arousal which leads to more aggressive behavioral responses. Therefore, the absence of visual and verbal cues in email may defuse such triggers. Second, email may also reduce the salience of group differences. By masking or deemphasizing gender, race, accent, or national origin, to name just a few, email may actually reduce the impact of unconscious bias on negotiation. Deemphasizing group membership may also suppress coalition formation. In addition, because negotiators are physically isolated and the social presence of others is diminished, they can take time to "step out" of the discussion and thoughtfully respond rather than merely react to the other party's behavior, potentially limiting escalation of social conflict even further.

2) Diminished Inter-Party Cooperation

Experiments in email negotiation have explored two connected concepts: the measure of inter-party cooperation throughout the negotiation process, and the degree to which resulting outcomes are integrative at the end of the negotiation. The connection between the two is obvious: the potential for integrative outcomes grows as parties become more aware of each other's needs and capabilities, and areas of potential joint gain emerge.

Email negotiations make information exchange likely to be constrained, analytical, and contentious. This diminishes negotiators' ability to accurately assess differential preferences and identify potential joint gains. Indeed, one comparison of face-to-face and computer-mediated negotiations revealed that negotiators interacting electronically were less accurate in judging the other party's interests. . . .

However, when used properly, email could *increase* information exchange. Lean media may work to promote more equal participation among negotiators. Diminished social context cues and resulting reduction in the salience of social group differences can reduce social influence bias among individuals and encourage lower-status individuals to participate more . . . Attention to this "new" information may subsequently enable negotiators to identify optimal trades and create more integrative agreements. . . .

3) Reduction in Integrative Outcomes

As previously mentioned, reduced process cooperation is expected to result in a lower level of integrative agreements. Many experiments measuring these two indicators — cooperative behavior and integrative outcomes — have shown that in e-negotiation, as opposed to face-to-face negotiation, one is less likely to encounter cooperation in the process, and less likely to achieve integrative outcomes. Additionally, the potential for impasse appears to be greater than in face-to-face negotiation. . . .

Why, we might ask, should email bargaining be less integrative than face-to-face encounters (if in fact the trend goes in this direction)? We believe that a reduction in the likelihood and degree of integrative solutions could result from lower levels of process cooperation and the difficulty of building rapport in email negotiation. If email somehow encourages negotiators to become more contentious and confrontational in the way they communicate, this can lead to spiraling conflict and the hardening of positions. This problem is made even more severe by the difficulty of establishing rapport in email. . . .

On the other hand, the media effects of email negotiation include one feature that might promote integrative thinking and outcomes. As we have seen, negotiators tend to exchange long messages that include multiple points all in one "bundle" when using asynchronous media like email. Argument-bundling may facilitate integrative agreements by encouraging negotiators to link issues together and consider them simultaneously rather than sequentially. This can promote log-rolling, a classic tool for reaching integrative outcomes. However, negotiators should avoid "over-bundling:" too many issues and too much information delivered at one time can place higher demands on the receiver's information processing capabilities. . . .

4) Diminished Degree of Inter-party Trust

Trust between negotiating parties has been identified as playing a key role in enabling cooperation, problem solving, achieving integrative solutions, effectiveness, and resolving disputes.

Communication via email, however, is fraught with threats to trust that are inherent in the medium and in the way parties approach and employ it. It has been suggested that lack of trust in online opposites is the factor responsible for the low levels of process cooperation and of integrative outcomes. Low levels of inter-party trust in email negotiation have been measured not only through indirect indicators, such as low process cooperation and infrequently integrative outcomes, but also directly: when questioned about the degree of trust they felt in negotiation processes, e-negotiators reported lower levels of trust than face-to-face negotiators did. . . .

5) Increased Tendency Towards Sinister Attribution

The media effects of email negotiation exacerbate the tendency toward the sinister attribution error: the bias toward seeing negative events as the outgrowth of others' negative intentions rather than unintended results or conditions beyond their control. The lack of social presence and of contextual cues lends a sense of distance and of vagueness to the interaction. The asynchronous dynamic of email negotiations adds to this challenge. Research shows that e-negotiators ask fewer clarifying questions than face-to-face negotiators do. Instead of gathering information from their counterparts, email negotiators may be more likely to make assumptions; if those assumptions later prove unfounded, the negotiators may perceive the other's inconsistent actions or preferences as a breaking of trust. The power of the sinister attribution error in e-negotiation is clearly demonstrated by experiments showing that e-negotiators are more likely to suspect their opposite of lying than are face-to-face negotiators, even when no actual deception has taken place.

REPACKING THE NEGOTIATOR'S TOOLBOX: RECOMMENDED SKILL-SETS FOR EMAIL NEGOTIATORS

In this section, we will briefly introduce four basic skill-sets that email negotiators need to acquire in order to cope with the media effects of email discussed in the last section. These four skills are discussed as initial proposals, and are certainly not suggested as an exhaustive list; no doubt, others will emerge.

Skill-Set #1: Writing Ability

A central skill that may seem both so obvious and so crucial that we need not address it is the ability to write — clearly, persuasively, and (at times) movingly. . . . Particularly when it comes time to establish rapport, defuse tension, or even apologize, some email negotiators may find that their writing skills are simply not up to the task at hand. Thus, a central skill set for effective email negotiation may be to improve the clarity and emotional power of writing. And when writing skills fall short of the task's requirements, email negotiators need the wisdom to discern their own limitations, pick up a phone, or make an appointment to meet in person with their negotiation counterparts.

Skill Set #2: Message Management

Managing Our Own Anxiety

The art of negotiating solely by exchanging written messages through postal mail is a long-forgotten one. We have become accustomed to exchanging opinions through synchronous communication, either face-to-face or over the telephone. Email negotiators need to relearn the art of asynchronous communication. This may not be intuitive, for one of the Internet's promises is instant access to anything and anyone. Our synchronous-communication upbringing, combined with our expectations of instant access, clash with the basic nature of asynchronous communication. As a result, email communication often involves an anxiety that blends distrust of the channel with distrust of the other. When we send messages and do not receive responses promptly, not only do we question whether our counterparts received the messages, we begin to wonder why (if indeed they *have* received them) they are taking so long to respond. To manage this anxiety and prevent a downward spiral of distrust, e-negotiators need to understand and bear in mind the limitations of the medium they are using.

Managing the Other's Anxiety

Research has shown that frequent message exchanges, as opposed to communication broken by intervals, are conducive to trust-building within groups. This is also true for the dyadic group formed by two people negotiating. Responding to an email within 24 hours, even if only to say that we are considering what a negotiation counterpart has written, might be a useful standard. On the other hand, delivering a strongly negative response or a total rejection of the counterpart's proposal should not be done too hastily.

Utilizing Asynchronicity

Once we become aware of, and overcome, the challenging characteristics of asynchronous communication, we can focus on the potential it offers for improved communication dynamics. It can be a very conducive channel for reasoned discussion, careful responses, and trust-building moves. It can help control our response time — to our own advantage. Asynchronous communication allows us to avoid knee-jerk reactions or escalatory cycles of contentious behavior, and to think pro-actively. The slower pace allows us to fashion and frame our response thoughtfully and productively. It enables us to verify details instead of giving off-the-cuff responses that may later turn out to be inaccurate — providing for more exact information-sharing. Email creates a searchable thread of exchanged email messages so that we can hold others accountable for representations and commitments. And, we can check our own past communications if they over-claim something we have allegedly promised. We can read a received message twice, or ask a colleague to take a look at it and tell us what she thinks, before we reply to it, lowering the effect of sinister attribution. We can do the same with a message we have written, before sending it. By learning when *not* to click "Reply," and when to delay clicking "Send," email negotiators can use the medium to maximum effect.

Skill-Set #3: Relationship Management

Setting the Stage: Unmasking

As we have seen, the mutual invisibility inherent in email negotiation facilitates adversarial, contentious, and trust-breaking behavior. It is easier to cause damage to a faceless other, particularly when we feel protected by a shield of anonymity and physical distance. The sense of anonymity and distance created between email negotiators leads both to assumptions that one can get away with aggressive or trust-breaking behavior, and to a lowering of moral inhibitions against doing so. This necessitates that negotiators consciously adopt a proactive agenda of unmask-ing themselves *toward* the other. The more negotiation counterparts perceive us as *people they know* rather than anonymous, faceless email addresses, the more likely they are to share information, rely on us, and trust in us.

Building Rapport

The concept of using pre-negotiation social interaction to create a positive and unmasked environment for an upcoming negotiation process is widely discussed and advocated in the negotiation literature that focuses on face-to-face interactions.

In face-to-face encounters, introductions and light, social conversations come naturally; in e-negotiation, this tendency diminishes. As we have discussed, negotia-tors tend to remain on topic, task-oriented, and analytic, leaving little room for social lubrication. As a result, e-negotiators need to *consciously* dedicate time and effort to the unmasking process. Experiments have indicated that even minimal pre-negotiation contact, at the most basic level of "schmoozing" via preliminary email introductory messages or brief telephone exchanges, has the potential for building trust, improving mutual impressions, and facilitating integrative outcomes. By inviting the other to reply, we are initiating a cycle of unmasking which not only transcends physical distance but also reshapes the process into one allowing for recognition and empathy, which can continue to develop as the negotiation progresses.

We would suggest building rapport through words rather than emotions. A negotiator could write the business part of the email first — working for absolute clarity and thoroughness — and then go back to insert the schmooze factor at the beginning of the email, e.g., "lovely to see you last week," "thanks much for getting back to me," etc.

Showing E-empathy

Demonstrating empathy is universally described as a powerful tool and important skill for any negotiator. This has been found to hold true in online communication as well: e-negotiators who show empathy are trusted by their negotiation opposites more than those who do not. This trust might cause the empathic negotiator's actions and intentions to be construed more positively, diminishing the tendency towards sinister attribution. Negotiators will be more likely to share information with a trusted counterpart, opening the door for more integrative agreements.

Skill-Set #4: Content Management

The absence of contextual cues focuses email negotiators on the actual *content* of messages. This necessitates particular skills with regard to three issues:

Clarity

As we have seen, message clarity helps avoid sinister attribution and allows for precise information sharing. Clear messages allow e-negotiators to focus on what their counterparts have written, reply to their points and consider their proposals. Clarity in reply creates a virtuous cycle.

Bundling

Email negotiators tend to bundle multiple points and multiple arguments in a single message. While on the one hand we have noted how this tendency might potentially facilitate the identification of integrative agreements by encouraging negotiators to link issues together and consider them simultaneously rather than sequentially, it might also clash with basic message clarity. Additionally, even if clearly written, an excessive amount of data might send the message recipient into an information overload. Email negotiators need to learn and practice balanced bundling. Judicious use of the "subject" line in an email helps both negotiators and their counterparts to search for and to frame the content of emails they receive. Thus, negotiators should craft subject lines that are sufficiently general that a broad search will produce a list that includes them (e.g., "Smith v. Jones") but also specific enough that they alert the recipient to what they contain and facilitate targeted searches (e.g., "Smith v. Jones — concerns about Smith deposition").

Framing

With the bulk of a message's impact shifted to its content, language and wording become paramount. This is especially important in the framing of issues and discussion topics. Asynchronous communication allows for careful framing of issues and well thought-out revision of frames proposed by the other party.

Part of framing is also thinking about the formatting of the email, which affects the perceptual frame through which the other recipient takes in the message content. In the body of the email, negotiators should alter default settings for style and font with caution and only for good reason. . . . A negotiator should also think carefully about using all caps — IT IS THE EQUIVALENT OF SCREAMING in email. Finally, we would suggest not using too many !!! to make a point or too many ☺ to try and lend "tone" to a particular comment — unless negotiators are certain that the relationships they have with their opposites make this suitable.

Problem 12-5.   *Try it Out Yourself!*

The next time you make a less-than-pleasing purchase on the Internet, try contacting one of the ODR services and keep a record of your inter-actions. Does dispute resolution over the Internet feel different from in-person dispute resolution? Do you have any way of knowing how many people were involved in the dispute?

B. PUBLIC HYBRIDS

This section traces the development of alternative processes in the public sphere — in courts and government agencies. One of the key questions to examine is whether the use of these processes is mandatory in either of two senses. First, *can* the judge or administrative agency require disputants to use or participate in the alternative process? Second, *must* the judge or administrative agency require disputants to use the alternative process as a condition for use of more traditional processes? Another significant question to consider is whether, if an agreement is reached in an alternative process, *must* some *public approval* (by a judge or agency) still be granted to assure full compliance with, and enforcement of, any agreement reached. And, what kind of *review*, if any, should there be of the quality, or commitment, to participation by the parties, in the alternative process?

The institutionalization of alternative approaches to litigation has increased with the passage of several important pieces of federal legislation. First, the Civil Justice Reform Act of 1990 encourages all federal courts to reduce cost and delay. As part of this effort, the Act authorizes each district court to "refer appropriate cases to alternative dispute resolution programs that . . . have been designated for use in a district court; or the court may make available, including mediation, minitrial, and summary jury trial." 28 U.S.C. §473(a)(6). Two other important pieces of legislation were also passed in 1990 to encourage the use of ADR approaches in the adminis-trative context. The Negotiated Rulemaking Act of 1990, 5 U.S.C. §§561-570, per-mits federal agencies to bring together public and private entities and individuals to draft federal regulations. The Administrative Dispute Resolution Act of 1990, 5 U.S.C. §§571-584, permits and encourages federal agencies to use mediation, arbi-tration, and other alternative processes to resolve disputes quickly and informally. Finally, the Alternative Dispute Resolution Act of 1998, 28 U.S.C. §§651-658, focuses again on the courts, but this time mandates, rather than encourages, the use of alternative processes. In particular, the Act requires "[e]ach United States district court . . . to authorize, by local rule . . . the use of alternative dispute resolution processes in all civil actions. . . ." 28 U.S.C. §651(b).

1. Mandatory Judicial Settlement Conferences

Even prior to the passage of the laws outlined above, many federal and state judges sought to require disputants to attend settlement conferences or use ADR processes. In issuing such orders, judges often relied on Rule 16 of the Federal Rules of Civil Procedure and its state equivalents. The initial version of Rule 16, entitled "Pre-Trial Procedures; Formulating Issues," authorized courts to require attorneys to appear before them for pre-trial conferences. In 1983, the rule was amended to specify that such conferences might "facilitat[e] the settlement of the case." Fed. R. Civ. P. 16(a)(5). The current version of the rule makes even clearer that judges may "take appropriate action, with respect to . . . settlement and the use of special procedures to assist in resolving the dispute when authorized by statute or local rules." Fed. R. Civ. P. 16(c)(9). It specifically allows courts to "require that a party or its representative be present or reasonably available by telephone in order to consider possible settlement of the dispute." Fed. R. Civ. P. 16(c).

The institutionalization of settlement and other forms of dispute resolution is controversial. Judges have authority and experience that make them particularly expert in predicting probable outcomes in an evaluative context, and they are usually well respected as "wise neutrals" because of their selection process and the formal rules that govern judicial neutrality, recusals, and conflicts of interest. On the other hand, some analysts argue that judges, who are supposed to perform adjudicatory roles, should not be involved in the settlement process — most certainly, when the judge at the settlement conference might be the same one to ultimately find the facts or rule on the legal issues. These critics argue judges are not trained to act as facilitative mediators, and adjudication (with rules of evidentiary admissibility) should be separated from efforts to settle the case — often on grounds different from the legal merits, even though we know that judges do engage in these efforts to settle cases.[13] A second controversy surrounds the question of whether institutionalizing settlement or other forms of dispute resolution actually serves the intended purpose of saving time and money. And more recently, questions have been raised about what legal duty lawyers might have to participate in mandatory settlement conferences (and other court required or suggested forms of ADR) — what would it mean to require "good faith participation"?[14] Carrie Menkel-Meadow discusses some of these issues below.[15]

---

13. Peter Robinson, Judicial Settlement Conference Practices and Techniques, 33 Am. J. of Trial Advocacy 113-165 (2009).

14. John Lande, Using Dispute System Design Methods to Promote Good-Faith Participation in Court-Connected Mediation Programs, 50 UCLA L. Rev. 69 (2002).

15. See also, Carrie Menkel-Meadow & Bryant Garth, Courts and Civil Procedure in Oxford Handbook of Empirical Legal Studies (2010).

❖   *Carrie Menkel-Meadow*, FOR AND AGAINST
SETTLEMENT: USES AND ABUSES OF THE
MANDATORY SETTLEMENT CONFERENCE

33 UCLA L. Rev. 490-494, 497-498, 503-504, 506-511, 513-514 (1985)

THE EVIDENCE ON SETTLEMENT CONFERENCES: WHAT DO THE DATA DEMONSTRATE?

. . . The first systematic study of the pretrial conference was undertaken by Maurice Rosenberg on mandatory conference, voluntary conference, and nonconference cases in New Jersey. That study reported findings, as yet uncontradicted, that mandatory pretrial conferences improved the quality of trial proceedings, but actually reduced the efficiency of the court by consuming judges' time in handling conferences, rather than in trying cases. Plaintiff "victories" were as frequent (all cases were personal injury cases) in mandatory conference cases as in other cases, though pretried cases were likely to result in higher recoveries. Most significantly, cases submitted to mandatory pretrial conferences were no more likely to result in settlements than those that were not. . . . In addition to quantitative analysis of the data collected, the Rosenberg study also consisted of interviews with and observations of judges with a variety of views on the judicial role in settlement conferences. Some judges participated as passive, neutral referees of the dispute; others were actively engaged in case management (i.e., issue clarification); still others saw settlement as one of their most useful functions. One of the most interesting and seldom noted implications of the Rosenberg study is that if parties achieve settlement with equal frequency in mandatory, voluntary, and nonconference cases, judicial settlement management may indeed be an inefficient use of judicial time. . . .

THE ROLE FOR SETTLEMENT CONFERENCES IN PROVIDING SUBSTANTIVE JUSTICE: WHEN SETTLEMENT?

Those who criticize the role of the judge in settlement functions assume the judge's proper role is purely adjudicative. Owen Fiss has stated starkly: "Courts exist to give meaning to public values, not to resolve disputes." Judith Resnik has argued that judges are required to provide reasoned explanations for their decisions, are supposed to rule without concern for the interests of particular constituencies, are required to act with deliberation, and are to be disinterested and disengaged from the dispute and disputants. Those who criticize the settlement function, I fear, have enshrined the adjudicative function based on an unproven, undemonstrated record of successful performance, just as the efficiency experts have exalted settlement conferences relying on unconvincing statistics. For me, the more fruitful inquiry is to ask under what circumstances adjudication is more appropriate than settlement, or vice-versa. In short, when settlement? . . .

On a historical level we know that courts have often done more than adjudicate in the pristine fashion described by Fiss and Resnik. Professors Schwartz, Eisenberg, Yeazell, and Chayes tell us that courts have always managed and administered not only themselves, but also the criminal justice system, probate matters, and other matters as well. Courts have promulgated rules, acting as a super legislature on occasion. Judges have been asked to mediate or settle important public issues outside the formal structure of adjudication. Contrary to Fiss's restrictive view, courts and the judges who sit in them historically have filled more roles than solely authoritative norm explicators.

THE FUNCTIONS AND PURPOSES OF THE MANDATORY SETTLEMENT CONFERENCE: THE HOW AND WHY OF SETTLEMENT PRACTICES

As greater numbers of judges and courts use settlement conferences, our information about particular practices increases. . . . What emerges from the data is a variety of role conceptions that parallel the various conceptions of the goals of settlement. For some, efficient case management is the primary role; for others, the primary role is the facilitation of substantive or procedural justice. For others still, the primary role is simple brokering of what would occur anyway in bilateral negotiations. Some judges avoid active settlement activity because they view adjudication as their primary role.

The Dangers of Efficiency-Seeking Settlement Techniques

For those who seek to use the settlement conference as a docket-clearing device, the conference becomes most problematic in terms of the substantive and process values (i.e., *quality* of solution) previously discussed. Judges see their role as simplifying the issues until the major issue separating the parties (usually described as money) is identified and the judge can attempt to "narrow the gap." In one study judges and lawyers were asked to report on judicial settlement activity. Seventy-two percent of the lawyers reported that they participated at least once in settlement conferences in which the judge requested the parties to "split the difference." The same study noted that when local rules require settlement conferences judges tend to be more assertive in their settlement techniques (using several techniques that some of the lawyers considered to be unethical). According to the study, jurisdictions with mandatory settlement conferences took more time in moving cases toward trial. This confirms the findings of earlier studies.

   A much touted settlement technique is the use of the "Lloyds of London" formula: The settlement judge asks the parties to assess the probabilities of liability and damages and, if the figures are within reasonable range, to split the difference. The difficulty with such settlement techniques is that they tend to monetarize and compromise all the issues in the case. Although some cases are reducible to monetary issues, an approach to case evaluation on purely monetary grounds may decrease the likelihood of settlement by making fewer issues available for trade-offs. Furthermore, a wider definition of options may make compromise unnecessary. . . . The irony is that settlement managers, who think they are making settlement easier by reducing the issues, may in fact be increasing the likelihood of deadlock by reducing the issues to one. Furthermore, as I have argued at length elsewhere, using money as a proxy for other interests the parties may have, may thwart the possibilities for using party interests for mutual gain.

In addition to foreclosing a number of possible settlements, the efficiency-minded settlement officer seems prone to use coercive techniques such as suggesting a particular result, making threats about taking the case off the docket, directing meetings with clients or parties. Lawyers find these techniques problematic. Thus, the quest for efficiency may in fact be counterproductive. . . .

To the extent that settlement procedures are used to achieve substantive outcomes that are better than court-defined remedies, they have implications for how the settlement conference should be conducted and who should conduct it. First, those with knowledge about the larger implications of the litigation — the parties — should be present (this is the principle behind the mini-trial concept with business personnel in attendance) to offer or accept solutions that involve more than simple money settlements. Second, such conferences should be managed by someone other than the trial judge so that interests and considerations that might effect a settlement but would be inadmissible in court will not prejudice a later trial. Some argue for a separate "settlement officer" because the skills required for guiding negotiations are different from those required for trying cases. Third, some cases in which issues should not be traded off should not be subjected to the settlement process at all. For example, in employment discrimination cases, parties should not be asked to accept monetary settlements in lieu of a job for which they are qualified. Finally, a more traditional mediator's role may be more appropriate when the substantive process (i.e., direct communication between the parties) may be more important than the substantive outcome (i.e., employer-employee disputes, some civil rights cases).

CONCLUSION

. . . The settlement conference is a process that can be used to serve a number of different ends. How we evaluate its utility depends on whether we are looking at the individual dispute being settled, the numbers of cases on the docket, the quality of the results (measured against cases that would have settled anyway and cases that would have gone on to trial), the effect of the number and types of settlements on the number and types of cases that remain in the system, or the alternatives available. These considerations do not all point in the same direction. The evaluation of settlement conferences is something we will have to keep watching. . . .

Problem 12-6.   *Uniformity or Variety*

Do you think there should be uniformity in how judges and courts approach settlement and other ADR practices, or is it appropriate for there to be local variation and discretion (whether at the level of court or individual judge)? See John Maull, ADR in the Federal Courts: Would Uniformity be Better?, 34 Duq. L. Rev. 245 (1996).

In a variant on the settlement conference, some courts use a special form of ADR known as "settlement week." During a specified period of time, regular trial assignments are suspended for an entire courthouse, and judges, magistrates, and often volunteer lawyers spend the entire period meeting with lawyers and parties in "settlement conferences" that may resemble either mediation, in its facilitative or evaluative forms, or non-binding arbitration. As you might imagine, some argue that this suspension of the trial docket for judges to perform other roles is *ultra vires* judicial roles and unauthorized by statutes or court rules. Despite such objections, many courts (mostly at the state level) still pursue this settlement device in an effort not only to settle particular cases and reduce court caseloads (the efficiency criterion) but also to educate lawyers and parties about negotiation, mediation, and other settlement techniques and theories (the qualitative approach). What do you think of the practice? What advantages and disadvantages do you see?

2. Special Masters

Just as settlement conferences have long been part of the traditional judicial repertoire, so too have "special masters," appointed by judges to assist them in resolving cases. In 1983, as judges began to experiment in broadening their procedural approaches, Fed. R. Civ. P. 53 was amended to permit individual judges, rather than whole courts, to appoint a "master" to serve as a "referee, an auditor, an examiner [or] an assessor." Fed. R. Civ. P. 53(a) (1983, amended 2003). In 2003, Rule 53 was "revised extensively" because special masters had come to perform a "variety of pretrial and post-trial functions." Fed. R. Civ. P. 53, Advisory Committee's Note on 2003 Amendments. While many special masters simply assist in gathering data or organizing discovery in complex cases, some judges have used special masters far more creatively, bringing in ADR concepts. Some special masters have served as mediators (Kenneth Feinberg in the *Agent Orange* litigation), developed data for rationalized grids of predictable settlement awards, or made factual or legal findings that helped disputants reach an amicable agreement. The role of special masters, like that of the judge in settlement conferences, is controversial. Some question the propriety of using non-Article III court personnel to affect the legal rights and remedies of parties before the courts. Others criticize the wide-ranging and essentially unregulated nature of special masters' activities. Although proponents justify the use of special masters on both efficiency and case management grounds, critics are concerned about whether special masters are sufficiently sensitive to justice and legal rights issues, and question how they are appointed and held accountable.

In the reading below, Francis McGovern examines one judge's early creative use of the special master provision in existing litigation. As the use of special masters in formal litigation, especially in class actions increased, it has become more common for special masters to be appointed, not only by judges but by the executive branch, including the President. These special masters perform a variety of dispute resolution roles, including the power, even before or during litigation, to make full awards of compensation (as in the September 11 Victim Fund and the recently announced special fund for compensation for personal and economic injuries due to the British Petroleum oil leak in the Gulf of Mexico, with Kenneth Feinberg serving as the Special Master in both cases).

 Francis E. McGovern, **TOWARD A FUNCTIONAL APPROACH FOR MANAGING COMPLEX LITIGATION**

53 U. Chi. L. Rev. 440, 456-463, 465-468 (1986)

In 1979 Judge Fox of the Eastern District of Michigan ruled that the Treaty of 1836 between the United States and the Ottawa and Chippewa peoples reserved to the tribes the right to fish in the treaty waters of the Great Lakes unfettered by regulation by the State of Michigan. The U.S. Department of the Interior subsequently ceased regulating Great Lakes fishing, leaving two independent sovereigns to govern a common natural resource. The tribal commercial fishers and other Michigan commercial and sport fishers competed for fish in most of the Michigan waters of Lakes Superior, Huron, and Michigan.

This competition triggered significant resource depletion and violence among the competitors. In an attempt to save the basic stocks of fish, the tribes, the state, and the United States agreed to close the fishery each year as soon as a certain amount of fish had been caught. As the competition increased, closure occurred earlier and earlier each year, and the tribes took a smaller and smaller percentage of the catch. The tribes could not compete technologically with the state commercial fishers, nor were they numerous enough to compete with the burgeoning state sport fishers. . . .

The treaty itself contained little guidance for resolving the allocation issue.

Given the paucity of precedent for any allocation scheme, the parties' wildly differing approaches, the extreme volatility of the situation, the complexity of any allocation process, and institutional weaknesses associated with continuing judicial management, Judge Enslen decided that if allocation was appropriate, the parties preferably should do it. He also believed that an expeditious decision was necessary to minimize the potential for violence in the uncertain situation. Judge Enslen appointed a special master to prepare the case for trial within eight months and explore the possibilities for settlement. The master's duties did not include ruling on substantive issues, and all his decisions were subject to de novo review by the judge.

United States v. Michigan was relatively complex litigation; the five named parties represented virtually all Michigan citizens. The issues and information involved every conceivable problem associated with managing the largest lakes in the world. From one perspective the case was a generic conflict — a distributional dispute to divide a common pool among competing users. Large numbers of equally situated parties, the fishers, had similar incentives to use a common asset, the Great Lakes, as much as possible. Without intervention, the cumulative use would destroy the resource through massive overfishing. The essential problem was to determine what kind of intervention would help to resolve the dispute.

Under this view of the lawsuit, its big issues were polycentric, not susceptible to the yes-or-no answers or mutually exclusive inquiries typical of special interrogatories posed to juries. The solution to any given question concerning resource division was dependent upon the solutions reached on the other questions: no issues were independent. This complex interrelationship of issues created difficulties which were compounded by the lack of any — much less clear — legal standards. The court was being asked to make extremely complex management decisions by using policy differences unreflected in the substantive law — "reasonable living standards," "subsistence," "maximizing value," and "equal distribution." Because of the continuing relationship among the parties, any court-imposed solution would probably generate future conflict. Even under optimal conditions, changes in the resource itself would breed future controversies.

Judge Enslen concluded that these characteristics begged for an allocation plan developed by the parties themselves. It was a classic case for integrative bargaining. The parties could identify their respective interests, share information concerning how they valued those interests, and reach for a combination of trade-offs that would maximize each side's use of the resource. Under an economic analysis of integrative bargains, they could seek superior allocations, reduce conflicts of interest, and possibly achieve an optimal solution. Given constraints on a court's ability to gather and evaluate this type of information, the parties would be in a superior position to locate an optimal allocation plan. A party-developed plan would also eliminate any dislocation that could accompany a court-ordered resolution . . .

The first task was to determine the likelihood of success for any bargain at all. In conjunction with the Program on Negotiation at Harvard, the master attempted to develop a scorable game that would mimic the actual dispute. The task involved identifying each party's interests, selecting all feasible elements to any allocation plan, stating the parties' priorities, and determining the variety of systems that could be used to organize those interests and elements. Each priority was then quantified in regard to each issue. The negotiation theory applied to the game was so-called differences orientation. For example, each party might value the same portion of Lake Michigan differently. The tribes living in the northern Michigan peninsula would probably prefer unlimited access to waters close to their homes. In contrast, the sports fishers generally lived in southern Michigan and would value the southern waters more highly. Differences orientation was particularly valuable here because of the economic and cultural disparities among the parties: what appeared in the litigation context to be a major problem of fundamental value differences was actually an asset in developing a mutually acceptable allocation plan. Once relative differences had been identified, they were entered into a computer.

A program was run to determine if any scenario would satisfy each party's minimum priorities. When the game was limited to the case's legal issues, no negotiated outcome seemed possible. If, however, the issues were expanded to include other items that might be subject to negotiation, some solutions might satisfy the hypothetical minimum interests of the parties. A court, for example, was limited to interpreting the treaty in perpetuity; an agreement by the parties could be for a term of years. A negotiated disposition, unlike a typical court decision, could also include provisions for plantings of fish, monetary payments, and market development.

When these and other issues were added to the computer, there emerged combinations of components which indicated different possible solutions where agreement was feasible. . . .

The court then assigned the special master to mediate among the named parties and the litigating amici. Because the case would eventually be tried to the judge, his ability to facilitate negotiation was limited by his strong ethical constraints against prejudging the outcome of the case. Therefore, the master performed this role while insulating the judge from the details of any bargaining. As a part of the mediation role, the master also kept the parties' critical decision makers aware of the progress of the litigation and the negotiations. He met with the leaders and sometimes virtually all the members of the tribes, officials of the U.S. Department of the Interior, and Michigan's Governor, Attorney General, and the Director of its Department of Natural Resources.

. . . After three days of negotiations the parties reached a settlement on March 28, four weeks before the scheduled trial. The settlement agreement closely paralleled one of the scorable game solutions that indicated possible areas of compromise. The court approved the settlement, but one of the tribes overruled its leaders on a subsequent 31-29 vote and decided to proceed with the litigation. All the other parties ratified the negotiated agreement. The judge severed the two alternative management plans for trial, conducted a trial, and ruled on the merits in favor of the negotiated plan. . . .

The court has requested the special master to evaluate the trial preparation and settlement process, and a report should issue after the next fishing season. Any evaluation will be extremely difficult to accomplish. An economic analysis suggests that the direct expenses were significant — approximately $200,000 for master, experts, and expenses. Attorneys for the parties worked almost full-time on the case from January to March and during May of 1985. Policy leaders and support personnel were also substantially involved during this time. Yet most of these expenses would have been incurred in traditional litigation. The cost to the court in time and money was minimal: only four conferences and a four-day trial. None of the master's rulings was appealed to the court. On balance there was a trade-off between identifiable additional expenses associated with the master's work and unidentifiable savings because of the expedited trial preparation. . . .

Were the deviations from the traditional trial model — the special master, scorable game, abbreviated discovery schedule, computer-assisted negotiations, and presentation from *United States v. Washington* — justified? Would the parties have settled anyway? Was the settlement "better" than an adjudicated outcome? Given the stated criteria, an ex post analysis suggests that the intervention was worthwhile. Ex ante, however, with the extremely high risk of no settlement, the answers are less clear.

> **Problem 12-7.   *Games Instead of Trials?***
>
> What do you think of the appointment of a special master in a complex case like this? Is this appropriate under the Federal Rules of Civil Procedure? Is this an abdication of judicial authority by the judge or the proper use of a court to facilitate a more lasting, pleasing settlement to all parties? Was it appropriate for the special master to use a scorable game (or simulation or economic model) to help the parties quantify their preferences and priorities and to rationalize the negotiation process, as you have studied it here? Explain your answer.

Perhaps the most dramatic use of a Special Master in recent years was the appointment of private attorney mediator and arbitrator, Kenneth Feinberg, to allocate government funds to victims and survivors of the attack on the World Trade Center on September 11, 2001, pursuant to special statutory authority and subsequent authorizing regulations, see 28 C.F.R. §§104.2 et seq. (2003). Acting relatively alone and *pro bono publico* (without pay but with assistance from his firm and members of the Department of Justice), Mr. Feinberg allocated millions of dollars on behalf of the government to compensate those who no longer had the legal ability to sue airlines and the government (though a few lawsuits are still pending). Mr. Feinberg used a special master-arbitral process in which parties presented documents of their claims and were allocated amounts based on a regularized grid of death benefits, injury, pain and suffering, and some remit for secondary coverage and other benefits. Those who requested a personal hearing with Mr. Feinberg were granted one and could tell the story of the harm they had suffered, though this rarely, or seldom, changed the amount they received. In a subsequent memoir about the experience, Special Master Feinberg suggested that perhaps a more mediative, rather than arbitral, process would have been appropriate, given the extreme pain and suffering, and need for expression and catharsis expressed by the claimants. He also opined that the government should never again provide for a special compensation scheme (based on tort principles of recovery) in extreme catastrophes like this one. Instead, he would favor something closer to equal payments for all victims.[16] Is Special Master Feinberg feeling the "weight" of judicial authority in allocating funds, without the full structure of adjudication or is he suggesting something else is troubling about the process? Feinberg is now allocating funds in a "private" setting as British Petroleum pays damages to those hurt (personally and economically) by a large oil spill in the Gulf of Mexico. Since this appointment was "approved" by President Obama it demonstrates how "hybrid" (public and private together) ADR processes have become.

---

16. Kenneth Feinberg, What Is a Life Worth? The Unprecedented Effort to Compensate the Victims of 9/11 (2006).

Problem 12-8.   *A New Special Master? The BP Oil Spill*

In June 2010, President Obama asked Kenneth Feinberg to serve as a special master, mediator, and manager of a special fund of $20 billion provided by BP to be paid to victims of a massive oil leak in the Gulf of Mexico, affecting millions of people, their homes, businesses, and recreation in at least five states. See Kenneth Feinberg — Administering a Fund, A Master Mediator, N.Y. Times, June 16, 2010.

By what authority was this role created? What is the purpose of such a process? What do you think will happen in this process and outside of it?

3. Disputes Involving Groups: Aggregate Claims and Class Actions

Disputes involving groups offer unique problems and opportunities. In this section we examine some of the hybrid processes that have been developed to handle such disputes. As we discuss hybrid processes for resolving group claims, we explore both claims that begin with litigation and group disputes that have not yet been and might never be filed in a court. Alternative procedural processes can be useful in both contexts. (Chapter 13, on multiparty processes, further examines some of the unique aspects of disputes involving groups.)

From the litigation standpoint, group claims are sometimes desirable but potentially difficult to handle. The class action was developed in the United States as one means of handling special aspects of group claims. Under Rule 23 of the Federal Rules of Civil Procedure and its state law equivalents, one or more named plaintiffs can bring claims on behalf of other unnamed, often unidentified, class members. Compared to individual litigation, proponents of the class action believe it is more efficient, improves access to the litigation system, and serves the public interest.[17] At the same time, class actions can be slow and expensive. Questions also arise as to whether class representatives or their lawyers adequately represent absent class members.

The increasing recognition that mass torts can be handled as group claims has increased the pressure on courts to find alternative means to handle such claims. Hundreds and sometimes thousands of people claim to have been injured in natural disasters, through the mass production of defective products, or by actions taken against large groups (as in employment discrimination, securities litigation, antitrust,

---

17. The American Law Institute has recently completed a review of legal guidelines for mass and group litigation, in both class action and other aggregative forms, see ALI, Principles of the Law of Aggregate Litigation (Samuel Issacharoff, Robert H. Klonoff, Richard Nagareda & Charles Silver, Reporters, 2010).

and consumer protection actions). Courts need to find ways to manage these complex suits.[18] Sometimes alternative processes are used in conjunction with litigation of mass claims; at other times the alternative processes take the place of litigation. This section provides examples of several of these different approaches, starting with those most closely connected to litigation. First, it examines uses of ADR in connection with mass personal injury litigation. Second, it considers how ADR has been used in connection with employment class actions.

As you read these excerpts, consider that managing group claims has itself become a subfield of dispute resolution professionals who help courts, government agencies, or private institutions design dispute resolution systems for mass claims. These processes raise special concerns and often engender controversy, as they try to balance such interests as efficiency, equity, fairness, justice, and the desire for individualized treatment. Note that more informal versions of ADR can be devised to resolve group disputes.

 Deborah R. Hensler, **A GLASS HALF FULL, A GLASS HALF EMPTY: THE USE OF ALTERNATIVE DISPUTE RESOLUTION IN MASS PERSONAL INJURY LITIGATION**

73 Tex. L. Rev. 1587, 1596, 1598-1600, 1606-1609, 1612-1616, 1619-1623
(1995)

Although mass torts may constitute only a small fraction of the total national civil caseload in any given year, litigation arising out of the use of — or exposure to — mass-marketed products has accounted for as much as one-fourth of civil money suits in some courts.

In addition to their sheer numbers, these cases challenge the civil justice system because of the grave significance of their results to the plaintiffs — who often seek compensation for alleged life-threatening and other severe injuries — and to the defendants — whose financial viability may ride on the outcome of the litigation. Moreover, because the costs of this type of litigation are measured in the billions of dollars and because a large fraction of these dollars are attributable to "transaction costs" — that is, legal fees and expenses — the management of the litigation by judges and attorneys attracts considerable attention. . . .

Mass torts involve a common set of injuries that occurred in the same or similar circumstances — for example, a hotel fire, a building collapse, or widespread product use — and that are allegedly linked to the actions of a single or small number of defendants. Plaintiffs and defendants are represented by a small number of law firms (relative to the magnitude of the litigation), and a single or small number of judges

---

18. See Eric D. Green, What Will We Do When Adjudication Ends? We'll Settle in Bunches, Bringing Rule 23 into the Twenty-First Century, 44 UCLA L. Rev. 1773 (1997); Francis E. McGovern, Settlement of Mass Torts in a Federal System, 36 Wake Forest L. Rev. 871 (2001); Carrie Menkel-Meadow, Ethics and the Settlements of Mass Torts: When the Rules Meet the Road, 80 Cornell L. Rev. 1159 (1995).

frequently manage the litigation because of aggregative procedures such as multi-districting and class action certification. . . .

In addition to numerosity, commonality, and interdependence of case values, many mass personal injury torts share three other features: controversy over scientific evidence of causation, emotional or political heat, and higher than average potential for claiming by allegedly injured parties. . . .

Mass personal injury litigation also appears to stimulate a higher rate of claiming than is associated with ordinary personal injuries. Contrary to conventional wisdom, most Americans do not bring legal claims when they are injured in accidents. . . .

These distinguishing features of mass tort litigation — numerosity, commonality, interdependence of case values, scientific controversy, heated emotional atmosphere, and increased propensity to claim — set the conditions for the resolution of all mass torts. They create the incentives for plaintiffs' attorneys to invest in mass litigation, for defendants to settle cases, and for judges to adopt novel disposition practices. . . .

Courts have responded to the challenges posed by mass personal injury litigation by devising streamlined procedures to resolve individual cases, informally aggregating and formally consolidating cases for settlement or trial, facilitating global settlements, and facilitating the design and implementation of administrative processes for delivering compensation to individual claimants. These approaches have been used alone in some litigation, but many mass tort cases have involved the use of two or more of these approaches concurrently or sequentially. These techniques have resolved litigation in trial courts, bankruptcy courts, and private fora. Over time, courts, and some attorneys, appear to have developed a preference for collective mechanisms, such as consolidation and aggregate settlements, over streamlining individual case disposition, and for global settlements resolving all current and future cases. . . .

INFORMAL GROUPING AND FORMAL CONSOLIDATION OF CASES

Because of the scale of the asbestos caseload, some courts have substituted group settlements of large blocks of cases for the more traditional case-at-a-time settlement. For example, in the Los Angeles Superior Court, judges assigned to the special asbestos calendar organized their caseload by date of filing and plaintiff's law firm. Judicial settlement conferences were scheduled to negotiate the disposition of all of a particular law firm's cases from a specified period. The Los Angeles approach to asbestos case disposition built on a long tradition of judicial settlement conferences in that court, as well as on asbestos lawyers' practice of settling large blocks of cases in mass disposition sessions outside the court.

As some judges experimented with mass settlement strategies, others experimented with consolidating cases for trial under Federal Rule of Civil Procedure 42 or state court equivalents. . . . When the juries reached different verdicts on the same liability evidence, the experiments were abandoned.

Devising Global Settlements

1. Settlement Strategies

Many judges have tried to settle, rather than adjudicate, the cases that have been consolidated before them. In some instances, judges have played a strong role in developing the settlement plan; in others, judges have relied heavily on a special master appointed to help the attorneys shape the plan. The attorneys in turn are usually organized into committees either appointed by the judge or formed voluntarily. . . .

2. Elements of Global Settlement Plans

Judges, special masters, and attorneys have fashioned settlement strategies that have three central components.

    a. Aggregate settlement amounts that cap defendants' damages exposure — the aggregate value of the settlement fund (and the allocation of shares among defendants) is a negotiated amount, which is sometimes determined more by what defendants are willing to pay and plaintiffs' attorneys are willing to accept than by any systematic data on the total size of the claimant population and the severity of their injuries.

    b. Rules for allocating the settlement fund among claimants. The allocation of dollars from a fund is determined by a grid or matrix — also arrived at through negotiation — that assigns potential claimants to categories with different cash values on the basis of evidence of causation, disease, or injury severity. The development of compensation grids is closely linked to the concept of a limited fund, which seems to lend itself to a rule-based system for allocating compensation. The criteria that underlie compensation grids or matrices are derived from an amalgam of scientific or medical information about the nature of injuries and their appropriate treatment, information about the factors that have determined settlement or trial value before the aggregate settlement, and the amount for which negotiators will settle.

In some early global settlements of mass toxic torts, the details of the grid were not worked out until after the attorneys had agreed on the total value of the settlement. In the Agent Orange litigation, special master Kenneth Feinberg suggested criteria for distributing compensation funds in a draft settlement plan that was shared with attorneys before the $180 million settlement was reached, but the final distribution plan was apparently devised subsequently. . . . The Dalkon Shield bankruptcy plan laid out a framework for allocating compensation that included four options — or tracks — for obtaining payment, but did not indicate what injuries would be compensated or what amounts would be paid under each option. It was left to the trustees of the fund established under the plan to develop specific eligibility criteria and payment levels. Perhaps in response to criticism of the operation of the Dalkon Shield Claimants' Trust, more recent global settlement plans have laid out detailed injury and disease categories and specified exact payments or payment ranges for each category. . . .

   c. Procedures for distributing compensation.   Once global settlements are final-ized, the daunting task of distributing funds to claimants begins. Most global settlement plans have established a claimants' trust facility to manage the corpus of funds and a claims resolution facility to distribute compensation to claimants. These facilities differ from case to case in many respects, including the options they offer for dispute resolution. Some payment schemes, such as those devised by the DDT settlement and the Agent Orange settlement, are wholly administrative. Recognizing the essentially administrative task of claims payment under the Agent Orange scheme, Judge Weinstein contracted with the Aetna insurance company to distribute compensation. At the other extreme, the first Manville Trust, although intended to rely primarily on negotiation, mediation, and arbitration to decide payment amounts, found itself embroiled in litigation and sank under the pressure of an unanticipated number of filings and size of damage awards. . . .

   In an effort to balance efficiency and equity concerns, the Dalkon Shield Claims Facility offered claimants a combination of administrative processes, for no injury and minor injury claims, and ADR processes, for more serious claims, with trial available for those who rejected other options. Under Option 1 of the bankruptcy plan, claimants could receive a flat amount of $725 simply for filing an affidavit that they were Shield users and had sustained injury. More than half of the claimants availed themselves of this option. Under Option 2 of the plan, claim-ants who presented minimal medical evidence of use and injury could receive scheduled damages ranging from $850 to $5500, depending on the nature of the injury. Under Option 3, claimants who thought they had stronger evidence of causation and damages above the Option 2 cap could enter into more traditional negotiations, including a settlement conference, with the Trust. Plaintiffs' lawyers expected that Option 3 offers would be in line with historical settlement values of Dalkon Shield legal claims. Finally, under Option 4, claimants could elect binding arbitration or trial. To implement the Option 4 portion of the plan, the Trust contracted with the Duke University Private Adjudication Center [to provide arbitration services]. . . .

   Since ADR is so often used to manage complex litigation, its forms and prac-tices may have to be adapted and modified for such uses. The article below explores how mediators may have to adapt their techniques in class actions.

The Honorable Myron S. Greenberg & Megan A Blazina,
**WHAT MEDIATORS NEED TO KNOW ABOUT CLASS
ACTIONS: A BASIC PRIMER**

27 Hamline L. Rev, 220-224 (2004)

OPPORTUNITIES FOR USE OF MEDIATION AND OTHER ADR MECHANISMS IN MASS TORT AND CLASS ACTIONS

A. Use of Mediation to Reach Resolution

Though it should be obvious, mediation and other forms of ADR provide parties an excellent opportunity to reach a resolution. For example, mediation can be utilized to resolve potential mass tort claims or class actions prior to judicial involvement or intervention. In such cases, mediation may be utilized to settle individual claims, as well as class-wide issues.

Due to the lengthy amount of time needed to prepare a class action suit for trial, there are many opportunities to employ the use of mediation in an effort to secure a comprehensive resolution of the dispute. Parties may wish to minimize the costs involved in the suit and elect to participate in mediation before discovery has been completed, or even initiated. If the opposing party hotly contests that the dispute is appropriate for class action treatment, parties may be better served to wait until after the court has ruled on class certification before attempting to negotiate a resolution. While many forums have a high success rate associated with mediation, the process is often considered beneficial for the parties even when resolution is not reached and can help facilitate the ongoing litigation.

B. Mediation to Facilitate Case Management

Even when mediation does not result in the resolution of a case, mediation is still successful if it helps to obtain a partial resolution to the case, narrow the issues, or provide other direction or assistance to the parties as they prepare to proceed to trial. As the litigation progresses, the opportunities for the use of mediation only increases. Mediation can be useful in managing the litigation and helping the parties identify the core issues of the dispute. It can help the parties narrow the issues and coordinate proposals for litigating these key issues. Mediation can also define the scope of discovery and facilitate communication among the parties. ADR can also be used to narrow the problems of scientific and medical causation, which are frequently at issue in mass torts and class actions.

In addition to the management benefits, the mediation process provides an excellent opportunity for the parties to examine their respective positions and perform a risk assessment of their claims. Mediators are in a unique position to provide parties with a neutral's evaluation of the merits of their position. Further, the parties may be able to gauge the opposing party's credibility while simultaneously obtaining an independent assessment of their own position. Additionally, the discovery gained through mediation can assist in evaluating the merits of the parties' positions and the potential settlement value of the case. Finally, the use of mediation for purposes of case management and evaluation, provides an on-going opportunity for the parties to explore a resolution even as the case progresses.

C. Use of Mediation Following Settlement and Resolution

Mediation and other ADR mechanisms can also serve an important function in the administration and implementation of a settlement following court approval. It is often difficult to anticipate all categories of claims, injuries or defenses when seeking to obtain a class wide settlement. However, "neutrals can assist in ascertaining fair formulas for allocating a fixed amount of money and in determining procedures for addressing fairness issues." These mechanisms are extremely beneficial in the context of class actions and mass torts, as settlements often entail complex administration of settlement funds and recovery. Of key concern is finding a system which will deal with claims quickly enough so that claimants can benefit from the compensation they receive, and cheaply enough so that the funds are not significantly drained by fees and transaction costs incurred in obtaining the compensation. Through mediation, claimants receive their portion of the recovery, and often just as importantly, feel they had an opportunity to be involved in their own claim and tell their story before a third-party and the defendants.

HELPFUL TOOLS AND METHODS FOR USE OF MEDIATION IN CLASS ACTIONS AND MASS TORTS

Before settlement negotiations can begin on the substantive issues involved in a dispute, the parties need to determine the procedures under which the negotiations will proceed. Who has the authority to decide any outstanding procedural and substantive issues and in what way these issues will be resolved should be addressed as early as possible. This will help define both the process itself and the mediator's role. Ensuring that the right people, i.e., those with authority to settle, are in attendance, will also go a long way in establishing a productive session.

Once the mediation commences, the mediator should ensure that the parties are prepared for each negotiating session. Set an agenda for each session, outlining the issues that are to be tackled, and ask the parties to be prepared to cover these topics. At the same time, the mediator should begin and end each negotiation by describing what has already been achieved. It can also be beneficial to start with small issues before tackling larger issues to help establish momentum in the negotiations. Disputes involving multiple parties and multiple issues are especially fit for mediation as the parties can seek resolution through a series of trade-offs or compromises. However, mediators should bear in mind that counsel in these suits are often highly skilled and may be highly confident about their ability to obtain an advantageous result. Recognizing the often large egos of the participants is part of the process that cannot be ignored.

Due to the complexities of mass tort and class actions, mediators should also be cautious regarding the use of marathon sessions during negotiations. This is particularly true when scientific or analytical data is at issue due to the nature of the material under examination. The parties may have difficulty understanding technical matter, but limiting the length of the mediation will allow the session to be productive, yet ease any frustration that may occur in complex cases.

When interacting with claimants, mediators should recognize that they may need to relate to claimants interpersonally, listen well, and empathize, in addition to making a determination of facts.

Some specific, if obvious, suggestions have been made which may help to facilitate a settlement of class actions and mass torts. First, work to build areas of agreement. Second, manage the communications process. A lack of good communication can be a deterrent to resolution, but ADR can help to ensure that communications are managed effectively. Third, work to diffuse emotional attachment. Mass torts, in particular, often involve heightened emotions due to the injuries suffered by the plaintiffs and their loved ones. Fourth, attempt to align expectations. "The ADR process should challenge each party's expectations relative to resolution of the case." Finally, make sure that the appropriate ADR process is employed.

Creative dispute resolution techniques are also used in the context of employment discrimination class actions. The settlement agreements in such class actions often create special procedures for awarding relief to class members. Some settlements cap the monetary awards made available; other settlements simply consider class members' individual claims. Of course, the process of designing these systems leads to interesting dispute resolution problems. Dispute resolution professionals often help design these systems, although given the adversarial nature of the conflict, their role may be more to facilitate than to serve as experts in process design.[19]

As discussed in Chapters 9 and 10, some companies try to prevent claims from being resolved on a group basis by using mandatory arbitration. Specifically, some arbitration clauses proscribe claimants from presenting their claims on a group basis either in arbitration or in litigation. This interaction between ADR and group claims is very different from what we discuss in this section. Lower courts have sometimes held such class action prohibitions in arbitration clauses to be unconscionable or impermissible under a particular statute. The Supreme Court continues to consider this issue of whether class actions can be permitted or prohibited in arbitration in several different forms, see, e.g., Stolt-Nielsen S.A. et al. v. Animal Feeds International Corp. (2010), discussed in Chapter 10.

---

19. See Lisa Bingham, Cynthia J. Hallberlin, Denise A. Walker, Won-Tae Chung, Dispute System Design and Justice in Employment Dispute Resolution: Mediation at the Workplace, 14 Harvard Negot. L. Rev. 1 (2009); Margaret L. Shaw & Lynn P. Cohn, Employment Class Actions Provide Unique Context for ADR, 5 Disp. Resol. Mag. 10 (Summer 1999), for further discussion of these processes and of the role neutrals can play in helping to devise ADR systems in this special context. For a recent survey of comparative approaches to dispute resolution in employment discrimination, see Jean R. Sternlight, In Search of the Best Procedure for Enforcing Employment Discrimination Laws: A Comparative Analysis, 78 Tulane L. Rev. 1401 (2004).

While many forms of ADR in mass cases appear to create global settlements or grids or simple monetary compensation schemes, without a full hearing, some of these forms provide for individualized mediation or arbitration hearings.

Problem 12-9.   *What's the Best Process?*

Where many people are hurt or injured at the same time, do you think ADR can deal appropriately with legal damages, the need for catharsis, and other forms of redress, or should claimants retain their rights to go to trial? Does it depend on the kind of case — death or bodily injury, employment discrimination or civil rights violations, economic harm?

For the view that some claimants may find it more cathartic and therapeutic to have a hearing, see Carrie Menkel-Meadow, Taking the Mass Out of Mass Torts: Reflections of a Dalkon Shield Arbitrator on Alternative Dispute Resolution, Judging, Neutrality, Gender, and Process, 31 Loy. L.A. L. Rev. 513-550 (1998).

In addition to efforts to develop class action, global settlements, and institutional settlement facilities like the Dalkon Shield Trust and the Wellington Asbestos Program at the national level, there have also been international efforts to construct programs for compensating people when there are mass injuries or many claims arising out of the same events. For example, the UN established a United Nations Compensation Commission in 1991 to compensate people who were injured in the Iraqi invasion of Kuwait in 1990.[20] And for many years a compensation program, primarily using arbitration to adjudicate claims arising out of the hostage-taking by Iran of Americans (and the subsequent freezing of Iranian assets in the United States), operated out of a special tribunal in The Hague. For many years, until relations deteriorated again, Israel and Lebanon maintained a public arbitral body (outside of formal courts) to adjudicate and order compensation for claims arising out of border disputes between citizens of both countries.[21]

---

20. Francis McGovern, Dispute System Design: The United Nations Compensation Commission, 14 Harv. Negot. L. Rev. 171 (2009).
21. Gabriella Blum, Islands of Agreement: Managing Enduring Armed Rivalries (2007).

Problem 12-10.   *ADR for Aggregate Harm?*

Should the government have provided for an ADR process for claims arising out of the harm caused by Hurricane Katrina in the Gulf Coast region? Was the government responsible for any of the harm? What kind of substantive compensatory program, with what kind of process, would have been appropriate? Should the government develop an ADR program for resolving the mass mortgage foreclosure and home finance issues arising out of the recent recession? Is this a different kind of mass or group dispute? Is it "private" or "public"? Is it a "mass" dispute or a series of private individual disputes? Who is responsible? Who should "resolve" these disputes? See Symposium, 11 Nev. L.J. (2011).

4. The Summary Jury Trial

As the ADR movement gained momentum, judges began to use new procedural techniques more creatively. The private mini-trial was so successful in the late 1970s and early 1980s that federal judge Thomas Lambros of Ohio imported aspects of it for use in federal courts. The practice spread to state courts as well.[22] In summary jury trials, used in jury cases containing contested factual or legal liability questions, lawyers present shortened versions of their cases (usually no more than part of a day), drawing on argument, testimony, or summarized depositions and documentary evidence. The audience, members of a regular jury venire who don't actually serve as jurors, deliberates and offers what is only an advisory verdict. The verdict is then communicated to the parties to encourage more realistic negotiations. This process was credited with providing lodestar damage assessments in certain repeat cases such as those involving asbestos. Further, it reduced caseloads and offered individualized assessments in cases with conflicting lawyer or party demands. As the excerpt below makes clear, however, this process also creates controversy because of its mandatory nature, its unorthodox use of jurors (who often don't know they are not "real" jurors), and its use of public courtrooms to facilitate private settlements. Judge Richard Posner's criteria for evaluating alternative procedures are also useful as you consider other court-adopted ADR programs.

---

22. Thomas D. Lambros, The Summary Jury Trial and Other Alternative Methods of Dispute Resolution: A Report to the Judicial Conference of the United States Committee on the Operation of the Jury System, 103 F.R.D. 461(1984).

Richard A. Posner, THE SUMMARY JURY TRIAL AND
OTHER METHODS OF ALTERNATIVE DISPUTE
RESOLUTION: SOME CAUTIONARY OBSERVATIONS

53 U. Chi. L. Rev. 366-369, 374-375, 385-389 (1986)

THE SUMMARY JURY TRIAL

A. Description

After pretrial discovery is completed and a pretrial conference held, a jury case that seems unlikely to settle on the eve of trial (as so many cases do) will be set for summary jury trial before a district judge or a magistrate. At the appointed time a jury is empanelled in much the usual manner, although in a summary jury trial the lawyers are not allowed as many challenges. The jurors are told it will be a summary jury trial but not — not yet anyway — that their decision will have no binding effect. The lawyers then present summaries of witness testimony plus their own argument. No live witnesses are called, but in summarizing the testimony that the witnesses would give if called the lawyers may not contradict any facts stipulated to or otherwise established in pretrial discovery. The jury is charged and deliberates, and returns a verdict in the usual way. The lawyers and their clients — for the parties themselves are required to attend the summary jury trial, the hope being that this will encourage settlement — can then talk to the jurors. The trial is intended to take the better part of a day, although I have been told of one that lasted six days.

The idea behind the summary jury trial is to facilitate settlement by giving parties and counsel a sense of how a jury is likely to evaluate their case. The verdict is in no way binding, and the parties can have a regular jury trial if they wish. But the summary jury trial is not voluntary; it is a compulsory part of the pretrial phase of the lawsuit, like a pretrial conference. . . .

B. Evaluation

1. The requirement of Rational Behavior.   Hence the summary jury trial should, as its advocates contend, increase the likelihood of settlement, though the effect may not be great because the reduction in uncertainty brought about by the summary jury trial may not be great:

(1) The jury's principal function is to determine the credibility of witnesses, yet there are no witnesses in the summary jury trial. The credibility assessed is that of the lawyers. A jury may react quite differently when confronted with the actual witnesses. We do not need a jury of laymen to decide which of two lawyers is more credible.

(2) If there is substantial variance in verdicts among different juries deciding the same case, the verdict in the summary jury trial will convey only limited information about the likely verdict of the real jury that will hear the case if the parties do not settle.

(3) As lawyers become more experienced in conducting summary jury trials, we may see more "strategizing" — lawyers holding back some of their best evidence or arguments in an effort to surprise the opponent at the real trial, should the summary jury trial not lead to settlement. Maybe a summary *bench* trial, which would avoid problems (1) and (2) as well as some of the legal problems discussed later, deserves consideration as an alternative device for facilitating settlement. . . .

2. Verifiability of Effects.   My second criterion for a proposed alternative to the conventional trial was that its effects be verifiable. This ideally would require that cases be assigned randomly for summary jury trial, with other cases receiving the usual treatment. . . .

No such study has been attempted. Judges who like the idea of the summary jury trial use it in cases they think will benefit from it. Neither the presiding judge nor the case is chosen randomly. So the fact that many judges who use the summary jury trial are enthusiastic about it may tell us little about its effectiveness. . . .

3. Legal and Prudential Constraints.   My third criterion is that any proposed alternative respect legal and prudential constraints on judicial power. Although Congress has empowered lower federal courts to issue supplementary rules of procedure, I am not sure it has authorized them to order summary jury trials. Admittedly, federal judges have long had the power to convene advisory juries. But the summary jury is not an advisory jury. It does not advise the judge how to decide the case, but is used to push the parties to settle. It is therefore outside the scope of Rule 39(c) of the Federal Rules of Civil Procedure, which deals with advisory juries. . . .

An important issue is what the jury in a summary jury trial is told, and when. Some judges tell the jury at the outset that its verdict will only be advisory — which is likely to reduce the verdict's informational value; other judges tell the jury after it has rendered its verdict; some never tell it. Never telling the jury worries me. The jury, especially in commercial litigation, is a curious institution, a vestige, many believe, of a previous epoch in legal evolution. If it works at all, this may be because jurors are impressed by being told that they are exercising governmental power. That makes them act more responsibly than one might have thought likely given the nature of the selection process and the lack of incentives for jurors to perform well. (The same, by the way, can and should be said about judges.) If word got around that some jurors are being fooled into thinking they are deciding cases when they are not, it could undermine the jury system.

Telling the jurors after they have delivered the summary verdict that the verdict is not legally binding is only a partial anodyne for my concern. (Telling them in advance eliminates the principal advantage of the summary jury trial over a mock proceeding, where the lawyers hire people off the street to be the jurors. Thus, advance notice calls in question the entire rationale of the device.) The jurors are still being fooled; and they are learning that juries sometimes make decisions and at other times simply referee fake trials. As word spreads, the conscientiousness of jurors could decline; it is almost a detail that the utility of the summary jury trial would also decline.

These reflections lead me to wonder, again, why we don't see proposals for summary *bench* trials. The answer may be that since the average bench trial in the federal system is only half the length of the average jury trial, the potential benefits of settlement are smaller.

Benefit to Society.   My last criterion for a proposed alternative to the conventional trial is that it move us in the right direction. Supposing that with the summary jury trial a higher fraction of cases is settled (at this moment a highly uncertain prediction), is this a good thing from the standpoint of society as a whole? It benefits the parties to cases that would otherwise have been tried (at least if coerced settlement is not a serious problem), because settlement is cheaper than trial. But is it a good or a bad thing for the rest of society?

The object of policy, even narrowly conceived, is not to maximize the settlement rate; it is to minimize the total costs of the system of dispute resolution. These include costs of legal error as well as the direct costs, to the parties and the judicial system, of dispute resolution. Raising the settlement rate will reduce the direct costs, in the short run, because litigation is more costly than settlement. But in the long run the litigation rate may rise. With few suits being tried and therefore few decisions being made, parties will find it difficult to predict how courts will resolve their disputes. . . . [C]ases will be litigated that would be settled if parties had better information about how their cases would be decided if they went to trial. Raising the settlement rate may also, as suggested earlier, increase the number of cases filed, by lowering the expected cost of litigating (which includes settlement, the terminating event of most lawsuits); if so, the total costs of resolving disputes may rise even if the average cost falls because more cases are settled.

Problem 12-11.   *Should Summary Jury Trials Be Public?*

Should summary jury trials that take place in a public courtroom be open to the public, or can the parties claim they are merely engaged in a "private" negotiation session that is not open to the public? The Sixth Circuit faced this question in Cincinnati Gas & Elec. Co. v. General Elec. Co., 854 F.2d 900 (6th Cir. 1988). It held that courts "have the power to conduct summary jury trials under either Fed. R. Civ. P. 16, or as a matter of the court's inherent power to manage its cases." Id. at 903 n.4. It then went on to reject the idea that the public or press had a right to observe the summary jury trial under the First Amendment, reasoning that summary jury trials are analogous to settlement negotiations that are shielded from the public eye. Do you think this is a good analogy?

5. Early Neutral Evaluation

Instead of using jurors or judges to help facilitate a settlement within the court system, some courts have developed hybrids that draw on mediation, arbitration, and case management and valuation practices. Early Neutral Evaluation (ENE) uses volunteer or paid lawyers to help parties assess the value of a case before trial and, in some cases, assist in fact development and discovery issues. ENE was first developed in the federal courts in the Northern District of California (San Francisco), while a similar system, called "Michigan mediation," was developed in the state trial courts in Michigan. In both settings, the practice involves shortened case presentations (with varying degrees of documentary or witness evidence, discovery completion, and argumentation) to either a single lawyer (California federal practice) or a panel of three lawyers (in Michigan), who then evaluate the case. The evaluation may suggest either substantive strengths or weaknesses in the case or attach a numerical value to what a likely verdict would be. This non-binding evaluation is then used to facilitate settlement negotiations by the parties and their lawyers. In some cases, if the evaluation does not result in a settlement, the neutral evaluators may assist the parties with other matters, such as developing a discovery schedule, streamlining issues for trial, or planning other settlement events.

The Federal District Court for the Northern District of California sets out its process on its website, *www.adr.cand.uscourts.gov.* It explains that the goals of ENE are to:

> "Enhance direct communication between the parties about their claims and supporting evidence;
> Provide an assessment of the merits of the case by a neutral expert;
> Provide a "reality check" for clients and lawyers;
> Identify and clarify the central issues in dispute;
> Assist with discovery and motion planning or with an informal exchange of key information;
> Facilitate settlement discussions, when requested by the parties."

The district court's website explains that "settlement is not the major goal of ENE, but the process can lead to settlement." Under the district court's plan, the evaluator provides a written assessment (samples are provided on the website), and parties are given the opportunity to negotiate a resolution either prior or subsequent to hearing the evaluation. The neutral may also help facilitate these negotiations. Attendance at the ENE is mandatory not only by the lead trial attorney for each side, but also by "clients with settlement authority and knowledge of the facts" and by "insurers of parties," if their agreement would be necessary for a settlement to occur. Id.[23]

---

23. For further discussion of the ENE process, see Stephanie Smith & Jan Martinez, An Analytic Framework for Dispute System Design, 14 Harv. Negot. L. Rev. 123, 146-151 (2009); W.D. Mich. L. Civ. R. 16.4; Wayne D. Brazil, A Close Look at Three Court-Sponsored ADR Programs: Why They Exist, How They Operate, What They Deliver, and Whether They Threaten Important Values, 1990 U. Chi. Legal F. 303; Robert J. Niemic, Donna Stienstra & Randall E. Ravitz, Guide to Judicial

6. Court-Connected Mediation and Non-binding Arbitration

Other than settlement conferences, the most prevalent forms of court-connected ADR are mediation and non-binding arbitration. In non-binding arbitration the award usually only becomes final if it is voluntarily accepted by the parties. The primary purpose of this form of arbitration would be, like summary jury trials or mini-trials, to give the parties (and their lawyers) some prediction of how the claim would be resolved if it went to trial. The hope being that once the disputants learn this prediction and have an opportunity to go through a process which is much like court litigation, they would abide by the arbitrator's decision. Cases are classified by monetary amount at stake, and are then assigned by state statute, court order, or procedural rule to an arbitration proceeding. The arbitration is "non-binding" in the sense that often a de novo appeal is possible, but court fees and bonds often "tax" such awards to make them feel more "binding." So far, most challenges to this form of "non-binding" arbitration as infringing on the Seventh Amendment right to civil jury trial have failed.[24]

Many courts have adopted non-binding arbitration programs with the hope that they will provide a quicker, cheaper form of justice than litigation. Certain jurisdictions, such as Pennsylvania, have used mandatory court-supervised non-binding arbitration for a long time. Other state and federal jurisdictions adopted mandatory non-binding arbitration programs during the 1980s and 1990s. Many of the federal programs were established in response to the Civil Justice Reform Act of 1990. Over half of the states had rules allowing or requiring non-binding arbitration. About a quarter of the federal district courts had a non-binding arbitration program, with ten of them requiring non-binding arbitration.[25] However, a number of federal court programs recently have replaced their mandatory non-binding arbitration programs with mediation.[26] Court-connected arbitration programs require that certain categories of disputes be heard by arbitrators before they can be aired in court. For example, Local Rule 53.2 of the Eastern District of Pennsylvania requires that virtually all suits brought for less than $150,000 proceed initially to non-binding arbitration. Nevada Arbitration Rule 3 provides that, with certain exceptions, all civil cases brought for $50,000 or less must be handled first through non-binding arbitration.

In most programs, the arbitrators are local attorneys or retired judges, but the ways in which they are chosen and conduct the arbitration may vary substantially.

Management of Cases in ADR (2001); Elizabeth Plapinger & Donna Stienstra, ADR and Settlement in the Federal District Courts: A Sourcebook for Judges & Lawyers (1996).

24. Jean Sternlight, Mandatory Binding Arbitration and the Demise of the Seventh Amendment Right to Jury Trial, 16 Ohio St. J. on Disp. Resol. 669 (2001); Dwight Golann, Making Alternative Dispute Resolution Mandatory: The Constitutional Issues, 68 Or. L. Rev. 487-568 (1989). See also Zamaro v. Price, 213 P.3d 490 (2009) (finding no right to trial by jury violated even though arbitrator's decision was shown to the jury in a de novo hearing).

25. Amy J. Schmitz, Nonconsensual + Nonbinding = Nonsensical? Reconsidering Court-Connected Arbitration Programs, 10 Cardozo J. Conflict Resol. 587 (2009).

26. Wayne Brazil, Should Court Sponsored ADR Survive? 21 Ohio St. J. on Disp. Resol. 241 (2006); Lisa B. Bingham, Why Suppose? Let's Find Out: A Public Policy Research Program on Dispute Resolution, 2002 J. Disp. Resol. 101, 120.

Some programs assign the arbitrators to a case and afford the litigants little or no opportunity to choose or even reject arbitrators, whereas other programs allow disputants to select their own arbitrators. In some programs, as in Pennsylvania, arbitrators sit in panels and hear several cases in a day. But in Nevada, court-annexed arbitrators hear cases individually and typically hear only a single matter in a day.

The economics of court-annexed arbitration also varies quite a bit. In some jurisdictions, the program is provided free to disputants, and the arbitrators serve on a volunteer basis or receive merely a small honoraria, such as $100 per case. In other jurisdictions, such as Nevada, the disputants are required to pay for court-annexed arbitration. The Nevada Arbitration Rules require disputants to pay arbitrators $100 per hour to a maximum of $1,000 per case (unless otherwise authorized by the ADR commissioner) and further require payment of up to $250 in costs to the arbitrator. These fees and costs are to be shared equally among the disputants.

The non-binding arbitration rules of many jurisdictions provide that the arbitration award becomes final and binding unless either party demands a trial de novo within a short period of time, such as 30 days. Thus, although the award is non-binding, it can easily become binding. Some jurisdictions seek to discourage parties from seeking a trial de novo by providing that a party who seeks trial de novo and secures a result less favorable than the arbitrator's award must pay a significant amount. In California a party who is unsuccessful on appeal must pay the opposing party's court costs and expert fees, and also reimburse the county or opposing party for fees paid to the arbitrator. In Nevada, where the party requesting the trial de novo fails to obtain a judgment that exceeds the arbitration award by at least 20 percent, the non-requesting party is entitled to its attorneys' fees and costs associated with the proceedings following the request for trial de novo. In other jurisdictions, the risk is far less since the party who unsuccessfully pursues a trial de novo loses only the arbitrator fees of $100 or so. E.D. Pa. Local Rule 53.2(7)(E).

Although court-mandated non-binding arbitration remains popular in some jurisdictions, it is unclear whether these programs meet the goal of resolving disputes more cheaply and quickly than through a combination of litigation and negotiation.[27]

Interestingly, non-binding arbitration was originally more popular, but today, more jurisdictions opt for mediation. Can you explain this trend? When mediation and non-binding arbitration are handled through the courts rather than privately, several interesting policy issues inevitably arise. Not surprisingly, similar issues arise with respect to other court-connected processes that we have already discussed:

---

27. Some books and articles discussing nonbinding arbitration include Amy Schmitz, supra note 25, Jane W. Adler et al., Simple Justice: How Litigants Fare in the Pittsburgh Court Arbitration Program (1983); Lisa Bernstein, Understanding the Limits of Court-Connected ADR: A Critique of Federal Court-Annexed Arbitration Programs, 141 U. Pa. L. Rev. 2169 (1993); Deborah Hensler, What We Know and Don't Know About Court-Administered Arbitration, 69 Judicature 270 (1986); Judge William P. Lynch, Problems with Court-Annexed Mandatory Arbitration: Illustrations from the New Mexico Experience, 32 N.M. L. Rev. 181 (2002); Barbara S. Meierhoefer, Court-Annexed Arbitration in Ten District Courts (1990); Note, L. Christopher Rose, Nevada's Court-Annexed Mandatory Arbitration Program: A Solution to Some of the Causes of Dissatisfaction with the Civil Justice System, 36 Idaho L. Rev. 171 (1999).

- Should the process be voluntary or mandatory from the perspective of the parties?
- Should the judge have discretion concerning which cases to order to mediation or arbitration, or should there be a set rule?
- Should mediation or arbitration be free, or should the parties pay a fee?
- What qualifications should be required of the mediators and arbitrators, and how should these be monitored?
- If mediation or arbitration is mandatory, who should be required to attend? Attorneys? Parties?
- Should the parties be required to participate in good faith? If so, how should good faith be determined?
- Should the proceedings be protected by rules regarding confidentiality or privilege?
- Should the practice of having volunteer neutrals in court-sponsored programs continue, or should neutrals be compensated like other professionals?

7. Restorative Justice: ADR in Criminal Contexts

Although most people think of using ADR only with respect to civil disputes, it is also used to handle conflicts arising in the criminal context. "Restorative justice" and "victim-offender" mediation aim to make the victim whole (or at least more whole), to instill some sense of remorse and responsibility in the offender, and, more generally, to heal the conflict and restore the fabric of communities torn apart by crime. While some programs focus on caseload reduction, most programs focus on the broader themes of forgiveness and reconciliation, with reconciliation being sought not only for its own sake but to prevent vengeance and vigilantism. These forms of ADR are used in settings ranging from neighborhood disputes and minor misdemeanors all the way up the criminal ladder to serious felonies and murder. Proponents of restorative justice advocate approaching crime and punishment from more than just a legalistic perspective.

 Marty Price, **PERSONALIZING CRIME: MEDIATION PRODUCES RESTORATIVE JUSTICE FOR VICTIMS AND OFFENDERS**

7 Disp. Resol. Mag. 8-11 (2000)

Our traditional criminal justice system is a system of retributive justice — a system of institutionalized vengeance. The system is based on the belief that justice is accomplished by assigning blame and administering pain. If you do the crime, you do the time. If you do the time, then you've paid your debt to society and justice has been done. But justice for whom?

In our system, crime is defined as an act against the state (e.g., State v. John Jones) rather than an act against individuals and their community. The prosecutor is the attorney for the state, not the harmed individuals. Victims may be viewed, at worst, as impediments to the prosecutorial process — at best, as valuable witnesses for the prosecution of the state's case. Only the most progressive prosecutor's offices view crime victims as their clients and prioritize the needs of victims.

The criminal justice system is offender-centered, placing its emphasis upon guilt, punishment and the rights of the accused. Crime victims' so-called rights are violated as often as they are honored. In most victims' rights amendments and statutes, these are rights without remedies.

Incarceration may be said to serve functions other than retribution: incapacitation, deterrence and rehabilitation. Public safety requires incapacitation of the minority of incarcerated offenders who are violent and dangerous. Intuitively, incarceration (or the threat of incarceration) may seem like a deterrent, but its proven deterrent effects are extremely limited. It is generally agreed that some rehabilitation programs work (notably, drug treatment), but rehabilitation as a goal of imprisonment has been widely abandoned by the corrections system in the United States since the 1970s. Although it is difficult to justify empirically on a broad scale, punishment appears to be a societal value in and of itself. Politicians cry out for more and longer prison terms; the building of prisons has become a major growth industry. In some states, the corrections budget exceeds the education budget.

PUNISHMENT OFTEN UNSATISFYING FOR MANY VICTIMS OF CRIME

Because our society defines justice in terms of guilt and punishment, crime victims often seek the most severe possible punishment for their offenders. Victims believe this will bring them justice, but it often leaves them feeling empty and unsatisfied. Retribution cannot restore their losses, answer their questions, relieve their fears, or help them make sense of their tragedy or heal their wounds. And punishment cannot mend the torn fabric of the community that has been violated.

FOCUS ON INDIVIDUALS, HEALING

Restorative justice has emerged as a social movement for justice reform. Virtually every state is implementing restorative justice at state, regional and/or local levels. A growing number of states that have officially adopted restorative justice principles and policies require any justice program that receives state funding to adhere to these principles.

Instead of viewing crime as a violation of law, restorative justice emphasizes one fundamental fact: crime damages people, communities and relationships. Retributive justice asks three questions: who did it, what laws were broken and what should be done to punish or treat the offender? Contrast a restorative justice inquiry, in which three very different questions receive primary emphasis. First, what is the nature of the harm resulting from the crime? Second, what needs to be done to "make it right" or repair the harm? Third, who is responsible for the repair?

Traditionally, accountability has been viewed as compliance with program rules or as taking one's punishment. But accepting punishment is passive, requiring nothing from the offender. A restorative justice system holds the offender accountable by facilitating and enforcing reparative agreements, including restitution. Restorative justice recognizes that we must give offenders the opportunity to right their wrongs and redeem themselves, in their own eyes and in the eyes of the community.

A DIFFERENT PARADIGM

Restorative justice is not any one program. It is a different paradigm for understanding and responding to issues of crime and justice. Restorative justice takes its most familiar forms in victim-offender mediation (VOM) programs and victim-offender reconciliation programs (VORP). Other restorative justice responses to crime include family group conferencing, community sentencing circles, neighborhood accountability boards, reparative probation, restitution programs, restorative community service, victim and community impact statements and victim awareness panels.

As the most common application of restorative justice principles, VOM/VORP programs warrant examination in detail. These programs bring offenders face to face with the victims of their crimes, with the assistance of a trained mediator, usually a community volunteer. Victim participation is always voluntary; offender participation is voluntary in most programs.

In mediation, crime is personalized as offenders learn the human consequences of their actions, and victims have the opportunity to speak their minds and their feelings to the one who most ought to hear them, contributing to the victim's healing. Victims get answers to haunting questions that only the offender can answer. The most commonly asked questions are "Why did you do this to me? Was this my fault? Could I have prevented this? Were you stalking or watching me?" Victims commonly report a new peace of mind, even when the answers to their questions were worse than they had feared.

Offenders take meaningful responsibility for their actions by mediating a restitution agreement with the victim to restore the victims' losses in whatever ways possible. Restitution may be monetary or symbolic; it may consist of work for the victim, community service or other actions that contribute to a sense of justice between the victim and offender.

FULFILLING RESTITUTION

VOM programs have been mediating meaningful justice between crime victims and offenders for more than 25 years. There are now more than 300 programs in the United States and Canada and more than 700 in England, Germany, Scandinavia, Eastern Europe, Australia and New Zealand. Remarkably consistent statistics from a cross-section of the North American programs show that about two-thirds of the cases referred resulted in a face-to-face mediation. More than 95 percent of the cases mediated resulted in a written restitution agreement. More than 90 percent of those restitution agreements are completed within one year. In contrast, the rate of payment of court-ordered restitution is typically only from 20 to 30 percent. Recent research has shown that juvenile offenders who participate in VOM subsequently commit fewer and less serious offenses than their counterparts in the traditional juvenile justice system. . . .

CAREFUL PREPARATION REQUIRED

Mediation is not appropriate for every crime, every victim or every offender. Individual, preliminary meetings between mediator and victim, mediator and offender permit careful screening and assessment according to established criteria. Premeetings are essential to case development, allowing for thorough preparation of participants to assure safe and successful mediation. In situations as emotionally charged as crimes, it would be difficult — in many cases impossible — to bring victims and offenders into dialogue if not for the trust each builds with the mediator.

At their best, mediation sessions focus upon dialogue rather than the restitution agreement (or settlement), facilitating empathy and understanding between victim and offender. Ground rules help assure safety and respect. Victims typically speak first, explaining the impact of the crime and asking questions of the offender. Offenders acknowledge and describe their participation in the offense, usually offering an explanation and/or apology. The victim's losses are discussed. Surprisingly, a dialogue-focused (rather than settlement-driven) approach produces the highest rates of agreement and compliance.

Agreements the victim and offender make together reflect justice that is meaningful to them, not limited by narrow legal definitions. In multistate and international (United States, Canada and United Kingdom) studies, the overwhelming majority of participants — both victims and offenders — have reported in postmediation interviews and questionnaires that they obtained a just and satisfying result. Victims who feared re-victimization by the offender before the mediation typically report this fear is now gone.

Forgiveness is not a focus of VOM, but the process provides an open space in which participants may address issues of forgiveness if they wish. Forgiveness is a process, not a goal, and it must occur according to the victim's own timing, if at all. For some victims, forgiveness may never be appropriate.

Restorative justice requires an offender who is willing to admit responsibility and remorse to the victim. Where a defendant maintains a not guilty plea in contemplation of a genuine defense — "I didn't do it," self-defense, diminished capacity, etc. — there is no place for mediation until such issues are resolved. Where a defendant maintains a pro forma not guilty plea only to preserve the possibility for plea negotiations, a restorative justice process may be appropriate.

DIFFERENT CONCEPT OF NEUTRALITY

. . . VOM requires specialized training beyond the basic skills of conflict resolution. Mediators are trained to guide the sensitive process of preparing victims and offenders to come face to face. Further advanced training is needed to mediate in crimes involving severe violence. Most victim-offender programs limit their service to juvenile offenses, crimes against property and minor assaults, but a growing number of experienced programs have found that a face-to-face encounter can be invaluable even in heinous crimes.

A number of programs have now mediated violent assaults, including rapes, and mediations have taken place between murderers and the families of their victims. Mediation has been helpful in repairing the lives of surviving family members and the offender in drunk-driving fatalities. In severe crime mediations, case development may take a year or more before the mediation can take place.

VOM may be useful at any stage of the criminal justice process. For young offenders and first- or second-time offenders, mediation may provide diversion from prosecution. In these cases, charges may be dismissed if the offender mediates an agreement with the victim and complies with its terms. After a guilty plea or a conviction, a court may refer an offender to VOM as a part of the sentence or as a term of probation. In cases of severely violent crime, VOM has not been a substitute for a prison sentence, and prison terms have seldom been reduced following mediation. Mediations have even taken place in prison. Impending release of an offender may motivate victims to seek mediation, and mediations have taken place after release from prison.

THE POWER OF REMORSE

As societal values, we want those who offend to "fess up, make amends and change their ways." Ironically, our adversarial criminal justice system conspires against these values. A defendant's role in the system is to assist his attorney in denying responsibility and avoiding consequences. The defense attorney properly advises the client to "admit nothing, say nothing." The understandable anger and bitterness that crime victims feel is often exacerbated because the defendant's stance (silence, avoidance of eye contact) communicates denial of responsibility and lack of remorse. Sadly, in many cases the defendant has, on advice of counsel, stifled a sincere desire to approach the victim in apology and contrition.

After the criminal justice system has validated such behavior as a defendant's proper role, the defendant may eventually negotiate a guilty plea or be found guilty. The issue of guilt resolved, we as a society now want the offender to shift gears and admit responsibility for the offense. Not surprisingly, such admissions are not often forthcoming.

WHAT CAN WE LEARN?

The most important lesson learned from restorative justice practice may be the realization that the key to justice is found not in laws but in the recognition and honoring of human relationships. If the application of restorative justice principles can bring justice and healing to some of the most grievous losses that human beings can suffer, the potential for more effective conflict resolution in other arenas must be considered. If crimes or disputes are not resolved with relationship values guiding the process, it is predictable that all parties may walk away feeling like losers or like victims — feeling that justice has not been done.

When lawyers are viewed as healers of conflicts, it will be a clear indicator that our justice system has become restorative in its assumptions, goals and priorities.

Regrettably, there will always be a need for adversarial processes for resolution of the situations where, sadly, the conflicts cannot be healed restoratively. In these intractable cases, we will employ the adversarial contest as the means for "alternative dispute resolution."

Problem 12-12.   *Integrating Restorative Justice*

Are there particular kinds of cases that you think are appropriate or inappropriate for this form of dispute resolution? Why? Is restorative justice possible in a world of determinate sentencing? ADR and restorative justice require discretion, flexibility, and degrees of "softness" in the system, qualities that determinate sentencing seeks to remove for reasons of justice and equity. How do we resolve these tensions? For a moving description of how restorative justice clinical instruction can address these questions in a law school setting, see Janine Geske, Symposium: Restorative Justice in Action, Why Do I Teach Restorative Justice to Law Students, 89 Marq. L. Rev. 327 (2005).

---

8. Problem-Solving Courts

With the success of restorative justice programs and the increasing emphasis on alternative forms of problem solving, some courts in the late 1980s and early 1990s developed new "multidisciplinary" or "multijurisdictional" courts to deal with and supervise more rehabilitative systems of justice. Recognizing that criminal activity often has its roots in other social problems such as drug addiction, homelessness, and family violence, such courts sentence offenders to community service rather than to jail, and provide each defendant with a detailed assessment on matters that include substance use, work record, health, and homelessness. These specialty or "unified" courts have been used in matters such as child abuse, neglect, delinquency, child custody, divorce, gun violations, drugs, and victimless crimes such as prostitution. Judge Judith Kaye, of the New York Court of Appeals, reports that preliminary evaluations of such programs in the criminal and family court contexts show signs of decreasing recidivism and changing behavior.[28] What are some of the advantages and disadvantages of courts that seek to do more than "merely" adjudicate? Has ADR come full circle when judges attempt to co-opt methods that were designed to be used outside of the courts? Can judges be remedial problem solvers, looking toward the future, as well as adjudicating the past? Note that many criminal defense and juvenile lawyers have been somewhat critical of problem-solving courts, which are seen as extensions of state power without full protection of conventional legal rights.[29] On

---

28. Judith S. Kaye, Changing Courts in Changing Times: The Need for a Fresh Look at How Courts Are Run, 48 Hastings L.J. 851 (1997).

29. Anthony C. Thompson, Courting Disorder: Some Thoughts on Community Courts, 10 Wash. U. J.L & Poly. 63 (2002). For an eloquent description and defense of these courts, see Greg Berman, John Feinblatt & Sarah Glazer, Good Courts: The Case for Problem Solving Justice (2005).

the other hand, where defendants opt to accept a diversion to "rehab" and thereby regain their sobriety, both the individual and society are winners.

C. CONCLUDING THOUGHTS ON HYBRID PROCESSES

Modifications of the four foundational processes are limited only by the imaginations of the users and designers, and we have not covered all of the possibilities here. Among other existing processes are appellate mediation/settlement conferences and consensus-building fora for public policy disputes (discussed more fully in the next chapter).

In concluding this chapter, let us recapitulate a few themes of this book by asking these questions: If "appropriate" or "alternative" forms of dispute resolution are suggested to compensate for or supplement problematic aspects of the conventional legal system, what happens when the alternatives present problems of their own? Should we revert to traditional litigation or seek to fix the problems with alternative processes? Or should we create new alternatives? Are there some basic fault lines we should continue to observe between private and public institutions? Between consensual and mandated processes? In respecting the neutrality of the third party? Carrie Menkel-Meadow raises below the question of whether the hybrid blending and institutionalization of ADR processes may, in fact, jeopardize the values underlying the ADR processes.

 Carrie Menkel-Meadow, **PURSUING SETTLEMENT IN AN ADVERSARY CULTURE: A TALE OF INNOVATION CO-OPTED OR "THE LAW OF ADR"**

19 Fla. St. U. L. Rev. 1, 13-14, 16-17, 32-33, 35-39 (1991)

What has this "institutionalization" meant? Has the growth and expansion of alternative dispute resolution institutions changed the consciousness of those whose job it is to solve legal problems? In my view, the qualified answer to these questions is no. This is illustrated by the cases which are now beginning to deal with some of the difficult legal issues raised by the uses of ADR. As we survey some of these developments, I suggest that attempts to innovate have been partly, if not totally, "captured" and co-opted by the uses to which advocates have put these new procedures. At the same time, advocates "attacking" or "manipulating" ADR may tell us something about its limits and abuses in the court system and alert us to the regulatory boundaries that may be necessary to keep each process working within its proper sphere.

I was first struck by the omnipresence of the adversary model when, as a mediator for the Asbestos Claim Facility, I received a copy of a letter in which one party had "filed an ADR proceeding *against*" the other party. The fact that the process had been labeled a mediation process did nothing to move the parties away from their adversarial perceptions of each other. The ADR proceeding of "mediation" was just a condition precedent to be attended to on the way to litigation. As the parties engaged in more disputing about the rules of the proceedings, it became clear that ADR was just another stop in the "litigation" game which provides an opportunity for the manipulation of rules, time, information, and ultimately, money.

As ADR has been increasingly used by courts and by private institutions of dispute resolution, it has been increasingly "legalized" — made the subject of legal regulation, in both private and public rules systems. Skillful lawyers are raising legitimate claims regarding the constitutionality of some of the aspects of ADR — such as infringements of the right to a jury trial, separation of powers, due process, and equal protection. Other claims which may not be as legitimate — such as refusing to participate in arbitration by claiming that it is coerced discovery — demonstrate that ADR has become just another battleground for adversarial fighting rather than multi-dimensional problem-solving.

For those of us who have sought to improve the quality of justice by changing orientations of lawyers and parties about how to solve legal problems, the use of new forms of dispute resolution within the courts has been a mixed blessing. . . . The use of settlement activity in the courts should be understood as the clash of two cultures. To the extent that settlement activity seeks to promote consensual agreement through the analysis of the point of view of the other side, it requires some different skills and a very different mind-set from what litigators usually employ. Thus, the issue is whether judges and lawyers in the courts can learn to reorient their cultures and behaviors when trying to settle cases or whether those seeking settlement continue to do so from an adversarial perspective. To the extent that we cannot identify different behaviors in each sphere, we may see the corruption of both processes. If one of the purposes of the legal system is to specify legal entitlements from which settlements may be measured, or from which the parties may depart if they so choose, then having adjudicators engage in too much mediative conduct may compromise the ability of judges to engage in both fact-finding and rulemaking. If courts fail to provide sufficient baselines in their judgments, we will have difficulties determining if particular settlements are wise or truly consensual. There is danger in the possibility that good settlement practice will be marred by over-zealous advocacy or by over-zealous desire to close cases that may require either full adjudication or a public hearing. . . .

In an important sense, the ADR movement represents a case study in the difficulties of legal reform when undertaken by different groups within the legal system. At the beginning were the *conceptualizers* — academics and judicial activists who developed both the critique of the adversary system and, in some cases, the design of alternative systems of dispute resolution. The *implementers* developed the concrete forms these innovations took when they moved into the legal system. Some of the *conceptualizers* — Frank Sander and several of the judges — were also *implementers*. In addition, other judges and judicial administrators principally concerned about case load management, and about the quality of solutions or decisions, became *implementers*. Support for the implementation of these ADR programs came from the principal foundation and government funding sources, as well as from groups of change-oriented practicing lawyers who played an important catalytic role in supporting and using some of the first alternative procedures.

Finally, the *constituents* of these ADR systems — lawyers and their clients as consumers — were "acted upon," sometimes somewhat consensually, by the force of court rules or judicial encouragement. We are just beginning to see some of their reactions in the litigation developing from ADR innovation and in evaluation research.

Each of these groups of actors within the ADR legal reform movement inhabit different cultural worlds — academia, the judiciary, law practice, the business world, and everyday life. Each group uses, transforms, and "colonizes" the work of the others. The research of academics is ignored or simplified; judges move cases along and adopt the language of case management rather than justice; lawyers "infect" clients with a desire for adversarial advantage, or in other cases clients do the same to lawyers; and professionals argue about credentialing and standards for the new profession.

In my view, productive discourse about ADR will have to transcend the language of these cultural differences. Academics, and particularly those who theorize about jurisprudential concerns, need to root their views in the practicalities of our empirical world. Occasionally, judges and legal practitioners need to step back and review the larger jurisprudential and policy issues implicated in "quick-fix" reforms. Practitioners and clients need to consider new forms of practice and process while diminishing their adversarial ways of thinking. A professional life should be one of re-examination, growth, and change. If we are really looking for new ways to process disputes — both to increase case-processing efficiency and to promote better quality solutions — then we have to be willing to look critically at the innovations and their effects from all quarters. I believe that social innovation and transformation are possible here — the issues are whether conventional mind-sets will "infect" these innovations on the one hand, or whether the "cure" will be worse than the disease on the other.

Problem 12-13.   *Multi-Doors Under One Courthouse Roof?*

To what extent will courts lose their legitimacy as courts if they perform too many other kinds of case processing within their walls? If the "other" processes are not considered legitimate within public institutions, they may be legally challenged and transformed into watered-down versions of court adjudication. No longer "alternatives," these watered-down versions may violate the legal rights and rules our courts are intended to safeguard. Can theorists, practitioners, and citizens change our views of what courts should do? What forms of ADR should be institutionalized?

Further Reading

James J. Alfini, *Summary Jury Trials in State and Federal Courts: A Comparative Analysis of the Perceptions of Participating Lawyers*, 4 OHIO ST. J. ON DISP. RESOL. 213-233 (1989).

Greg Berman, John Feinblatt & Sarah Glazer. (2005). *Good Courts: The Case for Problem Solving Justice.* New York: New Press.

Robert C. Bordone, *Electronic Online Dispute Resolution: A Systems Approach — Potential Problems, and a Proposal*, 3 HARV. NEGOT. L. REV. 3:175-193 (1998).

Wayne D. Brazil, *A Close Look at Three Court Sponsored ADR Programs: Why They Exist, How They Operate, What They Deliver, and Whether They Threaten Important Values*, 1990 UNIV. OF CHICAGO LEGAL F. 303 (1990).

CPR Corporate Dispute Management (E. Green, Ed.). (1982). *The CPR Legal Program Mini-Trial Handbook.* New York: CPR.

Kenneth Feinberg. (2005). *What's a Life Worth?: The Unprecedented Program to Compensate Victims of 9/11.* New York: PublicAffairs.

Harvard Negotiation Law Review. (2009). *Symposium on Dispute System Design.* 14 HARV. NEGOT. L. REV. 1-342.

James S. Kakalik, Terence Dunworth, Laural Hill, Daniel McCaffrey, Marian Oshiro, Nicolas Pace & Mary, E. Vaiana. (1996). *An Evaluation of Mediation and Early Neutral Evaluation Under the Civil Justice Reform Act.* Santa Monica, Calif: RAND.

Ethan Katsh & Janet Rifkin. (2001). *Online Dispute Resolution: Resolving Conflicts in Cyberspace.* San Francisco: Jossey-Bass Publishers.

John Maull, *ADR in the Federal Courts: Would Uniformity Be Better?*, DUQ. L. REV. 34: 245 (1996).

Carrie Menkel-Meadow. (2007). Restorative Justice: What Is It and Does it Work? In *Annual Review of Law and Social Science.* Palo Alto, California: Annual Reviews.

Michael L. Moffitt & Robert C. Bordone (Eds.). (2005). *Handbook of Dispute Resolution.* San Francisco: Jossey-Bass Publishers.

Mary Rowe, *The Ombudsman's Role in a Dispute Resolution System*, 7 NEGOTIATION J. 353 (1991).

Elizabeth Plapinger & Donna Stienstra. (1996). *ADR and Settlement in the Federal District Courts.* Washington, D.C.: Federal Judicial Center.

Andrea Kupfer Schneider, *The Intersection of Dispute Systems Design and Transitional Justice,* 14 HARV. NEGOT. L. REV. 289 (2009).

Andrea Kupfer Schneider, *Not Quite a World Without Trials: Why International Dispute Resolution Is Increasingly Judicialized,* J. DIS. RESOL., 119 (2006).

Jeffrey M. Senger. (2003). *Federal Dispute Resolution: Using ADR with the U.S. Government.* San Francisco: Jossey-Bass Publishers.

William Ury, Jeanne Brett & Stephen B. Goldberg. (1988). *Getting Disputes Resolved: Designing Systems to Cut the Cost of Conflict.* San Francisco: Jossey-Bass Publishers.

Douglas H. Yarn. (1999). *Dictionary of Conflict Resolution.* San Francisco: Jossey-Bass Publishers.

Chapter 15 | # Multiparty Dispute Resolution

Many disputes involve more than just two parties (a plaintiff and a defendant) and more than one or two issues. Even a seemingly simple personal injury case often involves multiple parties, including those who are not formally part of any lawsuit — the injured party, his or her family members, insurance companies, employers, manufacturers, or retailers. Complex cases or disputes such as class actions, mass torts, civil rights cases, environmental matters, corporate cases, and regulatory matters always involve more than two parties. Sometimes the number, complexity, and importance of issues and parties call for new approaches to dispute resolution.

Increasingly, those who study dispute resolution analyze how what they know about negotiation, mediation, arbitration, and adjudication might have to be adapted when there are more than two parties. Many new forms of conflict resolution are specially designed to deal with multiparty processes, both in public or governmental settings, and in private disputes. Negotiated rule making ("reg-neg") in the administrative context and consensus-building fora for public policy disputes (such as in environmental siting or community disputes) are two examples. Consider how the Obama administration has attempted to broaden democratic participation by using town hall meetings throughout the country to discuss proposals for reform of the health care system, the economy, and financial crises and other important policy changes.[1]

This chapter will introduce new concepts and principles for multiparty contexts. The formation of coalitions and alliances between some parties and "defections" by others change the dynamics of negotiation. With more people and complexity, organizational challenges are compounded, calling for more formal management of dispute resolution processes. At an institutional level, the field of Dispute System Design seeks to develop organizational, systematic, and rationalized means of handling conflict in complex and iterated settings. Applying dispute resolution theory and skills to complex transactions is another emerging field that is addressed in this chapter.

New practice and skill sets are required for managing meetings and facilitating group process. The "appropriateness" of particular processes must be considered. Do

---

1. See *www.whitehouse.gov* for announcements of "public comments," "public listening," and "town hall" events.

they work? Are they ethical? For example, who decides who participates? What sort of discourse is permitted or encouraged? What is the relation between our democratic principles and the processes we create?

Consider these additional questions as you read this chapter:

1. Are all relevant stakeholders able to participate in the particular form of multiparty dispute resolution?
2. How does this form of dispute resolution fit within our constitutional framework of government?
3. When might these new or different processes be "better" at solving some legal, political, or human problems than the processes we are currently using?

A. MULTIPARTY DISPUTE PROCESSES: HOW ARE THEY DIFFERENT?

The readings in this section suggest some of the ways in which multiparty dispute resolution may differ from dyadic (negotiation) or triadic (mediation or arbitration) processes. See if you can think of particular ways in which adding more parties changes some of the basic principles of negotiation, mediation, and arbitration practices, processes, and law.

This first section explores how some negotiation theorists (Robert Mnookin, Leigh Thompson, and James Sebenius) describe differences in two-party versus more-than-two-party negotiations. These authors provide guidance for thinking about and making choices in situations where coalitions are likely to form. It then presents some of the problems that can develop in group negotiations (including the two extremes of "groupthink" or more divergent and extreme positions). It then presents some of the ways in which multiparty negotiations have been organized and institutionalized in different settings, and considers their legitimacy in legal and constitutional terms.

1. Negotiating with More Than Two Parties: Coalitions and Groups

 Robert H. Mnookin, **STRATEGIC BARRIERS TO DISPUTE RESOLUION: A COMPARISON OF BILATERAL AND MULTILATERAL NEGOTIATIONS**

159 J. Institutional & Theoretical Econ. 200-201, 219 (2003)

I suggest that Pareto-criterion[2] may not provide an appropriate standard to evaluate issues of efficiency in multiparty bargaining. In a two party case, any negotiated deal

---

2. The Pareto-criterion is that gains or improvements to negotiated outcomes should be pursued if any continue to cause benefit for one party without harm to the other. This criterion may assume only

presumably better serves the parties than the *status quo*. The same could be said in a multiparty negotiation only if the consent of *every party* were necessary. A requirement of unanimity in multilateral negotiation, however, creates potential holdout problems that may pose severe strategic barriers to resolution. This problem can be mitigated if the consent of less than all the parties can permit action. But other problems may arise. If conditions of less than all are able to change the *status quo*, this necessarily means that a party left out of a coalition may potentially be made worse off.

A variety of procedural rules may permit decision-making without unanimity in multiparty negotiations. Majority voting is but one of many possible mechanisms to allocate decision-making authority. The outcome of any multilateral negotiation can be profoundly affected by these procedural rules and various decisions concerning agenda. [Another part of this paper] briefly explores the application of an unusual procedural rule — the "sufficient consensus" standard — that was employed in the multiparty "constitutional" negotiations in South Africa and in Northern Ireland . . .

[M]y own belief is that no theoretical perspective, and no single discipline, has a monopoly on useful insights concerning the barriers to the fair and efficient resolution of conflict. Indeed, I suspect that progress will turn very fundamentally on the ability of people from different disciplines to learn from one another and to work together to improve theory and practice. Our goal should ultimately be to go beyond simply understanding why negotiations sometimes fail and sometimes succeed — it should be to help us overcome the barriers and achieve more consistent success in the negotiated resolution of conflict.

 Leigh L. Thompson, **THE MIND AND HEART OF THE NEGOTIATOR**

221-227, 230-236 (4th ed. 2009)

KEY CHALLENGES OF MULTIPARTY NEGOTIATIONS

There are several challenges at both the cognitive (mind) and the emotional (heart) level that crop up in multiparty negotiations. We present four key challenges of multiparty negotiations and follow with some practical advice [on dealing with coalitions, formulating trade-offs, voting and majority rule, and communication breakdowns].

Dealing with Coalitions

A key difference between two-party and group negotiations is the potential for two or more parties within a group to form a coalition to pool their resources and have a greater influence on outcomes. A **coalition** is a (sub) group of two or more individuals who join together in using their resources to affect the outcome of a

---

two parties. Gains and harms may become more difficult to hold constant or without affecting other parties if there are more than two parties.

decision in a mixed-motive situation involving at least three parties. For example, parties may seek to maximize control over other members, maximize their status in the group, maximize similarity of attitudes and values, or minimize conflict among members. Coalition formation is one way that otherwise weak group members may marshal a greater share of resources. Coalitions involve both cooperation and competition: Members of coalitions cooperate with one another in competition against other coalitions, but compete against one another regarding the allocation of rewards the coalition obtains. . . .

Formulating Trade-Offs

Integrative agreements are more difficult to fashion in multiparty negotiations because the trade-offs are more complex. In a multiparty negotiation, integrative trade-offs may be achieved either through circular or reciprocal logrolling. **Circular logrolling** involves trade-offs that require each group member to offer another member a concession on one issue while receiving a concession from yet another group member on a different issue. A circular trade-off is typified by the tradition of drawing names from a hat to give holiday gifts to people. People receive a gift from one person and give a gift to yet another person. Ideally, we give gifts that are more appreciated by the recipient than by the giver. In contrast, **reciprocal trade-offs** are fashioned between two members of a larger group. Reciprocal tradeoffs are typified in the more traditional form of exchanging presents. Circular tradeoffs are more risky than reciprocal trade-offs because they involve the cooperation of more than two group members.

Voting and Majority Rule

Groups often simplify the negotiation of multiple issues among multiple parties through voting and decision rules. However, if not used wisely, decision rules can thwart effective negotiation, both in terms of pie expansion and pie slicing. There are a number of problems associated with voting that we will now describe.

Problems with Voting and Majority Rule

Voting is the procedure of collecting individuals' preferences for alternatives on issues and selecting the most popular alternative as the group choice. The most common procedure used to aggregate preferences of team members is **majority rule**. However, majority rule presents several problems in the attainment of efficient negotiation settlements. Despite its democratic appeal, majority rule fails to recognize the strength of individual preferences. One person in a group may feel very strongly about an issue, but his or her vote counts the same as the vote of someone who does not have a strong opinion about the issue. Consequently, majority rule does not promote integrative trade-offs among issues. In fact, groups negotiating under unanimous rule reach more efficient outcomes than groups operating under majority rule.

   Although unanimity rule is time consuming, it encourages group members to consider creative alternatives to expand the size of the pie and satisfy the interests of all group members. Because strength of preference is a key component in the fashioning of integrative agreements, majority rule hinders the development of mutually beneficial trade-offs.

There are other problems with voting. Group members may not agree upon a method for voting; for example, some members may insist upon unanimity, others may argue for a simple majority rule, and still others may advocate a weighted majority rule. Even if a voting method is agreed upon, it may not yield a choice. For example, a group may not find a majority if there is an even split in the group. Voting does not eliminate conflicts of interest, but instead, provides a way for group members to live with conflicts of interest; for this reason, majority rule decisions may not be stable. In this sense, voting hides disagreement within groups, which threatens long-term group and organizational effectiveness.

Voting Paradoxes

Consider a three-person (Raines, Warner, and Lassiter) product development team. The three are in conflict over which design to use — A, B, or C.

The preference ordering is depicted in Table 9-3. Everyone is frustrated, and the group has argued for hours. As a way of resolving the conflict, Warner suggests voting between designs A and B. In that vote A wins, and B is tossed in the trash. Warner then proposes that the group vote between A and C. In that vote, C wins. Warner then declares that design C be implemented. Lassiter concludes that the group vote was fair and agrees to develop design C. However, Raines is perplexed and suggests taking another vote. Warner laughs and says "We just took a vote and you lost — so just accept the outcome!" Raines glares at Warner and says, "Let's do the vote again, and I will agree to accept the outcome. However, this time I want us to vote between B and C first." Warner has no choice but to go along. In this vote B is the clear winner, and C is eliminated. Next, the vote is between A and B, and A beats B. Raines happily declares A the winner. Lassiter then jumps up and declares that the whole voting process was fraudulent, but cannot explain why.

Table 9-3
Managers' Preferences for Product Designs

MANAGER	DESIGN A	DESIGN B	DESIGN C
Raines	1	2	3
Warner	2	3	1
Lassiter	3	1	2

Raines, Warner, and Lassiter are victims of the **Condorcet paradox**. The Condorcet paradox demonstrates that the winners of majority rule elections will change as a function of the *order* in which alternatives are proposed. Alternatives that are proposed later, as opposed to earlier, are more likely to survive sequential voting. Thus, clever negotiators arrange to have their preferred alternatives entered at later stages of a sequential voting process.

The unstable voting outcomes of the product development team point to a larger concern, known as the **impossibility theorem**, which states that the derivation of group preference from individual preference is indeterminate. Simply put, there is no method of combining group members' preferences that guarantees that group preference has been maximized when groups have three or more members and there are three or more options. That is, even though each manager's preferences are transitive, the group-level preference is intransitive.

Strategic Voting

The problem of indeterminate group choice is further compounded by the temptation for members to **strategically misrepresent** their true preferences so that a preferred option is more likely to be favored by the group. For example, a group member may vote for his least-preferred option to ensure that the second choice option is killed. Raines could have voted strategically in the first election to ensure that his preferred strategy was not eliminated in the first round.

Consensus Decisions

Consensus agreements require the consent of all parties to the negotiation before an agreement is binding. However, consensus agreements do not imply unanimity. For an agreement to be unanimous, parties must agree inwardly as well as outwardly. Consensus agreements imply that parties agree *publicly* to a particular settlement, even though their *private* views about the situation may be in conflict.

Although consensus agreements are desirable, there are several problems with them. They are time consuming because they require the consent of all members, who are often not in agreement. Second, they often lead to compromise, in which parties identify a lowest common denominator acceptable to all. Compromise agreements are an extremely easy method of reaching agreement and are compelling because they appear to be fair, but they are usually inefficient because they fail to exploit potential pareto-improving trade-offs.

Communication Breakdowns

Most people take communication for granted in their interactions with multiple parties. In a perfect communication system, a sender transmits or sends a message that is accurately received by a recipient. There are at least three points of possible error: The sender may fail to send a message; the message may be sent, but is inaccurate or distorted; or an accurate message is sent, but is distorted or not received by the recipient. In a multiparty environment, the complexity grows when several people are simultaneously sending and receiving messages.

Private Caucusing

When groups grow large, communication among all parties is difficult. One way of simplifying negotiations is for negotiators to communicate in smaller groups, thereby avoiding full-group communication. Group members often form private caucuses for strategic purposes. However, private caucusing may cause problems. Full-group communication is more time consuming but enhances equality of group members' outcomes, increases joint profitability, and minimizes perceptions of competition. However, there is a caveat to the benefits of full communication. When the task structure requires group members to logroll in a reciprocal fashion (as opposed to a circular fashion), restricted communication leads to higher joint outcomes than full communication . . .

Perspective-Taking Failures

People are remarkably poor at taking the perspective of others. For example, people who are privy to information and knowledge that they know others are not aware of nevertheless act as if others are aware of it, even though it would be impossible for the receiver to have this knowledge. This problem is known as the **curse of knowledge**. For example, in a simulation, traders who possessed privileged information that could have been used to their advantage behaved as if their trading partners also had access to the privileged information. Perspective-taking deficiencies also explain why some instructors who understand an idea perfectly are unable to teach students the same idea. They are unable to put themselves in their students' shoes to explain the idea in a way the students can understand. . . .

Multiple Audience Problem

In some negotiation situations, negotiators need to communicate with another person in the presence of someone who should not understand the message. For example, consider a couple selling a house having a face-to-face discussion with a potential buyer. Ideally, the couple wants to communicate information to one another in a way that the spouse understands but the buyer does not — better yet, in such a way that the buyer is not even aware that a surreptitious communication is taking place. [This is called] the **multiple audience problem**. . . .

COALITIONS

Coalitions face three sets of challenges: (1) the formation of the coalition, (2) coalition maintenance, and (3) the distribution of resources among coalition members. Next, we take up these challenges and provide strategies for maximizing coalition effectiveness.

KEY CHALLENGES OF COALITIONS

Optimal Coalition Size

What is the ideal size for a winning coalition? Ideally, coalitions should contain the minimum number of people sufficient to achieve a desired goal. Coalitions are difficult to maintain because members are tempted by other members to join other coalitions, and agreements are not enforceable.

Trust and Temptation in Coalitions

Coalitional integrity is a function of the costs and rewards of coalitional membership; when coalitions are no longer rewarding, people will leave them. Nevertheless, there is a strong pull for members of coalitions to remain intact even when it is not rational to do so. According to the **status quo bias**, even when a new coalition structure that offers greater gain is possible, members are influenced by a norm of

coalitional integrity, such that they stick with their current coalition. The implication is that negotiators should form coalitions early so as to not be left without coalitional partners.

Dividing the Pie

The distribution of resources among members of coalitions is complex because a normative method of fair allocation does not exist. To illustrate this consider the following example. Lindholm, Tepe, and Clauson are three small firms producing specialized products, equipment, and research for the rehabilitation medicine community. This area has become a critical, high-growth industry, and each firm is exploring ways to expand and improve its technologies through innovations in the research and development (R&D) divisions. Each firm has recently applied for R&D funding from the National Rehabilitation Medicine Research Council (NRMR).

The NRMR is a government agency dedicated to funding research in rehabilitation medicine and treatment. The NRMR is willing to provide funds for the proposed research, but because the firms' requests are so similar, they will fund only a **consortium** of two or three firms. The NRMR will not grant funding to Lindholm, Tepe, or Clauson alone.

Table 9-5
Maximum Funding Caps as a Function of Parties in Consortium

ORGANIZATIONS IN CONSORTIUM	CAP FOR R&D FUNDING
Lindholm alone	0
Tepe alone	0
Clauson alone	0
Lindholm and Tepe	$220,000
Lindholm and Clauson	$190,000
Tepe and Clauson	$150,000
Lindholm, Tepe, and Clauson	$240,000

The largest of the three firms is Lindholm, followed by Tepe, and then Clauson. The NRMR took a variety of factors into consideration when they set caps on funding, as shown in Table 9-5.

The NRMR has strictly stipulated that for a consortium of firms to receive funding, the parties in the consortium (either two or three firms) must be in complete agreement concerning the allocation of resources among firms.

If you are Lindholm, what consortium would you consider to be the best for you? Obviously, you want to be in on some consortium, with either Tepe or Clauson or both, to avoid being left out in the cold. But what is the best division of resources within each of those consortiums? Suppose that you approach Tepe about a two-way venture, and Tepe proposes that she receive half of the $220,000 or $110,000 for herself. You argue that because you are bigger, and bring more synergy to the agreement, you should earn more. You demand $200,000 for yourself, leaving $20,000 for Tepe. At this point, Tepe threatens to leave you and approach Clauson. Tepe argues that she and Clauson can command $150,000 as a consortium without you, and each can receive $75,000. At this point, you argue that you can outbid her offer to Clauson with $80,000 and keep $110,000 for yourself. Just as Tepe is threatening to overbid you for Clauson, Clauson steps in and tells Tepe that she would want at least $100,000 of the $150,000 pie that she and Tepe could command. Tepe is frustrated, but relents.

You get nervous in your role as Lindholm. You certainly do not want to be left out. You could attempt to get Clauson or Tepe in a consortium. But, then, a thought occurs to you: Maybe all three of you can be in a consortium. After all, all three firms command the greatest amount of funding ($240,000). But how should the $240,000 be divided [among] the three of you? You are the biggest firm, so you propose that you keep half of the $240,000 (or $120,000), that Tepe get $80,000, and that Clauson get $40,000. This strikes you as fair. At this point, Clauson gets upset and tells you that she and Tepe can go it alone and get $150,000. She thinks that your share is unfair and should be reduced to something less than $90,000. You then remind Clauson that you and Tepe can get $190,000 together, of which you certainly deserve at least half, which is better than the $90,000 offer. Then the three of you are at it again in a vicious circle of coalition formation and demolition.

The negotiation between Lindholm, Tepe, and Clauson illustrates the unstable nature of coalitions. In this example, the left-out party is always able to approach one of the two parties in the coalition and offer him or her a better deal, which can then be beaten by the remaining party, ad infinitum. Furthermore, splitting the pie three ways seems to offer no obvious solution. So, what should the three parties do? Is there a solution? Or are the parties destined to go around in circles forever?

Getting Out of the Vicious Circle

As a way out of the vicious circle, let's conceptualize the problem as a system of simultaneous equations to solve. Namely,

$$
\begin{aligned}
L + T &= \$220,000 \\
L + C &= \$190,000 \\
T + C &= \$150,000 \\
L + T + C &= \$240,000 \\
L + T + C &= (\$220,000 + \$190,000 + \$150,000)/2 \\
&= \$560,000/2 \\
&= \$280,000 \text{ total funds needed}
\end{aligned}
$$

However, it is impossible to solve all simultaneous equations. We are $40,000 short of satisfying each party's minimum needs. What should we do? Consider the following three solutions: the core solution, the Shapley solution, and a hybrid model.

The Core Solution.   The core solution is a set of alternatives that are undominated. An alternative is in the core if no coalition has both the power and desire to overthrow it.

The first step in computing the core solution is to determine what would be each party's share if there were no shortage of funds. Thus, we solve for L, T, and C shares as follows:

$$(L + T) - (L + C) = \$220,000 - 190,000$$
$$= (T - C) = \$30,000$$
$$(L + T) - (T + C) = \$220,000 - \$150,000$$
$$= (L - C) = \$70,000$$
$$(T + C) + (T - C) = \$150,000 + \$30,000$$
$$2T = \$180,000$$
$$T = \$90,000$$
$$L + T = \$220,000$$
$$L + \$90,000 = \$220,000$$
$$L = \$220,000 - \$90,000$$
$$L = \$130,000$$
$$L + C = \$190,000$$
$$\$130,000 + C = \$190,000$$
$$C = \$190,000 - \$130,000$$
$$C = \$60,000$$

check:
$$L = \$130,000$$
$$T = \$90,000$$
$$C = \$60,000$$
$$\text{Total} = \$280,000$$

Thus, if we had a total of $280,000, we could solve each equation. But, the harsh reality is that we do not. So, the second step is to get the total down to $240,000 by deducting $40,000 from somewhere. In the absence of any particular argument as to why one party's share should be cut, we deduct an equal amount, $13,333, from each party's share. In the final step, we compute the "core" shares as follows:

Lindholm: $116,670
Tepe: $76,670
Clauson: $46,670

As Lindholm, you are delighted. Tepe agrees, but Clauson is not happy. She thinks that $46,670 is too little. She hires an outside consultant to evaluate the situation. The consultant proposes a different method, called the Shapley model.

The Shapley model. Consider a coalition formation in which one player starts out alone and then is joined by a second and third player. The Shapley model determines the overall payoff a player can expect on the basis of his or her **pivotal power**, or the ability to change a losing coalition into a winning coalition. The consultant considers all possible permutations of players joining coalitions one at a time. The marginal value added to each coalition's outcome is attributed to the pivotal player. The Shapley value is the mean of a player's added value (see Table 9-6). When all players bring equal resources, the Shapley value is the total amount of resources divided by the total number of people. This, of course, is the "equal division" principle, as well as the "equity principle."

Table 9-6
Analysis of Pivotal Power in Shapley Model

ORDER OF JOINING	LINDHOLM ADDED VALUE	TEPE ADDED VALUE	CLAUSON ADDED VALUE
LTC	0	$220,000	$ 20,000
LCT	0	50,000	190,000
TLC	$220,000	0	20,000
TCL	90,000	0	150,000
CLT	190,000	50,000	0
CTL	90,000	150,000	0
Shapley (average)[2]	98,333	78,333	63,333

[2]These figures are rounded slightly.

When Clauson's consultant presents this report, Clauson is delighted — her share has increased by almost $20,000. Lindholm is nonplussed because her share has decreased. Tepe is tired of all the bickering and proposes that they settle for something in between the two proposed solutions.

Raiffa's hybrid model. We have presented two models to solve for shares in coalition situations. The medium-power player's share in both models is identical, but the high- and low-power player's shares fluctuate quite dramatically. It is possible that an egocentric argument could ensue between Lindholm and Clauson as to which model to employ. One solution is a hybrid model in which the mean of the Shapley and core values is computed. This model yields the following shares:

Lindholm: $107,500
Tepe: $77,500
Clauson: $55,000

Tips for Low-Power Players.   We presented three different models of fair solutions. Each is compelling and defensible because each makes explicit the logic underlying the division of resources. It is easy to be a high-power player in coalition situations. However, the real trick is to know how to be an effective low-power player. Weakness can be power if you can recognize and disrupt unstable coalitions.

Power is intimately involved in the formation of coalitions and the allocation of resources among coalition members. Power imbalance among coalition members can be detrimental for the group. Compared to egalitarian power relationships, unbalanced power relationships produce more coalitions defecting from the larger group, fewer integrative agreements, greater likelihood of bargaining impasse, and more competitive behavior. Power imbalance makes power issues salient to group members, whose primary concern is to protect their own interests. What is best for the coalition is often not what is best for the organization.

Is there an optimal way for multiple parties to allocate resources so that group members are not tempted to form coalitions that may hinder group welfare? Usually not. Whereas there are several defensible ways to allocate resources among coalition members, there is no single best way.

STRATEGIES FOR MAXIMIZING COALITIONAL EFFECTIVENESS

Make Your Contacts Early

Because of the commitment process, people tend to feel obligated to others with whom they have made explicit or implicit agreements. For this reason, it is important to make contact with key parties early in the process of multiparty negotiation before they become psychologically committed to others.

Seek Verbal Commitments

One of the most effective strategies for enhancing coalitional effectiveness is to obtain verbal commitments from people with whom you want to develop trust and follow-through. Most people feel obligated to follow through with promises they make to others, even when verbal commitments are not legally binding in any sense.

Allocate Resources among Coalitional Members Fairly

If one or more members of the coalition regard the proposed allocation of resources to be unfair, the coalition will be less stable and they will be likely to renege. To the extent to which coalitional members feel that the distribution of the coalition pie is fair, they are more likely to resist persuasion from others to break away from the coalition.

James K. Sebenius, **MAPPING BACKWARD: NEGOTIATING IN THE RIGHT SEQUENCE?**

Negotiation 7, No. 6 (June 2004). Reprinted as "A Better Way to Negotiate: Backward" in Working Knowledge, July 26, 2004

How often have you heard that, when entering a negotiation, you should get your allies onboard first? Conventional wisdom, but not always the best advice. When the United States sought to build a global anti-Iraq coalition following Iraq's 1990 invasion of Kuwait, for instance, Israel appeared to be its strongest regional ally. Yet because Israel's formal membership might have kept numerous Arab states from joining the coalition, the U.S. government pointedly excluded the Israelis, starting negotiations elsewhere. Careful sequencing plus tacit Israeli membership avoided a potential setback.

Here's another bit of conventional wisdom on proper sequencing: "Get your own house in order first." Yet this was not the path that President George H. W. Bush followed in preparing for the first Gulf War. Instead of approaching Congress first, Bush committed U.S. troops to the region, built international political and military coalitions, and negotiated a U.N. Security Council Resolution authorizing "all necessary means" to eject Iraq from Kuwait. Only after these steps were taken did the Bush administration begin negotiating in earnest for congressional approval to use force in the Gulf.

Had Bush first approached a deeply skeptical Congress, agreement on the use of force would have been unlikely. A negative vote would have stymied any subsequent American efforts to build an international coalition. Getting the right players involved at the right moment opened the door to success. Getting the sequence wrong could have led to failure.

Though often overlooked, sequencing matters greatly in negotiation. Whether you're trying to get the "right" people to attend a charity event, invest in a new venture, or sign onto a complex deal, you'll face elaborate sequencing choices. With whom should you speak first? Whom next? Rules of thumb such as "allies first" or "negotiate internally, then externally" are unreliable guides. Yet a more effective approach, the logic of backward mapping, can help you choose your partners wisely — and negotiate in the right order.

SORTING OUT THE POSSIBILITIES

When Steve Perlman was preparing to launch WebTV in 1996, he faced a critical sequencing dilemma. He had obtained seed funding, developed the technology to bring the Internet to ordinary television sets, created a prototype, and hired core technical and management team members. Now running desperately low on cash, Perlman had to contend with many potential deal partners, including VCs, angels, and industrial partners (as potential sources of cash); consumer electronics firms, Internet service providers (ISPs), and content providers (for possible alliances and partnerships); manufacturers (for manufacturing set-top boxes); non-U.S. licensees; and wholesale and retail distributors (for sales). With his promising venture running on fumes, Perlman's next obvious negotiation might have been with venture capital firms for funding. Yet Perlman knew that, while VCs might have been willing to make small investments in his new firm, they were, at the time, quite wary of making major financial commitments to consumer electronics plays such as WebTV.

Instead, Perlman mapped backward from his VC target, reasoning that WebTV's appeal and value to the VCs would be greatly enhanced by partnership with a prominent consumer electronics firm. Perlman started by pitching his product to Sony, his first choice, which initially turned him down. But he then negotiated successfully with Philips and used the agreement to forge a complementary deal with Sony. With Sony and Philips onboard, Perlman was able to negotiate for VC money — at a far higher valuation. With this additional funding, Perlman had little difficulty threading a path of supporting agreements through manufacturers, wholesale and retail distribution channels, content providers, ISPs, and alliance partners abroad — and ultimately sold his young but thriving business to Microsoft for $425 million.

THE LOGIC OF BACKWARD MAPPING

When you map a negotiation backward, you envision your preferred outcome and think in reverse about how to get there. Here are the basic steps:

1. Draw a "map" of the parties who are currently involved and those who might potentially get onboard, along with their interests and their no-deal options.
2. Estimate the difficulty and cost of gaining agreement with each party as well as the value of having that person or group onboard.
3. Identify key relationships among the parties: who influences whom, who tends to defer to whom, who owes something to whom, and so on.
4. Focus on the most-difficult-to-persuade player — your ultimate target or someone else who's critical to the deal. Ask these questions: Which *prior* agreement or agreements among which set of the other players — if such agreements were in place — would maximize the chances of the target saying yes on your terms? Whom would you like to have onboard when you initiate negotiations with the target?
5. Ask analogous questions about the player(s) at this next-to-final stage: Whom would you ideally like to have onboard to maximize the chances of the most difficult player at this stage saying "yes"? How can you win that party over? Map backward in this fashion until you have found the most promising path through the cloud of possibilities.

To better understand the logic of backward mapping, consider the logic of project management. When deciding how to undertake a complex project, you focus first on your endpoint, then develop a critical path and a timeline by working backward to the present. A successfully completed project is comparable to a value-creating agreement supported by a sustainable coalition.

Once you begin applying the logic of backward mapping, you'll find yourself facing a number of questions: How can you identify critical players? Should your negotiations be secret or open, separate or collective? How can you avoid being harmed by the sequencing tactics of others?

HERE'S SOME ADVICE:

Study patterns of influence and deference. Would-be coalition builders learn quickly that approaching the most difficult — and perhaps most critical — party first may offer slim chances for a deal. To improve the odds, try to discern who influences the target player and to whom that player defers. In a 1993 *New Yorker* article, Sidney Blumenthal described how Bill Daley, then President Clinton's key strategist for congressional approval of the North American Free Trade Agreement, went about securing buy-in: "News might arrive that a representative who had been leaning toward yes had come out as a no. . . . When he heard the bad news, [Daley went into action]. . . . 'Can we find the guy who can deliver the guy? We have to call the guy who calls the guy who calls the guy . . .' ".

Careful sequencing can help manage sensitive information. For a building developer worried about being squeezed on price if her intentions become public, the property acquisition sequence may depend on the likelihoods of different paths. Other factors involve the physical relationship of the parcels acquired to those remaining. Rather than waiting for a later acquisition, can the developer use parcels already obtained to push forward some version of the project?

The answer to this question might drive the order of approach. Similar sequencing calculations face investors who seek to quietly purchase a series of blocks of stock for a possible acquisition or take positions in various debt securities to improve their position in a bankruptcy negotiation.

BEWARE SNEAKY SEQUENCERS

Be cautious: others may try to pull devious sequencing moves on you. Most parents quickly wise up to the household version of this gambit: to get Dad to say "yes," Junior will claim that "Mom said it was OK," then scurry to tell Mom that Dad has given the green light. Some children grow up to use these time-honored tactics in the workplace. For example, when a private equity firm negotiates with a major institutional investor, the investor might informally commit capital, relying on the supposed commitments of another investor known to be savvy. Knowing of this reliance, a less than scrupulous firm may be tempted to keep the two negotiations separate, using Party A's alleged agreement as a reason for Party B to close — and vice versa. Advice: explicitly verify the assertions of anyone who claims to have secured a prior commitment from another negotiator — who may be under the false impression that you've already said "yes."

OPENING UP THE PROCESS

The secrecy that surrounds some sequenced deals can make them appear manipulative. By contrast, a group of negotiators who know and trust one another and who are skilled at joint problem solving may find that an open, collective process generates better, more creative options than a separated, sequential approach. Open negotiations can also enhance feelings of legitimacy and group ownership of an eventual agreement.

Yet relying on inclusive meetings can be risky. Interests and agendas may surface that are better dealt with privately in a careful order. Large, open meetings may help opponents to identify each other, meet, join forces, and thus mount a more powerful combined challenge.

With each negotiation, you should consider whether to create a private or public sequential strategy, launch a group process, or opt for a hybrid. When sequencing appears to have an advantage — in coalition building, managing sensitive information, and dealing with potential opponents — the logic of backward mapping will help guide your path.

Problem 13-1.   *Drawing a "Backward Map"*

Think of a current multiparty dispute (either domestic or international) and see if you can draw a "backward map" of the "deference patterns" of the parties.

The question of how people behave in groups, whether forming coalitions or seeking to achieve something as a group, has long been the subject of study by sociologists and social psychologists. Not surprisingly, scholars have differed on whether people within a group become more solidified in their views,[3] especially as "against" other groups, or whether individuals within groups resist collective thinking. This has important implications for forming coalitions among individuals and is even more complex when one tries to bring groups, organizations, or nations together for multiple-party negotiations in the political, commercial, policy, or international arenas. Legal scholar Cass Sunstein explores some of the implications of this research next.

 ### *Cass R. Sunstein,* DELIBERATIVE TROUBLE? WHY GROUPS GO TO EXTREMES

110 Yale L.J. 71, 73-78, 82, 85-86, 88-90, 105-106, 113-116 (2000)

Every society contains innumerable deliberating groups. Church groups, political parties, women's organizations, juries, legislative bodies, regulatory commissions, multimember courts, faculties, student organizations, those participating in talk radio programs, Internet discussion groups, and others engage in deliberation. It is a

---

3. Irving L. Janis, Groupthink (2d ed. 1982); Robert B. Cialdini, Influence: The Psychology of Persuasion (rev. ed. 1993).

simple social fact that sometimes people enter discussions with one view and leave with another, even on moral and political questions. Emphasizing this fact, many recent observers have embraced the traditional American aspiration to "deliberative democracy," an ideal that is designed to combine popular responsiveness with a high degree of reflection and exchange among people with competing views. But for the most part, the resulting literature has not been empirically informed. It has not dealt much with the real-world consequences of deliberation, and with what generalizations hold in actual deliberative settings, with groups of different predispositions and compositions.

The standard view of deliberation is that of Hamilton and Rawls. . . . Group discussion is likely to lead to better outcomes, if only because competing views are stated and exchanged. Aristotle spoke in similar terms, suggesting that when diverse people

> all come together . . . they may surpass — collectively and as a body, although not individually — the quality of the few best. . . . [W]hen there are many [who contribute to the process of deliberation], each has his share of goodness and practical wisdom. . . . Some appreciate one part, some another, and all together appreciate all.

But an important empirical question is whether and under what circumstances it is really true that "some appreciate one part, some another, and all together appreciate all."

My principal purpose in this Essay is to investigate a striking but largely neglected statistical regularity — that of group polarization — and to relate this phenomenon to underlying questions about the role of deliberation in the "public sphere" of a heterogeneous democracy. In brief, group polarization means that members of a deliberating group predictably move toward a more extreme point in the direction indicated by the members' predeliberation tendencies. "Like polarized molecules, group members become even more aligned in the direction they were already tending." . . . Notably, groups consisting of individuals with extremist tendencies are more likely to shift, and likely to shift more; the same is true for groups with some kind of salient shared identity (like Republicans, Democrats, and lawyers, but unlike jurors and experimental subjects). When like-minded people are participating in "iterated polarization games" — when they meet regularly, without sustained exposure to competing views — extreme movements are all the more likely.

Two principal mechanisms underlie group polarization. The first points to social influences on behavior and in particular to people's desire to maintain their reputation and their self-conception. The second emphasizes the limited "argument pools" within any group, and the directions in which those limited pools lead group members. An understanding of the two mechanisms provides many insights into deliberating bodies. Such an understanding illuminates a great deal, for example, about likely processes within multimember courts, juries, political parties, and legislatures — not to mention ethnic groups, extremist organizations, criminal conspiracies, student associations, faculties, institutions engaged in feuds or "turf battles," workplaces, and families. At the same time, these mechanisms raise serious questions about deliberation from the normative point of view. If deliberation predictably pushes groups toward a more extreme point in the direction of their original tendency, whatever that tendency may be, is there any reason to think that deliberation is producing improvements? . . .

HOW AND WHY GROUPS POLARIZE

There have been two main explanations for group polarization. Both of these have been extensively investigated and supported. The first explanation of group polarization — social comparison — begins with the claim that people want to be perceived favorably by other group members and also to perceive themselves favorably. . . .

The second explanation is based on the commonsense intuition that any individual's position on an issue is partly a function of which arguments presented within the group seem convincing. The choice therefore moves in the direction of the most persuasive position defended by the group, taken as a whole. Because a group whose members are already inclined in a certain direction will have a disproportionate number of arguments going in that same direction, the result of discussion will be to move people further in the direction of their initial inclinations. The key is the existence of a limited argument pool, one that is skewed (speaking purely descriptively) in a particular direction. Hence there will be a shift in the direction of the original tilt.

There is a related possibility, not quite reducible to either of the two standard arguments, but incorporating elements of each. In their individual judgments, people are averse to extremes; they tend to seek the middle of the relevant poles. It is possible that when people are making judgments individually, they err on the side of caution, expressing a view in the direction that they really hold, but stating that view cautiously, for fear of seeming extreme. Once other people express supportive views, the relevant inhibition disappears, and people feel free to say what, in a sense, they really believe. There appears to be no direct test of this hypothesis, but it is reasonable to believe that the phenomenon plays a role in group polarization and choice shifts. . . .

DELIBERATIVE TROUBLE?

The central problem is that widespread error and social fragmentation are likely to result when like-minded people, insulated from others, move in extreme directions simply because of limited argument pools and parochial influences. As an extreme example, consider a system of one-party domination, which stifles dissent in part because it refuses to establish space for the emergence of divergent positions; in this way, it intensifies polarization within the party while also disabling external criticism.

In terms of institutional design, the most natural response is to ensure that members of deliberating groups, whether small or large, will not isolate themselves from competing views — a point with implications for multi-member courts, open primaries, freedom of association, and the architecture of the Internet. Here, then, is a plea for ensuring that deliberation occurs within a large and heterogeneous public sphere, and for guarding against a situation in which like-minded people wall themselves off from alternative perspectives. . . .

It is important to ensure social spaces for deliberation by like-minded persons, but it is equally important to ensure that members of the relevant groups are not isolated from conversation with people having quite different views. The goal of that conversation is to promote the interests of those inside and outside the relevant enclaves, by subjecting group members to competing positions, by allowing them to exchange views with others and to see things from their point of view, and by ensuring that the wider society does not marginalize, and thus insulate itself from, views that may turn out to be right or at least informative . . .

Problem 13-2. *Design a Process!*

From these descriptions of the complexities of multiparty decision-making processes, including negotiation for consensual agreements or voting to resolve conflicts, imagine how you might structure processes to facilitate the following:

a. The best possible process for a "good" decision;
b. The best possible process for "maximum stakeholder participation";
c. The best possible process to avoid bad "group polarization" and promote optimal heterogeneity in participation.

Are these processes all the same, or do different values suggest different process design?

---

2. Organizing and Legitimizing Group Negotiations: New Processes and Deliberative Democracy

As complex legal and social problems have increased, many participants and decision makers have used dispute resolution processes in official governmental, private, and hybrid settings. Those who have designed these processes are hoping to broaden party participation, achieve better substantive solutions, and create greater legitimacy, compliance with, and acceptance of the outcomes reached. In many cases, parties agree to "contingent" solutions that can be revisited, using these new multiparty processes, variously called consensus building, deliberative democracy, or public policy fora.

The excerpts below explore the use of some of these new "deliberative democracy" enhancing processes to resolve political and policy issues, by looking at different kinds of deliberations (principled argument, bargaining, and appeals to emotions, ethics, and values) that can be organized into different forms of processes. Consider how these processes could be used to deal with such issues as land use, water allocation, community disputes, budget decisions, and highly conflictual policy disputes, such as health care, abortion, and gun control.

 Carrie Menkel-Meadow, THE LAWYER'S ROLE(S) IN DELIBERATIVE DEMOCRACY

5 Nev. L.J. (2005)

To the extent that participation remains a cornerstone of democratic theory, new forms of participation may require the creation of new institutions or modifications of old forms to permit optimum and appropriate levels of participation for effective and legitimate outcomes. Whether tied to traditional constitutional and legal institutions, like courts, legislatures, and administrative agencies, or created new out of the particularities of specific situations, lawyers have knowledge, skills, craft and wisdom . . . to help craft and manage such institutions. . . .

The terrain has shifted to what kinds of processes or procedures may best facilitate either partial or more global "agreements" about the good and the just. What is fair becomes the principal concern in these process-oriented theories. Thus, some political theorists look to "reasoned deliberation" focused on rationality, principled and rational discourse, others on explicit models of bargaining and interest or preference trading or negotiation, and still others, on the recognition of emotional or subjective sensibilities (such as empathy and "imaginative identification") in the processes by which modern political actors must get things done. Some insist that foundational principles like American constitutionalism are essential to the legitimacy and fairness of any dispute resolution and political governance system, while others suggest that constitutionalism is too rigid and prevents important procedural flexibility from letting process rules be negotiated along with substantive outcomes, as particular parties and problems require. Modern political theorists seek to describe, elaborate and in some cases, prescribe "ideal speech conditions," "ideal proceduralism," "procedural justice," "fairness in procedure as an invariable value" or "discourse ethics" at various levels of theoretical complexity. Others have focused on "new institutions" or new understandings or reconfigurations of existing governmental institutions or structures, like courts, legislatures and agencies, often by focusing on new public and private collaborations. Still others suggest that new forms of participation will themselves generate new substantive solutions or at least contingent accommodations, recognizing that the tools used to solve problems may influence the resolutions that may be recognized." . . .

Those that describe such processes don't always agree about their purposes, structures or operation. Thus, for some "consensus," or some form of agreement by participants, beyond a majority, is an essential part of the commitment, for others, consensus may never be possible or desirable (especially about pre-deliberation commitments) and thus new democratic institutions are "pragmatic" because they may develop issue specific resolutions or develop collaboration out of necessity, rather than "real" and deep agreement. For still others, democratic discourse doesn't even produce policy or decisional "outcomes," just the possibility of increased conversation and "understanding."

In the world of politics, different kinds of problems call up different kinds of participants who may speak in different "languages" (for example, appeals to principles, reasons, logic, emotions, utilitarian interests or preferences, moral, ethical, or religious suasion). To make conflict resolution legitimate and effective in a wide variety of public and private settings, we have to marry conflict resolution theory and its process pluralism to political theory. Political scientist Jon Elster compares the processes of public-open and plenary processes, which employ highly principled and politicized rhetoric (as was used in the French constitutional process) to the more "secret," committee-based, and "pragmatic bargaining" rhetoric of the American constitutional process, suggesting that sometimes "second-best processes" (less transparent, more compromising, and less "principled") make for more robust outcomes or conclusions. (The American Constitution, even with its Civil War and amendments, has lasted far longer than the French.[4]) Drawing on Elster's work, Carrie Menkel-Meadow has elaborated a taxonomy of different modes of processes to use in conflict resolution and political deliberation. Her chart below describes and separates modes of discourse with different structures of process and different kinds of parties. She then provides examples of different kinds of group process and decision making.

---

4. Jon Elster, Strategic Uses of Argument, in Kenneth J. Arrow et al. eds., Barriers to Conflict Resolution (1995).

Carrie Menkel-Meadow, **INTRODUCTION: FROM LEGAL DISPUTES TO CONFLICT RESOLUTION AND HUMAN PROBLEM SOLVING**

in Dispute Processing and Conflict Resolution (2003), at xi, xxxi

MODES OF CONFLICT RESOLUTION

MODE OF DISCOURSE	PRINCIPLED (REASONS) (appeals to law, rules, universals)	BARGAINING (INTERESTS) (trades of interests, preferences, compromises)	PASSIONS (NEEDS/ EMOTIONS/RELIGION)
FORMS OF PROCESS:			
Closed (Confidential)	Some court proceedings; arbitration	Negotiation-U.S. Constitution; diplomacy	Mediation (e.g., divorce)
Open (Public)	French Constitution; courts; arbitration	Public negotiations; some labor	Dialogue movement
Plenary	French Constitution	Reg-Neg	Town meetings
Committees	Faculty committees; task groups	U.S. Constitution/ U.S. Congress	Caucuses-interest groups
Expert/ Facilitator	Consensus building	Mini-trial	Public conversations
Naturalistic (Leaderless)			Grassroots organizing/ WTO protests
Permanent	Government, institutions	Business organizations, unions	Religious organizations, Alcoholics Anonymous, Weight Watchers
Constitutive	UN, national constitutions	National constitutions/ professional associations	Civil justice movements, peace
Temporary/Ad Hoc	Issue organizations/ social justice	Interest groups	Yippies, New Age, vigilantes

> ## Problem 13-3.   *Sources of Legitimacy*
>
> When should we let "a thousand flowers bloom" (Chairman Mao) in governmental decision making and when do we need uniformity? Should localities be allowed to create their own zoning rules, educational requirements, policing standards, environmental regulations, water usage, or health standards, or should these decisions be made at higher levels of government? What is the appropriate level of governmental authority — national-constitutional? Federalism (state or local control)? Who should decide? Should we stick to textual commitments, as in the Constitution, or can who decides these questions be subject to bargaining processes?

Philip Harter combined the insights of problem-solving dispute resolution theory with the formal governmental processes used in multiparty disputes and public policy settings to devise a process called negotiated rule making ("reg-neg"). Reg-neg uses negotiation by the regulated and regulators, rather than top-down rulemaking, to produce new government regulations. Following Harter's publication of the article below, Congress permitted these processes in the Negotiated Rulemaking Act of 1990, 5 U.S.C. §§561-570, and multiparty negotiations in the form of "negotiated rule making" or reg-neg began to be employed in a variety of regulatory settings (occupational health and safety, food and drug administration, and environmental, to name a few). In 1996 these processes were more formally legitimated in the Administrative Dispute Resolution Act, 5 U.S.C. §§571-584. Though Harter's pathbreaking work has been primarily influential in federal policy making, many states have employed these processes as well.[5] Variations on this multiparty participation in negotiated rule making have also been used in private disputes, such as those over land use or development and racial or ethnic conflicts.

 Philip J. Harter, NEGOTIATING REGULATIONS: A CURE FOR MALAISE

71 Geo. L.J. 1, 28-31, 33-34, 42, 82-86, 112-113 (1982)

This article proposes that a form of negotiation among representatives of the interested parties, including administrative agencies, would be an effective alternative procedure to the current rulemaking process. Although virtually every rulemaking includes some negotiation, it is almost never the group consensus envisioned here. Negotiations among directly affected groups, conducted within both the existing policies of the statute authorizing the regulation and the existing policies of the agency, would enable the parties to participate directly in the establishment of the rule. . . .

---

5. For some examples, see Consensus Building Institute, *http://www.cbuilding.org*, and Policy Consensus Institute, *http://www.policyconsensus.org*.

THE ADVANTAGES OF RULEMAKING BY NEGOTIATION

Negotiating has many advantages over the adversarial process. The parties participate directly and immediately in the decision. They share in its development and concur with it, rather than "participate" by submitting information that the decision maker considers in reaching the decision. Frequently, those who participate in the negotiation are closer to the ultimate decision-making authority of the interest they represent than traditional intermediaries that represent the interest in an adversarial proceeding. Thus, participants in negotiations can make substantive decisions, rather than acting as experts in the decision-making process. In addition, negotiation can be a less expensive means of decision making because it reduces the need to engage in defensive research in anticipation of arguments made by adversaries.

Undoubtedly the prime benefit of direct negotiations is that it enables the participants to focus squarely on their respective interests. They need not advocate and maintain extreme positions before a decision maker. Therefore, the parties can develop a feel for the true issues that lie within the advocated extremes and attempt to accommodate fully the competing interests. An example of this benefit occurred when a group of environmentalists opposed the construction of a dam because they feared it would lead to the development of a nearby valley. The proponents of the dam were farmers in the valley who were adversely affected by periodic floods. Negotiations between the two groups, which were begun at the behest of the governor, revealed a common interest in preserving the valley. Without the negotiations the environmentalists would have undoubtedly sued to block construction, and necessarily would have employed adversarial tactics. Negotiations, however, demonstrated the true interests of the parties and permitted them to work toward accommodation. . . .

Rulemaking by negotiation can reduce the time and cost of developing regulations by emphasizing practical and empirical concerns rather than theoretical predictions. In developing a regulation under the current system, an agency must prove a factual case, at least preliminarily, and anticipate the factual information that will be submitted in the record. Because the agency lacks direct access to empirical data, the information used is often of a theoretical nature derived from models. In negotiations, the parties in interest decide together what information is necessary to make a reasonably informed decision. . . .

Negotiation also can enable the participants to focus on the details of a regulation. In the adversary process, the big points must be hit and hit hard, while the subtleties and details frequently are overlooked. Or, even if the details are not overlooked, the decision maker may not appreciate their consequences. In negotiations, however, interested parties can directly address all aspects of a problem in attempting to formulate workable solutions.

Overarching all the other benefits of negotiations is the added legitimacy a rule would acquire if all parties viewed the rule as reasonable and endorsed it without a fight. Affected parties would participate in the development of a rule by sharing in the decisions, ranking their own concerns and needs, and trading them with other parties. . . .

NEGOTIATING REGULATIONS

1. Establishing the Groundrules

Because the parties are unlikely to have previously engaged in negotiations among themselves, they need to establish the groundrules that will govern, or at least guide, the negotiations. . . . Therefore, defining the rules of acceptable conduct and the procedures under which negotiations will be conducted is important if the benefits of negotiation are to be realized. Although creative problem-solving can develop only with time, the rules can foster that process.

2. Rule of Reason

Milton R. Wessel has developed a set of dispute resolution principles that he calls the "Rule of Reason." Perhaps the fundamental application of the guidelines to negotiations is to remind the participants periodically that their purpose is to reach a mutually acceptable agreement when possible, not to seek victory for their positions. The parties should keep in mind that they must sort out, weigh, and accommodate conflicting interests. Thus, they need to be reminded of the give and take and good faith of the negotiation process.

3. Confidentiality

One significant issue the participants must face at the outset of negotiations is the extent to which the process will be open to public inspection. Under current theories agencies are accountable for reaching rational results based on the neutral exercise of their discretion. Thus, the rulemaking process is subject to public scrutiny at virtually every stage. For example, ex parte rules prohibit discussions and transmittal of data unavailable to others; advisory committees are open to public attendance; the Sunshine Act requires that meetings of collegial agencies be open to the public, and the Freedom of Information Act requires agencies to provide the public with many of their internal documents. In short, the current political climate distrusts meetings and other communications between agency officials and members of the private sector unless they are open to all. Therefore, confidential exchanges are frowned upon, if not banned outright. In keeping with this theory, the parties to a regulatory negotiation may agree to conduct their affairs in public.

Several experts, however, believe that negotiation is a process best carried on in private. Several examples demonstrate the benefits of privacy. First, the negotiators must make concessions on different issues to permit maximization of their own goals. Moreover, negotiators must be able to explain the results of their negotiations to their constituents and the reasons for conceding a particular issue that the negotiator believes is not of central importance. Second, a party may be reluctant to yield confidential data that can be useful to negotiations, if doing so will destroy its confidentiality. Third, a party reasonably could be reluctant to engage in the give and take of the negotiation process if it thought that a tentative position it raised in the negotiations subsequently would be held against it in another forum, such as litigation or an ensuing rulemaking process. Finally, and perhaps most significantly, a public forum may cause some of the parties to continue to posture and to take a hard, unyielding position. In short, public scrutiny could mean that the detrimental aspects of the adversarial process result without the correlative benefits of a neutral decisionmaker.

The negotiators therefore should be able to close their meetings in appropriate circumstances. The procedures of the negotiation process itself provide the safeguards that accrue from public meetings. The political legitimacy of the resulting rule derives from the acceptance of the rule by the parties in interest, and not on the public procedures by which it was developed. Further, the parties should feel no inhibition from meeting on a confidential basis with the mediator or other parties to the negotiation.

Since Harter's original suggestion, many reg-negs have occurred. However, these reg-neg processes have inspired heated academic and evaluative debate about their effectiveness and how that effectiveness should be measured.[6]

Problem 13-4.   *How Well Does Reg-Neg Work?*

What evaluative criteria would you use to assess whether stakeholder negotiations, held before formal rule making, are more or less successful than the more conventional draft rule, publish notice and comments, promulgation of regulation, and litigation model of administrative law (see Administrative Procedure Act, 5 U.S.C. §§551 et seq.)? How can we evaluate different kinds of processes when the subject matter of each process may be different and, unlike experimental evaluation, we cannot assign the same "issue" to several different treatments simultaneously for evaluation?

---

3. Legal Issues in Use of Consensus-Building and Group Negotiations

As government agencies, whether federal or state, legislative, executive or administrative, use more of these consensus-building and negotiated processes, there are many legal questions about when and how negotiated solutions actually become legal enactments with binding legal authority. These are complicated questions involving how the negotiation or consensus-building event was convened, who participates, and whether processes must be open to the public or can be conducted in private. The following excerpt explores some of these legal issues.

---

6. See, e.g., Cary Coglianese, Assessing Consensus: The Promise and Performance of Negotiated Rulemaking, 46 Duke L.J. 1255 (1997); Jody Freeman, Collaborative Governance in the Administrative State, 45 UCLA L. Rev. 1 (1997); Jody Freeman & Laura I. Langbein, Regulatory Negotiation and the Legitimacy Benefit, 9 N.Y.U. Envtl. L.J. 60 (2000); Philip J. Harter, Assessing the Assessors: The Actual Performance of Negotiated Rulemaking, 9 N.Y.U. Envtl. L.J. 32 (2000).

Dwight Golann & Eric E. Van Loon, **LEGAL ISSUES IN CONSENSUS BUILDING**

in The Consensus Building Handbook: A Comprehensive Guide to Reaching Agreement, 495-497 (Lawrence Susskind, Sarah McKearnan & Jennifer Thomas Larmer eds., 1999)

. . . With so many state legislatures, courts, and systems of legal rules in the United States, it is impossible to offer a single answer to most legal questions. Responses are likely to depend on the state(s) in which a consensus building effort takes place and the terms of the ground rules that govern a process. Precise answers are also difficult for the more fundamental reason that lawmakers themselves are sometimes unclear; the laws they pass and the rules they write often create more ambiguities than they resolve. For some issues, no statute or regulation exists, forcing individual courts to make law on an ad hoc basis. As a result, it can take decades before a particular issue is addressed in the legal system — and even then the answer may vary from one place to another.

Despite these limitations, it *is* possible to provide general guidance on legal challenges that may arise in the course of consensus building. We have identified six categories of challenges. Many of the issues within these categories proceed from the fact that consensus processes often involve public officials, who are subject to special constraints because of their role in government.

1. Relationship to government agencies and the courts. Disputes that are the subject of consensus building are sometimes simultaneously the focus of legal proceedings before agencies or courts. This raises the question of how the two processes should be coordinated.

2. Procedural requirements imposed by laws and regulations. Government employees often must follow specific procedures, which may prevent them from making binding commitments during a negotiation. For example, agency officials usually cannot commit to change regulations as part of a settlement, because they must first consider comments from the general public.

3. Substantive restrictions on the power of government representatives. Some limitations on government negotiators cannot be resolved even by following the right procedures because they arise from fundamental constraints embedded in the U.S. system of government. An example is the concept of separation of powers. The head of a federal agency, for example, cannot make commitments that bind Congress to take action. Similarly, state agencies are limited in how they can control the activities of municipalities on topics such as education or zoning.

4. Disclosure requirements and confidentiality protections. Participants in sensitive negotiations often prefer to hold their discussions in private, and many states bar participants from revealing what was said during a mediation process. Other states, however, require that meetings in which public officials participate be open to citizens and the press. Because consensus building is a mediative process that often involves public officials, both sets of laws may apply, creating confusion.

5. Liability considerations.   Mediators and facilitators can be held legally liable for their actions in a consensus-based process and should therefore take appropriate precautions. Certain risky behaviors should be avoided, for example, and liability insurance should be obtained.

6. Implementation concerns.   Once an agreement has been reached, everyone involved presumably wants to see it carried out. Nonetheless, implementation problems may arise over time, prompting two legal questions. One concerns the minimum requirements for a contract to be legally binding. For instance, must an agreement be written in "legalese" to be enforceable? The other question involves how to structure the terms of an agreement so that, if necessary, it can be enforced by court order. . . .

B. STRUCTURES, PROCEDURES, AND SKILLS FOR MULTIPARTY PROCESSES

Because multiparty processes occur in so many different contexts, it is hard to specify in advance what a particular multiparty process does or should do. A new field within dispute resolution has formed to develop structures, procedures, rules, protocols, and training models to guide both formal and informal multiple-party negotiations.

In the more formal multiparty processes, these organizing rules and protocols focus on both *rules of process* or *procedure* and *rules of decision* (such as voting procedures, definitions of key terms such as *consensus*, or majority rules). In informal processes too, including those in which "resolution" is not a goal (such as facilitated dialogues about controversial issues such as abortion or gun control), protocols or guided questions organize potentially complex and unstructured multiparty processes.

One of the founders of this new field, Lawrence Susskind, professor of urban planning at MIT and founder of the Consensus Building Institute, has pioneered the development of facilitated processes in complex public policy matters and disputes. In a handbook for this new practice, Susskind and several colleagues develop guidelines for conducting facilitated processes in both formal and ad hoc settings. The protocols and processes described below are intended to replace the more complex Robert's Rules of Order[*] for parliamentary and other organized meetings.

---

[*] Robert's Rules of Order, written in 1876, by Henry M. Robert, a military engineer, was a compendium of the procedural rules used in congress. Robert hoped these rules would be used not only in formal parliamentary proceedings, but in "non-legislative assemblies . . . to assist an assembly to accomplish the work for which it was designed." ROBERT'S RULES OF ORDER (Darwin Patnode ed., 1993) at 13-14.

Lawrence Susskind, **AN ALTERNATIVE TO ROBERT'S RULES OF ORDER FOR GROUPS, ORGANIZATIONS, AND AD HOC ASSEMBLIES THAT WANT TO OPERATE BY CONSENSUS**

in The Consensus Building Handbook: A Comprehensive Guide to Reaching Agreement 3, 3-13, 20-35, 55-56 (Lawrence Susskind, Sarah McKearnan & Jennifer Thomas-Larmer eds., 1999)

Let's compare what this "Short Guide" has to say with what *Robert's Rules of Order* requires. Assume that a few dozen people have gotten together, on their own, at a community center because they are upset with a new policy or program recently announced by their local officials. After several impassioned speeches, someone suggests that the group appoint a moderator to "keep order" and ensure that the conversation proceeds effectively. Someone else wants to know how the group will decide what to recommend after they are done debating. "Will we vote?" this person wants to know. At this point, everyone turns to Joe, who has had experience as a moderator. Joe moves to the front of the room and explains that he will follow *Robert's Rules of Order*. From that moment on, the conversation takes on a very formal tone.

Instead of just saying what's on their mind, everyone is forced to frame suggestions in the cumbersome form of *motions*. These have to be *seconded*. Efforts to *move the question* are proceeded by an explanation from Joe about what is and isn't an acceptable way of doing this. Proposals to *table* various items are considered, even though everyone hasn't had a chance to speak. Ultimately, all-or-nothing votes are the only way the group seems able to make a decision.

As the hour passes, fewer and fewer of those in attendance feel capable of expressing their views. They don't know the rules, and they are intimidated. Every once in a while, someone makes an effort to restate the problem or make a suggestion, but the person is shouted down ("You're not following *Robert's Rules!*") No one takes responsibility for ensuring that the concerns of everyone in the room are met, especially the needs of those individuals who are least able to present their views effectively. After an hour or so, many people have left. A final proposal is approved by a vote of 55 percent to 45 percent of those remaining.

If the group had followed the procedures spelled out in this "Short Guide to Consensus Building," the meeting would have been run differently and the result would probably have been a lot more to everyone's liking. The person at the front of the room would have been a trained facilitator or mediator — a person adept at helping groups build consensus — not a moderator with specialized knowledge about how motions should be made or votes should be taken. His or her job would have been to get agreement at the outset on how the group wanted to proceed. Then, the facilitator would have focused on producing an agreement that could meet the underlying concerns of everyone in the room: no motions, no arcane rituals, and no vote at the end. Instead, the facilitator might have pushed the group to brainstorm (e.g., "Can anyone propose a way of proceeding that meets all the interests we have heard expressed thus far?"). After as thorough a consideration of options as time permitted, the facilitator would ask, "Is there anyone who can't live with the last version of what has been proposed? If so, what improvement or modification can you suggest that will make it more acceptable to you, while continuing to meet the interests of everyone else with a stake in the issue?" The group would have likely developed a proposal that everyone — or nearly everyone — in the, room could support. And participants would leave satisfied that their opinions and needs had been heard, understood, and taken into account.

DEFINITIONS

Consensus Building (An Agreement-Seeking Process)

Consensus building is a process of seeking unanimous agreement. It involves a good-faith effort to meet the interests of all stakeholders. Consensus has been reached when everyone agrees they can live with whatever is proposed after every effort has been made to meet the interests of all stakeholding parties. Thus, consensus building requires that someone frame a proposal after listening carefully to everyone's concerns. Participants in a consensus building process have both the right to expect that no one will ask them to undermine their interests and the responsibility to propose solutions that will meet everyone else's interests as well as their own.

Most consensus building efforts set out to achieve unanimity. Along the way, however, there are sometimes *holdouts*: people who believe that their interests are better served by remaining outside the emerging agreement. Should the rest of the group throw in the towel? No, this would invite blackmail (i.e., outrageous demands by the holdouts that have nothing to do with the issues under discussion). Most dispute resolution professionals believe that groups or assemblies should seek unanimity, but settle for overwhelming agreement that goes as far as possible toward meeting the interests of all stakeholders. This effort to meet the interests of all stakeholders should be understood to include an affirmative responsibility to ensure that those who are excluded really are holdouts and are rejecting the proposal on reasonable grounds that would seem compelling to anyone who found themselves in the holdouts' shoes. It is absolutely crucial that the definition of success be clear at the outset of any consensus building process.

Facilitation (A Way of Helping Groups Work Together in Meetings)

Facilitation is a meeting management skill. When people are face-to-face, they need to talk and to listen. When there are several people involved, especially if they don't know each other or they disagree sharply, getting the talking-listening-deciding sequence right is hard. Often, it is helpful to have someone who has no stake in the outcome assist in managing the conversation. Of course, a skilled group member can, with the concurrence of the participants, play this role, too. As the parties try to collect information, formulate proposals, defend their views, and take account of what others are saying, a facilitator reminds them of the ground rules they have adopted and, much like a referee, intervenes when someone violates the ground rules. The facilitator is supposed to be nonpartisan or neutral.

There is some disagreement in various professional circles about the extent to which an effective facilitator needs to be someone from outside the group. Certainly in a corporate context, work teams have traditionally relied on the person "in charge" to play a facilitative role. The concept of facilitative leadership is growing in popularity. Even work teams in the private sector, however, are turning more and more to skilled outsiders to provide facilitation services. In the final analysis, there is reason to worry that a stakeholder might use facilitative authority to advance his or her own interests at the expense of the others. . . .

Before the parties in a consensus building process come together, mediators (or facilitators) can play an important part in helping to identify the right participants, assist them in setting an agenda and clarifying the ground rules by which they will operate, and even in "selling" recalcitrant parties on the value of participating. Once the process has begun, mediators (and facilitators) try to assist the parties in their efforts to generate creative resolution of differences. During these discussions or negotiations, a mediator may accompany a representative back to a meeting with his or her constituents to explain what has been happening. The mediator might serve as a spokesperson for the process if the media are following the story. A mediator might (with the parties' concurrence) push them to accept an accord (because they need someone to blame for forcing them to back off some of the demands they made at the outset). Finally, the mediator may be called on to monitor implementation of an agreement and reassemble the parties to review progress or deal with perceived violations or a failure to live up to commitments.

Facilitation and *mediation* are often used interchangeably. We think the key distinction is that facilitators work mostly with parties once they are at the table, while mediators do that as well as handle the prenegotiation and postnegotiation tasks described above. Also, mediators tend to be called on in particularly conflictual situations. In addition, some facilitators do not necessarily strive for agreement as mediators always do, but rather seek to ensure productive deliberation. Some professionals have both sets of skills; many do not. Neither form of consensus building assistance requires stakeholders to give up their authority or their power to decide what is best for them.

Recording (Creating a Visual Record of What a Group Has Discussed and Decided)

Recording involves creating a visual record that captures the key points of agreement and disagreement during a dialogue. Some facilitators (and mediators) work in tandem with a recorder. Recording can be done on large sheets of paper, often called flip charts, tacked up in front of a room. With the introduction of new computer and multimedia technologies, this can be done electronically as well. The important thing is to have an ongoing visual representation of what the group has discussed and agreed. Unlike formal minutes of a meeting, this "group memory" may use drawings, illustrations, maps, or other icons to help people recall what they have discussed. Visual records prepared by a recorder ultimately need to be turned into written meeting summaries. Like minutes, these summaries must be reviewed in draft by all participants to ensure that everyone agrees with the review of what happened.

Convening (Bringing Parties Together)

Convening, or the gathering together of parties for a meeting or a series of meetings, is not a skill that depends on training. An agency or organization that has decided to host a consensus building process (and wants to encourage others to participate) can play an important convening role. In a private firm, for example, a senior official might be the convener. In the public arena, a regulatory agency might want to convene a public involvement process. There is some disagreement about whether or not the convener or the convening organization is obliged to stay at the table as the conversation proceeds. In general, convening organizations want to be part of the dialogue, but we do not feel they must commit to ongoing participation in a consensus building process.

Someone has to finance a consensus building process. When it takes place inside an existing organization, financial arrangements are reasonably straightforward. When consensus building involves a wide range of groups in an ad hoc assembly, it is much less obvious who can and will provide the financial support. If costs are not shared equally by the parties, for example, and if they are covered by the convening organization, special steps must be taken to ensure that the facilitator or mediator has a contract with the entire group, and not just the convener, and that the organization(s) providing the financing do not use that sponsorship to dictate the outcome.

Conflict Assessment (An Essential Convening Step)

A conflict assessment is a document that spells out what the issues are, who the stakeholding interests are, where they disagree, and where they might find common ground. It is usually prepared by a neutral outsider based on confidential interviews with key stakeholders. There is some disagreement over whether the same neutral who prepared the conflict assessment should then be the one to facilitate or mediate, if the process goes forward. Typically, after interviewing a wide range of stakeholders, a neutral party will suggest whether or not it makes sense to go forward with a consensus building process and, if so, how the process ought to be structured. . . .

Circles of Stakeholder Involvement (A Strategy for Identifying Representative Stakeholders)

Stakeholders are persons or groups likely to be affected by (or who think they will be affected by) a decision — whether it is their decision to make or not. When we talk about "circles of stakeholders," we are talking about individuals or groups that want or ought to be involved in decision making, but at different levels of intensity. Some stakeholders may be involved in a core negotiating team, others may have their interests represented on that team, and still others may choose to observe the process from the sidelines.

Some stakeholders are very hard to represent in an organized way. Think about "future generations," for example. Who can represent them in a dialogue about sustainable development? In the law, various strategies have evolved so that surrogates or stand-ins can represent hard-to-represent groups (such as the members of a class of consumers who have been hurt by a certain product or children who have no capacity to speak for themselves in a court proceeding).

Sometimes, it is necessary to caucus all the groups or individuals who think they represent a certain set of stakeholders for the purposes of selecting a representative for a particular dialogue or problem-solving purpose. Such meetings typically need to be facilitated by an outside party. Finally, there are various statutes that govern who may and who must be invited to participate in various public and private dialogues. Ad hoc consensus building processes must take these laws into account.

[Susskind's Suggestions for Convening and Leading a Consensus Building Process can be found as an Appendix at the end of this chapter.]

Problem 13-5.   *Who Makes the Ground Rules?*

Consider whether, in Susskind's view, participants or facilitators should set ground rules. Does he believe rules should be "laid down" by facilitators or themselves be negotiated by the participants? What might be the consequences (both on the process and on ultimate outcomes) of ground-rule setting by the parties versus the facilitators? Are Susskind's rules flexible enough for use in a number of different contextual settings?

What, if anything, would you add to these guidelines (found in the appendix to this chapter)?

These excerpts contemplate a very particular kind of process, a relatively formal multiparty negotiation or policy-setting consensus-building environment. There are many other ways to organize multiparty negotiations, running from no rules at all to very formal rules of speaking and participation. Similarly, there are many schools of thought about how to be an effective third-party neutral in facilitating such meetings, depending on whether a decision or action is required at the end or whether a group is being convened for different purposes, such as to foster understanding across divisive value differences.[7]

---

7. For some other sources on how to facilitate such negotiations or group discussions, see, e.g., Lawrence Susskind & Jeffrey Cruickshank, Breaking Robert's Rules: The New Way to Run Your Meeting, Build Consensus and Get Results (2006); Center for Conflict Resolution, Manual for Group Facilitators (1977); Tim Hindle, Managing Meetings (1998); Public Conversations Project, Constructive Conversations about Challenging Times: A Guide to Community Dialogue, at *http://www.publicconversations.org/pcp/UploadDocs/CommunityGuide3.0/pdf*; Roger Schwarz, The Skilled Facilitator (2d ed. 2002).

C. DISPUTE SYSTEM DESIGN: PLANNING AND STRUCTURING REPEATED DISPUTE RESOLUTION

As dispute resolution processes and possibilities have become more complex, an entire new field, Dispute System Design, has developed to help organizations create processes to help prevent conflicts and manage disputes before they ripen into full-scale grievances or lawsuits. Organizations face both internal disputes and grievances involving their own employees, and external disputes, with either one-shot or repeat customers, suppliers, vendors, or constituents. For some organizations, these disputes are now referred to as "streams of disputes" because they involve large numbers of people (for example, in matters of defective products, employment discrimination, and price fixing). Claimants may experience one-shot or repeat disputes (such as when an operation fails to fix something adequately). The challenge is to create processes that treat individual complaints non-bureaucratically and also fairly, and efficiently deal with repetitive issues. The principles and skills used in Dispute System Design are now relevant in a number of different contexts — organizational, administrative, class action and aggregate litigation, and in a variety of international claims settings.

Good Dispute System designers recognize that "one size does not fit all" and that a tiered system is often optimal. Tiered systems may begin with informal conversation and negotiation, then use consensual mediation with a third party, and finally offer a system for hearing arguments and legal rights claims, with appropriate remedial possibilities (for example, non-binding arbitration). Of course, dispute mechanisms vary, according to the relationship between the disputants and the issues that arise.

The excerpt that follows explores the basic principles of Dispute System Design.

 William L. Ury, Jeanne M. Brett & Stephen B. Goldberg,
GETTING DISPUTES RESOLVED: DESIGNING SYSTEMS TO CUT THE COSTS OF CONFLICT

41-45, 52-56, 58-64 (1988)

DESIGNING AN EFFECTIVE DISPUTE RESOLUTION SYSTEM

Two oil companies, about to engage in a joint venture, agree in advance on a dispute resolution system. They will try to resolve all disputes in a partnership committee. Failing that, they will refer disputes to two senior executives, one from each company, both uninvolved in the joint venture. The executives' task is to study the problem and, in consultation with their respective companies, to negotiate a settlement. They thus act as mediators as well as negotiators. If the "wise counselors" cannot reach an agreement, the dispute will be sent to arbitration. Litigation will be avoided.

A statewide fire fighters union and an organization of cities and towns in the state are unhappy with the delay, unsatisfactory outcomes, and damaged relationships resulting from state-mandated arbitration to resolve disputes about the terms of fire fighters' collective bargaining contracts. They consult a dispute systems designer, who proposes that a joint committee of labor and management officials use mediation to break impasses. Both groups accept his proposal and successfully lobby the state legislature to add mediation to the statute. Arbitration remains available for disputes that cannot otherwise be resolved, but the favored procedure is to be mediation.

At the Catholic Archdiocese of Chicago, school administrators, looking for better ways to resolve disputes about teacher dismissals and student suspensions, designed a multistep dispute resolution procedure that requires negotiation between disputing parties; provides advice from a school conflict management board composed of teachers, parents, and principals from other schools; and offers the services of a trained mediator.

. . . [A] dispute resolution system is designed to reduce the costs of handling disputes and to produce more satisfying and durable resolutions. . . . [H]ow to design such a system — how to create an interests-oriented system, starting from a diagnosis of the existing system . . . — [involves] six basic principles of dispute systems design:

PRINCIPLE 1: PUT THE FOCUS ON INTERESTS . . .

Establishing a Negotiation Procedure

An established negotiation procedure becomes increasingly useful as the number of parties to the dispute grows, the complexity of the issues increases, and the parties grow larger and more bureaucratic. Such a procedure will designate, for example, who will participate in the negotiation, when it must begin and end, and what happens if it is unsuccessful. Such negotiation procedures exist in a variety of realms, from collective bargaining between labor and management to negotiation of federal environmental and safety regulations. . . .

Designing Multiple-Step Negotiation

In multistep procedures, a dispute that is not resolved at one level of the organizational hierarchy moves to progressively higher levels, with different negotiators involved at each step. One example is the contractual grievance procedure in the coal industry: step 1 is negotiation between the miner and his foreman, step 2 is negotiation between the mine committee and mine management, and step 3 is negotiation between the district union representative and senior management.

Multistep negotiation procedures, common in the labor-management context, are increasingly being used by parties to long-term business contracts. . . . In adding more negotiation steps, however, the designer needs to be careful. In some cases, the easy availability of a higher-level person will simply discourage people from reaching agreement at a lower level and will thus make lower-level negotiation a *pro forma* step. . . .

PRINCIPLE 2: BUILD IN "LOOP-BACKS" TO NEGOTIATION

Interests-based procedures will not always resolve disputes, yet a rights or power contest can be excessively costly. The wise designer will thus build in procedures that encourage the disputants to turn back from such contests to negotiation. These are what we call "loop-back" procedures. It is useful to distinguish such procedures on the basis of whether they encourage disputants to "loop back" from a rights contest or from a power contest.

Looping Back from a Rights Contest

Some loop-back procedures provide information about the disputants' rights and the likely outcome of a rights contest. The disputants can then use this information to negotiate a resolution. Rights are thus determined at the lowest possible cost, while the resolution remains consensual — usually enhancing the parties' satisfaction, the quality of the relationship, and the durability of the agreement. A brief description of some of these procedures follows:

Information Procedures

In recent years, thousands of claims against asbestos manufacturers have flooded the judicial system. Some innovative designers, working as agents of the court, have set up data bases containing information about the characteristics and results of asbestos claims that have been resolved either by trial or by settlement. When a new claim is filed, the designers identify similar claims in the data base and use the information about the outcomes of previously resolved cases to determine the range within which the new case is likely to be resolved. This information reduces uncertainty about the likely outcome of the case and provides an independent standard that can help the lawyers settle the case. . . .

Advisory Arbitration

Another way to provide information about rights is advisory arbitration. While the arbitrator's decision is not binding, it provides the parties with information about the likely result if the dispute is taken to arbitration or court. This information encourages a negotiated resolution by reducing the parties' uncertainty about an adjudicated decision. . . . The grievance mediation procedure that we designed for the coal industry . . . combines mediation with advisory arbitration. If mediation fails, the parties may request the third party to predict how an arbitrator would rule. Armed with this information, the parties may continue to negotiate or they may accept the predicted outcome. . . .

Looping Back from a Power Contest

The designer can also build in ways to encourage disputants to turn back from power contests and to engage in negotiations instead.

Cooling-Off Periods

Rarely does a negotiated agreement look so attractive as when the parties are on the verge of a costly power contest or are in the midst of one. One simple procedure designed to take advantage of this receptivity is a cooling-off period — a specified time during which the disputants refrain from a power contest. The Taft-Hartley Act and the Railway Labor Act both provide for *cooling-off periods* before strikes that threaten to cause a national emergency. During the cooling-off period, negotiations, while not required, normally take place. Cooling-off periods are also useful in small-scale disputes. In the Noel Coward play *Private Lives*, a bickering couple agree that, whenever an argument threatens to get out of control, one person will shout "Solomon Isaacs," which will bring all conversation to a halt for five minutes while each tries to calm down.

Crisis Negotiation Procedures

. . . Negotiation in times of crisis places special demands on negotiators. It may be useful therefore to provide crisis negotiation training — simulations, checklists, and standard operating procedures. It may also be helpful to establish a crisis communication mechanism. In disputes between the United States and the Soviet Union, the hotline serves this purpose.

Intervention by Third Parties

If violence breaks out during a strike or a family argument, the police intervene to stop the fighting. A form of third-party intervention is thus already built into many dispute resolution systems. In some cases, additional third-party intervention is useful. One example is the Conflict Managers Program in San Francisco schools, which trains children to intervene in playground disputes. Wearing bright orange T-shirts printed with the words "Conflict Manager," the children work in pairs during lunch and recess to spot and try to mediate emerging disputes. On the international scene, neutral United Nations peace-keeping forces separate hostile forces and buy time for negotiation and mediation. Such efforts require skills training as well as such resources as administrators and third-party interveners.

PRINCIPLE 3: PROVIDE LOW-COST RIGHTS AND POWER BACKUPS

A key part of an effective dispute resolution system is low-cost procedures for providing a final resolution based on rights or power. Such procedures serve as a backup should interests-based negotiation fail to resolve the dispute.

Low-Cost Procedures to Determine Rights

Conventional [and Hybrid] Arbitration

A less costly alternative to court is arbitration — in other words, private adjudication. Like court, arbitration is a rights procedure in which the parties (or their representatives) present evidence and arguments to a neutral third party who makes a binding decision. Arbitration procedures can be simpler, quicker, and less expensive than court procedures. Formal rules need not be followed, strict time limits can be agreed to, and restrictions can be placed on the use of lawyers and of expensive evidence discovery procedures. . . .

Low-Cost Procedures to Determine Power

Sometimes, even when interests and rights-based procedures are available, agreement is impossible because one or both parties believes it is more powerful than the other, and can obtain a more satisfactory resolution through a power contest. The designer, anticipating this situation, should consider building into the system a low-cost power procedure to be used as a backup to all other procedures. Getting the parties to accept such a procedure may be difficult, since each party is likely to oppose any new procedure that appears to give an advantage to the other. As a result such a design effort is likely to succeed only when the use of power procedures imposes high costs on all parties. There are a variety of relatively low-cost power contests including voting, limited strikes, and rules of prudence.

Voting

Before the National Labor Relations Act (NLRA) of 1935, disputes about workers right to engage in collective bargaining were handled through bitter strikes and violence. Some workers were killed; many were seriously injured. The NLRA did a great deal to end the violence by setting up a low-cost power contest — the union election — and by requiring employers to bargain in good faith with a union elected by a majority of the employees. . . .

Rules of Prudence

The parties may agree, tacitly or explicitly, to limit the destructiveness of tactics used in power contests. For example, youth gangs may agree to use only fists, not knives or guns in their fights. The United States and the Soviet Union observe certain rules of prudence — such as no use (explosion) of nuclear weapons, no direct use of force against the other side's troops, and no direct military action against the other's vital interests — in order to avert the highest-cost power contest, a thermonuclear war. . . .

PRINCIPLE 4: BUILD IN CONSULTATION BEFORE, FEEDBACK AFTER

A fourth design principle is to prevent unnecessary conflict and head off future disputes. This may be done through notification and consultation, as well as through post-dispute analysis and feedback.

Notification and Consultation

Notification refers simply to an announcement in advance of the intended action; consultation goes further and offers an opportunity to discuss the proposed action before it takes place. Notification and consultation can prevent disputes that arise through sheer misunderstanding. They can also reduce the anger and knee-jerk opposition that often result when decisions are made unilaterally and abruptly. Finally, they serve to identify points of difference early on so that they may be negotiated.

Post–Dispute Analysis and Feedback

Another goal is to help parties to learn from their disputes in order to prevent similar disputes in the future. Some disputes are symptomatic of a broader problem that the disputants or their organizations need to learn about and deal with. The wise designer builds into the system procedures for post-dispute analysis and feedback. At some manufacturing companies, lawyers and managers regularly analyze consumer complaints to determine what changes in product design might reduce the likelihood of similar disputes in the future. At the Massachusetts Institute of Technology, ombudsmen identify university practices that are causing disputes and suggest changes in those practices.

Where a broader community interest is at stake, the designer may include a different sort of feedback: a procedure for aggregating complaints and taking action to protect the community. For example, some consumer mediation agencies keep records of complaints against each merchant and alert the appropriate state authorities when repeated complaints are lodged against the same merchant.

Establishing a Forum

One means of institutionalizing consultation and post-dispute analysis is to establish a regular forum for discussion. The parties may benefit from meeting regularly to discuss issues that arise in a dispute but whose causes and implications range far beyond the dispute.

PRINCIPLE 5: ARRANGE PROCEDURES IN A LOW-TO-HIGH-COST SEQUENCE

The design principles above suggest creating a sequence of procedures from interests-based negotiation to loop-back procedures to low-cost rights and power backups. The sequence can be imagined as a series of steps up a "dispute resolution ladder." . . . The sequence used in the oil companies' joint venture contains three successive steps: first, try to catch disputes early by resolving them in the partnership committee; if that fails, bring in two uninvolved senior executives to negotiate; and, if that fails, turn to low-cost arbitration rather than to expensive litigation.

PRINCIPLE 6: PROVIDE THE NECESSARY MOTIVATION, SKILLS, AND RESOURCES

A final principle cuts across all others: Make sure the procedures work by providing the motivation to use them, the relevant skills, and the necessary resources. In designing a system, for example, to deal with disputes over the location of hazardous waste treatment facilities, as described earlier . . . one state legislature makes negotiation mandatory and provides resources in the form of technical assistance to aid the negotiation process. Without the necessary motivation, skills, and resources, procedures might well fail.

> **Problem 13-6.**   *Designing Systems for Different Contexts*
>
> What role does context play in designing a system? Design a dispute resolution system for (1) grade disputes at your school, (2) employment grievances at your workplace, (3) disputes within your living unit or family. How do your systems differ? Why? What values are expressed in each? Who are the decision makers or third-party neutrals in each system? How much direct negotiation or interaction have you designed for the principal disputants?

D. TRANSACTIONAL DISPUTE RESOLUTION: BEFORE THE DISPUTE

If mediators, facilitators, and other third-party neutrals help disputing parties find solutions to their conflicts, or facilitate the making of complex public policy decisions, why shouldn't they also devote their skills to crafting good deals or transactions at the beginning of relationships? Increasingly, business lawyers and clients are seeing the benefits of inviting in a third party to create value, prevent waste, or remove strategic barriers to information asymmetries, as well as to deal with emotional, cognitive, and other barriers to agreement and to facilitate Pareto-efficient (most gain with least harm to parties) and relationally satisfying arrangements in complex transactions. This creative use of ADR-like techniques to prevent disputes and create new transactions and entities is gaining more and more attention, especially in complex deals involving partnerships of venture capitalists in the private sector, public funding sources, governments, insurers, lenders, suppliers, developers, and consumers. This kind of managed transactional dispute resolution can be used in multiparty business deals, siting and design issues,[8] major construction projects,[9] and in the development of new projects (land use, joint fundraising) and entities (joint public and private agencies, such as Redevelopment and Stadium Authorities in many localities). The article below outlines some of the advantages of using multiparty mediation techniques in forming contracts and facilitating complex multiparty transactions.

---

8. For example, multiparty efforts were employed to develop designs for the rebuilding of the World Trade Center in New York. See Rebuilding the World Trade Center Site (Program on Negotiation, Harvard Law School and International Institute for Conflict Prevention and Resolution, featuring Lawrence Susskind, 2007).

9. See ConsensusDocs.org, Construction Contracts Built by Consensus, *http://consensusdocs.org/* (2009); Frank Carr, Kim Hurtado, Charles Lancaster, Charles Markert & Paul Tucker, Partnering in Construction: A Practical Guide of Project Success (1999).

Scott R. Peppet, **CONTRACT FORMATION IN IMPERFECT MARKETS: SHOULD WE USE MEDIATORS IN DEALS?**

19 Ohio St. J. on Disp. Resol. 283, 285-286, 298-301, 304-310, 314-321, 325-337, 339 (2004)

Much of [the] scholarship [on the lawyer's role in transactional bargaining] has its roots in Ronald Gilson's now classic article, *Value Creation by Business Lawyers: Legal Skills and Asset Pricing.*[10] In that article, Gilson asks how lawyers create value for their transacting clients. If the market is perfect and prices capital assets efficiently — as finance theory often assumes — there is little for a lawyer to do in a commercial transaction other than engage in distributive bargaining and add transaction costs. Gilson hypothesized, however, that the market does not always price transactions efficiently. In the real world, transaction costs, information asymmetries, strategic behavior, and other barriers to efficient asset pricing sometimes stand in the way of closing deals. And in those market imperfections lie a lawyer's opportunity. A business lawyer can use representations, warranties, and other contractual devices to bring the real world's imperfect market closer to the idealized world of efficient markets.

Gilson labeled this role "transaction cost engineering." For example, whereas in a perfect world transacting parties would have similar information and forecasts about the future performance of a commercial asset to be traded, in the real world expectations often differ. This makes it difficult to price that asset. One side may think the asset is worth a lot because the future looks bright; the other side argues that future prospects are grim. Such differences may lead to a negotiation breakdown and no deal. Lawyers can bridge such gaps, however, using an "earnout contract" that makes payment contingent on performance. By using legal devices to minimize the impact of market imperfections, a lawyer can add value to a transaction.

This Article takes Gilson's powerful explanation of the role of lawyers in commercial transactions as the jumping-off point for a slightly different inquiry into the dynamics of dealmaking. It focuses on the following paradox implicit within Gilson's article. On the one hand, Gilson recognizes that transaction costs, information asymmetries, and strategic behavior may keep parties from consummating deals. This is what creates an opportunity for lawyers to craft contracts that correct for these market imperfections. On the other hand, *lawyers* may also fall prey to the *same* transaction costs, information asymmetries, and strategic behavior as *they* negotiate. In other words, as lawyers try to negotiate contracts to help clients overcome these barriers to reaching a deal, these same barriers may compromise the lawyers' ability to do so.

---

10. Ronald J. Gilson, Value Creation by Business Lawyers: Legal Skills and Asset Pricing, 94 Yale L.J. 239 (1984).

Is there a role for a different kind of player in transactions — a player who could help parties, including business lawyers, to overcome these various market imperfections as they negotiate the terms and conditions of a deal? In particular, is there a role for *neutral* intermediaries — or mediators — in dealmaking? . . .

ECONOMIC JUSTIFICATIONS FOR TRANSACTIONAL MEDIATION

Discovering and Optimizing Gains from Trade

Transactional negotiators theoretically face similar adverse selection problems to those faced by disputing parties. First, the parties may not discover that trade is possible. Just as a litigating defendant may posture and bluff to try to low-ball a plaintiff, a buyer in a transaction may be tempted to try to get a better deal by "looking cheap." In other words, even if a buyer is willing to pay a high price, she may do better by looking as if she will only pay a low one. The opposite is true of sellers. One common example from the transactional context illustrates the problem. Because a high-value buyer does not want to signal his type to the seller, and because a seller is likely to equate having deep pockets with a willingness to spend, a deep-pocketed buyer may seek to hide its identity to prevent giving away too much to the seller. In this case an agent — such as an attorney — can be used to present an anonymous offer, thereby eliminating any signal about reservation price that might be inferred from the buyer's identity. An agent cannot, however, overcome the more basic adverse selection problem caused by the simple fact that making *any* offer sends information about the offeror's previously private reservation price. Information asymmetries may thus lead parties to exaggerate offers and demands in order to get a better deal. . . .

For example, as part of a larger project on fair division procedures, Steven Brams and Alan Taylor note that a mediator should theoretically be able to help merging companies resolve disagreements over "social issues," such as how to name the post-merger corporation, how to resolve status and position questions (e.g., who will be CEO), and where to locate the new company's headquarters. After reviewing a sample of large mergers that collapsed because of disputes over such issues, they concluded that "[t]hese deals highlight the need for effective dispute-resolution techniques in merger negotiations." Their "adjusted winner" procedure is designed to reduce deal failure and optimize the efficiency of trades about these social issues. The parties assign points to the various issues in contention and a mediator referee then uses their assignments to plumb for the most value-creating solutions to their disagreements.

Howard Raiffa also suggests that a mediator might serve as a "contract embellisher" in transactions. He suggests that at the start of bargaining a mediator could privately interview each party about its needs, priorities, and perceptions. The mediator would lock away that information and the parties would be left alone to negotiate a deal. At the conclusion of their negotiation, but prior to closing the deal, the intervener would return. After examining the terms of the parties' agreement, the intervener would try to use his private information about the parties' interests to craft a superior deal. He would then show his substitute agreement to each party privately. If both sides agreed that the mediator's suggestion was superior to their own contract, the substitution would be made. There would be no haggling about the terms of the mediator's proposal — it would be a take-it-or-leave-it situation.

Transactional Bargaining and Bilateral Monopoly

[Peppet goes on to suggest ways that mediators might help parties in various stages of complex deals ("matching," "pricing," "closing," and "renegotiation") where "bilateral monopoly characteristics" — as opposed to an open competitive market — surface.]

Matching

. . . Some transactions require that parties share confidential information to determine whether a match is possible. . . . A mediator could help parties in these circumstances. By comparing information, the mediator could determine whether a deal is possible or whether further discussions would be worthwhile. As long as the parties trust that the mediator can and will keep such information confidential, and so long as the mediator is sufficiently expert to render an opinion on the viability of a deal, the parties might use a mediator to overcome . . . matching stage strategic difficulties. . . .

Pricing

After finding each other, the parties must set a basic deal price. This often takes place through direct negotiation by the principals. Can a mediator add value in pricing? Some transactional contexts are true bilateral monopolies. In such deals, pricing may become strategic, as each side tries to conceal its reservation price to negotiate for a better deal. As in litigation, mediator services have arisen to help transacting parties deal with strategic problems in some bilateral monopoly bargaining. Collective bargaining is a common example of bilateral monopoly contracting — the presence of a union serves to limit the employer's market alternatives — and mediators often assist in this domain. Similarly, the sale of an Internet domain name is a modern bilateral monopoly transaction prone to strategic bargaining. Again, mediation and arbitration are used to overcome these strategic problems. . . . In addition to such bilateral monopolies, one would expect to see strategic bargaining — and the potential for mediator intervention — in pricing transactions in any sort of thin market. . . .

Closing

. . . A lawyer-mediator might prevent the parties' lawyers from blowing up the deal unnecessarily, and, perhaps more importantly, from reaching an inefficient set of contract terms. As lawyers and clients allocate legal risks and opportunities, possibilities for gains from trade arise because of differences in the parties' preferences and relative valuations. Although the bargaining about a single contract term may be largely distributive — I want a more restrictive allocation of responsibility for an environmental cleanup, you want a more expansive term — contracting attorneys can generally create value by trading between terms. For example, if a contract contains ten legal provisions (A, B, . . . J), parties X and Y will value those terms differently. If X finds term A extremely important and Y term B, they can create joint gains by allocating the risk in term A as X prefers and the risk in term B as Y prefers. And so on.

If transacting lawyers shared information openly, they would find such trades (at least to the extent that doing so was justified in light of the transaction costs incurred through the additional bargaining that would be required). As a result, one would expect to see highly tailored contractual provisions in complex deals — tailored terms would reflect these tailored trades. . . .

A mediator might help the parties to overcome these strategic difficulties, thereby permitting more complex contracting. Again, a mediator can solicit and compare information from each side, potentially finding value-creating trades. The mediator might test the viability of various packages of trades of legal terms, asking each side in confidence which of several sets of terms the party would accept, but not revealing the origin of the various packages. In this way, the mediator can surmount the adverse selection problems that might otherwise prevent tailoring contract language during the deal's closing stage.

Renegotiation (and Planning for Renegotiation During Closing)

Many deals do not end at closing. Instead, in complex transactions the parties may revisit their initial agreement and renegotiate key terms that were either originally left open or have become inefficient or outdated. . . . [D]isputes that arise during renegotiation can be difficult for parties to resolve because of the temptation to extract opportunistic gains as soon as both parties are locked into a long-term relationship by relationship-specific investments. . . .

In addition to using mediators during the renegotiation stage to resolve disputes, parties may also try to mitigate post-contractual opportunism through tailored contract terms that create incentives to comply. A contract without such safeguards will impose greater costs on a party expecting to make transaction-specific investments, and that party will therefore set a higher price for the transaction. To the extent that contract terms can be used to constrain the threat of opportunism, it will increase the surplus available in the transaction. . . .

Parties, however, may not always avail themselves of such opportunism-constraining terms. First, by the time negotiating parties (or their lawyers) conclude their closing stage negotiations, they may not sufficiently trust each other to rely on contractual solutions to future moral hazard problems. Anecdotal evidence suggests that "earnouts," for example, even if negotiated carefully, are often bought out from M&A deals just prior to closing. The parties know that the "earnout" provision's legal constraints on future opportunism will be imperfect, and by the closing date the parties may no longer trust each other enough to overcome doubts about such opportunism. To the extent that using a mediator throughout a transaction can help the parties better maintain trust, the parties might be more inclined to rely on such potentially value-creating terms.

Second, even if the parties *do* trust each other, they may avoid discussing such opportunism-constraining terms for fear of destroying that trust. Edward Bernstein has described the problem of "attitudinal costs" in transactional bargaining. When a party suggests crafting tailored contract provisions that are obviously intended to minimize the threat of future opportunism by the other party, that other party may receive the suggestion badly. The receiving party may perceive the suggestion as a signal that future disagreements will have to be resolved through formal contracting rather than more informal, friendly means. This may cause mistrust or suspicion and lead the receiving party to become more guarded or adversarial. This, in turn:

> [M]ay reduce the value of the transaction if it contemplates a continuing relationship or performance over time, such as a partnership, joint venture or construction contract. If negotiations are hostile, each party can expect a reduced probability of voluntary performance by the other who, if he has concluded that acting in the spirit of the transaction will not be reciprocated, will be more inclined to base his breach or perform decisions upon a comparison of legal sanctions against the benefit of breach (quoting Edward A. Bernstein, Law and Economics and the Structure of Value Adding Contracts: A Contract Lawyer's View of the Law & Economics Literature, 74 Or. L. Rev. 189, 231 (1995)).

Bernstein has analogized this to the risk for a personal relationship created by suggesting the negotiation of a prenuptial agreement. . . .

BEHAVIORAL JUSTIFICATIONS FOR TRANSACTIONAL MEDIATION

Managing Attributions, Emotions, and Relationships

Attributions and Emotions in Transactions

Like disputes, transactional negotiations are certainly not immune from emotions and attributions. Tempers flare, accusations are made, and relationships sour. Mergers and acquisitions, for example, can give rise to intense emotional disagreements that put great strain on the underlying business relationships. As Robert Kindler, an M & A partner at Cravath, Swaine & Moore has said, "Even transactions that make absolute economic sense do not happen unless the social issues work." Particularly if one party is more accustomed to negotiations than another or more sophisticated with doing deals in a particular context, transacting parties may spend a great deal of time and energy on these relational issues.

A neutral positioned between two parties can often help them to gain . . . perspective. As discussed above, anger is often driven by mis-attributions about another person's motivations. In strategic situations it is easy to assume that when the other bargainer "starts high" or "holds out," they do so because they intend to harm you or to treat you unfairly. Bargainers are less likely to attribute such actions to the exigencies of circumstance. By screening some overly opportunistic offers and at times sending fuzzy rather than clear information between the parties, a mediator can blunt such emotions and thereby keep the negotiations on track. Over time, avoiding emotional disagreements may help the parties to establish trust.

This not only leads to more amiable negotiations, but also has serious substantive benefits. As mentioned above, if the parties trust each other they may be better positioned to find value-creating solutions to their substantive differences. They may be able to rely more on informal agreements rather than contractual obligations and may be more flexible in the face of unexpected bumps in the road. Perhaps most importantly, they may avoid the destructive cycle of mis-attributions that can lead parties to "blow up" a deal or reach a Pareto-inefficient agreement.

Problem 13-7. *The Deal Mediator*

What kinds of transactions lend themselves to "deal mediators" (third-party neutrals who help put together the transaction)? What qualities would you look for in a deal mediator?

Peppet argues elsewhere in his article that "neither most existing [state] regulations nor the new [Uniform Mediation Act] extend sufficiently clear confidentiality protections to transactional mediation to foster mediator intervention in deals. . . . As a result, this regulatory regime may inhibit the development of transactional mediators." This conclusion arises from language in regulations that define mediation — and the scope of confidentiality protections — to mean a neutral's assistance with *disputes*. To remedy this shortcoming, Peppet proposes that "[s]tates should modify their existing statutes or their adoption of the UMA to account for transactional mediators. . . . States could simply replace 'dispute' with 'dispute or other matter' [in definitions of privileged mediation] per Rule 2.4's [Model Rules of Professional Conduct] approach. Like the new Rule 2.4, the comments to the state's mediation privilege statute could then clarify that 'other matter' includes transactional mediation."

You have now seen many of the creative ways in which dispute resolution processes are being expanded, modified, and adapted to facilitate human action in a variety of contexts, including private and public dealings and decision making. In the final chapter that follows we ask you to think about what new uses might be made of these processes that you have studied. What are some of the opportunities and challenges presented by the use of these different methods of dispute resolution and problem solving in the wide variety of contexts in which they might be employed?

Further Reading

Max Bazerman (Ed.). (2005). *Negotiation, Decision Making and Conflict Management.* International Critical Library on Business and Management.

Lisa Blomgren Bingham, Cynthia J. Halberlin, Denise Walker & Won-Tae Chung, *Dispute System Design and Justice in Employment Dispute Resolution: Mediation in the Workplace,* 14 HARV. NEGOT. L. REV. 1-50 (2009).

Susan L. Carpenter & W.L.D. Kennedy. (2001). *Managing Public Disputes: A Practical Guide for Professionals in Government, Business and Citizen Groups.* San Francisco: Jossey-Bass Publishers.

Cathy Costantino & Christina Sickles Merchant. (1996). *Designing Conflict Management Systems.* San Francisco: Jossey-Bass Publishers.

E. Franklin Dukes, Marina A. Piscolish & John B. Stephens. (2000). *Reaching for Higher Ground in Conflict Resolution: Tools for Powerful Groups and Communities.* San Francisco: Jossey-Bass Publishers.

John Forester. (2009). *Dealing with Differences: Dramas of Mediating Public Disputes.* New York: Oxford University Press.

Ronald Gilson & Robert H. Mnookin (eds.), *Business Lawyers and Value Creation for Clients,* 74 OREGON L. REV. 74: 1-13 (1995).

L. Michael Hager & Robert Pritchard, *Deal Mediation: How ADR Techniques Can Help Achieve Durable Agreements in Global Markets,* 14 ICSID REV. FOREIGN INVESTMENT L. J. 1 (1999).

Harvard Negotiation Law Review. (2009). *Symposium on Dispute System Design* 14: 1-342.

Carrie Menkel-Meadow, *Are There Systemic Ethics Issues in Dispute System Design? And What We Should [Not] Do About It: Lessons from International and Domestic Fronts,* 14 HARV. NEGOT. L. REV. 195-231 (2009).

Carrie Menkel-Meadow (Ed.). (2011). *Complex Dispute Resolution.* Farnham, UK and Burlington, VT: Ashgate Press.

Hallum Movius & Lawrence Susskind. (2009). *Built to Win: Creating a World Class Negotiating Organization.* Boston, Mass: Harvard Business School.

Roger Schwarz. (2002). *The Skilled Facilitator.* San Francisco: Jossey-Bass Publishers.

Stephanie Smith & Jan Martinez, *An Analytic Framework for Dispute Systems Design,* 14 HARV. NEGOT. L. REV. 123-170 (2009).

Lawrence Susskind, Sarah McKearnan & Jennifer Thomas Larmer. (1999). *The Consensus Building Handbook: A Comprehensive Guide to Reaching Agreement.* Thousand Oaks, Calif: Sage Publications.

Lawrence Susskind & Jeffrey Cruickshank. (2006). *Breaking Robert's Rules: The New Way to Run Your Meeting, Build Consensus and Get Results.* New York: Oxford Univ. Press.

APPENDIX

(Guidelines for Convening and Leading Consensus-Building Fora, from

Lawrence Susskind, *An Alternative to Robert's Rules of Order For Groups, Organizations and Ad Hoc Assemblies That Want to Cooperate by Consensus* (1999))

Section I. Helping an Ad Hoc Assembly Reach Agreement

We have identified five steps in the consensus building process: convening, clarifying responsibilities, deliberating, deciding, and implementing agreements. The key problems for ad hoc assemblies (as opposed to permanent entities) are organizational. Selecting the relevant stakeholders, finding individuals who can represent those interests effectively, getting agreement on ground rules and an agenda, and securing funding are particularly difficult when the participants have no shared history and may have few, if any, interests in common.

[The basic rules are provided below. For full elaboration on how to implement these rules, consult the original source, *The Consensus Building Handbook*.]

Step 1: Convening
1.1   Initiate a Discussion about Whether to Have a Consensus Building Dialogue.
1.2   Prepare a Written Conflict Assessment.
    1.2.1   Assign responsibility for preparing the conflict assessment.
    1.2.2   Identify a first circle of essential participants.
    1.2.3   Identify a second circle of suggested participants.
    1.2.4   Complete initial interviews.
    1.2.5   Prepare a draft conflict assessment. A draft conflict assessment ought to include a clear categorization of all the relevant stakeholders, a summary of the interests and concerns of each category (without attribution to any individual or organization), and — given the results of the interviews — a proposal as to whether the assessor thinks it is worth going forward with a consensus building process. If the assessor believes such a process should be organized, he or she also ought to recommend a possible agenda, timetable, and budget for the process.
    1.2.6   Prepare a final conflict assessment. Every interviewee ought to receive a copy of the draft conflict assessment and be given adequate time to offer comments and suggestions. The assessor ought to use this period as an occasion to modify the conflict assessment in a way that will allow all the key stakeholders to agree to attend at least an organizational meeting, if a recommendation to go forward is accepted by the convening entity. If key stakeholding groups refuse to participate, the process should probably not go forward. The final conflict assessment ought to include an appendix listing the name of every individual and organization interviewed. In appropriate instances, especially those involving public agencies, the final conflict assessment ought to become a public document.

        1.2.7   Convene an organizational meeting to consider the recommendations of the conflict assessment.

1.3   If a Decision Is Made to Proceed, Identify Appropriate Representatives.

        1.3.1   Identify missing actors likely to affect the credibility of the process.

        1.3.2   Use facilitated caucusing, if necessary.

        1.3.3   Use proxies to represent hard-to-represent groups.

        1.3.4   Identify possible alternate representatives.

1.4   Locate the Necessary Funding.

Step 2: Clarifying Responsibilities

2.1   Clarify the Roles of Facilitators, Mediators, and Recorders.

        2.1.1   Select and specify responsibilities of a facilitator or a mediator.

        2.1.2   Select and specify the responsibilities of a recorder.

        2.1.3   Form an executive committee.

        2.1.4   Consider appointing a chair.

2.2   Set Rules Regarding the Participation of Observers.

2.3   Set an Agenda and Ground Rules.

        2.3.1   Get agreement on the range of issues to be discussed.

        2.3.2   Specify a timetable.

        2.3.3   Finalize procedural ground rules. The final version of the conflict assessment should contain a set of suggested ground rules. These should address procedural concerns raised in the interviews undertaken by the assessor. The suggested ground rules should be reviewed and ratified at the opening organizational meeting. Most ground rules for consensus building cover a range of topics including (a) the rights and responsibilities of participants, (b) behavioral guidelines that participants will be expected to follow, (c) rules governing interaction with the media, (d) decision making procedures, and (e) strategies for handling disagreement and ensuring implementation of an agreement if one is reached.

        2.3.4   Require all participants to sign the ground rules.

        2.3.5   Clarify the extent to which precedents are or are not being set.

2.4   Assess Computer-Based Communication Options.

2.5   Establish a Mailing List.

Step 3: Deliberating

3.1   Pursue Deliberations in a Constructive Fashion.

        3.1.1   Express concerns in an unconditionally constructive manner.

        3.1.2   Never trade interests for relationships.

        3.1.3   Engage in active listening.

        3.1.4   Disagree without being disagreeable.

        3.1.5   Strive for the greatest degree of transparency possible.

3.2   Separate Inventing from Committing.

        3.2.1   Strive to invent options for mutual gain.

        3.2.2   Emphasize packaging.

        3.2.3   Test options by playing the game of "what if?"

3.3   Create Subcommittees and Seek Expert Advice.

     3.3.1   Formulate joint fact-finding procedures. If left to their own devices, participants in a consensus building process will produce their own versions of the relevant facts (or technical data) consistent with their definition of the problem and their sense of how the problem or issue should be handled. This often leads to what is called adversary science. It is better if all participants can agree on the information that ought to be used to answer unanswered or contested questions. An agreement on joint fact-finding should specify (a) what information is sought, (b) how it should be generated (i.e., by whom and using which methods), and (c) how gaps or disagreements among technical sources will be handled. It is perfectly reasonable for there to be agreement on facts while substantial disagreement on how to interpret such facts remains.

     3.3.2   Identify expert advisers.

     3.3.3   Organize drafting or joint fact-finding subcommittees.

     3.3.4   Incorporate the work of subcommittees or expert advisers.

3.4   Use a Single-Text Procedure.

     3.4.1   Draft preliminary proposals.

     3.4.2   Brainstorm.

     3.4.3   Withhold criticism.

     3.4.4   Avoid attribution and individual authorship. Consensus building is best viewed as a group enterprise. When individuals or a single group insists on claiming authorship of a particular proposal (i.e., in an effort to enhance its standing with its own constituents), they are likely to provoke criticism or counter proposals. Consensus is much more likely to emerge if participants avoid attributing or claiming authorship of specific ideas or packages.

     3.4.5   Consolidate improvements in the text. As the dialogue proceeds, participants should focus on "improving" a consolidated single text prepared by a drafting subcommittee or a neutral party. Avoid competing texts that seek to maximize the interests of one or just a few parties. When changes to a text are made, do not indicate where they originated. All revisions to the single text need to be acceptable to the group as a whole.

     3.4.6   Search for contingent options. As the discussion proceeds, participants should search for ways of bridging differences by suggesting contingent agreements. Using an "if . . . then" format is likely to be helpful. That is, if a set of participants is opposed to the prevailing draft of a recommendation or a consolidated agreement, then the set of participants should suggest the changes necessary for it to accept that proposal.

3.5   Modify the Agenda and Ground Rules (if necessary).

     3.5.1   Reconsider the responsibilities, obligations, and powers of sponsoring agencies and organizations. During the course of a consensus building process, it is not inappropriate to revisit the assignment of responsibilities and obligations of sponsoring agencies and organizations set by the participants at the outset. Changes should be made only if consensus can be reached on suggested revisions.

    3.5.2   Consider the obligations and powers of late arrivals. During the course of a consensus building process, as unanticipated issues or concerns arise, it may be desirable to add new participants. With the concurrence of the group, representatives of new stakeholding groups — attracted or recruited because of the emerging agreement or shifts in the agenda — can be added. The obligations and powers of latecomers (especially with regard to requesting that issues already covered be reconsidered) should be considered by the full group upon the arrival of new participants. Changes in the agenda or the ground rules should be made only with the concurrence of all parties.

3.6   Complete the Deliberations.

Step 4: Deciding

4.1   Try to Maximize Joint Gains.

    4.1.1   Test the scope and depth of any agreement. The results of every effort to maximize joint gains should be continuously assessed. This is best accomplished by having a neutral party ask whether the participants can think of any "improvements" to the proposed agreement. In addition, it is important to ask whether each representative is prepared to "sell" the proposal to his or her constituents and whether each can "live with" the group's recommendation.

    4.1.2   Use straw polls.

    4.1.3   Seek unanimity.

    4.1.4   Settle for an overwhelming level of support. It is appropriate to settle for an overwhelming level of support for final recommendations or decisions, if unanimity cannot be achieved within the agreed-on time frame. While it is not possible to specify an exact percentage of support that would constitute an overwhelming endorsement, it would be hard to make a claim for consensus having been reached if fewer than 80 percent of the participants in a group were not in agreement.

    4.1.5   Make every effort to satisfy the concerns of holdouts. Prior to making its final recommendations or decisions, a consensus building group should make one final attempt to satisfy the concerns of any remaining holdout(s). This can be done by asking those who can't live with the final recommendations or decisions to suggest modifications to the package or tentative agreement that would make it acceptable to them without making it less attractive to anyone who has already expressed support for it.

4.2   Keep a Record.

    4.2.1   Maintain a visual summary of key points of agreement and disagreement.

    4.2.2   Review written versions of all decisions before they are finalized. A written draft of the final report of a consensus building process should be circulated to all participants before they are asked to indicate support or opposition. Initial drafting responsibility may be allocated to the neutral, but ultimately all parties must take responsibility for a final report if one is produced.

4.2.3   Maintain a written summary of every discussion for review by all participants.

Step 5: *Implementing Agreements*

5.1   Seek Ratification by Constituencies.

5.1.1   Hold representatives responsible for canvassing constituent responses to a penultimate draft.

5.1.2   Hold representatives responsible for signing and committing to a final agreement in their own name.

5.1.3   Include the necessary steps to ensure that informal agreements are incorporated or adopted by whatever formal mechanisms are appropriate. Often, the results of a consensus building process are advisory. Sometimes they must be ratified by a set of elected or appointed officials. Any agreement resulting from a consensus building process should contain within it a clear statement of the steps that will be taken (and who they will be taken by) to ensure that the informal agreement will be incorporated or adopted by whatever formal means are appropriate. For example, informally negotiated agreements can be stipulated as additional conditions when a permit is granted by a government agency or the head of an organization. This must be done according to the rules of the permitting agency or the organization.

5.1.4   Incorporate appropriate monitoring procedures.

5.1.5   Include reopener and dispute resolution procedures.

5.1.6   Evaluate.

 *Chapter 14*

Choosing an Appropriate Process: Your Clients and the Future of ADR

Never underestimate the power of a small group of committed people to change the world. In fact, it is the only thing that ever has.

— Margaret Mead

Justice cannot be for one side alone but must be for both.
— Eleanor Roosevelt (and engraved in the Supreme Court of the United Kingdom)

You have now studied a wide variety of processes used to resolve conflicts and solve problems in many different settings. These processes offer opportunities and challenges. Opportunities include continuing to develop new processes to deal with increasingly diverse sets of disputes and parties, and engaging in the evolution of process pluralism. As you have seen in Chapter 13, a new part of the field of dispute resolution, called *dispute system design*, focuses on developing appropriate processes for different kinds of disputes in a variety of repetitive and organizational settings. But challenges also exist. While the modern dispute resolution processes have grown out of dissatisfactions with the cost, duration, rigidity, and complexity of conventional litigation processes, some worry that those new processes also have limitations and difficulties, such as in "privatizing" justice or reinforcing party inequalities. In this final chapter we ask you to reflect on how we should evaluate and assess the effectiveness of particular processes and to try to imagine what new processes might be developed in the future. Assessing and evaluating which process is appropriate for a particular legal matter or problem has at least two important components:

1. How to advise your own client about what process is appropriate for his or her particular matter, some of which we have already previewed in Chapters 2 (counseling your client) and 3 (choosing among different negotiation approaches in particular settings). In a sense this can be labeled the *"private"* side of ADR — lawyers assisting their clients with choices about which process is most likely to help the client achieve his or her goals and objectives.

2. As a matter of more *public policy*, which processes are best for achieving societal or institutional goals? Which processes should public institutions like courts, legislatures, and administrative agencies encourage and support? When should public institutions control private problem solving? In what circumstances should legal, political, or social disputes remain in the public eye for transparency, political debate, and formal resolution.

Both of these questions require us to think about parties' goals and what public interests are involved. Considering these questions requires us to be rigorous in how we evaluate the processes, empirically, strategically, and jurisprudentially. We will examine these issues in this chapter, looking first at how lawyers help clients evaluate particular processes, then at how these processes have been studied and evaluated so far. Finally, we return to the issues with which we began in Chapter 1. As we contemplate a future of further ADR use and development, what are the basic values we hope to express in our process designs and choices?

You are the next generation of dispute resolution professionals. We hope, through the learning you have done with this book, and in this course, you will rise to the possibilities of creating new processes for the resolution of new problems and conflicts that we cannot even imagine today.

A. CHOOSING AMONG DISPUTE RESOLUTION PROCESSES: PRIVATE INTERESTS

1. Comparing the Processes

The following excerpt from two founders of the modern dispute resolution movement is considered "a classic" in how to advise clients about the variety of dispute resolution options and how to ensure that clients' problems are addressed in the most appropriate process.

 Frank E. A. Sander & Stephen B. Goldberg, **FITTING THE FORUM TO THE FUSS: A USER-FRIENDLY GUIDE TO SELECTING AN ADR PROCEDURE**

10 Negot. J. 49 (1994)

CLIENT GOALS

In the hypothetical [sexual harassment] case with which we began this article, how do you, as [her] attorney, prepare for your initial interview with your client? Is she eager to remain at the company (perhaps because alternative employment opportunities are scarce) and hence wants to resolve this situation with the least disruption and fuss? Or is she so angry that she is determined to have some outside neutral pronounce her "right," and thus vindicate her position?

Answers to questions like these are critical in determining what dispute resolution procedure is appropriate in this case. The fact that [she] has decided to come to an attorney indicates that she is dissatisfied with the present posture of the dispute. But should she file a lawsuit or seek some other way of resolving the problem? If she has an emotional need for vindication, she will have to resort to some form of adjudication, either in court or — if the company is willing — through private means, such as arbitration or private judging. Private adjudication, in addition to assuring confidentiality, is often faster and cheaper than a court decision. In arbitration and private judging, there is also an opportunity to participate in the selection of the adjudicator and thus to obtain particular expertise. In addition, arbitration almost guarantees finality, since a reviewing court will hardly ever overturn an arbitrator's decision. If [she] wants public vindication, however, or a binding precedent, only court will do. . . .

These, then, are some of the considerations that lawyers and clients must examine with regard to processes that might meet client objectives. The value of various procedures in meeting specific client objectives is set forth in Table 1.

An important point to note is that the values assigned to each procedure in Table 1 . . . are not based on empirical research but rather upon our own experience, combined with the views of other dispute resolution professionals. Moreover, the numerical values assigned to each procedure are not intended to be taken literally, but rather as a shorthand expression of the extent to which each procedure satisfies a particular objective. . . .

The next step in the analysis is to list the client's goals in order of priority. If the client is primarily interested in a prompt and inexpensive resolution of the dispute that also maintains or improves the parties' relationship — which is typical of *most* clients in *most* business disputes — mediation is the preferred procedure. Mediation is the only procedure to receive maximum scores on each of these dimensions — cost, speed, and maintain or improve the relationship — as well as on assuring privacy, another interest which is present in many business disputes. It is only when the client's primary interests consist of establishing a precedent, being vindicated, or maximizing (or minimizing) recovery that procedures other than mediation are more likely to be satisfactory. . . .

		PROCEDURES				
	NONBINDING		SUMMARY JURY TRIAL	EARLY NEUTRAL EVALUATION	BINDING ARBITRATION/ PRIVATE JUDGING	COURT
	MEDIATION	MINITRIAL				
OBJECTIVES						
Minimize costs	3	2	2	3	1	0
Speed	3	2	2	3	1	0
Privacy	3	3	2	2	3	0
Maintain/ improve relationship	3	2	2	1	1	0
Vindication	0	1	1	1	2	3
Neutral opinion	0	3	3	3	3	3
Precedent	0	0	0	0	2	3
Maximizing/ minimizing recovery	0	1	1	1	2	3

0 = Unlikely to satisfy objective
1 = Satisfies objective somewhat
2 = Satisfies objective substantially
3 = Satisfies objective very substantially

One final point concerning client goals: Some contend that ADR should be avoided altogether when one party will be sure to win if the matter is litigated. We disagree. First, the likely loser may be persuaded, through the use of one of the evaluative ADR procedures, to concede, thus sparing both parties the costs of litigation. An agreed-upon outcome is also more likely to be fully complied with than a court order. Alternatively, the likely loser may offer, in ADR, a settlement that is better in non-monetary terms than what could be achieved in litigation; such a settlement preserves, and often enhances, the parties' relationship. Thus, the prospect of a victory in litigation is not reason enough for avoiding ADR.

IMPEDIMENTS TO SETTLEMENT AND WAYS OF OVERCOMING THEM

In some circumstances, a settlement is not in the client's interest. For example, the client may want a binding precedent or may want to impress other potential litigants with its firmness and the consequent costs of asserting claims against it. Alternatively, the client may be in a situation in which there are no relational concerns; the only issue is whether it must pay out money; there is no pre-judgment interest; and the cost of contesting the claim is less than the interest earned on the money. In these and a small number of other situations, settlement will not be in the client's interest.

Still, a satisfactory settlement typically is in the client's interest. It is the inability to obtain such a settlement, in fact, that impels the client to seek the advice of counsel in the first place. The lawyer must consider not only what the client wants but also why the parties have been unable to settle their dispute, and then must find a dispute resolution procedure that is likely to overcome the impediments to settlement. . . .

Poor Communication

The relationship between the parties and/or their lawyers may be so poor that they cannot effectively communicate. Neither party believes the other, and each searches for hidden daggers in all proposals put forth by the other. An inability to communicate clearly and effectively, which impedes successful negotiations, is often, but not always, the result of a poor relationship. . . .

The Need to Express Emotions

At times, no settlement can be achieved until the parties have had the opportunity to express their views to each other about the dispute and each other's conduct. . . .

Different Views of Facts

Did the defendant engage in the conduct that forms the basis of the plaintiff's complaint? Whose version of the facts is the finder of fact likely to believe? The greater the parties' disagreement on these matters, the more difficult settlement is likely to be. . . .

Different Views of Legal Outcome If Settlement Is Not Reached

Disputants often agree on the facts but disagree on their legal implications. The plaintiff asserts that, on the basis of the agreed-upon facts, he has a 90 percent likelihood of success in court; the defendant, with equal fervor, asserts that she has a 90 percent chance of success. While there may be a legitimate dispute over the likely outcome, both these estimates cannot be right. . . .

Issues of Principle

If each of the disputing parties is deeply attached to some "fundamental" principle that must be abandoned or compromised in order to resolve the dispute, then resolution is likely to be difficult. Two examples: a suit challenging the right of neo-Nazis to march in a town where many Holocaust survivors live; and a suit by a religious group objecting to the withdrawal of life support systems from a comatose patient. . . .

Constituency Pressures

If one or more of the negotiators represents an institution or group, constituency pressures may impede agreement in two ways: different elements within the institution or group may have different interests in the dispute, or the negotiator may have staked her political or job future on attaining a certain result. . . .

Linkage to Other Disputes

The resolution of one dispute may have an effect on other disputes involving one or both parties. If so, this linkage will enter into their calculations, and may so complicate negotiations as to lead to an impasse. . . .

Multiple Parties

When there are multiple parties, with diverse interests, the problems are similar to those raised by diverse constituencies and by issue linkages. . . .

Different Lawyer/Client Interests

Lawyers and clients often have divergent attitudes and interests concerning settlement. This may be a matter of personality (one may be a fighter, the other a problem solver) or of money. An attorney who is paid on an hourly basis stands to profit handsomely from trial, and may be less interested in settlement than the client. On the other hand, an attorney paid on a contingent fee basis is interested in a prompt recovery without the expense of preparing for or conducting a trial, and may be more interested in settlement than is the client. It is in part because of this potential conflict of interest that most processes that seek to promote settlement provide for the client's direct involvement. . . .

The "Jackpot" Syndrome

An enormous barrier to settlement often exists in those cases where the plaintiff is confident of obtaining in court a financial recovery far exceeding its damages, and the defendant thinks this is highly unlikely. . . .

The Public Perspective

For either a judge or a court employee responsible for recommending an ADR procedure, the question regarding barriers to settlement and how they can be overcome is the same as it is for individual disputants. The other question concerning goals is similar, but with a broader perspective. In lieu of asking what are the objectives one party wishes to achieve, as would counsel, the question is what both parties want to achieve. Under an ADR program in the Superior Court of the District of Columbia, for example, each party is asked to select, in order of importance, three goals for the processing of its case. These goals can then be considered in making an ADR recommendation.

    When a process selection is made from a public perspective, the public interest must also be considered. If the dispute is one in which a trial is likely to be lengthy, and so consume precious court time, there may be a public interest in referring the dispute to *some* form of ADR. Beyond that, one must ask if there is a public interest in having the dispute resolved pursuant to a *particular* procedure. For example, the referral of child custody disputes to mediation is required by law in several jurisdictions. The disputing parents may believe that they have no interest in a better relationship, but only in vindication, and hence prefer court to mediation. However, many states believe that a better relationship between the parents serves the public interest by improving the life of the child, and so mandate that child custody disputes go first to mediation.

The final question that must be asked in the public context is whether the public interests will be better served by a court decision than by a private settlement. If, for example, the dispute raises a significant question of statutory or constitutional interpretation, a court resolution might be preferable to a private settlement. While a court normally has no power to prevent parties from settling their own dispute, it does not follow that the court, as a public agency, should encourage or assist settlement in such a case.

Litigation may also serve the public interest better than mediation in cases of consumer fraud, which are often handled by the consumer protection division of an attorney general's office. Here not only the issue of *precedent*, but also the related issue of *recurring violations*, is key. The establishment of a general principle or a class remedy, by means of a class action, is clearly preferable to a series of repetitive and inconsistent mediations. . . .

Finally, two more situations may militate against any use of ADR. First, *one or more of the parties may be incapable of negotiating effectively.* An unsophisticated pro se litigant, for example, may be vulnerable to exploitation in an ADR process. (On the other hand, such an individual, if not represented by a lawyer, may not fare better in court.) Second, court process may be required for some other reason: for example, *when serious issues of compliance or discovery are anticipated.*

Conclusion

In addressing the problem of "fitting the forum to the fuss," we have suggested two lines of inquiry: What are the disputants' goals in making a forum choice? And, if the disputants are amenable to settlement, what are the obstacles to settlement, and in what forum might they be overcome?

The fact that these inquiries rarely lead to a clear answer to the question of forum selection does not, we think, indicate that the analysis is faulty. Rather, it indicates that the question of forum selection ultimately turns on the extent to which the interests of the disputing parties (and sometimes of the public) will be met in various forums. Thus, the most that analysis can offer is a framework that clarifies the interests involved and promotes a thoughtful weighing and resolution of those interests.

Moreover such an inquiry concerning goals and impediments is often independently helpful in clarifying the dimensions of the basic dispute. When it then comes to exploring the ADR implications of that analysis, a sophisticated ADR user might well ask: "If these are my goals and my impediments, what kinds of third-party help do I need, and how can I design a procedure that provides that kind of help?"

Problem 14-1. *Counseling a Client About Process Choice*

Considering the case type Professors Sander and Goldberg use at the beginning of this excerpt, sexual harassment, how would you counsel: (a) a plaintiff and, (b) a defendant in such a matter about which processes might be most appropriate for their needs and objectives?

Do you think the authors' analysis is correct? Complete?

---

2. Assessing the Impact of Processes on Clients

The next author interweaves therapeutic jurisprudence into dispute process choice. Advocates of therapeutic jurisprudence argue that lawyers must consider the emotional and mental impact of legal processes on their clients. Thus, Andrea Schneider encourages attorneys to examine the emotional or therapeutic impact of each dispute resolution process, rather than merely narrower legal concerns, arguing that this broader approach is more consistent with the ideals of dispute resolution itself. This advice also builds on the counseling concepts discussed in Chapter 2, specifically that lawyers should seek to understand a client's non-legal concerns.

 Andrea K. Schneider, **BUILDING A PEDAGOGY OF PROBLEM-SOLVING: LEARNING TO CHOOSE AMONG ADR PROCESSES**

5 Harv. Negot. L. Rev. 113 (2000)

A NEW MODEL FOR CHOOSING AMONG THE ADR PROCESSES

Therapeutic jurisprudence and preventive law [TJPL] provide a coherent methodology for choosing among the ADR processes of negotiation, mediation and arbitration. Given that ADR was developed with the goal of increasing parties' satisfaction, ADR practitioners should be advising their clients on that basis. An intellectual framework for choosing the process could achieve the qualitative-justice advantages that ADR's founders intended. This approach adds a needed layer to the current analysis of ADR choices by explicitly adding emotional and psychological concerns to that of the traditional legal and financial analysis. TJPL can help us look at additional factors in order to make a fully educated and beneficial choice for the client.

Finally, lawyers must examine the result of the ADR process for the impact on the client. Again, TJPL provides a framework for this analysis that is comprehensive and informative.

PROCESS/CLIENT INTEREST	NEGOTIATION	MEDIATION	ARBITRATION
Emotional (stress, speed, relationship, vindication)			
Legal (precedent, neutral opinion)			
Financial (costs, speed, recovery)			

APPLYING THE MODEL

To demonstrate the usefulness of applying TJPL, [we assume the following facts, outlined in Leonard Riskin, James Westbrook & James Levin, Instructor's Manual to Accompany Dispute Resolution and Lawyers 119 (1998)]. . . .

Dr. John Roark sued the *Daily Bugle*, its editor, and reporter Terry Ives for defamation. Terry Ives wrote a front page article about a fire in slum housing owned by Dr. John Roark. The article reports that a source in the Fire Marshall's office has indicated that the office is not ruling out the possibility of arson. The article also alleges that it is not uncommon for owners of tenements to intentionally burn their properties to collect insurance. When Roark called to complain, the editor said he stood by the story.

Roark insists that the reporter was negligent because property records show that Roark was only a limited partner in a group owning the property. Roark also believes that the reporter acted with malice because Ives had once before written a story about Roark's youngest son when the son was arrested for drug possession. Roark seeks $250,000 in actual damages for harm to his reputation, lost income in his medical practice, aggravation of a serious health problem, and mental anguish. He also seeks punitive damages of $1 million.

A. Step One: Counseling & Interviewing — Identifying Emotional Concerns

As part of the initial meeting with Roark, the lawyer should discuss, in addition to legal and financial concerns, the emotional impact of various dispute resolution processes. These concerns could range from broad issues applicable to every client to the more specific concerns that Roark might have in this case. The lawyer should first determine general issues such as how much Roark would like to participate in resolving the dispute, whether he is comfortable in formal settings, and how at ease he is with the legal process in general. The lawyer should review Roark's desire to tell his story and determine whether he (a) wishes to confront the other side; (b) wants to tell his story to a neutral third party; (c) would want to testify (and would be good at testifying) in a courtroom; or (d) would like to detach from the process as much as possible.

The lawyer should also look for emotional concerns particular to this client. In a defamation case with a claim of mental anguish, these issues should not be ignored. . . .

First, Roark's feelings of anger at the paper and hurt at his subsequent treatment need to be considered. . . . Second, this event has aggravated Roark's medical condition. . . . Finally, Roark could have more general emotional concerns. He might be worried about the impact of this situation on his reputation. He might be concerned about the impact that dealing with this situation would have on his quality of work and his quality of life. . . .

B. Step Two: Choosing a Process — Determining Legal Procedures That Would Be Therapeutic

In light of Roark's emotional concerns, each of the ADR processes should be assessed in terms of their ability to provide therapeutic, or emotionally beneficial, results. They should also be judged by whether any of these processes could also have nontherapeutic, or emotionally harmful, effects.

Again, this analysis is intended to augment, not supplant, traditional consideration of legal and financial ramification. Indeed, given the facts of this particular claim, it is plausible that only litigation would vindicate Dr. Roark's desires. Defamation is a complex legal claim and he might trust a court to better apply the relevant standards. . . .

1. Negotiation

Negotiation has the advantage of allowing clients to be more detached from legal proceedings because most negotiations occur solely between the lawyers outside the presence of the clients. Thus, if the client is relatively uninterested in participating, negotiation [without clients present] may provide the most therapeutic effects.

A problem-solving approach to negotiation can also have therapeutic effects on both lawyers and the clients. Since problem solving focuses on the interests of the client, the client must be more involved in the preparation of the case. . . .

2. Mediation

Mediation can have excellent therapeutic effects for clients. Numerous articles on mediation have discussed the value of being heard or meeting face-to-face to resolve disputes. The strength of mediation lies in providing the client the opportunity to tell her story in a setting that is safe and helpful. The opportunity to be heard is cathartic for many clients. Also, simply sitting across from the person whom the client perceives as having wronged him can be helpful in resolving and overcoming the dispute. Mediation allows parties the opportunity to face one another and to have a true conversation together. In addition, the ability to hear the plaintiff's story, perhaps even apologize, and to tell the other side of the dispute can be important for the defendant as well. . . .

In the *Daily Bugle* example, mediation would allow Roark to tell his story. A face-to-face meeting with the editor who ignored him could be of great psychological benefit. It might also provide the opportunity for the editor or reporter to apologize. Nevertheless, an unproductive mediation could be even more aggravating to Roark. If the editor is intransigent or the reporter admits no fault, Roark could leave even more infuriated.

3. Arbitration

Arbitration provides a different array of therapeutic advantages and disadvantages. Roark might want the whole world to know what has happened. If Roark feels that the paper has a history of sloppy reporting, he might opt for litigation to obtain a public ruling condemning their actions.

He might, however, be content with a private adjudication of his rights. In arbitration, a decision is made on the merits of the case, but with more speed and confidentiality than litigation. This might be a great benefit to him and his family given the situation between Roark and his son, as well as the family's general desire to keep its name out of the paper. . . .

C. Step Three: Looking to Settlement — Implementing Preventive Law for Therapeutic Outcomes

1. Negotiation & Mediation

Negotiation and mediation . . . can implement ideas from preventive law by looking beyond the specific litigation issue. If the goal is to prevent further disputes between the parties, then the ability of mediation to deal with these issues is more likely to work to clients' benefit than litigation. Settlements can be structured so that all of the elements of the dispute are discussed, evaluated, and dealt with in a final agreement. . . .

In Roark's case, the settlement agreement should be written with an eye toward the future. If payment is agreed upon, the settlement should specify how and when that payment will arrive. What if payment does not occur? If a public apology or retraction is part of the settlement, the settlement should include details such as timing and placement of such retraction. Is the apology on behalf of the paper, or will the apology come from the reporter? The settlement might include internal changes within the paper — a punishment for the reporter or new procedures for fact-checking. The where, when, and how of each of these elements should be covered in the settlement agreement. By dealing with these issues as part of the ADR process and settlement, Roark's lawyer can help him avoid disturbing legal problems down the road.

2. Arbitration

Arbitration can provide different preventive law opportunities, although there is often little opportunity to do so in the process. Frequently, individual arbitrators feel constrained to keep to the dispute at hand and not look down the road. This, however, should not prevent the parties from doing so. The parties can do this in two ways. First, they can agree to widen the scope of the questions presented to the arbitrator or perhaps give the arbitrator broader remedial powers. This would allow the arbitrator to employ preventive law ideas in crafting the decision by examining future interactions between the parties.

Problem 14-2.   *Is the Therapeutic Model Always Appropriate?*
Why does the author suggest that the Therapeutic Jurisprudence approach is consistent with dispute resolution principles? What, if any, disadvantages do you see in including this kind of approach in client counseling?

B. EVALUATING AND ASSESSING ADR PROCESSES: PUBLIC INTERESTS

Over time there have been many claims about the advantages and disadvantages of different forms of ADR and some efforts to examine these claims empirically. There is not yet an empirical consensus on the strengths and weaknesses of the various processes, including adjudication, but the following is one of the leading efforts to evaluate the use of ADR processes in court settings. Think about how you would design a study to test whether particular processes are meeting the needs of the parties and/or the interests of the public. Think about whether you would use different techniques to study whether a process was appropriate for the users (the parties) or for the larger system (the court system, society, a particular industry, or type of dispute).

  James S. Kakalik, Terence Dunworth, Laural A. Hill, Daniel McCaffrey, Marian Oshiro, Nicholas M. Pace & Mary E. Vaiana, **AN EVALUATION OF MEDIATION AND EARLY NEUTRAL EVALUATION UNDER THE CIVIL JUSTICE REFORM ACT**

v, xxvii–xxxiv (1996)

This report is one of four RAND reports evaluating the pilot program of the Civil Justice Reform Act (CJRA) of 1990. . . . The study was undertaken at the request of the Judicial Conference of the United States. . . .

The Civil Justice Reform Act (CJRA) of 1990 emerged from a multi-year debate about ways to reduce delay and litigation costs in federal courts. The legislation required each federal district court to develop a case management plan to reduce costs and delay. . . .

This study's objective is to assess the implementation, costs, and effects of mediation and neutral evaluation programs for civil cases in the six CJRA pilot and comparison federal district courts that had mediation or neutral evaluation programs in 1992-93 involving a sufficient number of cases to permit detailed evaluation. The districts studied were California (Southern), New York (Eastern),

Table S.1
Characteristics of ADR Programs Studied

District Program	Type of Referral	When Referred	Program Emphasis	Cases Included	Typical Session	ADR Provider	Median Fee
Mediation							
NY(S)	Mandatory	After mgmt. track is assigned	Settlement	Random experimental design	5 hours over 2 days	Lawyers	None
PA(E)	Mandatory	90 days from filing	Case issues, settlement	Random experimental design	Single 90-minute session	Lawyers	None
OK(W)	Voluntary; or mandatory at judicial discretion	Initial pretrial conference	Settlement	All cases required to have pretrial conference	Singe 4-hour session	Lawyers	$660, split by parties
TX(S)	Voluntary, tougher cases encouraged; or mandatory at judicial discretion	Initial pretrial conference or later	Settlement	All cases required to have pretrial conference	Singe 8-hour session	Lawyers	$1,800, split by parties
Neutral Evaluation							
CA(S)	Mandatory	Before initial pretrial conference	Evaluation, settlement	All cases required to have pretrial conference	2.5 hours over 2 days	Magistrate judges handling pretrial case mgmt.	None
NY(E)	Mandatory at judicial discretion; or voluntary	Initial pretrial conference or later	Settlement	Any eligible case with value >$100,000	Single 3.5-hour session	Lawyers	None

New York (Southern), Pennsylvania (Eastern), Oklahoma (Western), and Texas (Southern).

CHARACTERISTICS OF THE ADR PROGRAMS

[K]ey design features of the programs . . . assessed . . . vary considerably on a number of dimensions, including whether the program is mandatory or voluntary, the point in the litigation at which referral occurs, the purpose of the program, the length of sessions, the type of provider, and the cost to parties. . . .

DESIGN OF THE EVALUATION

We selected approximately 150 representative cases that were referred to the ADR program in each district and a comparison group of about 150 cases in the same district. . . .

We analyzed each district separately. Within each district, we compared the cases referred to ADR with the comparison group, using both bivariate tabulations and multivariate statistical analyses.

The primary measures used to evaluate the cases were:

- Time to disposition, defined as the interval from first filing of the case to case closing;
- Cost of litigation, defined primarily as lawyer work hours per litigant, but also including monetary legal fees and costs and litigant hours spent on the case;
- Cost to the court for administering the ADR program;
- Monetary outcomes;
- Provider, litigant, and lawyer views of satisfaction with case management that includes ADR; and
- Provider, litigant, and lawyer views of the fairness of case management that includes ADR.

The evaluation draws on subjective and objective case-level data from the period January 1991 through December 1995, depending on the district. We followed the cases from filing to termination, or until December 1995 when our data collection stopped if they were still open then. Data sources include:

- Court records, including summary data on each of the sample cases;
- Records and reports of CJRA advisory groups;
- Pilot and comparison districts' cost and delay reduction plans;
- Detailed case processing and complete docket information on our samples of cases;
- Mail surveys of ADR providers on the sample of ADR cases selected;
- Mail surveys of attorneys and litigants on closed ADR and comparison cases about costs, time, satisfaction and views of the fairness of the process; and
- Personal interviews with judges, court staff, lawyers, and ADR providers during site visits to each of the six districts.

About two-thirds of the ADR providers, half of the lawyers, and one-ninth of the litigants responded to our surveys. Because so few litigants responded, we excluded litigant data from our statistical analyses and view these data as merely supportive of our other analyses.

OVERVIEW OF PRIOR RESEARCH ON COURT-RELATED ADR

It is useful to view the results of the current study in the broader context of previous research on court-related ADR of all types.

The rationale for ADR programs is the hope that they will be faster, cheaper, and/or more satisfactory to participants than formal court adjudication. Although past research has not confirmed all of these putative benefits, it does seem to suggest that litigants are more satisfied when ADR has taken place, even if they do not settle their case at that time.

Unfortunately, sound empirical research on various ADR mechanisms is quite thin. Much of the literature is descriptive and, often, hortatory, with the latter tending to rely on anecdotal data or individual experiences, which may or may not be representative. Court-related arbitration and family mediation programs have been most extensively studied, using accepted academic research methods, including randomized experimentation. Early neutral evaluation has also been the subject of some field experimentation. Mediation outside of the family law context has not often been examined, nor have most private ADR programs been scrutinized closely.

The previous empirical research on court-annexed arbitration suggests that these programs have, at best, modest contributions to make to managing civil litigation more expeditiously and more economically. However, they offer litigants a more satisfying form of justice than is accorded through the combination of bilateral negotiation and judicially facilitated settlement that is their practical alternative in today's trial courts.

Previous empirical research on other forms of court-annexed ADR such as mediation and neutral evaluation is much more limited in volume than research on arbitration; the available findings do not provide an adequate basis on which to make definitive policy recommendations.

KEY FINDINGS OF THIS STUDY

Time to Disposition

We have no strong statistical evidence that time to disposition is significantly affected by mediation or neutral evaluation in any of the six programs studied.

There was no statistically significant difference in the time to disposition between the ADR sample cases and the comparison cases in five of the six ADR programs. TX(S) referrals to ADR were significantly slower (by about three months) to terminate than comparison cases. We believe the ADR cases terminate more slowly because judges encourage cases that appear more difficult to settle to volunteer for mediation.

Costs of Litigation

We have no strong statistical evidence that lawyer work hours are significantly affected by mediation or neutral evaluation in any of the six programs studied. . . .

As we discussed above with respect to time to disposition, TX(S) cases that appear tougher to settle receive more judicial encouragement to volunteer for mediation; these more difficult cases may have higher costs.

There are also confounding factors at work in CA(S). In addition to instituting a policy of early neutral evaluation, this district expanded the role of magistrate judges for civil cases and increased the use of early management. Policy changes other than neutral evaluation could have increased lawyer work hours. For example, in our main CJRA evaluation, we found that early management was associated with significantly increased lawyer work hours. Because of these other potential influences on the time that lawyers spend, we do not believe that the data from CA(S) provide any clear evidence that neutral evaluation, by itself, will necessarily lead to increased lawyer work hours.

Cost to Court for ADR Program Administration

The court's cost for ADR program administration includes the startup and recurring personnel cost of providing the program (including clerk's office personnel and judicial officer time), and any non-personnel costs such as for training programs, telephone, reproduction, and mailing. For CA(S), the cost of the magistrate judge's time spent providing the early neutral evaluation must also be included. Personnel time estimates include all full-time-equivalent (FTE) personnel actually working on the specific ADR program, whether they are paid by CJRA funds or not. Cost estimates, measured in 1995 dollars, include salaries, fringe benefits, and operations and maintenance expenses. . . .

The annual number of FTE court personnel devoted to ADR ranges from 0.8 to 3.15 for the six programs. . . .

The total annual cost to the district court of providing the ADR program being evaluated ranges from about $47,000 for 100 referred cases in NY(E) to about $384,000 for 1,070 referred cases in CA(S). . . .

These totals translate into a cost per case referred ranging from $130 to $490. . . . About $500, the highest administrative cost per case referred to ADR, contrasts with the substantially higher median cost of litigation per litigant, which ranges from $5,000 to $17,000. . . .

The total startup cost to district courts ranged from $10,000 to $69,000. . . .

Monetary Outcome

Money appears more likely to change hands when mediation or neutral evaluation is involved. ADR cases in all six programs have a higher percentage of monetary outcomes than comparison cases have. The difference in the likelihood of a monetary outcome is statistically significant in three of four mediation programs and nearly significant in the fourth.

A plausible explanation for this pattern is that the mediation process is designed to facilitate settlement and does indeed increase the number of cases that settle. When parties reach an agreement and settle the case, that disposition is likely to involve a monetary outcome.

Settlement as a Result of Mediation or Neutral Evaluation

The likelihood that a case referred to mediation or neutral evaluation settles just before or as a result of the ADR session ranges from 31 percent to 72 percent across the six districts. There appears to be a correspondence between settlement and when the session is held: Settlement is more likely to occur just before or after the ADR session when the session is held later in the life of the case. The programs ranked from lowest to highest percentage of ADR-related settlements are PA(E), CA(S), OK(W), TX(S), NY(E), and NY(S). We obtain the same sequence of programs if we rank them from the shortest to longest time from case filing to holding the ADR session. Discovery may be completed and cases may be more ready to settle by the time of the later sessions; thus, the fact that the lawyers and parties must meet for mediation or neutral evaluation may be the precipitating event required to finalize agreement.

Perceptions of Fairness

There was no statistically significant difference in lawyers' perception of how fairly the cases were managed. Lawyers on about nine out of ten cases in all programs felt that the mediation or neutral evaluation process was fair. A slightly lower percentage of litigants agreed, but the low completion rate for our litigant surveys does not allow us to confidently make statistical inferences from the litigant data.

Satisfaction

We found no statistically significant effects for *mediation* referral in terms of lawyer satisfaction with case management.

Overall, a smaller percentage of litigants than lawyers report being satisfied with case management. However, in three of the four mediation districts studied, a greater percentage of litigants from mediation cases report satisfaction than from the comparison cases.

Our findings with respect to litigant and lawyer satisfaction with case management that includes *neutral evaluation* are inconclusive. As noted above, the difference between our two CA(S) samples might be attributed to other factors, including the increased role of magistrate judges and the wider use of early management. We cannot distinguish between these confounding effects. . . .

Focusing on the ADR session itself, only a minority of the respondents were dissatisfied with ADR; the majority were either neutral or satisfied.

Opinions and Recommendations of Participants

We asked mediation and neutral evaluation program participants (litigants, lawyers, and ADR providers) for their opinions on a variety of topics, including the appropriateness and timing of the ADR session, possible problems, and the session's effects.

Participants in these programs are generally supportive of them. Most of the lawyers involved feel the programs are worthwhile in general as well as valuable for their individual cases. Only a small percentage in any district thought the referral to ADR was inappropriate or that the program should be dropped.

Litigants also generally thought that referral to mediation or neutral evaluation was appropriate for their case and that the program should be retained. However, they were a little less positive than lawyers, and up to one-fourth of the litigants in some programs felt that referral was inappropriate or that the program should be dropped.

The vast majority of lawyers in every program were satisfied with the ADR process itself and thought it was handled fairly. In no district did we find a local bar that strongly opposed a program of mediation or neutral evaluation.

This general satisfaction with the ADR process does not mean that it was perfect. The problem cited most often by lawyers and ADR providers was that the parties were not ready to settle. The timing of the ADR session could be a major factor in this lack of "readiness." It may be best to conduct the sessions in an atmosphere where at least the basic facts and positions on issues are known to both sides and the ADR provider as well. Substantial numbers of lawyers in some districts felt that the sessions were held too early to be useful. Lawyers and ADR providers also thought that in a minority of cases, settlement eluded them because critical persons with authority to settle did not participate in the session.

ASSESSMENT

Our evaluation provided no strong statistical evidence that the mediation or neutral evaluation programs, as implemented in the six districts studied, significantly affected time to disposition, litigation costs, or attorney views of fairness or satisfaction with case management. The low completion rate for our litigant surveys does not allow us to confidently make statistical inferences from the litigant data. Our only statistically significant finding is that the ADR programs appear to increase the likelihood of a monetary settlement.

We conclude that the mediation and neutral evaluation programs as implemented in these six districts are not a panacea for perceived problems of cost and delay, but neither do they appear to be detrimental. We have no justification for a strong policy recommendation because we found no major program effects, either positive or negative. This lack of a demonstrated major effect on litigation cost and delay is generally consistent with the outcomes of prior empirical research on court-related ADR. . . .

Given that most mediation and neutral evaluation programs have been in place in federal court for only a few years, refinements should be expected as time progresses. The problems noted by the participants in the ADR sessions suggest the need to consider ensuring that each side has some basic information about the other side's case before the session is held, adjusting the timing of the session to maximize its utility for the case, and enforcing the requirement that the sessions involve not only the lawyers but also those who hold the keys to the litigation's resolution.

At the time that the RAND studies were completed, the Federal Judicial Center also completed a study of five courts using various forms of ADR to evaluate the effects of various forms of court reform under the Civil Justice Reform Act. That study found there was some cost and delay reduction in several of the court-sponsored ADR programs.[1] The somewhat contradictory, or less than consistent, findings on the question of whether ADR processes increased court efficiency led to a spirited debate about evaluation studies and their outcomes in the literature and at policy and judicial conferences.[2]

---

1. Donna Stienstra et al., A Study of the Five Demonstration Programs Established Under the Civil Justice Reform Act of 1990 (1997).
2. Craig A. McEwen & Elizabeth Plapinger, RAND Report Points Way to Next Generation of Research, 3 Disp. Resol. Mag. 10 (1997); Carrie Menkel-Meadow, When Dispute Resolution Begets Disputes of Its Own: Conflicts Among Dispute Professionals, 44 UCLA L. Rev. 1871 (1997); Deborah Hensler, In Search of "Good" Mediation in Handbook of Justice Research in Law 258 (Joseph Sanders & V. Hamilton eds., 2001).

The next two articles report on and summarize a variety of studies that have empirically tested the claims made about both "alternative" forms of dispute resolution and adjudication. After you read these articles we ask you to think about what methods and variables might be used to evaluate the performance of different forms of process for different audiences. Different kinds of clients and different institutions may value different things in processes for dispute resolution, so it may be hard to use single or simple measures.

 Carrie Menkel-Meadow, **DISPUTE RESOLUTION**

in Oxford Handbook of Empirical Legal Research (Peter Cane & Herbert Kritzer eds., 2010)

Stark political, practical, and policy debates about the appropriate uses of various forms of "non-litigative," "non-adversarial," or "alternative-to-court" processes have led to heated debates about definitions, categorizations, methodologies, measurements, and conclusions from a wide range of studies attempting to "settle the scores" on practical issues of cost, fairness, efficiency, consumer satisfaction, and more jurisprudential issues such as voice, democracy, self-determination, rule of law, and the "justice" produced by the use of different processes. There are a variety of contested issues such as;

- whether there should be voluntary or mandatory assignment to a particular form of dispute resolution,
- whether the privacy of the parties is more important than or should be measured against the transparency to others of both processes and outcomes,
- whether vesting of power in privately paid professionals, rather than state officials, for dispute decisions is desirable,
- whether some forms of dispute resolution are more likely to serve the empowerment of parties, communities, and other non-elites, rather than those in the more expensive and elite controlled litigation systems,
- whether the resources invested in alternative systems are justified or improve compliance and enforcement of outcomes over commanded litigation results, and
- whether institutional design of alternative justice systems at very advanced stages of legal development can serve as a model in more newly created legal systems and political orders.

All of this has led to a serious "baseline" problem in empirical analysis of dispute resolution processes. With so many issues about how processes deliver fairness and justice being so hotly contested, it is difficult, if not impossible, to know what is being compared to what. Litigation varies as much in different venues (e.g., civil law versus common law, or federal versus state courts) as mediation does in private or court-annexed settings or, as arbitration does in domestic and international settings. Whenever I read any attempt to "compare" and "contrast" the efficacy or quality of different processes, I always ask, "compared to what?" Close scrutiny of virtually any comparison will dampen one's confidence in the conclusions reached. Put simply, truly experimental methods are virtually impossible in this field; one cannot submit the same actual dispute to two treatments. At best, so-called "like" cases in one "treatment" are compared to "like (similar) cases" in another "treatment" and therein lies the problem.[3]

In large aggregate studies, such as in the "Vanishing Trial" statistics demonstrating decreasing uses of full civil trials,[4] we can see general trends in processes used and in variations in gross outcomes. But when the focus is more on "internal" experiences of fairness of process and outcomes in particular cases, it is much harder to match totally homologous case types. Processes with the same name are practiced differently; different private ADR institutions and providers use different rules, standards, procedures, and definitions. Even in the public sector, when courts or administrative agencies use various forms of ADR, they do so with different intentions, different requirements, and different effects such as whether or not negotiated agreements can serve as public outcomes without formal governmental ratification.

. . . [M]y theme is one of skepticism that we can ever truly determine with any degree of confidence whether one particular process is "better" or "worse" than another in a specific case.

This is related to another theme illustrated here. In some cases there are "communities" of interest in promoting particular forms of ADR. It is often argued that big business prefers the control and economic efficiency of arbitration against individual employees, consumers, and investors, and that some courts prefer to deflect "smaller" cases to arbitration or mediation. Yet it is also often true that individual disputants might have very different motivations for seeking a particular kind of process. Thus, we have an additional measurement problem of aggregating individual preferences when those preferences may not be uniform, either for individuals or for organizations.

Those engaged in design of dispute-resolution institutions (whether in courts or private organizations) often ask instrumental questions, wanting to know what forms of process are "better" in terms of factors such as efficiency or fairness for a particular type of conflict. Existing studies seldom provide clear answers to such questions. In ADR some criteria of quality measurement for some factors such as efficiency can be quantitative, while other factors — fairness, availability of tailored and flexible solutions, and the degree of self-determination in such processes — resist quantitative measurement and must be assessed in a more qualitative fashion. Thus, the core question is not "which process is better?" but "which process is better for what and for whom?" Some form of "process pluralism" and choice is usually the answer.

---

3. The closest to this is a study which attempted to "match" similar types of cases in the formal justice system which were then assigned to different "treatments" — arbitration, litigation, or some form of negotiation or mediation, see E.A. Lind, R.J. MacCoun, P.A. Ebener, W.L. F. Felstiner, D.R. Hensler, J. Resnik & T. R. Tyler, (1989), The Perception of Justice: Tort Litigants' Views of Trial, Court-Annexed Arbitration and Judicial Settlement Conferences, Santa Monica, Cal.: RAND.

4. Marc Galanter, The Vanishing Trial: An Examination of Trials and Related Matters in Federal and State Courts, 1 J. Empirical Legal Studies 459-570 (2004).

To summarize, as we try to understand the meaning of many attempts to weigh and evaluate the successes and failures of ADR processes it is useful to always ask — *what is the baseline — compared to what*? In assessing what we know, don't know, and should know about ADR's actual empirical practices, it is important to recognize that ADR is itself variable, and it may be difficult, if not impossible, to specify with any degree of reliability what is going on inside particular processes and how particular processes can be compared to each other. But many have tried.

As the field of ADR has grown to include more kinds of disputes and a greater variety of processes, other structural and policy issues have been raised. Early on, one of the most important claims made against ADR was that compared with formal adjudication, it was likely to cause unfair or unequal outcomes for subordinated or disempowered parties (especially women, and various racial and ethnic minority groups). A variety of studies have been designed to test whether there are systematic biases and structural inequalities in how different parties and groups experience various dispute resolution processes,[5] including arbitration, and mediation in court and in private settings.

Related to claims about the effects of differences in power or resources between the parties, debates in the ADR literature have focused on the "repeat player effect." The argument is that parties who participate often in the same process (e.g., company-controlled arbitration) or third-party neutrals (whether arbitrators or mediators) who work often for the same parties produce unfair or structurally biased outcomes. . . . [T]he many recent attempts to evaluate this assertion have produced decidedly mixed and contested results.[6]

In studies which attempt to evaluate ADR processes there is always the question of what the yardstick of "measurement" of fairness, justice or efficiency should be, which has given rise to another important dispute: Should the outcomes of all dispute resolution conform to legal rules or precedents or are the parties free to resolve their disputes in creative, tailored ways that might provide fair or just outcomes for particular parties but might depart from formal legal rules or precedents (without themselves constituting unlawful outcomes)? This important jurisprudential question is not easily studied in direct form but some surrogates of measurement, such as compliance with agreements as opposed to commanded or law-based rulings, are increasingly the subject of evaluation in some areas such as in environmental and land-use, divorce and family, and labor and employment matters.

A variety of other controversial claims about the comparative value of different processes have also spawned inconclusive and contradictory studies. Cary Coglianese[7] has long questioned whether the use of negotiated-rule making or public policy consensus building processes has in fact decreased the cost of administrative rulemaking or bolstered its "consensual" and non-contested quality, against

---

5. G. LaFree & C. Rack, The Effects of Participants' Ethnicity and Gender on Monetary Outcomes in Mediated and Adjudicated Civil Cases, 30 Law & Society Rev. 767-797 (1996).

6. C.R. Drahozal & S. Zyontz (2009). An Empirical Study of AAA Consumer Arbitration, available at SSRN *http://ssrn.com/abstract=1365435*.

7. Cary Coglianese, Assessing Consensus: The Promise and Performance of Negotiated Rulemaking, 46 Duke L. J. 1255-1337 (1997).

continuing claims by its proponents that well managed multi-party negotiation processes can provide rulemaking in administrative contexts that is less likely to be challenged in post-hoc litigation. Jody Freeman[8] has provided one of the most in-depth empirical case studies of several collaborative rule-making efforts, but her work is challenged by Coglianese who insists on the need for more aggregate data and for comparisons with more conventional rule-making administrative processes before drawing conclusions about relative costs, compliance, and other post-hoc effects. In my own view, attempts to study and compare these particular uses of ADR are even more problematic than attempts to match aggregate cases in traditional litigation settings. Rule-making proceedings in front of different U.S. federal agencies (Environmental Protection Agency, Federal Drug Administration, Departments of Labor, Interior, etc.) are so factually, scientifically, legally and historically complex that comparisons across case types and are quite resistant to rigorous comparisons.

In my view, one of the few rigorously successful studies of comparability of process is the Metro Court study[9] of outcomes and satisfaction rates among adjudication and mediation users in New Mexico state courts. In an attempt to test Delgado, et al.'s[10] thesis that private processes would be adversely experienced by minority litigants, Michelle Hermann and her colleagues found far more complex relationships in the mix of process used, demographics of litigants and third party neutrals, and case types. Some women, for example, fared "better" in mediation outcomes, but were more skeptical of that process, and somewhat distrusting of its informal quality. Hispanics and some Blacks preferred mediation, even when their outcomes were relatively inferior to what they might have achieved in litigation, demonstrating some distrust of formal justice systems (particularly among immigrants who carry memories of corrupt courts from their native lands). This study generally refuted Delgado's "informality" hypotheses by demonstrating that factors other than race, gender and ethnicity such as case-type, repeat player effects, and whether parties had representatives or not, accounted for more of the differences in both outcomes and satisfaction rates. One important finding was that, in general, parties were more satisfied with processes in which the third party neutral, whether a judge or mediator, "matched" their own ethnicity.

Recent extensions of ADR to "on-line dispute resolution," truth and reconciliation commissions, transactional mediation in contract formation, not to mention such conventional uses of various forms of dispute resolution in diplomacy, market transactions, family relations, and ordinary day-to-day disputes and conflicts, suggest that the domain of dispute-resolution research is far more capacious than assessing how disputes are managed in formal legal arenas such as lawsuits or courts. These new domains of dispute resolution suggest a number of new and interesting research questions, combined with the still unresolved "older" research questions explored in

---

8. J. Freeman, Collaborative Governance in the Administrative State, 45 UCLA L. Rev. 1-98 (1997).
9. Michele Hermann et al., The Metro Court Project Final Report. University of New Mexico Center for the Study and Resolution of Disputes (1993); La Free & Rack, supra note 5.
10. R. Delgado, C. Dunn, P. Brown, H. Lee & D. Gubert, Fairness and Formality: Minimizing the Risk of Prejudice in Alternative Dispute Resolution, 1985 Wisconsin L. Rev. 1359-1405.

this essay — some descriptive, others comparative, still others relevant to normative or prescriptive issues:

1. Must dispute resolution be conducted face-to-face to be effective? What will the role of new technologies be in dispute resolution?
2. When can disputing "culture" be changed? Can people be taught to "collaborate" or is the assumption of scarcity and competition the human default? What difference would it make in lawyering behavior if legal rules allowed "apologies" to be admitted as evidence? Can publicity about alternative forms of dispute resolution (e.g. South Africa's Truth and Reconciliation Commission) change political or disputing cultures?
3. Do particular domains (e.g., transnational and inter-organizational) or subject matters (e.g. ongoing relationships) require particular forms of dispute processing? In other words, is "trans-substantive" process a misconceived or impossible notion?
4. What factors influence party choice in dispute processes?
5. Does any form of dispute resolution require particular expertise?
6. When should dispute processing be public and transparent and when should parties be permitted to resolve disputes privately? Does a legal system require totally public dispute processes for all of its conflicts?
7. Finally, as this essay began, can we ever fully study and know whether particular structural patterns of parties, case types, and processes are "better" for the parties or for outsiders than any other set of process structures or choices

 Bobbi McAdoo, Nancy A. Welsh & Roselle L. Wissler,
INSTITUTIONALIZATION: WHAT DO EMPIRICAL STUDIES TELL US ABOUT COURT MEDIATION

Disp. Resol. Mag. 8-9 (Winter 2003)

This article focuses on the lessons that seem to be emerging from the available empirical data regarding best practices for programs that mediate non-family civil matters. Throughout the article, we consider the answers provided by research to three questions: (1) How does program design affect the success of the institutionalization of mediation? (2) In what ways do design choices affect the likelihood of achieving settlement of cases? and (3) Which program design choices affect litigants' perceptions of the procedural justice provided by court connected mediation? Because these issues of institutionalization, settlement and justice are so important to the success and quality of court-connected mediation, they must be considered carefully in deciding both how to structure new court-connected mediation programs and how to improve existing programs.

DESIGN AND INSTITUTIONALIZATION

Most court-connected mediation programs seek successful institutionalization, which we define here as regular and significant use of the mediation process to resolve cases. Voluntary mediation programs rarely meet this goal because they suffer from consistently small caseloads. In contrast, programs that make mediation mandatory (at the request of one party or on a judge's own initiative) have dramatically higher rates of utilization. Significantly, mandatory referral does not appear to adversely affect either litigants' perceptions of procedural justice or, according to most studies, settlement rates. Further, judicial activism in ordering parties into mediation triggers increased voluntary use of the process, as lawyers begin to request it themselves in anticipation of court referral. An additional benefit of exposing lawyers to mediation is that they are more likely to discuss and recommend the process to their clients.

Another program design option involves requiring lawyers to consider mediation as an integral part of their usual litigation planning. For example, some courts require lawyers to discuss the potential use of mediation or other ADR processes and report the results of that discussion to the court early in the life of a case. Other courts require lawyers to discuss ADR with their clients. These court rules face less lawyer opposition than mandatory case referral and can give lawyers more control over the logistics of mediation (e.g., choice of mediator and timing). Adopting these rules (combined with active judicial support and willingness to order mediation when deemed appropriate) tends to increase requests to use mediation. . . .

WHICH CASES SHOULD MEDIATE

Although it has been suggested that certain general categories of civil cases (e.g., employment, contract) are "best" handled by mediation, there is no empirical support for this notion. Neither settlement rates nor litigants' perceptions of the procedural justice provided by mediation vary with case type. (There is some limited evidence, however, that medical malpractice and product liability cases may be somewhat less likely to settle than other types of tort cases.) Interestingly, the level of acrimony between the litigants in non-family civil cases does not seem to affect the likelihood of settlement in mediation. Not surprisingly, the cases most likely to settle in mediation are those in which the litigants' positions are closer together, the issues are less complex, or the issue of liability is less strongly contested. Litigants' perceptions of procedural justice do not seem to vary with the tenor of the relationship between the litigants or with these other case characteristics. Thus, because no case characteristics have been identified for which mediation has detrimental effects, mediation programs do not need to exclude certain types of cases. Some programs may be tempted to exclude the cases that seem likely to reach settlement on their own, without the assistance of a mediator. This choice, however, is likely to limit not only the rate of settlement achieved but also the opportunity to improve litigants' perceptions of the procedural justice of the settlement process and to enhance their views of the courts. . . .

WHO THE MEDIATORS SHOULD BE

Mediation is most likely to be successfully institutionalized if the mediators are drawn from the pool that is preferred by lawyers: litigators with knowledge in the substantive areas being mediated. But neither mediators' knowledge of the subject matter of the dispute nor the number of years they have practiced law has proved to be related to settlement or to litigants' perceptions of procedural justice. One characteristic of the mediators, namely having more mediation experience, is related to more settlements. However, several aspects of mediator training, such as the number of hours of training or whether it included role play, tend not to affect settlement. None of these mediator characteristics seem to be related to litigants' perceptions of the procedural justice of mediation. . . .

WHAT THE MEDIATORS SHOULD DO

The approach that mediators ought to use (facilitative, evaluative, transformative) has been the subject of much debate. Both active facilitation and some types of evaluative interventions tend to produce more settlements as well as heighten perceptions of procedural justice. For example, when mediators disclose their views about the merits or value of a case, cases are more likely to settle and litigants are more likely to assess the· mediation process as fair. By contrast, when mediators keep silent about their views of the case, cases are less likely to settle and litigants' views of procedural justice are not enhanced. But when mediators recommend a particular settlement, litigants' ratings of the procedural fairness of the process suffer, notwithstanding an increased rate of settlement. When litigants or their lawyers participate more during mediation, cases are more likely to settle than when they participate less. Moreover, the litigants evaluate the mediation process as more fair. In addition, when the lawyers behave more cooperatively during mediation sessions, both the likelihood of settlement and litigant perceptions of procedural fairness increase.

––––––––––

Controversies abound about how to collect data, how to categorize inputs and outputs, how to evaluate inside processes, how to define program and process objectives (cost savings to systems versus party satisfaction or self-determination for individuals), and how to find appropriate baseline comparisons of alternative treatments. It is difficult to measure ultimate consequences for parties inside a dispute, as well as the larger systems or societies in which particular disputes or dispute processing systems are located. There may also be "bystander" effects on other users of dispute resolution systems or on those who stand near or are affected by a particular dispute or outcome.

Because the evaluation of "success" of such processes entails both objective and quantitative measures (time and cost savings, transaction costs of systems used, number of cases settled) and qualitative and more subjective assessments (client satisfaction, better ongoing relationships, greater worker productivity, self-determination, and development of better human skill sets for communication), it is difficult to reach agreement about how to develop mutually agreed-on metrics in the field. This remains an important and ongoing project since increasingly funding agencies, both public and private, seek objective demonstrations of the effectiveness of these processes and programs. Below is a list of possible metrics that various studies have used to measure these aspects of dispute resolution processes. Developing a sound evaluation and research protocol requires some conceptualization of more "composite" formulas and measurement tools in order to capture both the quantitative and qualitative richness of what conflict resolution processes both promise and actually deliver. No single program evaluation has made use of all of these possible metrics (collection of all of this kind of data would be prohibitively expensive). Some possible variables and criteria for measurement are listed below.

QUANTITATIVE OR "OBJECTIVE" MEASURES

- Number of conflicts or disputes in relevant "universe" (which and how many form into formal claim or complaint)
- Number of contacts or cases (in a particular process, as compared to the full "universe" of possible cases or comparable cases in another process)
- Numbers of issues
- Number of cases resolved/settled/closed/disposed of ("settlement rates")
- Number of cases referred to another process
- Number of cases dropped
- Case types (categories within systems, e.g., employment promotion, dismissal, communication, etc.)
- Numbers of parties
- Types of agreements, resolutions, outcomes
- Time to process case
- Cost of processing case — to complainant, to (third-party neutral), to program or system
- Comparisons (where possible) of all of above of comparable cases in different systems
- Comparisons of pre-conflict resolution program claiming (grievance systems, litigation) or violence with post-programmatic claiming
- Comparisons of rates of compliance with agreements, judgments, or orders
- Durability/longevity of outcomes
- Longitudinal comparisons of changes in usage, time for processing, case types, etc.
- Demographic data on users, third-party neutrals, and other facilitators or professionals
- Variations in usage, outcomes, solutions by demographics, and differential characteristics of disputants and third-party neutrals, e.g., "experience" ratings
- Awareness of ability to choose different processes (an attitudinal measure)

QUALITATIVE OR SUBJECTIVE MEASURES

- Client satisfaction
- Criteria for selecting particular processes

- Improved relationships (post-conflict societies (e.g., Rwanda), families, work-places, commercial relations)
- Improved communication
- Enhanced workplace productivity
- Learned conflict resolution/communication/relational skills ("transforma-tive" mutual intersubjective understandings or learned use of new processes, e.g., lawyers using mediation and other forms of problem solving)
- "Better" outcomes (more creative, individually tailored, deeper solutions)
- Perceived self-determination/autonomy/control over decision making
- Compliance with national, systemic, family, company, workplace, contractual norms/rules when legitimacy less questioned
- Perceptions of fairness, justice, and legitimacy of process
- Trust in institutions, both dispute processing and others
- Resolution of systemic issues (proactive conflict resolution, policy changes)
- "Value added" to organization or institution

Problem 14-3. *What Metrics for ADR Evaluations?*

Can you think of any other measures in addition to those above? How would you combine both quantitative and qualitative measures to develop an accurate assessment of how a particular process is working (in compari-son to others)?

Choose a particular form of dispute resolution you are familiar with and design a study to evaluate its effectiveness. What measures will you choose? How will you collect data? For whom are you conducting your evaluation? The users? An organization? A client deciding what process to use in a particular dispute?

C. FUTURE USES OF DISPUTE RESOLUTION PROCESSES: PEACE AND JUSTICE REDUX

This text focuses on the foundational forms and some hybrid forms of dispute resolution found primarily in the domestic American context. Currently, these primary forms of dispute resolution are being extended to various forms of deliberative democracy and policy decision making, borrowing from basic media-tion and facilitation techniques.[11] Some of you may be interested in international and transnational forms of dispute resolution, which include formal courts, new

---

11. The recently passed legislative reforms to American health care were preceded by facilitated Town Hall meetings in a variety of locations throughout the country (to rather mixed reviews we might add). Large-number ADR is still a work in progress, Carrie Menkel-Meadow, Scaling Up Dispute Resolu-tion and Deliberative Democracy in Health Care Reform: A Work in Progress, Law & Contemporary Problems (forthcoming 2011).

special-jurisdiction international tribunals (like the World Trade Organization Appellate Body, the International Criminal Courts for the former Yugoslavia and Rwanda), international arbitration, mediation, and new hybrid forms of conflict resolution and peacekeeping or nation building, such as Truth and Reconciliation Commissions in South Africa, Chile, Liberia, Guatemala, East Timor, and many other places where there have been civil wars, genocides, post-military dictatorships, and other major conflicts.[12]

In the years to come ordinary legal conflicts will likely continue to proliferate, putting more stress on formal court systems. In many states, criminal laws like California's "three strikes and you're out" (after third conviction, long or life sentences in prison are mandated) make access to courts for civil matters very difficult, if not impossible, because virtually all courts are being used for criminal trials.

Changes in the general economy and the economy of dispute resolution will also affect what forms of process can be used. Costs of litigation are likely to continue to rise. Fluctuations in the legal economy affect how law firms are structured (whether you will find it harder or easier to find a job), and how clients assess what legal actions they want to take. Do shaky economies produce more or less litigation? More transactional, bankruptcy work-outs? Will troubled corporations downsize outside counsel and use more in-house counsel? Will government agencies seek more collaborative forms of regulation and joint problem solving?

The rapidly changing technology we use (e.g., laptops, mobile phones, other electronic devices) has already affected some of the ways we engage with each other (as we have explored in many of the chapters here), and undoubtedly there will be many new forms of technology-assisted communication and market transactions. There continues to be a relatively serious "digital divide" by income, which is likely to contribute to another form of "haves" and "have nots" in dispute resolution activity, as in other spheres of human endeavor.

As the legal system becomes more complex, it is also true that the Internet and other forms of modern communication make it possible for people to do things directly for themselves, where before, they might have relied on professionals. Think about how many times you or a family member resolved your own dispute or solved your own problem by computer or telephone or other direct action, without consulting an attorney or other professional. So, will we all become dispute resolution and problem-solving experts in the years to come, without need of formal counsel? While the possibility exists, we believe there will still be a role for well-educated and skilled professionals to assist other human beings in solving problems and managing or handling disputes. Think about the "added value" that a well-schooled dispute resolution professional can bring to solving human and legal problems.

You will be the practitioners and designers of new forms of dispute resolution. Some of you will be handling local disputes in your communities, with your local, state, or federal governments, on behalf of institutions, whether for profit or non-profit, local or multinational, and on behalf of victims of crime, violence, war, or

---

12. See, e.g., Jane Stromseth, David Wippman & Rosa Brooks, Can Might Make Rights? (Cambridge Univ. Press, 2006), Ch 7.

mal-distributions of wealth or other benefits. Some of you will represent individuals seeking some form of compensation, apology, or other relief for some forms of injustice or wrongs. Others of you will seek to form new entities or engage in transactions to produce more wealth, new products, or new social services. Some of you will seek positions in government, whether as politicians or civil servants, or on the larger world stage. Others of you may cease to practice law and become managers, entrepreneurs, teachers, or artists. Many of you will eventually become judges, arbitrators, mediators, or other forms of legal decision makers. Most of you will form new relationships and families in your professional and personal lives. All of you will be involved in conflicts or disputes of some sort. We hope you have learned enough about the different methods of conflict resolution that you will be able to assist your clients, constituencies, and loved ones in resolving their conflicts by employing a dispute resolution process.

We hope that you have learned to analyze some basic features of dispute resolution:

- Who are the parties to a conflict?
- What are the parties' needs, interests, and goals?
- What is the substance of the conflict?
- Are there applicable precedents, rules, laws, or customs for resolving the conflict?
- What are the resource-expanding possibilities for solving the problem?
- How should scarce or divisible materials be allocated?
- Do the parties need help (from representatives or third-party neutrals) to resolve their conflicts?
- Are particular disputes unique or repetitive?
- Do the parties desire privacy to resolve their dispute?
- Does someone else (the "public") require transparency or precedents or other guidance from particular disputes?
- Is a possible "resolution" likely to be final or to need some contingency planning and reopening provisions?
- Is the conflict an ad hoc (one-shot) conflict, or is there a need for some more institutionalized dispute handling?
- What kind of process seems most appropriate for the particular dispute (consensual, party-controlled, command decision with enforcement, informal or formal, intimate or private setting or public transparent process)?

Whatever the conflicts, disputes, and problems you encounter, some of the themes and issues presented in this book will continually arise, even if the contexts change. When is there a need for public, authoritative, legal rulings? When can/should parties be allowed to create their own solutions to problems, with their own forms of justice? When should parties deal with each other directly and when through intermediaries or representatives? Are there only two sides to a dispute, or should all who are affected by a decision be able to participate in making that decision? Can conflict resolution operate effectively across cultural, class, religious, and political divides, or does it require some basic value agreements?

It is all too common in current debates about what is appropriate in dispute resolution for the "sides" to become unduly polarized. It is claimed by some that formal, public, and mostly adversarial, legal processes bring justice, and informal processes bring "only" peace or better communication. Some of us (the authors of this book) cling to a belief that we are in the middle of an evolutionary process in which human beings are seeking new forms of "non-adversarial justice"[13] that go beyond the improvements of evidentiary legal trials over "trials by ordeal."[14] We think that modern dispute resolution is likely to be characterized by on-going "process pluralism," whether denominated a "multi-door courthouse"[15] or a "house of justice."[16] What is less clear is how parties, system designers, and our society should allocate where particular disputes should go.

We conclude this chapter with a few last words on the conundrums presented by making such choices. When is the primary purpose of dispute resolution "justice"[17] — and for whom (*just* us, the parties?, or a larger constituency)[18] — or peace, or can we have both? What are some of the opportunities (and limits) in creating new forms of dispute resolution?

 Julie Macfarlane, **THE NEW LAWYER**

1-2 (2008)

If lawyers do not represent conflict resolution in our public culture, then what is their function? There is an urgent need for lawyers to modify and evolve their professional role consistent with changes in their professional environment. The most important of these changes are widespread public dissatisfaction with the delays and costs associated with traditional legal processes, and the disappearance of full trials in all but a fraction of cases — the so-called "vanishing trial." Articulating a widespread experience, one Ontario lawyer points out, "It's considered exceptional now if we actually litigate something to trial." Despite the centrality of trial advocacy in the popular image of lawyering, it is now not uncommon for a partner in a law firm to have had little trial experience — and occasionally none.

While lawyers often assert that the declining trial rate demonstrates their ability to ultimately settle almost all their cases before trial, even beginning litigation may be an unattractive and unrealistic option for a client who wants an expeditious and practical solution at a reasonable cost. To be effective and successful in practice, the

---

13. Michael King, Arie Freiberg, Becky Batagol & Ross Hymes, Non-Adversarial Justice (2009).

14. Carrie Menkel-Meadow, Is the Adversary System Really Dead? Dilemmas of Legal Ethics as Legal Institutions and Roles Evolve in Current Legal Problems (J. Holder, C. O'Cinneide & M. Freeman eds., 2005).

15. Frank Sander, see Chapter 1.

16. Carrie Menkel-Meadow, Peace and Justice: Notes on the Evolution and Purposes of Legal Processes, 94 Geo. L.J. 553 (2006).

17. For a compelling account of the many forms of justice (with no realizable universal ideal) see Amartya Sen, The Idea of Justice (2009).

18. Carrie Menkel-Meadow, Whose Dispute Is It Anyway? A Philosophical and Democratic Defense of Settlement (in some cases), 83 Geo. L.J. 2663 (1995).

lawyers of the twenty-first century must find other ways to meet their clients' best aspirations — the achievement of effective, appropriate, and sustainable outcomes within a reasonable time frame rather than years tied up in legal procedures, draining their resources, and chasing an apparition of vindication and victory.

There is a growing realization among lawyers and their professional organizations that they are in danger of rendering themselves irrelevant to many ordinary people. At the same time, they are concerned that the types of conflict resolution service that they have traditionally provided for commercial and institutional clients — specialized legal advice and file management through the shoals of litigation — often looks inappropriate and even irrelevant in the face of business realities. Spending vast sums of money and swatches of time on "fighting" is no longer acceptable to major corporations and institutions and may never have been compatible with business culture. The demand for value for money is coming through loud and clear from all client groups, probably accelerated by the phenomenal explosion of access to legal information facilitated by the World Wide Web.

Governments and policy makers have already begun to act. Placing a high priority on cost-savings and efficiency, jurisdictions across North America have introduced earlier, informal, and simpler processes into civil and criminal justice systems, many focused on reaching an agreed bargain or resolution. Some of these new approaches have been forced on lawyers by policy makers who recognize the inefficiency of a conflict resolution model in which almost everything resolves before trial, but only after years of expending vast amounts of money on lawyers' fees and accumulating enormous amounts of paperwork, much of which is never used in the construction of a settlement.

The signs are clear and incontrovertible. Change is needed. And change is coming.

 Jean Sternlight, **ADR IS HERE: PRELIMINARY REFLECTIONS ON WHERE IT FITS IN A SYSTEM OF JUSTICE**

3 Nevada L. Rev. 289, 291, 293, 294, 296, 299, 300, 301, 303-304 (2002/2003)

For twenty five years or more we have been debating the proper role of alternative dispute resolution (ADR) in our system of justice. While the birth of the modern ADR movement is often linked to the 1976 Pound Conference, heated discussions as to the desirability of ADR continued long after that date. . . . Today it is clear that far more disputes in the United States are resolved through negotiation, mediation, and arbitration, than through trial. But the arrival of ADR does not mean that the questioning and critiquing has ended or must end, but rather that it should take a different form. . . .

Reviewing some of the anthropological and other literature regarding other societies' resolution of disputes, I saw that historically many societies have placed far greater emphasis on harmony and healing, and far less emphasis on individualistic adversarial approaches, than we do in the United States today. I also saw that a society's approach to dispute resolution will depend on a number of geographic, historic and other factors, and that the emphasis on harmony and community has both positive and negative aspects.

In pondering the comments of the various participants, I find myself attracted to aspects of each analysis. I am searching for ways to synthesize their perspectives. This attempt at synthesis leads me to offer five insights regarding how a society should go about deciding what type of dispute resolution process it ought to establish:

A. It is a Mistake to Distinguish Litigation from other forms of Dispute Resolution in an Either/Or Fashion.

B. Despite the Entanglement of Various Forms of Dispute Resolution, Significant Choices Must be Made Among the Forms of Dispute Resolution.

C. More Research is Needed Regarding What Disputants Want in a Dispute Resolution System.

> Once this research has been conducted, I believe it will ultimately show that disputants are generally looking for three benefits from a dispute resolution system: (1) a system that provides them with a substantively fair/just result; (2) a system that meets the procedural justice criteria of voice, participation, and dignity . . . and (3) a system that helps them to achieve other personal and emotional goals, such as reconciliation, or that at least does not leave them feeling worse, emotionally and psychologically.

D. We Need to Consider Societal as Well as Individual Interests in Setting Up a System of Justice.

E. We Can Ask a System of Justice to Do More than Just Resolve Disputes or Enforce Rights.

It may well be appropriate to have a procedural system with multiple components in order to serve our multiple goals. Of course, if we devise a system that contains multiple procedures (e.g. both litigation and mediation), we will also have to solve the additional problem of determining how and by whom the choice should be made as to which disputes should be handled under which process. . . . Who decides which disputes go where? . . . I have called this the problem of finding the appropriate "switching" mechanism, to choose between multiple dispute resolution tracks. . . . If we do not use pre-determined criteria, we must at least decide who will make these determinations, and on what basis. . . .

ADR is exciting in part because it allows and encourages us to move beyond our existing conceptions. Without abandoning what is precious about our legal system, we must also be open to new possibilities as we begin to rethink our approach to procedural justice.

Carrie Menkel-Meadow, **PEACE AND JUSTICE: NOTES ON THE EVOLUTION AND PURPOSES OF LEGAL PROCESSES**

94 Geo. L.J. 553, 555-556, 557, 576-579 (2006)

Process pluralism means paying attention to a variety of different systemic values (some of which may seem oppositional to each other) and party needs at the same time, and offering variegated possibilities of process for engagement and decision making. Such values include the attempt to achieve peace with justice, choice and self determination of the individual with care and responsibility for others, and recognition of the harms of the past with hopes for reconciliation in the future. . . . Some of the nettlesome issues to explore here include: (1) the relation of principle and social justice to compromise and consensus; (2) the need to include at least three forms of human discourse in human problem solving and legal decision making: principled argument, traded or bargained for preferences, and passionate commitments of emotion, religion, and moral values; (3) the tensions presented by needing rules of process and (perhaps different) rules of decision; and finally, (4) what I call the Oscar Wilde problem — if socialism takes up too many evenings,[19] imagine what process pluralism and participatory democracy will do to our social lives. Do we have the time, desire, and commitment to fully participate in the processes of our polities and personal lives? . . .

The British social philosopher Stuart Hampshire, in what turned out to be his last major work, *Justice Is Conflict*, (2000) opined that because we are unlikely ever to reach any real, uniform consensus on what constitutes the "substantive good" in a deeply pluralist and divided world, perhaps we can, at best, arrive at some close-to-universal principles for processes that enable us to live together within these differences. For him, this process is *audi alterum partum* ("hear the other side," or the Anglo-American adversary principle). For me, . . . it is closer to "understand *all* sides" of our modern multi-partied and multi-issued disputes. So I substitute "understand" for Hampshire's "hear" (a deeper level of human engagement and empathy, as well as reason) and "all" sides for Hampshire's "other" or "two" sides. Modern social and legal life needs to get beyond the binary, adversarial idea that there are only two sides to an argument or the "truth." "Understanding" and "coexistence" as aspirational values of peace give us some goals and end-states but do not tell us much about how to get there. Political theorists and philosophers over the years have elaborated many theories of political and social organization, from Hobbes's *Leviathan* and Rawls's "veil of ignorance"[20] to Habermas' "ideal speech conditions for uncoerced communicative action."[21] Most recently, a movement and plea for "deliberative democracy" harkening back to Aristotelian notions of participatory democracy and argument have inspired much writing on how we can achieve legitimate and fair consensus and good decisions at all levels of human

---

19. Oscar Wilde, A Life in Quotes 238 (Barry Day ed., 2000).
20. John Rawls, A Theory Of Justice 136-42 (1971).
21. Jürgen Habermas, A Theory of Communicative Action 72-74 (1985).

interaction and conflict, even when we have deep conflicts about facts and values. These recent efforts seek to provide a legitimating and explanatory framework for how to seek fair and "just" outcomes in highly conflictual situations of disputes, conflicts, policy, and law-making. It is my hope to marry this work on deliberative democracy to conflict resolution theory and practice so that we might seek peace and justice (always provisional and evolving in a postmodern world) simultaneously. . . .

THE WAY FORWARD

In the last ten years or so we have seen the flowering of process creativity in attempts to create whole new processes for human governance. Out of the horrors of apartheid, political oppression, genocide, and civil and ethnic wars, we, as a species, have created truth and reconciliation commissions and have adapted traditional community justice systems like *gacaca* in Rwanda, while using more traditional forms of adjudicated justice in the international war crimes tribunals of the former Yugoslavia, Rwanda, and other sites.

These new processes are intended to work on the levels of the most aspirational — of what could be best in our human species, often after what has been the worst — terrible violence. Intended to provide "truth" and "answers" for those who have been killed or seriously harmed (and their families), these processes "triage" cases so that the "least" serious can be dealt with by offering forgiveness, healing, and the possibility of reconciliation and the creation of a new and more peaceful society. These processes are the first I have seen to really take the emotional life of humans seriously. By use of narrative, storytelling, and some confrontation, victims and perpetrators meet head-on in a protected setting in which they are called to account on legal, emotional, and, ultimately, human levels.

These new processes are also quite controversial, and their successes and limits are being explored by participants and scholars. Nevertheless, political scientist James Gibson has concluded, after rigorous public opinion research, that those who participated in (or even only watched) the South African truth and reconciliation processes, even with all their weaknesses, were more likely to have internalized a "human rights consciousness" with an enhanced belief (or hope) in the rule of law to improve human relations and achieve justice.[22] This is consistent with decades of research in what is called "procedural justice," by social psychologists Tom Tyler and Allan Lind, finding that people judge their satisfaction with legal processes by their participation in and perceptions of fairness of those processes, irrespective of the outcomes.

In many settings, these new processes of forgiveness, reconciliation, and new-constitution-drafting have come from new participants in the process design. Women and disempowered racial, ethnic, or religious groups are increasingly finding their voices, after great catastrophe, in the creation of new communities and governments, and seeking new processes to participate in, so that old factions and patterns of power domination will not be repeated. Those who are creating these

---

22. James L. Gibson, Overcoming Apartheid: Can Truth Resolve a Divided Nation? (2004).

new processes are interested in justice, but they also want peace — to live together with mutual respect, to have sufficient resources to be free from want or illness and to be able to seek their own forms of human flourishing. But many of these processes have still come too late — post hoc or after terrible conflict and violence and injustice. Can we imagine the use of such processes before the terrible conflict, violence, and injustice happens, preventing the Rwandan genocide, the Holocaust, Darfur, and more unnecessary killing in the Mideast? What processes can we develop for preventative dispute resolution, when our legal education and processes are so currently focused on the past (lawsuits and judicial decision making from past disputes)? . . .

The challenges for us are many in creating and sustaining new forms of processes with which to seek peace and justice:

1. What should the role of emotions/passions/beliefs be in our conflicts and deliberations with each other? Transformative empathy is among the most significant and important ways of grounding justice and moving people to new places. (Think Martin Luther King, Jr., the Civil Rights Movement, and parents of gays whose love for their children teaches them to change their views; think contra the emotional appeals of fascists and demagogues that tap into the baser forms of group identity and values).

2. How do we reconcile the need to adjudicate and punish the past, with correction of injustice, with reintegration of the future with peace and forgiveness, if not forgetfulness?

3. Do we need "rules" of process and decision rules "laid down" in advance, or can we negotiate and deliberate about the very processes we will use to achieve peace and justice in different contexts (historically, geographically, and culturally)?

4. How do we deal with the tyranny of the majority in a democracy and the needs of minorities for recognition and fulfillment (whether temporary, by issue or politics, or more permanent, by group or other identification)?

Problem 14-4.   *What is Justice? What is Peace?*

Imagine yourself a person grievously wronged — a terminated employee, an abandoned spouse, a victim of an urban American police beating, a victim of discrimination, a released political prisoner from an opposition party in a dictatorial state, a family member of a murder victim, a property owner in a former Communist state whose property was confiscated, an aged surviving Korean "comfort woman," or a survivor of the German Holocaust or the Rwandan genocide.

What kind of process would you want in order to feel you had been "justly" dealt with?* Would you want a public process to give testimony? A private ceremony of grief? Would you require compensation? An apology? Retribution? A formal determination of guilt with punishment? Would you want to create your own process, or would you be willing to use the same process as other people who suffered the same wrongs? How likely do you think it will be that all people who suffer these injuries would agree to the same process?

*From, Carrie Menkel-Meadow, Remembrance of Things Past? The Relationship of Past to Future in Pursuing Justice in Mediation, 5 Cardozo J. Conflict Resol. 97, 105 (2004).

As you go out into the world to ponder these questions in new settings, with new conflicts, problems, and disputes unimaginable to us, we hope you will remember the questions and issues that you have studied here. We wish you great wisdom and good luck in solving problems and resolving disputes.

Further Reading

Peter Adler. (2008). *Eye of the Storm Leadership: 150 Stories, Quotes and Exercises on the Art and Politics of Managing Human Conflicts.* Keystone: Colorado.

Stuart Hampshire. (2000). *Justice as Conflict.* Princeton: Princeton University Press.

Priscilla Hayner. (2001). *Unspeakable Truths: Confronting State Terror and Atrocity.* Routledge.

Michael King, Arie Freiberg, Becky Batagol & Ross Hyams. (2009). *Non-Adversarial Justice.* Sydney, Australia: Federation Press.

Carrie Menkel-Meadow. (2010). Dispute Resolution. In Peter Cane & Herbert Kritzer (Eds.), *Oxford Handbook of Empirical Legal Research.* Oxford: Oxford University Press.

Carrie Menkel-Meadow, *Chronicling the Complexification of Negotiation Theory and Practice,* 25 Negotiation J. 415-429 (2009).

Frank Sander. (2000). *The Future of ADR,* 2000 J. Dispute Resol. 1 (2000).

Frank Sander, *Ways of Handling Conflict: What We Have Learned, What Problems Remain,* 25 Negotiation J. 533-537 (2009).

Andrea Kupfer Schneider, *Bargaining in the Shadow of (International Law),* 41 N.Y. U. J. INT'L L. & POL. 789 (2009).

Andrea Kupfer Schneider, *The Day After Tomorrow: What Happens Once a Middle East Peace Treaty Is Signed?,* 6 NEV. L.J. 401 (2006).

Amartya Sen. (2009). *The Idea of Justice.* Cambridge, Mass: Belknap Press of Harvard University Press.

Jane Stromseth, David Wippman & Rosa Brooks. (2006). *Can Might Make Rights?* Cambridge and New York: Cambridge University Press.

Lawrence Susskind, *Twenty-Five Years Ago and Twenty-Five Years From Now: The Future of Public Dispute Resolution,* 25 NEGOTIATION J. 551–557 (2009).

Roselle L. Wissler, *Representation in Mediation: What We Know from Empirical Research,* 37 FORDHAM URB. L. J. 419 (2010).

Roselle L. Wissler, *Court-Connected Settlement Procedures: Mediation and Judicial Settlement Conferences,* 26 OHIO ST. J. ON DISP. RESOL. (2011).

Craig Zelizer & Robert A. Rubenstein. (2009). *Building Peace: Reflections from the Field.* Kumarian Press.

Table of Online Resources

Table of Principal Cases

Collected References

AARON, Marjorie Corman (1996). "ADR Toolbox: The Highwire Art of Evaluation," 14 *Alternatives to High Cost Litig.* 62.

ABEL, Richard L. (1982). "The Contradictions of Informal Justice," in Richard L. Abel, ed., 1 *The Politics of Informal Justice: The American Experience.* 2 vols. New York: Academic Press.

_____ (1973). "A Comparative Theory of Dispute Institutions in Society," 8 *Law & Socy. Rev.* 217.

ABRAMS, Roger I. (2000). *The Money Pitch: Baseball Free Agency and Salary Arbitration.* Philadelphia, PA: Temple University Press.

_____ (1999). "Inside Baseball's Salary Arbitration Process," 6 *U. Chi. L. Sch. Roundtable* 55.

ABRAMSON, Harold I. (2010). *Mediation Representation: Advocating in a Problem-Solving Process* (2d ed.). South Bend, Ind.: National Institute for Trial Advocacy.

_____ (1999). "Protocols for International Arbitrators Who Dare to Settle Cases," 10 *Am. Rev. Intl. Arb.* 1.

ADLER, Jane W., HENSLER, Deborah R., and Charles E. NELSON (1983). *Simple Justice: How Litigants Fare in the Pittsburgh Court Arbitration Program.* Santa Monica, CA: Rand.

ADLER, Peter S. (2008). *Eye of the Storm Leadership: 150 Stories, Quotes and Exercises on the Art and Politics of Managing Human Conflicts.* Colorado: Keystone.

_____ (2006). "Protean Negotiation" in Andrea Kupfer Schneider, and Christopher Honeyman, eds., *The Negotiator's Fieldbook.* Washington D.C.: ABA Section on Dispute Resolution.

AIBEL, Howard J., and George H. FRIEDMAN (1996). "Drafting Dispute Resolution Clauses in Complex Business Transactions," *Disp. Resol. Mag.* 17 (January-March).

ALBIN, Cecilia (1993). "The Role of Fairness in Negotiation," 9 *Negot. J.* 223.

ALEXANDER, Janet Cooper (1991). "Do the Merits Matter? A Study of Settlements in Securities Class Actions," 43 *Stan. L. Rev.* 497.

ALFINI, James J. (1991). "Trashing, Bashing, and Hashing It Out: Is This the End of 'Good Mediation'?," 19 *Fla. St. U. L. Rev.* 47.

_____ (1989). "Summary Jury Trials in State and Federal Courts: A Comparative Analysis of the Perceptions of Participating Lawyers," 4 *Ohio St. J. on Disp. Resol.* 213.

ALLRED, Keith G., et al. (1997). "The Influence of Anger and Compassion on Negotiation Performance," 70 *Organizational Behav. & Hum. Decision Processes* 175.

AMERICAN ARBITRATION ASSOCIATION (2007). "2007 Annual Report." New York: American Arbitration Association. Retrieved from http://www.adr.org/annual_reports.

_____ (2004). *Drafting Dispute Resolution Clauses: A Practical Guide.* New York: American Arbitration Association. Retrieved from http://www.adr.org/si.asp?id=2424.

_____ (2002). "Statement of Ethical Principles." New York: American Arbitration Association. Retrieved from http://www.adr.org.

_____ (2003). "Supplementary Procedures for Consumer-Related Disputes." American Arbitration Association. Retrieved from http://www.adr.org.

AMERICAN ARBITRATION ASSOCIATION, AMERICAN BAR ASSOCIATION, and AMERICAN MEDICAL ASSOCIATION (1998). "A Due Process Protocol for Resolution of Health Care Disputes," in *Commission on Health Care Dispute Resolution: Final Report* (July 27). New York: ABA. Retrieved from http://www.adr.org/upload/livesite/focusArea/Healthcare/healthcare.pdf.

AMERICAN BAR ASSOCIATION, AMERICAN ARBITRATION ASSOCIATION, and ASSOCIATION FOR CONFLICT RESOLUTION (2005). "Model Standards of Conduct for Mediators." Washington, D.C.: ABA. Retrieved from http://www.abanet.org/dispute/news/ModelStandardsofConductforMediatorsfinal05.pdf.

AMERICAN BAR ASSOCIATION (2004). "Resolution on Good Faith Requirements for Mediators and Mediation Advocates in Court-Mandated Mediation Programs." Washington, D.C.: ABA, Section of Dipsute Resolution. Retrieved from http://www.abanet.org/dispute/webpolicy.html#9/.

_____ (2002). "Resolution on Mediation and the Unauthorized Practice of Law." Washington, D.C.: ABA, Section of Dispute Resolution. Retrieved from http://www.abanet.org/dispute/resolution2002.pdf.

_____ (2001). "Standards for the Establishment and Operation of Ombuds Offices." Washington, D.C.: American Bar Association. Retrieved from. http://www.abanet.org/poladv/letters/107th/adminlaw072602/attach.pdf.

_____ (1998). Preamble to "Guidelines for Litigation Conduct." Washington, D.C.: American Bar Association. Retrieved from http://www.abanet.org/dispute/ lawcivil.html.

AMERICAN LAW INSTITUTE (1981). *Restatement of the Law of Contracts (Second)* §161. 164.

_____ (1977). *Restatement of the Law of Torts (Second)* §525.

ANDERSON, Mary B. (1999). *Do No Harm: How Aid Can Support Peace–Or War.* Boulder, CO: Lynne Rienner Publishers.

ANGIER, Natalie (2002). "Why We're So Nice: We're Wired to Cooperate," *N. Y. Times,* July 23, p. F1.

ANONYMOUS (1981). Note, "The California Rent-a-Judge Experiment: Constitutional and Policy Considerations of Pay-As-You-Go Courts," 94 *Harv. L. Rev.* 1592.

APPLBAUM, Arthur Isak (1999). *Ethics for Adversaries.* Princeton, NJ: Princeton University Press.

ARNOLD, Tom (1995). "20 Common Errors in Mediation Advocacy," 13 *Alternatives to High Cost Litig.* 69.

AUERBACH, Jerold S. (1983). *Justice Without Law?* New York: Oxford University Press.

AUVINE, Brian, et al. (1977). *A Manual for Group Facilitators.* Madison, WI: Center for Conflict Resolution.

AXELROD, Robert (1984). *The Evolution of Cooperation.* New York: Basic Books.

AYRES, Ian (1995). "Further Evidence of Discrimination in New Car Negotiations and Estimates of Its Cause," 94 *Mich. L. Rev.* 109.

_____ (1991). "Fair Driving: Gender and Race Discrimination in Retail Car Negotiations," 104 *Harv. L. Rev.* 817.

BABCOCK, Linda, and Sara LASCHEVER. (2003). *Women Don't Ask: Negotiation and the Gender Divide.* Princeton, NJ: Princeton University Press.

BAKER, C. Mark, and Arif Hyder ALI (2002). "A Cross-Comparison of Institutional Mediation Rules," *Disp. Resol. J.* 72 (May–July).

BARKAI, John (1984). "How to Develop the Skill of Active Listening," 30 *Practical Lawyer.* 73.

BARRETT, Jerome T., and Joseph BARRETT. (2004). *A History of Alternative Dispute Resolution: The Story of a Political, Social and Cultural Movement.* San Francisco, CA: Jossey-Bass Publishers.

BARON, Robert A. (1990). "Environmentally Induced Positive Affect: Its Impact on Self-Efficacy, Task Performance, Negotiation, and Conflict," 20 *J. Applied Soc. Psychol.* 368.

BARTOS, Otomar J. (1978). "Simple Model of Negotiation: A Sociological Point of View," in I. William Zartman, ed., *The Negotiation Process: Theories and Applications.* Beverly Hills, CA: Sage Publications.

BASTRESS, Robert M., and Joseph D. HARBAUGH (1990). *Interviewing, Counseling, and Negotiating: Skills for Effective Representation.* Boston: Little, Brown.

BAUM, Simeon (2005). "Top 10 Things Not to Do in Mediation," *N.Y. L.J.* Col. 78.

BAZERMAN, Max H., ed. (2005). *Negotiation, Decision Making and Conflict Management.* Cheltenham, UK: Edward Elgar Publishing.

BAZERMAN, Max H., and Margaret A. NEALE (1992). *Negotiating Rationally.* New York: Free Press.

BEGLEY, Sharon (2000). "The Stereotype Trap," *Newsweek,* November 6, p. 66.

BERCOVITCH, Jacob (1992). "The Structure and Diversity of Mediation in International Relations," in Jacob Bercovitch and Jeffrey Z. Rubin, eds., *Mediation in International Relations: Multiple Approaches to Conflict Management.* New York: St. Martin's Press.

BERCOVITCH, Jacob, ed. (1996). *Resolving International Conflicts: The Theory and Practice of Mediation.* Boulder, Colo.: Lynne Rienner Publishers.

BERMAN, Greg, and John FEINBLATT (2001). "Problem-Solving Courts: A Brief Primer," 23 *Law & Poly.* 125.

BERMAN, Greg, John FEINBLATT, and Sarah GLAZER (2005). *Good Courts: The Case for Problem Solving Justice.* New York: New Press.

BERNARD, Phyllis, and Bryant GARTH, eds. (2002). *Dispute Resolution Ethics: A Comprehensive Guide.* Washington, D.C.: ABA, Section of Dispute Resolution.

BERNER, Robert, and Brian GROW (2008). "Banks vs. Consumers (Guess Who Wins)," *Business Week,* June 5. Retrieved from http://www.businessweek.com/magazine/content/08_24/b4088072611398.htm.

BERNSTEIN, Edward A. (1995). "Law & Economics and the Structure of Value Adding Contracts: A Contract Lawyer's View of the Law & Economics Literature," 74 *Or. L. Rev.* 189.

BERNSTEIN, Lisa (1993). "Understanding the Limits of Court-Connected ADR: A Critique of Federal Court-Annexed Arbitration Programs," 141 *U. Pa. L. Rev.* 2169.

_____ (1992). "Opting Out of the Legal System: Extralegal Contractual Relations in the Diamond Industry," 21 *J. Legal Stud.* 115.

BEZANSON, Randall P., Gilbert CRANBERG, and John SOLOSKI (1987). *Libel Law and the Press: Myth and Reality.* New York: Free Press.

BIBLE (Old Testament). "Then Came There Two Women [Before Solomon]," 1 *Kings* 3:16.

BICKERMAN, John (1996). "Evaluative Mediator Responds," 14 *Alternatives to High Cost Litig.* 70.

BINDER, David A., Paul BERGMAN, and Susan C. PRICE (2d ed. 2004). *Lawyers as Counselors: A Client-Centered Approach.* St. Paul: West Group.

BINGHAM, Lisa B. (2003). "Mediation at Work: Transforming Workplace Conflict at the United States Postal Service." Washington, D.C.: IBM Center for The Business of Government. Retrieved from http://www.businessofgovernment.org/pdfs/Bingham_Report.pdf.

_____ (2002). "Self-Determination in Dispute System Design and Employment Arbitration," 56 *U. Miami L. Rev.* 873.

_____ (2002). "Why Suppose? Let's Find Out: A Public Policy Research Program on Dispute Resolution," 2002 *J. Disp. Resol.* 101.

BINGHAM, Lisa, Cynthia J. HALLBERLIN, Denise A. WALKER, and Won-Tae CHUNG (2009). "Dispute System Design and Justice in Employment Dispute Resolution: Mediation at the Workplace," 14 *Harvard Negot. L. Rev.* 1.

BIRKE, Richard, and Craig FOX (1981). "Psychological Principles in Negotiating Civil Settlements," *Acad. of Mgmt. Rev.* 23.

BITTING, Melissa R. (1998). "Mandatory, Binding Arbitration for Olympic Athletes: Is the Process Better or Worse for 'Job Security'?," 25 *Fla. St. U. L. Rev.* 655.

BLACKER, Neal (2000). "Drafting the Arbitration/ADR Clause: A Checklist for Practitioners," *Prac. Law.* 55 (March).

BLAKE, Robert R., Herbert A. SHEPARD, and Jane S. MOUTON (1964). *Managing Intergroup Conflict in Industry.* Houston: Gulf Publishing.

BLAND, F. Paul, Jr., Michael J. QUIRK, Kate GORDON, and Jonathan SHELDON (2003). "The Supreme Court Does Not Require Preemption of Procedural Provisions," in *Consumer Arbitration Agreements: Enforceability and Other Topics* §2.2.2.2 (3d ed.). Boston: National Consumer Law Center.

BLUM, Gabriella (2007). *Islands of Agreement: Managing Enduring Armed Rivalries.* Cambridge, MA: Harvard University Press.

BOHMAN, James (1996). *Public Deliberation: Pluralism, Complexity, and Democracy.* Cambridge, Mass.: MIT Press.

BOLDUC, Danielle Sheri (1990). *Mediator Style Perspectives: An Innovative Look at Mediator Behavior* (unpublished master's thesis, Arizona State University).

BORDONE, Robert C. (1998). "Electronic Online Dispute Resolution: A Systems Approach—Potential, Problems, and a Proposal," 3 *Harv. Negot. L. Rev.* 175.

BORN, Gary B. (2009). *International Commercial Arbitration.* The Hague, The Netherlands: Kluwer Law International.

_____ (2001). *International Commercial Arbitration: Commentary and Materials* (2d ed.). Ardsley, N.Y.: Transnational Publishers.

BOULLE, Laurence J., Michael T. COLATRELLA, Jr., and Anthony P. PICCHIONI (2008). *Mediation: Skills and Techniques* (1 ed.). LexisNexis Matthew Bender.

BRAMS, Steven J., and Alan D. TAYLOR (1996). *Fair Division.* Cambridge, MA: Cambridge University Press.

BRAZIL, Wayne D. (2006). "Should Court Sponsored ADR Survive?" 21 *Ohio St. J. on Disp. Resol.* 241.

_____ (2000). "Continuing the Conversation About the Current Status and the Future of ADR: A View from the Courts," 2000 *J. Disp. Resol.* 11.

_____ (1990). "A Close Look at Three Court-Sponsored ADR Programs: Why They Exist, How They Operate, What They Deliver, and Whether They Threaten Important Values," 1990 *U. Chi. Legal F.* 303.

_____ (1984). "Settling Civil Cases: What Lawyers Want from Judges," *Judges' J.* 14 (Summer).

BREGER, Marshall J. (2000). "Should an Attorney Be Required to Advise a Client of ADR Options?," 13 *Geo. J. Legal Ethics* 427.

BRETT, Jeanne M. (2001). *Negotiating Globally: How to Negotiate Deals, Resolve Disputes, and Make Decisions Across Cultural Boundaries.* San Francisco: Jossey-Bass Publishers.

BROWN, Jennifer Gerarda (2006). "Creativity and Problem-Solving" in Andrea Kupfer Schneider and Christopher Honeyman, eds., *The Negotiator's Fieldbook.* Washington, D.C.: ABA Section on Dispute Resolution.

_____ (2004). "Creativity and Problem-Solving," 87 *Marq. L. Rev.* 697.

_____ (1997). "The Role of Hope in Negotiation," 44 *UCLA L. Rev.* 1661.

BRUNET, Edward (1999). "Replacing Folklore Arbitration with a Contract Model of Arbitration," 74 *Tul. L. Rev.* 39.

BRUNET, Edward, Richard E. SPEIDEL, Jean R. STERNLIGHT, and Stephen J. WARE. (2006). *Arbitration Law in America: A Critical Assessment.* New York, NY: Cambridge University Press.

BRYAN, Penelope E. (1992). "Killing Us Softly: Divorce Mediation and the Politics of Power," 40 *Buff. L. Rev.* 441.

BURGER, Warren E. (1982). "Isn't There a Better Way?," 68 *A.B.A.J.* 274.

_____ (1971). "The Necessity for Civility," 52 F.R.D. 211.

BURNS, Stacy Lee (2000). *Making Settlement Work: An Examination of the Work of Judicial Mediators*. Aldershot, UK: Ashgate.

BURRESSE, Alain (2006). "Listen Up," *Mont. Law.* 22.

BURTON, John W. (1987). *Resolving Deep-Rooted Conflict: A Handbook*. Lanham, MD: University Press of America.

BUSH, Robert A. Baruch (2002). "Substituting Mediation for Arbitration: The Growing Market for Evaluative Mediation, and What It Means for the ADR Field," 3 *Pepp. Disp. Resol. L.J.* 111.

_____ (1989-90). "Mediation and Adjudication, Dispute Resolution and Ideology: An Imaginary Conversation," 3 *J. Contemp. Legal Issues* 1.

BUSH, Robert A. Baruch, and Joseph P. FOLGER (2005 rev. ed.). *The Promise of Mediation: Responding to Conflict Through Empowerment and Recognition*. San Francisco: Jossey-Bass Publishers.

CARBONNEAU, Thomas E. (2004). *The Law and Practice of Arbitration*. Huntington NY: JurisNet, LLC.

CARPENTER, Susan L., and W.L.D. KENNEDY (2001). *Managing Public Disputes: A Practical Guide for Professionals in Government, Business and Citizen Groups*. San Francisco: Jossey-Bass Publishers.

CARNEVALE, Peter J.D., and Alice M. ISEN (1986). "The Influence of Positive Affect and Visual Access on the Discovery of Integrative Solutions in Bilateral Negotiation," 37 *Organizational Behav. & Hum. Decision Processes.* 1.

CARNEVALE, Peter J.D., Donald E. CONLON, Kathy A. HANISCH, and Karen L. HARRIS (1989). "Experimental Research on the Strategic-Choice Model of Mediation," in Kenneth Kressel and Dean G. Pruitt, eds., *Mediation Research: The Process and Effectiveness of Third-Party Intervention*. San Francisco: Jossey-Bass Publishers.

CARR, Albert H.Z. (1968). *Business as a Game*. New York: New American Library.

_____ (1968). "Is Business Bluffing Ethical?," *Harv. Bus. Rev.* 143 (January-February).

CARR, Frank, with Kim HURTADO, Charles LANCASTER, Charles MARKERT, and Paul TUCKER (1999). *Partnering in Construction: A Practical Guide to Project Success*. Chicago: Forum on the Construction Industry, ABA.

CARRINGTON, Paul D., and Paul H. HAAGEN (1996). "Contract and Jurisdiction," 1996 *Sup. Ct. Rev.* 331.

CARTER, James H. (2000). "Improving Life with the Party-Appointed Arbitrator: Clearer Conduct Guidelines for 'Nonneutrals,' " 11 *Am. Rev. Intl. Arb.* 295.

CARTER, Jimmy (1982). *Keeping Faith: Memoirs of a President*. Toronto: Bantam Books.

CENTER FOR CONFLICT RESOLUTION (1977). *Manual for Group Facilitators*. Madison, WI: Center for Conflict Resolution.

CENTER FOR PUBLIC RESOURCES. (1995). "The ABC's of ADR: A Dispute Resolution Glossary. 13 (11) *Alternatives (to the High Cost of Litigation)* 1.

CHAYES, Abram J. (1999) Preface to Robert H. Mnookin, Lawrence E. Susskind, eds., with Pacey C. Foster, *Negotiating on Behalf of Others: Advice to Lawyers, Business Executives, Sports Agents, Diplomats, Politicians, and Everybody Else*. Thousand Oaks, CA: Sage Publications.

CHAYES, Antonia, and Martha MINOW, eds. (2003). *Imagine Coexistence: Restoring Humanity After Violent Ethnic Conflict*. San Francisco: Jossey-Bass Publishers.

CHERNICK, Richard, Helen I. BENDIX, and Robert C. BARRETT, with Roger CLEGG, ed. (1997). *Private Judging: Privatizing Civil Justice*. Washington, D.C.: National Legal Center for the Public Interest.

CHRISTENSEN, Barlow F. (1982). "Private Justice: California's General Reference Procedure," 1982 *Am. B. Found. Res. J.* 79.

CIALDINI, Robert B. (1993). *Influence: The Psychology of Persuasion* (rev. ed.). New York: William Morrow.

CLERMONT, Kevin M., and Stewart J. SCHWAB (2004). "How Employment Discrimination Plaintiffs Fare in Federal Court," 1 *J. of Empirical Legal Studies* 429.

CLINTON, William J. (2001). Acceptance Speech for the International Advocate for Peace Award, March 19. Benjamin N. Cardozo School of Law. Retrieved from http://www.cardozo.yu.edu/cojcr/final_site/IAP_Award/2001/clintpdf.pdf.

COBEN, James R. (2000). "Mediation's Dirty Little Secret: Straight Talk About Mediator Manipulation and Deception," *J. Alternative Disp. Resol. Emp.* 4 (Winter).

COBEN, James R., and Peter N. THOMPSON (2006). "Disputing Irony: A Systematic Look at Litigation About Mediation," 11 *Harv. Neg. L. Rev.* 4,

COCHRAN, Robert F., Jr. (1990). "Legal Representation and the Next Steps Toward Client Control: Attorney Malpractice for the Failure to Allow the Client to Control Negotiation and Pursue Alternatives to Litigation," 47 *Wash. & Lee L. Rev.* 819.

_____ (2003). "Introduction: Three Approaches to Moral Issues in Law Office Counseling," 30 *Pepp. L. Rev.* 592.

COFFEE, John C., Jr. (1995). "Class Wars: The Dilemma of the Mass Tort Class Action," 95 *Colum. L. Rev.* 1343.

COGLIANESE, Cary (1997). "Assessing Consensus: The Promise and Performance of Negotiated Rulemaking," 46 *Duke L.J.* 1255.

COHEN, Herb (2003). *Negotiate This!: By Caring, but Not T-H-A-T Much.* New York: Warner Books.

COHEN, James R. (2000). "Mediation's Dirty Little Secret: Straight Talk About Mediation Manipulation and Deception," 2 *J. Alternative Disp. Resol. Emp.* 4.

COHEN, Jonathan R. (2003). "Adversaries? Partners? How About Counterparts? On Metaphors in the Practice and Teaching of Negotiation and Dispute Resolution," 20 *Conflict Resol. Q.* 433.

_____ (2001). "When People Are the Means: Negotiating with Respect," 14 *Geo. J. Legal Ethics* 739.

_____ (2000). "Apology and Organizations: Exploring an Example from Medical Practice," 27 *Fordham Urb. L.J.* 1447.

COHEN, Julius Henry (1918). *Commercial Arbitration and the Law.* New York: D. Appleton.

COHEN, Julius Henry, and Kenneth DAYTON (1926). "The New Federal Arbitration Law," 12 *Va. L. Rev.* 265.

COLE, Sarah Rudolph (2005). "Arbitration and State Action," 2005 *B.Y.U. L. Rev.* 1.

COLE, Sarah R., Nancy H. ROGERS, and Craig A. McEWEN (2001). "Dilemmas Presented by Institutionalization of Mediation," in 1 *Mediation: Law, Policy & Practice* ch. 2 (2d ed.). 3 vols. St. Paul: West Group.

COLE, Sarah R., Nancy H. ROGERS, and Craig A. McEWEN (2001). "Legal Services by Mediator: Conflict of Interest, Advertising, Joint Practice, and Unauthorized Practice," in 1 *Mediation: Law, Policy & Practice* ch. 10 (2d ed. & Supp. 2002). 3 vols. St. Paul: West Group.

COLE, Sarah R., Nancy H. ROGERS, and Craig A. McEWEN (2001). "Regulating for Quality, Fairness, Effectiveness, and Access: Mediator Qualifications, Certification, Liability and Immunity, Procedural Requirements, and Other Measures," in 1 *Mediation: Law, Policy & Practice* ch. 11 (2d ed. & Supp. 2002). 3 vols. St. Paul: West Group.

COLEMAN, Peter T., and Morton DEUTSCH (2000). "Some Guidelines for Developing a Creative Approach to Conflict," in Morton Deutsch and Peter T. Coleman, eds., *The Handbook of Conflict Resolution: Theory and Practice.* San Francisco: Jossey-Bass Publishers.

COMMITTEE ON COMMERCE, TRADE AND COMMERCIAL LAW (1925). "The United States Arbitration Law and Its Application," 11 *A.B.A.J.* 153.

CONA, Frank A. (1997). "Application of Online Systems in Alternative Dispute Resolution," 45 *Buff. L. Rev.* 975.

CONDLIN, Robert J. (2010). "Bargaining Without Law." Retrieved from http://ssrn.com/abstract=1649467.

_____ (1985). " 'Cases on Both Sides': Patterns of Argument in Legal Dispute-Negotiation," 44 *Md. L. Rev.* 65.

CONNOR, Lawrence D. (1996). "How to Combine Facilitation with Evaluation," 14 *Alternatives to High Cost Litig.* 15.

COOLEY, John W. (2005). *Creative Problem Solver's Handbook for Negotiators and Mediators* (Vol. 1 & 2). Washington, D.C.: ABA Section of Dispute Resolution.

_____ (1997). "Mediation Magic: Its Use and Abuse," 29 *Loy. U. Chi. L.J.* 1.

COOLEY, John W., and Steven LUBET (2003). *Arbitration Advocacy* (2d ed.). South Bend, Ind.: National Institute for Trial Advocacy.

COOPER, Laura, Dennis NOLAN, and Richard A. BALES (2005). *ADR in the Workplace.* St. Paul, MN: The West Group.

CORTINA, Lilia M., et al. (2002). "What's Gender Got to Do with It? Incivility in the Federal Courts," 27 *Law & Soc. Inquiry* 235.

COSTANTINO, Cathy (2009). "Second Generation Organizational Conflict Management Systems Design: A Practitioner's Perspective on Emerging Issues," 14 *Harv. Negot. L. Rev.* 81.

COSTANTINO, Cathy A., and Christina Sickles MERCHANT (1996). *Designing Conflict Management Systems: A Guide to Creating Productive and Healthy Organizations.* San Francisco: Jossey-Bass Publishers.

COVEY, Stephen R. (1989). *The Seven Habits of Highly Effective People: Restoring the Character Ethic.* New York: Simon and Schuster.

CPR INSTITUTE FOR DISPUTE RESOLUTION (1995). "The ABCs of ADR: A Dispute Resolution Glossary," 13 *Alternatives to High Cost Litig.* 147.

_____ (2001). "CPR's Online Seminar: Transactional ADR," 19 *Alternatives to High Cost Litig.* 173.

_____ (2000). *Rules for Non-Administered Arbitration.* CPR Institute for Dispute Resolution. Retrieved from http://www. cpradr.org/arbruleswappeal.pdf.

CPR-GEORGETOWN COMMISSION ON ETHICS AND STANDARDS IN ADR (2002). *Proposed New Model Rule of Professional Conduct Rule 4.5: The Lawyer as Third-Party Neutral.* New York: CPR Institute for Dispute Resolution. Retrieved from http://www.cpradr.org/pdfs/cprgeorge-modelrule.pdf.

CPR-GEORGETOWN COMMISSION ON ETHICS AND STANDARDS OF PRACTICE IN ADR (2002). *Principles for ADR Provider Organizations.* New York: CPR Institute for Dispute Resolution. Retrieved from http://www.cpradr.org/finalProvider.pdf.

CRAVER, Charles B., and David W. BARNES (1999). "Gender, Risk Taking, and Negotiation Performance," 5 *Mich. J. Gender & L.* 299.

CROCKER, Chester A., Fen Osler HAMPSON, and Pamela AALL, eds. (2001). *Turbulent Peace: The Challenges of Managing International Conflict.* Washington, D.C.: United States Institute of Peace Press.

_____ (1999). *Herding Cats: Multiparty Mediation in a Complex World.* Washington, D.C.: United States Institute of Peace Press.

CROSON, Rachel, and Robert H. MNOOKIN (1997). "Does Disputing Through Agents Enhance Cooperation? Experimental Evidence," 26 *J. Legal Stud.* 331.

CURRAN, Daniel, and James K. SEBENIUS (2003). "The Mediator as Coalition Builder: George Mitchell in Northern Ireland," 8 *Intl. Negot.* 111.

DAY, Barry, ed. (2000). *Oscar Wilde, A Life in Quotes.* London: Metro.

DE BONO, Edward (1999). *Six Thinking Hats* (rev. ed.). Boston: Little, Brown.

DEASON, Ellen E. (2004). "Procedural Rules for Complementary Systems of Litigation and Mediation — Worldwide," 80 *Notre Dame L. Rev.* 533.

_____ (2001). "Enforcing Mediated Settlement Agreements: Contract Law Collides with Confidentiality," 35 *U.C. Davis L. Rev.* 33.

DELGADO, Richard, Chris DUNN, Pamela BROWN, Helena LEE, and David HUBBERT (1985). "Fairness and Formality: Minimizing the Risk of Prejudice in Alternative Dispute Resolution," 1985 *Wis. L. Rev.* 1359.

DEMAINE, Linda J., and Deborah R. HENSLER (2004). "Volunteering to Arbitrate Through Predispute Arbitration Clauses: The Average Consumer's Experience," 67 *Law & Contemp. Probs.* 55.

DEUTSCH, Morton (1973). *The Resolution of Conflict: Constructive and Destructive Processes.* New Haven: Yale University Press.

DEUTSCH, Morton, and Peter T. COLEMAN, eds. (2000). *The Handbook of Conflict Resolution: Theory and Practice.* San Francisco: Jossey-Bass Publishers.

DEZALAY, Yves, and Bryant G. GARTH (1996). *Dealing in Virtue: International Commercial Arbitration and the Construction of a Transnational Legal Order.* Chicago: University of Chicago Press.

DICKENS, Charles (1853) *Bleak House* (1956 ed.). Boston: Houghton Mifflin.

DINERSTEIN, Robert D. (1990). "Client-Centered Counseling: Reappraisal and Refinement," 32 *Ariz. L. Rev.* 501.

DOERRE, Sharon (2001). "Negotiating Gender and Authority in Northern Syria," 6 *Intl. Negot.* 251.

DONAHEY, M. Scott (1992). "The Independence and Neutrality of Arbitrators," *J. Intl. Arb.* 31 (December).

DONEGAN, Frederick N. (1994). "Examining the Role of Arbitration in Professional Baseball," 1 *Sports Law. J.* 183.

DONNELL, Susan M., and Jay HALL (1980). "Men and Women as Managers: A Significant Case of No Significant Difference," *Organizational Dynamics* 60 (Spring).

DORF, Michael C., and Charles F. SABEL (2000). "Drug Treatment Courts and Emergent Experimentalist Government," 53 *Vand. L. Rev.* 831.

_____ (1998). "A Constitution of Democratic Experimentalism," 98 *Colum. L. Rev.* 267.

DRAHOZAL, Christopher R. (2006). *Commercial Arbitration: Cases and Problems.* Newark, NJ: LexisNexis Matthew Bender.

_____ (2005). "Contracting Out of International Law: An Empirical Look at the New Law Merchant," 80 *Notre Dame L. Rev.* 523.

_____ (2004). "Federal Arbitration Act Preemption," 79 *Ind. L.J.* 393

_____ (2003). "Contracting Around RUAA: Default Rules, Mandatory Rules, and Judicial Review of Arbitral Awards," 3 *Pepp. Disp. Resol. L.J.* 419.

_____ (2002). "In Defense of *Southland*: Reexamining the Legislative History of the Federal Arbitration Act," 78 *Notre Dame L. Rev.* 101.

DRAHOZAL, Christopher R., and Quentin R. Wittrock (2008). "Is There a Flight from Arbitration?," 37 *Hofstra L. Rev.* 71.

DRAHOZAL, Christopher R., and S. ZYONTZ (2009). "An Empirical Study of AAA Consumer Arbitration." SSRN. Retrieved from http://ssrn.com/abstract=1365435.

DRYZEK, John S. (2000). *Deliberative Democracy and Beyond: Liberals, Critics, Contestations.* New York: Oxford University Press.

DUKES, E. Franklin, Marina A. PISCOLISH, and John B. STEPHENS (2000). *Reaching for Higher Ground in Conflict Resolution: Tools for Powerful Groups and Communities.* San Francisco: Jossey-Bass Publishers.

DUNLOP, John T., and Arnold M. ZACK (1997). *Mediation and Arbitration of Employment Disputes.* San Francisco: Jossey-Bass Publishers.

EBNER, Noam, Anita D. BHAPPU, Jennifer BROWN, Kimberlee K. KOVACH, and Andrea Kupfer SCHNEIDER (2009). "You've Got Agreement: Negoti@ting via email" in

Christopher Honeyman, James Coben, and Giuseppe de Palo, eds, *Rethinking Negotiation Teaching: Innovations for Context and Culture.* St. Paul, MN: DRI Press.

EDELMAN, Lauren B., Howard S. ERLANGER, and John LANDE (1993). "Internal Dispute Resolution: The Transformation of Civil Rights in the Workplace," 27 *Law & Socy. Rev.* 497.

EDMONDS, David, and John EIDINOW (2001). *Wittgenstein's Poker: The Story of a Ten-Minute Argument Between Two Great Philosophers.* New York: Ecco.

EISENBERG, Theodore, and Elizabeth HILL (2003-2004). "Arbitration and Litigation of Employment Claims: An Empirical Comparison," *Disp. Resol. J.* 44 (November-January).

ElKOURI, Frank (2003). *How Arbitration Works.* Washington, D.C.: Bureau of National Affairs.

ELLMANN, Stephen (1987). "Lawyers and Clients," 34 *UCLA L. Rev.* 717.

ELLMAN, Stephen, Robert D. DINERSTEIN, Isabelle R. GUNNING, Katherine R. KRUSE, and Ann. C. SHALLECK (2009). *Lawyers and Clients: Critical Issues in Interviewing and Counseling.* Eagan, MN: Thomson West.

ELLMAN, Stephen, Isabelle GUNNING, Robert DINNERSTEIN, and Ann Schalleck (2003). "Legal Interviewing and Counseling: An Introduction," 10 *Clinical L. Rev.* 281.

ELSTER, Jon (1995). "Strategic Uses of Argument," in Kenneth J. Arrow, et al., eds., *Barriers to Conflict Resolution.* New York: W. W. Norton.

ESTREICHER, Samuel (2001). "Saturns for Rickshaws: The Stakes in the Debate over Predispute Employment Arbitration Agreements," 16 *Ohio St. J. on Disp. Resol.* 559.

_____ (1997). Predispute Agreements to Arbitrate Statutory Employment Claims. 72 *N.Y.U. L. Rev.* 1345.

EWALT, Henry W. (2002). *Through the Client's Eyes: New Approaches to Get Clients to Hire You Again and Again* (2d ed.). Chicago: ABA, Law Practice Management Section.

FALK, David B. (1992). "The Art of Contract Negotiation," 3 *Marq. Sports L.J.* 1.

FEERICK, John D. (1997). "Toward Uniform Standards of Conduct for Mediators," 38 *S. Tex. L. Rev.* 455.

FEINBERG, Kenneth (2006). *What Is a Life Worth? The Unprecedented Effort to Compensate the Victims of 9/11.* New York: Public Affairs.

FEINBLATT, John, Greg BERMAN, and Aubrey FOX (2000). "Institutionalizing Innovation: The New York Drug Court Story," 28 *Fordham Urb. L.J.* 277.

FELSTINER, William L.F., Richard L. ABEL, and Austin SARAT (1980-81). "The Emergence and Transformation of Disputes: Naming, Blaming, Claiming . . . ," 15 *Law & Socy. Rev.* 631.

FEUILLE, Peter (1975). "Final Offer Arbitration and the Chilling Effect," 14 *Indus. Rel.* 302.

FINKIN, Matthew W. (2008). "Privatization of Wrongful Dismissal Protection in Comparative Perspective," 37 *Indust. L. J.* 149 .

_____ (1997). "Employment Contracts Under the FAA- Reconsidered," 48 *Lab. L. J.* 328.

_____ (1996). " 'Workers' Contracts' Under the United States Arbitration Act: An Essay in Historical Clarification," 17 *Berkeley J. Emp. & Lab. L.* 282.

FISHER, Roger (1969). *International Conflict for Beginners.* New York: Harper & Row.

FISHER, Roger, Elizabeth KOPELMAN, and Andrea Kupfer SCHNEIDER (1994). *Beyond Machiavelli: Tools for Coping with Conflict.* Cambridge, Mass.: Harvard University Press.

FISHER, Roger, Andrea Kupfer SCHNEIDER, Elizabeth BORGWARDT, and Brian GANSON (1997). *Coping with International Conflict: A Systematic Approach to Influence in International Negotiation.* Upper Saddle River, N.J.: Prentice Hall.

FISHER, Roger, William URY, and Bruce PATTON (1991). *Getting to Yes: Negotiating Agreement Without Giving In* (2d ed.). Boston: Houghton Mifflin.

FISS, Owen M. (1984). "Against Settlement," 93 *Yale L.J.* 1073.

_____ (1979). "The Supreme Court 1978 Term — Foreword: The Forms of Justice," 93 *Harv. L. Rev.* 1.

FOLGER, Joseph P., and Robert A. Baruch BUSH (1996). "Transformative Mediation and Third-Party Intervention: Ten Hallmarks of a Transformative Approach to Practice," 13 *Mediation Q.* 263.

FOLLETT, Mary Parker (1995). "Constructive Conflict," in Pauline Graham, ed., *Mary Parker Follett — Prophet of Management: A Celebration of Writings from the 1920s.* Boston: Harvard Business School Press.

FORDHAM LAW REVIEW. (2009). Symposium: Against Settlement: Twenty Five Years Later. 78 *Fordham L. Rev.* 1117.

FOREST, Heather (1996). *Wisdom Tales from Around the World.* Little Rock, Ark.: August House Publishers.

FORESTER, John (2009). *Dealing with Differences: Dramas of Mediating Public Disputes.* New York: Oxford University Press.

FORGAS, Joseph P. (1998). "On Feeling Good and Getting Your Way: Mood Effects on Negotiator Cognition and Bargaining Strategies," 74 *J. Personality & Soc. Psychol.* 565.

FRANK, Jerome (1950). *Courts on Trial: Myth and Reality in American Justice.* Princeton: Princeton University Press.

FREEMAN, Jody (1997). "Collaborative Governance in the Administrative State," 45 *UCLA L. Rev.* 1.

FREEMAN, Jody, and Laura I. LANGBEIN (2000). "Regulatory Negotiation and the Legitimacy Benefit," 9 *N.Y.U. Envtl. L.J.* 60.

FRENCH, Hilary F. (1993). *Costly Tradeoffs: Reconciling Trade and the Environment* (Worldwatch Paper No. 113). Washington, D.C.: Worldwatch Institute.

FRESHMAN, Clark (1997). "Privatizing Same-Sex 'Marriage' Through Alternative Dispute Resolution: Community-Enhancing Versus Community-Enabling Mediation," 44 *UCLA L. Rev.* 1687.

FRESHMAN, Clark, Adele HAYES, and Greg FELDMAN (2002). "The Lawyer-Negotiator as Mood Scientist: What We Know and Don't Know About How Mood Relates to Successful Negotiation," 2002 *J. Disp. Resol.* 1.

FREUND, James C. (1992). *Smart Negotiating: How to Make Good Deals in the Real World.* New York: Simon & Schuster.

FRIEDMAN, Gary, and Jack HIMMELSTEIN (2008). *Challenging Conflict: Mediation Through Understanding.* Washington, D.C.: ABA.

_____ (2004). "The Understanding-Based Approach to Mediation." The Center for Mediation in Law. Retrieved from http://www.mediationinlaw.org/about.html.

_____ (2003). "Memo, No.2, Elements of Mediator-Parties Contract." The Center for Mediation in Law. Retrieved from http://www.mediationinlaw.org/about.html.

FUKUYAMA, Francis (1992). *The End of History and the Last Man.* New York: Free Press.

FULLER, Lon L. (2001). "The Forms and Limits of Adjudication," in Kenneth I. Winston, ed., *The Principles of Social Order: Selected Essays of Lon L. Fuller* (rev. ed.). Oxford, UK: Hart Publishing.

_____ (1971). "Mediation–Its Forms and Functions," 44 *S. Cal. L. Rev.* 305.

_____ (1963). "Collective Bargaining and the Arbitrator," 1963 *Wis. L. Rev.* 3.

_____ (1962). "Collective Bargaining and the Arbitrator," in Mark L. Kahn, ed., *Collective Bargaining and the Arbitrator's Role: Proceedings of the Fifteenth Annual Meeting, National Academy of Arbitrators.* Washington, D.C.: BNA.

GADLIN, Howard (2000). "The Ombudsman: What's in a Name?," 16 *Negot. J.* 37.

GALANTER, Marc S. (2004). "The Vanishing Trial: An Examination of Trials and Related Matters in Federal and State Courts," 1 *J. of Empirical Legal Studies* 459.

_____ (1984). "Worlds of Deals: Using Negotiation to Teach About Legal Process," 34 *J. Legal Educ.* 268.

_____ (1983). "Reading the Landscape of Disputes: What We Know and Don't Know (and Think We Know) About Our Allegedly Contentious and Litigious Society," 31 *UCLA L. Rev.* 4.

_____ (1974). "Why the 'Haves' Come Out Ahead: Speculations on the Limits of Legal Change," 9 *Law & Socy. Rev.* 95.

GALTON, Eric (2000). "Mediation of Medical Negligence Claims," 28 *Cap. U. L. Rev.* 321.

GALTON, Eric, and Tracie McFadden BURNS, eds. (1993). *Mediation: A Texas Practice Guide.* Dallas: Texas Lawyer Press.

GANDHI, Mohandas K. (1948). *Autobiography: The Story of My Experiments with Truth.* Trans. Mahadev Desai. Washington, D.C.: Public Affairs Press.

GARCIA, Patricia A. (2003). *Problem Solving Courts.* Chicago: ABA.

GARDNER, Howard, Mihaly CSIKSZENTMIHALYI, and William DAMON (2001). *Good Work: When Excellence and Ethics Meet.* New York: Basic Books.

GARTH, Bryant G. (1992). "Privatization and the New Market for Disputes: A Framework for Analysis and a Preliminary Assessment," 12 *Stud. L. Pol. & Socy.* 367.

GAUTHIER, David (1986). *Morals by Agreement.* Oxford, UK: Clarendon Press.

GAZER, B., R. HOWARD (Producers), R. HOWARD, and T. HALLOWELL (Directors). 2001. *A Beautiful Mind* [Motion picture]. United States: Universal Pictures and DreamWorks.

GESKE, Janine (2005). "Why Do I Teach Restorative Justice to Law Students?" in Symposium: "Restorative Justice in Action," 89 *Marq. L. Rev.* 327.

GETMAN, Julius G. (1979). "Labor Arbitration and Dispute Resolution," 88 *Yale L.J.* 916.

GIBSON, James L. (2004*). Overcoming Apartheid: Can Truth Resolve a Divided Nation?* New York: Russell Sage Foundation.

_____ (2004). "Truth, Reconciliation, and the Creation of a Human Rights Culture in South Africa," 38 *Law & Socy. Rev.* 5.

GIFFORD, Donald G. (1987). "The Synthesis of Legal Counseling and Negotiation Models: Preserving Client-Centered Advocacy in the Negotiation Context," 34 *UCLA L. Rev.* 811.

_____ (1985). "A Context-Based Theory of Strategy Selection in Legal Negotiation," 46 *Ohio St. L.J.* 41.

Gilles, Myriam (2005). "Opting Out of Liability: The Forthcoming, Near Total Demise of the Modern Class Action," 104 *Mich. L. Rev.* 373.

GILLIGAN, Carol (1982). *In a Different Voice: Psychological Theory and Women's Development.* Cambridge, Mass.: Harvard University Press.

GILSON, Ronald J. (1984). "Value Creation by Business Lawyers: Legal Skills and Asset Pricing," 94 *Yale L.J.* 239.

GILSON, Ronald J., and Robert H. MNOOKIN (1995). "Foreword: Business Lawyers and Value Creation for Clients," 74 *Or. L. Rev.* 1.

_____ (1994). "Disputing Through Agents: Cooperation and Conflict Between Lawyers in Litigation," 94 *Colum. L. Rev.* 509.

GINSBURG, Tom, and Richard H. McADAMS (2004). "Adjudicating in Anarchy: An Expressive Theory of International Dispute Resolution," 45 *Wm. & Mary L. Rev.* 1229.

GOBODO-MADIKIZELA, Pumla (2003). *A Human Being Died That Night: A South African Story of Forgiveness.* Boston: Houghton Mifflin.

GOH, Bee Chen (2006). "Typical Errors of Westerners," in Andrea Kupfer Schneider and Christopher Honeyman, eds., *The Negotiator's Fieldbook.* Washington D.C.: ABA Section on Dispute Resolution.

GOLANN, Dwight (1996). *Mediating Legal Disputes: Effective Strategies for Lawyers and Mediators.* New York: Aspen Law and Business.

_____ (1989). "Making Alternative Dispute Resolution Mandatory: The Constitutional Issues," 68 *Or. L. Rev.* 487.

GOLANN, Dwight, and Eric E. VAN LOON (1999). "Legal Issues in Consensus Building," in Lawrence Susskind, Sarah McKearnan, and Jennifer Thomas-Larmer, eds., *The Consensus Building Handbook: A Comprehensive Guide to Reaching Agreement.* Thousand Oaks, CA: Sage Publications.

GOLDBERG, Stephen B. (1989). "Grievance Mediation: A Successful Alternative to Labor Arbitration," 5 *Negot. J.* 9.

GOLDSTEIN, Joseph, and Jay KATZ (1965). *The Family and the Law: Problems for Decision in the Family Law Process.* New York: Free Press.

GOODPASTER, Gary (1996). "A Primer on Competitive Bargaining," 1996 *J. Disp. Resol.* 325.

GOODWYN, Wade (Reporter). (2002, Dec. 4). "Morning Edition: Profile: Success of Southwest Airlines," Washington, D.C.: National Public Radio.

GREATBATCH, David, and Robert DINGWALL (1989). "Selective Facilitation: Some Preliminary Observations on a Strategy Used by Divorce Mediators," 23 *Law & Socy. Rev.* 613.

GREEN, Eric D. (1997). "What Will We Do When Adjudication Ends? We'll Settle in Bunches, Bringing Rule 23 into the Twenty-First Century," 44 *UCLA L. Rev.* 1773.

_____ (1986). "A Heretical View of the Mediation Privilege," 2 *Ohio St. J. on Disp. Resol.* 1.

GREEN, Eric D., et al., eds. (1982). "The CPR Legal Program Mini-Trial Handbook," in CPR, *Corporate Dispute Management 1982: A Manual of Innovative Corporate Strategies for the Avoidance and Resolution of Legal Disputes.* New York: M. Bender.

GREEN, Eric D., Jonathan B. MARKS, and Ronald L. OLSON (1978). "Settling Large Case Litigation: An Alternate Approach," 11 *Loy. L.A. L. Rev.* 493.

GREENBERG, Melanie C., John H. BARTON, and Margaret E. McGUINNESS, eds. (2000). *Words over War: Mediation and Arbitration to Prevent Deadly Conflict.* Lanham, Md.: Rowman & Littlefield Publishers.

GREENBERG, the Honorable Myron S., and Megan A. BLAZINA (2004). "What Mediators Need to Know about Class Actions: A Basic Primer." 27 *Hamline L. Rev.* 220.

GREENHALGH, Leonard (1987). "Relationships in Negotiation," 3 *Negot. J.* 235.

GRENIG, Jay E., and R. Wayne ESTES (1989). *Labor Arbitration Advocacy: Effective Tactics and Techniques.* Stoneham, Mass.: Butterworths.

GRILLO, Trina (1991). "The Mediation Alternative: Process Dangers for Women," 100 *Yale L.J.* 1545.

GULLIVER, P. H. (1979). *Disputes and Negotiations: A Cross-Cultural Perspective.* New York: Academic Press.

GUNNING, Isabelle R. (1995). "Diversity Issues in Mediation: Controlling Negative Cultural Myths," 1995 *J. Disp. Resol.* 55.

GUTHRIE, Chris (2003). "Panacea or Pandora's Box?: The Costs of Options in Negotiation," 88 *Iowa L. Rev.* 601.

_____ (2001). "The Lawyer's Philosophical Map and the Disputant's Perceptual Map: Impediments to Facilitative Mediation and Lawyering," 6 *Harv. Negot. L. Rev.* 145.

GUTMANN, Amy, and Dennis THOMPSON (1996). *Democracy and Disagreement.* Cambridge, Mass.: Belknap Press of Harvard University Press.

GWARTNEY, James D., et al. (2003). *Economics: Private and Public Choice* (10th ed.). Australia: Thomson/ South-Western.

HABERMAS, Jürgen (1984). *The Theory of Communicative Action,* Trans. Thomas McCarthy. 2 vols. Boston: Beacon Press.

HACKETT, Donald, and Charles L. MARTIN (1993). *Facilitation Skills for Team Leaders.* Menlo Park, CA: Crisp Publications.

HADFIELD, Gillian K. (2004). "Where Have All the Trials Gone? Settlements, Non-Trial Adjudications and Statistical Artifacts in the Changing Disposition of Federal Cases," 1 *J. of Empirical Legal Studies.*

HAGER, L. Michael, and Robert PRITCHARD (1999). "Deal Mediation: How ADR Techniques Can Help Achieve Durable Agreements in the Global Markets," 14 *ICSID Rev.- Foreign Investment L.J.* 1.

HAMPSHIRE, Stuart (2000). *Justice Is Conflict.* Princeton: Princeton University Press.

HARTER, Philip J. (2000). "Assessing the Assessors: The Actual Performance of Negotiated Rulemaking," 9 *N.Y.U. Envtl. L.J.* 32.

_____ (1982). "Negotiating Regulations: A Cure for Malaise," 71 *Geo. L.J.* 1.

HAWKINS, Lee, Jr. (2004). "GM's Finance Arm is Close to Settling Racial-Bias Lawsuit," *Wall St. J.,* January 30, p. A1.

HAYFORD, Stephen L. (2000). "Unification of the Law of Labor Arbitration and Commercial Arbitration: An Idea Whose Time Has Come," 52 *Baylor L. Rev.* 781.

HAYNER, Priscilla (2001). *Unspeakable Truths: Confronting State Terror and Atrocity.* New York: Routledge.

HAYNES, John M. (1993). *The Fundamentals of Family Mediation.* Albany, NY: State University of NY Press.

_____ (1992). "Mediation and Therapy: An Alternative View," 10 *Mediation Q.* 21.

_____ (1981). *Divorce Mediation: A Practical Guide for Therapists and Counselors.* New York: Springer Publishing.

HAZARD, Geoffrey C., Jr. (1978). "Lawyer for the Situation," in *Ethics in the Practice of Law.* New Haven: Yale University Press.

HEEN, Shelia, and Douglas STONE (2006). "Perceptions and Stories," in Andrea Kupfer Schneider and Christopher Honeyman, eds., *The Negotiator's Fieldbook.* Washington, D.C.: ABA Section on Dispute Resolution.

HECHLER, David (2004). "Arbitration Not Such a Sure Thing?," *Natl. L.J.,* May 3, p. 1.

HEGLAND, Kenny (1982). "Why Teach Trial Advocacy? An Essay on Never Ask Why," in Jack Himmelstein and Howard Lesnick, eds., *Humanistic Education in Law* (Monograph 3: Project for the Study and Application of Humanistic Education in Law). New York: Columbia University School of Law.

HENKIN, Louis (1979). *How Nations Behave: Law and Foreign Policy* (2d ed.). New York: Columbia University Press.

HENSLER, Deborah R. (2002). "Suppose It's Not True: Challenging Mediation Ideology," 2002 *J. Disp. Resol.* 81.

_____ (2000). "In Search of 'Good' Mediation: Rhetoric, Practice, and Empiricism," in Joseph Sanders and V. Lee Hamilton, eds., *Handbook of Justice Research in Law.* New York: Kluwer Academic/Plenum Publishers.

_____ (1995). "A Glass Half Full, a Glass Half Empty: The Use of Alternative Dispute Resolution in Mass Personal Injury Litigation," 73 *Tex. L. Rev.* 1587.

_____ (1994). "Does ADR Really Save Money? The Jury's Still Out," *Natl. L.J.,* April 11, p. C2.

_____ (1986). "What We Know and Don't Know About Court-Administered Arbitration," 69 *Judicature* 270.

HERMANN, Michelle et al. (1993). *Metro Court Project Final Report.* Albuquerque, New Mexico: University Of New Mexico Center for the Study and Resolution of Disputes.

HILL, Marvin F., Jr., Anthony V. SINICROPI, and Amy L. EVENSON (1997). *Winning Arbitration Advocacy.* Washington, D.C.: BNA.

HINDLE, Tim (1998). *Managing Meetings.* London: Dorling Kindersley.

HINSHAW, Art, and Jess K. ALBERTS (forthcoming 2011). "Doing the Right Thing: An Empirical Study of Attorney Negotiation Ethics," 16 *Harv. Negot. L. Rev.*

HOFSTADTER, Douglas R. (1985). *Metamagical Themas: Questing for the Essence of Mind and Pattern.* New York: Basic Books.

HOLDING, Reynolds (2001). "Judges' Action Cast Shadow on Court's Integrity: Lure of High-Paying Jobs as Arbitrators May Compromise Impartiality," *S.F. Chron.,* October 9, p. A13.

_____ (2001). "Private Justice: Can Public Count on Fair Arbitration? Financial Ties to Corporations Are Conflict of Interest, Critics Say," *S.F. Chron.,* October 8, p. A15.

_____ (2001). "Private Justice: Millions Are Losing Their Legal Rights: Supreme Court Forces Disputes from Court to Arbitration–A System with No Laws," *S.F. Chron.,* October 7, p. A1.

HOLLANDER-BLUMOFF, Rebecca, and Tom R. TYLER (2008). "Procedural Justice in Negotiation: Procedural Fairness, Outcome Acceptance, and Integrative Potential," 33 *Law & Soc. Inquiry.* 272.

HOMANS, George Caspar (1974). *Social Behavior: Its Elementary Forms* (rev. ed.). New York: Harcourt, Brace, Jovanovich.

HONEYMAN, Chris (1990). "On Evaluating Mediators," 6 *Negot. J.* 23.

HORWITZ, Morton J. (1977). *The Transformation of American Law, 1780-1860.* Cambridge, Mass.: Harvard University Press.

HOWARTH, Joan W. (2000). "Toward the Restorative Constitution: A Restorative Justice Critique of Anti-Gang Public Nuisance Injunctions," 27 *Hastings Const. L. Q.* 717.

HUGHES, Scott H. (2004). "Mediator Immunity: The Misguided and Inequitable Shifting of Risk," 83 *Or. L. Rev.*

_____ (2001). "The Uniform Mediation Act: To the Spoiled Go the Privileges," 85 *Marq. L. Rev.* 9.

HUNTINGTON, Samuel P. (1994). "The Clash of Civilizations?," in Armand Clesse, Richard Cooper, and Yoshikazu Sakamoto, eds., *The International System After the Collapse of the East-West Order.* Dordrecht, Netherlands: Martinus Nijhoff Publishers.

HYMAN, Jonathan M., and Lela P. LOVE (2002). "If Portia Were a Mediator: An Inquiry into Justice in Mediation," 9 *Clinical L. Rev.* 157.

IGNATIEFF, Michael (1994). *Blood and Belonging: Journeys into the New Nationalism* (1st Am. ed.). New York: Farrar, Straus & Giroux.

IKLÉ, Fred Charles (1964). *How Nations Negotiate.* New York: Harper & Row.

INTERNATIONAL OLYMPIC COMMITTEE (2003). "Arbitration," in *Olympic Charter* art. 74. Lausanne: International Olympic Committee.

ISSACHAROFF, Samuel, Robert H. KLONOFF, Richard NAGAREDA, and Charles SILVER (Reporters) (2010). *Principles of the Law of Aggregate Litigation.* St. Paul, MN: American Law Institute Publishers.

ISEN, Alice M., Kimberly A. DAUBMAN, and Gary P. NOWICKI (1987). "Positive Affect Facilitates Creative Problem Solving," 52 *J. Personality & Soc. Psychol.* 1122.

ISEN, Alice M., P.M. NIEDENTHAL, and N. CANTOR (1992). "An Influence of Positive Affect on Social Categorization," 16 *Motivation & Emotion* 65.

IZUMI, Carol L., and Homer C. LA RUE (2003). "Prohibiting 'Good Faith' Reports Under the Uniform Mediation Act: Keeping the Adjudication Camel Out of the Mediation Tent," 2003 *J. Disp. Resol.* 67.

JACOBS, Margaret A. (1997). "Legal Beat: Private Jury Trials: Cheap, Quick, Controversial," *Wall St. J.,* July 7, p. B1.

_____ (1994). "Men's Club: Riding Crop and Slurs: How Wall Street Dealt with a Sex-Bias Case," *Wall St. J.,* June 9, p. A1.

JANIS, Irving L. (1982). *Groupthink: Psychological Studies of Policy Decisions and Fiascoes* (2d ed.). Boston: Houghton Mifflin.

JONES, William Catron (1956). "Three Centuries of Commercial Arbitration in New York: A Brief Survey," 1956 *Wash. U. L. Q.* 193.

KAHNEMAN, Daniel, and Amos TVERSKY (1995). "Conflict Resolution: A Cognitive Perspective," in Kenneth J. Arrow, et al., eds., *Barriers to Conflict Resolution.* New York: W. W. Norton.

KAKALIK, James S., Terence DUNWORTH, Laural A. HILL, Daniel McCAFFREY, Marian OSHIRO, Nicholas M. PACE, and Mary E. VAIANA (1996). *An Evaluation of Mediation and Early Neutral Evaluation Under the Civil Justice Reform Act.* Santa Monica, CA: Rand.

KAPLINKSY, Alan S., and Mark J. LEVIN (1998). "Excuse Me, but Who's the Predator? Banks Can Use Arbitration Clauses as a Defense," *Bus. L. Today.* 24.

KATSH, Ethan (2000). "The New Frontier: Online ADR Becoming a Global Priority," *Disp. Resol. Mag.* 6 (Winter).

KATSH, Ethan, and Janet RIFKIN (2001). *Online Dispute Resolution: Resolving Conflicts in Cyberspace.* San Francisco: Jossey-Bass Publishers.

KATZ, Lucy V. (1993). "Compulsory Alternative Dispute Resolution and Voluntarism: Two-Headed Monster or Two Sides of the Coin?," 1993 *J. Disp. Resol.* 1.

KAUFMANN-KOHLER, Gabrielle (1997). "Arbitration and the Games or The First Experience of the Olympic Division of the Court of Arbitration for Sport," *Mealey's Intl. Arb. Rep.* 20 (February).

KAYE, Judith S. (1997). "Changing Courts in Changing Times: The Need for a Fresh Look at How Courts Are Run," 48 *Hastings L.J.* 851.

KELLEY, Tom, with Jonathan LITTMAN (2001). *The Art of Innovation: Lessons in Creativity from IDEO, America's Leading Design Firm*. New York: Currency/Doubleday.

KELLY, Loretta (2006). "Indigenous Experiences in Negotiation," in Andrea Kupfer Schneider and Christopher Honeyman, eds., *The Negotiator's Fieldbook*. Washington, D.C.: ABA, Section on Dispute Resolution.

KELMAN, Herbert C. (1972). "The Problem-Solving Workshop in Conflict Resolution," in Richard L. Merritt, ed., *Communication in International Politics*. Urbana, Ill.: University of Illinois Press.

KENNEDY, Desiree A. (1995). "Predisposed with Integrity: The Elusive Quest for Justice in Tripartite Arbitrations," 8 *Geo. J. Legal Ethics* 749.

KENTRA, Pamela A. (1997). "Hear No Evil, See No Evil, Speak No Evil: The Intolerable Conflict for Attorney-Mediators Between the Duty to Maintain Mediation Confidentiality and the Duty to Report Fellow Attorney Misconduct," 1997 *BYU L. Rev.* 715.

KESSLER, Joan F., Allan R. KORITZINSKY, and Stephen W. SCHLISSEL (1997). "Why Arbitrate Family Law Matters?," 14 *J. Am. Acad. Matrimonial Law.* 333.

KICHAVEN, Jeff (2003). "Apology in Mediation: Sorry to Say, It's Much Overrated." International Risk Management Institute. Retrieved from http://www.irmi.com/Expert/ Articles/2003/Kichaven09.aspx.

KIM, Anne S. (1994). Note, "Rent-a-Judges and the Cost of Selling Justice," 44 *Duke L.J.* 166.

KING, Michael, Arie FREIBERG, Becky BATAGOL, and Ross HYAMS (2009). *Non-Adversarial Justice*. Sydney, Australia: Federation Press.

KIRTLEY, Alan (1995). "The Mediation Privilege's Transition from Theory to Implementation: Designing a Mediation Privilege Standard to Protect Mediation Participants, the Process and the Public Interest," 1995 *J. Disp. Resol.* 1.

KISSINGER, Henry (1979). *White House Years*. Boston: Little, Brown.

KLONOFF, Robert H., and Edward K.M. BILICH (2000). "Resolution of Class Actions," in *Class Actions and Other Multi-Party Litigation: Cases and Materials,* ch. 8. St. Paul: West Group.

KNAPP, Charles L. (2009). "Unconscionability as a Signaling Device," 46 *San Diego L. Rev.* 609.

KNAUER, Nancy J. (2002). "The September 11 Attacks and Surviving Same-Sex Partners: Defining Family Through Tragedy," 75 *Temp. L. Rev.* 31.

KOLB & Associates (1994). *When Talk Works: Profiles of Mediators*. San Francisco, CA: Jossey-Bass Publishers.

KOLB, Deborah M., and Judith WILLIAMS (2003). *Everyday Negotiation: Navigating the Hidden Agendas in Bargaining* (rev. ed.). San Francisco: Jossey-Bass Publishers.

KOROBKIN, Russell (2002). "Aspirations and Settlement," 88 *Cornell L. Rev.* 1.

_____ (2000). "A Positive Theory of Legal Negotiation," 88 *Geo. L.J.* 1789.

KOROBKIN, Russell, and Chris GUTHRIE (2006). "Heuristics and Biases at the Bargaining Table," in Andrea Kupfer Schneider and Christopher Honeyman, eds., *The Negotiator's Fieldbook*. Washington, D.C.: ABA Section on Dispute Resolution.

_____ (1994). "Psychological Barriers to Litigation Settlement: An Experimental Approach," 93 *Mich. L. Rev.* 107.

KOVACH, Kimberlee K. (2001). "New Wine Requires New Wineskins: Transforming Lawyer Ethics for Effective Representation in a Non-Adversarial Approach to Problem Solving: Mediation," 28 *Fordham Urb. L.J.* 935.

_____ (1997). "Good Faith in Mediation — Requested, Recommended, or Required? A New Ethic," 38 *S. Texas L. Rev.* 575.

KOVACH, Kimberlee K., and Lela P. LOVE (1996). " 'Evaluative' Mediation Is an Oxymoron," 14 *Alternatives to High Cost Litig.* 31.

KRAMER, Roderick M., E. NEWTON, and P.L. POMMERENKE (1993). "Self-Enhancement Biases and Negotiator Judgment: Effects of Self-Esteem and Mood," 56 *Organizational Behav. & Hum. Decision Processes* 110.

KRITEK, Phyllis Beck (1994). *Negotiating at an Uneven Table: A Practical Approach to Working with Difference and Diversity.* San Francisco: Jossey-Bass Publishers.

KRUSE, Katherine R. (2010). "Beyond Cardboard Clients in Legal Ethics." 23 *Georgetown J. Legal Ethics.* 1.

KUFLIK, Arthur (1979). "Morality and Compromise," in J. Roland Pennock and John W. Chapman, eds., *Compromise in Ethics, Law, and Politics* (Nomos 21). New York: New York University Press.

LaFREE, Gary, and Christine RACK (1996). "The Effects of Participants' Ethnicity and Gender on Monetary Outcomes in Mediated and Adjudicated Civil Cases," 30 *Law & Socy. Rev.* 767.

LALIVE, Pierre (1984). "Enforcing Awards," in International Chamber of Commerce, *60 Years of ICC Arbitration: A Look at the Future.* Paris: ICC Publishing.

LAMBROS, Thomas D. (1984). "The Summary Jury Trial and Other Alternative Methods of Dispute Resolution: A Report to the Judicial Conference of the United States Committee on the Operation of the Jury System," 103 F.R.D. 461.

LANDAU, Sy, Barbara LANDAU, and Daryl LANDAU (2001). *From Conflict to Creativity: How Resolving Workplace Disagreements Can Inspire Innovation and Productivity.* San Francisco: Jossey-Bass Publishers.

LANDE, John (2003). "Possibilities for Collaborative Law: Ethics and Practice of Lawyer Disqualification and Process Control in a New Model of Lawyering," 64 *Ohio St. L.J.* 1315.

_____ (2002). "Using Dispute System Design Methods to Promote Good-Faith Participation in Court-Connected Mediation Programs," 50 *UCLA L. Rev.* 69.

LANDES, William M., and Richard A. POSNER (1979). "Adjudication as a Private Good," 8 *J. Legal Stud.* 235.

LANDRY, Sherry (1996). "Med-Arb: Mediation with a Bite and an Effective ADR Model," 63 *Def. Couns. J.* 263.

LAO-TZU (1991). *Tao Te Ching.* Trans. Steven Mitchell. New York: Harper & Row.

LARSON, David (2010). "Robots, Avatars, and the Demise of the Human Mediator," 25 *Ohio State J. on Disp. Res.* 105.

LAX, David A., and James K. SEBENIUS (2006). *3D Negotiation.* Cambridge: Harvard Business Press.

_____ (1986). *The Manager as Negotiator: Bargaining for Cooperation and Competitive Gain.* New York: Free Press.

LEDERACH, John Paul (2003). "Cultivating Peace: A Practitioner's View of Deadly Conflict and Negotiation," in John Darby and Roger Mac Ginty, eds., *Contemporary Peacemaking: Conflict, Violence and Peace Processes.* New York: Palgrave Macmillan.

_____ (1995). *Preparing for Peace: Conflict Transformation Across Cultures.* Syracuse, N.Y.: Syracuse University Press.

LEHMAN, Warren (1979). "The Pursuit of a Client's Interest," 77 *Mich. L. Rev.* 1078.

LERMAN, David (1999). "Restoring Justice," *Tikkun* 13 (September-October).

LeROY, Michael H. (2009). "Do Courts Create Moral Hazard? When Judges Nullify Employer Liability In Arbitrations: An Empirical Analysis," 93 *Minn. L Rev.* 998.

LeROY, Michael H., and Peter FEUILLE (2003). "Judicial Enforcement of Predispute Arbitration Agreements: Back to the Future," 18 *Ohio St. J. on Disp. Resol.* 249.

_____ (2002). "When Is Cost an Unlawful Barrier to Alternative Dispute Resolution? The Ever Green Tree of Mandatory Employment Arbitration," 50 *UCLA L. Rev.* 143.

LEVIN, Murray S. (2001). "The Propriety of Evaluative Mediation: Concerns About the Nature and Quality of an Evaluative Opinion," 16 *Ohio St. J. on Disp. Resol.* 267.

LEVITT, Matthew A. (1997). "Kilometer 101: Oasis or Mirage? An Analysis of Third-Party Self-Interest in International Mediation," 15 *Mediation Q.* 155.

LEVY, Jerome S., and Robert C. PRATHER (1999). "Fly on the Wall," in *Texas Practice Guide: Alternative Dispute Resolution* app. A. St. Paul: West Group.

LEWICKI, Roy J., and Barbara Benedict BUNKER (1995). "Trust in Relationships: A Model of Development and Decline," in Barbara Benedict Bunker, Jeffrey Z. Rubin, et al., eds., *Conflict, Cooperation, and Justice: Essays Inspired by the Work of Morton Deutsch.* San Francisco: Jossey-Bass Publishers.

LEWIS, Michael (1989). *Liar's Poker: Rising Through the Wreckage on Wall Street.* New York: W.W. Norton.

LIEBMAN, Carol B. (2000). "Mediation as Parallel Seminars: Lessons from the Student Takeover of Columbia University's Hamilton Hall," 16 *Negot. J.* 157.

LIND, E. Allan, and Tom R. TYLER (1988), *The Social Psychology of Procedural Justice.* New York: Plenum Press.

LIND, E. Allan, Robert J. MacCOUN, Patricia A. EBENER, William L.F. FELSTINER, Deborah R. HENSLER, Judith RESNIK, and Tom R. TYLER (1989). *The Perception of Justice: Tort Litigants' Views of Trial, Court-Annexed Arbitration, and Judicial Settlement Conferences.* Santa Monica, CA: Rand.

LIPSKY, David B., Ronald L. SEEBER, and Richard D. FINCHER (2003). *Emerging Systems for Managing Workplace Conflict: Lessons from American Corporations for Managers and Dispute Resolution Professionals.* San Francisco: Jossey-Bass Publishers.

LOPEZ, Gerald (1984). "The Internal Structure of Lawyering: Lay Lawyering," 32 *UCLA L. Rev.* 1.

LOVE, Lela P. (2000). "Images of Justice," 1 *Pepp. Disp. Resol. L.J.* 29.

_____ (2000). "Training Mediators to Listen: Deconstructing Dialogue and Constructing Understanding, Agendas, and Agreements," 38 *Fam. & Conciliation Cts. Rev.* 27.

_____ (1997). "The Top Ten Reasons Why Mediators Should Not Evaluate," 24 *Fla. St. U. L. Rev.* 937.

_____ (1993). "Glen Cove: Mediation Achieves What Litigation Cannot," *Consensus* (MIT-Harvard Public Disputes Program) 1 (October).

LOVE, Lela P., and Joseph B. STULBERG (2004). "Targets and Techniques to Generate Movement." Training Materials (unpublished).

LOVE, Lela P., and John W. COOLEY (2005). "The Intersection of Evaluation by Mediators and Informed Consent: Warning the Unwary," 21 *Ohio St. J. on Disp. Resol.* 45.

LOVE, Lela P., and Kimberlee K. KOVACH (2000). "ADR: An Eclectic Array of Processes, Rather than One Eclectic Process," 2000 *J. Disp. Resol.* 295.

LOVE, Lela P., and Cheryl B. McDONALD (1997). "A Tale of Two Cities: Day Labor and Conflict Resolution for Communities in Crisis," *Disp. Resol. Mag.* 8 (Fall).

LOWENFELD, Andreas F. (1995). "The Party-Appointed Arbitrator in International Controversies: Some Reflections," 30 *Tex. Intl. L.J.* 59.

LOWENTHAL, Gary (1982). "General Theory of Negotiation Process, Strategy and Behavior," 31 *Kansas L. Rev.* 96.

LUBAN, David (1995). "Settlements and the Erosion of the Public Realm," 83 *Geo. L.J.* 2619.

_____ (1988). *Lawyers and Justice.* Princeton, NJ: Princeton University Press.

_____ (1987). "Some Greek Trials: Order and Justice in Homer, Hesiod, Aeschylus and Plato," 43 *Tenn. L. Rev.* 279.

LUBET, Steven (1996). "Notes on the Bedouin Horse Trade or 'Why Won't the Market Clear, Daddy?,' " 74 *Tex. L. Rev.* 1039.

LUBMAN, Stanley B. (1997). "Dispute Resolution in China After Deng Xiaoping: 'Mao and Mediation' Revisited," 11 *Colum. J. Asian L.* 229.

LUI-KWAN, Kalama, and Kurt OPSAHL (1999). "Foreword: The Legal and Policy Framework for Global Electronic Commerce," 14 *Berkeley Tech. L.J.* 503.

LYNCH, William P. (2002). "Problems with Court-Annexed Mandatory Arbitration: Illustrations from the New Mexico Experience," 32 *N.M. L. Rev.* 181.

LYONS, James (1985). "Arbitration: The Slower, More Expensive Alternative?," *Am. Law.* 107 (January-February).

MACFARLANE, Julie (2008). *The New Lawyer.* Vancouver: UBC Press.

MACHIAVELLI, Niccolò (1998). *The Prince* (2d ed.), Trans. Harvey C. Mansfield. Chicago: University of Chicago Press.

MACNEIL, Ian R. (1992). *American Arbitration Law: Reformation, Nationalization, Internationalization.* New York: Oxford University Press.

MACNEIL, Ian R., Richard E. SPEIDEL, and Thomas J. STIPANOWICH (1994). "A Modest Proposal," in 4 *Federal Arbitration Law: Agreements, Awards, and Remedies under the Federal Arbitration Act* §40.7.2.6 (Supp. 1999). 5 vols. Gaithersburg, Md.: Aspen Law & Business.

MALLEY, Robert, and Hussein AGHA (2001). "Camp David: The Tragedy of Errors," *N.Y. Rev. Books,* August 9, p. 59.

MALLOY, Brian J. (2003). "Binding Interest Arbitration in the Public Sector: A 'New' Proposal for California and Beyond," 55 *Hastings L.J.* 245.

MANN, Bruce H. (1984). "The Formalization of Informal Law Arbitration Before the American Revolution," 59 *N.Y.U. L. Rev.* 443.

MANNIX, Margaret (1999). "No Suits for You: Mad at a Firm? Arbitration Could Be Your Only Recourse," *U.S. News & World Rep.,* June 7, p. 58.

MARCUS, Mary G., Walter MARCUS, Nancy A. STILWELL, and Neville DOHERTY (1999). "To Mediate or Not to Mediate: Financial Outcomes in Mediated Versus Adversarial Divorces," 17 *Mediation Q.* 143.

MARGALIT, Avishai (2010). *On Compromise and Rotten Compromises.* Princeton, NJ: Princeton University Press.

MAULL, John (1996). "ADR in the Federal Courts: Would Uniformity Be Better?," 34 *Duq. L. Rev.* 245.

MAUTE, Judith L. (1991). "Public Values and Private Justice: A Case for Mediator Accountability," 4 *Geo. J. Legal Ethics* 503.

MAY, Kenneth (1996). "Labor Lawyers at ABA Session Debate Role of American Arbitration Association," *Daily Lab. Rep.* (BNA) No. 31, February 15, p. A-11.

MAYER, Bernard (2000). *The Dynamics of Conflict Resolution: A Practitioner's Guide.* San Francisco: Jossey-Bass Publishers.

MAYER, Caroline E. (1999). "Hidden in Fine Print: 'You Can't Sue Us': Arbitration Clauses Block Consumers from Taking Companies to Court," *Wash. Post,* May 22, p. A1.

MAZADOORIAN, Harry N. (2004). "To Draft or Not to Draft: The Rights and Wrongs of Drafting and Signing Settlements," *Disp. Resol. Mag.* 31 (Spring).

McADOO, Nancy A. WELSH, and Roselle L. WISSLER (2003). "Institutionalization: What do Empirical Studies Tell Us about Court Mediation," *Disp. Resol. Mag.* 8 (Winter).

McEWEN, Craig A. (1998). "Managing Corporate Disputing: Overcoming Barriers to the Effective Use of Mediation for Reducing the Cost and Time of Litigation," 14 *Ohio St. J. on Disp. Resol.* 1.

_____ (1996). "Mediation in Context: New Questions for Research," 3:2 *Disp. Resol. Mag.* 16.

McEWEN, Craig A., and Elizabeth PLAPINGER (1997). "RAND Report Points Way to Next Generation of ADR Research," *Disp. Resol. Mag.* 10 (Summer).

McEWEN, Craig A., and Richard J. MAIMAN (1981). "Small Claims Mediation in Maine: An Empirical Assessment," 33 *Me. L. Rev.* 237.

McEWEN, Craig, and Nancy H. ROGERS (1994). "Bring the Lawyers into Divorce Mediation," *Disp. Resol. Mag.* 8 (Summer).

McGOVERN, Francis E. (2009). "Dispute System Design: The United Nations Compensation Commission, 14 *Harv. Negot. L. Rev.* 171

_____ (2001). "Settlement of Mass Torts in a Federal System," 36 *Wake Forest L. Rev.* 871.

_____ (1997). "Beyond Efficiency: A Bevy of ADR Justifications (An Unfootnoted Summary)," *Disp. Resol. Mag.* 12 (Summer).

_____ (1986). "Toward a Functional Approach for Managing Complex Litigation," 53 *U. Chi. L. Rev.* 440.

MEIER, Barry (1997). "In Fine Print, Customers Lose Ability to Sue," *N.Y. Times,* March 10, p. A1.

MEIERHOEFER, Barbara S. (1990). *Court-Annexed Arbitration in Ten District Courts.* Washington, D.C.: Federal Judicial Center.

MELTSNER, Michael, and Philip G. SCHRAG (1974). "Negotiation," in *Public Interest Advocacy: Materials for Clinical Legal Education.* Boston: Little, Brown.

MENDENHALL, Robert W. (1996). "Post-Settlement Settlements: Agreeing to Make Resolutions Efficient," 1996 *J. Disp. Resol.* 81.

MENKEL-MEADOW, Carrie (forthcoming 2011). "Scaling Up Deliberative Democracy as Dispute Resolution in Health Care Reform: A Work in Progress," 74(3) *Law and Contemporary Problems* .

_____ (2010). "Why and How to Study Transnational Law," 1 *University of California Irvine Law Review.*

_____ (2010). "Compromise, Negotiation, and Morality," 26 *Negot. J.* 481.

_____ (2010). "Dispute Resolution" in Peter Cane & Herber Kritzer, eds., *Oxford Handbook of Empirical Legal Research.* Oxford: Oxford University Press.

_____ (2009). "Are There Systemic Ethics Issues in Dispute System Design? And What We Should [Not] Do About It: Lessons from International and Domestic Fronts," 14 *Harv. Negot. L. Rev.* 195.

_____ (2009). "Chronicling the Complexification of Negotiation Theory and Practice," 25 *Negot. J.* 415.

_____ (2009). "Maintaining ADR Integrity," 27(1) *Alternatives (to High Cost of Litigation)* 1.

_____ (2008). "Are Cross-Cultural Ethics Standards Possible or Desirable in International Arbitration?," in Peter Gauch, Franz Werro, Pascal Pichonnaz eds., *Melangés en l'honneur de Pierre Tercier.* Geneva, Switzerland: Schutheis Pub.

_____ (2007). "Know When to Show Your Hand," 10 *Negot. Newsletter.* 6.

_____ (2007). "Restorative Justice: What Is It and Does It Work?," 3 *Annual Review of Law and Social Science.* 10.1.

_____ (2006). "Peace and Justice: Notes on the Evolution and Purposes of Plural Legal Processes," 94 *Geo. L. J.* 553.

_____ (2005). "Is the Adversary System Really Dead? Dilemmas of Legal Ethics as Legal Institutions and Roles Evolve," in J. Holder, C. O'Cinneide, and M. Freeman, eds., 57 *Current Legal Problems.* New York: Oxford University Press.

_____ (2005). "The Lawyer's Role(s) in Deliberative Democracy," 5 *Nev. L.J.* 347.

_____ (2004). "Legal Negotiation in Popular Culture: What Are We Bargaining For?," in Michael Freeman, ed., *Law and Popular Culture.* Oxford, UK: Oxford University Press.

_____ (2004), "Remembrance of Things Past? The Relationship of Past to Future in Pursuing Justice in Mediation," 5 *Cardozo J. Conflict Resol.* 97.

_____ (2004), "What's Fair in Negotiation? What is Ethics in Negotiation?," in Carrie Menkel-Meadow and Michael Wheeler, eds., *What's Fair: Ethics for Negotiators.* San Francisco: Jossey-Bass Publishers.

_____ (2003). "Conflict Theory," in Karen Christensen and David Levinson, eds., 1 *Encyclopedia of Community: From the Village to the Virtual World.* 4 vols. Thousand Oaks, CA: Sage Publications.

_____ (2003). "Correspondences and Contradictions in International and Domestic Conflict Resolution: Lessons from General Theory and Varied Contexts," 2003 *J. Disp. Resol.* 319.

_____ (2003). "Introduction: From Legal Disputes to Conflict Resolution and Human Problem Solving," in Carrie Menkel-Meadow, ed., *Dispute Processing and Conflict Resolution: Theory, Practice and Policy.* Aldershot, UK: Ashgate/Dartmouth.

_____ (2002). "Ethics Issues in Arbitration and Related Dispute Resolution Processes: What's Happening and What's Not," 56 *U. Miami L. Rev.* 949.

_____ (2002). "Ethics, Morality and Professional Responsibility in Negotiation," in Phyllis Bernard and Bryant Garth, eds., *Dispute Resolution Ethics: A Comprehensive Guide.* Washington, D.C.: ABA, Section of Dispute Resolution.

_____ (2002). "The Lawyer as Consensus Builder: Ethics for a New Practice," 70 *Tenn. L. Rev.* 63.

_____ (2002). "Practicing 'In the Interests of Justice' in the Twenty-First Century: Pursuing Peace as Justice," 70 *Fordham L. Rev.* 1761.

_____ (2001). "Aha? Is Creativity Possible in Legal Problem Solving and Teachable in Legal Education?," 6 *Harv. Negot. L. Rev.* 97.

_____ (2001). "Ethics in ADR: The Many 'Cs' of Professional Responsibility and Dispute Resolution," 28 *Fordham Urb. L.J.* 979.

_____ (2000). "The Limits of Adversarial Ethics," in Deborah L. Rhode, ed., *Ethics in Practice: Lawyers' Roles, Responsibilities, and Regulation.* New York: Oxford University Press.

_____ (2000), "Mothers and Fathers of Invention: The Intellectual Founders of ADR," 16 *Ohio St. J. on Disp. Resol.* 1.

_____ (2000). *Mediation: Theory, Practice and Policy.* Aldershot: UK and Burlington, Vt.: Ashgate Press.

_____ (1999). "Ethics and Professionalism in Non-Adversarial Lawyering," 27 *Fla. St. U. L. Rev.* 153.

_____ (1999). "The Lawyer as Problem Solver and Third-Party Neutral: Creativity and Non-Partisanship in Lawyering," 72 *Temp. L. Rev.* 785.

_____ (1998). "Taking the Mass Out of Mass Torts: Reflections of a Dalkon Shield Arbitrator on Alternative Dispute Resolution, Judging, Neutrality, Gender, and Process," 31 *Loy. L.A. L. Rev.* 513.

_____ (1997). "Ethics in Alternative Dispute Resolution: New Issues, No Answers from the Adversary Conceptionawyers' Responsibilities," 38 *S. Tex. L. Rev.* 407.

_____ (1997). "The Silences of the Restatement of the Law Governing Lawyers: Lawyering as Only Adversary Practice," 10 *Geo. J. Legal Ethics* 631.

_____ (1997). "When Dispute Resolution Begets Disputes of Its Own: Conflicts Among Dispute Professionals," 44 *UCLA L. Rev.* 1871.

_____ (1996). "Is Mediation the Practice of Law?," 14 *Alternatives to High Cost Litig.* 57.

_____ (1996). "The Trouble with the Adversary System in a Postmodern, Multicultural World," 38 *Wm. & Mary L. Rev.* 5.

_____ (1995). "Ethics and the Settlements of Mass Torts: When the Rules Meet the Road," 80 *Cornell L. Rev.* 1159.

_____ (1995). "Whose Dispute Is It Anyway?: A Philosophical and Democratic Defense of Settlement (in Some Cases)," 83 *Geo. L.J.* 2663.

_____ (1993). "Public Access to Private Settlements: Conflicting Legal Policies," 11 *Alternatives to High Cost Litig.* 85 (1993).

_____ (1991). "Pursuing Settlement in an Adversary Culture: A Tale of Innovation Co-Opted or 'The Law of ADR,' " 19 *Fla. St. U. L. Rev.* 1.

_____ (1985). "Feminist Discourse, Moral Values, and the Law—A Conversation," 34 *Buff. L. Rev.* 11.

_____ (1985). "For and Against Settlement: Uses and Abuses of the Mandatory Settlement Conference," 33 *UCLA L. Rev.* 485.

_____ (1985). "The Transformation of Disputes by Lawyers: What the Dispute Paradigm Does and Does Not Tell Us, 1985 *Missouri J. Dispute Res.* 25.

_____ (1984). "Toward Another View of Legal Negotiation: The Structure of Problem Solving," 31 *UCLA L. Rev.* 754.

_____ (1983). "Legal Negotiation: A Study of Strategies in Search of a Theory," 1983 *American Bar Foundation Research J.* 905.

MENKEL-MEADOW, Carrie, ed. (forthcoming 2011). *Complex Dispute Resolution.* 3 vols. Farnham, U.K. and Burlington, Vt.: Ashgate Press.

_____ (2001). Introduction to *Mediation: Theory, Policy, and Practice.* Aldershot, Eng.: Ashgate/Dartmouth.

MENKEL-MEADOW, Carrie, and David BINDER (1983). *The Stages and Phases of Negotiation.* Chicago: ABA Lawyering Skills Institute.

MENKEL-MEADOW, Carrie, and Bryant GARTH (2010). "Process, People, Power and Policy: Empirical Studies of Civil Procedure and Courts," in Peter Cane and Herbert Kritzer, eds., *Oxford Handbook of Empirical Legal Research.* New York: Oxford University Press.

MENKEL-MEADOW, Carrie and Michael WHEELER (2004). *What's Fair? Ethics for Negotiators.* San Francisco: Jossey-Bass Publishers.

MENTSCHIKOFF, Soia (1961). "Commercial Arbitration," 61 *Colum. L. Rev.* 846.

MIALL, Hugh (1992.) *The Peacemakers: Peaceful Settlement of Disputes Since 1945.* New York: St. Martin's Press.

MILNER, Neal (2002). "Illusions and Delusions About Conflict Management–In Africa and Elsewhere," 27 *Law & Soc. Inquiry* 621.

MINOW, Martha (1998). *Between Vengeance and Forgiveness: Facing History After Genocide and Mass Violence.* Boston: Beacon Press.

MITCHELL, George J. (1999). *Making Peace.* New York: Knopf.

MNOOKIN, Robert H. (2010). *Bargaining With the Devil: When to Negotiate, When to Fight.* New York: Simon & Schuster..

_____ (2003). "Strategic Barriers to Dispute Resolution: A Comparison of Bilateral and Multilateral Negotiations," 159 *J. Institutional & Theoretical Econ.* 199.

_____ (2003). "When Not to Negotiate: A Negotiation Imperialist Reflects on Appropriate Limits," 74 *U. Colo. L. Rev.* 1077.

_____ (1993). "Why Negotiations Fail: An Exploration of Barriers to the Resolution of Conflict," 8 *Ohio St. J. on Disp. Resol.* 235.

MNOOKIN, Robert H., and Jonathan R. COHEN (1999). Introduction to Robert H. Mnookin, Lawrence E. Susskind, eds., with Pacey C. Foster, *Negotiating on Behalf of Others: Advice to Lawyers, Business Executives, Sports Agents, Diplomats, Politicians, and Everybody Else.* Thousand Oaks, CA: Sage Publications.

MNOOKIN, Robert H., and Lewis KORNHAUSER (1979). "Bargaining in the Shadow of the Law: The Case of Divorce," 88 *Yale L.J.* 950.

MNOOKIN, Robert H., Scott R. PEPPET, and Andrew S. TULUMELLO (2000). *Beyond Winning: Negotiating to Create Value in Deals and Disputes.* Cambridge, Mass.: Belknap Press of Harvard University Press.

MOBERLY, Robert B. (1994). "Ethical Standards for Court-Appointed Mediators and Florida's Mandatory Mediation Experiment," 21 *Fla. St. U. L. Rev.* 701.

MOFFITT, Michael L. (2003). "Suing Mediators," 83 *B.U. L. Rev.* 147.

_____ (2003). "Ten Ways to Get Sued: A Guide for Mediators," 8 *Harv. Negot. L. Rev.* 81.

_____ (2000). "Will This Case Settle? An Exploration of Mediators' Predictions," 16 *Ohio St. J. on Disp. Resol.* 39.

_____ (1997). "Casting Light on the Black Box of Mediation: Should Mediators Make Their Conduct More Transparent?," 13 *Ohio St. J. on Disp. Resol.* 1.

MOFFITT, Michael L., and Robert C. BORDONE (2005). *The Handbook of Dispute Resolution.* San Francisco: Jossey-Bass Publishers.

MOOHR, Geraldine Szott (1999). "Arbitration and the Goals of Employment Discrimination Law," 56 *Wash. & Lee L. Rev.* 395.

MOORE, Christopher W. (2003). *The Mediation Process: Practical Strategies for Resolving Conflict* (3rd ed.). San Francisco: Jossey-Bass Publishers.

MORAWETZ, Nancy (1993). "Bargaining, Class Representation, and Fairness," 54 *Ohio St. L.J.* 1.

MORRILL, Calvin (1995). *The Executive Way: Conflict Management in Corporations.* Chicago: University of Chicago Press.

MORRIS, Michael, Janice NADLER, Terri KURTZBERG, and Leigh THOMPSON (2002). "Schmooze or Lose: Social Friction and Lubrication in E-Mail Negotiations," 6 *Group Dynamics* 89.

MOSES, Margaret (2004). "Can Parties Tell Courts What to Do? Expanded Judicial Review of Arbitral Awards," 52 *U. Kan. L. Rev.* 429.

MOVIUS, Hallum, and Lawrence SUSSKIND (2009). *Built to Win: Creating a World Class Negotiating Organization.* Boston, Mass.: Harvard Business School.

MURRAY, Daniel E. (1961). "Arbitration in the Anglo-Saxon and Early Norman Periods," 16 *Arb. J.* 193.

NABATCHI, Tina, and Lisa BINGHAM (2003). *Expanding Our Models of Justice in Dispute Resolution: A Field Test of the Contribution of Interactional Justice.* Paper presented at meeting of American Society for Public Administration, Philadelphia, PA.

NADER, Laura (1993). "Controlling Processes in the Practice of Law: Hierarchy and Pacification in the Movement to Re-Form Dispute Ideology," 9 *Ohio St. J. on Disp. Resol.* 1.

_____ (1984). "The Recurrent Dialectic Between Legality and Its Alternatives: The Limitations of Binary Thinking," 132 *U. Pa. L. Rev.* 621.

_____ (1979). "Disputing Without the Force of Law," 88 *Yale L.J.* 998.

NADER, Laura, and Elisabetta GRANDE (2002). "Current Illusions and Delusions About Conflict Management–In Africa and Elsewhere," 27 *Law & Soc. Inquiry* 573.

NADER, Laura, and Christopher SHUGART (1980). "Old Solutions for Old Problems," in Laura Nader, ed., *No Access to Law: Alternatives to the American Judicial System.* New York: Academic Press.

NADLER, Janice (2001). "Electronically-Mediated Dispute Resolution and E-Commerce," 17 *Negot. J.* 333.

NALEBUFF, Barry, and Ian AYRES (2003). *Why Not? How to Use Everyday Ingenuity to Solve Problems Big and Small.* Boston: Harvard Business School Press.

NATIONAL ARBITRATION FORUM (2009). "National Arbitration Forum to Cease Administering All Consumer Arbitrations in Response to Mounting Legal and Legislative Challenges." Minneapolis, MN: National Aribitration Forum. Retrieved from http://www.adrforum.com/newsroom.aspx?itemID=1528.

_____ (2003). "Arbitration Bill of Rights with Commentary." National Arbitration Forum. Retrieved from http://www.arb-forum.com/articles/pdfs/BOR-Com-1-2-03.pdf.

NELKEN, Melissa L. (1996). "Negotiation and Psychoanalysis: If I'd Wanted to Learn About Feelings, I Wouldn't Have Gone to Law School," 46 *J. Legal Educ.* 420.

NIEMEC, Robert J. (1997). *Mediation & Conference Programs in the Federal Courts of Appeals: A Sourcebook for Judges and Lawyers.* Washington, D.C.: Federal Judicial Center.

NIEMEC, Robert J., Donna STIENSTRA, and Randall E. RAVITZ (2001). *Guide to Judicial Management of Cases in ADR.* Washington, D.C.: Federal Judicial Center.

NISBETT, R., and L. ROSS (1980). *Human Inference: Strategies and Shortcomings of Social Judgment.* Englewood Cliffs, NJ: Prentice Hall.

NOESNER, Gary W., and Mike WEBSTER (1997). "Crisis Intervention: Using Active Listening Skills in Negotiations," *FBI L. Enforcement Bull.,* August 1, p. 13.

NOLAN-HALEY, Jacqueline M. (1999). "Informed Consent in Mediation: A Guiding Principle for Truly Educated Decisionmaking," 74 *Notre Dame L. Rev.* 775.

OLSON, Ronald L. (1980). "Dispute Resolution: An Alternative for Large Case Litigation," *Litig.* 22 (Winter).

ORR, Dan and Chris GUTHRIE (2006). "Anchoring, Information, Expertise, and Negotiation: New Insights from Meta-analysis," 2006 *Ohio J. Disp. Resol.* 597.

ORWELL, George (1949). *1984: A Novel.* London: Secker & Warburg.

PALEFSKY, Cliff (2001). "Only a Start: ADR Provider Ethics Principles Don't Go Far Enough," *Disp. Resol. Mag.* 18 (Spring).

PARK, William W. (2003). "The Contours of Arbitral Jurisdiction: Who Decides What?," *Mealey's Intl. Arb. Rep.* 14 (August).

PAUL, Roland A. (1976). "A New Role for Lawyers in Contract Negotiations," 62 *A.B.A. J.* 93.

PEARSON, Jessica, and Nancy THOENNES (1989). "Divorce Mediation: Reflections on a Decade of Research," in Kenneth Kressel and Dean G. Pruitt, eds., *Mediation Research: The Process and Effectiveness of Third-Party Intervention.* San Francisco: Jossey-Bass Publishers.

PEPPET, Scott R. (2004). "ADR Ethics," 54 *J. Legal Educ.* 72.

_____ (2004). "Contract Formation in Imperfect Markets: Should We Use Mediators in Deals?," 19 *Ohio St. J. on Disp. Resol.* 283.

_____ (2003). "Contractarian Economics and Mediation Ethics: The Case for Customizing Neutrality Through Contingent Fee Mediation," 82 *Tex. L. Rev.* 227.

PETER, James T. (1997). "Med-Arb in International Arbitration," 8 *Am. Rev. Intl. Arb.* 83.

PHILBIN, Donald R. (1999). "The One Minute Manager for Mediation: A Multidisciplinary Approach to Negotiation Preparation," *Harv. Negot. L. Rev.* 281.

PHILLIPS, Barbara A. (1997). "Mediation: Did We Get It Wrong?," 33 *Willamette L. Rev.* 649.

PLAPINGER, Elizabeth, and Donna STIENSTRA, with the assistance of Laural HOOPER and Melissa PECHERSKI (1996). *ADR and Settlement in the Federal District Courts: A Sourcebook for Judges & Lawyers.* Washington, D.C.: Federal Judicial Center.

PLOUS, Scott (1993). *The Psychology of Judgment and Decision Making.* Philadelphia: Temple University Press.

POSNER, Richard A. (1986). "The Summary Jury Trial and Other Methods of Alternative Dispute Resolution: Some Cautionary Observations," 53 *U. Chi. L. Rev.* 366.

POU, Charles, Jr. (2003). " 'Embracing Limbo': Thinking About Rethinking Dispute Resolution Ethics," 108 *Penn. St. L. Rev.* 199.

POUNDSTONE, William (2003). *How Would You Move Mount Fuji?* Boston: Little, Brown.

POWELL, Gary N. (1990). "One More Time: Do Female and Male Managers Differ?," *Acad. Mgmt. Executive* 68 (August).

PRESS, Sharon (1997). "Institutionalization: Savior or Saboteur of Mediation?," 24 *Fla. St. U. L. Rev.* 903.

PRICE, Marty (2000). "Personalizing Crime: Mediation Produces Restorative Justice for Victims and Offenders," *Disp. Resol. Mag.* 8 (Fall).

PRICEWATERHOUSE COOPERS (2008). "*International Arbitration: Corporate Attitudes and Practices 2008.*" London: Pricewaterhouse Coopers. Retrieved from http://www.pwc.co.uk/pdf/PwC_International_Arbitration_2008.pdf.

PRIEST, George L. (1989). "Private Litigants and the Court Congestion Problem," 69 *B.U. L. Rev.* 527.

PROGRAM ON NEGOTIATION AND INTERNATIONAL INSTITUTE FOR CONFLICT PREVENTION AND RESOLUTION (Producer) (2007). *Rebuilding the World Trade Center Site: An Exercise in Multi-Party Negotiation, featuring Lawrence Susskind* [film]. Cambridge, Mass.: PON at Harvard University.

PRUITT, Dean G. (1983). "Achieving Integrative Agreements," in Max H. Bazerman and Roy J. Lewicki, eds., *Negotiating in Organizations.* Beverly Hills, Cal.: Sage Publications.

_____ (1981). *Negotiation Behavior.* New York: Academic Press.

PRUITT, Dean G., and Steven A. LEWIS (1977). "The Psychology of Integrative Bargaining," in Daniel Druckman, ed., *Negotiations: Social-Psychological Perspectives.* Beverly Hills, Cal.: Sage Publications.

PUBLIC CITIZEN (2007). "The Arbitration Trap: How Credit Card Companies Ensnare Consumers." Washington, D.C.: Public Citizen. Retrieved from http://www.citizen.org/documents/ArbitrationTrap.pdf.

PUBLIC CONVERSATIONS PROJECT (2003). "Constructive Conversations About Challenging Times: A Guide to Community Dialogue" (version 3.0). Public Conversations Project. Retrieved from http://www.publicconversations.org/pcp/uploadDocs/CommunityGuide3.0.pdf.

PUTNAM, Linda L. (2006). "Communication and Interaction Patterns" in Andrea Kupfer Schneider and Christopher Honeyman, eds., *The Negotiator's Fieldbook*. Washington D.C.: ABA Section on Dispute Resolution.

PUTNAM, Robert D. (1993). "Diplomacy and Domestic Politics: The Logic of Two-Level Games," in Peter B. Evans, Harold K. Jacobson, and Robert D. Putnam, eds., *Double-Edged Diplomacy: International Bargaining and Domestic Politics*. Berkeley: University of California Press.

RABER, Nancy K. (1998). "Dispute Resolution in Olympic Sport: The Court of Arbitration for Sport," 8 *Seton Hall J. Sport L.* 75.

RACHLINSKI, Jeffrey J., Sheri Lynn JOHNSON, Andrew J. WISTRICH, and Chris GUNTHRIE (2009). "Does Unconscious Racial Bias Affect Trial Judges?," 84 *Notre Dame L. Rev.* 1195.

RAIFFA, Howard (1985). "Post-Settlement Settlements," 1 *Negot. J.* 9.

_____ (1982). *The Art and Science of Negotiation*. Cambridge, Mass.: Belknap Press of Harvard University Press.

RAIFFA, Howard, with John RICHARDSON and David METCALFE (2002). *Negotiation Analysis: The Science and Art of Collaborative Decision Making*. Cambridge, Mass.: Belknap Press of Harvard University Press.

RALSTON, Jackson H. (1929). *International Arbitration from Athens to Locarno*. Stanford, CA: Stanford University Press.

RAU, Alan Scott (2003). "Everything You Really Need to Know About 'Separability' in Seventeen Simple Propositions," 14 *Am. Rev. Intl. Arb.* 1.

_____ (1999). " 'The Arbitrability Question Itself,' " 10 *Am. Rev. Intl. Arb.* 287.

_____ (1997). "Integrity in Private Judging," 38 *S. Tex. L. Rev.* 485.

RAWLS, John (1971). *A Theory of Justice*. Cambridge, Mass.: Harvard University Press.

REED, Lucy F. (2002). "Drafting Arbitration Clauses," 670 *Practising L. Inst., Litig. & Admin. Prac. Course Handbook Series* 553.

REHNQUIST, William H. (1977). "A Jurist's View of Arbitration," *Arb. J.* 1 (March).

REILLY, Peter (2009). "Was Machiavelli Right? Lying in Negotiation and the Art of Defensive Self-Help," 24 *Ohio St. J. on Disp. Resol.* 3.

REIMUND, Mary Ellen (2003). "Mediation in Criminal Justice: A Restorative Approach," *Advoc. (Idaho)* 22 (May).

RELIS, Tamara (2009). *Perceptions in Litigation and Mediation: Lawyers, Defendants, Plaintiffs and Gendered Parties*. Cambridge, UK: Cambridge University Press.

RESNIK, Judith (1995). "Many Doors? Closing Doors? Alternative Dispute Resolution and Adjudication," 10 *Ohio St. J. on Disp. Resol.* 211.

_____ (1982). "Managerial Judges," 96 *Harv. L. Rev.* 374.

REUBEN, Richard C. (2003). "*First Options,* Consent to Arbitration, and the Demise of Separability: Restoring Access to Justice for Contracts with Arbitration Provisions," 56 *SMU L. Rev.* 819.

_____ (1997). "Public Justice: Toward a State Action Theory of Alternative Dispute Resolution," 85 *Cal. L. Rev.* 577.

REYES, Robert M., William C. THOMPSON, and Gordon H. BOWER (1980). "Judgmental Biases Resulting from Differing Availabilities of Arguments," 39 *J. Personality & Soc. Psychol.* 2.

RHODE, Deborah L. (2000). *In the Interests of Justice: Reforming the Legal Profession.* New York: Oxford University Press.

RICHMAN, Barak D. (2002). "Community Enforcement of Informal Contracts: Jewish Diamond Merchants in New York" (Discussion Paper No. 384). Harvard University, John M. Olin Center for Law, Economics, and Business. Retrieved from http://www.law.harvard.edu/programs/olin_center/papers/pdf/384.pdf.

RICIGLIANO, Robert (2003). "Networks of Effective Action: Implementing an Integrated Approach to Peacebuilding," 34 *Security Dialogue* 445.

RISKIN, Leonard L. (2003). "The New Old Grid and the New New Grid System," 79 *Notre Dame L. Rev.* 1.

―――― (1994). "Mediator Orientations, Strategies and Techniques," 12 *Alternatives to High Cost Litig.* 111.

―――― (1991). "The Represented Client in a Settlement Conference: The Lessons of *G. Heileman Brewing Co. v. Joseph Oat Corp.,*" 69 *Wash. U. L. Q.* 1059.

―――― (1984). "Toward New Standards for the Neutral Lawyer in Mediation," 26 *Ariz. L. Rev.* 329.

―――― (1982). "Mediation and Lawyers," 43 *Ohio St. L.J.* 29.

RISKIN, Leonard L., James E. WESTBROOK, and James LEVIN (1998). *Instructor's Manual with Simulation and Problem Materials,* accompanying *Dispute Resolution and Lawyers* (2d abr. ed.). St. Paul: West Group.

RISKIN, Leonard L., and Nancy WELSH (2008). "Is That All There Is? 'The Problem' in Court-Oriented Mediation," 15 *Geo. Mason L. Rev.* 863.

ROBBENNOLT, Jennifer K. (2006). "Apologies and Settlement Levers," 3 *J. Empirical Stud.* 333.

―――― (2003). "Apologies and Legal Settlement: An Empirical Examination," 102 *Mich. L. Rev.* 460.

ROBERT, Henry M. (2000). *Robert's Rules of Order Newly Revised* (10th ed.). Sarah Corbin Robert et al., eds. Cambridge, Mass.: Perseus Publishing.

ROBINSON, Peter (2009). "Judicial Settlement Conference Practices and Techniques," 33 *Am. J. of Trial Advocacy.* 113.

ROGERS, Catherine A. (2011). *Ethics in International Arbitration.* New York: Oxford University Press.

―――― (2002). "Fit and Function in Legal Ethics: Developing a Code of Conduct for International Arbitration," 23 *Mich. J. Intl. L.* 341.

ROME, Donald Lee (2003). "Business Mediation's Orientation Focuses Detail on Printed Words," 21 *Alternatives to High Cost Litig.* 21.

ROSE, Carol M. (1995). "Bargaining and Gender," 18 *Harv. J.L. & Pub. Poly.* 547.

ROSE, L. Christopher (1999). Note, "Nevada's Court-Annexed Mandatory Arbitration Program: A Solution to Some of the Causes of Dissatisfaction with the Civil Justice System," 36 *Idaho L. Rev.* 171.

ROSE, Laurel L. (1996). "Are Alternative Dispute Resolution (ADR) Programs Suitable for Africa?," *Africa Notes* (Cornell University) 5 (September).

ROSENTHAL, Robert, and Lenore JACOBSON (1968). *Pygmalion in the Classroom: Teacher Expectation and Pupils' Intellectual Development.* New York: Holt, Rinehart and Winston.

ROSS, Dennis (2004). *The Missing Peace: The Inside Story of the Fight for Middle East Peace.* New York: Farrar, Straus and Giroux.

ROSS, Lee (1995). "Reactive Devaluation in Negotiation and Conflict Resolution," in Kenneth J. Arrow, et al., eds., *Barriers to Conflict Resolution.* New York: W.W. Norton.

ROWE, Mary P. (1991). "The Ombudsman's Role in a Dispute Resolution System," 7 *Negot. J.* 353.

RUBEN, Alan Miles, Frank ELKOURI, and Edna Asper ELKOURI (2003). *How Arbitration Works: Elkouri & Elkouri.* Washington D.C.: Bureau of National Affairs.

RUBIN, Jeffrey Z., and Frank E.A. SANDER (1991). "Culture, Negotiation, and the Eye of the Beholder," 7 *Negot. J.* 249.

_____ (1988). "When Should We Use Agents? Direct vs. Representative Negotiation," 4 *Negot. J.* 395.

RULE, Colin (2002). *Online Dispute Resolution for Business: B2B, Ecommerce, Consumer, Employment Insurance, and Other Commercial Conflicts.* San Francisco: Jossey-Bass Publishers.

RUSSO, J. Edward, and Paul J.H. Schoemaker (1989). *Decision Traps: The Ten Barriers to Brilliant Decision-Making and How to Overcome Them.* New York: DoubleDay Business.

RUTLEDGE, Peter B. (2009). "The Case Against the Arbitration Fairness Act," 16 *Disp. Resol. Mag.* 4.

_____ (2008). "Who Can Be Against Fairness? The Case Against the Arbitration Fairness Act," 9 *Cardozo J. Conflict Resol.* 267

SALACUSE, Jeswald W. (1998). "Ten Ways that Culture Affects Negotiating Style: Some Survey Results," 14 *Negot. J.* 221.

SANDER, Frank E.A. (2009). *"Ways of Handling Conflict: What We Have Learned, What Problems Remain,"* 25 *Negot. J.* 533.

_____ (2000). "The Future of ADR," 2000 *J. Dispute Resol.* 1.

_____ (1976). "Varieties of Dispute Processing," 70 *F.R.D.* 111.

SANDER, Frank E.A., and Jeffrey Z. RUBIN (1988). "The Janus Quality of Negotiation: Dealmaking and Dispute Settlement," 4 *Negot. J.* 109.

SANDER, Frank E.A., and Michael L. PRIGOFF (1990). "Professional Responsibility: Should There Be a Duty to Advise of ADR Options?," *A.B.A. J.* 50 (November).

SANDER, Frank E.A., and Stephen B. GOLDBERG (1994). "Fitting the Forum to the Fuss: A User-Friendly Guide to Selecting an ADR Procedure," 10 *Negot. J.* 49.

SAUNDERS, Harold H. (1999). *A Public Peace Process: Sustained Dialogue to Transform Racial and Ethnic Conflicts.* New York: St. Martin's Press.

SCANLON, Kathleen M. (2002). *Drafter's Deskbook for Dispute Resolution Clauses.* New York: CPR Institute for Dispute Resolution.

SCARDILLI, Frank J. (1997). *"Sisters of the Precious Blood v. Bristol-Myers Co.*: A Shareholder-Management Dispute," reprinted in Leonard L. Riskin and James E. Westbrook, *Dispute Resolution and Lawyers* (2d ed.). St. Paul: West Group.

SCHELLING, Thomas C. (1960). *The Strategy of Conflict.* Cambridge, Mass.: Harvard University Press.

SCHILTZ, Patrick J. (1999). "On Being a Happy, Healthy, and Ethical Member of an Unhappy, Unhealthy, and Unethical Profession," 52 *Vand. L. Rev.* 871.

SCHMITZ, Amy J. (2009). "Nonconsensual + Nonbinding=Nonsensical? Reconsidering Court-Connected Arbitration Programs," 10 *Cardozo J. Conflict Resol.* 587.

_____ (2002). "Ending a Mud Bowl: Defining Arbitration's Finality Through Functional Analysis," 37 *Ga. L. Rev.* 123.

SCHNEIDER, Andrea Kupfer (2009). "Bargaining in the Shadow of (International Law)," 41 *N.Y.U. J. Int'l L. & Pol.* 789.

_____ (2009). "The Intersection of Dispute Systems Design and Transitional Justice," 14 *Harv. Negot. L. Rev.* 289.

_____ (2006). "Aspirations" in Andrea Kupfer Schneider and Christopher Honeyman, eds., *The Negotiator's Fieldbook.* Washington D.C.: ABA Section on Dispute Resolution.

_____ (2006). "Not Quite a World Without Trials: Why International Dispute Resolution Is Increasingly Judicialized," *J. Disp. Resol.* 119.

_____ (2006). "The Day After Tomorrow: What Happens Once a Middle East Peace Treaty Is Signed?," 6 *Nev. L. J.* 401.

_____ (2002). "Shattering Negotiation Myths: Empirical Evidence on the Effectiveness of Negotiation Style," 7 *Harv. Negot. L. Rev.* 143.

_____ (2000). "Building a Pedagogy of Problem-Solving: Learning to Choose Among ADR Processes," 5 *Harv. Negot. L. Rev.* 113.

_____ (1999). "Getting Along: The Evolution of Dispute Resolution Regimes in International Trade Organizations," 20 *Mich. J. Intl. L.* 697.

SCHNEIDER, Andrea Kupfer, and Christopher HONEYMAN, eds. (2006). *The Negotiator's Fieldbook.* Washington D.C.: ABA Section on Dispute Resolution.

SCHÖN, Donald A. (1983). *The Reflective Practitioner.* New York: Basic Books.

SCHUCK, Peter H. (1987). *Agent Orange on Trial: Mass Toxic Disasters in the Courts.* Cambridge, Mass.: Belknap Press of Harvard University Press.

SCHUMACHER, E.F. (1977). *A Guide for the Perplexed.* New York: Harper & Row.

SCHWARTZ, David S. (2009). "Mandatory Arbitration and Fairness," 84 *Notre Dame L. Rev.* 1247.

_____ (2004). "Correcting Federalism Mistakes in Statutory Interpretation: The Supreme Court and the Federal Arbitration Act," 67 *Law & Contemp. Probs.* 5.

_____ (1997). "Enforcing Small Print to Protect Big Business: Employee and Consumer Rights Claims in an Age of Compelled Arbitration," 1997 *Wis. L. Rev.* 33.

SCHWARZ, Roger (2002). *The Skilled Facilitator: A Comprehensive Resource for Consultants, Facilitators, Managers, Trainers, and Coaches* (2d ed.). San Francisco: Jossey-Bass Publishers.

SEARLE CIVIL JUSTICE INSTITUTE AT NORTHWESTERN LAW SCHOOL (2009). "Consumer Arbitration Before the American Arbitration Association." Everston, IL: Northwestern University.

SEBENIUS, James K. (2004). "Mapping Backward: Negotiating in the Right Sequence?," 6 *Negotiation* 7.

_____ (1996). "Sequencing to Build Coalitions: With Whom Should I Talk First?," in Richard J. Zeckhauser, Ralph L. Keeney, and James K. Sebenius, eds., *Wise Choices: Decisions, Games, and Negotiations.* Boston: Harvard Business School Press.

SELTMAN, Lee (1993). "Appointments of Special Masters to the Supreme Court and the Ninth Circuit" (working paper of the Ninth Circuit Gender Bias Task Force).

SEMINAR (1997). "Efficient Organization of International Arbitrations" (pts. 1 & 2), 8 *World Arb. & Mediation Rep.* 61 and 8 *World Arb. & Mediation Rep.* 82.

SEN, Amartya (2009). *The Idea of Justice.* Cambridge, Mass.: Belknap Press of Harvard University Press.

SENGER, Jeffrey M. (2004). "Decision Analysis in Negotiation," 87 *Marq. L. Rev.* 723.

_____ (2003). *Federal Dispute Resolution: Using ADR with the U.S. Government.* San Francisco: Jossey-Bass Publishers.

SEUL, Jeffrey R. (1999). "How Transformative Is Transformative Mediation?: A Constructive-Developmental Assessment," 15 *Ohio St. J. on Disp. Resol.* 135.

SHAPIRO, Daniel L. (2006). "Untapped Power" in Andrea Kupfer Schneider and Christopher Honeyman, eds., *The Negotiator's Fieldbook.* Washington D.C.: ABA Section on Dispute Resolution.

SHAPIRO, Justine, and B.Z. GOLDBERG (Directors and Producers). (2001). *Promises* [Motion picture].). New York: Cowboy Pictures.

SHAPIRO, Martin (1981). *Courts: A Comparative and Political Analysis.* Chicago: University of Chicago Press.

SHAW, Margaret L., and Lynn P. COHN (1999). "Employment Class Actions Provide Unique Context for ADR," *Disp. Resol. Mag.* 10 (Summer).

SHELL, G. Richard (1999). *Bargaining for Advantage: Negotiation Strategies for Reasonable People.* New York: Viking.

SHERMAN, Edward F. (1993). "Court Mandated Alternative Dispute Resolution: What Form of Participation Should Be Required?," 46 *SMU L. Rev.* 2079.

SHESTOWSKY, Donna (2006). "Psychology and Persuasion," in Andrea Kupfer Schneider and Christopher Honeyman, eds., *The Negotiator's Fieldbook*. Washington D.C.: ABA Section on Dispute Resolution.

SHULMAN, Harry (1955). "Reason, Contract, and Law in Labor Relations," 68 *Harv. L. Rev.* 999.

SILBEY, Susan S., and Sally E. MERRY (1986). "Mediator Settlement Strategies," 8 *Law & Poly.* 7.

SLAIKEU, Karl A. (1989). "Designing Dispute Resolution Systems in the Health Care Industry," 5 *Negot. J.* 395.

SMITH, Linda F. (2007). "Was it Good for You Too? Conversation Analysis of Two Interviews," 96 *Kentucky L.J.* 579.

SMITH, Stephanie, and Jan MARTINEZ (2009). "An Analytic Framework for Dispute System Design," 14 *Harv. Negot. L. Rev.* 123.

SPECIAL COMMITTEE ON GENDER (1996). "Final Report of the Special Committee on Gender to the D.C. Circuit Task Force on Gender, Race, and Ethnic Bias," in 1 *The Gender, Race, and Ethnic Bias Task Force Project in the D.C. Circuit* (1995), reprinted in 84 *Geo. L.J.* 1657.

SPILLENGER, Clyde (1996). "Elusive Advocate: Reconsidering Brandeis as People's Lawyer," 105 *Yale L.J.* 1445.

SPORS, Kelly K. (2004). "Tip of the Week: Don't Sign Car Clause," *Wall St. J.*, January 11, p. 1.

STEMPEL, Jeffrey W. (2004). "Arbitration Unconscionability and Equilibrium: The Return of Unconscionability Analysis as a Counterweight to Arbitration Formalism," 19 *Ohio St. J. on Disp. Resol.* 757.

_____ (2000). "The Inevitability of the Eclectic: Liberating ADR from Ideology," 2000 *J. Disp. Resol.* 247.

_____ (1991). "Reconsidering the Employment Contract Exclusion in Section 1 of the Federal Arbitration Act: Correcting the Judiciary's Failure of Statutory Vision," 1991 *J. Disp. Resol.* 259.

STERNLIGHT, Jean R. (2010). "Lawyerless Dispute Resolution: Rethinking a Paradigm," 37 *Fordham Urban Law J.* 1.

_____ (2009). "Fixing the Mandatory Arbitration Problem: We Need the Arbitration Fairness Act of 2009." 16 *Disp. Resol. Mag.* 5.

_____ (2005). "Creeping Mandatory Arbitration: Is It Just?," 57 *Stan. L. Rev.* 1631.

_____ (2004). "In Search of the Best Procedure for Enforcing Employment Discrimination Laws: A Comparative Analysis," 78 *Tulane L. Rev.* 1401.

_____ (2003). "ADR Is Here: Preliminary Reflections on Where It Fits in a System of Justice," 3 *Nev. L.J.* 289.

_____ (2003). "The Rise and Spread of Mandatory Arbitration as a Substitute for the Jury Trial," 38 *U.S.F. L. Rev.* 17.

_____ (2002). "Is the U.S. Out on a Limb? Comparing the U.S. Approach to Mandatory Consumer and Employment Arbitration to That of the Rest of the World," 56 *U. Miami L. Rev.* 831.

_____ (2001). "Mandatory Binding Arbitration and the Demise of the Seventh Amendment Right to a Jury Trial," 16 *Ohio St. J. on Disp. Resol.* 669.

_____ (2000). "As Mandatory Binding Arbitration Meets the Class Action, Will the Class Action Survive?," 42 *Wm. & Mary L. Rev.* 1.

_____ (1999). "Lawyers' Representation of Clients in Mediation: Using Economics and Psychology to Structure Advocacy in a Nonadversarial Setting," 14 *Ohio St. J. on Disp. Resol.* 269.

_____ (1997). "Rethinking the Constitutionality of the Supreme Court's Preference for Binding Arbitration: A Fresh Assessment of Jury Trial, Separation of Powers, and Due Process Concerns," 72 *Tul. L. Rev.* 1.

_____ (1996). "Panacea or Corporate Tool?: Debunking the Supreme Court's Preference for Binding Arbitration," 74 *Wash. U. L.Q.* 637.

STERNLIGHT, Jean R., and Elizabeth J. JENSEN (2004). "Using Arbitration to Eliminate Consumer Class Actions: Efficient Business Practice or Unconscionable Abuse?," 67 *Law & Contemp. Probs.* 75.

STERNLIGHT, Jean R., and Jennifer ROBBENNOLT (2008). "Good Lawyers Should be Good Psychologists: Insights for Interviewing and Counseling Clients." 23 *Ohio St. J. on Disp. Resol.* 437.

STIENSTRA, Donna, Molly JOHNSON, Patricia LOMBARD, with Melissa PECHERSKI (1997). *Report to the Judicial Conference Committee on Court Administration and Case Management: A Study of the Five Demonstration Programs Established Under the Civil Justice Reform Act of 1990.* Washington, D.C.: Federal Judicial Center.

STILLINGER, C., M. EPELBAUM, D. KELTNER, and L. ROSS (1990). "The 'Reactive Devaluation' Barrier to Conflict Resolution" (unpublished manuscript, Stanford University).

STIPANOWICH, Thomas J. (2010). "Arbitration: 'The New Litigation,' " 2010 *Ill.. L. Rev.* 1.

_____ (1998). "Reconstructing Construction Law: Reality and Reform in a Transactional System," 1998 *Wis. L. Rev.* 463.

STIPANOWICH, Thomas J., and Peter H. KASKELL, eds. (2001). *Commercial Arbitration at Its Best: A Report of the CPR Commission on the Future of Arbitration.* Chicago: ABA.

STOLBERG, Sheryl Gay (2010). "Administering Fund, A Master Mediator," *N.Y. Times,* June 16, p. A18.

STONE, Douglas, Bruce PATTON, and Sheila HEEN (1999). *Difficult Conversations: How to Discuss What Matters Most.* New York: Viking.

STONE, Katherine Van Wezel (1996). "Mandatory Arbitration of Individual Employment Rights: The Yellow Dog Contract of the 1990s," 73 *Denv. U. L. Rev.* 1017.

STRAIN, Jason, and Elizabeth KEYES (2003). "Accountability in the Aftermath of Rwanda's Genocide," in Jane E. Stromseth, ed., *Accountability for Atrocities: National and International Responses.* Ardsley, N.Y.: Transnational Publishers.

STRAUS, David A. (1999). "Managing Meetings to Build Consensus," in Lawrence Susskind, Sarah McKearnan, and Jennifer Thomas-Larmer, eds., *The Consensus Building Handbook: A Comprehensive Guide to Reaching Agreement.* Thousand Oaks, CA: Sage Publications.

STRINE, Leo E., Jr. (2003). " 'Mediation-Only' Filings in the Delaware Court of Chancery: Can New Value Be Added by One of America's Business Courts?," 53 *Duke L.J.* 585.

STROMSETH, Jane, David WIPPMAN, and Rosa BROOKS (2006). *Can Might Make Rights?* Cambridge and New York: Cambridge University Press.

STULBERG, Joseph B. (1998). "Fairness and Mediation," 13 *Ohio St. J. on Disp. Resol.* 909.

_____ (1987). *Taking Charge/Managing Conflict.* Lexington, Mass.: Lexington Books.

_____ (1981). "The Theory and Practice of Mediation: A Reply to Professor Susskind," 6 *Vt. L. Rev.* 85.

STULBERG, Joseph B., and Lela P. LOVE (2009). *The Middle Voice: Mediating Conflict Successfully.* Durham, NC: Carolina Academic Press.

STURM, Susan, and Howard GADLIN (2007). "Conflict Resolution and Systemic Change," 2007 *J. Disp. Resol.* 2.

SUBRIN, Stephen N. (2002). "Discovery in Global Perspective: Are We Nuts?," 52 *DePaul L. Rev.* 299.

SUNSTEIN, Cass R. (2000). "Deliberative Trouble? Why Groups Go to Extremes," 110 *Yale L.J.* 71.

SUSSKIND, Lawrence (2009). "Twenty-Five Years Ago and Twenty-Five Years From Now: The Future of Public Dispute Resolution," 25 *Negot. J.* 551.

_____ (1999). "An Alternative to *Robert's Rules of Order* for Groups, Organizations, and Ad Hoc Assemblies that Want to Operate by Consensus," in Lawrence Susskind, Sarah McKearnan, and Jennifer Thomas-Larmer, eds., *The Consensus Building Handbook: A Comprehensive Guide to Reaching Agreement.* Thousand Oaks, CA: Sage Publications.

———— (1981). "Environmental Mediation and the Accountability Problem," 6 *Vt. L. Rev.* 1.

SUSSKIND, Lawrence, and Gerald McMAHON (1985). "The Theory and Practice of Negotiated Rulemaking," 3 *Yale J. on Reg.* 133.

SUSSKIND, Lawrence, and Jeffrey CRUICKSHANK (2006). *Breaking Robert's Rules: The New Way to Run Your Meeting, Build Consensus and Get Results.* New York: Oxford University Press.

SUSSKIND, Lawrence, and Liora ZION (2002). "Can America's Democracy Be Improved?" (working paper). Consensus Building Institute and MIT-Harvard Public Disputes Program. Retrieved from http://www.susskind.info/ content/contributions/democracy.pdf.

SUSSKIND, Lawrence, Sarah McKEARNAN, and Jennifer Thomas LARNER (1999). *The Consensus Building Handbook: A Comprehensive Guide to Reaching Agreement.* Thousand Oaks, Calif.: Sage Publications.

SWARD, Ellen E. (2003). "A History of the Civil Trial in the United States," 51 *U. Kan. L. Rev.* 347.

SYMPOSIUM (2010). *Nev. L. J.* ADR and the Financial Crisis.

SYMPOSIUM (2009). "Dispute System Design." 14 *Harv. Neg. L. Rev.* 1.

SYMPOSIUM (2009). "Against Settlement: Twenty Five Years Later," 78 *Fordham L. Rev.* 1117.

SYMPOSIUM (2008). "Empirical Studies of Mandatory Arbitration," 41 *U. Mich. J. L. Reform.* 777.

SYMPOSIUM (2004). "The Vanishing Trial," 3 *J. of Empirical Studies.* 1.

SYMPOSIUM (2003). "Beyond Belonging: Challenging the Boundaries of Nationality," 52 *DePaul L. Rev.* 759.

SYMPOSIUM (2000). "ADR in Cyberspace," 15 *Ohio St. J. on Disp. Resol.* 589.

TANNEN, Deborah (1998). *The Argument Culture: Moving from Debate to Dialogue.* New York: Random House.

———— (1990). *You Just Don't Understand: Women and Men in Conversation.* New York: Morrow.

TASK FORCE ON ALTERNATIVE DISPUTE RESOLUTION IN EMPLOYMENT (1995). "A Due Process Protocol for Mediation and Arbitration of Statutory Disputes Arising Out of the Employment Relationship." ABA, Section of Labor and Employment Law. Retrieved from http://www.bna.com/bnabooks/ ababna/special/protocol.pdf.

TESLER, Pauline H. (2001). *Collaborative Law: Achieving Effective Resolution in Divorce Without Litigation.* Chicago: ABA, Section of Family Law.

THALER, Richard H. (1980). "Toward a Positive Theory of Consumer Choice," 1 *J. Econ. Behav. & Org.* 39.

THOMAS, Kenneth (1976). "Conflict and Conflict Management," in Marvin D. Dunnette, ed., *Handbook of Industrial and Organizational Psychology.* Chicago: Rand McNally College Publishing.

THOMPSON, Anthony C. (2002). "Courting Disorder: Some Thoughts on Community Courts," 10 *Wash. U. J.L. & Poly.* 63.

THOMPSON, Leigh L. (2009). *The Mind and Heart of the Negotiator* (4th ed.). Upper Saddle River, N.J.: Prentice Hall.

THOMPSON, Leigh, and Janice NADLER (2002). "Negotiating via Information Technology," 58 *J. Soc. Issues* 109.

THOMSON, Dean B. (1994). "Arbitration Theory and Practice: A Survey of AAA Construction Arbitrators," 23 *Hofstra L. Rev.* 137.

THORNBURG, Elizabeth G. (2000). "Going Private: Technology, Due Process, and Internet Dispute Resolution," 34 *U.C. Davis L. Rev.* 151.

TICKELL, Shari, and Kate AKESTER (2004). *Restorative Justice: The Way Ahead.* London: Justice.

TONN, Joan C. (2003). *Mary P. Follett: Creating Democracy, Transforming Management.* New Haven: Yale University Press.

TRANTINA, Terry L. (2001). "How to Design ADR Clauses that Satisfy Clients' Needs and Minimize Litigation Risk," 19 *Alternatives to High Cost Litig.* 137.

TREMBLAY, Paul, R. (2006). ""Pre-Negotiation" Counseling: An Alternative Model," 13 *Clinical L. Rev.* 541.

UMBREIT, Mark S. (1988). "Mediation of Victim Offender Conflict," 1988 *J. Disp. Resol.* 85.

URY, William (1991). *Getting Past No: Negotiating with Difficult People.* New York: Bantam Books.

URY, William L., Jeanne M. BRETT, and Stephen B. GOLDBERG (1988). *Getting Disputes Resolved: Designing Systems to Cut the Costs of Conflict.* San Francisco: Jossey-Bass Publishers.

UTZ, Pamela J. (1978). *Settling the Facts: Discretion and Negotiation in Criminal Court.* Lexington, Mass.: Lexington Books.

VOLTAN, Vamik (1997). *Blood Lines: From Ethnic Pride to Ethnic Terrorism.* New York: Farrar, Straus & Giroux.

VONNEGUT, Kurt (1965). *God Bless You, Mr. Rosewater.* New York: Holt, Rinehart and Winston.

WALDMAN, Ellen A. (2001). "Credentialing Approaches: The Slow Movement Toward Skills-Based Testing Continues," *Disp. Resol. Mag.* 13 (Fall).

_____ (1997). "Identifying the Role of Social Norms in Mediation: A Multiple Model Approach," 48 *Hastings L. J.* 703.

WALDMAN, Ellen A., ed. (2010). *Practical Ethics for Mediators.* San Francisco: Jossey-Bass Publishers.

WALDMEIR, Patti (2003). "How America is Privatising Justice by the Back Door," *Fin. Times,* June 30, p. 12.

WALKER, Laurens, et. al. (1975). "Reactions of Participants and Observers to Modes of Adjudication," *4 J. Applied Soc. Pyschol.* 295

WARE, Stephen J. (2006). "The Case for Enforcing Adhesive Arbitration Agreements — with Particular Consideration of Class Actions and Arbitration Fees," 5 *J. Am. Arb.* 251.

_____ (2001). "Paying the Price of Process: Judicial Regulation of Consumer Arbitration Agreements," 2001 *J. Disp. Resol.* 89.

_____ (2001). "State Law Making Arbitration Agreements in Certain Types of Transactions Unenforceable," in *Alternative Dispute Resolution* §2.13. St. Paul: West Group.

_____ (2001). "State Law Raising the Standard of Assent for Contract Formation," in *Alternative Dispute Resolution* §2.14. St. Paul: West Group.

_____ (2001). "Unconscionability," in *Alternative Dispute Resolution* §2.25. St. Paul: West Group.

WATKINS, Michael, and Susan ROSEGRANT (2001). "Introduction: Seven Principles of Breakthrough Negotiation," in *Breakthrough International Negotiation: How Great Negotiators Transformed the World's Toughest Post-Cold War Conflicts.* San Francisco: Jossey-Bass Publishers.

_____ (2001). "Managing Conflict," in *Breakthrough International Negotiation: How Great Negotiators Transformed the World's Toughest Post-Cold War Conflicts* ch. 6. San Francisco: Jossey-Bass Publishers.

WATSON, Lawrence M., Jr. (2002). *Effective Advocacy in Mediation: A Planning Guide to Prepare for a Civil Trial Mediation.* Upchurch Watson White & Max Mediation Group. Retrieved from http://www.uww-adr.com/2002/pdfs/effectiveadvocacy.pdf.

WEINSTEIN, Janet, and Linda MORTON (2003). "Stuck in a Rut: The Role of Creative Thinking in Problem Solving and Legal Education," 9 *Clinical L. Rev.* 835.

WEISBERG, Robert (2003). "Restorative Justice and the Danger of 'Community,' " 2003 *Utah L. Rev.* 343.

WELSH, Nancy A. (2010). "What is '(Im)Partial Enough,' in a World of Embedded Neutrals?," 52 *Arizona L. Rev.* 395.

_____ (2008). "Looking Down the Road Less Traveled: Challenges to Persuading the Legal Profession to Define Problems More Humanistically." 2008 *J. Disp. Resol.* 45.

_____ (2004). "Remembering the Role of Justice in Resolution: Insights from Procedural and Social Justice Theories," 54 *J. Legal Educ.* 49.

_____ (2001). "Making Deals in Court-Connected Mediation: What's Justice Got to Do With It?," 79 *Wash. U. L. Q.* 787.

_____ (2001). "The Thinning Vision of Self-Determination in Court-Connected Mediation: The Inevitable Price of Institutionalization?," 6 *Harv. Negot. L. Rev.* 1.

WESTON, Maureen A. (2009). "Doping Control, Mandatory Arbitration, and Process Dangers for Accused Athletes in International Sports," 10 *Pepp. Disp. Res. L. J.* 5.

_____ (2004). "Reexamining Arbitral Immunity in an Age of Mandatory and Professional Arbitration," 88 *Minn. L. Rev.* 449.

_____ (2001). "Checks on Participant Conduct in Compulsory ADR: Reconciling the Tension in the Need for Good-Faith Participation, Autonomy, and Confidentiality," 76 *Ind. L .J.* 591.

WHITE, James J. (1980). "Machiavelli and the Bar: Ethical Limitations on Lying in Negotiation," 1980 *Am. B. Found. Res. J.* 926.

WIGMORE, John Henry (1923). "General Principle of Privileged Communications," in 5 *A Treatise on the Anglo-American System of Evidence in Trials at Common Law* §2285 (2d ed.). 5 vols. Boston: Little, Brown.

WILDE, O. (2000). *A Life in Quotes.* (Barry Day, ed.)

WILLIAMS, Gerald R. (1996). "Negotiation as a Healing Process," 1996 *J. Disp. Resol.* 1.

_____ (1983) *Legal Negotiation and Settlement.* St. Paul: West Group.

WINSLADE, John and Gerald MONK (2001). *Narrative Mediation: A New Approach to Conflict Resolution.* San Francisco: Jossey-Bass Publishers.

WISSLER, Roselle L. (forthcoming 2011). "Court-Connected Settlement Procedures: Mediation and Judicial Settlement Conferences," 26 *Ohio St. J. on Disp. Resol.*

_____ (2010). "Representation in Mediation: What We Know from Empirical Research," 37 *Ford. Urb. L. J.* 419.

_____ (2004). "Barriers to Attorneys' Discussion and Use of ADR," 19 *Ohio St. J. on Disp. Resol.* 459.

_____ (2000). "Attorneys' Use of ADR is Crucial to Their Willingness to Recommend It to Clients," *Disp. Resol. Mag.* 36 (Winter).

_____ (1997). "The Effects of Mandatory Mediation: Empirical Research on the Experience of Small Claims and Common Pleas Courts," 33 *Willamette L. Rev.* 565.

WISSLER, Roselle L., and Robert RACK (2004). "Assessing Mediator Performance: The Usefulness of Participant Questionnaires," 2004 *J. Disp. Resol.* 229.

WORKING GROUP ON HUMAN NEEDS AND FAITH-BASED AND COMMUNITY INITIATIVES, facilitated by THE CONSENSUS COUNCIL, INC., and coordinated by SEARCH FOR COMMON GROUND (2003). *Harnessing Civic and Faith-Based Power to Fight Poverty.* The Consensus Council, Inc. Retrieved from http://www.agree.org/upload/projects/SFCGbook2003.pdf.

WU, Jianzhong, and Robert AXELROD (1995). "How to Cope with Noise in the Iterated Prisoner's Dilemma," 39 *J. Conflict Resol.* 183.

YARN, Douglas H. (1999). *Dictionary of Conflict Resolution.* San Francisco: Jossey-Bass Publishers.

YOUNG, Gary M. (2002). "Malpractice Risks of Collaborative Divorce," *Wis. Law.* 14 (May).

YOUNG, Michael (2010). "Mediation Gone Wild: How Three Minutes Put an ADR Party Behind Bars," 25 *Alternatives* 97.

ZARTMAN, I. William (2003). "The Timing of Peace Initiatives: Hurting Stalemates and Ripe Moments," in John Darby and Roger Mac Ginty, eds., *Contemporary Peacemaking: Conflict, Violence and Peace Processes.* New York: Palgrave Macmillan.

ZELIZER, Craig, and Robert A. RUBENSTEIN (2009). *Building Peace: Reflections from the Field.* Sterling, VA: Kumarian Press.

Index